THE CAMBRIDGE HISTORY
OF THE NATIVE PEOPLES OF
THE AMERICAS

VOLUME III:

South America

THE CAMBRIDGE HISTORY
OF THE NATIVE PEOPLES OF
THE AMERICAS

VOLUME I: NORTH AMERICA
Edited by Bruce G. Trigger and Wilcomb E. Washburn

VOLUME II: MESOAMERICA
Edited by R. E. W. Adams and Murdo MacLeod

VOLUME III: SOUTH AMERICA
Edited by Frank Salomon and Stuart B. Schwartz

THE CAMBRIDGE HISTORY
OF THE NATIVE PEOPLES OF
THE AMERICAS

VOLUME III

SOUTH AMERICA

PART 1

Edited by

Frank Salomon
University of Wisconsin-
Madison

Stuart B. Schwartz
Yale University

CAMBRIDGE
UNIVERSITY PRESS

PUBLISHED BY THE PRESS SYNDICATE OF THE UNIVERSITY OF CAMBRIDGE
The Pitt Building, Trumpington Street, Cambridge, United Kingdom

CAMBRIDGE UNIVERSITY PRESS
The Edinburgh Building, Cambridge CB2 2RU, United Kingdom http://www.cup.cam.ac.uk
40 West 20th Street, New York, NY 10011-4211, USA http://www.cup.org
10 Stamford Road, Oakleigh, Melbourne 3166, Australia
Ruiz de Alarcón 13, 28014 Madrid, Spain

First published 1999

Printed in the United States of America

Typeface Adobe Garamond 11/13 pt.   *System* DeskTopPro/UX® [RF]

Library of Congress Cataloging in Publication data
South America / edited by Frank Salomon, Stuart B. Schwartz
p.   cm. – (Cambridge history of the Native peoples of the Americas)
Includes bibliographical references and index.
ISBN 0–521–33393–8
1. Indians of South America–History.
I. Salomon, Frank.   II. Schwartz, Stuart B.   III. Series.
E77.N62   1999
970.004'97–dc20   95-46096
                                                          CIP

A catalog record for this book is available from the British Library.

Volume I: North America   ISBN 0 521 34440 9   hardback complete set
   Volume I: North America, Part 1   ISBN 0 521 57392 0
   Volume I: North America, Part 2   ISBN 0 521 57393 9
Volume II: Mesoamerica   ISBN 0 521 65205 7   hardback complete set
   Volume II: Mesoamerica, Part 1   ISBN 0 521 35165 0
   Volume II: Mesoamerica, Part 2   ISBN 0 521 65204 9
Volume III: South America, Part 1   ISBN 0 521 63075 4
   Volume III: South America, Part 2   ISBN 0 521 63076 2
   Volume III: South America   ISBN 0 521 33393 8 hardback complete set

CONTENTS

v

ILLUSTRATIONS

FIGURES TO PART I

MAPS TO PART 2

FIGURES TO PART 2

INTRODUCTION

FRANK SALOMON AND STUART B. SCHWARTZ

This volume, the third in the *Cambridge History of the Native Peoples of the Americas*, presents the history of the indigenous peoples of South America from the earliest peopling of the continent to the 1990s. It concentrates on continental South America but also makes some reference to peoples of the Caribbean and lower Central America who were linguistically or culturally connected to South America. A volume of such chronological, geographical, and ethnographic scope is a daunting challenge. It has rarely been attempted. The last great benchmark compilation on the peoples of South America, Julian Steward's *Handbook of South American Indians* (1946), which was digested but also denatured in Steward and Faron's (1959) *Native Peoples of South America*, influenced a generation of scholarly inquiry. As editors, we looked upon the present volume as a way of integrating much of what has been learned and altered in the half century since the publication of that work, and as a means of making these new findings and studies available to a wide readership.

The *Handbook*, although it contains some excellent historical research, was evolutionist rather than historical in its overarching intention. We are concerned with presenting South Americans as historical actors in the full sense.

The present volume is not a handbook or an encyclopedia but rather an idea-oriented history. It does aim at broad coverage, but it emphasizes development of general themes rather than completeness. Not every group will be mentioned, nor every society explained, but the broad patterns and general processes that large clusters of them shared will be delineated and discussed. Some authors have questioned habitual analytical blocs, some have reconceptualized periodizations, and many have problematized the common labels under which South American peoples are grouped. Among the idea-oriented approaches we encouraged were those that sought to relate indigenous peoples' own reported or self-documented ideas about the past with the record as constructed through exterior views. This volume marks an early stage in the encounter between "histories of Indians" and "Indian histories," which are gradually taking shape as native peoples overcome their longstanding marginalization from the orbit of Spanish/Portuguese literacy and win the standing of conceptual protagonists.

It may be useful for readers to know the process by which this book came into being. The editors of the present volume first drew up a detailed prospectus outlining their understanding of the general trajectory of the history of the indigenous peoples of the continent including the basic processes as well as the regional and chronological divisions that could best present that history. Authors were then sought to write specific chapters within that framework. Because much of the scholarship on indigenous peoples of South America had been written within the framework of modern national boundaries, the editors sought authors who were willing to break out of that tradition and conceive of their task in terms of broader regional or conceptual frameworks. All of the authors were already recognized specialists, but this approach often placed on them an added burden of mastering somewhat unfamiliar scholarship while broadening the temporal or geographic scope of their inquiry. This slowed the volume's progress, and we hope that the final result reflects the advantages of this approach. The editors paid no attention to the ethnic or national background of the potential contributors, but an early decision was made to make sure that the important research advances made by South American scholars, many of which were not familiar to the general English-reading public, be represented in the volume as fully as possible. The result has been the inclusion of authors from Europe, the United States, Canada, and various Latin American countries. Within the editorial framework, authors were given free rein to design their chapters and present their conclusions and interpretations. The reader will notice a certain overlapping of chapters as well as differences of interpretation between authors. We believe that this is appropriate given the state of the field and the nature of historical inquiry. Finally, wherever possible, authors have been urged to integrate indigenous "voices" and to reckon with individual Native Americans rather than with Native America as a reified category.

Certain principles served as the basis of the organization of this volume. First, we have sought to make more permeable the old distinctions between "highland" and "lowland" societies. In light of archaeological discoveries showing that complex South American society is rooted in lowland antiquity, many authors have repudiated the common distinction between "civilized" Andean empires and "primitive" or "simple" lowland societies. Moreover, both typological studies and historical evidence now indicate that the histories of highland and lowland societies were not separate spheres but were profoundly interconnected. Small scale and simple organization, it becomes more and more clear, often replaced complexity only when the protracted emergencies of colonial times made re-adaptation necessary. We also (within the limitations of the evidence available) reject the implicit assumption that lowland societies because of ecological constraints or because of their lack of dynamism or unhistorical cultural character reward historical study less than highland ones. Looking at complex formations, we avoid the traditional use of European states and empires as prefabricated "types" for understanding indigenous states, especially highland societies like the Inka. Cultural analysis and methodological critiques have undercut the assumptions that underlay such approaches. Second, although we recognize that the European conquest, especially in its biological and demographic impact, was a singular event, we have emphasized native peoples' agency and individuality, which extended through and beyond the conquest. Colonial domination was important, but to emphasize it to the exclusion of all other processes is to lose too much of Native American history. Counteracting the apocalyptic emphasis on 1492 typical of quincentennial-period historiography, several authors treat the European onslaught as an episode in the changing story of native institutions rather than the cutoff date for whole ways of life. Third, we have sought in the organization of this volume to avoid the common anachronistic mistake of setting modern national boundaries across the path of comparison and synthesis. Above all, our objective is to bring the diverse indigenous societies into equitable focus, to unfold their histories in terms of their internal dynamics, their connections, and their conflicts. Rather than typologizing South American indigenous societies in terms of geographical region, cultural area, or period, we prefer to seek the crucial conflicts, movements, encounters, and innovations within which native achievement has been framed.

To do this, the authors have drawn on archaeological, ethnographic, and documentary sources, on historical linguistics, demography, biocultural studies, and on other fields and methods, many of which have made great advances since the publication of the *Handbook of South American Indians*. These have been integrated here within the framework of history – unfolding social reality in terms of change. Readers will note some differences in the approach and the mix of sources dependent on the current state of research. For the highland areas, much of the archaeological and documentary evidence has accumulated since the 1960s and is still awaiting comparative synthesis. Most of it – especially the huge bulk of native testimony written into litigation and bureaucratic records – is little known in the English-speaking world. For the lowlands, ethnohistorical literature is smaller in volume but fast growing and sufficient to reveal the variety and complexity of those cultures.

Traditional ways of thinking about the indigenous peoples of South America have often led to misunderstanding and misconception. Emphases on "tribal" peculiarities in distinction to "European" commonalities led to a fragmented vision of indigenous societies that lost sight of larger relationships. Older regional historiographical approaches often ignored important networks of alliance, trade, pilgrimage, and migration cutting across traditional frameworks of study. Overemphasis on the cataclysm of European conquest detracted from the study of social projects, institutions, and processes that developed through and beyond the invasion, and it downplayed the internal dynamic of native communities as historical actors in their own right. The organization of this volume and the approach of most of its authors who deal with the period after 1492 is based on seeing indigenous societies not as isolated, inward-looking, and "resistant" in a simplistic sense but as participants in early modern transatlantic history – in the making of mercantile capitalism, the breakdown of the *ancien régime*, and the formation of some of the world's earlier postcolonial independent states. Wherever possible, the volume tries to emphasize research that allows us to see how the indigenous peoples of South America conceived of their social universe – of personhood, identity, gender, freedom, obligation, and constraint at different historical moments and under varying conditions.

Finally, this volume also departs from approaches that emphasized traditional notions of "authenticity" and from attempts to find the "real" Inka or Tupinambá. Instead, we have placed much more emphasis on the shifting historical nature of such categories and on mixed and interstitial groups. Priority has also been given to large periods often neglected in the traditional historiography in regard to indigenous societies. Thus the reader will find much here on the nineteenth century as well as the later seventeenth and early twentieth centuries, periods too long left relatively blank in the historiography of the native peoples of South America.

We hope that the effect will be to counteract the facile assumption of continuity between "ancient" lifeways recorded at early dates, and modern "tradition" or "identity." Rather than tolerating any longer the supposition that modern indigenous South Americans embody archetypes of changeless culture – an idea that still saturates semischolarly and popular literature – we ask readers to recognize them as contemporaries in every sense: as products of recent pasts as well as remote exotic ones, and as protagonists of their own affairs in every period.

Within the twenty-six chapters that constitute this book, authors have taken a variety of approaches. Some have organized their materials chronologically, others by region, and still others around key problems or concepts. The volume begins with a short section on Native American and European ways of historical thinking. Chapters 1 and 2 are reflexive inquiries into the modes of thinking and the failures of knowledge about the peoples of South America. They seek to begin to understand why South America – the continental landmass with the longest colonial and neo-colonial history – could still be seen in the 1970s as what Patricia Lyon called, "the least known continent." Salomon explores the variety of "Indian" ways of reconstructing the past, often through myth, ritual, oral testimony, or other means, all of which present challenges for connecting such approaches to Western understandings and historiography. Sabine MacCormack in Chapter 2 examines the mental frameworks that Europeans developed for seeing South Americans in the first two centuries of contact. Chapters 3 and 4 offer contrasting perspectives on the peopling of the continent and the foundation of regional cultures, reflecting both sides of the hotly debated issues of how long humans have lived in South America and how soon they domesticated its biota. In the first of these, Thomas Lynch considers the evidence of the preceramic hunter-gatherers and maritime peoples who occupied the continent for most of its prehistory. He emphasizes the critical use of data and is skeptical of proposal for very early dating. Anna Roosevelt in Chapter 4, on the other hand, favors the early chronology model and emphasizes the emergence of sedentary societies based on cultivation. She argues that social complexity had little to do with political centralization.

Chapters 5 to 9 are primarily archaeological syntheses of different parts of the continent, tracing the historical record from the emergence of village societies to the arrival of Inka or Spanish invaders. Izumi Shimada examines Andean and Pacific coast diversity in Chapter 5 including the "Chavín" horizon, but balances the "horizon" approach by emphasizing the multicentric nature of Andean prehistory. Luis Lumbreras in Chapter 6 on "Andean Urbanism and Statecraft" discusses the interrelation of large polities like Wari and Chimor with the other peoples of the region. In Chapter 7, Juan and Judith Villamarín combine ethnohistorical and archaeological evidence of "chiefdoms," or "intermediate societies," from the Caribbean to northern Argentina, presenting a rich array of evidence that permits broad comparisons of those social formations across the continent. The huge number of cases embraced emphasizes that politically organized "intermediate societies," long treated as stunted states, constituted a large and long-lasting proportion (perhaps a majority) of societies, and might better be thought of as a characteristic social form in their own right than as incipient states. The archaeological evidence of migratory waves in the Caribbean forms the basis of Allaire's discussion in Chapter 8. Rivera in his Chapter 9 on the Southern Cone is concerned to question the stigma of the term "marginal," which the *Handbook* attached to the Southernmost peoples.

Chapters 10 through 14 outline the impact of indigenous imperial expansions on the peoples of South America. Rostworowski and Morris analyze the indigenous empire of the Inka in Chapter 10, emphasizing distinctive organizing premises of economy and ideology. They are followed by a set of regional studies of the crisis and transformation of indigenous societies in the face of European contact to about 1580: Whitehead on the Caribbean, Spalding on the Andean region, Monteiro on Brazil, and Garavaglia on Paraguay and the pampas. This organization invites comparisons. Inka expansion operated within an economic and ideological framework that combined domination with managed and idealized concepts of complementarity and centralized redistribution. The Iberian empires driven by the expansive dynamism of Mediterranean mercantile-military society and religious fervor expanded throughout the Americas, at first by harnessing the impetus of internal political and social changes that the conquest itself set in motion. These transformations and innovations took different forms, dependent in large part on the nature of the indigenous societies. In the Caribbean islands and the northern mainland of South America, where Cariban and Arawakan groups culturally predominated, invasion entailed not only the notorious demographic disaster and depopulation of the island peoples but also the fateful initial development of Spanish techniques and institutions and practices for dealing with indigenous peoples. It yielded a pattern of significant settlement in a few principal ports but virtually no European settlement in the interior except on the Orinoco. Although those societies in direct contact with the Spanish suffered profound transformations, Whitehead points out in Chapter 11 that many peoples of northern South America were little affected prior to 1580. In contrast, Karen Spalding shows in Chapter 12 that in the Andean region the Spanish conquerors appropriated a gigantic preexisting power structure and made rapid use of indigenous means of centralization. At the same time, however, the entanglement of individual Spaniards in the politics of local chiefdoms created webs of collaboration, factionalism, and resistance that limited Spain's early attempts at centralization. The Portuguese and to a lesser extent the French on the Brazilian coast, both in contact with predominantly Tupí-Guaraní peoples, depended on alliance and barter in early relations. Here there was no political centralization and "acute and persistent" political fragmentation as well as cultural diversity, which was appropriated and manipulated by the Europeans. John Monteiro's Chapter 13 describes an intermittent and slow process, a pattern of trade and alliance shifting to warfare, enslavement, and conversion and eventually accompanied by demographic collapse and cultural disruption among the peoples of the Brazilian littoral. They responded by retreat, resistance, and revitalization movements. In the Río de la Plata, the extension of European conquests of Peru and Brazil encountered stateless societies and inherited kinship-based forms of alliance and inequality. Juan Carlos Garavaglia shows that the process of conquest stimulated new mutations of a prophetic and rebellious tradition among Tupían and Guaranían peoples and created a contested rather than compliant background for their participation in the coercive utopias of the Franciscan and Jesuit missions.

Chapters 15 to 20 move beyond the period of crisis to deal with the colonial condition, extending, in fact, in some places well beyond the formal "colonial" period and into the era of the independent nation-states of the region. For the Andean region, the late Thierry Saignes in Chapter 15 shows how "the people called Indians" replaced their demolished overarching indigenous institutions by demanding that native lords mediate skillfully with the colonial regime. Under that mediation, they developed networks of commerce and used Catholic institutions like godparentage and confraternities to build locally controlled frameworks of solidarity, inventing forms of legitimacy to preserve magico-religious as well as legal and public land rights. For Araucania, the Chilean and Argentine terrain of the peoples whose major descendants are the Mapuche, Kris Jones in Chapter 16 shows that active resistance and techniques of adaptation and incorporation of intrusive material goods and individuals fostered a resistance so successful that it provided a continuity extending to the end of the nineteenth century. A similar approach is taken by Anne Christine Taylor in Chapter 17 on the Andean-Amazonian area of interaction where there was no decisive period of colonial transformation. She argues that the traditional division between "civilized" highlands and "primitive" lowlands is itself a reflection of these colonial failures. James Saeger in Chapter 18 considers the people of Paraguay and the Chaco from the late sixteenth century to 1882. Counterposing the cultures of the Guaraní and Guaicuruan peoples and their subsequent histories under colonial rule, he emphasizes the similarity of their history to that of other indigenous peoples of the continent. In Chapter 19, Robin Wright and his collaborators, using a variety of examples from the Amazon basin and coastal and southern Brazil, trace the destruction, retreat, and survival of various indigenous groups. Reflecting recent historiographical trends, this chapter is able to document continuities in indigenous-white relations extending from the colonial to the national periods through the end of the Brazilian empire in 1889. Finally, Neil Whitehead in Chapter 20 carries the story of the peoples of northeastern South America from the Orinoco to the Caribbean from the sixteenth to the twentieth century. His emphasis is on the complexity of indigenous responses and on changes within indigenous societies themselves in an area where the competition between Europeans often created unsuspected latitude and opportunities for indigenous autonomy.

We close the colonial and neo-colonial era with a double retrospective that presages both the conceptual collapse of colonial ethnic definitions and the end of the colonial order. In Chapter 21, Schwartz and Salomon emphasize the way in which the colonial era undid the simple idea of "native" America by generating new peoples in the interstices of officially visible social organization. A process of ethnogenesis created new social types – mestizos, "tribes," individuals who crossed cultural frontiers – and created still less-recognized categories hard to define in colonial or modern ethnic terms. In Chapter 22, Luis Miguel Glave examines the political breakdown of colonial arrangements, which provoked indigenous rebellions in the core Andean colonies, bringing the "Republic of the Indians," into revolt during the era of the Atlantic Revolutions.

Chapters 23 and 24 are broad, synthetic overviews of the era of Independence and the nineteenth century, roughly divided between "highland" and "lowland" South America. Brooke Larson first contrasts the quite different fortunes of the respective peoples of Colombia, Ecuador, Peru, and Bolivia in the face of these would-be-national state-building projects. Jonathan Hill views the northern and southern lowlands in the era of nation-building and through the disastrous rubber boom. In both of these chapters, we see how the equivocally "national" character of the creole patriotic movements for independence, and their racial exclusivism, led the beneficiaries of colonial failure to build independent states hostile to indigenous peoples. These processes created an alienation between official nationhood and on-the-ground cultural diversity that is still historiographically difficult to penetrate.

The final two chapters concern the recent era, for which ethnography and the self-scholarship of modern native South Americans each complement exterior historiography. The central theme of these chapters is the modern search for organizational forms capable of asserting ethnic interests against the grain of most state and church institutions. In Chapter 25, Xavier Albó examines the Andean countries where most Quechua and Aymara societies by 1900 had been compressed into a single social class, the peasantry. He describes the breakdown of the old agrarian order and the remarkable consequences, diversifying throughout the Andean countries: syndicalism and revolution in Bolivia; migration and "de-Indianization" amid a failing "revolution from above" in Peru, and federative ethnic movements in Ecuador among others.

In Chapter 26, David Maybury-Lewis views the lowland peoples of the continent. Outlining the development of indigenous federations and other institutions, he emphasizes how they have succeeded in expressing their desire for rights to land and local autonomy as a way to safeguard their own cultures. The lowlanders have stressed the ethnic and cultural dimensions of their struggle as corporate entities within and across modern national states. By doing so, they have underlined the participation of the indigenous peoples of South America in the global issue of ethnic pluralism within and beyond the nation-state.

This historical turn itself has affected (and been influenced by) shifts in the practice of historiography and historical anthropology. The shifts are reflected in this volume and deserve a short commentary. Until the

1970s, history "proper" usually dealt with native South Americans as the objects or victims of colonial history, and in many areas dismissed the intranative past (beyond canonical chronicles) as simply unresearchable or unimportant. This mindset tended especially to go unchallenged in regard to Amazonia, where the impressive achievements of essentially ahistorical or synchronic-minded ethnographic modeling (whether social-anthropological in the British mold, Lévi-Straussian, or ecologically systematic) allowed a continuing misattribution of timelessness to the peoples rather than to the reigning analytical postulates about them. However, scholars who aspired to anthropological modeling of change and dynamism had already begun by the 1960s to generate a body of studies loosely self-labeled as "ethnohistory" or *etnohistoria*, using a term of older North American origin. (It occurs in Peruvian Spanish context, however, before World War II.) The "ethnohistory" label stuck to conceptually diverse studies that had in common only the indigenous focus. When used thoughtfully, it was sometimes defined as historiography, which uses concepts derived from ethnology as its heuristic, but many writers applied it too broadly to any historical study of peoples lacking a published or official historiography. The popularity of "ethnohistory" in this broad sense grew quickly, notably in the Andes, especially as the 1970s brought surges of indigenous activism in Ecuador and Bolivia and political restructuring in Peru. However, the very successes of indigenous revindication, as well as the research findings themselves, undercut the equation between "history of Indians" and "ethnohistory." For one, the increasingly clear view of native peoples as protagonistic within a multi-ethnic history, rather than acting in segregated parallel alongside a Euro-American history, demanded a more integrating historiography. To put it bluntly, there was nervousness lest ethnohistory become a kind of intellectual apartheid. Once research had overcome the image of natives as a "people without history," it became possible to ask, as one historian acidly did, whether those who had formerly been labeled "without history" would feel any better on hearing themselves described as peoples "with ethnohistory." The legitimate force of this concern caused the present editors to discourage the use of "ethnohistory" as a synonym for indigenous history.

However, at the same time, the term "ethnohistory" in a narrower sense has retained an equally legitimate vitality. The narrow sense is the sense analogous to terms like "ethnobotany" and "ethnoastronomy": that is, the study of various cultures' local understandings of time, change, and human causation. Cultural anthropological theory in the last two decades of the twentieth century has been strongly concerned with the question of how culturally framed apperceptions of the unforeseen condition (or "structure") historic response. Those who think peoples differ radically in their understandings of how the world changes (for example, because they see change as shaped by archetypal relations among divinities rather than by human practice) are also likely to think that "ethnohistory" in this narrow sense is a crucial determinant of the way peoples respond to crisis and the way historic societies actually turn out. The limelighted stage of this debate has been Polynesia (with Marshall Sahlins and Gananath Obeyeskere as the leading antagonists). But for reasons sometimes autonomous from the "Captain Cook" debate, South Americanists have also attended ever more closely to folk theories or premises about change and to indigenous genres expressing them. In most areas of South America at the end of the twentieth century, ethnohistory in the narrow sense is a true research frontier, and several of the contributors to this volume have given what is known about it notable emphasis. The movements of ethnic self-assertion described in the final two chapters are particularly interesting in this regard insofar as they make us contemporary witnesses to native efforts at remobilizing local or ethnic memory within a political conjuncture that demands formulation compatible with metropolitan ideologies and the folk historical sense they carry. As contemporaries studying with and in, not just about, indigenous South America, researchers become interlocutors in the creation of new ethnohistories.

South Americans who consider themselves indigenous in one way or another often express concern with the discord between their ethnohistorical identities in the strict sense, and the social taxonomy assigned from without. Contemporary senses of peoplehood have become acutely self-conscious and controverted as groups debate, for example, whether to embrace or repudiate categories like "mestizo" or broad generalities like "Quechua," which submerge the more local identities to which feelings of "we" actually attach. In this matter, too, researchers are witness to processes that are not unique to our time. But in the historic record, the processes of social taxonomy take place off stage, and we rarely know just how a certain word became accredited as the name of a "real" social entity. The resultant problems of terminology demand some methodological attention.

The editors regard the problem of standardizing names of groups as an insoluble one, not merely because of the vast number of overlapping terms in print but because the notion that inherently correct taxa could exist at all, or that they lie "out there," scattered like needles in the ethnographic haystack, is a theoretical chimera. Anyone who has browsed Timothy J. O'Leary's *Ethnographic Bibliography of South America* (New Haven: Human Resources Area Files, 1963), James S. Olson's *The Indians of Central and South America* (New York, 1991), or the comprehensive current website Ethnologue, will have been startled by the huge number of bewildering names that attach to each seemingly discrete "tribe" and to its subgroups. The task of bringing legible order to this unmanageable lexicon can be carried only at the level of providing artificial conventions, and even then it faces several kinds of difficulties.

For one, group naming at its root in local folk process is not done for the sake of standardization or objective mapping but for local pragmatic reasons. Only in sorting out the products ex post facto does scholarship impose taxonomic order, and this process has inherent ingredients of reification and spurious accuracy. As Audrey Butt Colson reported from cases in the Guiana Highlands, most speakers see themselves and others as members of more or less large collectivities – "my people the Pemon," "another people, the Kapon" – which possess "folk unity" based on a language and a shared sense of "peoplehood." And at the most local scale, they tend to see themselves and others as belonging to small localized groups associated with a territory, a river segment, a village, and so on – "my group, the people along Red Earth Bend." These large- and small-scale terminologies tend to form relatively consensual mappings acceptable to both members and nonmembers of the groups named. But at the intermediate levels, naming processes are different, because the social encounters among aggregates at medial level are typically not consensual. For example, the regional clusters of local groups that dispute resources are often the ones that states and informal observers call separate "tribes" even though cultural differences between them may be small. Boundary relations among them include warfare, shamanic or other magical disputes, and ideological disagreements. At such medial levels, most speakers describe their own groups as the "real *x*'s" ("real Pemon") and vilify their rivals, including those who belong to the same maximal "people," with what Colson calls "nicknames." Nicknames are often pejoratives meaning such things as "Those who do not know how to speak" (*Taurepan*, a Carib nickname taken as a valid ethnonym by Koch-Grünberg). These terms function taxonomically only in relation to the speaker's pragmatic interests and local shibboleths.

So a first problem in making sense of ethnonyms arises from sorting out the innumerable "nicknames" in written records. Many are synonyms. It takes great local expertise to filter them, and in the case of historic sources from past centuries, the knowledge needed to do so is often no longer available.

A second problem arises from the indiscriminate proliferation of seeming "peoples" which in many cases are really just the names of very small units such as the inhabitants of a river segment. As for their culture and ethnic sense of selfhood, they would better have been classified under more inclusive terms. Nonetheless, the historical record swarms with names of supposed "nations" or "extinct tribes" or "peoples" heard about vaguely and rarely, sometimes only once.

A third problem arises from graphophonemic inaccuracy. It is usual to find South American peoples referred to under varying spellings: Machiguenga/Matsiguenka; Caingang/Kaingang/Kainjgang; Quechua/Kechwa/Qheshwa/Kkechua/Qquichua, and so on, depending on the native language habits of the writer and on the ethnographic norms of the era, among other factors.

A fourth problem lies in the politics of naming. Many names in print, including some of the most widely used, are distasteful to those named (like "Campa" for Asháninka in Peru or "Jívaro" for Shuar and "Auca," meaning 'enemies,' for Wao in Ecuador). When an attributed name is plainly the expression of hostility or incompetent testimony, many of our authors have disposed of it with a reference pointing to a more acceptable name. In recent years, many or most indigenous groups have demanded the replacement of stigmatizing names (usually nicknames in origin) by ethnonyms of their own choosing, and we generally favor such reforms. Reforms can, however, bring difficulties anew. For example, many Ecuadorian Quichua speakers would today prefer to be called by a broad autodenomination, *Runa*, meaning 'men' or 'people'. But this word has problems of its own. It carries an implicit message of gender inequality unwelcome to the increasingly active feminist sector within this population. Also, some Quichua speakers dislike it because it is homonymous with the local Spanish-language usage of *runa*, which is a racist pejorative; and finally, anyone who knows the region will wonder whether it also includes Peruvian Quechua speakers, who could also be called *Runa*, but who avoid the term in ethnic autodenomination.

A fifth problem arises at this point. The never-ceasing historic process of coining names does not simply relabel peoples; it retaxonomizes them, merging or dividing previous ethnic categories. These new taxa are themselves sometimes historical facts of great importance, especially when the power that impose them could impose roles corresponding to them. The word *indio* is the standout case. Throughout South America today, it is used primarily to impose a "racial" stigma. It is much more demeaning than the English word "Indian." However, no purpose would be served by simply suppressing this word, because the imposition of the *indio* category, merging all native distinctions, was itself a historically efficacious act with whose consequences this book is greatly concerned. In making diverse South Americans into "Indians," Iberians imposed social roles that millions of people actually did, unwillingly, carry out. The social fact of being Indian constituted a framework for all resistance as well as compliance.

Thus we do not think a standardized, consensual, or ethically purified ethnonymy is possible for historiographic purposes – not even if a genie were to grant the editors linguistic omnipotence. In the end, discrepancies are not chiefly due to lack of sound conventions about how to register norms "out there." They are due to the fact that naming, as sedimented in the document record, registers real-world dissensus; the sum of ethnonyms is not a map but the mess left behind on a semantic battlefield.

In the face of these problems, we limit ourselves to the modest goal of providing conventions without totally postponing the job of problematizing conventions.

We allowed authors to choose the level of detail they judged essential to recognition of indigenous agency. In some chapters, this includes names of small and unfamiliar groups, because the small group, like the indigenous individual, is an underrecognized social actor. But we have tried to provide signposts for major names that the reader will want to follow through the literature.

In collating the ethnonyms that authors chose to use, we tried to serve readers' needs by choosing a standardized spelling of each. The criteria for standardization were:

1. We retained linguistically well-informed spelling when the authors supplied them, but we disclaim uniform linguistic accuracy, which is usually impossible to attain from historic sources. We have not attempted phonological reconstruction of the forms (mis)recorded in sources.
2. Where it was possible to do so without violating other criteria, we used a form that is recognizable in relation to extant literature.

3. Where possible we used forms cited as index standards in O'Leary's *Ethnographic Bibliography of South America* because his bibliography (together with CD-ROM databases such as *Latin American Studies, Handbook of Latin American Studies*, and so forth) offers a major gateway into the literature and helps readers connect with writings that describe the group in question under other names.

4. Wherever possible, our authors discarded objectionable nicknames, even those common in the literature. In the case of nicknames widely diffused in literature, such as "Campa" or "Jívaro," we sought to mention equivalences with more acceptable terms. Some articles include current reformed ethnonyms if they are becoming well established. We avoided proposals for renaming that may prove ephemeral.

One of the most troublesome problems concerns exogenous "lumping" terms. We treat them in the following ways: We admit the word *indio* and its imperfect gloss 'Indian' as the name of a colonial social role. In general, we avoid it as a generic modern term for Native South Americans because its predominant function is to impute racial inferiority. However, Xavier Albó, in Chapter 25, has taken sides with those who hope to transvalue the word *indio*, translated 'Indian,' somewhat as "black" was transvalued in the American English of recent times.

We admitted exogenous broad terms that are generally intended nonprejudicially. These include *indígena* and 'indigenous', *natural* (a colonial usage) and its gloss 'native', "Native American," "autochthonous," "aboriginal," and "Amerindian."

In treating other terms that arose within Latin American folk models of inequality, such as *blanco* 'white', *mestizo* 'mixed blood', *negro (moreno, preto)* 'black', we deal with them as cultural classifiers typical of the periods in question. Chapter 21 explicitly problematizes the degree to which they denominated self-recognized groups.

Regarding terms that bracket types of societies, this volume, unlike the *Handbook of South American Indians*, is not keyed to any theory about levels of sociocultural complexity and does not seek to establish disciplinary benchmarks for the meaning of words such as "band," "state," or "chiefdom." We have requested authors to provide definitions within their respective frameworks where necessary. However, one term requires comment because its many usages in the extant literature produce confusion. This, of course, is the word "tribe." In both old and recent sources about (mostly lowland) peoples, the Spanish *tribú* and Portuguese *tribu* are used indiscriminately as terms for any group of people that putatively possesses a culture and language and coheres endogamously within a territory or along paths of movement; the political implications are vague, ranging from acephaly to strong chiefdom, and often include a notion of military rivalry with similar units. Although the Church, the Iberian empires, and the successor states did sometimes make use of this poorly considered bracketing term in sorting out indigenous subjects, in most South American periods and places "tribes" were not officially recognized as corporations with separate territorial treaty rights the way they were in North America. Certain South American peoples, notably in Colombia, Chile, and Brazil, have at varied periods been accorded politically defined territories, but these were not consistently keyed to notions of capital-T Tribe (see Chaps. 23–26). None of the usual vernacular North American usages of "tribe," then, are useful descriptors for this book.

But in modern research, the word does have one relatively precise and useful ethnographic sense, namely, the concept of "colonial tribe." A "colonial tribe" is a political formation growing around alliances between state/Church power (whether imperial or that of the Republics) and selected leaders of native groups around the fringes of the state's effectively governed space. What state agents and missionaries vaguely perceived as "tribes" did indeed become effective polities whenever alliances conferred privileged access to weapons and trade goods. The resultant politico-military groupings (which could well crosscut older cultural or endogamous boundaries) did form a definable sort of society, and it is this formation that the work in hand calls "tribes."

Regarding names of persons, we let stand the best-known forms proper to the context even when it might be possible to reconstruct a more linguistically transparent form. So, for example, the colonial rebel Juan Santos Atahualpa retains his hispano-Quechua name, although we also register its Quechua component as Atawallpa in the chapter on prehispanic Inkas. In Chapter 10, on Inka rule, the editors have made heavier use of reconstruction so as to restore a number of important Inka names; because the context is prehispanic, no point would be served by inserting anachronistic hispano-Quechua forms. In quotations from earlier authors, we let stand the earlier spellings of all non-English words.

The use of non-European common nouns also presents diachronic problems that have no single "correct" solution. For example, many

Inka-era words, which up to 1532 had a Quechua context and therefore require a rephonologized orthography accurate to that language (e.g., *wak'a* 'superhuman being, shrine'), became hispano-Quechua colonial words after 1532 and were written in nonstandardized Spanish orthography (e.g., *huaca, guaca,* 'idol, pagan object of worship' or, later, 'prehispanic burial'). Rather than standardize anachronistically, and thereby obscure the fact that meaning changed along with spelling, we have used standards appropriate to the respective eras.

For rephonologizations toward Inka-era southern Quechua, we use the Peruvian Ministry of Education's "official" orthography as published in its 1976 set of reference works. For hispano-Quechua terms we have chosen the most commonly recognized form. Rephonologization is less feasible for place names than for other words, either because the accurate prehispanic form is unknown or because it would inconvenience readers. For significant instances of this kind, we often use the ex-colonial forms found on official national maps. For example, the sacred city of the Inka, Qusqu, was colonially spelled Cuzco or Cusco and is today sometimes written Qosqo. Although Qusqu would be defensible for pre-1532 context, few readers recognize it, so we reluctantly and anachronistically standardize the form to Cusco, which appears on the well-known national map published by Peru's Instituto Geográfico Nacional (1988). For archaeological site names and typological terms, we use the forms common to archaeological literature, although it often deviates from the work of philologists and historians. Following common usage, the major Andean language is called Quichua in north Andean (today Ecuadorian) context and Quechua everywhere else.

Lastly, readers should be aware of the differences between Spanish and Portuguese orthography. Thus some authors may use *guaraní* (Sp.) while those who concentrate on Brazil will use *guarani* (Port.). We have sought to insure consistency within chapters but not between them. Individual authors usually write within a Spanish or Portuguese language framework, and an attempt to standardize usage throughout the volume would create anomalies.

Finally, by way of acknowledgments, we wish to thank Cambridge University Press' history editor Frank Smith for his patience and attention to the project's complex needs. A vote of thanks is also due to the translators identified at the beginning of each originally non-English chapter. Blenda Femenias, the translator of Chapter 25, also provided valuable help in the overall editing of several other chapters. Sinclair

Thompson and Mark Goodale gave valuable help in the editorial process. We thank our authors for their remarkable patience. And we thank our myriad educators, the innumerable South Americans whose testimonies, whether anonymous or attributed, have accrued in writing and become the actual foundation of the work.

1

TESTIMONIES: THE MAKING AND READING OF NATIVE SOUTH AMERICAN HISTORICAL SOURCES

FRANK SALOMON

This introductory chapter surveys writings that contain native South American versions of the past and problematizes the way they contain them. Its main purpose is to afford readers a "feel" for native sources' diverse viewpoints, their verbal textures, their transformations during editing into non-native genres, and their historiographic promise. Secondarily, it raises questions about making a *History* out of materials that mobilize memory in ways more or less distant from Euro-American historiography. In what sense is a chant in praise of mummified ancestors or a Kogi origin story a historical source? What reading shall we give them? Aside from writing histories of South American Indians, a still-underdeveloped but basically conventional part of the academic agenda, has anyone written South American Indian histories? What sorts of textual pasts are indigenous South American writers producing now?

The first five parts sketch the literature of colonial native testimonies. The next three sections concern modern sources in their relation to ethnography (see Map 1.1). The final two sections concern methodological issues about oral tradition, literacy, and the material record. Overall, and especially from page 51 onward, the chapter is concerned with some critical questions that arise in the effort to imbue historiography with ethnographic insight: How different and how separate are mythic and historical "past-discourses"? Why has the West been slow to recognize South American social memory? What difference does the introduction of writing make to indigenous treatments of the past? Where local uses of the past differ fundamentally from literate historiography, how can historians handle them with authenticity?

RECORDING OF EVENTS AND MEMORIES IN NATIVE
MNEMOTECHNOLOGIES

South America offers nothing similar to Mesoamerican codices because
no native South American culture practiced writing in the common sense
of the word before Iberian contact. To be sure, before 1492, most South
Americans expressed thoughts about descent, time, and change in innumerable mnemonic practices, which, without resembling writing, were
taken as legible remembrances. Some groups encoded the past in bodily
actions: dances with costumes representing ancient beings, or chants, or
pilgrimages to origin places. Others inscribed the past in sacred artifacts,
some meant to eternalize evocative bodily action: lifelike ancestor mummies, trophies such as masks made from human faces (in Peru) or skins
of enemies stuffed with ash (in Colombia) to commemorate victories.
Other mnemonic objects aggrandized a historic person or kin group in
tomb architecture, including (in Peru) palatial structures holding dead
sovereigns. These methods of remembrance accompanied an idea of the
past as a parallel reality into which one could enter by ritual means,
retrieving powerful knowledge and thereby influencing the future.

"Legible" images of the ancients occurred on figurative ceramic,
which, in several cultures of the Pacific shore, reached an iconography of
encyclopedic complexity and included portraits of human individuals.
Complex iconography, especially when presented in striplike series of
images (as occurs in northern Moche ceramics) were visible scenarios of
human-divine interaction. Some have been convincingly explicated.
However suggestions that arrays of colored "beans" painted on Mochica
ceramic or of geometrical *tuqapu* (written *tocapu*, etc.) emblems on Inka
garments encode language remain speculative.

One system of graphic language that endured into modernity may
derive from prehispanic precedent: the "picture writing" of the San Blas
(Panamanian) Cuna. Cuna "writing" uses chains of partly semasiographic
and partly logographic symbols to help readers memorize long song texts,
narratives, and lists of shrines. Its principles may well be of prehispanic
derivation, though no prehispanic example is known.

In the Inka heartland, pictures may have served to convey information
across language boundaries. An early source close to the Inka royalty tells
us newly conquered provinces had to send "pictures of what they possessed and of what kind and usefulness their respective lands were."
Cristóbal de Molina "Cuzqueño" said the Inka "had in a house of the

Map 1.1.

Sun called Poquen Cancha, which is close to Cusco, the life of each one of the Inka [sovereigns], and of the lands he conquered, and what was their origin, painted as figures on certain panels [*tablas*]." Through three colonial centuries, pictorial genealogies using combined Inka and Spanish iconographic conventions remained popular among natives.

Starting in 1940, D. E. Ibarra Grasso documented in the area of Lake Titicaca and as far south as Potosí, many examples of pictorial mnemonic texts drawn on leather or paper. Some examples of Bolivian "visible language" took the form of three-dimensional clay models. All known examples served as aids to learning catechism rather than history. Whether they belong, as Ibarra Grasso thought, to a continuous tradition derived from prehispanic models is far from certain. Early attestations are ambiguous, and the first clear description was published in 1869.

The foregoing mnemotechnologies afford clues to "Indian histories" even before 1492, but only one medium so far discovered gives a clear precolumbian toehold for a "history of Indians": the Andean *khipu* or knotted cord record. Hundreds of ancient *khipu*s exit in collections, mostly looted from prehispanic tombs and therefore lacking archaeological context. The art of making *khipu*s to record quantitative data (such as tribute quotas, censuses, or herd records) is fairly well understood. It resembles the use of the abacus but is also adaptable to tree-structures and other complex arrays of data. Its arithmetic rests on a system of base-ten positional notation. The meaningful features of numerical knots included color, knot position, knot type, and left- or rightward motion in making cord and knot. Large *khipu*s could hold vast statistical matrices in complex formats, such as, for example, a census of an imperial province, or the inventory of a vast warehousing complex. The largest known example, from northern Chile, has 1,404 data cords.

Could *khipu*s represent nonnumerical data such as narrations? One early and well-informed witness mentions a variant of the *khipu* that used "long strings of beads" to record the decrees of the Inka ruler "Ynga Yupangue." Early colonial natives generally agreed *khipu*s encoded narratives, and in early colonial Cusco, *khipu* experts were considered repositories of dynastic knowledge. As early as 1542, the Licentiate Vaca de Castro collected a seemingly historic narrative that has become known as the "chronicle of the *khipu* masters." But we do not know much about how "*khipu* masters" like Callapiña and Supno, the 1542 sources, encoded nonnumerical data. The leading modern students of *khipu* technique, Robert and Marcia Ascher, see historical *khipu*s as technically possible. If certain *khipu* number/knot combinations were assigned to represent certain opening formulas, each of which introduced an episode of a stereotyped sort, then a *khipu* indicating order of formulaic introductions would serve as a key to correct ordering of events and persons. Royal oral chronicles from Burundi are analogously organized upon a pattern of semirhythmically recurring introductory formulas each of which calls forth a given type of episode (e.g., a rebellion by a court diviner). Such a system would record the structure, not the content, of a narrative, and reading it would depend on personally knowing a priori what structures belong to what narratives and what particulars should fill them. Gary Urton, however, argues that *khipus* were more like writing than this, in the double sense that they functioned as standardized rather than personalized aids to memory, and that they encoded syntactical relations among elements of a narrative rather than merely listing its raw ingredients.

Early colonial chroniclers respected *khipu*-based historical testimony. When Pedro Sarmiento de Gamboa researched what was to be the official history of Inka rule endorsed by Viceroy Francisco de Toledo's regime (1572), he knew no better way to legitimate it than to present it as the fruit of interviews with over a hundred *khipu* masters. Until the late sixteenth century, colonial courts also readily received *khipu*-based testimony, especially records regarding economic transfers. When the native lords of Hatun Xauxa in 1561 sued for recovery of the goods and services they had given Pizarran armies in the early days of the European invasion, the Xauxa lords were able to account to the court's satisfaction for transfers that had taken place a quarter century earlier, down to the last "partridge" (actually the Andean bird is a tinamou) and pair of sandals.

ORAL TESTIMONY EMBEDDED IN IBERIAN CHRONICLES

What little we know about oral representations of the past in pre-European times comes mostly from the viceroyalty of Peru. In Amazonian and Pampean regions, early testimonial data are very scarce, because there was no period of "indirect rule" during which translation, transculturation, and writing could develop within native society. In all cases, the dubious translating process and the intense though often hidden political agenda of postinvasion historiography require cautious reading. Some early chroniclers talked with Inka princes and soldiers even before Spanish victory was secure. Yet because their nascent "history of Indians" was framed within the theme of Spanish victory, all but a few made it hard to isolate elements of "Indian history" apart from European concerns.

Rightly or wrongly, most chroniclers thought that the Inka state, like European kingdoms, sponsored official intellectual authorities: *amautas*, as they were called in hispano-Quechua, because their work was *hamutani* ("to conjecture and bring out in speech what will be good and turn out well and what will not"). *Amautas* supposedly created short historico-mythic narratives for the edification of Inka youth. At major Inka ceremonies, *harauicos*, sometimes glossed 'poets', performed ballads of the deeds of the mummified ancestors.

In the courses of their reigns, Inka rulers authorized chants of their victories. Juan de Betanzos, an early conquistador of Cusco who married an Inka princess and knew Quechua well enough to appreciate what she told him, wrote down in 1551 a seeming paraphrase of the heroic poems (*cantares*; the word was the then-current Spanish term for *chansons de geste*) that Inka rulers and commanders sang. His chapter 19 describes the début of a new *cantar* in honor of Inka victory over the Soras people. It suggests the ceremonial matrix of official Inka historical knowledge.

The sovereign "Ynga Yupangue" ordered captive Sora lords and all their insignia displayed before him. He had red fringes attached to each garment and then trod them underfoot. He dedicated a new refrain to the occasion: "Ynga Yupangue, Child of the Sun, conquered the Soras and put fringes on [them]." This refrain formed a leitmotif to a month-long triumph in whose later stages the Inka nobility re-performed "histories":

They would enter into the city [of Cusco] singing, each one in order, the things that had happened to them, all of which they went chanting, starting first, with the ones who had been with Ynga Yupangue and with the chant you already heard, about the conquest of the Soras. And when these had finished, the other captains started to chant what had happened to them in Condesuyo Province, and the other captains who had subjected the lowlands did the same, and likewise [the Inka] ordered that the prisoners should go along weeping and reciting their faults and crimes in a loud voice, as they were subjects and vassals of the Sun's child.[1]

The greatest recitals of Inka history were associated with mortuary rituals and the honors done for the preserved bodies of dead rulers. The

---

[1] Juan de Betanzos' *Suma y narración de los Incas* [1551], María del Carmen Rubio, ed. (Madrid, 1987), 93–97.

brilliant soldier-chronicler Cieza de León explains how, at royal funerals, *khipu* masters recounted the administrative chronicle of the deceased's reign to "those who were the best in rhetoric and richest in words." These specialists would compose them into popular songs with refrains (*villancicos*) or ballads (*romances*).

And so, knowing what had to be said because of what had occurred in similar ceremonies for dead lords . . . they would sing in elegant order the many battles that were fought in this and that part of the kingdom; and consequently they had at hand appropriate chants or ballads for each undertaking, which, when such were needed, they could sing so that the people would rally on hearing them and understand what happened in other times. . . . Those Indians who by the kings' order knew these ballads were honored and were favored, and they took great care to teach the ballads to their children and to men of their own provinces, the best-informed and most astute ones to be found; and so, by passing knowledge from one mouth to another, they became able today to tell what happened five hundred years ago as if it were ten.[2]

When an Inka sovereign died, his mummy was considered the permanent owner of the estate built up during his reign. Oral traditions formed part of this estate. Poet-performers representing the sovereigns' respective descent groups sang their ballads or chants to the reigning sovereign whenever the mummies attended ceremonies at the plazas of Cusco.

Many Spanish writers, particularly from the 1560s through the 1590s, compiled versions of Inka oral tradition. In laying the jural bases of Spanish rule, Viceroy Francisco de Toledo (1569–1581) commissioned the compilation and tendentious interpretation of much Inka lore. The jurists Juan de Matienzo and Juan Polo de Ondegardo wrote down what they believed to be both pre-Inka customary law and details of Inka legislation.

The art of eliciting South American folk history and braiding it into chronicles of European type was practiced far into the seventeenth century, not only in Inka lands but also in peripheries where less centralized native societies were less easily compared to European models of statecraft and worship. However, much less is known about the lore of the past among non-Inka peoples. Cieza de León began writing down his observations about northern South American peoples while in Venezuela in 1541; from 1548 on, he traveled southward through Colombian regions where the Inka never ruled. On this route, and then as he continued

---

[2] Pedro Cieza de León, *The Incas of Pedro Cieza de León*, Harriet de Onís, trans. (Norman, Oklahoma, 1959), 187–188.

deeper into the former Inka empire, he noted that some people whom his contemporaries considered savage nonetheless possessed a form of history. Among the Quimbaya, a Colombian people dwelling far outside Inka rule, he observed that:

When they went out to their festivals and pleasures in some plaza, they used to get all the Indians together, and two of them with two drums would beat out the rhythm; with another one taking the lead, they start to dance and perform, and all follow; and each carries a jar of wine in the hand; because drinking, dancing and singing are things they do all at once. Their songs consist of reciting in their own style their undertakings of the moment, and retelling the past fortunes of their elders.[3]

Fray Pedro Simón's huge Colombian-Venezuelan chronicle contains large stretches of what must be in origin native testimony. In such sources, it is usually difficult to isolate native testimony, because European suppositions and rhetoric not only frame but suffuse and transmute virtually all the information originally gathered from natives.

Few soundings of historical consciousness are available for people who lived beyond European frontiers. What we know of Amazonian peoples' sense of the past usually comes from outsiders: missionaries, ex-captives, and travelers. The coastal Brazilian Tupinamba, whose cannibalism inspired Montaigne's great essay, practiced cannibalism for reasons closely related to their sense of historicity. Visitors saw the warlike coastal Brazilians as preoccupied with their past; leaders chanted ancestors' warlike and heroic deeds as well as origin myths, while the group responded in refrain. In 1555, André Thévet heard and recorded performances that included not only myths of origin but an oratorical tirade by a Tupinamba chief in which he recounted his victories and acts of ritual cannibalism. This complex of war and vengeance has been interpreted as the armature of a disinctive mode of historical consciousness (see p. 57, pp. 109–21).

CIVIL GOVERNANCE AND NATIVE TESTIMONY

Fortunately chronicles make up only a small portion of the record fashioned from native speech. The mass of the documentary iceberg consists of material generated in the work of both civil and church bureaucracies: letters from native leaders, lawsuits, claims of nobility, and so forth.

[3] Pedro Cieza de León, *La crónica del Perú* [1553] (Buenos Aires, 1962), 88.

Though this material was hardly meant to be read as history, most of the progress historical ethnology has made since the 1946–1959 *Handbook of South American Indians* derives from its analysis. Martin Lienhard's useful studies on the capture of literacy by American peoples place the sources into a dramatically expanded history of New World literature.

This largely unpublished universe of writing freshens vistas of the indigenous past. Indeed, lawyers' and administrators' relative unconcern with scholastic norms of historiography, their lack of edifying purpose, and their cold adherence to the goal of managing native society opened their work to considerations that sometimes approach the ethnographic. Administrative paper and litigations focus on house-to-house scale detail, they seek to learn local customary laws, they mobilize the testimony of thousands of people too low-ranking to interest chroniclers of state and empire, and they deal with the domains of work and family, not just warfare and worship. Law, as understood circa 1600, embraced a wider sweep of social relationships than did history as then understood.

The civil governance of thickly settled regions like the Andes generated, for example, detailed house-to-house inspections (*visitas*) the better to levy tribute. When well executed, these proceedings yielded not only controlled sets of field notes on native society from 1548 onward, but penetrating inquiries on the norms obtaining before Spanish rule. *Visitas* also often contain detailed questionnaires about the local administration of Inka institutions. The data are incomparably more detailed than anything chroniclers recorded. John Murra pioneered the use of such data to clarify the fine structure of Inka rule. Each community spelled out its tribute obligations to the Inka in what are probably local categories. When asked to read out their *khipu*s in 1559, the native lords of Urin Chillo, on the Ecuadorian periphery of the Inka domains, explained that

[Urin Chillo] used to serve the Inkas by bringing firewood and straw for them to the city of Quito, and gave them some Indians who took care of some llamas on their own land, and they used to sow some maize fields for them, and they carried what they harvested to the storage deposit in the city of Quito, and some Indians who know how to make *cunbi* [luxury] clothing made some clothing with wool that the [Inka's] managers gave them, and they also used to give [the Inkas] some Indians for warfare when asked, and an Inka manager together with the cacique of the town used to parcel out all the abovementioned [duties] according to the town's ability and that of each Indian.[4]

---

[4] *Visita y numeración de los pueblos del valle de los Chillos 1551–1559*, Cristóbal Landázuri, ed. (Quito, 1990), 201.

Another way in which the state sometimes sucked native historical memories into the written current was to require "Geographical Reports" about provincial regions. Questionnaires from the 1570s onward elicited a crown data base about lands where benefices and saleable office could be purveyed. Some curates and administrators responded to the call for reports with almost ethnographic thoroughness, occasionally embedding local accounts of the remote past. Such documents provided historic testimonies from low-status peoples rarely consulted by chroniclers, such as the ethnically stigmatized Cañaris:

In the time of their paganism, each sector (*parcialidad*) had its own lordship (*señorío*) . . . and the lord of this town of Azogue before the Inka came was called Pueçar, which means 'broom', and we don't know the meaning of his being called so. This chieftain Pueçar had a son called Guichannauto, which means "heavy head" because he had a very large head. . . . Before the Inka conquered them they didn't pay as tribute anything more than what constituted recognition of the chief, namely food and drinks for him and work on his fields in their seasons and on his houses.[5]

The thickest vein of oral-historical tradition about secular matters is the lore embedded in litigation. Especially valuable are the dynastic traditions adduced during lawsuits between claimants to colonial chiefdoms, and the agrarian history adduced in resource fights between communities. When native litigants took the stand, they readily recited power conflicts, successions, and genealogies from two or three generations previous to Spanish conquest. If one adds in the autobiographical papers colonial lords tendered in applications for pensions, the native record appears anything but scarce. Indeed, the tidal wave of native litigation that began to swamp Spanish courts from the 1570s onward has opened windows invisible in the chronicle record.

One example is the coast of Peru, illuminated by the researches of María Rostworowski. Up to about 1970, the area seemed ethnohistorically unresearchable because epidemics demolished native polities before many chronicles were written. Yet the long memory mobilized in lawsuits kept retrieving the prehispanic past even when its "owners" were almost gone. The following is a fragment of a lawsuit about coca fields that were contested among three non-Inka ethnic groups, the Inka state, and, later, Spanish neo-feudal interests. In 1558, the witness Cristóbal Malcachagua

---

[5] Gaspar de Gallegos, "Sant Francisco Pueleusí del Azogue" [1582] in *Relaciones Geográficas de Indias*, Marcos Jiménez de la Espada, ed. (Madrid, 1965), 275.

remembered how, as a youth, in Inka times, he had played a small part in native lords' diplomacy:

In the time of Guascar Ynga, Vilcapoma was the cacique [native lord] of the said town of Chacalla, which was before the Christians came to this land. Sometimes he used to go to Guarocheri, of which this witness is a native, to visit the Guarocheri cacique, whose name was Nynaguilca, father of Don Sebastian who is the cacique now. He used to carry cobs of corn and coca and red pepper and other foods for the said cacique Nynaguilca, and he would say: "This is what I've brought from my field called Quybi." In Inka times the lord of Guarocheri used to have fields in Quibi and when this witness was a boy of twelve or thirteen years, he went by order of cacique Nynavilca from Guarocheri town to Quybi to see and visit the fields the cacique had there. And as he walked through them visiting and looking them over, this witness . . . heard some Indians from Chaclla say, as they were coming to the said Nynabilca, that the Indians of Canta also wanted to take over their lands at the time of a native insurrection. Nynabilca said they should sell their lands and fields to the Indians from Canta and if [Canta] inflicted any more nuisances or damages, all the Yauyo Indians would go out against the Canta Indians.[6]

Papers of this genre (although not always of this quality) accumulated in all areas where native societies were transformed into colonial peasantries.

Notarial copybooks from colonial cities, too, almost always contain papers about the mundane business conducted by Indian urbanites or visitors. The most rewarding protocols are wills, in which native women as well as men detailed their lands, clothes, furniture, and finances and outlined their most important familial relationships. Insofar as wills look backward at genealogical relationships and forward via estate planning, they are testimonies of diachronic reasoning. Also, they sometimes mention older regalia whose display embodied traditional legitimacy. When Don Diego Collín, ruler of a community in highland Ecuador, made his will in 1598, he left an important clue to his group's concept of legitimate continuity, namely, that the succession required inheritance of regalia including exotic Amazonian costume:

Item, I declare that I have a blowgun and I order that the said Don Miguel Zumba my nephew is to have and inherit it together with its staffs.

Item, I declare that I have three feather diadems and I order that they be divided among Don Miguel my nephew and the said Don Diego and Don Luis my

---

[6] *Conflicts over coca fields in XVIth-century Peru*, María Rostworowski de Diez Canseco, ed. (Ann Arbor, 1989), 94.

sons – with other small feathers of birds which I have, each of them two feathers with its diadem.

Item, I declare that I have a string of shells which natives call *catuc* ['finger-bone'?] and I order that my son Don Diego Cullin is to have and inherit it.

Item, I declare that I have two drums from the Quijos [an Amazonian region] and I say that they may never be taken from my house forever but are to be left on display.[7]

Natives also took part in the politico-legal battles that raged in the wake of the civil war between Pizarran conquistador elites and the Spanish crown. When Indians sought redress for what was confiscated in war, or when Spanish warlords asked to be reimbursed for their services against rebel *encomenderos*, they often mobilized native memories reaching back to the early moments of contact. One memorable trial in 1573 interviewed eighteen veterans of the Inka armies that vainly defended Tawantinsuyu. Don Diego Chuqui Xulca remembered the first rumors of the "sons of the sea," and then their desecration of the supreme shrine:

It was told and became well known here in the province of Yauyos that Atahuallpa [the Inka prince victorious in a war of succession] was in Caxamarca with armed forces, and that Spaniards and Christians called Capacochas [meaning 'sons of the sea', according to other witnesses] were coming against him. This witness went there in the company of his father . . . and as [they] were going along the road . . . they ran into Hernando Pizarro and other Spaniards who were coming with him, and an Inka envoy sent with him by Atahuallpa called Inga Mayta. Hernando Pizarro made him return to [the great sanctuary at] Pachacamac . . . and there this witness saw how Hernando Pizarro made them collect all the gold and silver, vases and pitchers and the consecrated women and vessels and objects of service and bowls and many other golden and silver and gilded objects which were in the houses of the Sun and the idol Pachacama, and the belongings of the nuns or mamaconas.[8]

Obviously, this is not exactly first-person testimonial language. How freely did native discourse pass through the filter of legalistic form? Legal papers appear at first glance dryly formulaic. Lawyers, stage-managing witnesses for clients' ends, used questionnaires to cut and frame oral

[7] Chantal Caillavet, "Ethno-histoire équatorienne: un testament indien inédit du XVI siècle," *Caravelle* 41 (1983), 16.
[8] *Versión Inca de la conquista*, Edmundo Guillén Guillén, ed. (Lima, 1974), 20.

tradition inauthentically. Colonial judges let lawyers mold testimony through leading questions. In the process, they snipped "Indian histories" to fit such "histories of Indians" as clients' interests required.

With a few exceptions, such as the innovative lawyer-researcher Polo de Ondegardo, legally trained questioners generally limited witnesses to points of preconceived legal interest rather than expanding the reach of law by exploring Andean ideas. Even though witnesses probably drew on diverse genres (dynastic titles, *khipu* readouts, etc.), native stylistics were silenced. First-person diction and native-language tropes got flattened to a characteristic run-on reportorial style. Translators were usually present but almost never explored the semantics of non-Spanish words, and opponents almost never questioned each other's translations. Even at early dates, legal writing took place within well-established codes of inaccurate but rigid cross-cultural correspondence. And although Quechua discourse must underlie most of these papers, written Quechua is scarce. (The exceptions are typically native-to-native exchanges: transactions prepared by "scribes for natives," whose work was important but rarely preserved, or political correspondence such as the out-of-court letters of two native lords studied by Itier.) Given these facts, all except the most sensitive civil papers look ethnographically unpromising.

But other factors point in the opposite direction. For one, litigation was in one sense a more natural context for the recitation of native genres than was that most acculturated of all activities, book writing. We know from African studies that disputes were among the few contexts in which the otherwise separate proprietary traditions belonging to different lineages would normally be juxtaposed and contrasted. A trial, even a colonial one, falls in part within the context proper to the native mnemotechnology. Also, besides trial records' evident advantages for "history of Indians" (they allow one to weigh contrary native opinions and collate them with exterior testimony), trials also have advantages for capturing properties of "Indian history," such as the ways in which opposing villages argued overlapping but discrepant genealogical histories.

The following is a sworn genealogy given by Martyn Choquesapinti, a 1623 litigant for a Peruvian chiefdom. In order to give it, someone (probably Choquesapinti) drew onto a paper a diagram of interconnected circles representing persons (lawyers called it a family tree). A scribe then wrote Choquesapinti's explanations onto the paper, superimposing script on diagram:

Apo Chata [interlineated: Yauri] was the paramount cacique of this thousand of Quinti [illegible word] since the time of the Inka and he had three sons who are the following.

the oldest son of Apochata Yauri was Maca Guaman who merited [i.e., succeeded to rule through his achievements] in Inka times;

This man was the son of the said Maca Guaman who was named Yauri Villca, who merited in Inka times;

This [is] the son of the said Yauri Villca who was called Don Miguel Marcos.

Don Miguel Marcos had as his legitimate son Don Miguel Chumbi Ricçi. This said Don Miguel Chumbi Ricçi had a lawsuit about his office of cacique with Don Pedro Anchivillca, Don Miguel Guamanchata's father, and with Don Fernando Llacsavillca.[9]

South Americans did not take long to incorporate institutions and concepts of colonial origin into their testimonies, and thus accredit them as traditional. For example, the concept of the *cacique principal* or paramount colonial chief, although it was at first recognized by natives as an innovative Spanish transformation of *curacazgo* or kinship-modeled political primacy, became by the 1560s a model for native political action. Native lords made use of it retroactively in explaining ancient as well as recent succession. It only took one generation to learn that exogenous "histories of Indians" were themselves valuable in building effective "Indian histories."

THE CHURCH AND NATIVE TESTIMONY

State functionaries normally paid little attention to the realms of belief and symbolism. When native litigators adduced mythohistoric material in support of claims, they washed it of obviously miraculous features and substituted legally recognizable motifs; for instance, the magical creator of a fertility-giving lake would be recast as the political sponsor of a lake-fed irrigation system. It is primarily via churchmen that we have some testimony about native belief and rite. In another respect, too, Church records tend to be strong where state records are weak: The Church often put resources into mission frontiers (Amazonia, the Orinoco, the Mojos,

---

[9] Lilly Library, Indiana University. Latin American Manuscripts: Miguel Huaman Chata, cacique, et al. Causas sobre el cacicazgo del pueblo de Quinti [1596–1626] f.145r–146v.

and Paraguay), which had lacked prehispanic states and which Iberian statecraft neglected or avoided.

The earliest Christian missionaries took little interest in "Indian" belief. It was only in the middle 1560s that an intense native religious ferment, itself provoked by Spanish depredations, stimulated Spanish interest in "idolatry." Unintentionally, persecution opened Spanish eyes to the deepest and least familiar concerns of "Indian history": the nexus uniting cosmology, landscape, and social organization in a single all-explanatory model.

In the area of Huamanga (now Ayacucho, Peru), a nativist religious revival called *Taki Unquy* (other common spellings: Taki Onqoy, Taqui Oncoy) demanding return to the cults of the prechristian *huacas*, evoked a series of persecutions whose trial records contain a poorly processed but still invaluable group of testimonies about what natives believed to be their vital link to a prehispanic past. Taki Unquy has itself been taken (by Steve Stern) as a revolution in the uses of memory. It required its converts to hark back to their oldest and most localistic pre-Inka deities, but at the same time to begin thinking of them as emblems of a new macro-category – the indigenous – as opposed to the global domain of the foreign. No texts of actual Taki Unquy sermons have been found. Father Luis de Olvera, the original instigator of persecution, said its adherents believed

that God was powerful enough to have created Castile and the Spaniards, and the crops that grow in Castile, but that the *huacas* had been powerful enough to have made this land and the Indians, and the crops and the things that grew in it, and that the Marqués Pizarro, when he entered Caxamarca and conquered the Indians and subjected this kingdom, had done so because God had at that time overcome the *huacas*, but that now, they had all come back to life to do battle with Him and conquer Him, and that the said *huacas* no longer embodied themselves in stones nor in trees nor in springs, as in Inka times, but instead put themselves into the Indians' bodies and made them speak and then seized them so they trembled saying that they had the *huacas* in their bodies, and they took many of them and painted their faces with a red pigment and put them in enclosures and the Indians went there to adore them as the idol and *huaca* which had gotten into their body.[10]

Does South America offer anything comparable with the Mayan *Popol Vuh* – a book of non-Christian religious testimony written in an Ameri-

---

[10] *El retorno de las huacas. Estudios y documentos del siglo XVI*, Luis Millones, ed. (Lima, 1990), 178.

can language? One such work exists. Toward the end of the sixteenth century, Spaniards had already wrecked the Inka shrines and the major sanctuaries that united belief over huge regions. At the same time, the Church excluded Andeans more and more from its clergy. This squeeze fostered tension between village religious leaders and the swelling colonial clergy. The intranative religious processes of the time are obscure, but it seems some natives clandestinely revivified and rethought the cults of ancient divinities (*huacas*). Renewal of *huaca* leadership and protest against clerical exploitation threatened the early colonial modus vivendi, which winked at surviving local cults in exchange for toleration of curates' carnal and business excesses. It was in the midst of this ambience, in 1597, that the brilliant bilingual cuzqueño Francisco de Avila took up an important parish in Huarochirí Province. In a few years, he made enemies among local natives by busying them with his illegal enterprises and outraging their persons. When they denounced him to an ecclesiastical court – he was jailed briefly – Avila took revenge by publicizing their adherence to *huacas*. He organized the first of several persecutions that would lash the western Andes through most of the seventeenth century.

In 1607 or 1608, he persuaded someone fully literate in Quechua to compile a detailed report on the Andean religions of his parish and its region, upvalley from the Lima coast. The result, apparently after some editing, was the untitled, undated, and anonymous text known as the *Huarochirí Quechua Manuscript* (preserved in Spain's National Library with a group of other manuscripts Avila once owned). Although Avila used it as a guide to his sleuthing against native priests, and wrote a "Treatise on False Gods" based on part of its content, he never mentioned it explicitly. It was first published in 1939.

Written in Quechua, which had been transformed from the political language of the Inka empire to the "general language" of Spanish missionary campaigns, the Huarochirí manuscript holds a summation of native religious practice and an image of the superhuman powers as imagined around C.E. 1600. Its editor or redactor clearly intended it to be a synthetic, treatise-format totalization of an Andean sacred history, suitable for comparison with Spanish chronicles:

If the ancestors of the people called Indians had known writing in earlier times, then the lives they lived would not have faded from view until now.

As the mighty past of the Spanish Vira Cochas is visible until now, so, too, would theirs be.

But since things are as they are, and since nothing has been written until now,

I set forth here the lives of the ancestors of the Huaro Cheri people, who all descend from one forefather:

What faith they held, how they live up until now, those things and more;

Village by village it will be written down: how they lived from their dawning age onward.[11]

The oral authors were provincial Indians corraled into "reduction" villages by the 1580s. Few if any of them had been alive when the Spanish invaded. Their lands, stretching from the snowcaps of the western cordillera down toward the river canyons and deltas of the Pacific shore, had by 1600 become thoroughly enmeshed in colonial economy. They vividly remembered the Inka – some of their ancestors had been Inka allies – but their own divinities sacralized local agropastoral, rather than imperial, experience.

The Huarochirí tellers envisioned history as an interaction between humans and their patron *huacas*, beginning long before Inka invasion and continuing long after Spanish conquest. A primordial world once belonged to protohumans who won immortality by sacrificing half their children. But new deities with other human allies built a world of war and mortality. Its axis of conflict and synthesis set the stormy powers of the heights, and their human progeny the Yauyos, against the ancient powers of the irrigated coastal valleys whose rich aborigines were the Yuncas. The paramount power of the mountains was Paria Caca (Jaqaru? Paria Kaka?), master of rainstorms, who appeared on a mountain as five eggs, which became five falcons that then became five men. The men were the progenitors of five victorious descent groups. The powers of the coastal valleys, on the other hand, were incarnated in a fivefold female power, Chaupi Ñamca. Some chapters detail a village-level ritual regimen based on balanced interlacing of the two traditions.

Other chapters tell how strange invaders – the Inka, and after them the Spanish – encountered the children of Paria Caca and of Chaupi Ñamca. The chapters about Inkas can to some degree be correlated with politically and legally documented events and with archaeological landmarks. The following episode tells how a highland herdsman who cared

---

[11] *The Huarochirí manuscript, a testament of ancient and colonial Andean religion*, Frank Salomon and George Urioste, trans. (Austin, 1991), 42–43.

for Paria Caca's llama flock prophesied the Spanish invasion; it reflects, in hindsight, desperation about early-colonial epidemics and defeats.

One day they sacrificed one of [Paria Caca's] llamas, a llama named Yauri Huanaca.

When those thirty [priests] examined the heart and entrails of the llama, one of the thirty, a fellow called Quita Pariasca the Mountain Man, spoke up and said, "Alas, brothers, the world is not good! In coming times our father Paria Caca will be abandoned."

"No," the others retorted, "you're talking nonsense!"

"It's a good augury!"

"What do you know?"

One of them called out, "Hey, Quita Pariasca! What makes you think that? In these llama innards our father Paria Caca is foretelling something wonderful!"

But at the time he said that, the mountaineer hadn't even approached the llama to inspect its innards. He had prophesied so just by watching from afar.

The mountaineer spoke out and rebuked them: "It's Paria Caca himself who says it, brothers."

Then they derided Quita Pariasca with spiteful words:

"That smelly mountain man, what could he know?"

"Our father Paria Caca has subjects as far away as the limits of the land called Chinchay Suyo. Could such a power ever fall desolate?"

"What does a guy like that know?"

They talked in great anger.

But just a very few days after the day when he'd said these things, they heard someone say, "Vira Cochas have appeared in Caxa Marca!"

A certain man who was also from Checa, named Tama Lliuya Casa Lliuya, a member of the Caca Sica *ayllu*, is known to have dwelt as one of Paria Caca's retainers.

At that time, they say, there were thirty priests at Paria Caca and this Casa Lliuya Tama Lliuya was the eldest of them all.

When the Vira Cochas, the Spaniards, arrived there, they kept asking insistently, "What about this *huaca*'s silver and garments?"

But the thirty refused to reveal anything.

Because they did, the Spanish Vira Cochas got furious, and, ordering some straw piled up, they burned Casa Lliuya.

When half the straw had burned, the wind began to blow it away.

And so although this man suffered horribly, he did survive.

But by that time the others had handed the clothing and the rest of the things over to the Spaniards.

It was then that all the men said, "Very truly indeed were we warned by this mountain man Quita Pariasca!"

"Brothers, let's go away, let's disband."

"The world is no longer good," they said. And so they dispersed, each going back to his own village.

When the burned man from Checa healed up, he arrived at a village called

Limca in the territory of the Quinti, carrying along a child of Paria Caca named Maca Uisa.[12]

The story is not a counsel of despair. On the contrary, it – like much of the "Indian history" submerged in the convert editor's "history of Indians" – carries a muffled message of cultural revitalization. The text goes on to tell how Quita Pariasca, by rescuing a *huaca*, brought prosperity to those who carried on cult clandestinely.

Even though some of the people mentioned can be firmly correlated to exterior documents of the period, the chronology of the Huarochirí mythology is hard to assess. The editor or redactor has spliced together data of several time strata to project a fake simultaneity. Remembrances of antiquity share pages with descriptions of priestly law and ritual as practiced in early colonial times and even with reports of contemporary clandestine practice circa 1600. The manipulative editing seems designed to make certain people alive in 1608 look as unambiguously "idolatrous" as possible.

But even if the sources had been spared such manipulation, they would not have embodied a view of diachrony much like that of European historians. The tellers were not chiefly interested in compiling a chain of human causes for human events. Rather, their main preoccupations were "mythohistoric": They developed a view of time in which the ancestry of living people connected, by a seamless genealogical web, to mummified "ancients," to *huaca*s, thence to deified features of the landscape, and finally to forces of the cosmos itself. To speak of change and genealogy was not a matter of tracing past cause and effect but of mapping out hierarchies of power and sacredness upon a unified pattern that both humanity and nature exemplified.

Ecclesiastical governance like secular governance embedded thousands of other, less massive, native testimonies into administrative papers and lawsuits. The most celebrated are trial records from the "extirpation" campaigns that followed on Avila's spectacular 1607–1608 exposé about Huarochirí. During several discontinuous campaigns, the last large one being that of the 1660s, squads of Jesuit-trained persecutors wrung origin stories and ancestor-cult data from provincial natives of Lima Archdiocese and, less commonly, other areas. Sporadic persecutions continued past 1700.

"Extirpating judges" learned to pick vulnerable witnesses first. By blackmailing them, or by exploiting their political ambitions and medical

---

[12] *The Huarochirí manuscript, a testament of ancient and colonial Andean religion*, Frank Salomon and George Urioste, trans. (Austin, 1991), 96–98.

problems, they wrung out secret denunciations. "Extirpators" then captured priests or even humble devotees of clandestine cults. Confession by torture was frequent and legal. The accused typically included local officiants and priestesses of sacred mountains or other place deities, as well as curators of ancestor mummies preserved in caves or "houses of the dead." There existed, so clerical experts wrote, hierarchies of "ministers," "masters," "priests," and "preachers" dedicated to upholding the faith of the *huaca*s during the age of coercive evangelism.

Despite the deformation caused by coercion and the requirement that witnesses explain their culture under the rubric of Satanic deception, "extirpation" trials contain the fullest accounts of ritual and even of visionary experience posterior to the Huarochirí manuscript. They are also one of the few sources rich in information about Andean women as religious actors.

Extirpation records make it clear that remembering what Lima-area natives took to be their history was a main feature of non-Christian worship. In the mid-seventeenth century, over 120 years after the Spanish invasion, a clandestine but major ritual in the town of San Pedro de Hacas evoked public recitations of the deeds of ancestors. Hernando Hacas Poma said that as "indoctrinator" of those who remained faithful to the *huaca*s, he organized nighttime rituals during the Christian festivals of Saint Peter and Corpus Christi. Celebrants were careful to assure the *huaca*s that despite the daytime rites of the Saints, the festival really honored them.

And this witness [Hacas Poma] and the other old men would pour out a little coca in the plaza and on the night of the festival day, they would perform the *vecochina*, which means that all the local kindreds and residential sectors would go forth, with the priests and ministers of idols in the lead, and the old ladies who accompanied them with small drums would beat them along all the streets, singing chants [*cantares*] and dance-songs of remembrance [*taquies*] in their language and in their ancient style. [They would] recount the stories and ancient deeds of their mummies and their *huaca*s, and entering into the houses of the standardbearer[s] of the sodalities, they would drink and get drunk. Until sunrise they continued in these exercises, engaging in contests and team matches between one residential sector and another, without sleeping the whole night through. According to this superstitious belief, the sector or team that fell asleep first, lost, and would suffer affronts about not knowing how to worship their idols right. The team that didn't sleep would carry off the victory and enjoy high regard, because this was the rite and the ceremony of their paganism.[13]

[13] *Cultura andina y represión. Procesos y visitas de idolatrías y hechicerías, Cajatambo, siglo XVII*, Pierre Duviols, ed. (Cusco, 1986), 227.

What was the content of *vecochina* recitals? We do not have a full text, but some of the "extirpators" left detailed notes on the genealogies, which perhaps made up the implicit frame of the songs of remembrance. When Hernando Rodríguez Príncipe visited the Allauca "hundred" of Recuay, he succeeded in recording a coordinated genealogy of ancestors and *huaca*s. A small part reads:

The *visitador* [inspector] spent ten days stuck in a shack under the inclemencies of winter's harshness and the frigid climate without these stubborn people's being moved to declare the main *huaca* which they have hidden there, whose heirs and first possessors are the following:

Choque Cochachin, whom they falsely claim to be the first who came from Yaro Titicaca, made his mansion in this Allauca. He had as sons Chuchu Lliviac, Hanampa Lliviac, Machacuay, with whom paganism expired. His sons Juan Ympe and the father of Don Francisco Machacuay, Juan Bautista, Juan Chuquis, and the other consultants [i.e., officiants of *huaca* cults] entered into Christianity.

These had as their main *huaca* Carachuco, an idol of vermillion stone with hands and feet and features representing Lightning, whose children these [people] falsely claim to be. Deceived by the demon, they have hidden him with all his instruments, costumes, and subaltern idols.[14]

After such researches, "extirpators" punished *huaca*-worshipers with whippings, exile, or the galleys and with public burning of the mummies and their sacred paraphernalia. Trials that led to the burning of ancestor mummies have a particular importance in understanding the transformation of native understandings of the past because in them a central mnemonic system was consumed. (Not that burning always led to forgetfulness; sometimes the ashes were gathered to make a special kind of holy object called a "burned father.")

The renown of "extirpation" sources obscures other types of canon-law proceedings, which also preserve native voices: trials of priests accused of misconduct by native parishioners, "visits" of inspection to parishes, suits in which natives demand reorganizations to accommodate their agropastoral systems, disputes about payments for the making of ritual objects, records of appointment to civil-religious hierarchies, and many other sorts of grass-roots paperwork.

Only in the viceroyalty of Peru did the church undertake systemati-

---

[14] *Cultura andina y represión. Procesos y visitas de idolatrías y hechicerías, Cajatambo, siglo XVII*, Pierre Duviols, ed. (Cusco, 1986), 494.

cally to record "diabolical deceptions," that is, native cults and beliefs. From the period of the extirpations onward, however, many other parts of South America have a relatively copious record of missionary sources. These include Jesuit Annual Letters and field reports, draft catechisms and vocabularies in diverse languages, regimens for compressing tropical forest societies into mission villages, biographical testimonies about missionaries, and papers concerning disputes among rival orders. Despite considerable progress in archival organization and publication (particularly the outstanding series *Monumenta Amazonica*), the literature about colonial concepts of the past in such mission frontiers as Amazonia, Paraguay, the Orinoco, or the Venezuelan-Colombian *llanos* remains scarce.

All such literature presents tricky critical problems. It is never easy, and rarely even possible, to separate originally South American models of the past from those adapted to Christianity, or (a less studied possibility) composed in apologetic reaction to it. In colonial America, there was no way a religion could become a text except by answering the discourse of Christendom. Because Christians understood the activity of the superhuman to be precisely a historical kind of action – the drama of creation, fall, salvation, and *eschaton* – those who recorded American testimony utilized salvation history as the unconscious or conscious matrix of their enterprise. In the sixteenth and seventeenth centuries, it was a common opinion among learned people that pagan beliefs, though confused by diabolic deception, had a fundament referring back to humanity's true (i.e., biblical) history. Reconciling elements of the folk past to biblical history by comparison and extrapolation (e.g., by seeking synchronisms and verbal likenesses with Hebrew antiquity) was seen as the way to recuperate whatever truth value the beliefs of Americans held. To the degree that priests, converts, and native lay writers considered paganism worth studying at all, they could not help but produce bibles of paganism.

It is, however, far from certain that generic biblicizing was simply a matter of the "colonization of the imaginary" (as Gruzinski calls it). Bible-like narrative strategies, such as a continuous structure uniting cosmogony to miraculous deeds of mythic founders, then to legendary human events, and finally to historic transformations in recent time, may have been invented more than once. Not all human-divine histories are necessarily consequences of a unique historiographic Big Bang in the ancient Near East. Terence Turner has argued that the mythic-cum-historical form of consciousness conspicuous in the Huarochirí manuscript may arise anytime a partly self-sufficient society is perceived by its own people as "relatively incomplete, because part of a larger imperial or other form of inter-ethnic political system," and therefore subject to partly self-made, but partly imponderable and mysterious, mutation. Whether literacy, or confrontation between discrepant theories of society, are necessary conditions to the development of what might be called generic bibles, remains as a research area uncharted in South America. If it were to be shown that the development of bible-like architecture in synthesized mythology and memory occurs as endogenous process in America, one could interpret in a new way the "native chroniclers'" insistence that before 1492 natives had already attained the equivalent of biblical revelation.

Beyond the Andean region, it is harder still to recapture "Indian history," even where missionary authors did penetrate. In most jungle and grassland areas, the lethal politics of conquest, and the crushing paternalism of missions where no native could aspire to leadership, prevented the emergence of that stratum of *ladino* (bicultural) mediators which elsewhere spoke for the church and state within native society and vice versa. It was this stratum that in the Andes gave rise to routine native paperwork, and which occasionally produced dissident native chroniclers able to report nonroutine ideas.

To some degree the Jesuit missions in Paraguayan Guaraní lands constituted an exception. Jesuit teaching did bring many Guaraníans to literacy. Paraguayan Guaraníes under Jesuit mission rule convened village councils responsible for several kinds of documentation. No Guaranían historical text is now known, but Melià and others have recovered council documents in which Guaraní Christians report abuses suffered in the recent past, denounce attacks on priests by neighboring "infidels," and, toward the end of the mission era, defend century-old villages threatened by a 1750 land cession to Portugal. Lienhard has studied seven 1753 letters from Guaraní mission notables denouncing the handover. Their texts, though influenced and perhaps even edited by Jesuits, nonetheless voice what was apparently a widely felt native sentiment: that Guaraní Christendom arose from an endogenous sacred history, and therefore constituted not just a neophyte group but a nation contributing in its own right to salvation history. One of the Guaraní letters, which Jesuits presented in Spanish, came from Nicolás Ñenguiru of La Concepción mission:

Sir, listen to the true words of these our children: in this same way they speak to us [the mission village council]. They say: "In the old times, our holy father named Roque González de Santa Cruz, after he came to our land, showing us God's being and the Christian way of being [*sic*]. By our own will alone we gave ourselves, to God in the first place, and afterward also to our king, so he would always be our protector. Only for this reason do we subject and humiliate ourselves: and this too is something we choose to do. . . . With our hands alone have we worked and improved this land. Neither the Portuguese nor any Spaniard have given us anything."[15]

Guaranían letters afford a glimpse of how colonial process often engenders "new peoples" with distinctive views of history. Unfortunately their authors' cause was lost, resistance being crushed by 1756, and the victims eventually peonized. Other examples of Guaranían-related colonial drama and polemic exist, but the expulsion of the Jesuits (1759 from Brazil and 1767 from Spanish domains) attenuated native access to literate traditions at least as much as did the repression of the Andean rebellions in the viceroyalty of Peru slightly later. By 1800, Paraguayan Guaraní villagers were struggling merely to place a few of their own would-be teachers in local secondary schools.

NATIVE CHRONICLERS AND NATIVE HISTORICAL ENQUIRY

For a short time, coinciding with part of Spain's "golden century" of literature, Andean society produced a spurt of dissident native historiography. These "native chroniclers," unlike their predecessors, consciously intended an "Indian history" that would not only challenge the "history of Indians" but explain Europe within "Indian history." All the same, they were not neo-traditionalists. On the contrary, they meant to learn and subsume European literary forms, epistolary and poetic as well as historiographic. They meant to reframe Andean tradition in the context of what were then controversies of European modernity. The earliest such work, Titu Cusi Yupanqui's 1570 *Relación de la conquista del Perú*, already constitutes a radical reworking of Inka tradition. The author, a scion of an Inka line that had fought on against Spanish rule for 40 years from a redoubt at Vilcabamba, prepared his history in support of a project for negotiated peace and permanent recognition of Inka royalty. Its actual composition was probably molded by the author's Catholic

---

[15] *Testimonios, cartas, y manifiestos indígenas*, Martin Lienhard, ed. (Caracas, 1992), 333.

confessor and his scribe. Nonetheless Titu Cusi's text has points of unique interest. For one, it is a clear manifesto of resistance in form as well as content; unlike papers written *for* natives, it firmly seizes the authorial role of protagonist. For another, Lienhard suggests, "it seems like a written 'script' of a *qaylli*, a ritual homage to an Inka," namely, the author's mummified father, who had led the first anti-Spanish resistance. Titu Cusi's narrative contains an early version of a tradition that diffused all over the Andes and that twentieth-century tellers, perhaps influenced by re-oralized stories from published versions, still adduce to explain Quechua alienation from official media:

My uncle [the Inka sovereign] Ataguallpa ... received [the Spanish] very well, and when he gave one of them a drink of the drink we use, in a golden beaker, the Spaniard as he received it from his hand, poured it on the ground, because of which my uncle became very angry. . . . The [Spanish] showed my uncle a letter or book or some such, I don't know what, saying that it was the *quillca* [drawing, inscription] of God and the King, and my uncle, since he felt offended about the spilling of the *chicha*, which is what our drink is called, took the letter or whatever it was, and threw it away, saying "What do I know about what you give me? Get going, leave."[16]

The Titu Cusi account, a crucial chapter in how Inka nobles gained command of European historiographic discourse for their own purposes, is nonetheless misleading as a sample of Andean historic discourse. (Note, for example, the false exoticism of the '*chicha*' gloss. *Chicha* is not an Andean word but a possibly Arawakan one introduced by Spaniards arriving from the Caribbean.)

Only one Andean history book attained enough influence to shape the dominant "history of Indians." It did so by canonizing a privileged "Indian history" – that of certain royal Cusco lineages – as equal in worth to European histories of kingdoms. Garcilaso Inca de la Vega, born in Cusco in 1539 of a conquistador father and a royal Inka mother, published in 1609 the first part of the *Royal Commentaries of the Incas*. In some of the "golden century's" most seductive prose, the half-Inka Garcilaso purported to record what he had learned as a youth among other children of the newly converted Inka royalty. His predominant ideological effort, the vindication of Inka descent as a noble title equal in worth to European ones, fought in vain the increasingly anti-Inka tenor of decrees from Spain. But his lavish idealizations of Inka rule as an age of

[16] Titu Cusi Yupanqui's *Relación de la conquista del Perú* (Lima, 1973), 15–16.

wisdom and social justice were to grow in European influence through the eighteenth century, when, taken up by Voltaire and many lesser critics of the *ancien régime*, the Inka acquired a utopian halo. Garcilaso retains primary interest for study of Inka historical thought, less for factual verity than because he expressed, and powerfully perpetuated, the historical opinions of a colonial Inka stratum persisting with declining wealth and power but great local prestige until 1780.

We know Garcilaso was not completely unique because he incorporated and acknowledged sections of a manuscript by another gifted half-Inka researcher, Blas Valera. Valera's original manuscript was lost in a British maritime bombardment. He seems to have shared Garcilaso's political viewpoint. His image of Inka tribute extraction, for example, is a pointed attempt to shame Spaniards about abuses postdating the Toledan reforms:

> The burden of the tributes imposed by the [Inka] kings was so light that what we are about to say may well appear to the reader to have been written in jest. Yet, not content or satisfied with all these things, the Inkas distributed all that was needful for clothes and food with abundant liberality and gave away many other gifts not only to lords and nobles but also to taxpayers and the poor. They might therefore more properly be called diligent fathers of families or careful stewards than kings, and this gave rise to the title *Cápac Titu* which the Indians applied to them. *Cápac* is 'a prince powerful in wealth and greatness' and *titu* means 'a liberal, magnanimous prince, august demi-god.' This is also the reason why the kings of Peru were so beloved by their vassals that even today the Indians, though converted to Christianity, do not forget them, but rather call upon them in turn by their names with weeping and wailing, cries and shouts, whenever they are in trouble or need.[17]

The claim that Inka tribute was a light burden does not survive study of *visitas* in which ex-subjects of Inka rule explained their former obligations.

A third half-Inka history of perhaps equal importance was written in Quito, by the mestizo priest Diego Lobato de Sosa (similarly born of a royal Inka mother). He testified at a hearing in 1600 that he had been interviewing many aboriginal and Inka veterans of the Inka wars in what is now Ecuador, and was working on a book about Inka conquests in the north. The manuscript has not yet been found.

The fully Andean "native chroniclers" of the early seventeenth century

---

[17] Garcilaso Inca de la Vega, *Royal commentaries of the Incas* [1609], Harold Livermore, ed. (Austin, 1966), Vol. 1, 266.

never won such influence. Felipe Guaman Poma de Ayala and Juan de Santacruz Pachacuti Yamqui Salcamaygua both were native nobles who learned under monastic influences to write Spanish and Quechua. Their astonishing works are in some respects apologia for provincial native dynasties, never fully reconciled to Inka rule and now threatened as well by post-Toledan demotion of ethnic nobility.

Losing a lawsuit (recently published) was the experience that moved Guaman Poma to expand his concept of writing-as-vindication from litigation, to "Indian history," to a world history built around the Indies, and finally to metahistorical prophecy. Both writers, Guaman Poma and Pachacuti Yamqui, felt their families' pre-Inka roots linked them with the primordial virtues of golden or revelatory ages imagined in Joachinist metahistories. Indeed, they justified non-Inka Andean culture by arguing that it had status parallel to that of Hebrews. They seek to organize American epochs in stages paralleling contemporary models of "universal history," the better to liken their titles to those of European nobility. But at the same time, as Adorno has shown, these authors courageously challenged Christendom's failures in America with polemics and stinging satire. Guaman Poma warned that Christendom's failure to bind the parallel New and Old World parts of human history into a just world order condemned it to an apocalyptic retribution.

In no sense, then, were "native chroniclers" living fossils of preconversion intellectuality. Nonetheless, even after cautiously observing their engagement with contemporaneity, no reader can fail to be amazed by the detail and variety of colonial Andean folk history these writers recorded.

Guaman Poma's vast (1,100-page) *New Chronicle and Good Government of Peru* contains a detailed account of Inka-era social organization. It is unique for its over 300 drawings (see pp. 781, 813, 829, 837) and for its provincial's-eye viewpoint. Guaman Poma retells the lore of his "Yarovilca Allauca Huánuco" ancestors as well as giving an exceptionally full Inka history notable for its coverage of Inka 'queens' (*coyas*) and 'princesses' (*ñustas*). He did not live to see his work read much. He was considered an eccentric and troublemaker in his own time, and when, in impoverished old age, he brought his *New Chronicle and Good Government of Peru* (probably finished in 1613 or 1615) to Lima, no Spanish official endorsed it. It gathered dust unread until 1908, when Richard Pietschmann found it in the Royal Library of Copenhagen.

Guaman Poma believed all humanity derived from Adam and Eve but had divided into Old and New Worlds streams. The two human histories ran in parallel in mutual ignorance through four numbered "ages" of increasing sophistication and declining moral stature. The American Fourth Age was:

AUCA RUNA ['Warlike People']. Of this fourth age of Indians called Auca Pacha Runa ['Warlike Age People'], descendants of Noah and of his progeny, of Uari Uiracocha Runa ['Ancient Uiracocha people', the first age] and of Uari Runa ['Ancient People', the second age] and of Puron Runa ['Desolation People', the third age]:

These people lasted and multiplied for two thousand one hundred years. These Indians went forth and emptied their population out of the good sites, for fear of war and insurrection and the conflicts they had among themselves.

From their lowland towns they went to settle on the heights and hills and cliffs and to defend themselves and they began to make fortresses with they call [*sic*] *pucara*. They built walls and fences and inside them houses and fortresses and hiding places and wells to get drinking water . . .

And they had a lot of gold and silver. . . .

And they became great captains and valiant princes from valor alone. They say they turned into lions and tigers and foxes and buzzards and hawks and wildcats in battle.[18]

America's Age of Warlike People corresponded to the Fourth Age of Old World antiquity:

FOURTH AGE OF THE WORLD since King David. . . . In this age many kings rose up in rebellion and many lords and they multiplied and many people in the world [*sic*]. And in this time they entered into civilization, both in justice as in government and office, technique and mechanical work, and they obtained much capital and wealth and they went out to look for gold, silver, and they began to attack each other in greed for wealth.

They left what is good, entered into the evil of the world.[19]

Inka dominion appeared to Guaman Poma a tyrannical interlude (fortunately, one he chose to describe in intricate detail) and not a Fifth

---

[18] Felipe Guaman Poma de Ayala, *Nueva corónica y buen gobierno* [1615], John V. Murra, Rolena Adorno, and Jorge Urioste, eds. (México D.F., 1980) Vol. 1, 51–61.
[19] Felipe Guaman Poma de Ayala, *Nueva corónica y buen gobierno* [1615], John V. Murra, Rolena Adorno, and Jorge Urioste, eds. (México D.F., 1980) Vol. 1, 22–23.

Age. Christianity, the true Fifth Age, was destined to reunite the halves of world history and lead it toward its *eschaton*.

But because Spain had botched the task by oppressing Indians and denying the rights due their ancient nobility, the impending climax of history would take the form of a cataclysmic punishment. In prose and in drawings, the "Good Government" contains vitriolic attacks on abuses in conquest-era government: A Spanish lady bashes her native servant-girl with a flatiron, a priest ships his bastard babies off to Lima by the mule-load. Native lords get drunk with Spanish racketeers and half-breed criminals, then connive in the abuse of native women. Viceregal officials pillage the king's possessions. In old age, almost crazed with the weight of his witnessing, Guaman Poma cast himself as a messianic figure. In his autobiographical chapter, "The Author Walks," he becomes a charismatic wanderer leading "the Poor of Christ" toward a confrontation with injustice. He thought the act of writing his book and conveying it to the king and Holy Roman Emperor would itself hasten a climactic transformation.

Is Guaman Poma's stagewise history an Andean model? His way of dividing time shows clear affinities to Inka ways of dividing space, which he did use in trying to organize the suddenly doubled geography of humankind. One of his maps proves that he thought of "Castile" and "The Indies" as respectively the lower and upper moieties of a world space organized in ranked halves, just as the idealized territory of the Inka capital had been. But where temporal, as opposed to spatial, organization is concerned, the question becomes complicated. Innumerable New World peoples share the idea that time is filled by successive worlds, and in one form or another this notion crops up in Andean ethnographies. But Guaman Poma also had ample opportunity to learn European stagewise historical models. The idea of measuring historic teleology against the succession of bad and worse empires had roots as ancient as Hebrew prophecy (the Book of Daniel was a source popular among learned Europeans). Such ideas throve among European intellectuals circa 1600, and not just in America. Nor was Guaman Poma the first to modify five-age schemes making room for peoples of the New World, although the particular ethno-prehistory with which he fills the ages does appear unique.

If Guaman Poma departs from what was then a popular current among historians, it is not so much in the stagewise form of his argument, or in the postulate of periodic world-transforming cataclysms, which he calls *pachacutis* (*pacha kuti*, 'turn of space/time'), as in the supreme value he sets on Amerindians' role in universal history. Guaman Poma may have shared with a native elite his vision of South American antiquity as being equal in unrecognized worth and glory to the Old World – as being in fact the complement on whose vindication the world's salvation waited. Certainly his book has close affinities to that of his contemporary and fellow native chronicler, Juan de Santa Cruz Pachacuti Yamqui Salcamaygua, and less conspicuous but important resemblances to the Huarochirí manuscript.

Andean aspirations reconceived in the guise of renaissance teleological history gave these authors occasion to write down enormous amounts of what appear to be orally transmitted memory. Local and Inka genealogy and politics, prehispanic institutions and beliefs, traditional agricultural knowledge, and fragments of what the authors believed to be ancient poetry or song come to life in Guaman Poma's pages and illustrations as nowhere else. It is in this heavy impasto of élite memories and local observations, epithets, and stylized narratives, that native chroniclers seem most native – richest in unfamiliar detail about the past as "the people called Indians" imagined it:

THE TWELFTH COIA [Inka Queen] Chuqui Llanto, *coya*: They say she was many times over beautiful and pale, that she had not a blemish on her body. And in her appearance and very happy [*sic*] and full of song, given to raising little birds. And she had nothing of her own, although her husband was avaricious; from pure avarice he ate half the night through and in the morning woke up with coca leaves in his mouth. . . . [A description of her regalia follows.]

First her husband died, Guascar Ynga. She covered herself completely in mourning. And she died in Yucay at the time of the Christian conquest. And nothing is written of her son nor daughter, legitimate nor bastard, nor did she have any.

And so with this king and queen, *Ynga* and *Coya*, the kings, the *capac apu Ynga*s, came to an end. And she died at 59 years. The sad life of this lady came to an end.[20]

Although Guaman Poma and Pachacuti Yamqui were marginal figures, they stood at the margins of a colonial establishment rich in native-language literacy. During the midcolonial florescence of Quechua, Peru's "general language" (with a dialectological tilt toward Cusco norms) en-

[20] Felipe Guaman Poma de Ayala, *Nueva corónica y buen gobierno* [1615], John V. Murra, Rolena Adorno, and Jorge Urioste, eds. (México D.F., 1980) Vol. I, 120–121.

joyed a literary florescence as well. Regional élites not only heard baroque sermons and devotional poetry in Quechua but also enjoyed plays on Inka themes in Quechua versions of Spanish baroque dramaturgy. The most famous, the drama *Ollantay*, was a perennial favorite. Rivet and Créqui-Montfort's great Quechua-Aymara bibliography lists 139 works containing matter in these languages prior to 1780.

Many researchers have concurred with Rowe in recognizing the recollection of Inka times as a key process in the "Inka national movement," with its search for a revolutionary utopia that might vindicate native nobility and at the same time create a modern Peru equal to challenges Spain could no longer meet (see Chap. 22). Families of Inka nobility, demoted by colonial change and much acculturated, but still venerated by many natives, fed nostalgia with portraits, plays, and processions in ancient regalia. As early as 1667, the government of Quito (Ecuador) panicked over the case of a part-Inka official who unintentionally set off an anticolonial movement by displaying genealogical paintings that seemed to prove connections between local lords and Inka royalty. What makes the case especially telling is the fact that, just before Spanish invasion, the ethnic group in question had all but exhausted Inka armies with its fierce resistance. A century after he wrote them, Garcilaso Inca's *Royal Commentaries* enjoyed unprecedented popularity. Amid this climate, ideologues claiming Inka descent mobilized numerous small but bloodthirsty plebeian revolts (especially in what is now Ecuador) and a few major, broad-based upheavals (in Peru and Bolivia). The key to their ideological success was a program to reverse historic identities. They urged those discontent with the Bourbon regime to crown neo-Inka sovereigns and attack centers of local power. The greatest of these revolts developed innovative multiethnic coalitions around the theme of Inka resurgence. The 1780 Túpac Amaru II rebellion in Peru and the slightly later Catari rebellions in Bolivia could, had they not been suffocated in blood, have marked a decisive turn in the evolution of Quechua-Aymara modernity. Absorbing "history of Indians" and reformulating the problems of Indian servitude as the exemplar of a broader colonial problem, Quechua élites seemed on the verge of developing a version of history broad in reach and yet predominantly indigenous.

But repression proved the more powerful turn. From Cusco, governors tried to stamp out every vehicle of seditious memory: New laws banned Quechua-language publishing, teaching of the tongue, drama on Inka themes, pictures of Inka peoples, and even music for ancient instruments.

Unenforceable at face value, the repressive decrees did expel Andean languages from the orbit of popular literacy. They put an end to Quechua academic life and set American speech into a trajectory as the specialized speech of disenfranchised peasants. The degradation of Quechua to a nonwritten language characteristic of lower peasantries deepened through the succeeding century. In some cities, written Quechua held on as a literary pastime of provincial aristocracies, but explicit "Indian history" was deeply muted.

Partly for this reason, the last years of Iberian dominion, and the Republican era from Bolivarian times to the late nineteenth century, remain difficult intervals for the study of indigenous viewpoints. Although dissident projects within bilingual creole élites occasionally harked back to Inka memories, the grass-roots paperwork of the native majority had to speak, of necessity, the deindigenized political language of a Europhile period. Typical nineteenth-century text production occurred within positively anti-indigenous projects of creole state-building. Enlightened opinion, aspiring to a republic of free individual citizens, saw the persistence of institutionalized *ayllu* corporations as an unacceptable *ancien régime* vestige. Indeed, increasingly racist thinking blamed the shortcomings of the new states on their "burden" of Indian population.

Tristan Platt has argued that when political élites pressed for the elimination of native group rights, because these made "Indian" communities exceptions to the ideal of individual ownership and land commoditization, Andean (especially Bolivian) *kuraka*s mounted a resistance based on the premise of a historic "pact" or "covenant" between *ayllu* and state. They understood traditional practices to imply that communal tribute payment entailed permanent recognition of *ayllu*-based communities. Their protests (which sometimes included a puzzling native insistence on paying colonial taxes from which liberals proposed to "emancipate" them) only rarely smacked of the Inka utopia. More usually, native leaders appealed to detailed legal and moral precedents defining a "moral economy" between *ayllu* and state.

The defense of these positions demanded historical research. Command of old records became ever more pressing as, later in the nineteenth century, latifundist land-grabbers threatened basic livelihoods. Self-defense, then, had much to do with Andean communities' attachment to archival work. Self-taught rural intellectuals developed impressive research skills with or without help from lawyers. Because bilingual urban élites in Cusco and elsewhere tended to monopolize the spotlight in public indigenist fora of the early twentieth century (both local ones saturated with Inka nostalgia, and metropolitan ones tending toward Mexican-style nationalist programs), it is only now becoming possible to recover the work of independent peasant intellectuals. Some belonged to radical organizations like Peru's Tawantinsuyu Association, which both the state and regional élites disfavored; others belonged only to village councils. Clearly, their effort was massive; when twentieth-century legislation in several republics gave communities the option of seeking jural recognition, villagers, sometimes with minimal professional help, tendered document packages including locally preserved titles from the early seventeenth century. Lawsuits remained a constant wellspring of historical inquiry. Up to the present, community leaders – whether dissident *kuraka*s as in Bolivia or the conventional presidents of village councils found all over South America – derive a large share of their legitimacy from the ability to find and safeguard papers that prove the unique truth of communal claims. It is not unusual to hear modern peasants proudly call a trunk of papers in an adobe council house their *magna charta*.

THE "MYTH/HISTORY" DEBATE IN THE STUDY OF
COLONIAL NATIVE TESTIMONY

Given these strata of primary sources, how are researchers to fashion these sources into a history at once intelligible in the non-native orbit, and authentic to native categories? An underlying tension between respect for the "otherness" of "Indian history" (which demands epistemological caution about representing native viewpoints), and recognition of indigenous peoples' "agency" in the making of early modernity (which demands bold synthetic representations), runs through the literature. The period leading up to the Columbian quincentennial brought these imperatives into friction. Faced with both imperatives, South American research worked itself into methodological difficulties.

Merely including the native into a historiography whose overall direction was to chronicle the triumph of Europe did not satisfy Americanists for long. In 1959, Miguel León-Portilla published his project for a "vision of the vanquished" containing the Mesoamerican people's accounts of events as a counterweight to triumphalist historiography. The momentum of native action as a force in making America, the shaking off of a view of Native Americans as historically passive victims, became durably appealing themes in the historiography of resistance. The resistance theme, in tandem with Marxian concentration on production and conflict, underlay path-breaking research on rebellions and inequalities in many societies – for instance, Spalding's early studies on rural Peru or Bengoa's detailed research on Mapuche Chile.

However, resistance history by itself tends to become the mere inverse of triumphalism. Cultural anthropology proposed other paths toward the capture of "vision." Twelve years after León Portilla, Nathan Wachtel gave his pioneering study of Andean folk-historical ideas a pointedly similar title. Putting structuralist techniques at the service of *mentalités* analysis, he proposed to reveal what conquest events looked like when framed by non-European premises. "Vision," of course, was not directly available. The goal rather was to infer past cultural principles of structure, then compare cultural orderings of time and change as they looked prior to conquest, when "destructured" in conquest, and when "restructured" in response to it. The proposed history was in effect that of a cultural logic in dialogue with events; understanding it was to help us make ethnographically grounded sense of otherwise opaque actions.

This cue has proven fruitful. Yet the vertiginous chase after ever-deeper kinds of ethnographic rapport with the past has a tendency to produce prickly evidential paradoxes. The more seriously one entertained differences of "vision" between nonliterate Americans and literate *conquistadores*, the more one had to suspect the written record of falsifying the native experience one sought, and the more complex and epistemologically risky the source-critical or explanatory route became.

This situation has deep roots in intra-anthropological debate about the accessibility of non-European history. From the publication of the *Handbook of South American Indians* through the late 1960s and early 1970s, it was maintained by scholars of otherwise diverse convictions that in certain whole classes of South American societies historical thought simply does not occur, or is too fantastic to be of use for historical "reconstruction." In their 1959 summation of the *Handbook*, Steward and Faron, echoing Lowie's strictures of the 1920s, counseled Amazonianists to content themselves with the same sort of highly generalized, event-less history, which in Africa is associated with the work of George Peter Murdock:

The prehistory of the tropical forest peoples can be reconstructed only in the most inferential and uncertain manner. . . . The Indians lacked a sense of history and took no interest in genealogies. Even those societies whose principal religious activity centered in a cult of the dead were concerned with ancestors in a general sense and not as identifiable individuals. There is no group whose oral history extended back more than one hundred years. The culture history of the tropical-forest people can be inferred only from the distribution of linguistic groups and of cultural features. The linguistic evidence, together with some oral history, permits the reconstruction of certain migrations.[21]

This longstanding North American skepticism about "history of Indians" coincided with a theoretical critique from a different quarter, hostile as well to attempts at "Indian history." For Lévi-Strauss, historicity itself was a local peculiarity of the West. Societies lacking Europe's attachment to change as a source of meaning (its historical "hotness") demanded a form of empathy less captive to time and more similar to the schematisms of mathematics. Lévi-Strauss's 1962 *The Savage Mind* persuaded many that Amazonian narratives, irrespective of narrative tense, used the past only as an idiom and were meaningful rather as repositories of logical relationships among elementary categories. Like the steps in solving an algebraic equation, structuralists suggested, narratives are sequential in form but express a total set of relationships that is simultaneous or timeless. What facts or fictions a historically "cold" narrative uses as tokens is by this argument all but irrelevant both to its local meaning and to its scientific value.

In the resulting debate – the "myth and history" debate – "myth" was usually taken to mean a class of narratives that explain the categorical makeup of the world as it is by referring to a time when the laws of nature did not operate as they do now and categories were labile. In mythic time, prototypical events usually described as ancient (but perhaps outside time altogether, insofar as mythic reality remains accessible through dreams or visions), set the world into a shape on which human events only embroider finite variations. Myth was usually understood as a form of social self-consciousness, that is, a story a society tells about itself in more or less fantastic idiom but with more or less conscious reference to received truths. Relations among mythic beings often compactly and concretely express what more complex societies would express as ideological abstractions.

In this view, myth sets a limit on consciousness: It cannot make culture an object to itself. The mythic outlook, which treats natural beings as cultural (e.g., mythic animals and humans form a single society), in the end clothes cultural forms in seemingly unquestionable, unanswerable naturalness.

Lévi-Strauss developed this view around Amazonian village societies.

---

[21] Julian Steward and Louis Faron, *Native peoples of South America* (New York, 1959), 287.

For students of the state-centered Inka society, however, the native discourse about the past, discussed above, presented challenges both to Lévi-Straussian and to positivistic views. The long debate on the historicity of Inka dynastic tradition as relayed by chroniclers affords an important case study. Until the 1950s, scholarly readings of "Inka history" treated it in parallel to Mediterranean ancient history. Rowe founded an influential "absolute chronology in the Andean area" (1945) on a reading of Inka dynastic lore as chronicling in a European-like sense.

The structuralist critique of "straight" historicism in the Andean orbit was in large part the work of R. T. Zuidema. Grounded in the Dutch structuralism of de Jong, and concerned much more than Lévi-Strauss with the consciously elaborated use of kinship and categorical models, Zuidema argued that the seemingly historical texture of Inka discourse as presented by Spanish authors is wholly misleading.

A roughly standardized list of Inka names, which the Spanish understood as a royal succession list, forms the armature of most Spanish renderings of "Inka history." But, Zuidema argued, what the Spanish took to be a chronological series of Inka rulers was actually something quite different: a finite set of titles in fixed hierarchical relation, each of which was occupied at successive times by different individuals. The deeds attributed to the respective names are not unique historical events but archetypes associated with their structural positions. The order this schema described was not diachronic at all. "History" was an elaborate temporal metaphor for the synchronic array of rank in the Inka capital of Cusco. Relative antiquity was a trope for relative standing in a unified schema of ritual kinship. Given this reading, seemingly individualistic images, like that of Chuqui Llanto quoted from Guaman Poma earlier, become attributes of structural positions in a static scheme; any person occupying Chuqui Llanto's position in society would have been described as a person with these traits.

Today such schemes of "positional succession" are not especially mysterious, having been documented in Africa, but Spaniards with views fixed on the historicist horizon of the sixteenth century could not find any terms faithful to the Inka concept. Zuidema concluded:

Given this situation, I would consider the whole of Inka history up to the time of the Spanish conquest, and even to a certain extent beyond, as mythological. Inka "history" then, integrated religious, calendrical, ritual, and remembered facts into one ideological system, which was hierarchical in terms of space and time. This Inkaic hierarchical ideology should not be confused with the Western linear conception of history imposed by the Spanish. . . . An historical chronology up to the Spanish conquest will have to be established independently by archaeology.[22]

In structuralism, the observation that seemingly historic discourse often expresses the logic of an ahistorical model of social structure went along – in what now seems a non sequitur – with a tendency to see such ideal structures as inherently more enduring than their merely behavioral instantiations. Modern narratives and ideal renderings of social organization – for example, village social structures observed in the 1960s – were taken as reincarnations of models from the Andean past, which held essentially constant and constituted "The Andean" (*lo andino*). Modern Peruvian tradition, too, was analyzed as reprocessing such pre-Inka basics as endogamous moiety ideology and the fourfold partitioning of space and time.

The structuralist project was criticized by Marxists and by non-Marxist historicists as reinstating in new terms an old indigenist fallacy: the image of the Indian whose culture, bound by "unchanging tradition" intrinsically repels change in a way that "modern" culture does not. From 1980 to 1990, convulsive historical transformations – especially local Shining Path and village militia warfare in the same Ayacucho villages that had so recently been the forge of structuralist research – cast a deep shadow over any such rendering.

The heirs of first-generation structuralism sought to revise structure as an image of intelligible change – in fact, as "Indian history." In the Andes as in many other quarters (most notably Oceania), ritual came to be reinterpreted as history-making, not history-defying, action. Native sources were reread no longer as sources about what happened before writing was learned, but as sources about how Andeans reorganized the lore of prehispanic origins in the course of dealing with the colonial situation.

An Andean case study, Urton's 1990 *The History of a Myth*, argues that the reason a certain village, Pacariqtambo, is today considered the origin shrine of the Inka is that on an identifiable occasion – a judicial hearing in 1569 – an Andean noble, Don Rodrigo Sutiq Callapiña, persuasively "concretized" a preexisting Inka origin myth in terms of local geographical detail. Increasingly, even the most abstract or ritualistic

[22] R. Tom Zuidema, "Myth and history in ancient Peru," in *The logic of culture*, Ino Rossi, ed. (South Hadley, Mass., 1982), 173–174.

schemes of Inka culture are understood as realized in the logic of practical action. For example, the *ceque* system of Cusco, an Inka schema coordinating kinship corporations to a ranked ensemble of shrines aligned on lines from the sacred center, can now be partly understood in relation to practical projects – historical facts in the usual sense – such as the administration of Cusco's irrigation infrastructure.

The advancing debate about structuralism had the effect of undercutting the original stage on which it began. The original ground for skepticism about the chances for knowing native history was a seemingly clear distinction between historical and unhistorical views of the past. But the main casualty of debate was not the idea of "Indian history". It was the myth/history antithesis itself.

In the overwhelming bulk of printed literature on South America, most of what South Americans are reported as saying about the past is said in what appears as a strongly mythic idiom. Especially where Amazonia is concerned, for every native text about "history" in the sense of human causation, one can easily find ten texts about miraculous origins of institutions, landscape features, human inequalities, and so on. Yet by the 1970s, for many reasons both theoretical and political, it was no longer defensible to assume that native collectivities had arrived in modernity by sleepwalking through history. It became incumbent to explain how the cultures that produced these discourses had interpreted and faced human transformations.

A 1988 collection of South Americanist comment on the debate, *Rethinking History and Myth*, takes as its point of departure two assumptions: that regardless of genre variation and the binding of memory into idealized social patterns, changing contingency elicits and informs every performance of tradition. None is in principle ahistoric. Second, the common myth/history distinction in regard to genre analysis rests on ethnocentric suppositions. The contributors generally retain an analytical distinction between myth and history but do not purport to find the two as separate facts in the real world. Myth is defined as discourse that gives priority to structure, and which guarantees (in Hill's words) that "relations of contrast and difference of major social importance will not be forgotten." History "gives greater weighting to agency and social action in the present, which is informed by knowledge of past times that are qualitatively the same as the present. . . . Historical consciousness includes a sense of the indeterminate and processual nature of one's own social order." But the difference between the two modes is only "a

relative contrast between complementary ways of interpreting social processes." They inform each other reciprocally. In nonliterate societies, the
telling of the past is radically elliptical; history is understood in relation
to a few crucial moments of rapid change, with little attention to the
idea of constantly chronicled time. But these archetypal moments frame
the world of the possible when real choices are taken.[23]

The effort to develop ethnohistories in the strict sense – that is,
"Indian histories" as opposed to "histories of Indians" – now concentrates in good measure on efforts to transcend habitual dichotomies like
"myth" versus "history," and to imagine how human continuity appeared when memories were grouped under less familiar premises. Today
one must take local categories of genre and the internal properties of
narratives – not imported dichotomies like myth/history – as the points
of departure. In their studies of the Tupinamba as described by early-
colonial Europeans, Manuela Carneiro da Cunha and Eduardo Viveiros
de Castro have developed a nonmythological model around a problem
no less classic than Inka succession: Tupinamba cannibalism, as observed
on the Brazilian coast early in the sixteenth century (see pp. 109–121).
Tupinamba communities engaged constantly in warfare and in gatherings
to remember peers killed by enemies. For Carneiro and Viveiros, revenge
raids were not a matter of restoring prior integrity to society but one of
constituting society in the first place. No other institution *but* war located
past, present, and future in an intelligible world of change. The Tupinamba lacked lineages, ceremonial groupings, prescriptive marriage rules
or inherited names and ranks. Instead, they ordered action over time
through the "eternal perpetuation" of combat. Warriors vindicated their
group's dead by taking captives, incorporating and even glorifying enemy
warriors, then killing and eating them so as to restore honor – and so as
to garner the enmity of others, which was itself the sine qua non of
intelligible social action. Only raiding built up continuity of action and
infused social action with meaning over time. "It is vengeance which
alone connects those who have lived (and died) and those who will live
(to die). . . . The memory of each group, its very future is achieved
through its enemies."[24]

---

[23] Jonathan D. Hill, "Introduction: Myth and History," in *Rethinking history and myth*, Jonathan
D. Hill, ed. (Champaign, Ill., 1988), 1–17.
[24] Manuela Carneiro da Cunha and Eduardo Viveiros de Castro, "Vingança e temporalidade,"
Journal de la Société des Américanistes 71 (1985), 191–208.

THE HISTORICAL DIMENSION IN ETHNOGRAPHIES AND
EX-ORAL BOOK GENRES

Heightened debate about whether native South American testimony belonged in any genre category similar to history coincided with debate
elsewhere about the genre properties of history itself. Throughout the
1980s, critics aligned with Hayden White argued that regardless of who
sets about interpreting the past – European or Indian – the processual
reality called "history" is in any case no more objectively "real" than the
genre vessels within which the teller opts to construct it.[25] By prioritizing
study of rules of "emplotment" and conventions of narrative authority,
literary criticism made of history, as Stephen Bann said, a "reverse emperor" whose purported factual nudity can never be glimpsed because we
know him only through his poetic dress anyway.[26]

This debate suggests that the apparent paucity of historic testimony in
South American lore may be due to specific Euro-American disabilities
in recognizing South American ways of referring to past human action.
Until conscious regard for the South American "poetics" of history
entered, historians were ill-equipped even to recognize the local genre
vessels of "past-discourse". Academic conventions for studying "tribes"
undergeneralized South American interest in historic change at least as
much as renaissance historicism in the seventeenth-century Andes over-
generalized it.

Yet, paradoxically renaissance historicism and modern studies of "oral
tradition" or "folklore" sent remarkably similar products to the scholarly
marketplace. In modern scholarship, testimonies individually edited as
myths, folktales, or traditional stories are rarely left to stand in unhistorical simultaneity. Instead, compilers recompose "historyless" texts into
editorial wholes with bible-like plot lines almost entirely parallel to the
bibles of paganism that dominated seventeenth-century historiography in
the Andes.

When Susan Niles in 1981 published her annotated bibliography,
South American Indian Narrative, she found 651 substantial sources. Had
she set criteria more inclusive of colonial writings, the list would have

---

[25] Hayden White, *Metahistory: The historical imagination in nineteenth-century Europe* (Baltimore, 1973).
[26] Stephen Bann, *The clothing of Clio: A study of the representation of history in nineteenth-century Britain and France* (Cambridge, England, 1984).

been much longer. Clearly the connection between literacy and the oral traditions of South America is by no means slight. Yet only a few of these volumes contain any narratives of history in the sense of narratives about change as a humanly made phenomenon. Almost all restrict themselves to material neatly bounded by the definition of myth as narrative of prototypical events in a primordial time. Is this because South Americans are "cold" to history, or because researchers were "cold" to South American history?

Biased genre preferences play a part. Certain local genres expressive of historic concerns in the Western sense tend to be omitted because they seem banal or incoherent to outsiders. For example, ethnographers in the Andean highlands have recorded innumerable folk narratives about deified land features but hardly any of the narratives about secular change like price fluctuations and the physical form and value of currency, or the succession of claims on disputed lands. The latter are in fact much more common and central areas of discourse than are "mythic" stories as such.

Similarly, in lowland societies, narratives of village fission, war, and migration express a microscopic historicism reminiscent of that "little history" Rosaldo considers the core of Philippine Ilongot consciousness.[27] These texts usually interest ethnographers less than do myths of origin. War stories – for example, the war tale Harald Schultz collected among the central-Brazilian Waurá – seem to be a separately important genre from stories about sacred or superhuman beings in many tropical forest societies. Indeed, a Brazilian Xavante, Carlos Wahubtedewa, told Salesian researchers that one of the purposes of war is to propagate stories:

When only a few of the [enemy] were left, [the Xavante] began to shout "If they get finished off like this, nobody will tell the story about them!" So the [Xavante] let some of them escape, because if they had all died, nobody would ever have heard what happened to them.[28]

War stories seem particularly well documented in the Orinoco and Roraima basins of northern South America. Im Thurn printed some in 1883, and Reverend William Henry Brett, in an 1879 book of legends

[27] Renato Rosaldo, *Ilongot headhunting 1883–1974. A study in society and history* (Stanford, 1980), 54–58
[28] Bartolomeu Giaccaria and Adalberto Heide, *Jerônimo Xavante conta mitos e lendas* (Campo Grande, Mato Grosso, Brazil, 1975), 249.

from British Guiana, perhaps trying to capture oral versification, trans-
muted similar material into aboriginal "patriotic gore":

> *The Fight on the Bowruma.*
> Caribs from Essequibo banks to our Bowruma came,
> In one special season; which was every year the same.
> And more and more they harried sore all who were living there,
> And made them cry, "O let us die, 'tis more than man can bear!"

The defenders lure the Caribs into a seemingly defenseless village, then
punish them from without:

> Swiftly those arrows are poured in; they shoot with might and main,
> And all the foremost Caribs are by those keen arrows slain.
> The others to the river fly; but foes are there before;
> And sternly in the forest they pay off the ancient score,
> Till each red-painted warrior there lies redder in his gore![29]

Koch-Grünberg, who studied three peoples of the Orinoco and Roraima in 1911–1913, observed that "stories about ancient struggles are
numerous and independent of myths." He seems to have paraphrased
the following narrative about how the Taulipáng and Arekuná fought
their Pischaukó enemies, but it remains vivid enough:

Manī-kuʒá, the paramount chief and two subchiefs, Aliah, who was a small, fat
man but very brave, and his brother [led the attack on the Pischaukó saying]
. . . "Forward, forward, forward!" [Manī-kuʒá] urged them on. They came close
to the [enemy] house. It was night. In the house there was a shaman who was
blowing on a sick man [to cure him]. This man said, "People are coming" and
warned the dwellers in the house. Then the master of the house, the chief of the
Pischaukó, said "Let them come. I know who it is, it's Manī-kuʒá, but he'll
never get out of here." The shaman kept on warning him, and said "The people
are already here." The chief said, "It's Manī-kuʒá, he'll never get out of here,
he'll end his life here." Then Manī-kuʒa cut the vine that was holding up the
palisade. Two women got in and set the house on fire, one through the entrance
door, the other through the exit. There were a whole lot of people in the house.
Then the women withdrew back outside the palisade. The fire caught on in the
house. An old man climbed up to douse it. A lot of people got inside. They
fired their shotguns, but without aiming, because they couldn't see anybody, it
was just to scare the enemy. The old Taulipáng chief wanted to shoot his arrow
at a Pischaukó but he missed. The Pischaukó was in a hole in the ground. While
the oldster put a second arrow [to his bow] the Pischaukó felled him with a

---

[29] William Henry Brett, *Legends and myths of the aboriginal Indians of British Guiana* (London,
1879), 35–38.

shotgun blast. Mani-kuẓa saw that his father was dead. Then the warriors fired. They had the whole house surrounded and the Pischaukó had nowhere to flee to.[30]

A formidable Jesuit ethnographer of the mid–eighteenth century, Martin Dobrizhoffer, described the chanting of war narratives among the Paraguayan Abipones as an elaborate musical performance of history inspired by "poetic rage":

They never sing all at once, but only two at a time, always greatly varying their voices from high to low, one either taking up, or following, or interrupting the other, and sometimes accompanying him. Now one, now the other is silent for a short interval. The tones vary according to the subject of the song, with many inflexions of the sound, and, if I may so express myself, a good deal of shaking. He who, by a quicker motion of the throat can now suspend the song for a while, now protract, and now interrupt it with groans, or laughter, or can imitate the bellowing of a bull, or the tremulous voice of a kid, – he will gain universal applause. No European would deny that these savage singers inspired him with a kind of melancholy and horror, so much are the ears, and even the mind, affected by that deadly chanting, the darkness adding greatly to the mournful effect.

. . . They do not sing extemporaneously, but what has been long studied beforehand. The songs are restricted by no metrical laws, but sometimes have a rhythmical sound. The number of verses is regulated, not according to the pleasure of the singer, but according to the variety of the subject. Nothing but warlike expeditions, slaughters, and spoils of the enemy, taking of towns, plundering of waggons and estates, burning and depopulating colonies of the Spaniards, and other tragedies of that kind furnish the savages with subjects for singing and rejoicing. These events, together with the place and time, where, and when they happened, they describe; not rudely, but with considerable elegance. . . . During the time that these songs are chaunted, a period of many hours, not one of the auditors dares utter a word, and though night itself persuades sleep, you will not see one of them even yawn. . . . They conclude the magnificent commemoration of their mighty deeds with *Gramackka akam*: Such then we are.[31]

Considerable elaborations of folk-historical thinking come to light whenever ethnographers allow them to. Protásio Frikel's 1970 study, *Os Kaxúyana, notas etno-históricas*, credits a corpus of folk history from a Cariban people of the Trombetas River area in Brazil with a double intelligibility: both relative to exterior testimonies recorded during at

---

[30] Theodor Koch-Grünberg, *Del Roraima al Orinoco* [1924] (Caracas, 1979–82), Vol. 3, 100–101.
[31] Martin Dobrizhoffer, *An account of the Abipones, an equestrian people of Paraguay* [1784] (3 vols., London, 1822), Vol. 2, 429–430.

least 200 years, and as a Kaxúyana interpretation of what appear to the Kaxúyana themselves as anomalous features of their own culture. The section "ethnohistoric traditions" in Reichel-Dolmatoff's 1949 ethnography of the Kogi of the Santa Marta Peninsula, Colombia, contains detailed lore about the history of the surrounding non-Kogi peoples. It begins with "mythic tribes" representing the major divisions of native humanity:

> In those times the Universal Mothers shared out the lands of the Sierra Nevada [de Santa Marta] among all the Indians. Every *Túxe* [group of males] lived in a different settlement. There were four *Túxe*s who went to distant lands. The first two . . . went to the South and arrived almost at the land of Bokotá. The other two went to the West. . . . They got to a land called Panama. None of these four *Túxe*s took along women with them. Rather they went alone, just the men. They married other women they found there.[32]

From this half-mythic point of departure, taking the Panamanian Cuna and the capital of Bogotá as outermost poles of orientation, an expansively detailed classification and "history" of many groups is unfurled. The scheme of ethnographic categories and the details of human movement and conflict are much more detailed than the equivalent part of the *Handbook of South American Indians*.[33]

Unfortunately for readers of most ethnographies, setting myth in a class by itself tends to obscure its historic matrix. When ethnographers comment on the way oral lore actually came to their ears and microphones, they generally note that although myth may emerge as a delimited genre, the occasions for reciting it are a complex skein that includes among other factors discussion of political circumstances, affairs of living members and outsiders, satirical intentions, momentary events reminiscent of ancient analogues, and the ethnographer's own "observer effect."

For example, when Johannes Wilbert set about to re-edit Gusinde's Fuegian Yámana ethnography in the format used by folklorists, Wilbert perceived as an obstacle the Yámana oral authors' tendency to surround the "red thread" of mythic plot with a tangled skein of "true-life episodes." Among both the Selk'nam and the Yámana, it proved "impossible to transcribe neat stories with a beginning, a climax, and an end. Interfering with this were not so much the variations in style of the different informants, but the storytellers' inclination to insert personal

---

[32] Gerardo Reichel-Dolmatoff, *Los Kogi* [1949] (Bogotá, 1985) Vol. 1, 158–159.
[33] Gerardo Reichel-Dolmatoff, *Los Kogi* [1949] (Bogotá, 1985) Vol. 1, 254–264.

experiences that often run longer than the actual narrative." "There existed but a fine line between the mythological past and the present, and . . . mundane acts acquired meaning and validity through relating them to prominent mythological personages and events of the traditional past."[34] Each of Gusinde's myths, as Gusinde himself pointed out, is a composite made by the oral authors' choices about what episodes fitted together in light of the concerns of the moment of telling. Although the personages of antiquity stood in genealogical relation to each other, the relations were implicit and malleable; only an outsider would need to fix them in static synthesis, and this would falsify the spirit of the telling. In the magnificent synthesis of his 1918–1924 field expedition, Gusinde dodged falsification by presenting the Selk'nam society of the "ancestors" twice. First he shows them as a gallery of sharply individuated archetypal persons:

Čẽnuke was a very dangerous man. . . . in his youth [he] was antisocial and unpopular, of an unsympathetic and repellent mentality. He always used to try to cause the other children harm and mistreat them. . . . He became stronger and more powerful . . . he tried to overpower everyone and put them under his power, but all united and successfully resisted him.

Then Gusinde re-presents them in a hypothetical chronology of his own devising:

The arrogant behavior of Čẽnuke can probably be intercalated after the departure of [the first of the primordials]. . . . The ambitious schemes of Čẽnuke and other events of the sort make up the first clear indices presaging imminent disorder . . . which ends with a violent revolution [and new mythic persons].[35]

The latter analysis generates a stagewise ordering reminiscent of Guaman Poma.

Few had the patience to sustain such innovative ambiguity. The art by which recorded chunks of narrative are stitched into book format, and edited as Euro-American prose, shows striking uniformity across the colonial and republican centuries. Although modern editors have long since abandoned the supposition that the more mythic a text is, the earlier the literal time it refers to, many nonetheless organize narratives through tables of contents similar to those of biblicizing renaissance

---

[34] *Folk literature of the Yamana Indians: Martin Gusinde's collection of Yamana narratives*, Johannes Wilbert, ed. (Berkeley, 1977), 9–10.
[35] Martin Gusinde, *Los indios de tierra del fuego. Tomo primero volumen I y II. Los Selk'nam* [1931] (Buenos Aires, 1982) Vol. 2, 555–556, 669.

works. They seem to retain the concept of the book as representing a totality of belief, in a coherent outline accessible through cumulative linear reading.

The outline itself varies little. It runs from mythic fiat of deities through to intelligible human action, generally beginning with myths that contrast the human condition with an imagined alternative, a time when the relation between humans and deity were radically different. Typically there follows a myth about a disaster or other break (e.g., a flood), which signals the end of this era. Like the Bible, the work then tells in more or less depth of an antiquity when early but definitely human persons, or hero-ancestors, who share a common descent, gave society its form and achieved heroic deeds. From here on, society as collective subject is considered as a set of groups often associated with eponymous ancestors. As with the biblical tribes and nations, these groups relate to each other on terms of kinship or of hereditary enmity patterned on social realities at the time of telling. Their stories are intensely concerned with control over specific places and resources, often sacralized. Some stories encode specific political struggles with surrounding peoples or create archetypes of struggle in which superhumans intervene. Also like the Bible, these works in later parts become concerned with the relation between the local sacra and the power of invading empires – sometimes the Inka, always the Spanish, Portuguese, Dutch, and so on. And also as in prophetic portions of scripture, one clearly senses the pressure of a perceived crisis – a crisis of survival for the collective subject – contemporary with the recension.

In the introduction to a book whose Spanish title means *The Real Bible of the Cashinahua*, one researcher of Amazonian Peru explains with candor why even a modern anthropologist well aware that biblicizing is a part of the colonial enterprise, feels obliged to practice it:

Preparing a compilation implies the need to order the stories. Nothing could be more contradictory in relation to their function in oral tradition, where each narrative (*relato*) is freestanding and where it would be useless to try to discover among them any thread of logical or chronological continuity.

. . . any intent to establish chronological sequences beyond those implicit in a given story's coherence, is visibly considered by the informants as inopportune.

So it is appropriate to turn one's back on a method of work which consists in seeking to integrate all the narratives as one super-narrative and incorporating them as episodes. On this point, the comparison which we establish with the Bible through our title risks leading the reader into an error: The Bible is, and has been for a long time, essentially one book. As such it can be read practically from start to finish.

It would be a serious error to read *The Real Bible of the Cashinahua* from cover to cover, thinking that story 1 precedes story 2 logically or chronologically . . . all [the stories] coexist absolutely in parallel in mythic time.

. . . Knowing all this, how should one group the narratives, in the absence of a temporal framework, specific spatial domains, or even social or ceremonial criteria? . . .

Finally I opted for a thematic grouping which implies a certain categorization of the narratives. This categorization is correctly taken as completely foreign to the situation in which myth, through its orality, develops and adapts itself.[36]

The compiler then goes on to set the texts into the normal bible-like sequence beginning with "myths proper" and ending with "historic myths."

The same pattern, in varied disciplinary garb, dominates many sequential unifications of South American texts. Not only compilations of "folklore" like León Cadogan's Guaraní compilations, but also ethnographic compilations like Siro Pellizaro's Ecuadorian *Mundo Shuar*, tend to group what are called "sacred histories" into preconceived themes (creation, cataclysm, etc.) and then submit these to an aprioristic outline proceeding from creation myths through primordial age, cataclysm, to political and genealogical diversification, culminating in Christian conversion and imminent revival (now usually pictured as ethnic revival).

Not all the genres that guide the capture and transformation of South American memories are biblical. In some African and Asian studies, epic and the notion of mythic cycle guide the establishment of sequence, and this is occasionally the case in South America too; for example, in a distinguished compilation of Aguaruna (Peruvian "Jívaroan" or Shuar) texts, the section on the spirits of people unjustly killed is organized as "the Iwanch cycle."[37] Other editors have chosen as common ground between European library and oral repertory models of successive cataclysm and re-creation influenced by the deluge, Plato's Atlantis, Greco-Roman cyclical models, and stagewise transformational schemes rooted in Joachinism. Some works seem to be influenced by an encyclopedism, which equates generality with priority and proceeds from origins of the world, to specific origins, to gender origins and so forth toward ramifying sets like animal stories, stories of Toad, and so on. All these editorial techniques sacrifice the oral contribution to "history of Indians" without gaining any advantage for "Indian histories."

---

[36] André Marcel D'Ans, *La verdadera Biblia de los Cashinahua* (Lima, 1975), 39–41.
[37] Aurelio Chumap Lucía and Manuel García-Renduelas, *"Duik Múun . . ."* (2 vols., Lima, 1979), Vol. 2, 601–645.

But what might a holistic South American image of the past – a major "Indian history" – look like if built up through its local constituents rather than crammed into imported genres?

Although no extant work does so on any large scale, Amazonian research gives illuminating leads. (The works of Sally and Richard Price afford a related corpus based on African-descended Guyana maroon populations.) In her ethnographies of the central-Brazilian, Cariban-speaking Kalapalo (notably *A Musical View of the Universe* and *The Last Cannibals, A South American Oral History*), Ellen Basso begins with the premise that, at the finest-grained level, a story is a series of speech events. The way the flow of speech is segmented is itself an image of the way "distinct events are isolated from each other" and also of the way they are connected. Therefore the detailed fashion in which transcription and translation reflect verbal features, such as emphasis, pause, minor and major divisions among parts, no less than large divisions like "myth" or "chapter," are matters of content as much as of form.

For example, Basso translates a story told by Muluku, a Kalapalo resident in the Xingu National Park, Brazil, segmenting the flow into stanzas, verses, segments, and lines according to Kalapalo grammatical discourse markers. One episode tells how Christians took away the protagonist Saganafa:

It was still very early, before dawn.
While they continued to do that others were coming toward them
some Christians were coming toward them.
They saw something white on the sandbar, a lot of them,
some distance from where they were just then.
"Look at all the jabiru storks," he said to him,
to his grandson.
"Grandfather," Saganafa answered,
"At night I'm not well because of that very thing,
not well at all.
At night that's how I am."
"I see."
He continued to go, shooting *wagiti*.
Toward Tefupe.
While he was doing that the Christians had already come there.
"Hey, Grandfather. Some Christians are here!"
They held onto their canoe, the Christians did.
"Well, where are you two going?" the Christians asked.
"We've come here for fish."
"Well, come along with me."

"All right!" Saganafa answered.
"Well, come with me, come be my daughter's husband."
"I will! Grandfather, I really am going now, I'm going away."
    "Very well."
"I came here because of the pain of my father's speech,
Grandfather," he said.
"I arrived because he was never pleased with me
        Now that is how I will leave.
    Tell the others. You will tell our descendants the story of my
    departure," Saganafa said.
        "Now that's how I will leave."
    How sad he was when he said that!

The Christians then give Saganafa's grandfather three metal tools in payment for Saganafa and depart.

So, payment was given to him,
    Payment for Saganafa was given by the Christian.
    "Take this, because now I'm taking this boy of yours with me for
good,
        I'm taking your grandson away.
        I'm leaving right now."[38]

Among the evil Christians, Saganafa becomes the father of four Christian boys. By accident he learns that Christians sacrifice Indians to their ancestor and that the victims' blood is what metal tools are made from. He flees. But his Christian sons return over and over looking for him, harming Kalapalo people. When the Kalapalo avenge themselves by killing the most beautiful of them, Saganafa's other sons break their relation with the Kalapalo forever.

Basso argues that segment breaks and other linguistic signals in the text are what make relations among the events intelligible; Kalapalo historicity inheres in them. Both in verbal form and in explanatory logic, the hinge of every action is a discontinuity corresponding to a linguistically signaled change of the actor's mood and motive.

Is a story made this way history? Yes, says Basso, but not by virtue of correlation with "facts" of Brazilian archival history. That is a separate matter. To appreciate a testimony's *local* historicity, one must highlight variation in the principles by which different cultures make the connectedness of events meaningful. Kalapalo people might not attach much importance to recovering whatever real-life incident lay behind the story

[38] Ellen Basso, *A musical view of the universe* (Philadelphia, 1985), 37–62.

of Saganafa's abduction. Instead, they have elaborated the facts into "symbols that stand for the abstractly conceived contrast between Europeans and Kalapalo." Items like blood that coagulates into steel appear miraculous and eminently mythical. But classifying "Saganafa" as myth would be misleading, because what connects one symbolic event to the next is an aspect of human action, namely, feeling and motive. The Kalapalo, like European historians who esteem individual "great men" as the source of innovation, see the feelings of the principles as the causal link that explains why the world is as it is.

Insofar as "Saganafa" is an explanatory text emphasizing change that is intelligible because it is humanly made, the story resembles history. But the rules by which remembered experience is made into an explanatorily usable event are so different that the textual products do not bear on their surface easy clues about how to transpose histories cross-culturally.

HEIRS OF THE NATIVE CHRONICLERS: ETHNICITY AND AUTHORITY IN THE TWENTIETH CENTURY

The nineteenth and early twentieth centuries are so little researched in regard to native South America that it is still unsafe to guess how much native written or taped testimony from those times exists. At least one source defined by its author as a native chronicle is known to have been written in the modern era. The Colombian insurgent Quintín Lame, who grew up in the later nineteenth century as an assimilated sharecropper, emerged in 1910–1920 as a rebel ethnic leader of the Páez and in 1939 finished a 118-page manuscript entitled "Thoughts of the Indian Educated in the Colombian Forest." It went unpublished until 1971 but is now available in both Spanish and English. Rappaport summarizes this "extremely cryptic" work as containing Lame's "prophetic philosophy, personal reminiscences, denunciation of specific abuses against Indians, and his vision of Páez history." Like Felipe Guaman Poma de Ayala three centuries earlier, Quintín Lame took an interest in European absolute chronology primarily as a measure of semi-millennial intervals that climax in the author's emergent role as native author-messiah:

But after 447 years, among the descendants of the Indian race [there appears] the great-grandson of the Indian Juan Fama [*sic*, for Tama] de Estrella. . . . And so tomorrow a communion of Indians will be born, the legitimate descendants of our Guananí land, the descendants of those hated tribes persecuted by the non-Indian; but the Law of Compensation exists, gentlemen, and in itself is avenging justice, because the deed of old Adam and the caprice of old Eve were paid for after four thousand years.[39]

There may well be other such manuscripts. But in one sense the question of whether postcolonial "native chroniclers" exist as named authors is misleading, because during native languages' centuries of margination from the orbit of literacy, native authorship itself became largely invisible. The overwhelming bulk of oral-authorial work was, and still is, hidden under the invidious title of "informant."

The task of recovering "Indian history" is therefore often a matter of recognizing "informants" as authors. The minority of ethnographers who choose to print accounts based on only one or a very few native teachers, and present their testimony in near-verbatim form, do afford native experts a sometimes explicit authorship.

A few modern researchers address the difficult task of building into their volumes some of local experts' ideas about the kinds of knowledge that exist and the proper relations among them. Reichel-Dolmatoff's *Amazonian Cosmos*, based on the testimony of the young Desana Antonio Guzmán, opened methodological debate about the representation of "cultures" via the unique subjectivities of persons. Landaburu and Pineda Camacho in *La Gente del Hacha*, an edition of the Andoke oral works of Yiñeko and Fisi, have followed the European tradition in chronologizing testimonies overall, so that they run from creation to "the captains of my [Yiñeko's] youth." Like D'Ans they acknowledge that this is an extraneous convention. But in clustering the component testimonies, they also tried to convey Andoke understandings about what sorts of stories belong together. A good reading, Andoke-style, is not so much one that catalogues the story or contextualizes it as one that artfully plays on its ganglion-like connections to realms widely diverse from the one the text is primarily "about." For example, the teller of a story about the jaguar Sindi presupposes that the audience possesses

fy5674,1,11,13acquaintance with the linguistic meaning of his name, here 'the carnivore';

acquaintance with his acts, relatives, allies, and enemies in myth;

[39] Manuel Quintín Lame, *Los pensamientos del indio que se educó dentro de las selvas colombianas* [1939] in *En defensa de mi raza*, Gonzalo Castillo Cárdenas, ed. (Bogotá, 1971), 24.

acquaintance with the jaguar, its properties and behavior, since Sindi is the "owner" of jaguars;

acquaintance with the real attitude of the Andoques toward the jaguar and the feeling it arouses in them;

awareness that the Carijones call the Andoques "Sindi's people"; etc.[40]

If the last of these associations is heavily played upon, the story, however "mythic" it appears, has meanings intelligible to Euro-Americans as ethnological or historical. For the most part, sophisticated and candid editing of oral testimony remains an unfinished step in understanding the construction of the unwritten past.

Some important oral authors, who are not themselves literally writers, nonetheless resemble the "native chroniclers" of the early seventeenth century in their biographical trajectory and in their ambitions to originate self-conscious "Indian history." Today as in colonial times, there appears to be a link between the making of synthetic accounts of one's own culture for foreign ears, and a history of close association with Christian clergy followed by travel and/or alienation and return to a native "home." Aurelio Chumap Lucía, the Aguaruna co-author of *"Duik Múun..."* was swayed by an education in Protestant fundamentalism but later developed strong motives of ethnic revivalism.

Colombia is particularly fertile with this literature. A remarkable 1992 example, whose Spanish title means *My Feet Are in My Head*, contains a self-ethnography and mythohistory by an U'wa (Chibchan-speaking Tunebo) woman named Berichá or Esperanza Aguablanca. Berichá was born legless but, once missionary nuns helped her learn literacy, achieved a sophisticated career as writer and spokeswoman for native groups. Her campaign for the reclamation of U'wa memory included not only her own written mythohistory but also efforts to prevent or compensate the theft of sacred objects, the non-narrative vessels of memory. *Tradiciones de la gente del Hacha*, whose oral authors Yiñeko and Fisi are respectively a northwest Amazonian lineage elder and his heir-apparent, had a similar genesis. So did the Desana (Tukanoan) *Antes o mundo não existia* by Umúsin Panlõn Kumu and his son Tolamõn Kenhiri. Kenhiri, a mission school student, was (like the colonial "native chroniclers") exposed to

---

[40] Jon Landaburu and Roberto Pineda Camacho, *Tradiciones de la gente del Hacha* (Bogotá, 1984), 34.

Catholic libraries dominated by works on Greece, Rome, and medieval Europe; he had taken on himself the writing of his father's recitations before he began collaborating with his editor. Sometimes commerce and even anthropology itself play a part. Floresmiro Dogiramá, the main oral author of *Zroārā Nēbura*, an Emberá (Colombian Pacific littoral) "oral literary" collection, was the son of a partially bilingual *cacique*. At fourteen he learned to write while serving a merchant in Baudó, and in 1927 the Swedish pioneer ethnographer Baron Erland Nordenskiöld (who also initiated the study of Cuna "pictographic" literacy) employed him as an "informant." The Arawakan writer Maximiliano José Roberto underwent similar experiences probably in the early 1880s, and the modern Guajiro myth-writer Miguel Jusayú's biography partakes of the same motif. Both writers' works are described later.

A vogue for "testimonial literature" has greatly expanded the audience for written native autobiographies, and South American examples are fairly numerous. As early as 1927 Pascual Coña, a "quite educated" Chilean Mapuche according to his editor Father E. W. de Moesbach, concluded an oral autobiography detailing the Araucanian way of life in the late nineteenth century and recording the 1881 native war against the Chileans. While planning the insurrection, the Pehuenche (eastern) Araucanians sent a message to the Mapuche leader Neculmán:

"Well, there are the *huinca*s [Euro-Americans]; we will rise up against them; the Argentinian natives will finish off the foreigners; you should do the same with yours and attack them too. . . ."
. . . Neculmán addressed the Argentinian messenger, saying, "Here is my chiefs' reply, as you have heard."
[The messenger] replied "Just so. I have heard your word and I will pass it to my chiefs when I get there."
Then he handed over his *quipu* [the word is supplied as translation of a Mapuche phrase] or thread of knots, and said: "This is our signal, it contains the counted days, you must untie one every day; the day that comes out last there will be rallies of forces everywhere."
Having said that, the messenger made his farewell.[41]

Much later, the Quechua oral autobiography of the Cusco cargo porter Gregorio Condori Mamani found a wide audience in Valderrama and Escalante's Spanish translation. (It is now available in English as well.) In the wake of Peru's military nationalist "revolution from above,"

---

[41] Pascual Coña was the oral author of Ernesto Wilhelm de Moesbach, *Vida y costumbres de los indígenas araucanos en la segunda mitad del siglo XIX* (Santiago, Chile, 1930), 271.

the discovery of imaginative riches on the native side of the country's linguistic divide resonated widely among intellectuals. Perhaps most importantly, it gave the literate public a sense of the country's sociolinguistic stratification as felt from the viewpoint of those shut out. Condori Mamani remembers his conscription:

They taught me the alphabet there in the army. I was able to sign my name, and – a, o, i, p – I could also recognize some letters of the alphabet on paper. . . . They say that nowadays, whoever enters the army unable to see [i.e., illiterate], comes out with their eyes open and knowing how to read. And those unable to speak also come out with Spanish flowing off their tongues.

So it was. You'd enter the army sightless, and sightless you'd leave, because you'd never really get the alphabet right. And just the same you'd be unable to speak when you entered and unable to speak when you left, Spanish barely dribbling off your tongue. There in the army, those lieutenants and captains didn't want us speaking the runa [indigenous] tongue. They'd say:
"Dammit, Indians! Spanish!"
So the noncommissioned officers would beat Spanish into us.[42]

Native memoir literature has also acquired an important place in social history, above all in Bolivia with its powerful history of labor union-based politics. These books are at the same time "Indian histories" – written in Quechua or Aymara, they usually presuppose such familiarity with Andean culture that even the Spanish translations are hard for non-Bolivians to understand – and "histories of Indians" prepared for an ideologically self-conscious audience. Bolivian "testimonial" autobiographies – notably those of women – are perhaps the most widely read of all South American native texts. Most are by underdogs who achieved important roles in political or labor movements. Probably the most inclusive collections of testimonial autobiography of rank-and-file people are those prepared by Silvia Rivera Cusicanqui's Oral History Workshop, centering on Bolivian Aymara and Quechua labor and leadership. *Let Me Speak* by the tin miner Domitila Barrios de Chungara achieved popularity in Bolivia (and translation to English) well before the Nobel Prize recognized *I, Rigoberta Menchú*. The memoirs of the miner Juan Rojas are also available in English. Other examples include the autobiography of Ana Maria Condori, an Aymara-speaking domestic servant turned jungle "colonist,"[43] Juan H. Pévez, a leader of an early Peruvian indigenous organization,[44] the Bolivian peasant leader Enrique Encinas,[45] and

---

[42] Alejandro Condori Mamani and Asunta Quispe Huamán, *Andean lives* (Austin, 1996), 51–52.
[43] Ana María Condori, *Nayan uñatatawi. Mi despertar* (La Paz, 1988).
[44] *Memorias de un viejo luchador campesion: Juan H. Pévez*, Teresa Oré, ed. (Lima, 1983).
[45] Enrique Encinas, *Jinapuni. Testimonio de un dirigente campesino* (La Paz, 1989).

Martín Painemal Huenchual,[46] a pioneer Mapuche organizer in Chile. José Matos Mar's *Taquile en Lima*, unlike explicitly political testimonies, contains an encyclopedic Peruvian corpus of "daily life" testimonies about migration, perhaps the dominant fact of recent Andean experience: This huge book tells how the inhabitants of an island in Lake Titicaca came to live in the desert outskirts of Lima. On another side, native memoir literature shades into the genre of Protestant conversion testimonies (for example, the autobiography *Tariri*), which also appear heavily edited.

Studies of postindependence change in Amazonia also make use of autobiographical and oral-historical research. Brazil's best-known activist researchers, the Villas-Boas brothers, edited the memoirs of Káia, a Juruna elder from the upper Xingu. The old man recalls Juruna invasion of the territory and Juruna experience of many "national" events, such as the Prestes Column march, a revolutionary campaign of the 1920s.

Western Amazonia during the plagues, slave raids, and destructive rubber extraction that came with the age of independence yields some particularly powerful testimonies. Javier Comunyaro, an Aracuara (Witoto) told Roberto Pineda Camacho of an epidemic in the Caquetá:

The people didn't take refuge in the big ravines, but in little ravines; there in the gullies, in the hollows, that little bit of people. There the fever did reach. The fever doesn't nest in the forest; there it doesn't arrive. Fever only reaches the planted plot, the longhouse, the road. . . . This was before the Peruvian rubber tappers, now.

The people from one longhouse started to die. The same happened in another longhouse, in another, and so on.

All the people had hidden. . . . That day smoke was seen in the sky and all over, nothing but smoke . . . pure "fog"; the sun hardly showed through it. The smoke was pure sickness. It was all over the longhouses, on all sides.

Nobody shouted, nobody talked, they made no noise. Everybody kept silent.

A few people had hidden in the forest. Fever doesn't reach there; they were all right. But they couldn't make any fire there, so how could they live? They couldn't make smoke or fire, because when smoke comes out, Sickness sees the smoke and goes over there. Sickness spends its life looking for where smoke comes out, where fire is. Sickness goes around searching!

So a month went by, and nothing happened to them. Around midday, so the people say (and who knows if they're lying?), [voices] shouted in the sky. At twelve midday, they shouted loud, while everybody kept dead quiet. They shouted:

"Ah! Ah!"

---

[46] Martín Painemal Huenchual, *Vida de un dirigente mapuche* (Santiago, 1983?).

"Where are the people? Where are the people that there used to be so many of?"

"Where did they go?"

Here a shaman shouted. Sickness shouted like this:

"Where are the people who used to be here? Where did they go???

"I thought there were men here. Where are they?

"There are no men! I want to talk with a person, but where is he?"

The people all kept good and quiet. Afterwards, right there, Sickness set to singing:

> "I'm the one who went forth; I went to walk, to greet, to greet the
>   people.
> The people couldn't take it.
> Those people, they who said they were so strong!
> But it was no big thing, just an itch, that finished them off."

That's how he danced.

Nobody answered him. Then he headed down the road. The sickness was measles. The measles sang like that. . . . He wasn't a human being, he was pure sickness. When he went down there he walked every road. There no longer was anyone there. . . . He shouted on the road too. All the longhouses stood silent. . . . On the road he began singing again:

> "HU! HU! Where are the people?
> Where's the man who's a match for me?
> He's the one I want to talk with!
> Where are the people?"

And they didn't answer him. All were frightened. He sang again. When he went down to earth he searched for people here, there and everywhere, but there no longer were any people. . . .

And from then on sicknesses hardly come round any more. Because a lot of the shamans died. Who'd do that kind of damage now? Until the Peruvians arrived. After that came the Peruvian rubber tappers.[47]

And with them came another onslaught, *cauchu uras* 'the age of rubber,' also widely remembered in Amazonian oral tradition. The successive episodes of extractive frontier and mission expansion – gold, rubber, oil, each with attendant missionary incursions – are often remembered as epochs in Amazonian folk history. Rucuyaya Alonso Andi or Bandio, a Quijos Indian of the upper Napo River, furnished an oral memoir that forms the core of Blanca Muratorio's study of the Quijos 1850–1950:

---

[47] Roberto Pineda Camacho, *Historia oral y proceso esclavista en el Caquetá* (Bogotá, 1985), 129–131.

At the beginning, the two missions [Catholic and Evangelical] used to fight each other a lot. . . . Each Evangélico came with his wife. The first one who came was Ruben Larson, then came the one called Mr. John, whoever he was. Whenever a lot of them came, I carried the loads and the children who were very big and heavy gringos. For one of the biggest children we had to make a double box [wooden chair in which people were carried on the Indians' backs] with a roof. That's how we brought him, by carrying that huge box. Although the children of the gringos were young, they were as tall as can be. At the beginning, the Evangélicos only came to preach and they gave us some medicine, but later they started the schools. They would agree to baptize and marry people only after they had become believers. When the gringos arrived, the priests frightened us by saying that the gringos came from hell . . . we used to answer: "You are not from here either; you are from Italy, dominated by the Pope."[48]

In areas where substantial numbers of people who speak American languages have acquired literacy, and have been exposed to democratizing tendencies in historiography and literature, some members of the native intelligentsia publish as sole authors of works that combine oral-historical and documentary research. Usually these works consist of collected oral testimonies about crucial periods in the recent past of the researcher's own groups, drastically edited around an argument of political revindication and also framed within genre norms heavily influenced by academia. Examples include Yánez del Pozo's and Males' oral-based histories of Ecuadorian ethnic groups now transformed into literate peasants and urbanites. Their titles mean, respectively, *I'm Telling You Frankly* and *The Original Life of the Kindreds from Imbabura*. Males and Yánez del Pozo innovate in retaining the stigmatized dialect and the (to urbanites) boring detail of peasant microhistory. Segundo Cotacachi Terán told Males what the Depression era meant to a butcher in the countryside and in so doing gives a historical clue about the interdependence between Afro-Ecuadorian and Quichua groups characteristic of the area:

Business was bad in Urcuquí, it wasn't worth it. . . . For example, a pig that you killed, you couldn't finish selling in three or even four days, so we had to go around peddling it saying "Don't you want meat? Buy meat!" At that time, 1938, a pound of meat, seems like, went for a *real* or a *real* and a half, and you'd yell and yell, but as for selling, nothing. So that's why we used to go to the estate of San José to offer it on credit to the black people who worked there, so they'd pay us back in a couple of weeks. We couldn't sell here, so instead we'd go down there to Salinas, where the houses were made of straw, that's all, about ten little huts seems like it was. With our things loaded on the donkey, with the

[48] Blanca Muratorio, *The life and times of Grandfather Alonso* (New Brunswick, N.J., 1991), 97.

mutton, the pork, we'd keep peddling. . . . We used to return home the same
day, covering a lot of ground, and no chance we'd finish selling. What a job!
We had some real hard times.[49]

In a more assimilated genre, resembling the revisionism exemplified by
Dee Brown's *Bury My Heart at Wounded Knee*, Curapil Curruhuinca's
"Mapuche chronicles," from Chilean-Argentinian borderlands, seeks to
reverse perspective on the popular soldiers-and-Indians historiography of
the Southern Cone.

Some native South American authors have created extensive prose
reworkings of "traditional" oral lore. Among the most imposing is *Yurupary*, an 83-page retelling of an important northwest Amazonian mythic
and ritual complex, which a little-known Brazilian Indian of Manao or
Tariana (Arawakan) ancestry named Maximiliano José Roberto purportedly wrote in the "general language" of the Amazon lowlands (also called
Tupi-Guarani or Ñengatú) some time before 1890. Roberto served as
guide to visiting scientists, and this may have impelled him to start
writing. His original has been lost. Its textual character, which a modern
scholar considers "epic," is hard to estimate from the 1890 Italian translation or the 1983 Spanish retranslation. Bidou sees in *Yurupary* a comment on the emergence of an Amazonian historicity:

[*Yurupary*] breaks away from mythical tradition, which is premised on a non-
questioning of its origins. Out of the ruins of the "savage mind," a new form of
discourse is thus created, which can be considered, according to [the editor]
Stradelli, as legendary. Its main characteristics are that it implies a historical
perspective and is expressed in legislative terms, as distinct from mythical meta-
phors.[50]

Miguel Angel Jusayú, a Venezuelan Guajiro native ethnographer who
writes stories from oral tradition in an accomplished modern Spanish
prose showcasing some tropes from his mother tongue, was blinded at
thirteen and returned to the Guajiro after being sheltered in a mission.
In many parts of South America, literate first-language speakers of American tongues have undertaken editorial roles in connection with bilingual
education projects and educational NGOs; usually the first fruits are

[49] Antonio Males, *Villamanda ayllucunapac punta causai. Historia oral de los imbayas de Quinchuquí
    – Otavalo 1900–1960* (Quito, 1985), 47.
[50] "Du mythe à la légende," *Journal de la Société des Américanistes* 75 (1989), 64.

anthologies of favorite tales and children's books to foster bilingual literacy.

THE ETHNOGRAPHY OF LITERACY AND MEMORY

A family of influential arguments whose best known protagonists are the anthropologists Jack Goody and the literary critic Walter J. Ong have proposed that historical thinking in the European sense grew not from any particular social organization but from the technology of writing. Written language can endure beyond its context as speech cannot. Through writing, one's own culture becomes an object of distanced study. Discrepancies between past and present teachings open the door to skepticism, and to the realization that humans have constructed social norms over time rather than receiving them once and for all from deities.

If correct, this view would simplify understanding of how historical discussion does or does not arise among South Americans. Under Goody's view, as for early Lévi-Straussians, "Indian history" is not historic thinking at all until it acquires a written context. However, there are powerful objections of which the Africanist Vansina and the theorist Brian Street point out several. Social pressures tend to push readers to read the same books, which can just as well foster the illusion of closure as provoke dissonance; and in any case literacy does not necessarily set the discovered past in surprising contrast to present belief, because any text "means" what it is taken to mean in the light of current doxa. Brian Street goes on to question the reality of literacy effects as such. Effects of literacy, even unforeseen ones, depend on how any given society institutionalizes and ideologizes writing. Both critics observe that the oral-literate dichotomy is ethnographically unrealistic because much of humankind – certainly most of native South America post-1492 – has lived "paraliterately." Familiar with writing's unique place in politics, history, and religion, "paraliterate" people nonetheless see and use it in a narrow functional spectrum, developing broad fundamental meanings through orality and gesture. These broader discourses assign writing crucial but not general powers.

Does literacy really work a revolution on "Indian history"? Above all, what a fieldworker finds in modern native South American views of the past is polyphony and fragmentation: literacy-based knowledge of the past seems to add more "histories" to "past-discourses" that are already plural, with oral-genealogical, mythical, and secular ideological views of the past normally coexistent. Nobody insists on authoritative synthesis, even when "Indian histories" are logically incompatible, because past-discourse tends to be fractionated in the image of power relations that are themselves discontinuous fields.

One obstacle to understanding literacy effects is that ethnographers arrive too late to see them. In lowland societies that have learned to read recently, elders of the first literate generation first saw literacy as a new technique within a range of skills that already treated the world as a legible field of indexical signs. They liken reading to tracking footprints, criticizing body painting, or interpreting drug hallucinations, for example. In the 1950s, missionaries to the Piro (of Amazonian Peru) heard that a man named Sangama had, forty years before, found some printed papers discarded by traders and invented a shamanic art of reading them. The paper seemed to him a female being whose mouth (writing) offered knowledge. Early awareness of literacy may foster a generally textualizing image of the world, even on the part of people who cannot read, like those Andokes who told Landaburu and Pineda that prehistoric petroglyphs record, in the now-illegible script of prehuman giants, the original names of all creatures.

The Piro of the 1950s were hungry latecomers to a process that the Spanish, intensely writing-conscious by 1500 and disposed to erect huge inequalities on the basis of writing as privileged access to truth, had set in motion centuries before. Areas that experienced it early generated both reverence for texts (as guarantees of rights) and ambivalence toward scribes and teachers (who usually denigrated all languages but Spanish, and who made access to writing a costly and humiliating experience). The terrifying "School Myth," which Isidro Huamaní of Ayacucho told in the 1960s, expresses the conviction that the true meaning of writing can be known only by the unmasking of writing itself:

God the powerful, our father, used to travel around the world. He had two sons: the Inka and Sukristus [i.e., Jesus Christ]. Inka said to us: "Talk," and we learned to talk. Since then, we teach our children to speak. Inka asked Mother Earth to give us food, and we learned to plant. The llamas and the cows obeyed us. That was an age of abundance. . . .

Afterward [Inka] built a tunnel which is in Cusco. Through that passageway the Inka visited our Mother Earth. He talked to her, he brought her presents, he asked her favors on our behalf. When the Inka married Mother Earth, he had two children. Lovely babies they are. We don't know their names. Or whether they are still walking in those tunnels, or if they are hidden in the Cathedral in Lima. Sir, have you not seen them?

When they were born, Holy Jesus felt a lot of rage and pain. Since Jesus had already grown up and was a strong young man, he wanted to overcome his elder brother the Inka. "How shall I beat him?" he asked.

The Moon felt sorry. "I can help you," she said, and let fall a leaf with writing. Jesus said, "This will scare the Inka." On a dark field he showed the paper. The Inka was frightened at not understanding the writing, and said, "What sort of thing are these drawings? What does my brother want?" He ran away, he went far.

"How can I take the Inka captive?" [asked Jesus.] "Surely I'll never be able," he said, and started to cry. The puma felt sorry. He said "I will help you," and called all the pumas. The pumas chased the Inka, great ones and small ones. Every time the Inka went down to eat in the valley, the pumas chased him away. He was dying from hunger.

When the Inka could no longer do anything, Jesus Christ struck Mother Earth, and he cut her throat. Then he had churches built; there he is, he protects us and loves us.

The Ñaupa Machu ['Old One of Yore', (i.e. evil living survivor of a prehuman age)] was delighted when he found out that the Inka had died. The Ñaupa Machu had had to live hidden while the Inka was travelling about on Earth. Ñaupa Machu lived in a mountain which was named School. He was pleased that Jesus had struck Mother Earth.

Into this mountain the Inka's two children went, looking for their father and mother. Ñaupa Machu said to them, "Come, come, I'll show you where the Inka is and where Mother Earth is." They say the children went to school happy. Ñaupa Machu wanted to eat them. "Mother Earth no longer loves the Inka," he said. "The Inka has made friends with Jesus Christ and now they live together like two little brothers. Look at the writing, it's all said right here!" The children were very frightened, and they ran away. Since then all children must go to school. And just like Mother Earth's two children, almost all of them dislike school and run away.

Where could they be, those children of the Inka? They say that when the elder is fully grown, he will return. That will be the day of the final judgment. But we do not know if he will be able to return. The children, the babies, must look for him, and they are looking.[51]

The "School Myth" reflects on a historic reality: the extension of compulsory Spanish-language public education to a Quechua-speaking peasantry which was promised, but rarely received, social mobility in

---

[51] Alejandro Ortiz Rescaniere, *De Adaneva a Inkarrí. Una visión indígena del Perú* (Lima, 1973), 143–149.

exchange for acculturation. It is perhaps more than coincidental that the generation of Ayacucho-area children that Isidro Guamaní's story mentions grew up to include the first generation of Shining Path guerrillas around 1981. Shining Path ideology carried to its farthest extreme the cult of written authority. Its fundamentalist Communism has been seen by C. I. Degregori as attempting to seize for frustrated highlanders a scripture of historical truth hidden behind the false teachings of ordinary books.

The Colombian Páez as seen in Joanne Rappaport's ethnography *The Politics of Memory* also put writing near the center of the language of power, and therefore of conflict. But here, unlike Ayacucho, "Indian history" built a two-way bridge to a "history of Indians." Páez peasants revere colonial papers for possessing "supernatural power that arises out of [history's] written – and thus disembodied – form," regarding the fetish power the years have distilled into these papers, rather than their legal content, as the guarantee of the land claims they record. Páez set high value on writing as a special skill. They have employed it since the early twentieth century to project Páez traditional history and knit it together with a "national" history persuasive to outsiders. Yet all written knowledge is considered as only a secondary reflection of "truths" about Páez origins and achievements whose other "sources" are landmarks and oral myths, especially a genre of narratives about past *caciques*.

Indeed, modern Colombians, including many urbanites, feel that the history known from writing has meaning precisely because it contrasts with another set of "true" memories, one that lies beyond the reach of writing. The latter is distilled in the lore of Amazonian magic. Colombians associate shamanism with the historic Witoto and other Amazonian peoples, whom Euro-Americans and Europeans, in the epoch of the rubber boom, slaughtered and enslaved. The Amazonian shaman is popularly felt to be the curator of a repressed but still redemptive "savage" past, which the modern state has martyred to progress – at the expense of modern people's health and sanity. Modern people of western Amazonia are well aware of their standing as repositories of archaic power. Manuel Muyuy said that the Ingano [Colombian Quechua]-speaking people of the Sibundoy Valley owe their far-flung prestige as healers to knowledge that their ancestor took from a prehuman cannibal being:

> He killed that heathen,
> and he took the inheritance of that one,

the inheritance,
his knowledge he took for himself into his own mind.
Surely more, he took for himself his mind,
you see, that one was an owner of knowledge.[52]

In all the foregoing cases, from deeply colonialized peasantries to recent mission zones, representations of the past are divided and contested. The authority of state education tends to regulate discourse across class lines, using the Spanish language and writing. An oral stream fosters more inward-looking reflections on collective self and other. On the Bolivian highlands and in many other places, the field of past-discourse, like so much of culture created under colonialism, is divided into a superordinate, authorized, centralized field – the eurocentric authorized history of the republic, whose usual spokesperson is the schoolteacher, and which makes "history of Indians" a distinctly subaltern topic – and a subordinate, unoffical, locally varied field consisting of folk-historical memory. This unoffical history is typically concerned with a range of seemingly scattered themes: the *chullpa*s or pre-Christian dead, legendary founders of villages and localized kindreds, participation in wars both international and civil, the lore of past trade and currency, and past vicissitudes of village self-defense in litigation and combat. It is often emphatically "Indian history," in perennially unresolved relation to official history.

For centuries, the two currents have stood in a relationship of antagonistic interdependence. Each derives meaning from the other. But the terms of exchanged meaning are asymmetrical. The official past claims to be truer than folk memory and enjoys the privilege of displacing "backward" and "Indian" thought, or "folklorizing" it. In most of Andean South America, rural adults are generally literate, and indeed they produce large archives in the course of meticulously recorded village self-government. Yet if publicly asked about "history," villagers usually refer visitors to teachers. Local traditions and writings exert authority in subordinate contexts such as village ritual outside the church, pilgrimages, village council meetings, or family feasts. Unlike official history, it possesses no context in which it is synthesized into a totalizing, "true," and chronologically continuous past. Yet nonwritten symbols of continuity (costumes, crosses, venerated textile bundles) and handwritten Books of Acts, all of which connect people to this less-recognized past, are prized

---

[52] John Holmes McDowell, *Sayings of the ancestors* (Lexington, 1989), 119.

as links to a history more valuable than that enshrined in churches and schools. Fundamental claims to land and water rest, after all, on such local knowledge, not on imports. Expertise on "immemorial" tenure, of titles, genealogies, and boundaries, undergirds subsistence itself.

When communities fight for political recognition or productive resources, the ability to project this knowledge into outside fora becomes a precious resource. Villagers with a knack for writing (typically former secretaries of community councils) are pressed into service as brief-writers. Preparing petitions and claims, many marshal documents centuries old. Understanding of rural historical consciousness demands close study of papers like the ones the Bolivian "Scribe of the Delegated *Caciques*" Leandro Condori Chura appended to his Aymara autobiography. Condori Chura, who had only one year of schooling, worked in exchange for meals and went into debt to buy a typewriter: "Shit, lawyers are just people like me, can't I make documents?" Soon he became skilled in showing peasant *caciques* where the written record contained legal findings damaging to latifundists:

Morales annulled the decrees of [Mariano] Melgarejo [President 1865–1871]. I read citations, saying "the estate property is annulled." I always had the decrees where the *Caciques* were mentioned. "They're the authority, the *Caciques* have power," that's what I said. The decrees favorable to the *Caciques* are from before Melgarejo and that's what's in the record, in documents. . . . I would read and they'd pick it up from there, talking: "That's it, it's done," they would say.[53]

Relations between official historiography and local intellectual processes are changing rapidly. In Bolivia since the 1970s, and in Ecuador since the 1990 indigenous "uprising," some sectors of both the Church and academia have sought to infuse "popular" content into the authoritative current of published history by running contests for the best local history essays. The winning submissions often display fascinating new combinations of legal-based, school-based, and oral-based historical expression, with ancient history often taken as prefiguration of recent struggles. Lorenzo Inda, writing about his home community of Irohito Yanapata on the Bolivian side of Lake Titicaca, tells in illustrated "notebook" format about his ancestors' migrations:

According to what my grandfather Luis Ynta Waranqa told me, through his father's grandparents, there was drought in Lapaka in the year 1675 all over the

[53] Leandro Condori Chura, *El escribano de los caciques apoderados / Kasikinakan Purirarunakan Quilquiripa*, Esteban Ticona Alejo, ed. (La Paz, 1992), 84.

Macha high plains and other parts of our Bolivia, this drought was something to cry about, very sad . . .

. . . they had to eat skins of dried potato and the seed of wild grasses, animal skins and other things. The drought was a matter of seven years or even a little more, since there was this drought, well the URUs left this place of Yrohito Yanapata; in search of water to live . . . [and sought refuge for seven years] and afterward they returned home.

. . . this is before the discovery of America, that's why the URUs used to occupy great reaches of land, but they didn't know how to work agriculturally, they specialized in hunting and fishing wild animals of the lake . . . [for vegetable foods] they used to trade or barter.

. . . [after protracted struggles to secure land rights against Aymara rivals] in the year 1959, the URU community had their land registered by the engineer and topographer under the auspices of Felipe Vela Yuyaq[?] ylakata [Aymara: holder of staff of mayoral office] and bara [same, in Spanish] of the community of URUs. From that date it has a land area of 54 hectares [and] now the boundaries and limits are maintained.[54]

Home-made historiography reflects multiple forces now converging to change the ideology and institutions of literacy. Fast-growing Protestant movements and some new movements derived from Adventism consider literacy the threshold of sanctity. Bilingual schoolteachers and NGO (nongovernmental organization) activists encourage rural people to generate their own documentation. Each of these ideologies at the same time proposes a rupture with the past, and a recapture of "popular memory." Whether they will yield grass-roots revisions in the nexus of writing, authority, and memory, or influence South American intellectuality beyond village level, depends partly on constitutional decisions to be taken by states facing with uncertainty the question of pluralism.

CAN NON-EUROPEAN ACCOUNTS OF THE PAST BE COORDINATED TO EXTERIOR HISTORY?

How can anyone connect culturally diverse testimonies to the project of intercultural, intersocietal history? No one any more regards oral tradition as a directly exportable data base. Certainly folk history bears no simple relationship to absolute chronology. Is it then still worthwhile to treat such corpuses as deposits of historical fact?

It is sometimes possible, if not to dissolve such difficulties, at least to

---

[54] Lorenzo Inda C., *Historia de los Urus. Comunidad Yrohito Yanapata* (La Paz, 1988), fo.10–11, unnumbered folios.

define them in a way that shortens the distance between testimony and contextual facts of social organization. One still little-explored avenue is situating native testimony in local "sociologies of knowledge." Rosaleen Howard-Malverde, in a monograph on "Quechua ways of telling the past," emphasizes that between two neighboring Peruvian villages, the one that retained a detailed and peculiar oral history embodying memories of colonial events, independent of writings, was the one that lacked institutions claiming social authority over knowledge of the past via literacy; the difference in the locus of accepted knowledge profoundly affected peoples' notions of how society had changed.

In remote eras, too, institutional vessels affected historical contents. Early sources on the Inka empire differ irreconcilably in their royal genealogies and assertions about "the Inka constitution."[55] Previous synthesizers felt obliged to rank sources as to closeness to Inka "truth," without clearly explaining the causes of variation. Studies from Africa and India, however, undercut the assumption that there would normally have existed a uniquely authoritative royal account from which post-invasion narrators and chroniclers deviated. In societies where plural kinship corporations associate at the apex of power, historical truths are held to be plural, proprietary, and almost incommensurable. The attempt to reconcile or merge overlapping testimonies from different corporate sectors (e.g., lineages, castes) of a given society into a synthetic image of "what really happened" is misguided because in many cases historical truth is felt to be relative to, and the property of, the group "owning" a tradition.

In such societies, under ordinary circumstances different groups' historical narratives are assumed to be more or less mutually irrelevant. When mutually confronted in litigation, they are expected not to match, because each is "true" only of its "owners'" ancestors and the interests held in their names. D'Azevedo sums up historical debate among the Gola, a western Liberian people:

Regardless of what may appear to the outsider as inconsistencies between rival family versions of the past, all is taken as the truth until that situation arises in which the past must be entered as evidence in a matter of honour or litigation. Then one's own version is held up as the truth and all others are characterized as incompetent. Should one fail to press one's family's interests in terms of a partisan appeal to the events of the past, the ancestors will take their revenge.

[55] John H. Rowe "La constitución inca del Cuzco," *Histórica* (Lima) 9:1 (1985), 35–73.

Truth then, is that which brings about the desired results, and no man can be blamed for stating what it is in his interests to state.[56]

This will sound familiar to readers of colonial South American litigation. The genealogies given by rival contenders for colonial chieftaincies are normally irreconcilable in content. The same is true of discrepancies about superhuman genealogy, which differ even within one cultic community because they express in mythic idiom folk-sociological perceptions that differ with points of view.

> But the fact is that in each village, and even *ayllu* by *ayllu*, people give different versions, and different names, too. People from Mama say one thing and the Checa say another.
>   Some call Chaupi Ñamca Paria Caca's sister.
>   Others say, "She was Tamta Ñamca's daughter." . . .
>   Still others say, "She was the Sun's daughter."
>   So it's impossible to decide.[57]

Such discrepancies struck early Spanish inquirers, accustomed to centralized theological authority, as proof that Indians were either dishonest or mentally inferior. "None answered [the licentiate Vaca de Castro's 1542 questions] satisfactorily but instead very variously, each one according to his own group's interests." However, once one assumes that discrepancies reflect situations where segments of society each possess autonomous fora, they become intelligible problems in their own right. If this perception complicates use of traditions as chronological data or sources of "fact," it also enriches understanding of how memory is officialized and contested in nonwestern historical action. Treating Inka succession lists as proprietary histories of *panaka*s (corporations of people descended from past sovereigns) gives them greater though less tractable data value.

Similarly, we may never be able to turn testimony directly into dated chronologies. Here, too, African research points to more sophisticated avenues. When tested against external benchmarks, genealogies from African societies lacking absolute-dated calendars (i.e., those employing baselines like year C.E. 0) turn out to be difficult sources for chronology. In such societies, elapsed time is usually registered by comparison with reigns and the passage of age sets, but these are themselves subject to systematic "structural amnesias." The reason is that genealogies are normally maintained in only enough time depth to cover the demand for

[56] Warren D'Azevedo, "Uses of the past in Gola discourse," *Journal of African History* (1962), 26.
[57] *The Huarochirí manuscript* [1608?], Frank Salomon and George Urioste, trans. (Austin, 1991), 87.

crucial transitions and current relevance. Supererogatory data are "telescoped." In colonial Andean chieftaincies, relevancy was usually stereotyped as two or three generations prior to Spanish contact.

Moreover, in America as in Africa, multiple events that resemble each other are conflated into single archetypal events. The judicial murder of the Inka king at the time of Spanish invasion, that of the last resisting independent Inka forty years later, and the execution of a neo-Inka rebel leader two centuries later still, are conflated in the most widespread myth memorializing Spanish conquest. If these events are later reanalyzed into multiple episodes, tellers often feel them to represent "the same" event recurring after a patterned cycle. If pressed about dates, they provide patterned or even millenarian "round" numbers. Cultural logic overrides chronology.

Such hazards and many others impede generating absolute chronology from oral tradition but do not necessarily impede locating oral tradition in absolute chronology. At least where post-1492 events are concerned, synchronisms often help key tradition to exterior chronology. A synchronism is the mention of a person or event from outside the tradition's own orbit, for example, an astronomical event, a species or technological device whose introduction date is known (paper money, eucalyptus, steamboats), the appearance of a nonlocal person who is documented extralocally, or the mention of a local person known from dated records.

For example, an important collection of Makiritare sacred lore from the Venezuelan upper Orinoco, which de Civrieux and later Guss translated as the "creation cycle" *Watunna*, becomes historically intelligible through synchronisms with events and places known from Spanish, Dutch, and Venezuelan documentation. One passage of Guss's rendering tells how in remote times Makiritare went to meet a rich, benign child of the culture hero Wanadi. The child Iaranavi

was the rich man, Wanadi's shopkeeper, friend to the poor. He was always travelling around, trading goods. Our grandfathers travelled to Ankosturaña too to get goods from Iaranavi. They learned how to trade there, how to exchange their stuff for the things they didn't have.[58]

Ankosturaña can be linked to Angostura, an old toponym corresponding to Puerto Bolívar. Iaranavi's trade refers to an early and successful phase of Spanish trade with the Makiritare starting in 1759. The subsequent

---

[58] Marc de Civrieux and David M. Guss, *Watunna* (San Francisco, 1980), 154–156.

embitterment of Spanish-Makiritare relations leading to a successful re-bellion in 1775 has condensed into the mythicized figure of the evil Fañuru (*español* pronounced in local phonology). The story of a miracu-lous journey to the lake of heaven recalls in mythohistoric diction the Makiritare renewal of trade, this time via a Dutch seaport in Guyana. Because the colonial record in some parts of South America is among the world's longest, and because from the 1560s onward Spanish organization placed literate persons inside the hearths of many thousands of commu-nities, the prospect of finding synchronisms with local tradition is reason-ably favorable.

Sometimes testimonies not meant to set forth a chronological history do so unintentionally. Such information, unconsciously imparted and therefore relatively light of ideological cargo, can be retrieved by analyti-cal readings. Max Uhle's South American disciples realized this from the 1920s on, when propounding onomastic analysis ("the etymological method," focalizing names of places and people). A series of methodolog-ical errors casts a shadow over this work. Onomastics can, however, be modernized with appropriate linguistic and statistical controls. The en-semble of names of persons or of places in, for example, a tribute inspection or a census forms a natural distribution of cultural artifacts comparable with the distribution of archaeological artifacts over a land-scape. Like a ceramic distribution, an onomasticon can be analyzed to reveal continuities and discontinuities in time and space. In northern Peru, two recent studies have linked linguistic regularities in place names to prehispanic cultural movements rarely accessible via archaeology or the overt layer of colonial texts. Changes in distribution of personal names reveal how post-Inka Ecuadorians appropriated Inka name ele-ments, or how nineteenth-century Paraguayan nationalism undercut Guaranían expressions of personhood.

Perhaps the strongest link in the connection between native and exterior accounts of the past will eventually emerge from historical ar-chaeology. Accounts of Inka roads and waystations in the chronicles have been closely matched to remains on the ground. Probably the most complete archaeological-documentary synthesis occurs in Arno Kern's exploration of Jesuit missions in Guaraní lands. A few important early-colonial documentary reports, such as those describing deepwater seafar-ing based at Chincha, multiethnic coca exploitation in the Chillón Valley, the trading of "axe-monies" and "shell-monies" through wide swaths of the continent, and the long-distance traffic in *Spondylus* shell up and down the Pacific shore, have become the object of sustained archaeological research. Early colonial European objects such as glass beads, metal buttons, and glazed pottery are found all over the continent in indigenous archaeological context, and whole village sites showing colonial architecture have still-unexploited documentary correlates. But on the whole, the reconnection of the world of words with the world of things is still, in the South American theater, unfinished business.

CULTURAL DISTANCE AND HISTORIOGRAPHIC SYNTHESIS

Does the huge store of South American Indian lore about the past that already exists in writing allow a "history of Indians" that also embodies "Indian history"? The contributors to this book have taken varied approaches, but no one can yet claim that the exchange between Amerindian histories and the European historiographic tradition is as coherent as that between, for example, Amerindian folk botany and the life sciences. On the whole, five centuries after Europe discovered that it lacked historic orientation to a huge part of humanity, we are still in a position to make only modest claims for a transatlantic dialogue about human time and change.

In this volume, the contributors have strengthened "history of Indians" by synthesizing a great deal of research that postdates the *Handbook of South American Indians.* They have read older information with new awareness that colonial history, as much as any other, is history made by, and not just inflicted on, American peoples. It has become possible both to picture overarching linkages and dynamics across societies, where only tribal microhistories were once visible (such as in most of Amazonia). Conversely, it has become possible also to distinguish variety and microdynamics where vast imperial structures once monopolized research (as in most of the Andes). Little by little scholarship has allowed itself to be influenced by (and not just to be aware of) South American categorizations that organize the social universe in unfamiliar ways. The division of South America into parts defined aprioristically, by imposing European discriminators like level of sociopolitical complexity or ecological base, is starting to give way to distinctions built upward from knowledge of connection and discontinuity among Native American actors on the ground.

But in learning to work with the testimonies of native South America, the voices that form part of each collectivity's own dialogue with the past, we confront a cultural heterogeneity that we still need to respect as an unknown. The foregoing pages illustrate that the academic construct "history" is overspecialized for the purpose of apprehending South American discourses about the past. We can hold onto it as a heuristic device, but not as an imputed universal. In many cases, on any continent, people's motives and axioms in talking about the past are not primarily centered on creating registers of factual events and causal links among them. When South Americans speak of the past, they may be practicing mythopractical rehearsal of "primordial" categories, shamanic retrieval of a redemptive past, or the establishment of moral continuity through vengeance. Their pasts may work as images of proprietary claims in segmented society. They may be manifestos of ethnic resurgence. Their narratives may seek emotive catharsis in mourning, laughter, or fellow-feeling. Satire and subversion sometimes outrank the preservation of continuity as motives for rehearsing the past. The projection of collective "self" to foreigners, and many other steps in the protean dance of cultures, all seem like history-telling, but only from one of several possible angles.

That one can retrieve from all these doings statements which resemble the products of historiography is a small fact about a vast and exuberantly multifunctional domain of action. And installing such history-like statements as pieces within an overall occidental historiography is a means, not an end. The emerging armature of "history of Indians" might turn out to be useful mostly as a framework for understanding diversity in human ways of inhabiting time and change – not only other "emplotments" of memory, in Hayden White's terms, but other ways of inserting memory into social life. Ultimately, if the growth of academic historiography among peoples as distant from the European academic mainstream as native South Americans formerly were, is to have any benefit beyond filling out the grid of groups and centuries, it will be the benefit of expanding all parties' ability to imagine how human mutability functions and appears to its agents under varying cultural principles. The task remains almost as incomplete after the quincentennial as it was before. But the nature of the job becomes clearer.

BIBLIOGRAPHIC ESSAY

For the English-reader, entry points to the dispersed literature about South American folk history are Jonathan D. Hill's *Rethinking history and myth* (Champaign, Illinois, 1988) and Joanne Rappaport's *The politics of memory* (New York, 1990). Susan Niles' *South American Indian narrative* (New York, 1981), updated in the *Enzyklopädie des Märchens* (Berlin, 1991) covers the area of overlap between folklore and folk history. Hundreds of works listed in Timothy J. O'Leary's *Ethnographic bibliography of South America* (New Haven, 1963) contain fragments of Native American historic lore.

Readers of Spanish will find a much more concentrated introduction in Martín Lienhard's study of native South American literacy *La voz y su huella* (Hanover, New Hampshire, 1991) and the excellent sourcebook accompanying it, *Testimonios, cartas, y manifiestos indígenas* (Caracas, 1992). The excerpt from Ñenguiru's 1753 Guaraní letter comes from the latter.

Anne Marie Hocquenghem's *Iconografía mochica* (Lima, 1987), Jürgen Golte's *Iconos y narraciones* (Lima, 1994), and Christopher Donnan's *Moche art and iconography* (Los Angeles, 1976) clarify northern Peruvian image-narratives. Thomas A. Sebeok's *Native languages of the Americas*, vol. 2 (New York, 1977), contains Thomas S. Barthel's summation "Writing systems." In *Ethnological Studies* 6 (Gothenburg, Sweden 1938), Henry Wassén reproduces several examples of Cuna "picture writing." Dick Edgar Ibarra Grasso's *La escritura indígena andina* (La Paz, 1953) contains much of what is known about Bolivian pictorial texts. Robert and Marcia Ascher consulted nearly all known *khipu*s for *Code of the quipu* (Ann Arbor, 1981).

The triumph of writing over indigenous media has received critical attention in, among other works, Walter Mignolo's *The darker side of the Renaissance: Literacy, territoriality, and colonization* (Ann Arbor, 1995), and *Writing without words: Alternative literacies in Mesoamerica and the Andes*, edited by Elizabeth Hill Boone and Walter D. Mignolo (Durham, 1994).

The 1987 Madrid edition of Juan de Betanzos' 1551 *Suma y narración de los Incas*, edited by María del Carmen Rubio, contains important recently recovered chapters; it has been translated into English by Roland Hamilton as *Narrative of the Incas* (Austin, 1996). For 1542 *khipu* testimony, see Callapiña, Supno, et al. (baptismal names not stated), *Relación de la descendencia, gobierno, y conquista de los Incas* (Lima, 1974). Part of Cieza's work is available in English: *The Incas of Pedro Cieza de León* (Norman, Oklahoma, 1967). Father Bernabé Cobo's 1650 synthesis has been translated as *History of the Incas* (Austin, 1979) and *Inca religion and customs* (Austin, 1990), and a number of other chronicles containing data of indigenous origin are available in more or less responsible translations.

Among the most famous "bureaucratic" sources is Iñigo Ortiz de Zúñiga's *Visita de la provincia de León de Huánuco en 1562* (2 vols., Huánuco, 1972). María Rostworowski reprints perhaps the richest single lawsuit in *Conflicts over coca fields in XVIth-century Peru* (Ann Arbor, 1989) with valuable explanatory material. Luís Millones and collaborators reprint the whole *Taki Unquy* corpus in *El retorno de las Huacas* (Lima, 1990). Frank Salomon and George Urioste have translated *The Huarochirí manuscript* ([1608?] Austin, 1991).

Thomas Sebeok's *Native languages of the Americas* vol. 2 (New York, 1977) contains Jorge A. Suárez's conspectus on Latin America's "Classical languages." Many colonial works on native language are cited in Čestmír Loukotka's *Classification of South American Indian languages* (Los Angeles, 1986). For a history of Andean languages, see Bruce Mannheim, *The language of the Inka since the European invasion* (Austin, 1990). Paul Rivet and Georges de Créqui-Montfort's great *Bibliographie des langues aymará et kičua* (4 vols., Paris, 1951–1956) remains indispensable. The twin monuments of Andean lexicography are newly reprinted: Ludovico Bertonio's 1612 *Vocabulario de la lengua aymara* (Cochabamba, 1984) and Diego Gonçález Holguín's 1608 *Vocabulario de la lengua general de todo el Peru* (Lima, 1989). Their nearest lowland counterpart is the 1639 *Gramática y diccionario de la lengua tupi ó guaraní* by Antonio Ruiz de Montoya (Vienna, 1876). For colonial Guaraní, see Bartolomeu Melià's contribution to *America Latina en sus Lenguas Indígenas*, edited by Bernard Pottier (Caracas, 1983). An example of recent scholarship on written colonial Quechua is César Itier *Del siglo de oro al siglo de las luces* (Cusco, 1994).

Pierre Duviols reprints many "idolatry" trials in *Cultura andina y represión* (Cusco, 1986); recent English treatments are Nicholas Griffiths's *The cross and the serpent: Religious repression and resurgence in colonial Peru* (Norman, 1996) and Kenneth Mills' *Idolatry and its enemies* (Princeton, 1997). The three famous "native chronicles" are Titu Cusi Yupanqui's *Relación de la conquista del Perú* (Lima, 1973), Felipe Guaman Poma de Ayala's 1615 *Nueva corónica y buen gobierno* (3 vols., México D.F., 1980), and Joan de Santa Cruz Pachacuti Yamqui Salcamaygua's 1613 *Relación de antigüedades deste reyno del Perú* (Cusco, 1993). The translation of Guaman Poma by C. Dilke is unfortunately not accurate enough to be usable. Harold Livermore has handsomely translated Garcilaso Inca

de la Vega's 1609 *Royal commentaries of the Incas* (2 vols., Austin, 1966).
Rolena Adorno's *Guaman Poma, writing and resistance in colonial Peru*
(Austin, 1986) offers English commentary.

Miguel León-Portilla's *Visión de los vencidos* (México D.F., 1959) may
be compared with Nathan Wachtel's *Vision of the vanquished*, which
appeared in English in 1973 (New York). An outstanding example of
Marxian but also ethnographic-minded history of that period is Karen
Spalding's *De indio a campesino* (Lima, 1974); see also José Bengoa's
Historia del pueblo mapuche (Santiago, Chile, 1985).

Julian Steward and Louis Faron summarized the 1946–1950 *Handbook
of South American Indians* in their 1959 *Native peoples of South America*
(New York); Claude Lévi-Strauss's *The savage mind* (*La Pensée sauvage*)
(Paris, 1962) was republished in English in 1966 (London). John H.
Rowe's argument for "Absolute chronology in the Andean area" was
published in *American Antiquity* 10 (1945), 265–284. The quote from
Sabine MacCormack appears in "The fall of the Incas: A historiographi-
cal dilemma," *History of European Ideas* 6 (1985), 421–446. R. Tom
Zuidema's position is quoted from his 1982 "Myth and history in ancient
Peru," in *The logic of culture*, edited by Ino Rossi (South Hadley, Mass.,
1982). The Spanish original is 1977. Gary Urton studies "concretization"
in *The history of a myth* (Austin, 1990). Manuela Carneiro da Cunha and
Eduardo Viveiros de Castro's "Vingança e temporalidade" appears in
Journal de la Sociéte des Américanistes 71 (1985), 191–208; see also the
latter's *From the enemy's point of view* (Chicago, 1982).

Amazonian studies with more or less marked folk-historical content
include Harald Schultz, "Lendas waurá" in *Revista do Museu Paulista*
Nova Série 16 (1965–1966), 21–150; Bartolomeu Giaccaria and Adalberto
Heide, *Jerônimo Xavante conta mitos e lendas* (Campo Grande, Mato
Grosso, Brazil, 1975); Protásio Frikel, *Os kaxúyana: notas etno-históricas*
(Belén-Pará, 1970); Karin Hissink and Albert Hahn, *Die Tacana I: Erzäh-
lungsgut* (Stuttgart, 1961); Curt Nimuendajú, *Os Apinayé* [1939] (Belém-
Pará, 1983). Comparable works from Roraima and Orinoquia are Everard
Im Thurn, *Among the Indians of Guiana* [1883] (New York, 1967); Wil-
liam Henry Brett, *Legends and myths of the aboriginal Indians of British
Guiana* (London, 1879); Theodor Koch-Grünberg, *Del Roraima al Ori-
noco* [1924] (3 vols., Caracas, 1979–82). The Abipón material is from
Martin Dobrizhoffer, *An account of the Abipones, an equestrian people of
Paraguay* [1784] (3 vols., London, 1822). For other areas, see Gerardo
Reichel-Dolmatoff, *Los Kogi* [1949] (2 vols., Bogotá, 1985); Johannes

Wilbert, ed., *Folk literature of the Yamana Indians: Martin Gusinde's collection of Yamana narratives* (Los Angeles, 1977); Martin Gusinde, *Los indios de tierra del fuego. Tomo primero volumen I y II. Los Selk'nam* [1931] (Buenos Aires, 1982).

On the biblicized editing of oral lore, see André Marcel D'Ans' *La verdadera Biblia de los Cashinahua* (Lima, 1975). Sirio Pellizaro has edited the ever-growing *Mundo Shuar* (Sucúa, Ecuador) since 1976. Ellen Basso analyzes the Saganafa text in chapters 2 and 3 of *A musical view of the universe* (Philadelphia, 1985), and sets it into a broader exegesis of Kalapalo understandings of change in *The last cannibals. A South American oral history* (Austin, 1995).

Quintín Lame's book was published in Spanish as *En defensa de mi raza* (Bogotá, 1971) and reappears in English in Gonzalo Castillo Cárdenas, *Liberation theology from below* (Maryknoll, New York, Orbis, 1987). Berichá's *Tengo los pies en la cabeza* (Bogotá, 1992) merits the attention of Spanish readers. Amazonian works in which native oral authorship is to varying degrees respected are Jon Landaburu and Roberto Pineda Camacho, *Tradiciones de la gente del Hacha* (Bogotá, 1984); Aurelio Chumap Lucía and Manuel García-Renduelas, *"Duik Múun . . ."* (2 vols., Lima, 1979); Umúsin Paulõn Kumu and Tolamõn Kenhiri, *Antes o mundo não existia*, edited by Berta G. Ribeiro (São Paulo, 1980). Floresmiro Dogiramá's *Zroārā nēburā*, edited by Mauricio Pardo (Bogotá, 1984) was compiled on the Colombian Pacific littoral. Father Ernesto Wilhelm de Moesbach published Coña's autobiography under the title *Vida y costumbres de los indígenas araucanos en la segunda mitad del siglo XIX* (Santiago, Chile, 1930). For later oral autobiography, see Gelles's and Martínez Escobar's translation *Andean lives* (Austin, 1996) of the Quechua narrative *Alejandro Mamani* (Cusco, 1977), or Domitila Barrios de Chungara, *Let me speak*, edited by Moema Viezzer [1977] (New York, 1978). Lucy Briggs has resuscitated the Aymara/Spanish/English text of *Manuela Ari: An Aymara woman's testimony of her life*, originally collected by Harry Tschopik (Bonn, 1995). See also Ana María Condori, *Nayan uñatatawi. Mi despertar* (La Paz, 1988), *Memorias de un viejo luchador campesino: Juan H. Pévez*, Teresa Oré, ed. (Lima, 1983), Enrique Encinas, *Jinapuni. Testimonio de un dirigente campesino* (La Paz, 1989), and Martín Painemal Huenchual, *Vida de un dirigente mapuche* (Santiago, 1983?). The miner Juan Rojas's autobiography exists in English as *I spent my life in the mines* (New York, 1992). Emily Ethel Wallis edited a representative conversion autobiography, *Tariri* (London, 1965).

Among the few works of explicit oral historiography are Andean studies such as Silvia Rivera Cusicanqui and Zulema Lehm, *Los artesanos libertarios y la ética del trabajo* (La Paz, 1988) and José Matos Mar, *Taquile en Lima* (Lima, 1986). Amazonian examples are Claudio Villas-Bôas and Orlando Villas-Bôas' edition *Xingu. O velho Káia (conta a historia do seu povo)* (Porto Alegre, 1984), Roberto Pineda Camacho, *Historia oral y proceso esclavista en el Caquetá* (Bogotá, 1985), and Blanca Muratorio, *The life and times of Grandfather Alonso* (New Brunswick, N.J., 1991). Ecuador offers several works by native historical researchers: *Villamanta ayllucunapac punta causai* by Antonio Males (Quito, 1985), which is mostly in Spanish, and José Yánez del Pozo, *Yo declaro con franqueza* (Quito, 1986). Curapil Curruhuinca and Luís Roux have written several works on Araucanians including *Las matanzas de Neuquén* (Buenos Aires, 1984). *Yurupary*, an important Tupí-Guaraní literary working of myth, has been retranslated from Italian to Spanish by Susanna N. Salessi and includes comments by Héctor H. Orjuela (Bogotá, 1983). The modern Spanish-language works of Miguel Angel Jusayú include *Jukûjálairrua Wayú* (Caracas, 1976). *El escribano de los caciques apoderados / Kasikinakan Purirarunakan Qillqiripa* (La Paz, 1992) contains the memoirs of Leandro Condori Chura as edited by Esteban Ticona Alejo. An example of the homemade historiography evoked by publication contests is Lorenzo Inda C., *Historia de los Urus. Comunidad Yrohito Yanapata* (La Paz, 1988).

The "literacy thesis" was initially stated in Jack Goody and Ian Watt, *Literacy in traditional societies* (Cambridge, 1968) and Walter J. Ong, *Orality and literacy* (London, 1982). For critiques, see Jan Vansina, *Oral tradition as history* (Madison, 1985) and Brian Street's *Literacy in theory and practice* (New York, 1984). Alejandro Ortiz Rescaniere's *De Adaneva a Inkarrí* (Lima, 1973) is the source of the "School Myth." Cuna oral literature and related writings are the subject of a fascinating literature including James Howe, *The Kuna gathering* (Austin, 1986), Fritz W. Kramer, *Literature of the Cuna Indians* in *Etnologiska Studier* (Gothenburg, Sweden, 1970), Henry Wassén, *Original documents from the Cuna Indians of San Blas, Panama* in *Etnologiska Studier* 1938, and other products of Gothenburg-sponsored research. On Colombia's folk-historical tradition about Amazonia, see Michael Taussig's *Shamanism, colonialism, and the wild man* (Chicago, 1986) and John Holmes McDowell, *Sayings of the ancestors* (Lexington, 1989). Alcida Ramos has considered the refashioning of leadership tradition in "Indian voices" (see also Norman E.

Whitten Jr.'s "Historical and mythic evocations of chthonic power") in Jonathan Hill's *Rethinking history and myth* (Champaign, Ill., 1988). The same volume contains Mary Dillon and Thomas Abercrombie, "The destroying Christ: An Aymara myth of conquest." Peter Gow has contributed variously on vehicles of memory – for example, in "Gringos and wild Indians – Images of history in Western Amazonian cultures," *L'homme* 33 (1993), 327–347. Rosaleen Howard-Malverde's *The speaking of history: "Willapaakushayki" or Quechua ways of telling the past* (London, 1990) contains well-translated Quechua texts and a close analysis of a central Peruvian discourse of the past in relation to folk society and to literacy.

On the refashioning of Inka memories, see Kathleen Klumpp "El retorno del Inga: una expresión ecuatoriana de la ideología mesiánica andina" in *Cuadernos de Historia y Arqueología* (Guayaquil) 41 (1974), 99–135, and Alberto Flores Galindo, *Buscando un Inca* (Lima, 1987). Xavier Albó studies modern derivatives of remembered rebellion in "From MNRistas to Kataristas to Katari" in *Resistance, rebellion, and consciousness in the Andean peasant world*, edited by Steve J. Stern (Madison, 1987).

Vansina's *Oral tradition as history* contains many clues for comparison with other continents with respect to sociology of historic knowledge *inter alia*. The Gola example is from Warren D'Azevedo, "Uses of the past in Gola discourse," *Journal of African History* 3 (1962), 11–34. The retranslation of Makiritare narrative comes from Marc de Civrieux and David M. Guss, *Watunna* (San Francisco, 1980). English-language examples of onomastic method include Christina Bolke Turner's and Brian Turner's "The role of mestizaje of surnames in Paraguay in the creation of a distinct New World ethnicity," *Ethnohistory* 41 (1993), 139–165, and Frank Salomon and Sue Grosboll, "Names and peoples in Incaic Quito," *American Anthropologist* 88 (1986), 387–399. John Hyslop's *The Inka road system* (Orlando, Florida, 1984) and *Inka settlement planning* (Austin, 1990) exemplify detailed coordination of colonial literature with archaeological surface survey. Colonial missions to the Guaraní-speaking peoples are the object of both historical and archaeological study, of which a distinguished example is Arno Kern's *Missões, uma utopia politica* (Porto Alegre, 1982); see also José Antonio Gómez-Perasso, *Interpretación de estructuras en arqueología histórica* (Asunción, 1984).

2

ETHNOGRAPHY IN SOUTH AMERICA:
THE FIRST TWO HUNDRED YEARS

SABINE MACCORMACK

INTRODUCTION

The arrival of Europeans on the South American continent, and the wars of conquest and journeys of exploration that soon followed, occasioned much writing of diverse kinds. This chapter concerns the development of European ideas about "Indians," and some consequences of these ideas. Rough-hewn narratives by soldiers, fortune hunters, and explorers rub shoulders with historical works of sophistication and elegance. The Spanish crown issued administrative questionnaires about South American peoples, their religions, governments, and regional histories, and also about the continent's geography, fauna, and flora, thereby generating volumes of responses by colonial officials. Systematic lexical and grammatical studies of Amerindian languages written for and by missionaries can be supplemented by less learned but often valuable observations of a more casual nature. In addition, there are maps and itineraries, letters and lawsuits. Beyond all that, a voluminous literature soon came into existence in Europe to rearrange and reinterpret data found in eyewitnesses' original writings with a view to European tastes and predilections. And finally, there also exists a small but precious corpus of writings by Amerindians, recording how those who were at home on the continent perceived the destruction of much of their world and the transformation of what remained within the framework of foreign-created institutions.

Even so, however much we propose to focus on the cultures and histories of the native peoples of the Americas, it is impossible to get away from the productions of foreigners: Spaniards and Portuguese, Germans, Italians, Frenchmen, and Englishmen who wrote down their experiences of the newly discovered continent. Even as writing took place, writing supplanted, and as a result destroyed, alternative, indige-

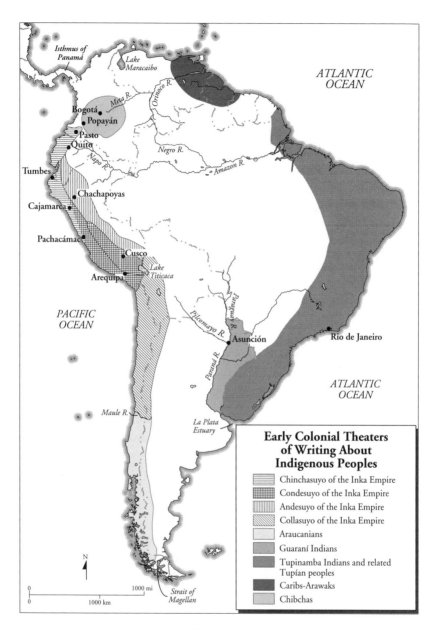

Early Colonial Theaters of Writing About Indigenous Peoples

- Chinchasuyo of the Inka Empire
- Condesuyo of the Inka Empire
- Andesuyo of the Inka Empire
- Collasuyo of the Inka Empire
- Araucanians
- Guaraní Indians
- Tupinamba Indians and related Tupían peoples
- Caribs-Arawaks
- Chibchas

Map 2.1

nous methods of handling and preserving information. Writing was a tool of the invaders, an instrument to organize and control subject populations, preserving, for the most part, only those aspects of their cultures, religions, and historical memories that were meaningful in the new colonial context. But that is not the whole story. For, as a tool, writing was in some respect neutral. Just as in early medieval Europe, it had been monks and other ecclesiastics who preserved within their Christian and Latin literary culture certain fragments, and sometimes more than fragments, of the Germanic cultures that Christianity destroyed or modified, so also in the Americas. Furthermore, a written text, once it leaves the writer's hands, acquires a certain autonomy because the contexts within which, and reasons for which, it will be read are inevitably independent of whatever a writer might have hoped for or intended. And finally, from the sixteenth century onward, writing has been and continues to be used by native Americans irrespective of what the many newcomers to the continent might say. In short, the plethora of voices that comes to us from sixteenth- and seventeenth-century South America does not sound a uniform melody, or even a coordinated set of themes. Instead, confusions of the moment, uncertainties in the writer's mind, arguments left pending or incomplete, all conspire to afford many a surprising glimpse of the continent's indigenous peoples, of their actions and words, their feelings and ideas.

With all that, we must understand that the South American continent as conceptualized by Europeans (see Map 2.1) was a very different entity from what the peoples who had lived there for millennia perceived. For the latter, the continent was experienced from within, and its land, however distant most parts of it were from the intimate and familiar world of any given observer, formed a continuous whole. In 1527, the Quirandíes Indians on the Paraná River were thus able to inform a Spaniard that they had heard about the ebb and flow of the Pacific Ocean. But it was not only by hearsay that the continent as such was known to its inhabitants. Consider the following events. In about 1522, the Inka ruler Huayna Cápac, who was at the time in Quito, received information that the heavily garrisoned and fortified stronghold of Cuzcotuyo in Charcas on the southeastern frontier of his empire had been captured by a nation whom the Inkas called Chiriguanos. The Inka sent one of his captains with an army, and for the time being, the disaster was remedied. It was, however, no isolated occurrence, for in 1549 a group of 300 Indians from Brazil who belonged to a group that was distantly related to the Chiriguano arrived in Chachapoyas in northeast Peru and told a story that caused considerable astonishment. They were the remnant of a host of some 12,000 persons who had set out ten years earlier under a religious leader who promised that at the end of their migration they would come to a land "of immortality and perpetual rest," a land without evil. By this time, the Portuguese were systematically occupying the Atlantic coast of Brazil and were organizing it into military and administrative districts, while the Inka empire was already in the course of being transformed into the Spanish viceroyalty of Peru. But the eastern slopes of the Andes, and the vast river valleys of the Amazon, the Orinoco, and the Río de la Plata with their many tributaries, remained largely inaccessible to Europeans. As a result, the long migrations, of which the destruction of the fortress of Cuzcotuyo and the arrival of the 300 "Brazilians" in Chachapoyas were distant reverberations, remained essentially unintelligible to them. By contrast Europeans, viewing the continent from the coasts inward, perceived it as novel and unitary. Also, they saw it not as lands that had been experienced over time and that could be traversed from one end to the other, but as lands capable of being rendered accessible only with difficulty and from a handful of heavily guarded sites, most of which were on the coast.

This reality is plain to see on all the early maps of South America, which provide much information about coastal regions and much less about the interior. Geographical expertise, or the absence of it, in turn conditioned what Europeans were able to learn about the people who inhabited the continent, how they came by their information, and how they organized it. Francisco López de Gómara, whose extremely influential and often-translated *History of the New World* was published in 1553, opened his work with a description of the coastlines of the Americas, beginning in the northeast with Greenland and Labrador, going to the Strait of Magellan and continuing northward along the Pacific coastline as far as California. Gómara collected this information from "the maps of the King's cosmographers" and used it as a framework within which to organize his history. Gonzalo Fernández de Oviedo, author of a history of the Americas in fifty books that are a veritable treasure trove of important information of all kinds, also circumnavigated, as it were, the South American continent in his narrative. Here, a loosely organized order of events in rough chronological sequence follows first the Atlantic hen the Pacific coast of South America, with the Strait of rving as a geographical matrix. It was not until the mid–

seventeenth century that Lucas Fernández Piedrahita, born in Bogotá of a Spanish father and a noble lady of Inka descent, described the cultural and physical geography of South America, as seen from within the continent, as a lived reality. For it was only in this way that he could adequately inform the reader of the geographical whereabouts of his own native land, the New Kingdom of Granada, which is now Colombia.

In the sixteenth century, such a vision was not yet possible. Instead, the geographical criteria that Europeans brought to their descriptions of South America were reinforced by political ones that meshed with the continent's indigenous cultural geography only to a certain extent and incidentally. The Atlantic coast of Brazil from the Río de la Plata to the Amazon was dominated during the earlier sixteenth century by the Tupinamba and related peoples, who shared much culture and spoke reciprocally intelligible dialects of the same language, although they did not form a coherent or coordinated political unit. It was members of this group of societies who reached the Inka empire in about 1522, and Spanish Peru in 1549. According to the treaty of Tordesillas of the year 1494, which assigned newly discovered lands and lands yet to be discovered to either Spain or Portugal, most of the territories occupied by the Tupinamba group and its peers fell to the Portuguese, whereas the Inka empire, Venezuela, the Guianas, and the Amazon Basin fell to Spain. Excepting the Inka empire, the information that Europeans gathered about South America during the sixteenth century came for the most part either from coastal regions or from river valleys, where the European hold tended to be strongest. In 1552, for example, a French Calvinist mission was sent to Brazil, and one of its members, Jean de Léry, wrote an account of the Tupinamba near Rio de Janeiro, among whom he spent some time. Another French mission, this one Catholic, was sent in the early seventeenth century to the Tupinamba on the Maranhão island in the mouth of the Amazon, and Claude d'Abbéville and Yves d'Évreux, who were members of the mission, produced further descriptions of this different group of the Tupinamba. Between 1541 and 1544, Alvar Núñez Cabeza de Vaca penetrated some 1,500 miles up the Paraguay river. Both Cabeza de Vaca and the German Ulrich Schmidel, who traversed part of a similar route between 1536 and 1552, were able to learn a surprising amount about the Indians whom they encountered. Another traveler who followed a river system, that of the Orinoco, was Sir Walter Raleigh, whose *Discoverie of the . . . empyre of Guiana*, published in 1596, describes his journey. There are also, for the sixteenth century, descriptions of the Amazon valley, which mention, all too briefly, the Indian societies that were encountered. All these journeys were motivated by plans of conquest, hopes of exploiting natural resources, or the search for precious metals. At the same time, however, human curiosity about the indigenous world on occasion displaced the tale of domination or acquisition from center stage.

Many of the early ethnographic works about South America were written by Spaniards. Unlike the Portuguese, most of whom were not greatly interested in the peoples of South America, a good many Spaniards, officials, and soldiers, men of significant learning as well as those who had no learning at all, proved eager observers and found much to say about the indigenous world that they encountered.

The ideas and preconceptions that these Spaniards brought to their observations, and that framed their observations in the first place, therefore constitute a fundamental component in what can now be learned about South America in the sixteenth and seventeenth centuries. Some Spaniards who fought in the Americas had earlier fought in Italy, and some of their fathers or grandfathers had participated in the conquest of Granada. Warfare was a part of their expected daily experience. They knew how to appreciate endurance and bravery, even if it was the bravery of their enemies. They had a sharp eye for the workings of different structures of command, and they were deeply interested in different forms of religious observance. Finally, they were acutely aware of questions of comportment, of honor and shame, and, thinking of these as visible via the body, were able to describe a person's physical appearance and physical presence even without the mediation of a shared language. It was from observations accumulated around themes such as these that over the decades, a body of information integrated perceptions of the different populations of South America into cognitive structures developed in Europe. Questions that had first been asked in Europe about Muslims and Jews, Greeks, Turks and Italians were asked again in new cultural contexts where they did not necessarily apply the same way they had earlier.

Meanwhile, both South America and Europe changed, and these changes in turn affected what Europeans were able to learn in South America. The absence in South America of clearly marked linear frontiers, such as were coming into existence in Europe at this time, heightened the fluid, generalized nature of much of the information that Europeans gathered. Frequently, adventurers or missionaries who were traveling beyond the well-trodden routes of the coast or the roads of the Inka empire barely knew where they were.

BRAZIL AND THE GUARANI

In 1500, a Portuguese fleet bound for India made an unplanned landfall in northeastern Brazil. The crews were greeted on the shore by a group of Indians who appear to have been Tupinamba. For over a week, Indians and Portuguese consorted with each other by resorting to sign language, all the while observing every detail of each other's behavior. Here, so it seemed to Pedro Vaz de Caminha, who described these encounters in a letter to King Manuel of Portugal, were people who were as innocent as Adam before the Fall and blissfully free from sexual self-consciousness. Men and women alike walked about naked wearing only red and black body paint and adornments of feathers and string, feeling no shame whatsoever. In addition, they apparently performed no agricultural labor, kept no domestic animals, and followed no discernible form of worship or idolatry. In short, their existence was as close as might be imagined to humankind's paradisal origins.

For Europeans, the years preceding and following the voyages of Columbus were years of millennial expectations: Jerusalem might be reconquered from the Turks; Antichrist might come; a utopian paradisal society might come into existence. This was why Vaz de Caminha, convinced that the Indians would be eager converts to Christianity, glimpsed in Brazil promise of a speedy realization of paradise recovered. The Portuguese would learn the Indians' language, and meanwhile, there were other forms of expression that transcended the limitations of words and sentences. One of the Indians, Vaz de Caminha thought, desired the captain's gold chain, and another liked a rosary of white beads, "but we did not wish to understand," writes Vaz de Caminha, "because we did not want to give them [the chain and rosary]." Some other objects, among them a cloth of feathers and European hats and shirts, did change hands. The Indians at first vomited the Portuguese food they were offered but later, sitting down side by side with the newcomers, became accustomed and swallowed it. Most important, because the Indians freely participated in the celebration of Mass, following and imitating every movement of the ceremony, the Portuguese thought that they in some way understood the ritual's meaning. For the moment, the complicated world of politics, of the exercise of power over persons and territories, which had motivated the voyage that accidentally brought the Portuguese to Brazil, appeared to have been suspended. What Vaz de Caminha observed was individuals and human innocence. He did not consider questions of daily survival, social relations, or political organization as they affected the Indians whom he saw.

But survival, social relations, and political organization moved to center stage as soon as Europeans came to South America to stay, or to exploit its resources. The people whom the Inka called Chiriguano and who invaded their empire in about 1522 had been accompanied on their expedition by a Portuguese, Alejo García, who was hoping to capture the fabled Inka treasures of which some rumor had reached him. There followed other European attempts to travel northward from the estuary of the Río de la Plata and then from the fort and later city of Asunción, which was founded on the Paraguay River in 1537. These expeditions depended for their success on Indian support; sheer necessity led the invaders to observe the indigenous world in much greater detail. The first and most basic need of the European adventurers was for food, which they either stole or exchanged for trade goods, especially metal tools that they had brought with them. It was the invaders' need for food, and also for shelter, for assistance in finding their way, and for military support that conditioned and guided their perceptions of the indigenous world.

The principal suppliers of food and also of military support were the Guaraní. They formed a continuous language group with the Tupinamba, who occupied much of the Atlantic coast of Brazil, and had recently come to dominate, in addition, the Río de la Plata estuary and the valleys of Paraná, Paraguay and Pilcomayo rivers. The Chiriguanos with whom Alejo García had traveled were still another branch of this same group of peoples, which is why Cabeza de Vaca, who encountered some survivors of this expedition in 1541, included them among the Guaraní. Another Spaniard who learned something about the Guaraní was Luis Ramírez, a member of Sebastian Cabot's expeditionary force of Río de la Plata explorers in 1527. Ramírez was aware that the Guaraní were akin to the Tupinamba, had come southward recently, and were widely feared, although on friendly terms with the Spanish.

They move about scattered throughout this land like corsairs, because they are at war with all these other nations. They are very treacherous and rule over a large expanse of this India, for their borders extend as far as the mountains. They exchange goods for metal that has been made into disks, ear ornaments and hatchets; with these latter they cut down vegetation in order to sow their crops.[1]

The crops of the Guaraní, these early travelers noted, consisted of maize, manioc roots, and different varieties of potatoes. They also gathered honey and raised ducks, chickens, and sometimes guanacos; inside their houses they kept large numbers of parrots, whose feathers were valued for personal adornment. The houses were built of wood, with thatched roofs, and were grouped in small settlements, each surrounded by a protective stockade. Other ethnic groups, like the Agaces, and the Yapirúes from the vicinity of Asunción, were nomadic hunters, whereas the Guaxarapos who lived on the Paraguay River near Itatín were transhumants. Between January and April, when the rivers flooded, transforming the entire region into lakes and swamps, the Guaxarapos took to their canoes. Cabeza de Vaca observed how in the center of each canoe

they put two or three loads of clay and make a hearth; which done, the Indian comes aboard with his wife, child and household, and they go with the current wherever they like, making a fire on the hearth for cooking and for warmth, and so they travel for four months of the year, going ashore on lands which remain dry, where they kill deer, tapirs and other wild animals.[2]

When the river banks became visible again, they returned to their houses and fisheries, "and they enjoy this good life, dancing and singing all day and all night," according to Cabeza de Vaca, "for they are people whose livelihood is assured."

Most Indians living in the Río de la Plata estuary and along the Paraná and Paraguay rivers wore no clothes that Europeans thought worthy of the name, but Europeans repeatedly commented on the diverse forms of personal adornment that they saw. According to the German Ulrich Schmidel, men among the Jerus or Xarayes, apart from wearing ear and lip ornaments,

are painted in blue on their bodies from the top down to the knees, and it is just as if one were to paint trousers. The women are painted in a different manner, also in blue, from their breasts down to their private parts. The painting is most handsome, and it would be very difficult here in Germany to find a painter as highly skilled.

---

[1] Luis Ramirez, *Carta a su padre*, in José Toribio Medina, *El Veneciano Sebastian Caboto al servicio de Espana*, vol. 1 (Santiago de Chile, 1908), p. 449.
[2] Alvar Núñez Cabeza de Vaca, *Comentarios*, in ed. R. Ferrando, Alvar Núñez Cabeza de Vaca, *Comentarios y Naufragios* (Madrid, 1984), p. 242.

Not that nudity was equivalent to ignorance of the art of making textiles, for

> their women weave large cotton shawls, very choice, like fine cloth from Arles, into which they work many kinds of figures, such as deer, ostriches [i.e. rheas], Indian sheep [i.e., llamas or guanacos] and all manner of other things that a woman might imagine. In such shawls they sleep when it is cold, or they sit on them and use them in whatever manner they see fit.[3]

As for the king of the Xarayes, Schmidel found him to be a deeply imposing personage, surrounded as he was by hunters, dancers, and musicians, while attendants cleaned his path and scattered flowers and herbs where he was to walk. At meal times, musicians played before the king, and at midday, he watched the most handsome dancers from among his people, both men and women, perform in his presence. In short, thought Schmidel, "he holds court, being the greatest lord in the land."

Cabeza de Vaca likewise witnessed some impressive displays of dignity and power, as when near Asunción, his force was joined by a group of Guaraní warriors. "It was a sight to behold, the order that they maintained, their warlike equipment, their arrows finely adorned with parrot feathers, their bows diversely painted . . . and their drums, trumpets and bugles." In accord with Guaraní custom, Cabeza de Vaca as leader of the expedition received from each Guaraní chief an artfully painted bow and an arrow from each of the Guaraní warriors, whereupon they all started on their march.

> They proceeded in a squadron which was easily a league long, all with their parrot feather ornaments, and their bows and arrows; they went in the vanguard, and behind them went the governor Cabeza de Vaca with the horse, and then the Spanish infantry, with the baggage, and the Indians had their own baggage. In this way they marched until noon, when they rested under some great trees. Having eaten and rested there, they continued along the paths where the Indians who knew the land guided them . . . They continued marching . . . in a squadron and in good order, being some ten thousand men, which was a sight to behold, how they all went painted in red ochre and other colors, with so many white beads around their necks, and with plumes over their heads, and with their copper disks, which, when the sun was reflected in them, spread such a radiance that it was a marvel to see.[4]

---

[3] This and the preceding quote are from Ulrich Schmidel, *Reise nach Süd-Amerika in den Jahren 1534 bis 1554 nach der Münchener Handschrift herausgegeben von Dr. Valentin Langmantel* (Tübingen, 1889), pp. 66 and 67.

[4] Alvar Núñez Cabeza de Vaca, *Comentarios* (ed. R. Ferrando), p. 193

Guides such as Cabeza de Vaca mentioned here were present in every expedition that Europeans undertook in South America. Indeed, without them, and without Indian interpreters, the European penetration of the continent would have been inconceivable. At the same time, these guides and interpreters afford a glimpse of relations among different societies, and of networks of communication that reached as far as the Inka frontiers and the Amazon Valley. Individuals who spoke Guaraní either as their mother tongue or as a second language are most frequently mentioned as translators in the European sources, and Guaraní appears to have been used as a *lingua franca* in the region of the Río de la Plata and the Paraguay. Some of the translators were prisoners of war who had learned a second language in captivity and were handed over to the Spanish along with items of food. Even without working as guides or translators in any formal sense, prisoners were useful sources of information to Indians and Spaniards alike. In addition, Cabeza de Vaca encountered a few Indians who had adopted Christianity, spoke some Spanish, and were known, to Spaniards at any rate, by a Christian name. Cabeza himself persuaded the nomadic Agaces to hand over some of their women to be taught Christianity in Spanish. On occasion, Spaniards learned to converse in an Indian language. Two Spaniards from Asunción, for example, had learned the language of the neighboring Guaycurú, who were hunter-gatherers at war with the Tapua Guaraní. Here, as on other occasions, Indians, in this instance the Tapua Guaraní, some of whom had become Christians, were able to exploit their friendship with the Spanish in order to pursue preexisting enmities. At times, the Spanish, to their own puzzlement, were simply treated like one further cultural group among many, as the following episode illustrates.

With the help of his Guaraní allies, Cabeza de Vaca had defeated the Guaycurú, and following his own principles as well as a recent law of Charles V, he set free the prisoners and made them the emperor's free subjects. But that was not the end of the story. As had been arranged, the Guaycurú warriors returned to Asunción with their dependents,

and about twenty men of their nation came before the governor Cabeza de Vaca, and in his presence sat down on one foot as is the custom among them, and said through their interpreter that they were leaders in their nation of the Guaycurúes, and that they and their forefathers had fought all the tribes of that land, and had always defeated and maltreated them, without being defeated and maltreated themselves. And that since now they had encountered men more valiant than themselves, they were going to put themselves into their power to be their slaves, to serve the Spanish.[5]

Cabeza de Vaca understood this transaction to mean that in the knightly idiom with which he was familiar, the Guaycurú were offering their submission to Charles V of Spain. But this is not quite what was happening. As Europeans learned in greater detail later, when an Indian warrior had been captured, he in some sense lost his affiliation with his group and became a member of the conqueror's, which is just what the Guaycurú warriors thought had occurred. These warriors viewed the Spanish as a newly arrived social group whose members could simply be integrated into preexisting systems of personal and interethnic relationships. Such transactions were possible because, during these early contacts, the irreversible and destructive impact that accompanied the European passion for gold and the control of territory remained unforeseen by the leaders of indigenous societies. This passion, however, guided almost every step that the Europeans took.

Some 500 miles North of Asunción, emissaries of Cabeza de Vaca's expedition encountered a delegation from the king of the Xarayes whose dignified court had so deeply impressed Ulrich Schmidel. Seated in a hammock, and surrounded by some 300 elders, the king conversed with Cabeza de Vaca's men with the help of a Guaraní interpreter. As transpired in the conversations that followed, the Guaraní was a lonely survivor of an expedition which years earlier his people, the Guaraní of Itatín, had sent to "the land further ahead." The king of the Xarayes, whose name appeared to be Camire, had also received news of this land, although he thought that access to it was blocked by a periodically flooded region. At the same time, however, the king knew about the expedition of Alejo García that had actually reached this elusive region. Cabeza de Vaca's emissaries thus thought they were on the right track, all the more so because the Guaraní interpreter informed them that in the "land further ahead" there was a lake with a "house of the Sun" on an island, where "the Sun enclosed itself." Furthermore, the land contained much "yellow and white metal," and finally, so the Spaniards understood, there were villages of women warriors who on occasion consorted with men but only raised their girl children, returning the boys to their fathers.

---

[5] Alvar Núñez Cabeza de Vaca, *Comentarios* (ed. R. Ferrando), pp. 204–205.

Fever and impassable swamps prevented the Spanish from reaching this land, but the fusion of Guaraní and Spanish mythic imaginations that contributed so much to European ethnographic speculation about the South American continent became that much more potent. Perhaps the Spanish misapplied the name Camire to the king of the Xarayes, because in other colonial sources, Candire is a name attributed to the ruler of the messianic land without evil. After all, this land was being sought not only by the Guaraní with whom Alejo García had traveled but also by the kinsfolk of the translator whom Cabeza de Vaca's Spaniards encountered, and by several other migrating groups of Guaraní and Tupinamba Indians. This land of millennial hope, where warfare and conflict would cease, was transformed by Europeans into a land of legendary wealth that would free individuals from the obligations of membership in political society in a quite different but equally uncompromising way. Endowing this land with concrete existence, the German publisher Levinus Hulsius, who in 1599 printed a Latin translation of Ulrich Schmidel's account of his experiences, included in the book a map of South America, which includes the land "Camire" as a place one might actually reach. The map locates Camire west of the Paraná River, which in turn is represented flowing northward into a region of lakes and swamps that matches the description of the king of the Xarayes, and thence into the Amazon River. The Paraná's southern end, on the other hand, headed into the Río de la Plata in the manner that was by then very well understood.

While Candire was a South American name that could be attributed to a place Europeans had long dreamed about under many different names, the women warriors spoken of by the Guaraní translator among the Xarayes lent substance to an ancient story that was quite specific. This was the account, recurring in the myths, histories, and geographical treatises of classical antiquity from Homer onward, that somewhere near the edges of the known world lived a group of warlike women known as Amazons. Sixteenth-century Spaniards could learn from the *Primera Crónica General de España* of Alfonso X that these women had created a fully articulated political society raising only their girl children while the fathers raised the boys. To look for Amazons in an actual social and historical reality thus amounted to more than satisfying an ancient curiosity about possible but improbable methods of government. Rather, it meant thinking that the human world was somehow capable of attaining a completeness in which even an imaginary social order could come to fruition. In a society like that of sixteenth-century Europe, which prized male heirs over girls, the women warriors who raised only girls constituted a reversal of the familiar order. Such reversals were frequently encountered in America. They appeared to be worthy of note because they seemed to correct features of European society, such as the subordination of women, which even at the time were on occasion viewed as flaws. Moreover, considerations of this kind were not altogether groundless, because concrete evidence to substantiate them did occasionally come to light. Cabeza de Vaca, for example, thought that the women of the Guaycurú enjoyed exceptional and exemplary privileges because they were permitted to exempt from death any of the captives their menfolk brought home. Such a captive would be accepted fully into their society. "For sure," concluded Cabeza de Vaca, "these women enjoy more freedom than our Lady Queen Isabel gave to the women of Spain."

What was at stake, however, was not merely the role of women in society but the larger question of how political and social authority was exercised in indigenous polities. Some nomadic groups like the Guaxarapos, whose free and easygoing river life Cabeza de Vaca regarded as enviable, appeared to have no chief at all. Other chiefs, whatever their ceremonial and military role might have been, were not obeyed in any way that Europeans found intelligible. Europeans were slow to understand both the internal traditions and the historical experience that defined relations between any given indigenous group and its leaders. The nature of political authority as exercised in South American societies remained opaque to most Europeans. As late as 1583, a Spaniard describing people living near Santiago del Estero in Tucumán thus noted succinctly, "they do have lords, but these lords are poorly obeyed." Political authority wielded in a fashion that Europeans found recognizable seemed to be the exception not the rule, which was why, when there did seem to exist some discernible sign of a hierarchy of power, it was at once noted. In this kind of world, ancient European myths and stories about reversals of the natural, social, and political order found a ready home, all the more so because they could merge with analogous indigenous myths.

THE TUPINAMBA

By the mid–seventeenth century, hardly a trace was left of the Tupinamba, whose sway had extended along the entire Atlantic coast of Brazil

and some considerable distance inland. Instead, Portuguese forts, settlements, and sugar plantations run by slaves brought from Africa covered
the land that the Tupinamba had once occupied. But in the sixteenth
and early seventeenth centuries, and indeed ever since, the Tupinamba
have provided the outside world much food for thought.

In 1553, the German gunner Hans Staden, who was serving among the
garrison of a Portuguese fort on Guanabara Bay, where Rio de Janeiro
had recently been founded, was captured by the Tupinamba. After nine
months of captivity, he managed to escape. His illustrated account of his
experiences, published in 1557, was incorporated into the extremely influential compilation of diverse writings about the Americas that appeared
in 1592 from the press of Theodore de Bry in Frankfurt. In 1554 and 1555,
André Thévet, the French Franciscan friar and cosmographer, spent some
time with the Tupinamba of the same region, and in 1557, the Calvinist
missionary Jean de Léry did likewise. Their work also was excerpted in
De Bry's compilation. By the time that Staden, Thévet, Léry, and the
Jesuit missionaries who were working among the Tupinamba put pen to
paper, the Indian world of South America was no longer the terra
incognita that it had been to Vaz de Caminha. Rather, the publications
of Amerigo Vespucci, of the Italian humanist Pedro Martir de Anglería,
and of Antonio Pigafetta who chronicled Magellan's circumnavigation of
the globe, and numerous other writings whether published or not, had
produced in Europe a certain familiarity with the "new" continent.
Much of what had been written was inevitably incomplete and in places
misleading, but at the same time, a certain typology of themes had been
established that led those who wrote about South America to order their
materials in accord with these themes and readers' expectations. Thus,
for example, Staden, having recounted his personal experiences in chronological order, concluded his work with a synthetic account of Tupinamba customs and material culture. An attentive reader of Schmidel
and Cabeza de Vaca might have deduced the importance of ceremonies
of greeting in the Tupí-Guaraní world. But Staden, Léry, and Thévet, all
of whom had learned to communicate in the language of the Tupinamba
to a greater or lesser extent, were specific and very articulate on this
subject. In the early seventeenth century, two further French missionaries, Claude d'Abbeville and Yves D'Évreux, who worked among the
Tupinamba in Maranhão, also learned the language and wrote in accord
with that knowledge. Beyond language, certain further topics, mentioned

casually earlier, had by then become de rigueur: These included religion, nudity, and anthropophagy.

At the same time, by the mid–sixteenth century, the world of the Tupinamba was beginning to change profoundly thanks to the presence of Europeans paying for various kinds of Tupinamba labor with metal tools such as knives, hatchets, and scissors. Hans Staden observed how, using a stone wedge with a small stone cutting board, the Tupinamba trimmed their hair, achieving the finely chiseled effect that Jean de Léry reproduced in his illustrations. The availability of scissors completely changed the nature of this job. Staden also noted that Tupinamba craftsmen when attaching stone axheads to wooden handles were now, instead of following their own traditional design, imitating the European method of joining axheads made of metal to wooden handles. Only a few years earlier, Ulrich Schmidel had exchanged axes and knives from Nuremberg for four golden discs and some silver armlets without giving any further thought to the transaction. Tools were one thing, however, and clothes were quite another. Over the long term, Schmidel's idea that body paint could be viewed as a form of dress found no resonance in writings about Indians: Instead, what struck Europeans was that Indians felt no shame and did not want to wear any clothes, even if they were presented with them.

For Europeans, nudity raised a host of difficulties. The feeling of shame at being naked, they thought, was the consequence of Adam's sin, which is why the nudity of Indians reminded so many Europeans of paradise and the golden age, before sin had brought labor, pain, and death into the world. On the other hand, it was inconceivable that the Indians were exempt from the Fall, and thus their nakedness and obliviousness to the feeling of shame remained problematic. Léry accordingly gave a meticulously detailed description of the physical appearance of Tupinamba men and women, of the adornments they did wear, of body painting, of the incisions men made into their skins to denote mourning and the number of enemies they had killed, and of all other aspects of caring for the body. Like the Dominican missionary Bartolomé de las Casas, who was at this same time writing about the nudity of Indians in the Caribbean, Léry also stressed that the women's nudity did not provoke lust. Instead, it was the women of France with their "elaborate attire, paint, wigs, curled hair, great ruffs and infinity of trifles," who occasioned social ills that did not exist among the Tupinamba. Nevertheless, the issue of nudity could not be laid to rest. Thévet suggested that Tupinamba nudity was comparable to nudity in classical antiquity, although it was also true that "we do not read anywhere that nudity is willed and commanded by God." Yves D'Évreux compared the Tupinamba warrior's slashing of his skin to a similar custom of the ancient Israelites, prohibited in Deuteronomy and Leviticus, while Claude d'Abbéville returned to the core of the problem, which was the Tupinamba's apparent obliviousness to shame. He proposed two answers. First, he thought that the feeling of shame was a matter of custom, and that it was thanks to custom that the Tupinamba "experience no more surprise at seeing the entire body uncovered than we do at seeing a person's hand or face." And second, he addressed the wider issue of law.

> Our first parents did not hide their nudity and felt no shame until their eyes were opened, that is, until they had knowledge of their sin and knew themselves to be despoiled of the beautiful cloak of original justice. For shame only arises from the knowledge that vice and sin are a deficiency, and knowledge of sin only arises from the knowledge of law. As Saint Paul says, "I do not know sin except by the law." Because the Tupinamba have never had knowledge of the law, they also cannot know that vice and sin are a deficiency, having had their eyes closed in the darkness of paganism.[6]

The "darkness of paganism" was another of the large issues that came to the forefront once Europeans gained a closer acquaintance with the people of the New World. At first glance, it seemed that the peoples of the Río de la Plata and the Tupinamba had no religion at all, because they had no places of worship and no religious rituals that Europeans could discover. Increased familiarity, however, produced a different and much more complicated picture.

Over time, it became clear that there were indeed no places of worship to be found among the Tupinamba. In addition, they had no priesthood, did not offer sacrifice or prayer to any deity, and observed no sacred calendar or any equivalent to the Christian day of rest. They reckoned time by the moon but, it appeared, had no way of telling one year from another; at any rate, Europeans did not ask questions that led Tupinamba men and women to explain how they knew their own age. As a result, it seemed that the much quoted dictum of Cicero – that there was no nation so barbarous that it did not follow some religion – was quite

---

[6] Claude d'Abbéville, *Histoire de la mission des pères Capucins en l'isle Maragnan et terres circonvoisins* (Paris, 1614, ed. A. Métraux and Jacques Lafaye, Graz, 1963), p. 270.

simply wrong. No sooner said, however, than Europeans began to have doubts about the absence of religion among the Tupinamba. For in effect, it appeared that the Tupinamba did have a concept of God. Jean de Léry thought that this concept focused on Toupan, who was in some sense identified with thunder. But the matter remained problematic, for when Léry attempted to convince his Tupinamba interlocutors that Toupan was indeed the Christian God who cared for all human beings, it became clear that the two concepts did not match:

> We would say to the Tupinamba that we believed in a sole and sovereign God, Creator of the world. Hearing us hold forth on this subject, they would look at each other saying "The!" – their customary interjection of astonishment – and be struck with amazement. When they hear thunder, which they call Toupan, they are much afraid. Adapting ourselves to their crudeness, we would seize the occasion to say to them that this was the very God of whom we were speaking, who, to show his grandeur and power, made heavens and earth tremble. Their resolution and response was that since he frightened them in this way, he was good for nothing.[7]

Similarly, episodes of Tupinamba myth and certain aspects of their beliefs resonated with European ideas. The Tupinamba told of a flood in which only one couple, from whom they claimed to be descended, had survived. Also, they thought that they had been instructed in the arts of civilization by a teacher who had come to them from abroad and who had then left. The flood resonated with Noah's flood, and Jesuit missionaries among the Tupinamba and other Brazilian societies were inclined to think that the teacher was one of Christ's original apostles who had preached the gospel throughout all the world. In addition, the Tupinamba were afflicted by visions of fearful spirits, whom missionaries identified with the devil, while nonetheless being aware that the correspondences between their own ideas and those of the Indians were imperfect. Yves D'Évreux, for example, who in 1613–1614 worked among the Tupinamba who had recently migrated from Guanabara Bay to Maranhão in order to escape from Portuguese oppression, asked if the malignant spirits had plagued them in their old homes. The answer was no. This seemed to contradict the Christian idea that the devil was omnipresent.

Another component of true religion, in European eyes, was belief in

---

[7] Jean de Léry, *History of a voyage to the land of Brazil, otherwise called America*, translation and introduction by Janet Whatley (Berkeley, 1990), p. 134.

an immortal soul. Clearly the Tupinamba believed in an afterlife, when "the souls of those who have lived virtuously go off behind the high mountains where they dance in beautiful gardens with the souls of their forebears." Wicked souls, on the other hand, would go to a place of horror. Missionaries could only agree that this anticipation of reward and punishment in the next life corresponded to their own teaching. But here also there were tensions. The virtue that the Tupinamba most admired was that of the warrior, who avenged himself on his enemies by capturing and then eating them. Such virtue, moreover, was socially rewarded because a victorious warrior was honored among his fellow villagers by being allowed to add his fallen enemy's name to his own. Successful vengeance was thus spelled out not only in warfare but also in the daily life of Tupí villages.

The demands of reciprocal vengeance endowed the life of these villages with a predictable content that Europeans disrupted and changed. The Portuguese occupation of the coast of Brazil pushed Indians inland and occasioned several migrations of Tupinamba Indians in search of a land without evil. Increasingly, this meant a land without Portuguese. Furthermore, the presence in Indian villages of missionaries, representatives of an alien and ever more dominant culture, changed the fabric of Indian life bringing it more in line with what Europeans expected. Throughout the Americas, missionaries were among the most careful and attentive observers of indigenous cultures. But unlike modern anthropologists, they were not participant observers: Rather, they observed in order to bring about change, and increasingly, change went hand in hand with the use of force. When Thévet and Léry lived among the Tupinamba of Guanabara Bay, they were not in a position to convey the Christian message by violence. It was perhaps for this reason that Léry was so profoundly moved by the sheer strangeness of the Tupinamba, a strangeness that he could do little to modify. "During that year or so when I lived in their country," Léry wrote,

I took such care in observing them all, great and small, that even now it seems that I have them before my eyes, and I will forever have the idea and image of them in my mind. But their gestures and expressions are so completely different from ours, that it is difficult to represent them well by writing or by pictures.[8]

Elsewhere, Léry remembered listening to the Tupinamba sing. The occasion was the ceremony in which the *maraca* rattles that were used to

[8] Jean de Léry, *Voyage*, p. 67 (tr. Whatley).

foretell outcomes of wars and the nature of harvests were endowed with a voice to prophesy. Initially, the collective singing, accompanied by ecstatic seizures and fainting, had frightened Léry. But then the quality of the singing changed and

> I received in recompense such joy, hearing the measured harmonies of such a multitude, and especially in the cadence and refrain of the song, when at every verse all of them would let their voices trail, saying *Heu, heuaure, heura, heuaure, heura, heura, oueh* – I stood there transported with delight. Whenever I remember it my heart trembles, and it seems their voices are still in my ears.[9]

Sixty years later, however, Claude d'Abbeville and Jean d'Évreux found themselves in a very different situation in Maranhão. With Tupinamba help, the French had constructed a trading settlement with a fort and chapel at São Luis in the expectation of maintaining a permanent presence in Brazil, so that their missionary endeavor was now reinforced with a certain degree of coercive power. Yves d'Évreux, observing that the Tupinamba believed in an afterlife, studied their funerary customs as an expression of this belief and of true religious feeling. Public mourning for a dead warrior was followed by a panegyric oration in which a chief or other respected personage recounted the noble deeds of the deceased. The warrior was placed in his grave in a seated position, surrounded with what he needed for his journey to the other world: flour, water, and meat, as well as his axes, his fishing hooks, his bow and arrows, and a fire in a small pit. Next,

> they ask him to remember them to their fathers and grandfathers, their kinsfolk and friends who dance beyond the mountains of the Andes, where they believe they will all go after their death. Some individuals give him trade goods to take to their friends, and finally, everyone exhorts him to be courageous on his journey, and remind him not to let his fire go out, not to walk through enemy territory and not to forget his fishing hooks and axes after he has slept in a place. Then they cover him gently with earth, and remaining on the grave for a while, they weep bitterly in bidding him good bye. The women return frequently by day and night in order to weep on the grave and ask if he has already left.[10]

This journey of the dead about which Yves d'Évreux heard from his Tupí interlocutors was the direct counterpart to the journey that the living Tupinamba could and did make to the "land without evil." Indeed, just before d'Évreux arrived in Maranhão, a *page*, or shaman, had

---

[9] Jean de Léry, *Voyage*, chapter 8, p. 67 (tr. Whatley).
[10] Yves d'Évreux, *Voyage au Nord du Brésil fait en 1613 et 1614*, with introduction and notes by Hélène Clastres (Paris, 1985), chapter 31.

led some followers toward the Amazon in search of this land. The difficulty for d'Évreux, however, was that the journey to the land without evil and the correspondingly concrete visualization of the journey of the dead did not match his own Christian concepts of the purpose of life and afterlife. He thus insisted that the dead be buried without grave goods in the Christian manner, in a Christian cemetery. This could only be achieved by resorting to a degree of coercion.

The Tupinamba were warlike people. The decision to go to war was often made by shamans who interpreted the voices of spirits speaking in the *maraca* rattles that every Tupí family owned. The dreams of individual warriors on the eve of a planned expedition were also relevant to the final decision about going to war or not. The primary reason for warfare was to avenge past wrongs, to bring prisoners back to the village, and to consume them according to an elaborate ritual procedure extending over several days. The prisoner's role was to conduct himself bravely, to defend himself to the very end, if possible by injuring his captors, and to know that his kinsfolk would in due course avenge him by capturing and eating those who had eaten him. As all the early observers noted, cannibalism was driven not by hunger but by the desire for vengeance. However, regardless of vengeance, Europeans found these doings hard to understand. The theologians and jurists of Salamanca, who were highly critical of the Spanish invasion and conquest of central and South America, conceded that war could justly be waged against cannibals in order to save the lives of the victims. But Europeans also learned that victims did not necessarily appreciate humanitarian intervention. A young slave told his French missionary master that, deprived of the chance to go to war with the great men of his country, he preferred to be dead:

When one is dead one no longer feels anything, whether they eat or do not eat, it is all the same to one who is dead. I would be grieved to die in my bed, not to die like a great man amidst dancing and drinking, not to avenge myself before dying on those who are about to eat me. Whenever I think that I am the son of a great man of my country, that my father was feared and that crowds gathered around him to listen to him when he went to the tribal meeting, but that now I am a slave and cannot, like great men's sons in our lands, paint my body and wear feathers on my head, my arms and ankles, I wish I were dead. In particular, when I ponder and remember that I was captured as a boy in my own land with my mother, and was taken to Comma where I saw my mother being killed and eaten, I can only regret my life, because I wanted to die with her who loved me tenderly.[11]

[11] Yves d'Évreux, *Voyage*, pp. 71–72.

The gulf of self-perception and feeling that separated Indians and Europeans on this issue of eating one's enemy was profound. The Tupinamba captured Hans Staden, whom they viewed as a Portuguese, and hence as their enemy, in order to eat him. For nine months, watching his captors' every thought, word, and movement, he eluded his fate, meanwhile acquiring a reputation for possessing extraordinary powers. He was asked to pray to his God that a storm might pass, and it did so; he observed that the moon looked angry and threw a chief into a panic; he correctly predicted that another chief would not die of a disease that had struck his household, but meanwhile, Staden was treated as a prisoner in the usual fashion. "You are my bound beast," the women shouted; on another occasion, when Staden was forced to hop with his legs tied together, as was customary for a prisoner, people laughed, "There comes our meat, hopping along." Other prisoners were eaten, and Staden watched, reaching his own private version of extreme wretchedness: "I had become so callous by misery that I no longer felt it." At the same time, however, his very existence raised doubts among the Tupinamba as to the viability of eating captives. On one occasion, a storm arose after a prisoner had been eaten. Some people felt that had Staden not watched, the weather would have remained fine. On another occasion, the chieftain Quoniambec, whom Francois Thévet included in his *Portraits of Illustrious Men*, invited Staden to share a human leg: "I responded: 'An unreasoning animal does not devour its own kind. Ought one man, therefore, to devour another?' [Quoniambec] bit into the leg and then said, 'Jauware sche, a jaguar am I. It tastes good.'" Tupinamba men were named after wild animals and imitated the cries of those animals when hunting. Quoniambec's response to the foreigner thus contained a twofold thrust: On the one hand, he countered Staden's logic by denying its premise, and on the other, he produced the information that in his capacity of eating his enemy he was a jaguar, thereby affording a glimpse into Tupí perceptions of identity that for the rest remained deeply opaque to Europeans.

A person was received in a Tupinamba village in one of two ways: as a prisoner who came as "our meat, hopping along," or as a valued visitor for whom an elaborate ceremony of welcome was performed. Staden and Léry both captured an aspect of Tupinamba life that was utterly lost in Theodore de Bry's influential review of American Indian cultures: the deep ceremoniousness of village life, the deference paid by one individual to another. What de Bry read in and reproduced from the accounts of

Staden and others was perspectives on the lives and manners of savages, of people who lacked most forms of decorous human exchange. But this is not really what Staden, Léry, d'Abbeville, and d'Évreux or the Jesuit missionaries described. Rather, they were struck by the harmony of domestic and village life, by the complex courtesies with which the Tupí greeted their visitors, and by the formalities of verbal exchange that had to be observed in conducting a conversation. Tradition decreed that women should greet a visitor in tears. They should speak of the hardship of his journey, remember deceased friends, and praise the visitor's kindness in coming. Words of welcome from the head of household followed. His task was to enquire after the visitor's name and purposes and to offer refreshment, all of which Jean Léry found to be "quite contrary to our embraces, hugs, kisses and handclasps upon the arrival of our friends." At the same time, however, Europeans themselves belonged to ceremonious societies in which gestures conveyed meaning, and this in turn rendered the gestures of the Tupinamba and others meaningful and intelligible. Furthermore, the Bible and the texts of classical antiquity spoke repeatedly about ceremonious actions that served as illuminating parallels and precedents for American analogs.

There was, however, one difficulty in the functioning of these parallels. Much of European ceremony, both past and present, served to establish and express hierarchy. Bending the knee and uncovering the head in worship or homage, or kissing a person's hand as an expression of respect conveyed subordination. Wearing tokens of power, such as crown and scepter, armor and rare clothing, communicated the superiority of the bearer in relation to the rest. But in the societies that Europeans encountered in the Río de la Plata and in Brazil, ceremonious expression rarely if ever served to articulate rank and hierarchy of this kind. Indeed, according to a frequently repeated refrain, the Indians of Brazil and many other parts of South America quite simply lacked any concept of law and authority.

There were palpable reasons for such an opinion. Children, so it seemed, grew up without formal education, and without chastisement. Private quarrels were rare, but if two individuals did come to blows, people would watch without intervening, and only when the fight was over would they assist in mediating a settlement for the offended party. Such a settlement followed no elaborate juridical principles but simply applied the law of retaliation. Most villages had more than one chief, but Europeans found it impossible to ascertain what precisely their powers were. Indeed, among the Indians of the Paraguay River, it was sometimes difficult for the Spaniards who were fighting in the region to learn who was the chief. Ulrich Schmidel went out of his way to point out that the Mbayá Indians had vassals who obeyed and served them in the same way that "here in Germany peasants are subject to a nobleman." This was, however, an exceptional situation. What Europeans usually noticed was a general absence of subordination and constraint of any kind. Frequently, this absence was perceived by Europeans as a deficiency, the conclusion being that with regard to political order as also in other respects, the Indians remained at a phase of development that the "polished nations" of Europe had transcended centuries ago. On the other hand, many observers were unable to withhold their admiration for the Indians' ability to live with each other in harmony and according to the law of nature in the absence of coercive power exercised by a ruler and by legitimately constituted civic authorities. In effect, among the Tupinamba, there existed no public domain of any kind. The result ought to have been, according to European ideas of the period, a state of nature such as Hobbes described.

No satisfactory answer was found as to why such a state did not prevail in the Americas. Instead, there exist a variety of descriptions of how the Tupinamba ran their collective life. Frequently, classical antiquity provided an explanatory context for the phenomena. Chiefs among the Tupinamba had little authority; rather, as among the ancient Spartans, men of experience were respected as a group and made decisions about war and peace. In a similar vein, the eulogy that was pronounced by a respected elder over a dead leader reminded Europeans of Roman funerary eulogies as described in a famous passage by the Greek historian Polybius. Finally, while the Tupinamba had no legal system, it was also the case that like the ancient gentiles, they lived by the law of nature, and moreover put into practice the precept of Justinian, *honeste vivere, alterum non laedere, suum cuique tribuere*, "to live honorably, to avoid harming one's neighbor, and to give to each his own." Not everything that the Tupinamba did, however, was explained by reference to the ancient world. Several Europeans noted, independently of each other, the importance of persuasion among the Tupinamba. Among people profoundly disinclined to obey orders, a good leader had to speak eloquently if his followers were to join in collective action such as hunting and warfare; he had to explain the traditions of the past as they applied to the present; and he had to create consensus with regard to each day's doings and plans for the next day. As Claude d'Abbeville wrote, a chief of the Tupinamba

has no authority other than giving advice, especially when they are in their assembly or *carbet* which they hold every evening in the open space where their houses are. Having made a good fire which serves them for light and to smoke, they bring their cotton hammocks which they hang in the air from poles fixed into the ground. Once each lies reclining in his hammock with a cigar in his hand, they discuss the events of the day and what is to come for peace or war and any other urgent matter, which they determine according to the resolution of their chief.[12]

Europeans glimpsed some further aspects of this egalitarian mentality among the Tupinamba. In Europe, wars were fought to gain territory, wealth, and power. The Tupinamba, however, did not appreciate wealth and power. They believed that there existed sufficient territory to meet everyone's needs. The only grounds for war was vengeance, which did not produce property or power but was an end in itself. The Tupinamba thus worked not to accumulate possessions but only for simple survival. They had no appreciation for the use of money and consequently were uninterested in learning what it was to buy and sell. The French, believing that the Tupinamba were educable in European and Christian ways, took some of them back to France. An episode that occurred on one such voyage revealed just how wide was the gulf between Tupinamba and European perceptions of value, and of virtuous behavior. Bad weather forced the ship to stop at Falmouth, where the Tupinamba learned to detest the port's traders as "*tapouytin*, worthless white enemies, petty and avaricious," because they would not part with goods for the value offered. A further difficulty was money, because the Indians saw no difference between coins of gold, silver, and base metals. One of the Indians, who had found a small blackened base metal coin, accordingly tried to use it to purchase oysters from a fisherman. On being told that a coin of "white metal" was needed for this transaction, he whitened his black coin with chalk, whereupon, amidst general hilarity, the fisherman also laughed and gave him some oysters. Even so, the Tupinamba Indian could not rid himself of the conviction that the *tapouytin* were both greedy and depraved.

At the beginning of the sixteenth century, Pedro Vaz de Caminha and

---

[12] Claude d'Abbeville, *Histoire* p. 329.

other Europeans had glimpsed in the Americas traces of paradisal freedom, of the golden age and primal innocence that had long been deeply rooted in the dreams and aspirations of the Old World. These were illusions, but not only illusions. What impressed the first Europeans in the New World was that here, human beings felt and behaved differently. They felt no shame, they seemed apathetic to the accumulation of property, and they seemed to need no coercive institutions in order to live in an abundance of "natural charity." On the other hand, the Tupinamba pursued their ideal of vengeance to an extreme that Europeans found repulsive. Yet even vengeance and anthropophagy were intelligible to those who had lived through the French Wars of Religion. It is no accident that Montaigne, who observed and abhorred the calculated atrocities of confessional warfare, found Indian man-eating less inhuman than the deeds of his own countrymen. Jean de Léry, who wrote so incisive and moving a description of the Tupinamba, was one of some 500 persons to survive the siege of Sancerre in 1573; there, during the last desperate months when all stores had been used up, human flesh was eaten. The Europe that had looked in hope to new horizons at the beginning of the century, at century's end struggled not only with religious division but also with the practical consequences of that newly described science, reason of state. This shift in the political and cultural life of the Old World also influenced the way Europeans perceived the Inka empire and the chiefdoms of the Pacific coast, of the Amazon Basin, and of Venezuela.

TAWANTINSUYU AND ITS NEIGHBORS

In September 1513, a group of Indians led the Spaniard Blasco Núñez de Balboa from the Caribbean across the Isthmus of Panamá. In a grand gesture that still fired the imagination of historians over a century later, Balboa took possession of the Pacific Ocean on behalf of King Fernando II of Aragón, regent of Castile. In 1519, the city of Panamá was founded. Very soon, expeditions of adventurers and servants of the Spanish crown set out from there in the hope of founding further cities and settlements, and of seizing the gold and silver treasures that were rumored to exist in lands that lay to the south. Initial explorations of the Pacific coast near Panamá progressed haltingly, even though indigenous people had been sailing up and down these thickly inhabited shores for centuries. It was thus from "Indian lords and merchants and their interpreters, whose trade penetrated much territory," that the royal inspector Pascual de Andagoya heard about the Inka empire.

A few years later, in 1525, an expedition headed by Francisco Pizarro captured an Indian trading raft just south of the equator near Túmbez. The raft was equipped with cotton sails, was manned by some twenty sailors, and carried an impressive cargo of

numerous objects of gold and silver for personal adornment which they intended to exchange with their trading partners. The objects included crowns, diadems, belts, bracelets, leg ornaments and breast plates, pincers and small bells and strings and bunches of beads, ruby silver and mirrors adorned with the said silver, cups and other drinking vessels. They carried many cloaks of wool and cotton, shirts and jackets, capes, head coverings and many other garments, most of them beautifully worked with elaborate craftsmanship, in colors of red, crimson, blue and yellow diversely worked into figures of birds, animals, fish and plants. They carried some small scales similar to the Roman kind for weighing gold, and many other things. Among the strings of beads were some containing small stones of emerald and chalcedony and other precious stones and pieces of crystal.[13]

This detailed list of trade goods reflects not only the affluence and sophistication of the Indian chiefdoms of the region but also the Spanish newcomers' ethnographic interests and powers of observation. During these very years, Catholic uniformity was being forcibly imposed in the peninsula, but Spaniards retained a lively interest in the appearance and the doings of their neighbors in divergent expressions of status, power, wealth, and personal dignity. Ambassadors and ecclesiastical emissaries had long traveled from the peninsula to northern Europe, Italy, and the eastern Mediterranean. Their accounts of what they had seen and experienced established a language of ethnographic enquiry that recurs in narratives written by *conquistadores* from the Americas, when in turn these men put pen to paper to describe or defend their actions. Such writings, whether produced simply for publication, or for purposes of litigation or requesting promotion, were usually designated as *relaciones*, or reports. Insofar as these works discussed the indigenous people of the Americas, a standardized set of themes to be treated emerged quickly, precisely because earlier Spanish travel literature had prepared the way in

[13] Relación Sámano, in Francisco de Xérez, *Verdadera relación de la conquista del Perú*, ed. Concepción Bravo (Madrid, 1985), pp. 179–180.

defining what to ask about and look for. Like their fifteenth-century ancestors in Europe, Spaniards of the sixteenth century in America were interested in jewels, clothing and personal appearance as expressions of status and hierarchy. The list of garments and of items for personal adornment and domestic consumption that were looted from the trading raft captured near Túmbez is far from unique. From these matters concerning the individual, *relaciones* about Panamá, the North Andes, and Peru usually proceed to mention domestic and familial rituals and customs, such as marriages, funerals, and rules of inheritance, and particulars of communal and public life, government, agriculture, warfare, architectural design, and religious belief and ritual. Just as in the Río de la Plata, so in the territories that now make up Panamá and Colombia, Ecuador, Peru, Bolivia, and Chile, the Spanish invaders were dependent for their very survival on their understanding of certain practicalities of life, in particular of indigenous methods of food production and warfare. No such practical concerns explain repeated and extended descriptions of Indian funerary customs, religious beliefs, and methods of exercising political authority. These did, however, raise more transcendental questions as to the nature of human life and society, and the extent to which European and American societies could be compared.

North of the city of Panamá and also in many regions of the North Andes, "tribes," "nations," or "peoples" seemed to be living by the law of nature, much as it had been envisioned by the Infante Don Juan Manuel in the early fourteenth century in a work describing his own Christian as compared to a gentile society. Exactly like Juan Manuel's imagined gentiles, so on the Isthmus of Panamá and in the North Andes, people appeared to observe "no ceremonies or worship" because they had no clear idea of the existence of an all-powerful deity. On the other hand, they lived together in a social life that was ordered "with much justice."

The law of nature was not merely an ethnographic stereotype that Spaniards arbitrarily imposed on alien societies; it was a general social theory. The concept of natural law provided a framework within which such societies could be observed and described. Thus, for example, Pascual de Andagoya described the Indians of the province of Cueva on the Isthmus of Panamá, whom he had encountered in 1514, in some detail. Each settlement, some consisting of only three or four houses, had its own headman.

The lords of this province were small, because there were many of them, and there was much conflict over fishing and hunting, in which many were killed. Lords in their language are known as *tiba*, and the headmen, who are nobly descended, were called *piraraylos*, because being valiant men, they gained fame in war. Those who left battle wounded were honored by the lord with the gift of a house and attendants and received the title *cabra*. They lived in much justice, in the law of nature, without any ceremony or worship. In these provinces the lords in person judged disputes without intervention of judge or bailiff, and also without information from witnesses, because they were convinced that the parties would tell the truth. In these provinces lords took no income or tribute from their subjects except for personal services whereby, whenever the lord needed assistance with building a house, with planting, fishing or warfare, everyone had to contribute without receiving remuneration from the lord beyond celebratory drinking and eating. In this way, neither did lords take from their vassals, nor did they lack for anything, and they were feared and loved.[14]

After mentioning marriage arrangements and inheritance, Andagoya wrote in some detail about shamanistic journeys, funerary rituals, and religious beliefs. All of this, he concluded, added up to "living by the law of nature, to keeping the precepts of not killing, stealing or taking another's wife." Andagoya was not the only one to notice that lordship and political authority as viewed by Indians of the isthmus and the North Andes had no real European equivalents, because they did not translate into any explicit forms of coercive power. Reference to the concept of natural law was one way to describe this state of affairs. Other observers felt that, however strange these Indian social arrangements might be, they nonetheless added up to a political life, something absolutely distinct from primal chaos.

So while many Indians lived "politically," and according to natural law, other Indian societies displayed no discernible signs of political hierarchy. These, according to Pascual de Andagoya, "we call *behetrías* because they have no lord at all." In medieval Castile, people inhabiting regions described as *behetrías* were free to choose their own lords or to omit doing so. In a *behetrías*, accordingly, rights of dominion could not be inherited, and therefore it was impossible to institutionalize power. This was precisely what Andagoya and other Spaniards thought they saw among indigenous societies that lacked a visible structure of authority. For the historian Pedro Cieza de León, who between 1541 and 1550 traveled extensively throughout the Andean world, the distinction be-

---

[14] Pascual de Andagoya, *Relación y documentos* ed. A. Blázquez (Madrid, 1986), pp. 89–90.

tween societies that were *behetrías* and those that were not seemed fundamental. As he saw it, in the region of Popayán in what is now southwestern Colombia, there existed *behetrías* and nothing else. "Above all," wrote Cieza, "these people hate providing service for others and living in subjection." The reason that this mode of existence, free of hierarchy and political obligation, could be sustained, Cieza thought, was essentially ecological and environmental.

These provinces are very fertile, and are surrounded on all sides by dense mountain jungle, swamps and other obstacles. And even if the Spanish invade, the Indians will burn the houses which they inhabit, which are of wood and straw, and remove themselves the distance of a league or two, or however far they see fit, and in three or four days they will have built a house, and in the same time they will plant the maize they need, which they harvest within four months. And if in this place also they are persecuted, they give it up and move on, or return, and wherever they go, they find food and fertile land that is suitable for producing a crop. Hence, they obey when they wish to do so, war and peace are in their own hands, and they never lack sustenance.[15]

Cieza perceived a profound contrast between these decentralized North Andean societies and the very different polities of the Central Andean highlands of Peru. The Indians of Peru, he thought,

serve well and are docile, both because they are more reasonable than the others and because they were all subject to the Inka kings, to whom they paid tribute and always obeyed them. Such were the circumstances in which they were born, and if they did not want to obey, necessity forced them to it. For the land of Peru is desolate, full of mountain highlands and snowy expanses. If thus they were to leave their villages and valleys for these wildernesses, they would not be able to survive because the land yields no fruit and there is no place to go other than their own valleys and provinces. As a result, to avoid death, given that they cannot live alone, they must be subject and not give up their lands.[16]

Cieza was not the first to perceive a fundamental difference between the Inka empire and its northern neighbors. Even the hardened soldiers of fortune who accompanied Pizarro on the expedition that resulted in the capture and murder of the Inka ruler Atawallpa in 1533 noticed that they were entering a very different world as they were approaching the Inka coastal settlement at Túmbez. Some of the settlements further north had indeed been sizable, but houses everywhere had been built of wood and

[15] Pedro Cieza de León, *Crónica del Perú. Primera Parte*, ed. F. Pease (Lima 1984), p. 58
[16] Pedro Cieza de León, *Crónica del Perú. Primera Parte*, ed. F. Pease (Lima, 1984), chapter 13, pp. 58–59.

thatch, whereas Túmbez, like most other Inka settlements and cities, possessed buildings constructed of stone that impressed many Europeans as being superior even to the admired architectural creations of the Romans. Although Túmbez was a mere outpost of the Inka empire, it was the seat of an Inka lord who administered justice and supervised the *corvée* labor that Inka subjects performed for the state. There was also a temple of the Sun, along with a house for chosen women who wove cloth for the Inka state and brewed maize beer for ceremonial uses. The place thus familiarized the invaders with institutions that they were to encounter again and again in their expedition southward. In the words of Miguel de Estete, a member of Pizarro's invading host, at Túmbez,

begins the peaceful dominion of the lords of Cuzco and the good land. For although the lords further North including the lord of Tumbala who was a great man were subject to the Inkas, they were not as peaceable as those to the South. For they only recognized the Inkas and gave certain tribute, but no more; whereas further South they were all Inka vassals and very obedient.[17]

Traversing the chiefdoms and *behetrías* of the North Andes, Spaniards had at times been impressed by a certain splendor of golden jewels and formal attire, and by elaborate rituals that served to distinguish important individuals from the rest. But all this was as nothing compared to the sheer refinement, the solemn and dignified ceremonial, and the hosts of male and female attendants that surrounded the Inka ruler. Traversing the Andes, most Spaniards used any vocabulary that came to hand in order to describe the phenomena they encountered. They thus referred to the maize beer that was brewed by the chosen women of the Sun, *aha* in Quechua, by the term *chicha*, picked up on the Isthmus of Panamá. Andean places of worship were often described as *mezquita* or 'mosque,' while Andean and Inka lords, *kuraka* in Quechua, were almost invariably referred to by the Caribbean term *cacique*. The Inka ruler Atawallpa was thus often described as a *cacique*, but in this instance it soon became clear that the term was a misnomer and that the Inka empire was not simply another chiefdom.

Men who had been trained in Spain to conduct themselves in accord with an elaborately orchestrated courtly ceremonial recognized the existence of a courtly code of conduct among the Inka and described it in

---

[17] Miguel de Estete, *Noticia del Perú*, in Horacio H. Urteaga, ed., *Historia de los Incas y conquesta del Perú. Coleccion de libros y documentos referentes a la historia del Perú*, second series, vol. 8 (Lima, 1924), p. 20.

some detail. But they considered themselves in no way bound by it. On the last day of Atawallpa Inka's freedom, representatives of the four parts of the empire carried him into the square of Cajamarca on his royal litter, the carrying poles of which were covered in silver. Dancers and musicians walked in front. Attendants cleaned the ground where the Inka was about to pass, "which was hardly necessary," wrote Miguel de Estete, "because the people of Cajamarca had already swept carefully." The Inka's sacred person was shaded by a parasol, and alongside his litter were carried the litters of the great lords of the empire, one of them being the lord of Chincha, the most powerful nobleman of Atawallpa's empire. Different groups of Atawallpa's followers wore tunics of varying patterns and colors, among which Miguel de Estete picked out the black and white checkerboard tunics that seemed to him to resemble the liveries worn by European courtiers. Some forty years later, the conqueror's brother Pedro Pizarro still remembered how the gold and silver ornaments of Atawallpa's followers had sparkled in the afternoon sunlight. Long after the Inka were gone, Andean people recalled with yearning the intense solemnity that had projected the ruler's majesty during royal journeys and processions. Inka pomp was a cherished symbol of a lost world of order, dignity, and abundance.

While the Inka ruler's interaction with the multitude of his subjects was articulated by one set of ceremonial rules, another governed the more intimate daily life of the Inka court. One *conquistador* from Extremadura noticed that when Atawallpa spat, he did so not on the ground but into the hands of a lady of his court. He wore his garments only once, and immediately changed if a garment was soiled; on one occasion, a Spaniard thus watched Atawallpa withdraw in the middle of his meal so as to change tunics. He ate alone, from gold dishes and goblets that were set aside for his exclusive use. No one touched the Inka's food once it had been placed before him. Everything that had come into contact with the Inka's person was subsequently burned.

Access to the Inka was carefully controlled. When Pedro Pizarro visited the Inka court stationed outside Cajamarca, he found Atawallpa hidden behind a ceremonial cloth through which he could see, while himself remaining unseen. Even great lords presented themselves before the Inka barefoot, just as they would only enter barefoot into a place of worship. Nobody entered the Inka's presence without carrying a burden or gift as a token of submission and reverence. The *conquistador* Juan de Mena had watched how individuals desiring to speak with Atawallpa would wait, standing at a distance. Francisco Pizarro's secretary Xérez had observed how, coming nearer, they would kiss the Inka's hands and feet. Andean people blew eyelashes to the divine Sun as an expression of veneration, and likewise to the Inka. Like the *huacas*, the Andean holy presences, the Inka was only addressed with lowered eyes. He himself rarely looked at anyone. When giving a command, the Inka did it merely with a gesture of his hands or a glance of his eyes, without speaking. He never raised his voice, expecting from his subject the most unquestioning and unconditional obedience.

Spaniards found the veneration with which Andean people approached the Inka ruler both awe-inspiring and unnerving. Nearly forty years after Atawallpa was killed in Cajamarca, Francisco Toledo, then viceroy of Peru, brought the Inka ruler Túpac Amaru I, who had ruled over a small Inka state in exile, to be executed in the old capital city of Cusco. According to a Spanish eyewitness,

on the day when the Inka was to be killed, a platform had been erected for the execution in the main square of Cuzco, which was filled with over a hundred thousand Indian men and women who were mourning loudly for their king and lord. And Túpac Amaru was so profoundly dismayed that he could hardly speak. Being close to so fearful an end, having been baptized at his own request on the very platform, and having been given the name Don Pablo, it seems that Our Lord bestowed on him his divine mercy and gave him courage and strength in his hour of great need. . . . Raising both his hands, the Inka Túpac Amaru made with them the sign that the Inkas customarily make when addressing their nobles. Turning his face to where most of the *kuraka*s were standing, he said in their language and in a loud voice, "Oiariguaichic!" [Quechua: 'Listen to me!'] Instantly, the shouting, mourning and crying out ceased, and a complete silence descended as though not a living soul had been present in the square. So great was the authority and monarchy of the Inkas, and the obedience that their subjects paid to them.[18]

Among other things, Túpac Amaru urged his subjects to become Christians, and he was then beheaded. "As soon as the Inka's speech was ended," continued our eyewitness,

the Indians began once more to grieve and mourn, even more so at the sight of the execution, in a way that, without having seen it, is impossible to imagine. The head was placed on the pillory, whence the Viceroy ordered it to be

---

[18] Antonio Bautista de Salazar, "Virey Don Francisco de Toledo," in *Colección de documentos inéditos, relativos al descubrimiento, conquista y organización de las antiguas posesiones espanolas de America y Oceania*, vol. 8 (Madrid, 1867), pp. 278–279.

removed the other night because a large multitude of Indians were worshiping and adoring it without even stopping to eat. Such was the veneration in which the Inkas were held, even after they had died.[19]

The death of Túpac Amaru in 1572 marked the end of an era. While he lived it had remained thinkable that the Inka élite and the *kuraka*s of the former Inka empire would retain some decisive position of leadership within Spanish governmental structures. The passing of this era also marked a profound shift in the methods and content of ethnographic and historical enquiry in the Andes. In 1560, the missionary friar Domingo de Santo Tomás, who as prior of the Dominican convent of Chincha had conversed with Pedro Cieza de León, published the first lexicon and grammar of Quechua, the language that the Inka had employed as the *lingua franca* of their empire. These volumes are not merely monuments of meticulous ethnographic enquiry and linguistic scholarship. In declaring that Quechua was as elegant, ordered, and articulate a language as Latin and Spanish, and that it could be described according to the same grammatical concepts, Fray Domingo was entering a plea for Andean self-government, with minimal interference from Spaniards. A capacity for self-government, in the eyes of sixteenth-century Spaniards, expressed itself in knowing how to delegate authority, how to distribute obligations, and how to organize a hierarchy of persons ensuring that a given set of tasks would be performed in an appropriate manner. The presence of such a hierarchy at the Inka court was what impressed the Spanish invaders who watched Atawallpa interact with those who served him, whether they were the ladies of his entourage, the lord of Chincha, or the great general Chalicuchima who stepped into Atawallpa's presence with downcast eyes, barefoot and carrying a burden.

Some ten years later, Cieza, passing through Xauxa, observed the workings of hierarchy in another context. How was it, he had been asking himself, that beyond the frontiers of the Inka empire, entire regions had been depopulated as a result of the wars and epidemics that attended the Spanish invasion, while in Peru, populations, although diminished in numbers, were continuing to exist? His answer was that the long practice of delegating authority and of distributing tasks in accord with the resources of different groups and individuals endowed

---

[19] Antonio Bautista de Salazar, "Virey Don Francisco de Toledo," in *Colección de documentos inéditos, relativos al descubrimiento, conquista y organización de las antiguas posesiones espanolas de America y Oceania*, vol. 8 (Madrid, 1867), p. 281.

the population of the former Inka empire with a resilience that was lacking in more decentralized societies. This perception, which Cieza was not the only one to express, also resounds in the lexicon of Domingo de Santo Tomás. This work abounds in vocabulary denoting levels of authority that range from the *capac çapa* (i.e., qhapaq sapa), the Inka "king or emperor," to the simple *yayanc*, or master of servants. The lexicon also provides terminology for professional specializations of merchants, weavers, embroiderers, potters, and many others, thus assembling, point by small point, the linguistic portrait of a many-layered and ordered society that easily matched European counterparts.

A similar argumentation speaks in the questionnaire that Domingo de Santo Tomás compiled for the use of royal visitors whose task it was to assess the tribute-paying capacities of different Andean regions. Questionnaires had long been used in peninsular litigation and were also used in Peru. During the second half of the sixteenth century, this same method of fact finding was employed in the Americas in order to assemble information desired for purposes of government and the collection of revenue. It was to replace official questionnaires compiled for such purposes by bureaucrats that Domingo de Santo Tomás produced a version of his own, which, so he thought, corresponded more appropriately to what Spaniards ought to learn about Peru and its Inka past. Here, as in the lexicon, the well-ordered quality of Andean society and its various traditions of delegating authority are highlighted. In the questionnaire, Domingo de Santo Tomás distinguishes the Inka or "sovereign lord" of Peru from his "governors," who in turn are not the same as "the lords whose personal vassals the Indians were." In addition, the questionnaire is designed to reveal the crucial point that "in former times" Indians worked for the Inka peoples but did not pay tribute or tax out of their own possessions. They owed work only, applying it to raw goods the Inka supplied. Another expert on Inka government who understood the centrality of this issue was the lawyer Juan Polo de Ondegardo, who was equally convinced that Inka governmental practices should be preserved in the colonial context whenever possible and should therefore be studied carefully. Although not all Spaniards in Peru held these same convictions, a veritable flood of official enquiries during the second half of the sixteenth century led to the amassing of information not only about taxation but also about the geography, climate, ecology, history, and customs of the different Andean regions. The simple and concise reports or *relaciones* that the first invaders had written were thus supplanted by more elaborate geographical and historical reports. Some of these were designed not only to serve the needs of government but also to be incorporated into official histories of the Spanish empire that were being commissioned at the time by Philip II and the Council of the Indies in Madrid.

Meanwhile, the nature of the information that was being searched for and collected in the Andes had also changed. Among the first to realize that Inka and Andean society could not be understood without some grasp of the history of the Inka was Pedro Cieza de León, who made extensive enquiries into this subject while he was in Cusco in 1550. Another diligent investigator of Inka history was the *conquistador* Juan de Betanzos; he lived in Cusco and, having married one of Atawallpa's cousins, learned about the Inka past from this lady's kinsmen. In addition, several lawyers, among them Juan Polo de Ondegardo and Hernando Santillán, pointed out that in order to govern in the Andes, historical knowledge was indispensable, because without it, Inka legislation and legal custom would inevitably remain unintelligible.

Cieza and Betanzos were the first to understand that, as the Inka and many of their subjects had viewed matters, the origin and earliest history of the Inka ruling clan, shrouded though this was in myth, constituted the raison d'être of Tawantinsuyu, the empire of the "four interdependent parts" of Peru. Several assertions converged on this issue. In many parts of the Andes and especially in Cusco, Spaniards were told that ordered political life had begun with the Inka. Previously, according to Cieza, "the nations of these regions lived without order, killing each other." "They were all *behetrías* without order, for they declare unambiguously that they had no lords, but only captains with whom they went forth to war." According to Polo, "each province defended its own land without help from anyone because they were *behetrías*." Various accounts were current according to which the Inka, who came from Pacaritambo near Cusco, obeyed the divine mandate of "their father the Sun." By teaching people everywhere skills of civilization such as agriculture and weaving, they gradually became masters of their empire. According to other versions of the story, the Inka resided in Cusco for many generations but emerged as an imperial power comparable to the Romans when an Inka ruler's younger son, who became known as Pachacuti (Pachakuti, 'turning of time/space,' 'reversal'), defeated an invading army of the neighboring Chancas. Before the decisive battle, Pachacuti Inca experienced a vision of "his father the Sun." During that battle, the Sun sent warriors who helped to gain the victory and were then metamorphosed into stone. Subsequently, Pachacuti initiated the construction of Quri Kancha (Coricancha in colonial usage), the "enclosure of gold," which became the central sanctuary of the Inka empire. One of the facts that convinced Spaniards that Inka statecraft was deeply and inextricably rooted in beliefs about Inka origins was that one portion of all conquered land in the empire was assigned to the maintenance of the state cult of the Sun, with a further portion subsidizing the ruling Inka and the rest being left to the people at large and their *kurakas*. In this way, the pattern of landholding in the empire articulated both that empire's religious foundations, and the sequence or succession of ruling Inka. In the words of the lawyer Hernando Santillán, the subjects of the Inkas still knew who their Inka rulers had been because

when one of these rulers conquered a province or valley, the natives built him a house and assigned fields to him with Indians to work them, and they gave him women as a token of being his subjects and vassals. To this day, the houses and fields which were assigned to and worked on behalf of each of these lords are known. And in this way it is known how many lords there were and who they were.[20]

As Spaniards viewed matters, however, there were some difficulties regarding all this information. For one thing, accounts of the origin of the Inka people contained many components that could only be viewed as legendary. Second, before the arrival of Europeans, writing had been unknown in the Andes. What the Inka peoples did have was a system of encoding information on knotted cords known as *khipus*, which were created and preserved by professional *khipu* makers. Many *khipus* recorded quantitative or numerical information: population statistics; varieties of *corvée* labor to be performed for the state in different regions; the content of Inka state storehouses for food supplies, cloth, sandals, and military equipment; and finally, sacrifices owed to regional and Inka deities. When Spanish officials conducted inspections during the early colonial period, assessing the tribute-producing capacities of different regions, the bulk of the information that they gathered came from *khipus*. Other information recorded on *khipus* was narrative and historical, as, for example, accounts of the origins of the Inka and the accounts of the deeds and accomplishments of different Inka rulers such as were collected

---

[20] Hernando Santillán, "Relación," in ed. E. Barba, *Crónicas peruanas de interés indígena* (Biblioteca de autores españoles, vol. 209, Madrid, 1968), p. 104.

by Pedro Cieza de León and other historians. Like every other early Spaniard who mentioned information from *khipus*, Cieza had the highest regard for its accuracy. At the same time, however, he like many others expressed unease about the nature and content of this information. For example, because historical narratives differed from one region to the next, Cieza decided to dismiss regional narratives and take what he learned from the Inka élite in Cusco as his guideline. Even in Cusco, however, some historical narratives were incompatible with each other. This difficulty was aggravated by the fact that as Spaniards perceived it, the Inka had not devised an absolute chronology with an agreed date from which years were counted. Hence, chronological criteria could not be used to evaluate conflicting versions of Inka history. Moreover, there appeared little possibility of correlating such Andean and Inka chronology as did exist with European equivalents, because in Europe ancient historical texts such as the Bible and the writings of classical and medieval historians and chronographers had served as the foundation of absolute chronology. In the Andes, by contrast, there were the *khipus*, along with recitations and songs about the past performed at Inka festivals, but this did not constitute an equivalent to European written traditions.

The conclusion that, in effect, no writing had existed in the Andes before the advent of Europeans had profound repercussions for all future European interpretations of Inka culture, especially when we consider it in the context of the political evolution of the Andean world during the later sixteenth century. By the time Túpac Amaru was killed in 1572, the project of fostering Andean self-government, so dear to Domingo de Santo Tomás and a number of like-minded missionaries and secular officials, had been shelved. It would be replaced by an interventionist policy that brought into existence a colonial state subordinating Andean interests to those of Spaniards.

The definitive implementation of this policy by Viceroy Toledo was accompanied by a significant shift in interpretations of the Inka past. Cieza and many of his contemporaries had regarded the Inka as the natural lords, the legitimate sovereigns of their people, just as the kings of Castile and other peninsular rulers were natural lords in the lands where they governed. This conclusion was underpinned by the perception that the Inka had ruled for a very long time and that their dominion had been exercised by persuasion and consent and not merely by military might. Before the Inka, so the Spanish believed, only *behetrías*, decentralized societies that were intermittently at war with each other and knew of no legitimately constituted political authority, had been known in the Andes. Indeed, beyond the frontiers of the Inka empire, to the north of Quito and to the south, in Chile, *behetrías* still held sway and were a living proof of the political and cultural achievements of the Inka.

Such appreciation of the Inka, however, did not mesh well with the colonial project of supplanting Inka with Spanish institutions wherever possible. A central premise of the extensive enquiries into the Inka past and Inka government that Toledo organized was that the Inka, far from ruling as natural lords, had ruled as tyrants. For the most part, so the theory ran, the Inka had prevailed by resorting to force and had displaced earlier polities whose rulers ought to be viewed as the true natural lords of Andean peoples, if indeed such a concept could be applied in the Andes at all. In 1572, Pedro Sarmiento de Gamboa completed a history of the Inka in light of these ideas. Like Cieza twenty years earlier, Sarmiento collected his information from Inka notables in Cusco. Toledo himself used these same individuals as informants, while also gathering data elsewhere and from other people. But the questions that were now asked were framed differently. Where Cieza had wanted to explain the achievement of the Inka, the information that was now looked for was about Inka tyranny. Toledo thus asked questions such as:

Whether it is true that the first Inka, who was called Manco Capac, tyrannically and by force of arms subjected the Indians who lived on the site of this city of Cusco and took their land. . . .

Whether it is true that they never willingly recognized or elected these Inkas or their successors as lord, but obeyed them from fear because of the great cruelties the Inkas inflicted on them and on others.[21]

These questions were posed to the descendants of groups whose ancestors, as Cieza had also understood, did live on the site of Cusco before the Inka arrived there. But where Cieza used the Spanish vocabulary of political legitimacy and consent to highlight the harmonious aspects of Inka governance, as well as its long duration, Toledo used this same vocabulary so as to highlight the opposite. As a result, the very survivors of the Inka élite of Cusco declared under oath that

---

[21] Marcos Jiménez de la Espada, ed., *Memorias antiguas historiales y políticas del Perú, por el licenciado D. Fernando de Montesinos, seguidas de las informaciones acerca del señorío de los Incas hechas por . . . D. Francisco de Toledo* (Madrid, 1882), pp. 224–225.

as regards tyranny, they heard Indians say that Topa Inka Yupanqui (the grand-father of Atawallpa) was the first who by force of arms made himself lord of all of Peru from Chile to Pasto, recovering also some provinces near Cusco which his father Pachacuti Inka had conquered, which had rebelled. Because until then, all Peru had been ruled as *behetrías*.[22]

There was thus nothing sacrosanct or worth preserving about such recent and shallow Inka institutions.

At the same time, however, a more difficult and complex issue speaks through the contrasting views of the Inka that emerged in Spanish historical and ethnographic enquiries during the 1550s and 1570s. This is that European political vocabulary, regardless of whether it was deployed in terms of appreciation of the Inka or confrontationally, could not fully describe Inka institutions because these institutions developed according to processes that had no European parallels. The late medieval vocabulary of natural lordship and natural law that underlies some peninsular politi-cal debates of the first half of the sixteenth century, and that also speaks in the enquiries of Cieza and his contemporaries, highlighted the benev-olent aspect of Inka dominion. The vocabulary of reason of state that came to prevail in Europe in the later sixteenth century, and that also underlies the enquiries of Viceroy Toledo, on the other hand, highlighted Inka ferocity and military prowess. Cieza and his contemporaries, who also noticed the military dimension of Inka governance, had considered it to be much less important than Inka success in creating and perpetu-ating institutions of peace. But the real issue was that European concep-tual categories and political experience of whatever period did not fully correspond to Andean equivalents. On the one hand, European catego-ries were instrumental in collecting, organizing, and interpreting consid-erable bodies of data about the Inka and their neighbors. On the other hand, however, these categories veiled from view some aspects of Andean culture, religion, and politics that did not readily fit the available frame-work.

The city of Cusco, for example, made a profound impact on the several Spaniards who recorded their impressions of it during the early decades after the invasion. Streets, open spaces, houses, temples, and palaces were all described in terms of high admiration, but very little was

[22] Marcos Jiménez de la Espada, ed., *Memorias antiguas historiales y políticas del Perú, por el licenciado D. Fernando de Montesinos, seguidas de las informaciones acerca del señorío de los Incas hechas por . . . D. Francisco de Toledo* (Madrid, 1882), p. 254.

said about the principles of political and social order that had brought
these spaces and structures into existence. Among the very first to contemplate these principles was Pedro Cieza de León, who conversed with
Cusco's Inka inhabitants in some detail. From them he learned that the
city was divided into an upper (*hanan*) and a lower (*urin*) region, which
were described as "Hanan Cusco" and "Urin Cusco," respectively; the
Inka lineages who resided in these two regions were likewise known as
"Hanan" and "Urin." Furthermore, so Cieza understood, Cusco was the
center of a network of roads that linked the city to the four parts of the
empire. In describing this road system, Cieza was reminded of the manner in which the Romans had administered Spain, and thus he wrote:

> Four royal roads issued from Cuzco's central square. On the road which they
> call Chinchasuyo, one goes to the lands of the coast and to the mountains that
> extend as far as the provinces of Quito and Pasto. On the second road, which
> they call Condesuyo, they travel to the provinces of that name which are subject
> to Cusco, and to the city of Arequipa. On the third royal road, which is called
> Andesuyo, one travels to the provinces which are situated on the slopes of the
> Andes and to some settlements which lie beyond this mountain range. On the
> last of these roads, which they call Collasuyo, people travel to the provinces
> which extend as far as Chile. In this way, just as in Spain the Romans made a
> division of the peninsula into provinces, so these Indians, by way of keeping
> control of the different parts of so vast a land, did by means of their roads.[23]

Roman analogies of this kind, which were cited repeatedly by Spanish
historians of the Inka, served to explain the sheer size of the Inka empire
and also the sophistication and equity of Inka administration that Cieza
and others admired so greatly. But while explaining one issue, such
analogies hid from view several others. It was thus only in the early
seventeenth century that it became evident that the Inka had conceptualized the four "provinces" of their empire as related to each other in
terms of *hanan* and *urin*, upper and lower, and that this relationship of
the provinces among each other mirrored relationships of dignity and
power among the inhabitants of the capital. The terms *hanan* and *urin*
were thus seen to describe not only, or even principally, geographical
location but also gender, status, cultural traits, and political and economic position. Hierarchy was one aspect of this method of taking stock
of the world, and complementarity was another. According to the historian Garcilaso de la Vega, who had grown up in Cusco as the son of a

---

[23] Pedro Cieza de León, *Crónica del Perú. Primera Parte*, p. 258.

royal Inka lady and a Spaniard, this cosmic and social order had been initiated in the legendary past, when the first Inka ruler and his consort had founded the city of Cusco.

The king desired that the settlers whom he had gathered together should populate Hanan Cuzco, which thus they called "Upper," while those who were gathered together by the queen were to populate Urin Cuzco, and hence they called it "Lower." This division of the city was not made for one half to surpass the other in privilege and advantages, but rather, all were to be equals as brothers, sons of one father and one mother. The king only desired that there should be this division of the people under the distinct names of Upper and Lower so as to preserve as an everlasting memory that one group had been brought together by the king and the other by the queen. There was to be only one difference and token of superiority, namely that those from upper Cusco should be respected as firstborn elder brothers, while those from below were to be like younger sons. With regard to position and status, they were to be like the right and left arms, because those from above had been gathered by the man, and those from below by the woman. In imitation of this model, the same division was later implemented in all other settlements of the empire, which were divided by region and lineage, calling them *Hanan ayllu* and *Urin ayllu*, which are the upper and the lower lineages; and *Hanan suyu* and *Urin suyu*, which are the upper and lower regions.[24]

Garcilaso published his history of the Inkas in 1609. By this time, officials of the Spanish government of Peru had discovered that dual organization was indeed ubiquitous in the Andes and that every Andean settlement consisted of upper and lower moieties, each moiety being headed by its own *kuraka*. In 1567, for example, during an official inspection of the province of Chucuito on Lake Titicaca, Don Martin Cari, who was principal *kuraka* of the upper moiety of Chucuito, informed the inspectors that they ought to ask not him but the *kuraka* of the lower moiety to provide information about that moiety. In addition, Don Martin Cari declared, the inspectors ought to collect the information they wanted about the constituent communities of his own moiety from the various lords of those communities. Like other enquiries of its kind, the inspection of 1567 thus documented a finely articulated dual hierarchy of regional lords who interacted with each other as interdependent participants in a larger whole. Such inspections also revealed that at times, the very nomenclature of people and places articulated a

---

[24] Garcilaso Inca de la Vega, *Comentarios reales de los Incas* ed. Carmelo Sáenz de Santa María (Biblioteca de autores españoles, 133 Madrid, 1963), p. 28.

hierarchy and duality of origin. In 1586, for example, an official enquiry conducted in the province of Collaguas, northwest of Arequipa, described the relationship between the two neighbouring settlements of Yanqui and Lare:

The town of Yanqui is thus called because *yanqui* is a venerable name; preeminent lords are described by this term, and because the preeminent lords resided and still reside in this town, which is head of this province, and has its name for the following reason. As an expression of courtesy and respect, the people of the region describe a preeminent lord as *lare*; a person is not free to describe himself by this term if he is not descended from a lord of preeminent and noble status, because the word means "uncle" or "kinsman." *Lares* and *yanquis* are thought to be brothers who originated from the mountain Collaguata, and then founded these two leading towns of *Yanque*, where the higher lords resided, and the other is *Lare*, where the lords who follow those of Yanque as uncles and nephews have their abode.[25]

Most representatives of Spanish government in the Andes experienced little reluctance in superimposing their own administrative system on Andean and Inka institutions, thereby modifying or destroying these institutions before they had been fully understood. Questionnaires that were sent from Spain to initiate official inspections in the Andes thus ranged widely over every conceivable detail of work, government, settlement pattern, and ecology, without ever enquiring explicitly into the workings of dual organization even after its rudiments and ubiquity were well understood. The fact that Andean societies were ordered and governed themselves as moieties thus did not occasion any reexamination of the categories that Europeans deployed in reflecting on possible varieties of political organization. Here also, an observation of Cieza's is indicative of a larger issue. Cieza was told that the third Inka ruler, Lloque (*lluqi*, 'left side') Yupangue, resided in the lower part of Cusco, and that according to some Indians, one Inka ruler had to be of the lower moiety, while another was to be of the upper one. In this case, the Inka empire would have been a dyarchy, ruled by a pair of rulers just as the provinces were ruled by pairs of *kuraka*s. However, in the wake of Aristotle, monarchies, aristocracies, and republics were the practicable forms of government that early modern Europeans were prepared to contemplate, which is why Cieza dismissed the information he had been given about

---

[25] "Relación de la provincia de las Collaguas para la discrepcion de las Indias que Su Magestad manda hacer," in *Relaciones Geográficas de Indias. Perú*, vol. 1, ed. Marcos Jiménez de la Espada (Biblioteca de autores españoles, vol. 183, Madrid, 1965), section 13, p. 329.

dyarchy with the words, "I do not think this is true and do not believe it."

Even so, the norms that Spaniards used to order and interpret information about the Andes did not constitute a watertight system. For even though dual organization lacked any notable parallels in contemporary Europe, it was perceived to be a crucial factor in the ordered delegation of authority and in the distribution of labor that differentiated the Inka empire from neighboring *behetrías*. These functions in turn made this empire recognizable as such in the eyes of men who regarded hierarchy and a certain ordered regularity as necessary manifestations of any form of political society.

This was why Europeans, when looking beyond the frontiers of the Inka empire, tended to perceive civilization on the side of the Inka and an absence thereof elsewhere. Indeed, at times the Spanish identified their own political goals with those of the Inka. During the later sixteenth century, for example, they noted that the conquest of Chile, of the frontier region between Paraguay and the former Inka empire, and of the Upper Amazon was emerging as infinitely more difficult than the conquest of the central lands of the Inka had been. These frontiers were the very regions where the Inkas had also suffered regular reverses, and where, possibly, the Inkas had perceived a set of natural boundaries. In 1574, Viceroy Toledo launched an unsuccessful campaign against the Chiriguanos on the Paraguayan frontier. Forty-two years earlier, as Polo de Ondegardo pointed out to the viceroy, ancestors of some of these same Indians had invaded the Inka empire and had captured the fortress of Cuzcotuyo. Similarly, Spanish observers noted that the Inka conquest of Chile had been costly and that the Inkas did not penetrate south of the River Maule. The historian Jerónimo de Vivar, who wrote in 1558, commented repeatedly on the indomitable qualities of the Indians of Chile, and the valor of the Araucanians as celebrated in Alonso de Ercilla's epic poem.

Similarly, the resistance that the Inkas had encountered on the northern frontier of the "kingdom of Quito" was remembered during subsequent generations. All these polities were chiefdoms whose people, as the Spanish viewed it, valued their freedom above all and admired bravery as the highest virtue their leaders could possess. In religious terms also, Spanish observers contrasted the Inka people and their neighbors, highlighting on the one hand the elaborate and centralized state cult of the Sun that the Inka had implanted throughout their empire, and on the other hand the absence of organized worship among the peoples who lived at and beyond the former Inka frontiers.

The contrasts that Spaniards perceived between sedentary Inka society, centralized, ordered, and governed from cities by religious and state institutions, and the often nomadic or seminomadic frontier societies that lacked cities and centralization, probably perpetuated the opinions that the Inka had earlier expressed about societies other than their own. All versions of the Inka myth of origins stress the Inka mission of teaching arts of civilization such as agriculture and weaving, which were not new to the Cusco region but, in the form that the Inka practiced them, were indeed new to the Amazonian lowlands, to Chile, and to regions on and beyond the northern frontiers of the empire. Such a vision helped to minimize or even conceal features that Inka society shared with other South American societies. These features spelled out certain cultural, religious, and political continuities prevailing across the South American continent. Sixteenth- and seventeenth-century European observers were unable to discern these continuities, even though European writings of the period indicate that they did exist. Let us consider some examples.

Spaniards in what is now Panama, Venezuela, Colombia, and Ecuador, among them Pedro Cieza de León, commented – often with puzzled fascination – on the funerary observances of the Indians with whom they came into contact. In particular, they wondered at the frequent custom of preserving dead bodies and keeping them among the living. On the Isthmus of Panamá, for example, Pascual de Andagoya observed how the corpse of a lord was ceremoniously dried out over a smoldering fire and subsequently received periodic offerings. According to Gonzalo Fernández de Oviedo, some indigenous groups in Venezuela observed a similar ritual, and Pedro Cieza de León described a further variant of it in Popayán. In the province of Arma, the bodies of deceased lords were kept inside the houses of the living, while near Cali, the skins of enemies who had been eaten were filled with ashes and preserved for purposes of divination. Similarly, during the conquest of Chile, Spaniards noted that dead bodies were preserved in or near the houses of the living, in fields, or in special enclosures above ground. These dead bodies continued receiving the attentions of the living. A formal separation between the living and the dead such as was customary in Christian Europe seemed to be unknown among the cultures that surrounded the Inka empire. Among the Inka, observances and rituals that likewise served to include the dead within the affairs of the living figured prominently, and at a state level they were elaborated into the formal cult of the mummified bodies of deceased rulers. These mummies retained ownership of the palaces, lands, herds of llamas, textiles, and ornaments that they had enjoyed during their lifetimes. Royal mummies received the services of their kinsmen and followers and participated in imperial celebrations. In 1533, a group of Spaniards who had been sent to raid Cusco for its treasures was surprised to encounter, in the convent of the chosen women of the Sun, two of these mummified bodies. "In this house," wrote one of these intruders,

there were many women; and there were two embalmed Indians, and next to them was a living woman with a mask of gold over her face, who was fanning away dust and flies with a fan. The embalmed bodies held in their hands very fine staffs of gold. The woman would not allow the Spaniards to enter unless they took off their shoes, and so they went in to see these dry figures, having first removed their shoes.[26]

Later during the same year, several of these royal mummies were carried in procession around Cusco to celebrate the inauguration of Manco Inca, whom the Spanish had chosen to succeed Atawallpa.

Casual observations by sixteenth-century Europeans thus reveal that rituals regulating interaction between the living and deceased rulers and other important individuals, as well as rituals that underpinned the continuing presence of the dead among the living, straddled cultural and political frontiers within and beyond the Andean highlands.

The same was the case regarding rituals surrounding living rulers. At Cajamarca, the Spanish observed how the path that was to be traversed by Atawallpa was carefully cleaned and swept, while on certain occasions in Cusco, feather work of diverse colors was spread out where the Inka was to walk. Such observances were not unique. Ulrich Schmidel and Alvar Nuñez Cabeza de Vaca both noted that on the Paraguay River, people honored their chiefs by sweeping the paths where they were to walk and by scattering flowers and scented herbs.

Such ritual particulars were anchored in larger patterns of social organization and the organization of work, and also in perceptions of the mythic past, which all point to cultural continuities that extend from one end of the South American continent to the other. Yves d'Évreux

---

[26] "The Anonymous de la conquista del Perú," ed. A. Pogo, *Proceedings of the American Academy of Arts and Sciences* 64: 8 (1930), pp. 256, 258.

observed that the Tupinamba viewed work as a cooperative enterprise in which chiefs labored side by side with their people, given that coerced work was unknown. Once a given task had been accomplished, a Tupinamba chief was expected to entertain with food and drink those who had worked with and for him. That was the purported reason why chiefs had larger gardens than the rest. Throughout the Inka empire, people observed similar rituals of cooperation, always involving public feasting at the expense of the individual for whom work had been performed. Indeed, frequently, the work itself was ritualized, with the Inka or principal lord inaugurating the task at hand, with those lower down in the social hierarchy taking their turns subsequently. Ritualized work was distributed to men and women by age groups, with each group ranging from the very young to the very old accomplishing tasks that corresponded to its strength and ability. The Tupinamba also organized themselves in age groups and distributed work accordingly. According to the historian Jeronimo de Vivar, the Indians near Concepción in Chile maintained a similar system of age groups; individuals received one name at birth, another at age twelve or fifteen, and a final name at age forty or fifty years.

Parallels of this kind, casually noted by European writers of the early modern period, document age-old networks of cultural, political, and economic interconnections that pervaded the South American continent. Such parallels existed not only between the Inka and their immediate neighbors, on the one hand, as well as with the societies of the Atlantic coast of South America on the other, but also between the Inka and the natives of the Amazon and of Venezuela. To these regions we now turn.

THE AMAZON RIVER AND VENEZUELA

The vast estuary of the Amazon River was first sighted by Europeans in 1500, but it took another forty years before it dawned on the newcomers that this body of fresh water issuing into the ocean was connected to a river system that originated on the eastern slopes of the Andes well over 2,000 miles away. The first Europeans to navigate the entire length of the river from the vicinity of Quito to its estuary were Francisco de Orellana and his fifty-four companions. Even after these men had reached the Atlantic Ocean in August 1542, at the end of a voyage lasting nearly eight months, some people insisted on thinking that the Amazon estuary was to be identified with that of the Orinoco River, which, in actual fact, is situated some thousand miles to the northwest, on the coast of Venezuela. However, this kind of error was hardly surprising given that the chronicler of Orellana's voyage, the Dominican friar Gaspar de Carvajal, provided little hard geographical information. He kept observing that "it was hidden from us what kind of journey we were making," or "we did not know what river it was that we were on," or "God helped us, lost human beings who did not know where we were."

The entire expanse of territory traversed by Orellana, as well as much of Venezuela and of the New Kingdom of Granada, was from the very beginning the home of legends and remained so for generations. These legends were all the more powerful because they were rooted in information that had been gathered from Indians who were believed to understand "the secrets" of their native land. It was from Indians near Quito that Orellana and others heard about a "land of cinnamon" where this much desired spice, which the Portuguese and others were importing to Europe from Asia, could be harvested from trees. Getting to these cinnamon trees had been one of the original purposes of Orellana's adventure. A 1561 voyage down the Amazon, by Pedro de Ursúa and Lope de Aguirre, was occasioned by an account of the kingdom of Omaguas, which supposedly rivaled the wealth of the Inka empire. This story had been picked up from the remnant of Tupinamba Indians who in 1549 had arrived in Peruvian Chachapoyas after their decade-long transcontinental trek from their homes in Brazil. Supporting information about Omaguas came from Germans and Spaniards in Venezuela who were fighting their way southward from the Caribbean coast and who, as best they were able, tried to learn what their Indian guides and interpreters were not necessarily willing to communicate. Another potent legend concerned El Dorado, "the gilded man." Some versions reported him among the Omagua, others on the northeastern cordillera of the Andes, or possibly in Guiana. Or maybe El Dorado was not a man but a place, even if, as the historian José de Oviedo y Baños wrote toward the end of the seventeenth century, it was "an imaginary place founded on pure fancy."

Furthermore, just as in the Río de la Plata region, so on the Amazon River the much repeated legend about women warriors who lived in an ordered polity without men circulated widely. This, at any rate, was what the Spanish believed they were being told by their indigenous interlocutors, at the same time reaching the conclusion that these women were to be identified with the Amazons of classical antiquity. So when, some distance west of the confluence of the Amazon and Tapajós rivers, Gaspar de Carvajal observed among male warriors some women appearing in proud heroic nudity, doing battle against the Spanish, he was convinced that these women had something to do with the noble Amazons who had been mentioned by classical historians. The suggestion that a society of Amazons was to be found in South America occasioned erudite ridicule among some scholars in Europe. Nonetheless, the Jesuit missionary Cristóbal de Acuña, who in 1639 undertook a voyage down the Amazon River, was convinced that they did exist. Acuña moreover gave thought not so much to the "gilded man" as to a gilded lake, which might yet be found somewhere along the Amazon River. Last but not least, in 1639, warrior Amazons conversing with the Spanish invaders of Peru made their appearance on the theatrical stage of Madrid. There a warrior woman explained in a long and dramatic monologue how her ancestors had voyaged from the Mediterranean to their new home on the American river that by this time Europeans were beginning to agree to call "Amazon."

Such legends found so ready a home not only in the Río de la Plata but also in the Amazonian valleys and lowlands and along the Orinoco River, because the societies of these regions remained inherently more alien and inaccessible to Europeans than the Inka or even the Tupinamba, the Chiriguano, or the indomitable Araucanians of Chile. The reason was that, up to the mid-colonial era, few really permanent and substantial European settlements grew in the forests and savannahs of these vast interior river systems. Except in the Río de la Plata, there was no effective conquest of inland South America. Europeans passed through as travelers or adventurers looking forward to some future period of settlement, but such a period had not as yet arrived. Men who wrote about the Inkas and the Tupinamba, or about the *behetrías* of the kingdom of Quito, and later about the Chibcha of Bogotá, did so in a context of European settlement and colonial government that allowed for contact over many years, and thus for sustained and detailed study of institutions, customs, and languages. Furthermore, "indirect rule" at the local level fostered a native bicultural stratum able to answer European questions in terms Europeans would listen to. Meanwhile, however, the cultures being studied and described in the new colonial context changed profoundly. As we have seen, these changes are embedded in the literature about them.

Conversely, in the valleys of the Amazon and the Orinoco, the writers' impact on the societies they described was at first considerably smaller than in the more colonized lands of coastal Brazil, riverine Argentina, the Andes, and Caribbean Venezuela. The inland-traveling authors produced travel literature, a genre of writing that was inevitably superficial because it consisted of a patchwork of passing scenes. It afforded little scope for observations requiring an understanding of a people's history, institutions, and language. Francisco de Orellana did compose alphabetized word lists of the languages of Indian nations he was passing on his voyage. But compilations of this kind, evidently most useful for purposes of finding one's way and obtaining food, cannot be compared to research such as that done by Domingo de Santo Tomás and Diego González Holguín on Quechua, or by Claude d'Abbéville on Tupí, works that stand handsomely alongside the best European scholarship of their time. Even so, sixteenth- and seventeenth-century European literature of travel and exploration does afford some surprisingly detailed and complex glimpses of Amazonian societies.

What drove the first Spaniards to see the Amazon and to make contact with indigenous peoples was primarily their need for food. The same situation obtained, during this same period, on the Río de la Plata and the Paraguay River, except that on the Amazon, there was no direct conquest and hence no coexistence between indigenous people and invaders. The Spaniards had little occasion and no desire to understand how the people they met governed themselves.

An encounter between Orellana's men and the Amazonian people of the Ymara (Omagua?) on the Napo River furnishes an example. After more than a week of floating by uninhabited river banks while fighting starvation with shoe leather and herbs, the Spaniards heard drums at a distance, distinguishing soprano, alto, and tenor tones, and hoped they would soon reach a settlement, as indeed they did. Finding that the Indians had "deserted their village leaving behind all the food that was in it," the Spaniards ate the food. When in due course the chief and some of his people returned, the most important matter to be recorded was that "the Indians brought in abundance what we needed, meat, partridges, turkeys and many kinds of fish." The chief of this group was described as "old Aparia" or "Aparia the lesser." Farther downstream, Orellana's expedition encountered a chief whom, without further explanation, Gaspar de Carvajal described as "Aparia the Great." This is a tantalizing and enigmatic piece of information, given that throughout the Inka empire and in early colonial Peru, *kurakas*, local lords, ruled in pairs, the upper and lower moiety of every community being represented by its own *kuraka*. Amazonia had, and has, its own paired power structures. Harrowed by hunger and uncertain of their whereabouts, however, the Spanish on the Amazon were not inclined to enquire about the intricacies of local governance. Information about foodstuffs, on the other hand, appears regularly in accounts of these journeys. Along the entire length of the river, the Spanish were able to exchange or steal turtles and "fish of various kinds," as well as partridges, manatees, and roasted monkeys. They even took parrots. The Indians kept them for their feathers and as pets, but the Spanish wanted them, as Carvajal bluntly put it, "for the pot."

Amazonian economy as described by the early travelers was capable of producing surpluses, and a number of societies developed techniques of storing their food. Among the Machiparo, for example, where Orellana's company ate meat, fish, and a kind of bread that was made, as elsewhere along the Amazon, of manioc, or of manioc mixed with maize, over a thousand tortoises were kept in small artificial lakes. Twenty years later, Lope de Aguirre's troops again noticed these lakes, which were enclosed by circles of heavy stakes. In addition, they saw the Machiparo storing some of their maize. The Amazonians also prepared an alcoholic beverage, ate turtle eggs, and produced what the Spanish called "pastries." East of the Rio Negro, Carvajal noted that maize was being stored in baskets, which in turn were set in ash in order to keep the contents dry. An account of Pedro Texeira's expeditions, undertaken during the years 1637–1639, describes how on Amazonian islands, apparently near the river's estuary, villagers kept manioc dry by storing it in silos dug into the ground. Repeatedly, the Spaniards admired the "handsome sight" of orchards of fruit trees and of cultivated fields of maize and vegetables. In short, many Amazonian societies were affluent, capable of creating large and well-organized settlements and of raising sizable armies of fighting men. About approaching the land of the "very great lord" Machiparo, for example, Gaspar de Carvajal wrote:

This Machiparo dwells on a ridge at the river's edge and rules over many large settlements which can raise fifty-thousand fighting men between the ages of thirty and seventy. Before reaching this settlement, from a distance of two leagues, we could see the light color of the villages, and we had not progressed far when a very large number of canoes came upstream, all splendidly fitted for war, with their shields made of lizard skin and of hides of manatees and tapirs, each shield the height of a man, covering him entirely. The warriors raised a loud noise, drumming numerous drums and blowing wooden trumpets, threatening that they would eat us.[27]

Farther downstream, Orellana's men encountered the Omagua and admired their pottery, "very well made, with different designs and glazed." Moreover, wrote Gaspar de Carvajal,

in a large house we saw two large idols, the height of giants, woven of palm fronds, and they had elongated ears like the Inkas of Cusco. We did not dare to sleep there because many wide and excellent roads led to the inland regions, indicating that this village was much frequented and that in this neighborhood or very close, there existed many settlements and people.[28]

Some three weeks later,

all the time passing very sizable settlements, we landed in a village where we found, in a square, in a shrine of the sun, a large relief plaque ten foot in circumference, all of one piece, from which the reader can imagine the size of the tree from which this piece had been cut. The design showed a round tower with two doors, in each door two columns, and on the sides of the tower were two lions of fierce aspect looking backwards, as though about to hide. In their paws and claws they held the entire sculpted relief, in the centre of which was a wheel with a hole where they poured chicha, which is the wine these people drink, as an offering to the sun, and the sun is whom they adore as their god. Beneath this plaque, the chicha flowed out to the ground. Finally, the building itself was a sight to behold, and a sign of the great cities that lie inland: this is what all the Indians gave us to understand. In the same square there was a house of the sun, large and standing to one side, where the Indians perform their rites and ceremonies. There we saw many garments of diversely colored very fine feathers, which were sewn and woven into cotton cloth. The Indians wear these garments to celebrate their festivals and to dance, when they gather there for some feast day or to rejoice before their idols.[29]

Travelers along the Amazon repeatedly mentioned solar worship without necessarily connecting such cults with the solar cult of the Inka. However, what was at issue in Carvajal's account of Omagua sun worship

[27] Gaspar de Carvajal, in José Toribio Medina ed., *Descubrimiento del Río de las Amazonas según la relación hasta ahora inédita de Fr. Gaspar de Carvajal con otros documentos referentes a Francisco de Orellana* (Madrid, 1894), p. 237.
[28] Gaspar de Carvajal, in Gonzalo Fernández de Oviedo, *Historia general y natural de las Indias*, ed. Juan Pérez de Tudela Bueso (Biblioteca de autores españoles vol. 221, Madrid, 1959), p. 386.
[29] Gaspar de Carvajal, in Gonzalo Fernández de Oviedo, *Historia general y natural de las Indias*, ed. Juan Pérez de Tudela Bueso (Biblioteca de autores españoles, vol. 221, Madrid, 1959) pp. 387–388.

was not merely a broad cultural similarity between an Amazonian culture and the Inka culture, because Carvajal noted the specific ritual of pouring maize beer, which the Spanish called *chicha*, into an opening that gave access to the earth. Such libations, ritual articulations of the connection between the world above and the world below, were a regular part of Inka religious practice. But Carvajal appears not to have thought of the Inka during this encounter with an Amazonian religious observance involving the sun. Instead, what occupied him here and elsewhere on his long journey along the Amazon was the future possibility of founding Spanish settlements, and of perhaps finding precious metals and those elusive "great cities inland," cities belonging to an empire rivaling that of the Inka.

The lure of some hidden empire of untold wealth and splendor colored European ideas not only about the Amazon and the Río de la Plata but also about Venezuela, the Orinoco, and the New Kingdom of Granada (Colombia). In origin, this idea had nothing to do with the Inka. Rather, it arose from Columbus's expectation that he would find the land of Cathay, which European travelers had sought during earlier centuries. Treasures sent to Seville by the invaders of the Inka empire merely reinforced the vigor of this idea. It served as one of several organizing principles underlying European ethnographic perceptions of South America during the sixteenth and seventeenth centuries. With such legends in mind, early European travelers along the Amazon (unlike later anthropologists) experienced little surprise that so inhospitable and inaccessible an ecology should have generated cultures of affluence and sophistication, because these cultures were simply thought of as outposts of an as yet undiscovered great civilization.

Such a civilization also figured prominently in the thoughts of Europeans who approached the South American continent from the Caribbean littoral. Between 1530 and 1546, German officials and soldiers of fortune undertook several expeditions to the interior. They had heard that a great empire awaited somewhere on the Meta River, a tributary of the Orinoco. It was thanks to this obsession, and the absence of a shared language, that the indigenous world remained somewhat alien and remote from these men. As one of their number, Nicholas Federmann, wrote about his expedition south of Coro, undertaken in 1530:

Traversing 73 miles, we encountered five nations, each of whom spoke a separate language, whence you will understand with what difficulty we communicated until we reached the Caquetíos Indians. For the language of the Caquetíos, I had with me two competent Christian translators. But among the Xideharas, we were constrained to communicate with help of two additional translators, among the Ayamanes with three, among the Cayones with four, and among the Xaguas with five different persons. And thus, without a doubt, before my statements had been translated into the fifth language, each of these men will have added or taken away something of what I had said, so that of every ten words that I spoke, hardly a single one will have been rendered according to my desire and our needs. This was no small hindrance in our endeavor to understand the secrets of the land through which we were journeying.[30]

Meanwhile, amidst general destruction, the Spanish worked their way inland from different sites including the Orinoco estuary, sending reports of their activities home to Spain. The authors and many of their reports along with materials and persons from all parts of Spanish America were examined by the historian Gonzalo Fernández de Oviedo, who, after a long career in the Indies, became governor of the fortress of Santo Domingo and resided there from 1533 until his death in 1557. All Spanish traffic to and from America passed through this island, and little of it escaped Oviedo's notice. He brought to his descriptions of indigenous societies not only a bent for the particular and the specific, for the characterizing marks of any given culture, but also his own wide-ranging personal culture, acquired in a lifetime of study, travel, and service to the Spanish crown. And he had chances to interview witnesses whose expertise nobody else tapped. As a result, Fernández de Oviedo was able to dispense with empires so far undiscovered as an ethnographic category. Instead, he resorted to the encyclopedic *Natural History* of the Elder Pliny, to ethnographic writings of classical antiquity, to the historical record of medieval Spain, and to his own experience by way of describing and classifying the New World.

Having read in Caesar's *Gallic War* that the ancient Britons painted their bodies, Fernández de Oviedo described this same custom as practiced south of Coro by the Guiriguana Indians, whose women "paint their breasts and arms with most handsome designs in indelible black. And how can we blame them," Oviedo continued, "when we look at other nations of the world who are now prosperous and live in a Christian republic, like the English of whom Julius Caesar writes?" On another occasion, he heard of body painting among the Indians of Caboruto on

---

[30] Nicolas Federmann, "Indianische Historia," in Arnold Federmann, *Deutsche Konquistadoren in Südamerika* (Berlin, 1938), pp. 112–113.

the Orinoco and was reminded of a North African parallel, bearing in mind all the time that painting the body was considered to be "a matter of elegance" and ought to be appreciated as such. Similarly, where Vaz de Caminha, Léry, and others had asked themselves why the Tupinamba felt no shame at being naked, Fernández de Oviedo viewed nudity as a matter of cultural convention. As a result, he thought that the cords being worn by women among the Onoto and Guiriguiri Indians on Lake Maracaibo in effect performed exactly the same function as elaborate European clothing. "Behind this wall," he explained, "their private parts are very well hidden."

Fernández de Oviedo's many comparisons between America and other parts of the world during different periods of their historical development enabled him to integrate what was new about the "New World" into a known and intelligible scheme of things. But that is only half the story. For in effect, these comparisons, and the tradition of encyclopedic history within which he wrote, provided Oviedo with a framework that was sufficiently capacious to take stock of a very large body of information without either losing track of his overall design or getting cramped by his own categories. A case in point is his descriptions of indigenous methods of predicting the future and curing diseases. Like other learned Europeans of his time, Oviedo did not believe these methods to be efficacious; he thought them a form of magic. However, having read Pliny's discussion about the ubiquity and power of the magic arts, which combined into a single fabric the persuasive force of medicine, religion, and astrology, Oviedo was able to describe "magic" as practiced in the Americas with considerable insight and acumen. Consider his account of a ritual of curing among the same Caquetíos Indians, about whom Federmann had not been able to learn a great deal. The story opens with a conversation between shaman and patient in which the patient declares that he is sick, that he wishes to be cured, and that he believes the shaman to be capable of curing him. The issue here is that Oviedo understood very clearly that the cure was a communal transaction – that is, it could not work unless the patient both cooperated and believed in the practicing shaman's power, and unless the performance of the curing ritual, which could last several days, was reinforced by sustained group participation. This was why the cure had to be preceded by a collective fast and was performed with much shouting and display. At the same time, the shaman's reputation had to be protected for the future. If the patient did not get better, the shaman would at a certain point abandon him explicitly and publicly by declaring that he had received a prophetic insight that no cure was possible, and with these words "he takes his leave and departs."

While at many junctures Fernández de Oviedo's wide reading guided his selection and presentation of South American materials, at other times he drew on his own understanding of the indigenous world. He set little store by stories that Europeans claimed to have picked up from Indians about some undiscovered wealthy empire, instead explaining such stories by reference to European greed. Among the reasons that Oviedo gave no credence to such stories was his own understanding of the sheer diversity of indigenous cultures. An example is his discussion of the Arawak and Carib nations of the Orinoco and Venezuela at large (see Chaps. 8 and 11). As Fernández de Oviedo understood matters, the two groups were bitter enemies and were in addition distinguishable by their customs. For example, he thought that the Caribs ate their captive enemies, while the Arawak made slaves of them. But the position was complicated, because Oviedo was uncertain whether the Aruacay people, also at home on the Orinoco River, were to be included among the Arawak. "I used to think," he wrote, "that the Arawak were from the settlement of Aruacay, and then, with time, I changed my mind. Whatever the position may be, I will give the information that is available about the Arawak." With this caution, he foresaw the hazards in European tendencies to pigeon-hole peoples in "Arawak" and similar pigeonholes. In short, Fernández de Oviedo recognized quite explicitly the difficulty that the Spanish and others encountered in distinguishing the many different indigenous peoples of Venezuela whose languages and cultures they only partially understood, and he endeavored as best he was able to make allowance for this difficulty.

Oviedo's distinction between Arawak and Caribs was, so it seemed, confirmed a few years later when a response to an official enquiry revealed that the Arawak considered themselves to be newcomers to the Orinoco region. They thought it had formerly been inhabited only by Caribs:

They say that they came in ships from where the sun rises and sailed along the coast and because they found that these rivers were so productive of food crops, they sailed along them and made friends with the Caribs who possessed the land. But then, seeing the evil customs of the Caribs and that they ate other Indians, the Arawak rose up against them and in great wars drove them from these same rivers and themselves remained as possessors and settlers. And so, today, they occupy the low lying territory and by warfare they manage to take the best land which formerly the Caribs occupied.

The same official enquiry recorded some Arawak religious beliefs, which resonate with themes that are familiar from other parts of South America. These traditions included a divine origin in the sky via cosmogonies that comprise both a male and a female dimension, and the ethical behest of not hoarding property:

Their belief and adoration is the sky, because they say that in the upper sky live a great lord and a great lady. They say that this great lord creates them and sends them water to the earth in order to create for them all the things which are on the earth. And they say that if an Arawak dies, and he is good, his soul, which they call *gaquche*, goes up to this great lord, and he who has been evil, his soul is taken by *Camurespitan*, which is how they call the devil. I asked them what an Arawak has to do to be good, and they say that he must not kill another Arawak, and not deny his property to him who asks for it, and to those who arrive at his house he must give something to eat. He must not take the possessions or wife of another Arawak, and must always live in peace and friendship with the other Arawak. Those who do this, their souls go to *Huburiri*, who is the great lord they mention.[31]

Oviedo thought that Arawak ear ornaments resembled those of the Inka. Perhaps it was observations such as this, along with the belief that the land of El Dorado must after all exist, that led the Englishman Sir Walter Raleigh to stick, through thick and thin, to his conviction that a remnant of the Inka had escaped from Peru and had founded in Guiana an empire even more splendid than their Andean one. In 1595, Raleigh undertook, in the name of Queen Elizabeth I, an expedition along the Orinoco that was designed to reach this empire; he came away believing that he had almost reached it, and that all that was needed was a simple further expedition. Having read and conflated the accounts of the Inka by Gómara, who had never left Europe, and by Cieza de León, who knew the Andes very well, Raleigh reached the conclusion that like Orellana, some surviving Inka had sailed down the Amazon River and had settled in Guiana. Confirmation of this story came from an aged Indian lord, with whom Raleigh conversed through an interpreter, who said that the lord

---

[31] This and the preceding quotation come from Rodrigo Navarrete and Antonio Barbudo, "Relación de las provincias y naciones de los Indios . . . Aruacos," in Antonio Arellano Moreno ed., *Relaciones geográficas de Venezuela* (Caracas, 1974), pp. 84–85.

remembered in his father's lifetime when he was very old, and himself a young man that there came down into that large valley of Guiana, a nation from so far off as the Sun slept (for such were his own words), with so great a multitude as they could not be numbered nor resisted, and that they wore large coats, and hats of crimson color, which color he expressed, by shewing a piece of red wood, wherewith my tent was supported, and that they were called Oreiones and Epuremei, those that had slain and rooted out so many of the ancient people as there were leaves in the wood upon all the trees and had now made themselves Lords of all.[32]

The "large coats," remembered by people who, as the Spanish put it "went naked," might have invited Raleigh to think of the fine Andean cloth mentioned in the Spanish sources he had read. The "hats of crimson color" may enshrine a memory of the crimson headband of sovereignty worn by Inka rulers. Finally, *orejones*, "long ears," was the term with which the Spanish often referred to Inka nobles because of the large ear spools they wore as a token of their status. And yet, Raleigh's fixed idea about an Inka empire in exile in Guiana may have much less to do with South American cultural and political history than it does with perennial attempts by outsiders at finding some principle of coherence and intelligibility in the continent' configuration.

REVIEWING THE PAST: ETHNOGRAPHY AS HISTORY

Almost always we learn about South American cultures during and following the period of contact through European voices, although on occasion it is possible to hear an indigenous voice within European narratives. Meanwhile, however, children were being born of unions between Europeans, especially Spaniards, and indigenous women. Other children were born of Spaniards for whom South America had become home. Some of the men among the early Euro-American generation in due course put pen to paper and wrote histories of their *patrias*, their homeland, where *patria* refers not to all of South America but to the regions, later to become nation-states, carved out during the period of invasion and settlement. In addition, we have a small body of Andean texts by men of indigenous ancestry and culture who wrote in order to take stock of the mythic and historical past of their own people and of

---

[32] Walter Raleigh, *The Discoverie of the large, rich and bewtiful empyre of Guiana, with a relation of the great and Golden Cities of Manoa (which the Spanyards call El Dorado* (London, 1596; Amsterdam, 1968), p. 63.

the destiny of these people under Spanish government. The official enquiries that had been undertaken on behalf of the Spanish crown during the second half of the sixteenth century, in order to organize the new colonial government, had been discontinued by the time the new century dawned: What information was wanted had been gathered. However, beginning in the earlier seventeenth century, the church organized its own set of enquiries, which were designed to reveal and "extirpate" indigenous religious ideas and practices. Customarily, the statements of Andean witnesses were recorded at length, albeit in Spanish translation. These documents give a unique insight into the ideas and actions of Andean people during this period.

Put differently, the religious, cultural, and political life of South America changed radically during the century that followed the first European landfall in Brazil, and concurrently, the nature and content of the written documents that were being produced also changed. Most of the sixteenth-century sources were written with a certain naiveté, a conviction that – notwithstanding all that was new, hard to describe, and hard to understand – it was genuinely possible to record something worth knowing and knowable. This conviction is absent in the later documentation. Instead, information was recorded, for a variety of different reasons, to correct earlier misapprehensions, to fill in missing items, and to explain what had remained unintelligible. From the vantage point of indigenous people, what had remained unintelligible was first of all the European invasion in itself, above all its destructive character. Pondering this problem led not only to a rethinking of the events but also to a series of new descriptions of indigenous cultures. Let us begin with the events.

Some sixteenth-century Spanish jurists and theologians, above all the Dominican friar Francisco Vitoria, who taught in Salamanca, had condemned armed aggression and found little to recommend in the Spanish wars of conquest in the Americas. It was in the face of such opinions that a number of historians of the "deeds of the Spanish in the Americas" sought to show that the *conquistadores* had often fought in self-defense, for sheer survival, and for long-term peace and prosperity.

By the early seventeenth century, it had become very clear that indigenous people in South America did not agree. The Andean nobleman Don Felipe Guaman Poma de Ayala, who completed a history of Peru in circa 1615, thus reported that his grandfather had been sent by the Inka as a peaceful emissary to meet the approaching Spaniards and to supply them with whatever they needed. A similar account, apparently

written a little later, comes from Don Joan Santacruz Pachacuti Yamqui
Salcamaygua, a nobleman from the vicinity of Cusco, who described not
only how his ancestor met the Spanish on behalf of the Inka but also
how the Spanish were ceremoniously welcomed in Cusco's temple of the
Sun, which was thereby transformed into a Christian sanctuary. During
these same years, Garcilaso Inca de la Vega, son of a *conquistador* and the
granddaughter of the Inka "Tupa Yupanqui," was living in Córdoba in
Andalucía. There he wrote a history of Inka and Spanish Peru, in which
he reflected on the needless violence of the Spanish takeover, Peaceful
coexistence would have been possible, he thought. Such reflections were
not confined to historians writing in or about Peru. In 1612, Ruy Diaz
de Guzmán, grandson of Domingo Martínez de Irala, governor of the
Río de la Plata, completed his history of Argentina. He collected his
information as much from documents as from the memories of men who
had taken part in the conquest and settlement of this region. From these
men, or from their descendants, he heard that before Pizarro had ever
reached Peru, Spaniards setting out from the Paraná River near the coast,

entered into a province populated by a multitude of people rich in gold and
silver who owned large herds of llamas, and from the wool they produced much
well woven cloth. These people obeyed a great Lord who ruled over them. Since
the Spanish thought it wise to place themselves under the protection of this
Lord they proceeded to where he was. Arriving in his presence, they stated their
errand with awe and reverence and as best they were able. They requested his
friendship on behalf of His Majesty who, so they explained, was a powerful
emperor on the other side of the sea who had no need of new lands and
dominions but desired his alliance, only wishing them to know the true god. In
this particular, the Spanish expressed themselves with much circumspection, in
order not to displease that great Lord, who received their message kindly,
treating them well and appreciating their customs and conversation. They stayed
there many days, until they requested leave to return, which the Lord generously
granted them, giving them many pieces of gold and silver and as much cloth as
they were able to carry.[33]

This account from far beyond the frontiers of the Inka empire, of a first
meeting between the Spanish and the Inka ruler whom the newcomers
could only dimly recognize, reformulates the actual events to allow for
the possibility of an alternative, less destructive period of invasion and
settlement. The story states, as if from an indigenous point of view, what
Europeans, who had so far held a virtual monopoly in the creation of

[33] Ruy Díaz de Guzmán, *La Argentina*, E. de Gandia ed. (Madrid, 1986), p. 106.

written historical narratives, did not know. More such stories followed. Garcilaso de la Vega and Guaman Poma both reported the death of the Inka Túpac Amaru in 1571, but with a new epilogue. According to Guaman Poma,

Don Francisco de Toledo, the viceroy, having completed his turn of duty in this kingdom of the Indies returned to Castile. When he wanted to enter to kiss the hands of his Majesty, the lord and king Philip II, the doorkeeper did not give him permission to come in. With this sorrow he went to his own house, sat down in a chair and did not eat. Thus seated he died intestate and bid farewell to this life.[34]

Garcilaso, who wrote in Spain, told the story a little differently:

Convinced of his merits, the viceroy Toledo came before his Majesty King Philip II to kiss his hands. His Catholic Majesty who had learnt in detail all that had occurred in Peru and in particular the death of the prince Túpac Amaru did not receive the viceroy with the approval the latter expected. With a few short words he told him to return to his house because his Majesty had not sent him to Peru to kill kings but to serve them.[35]

Historical traditions circulating in Quechua, as distinct from Spanish, communicated similar ideas, although here, it was the death of Atawallpa, sometimes fused with that of Túpac Amaru, that captured the imagination. The Quechua *Tragedy of the Death of Atawallpa*, versions of which were performed as early as the sixteenth century, thus ends with the return to Spain of Francisco Pizarro, who came into the presence of the king of Spain bringing, as a trophy, the Inka's head. To which the king responded:

> What do you tell me, Pizarro?
> You leave me dumbfounded.
> How have you done this thing?
> This face that you bring me
> is my own face.
> When did I command you to kill this Inka?[36]

The alternative versions of the advent of Europeans in South America that came into existence from the later sixteenth century were more than

[34] *Nueva Coronica y Buen Gobierno*, J. Murra, R. Adorno, J. Urioste eds. (Madrid, 1987), p. 459.
[35] Garcilaso Inca de la Vega, *Comentarios reales de los Incas*, ed. Carmelo Sáenz de Santa María (Biblioteca de autores españoles, 135, Madrid, 1963), p. 172.
[36] *Tragedia del fin de Atawallpa*, Jesus Lara ed. (Cochabamba, 1957), p. 188 (translation by Christopher Wallis).

revisions of historical events, more also than simple wishful thinking. What was at issue was not merely events but also the presuppositions that inevitably enter into descriptions and characterizations of cultures. During the sixteenth century, Bartolomé de las Casas, Juan Gines de Sepúlveda, the Jesuit José de Acosta, and the many writers who copied from or responded to their arguments had endeavored to locate indigenous American cultures on a map of cultures worldwide and across time. Like the definition of various South American polities as *behetrías*, these comparative descriptions of cultures worldwide were experiments in the applicability of existing European and Spanish concepts of political order, religious truth, and cultural attainment to the hitherto unknown societies of the Americas.

Attentive scrutiny of the admittedly fragmentary record of indigenous responses to such writings and ideas reveals that native South Americans frequently thought that Europeans were misinformed, or were asking the wrong questions, or were making wrong assumptions. It was in the face of the widely held assumption that indigenous societies had produced nothing corresponding to the European idea of law, for example, that as early as the mid–sixteenth century, kinsfolk of the Inka Atawallpa told a Spaniard in Cusco that the Inka Pachacuti had laid down "laws and ordinances." Topics he legislated upon include the administration of the empire, the storage and distribution of surplus goods, theft, rules of marriage, and the designation of status. Other laws deal specifically with Cusco, regulating the marketing of goods, the management of accidental fires, and the care of illegitimate children. Some of these regulations were reiterated elsewhere, but without making the point that there existed a corpus of Inka law. However, this point was raised again in the early seventeenth century by both Garcilaso and Guaman Poma, and also by the Mercedarian friar Martín de Murúa, who wrote a history of Peru that drew on some of Guaman Poma's information. A little later, Lucas Fernández Piedrahita, whose history of the New Kingdom of Granada comprises a number of indigenous traditions, wrote a review of laws obtaining in the prehispanic polity of Bogotá. Here, as in laws attributed to the Inka in seventeenth-century sources, Spanish and Christian ideas of what constituted law were deployed to define indigenous ones, because Andean people were interested in demonstrating to the invaders that their societies had conformed to the now-dominant culture's criteria of political order. The elaborate vocabulary covering concepts of law and justice that the lexicographer Diego Gonzalez Holguín compiled in his

Quechua dictionary of 1608 gives direct access to ongoing Andean traditions in this field.

Guaman Poma, like the other historians who argued for the existence of prehispanic law and legal thinking in the Andes, was a man of scholarly inclinations. The tone these historians adopted was, almost throughout, ironic, even if some of the opinions they contested were less so. Discussions about the nature of indigenous religious beliefs and practices, on the other hand, were a different matter, largely because here, Christian missionaries saw themselves, and were perceived, as rivals of indigenous bearers of religious authority. In this field, therefore, seventeenth-century indigenous revisions of established historical narratives resulted in a series of highly charged debates about the inherent worth of pre-Christian and non-Christian religious traditions persisting amid missionary Christianity. From the very moment of contact, Europeans in South America had been eager to recognize in the myths they were told, and even in some of the rituals that they observed, a certain resonance with their own Christian convictions. European retellings of myths from South America thus highlighted personages and events that seemed to echo the account of creation and human origins in the book of Genesis. This is why we are relatively well informed about figures like the Tupí creator Monan, who according to André Thévet was endowed "with the same perfections that we attribute to God," about the Tupí teacher and benefactor Maire-Monan, and about "Jeropary," whom missionaries tended to identify as the Tupí version of the devil. Jean de Léry and Yves d'Évreux, on the other hand, identified the biblical creator with the Tupí thunder deity Toupan, and this interpretation achieved long-lasting acceptance. Similarly, in the central Andes, several Spaniards focused on "Viracocha" (i.e., Wira Qucha) as in some sense equivalent to the biblical creator, while Garcilaso Inca argued at some length that the coastal deity Pacha Kamaq, whose name very roughly means 'maker of the world', was the god of whom the Christians spoke. A little later, Fernández Piedrahita recognized "an author of nature who made heaven and earth" among the Chibcha of the New Kingdom of Granada. In addition, myths dealing with prophets and culture heroes were regularly interpreted by Europeans as referring, in however indirect a way, to a Christian apostle who was thought to have reached the Americas shortly after the death of Jesus.

But there was a difficulty with all this: While recognizing some validity in indigenous concepts of deity and human origins, Europeans invariably described indigenous teachers and ritual specialists by the term "sorcerer" or others equally derogatory. The issue was that some Europeans came to the Americas as missionaries whose claim to social and spiritual authority conflicted with that of the so-called sorcerers. As the Tupí shaman Pacamont said to Yves d'Évreux:

You should know that before you arrived, it was I who purified the people of my land, just as you do for your own people, but I did it in the name of my own spirit, and you do it in the name of God, Toupan. I breathed on the sick and they became well. They told me what wrong they had done and I prevented Jiropari, the devil, from harming them. I caused prosperous years to come and avenged myself when those who despised me fell ill.[37]

On this basis, the shaman Pacamont thought that he should enjoy the same honors as the French missionary priests and should be admitted into their privileged society by being baptized. But Yves d'Évreux refused to perform the ceremony over him because "You are still too carnal to comprehend the Christian mysteries." This message was as unintelligible and unacceptable to Pacamont as it was to other shamans among the Tupinamba, because the assertion that they were carnal amounted to undermining the authority these men enjoyed among their own people. Put differently, Tupí shamans were being required to make way for Christian priests because, in actual practice, as distinct from theory, Tupí sacred knowledge was judged by the newcomers to be incompatible with Christian knowledge.

   An analogous conflict about the status of indigenous sacred knowledge was battled out in the Andes during the early and middle decades of the seventeenth century. Here, even more explicitly than among the Tupinamba, indigenous religious specialists took upon themselves the task of redefining the scope and status of Christianity, and thus of their own religious traditions. The core of their argument was that Christianity was an appropriate religion for Spaniards, and that Andean people were obliged to observe their own established rituals and were cared for by their own deities. As Francisco Poma explained to an ecclesiastical judge in 1657, the indigenous priests of his native village San Pedro de Hacas

gather offerings from their *ayllus*, kin groups, twice a year, when they prepare to till their fields and when the maize begins to ripen. Francisco Poma himself has frequently given guinea pigs, coca, llama fat and corn beer to the priest Her-

---

[37] Yves d'Évreux, *Voyage* II, chapter 15, p. 238.

nando Hacaspoma. Hacaspoma and the other priests offer these sacrifices to the ancestral mummies and deities and then they make the public crier call the Indians *ayllu* by *ayllu* to gather in the square, where they all make their confessions before the priest of their *ayllu*. Next, their heads are washed with maize flour, and thus they are absolved and are told to fast for five days. . . . During those five days the *ayllus* invite each other, and Francisco Poma has listened to how the priests taught and preached to all men and women that those who were born Indians ought not to adore the Christian god or the saints made of wood inside the church, because these were the images and *guacas*, deities, of Spaniards. Indians had their own different protectors who were their ancestral mummies and their deities whom they must adore with sacrifices, fasting and confession, because if they do not do this they will all die and their crops will be spoilt by frost and the irrigation canals and wells will dry up.[38]

This and many similar statements from elsewhere in the Andes testify to the ability of members of Andean priesthoods, which often included women, to confront not only Christian missionary efforts but also the cultural and political forces of hispanization. They clearly found renewed means of affirming indigenous identities. However, Andean religion, culture, and political norms had changed in over a century of colonial governance, because everything now had to be explained and justified in the face of an often critical and even hostile setting. Viewed from within an Andean universe, likewise, things were not the same. However much some individuals might wish to separate their lives and thoughts from Spanish influences, such a separation was simply no longer possible.

Take the example of writing. In the course of the sixteenth century, Europeans investigating the history and ethnography of South America had regularly commented on the difficulties of gathering information because the Indians had no writing. Some historians, like Pedro Cieza de León, thought that the Inka *khipus* were in some sense an equivalent to the Latin alphabet, while at the same time discovering that historical information stored on *khipus* did not afford the "reader" the same certainty as came from European written texts. There were thus grounds for supposing that the *khipus* did not amount to writing. As an Andean scribe wrote in Huarochirí during the early seventeenth century:

If the ancestors of the people called Indians had known writing in earlier times, then the lives they lived would not have faded from view until now. As the mighty past of the Spanish Vira Cochas is visible until now, so would theirs be.

---

[38] Pierre Duviols, *Cultura andina y represión. Procesos y visitas de idolatrías y hechicerías, Cajatambo siglo XVII* (Cusco, 1986), pp. 188–189.

But since things are as they are, and since nothing has been written down until now, I set forth here the lives of the ancestors of the Huarochirí people, who all descend from one forefather, what faith they held, how they live up until now, those things and more; village by village it will be written down, how they lived from their dawning age onward.[39]

An analogous project was at this same time undertaken by Guaman Poma, who wrote the history of all of Peru "from their dawning age" until his own present. Before reaching the time of the Inka, Guaman Poma described four ages of Andean history, which he correlated with four ages of biblical history, and the scribe of Huarochirí also connected his narrative with a biblical chronology, although less explicitly.

These ideas as to how to arrange Andean histories befitted the times. In 1589, the Dutch scholar Joseph Scaliger had published his work on historical chronology, in which he examined the interrelations between all the chronological systems known to him, thereby placing the study of antiquity on an entirely new footing. This book, along with other, lesser European works on historical chronology, was available in Peruvian libraries. Such writings provide a context for the chronological awareness of Guaman Poma and the Huarochirí scribe, and for their interest in differentiating distinct historical epochs in the Andes. In short, scholarly initiatives emanating from Europe, combined with the availability of the Latin alphabet as a means of communication, fostered a new Andean awareness of the importance of remote antiquity for understanding religious and political issues of the day. As viewed by the few seventeenth-century Andean thinkers of whom we know, Europe did not in any sense abrogate Andean culture, although it did introduce different themes and ideas. This reality found graphic expression in two of Guaman Poma's drawings that juxtapose *khipus* and European writing as complementary to each other.

Guaman Poma endowed remote Andean antiquity with a face by positing distinct phases of cultural, political, and religious evolution that progressed from primitive agriculture to irrigation agriculture, to the development of crafts such as weaving, onward to an age of warfare, and then to the Inka. Spanish scholars of the time likewise were groping for an Andean antiquity that predated the Inka, and they sought to match the awesome ancient buildings that Cieza had seen at Tiahuanaco and

---

[39] Frank Salomon and George L. Urioste, eds. and trans., *The Huarochiri manuscript. A testament of ancient and colonial Andean religion* (Austin, 1991), pp. 40–41.

Chavín with some form of historical narrative. It was in pursuit of such a narrative that around the mid–seventeenth century, Fernando de Montesinos collected Andean information – from what sources is not clear – about a series of dynasties predating the Inkas by way of arguing that Peru had first been populated in the time of King Solomon. This idea had been first propounded in 1578 by the Spanish biblical scholar Benito Arias Montano. It had been much elaborated upon since then and was to continue to occasion learned discussion until the end of the seventeenth century and beyond. Other scholars in South America adhered more explicitly to indigenous traditions in their endeavor to fill in the gaps left by earlier historical and ethnographic writings. In this context, the fabled figure of El Dorado surfaced once more in the work of Juan Rodríguez Freyle, who completed his history of the New Kingdom of Granada in 1636.

Like other historians of the period, Rodríguez Freyle sought out individuals who had access to information that was not otherwise known. He thus conversed with "Don Juan, lord of Guatavita, nephew of the lord who was ruling when the *conquistadores* arrived; he later succeeded his uncle and told me these antiquities." Guatavita was a sacred lake, and as Rodríguez Freyle understood it, the lord of this lake was at the same time overlord of the principality of Bogotá, in which by long tradition, the succession passed to the son of the ruler's sister, that is, matrilineally. At the time of the Spanish invasion, Don Juan was engaged in a six-year fast that was to prepare him to take up power. The fast, so Don Juan told Freyle, was followed by an elaborate ceremony of inauguration at Lake Guatavita. A raft was made ready that carried braziers of smoldering incense and perfumes, and the shores of the lake were crowded with people resplendent in their fineries. Next,

the heir was undressed, anointed with a viscous substance and powdered in gold dust, leaving him entirely covered in gold. He then boarded the raft, taking along a treasure of gold and emeralds as a sacrifice to his god. Four principal lords, also naked, accompanied him, and they were richly adorned in featherwork and golden jewels, each lord with his sacrificial offering. The raft being launched, the sound of diverse instruments, bugles and trumpets echoed through valleys and mountains and continued until those on the raft, having reached the centre of the lake, raised a flag as a sign for silence. Next, the gilded Indian offered his sacrifice, throwing all the gold at his feet into the lake, and the lords accompanying him did the same. Then they lowered the flag, and with the raft heading landward, the shouting, flutes and bugles resounded once more. With this ceremony, they received the newly elected lord as their acknowledged ruler, and from this same ceremony was derived the famous name of El Dorado, for the sake of which so many lives and so much property have been wasted.[40]

Graphic description, abounding in colorful detail, was a forte of creole historians of the earlier seventeenth century. These men studied in archives, perused earlier historical works, and supplemented their own lived experience by questioning members of the older generation. From Antonio de la Calancha, historian of the Augustinian Order in Peru, who was born in La Plata, we thus have careful descriptions of the pre-Inka and Inka oracular sanctuary of Pacha Kamaq, which he had visited, and of other ancient sites of which he had been told. In addition, Calancha was interested in Andean religious customs and beliefs, which he compared to those of classical antiquity. Alonso Ramos Gavilán, who was born in Huamanga, wrote a history of the image of Our Lady of Copacabana; the book begins with a detailed account of the pre-Inka history and culture of this pilgrimage center. Toward the end of the seventeenth century, José de Oviedo y Baños began collecting materials for his history of the conquest of Venezuela. This work also is steeped in particulars bearing on Venezuela's indigenous cultures. In Chile, the European Jesuit Alonso de Ovalle interspersed his account of Jesuit missions with frequent materials about the region's history and ethnography.

At the same time, it is not only the authors' interest in telling detail, and in South American antiquities, that differentiates these works from their sixteenth-century antecedents. When Cieza de León wrote about the Inka, and Léry wrote about the Tupinamba, these people were a living presence. Their culture could indeed be studied, but it also had to be reckoned with and accommodated. This was no longer the case as the seventeenth century drew to a close. Throughout South America, indigenous people and newcomers were increasingly separated into the two distinct "republics" that were posited in Spanish colonial legislation: place of residence, occupation, and social and cultural privilege all militated toward differentiating members of the republics of Indians and Spaniards from each other. As a result, when Europeans and creoles wrote about the history and the political and religious traditions of Indians, it was not equals that they were writing about. Rather, they wrote either about a precolumbian past that was becoming ever more irrelevant in practical terms, or else about the customs, whether laudable

---

[40] Juan Rodriguez Freyle, *Conquista y descubrimiento del Nuevo Reino de Granada*, ed. Jaime Delgado (Madrid, 1986), pp. 67–68.

or not, of people who in a political and economic sense counted as inferiors. The following example shows what was at issue.

In 1656, Antonio León Pinelo completed a large and very erudite manuscript that discussed once again the many theories about the origin of Indians. Like Cieza, who had reflected on the cultures of Chavín and Tiahuanaco without being able to learn anything specific about them, León Pinelo felt that cultures of some kind must have existed in the Andes before the Inka. It was not only the pre-Inka ruins of Tiahuanaco that impressed him but also the Inka fortress of Sacsayhuaman, which overlooks Cusco and which was begun by the Inka Pachacuti in the later fifteenth century. But the difficulty was that León Pinelo could not imagine that an edifice on so vast and majestic a scale as Sacsayhuaman could conceivably have been built by the ancestors of the Indians he knew. He therefore concluded that it must have been built by a generation of giants who were living in the Andes before Noah's flood. Giants had long been a problem in South American ethnohistory, and from time to time, bones thought to be those of giants were discovered. León Pinelo's conclusion about Sacsayhuaman thus satisfied the exigencies of European erudition. But it did nothing to advance the study and understanding of indigenous cultures and histories.

Although León Pinelo's work on the origin of Indians remained unpublished until 1943, it does mark a shift in South American, and especially in European, attitudes toward Amerindian cultures. Cieza, Polo de Ondegardo, Garcilaso, and the many others who interested themselves in Andean history and culture had described the Inka empire as a major civilization that was in some respect comparable to European civilizations. This view was maintained independently of the fact that the Inka empire had been destroyed by the invaders. Analogously, Juan Rodríguez Freyle viewed the lord of Guatavita as the head of a significant polity, a king who ruled over other major lords. In Venezuela, likewise, José de Oviedo y Baños described indigenous lords as men of notable stature, and he gave especial attention to the tragic history of the mestizo Francisco Fajardo, son of a Spaniard and the *cacica*, ruler, of the Guaiqueri Indians on the island of Margarita.

In Europe meanwhile, from the later seventeenth century, Indians were increasingly viewed as savages, whether noble or not: as people dressed in garments made of grass, leaves, and feathers. People of this kind had not yet arrived at the capacity to distinguish fact from fiction and history from myth, and therefore could not have possessed such cultural resources as were needed for the maintenance of reliable traditions and the formation of political societies. As a result, European study of Amerindian cultures became a very different discipline from the one that has occupied us here.

In South America, on the other hand, creole scholars and historians began to investigate what they believed to be ancient indigenous historical traditions by way of combating European criticisms of the precolumbian cultures of their homelands. In an eighteenth-century context, their ideas were considerably less "enlightened" than those of their European colleagues. Viewed from a South American standpoint, however, these ideas harmonized, at least to a certain extent, with the aspirations of Andean political leaders committed to gaining for their people the right of participating in public life as equals. And that also is a form of enlightenment.

BIBLIOGRAPHIC ESSAY

Introduction

Secondary works here cited may be consulted for further bibliography, most of which is not duplicated in these notes. I do, however, supply specific references to the writings of the sixteenth, seventeenth, and eighteenth centuries, which document my argument, in order to help the reader gain an insight into the nature of these texts and into how I have interpreted them. Translations are my own unless otherwise noted, and for the sake of brevity, most are condensed versions of the original. Also, I have tacitly supplied necessary contextual information and adjusted wordings for greater clarity.

John Alden and Dennis C. Landis, *European Americana: A chronological guide to works printed in Europe relating to the Americas 1493–1776*, 6 vols. (New York, 1980–1988) is invaluable. The following works may be consulted for an overview of themes and materials here discussed: Nicolás Sánchez-Albornoz, *La población de America latina. Desde los tiempos precolumbinos al ano 2025* (new revised edition, Madrid, 1994); Margaret T. Hodgen, *Early anthropology in the sixteenth and seventeenth centuries* (Philadelphia, 1964); J. H. Elliott, *The Old World and the New 1492–1650* (Cambridge, 1970); D. A. Brading, *The first America. The Spanish monarchy, Creole patriots and the liberal state 1492–1867* (Cambridge, 1991); Frauke Gewecke, *Wie die neue Welt in die alte kam* (Munich, 1992);

Anthony Grafton, *New worlds, ancient texts. The power of tradition and the shock of discovery* (Cambridge, Mass., 1992). *Los conquistados, 1492 y la población indígena de las Americas* (Bogotá, 1992), edited by Heraclio Bonilla, is an outstanding collection of essays; the volume *La imagen del indio en la Europa moderna* (Madrid, 1990) provides a useful survey of texts and materials, although different contributions vary in quality. Among earlier collections, see Fredi Chiapelli, *First images of America. The impact of the New World on the Old*, 2 volumes (Berkeley, 1976). The revised and expanded edition of Francisco Esteve Barba, *Historiografía Indiana. Segunda edición revisada y aumentada* (Madrid, 1992) surveys historical and other texts written in Spanish during the early colonial period. John H. Rowe, "The Renaissance Foundations of Anthropology," *American Anthropologist* 67 (1965), 1–20, remains fundamental. Arnaldo Momigliano's Sather lectures of 1961–1962, which helped to inspire this article, are now published: *The classical foundations of modern historiography* (Berkeley, 1990).

A great deal of early ethnographic writing about the Americas came from the pens of missionaries interested in understanding the people they were trying to convert. The missionaries were aware that a parallel process had earlier taken place in Europe; see S. MacCormack, "Ubi Ecclesia? Perceptions of Medieval Europe in Spanish America," *Speculum. A Journal of Medieval Studies* 69 (1994), 74–100. Luis Weckmann, *La herencia medieval del Brasil* (México D.F., 1993), a learned and far-ranging work, touches on medieval antecedents in missionary writing.

In sixteenth-century Spain, missionaries and others debated the "capacities" of Indians. See Anthony Pagden, *The fall of natural man. The American Indian and the origins of comparative ethnology* (Cambridge, 1982); *Francisco de Vitoria y la escuela de Salamanca. La ética en la conquista de America*, ed. Luciano Perena (Madrid, 1982); Berta Ares, Jesús Bustamante, Francisco Castilla, and Fermín del Pino-Diaz, *Humanismo y visión del otro en la España moderna* (Madrid, 1992); Gustavo Gutiérrez, *Las Casas. In search of the poor of Jesus Christ* (New York, 1993); Fermín del Pino-Diaz, "La Renaissance et le Nouveau Monde: José de Acosta, jesuite anthropologue (1540–1600)," *L'Homme* 122–124 (1992), 309–326. See also A. Pagden, "The forbidden food: Francisco de Vitoria and José de Acosta on cannibalism," *Terrae Incognitae. The Journal for the History of Discoveries* 13 (1981), 17–29; two opposing views on the credibility of sixteenth-century accounts of Tupí cannibalism: Peter Waldmann and others, "Die Tupinamba: Realität und Fiktion in den

Berichten des 16. Jahrhunderts," in Peter Waldmann and Georg Elwert, eds, *Ethnizität im Wandel. Spektrum* 21 Saarbrücken, 1989), 93–118; Donald Forsyth, "Three cheers for Hans Staden: The case for Brazilian cannibalism," *Ethnohistory* 32:1 (1985), 17–36.

On the historian Gonzalo Fernández de Oviedo in Italy, see A. Gerbi, *Nature in the New World. From Christopher Columbus to Gonzalo Fernández de Oviedo* (Pittsburgh, 1985), 137. The young Francisco Pizarro appears to have served in Italy; see J. Lockhart, *The men of Cajamarca: A social and biographical study of the first conquerors of Peru* (Austin, 1972), 140 f.; Pedro de Candía, who was Greek, had also served in Italy, Lockhart p. 129, and Hernando Pizarro had served in Navarre, p. 158. The father of Juan Ruiz de Arce, who joined Francisco Pizarro for the invasion of Peru, fought in Navarre, Portugal, and Granada; see Antonio del Solar y Taboada Marqués de Ciadoncha, "Relación de los servicios en Indias de don Juan Ruiz de Arce, conquistador del Perú," *Boletín de la Academia de la Historia* 102 (Madrid, 1933), 327–384.

For information about the ebb and flow of the Pacific picked up on the Paraná River, see "Carta de Luis Ramírez a su padre, 1528," in José Toribio Medina, *El Veneciano Sebastian Caboto al servicio de España*, vol. 1 (Santiago de Chile, 1908, hereafter Luis Ramírez, "Carta"), 442–457 at p. 449. For the fall of Cuzcotuyo, Pedro Sarmiento de Gamboa, *Historia índica* (Biblioteca de Autores Españoles 135, Madrid, 1965), 61; land of "immortality and perpetual rest," Pero Magalaes de Gandavo, *History of the Province of Santa Cruz*, chapter 14 (in John B. Statson, trans., *The histories of Brazil by Pero de Magalhaes*, New York, 1922, 117); Erland Nordenskiöld, "The Guaraní invasion of the Inka empire in the sixteenth century: An historical Indian migration," *Geographical Review* (New York, August 1917), 102–121; A. Métraux, "Migrations historiques des Tupi-Guarani," *Journal de la Société des Américanistes* 19 (1927), 1–41; Charles E. Nowell, "Aleixo Garcia and the White King," *Hispanic American Historical Review* 26 (1946), 450–466.

Francisco López de Gómara, *Historia general de las Indias*, ed. Pilar Guibelalde (Madrid, 1965), Part I, chapters 11–12, writes on American coastlines. This work may now be consulted in a facsimile edition of Garcilaso Inca de la Vega's copy in the Biblioteca Nacional of Lima, with his marginal notes: *La historia general de las Indias y nuevo mundo con más la conquista del Perú y de Mexico . . .* ([Zaragoza, 1555] Lima, 1993). The geographical outline in Gonzalo Fernández de Oviedo, *Historia general y natural de las Indias*, ed. Juan Pérez de Tudela Bueso, appears in Books 20–21 and 39–40 (Biblioteca de Autores Españoles, vols. 117–121, Madrid, 1959) with a very useful and carefully documented introductory study. The work opens with discussions of the flora and fauna of the Americas and an account of the Caribbean (Books 1–19). The historical narrative for the rest of Spanish America follows, with events relating to the Portuguese mentioned only in passing. The first part of Lucas Fernández Piedrahita, *Historia general de las conquistas del Nuevo Reino de Granada*, containing, in Book 1, chapter 1, the description of South America, was first published in 1668; the remainder of the work followed in 1881 (the whole reprinted, Bogotá, 1942).

Two late medieval Spanish travelers who produced highly informative narratives that are antecedents to Spanish descriptions of South American peoples were Clavijo and Tafur. See Ruy González Clavijo, *Embajada a Tamorlan*, ed. F. Estrada (Madrid, 1943), and Robert W. Edwards, "Armenian and Byzantine religious practices in early fifteen-century Trabzon: A Spanish viewpoint," *Révue des Études Armeniennes* 23 (1992), 81–90, giving an insight into Clavijo's powers of observation. See also Pero Tafur, *Andanças e viajes de un hidalgo español*, ed. Marcos Jiménez de la Espada (Madrid, 1995), as well as José Vives, "Andanças e viages de un hidalgo español (Pero Tafur 1436–1439) con una descripción de Roma," *Analecta Sacra Tarraconensia. Revista de ciencias histórico-eclesiásticas* 19 (1946), 123–215.

Brazil and the Guaraní

On Brazil, John Hemming, *Red gold. The conquest of the Brazilian Indians* (Cambridge, Mass., 1978), is authoritative and very well documented. The first Portuguese landfall in Brazil on 22 April 1500 was described in a letter to King Manuel of Portugal by Pero Vaz de Caminha; for the original text, see José Augusto Vaz Valente, *A carta de Pero Vaz de Caminha. Estudo critico, paleografico-diplomatico* (Coleção Museu Paulista, Serie de Historia 3, São Paulo, 1975), or a Spanish translation in Francisco Morales Padrón, *Primeras Cartas sobre América (1493–1503)* (Seville, 1990). Regarding the millennial hopes that stirred Europe during the later fifteenth and sixteenth centuries, see *The Libro de las profecias of Christopher Columbus*, with translation and commentary by Delno C. West and August Kling (Gainesville, 1991); Harry Levin, *The myth of the golden age in the Renaissance* (New York, 1972).

Among the older works on the Río de la Plata, Julián M. Rubio, *Exploración y conquista del Río de la Plata. Siglos XVI y XVII* (Barcelona, 1942) remains useful for its documentation and excellent illustrations; Guillermo Furlong, *Historia social y cultural del Río de la Plata 1536–1810. El trasplante cultural: ciencia* (Buenos Aires, 1969) reproduces over a dozen early maps of what is now Argentina, Uruguay, Paraguay, and southern Bolivia. They help in reading sixteenth-century descriptions of these territories. On Jesuit missions, see Dauril Alden, *The making of an enterprise. The Society of Jesus in Portugal, its empire, and beyond, 1540–1750* (Stanford, 1996).

The quotation about the Guaraní as "corsairs" is from Luis Ramírez, "Carta," p. 449. The text of Alvar Núñez Cabeza de Vaca, *Comentarios*, is cited from the edition by R. Ferrando, *Naufragios y Comentarios* (Madrid, 1984). Ulrich Schmidel's work appears in Spanish in ed. Lorenzo E. López, *N. Federmann: U. Schmidl. Alemanes en America* (Madrid, 1985). Passages here cited from Schmidel are translated from ed. V. Langmantel, *Ulrich Schmidels Reise nach Süd-Amerika in den Jahren 1534 bis 1554 nach der Münchener Handschrift herausgegeben* (Tübingen, 1889, hereafter *Reise*); this text is more or less the same as the sixteenth-century printed versions but in places offers more detail. Information about agricultural produce, domestic animals, hunting, fishing, houses, and personal adornment in the Río de la Plata region, and along the Uruguay, Paraná, and Paraguay rivers, is scattered throughout the texts of both Schmidel and Cabeza de Vaca. Less detailed information may be found in other early sources, such as Domingo de Irala, "Carta a S.M. . . . 1545," in *Colección de libros y documentos referentes a la historia de América*, vol. 6 (Madrid, 1906), 379–395; pages 361–377 also contain Irala's "Relacion" of 1541, and pages 1–98 contain a 1545 "Relación" by Cabeza de Vaca, condensing material that also appears in the *Comentarios*. See also Francisco Ortiz de Vergara's letter to Juan de Ovando in *Colección de documentos inéditos relatives al descubrimiento, conquista y organización de las antiguas posesiones españolas en America y Oceania*, ed. Luis Torres de Mendoza, vol. 4 (Madrid, 1865), 378–390; this document gives a lively impression of the sheer chaos brought about in the Chaco not only by the Spanish advance but also by that of the Guaraní.

The passage about the Guaxarapos is from Cabeza de Vaca, *Comentarios*, chapter 52; his description of the Guaraní warriors is in chapters 20–22; for guides and translators, who are mentioned very frequently, see, especially, Cabeza de Vaca, *Comentarios* 7; 12; 13; 17 (women of the Agaces); 19; 23; 44; 49–50; 58; 60. The submission of the Guaycurúes is described in *Comentarios*, chapter 30.

Ulrich Schmidel's descriptions of body painting and weaving are in his *Reise* chapter 36, where he also describes the dignity of the king of the Xarayes; in chapter 37 he mentions the Amazons; his chapters 45, 46, and 48 mention an entire series of guides and translators, for whom see also chapters 21 and 37. For the map showing Camire as a place, see Levinus Hulsius, *Vera historia admirandae cuiusdam navigationis quam Huldericus Schmidel, Straubingensis, ab anno 1534 usque ad annum 1554 in Americam vel novum mundum, iuxta Brasiliam et Rio de la Plata confecit . . . adiecta tabula geographica . . .* (Nuremberg, 1599). On the Guaycurúes, see Cabeza de Vaca, *Comentarios*, chapters 29–31; the comment about Queen Isabel is in chapter 26; on the Xarayes and the story of the Guaraní interpreter, see chapters 59–60.

The *Relación de Hernando de Ribera*, appended to A. Ferrando's edition of Cabeza de Vaca's *Comentarios*, mentions the island where "the sun enclosed itself" and the Amazons, for whom see further, Alfonso X, *Primera crónica general de España*, ed. R. Menéndez Pidal (Madrid, 1977), chapter 390, p. 219b. The same story recurs in Yves D'Évreux, *Voyage au Nord du Brésil fait en 1613 et 1614*, ed. H. Clastres (Paris, 1985). On Candire and related matters, see Isabelle Combès and Thierry Saignes, *Alter ego. Naissance de l'identité Chiriguano* (Paris, 191); also, ed. Marcos Jiménez de la Espada, *Relaciones geográficas de Indias – Perú*, vol. II (Biblioteca de Autores Españoles 184, Madrid, 1965), 96–98. The comment on the lords of Indians near Santiago del Estero is from the "Relación de las Provincias de Tucumán que dió Pedro Sotelo Narvaez," in Marcos Jiménez de la Espada ed., *Relaciones geográficas de Indias – Perú*, vol. I (Biblioteca de Autores Españoles 183, Madrid, 1965) p. 390; Ana Maria Lorandi, "El mestizaje interétnico en el noroeste argentino," in H. Tomoeda and L. Millones, eds., *500 años de mestizaje en los Andes. Senri Ethnological Studies* 33 (Osaka, 1992), 133–166. Thierry Saignes, *Los Andes orientales: historia de un olvido* (Lima, 1985), makes a widely relevant contribution to understanding political power in non-centralized South American societies.

For European ideas about strange and distant lands and about reversals of the familiar order, see James S. Romm, *The edges of the earth in ancient thought* (Princeton, 1992); Mary B. Campbell, *The witness and the other world. Exotic European travel writing, 400–1600* (Ithaca, 1988); on the

Amazons, J. J. Bachofen, *Myth, religion and mother right. Selected writings,* preface by George Boas, introduction by Joseph Campbell (Princeton, 1967); Enrique de Gandia, *Historia crítica de los mitos y leyendas de la conquista de America* (Buenos Aires, 1946) is a pioneering study; see further, Juan Gil, *Mitos y utopías del descubrimiento 3. El Dorado* (Madrid, 1989).

The Tupinamba

On the sources, see John Hemming, *Red gold,* and José Honorio Rodrigues, *Historia da historia do Brasil* (São Paulo, 1988); Donald W. Forsyth, "The beginnings of Brazilian anthropology: Jesuits and Tupinamba cannibalism," *Journal of Anthropological Research* 39:2 (1983), 147–178.

Frank Lestringant, *Mapping the Renaissance world* (Berkeley, 1994) describes European concepts of space and geography that conditioned writings about the Americas, especially those of André Thévet. On tools, see Schmidel, *Reise,* chapter 37, and for the Tupí context, Hans Staden, *Warhaftige Historia und Beschreibung eyner Landtschafft der wilden nackten grimmigen Menschenfresser Leuthen in der Neuenwelt America gelegen . . . Warhaftiger kurzer bericht, handel und sitten der Tuppin Inbas derer gefangener ich gewesen bin wonen in America . . .* (Marburg, 1557, facsimile with introduction by R. N. Wegner, Frankfurt, 1925; English translation by A. Tootal, *The captivity of Hans Stade of Hesse in* A.D. *1547–1555 among the wild tribes of Eastern Brazil,* Hakluyt Society, vol. 51, London, 1874), Part II, chapters 3; 9; 16. On nudity, Jean de Léry, *History of a voyage to the land of Brazil, otherwise called America,* translation and introduction by Janet Whatley (Berkeley, 1990), chapter 8 (quotations of Jean de Léry are taken from this translation); André Thevet, *Les singularités de la France antarctique autrement nommée Amérique et de plusieurs terres et îles découvertes de notre temps par frère André Thevet natif d'Angoulême* (Paris, 1558, facsimile with introduction by P. Gasnault and J. Baudry, Paris 1982), chapter 29; Yves D'Évreux, *Voyage,* chapter 14; Claude d'Abbeville, *Histoire de la mission des pères Capucins en l'îsle de Maragnan et terres circonvoisins* (Paris, 1614, facsimile with introduction by A. Métraux and J. Lafaye, Graz, 1963), chapter 46.

On religion among the Tupinamba, A. Métraux, *La réligion des Tupinamba et ses rapports avec celle des autres tribus Tupi-Guarani* (Paris, 1928) remains fundamental; Hélène Clastres, *La terre sans mal. Le Prophétisme*

Tupi-Guarani (Paris, 1975, now translated, *The Land-Without-Evil. Tupí-Guaraní Prophetism*, Urbana, 1995), and Pierre Clastres, *Le grand parler. Mythes et chants sacrés des Indiens Guarani* (Paris, 1974), pursue related themes into colonial and modern times.

Discussion about Toupan and reference to Cicero, *On the nature of the gods* II,4,12 in Jean de Léry, *Voyage*, chapter 16. A detailed rendering of the Tupinamba myth of creation and origins is given by André Thevet, *La cosmographie d'André Thevet, Cosmographe du Roy* (Paris, 1575), pp. 913 ff; part of this account is reproduced by A. Métraux, *La réligion des Tupinamba*, pp. 225 ff. On the strangeness of the Tupinamba, see Léry, *Voyage*, chapters 8; 16. D'Évreux on burials, *Voyage* I, chapter 31; in *Voyage* I, chapter 16, d'Évreux wrote about his own slave. On migration to the land without evil, see d'Abbeville, *Histoire*, chapter 52; d'Évreux, *Voyage* I, chapter 33.

"A jaguar am I" comes from Staden, *Warhaftige Historia*, Part I, chapter 44; Part II,3 on Tupinamba hunting and imitating animal noises and II,16 on Tupinamba naming their male children after wild animals. (But note that d'Abbeville, *Histoire*, chapters 32 ff., lists villages and chiefs of Maranhão indicating that many chiefs were not named after wild animals. Yves d'Évreux, *Voyage* I,20 expressed the opinion that the presence of the French in Maranhão curtailed the scope of ritual cannibalism. In claiming to be a jaguar, Quoniambec may at the same time have been claiming the powers of a shaman. See Lucas Fernández de Piedrahita, *Historia general de las conquistas del Nuevo Reino de Granada* (Bogotá, 1942), Book 1, chapter 3, p. 33 on shamans (described as *hechiceros*, 'sorcerers') appearing as jaguars. For ethnographers' views, see E. Jean Matteson Langdon and Gerhard Baer, eds., *Portals of power. Shamanism in South America* (Albuquerque, 1992).

On Theodore de Bry, see Bernadette Bucher, *Icon and conquest: A structural analysis of the illustrations of de Bry's Great Voyages* (Chicago, 1981); Michele Duchet, ed., *L'Amérique de Theodore de Bry. Une collection de voyages protestante du XVIè siècle. Quatre études d'iconographie* (Paris, 1987).

Welcome of tears, Léry, *Voyage*, chapters 18; 20; see also d'Évreux, *Voyage* I,24; 50; d'Abbeville, *Histoire*, chapter 48. The welcome of tears, along with other customs of the Tupinamba, was still observed in 1965 among the Tapirapé of central Brazil; see Charles Wagley, *Welcome of tears. The Tapirapé Indians of central Brazil* (New York, 1977). For ancient European precedents for ceremonious behavior, d'Évreux, *Voyage*

I, chapter 14, where the author mentions the issue explicitly; at the same time, the accounts of Indians are pervaded by comparisons to the ancient Israelites and classical antiquity too numerous to list.

On the absence of law and authority among Indians: Pero Magalhaes de Gandavo, *The histories of Brazil* (tr. John B. Stetson, New York, 1922), chapter 10, repeats the refrain that Indians have no "fe, ley, rey" (faith, law, king) – indeed, that their language lacks the letters f, l, and r. The work (chapters 10–14) also provides a well-informed but, in places, judgmental survey of the Tupinamba and neighboring peoples. Cabeza de Vaca, *Comentarios*, chapter 70, "the Indian who seemed to be chief, to judge by the respect with which the Indians treated him." Ulrich Schmidel, *Reise* 44, on the Mbayá and their subjects. The term "polished nations" (*nations policées*) is used by Yves d'Évreux, *Voyage* I, chapter 14. In chapter 19, d'Évreux suggests that the Tupinamba could be taught "virtue and the sciences," which he conceptualized in Stoic terms, quoting Seneca. The thoughts of d'Abbeville ran along similar lines. On the juridical precept of Justinian and the Tupí village meeting, see d'Abbeville, Histoire chapter 53; in chapter 50, d'Abbeville describes the Falmouth episode, which reveals, indirectly, the contradictions between Tupinamba and European concepts of virtue.

The phrase "natural charity" is used by d'Évreux I, chapter 28; Luis Ramírez, "Carta," p. 444, also commented on the harmony of Tupí social life: "Their best quality is that they never have disagreements among each other." On Montaigne, see David Quint, "A reconsideration of Montaigne's *Des cannibales*," in K. Ordahl Kupperman ed., *America in European consciousness* (Chapel Hill, 1994), 166–191. Jean de Léry himself described the siege of Sancerre in *Histoire mémorable de la ville de Sancerre. Contenant les entreprises, siège, approches . . . et autres efforts des assiégans: les résistances . . . la famine extrème et deliurance notable des assiégez . . .* (La Rochelle, 1574), see chapter 10 on eating human flesh; see also Geralde Nakham, *Au lendemain de la Saint-Barthelemy. Guerre civile et famine* (Paris, 1975).

On reason of state, see Friedrich Meinecke's classic, *Machiavellism; The doctrine of* raison d'état *and its place in modern history* (London, 1957); Pierre Clastres, *Society against the State. Essays in political anthropology* (New York, 1989) is a pioneering work of lasting significance on Amerindian political and social thought; further, on the creation of social order without the formation of a state, Fernando Santos-Granero, *The power of love: The moral use of knowledge amongst the Amueshua of central*

Peru (London, 1991); see also Elizabeth Rawson, *The Spartan tradition in European thought* (Oxford, 1969), especially chapter 12.

Tawantinsuyu: The Empire of the Four Parts and Its Neighbors

For a survey of Spanish historians of South America, see Francisco Esteve Barba, *Historiografía Indiana* chapters 7–10. D. A. Brading, *The first America*, about all of Spanish America, contains helpful chapters about the viceroyalty of Peru and its successor nations.

Blasco Núñez de Balboa surveying the Pacific Ocean was remembered by Antonio de la Calancha, *Corónica moralizada del Orden de San Agustín en el Perú* (Barcelona, 1639; Lima, 1974), Book I, chapter 4; see on this episode and early expeditions in search of the Inka empire, John V. Murra, " 'Nos hazen mucha ventaja:' The early European perception of Andean achievement," in K. Andrien and R. Adorno, eds., *Transatlantic encounters. Europeans and Andeans in the sixteenth century* (Berkeley, 1991), 73–89.

Pascual de Andagoya, *Relación y documentos*, ed. Adrián Blásquez (Madrid, 1986); the capture of the trading raft in 1525 was described in the so-called *Relación Samano*, which is reproduced, along with the *Relación* by Diego de Trujillo in the volume Francisco de Xérez, *Verdadera relación de la conquista del Perú*, ed. Concepción Bravo (Madrid, 1985). Another detailed description of a trading raft sighted off the north coast of Peru appears in Miguel de Estete, *Noticia del Perú*, in H. H. Urteaga and D. Angulo, eds., *Historia de los Incas y conquista del Perú* (Colección de libros y documentos referentes a la historia del Perú, 2nd series, vol. 8, Lima, 1924). The work of Raúl Porras Barrenechea remains fundamental for the study of early Peruvian historiography and ethnography; see, in particular, Raúl Porras Barrenechea, *Las relaciones primitivas de la conquista del Perú* (Paris, 1937) and his *Los cronistas del Perú (1528–1650) y otros ensayos*, ed. Franklin Pease G. Y. (Lima, 1986). Philip Ainsworth Means, *Biblioteca Andina* (New Haven, 1928; Detroit, 1973), remains valuable.

Infante Don Juan Manuel, *Libro de los estados*, ed. R. B. Tate and I. R. McPherson (Oxford, 1974); see Alain Milhou, "El indio americano y el mito de la religión natural," in *La imagen del indio en la Europa moderna* (Madrid, 1990), 179–196. On *behetría*, see Alfonso X of Castile, *Siete Partidas*, partida 4, title 25 law 3, and eds. Ignacio Jordán de Asso y del Río and Miguel de Manuel y Rodríguez, *El fuero viejo de Castilla*

(Madrid, 1771), Book I, title 8. On the functioning of *behetrías* in late medieval and sixteenth-century Spain, see A. Moreno Ollero, "Una behetría 'de mar a mar' en el siglo XVI: Melgar de Fernamental," *Anuario de estudios medievales* 19 (1989), 731–741. The comparison between *behetría* and the Inka empire by Pedro Cieza de León is in his *Crónica del Perú. Primera parte* (Lima, 1984), chapter 13, see also chapter 36; for a discussion, see Frank Salomon, *Native lords of Quito in the age of the Incas. The political economy of north Andean chiefdoms* (Cambridge, 1986), 21 ff.; I have consulted Salomon's translation of the passages from Cieza in making my own. See further, Jean-Paul Deler, *Genèse de l'éspace écuatorien. Essai sur le territoire et la formation de l'état national* (Paris, 1981) and Segundo Moreno Yánez, ed., *Pichincha. Monografía histórica de la region nuclear ecuatoriana* (Quito, 1981). On terminology such as "mezquita," see S. MacCormack, "The fall of the Incas: A historiographical dilemma," *History of European Ideas* 6 (1985), 421–445.

Research on the Inka and Andean cultures in general is proceeding apace; J. V. Murra, *The economic organization of the Inca state* (Greenwich, 1980, a published version of his 1955 dissertation) is a landmark. The following collections present important work by various scholars: G. Collier, R. I. Rosaldo, and J. D. Wirth, eds., *The Inca and Aztec states 1400–1800. Anthropology and history* (New York, 1982); J. V. Murra, N. Wachtel, and J. Revel, eds., *Anthropological history of Andean polities* (Cambridge, 1986); S. Masuda, I. Shimada, and C. Morris, *Andean ecology and civilisation. An interdisciplinary perspective on Andean ecological complementarity* (Tokyo, 1985); John Hemming, *The conquest of the Incas* (New York, 1970) is both gripping and superbly documented. For historiography, see Franklin Pease G. Y., *Las Crónicas y los Andes* (México, 1995).

Episodes in Inka courtly ceremonial are described in several accounts of the capture of Atawallpa in Cajamarca. These include: the *Relación* of Francisco de Xérez; the *Relación* by Diego de Trujillo; the *Relación* by Juan Ruiz de Arce; Estete's *Noticia* (all cited above); further information appears in ed. A. Pogo, The Anonymous *La conquista del Perú*, *Proceedings of the American Academy of Arts and Sciences* 64 (1930); Pedro Pizarro, *Relación del descubrimiento y conquista de los reinos del Perú*, ed. G. Lohmann Villena (Lima, 1978); Juan de Betanzos, *Suma y narración de los Incas* (Madrid, 1987); Pedro Cieza de León, *Crónica del Perú. Segunda Parte* (Lima, 1985). The account of the death of Túpac Amaru is by Antonio Bautista de Salazar, in *Colección de documentos inéditos, relativos al descubrimiento, conquista y organización de las antiguas posesiones españ-olas de America y Oceania*, vol. 8 (Madrid, 1867), 278 ff., passim. On Andean *behetrías* before the Inka, see Cieza's *Crónica del Perú. Segunda parte*, ed. F. Cantù (Lima, 1985), chapter 4; Juan Polo de Ondegardo, "Notables daños de no guardar a los Indios sus fueros," in *El mundo de los Incas*, ed. Laura González and Alicia Alonso (Madrid, 1990), chapter 1. Hernando Santillán's statement about the Inka's houses and fields is from his *Relación* in *Crónicas peruanas de interés indígena* ed. E. Barba (Biblioteca de Autores Españoles, vol. 209, Madrid, 1968), section 3. For a particularly insistent statement (with which Viceroy Toledo would likely have disagreed) contrasting the Inka as "natural lords of Cusco" and *behetrías* South of Quito, where no "general lords" were to be found, see "Descubrimientos, conquistas y poblaciones de Juan de Salinas Loyola" [1571] in *Relaciones geográficas de Indias. Perú* ed. M. Jiménez de la Espada, Biblioteca de Autores Españoles, vol. 185 (Madrid, 1965), 197–204. For Tawantinsuyu as "all of Peru or the four parts of it, which are Ante suyu, Collasuyu, Conti suyu and Chinchay suyu," see González Holguín, *Vocabulario* p. 336; Franklin Pease G. Y., *Del Tawantinsuyu a la historia del Perú* (Lima, 1989). Pedro Cieza de León's reflections about the delegation of authority in the Inka empire are in his *Crónica del Perú. Segunda Parte*, ed. Francesca Cantù (Lima, 1985), chapter 12.

On natural lords, consult R. S. Chamberlain, "The concept of the *señor natural* as revealed by Castilian law and administrative documents," *Hispanic American Historical Review* 19 (1939), 130–137. For Viceroy Toledo's inquiries, see ed. M. Jiménez de la Espada, *Memorias antiguas historiales y políticas del Perú, por el licenciado D. Fernando de Montesinos, seguidas de las informaciones acerca del señorío de los Incas hechas por . . . D. Francisco de Toledo* (Madrid, 1882). The quotes are from 224f.; 254. On *khipus*, see the important article of Gary Urton, "A new twist in an old yarn: Variation in knot directionality in the Inka khipus," *Baessler-Archiv* Neue Folge Band XLII (1994), 271–305.

Pedro Cieza de León's description of Cusco appears in his *Crónica del Perú. Primera Parte*, chapter 92; in *Crónica del Perú. Segunda Parte*, chapter 32, Cieza mentions the possibility that one Inka ruled in Hanan Cusco and another in Urin Cusco; see P. Duviols, "La dinastía de los Incas: monarquía o diarquía? Argumentos heurísticos a favor de una tesis estructuralista," *Journal de la Société des Américanistes* 64 (1979), 67–83. Garcilaso Inca de la Vega's account of the foundation of Cusco is in his

Royal Commentaries of the Incas (Biblioteca de Autores Españoles, vol. 133, Madrid 1963; English translation by H. Livermore, Austin, 1970), book I, chapter 16. R. T. Zuidema, *The ceque system of Cuzco. The social organization of the capital of the Inca* (Leiden, 1964), has oriented almost all subsequent research on the topic. See further, J. H. Rowe, "An account of the shrines of ancient Cuzco," *Ñawpa Pacha* 17 (1979), 1–80. The account of Yanqui and Lare is in the "Relación de la provincia de los Collaguas para la descripción de las Indias que Su Magestad manda hacer," in ed. M. Jiménez de la Espada, *Relaciones geográficas de Indias. Perú* (Biblioteca de Autores Españoles, vol. 183, Madrid, 1965), p. 329. For the Collaguas region, see Paul H. Gelles, "Channels of power, fields of contention: The politics of irrigation and land recovery in an Andean peasant community," in W. P. Mitchell and D. Guillet eds., *Irrigation at high altitudes: The social organization of water control systems in the Andes* (Society for Latin American Anthropology Publication Series, vol. 12, 1993), 233–273; see also, in the *Irrigation* volume, Jeanette Sherbondy's "Water and Power: The role of irrigation districts in the transition from Inca to Spanish Cusco," 69–97. See also Susan E. Ramírez, *The World upside down. Cross-cultural contact and conflict in sixteenth-century Peru* (Stanford, 1996). Don Martin Cari's answers to the inspectors of Chucuito are in ed. W. Espinoza Soriano, *Visita hecha a la provincia de Chucuito por Garci Diez de San Miguel en el año 1567* (Lima, 1964), 14–15. Dual organization in the Andes predates the Inkas: see R. Burger and L. Salazar-Burger, "The place of dual organization in early Andean ceremonialism: A comparative review," in L. Millones and Y. Onuki eds., *El mundo ceremonial andino. Senri Ethnological Studies* 37 (Osaka, 1993), 97–116. In the same volume, see G. Urton, "Moieties and ceremonialism in the Andes: The ritual battles of the carnival season in southern Peru," 117–142. María Rostworowski, *Estructuras andinas del Poder. Ideología religiosa y politica* (Lima, 1983) surveys a large body of material on dual organization under the Inka and during the early colonial period. See also her "Estratificación social y el Hatun Curaca en el mundo andino," in her *Ensayos de historia andina. Elites, etnias, recursos* (Lima, 1993), 41–88. Further resources are Patricia Netherly, "Organization through opposition. Dual division and quadripartition on the north coast of Peru," *Working Papers on South American Indians* no. 4 (Bennington, Vt., 1984). On dual organization in the contemporary Andes, see Salvador Palomino Flores, "La dualidad en la organización socio-cultural de algunos pueblos del area andina," *XXXIX Congreso Internacional de Americanistas. Lima*

1970, Actas y Memorias, vol. 3 (*Revista del Museo Nacional,* vol. 37, Lima, 1971), 231–260.

For the connection between Inka reverses in Paraguay and Viceroy Toledo's campaign in the same region, see Combès and Saignes, *Alter Ego,* 135–142. This work includes a French translation of Polo's *Informe,* addressed to the viceroy (the Spanish original being in Ricardo Mujia, *Bolivia-Paraguay. Anexos,* vol. II [La Paz, 1914], 82–98). On Inka and Spanish reverses in Chile, see Garcilaso Inca de la Vega, *Royal commentaries of the Incas,* translated by H. Livermore (Austin, 1966), Book 7, chapters 18–25. About Inka campaigns south to the River Maule, see Jerónimo de Vivar, *Crónica de los reinos de Chile,* ed. A. Barral Gómez (Madrid, 1988), chapter 93. In chapters 13 and 27, Vivar describes Quechua as a *lingua franca* in the part of Chile that the Inkas had controlled. In chapter 104, Vivar suggests the Indians of Concepción displayed bravery rivaling that of the ancient Iberians who fought Rome. On Ercilla's *Araucana,* Jaime Concha, see "El otro Nuevo Mundo," in *Homenaje a Ercilla* (Universidad de Concepción, 1969), 31–82; also Victor Raviola, "Elementos indígenas en 'La Araucana' de Ercilla," in *Don Alonso de Ercilla. Inventor de Chile* (Santiago de Chile, 1971), 81–136. On the continuity of Inka and Spanish colonial political and cultural frontiers, see F. M. Rénard-Casevitz, Th. Saignes, and A. C. Taylor-Descola, *L'inca, l'espagnol et les sauvages* (Paris, 1986). Alonso de Ovalle S. J., *Histórica relación del Reyno de Chile y de las missiones, y ministerios que exercita en el la Compañía de Jesús* (Rome, 1646), book I, provides an important historical and ethnographic survey of Chile, stressing Indian bravery; note especially chapter 2, which comments on Ercilla. See also José Bengoa, *Historia del pueblo Mapuche (Siglo XIX y XX)* (Santiago de Chile, 1985), for its substantial introductory chapter on the colonial period.

On funerary observances: Pascual de Andagoya, *Relación,* p. 92; Gonzalo Fernández de Oviedo, *Historia general y natural de las Indias,* book 25, chapter 9 (in Biblioteca de Autores Españoles, vol. 119, Madrid, 1959, p. 33); Cieza de León, *Primera Parte,* chapters 16; 19; 28; Francisco de Figueroa in Francisco de Figueroa, Cristóbal de Acuña and others, *Informaciones de jesuitas en el Amazonas 1660–1684* (Iquitos, 1986), 286. For Chile, Jerónimo de Vivar, *Crónica de los reinos de Chile,* ed. A. Barral Gómez (Madrid, 1988), chapters 8; 11; 17; 22; 90; 105; 110. This work was completed in 1558 and abounds in first-hand ethnographic information.

The deceased Inka in the convent of the chosen women (Acllahuasi) are described in *The Anonymous La Conquista del Perú*, ed. A. Pogo, *Proceedings of the American Academy of Arts and Sciences* 64: 8 (1930), 255 ff. Garcilaso Inca de la Vega was shown five of the royal bodies by Polo de Ondegardo in 1560. See *Royal Commentaries of the Incas*, Part I, Book 5, chapter 29; Book 8, chapter 8. For featherwork spread out where the Inka ruler would walk, see Cristóbal de Molina in *Fábulas y mitos de los Incas*, ed. H. Urbano and P. Duviols (Madrid, 1989), 71 (month of May). Also relevant are Cabeza de Vaca, *Comentarios*, chapters 11; 13 and Ulrich Schmidel, *Alemanes*, chapter 36. On age groups and organization of work, see d'Évreux, *Voyage* I, chapters 3; 13; 21–22; Vivar, *Crónica*, chapter 105; Inka age groups are discussed by J. H. Rowe, "The age-grades of the Inca census," *Miscelanea Paul Rivet octogenario dicata*, vol. II (México D. F., 1958), 499–522. A large-scale study, with useful documentation, of patterns of social and religious perceptions and practices that span South America is by Lawrence Sullivan, *Icanchu's drum. An orientation to meaning in South American religions* (New York, 1989). For an important earlier commentary on aspects of social organization to be encountered across South America (specifically among the Bororo of Brazil and among the Inka), see R. T. Zuidema, *The ceque system of Cuzco. The social organization of the capital of the Inca* (Leiden, 1964), 21–22; 242–246.

The Amazon River and Venezuela

On prehispanic Colombia, see G. Reichel-Dolmatoff, *Arqueología de Colombia. Un texto introductorio* (Bogotá, 1986); on Spanish penetration, Jane M. Rausch, *A tropical plains frontier. The llanos of Colombia 1531–1831* (Albuquerque, 1984); the opening chapter of Anthony McFarlane, *Colombia before independence. Economy, society and politics under Bourbon rule* (Cambridge, 1993) is also useful; David Block, *Mission culture on the upper Amazon. Native tradition, Jesuit enterprise, and secular policy in Moxos 1660–1880* (Lincoln, 1994) makes good on the promise of its title. Anna Curtenius Roosevelt, *Parmana. Prehistoric maize and manioc subsistence along the Amazon and Orinoco* (New York, 1980) is an excellent survey of the earlier literature on Amazonian cultures. The work argues that the populous settlements along the Amazon and Orinoco rivers that figure so regularly in the ethnohistorical literature of the sixteenth and seventeenth centuries were sustained by the cultivation of maize alongside the less nutritious manioc. This thesis is amply confirmed by Gaspar de Carvajal and other travelers along the Amazon who frequently mention maize as one of the food items that they obtained from Indians.

Gaspar de Carvajal's account of Orellana's voyage survives in two recensions that are similar but not identical. One was published by José Toribio Medina as *Descubrimiento del Río de las Amazonas segun la relación hasta ahora inédita de Fr. Gaspar de Carvajal con otros decumentos referentes a Francisco de Orellana* (Madrid, 1894, hereafter cited as Carvajal-Medina). The other recension was reproduced by Gonzalo Fernández de Oviedo in his *Historia general y natural de las Indias*, book 50, chapter 24 (Biblioteca de Autores Españoles, vol. 121, Madrid, 1959), 323–402 (hereafter cited as Carvajal-Oviedo). On the Amazons, Carvajal-Medina 262–265; Carvajal-Oviedo 392; 394; Cristóbal de Acuña in *Informaciones de Jesuitas en el Amazonas*, 71 ff.; the golden lake is mentioned on p. 60. Tirso de Molina's *Amazonas en las Indias*, part of his Pizarro trilogy, was first published in 1635 and appears in his *Obras dramáticas completas* (Madrid, 1968), 697–734. Shortly after Orellana, having completed his voyage down the Amazon River, arrived in Santo Domingo, the Italian traveler Galeotto Cei, who was also on the island at this time, heard about the voyage and the Amazons. Cei did not find Amazons credible but suggested, sensibly, that "these Indian women go to war with their husbands, carrying their arms and assisting them, just as the Germans and the Swiss do." See Francesco Surdich ed., *Viaggio e relazione delle Indie (1539–1553). Galeotto Cei* (Rome, 1992), p. 58.

On Orellana's alphabetized word lists, consult Carvajal-Medina 262 or Carvajal-Oviedo 379, where these dictionaries, which appear not to have survived, are described as *abecedarios*. Domingo de Santo Tomás, *Gramática o arte de la lengua general de los Indios de los reynos del Perú*, introduction and transcription by Rodolfo Cerron Palomino (Madrid, 1994; the accompanying facsimile reproduces both the grammar and the lexicon). For further references to works on Quechua, see Bruce Mannheim, *The language of the Inka since the European invasion* (Austin, 1991); the linguistic researches of Claude d'Abbeville are embedded in his *Histoire* of the Tupinamba. See further, Antonio Tovar and Consuelo Larruecea de Tovar, *Catálogo de las lenguas de America del Sur* (Madrid, 1984). Its bibliography includes works published during the colonial period.) Other important references include Cesmir Loukota, *Classification of South American Indian languages* (Los Angeles, 1968); Harriet E. Manelis Klein and Louisa R. Stark, eds. *South American Indian languages*.

Retrospect and prospect (Austin, 1985); Mary Ritchie Key, *Language change in South American Indian languages* (Philadelphia, 1991); eds. R. Escavy and others, *Actas del Congreso Internacional de Historiografía Linguistica. Nebrija V Centenario. Volumen II: Nebrija y las Lenguas Amerindias* (Murcia, 1994).

For the Aparia episode, see Carvajal-Medina 222–230; Carvajal-Oviedo 377–378; on dual organization among Amazonian peoples, see Claude Lévi-Strauss, "Les structures sociales dans le Brésil central et oriental," and his, "Les organisations dualistes, existent-elles?," both in his *Anthropologie structurale* (Paris, 1978), 133–145; 147–180, respectively. See also David Maybury-Lewis, "The analysis of dual organizations: A methodological critique," with the response by Claude Lévi-Strauss, "On manipulated sociological models," in *Bijdragen tot de Taal-, Land-en Volkenkunde* 116 (1960), 17–54. Discussion continues in David Maybury-Lewis ed., *Dialectical societies. The Gê and Bororo of central Brazil* (Cambridge, Mass., 1979); Jon Christopher Crocker, *Vital souls. Bororo cosmology, natural symbolism, and shamanism* (Tucson, 1985).

Regarding food storage, see Carvajal-Oviedo 383; 390; "parrots for the pot," p. 379. See also Francisco Vásquez, *El Dorado: Crónica de la expedición de Pedro de Ursúa y Lope de Aguirre* (Madrid, 1987), 69; *Relación del descubrimiento del Río de las Amazonas* in Rafael Diaz, ed. *La aventura del Amazonas* (Madrid, 1986), 234. This evidence, which could easily be expanded, merits consideration in regard to Anna Curtenius Roosevelt's comments (see above) on the difficulties of storing food in the humid Amazonian climate. Regarding orchards, see Carvajal-Oviedo p. 386; cultivated fields, Carvajal-Medina p. 261. For Machiparo military display, consult Carvajal-Medina p. 237; on the Omagua, p. 246, or Carvajal-Oviedo p. 386. The sculpted relief with tower and lions appears in Carvajal-Oviedo 387 ff. On *chicha* poured through an opening into the earth, see R. T. Zuidema, "El Ushnu," in José Alcina Franch ed., *Economía y sociedad en los Andes y Mesoamerica* (*Revista de la Universidad Complutense* 28, Madrid, 1979), 317–362.

On the Germans in Venezuela, see M. M. Lacas, "A sixteenth century German colonizing venture in Venezuela," *The Americas* 9 (1952–53), 275–290. Juan Friede, *Los Welser en la conquista de Venezuela* (Caracas, 1961) is a major documented study. One chapter of this work was published in English (but without the relevant reproductions of maps from the book) as "Geographical ideas and the conquest of Venezuela," *The Americas* 16 (1959–60), 145–159. Nicolás Federmann's account of his expedition, published in 1557 as *Indianische Historia,* appears in Arnold Federmann, *Deutsche Konquistadoren in Südamerika* (Berlin, 1938), 81–160; the passage here translated and quoted is on 112 f. A Spanish version appears in L. L. López trans. *N. Federmann; U. Schmidl. Alemanes en America* (Madrid, 1985); for the quotation, see chapter 8. Problems of translation are a classic theme in early writings about the Americas. See S. MacCormack, "Atahuallpa and the Book," *Dispositio. Revista Americana de Estudios Semióticos y Culturales* 14 (1989), 141–168.

The cited passages about body painting and nudity are from Gonzalo Fernández de Oviedo, *Historia general y natural de las Indias,* book 25,1; book 24,9 and book 25,9 (ed. Juan Pérez de Tudela Bueso, Biblioteca de Autores Españoles, vols. 117–121). On curing among the Caquetíos Indians, see Oviedo, *Historia,* book 25,9. The passage from Pliny the Elder that Oviedo had in mind is in *Natural History,* book 30,1,1. See Claude Lévi-Strauss, "Le sorcier et sa magie," in his *Anthropologie structurale* (Paris, 1974), 183–203. On Caribs, Arawak, and Aruacay, see Oviedo, *Historia,* book 24,3; 17. Arawak beliefs about their past and religion were recorded by Rodrigo Navarrete and Antonio Barbudo in "Relación de las provincias y naciones de los Indios . . . Aruacas," in Antonio Arellano Moreno ed., *Relaciones geográficas de Venezuela* (Caracas, 1974), 84–85. Sir Walter Raleigh described his expedition to South America in *The Discoverie of the large, rich and bewtiful empyre of Guiana, with a relation of the great and Golden Citie of Manoa (which the Spanyards call El Dorado)* (London, 1596, facsimile reprint Amsterdam, 1968). It appears with new contextual material in Neil Whitehead's 1998 edition (Norman, Oklahoma). The quote appears on p. 63 of the 1596 original.

Reviewing the Past: Ethnography as History

Several relevant essays appear in *Native traditions in the postconquest world,* edited by Elizabeth H. Boone and Tom Cummins (Washington, 1998). In his *Nueva Corónica y Buen Gobierno* edited by J. V. Murra, R. Adorno, and J. Urioste (Madrid, 1987), Felipe Guaman Poma de Ayala describes his view as to how the invasion did happen and how it ought to have happened (see especially 375 ff.). The *Relación de antigüedades deste reino del Perú* [1613] of Joan de Santacruz Pachacuti Yamqui has recently been edited by César Itier (Cusco, 1993) and also by H. Urbano and A. Sánchez, in *Antiguedades del Perú* (Madrid, 1992); see on this text Regina Harrison, *Signs, songs, and memory in the Andes. Translating*

Quechua language and culture (Austin, 1989). Garcilaso Inca de la Vega discussed the invasion in his *Royal commentaries of the Incas and general history of Peru*, Part II, tr. H. Livermore (Austin, 1966), Book I, chapters 16–25. Book VIII, chapter 20 is about Viceroy Toledo's return to Spain, for which see further Constance Classen, *Inca cosmology and the human body* (Salt Lake City, 1993), 120 ff. On the Spanish encounter with a "Lord" who is not named but evokes the Inka ruler, see Ruy Diaz de Guzmán, *La Argentina*, ed. E. de Gandia (Madrid, 1986), Book I, chapter 9. On contemporary Andean historical consciousness, see Joanne Rappaport, *Cumbe reborn. An Andean ethnography of history* (Chicago, 1994); see also Gonzalo Castillo-Cárdenas, *Liberation theology from below. The life and thought of Manuel Quintin Lame* (New York, 1987), with an English translation of Lame's *Pensamientos*.

See Charles Gibson, "Conquest and so-called conquest in Spain and Spanish America," *Terrae Incognitae. The Journal for the History of Discoveries* 12 (1980), 1–19 for a little-discussed aspect of the "debate" of the Indies. On laws of the Inkas, see Juan de Betanzos, *Suma y narración de los Incas*, part I, chapter 21; Garcilaso, *Royal Commentaries*, Part I, book 2, chapters 11–15; book 4, chapters 10; 19, reviewing earlier accounts of Inka law. See also Guaman Poma, *Nueva Corónica* 182 ff.; Martín de Murúa, *Historia general del Perú, origen y descendencia de los Incas*, ed. M. Ballesteros Gaibrois (Madrid, 1962), book 2, chapter 22. Murúa's earlier *Historia del origen y genealogía real de los Reyes Incas del Perú*, ed. C. Bayle (Mardrid, 1946), Book 3, chapter 73 contains very similar information. For laws of Bogotá, see Lucas Fernández Piedrahita, *Historia del Nuevo Reino de Granada* (Bogotá, 1942), written in the 1640s, book 2, chapter 5. Diego González Holguín, *Vocabulario de la lengua general de todo el Perú llamada Qquichua* (Lima [1608], 1952) illustrates on p. 552 that the Quechua semantic fields assembled under notions of justice do not coincide with Spanish ones.

On the creator among the Chibcha, consult Lucas Fernández Piedrahita, *Historia*, book I, chapter 3. Pedro Simón takes a more cautious view of Chibcha beliefs, although he did recognize a supreme deity in the indigenous religious traditions that he collected. See his *Noticias historiales de las conquistas de tierra firme en las Indias occidentales. Segunda parte* (Bogotá, 1891, completed before c. 1625) segunda noticia, chapter 3. A helpful collection of original sources with commentaries about Wira Qucha is by Henrique Urbano, *Wiracocha y Ayar. Héroes y funciones en las sociedades andinas* (Cusco, 1981). On Pacha Kamaq interpreted as the

Christian god, see Garcilaso Inca de la Vega, *Royal commentaries*, Part I, book 2, chapter 2. On the Andean apostle, in his incarnation as Tunupa, see Teresa Gisbert, *Iconografía y mitos indígenas en el arte* (La Paz, 1980). André Thévet's chapter about the Tupí creator and related matters is reproduced in Métraux' *La réligion des Tupinamba*, p. 225 ff. On the Tupí creator and Tupí shamans, see Jean de Léry, *Voyage*, chapter 16; Claude d'Abbeville, *Histoire*, chapters 11; 52; Yves d'Évreux, *Voyage*, Part I, 8–9; Part II, chapters 15–17. The passage here cited is in chapter 15.

On continuing indigenous religious practice during colonial times, see Pierre Duviols' now-classic work *La lutte contre les réligions autochtones dans le Pérou colonial. "L'extirpación de l'idolàtrie" entre 1532 et 1660* (Lima, 1971). Kenneth Mills offers an English treatment in *Idolatry and its enemies* (Princeton, 1997). Francisco Poma's testimony comes from Pierre Duviols ed., *Cultura andina y repression. Procesos y visitas de idolatrías y hechicerías, Cajatambo, siglo XVII* (Cusco, 1986), 188–189. For the study of documents of this kind, see Carlo Ginzburg, "The inquisitor as anthropologist," in his *Clues, myths, and the historical method* (Baltimore, 1989), 156–164; 220–221; Armando Guevara-Gil and Frank Salomon, "A 'personal visit': Colonial political ritual and the making of Indians in the Andes," *Colonial Latin American Review* 3,1–2 (1994), 3–36. On Andean women filling sacred functions, see Irene Silverblatt, *Moon, sun and witches. Gender ideologies and class in Inca and colonial Peru* (Princeton, 1987). Further documentation of Andean "idolatry" has been published by Ana Sánchez in *Amancebados, hechiceros y rebeldes (Chancay, siglo XVII)* (Cusco, 1991). See also the collection of essays, edited by Gabriela Ramos and Henrique Urbano, *Catolicismo y extirpación de idolatrías, siglos XVI–XVIII* (Cusco, 1993), which includes (205 ff.) Pedro Guibovich Pérez's study of a noted "extirpator's" library. For Peru before the Inkas according to Fernando de Montesinos, see his *Memorias antiguas históriales y políticas del Perú . . . seguidas de las informaciones acerca del señorío de los Incas hechas por mandado de D. Francisco de Toledo* (Madrid, 1882). On the ages of the world in Guaman Poma, Jan Szemiński, "Las Generaciones del mundo según Don Felipe Guaman Poma de Ayala," *Historica* 7 (Lima, 1983), 69–110. On Benito Arias Montano, who thought that Peru was the Ophir of the Hebrew Bible (a problematic view, even then; the texts being discussed were I Kings 9,28; 10,11), see Ben Rekers, *Arias Montano* (Madrid, 1973). Gregorio García, an acquaintance of Garcilaso Inca de la Vega, wrote an exhaustive treatise speculating about the origin of the Indians, *Origen de los indios de el nuevo mundo e indias occidentales*

(Valencia, 1607); the expanded version (Madrid, 1729) was reprinted with an introduction by Franklin Pease (México D. F., 1981); Diego Andrés de Rocha, *El origen de los indios* (Lima 1681, Madrid, 1988) returned to the same issue. "Indian" origins interested Jews of Amsterdam: see Menasseh Ben Israel, *Origen de los americanos, esto es, esperanza de Israel* (Amsterdam, 1650). A French translation with introduction by Henri Mechoulan and Gerard Nahon is *Éspérance d'Israel* (Paris, 1979). José de Acosta was the first to argue that the Indians reached America from Asia, in *Historia natural y moral de las indias* (Seville, 1590; México D. F., 1962), Book I, chapter 16. Elias Bickermann discussed Greek theories about the origins of nations that remained influential until the eighteenth century, in "Origines gentium," *Classical Philology* 47 (1952), 65–81. See also D. C. Allen, *The legend of Noah. Renaissance rationalism in art, science and letters* (Urbana, 1949) on what was at stake, from a European point of view, in biblical-historical theories about the origin of Indians.

For writing in the seventeenth-century Andes, see Frank Salomon and George L. Urioste, *The Huarochirí manuscript. A testament of ancient and colonial Andean religion* (Austin, 1991), with excellent introduction; the translation of the passage here cited is at 40–41. For correlations between Andean and biblical events, see chapter 3, p. 52, and chapter 4, p. 53. Also relevant is Rolena Adorno, *Guaman Poma. Writing and resistance in colonial Peru* (Austin, 1986); see as well her "Literary production and suppression: reading and writing about Amerindians in colonial Spanish America," *Dispositio* 11 (1988), 1–25. For Guaman Poma's ages of the world, see his *Crónica* 12 ff.; for his pictures of European writing on a sheet of paper or in a book, going hand in hand with *khipus*, see *Crónica* 202, 800. Essays collected in *Guaman Poma de Ayala. The colonial art of an Andean author* (New York, 1992) assemble new materials relevant to the interpretation of Guaman Poma's text and images. See also E. H. Boone and W. D. Mignolo eds., *Writing without words: Alternative literacy in Mesoamerica and the Andes* (Durham, 1994).

On the lord of Guatavita and his inauguration ceremony, with passage quoted, see Juan Rodríguez Freyle, *Conquista y descubrimiento del Nuevo Reino de Granada*, ed. Jaime Delgado (Madrid, 1986), book I, chapter 2. But note that Pedro Simón (*Noticias Historiales . . . Segunda parte*, segunda noticia, especially chapter 10) and Lucas Fernández Piedrahita (*Historia general*, book I, chapter 5) give very different accounts of the indigenous polities of Bogotá and Tunja. Antonio de la Calancha describes the site of "Pachacámac" in *Corónica moralizada*, book 2, chapter

19; see also book 2, chapter 4 on Tiahuanaco, which Calancha had also visited; book 3, and chapter 1 on the valley of Pacasmayo in Northern Peru. For Tiahuanaco, see Alonso Ramos Gavilán's 1621 *Historia del Santuario de Nuestra Señora de Copacabana* (Lima, 1988). Waldemar Espinoza Soriano comments on "Alonso Ramos Gavilán. Vida y obra del cronista de Copacabana" in *Historia y Cultura* 6 (Lima, 1972), 121–194. On Sacsayhuaman built by giants, see Antonio León Pinelo, *El Paraiso en el nuevo mundo* ed. Raúl Porras Barrenechea (Lima, 1943), book 2, chapter 15; book 2, chapter 11 assembles much of the earlier material to the effect that giants lived in the Americas before the flood. Cieza visited Chavín and Tiahuanaco; while realizing that these were not Inka sites, he was unable to learn more. See his *Crónica del Perú. Primera Parte*, chapter 87, on Chavín, and chapter 105, on Tiahuanaco.

Corneille de Pauw wrote the article on "Amérique" in Supplement I of Diderot's *Encyclopédie où dictionnaire raisonné des sciences, des arts et des métiers pour une société de gens de lettres* (Amsterdam, 1776). Reviewing eighteenth-century literature about the indigenous peoples of the Americas, he found that Indians of the Amazon existed "in an eternal childhood;" even in Inka Peru, social life had made "only a certain feeble progress." Altogether, he found American humanity retarded behind Europeans by 3,000 years. But see also, on François Lafitau and his context, S. MacCormack, "Limits of understanding: Perceptions of Greco-Roman and Amerindian paganism in early modern Europe," in K. O. Kupperman ed., *America in European consciousness, 1493–1750* (Chapel Hill, 1994), 79–129. Juan de Velasco, in his 1789 *Historia del reino de Quito en la América meridional*, referred to Jacinto Collahuazo, native lord of Ibarra, as one of his most important authorities; see the edition by Aurelio Espinosa Pólit (2 vols., Puebla, 1960). For earlier references to the importance of indigenous authorities, see Garcilaso Inca de la Vega, *Royal commentaries*, Book 1, chapters 15–17; Guaman Poma, *Nueva Corónica*, 883 ff. Pedro Simón also used indigenous sources. See, for example, *Noticias historiales. Segunda parte* segunda noticia, chapters 10 ff.

On indigenous political movements in the Andes, see the documentation assembled in ed. C. D. Valcárcel, *La Rebelión de Túpac Amaru* vols. 2–3 (Lima, 1971–1972); J. H. Rowe, "Genealogía y rebelión en el siglo XVIII," *Revista Histórica* 33 (Lima, 1981–1982), 317–336; Scarlett O'Phelan Godoy, *Rebellions and revolts in eighteenth century Peru and Upper Peru* (Cologne, 1985); Alberto Flores Galindo, *La utopía tupamar-*

ista (Lima, 1983); Segundo E. Moreno Yánez, *Sublevaciones indígenas en la audiencia de Quito. Desde comienzos del siglo XVIII hasta fines de la Colonia* (Quito, 1985); Alonso Zarzar, *Apo Capac Huayna, Jesús Sacramentado. Mito, utopía y milenarismo en el pensamiento de Juan Santos Atahualpa* (Centro Amazonico de Antropologia y Aplicación Práctica, Lima, 1989).

3

THE EARLIEST SOUTH AMERICAN LIFEWAYS

THOMAS F. LYNCH

INTRODUCTION

South America was the last of the continents to be discovered, invaded, and permanently settled by our species. It was a pristine land; thus the tale of settlement, as known through archaeology, has great potential both romantically and scientifically. However, in reaction to the excesses of European prehistory, in which migration and invasion were apparent at nearly every major cultural juncture, American archaeologists generally have eschewed migration as an explanatory mechanism and even failed to recognize it in the archaeological record. In the first case, the initial settlement of the Americas, obviously migration must be considered. Human radiation or migration was part and parcel of the exchange of Old and New World faunas – predominantly west to east – that took place between the Eurasian and North American Arctic in Cenozoic times (66 million years B.P. to present). During the last part of Cenozoic times, the Quaternary Period (2 million B.P. to present), when there was a Beringian land connection only part of the time, radiation and exchange took place among proboscideans (the order containing mammoths, etc.), horses, camels, mountain-sheep and goats, musk oxen, bison, moose, elk bears, foxes, wolves, and finally the predator that most concerns us – the members of our own species who had managed to adapt to the "mammoth steppe," to prey upon the Palearctic (and eventually Nearctic) fauna.

Archaeological evidence for Amerindian ancestors' migration through the Arctic is sketchy. There is still argument over the details of chronology and route, but it is clear that the human career in America is an extension of Eurasian Upper Paleolithic lifeways. From the beginning, the favored route has been an inland passage through Siberia, Alaska (either the Yukon Valley or the northern slopes of the Brooks Range), up the Canadian Firth and Mackenzie drainages, and finally, between the Keewatin-Laurentide and Cordilleran glacial lobes, into the North American heartland. Some have taken minority positions favoring maritime/coastal entries across the North Atlantic or the North Pacific glaciated shores, but these have found scant support. The similarities are striking between Paleoindian (American) and Upper Paleolithic (Eurasian) hunting and gathering adaptations, migratory behavior, and artifacts. The last include cylindrical, bevel-based bone points, bone needles, notched and grooved bone discs, bone and antler shaft wrenches (*bâton percé* or *bâton de commandement*), hooked *atlatls* or throwing boards, worked mammoth ivory, large flint blades, endscrapers for preparing hides, bifacial spear points, and red ochre-covered burials.

As herd-following hunters, the first Paleoindians had a "focal" subsistence strategy that depended on a narrow range of highly productive but relatively inelastic resources. Mammoth and possibly mastodon at first, perhaps horse and giant sloth, and increasingly bison, were critical prey, apparently subject to wasteful, if energetically efficient, exploitation. Societies with focal economies characteristically resort to long-distance migration, as they often deplete local resources more rapidly than societies making use of diffuse or broad-spectrum subsistence strategies. (The North American hunters of beaver pelts in recent historic times are an extreme example of long-distance migration associated with this sort of focal economy.) In his original model of "Pleistocene overkill," Paul S. Martin popularized, reiterated, and ably defended a wave-of-advance model, but a leapfrogging pattern of advance perhaps is even more likely, given the probably focal subsistence strategy, in which the most productive islands of resources are scattered but predictable.

In the 1980s, a younger generation of archaeologists crafted models of Paleoindian adaptive behavior that satisfied more of the archaeological data. Situations differed greatly between arctic and tropical latitudes, but everywhere Paleoindian sites suggest an emphasis on hunting and high residential, logistical, and range mobility. These first Americans made prominent use of high-quality flinty rock from large quarry sources, using a distinctive bifacial technique. They made only limited use of caves and rock shelters, and they undertook a markedly low level of food processing for storage – quite unlike most modern hunter-gatherers.

Archaeologists do not believe that the first Americans were primarily forest dwellers, living in small bands and foraging mainly on plants, as do some of our nearest primate relatives. This would be an unlikely or forced readaptation for a people that had adapted culturally to the mammoth steppe and managed to cross Beringia. A low-technology, static, forest adaptation (without fire or stone tools) would be unlikely as well for migrants who had come by the maritime or coastal route, even if there were archaeological justification for that scenario. Some doubt that the Clovis Horizon (about 11,500–11,000 years ago) represents the very first Paleoindians, preferring an entry a few thousand, rather than hundreds of, years earlier. However, virtually all archaeologists can agree with Martin's synoptic ecology: The first Americans were drawn "to grasslands or woodlands adjoining flood plains, to mineral springs, lake shores, and coastal marshes. Large herbivores frequented these places because they provided edible foliage, fruits, seeds, roots, and tubers. If the first Americans also relied on plant foods, the same habitats would have been equally attractive to them."[1]

One of the central debates about the peopling of America concerns the alleged presence of humans at dates much more than 12,000 years before the present. If people lived in America before 12,000 years ago, their remains have become extremely scarce and nearly impossible to authenticate. In the pages that follow, we critically examine evidence about the supposed very early populations known under the rubrics of pre-Paleoindian, pre-Clovis, or pre–projectile-point populations. (The first term refers generally to cultures predating the early Amerindian peoples known through their big-game subsistence; the second term more specifically implies an American point-making culture prior to the benchmark Paleoindian hunting-point technology; and the last posits a population that worked stone crudely prior to all point-making.) Dena Dincauze assessed the matter comprehensively, some years ago, and came to pessimistic conclusions on both the procedures of the advocates and their results. It has been patently obvious for many years that artifacts and human bones always are absent in paleontological sites and natural traps, some containing a full range of Rancholabrean animals that date to more than 12,000 years ago. Many of these would have been excellent hunting and scavenging places, and some were used later, during the extinction process and after 10,000 years ago, when the major extinctions

---

[1] Paul S. Martin, "Clovisia the beautiful," *Natural History* 97 (1987), No. 10, 10. For other migration models, see David W. Anthony, "Migration in archeology: The baby and the bathwater," *American Anthropologist* 92 (1990), 895–914, and Robert L. Kelly and Lawrence C. Todd, "Coming into the country: Early Paleoindian hunting and mobility," *American Antiquity* 53 (1988), 231–44

had run their course. Even Richard Morlan, a sometimes protagonist for pre-Clovis occupation, thinks that all the possibly earlier sites fall short of proving the case. He admits, "In fact, I am increasingly impressed by the contrast between the paucity and plethora of data before and after 11,500 years ago."[2]

A few years ago, when I reviewed the North American literature for human skeletal material that could be older than 12,000 years, there remained only two possibilities: the poorly documented remains from Warm Mineral Springs, Florida, and Natchez, Mississippi. The latter now has been sensibly evaluated and directly dated by radiocarbon to 5,580 ± 80 years ago (AA-4051).[3] As for cultural remains, there is no compelling evidence of human occupation before the Paleoindian or Clovis stage. Those who accept an earlier, usually "pre–projectile-point," stage have been fooled over and over by mixed and misdated sites, and they often have been forced to posit extremely simple, even stagnant, peoples who knew not the use of fire, burial customs, hunting technology, or stone artifacts elaborate enough to signal their identities to us or their contemporaries. To most of us, the best models of Paleoindian behavior, society, technological development, and resource use suggest that Paleoindians flourished in a previously unpopulated America. Likewise, the patterns of dental morphology, immunoglobulin allotypes, and linguistic diversification point to a colonization through eastern Siberia only 12,000 to 15,000 radiocarbon years ago. That chronology would allow the tentative inclusion of the three most popular of proto-Paleoindian sites to have survived close inspection – Bluefish Caves, Meadowcroft, and Fort Rock Cave – although all have detractors and none is entirely convincing.[4]

Just as the human colonization of North America would appear to set limits for the colonization of South America, the human occupation of eastern Siberia is a limiting factor, to most archaeologists, for human

---

[2] Richard E. Morlan, "Pre-Clovis people: Early discoveries of America," in *Americans Before Columbus: Ice-Age Origins*, Ronald C. Carlisle, ed. (Pittsburgh, 1988), 38.

[3] Thomas F. Lynch, "Glacial-age man in South America? A critical review," *American Antiquity* 55 (1990), 13; John L. Cotter, "Update on Natchez man," *American Antiquity* 56 (1991), 36–39.

[4] For example, C. Vance Haynes, Jr., "More on Meadowcroft radiocarbon chronology," *Review of Anthropoloy* 12 (1991), No. 1, 8–14; Kenneth B. Tankersley and Cheryl A. Munson, "Comments on the Meadowcroft Rockshelter radiocarbon chronology and the recognition of coal contaminants," *American Antiquity* 57 (1992), 321–326, but see also James M. Adovasio, Jack Donahue, and Robert Stuckenrath, "Never say never again: Some thoughts on could haves and might have beens," *American Antiquity* 57 (1992), 327–331.

presence in North America. Unfortunately, the uttermost regions of Siberia are less well known, and the date is less certain and actively disputed. The earliest secure radiocarbon dates are about 14,000 years ago for the Early Ushki culture, to the southeast on the Kamchatka Peninsula, and, thousands of kilometers east of Bering Strait, the Dyuktai Cave complex, of similar age (14,000–12,000 years), which may have spread east to Beringia by 13,000 years ago, when the Bering land bridge was giving way to the Bering Strait. There are technological arguments for deriving the bifacial Paleoindian flint points from these sources, but the precursors of Paleoindian points, bone tools, and burial customs can be seen even more clearly in the distant Malta complex, near Lake Baikal, dated conservatively by Vance Haynes to 14,750 years ago, but more generously to 18,000 years by geological associations.

MIGRATION TO SOUTH AMERICA

Beringia was not the only obstacle to mammalian radiation in the Americas. The pattern of exchanges (and lack of exchanges) observed by zoogeographers suggests that the Bering area cooled throughout the Tertiary Period (66 million–2 million years B.P.), with the cool zone progressively separating the ranges of many animal groups. In the Eocene Epoch (that is, the second part of the Tertiary), the exchange between Old World and New consists of large parts of the continental faunas, but by the Oligocene (or third part), major radiations of tropical and temperate mammals (such as pigs, giraffes, mongooses, higher primates) are failing to penetrate the Arctic filter. Through time the exchange involves smaller fractions of the total continental faunas, lower taxonomic categories, and ecologically less novel types. The most important selective factor seems to be zonation of climate, especially toward the end of the Tertiary Period, when the types exchanged belong generally to cool but not Alpine climates and those living in grasslands rather than forests. The migration of a single species of tropical primate (our own), during the Quaternary, signals a totally new *cultural* adaptation rather than reversal of the climate trend or biological adaptation.

The passage to South America was conditioned by very different, sometimes opposite, factors. Throughout the Tertiary, until nearly Pleistocene time (2 million–10,000 years B.P.), there was enough of a sea gap between North and South America to prevent exchange of the evolving mammalian faunas. As a result, in a situation somewhat similar to the

Australian marsupial mammals, some thirty families of South American land mammals evolved to occupy niches filled by Nearctic and Palearctic mammals in North America. When the sea gap was closed toward the end of the Pliocene Epoch (that is, the last part of the Tertiary Period, ending 2 million years ago), about twenty-four families became shared between the two continents, with the northern families usually dominating. (The opossum, armadillo, and porcupine are exceptions.) This invasion may well represent the first case of "yankee imperialism," involving as it did *Stegomastodon* and *Haplomastodon* (Fig. 3.1), two close relatives of what used to be known as *Archidiskodon imperator*, the "imperial mammoth."

It is entirely appropriate to see Paleoindian hunters (along with canid and felid predators, such as wolves and sabertooths) as coming on the heels of horses, camelids, deer, bovids, and mastodons as they radiated into South America earlier in the Pleistocene Epoch (2 million–10,000 B.P.). George Gaylord Simpson called this the great American interchange, one of the most remarkable faunal migrations in the geological record. Our lineage is "Johnny come lately," monkeys and higher primates having evolved separately since the Oligocene in the Old World, while New World monkeys evolved separately in South America due to the arctic filter and Panamanian sea gap. Although some Palearctic and Nearctic mammals were unable to adapt to lower Central America, and thus cross the Pleistocene land bridge to South America, human beings, as essentially tropical animals, crossed rapidly – indeed, instantaneously in geological terms – once they had achieved the cultural adaptations that allowed the Paleoindian florescence in North America.

Problematic Claims of Glacial-age Settlement

European researchers, more than Americans, have long been inclined to accept a Paleolithic period in South America. This occupation would have occurred long before the sudden and obvious appearance, about 11,000 years ago, of Paleoindian hunters. After more rigorous investigation, a pre-Paleoindian occupation of North America has come to be seen as increasingly unlikely, but, at the same time, a few North and South American archaeologists have returned to the turn-of-the-century European position of arguing for a much earlier settlement of the southern continent. Regardless of the merits of the putatively early sites themselves, still being hotly debated, this position presents practical difficul-

Figure 3.1. Late Pleistocene mammals, extinct in Postglacial time, that might have been hunted by hypothetical predecessors of the Paleoindians: (A) *Toxodon* (a notoungulate perhaps represented in the rock art of Bahia), (B) *Doedicurus* (a glyptodon or giant armadillo from La Moderna and Esperança), (C) *Megatherium* (the large ground sloth in various forms and contexts at Arroyo Seco, Cueva del Indio del Rincón, Esperança and Pikimachay), (D) *Macrauchenia* (a litoptern perhaps represented in the rock art of Bahia), (E) *Smilodon* (a placental sabertooth more likely to be the hunter than the hunted), (F) *Haplomastodon* (a gomphotheriid proboscidean in various forms and contexts at Monte Verde, Nochaco, Tagua-Tagua, Taima-Taima, and Tibitó). Drawings by Judy Spencer, after dust jacket and figure illustrations in *Splendid Isolation: The Curious History of South American Mammals*, by George Gaylord Simpson (1980), Yale University Press, New Haven.

ties, such as defining the nature of any earlier adaptation and finding a high latitude source for the earliest settlers.

Lamenting the absence of secure early sites in North America, James Dixon once postulated that early human beings arrived first in South America, whence they spread gradually northward (Map 3.1). This would appear to be a revival of Paul Rivet's long abandoned hypothesis. Even

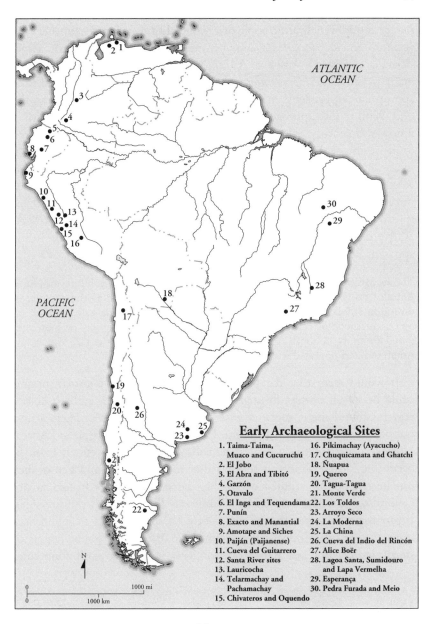

ATLANTIC
OCEAN

PACIFIC
OCEAN

Early Archaeological Sites

1. Taima-Taima,
   Muaco and Cucuruchú
2. El Jobo
3. El Abra and Tibitó
4. Garzón
5. Otavalo
6. El Inga and Tequendama
7. Punín
8. Exacto and Manantial
9. Amotape and Siches
10. Paiján (Paijanense)
11. Cueva del Guitarrero
12. Santa River sites
13. Lauricocha
14. Telarmachay and
    Pachamachay
15. Chivateros and Oquendo

16. Pikimachay (Ayacucho)
17. Chuquicamata and Ghatchi
18. Ñuapua
19. Quereo
20. Tagua-Tagua
21. Monte Verde
22. Los Toldos
23. Arroyo Seco
24. La Moderna
25. La China
26. Cueva del Indio del Rincón
27. Alice Boër
28. Lagoa Santa, Sumidouro
    and Lapa Vermelha
29. Esperança
30. Pedra Furada and Meio

N

0   1000 mi
0   1000 km

Map 3.1

today, some French anthropologists would bring *Homo erectus* to Brazil 200,000 to 300,000 years ago, by means of an invisible trail across Beringia and North America. A California anthropologist, Jeffrey Goodman, would have *Homo sapiens* evolve in America, despite the lack of appropriate antecedents in the fossil record, and then spread back to the Old World. His approach is reminiscent of that of the accomplished nineteenth-century paleontologist Florentino Ameghino, who attempted to prove the evolution of mankind on the banks of the Río de La Plata. Every logical possibility has been presented, even perfectly serious and recent proposals that bifacial and sometimes fluted Paleoindian points were developed independently in Venezuela or Ecuador, and perhaps spread north to become the characteristic American Paleoindian artifact. With tongue in cheek, Michael Moseley once suggested a solution to the apparent dilemma:

The recognition of a preprojectile point stage and phase in South but not North America can be interpreted in several ways. It may be seen as the product of diverging scholastic traditions separated not so much by theoretical biases [as by] . . . methodological standards. The alternative interpretation of man's reputed antiquity in South America would be that he entered the Hemisphere via Antarctica and migrated from south to north.[5]

It would seem that the problem of South American human origins could be solved simply, through a detailed analysis of the earliest skeletal remains found there, together with comparative analysis of likely ancestral populations in North America, East Asia, or even Europe and Africa. However, the putatively earliest remains have an inconvenient habit of becoming "lost," almost as soon as they are discovered and before they can be thoroughly studied or reliably dated. The bones from Garzón, Colombia, were lost before Hans Bürgl was able to report the site. Alan Bryan maintains that the robust calotte (skull cap) that he published, from the British Consul's depredations in the Lagoa Santa region of Brazil, has become lost. The most primitive Sumidouro skull, found and

[5] M. Edward Moseley, Review of *Prehistoria de Suramérica* (Juan Schobinger), *American Anthropologist*, 73 (1971), 932. Other forthright spokesmen of the pre-Clovis school include E. James Dixon, *Quest for the Origins of the First Americans* (Albuquerque, 1993) and "The origins of the first Americans," *Archaeology* 38 (1985), No. 2, 22–27; P. Rivet, "Recherche d'une voie de migration des Australiens vers l'Amerique," *Séances Publiques, Société Biogéographique* 3 (1926), 11–16; Henri de Lumley et al., "Découverte d'outils taillés associés à des faunes du Pleistocène moyen dans la Toca da Esperança, État de Bahia, Brésil," *C. R. Acad. Sci. Paris* 306 (1988), 241–247; Jeffrey Goodman, *American Genesis* (New York, 1981); Florentino Ameghino, *La antigüedad del hombre en La Plata* (Paris, 1880)

reported by Lund and Pöch, is unavailable now, but eventually it may be relocated in Europe. The Miramar dentition, found by Ameghino in Argentina, has been determined to be from a peccary, while LePaige's "Atacama Man" (Chile) may not even be from an animal.

According to Ernesto Salazar, who has taken the initiative of dispelling some of the myths of Ecuador's past, propagated mostly by Europeans and North Americans, the Punín skull has been dated by radiocarbon to 4950 B.C.E., Punín-2 to 1240 B.C.E., and the Paltacalo skull (an "Australoid" specimen touted by Rivet as proof of his oceanic migration) is nowhere to be found. Fortunately, it was possible to track down the Otavalo skull, which a medical doctor had removed to England and publicized as being of great primitiveness and age (22,800–36,000 years), using notoriously unreliable dating techniques. A more reliable technique, using bone proteins, indicates an age of about 2,500 years. The ratio of stable carbon isotopes suggests, as one would expect with such a date, that Otavalo Man was a heavy consumer of domesticated maize.

Anatomists continue to work with the cranial morphology of remaining South American specimens, none claimed to be older than 12,000 years and none dated directly by radiometric means. A recent study of eight Colombian specimens (Tequendama I and II, 7000–4000 B.C.E.) and thirty Brazilian skulls (from various Lagoa Santa excavations of the nineteenth and twentieth centuries) purports to show a relationship with Tasmanian, Tolai, and South Australian native peoples. The authors conclude that these skeletal remains, regardless of their ages, exhibit more similarities with modern South Pacific skulls than with those of people living in Asia and the north. This viewpoint holds that the Americas were settled before the classical "Mongoloid" type (characterized by the sinodent pattern and other features) evolved in Asia. The first Americans are claimed to resemble closely the racial stock that populated Australia. This would require a pre-Paleoindian migration much earlier than that accepted by most archaeologists. Moreover, such studies are subject to other possible interpretations, ranging from independent convergent evolution to statistical variation in the small, uncertain, and selected sample of human crania. Work by Gentry Steele nevertheless confirms that the earliest skeletal remains differ systematically and significantly from those of later Indians.

In their study of a broader but not larger sample of dated skulls, Isabel Martí and Francisco Rothhammer found that cranial indices varied insignificantly with age of specimen, but that the altitudes of the sites from which the skulls had come explained 16 percent of the variation. Whereas selective adaptation to the extreme altitudes of South America seems to have had a measurable effect on human differentiation, native South Americans do not show much consistent variation in skeletal morphology, certainly too little to prove the case for a separate and earlier migration from Asia or anywhere else. A majority of anthropologists follows the conclusions of Christy Turner, based on dental characteristics, that northeast Asia was the ancestral home for all American peoples. Well-documented dentitions, from cremations of twelve individuals found in caves in southern Chile, "suggest that paleo-Indians could easily have been ancestral to most living Native Americans, that very little dental evolution has occurred, and that the founding paleo-Indian population was small, genetically homogeneous, and arrived late in the Pleistocene."[6]

The bone evidence, then, for a pre-Paleoindian occupation of South America, is essentially nil. Every decade seems to have its "lucky strike," but none has yet panned out. As this was written, scientists were considering human bones from the Ñuapua paleontological site in the Gran Chaco of southeastern Bolivia, where they were found in very fragmentary condition, mixed with a fauna that may date from the transition of the Pleistocene to Holocene or Recent Epoch (10,000 B.P. to present). However, these bones were unaccompanied by artifacts, mostly superficial, and impossible to date.

From the beginning, many of the proponents of a South American Paleolithic stage have been European archaeologists, amateur or professional, who modeled their expectations on the Old World paleolithic sequence and relied principally on archaeological indications. Some were diplomats, others were businessmen and engineers (especially in mining and nitrates), who came and went. Missionaries and scientists (e.g., Gustavo LePaige) sometimes stayed and took citizenship in the American nations. Other scientists (Bürgl, Butzer, Guidon, de Lumley, Menghin) are known as much, or more, for their work elsewhere as that in South America. North and South American archaeologists generally have been more conservative in their assessments of the possibility of glacial-age human presence, with the notable exception of a few vocal and much

---

[6] Christy G. Turner, II and Junius Bird, "Dentition of Chilean Paleo-Indians and peopling of the Americas," *Science* 212 (1981), 1053–1055.

cited scholars. If one read only *Nature* rather than *Science*, or (British) *Antiquity* rather than *American Antiquity*, one might come away with a different picture of the settlement of South America. Elsewhere, I have reviewed at great length the sites upon which these divergent opinions are based, but here I can give only a synopsis.

Each year brings new and apparently startling discoveries, well publicized in the newspapers, press conferences, and professional congresses. The short half-life or shelf-life, which characterizes most of the pre-Paleoindian sites, has been much noted and even joked about. In a 1974 review, I focused on sites and complexes of the "early" Biface and Chopper tradition: Caracaraña, Ghatchiense, Chuquicamata, Ampajango, Manantial, Chivateros, Manzanillo, Rancho Peludo, and Garzón. None of these figures in today's argument. The technologically impoverished "Flake tradition" has fared nearly as badly, with the virtual disappearance from serious discussion of Pikimachay (Pacaicasa and Ayacucho), Oquendo, Tortuga, Achona, Exacto, Catalanense, Altoparanense, Riogalleguense, Oliviense, and Tandilense. Abrense (Colombia) is now considered usually to be either Paleoindian or, preferably, Archaic; Tagua-Tagua is firmly Paleoindian and Archaic; and only Guitarrero and Los Toldos retain flake industries and anomalous pre-Paleoindian dates. But those dates are only slightly early, are at variance with other dates on the same strata, and are associated with small collections, or collections that otherwise include projectile points of obviously later types.[7]

In Venezuela, the sites of Muaco and Cucuruchú, along with Cruxent's seriation of the Río Pedregal terrace collections, have been virtually ignored by other scholars, while Taima-Taima has been received skeptically. Nevertheless, Taima-Taima has been as thoroughly described, redescribed, and discussed as any of the pre-Clovis contenders, other than Meadowcroft in North America. Taima-Taima is a little tarnished, and it has its problems, but, to my mind, it is the best of the remaining possibilities. There are few suggestions of human activity, among the ample indications of other animals, but one or more artifacts are surely real. They may be intrusive, representing a later event than the slightly pre-Paleoindian radiocarbon dates. The claimed butchering of a juvenile

---

[7] Agusto Cardich, L. A. Cardich, and A. Hajduk, "Secuencia arqueológica de la Cueva 3 de Los Toldos (Santa Cruz, Argentina)," *Relaciones de la Sociedad Argentina de Antropología* 7 (1973), 85–123; Thomas F. Lynch, "Lack of evidence for glacial-age settlement of South America: Reply to Dillehay and Collins and to Gruhn and Bryan," *American Antiquity* 56 (1991), 348–355; Thomas F. Lynch et al., "Chronology of Guitarrero Cave, Peru," *Science* 229 (1985), 864–867.

mastodon, and its association with two artifacts and dated twigs, has not been illustrated in a convincing way. Thus there is a definite possibility of natural mixture and confusion of a Paleoindian visit with slightly earlier "natural" events at these Pleistocene waterholes and animal wallows, some of which include modern pottery and glass. Here, as at many similar sites, it may be that the bones, artifacts, and containing deposits form not a primary association but rather a secondary deposit, quite possibly mixed by the trampling and wallowing of the latest animals to use the waterholes. Some have flowing springs, while others, such as Taima-Taima, have a water table that rises and falls within the basin.

During the excavations, upwelling water still moved through the Taima-Taima deposits, creating what were described as "volcanoes" of sand and water that rose from the exposed surface. Each day the excavation pit was pumped anew, so that work in the bog could continue. Under these conditions, it would hardly be surprising if the associations became confused and the small, dense stone artifacts migrated downward. Even if no movement of bones and tools took place, it is highly likely that dissolved or suspended carbon has moved with the groundwater to contaminate the samples. Geochronologists warned of this in the beginning, yet some proponents still insist on the validity of the cultural associations and dates. Without denying the possibility, I would suggest that it is more likely that Taima-Taima is either a secondary combination of materials of slightly different ages, or an infrequently used Paleoindian kill site in which some of the dated remains have become contaminated. Rather than accepting the 13,000-year-old dates at face value, I have cautioned my colleagues to note, as well, "problems with stratigraphically inconsistent dates (reversals), inconsistencies among materials dated, the presence of coal in the bed below (from which water and sand are percolating), the general problem of carbon exchange in fluctuating and moving groundwater, the dating of soils (paleosols) and associating them with human events, and most importantly, the probabilities of mixture and intrusion."[8]

According to Jared Diamond, "1989's favorite" was the site of Monte Verde in southern Chile. Nevertheless, doubts and reservations have already been published by Gary Haynes, Dena Dincauze, Lautaro Núñez, and Calogero Santoro, as well as myself.[9] The main issues are the radio-

[8] Thomas F. Lynch, "Glacial-age man in South America?" *American Antiquity* 55 (1990), 18.
[9] Gary Haynes, "Review of new evidence for the Pleistocene peopling of the Americas," *North American Archeologist* 10 (1989), 258–262; Dena F. Dincauze, "Review of Monte Verde: A late

carbon dates (possibly misinterpreted or even systematically contaminated), the interpretation of the site's stratigraphy, the recognition of artifacts and other signs of human culture, the possible conflation of remains of different ages, and the possible conflation of cultural with noncultural remains. Some critics are troubled by one aspect, some by another. It will be interesting to see, after a few years have passed, how many archaeologists follow Tom Dillehay and Michael Collins in their interpretation of Monte Verde as an Archaic-like village, occupied year-round, in *pre*-Paleoindian times 13,000 and even 33,000 years ago. This would be an improbable coincidence in a continent where verifiable glacial-age sites have otherwise been as scarce as hen's teeth. Elsewhere, we see that such superpositions have happened mostly in strategic places, or those intrinsically valuable as scarce resources, such as caves or springs, or where nature makes secondary deposits, as in a river channel. To the contrary, Monte Verde was a damp and cool environment, at a rather poor camping place along a minor creek. Even a single pre-Paleoindian campsite is unlikely; rather, the settlement and extraction pattern proposed by the excavators might belong instead to the more recent Archaic pattern described later in this chapter. Moreover, many archaeologists are skeptical of most of the Monte Verde artifacts, including hearths, structures, and most of the wooden artifacts. The stone artifacts, which would fit later Archaic industries, may have been mixed with remains of a paleontological site.

If Monte Verde was the hot site of 1989, Alice Boër, Toca da Esperança, and Toca do Boqueirao da Pedra Furada were the favorites of the preceding few years. Disillusionment about the last of these Brazilian sites began in 1985 at Denver, when Pedra Furada was presented to American archaeologists, and doubts became widespread in 1989 after the "First World Summit Conference on the Peopling of the Americas," held in Maine. By then the claim of a 30,000-year-old tradition of cave art had already been withdrawn, many archaeologists were disappointed in their inspections of the quartz and quartzite "artifacts," and photographs of the claimed pre-Paleoindian hearths were found to be unconvincing. This is not to deny the reality or importance of Archaic and later art traditions, formal hearths, and lithic industry made on flinty rocks discovered at hundreds of sites in Piauí by the French art historians

Pleistocene settlement in Chile," *Journal of Field Archaeology* 18 (1991), 116–119; Lautaro Núñez and Calogero Santoro, "Primeros poblamientos en el cono sur de América (XII–IX milenio a.p.," *Revista de Arqueología Americana* 1 (1990), 91–139; Tom D. Dillehay and Michael B. Collins, "Early cultural evidence from Monte Verde in Chile," *Nature* 332 (1988), 150–152.

and archaeologists. Not only are the sites of Sao Raimundo Nonato said to be badly disturbed by termites, rodent burrows, and rockfalls – as at Pedra Furada and Toca do Meio – but the geomorphology and stratigraphy have been inconsistently described. To many observers it seems likely that the charcoal, perhaps 40,000 years old, might have resulted from natural brush fires in the surrounding semidesert *caatinga*, or thorn forest. In this environment charcoal and ash are often distributed and concentrated by wind and flash floods. The latest dates (> 47,000 years) and a "hearth" dated 42,400 ± 2,600 B.P. are no more credible than those presented before.

Several of us still hope that the region of Sao Raimundo Nonato will yield Paleoindian associations of indubitable artifacts with the bones of extinct animals. As I write this, there are rumors circulating that the bones of giant sloths have been found in rock shelters across the valley from the notorious sites – but no artifacts were yet found in association. In Bahia (also written Bahía), art historians and archaeologists have tried to demonstrate Pleistocene climate changes through rock paintings in which they claim to identify various extinct and locally extinct animals. The alleged representations of *Toxodon* (gigantic native notoungulate), *Sceliodotherium* (ground sloth), *Glyptodon* (giant armadillo) (Fig. 3.2), *Hippidion* and *Amerhippus* (native horse), *Arctodus* (short-faced bear), and *Palaeolama* (extinct precursor of the llama) could be argued from dawn to dusk but would hardly satisfy paleontologists.[10]

Indeed, human coexistence with a Middle Pleistocene fauna, at Toca da Esperança in Bahia, has been promulgated widely in Brazil and France. Even among those who would hope for an entry 20,000 or 30,000 years ago, this announcement has not been well received. The problems at Esperança are much the same as with Pedra Furada and Monte Verde. Although Beltrao and Danon have identified campfire structures, charcoal, bone tools (drills), and a few crude flake, pebble, and chopper tools – made of exotic quartz and quartzite from at least 10 kilometers' distance – many archaeologists distrust the associations or identifications. Still, the tools are said to be incontestably in place, together with an appropriate fauna of extinct horse, giant sloths, arma-

[10] Maria de Conceiçao de M. C. Beltrão and Martha Locks, "Climate changes in the archaeological region of Central, Bahia, Brazil, as shown by interpretation of pre-historic rock paintings," *Proceedings of the First International Congress of Ethnobiology, Belém, Brazil* 1 (1988), 99–112; Maria Beltrão et al., "Les representations pictographiques de la Sierra da Pedra Calcaria: Les Tocas de Buzios et de Esperança," *L'Anthropologie* 94 (1990), 139–154.

Figure 3.2. South American edentates found in equivocal archaeological contexts at La Moderna (glyptodon, foreground), in Fell's Cave and Rio Grande do Sul (mylodon, background), and in the rock art and cave sites of Bahia, such as Toca da Esperança (*Nothrotherium*, an archaic megalonychid or giant sloth, on the right). After restorations by Charles R. Knight and R. Bruce Horsfall, in *Prehistoric Life*, by Percy E. Raymond (1939), fig. 143, Harvard University Press, Cambridge.

dillo, camelid, and perhaps bear. Brocket deer and agouti are the only extant forms.[11]

On the face of it, there is no particular reason not to trust the alpha and gamma-ray spectrometry dates, ranging from 204,000 to 295,000 years, done in France and the United States at three highly respected laboratories. However, in this time range, *Homo erectus* is not considered to have mastered the Siberian adaptation, which would have required advanced hunting skills, clothing, and the facile and regular control of fire that might allow passage through Arctic Beringea.

In fact, it may be the very antiquity of Esperança that has caused most of my colleagues to reject it out of hand. This is not fair; the site should stand or fall on its own merits, like Pedra Furada, Monte Verde, Taima-Taima, and other marginally pre-Paleoindian sites. To my mind the greatest problems with Esperança Cave are its incomplete publication (which especially does not allow us to judge the artifacts and cultural features) and the lack of depth of its four strata (totaling only 100 to 150 centimeters) said to span 300,000 years. Given that Level I has a radio-carbon date of 2,020 ± 130 years B.P.; it may be that bonafide artifacts have somehow migrated down to the earlier levels. Again, the difficulties revolve around the identification of human culture and the trustworthiness of the stratigraphic associations.

Taima-Taima, Monte Verde, Pedra Furada, and Esperança are the sites that have been most discussed over the last few years. These, and the pre-Paleoindian sites of yesteryear, are reviewed in the major journals, but serious students should consult as well the primary sources cited therein.

Beyond the issues of chronology and validity of the sites lies the intrinsically more interesting question of what adaptation or adaptations might be represented by these disputed early sites. Unfortunately, even the most avid proponents of pre-Clovis occupation of the Americas have trouble discerning, much less agreeing upon, a consistent pattern. One obvious possibility is that the Paleoindians might not have come directly from Eurasia, as Upper Paleolithic big game hunters and gatherers, but have descended from a people already here, who might have had a more

---

[11] Maria Beltrão and J. Danon, "Evidence of human occupations during the Middle Pleistocene at the Toca da Esperança in Central archaeological region, State of Bahia, Brazil," *Anais da Academia Brasileira de Ciências* 59 (1987), No. 3, 275–276; de Lumley, "Découverte d' outils taillés," associés à des faunes du Pleistocène moyen dans la Toca de Esperança, État de Bahia, Brésil, C.R. Acad. Sci., Paris, 306 (1988), 241–247.

generalized adaptation. If they had adapted especially to the forests and marine edges of the continents, they might have stressed collecting, gathering, and scavenging, hunted but little, and left behind few distinctive projectile points. In some situations tools might have been made mostly of wood and scavenged bone.

Carl Sauer seminally introduced one hypothesis for low-tech gathering, the notion of the simple and contented beachcomber. This model seems destined to surface every generation or so. In this story the prehistorian places a few devolved maritime collectors and gatherers along the enlarged continental fringe, during the glacial maximum, allowing meltwater transgression conveniently to erase their archaeological record in the postglacial stage. Besides, say some, their tools might have been so simple that, next to those left by the Paleoindians, we would hardly notice them. Although postglacial maritime transgression, resulting from melting glaciers and rising sea level, will have destroyed many sites during the first few millennia of postglacial time, it is hard to believe that a people colonizing a world vacant of other people and apes would have not spread inland, at least along the river valleys. Our species and all our near relatives are essentially terrestrial. The maritime fringe is at the edge of our niche, is neither as productive nor healthy as it first seems, and requires its own distinctive and relatively advanced technology for efficient exploitation. To most of us, the maritime adaptation seems more characteristic of the Postpaleoindian Archaic stage, but there is no denying scattered precedents in the Old World. An initial maritime adaptation might explain potentially early sites, in which the bifacial projectile-point technology were absent, or an early settlement pattern that included no associations of cultural remains with extinct Pleistocene mammals.[12]

The other major alternative, for those who would believe in pre-Paleoindian sites, supposes precursors who were less narrowly adapted to the "mammoth steppe" but who still engaged in some hunting of large

---

[12] Carl O. Sauer, "Seashore – Primitive home of man?" *Proceedings of the American Philosophical Society* 106 (1962), 41–47; Alan L. Bryan, "Paleoenvironments and cultural diversity in late Pleistocene South America," *Quaternary Research* 3 (1973), 237–256; James B. Richardson, III, "Modeling the development of sedentary maritime economies on the coast of Peru," *Annals of the Carnegie Museum of Natural History* 50 (1981); Alan J. Osborn, "Strandloopers, mermaids, and other fairy tails: Ecological determinants of marine resource utilizations, the Peruvian case," in *For Theory Building in Archaeology*, Lewis R. Binford, ed. (New York, 1977), 157–243; Vivien Standen, Marvin Allison, and Bernardo Arriaza, "Osteoma del conducto auditivo externo: hipótesis en torno a una posible patología laboral prehispánica," *Revista Chungará* 15 (1985), 197–209.

mammals. Later, in specific times and places, their descendants might have become specialized Paleoindians. This hypothesis would accept at face value the dates and associations recorded at Meadowcroft, Taima-Taima, Tagua-Tagua, Monte Verde, Los Toldos, and Guitarrero. Such a people would have entered South America not as Paleoindians but, most probably, as a forest-adapted folk that would be harder to find archaeologically. Given a lack of attention to the efficiently hunted large game, they might also have been less numerous. Unfortunately, the supporting field data for such a proposal are too meager, as we have seen, to lend much confidence. In addition, the "cultural remains" from sites that might fit this hypothesis are all quite different. Even the stone tools are extremely disparate. For example, the bifaces at Monte Verde are very different from one another and completely different from the El Jobo (Taima-Taima) bifaces that I have handled. Elements at Meadowcroft, Taima-Taima, and Tagua-Tagua could be Paleoindian (and some, as well, Archaic), but the stone tools from Monte Verde, Los Toldos, and Guitarrero seem to relate most closely to types best known in Archaic and very late Paleoindian industries.

Climate, Environmental Change, and the Problem of Human Entry

Whatever the meteorological changes, and there has been considerable dispute, there is little doubt that large parts of South America were more hospitable to hunter-gatherers at the end of the glacial stage than they would be today. The most important variables and areas of confusion include the continental synchronism, or lack of it, of changes in temperature and precipitation; the displacement of storm tracks and regional precipitation belts at the close of the Pleistocene Epoch toward 10,000 B.P.; the correlation of glacial regimen with changes in lake levels, precipitation, evaporation, and vegetation; the onset of the El Niño (also called ENSO) phenomenon with its periodic augmentation of west-coast rainfall and other Andean climate changes; and the extent and direction of changes in Amazonia (temperature, precipitation, vegetation, speciation) and their relation to changes in the Andes and the northwestern fringe of the continent that connects to Central America.[13]

[13] Previously, I have discussed these environmental factors at length: Thomas F. Lynch, "The Paleo-Indians," in *Ancient South Americans*, Sesse D. Jennings, ed. (San Francisco, 1883), 87–137; "Quaternary climate, environment, and the human occupation of the South-Central Andes," *Geoarchaeology* 5 (1990), 199–228.

Panamanian studies of pollen and phytoliths taken from cores extracted from lake sediments show a minimum depression of vegetation zones of 800 meters (relative to present zones) between 14,300 and 11,100 years ago. In terms of change in mean annual temperature, this suggests that the late-glacial period in central Panama was some 5° Celsius cooler than now. A rapid change in vegetation began about 11,100 years ago, when the relatively cool and drier glacial climate was replaced, to judge by the invading plants and rising lake waters, by a distinctly wetter and warmer regime. This corresponds fairly well with similar changes recorded across the land bridge in Venezuela, Colombia, and Ecuador.

About 11,000 years ago human arrival and its effect on the structure and composition of the Panamanian forests is also marked. Suddenly, small particles of carbon (soot from widespread fires, probably Paleoindian fire drives) become common in the cores. At the same time, phytoliths of sedges and weedy plants, which follow fires, peak in frequency. Over 90 percent of the weed phytoliths are coated with carbon, indicating that they were burnt. These fires are not likely to have had natural causes, as there are no signs of volcanic eruption and the massive disturbance started suddenly and continued despite increases in rainfall. According to the investigators, "The increased abundance of secondary forest and disturbance taxa, and increasing charcoal influx, continuing across the postulated climatic boundary [of increasing precipitation], is strongly indicative of human disturbance."[14] It is impossible to ignore that this disturbance horizon coincides in time with the Paleoindian expansion into Central America, probably as the first human occupants began to prey upon the megafauna that had established itself in the savanna and thorn forest of the late-glacial Pacific watershed. "The La Yeguada data make it clear that drier and cooler climatic conditions lasted from at least 14,000 to 10,500 years B.P. Such conditions would have favored a mosaic of thorn scrub and grassland at the expense of deciduous forest, the present-day natural growth."[15]

Less than 100 kilometers further east, Mark Bush and Paul Colinvaux have reported on a core from a caldera lake, slightly lower (500 meters above sea level) than La Yeguada, that probably preserves a detailed

---

[14] Dolores R. Piperno, Mark B. Bush, and Paul A. Colinvaux, "Paleoenvironments and human occupation in late-glacial Panama," *Quaternary Research* 33 (1990), 108–116.

[15] Piperno et al., "Paleoenvironments and human occupation," 114; Mark B. Bush and Paul A. Colinvaux, "A pollen record of a complete glacial cycle from lowland Panama," *Journal of Vegetation Science* 1 (1990), 105–118.

climate record throughout the last 150,000 years, including a complete glacial cycle. Their reconstruction suggests lower precipitation and lake levels, despite cooler conditions, from 30,000 to 12,000 years ago. Cooling on the order of 4° Celsius, and as much as 6° below modern temperatures from 14,000 to 10,000 years ago, denied the Chiriqui highlands to tropical rain forest, keeping rain forest species confined to well below 500 meters of elevation. Studies coordinated by the international CLIMAP project effectively demonstrated that the glacial-age equatorial oceans were 2° to 6° Celsius cooler than now, while July air temperatures over northern South America were depressed about 5°. Rainfall may have increased over the equatorial oceans, but it seems generally to have decreased over the continents.

Glacially lowered sea level is an additional mechanism that might have provided a better corridor for the first migrations to South America, because the minimum sea-level stand occurred as late as 15,000 years ago. In Panama, lower sea level would have caused incision of the river and stream channels on the Pacific side of the isthmus, which has a dry season of as long as five months. As streams responded to lower base level by incising channels and lowering the water table of the interfluvial zone, a seasonally dry landscape would become susceptible to fire damage, especially where fire was used by Paleoindian hunters. Even without major reductions in precipitation, it is safe to postulate a late-glacial strip of savannah, cut by gallery forests in the incised river bottoms, along the Pacific coast of lower Central America. Biogeographers, working independently of modern palynological and archaeological studies, have long been aware that the exchange between North and South America of plants and animals that could not survive in tropical forests required such Pleistocene habitat changes, at least on a temporary basis.[16]

Lake-level records are especially good indicators of the interactions among precipitation, temperature, evapotranspiration, and albedo (atmospheric and earth surface). These in turn are important components of the changing climate, vegetation, and glaciation that characterize the end of the Pleistocene Epoch. From Lake Valencia, in northern Venezuela, there is a continuous 13,000-year record, showing that the lake and its environs were dry or nearly dry until 10,000 years ago, when a permanent lake of fluctuating salinity formed. According to biogeographers, extremely dry, even droughty conditions in late-glacial northern

[16] Lynch, "The Paleo-Indians," 99–103.

Venezuela are also indicated by the concentration and then extinction of large mammals around springs and waterholes, such as Taima-Taima.

Past climate in lowland Colombia, directly below the Isthmus of Panama, is unstudied, but from the highland savannah of Bogotá, and especially Lake Fuquene, there are excellent pollen and lake-level records. Although the first part of the last glacial stage in the Colombian highlands seems to have been wet, about 20,000 years ago a trend toward progressively drier types of vegetation began. This culminated about 13,000 years ago, when tall-grass prairies (*páramos*) were extensive and rainfall probably less than half what it is now. Lake levels were lower despite the simultaneous contrary effects of lower temperature and less evaporation. After some amelioration 13,000 to 11,000 years ago, cool dry conditions returned from 11,000 to 9,500 years ago. Temperatures at least 3° Celsius less than the present are indicated by pollen studies and tree line descent to 2,500 meters, but changes in lake levels of the savannah of Bogotá are difficult to interpret, as they were also influenced by tectonic movements of the structure of the basin.[17]

We have little direct knowledge of the vegetation of the western coastal strip of Colombia and Ecuador during the glacial period. However, models of worldwide changes in atmospheric circulation displace the moisture-laden southwesterly winds that now bring heavy rainfall to western Colombia and northwestern Ecuador, while cold ocean currents welling up along the coast would result in cooler onshore sea breezes and reduced precipitation near the coastline. The significant decrease in winter rainfall resulted in a relatively dry corridor connecting Panama and Ecuador, at the same time as lower sea level exposed a strip of infertile continental shelf. "The two factors may have combined to produce a narrow coastal strip of open savanna bordered inland by a dry forest. . . . When this corridor existed, species adapted to savanna and dry forest habitats would have been able to move southward from dry areas in Panama to those of southern Ecuador and Peru, and similarly in the opposite direction."[18] The exchange in biota is visible paleontologically

---

[17] Claudio Ochsenius, "Aridity and biogeography in northernmost South America during the late Pleistocene (peri-Caribbean arid belt, 62°–74° W)," *Zentralblatt für Geologie und Paläontologie* 1 (1983), 264–278; Vera Markgraf, "Palaeoclimates in Central and South America since 18,000 B.P. based on pollen and lake-level records," *Quaternary Science Reviews* 8 (1989), 1–24.

[18] Kenneth E. Campbell, Jr., "Late Pleistocene events along the coastal plain of northwestern South America," in *Biological Diversification in the Tropics*, G. T. Prance, ed. (New York, 1982), 423–440, 434.

throughout the Pleistocene and finally, in archaeological form, in the Paleoindian migration southward about 11,000 years ago. Direct evidence of glacial-age cooling and/or aridity comes from analysis of pollen, phytoliths, and wood samples collected at two sites (970 and 1,100 meters elevation) at the eastern edge of the Ecuadorean Andes. Consistent with Clapperton's estimate, on geomorphological features, of full-glacial cooling of 7.4° Celsius at high, glaciated elevations, the palynologists calculate 7.5° Celsius cooling to bring the sub-Andean forest down 1,500 meters to Mera and San Juan Bosco. A similar downslope movement of montane vegetation probably occurred again during the last glacial advance. In southern Ecuador, Andean deglaciation takes place some 12,000 years ago, followed by human forest disturbance at 10,500 B.P.[19]

Data on higher Andean glaciation to the south, in Peru, Bolivia, Chile, and Argentina, are numerous but often ambiguous and open to varying interpretations and chronologies. On the one hand, J. H. Mercer and C. M. Clapperton argue for globally synchronous glacial advances but date them differently, while on the other, many scholars stress the local topographic and atmospheric factors that may have caused advance and retreat to be time transgressive latitudinally or even hemispherically. In southern Peru and Bolivia, significant glacial advance took place as late as 12,000 to 11,000 years ago. Despite a general warming trend, locally greater precipitation may have fed "warm," rapidly advancing cordilleran glaciers.

More precipitation, combined with melting snow fields and melting and surging glaciers, fed an immense lake (Tauca) on the Peruvian/Bolivian/Chilean *altiplano* (high plain), as well as several moderate size lakes on the *punas* (high-altitude tundras) of northern Argentina and Chile. Several radiometric dates suggest that the Lake Tauca high stand persisted from about 12,500 years ago until 11,000 or perhaps 10,000 years ago, throughout the present Titicaca-Poopó-Coipasa-Uyuni basin. Stored Pleistocene groundwater might also have helped maintain the South-Central Andean lakes well into postglacial times. This is indicated by obsidian hydration dates showing relatively heavy Early Archaic settlement and use of now-dry *quebradas* and saline lake basins of northern Chile. In the same area of the Atacama Desert and dry *puna*, a Swiss

[19] Lynch, "The Paleo-Indians," 101; Mark B. Bush et al., "Late Pleistocene temperature depression and vegetation change in Ecuadorian Amazonia," *Quaternary Research* 34 (1990), 330–345; Mark B. Bush, personal communication, 1990.

team found, following arid conditions 15,000 to 13,000 years ago, a significant wet interval indicated by glacial advances on Volcan Llullaillaco and freshwater stands of the Laguna Lejía. These are dated tentatively by two radiocarbon tests (13,330 ± 110 B.P. and 11,700 ± 110 B.P.), as well as one discordant result (15,490 ± 160 B.P.). Varves and freshwater diatoms evidence the wet conditions, which they correlate with the Tauca-phase lake on the *altiplano*. The formation of paleosoils some 500 meters above the current vegetation maximum suggests conditions wetter and warmer (about 3.5° Celsius) sometime early in the Holocene.[20]

Springs, lakes, and generally more abundant vegetation and animal life, in combination with high-altitude temperatures higher than those of the present, help explain the very visible human presence that archaeologists find in this desert zone in late Paleoindian and Early Archaic times. It is interesting that the late-glacial desiccation that allowed Paleoindian entry to northern South America was accompanied, in the now-drier central and south central Andes, by the temporarily wetter and probably warmer conditions that allowed rapid human migration and adaptation to that part of the continent.

Progress has been slower in reconstructing the late-glacial climate of Amazonia, the Guiana and Brazilian highlands, and the lowlands of northern South America. A few pollen studies show savanna vegetation along the Guyana coast, during at least part of the last glacial period with dry and open conditions inland at Rupununi. Lower precipitation on the coastal lowlands corresponds to a reduction in temperature of the adjoining Caribbean waters, as measured in oxygen isotopic and micropaleontological sea cores. Sedimentological cores taken off the mouth of the Amazon on the northeastern edge of the continent suggest a much drier and/or colder climate, with rapid erosion aided by deforestation. Unweathered feldspar sands are thought to have been derived from the Guiana highlands in late-glacial times and washed into the Amazon by

---

[20] Lynch, "Quaternary climate," 200–209; Thomas F. Lynch and Christopher M. Stevenson, "Obsidian hydration dating and temperature controls in the Punta Negra region of northern Chile," *Quaternary Research* 37 (1992), 117–124; Bruno Messerli et al., "Climate change in the extreme arid altiplano of northern Chile (initial project report)," (Berne, 1990); Martin Grosjean and Lautaro Núñez Atencio, "Late-glacial, early and middle Holocene environments, and resource use in the Atacama (northern Chile)," *Geoarchaeology* 9 (1994), 271–285. Recent work in the central Andes is summarized by Lonnie G. Thompson, "Reconstructing the paleo-ENSO records from tropical and subtropical ice cores," *Bulletín de L'Institut Français d'Études Andines* 22 (1993), 65–83. My own summary, with particular reference to early settlement history, was given in Minneapolis, 1995, as "Changing adaptations to the Gran Despoblado of northern Chile."

south-flowing tributaries. However, in the delicately balanced ecotonal savannas of the Guiana highlands, erosion might have been initiated by relatively small climate changes, with precipitation patterns in most of the Amazon basin remaining static or varying independently.[21]

The sole consensus on Amazon vegetation and climate changes is that we must abandon the consensus inherited from the last generation – that is, the idea of an everlastingly stable forest and climate, with abundant warmth and moisture, protected from catastrophic glacial changes, in which new species constantly accumulated, but from which few were lost. Following Jürgen Haffer's suggestion that various corners of the Amazon basin became refuges for the forest plants and animals during glacial-age droughts, there has been much argument over the meaning of disjunctive centers of species variety, especially of birds and butterflies. The assumption was that areas lifted slightly above the main river basin would have received sufficient rain to maintain the tropical forest, while extreme aridity decimated most of the formerly continuous forest vegetation and inhabitants. The isolated endemic pockets were to preserve the old species and become centers of differentiation for new ones. But there are other explanations possible as well. In at least some lineages, the centers of diversity have also been centers of activity in collection. Another possibility is that upland areas have more edaphic and topographic variety, on which speciation might be based. In the "intermediate-disturbance hypothesis," the disjunct centers of speciation would be seen as rather the opposite of refugia; this hypothesis maintains that centers of variability will occur where habitat changes are frequent, but not excessive, rather than in climatically stable refugia.[22]

Although the data points are few, and mostly on the western rim of the Amazon, the vegetation of the Amazon basin seems to have been affected more by glacial-age cooling than aridity. In fact, hydrological processes, even massive seasonal flooding from at least 10,000 until 5,000 years ago, have been an important component of the intermediate-level disturbances that contribute to disjunct distributions and species richness in the Amazon Basin. The most important factor in the reorganization

---

[21] John E. Damuth and Rhodes W. Fairbridge, "Equatorial Atlantic deep-sea Arkosic sands and ice-age aridity in tropical South America," *Bulletin of the Geological Society of America*, 81 (1970), 189–206; Rhodes W. Fairbridge, "Effects of Holocene climate change on some tropical geomorphic processes," *Quaternary Research* 6 (1976), 529–556.

[22] Jürgen Haffer, "Speciation in Amazon forest birds," *Science* 165 (1969), 131–137; Paul A. Colinvaux, "Ice-age Amazon revisited," *Nature* 340 (1989), 188–189; Colinvaux, "The past and future Amazon," *Scientific American* 260 (1989), 102–108.

of the tropical forest community in glacial times would seem to be the better documented temperature depression, on the order of 6° Celsius, which may have brought killing frosts to much of the Amazon Basin. Rather than retreating intact to upland refugia, forest species must have survived at low elevation in plant communities for which we have no modern analogs. What we accepted a few years ago as primeval undisturbed Amazon forest looks now, to Colinvaux, to be an ephemeral product of the past few millennia, much like the forests of eastern North America. We do not know what the late-glacial and early Holocene Amazon Basin was like, or whether it had the resources that would make it attractive to Paleoindian or Early Archaic peoples. The work on the *varzea* lakes near Manaus is a start, but we need longer and more widely distributed records before we can connect the wide expanse of Amazonia to the emerging picture in Colombia, Peru, and especially Ecuador. In the absence of any late-glacial pollen records from the Amazon forest itself, it is risky to draw paleoenvironmental inferences, but Markgraf models the entire tropical American lowlands as cool and dry 12,000 years ago, becoming as wet or wetter than the present by 9,000 years ago. At this point, rather than generalizing on the basis of such limited evidence, I would follow Arthur Shapiro in arguing that any demonstration of the refugial theory, with its attendant desiccation of the Amazon Basin, would "depend as much on stronger, more compelling cross-correlation with the highlands as on evidence likely to be generated stratigraphically, genetically, or geographically in the lowlands alone."[23]

THE PALEOINDIANS

Before considering Paleoindian lifeways as they are known from archaeological sites, it is worth turning to anthropological and linguistic postulates on the condition of the migrants as they entered the continent. The most exciting new information about the bodies of the Paleoindians comes not from the scarce bones that have survived but rather from the

---

[23] Arthur M. Shapiro, "Iterated ontogenies reiterated (review)," *Paleobiology* 15 (1989), 67–73; Bush et al., "Late Pleistocene temperature"; Paul A. Colinvaux, "Amazon diversity in light of the paleoecological record," *Quaternary Science Reviews* 6 (1987), 93–114; Colinvaux and Kam-biu Liu, "The late Quaternary climate of the western Amazon Basin," in *Abrupt Climatic Change*, W. H. Berger and L. D. Labeyrie, eds. (New York, 1987), 113–122; Markgraf, "Palaeoclimates in Central and South America," 9.

DNA of their genes, which has been passed down to their descendants, the modern Native American peoples. Today's research focus is on the DNA of mitochondria, which are maternally inherited organelles that lie outside the nucleus of a cell. Nuclear DNA, carried by our forty-six chromosomes, is shuffled and recombined to make new gene arrangements, as sperm and egg unite to create the new individuals of each generation. To the contrary, the mitochondrial genes from the parents do not recombine. Instead, the mitochondrial DNA is passed down only by females to their children, mothers to daughters, along the human matrilineages.

Genetic Studies

Although there are no random recombinations, as affect the nuclear DNA, the mitochondrial DNA does change slowly, mutating from time to time, rather than always replicating exactly, as it passes from generation to generation. It is these sequential mutations, which progressively differentiate one lineage from another, that allow biologists to reconstruct a phylogenetic "tree" of evolution, and even to estimate the time of separation of the branches. As the mutations accumulate along maternal lineages, it is possible to track continental-scale migrations through the distinctive mitochondrial DNA of the descendants.

Studies by D. C. Wallace and others began with the Pimas, an isolated Maya population, and a relatively distinct and genetically unmixed Ticuna group from the Western Amazon. All three populations, but especially the Ticuna (44%), had high frequencies of a rare Asian mutation (HincII morph 6), suggesting that it was characteristic of a single founding Paleoindian group. Systematic search for an Asian population, with similarly high proportions of this and three other morphs, had not yet begun. Nevertheless, Wallace was confident that a single migration came across the Bering land bridge carrying these four lineages of mitochondrial DNA. In the peoples studied thus far, the morphs occurred in similar percentages, suggesting that the original Paleoindian group, as it separated from the Asian gene pool, was fairly small and similarly characterized by these four primary maternal lineages. It seemed possible that at some "bottleneck" of the movement across Beringia, the primal Paleoindian group had only four women whose children survived. Some

600 or 700 generations later, their DNA morphs survive in the blood of the people of South America.[24]

Other genetically carried characteristics are often more difficult to track through prehistoric time. All are subject to the randomness of sexual recombination; some are highly influenced by selective adaptation (e.g., blood antigens); many, especially those observed, are highly complex and plastic in their expression (skull shape, stature, skin color); and most preserve poorly. However, dental characteristics have been studied much longer than mitochondrial DNA and with great success. Teeth preserve well, are easily observed and measured, are relatively stable in evolution, are reasonably variable between populations, and have a high genetic component (as opposed to variable expression by the subject's age, sex, or environmental history). Turner recognizes three native American subgroups of the Sinodont pattern that is characteristic of northern Asia. From study of modern and archaeological dentitions, he concludes that the subpatterns are temporally and spatially stable and that they correspond culturally and linguistically with three cultural blocs: the Aleut-Eskimo peoples; the Na-Dene speakers (that is, the Athabaskan peoples of northwestern North America together with the Navajo and Apache); and all the rest of the North and South American native peoples, collectively called Amerindians. The third and by far the largest group is thought to be descended from the Paleoindian migration in late-glacial times. Turner and I are in agreement that "the early Palaeo-Indian hunters of mammoth and other large animals were in North America by 12,000 B.P. Their descendants reached the southern tip of Chile 1,000 years later. Evidence for human presence in the Americas prior to 12,000 B.P. is qualitatively poor, quantitatively insufficient or variously controversial."[25]

All New World dentitions are much alike, resembling each other more than they do Old World dentitions. Also, what variety there is occurs

---

[24] D. C. Wallace, K. Garrison, and W. C. Knowler, "Dramatic founder effects in Amerindian mitochondrial DNAs," *American Journal of Physical Anthropology* 68 (1985), 149–155; T. G. Schurr et al., "Amerindian mitochondrial DNAs have rare Asian mutations at high frequencies, suggesting they derived from four primary maternal lineages," *American Journal of Human Genetics* 46 (1990), 613–623. Further work shows greater complexity.

[25] Turner, Christy G., II, "The dental search for native American origins," in *Out of Asia: Peopling the Americas and the Pacific*, Robert Kirk and Emöke Szathmary, eds. (Canberra, 1985), 32, 31–78; Turner and Junius Bird, "Dentition of Chilean Paleo-Indians and peopling of the Americas," *Science* 212 (1981), 1053–1055.

mostly in the north, with a drift toward uniformity in modern and archaeological dentitions found southward. This, like the initial results from study of mitochondrial DNA, supports a rapid, expanding-front colonization, rather late in time, by an absolutely small original founding group. Skeletal remains from the first wave of population are rare. They may include the fragmented and cremated dentitions from eleven Paleoindians buried in Cerro Sota and Palli Aike Caves near the Strait of Magellan, in southernmost Chile. Although collected in 1936, these were thought to be reasonably securely dated and related to the Paleoindian artifacts and extinct horse and sloth remains recovered by Junius Bird in well-controlled excavations at Fell's Cave. The remains from Fell's Cave are still thought to date between 11,000 and 10,000 B.P., but at least one of seven individuals from Cerro Sota has been directly dated by AMS to less than 4,000 B.P.[26] Nevertheless, the Cerro Sota and Pali Aike dentitions provide a direct and diachronic Paleoindian link with north Asia, with very little divergence of eleven carefully studied traits.

Many workers have tried to make sense of the distributions of blood group antigens, proteins in blood serum, red blood cell enzymes, immunoglobulins, the ability to taste phenylthiocarbamide, and even earwax types. Results have been mixed, although the simple mode of inheritance, often well understood, has lent an aura of science to the laboratory procedures. Complex measures of relationship, based on stature, body type, skin color, and of course, cranial morphology, now generally are discounted, as they have led to discordant and sometimes unbelievable results. It would seem that random genetic drift in the small, often segregating genetic pools has confused the record. The rapid movement of small groups, budding off repeatedly one from the other, gave the "founder effect" ample room to express itself.

In the furor surrounding a study by a team of medical geneticists who claim to have shown that worldwide there is considerable parallelism between genetic and linguistic evolution, many have lost sight of their major contribution to human genetic history. Carefully eschewing anthropometric data, and other factors most likely to be sensitive to selective environmental pressures such as climate, they have compared the

---

[26] In 1991, on my suggestion, John Hyslop sent three samples of the Cerro Sota bone to the Oxford Radiocarbon Accelerator Unit and the Arizona Laboratory of Isotope Geochemistry. These were from the radius and mandible of a single individual, cataloged as 99.1/780 at the American Museum of Natural History. The AMS laboratory numbers and results are OxA-2850, 3380 ± 70 B.P.; AA-7788, 3645 ± 65 B.P.; AA-7789, 3755 ± 65 B.P.

frequency of 120 polymorphic genetic alleles in 42 populations to calculate Nei's genetic distance between the populations. This measure of overall genetic similarity is based on enough traits to be useful, even though we must not assume that, individually, any of these are neutral genetic markers. They may not be able to diagram an exact, branching family tree (cladogram), but their reconstruction is the best general guide yet drawn and, by all accounts, should be a fair approximation of our species' phylognetic tree. The Paleoindian (or general Amerind) genetic division from Northwest Amerind (Na-Dene) and especially Eskimo (Eskimo-Aleut) is clear, as is the more remote separation of these from populations in northeastern Asian.[27]

A Single History of Life

Neither does it matter, for our purposes, that the separation of breeding populations (subraces) is intrinsically a different process, potentially evolving on separate lines and studied in different ways than the evolution of linguistic stocks. Although the phylogenetic and linguistic trees were determined entirely independently (for once, we may be thankful for the isolation of specialized scholars), there is remarkable congruence, especially in the Americas. Although "political correctness" insists on constant reminders that biological and linguistic change are different processes, it is also important to notice that they intertwine historically. In the prehistoric American case, it is fairly obvious why, generally, there was "a single history of life." In both processes we have "the shared lack of intrinsic barriers to hybridisation and consequent reliance on extrinsic (geographical and, especially, behavioural) isolation."[28] The migrants came relatively late, passed through bottlenecks in Beringia and Panama, and met no other peoples. The single history of life, the convergence of biological and linguistic change, and the very speed of the process of change, are characteristic of human radiation into unpopulated lands. It may also be significant that class-ranked societies and conquest states were relatively slow to evolve in America, and then only in nuclear areas.

---

[27] L. L. Cavalli-Sforza et al., "Reconstruction of human evolution: Bringing together genetic, archaeological, and linguistic data," *Proceedings of the National Academy of Science* 85 (1988), 6002–6006; Richard Bateman et al., "Speaking of forked tongues: The feasibility of reconciling human phylogeny and the history of language," *Current Anthropology* 31 (1990), 1–24; Cavalli-Sforza et al., "Reply to speaking of forked tongues," *Current Anthropology* 31 (1990), 16–18.
[28] Bateman et al., "Speaking of forked tongues," 8–9.

Throughout most of their history, the Americas were hardly a multicultural society; values were shared, communication was easy, and neighbors were more remote than despised. Only in a few nuclear areas of resource diversity and concentration had there been opportunity for the development of a critical mass that would lead to the excesses – some beautiful, some brutal – of "civilization."

I think that a misunderstanding of the scale of time has been the major reason behind astonishment at, and resistance to, any reconciliation of human phylogeny and linguistic history. Richard Bateman complains that attempts to classify American languages comprehensively are bound to fail, because of the time depth, whereas European languages have been diverging for only a few thousand years, not enough time to mask their similarities but enough for development of clear-cut differences among the subbranches. But, I would argue, if we can follow the Indo-European divisions back so surely for 6,000 years, is it not reasonable to hope that the American languages can be tracked over 12,000 years, a mere 600 generations?[29] New World prehistory is a wonderful arena in which to practice reconstruction of biological phylogeny, historical linguistics, and cultural development – even though that task is not politically correct. Most likely, the first Paleoindians to reach Tierra del Fuego would still have been able to communicate with their cousins in the Arctic. They surely resembled them physically, and they knew how to use and make many of the same tools.

Through archaeology, we know already a fair bit about the far-ranging, big-game hunting way of life that is most characteristic of Paleoindians. Increasingly, we know something of the lifeways of their antecedents in northern Eurasia. To whom, in the Old World, were the Paleoindians related biologically and linguistically? There is no agreement, but still it is a problem worth study and consideration, especially as the scale of human biological and cultural evolution has shortened, in the eyes of many anthropologists, over the last generation or so.

---

[29] Those who believe in the extreme antiquity of humankind in America take, of course, the opposite point of view. They argue that diachronic linguistic reconstruction is impossible due to time depth. Probably they would argue, as well, that complex and open human language began long before the Upper Paleolithic. The "long chronology" adherents see American diversity as resulting from many migrations, great time depth, and mixture of populations and cultures. Genetic drift and linguistic diversification in small, isolated populations are puzzling concepts to them. Some even maintain, illogically, that the speed of Paleoindian dispersal resulted not from a new adaptation in unpopulated lands but from the contact diffusion of Paleoindian traditions across already densely settled continents.

Without rehashing all the arguments, many of which are still current, I should say that modern human beings, and most importantly the behavior that makes us what we are, no longer seem to go nearly so far back into the past. Not only are Piltdown man and early *Homo sapiens* dead, but a whole suite of cultural and behavioral traits may characterize only the last 30,000 to 40,000 years – 100,000 years at the very most – controlled use of fire, burial and other ritual, cooperative hunting, art styles, tailored clothing and footwear, and probably the sort of open and flexible languages spoken everywhere today.

Biologically modern and culturally complex human beings seem now to be fairly recent, and it is not ridiculous to hope that we can trace modern genes, languages, and "Upper Paleolithic" (also Late Stone Age and Paleoindian) cultures back to prototypes. Rather than depriving Native Americans of their antiquity, this viewpoint, in a relative sense, decreases the "youth" of American humanity and culture. If the *sapiens* stage of development is relatively recent, American roots go back closer to the beginning of our species history, making this nearly pristine cultural achievement that much more distinctive, interesting, and contributory to our human career.

In the high-latitude region where archaeology is best known (Europe), human beings became systematically successful and numerous, in seasonally frigid environments, only midway through the Upper Paleolithic. It is in the Solutrean, and sometimes almost indistinguishable early Magdalenian cultures that, in Europe, the Upper Paleolithic complex came together and flourished, some 20,000 years ago at the beginning of the last glacial maximum.[30] Although it was about 15,000 years earlier that technology and material culture enabled Aurignacian people to survive in fully continental climates, the Eurasian "mammoth steppe" was not exploited fully, if at all, before the last glacial maximum. The evidence is very tentative, circumstantial, and open to many interpretations. However, I would argue that band-level cooperative hunting, modern language, and complex social organization (accompanied by ritual and artistic display) evolved sometime between 35,000 and 20,000 years ago. If so, the placement of the Amerind (Paleoindian) divergence from the proposed Eurasiatic and Nostratic superphyla is on the right chronological scale.

---

[30] Lawrence G. Straus, "Southwestern Europe at the last glacial maximum," *Current Anthropology* 32 (1991), 189–199.

The biological similarities between early North Americans and northern Asians are most evident, but dentally, skeletally, and genetically there are increasing signs of Native American affiliations to Europe as well. In terms of archaeological material culture, and now perhaps linguistics, there are also hints of European relationships. My conclusion is that, regardless of the final disposition of the Amerind languages and the Eurasiatic superphylum by comparative historical linguistics, we had better look more seriously at the glacial-age mammoth steppe (northeastern Europe, northern Asia, across to northwestern America) as the cradle of virtually all North and South American peoples and civilizations.

Language and Cultural Relics

For generations some American linguists have tried to put order in the great diversity of American languages. Although other scholars had claimed that hundreds of mutually unintelligible languages were spoken in the Americas at the time of European contact, many languages had been collected from only a few selected informants, often elderly, sometimes of one sex only, who had spoken or heard the language only in childhood and who had imperfect memories of it. By 1930, Edward Sapir managed to group North American languages into six stocks. A generation later, Morris Swadesh put most native American languages in a single large phylum and proposed a time depth of about 15,000 years. Swadesh's method of calculating the time depth of the divisions – into Eskimo-Aleut, Na-Dene, and a third group covering all of South America and most of North America – was heavily criticized, but similar tripartite divisions have been well defended in recent years by Joseph Greenberg and Merritt Ruhlen, who use even more conservative chronological estimates.

Working mostly with lexical or etymological reconstructions (sound and meaning correspondences in the vocabularies), Ruhlen reconstructs all three American stocks back to Eurasiatic roots, with the South American languages being derived from a single early Amerind (presumably Paleoindian) migration. He relates Amerind to Greenberg's northern Eurasiatic phylum, which differs from Nostratic, as defined by the Russian linguists, in excluding Afro-Asiatic, Kartvelian, and Dravidian, while including Japanese, Ainu, Gilyak, Chukchi-Kamchatkan, and Eskimo-Aleut. However, Eskimo-Aleut is seen as only one constituent branch of the Eurasiatic phylum, while Amerind shows relationships to Eurasiatic as a whole, sharing etymological reconstructions with all its major branches, and presumably having broken away from the Eurasiatic complex before it had begun to differentiate.

Although few North American linguists are ready to accept Greenberg's Eurasiatic grouping unconditionally, or all of the hundreds of etymologies that support it, the correspondence between the independently derived linguistic, archaeological, dental, and genetic markers (as marshalled by Cavalli-Sforza) is both good and intuitively tempting. The case is stronger now than when first assembled by Greenberg, Turner, and Stephen Zegura.[31] Our Paleoindians, the first securely identified inhabitants of South America, came fairly directly, if at a great distance, out of the latter half of the North Eurasiatic Upper Paleolithic, whether or not Greenberg's reconstructions prove acceptable.

Aside from the problematic deep reconstruction of language, which through shared vocabulary items says something about the prototypical condition, most cultural information comes from archaeology. Before passing on to that, I should say something, nevertheless, about cultural relics, as collected by ethnographers and folklorists, particularly those who were trained in Europe. On the one hand, there are many customs and artifacts associated with curing that have wide if spotty distributions from northern Eurasia, into North America, and sometimes even South America. Examples are the use of hallucinogens, shamans with tambourines and hoof-rattles, the sucking out of disease through a hollow (often bone) tube, and the lifeline motif in art. Interesting though they are, usually it is only the wide distribution itself that suggests great antiquity. Rather than coming with the Paleoindians, these customs and artifacts might have been spread from group to group in later times. Unlike basic vocabulary, grammatical structure, and sound systems in language, many of the Panamerican traits could have been overlain on existing culture.

To my mind, though, there are a few exceptions that are so basic, so complex, or partially supported by archaeology that I must accept them. In the first and third groups, we have early coiled and twined basketry, *atlatl* (throwing board) hooks, and snares to catch small animals, known from the early Great Basin of North America and the Andes of South

---

[31] Joseph H. Greenberg, Christy G. Turner, II, and Stephen L. Zegura, "The settlement of the Americas: A comparison of the linguistic, dental, and genetic evidence," *Current Anthropology* 27 (1986), 477–497; Greenberg, *Language in the Americas* (Stanford, 1987); Merrit Ruhlen, *Linguistic Evidence for the Peopling of the Americas* (Orono, 1989); Ruhlen, "Voices from the past," *Natural History* 96 (1987), No. 3, 6–10; Zegura, "Blood test," *Natural History* 96 (1987), No. 7, 8–11.

America. Eyed needles are present in North American Paleoindian sites and sewn, moccasin-style footwear (accompanied by sewn skin clothing?) may have gone south early, to judge by footprints in Salvadorean and Nicaraguan mudflows. There, before the local extinction of bison, shod people tracked the same flows as unshod bison.

In northern Mexico and Texas, Early Archaic and sometimes Late Paleoindian cave sites contain, at times, seeds of Texas buckeye, soapberry, and red (mescal) beans, which may well have been ingested for their hallucinogenic effect. The use of other mind-altering drugs is very widespread in South America, although archaeological documentation is not good until the last few thousand years. American emphasis on hallucinogens probably derives from northern Eurasia, where their use is similarly prominent.

From folklore comes a good example of a trait so complex and yet so widespread that it is tempting to attribute it to the primary dispersal of Paleoindians, rather than diffusion across an already populated landscape. Olaf Blixen has called attention to the distribution of a mythical narrative about a man who transforms his leg into a bony piercing weapon with which he wounds or kills others. He attacks relatives and/or companions until he is killed finally by them, or by a hero who comes to their defense. This story has been collected among Timbiras, Kayapó, Chaqueños, and other South American peoples, but it is also widespread in North America, where it is known to a number of Siouxan and Algonquian groups, and, in variant form, the Pomo. It would be interesting to learn if the story has been collected in the Old World.[32]

The Archaeological Record of Paleoindian Culture

When Paleoindians entered South America, along the narrow front across part of the Isthmus of Panama and Darién, I presume a uniform culture. Only in the very unlikely case that they had simultaneously adapted to forest life on the wetter Atlantic side, would we be dealing with more than one initial cultural pattern. Even Tony Ranere, who believes in an early adaptation to closed forest, now thinks that Paleoindians passed through savannahs, thorn scrub, and open woodland, which would have

---

[32] Olaf Blixen, "El homocida de la pierna punzante," *Comunicaciones Antropológicas del Museo de Historia Natural de Montvideo*, 2 (1990), No. 15, 1–23.

covered the Guanacaste lowlands of northwestern Costa Rica and the enlarged plains bordering the Bay of Panama. There may have been patches of closed forest to cross, but Ranere and R. G. Cooke "see the pursuit of game as *the* original Paleoindian strategy, with large herbivores, if available, being the preferred prey. Other subsistence activities, while certainly pursued, were 'fitted' into the Paleoindian schedule."[33]

The move to exclude Paleoindians from tropical rain forests is in line with recent observations that modern hunters and gatherers, when found in tropical forests, are either there temporarily, supplement their foraging with some horticulture, or have been pushed recently into the forest by competing peoples. A recent global overview finds "no convincing ethnographic evidence and, with the possible exception of Malaysia, no archaeological evidence for pure foragers in undisturbed tropical rain forests."[34] It seems unlikely that humans have ever existed permanently in the rain forest, independently of some agriculture. Any Paleoindian use would likely have been nonagricultural, transitory, sporadic, or perhaps for some specialized purpose, such as raw material procurement.

Be that as it may, the largest Paleoindian site in lower Central America (Turrialba) would probably be covered with rain forest today, if it were not for agricultural land clearance. Located in the Atlantic drainage, to the east of the Cordillera Central, Turrialba has annual precipitation on the order of the 4,000 millimeters typical of tropical rain forest. In Paleoindian times, however, depression of temperature (c. 5° Celsius) and vegetation zones (c. 800 meters) may have brought the montane oak forest down from 1,500 meters above sea level to the 700-meter elevation of the site. Major prehistoric sites often are found at the ecotones between natural areas, which in this case also gave access to the cryptocrystalline flinty (siliceous) cobbles and boulders to be had from the stream beds of the Reventazón drainage. Whatever the reasons, many later peoples also camped, worked flint, and probably farmed here, creating an expansive mixed site, only 20 to 40 centimeters deep.

[33] Anthony J. Ranere and R. G. Cooke, *Early Human Migration through the Isthmus of Panama* (Seattle, Circum-Pacific Prehistory Conference, 1989), 11; Ranere, "Human movement into tropical America at the end of the Pleistocene," in *Anthropological Papers in Memory of Earl H. Swanson. Jr.*, L. B. Harten, C. N. Warren, and D. R. Tuohy, eds. (Pocatello, 1980), 41–47.
[34] Robert C. Bailey et al., "Hunting and gathering in tropical rain forest: Is it possible," *American Anthropologist* 91 (1989), 59–82, 59.

Plowing has scattered as well as mixed the artifacts and potsherds, but the site may have covered, in its many different occupations, some 10 hectares.

From the 28,000 pieces of flint collected, only a moderate number are diagnostically Paleoindian, including seventeen or eighteen fluted points, but also large blades, bifacial knives and scrapers, and snub-nosed scrapers, some with lateral spurs, that are typical of Paleoindian industries from large North American campsites. Two of the projectile points that are complete seem to be of the Western Clovis style, although not well fluted, while at least one other resembles the fishtail tanged points of South America. Known best from Bird's excavations in Tierra del Fuego, but with a wide distribution in southern and western South America, the fishtail Paleoindian points are often compared with "waisted" Cumberland, Quad, and other eastern North American Clovis subtypes. The similarity is fairly convincing. It is easy to imagine the concavity of the lanceolate point's waist becoming ever more accentuated, as Paleoindians spread South, to become eventually the stemmed fishtail type. In fact, the fluted, grooved, or at least thinned stems are sometimes so Clovis-like that, when first identified in Ecuador (El Inga), archaeologists confused the broken stems from fishtail points with bases of North American Clovis points. Be that as it may, Paleoindian points in Costa Rica (known from three sources) more often look northern than southern, but in Panama the ratio changes to a southern predominance (six of seven) in the surface finds from Alejuela or Madden Lake. At newly discovered La Mula West, though, the width of point bases and the contour of the lateral edges suggests a lanceolate, rather than stemmed, conformation. This site is near Parita Bay, along the Pacific fringe, where Paleoindians may have first penetrated Panama. Largely through the efforts of Ranere and Cooke, early Panamanian archaeology is better known, but there is only one radiocarbon date of Paleoindian age (10,440 ± 650 B.P. from the Corona Shelter).

Once past the bottleneck of Darién and into mainland South America, the climate, vegetation, and topography change rapidly, depending on direction taken. There are many opinions as to whether the Paleoindians went one way or another, or perhaps began adapting to a variety of environments. To the east, toward Venezuela, the coastal zone becomes drier, but also, inland to the south, the major valleys of the Cauca and Magdalena rivers look like ramps that might have conducted the first Paleoindians up and into Colombia's great intermontane valleys and high savannah-like formations. Writing of northern Venezuela, Colinvaux portrays a vivid *entrada*: "We are, therefore, given a tantalizing glimpse of a late glacial landscape, principally savanna land but with patches of woodland or even forest within a day or two's march. It might have been an easy land for people to penetrate if their culture was one already adapted to more open regions in the northern continent."[35]

Unfortunately, typical Paleoindian chipped-stone projectile points are exceedingly rare in northern South America. To my knowledge, none of the fishtail types has been found in central or eastern Venezuela, Guyana, Surinam, French Guiana, or northern Brazil. Across that vast area, there are no signs of Paleoindian dispersal past the Paraguaná Peninsula, 100 kilometers across the Gulf of Venezuela from Colombia's Guajira Peninsula. At El Cayude, fluted points made of chert resemble the Madden Lake specimens from Panama, as well as the stemmed fishtail points from Chile, and they are not associated with any quartzite artifacts of the El Jobo series. The El Jobo lanceolate points may yet prove to have been functionally equivalent, but they have yet to be found in a subsurface living site with a complete stone tool industry. The El Jobo "points" themselves may not be finished tools, but they resemble Mexican Lerma points and, as already discussed, may be associated with extinct animals at Taima-Taima and like sites. That is, the El Jobo complex may be Paleoindian in terms of adaptation and date. In the Guiana highlands, there are large stemmed points, not at all like the fishtail type, which are undated, not associated with extinct animals, and more likely to belong to the Archaic stage.

Two possible fishtail points are known in Colombia – one from the Manizales site and the other from Bahía Gloria, on the Gulf of Darién, which is fluted and said to resemble those from Alejuela Lake in Panama. A handful of additional stone points from surface finds, sometimes with basally thinned and indented tangs, cannot be dated directly. Some have triangular blades or roughly pentagonal outlines, reminiscent of early Archaic types in the Central and South Andes, and they generally are assumed to be fairly early. These come especially from La Tebaida on the eastern flank of the Cauca Valley, La Elvira near Popayán in the Upper Cauca, Restrepo in the Western Cordillera, El Espinal in the Tolima district, and a few other sites that Warwick Bray dates to the much later

---

[35] Paul A. Colinvaux, "Pollen from the Late Glacial of tropical South America: Vegetation and climate at first settlement," *Quarterly Review of Archaeology* (1981), 2.

ceramic period. In fact, so few projectile points have been recovered in Colombia that there is a common presumption that wood or bone points were preferred.[36]

This is not to say that there are no signs of Paleoindian occupation of highland Colombia. Stone tool typology, although a standard determinant of cultural affiliation from the earliest days of archaeology, is not the only consideration. El Abra, Tequendama, and Tibitó – all in the Sabana de Bogotá – have radiocarbon dates in the Paleoindian range. More importantly, perhaps, bones of extinct horse and mastodon were found at Tibitó, together with a few flakes, core fragments, and a keel-shaped scraper and knife-scraper. Given the date of 11,740 ± 110 years, all that is missing is a more complete and characteristic Paleoindian stone tool industry. Tibitó apparently is a small campsite, rather than a kill or butchering place, so it would not be at all surprising if the collection of 121 pieces of chert did not include bifacially worked pieces or snub-nosed endscrapers on blades.[37]

At Tequendama 1, where the earliest occupation has a date of 10,920 ± 260 B.P., the fauna is modern and composed mostly of white-tailed and brocket deer (*Mazama*), but also various rodents, armadillo, and canids. From fossil pollen, it seems the Sabana de Bogotá was cool and dry from 11,000 to 10,000 years ago, with some open woodland on a prairie-like high-altitude grassland (*páramo*). Again, the industry is small, but it includes one fragment of a projectile point, a bifacially worked flake, a finely worked steep scraper, and cores with prepared platforms. Some 50 percent of the specimens are cutting tools, including some long flakes or blades, 30 percent are scrapers that may have been used for preparing hides, and 7 percent are perforating tools. There is reason to categorize the Tequendama site either as early Archaic (Abriense) or Paleoindian. The latter alternative is attractive, additionally, because basalt artifacts or raw materials were transported from the Magdalena valley, neighboring areas of the Cordillera Central, or the eastern *altiplano*. Far-ranging travel and procurement of stone from a distance are more typical of the Paleoindians than Archaic peoples.

The sites of Sueva 1 and El Abra itself appear to me to be Archaic, not

[36] Gonzalo Correal Urrego, "Estado actual de las investigaciones sobre la etapa lítica en Colombia," *Antropológicas* (Colombia) 2 (1980), 11–30; Carlos H. Illera Montoya and Cristobal Gnecco Valencia, "Puntas de proyectil en el valle de Popayán," *Boletín del Museo del Oro* 17 (1986), 45–57; Warwick Bray, *Projectile Points from the Colombian Andes* (London, 1982).

[37] Gonzalo Correal Urrego, "Apuntes sobre el medio ambiente pleistocénico y el hombre prehistórico en Colombia," in *New Evidence for the Pleistocene Peopling of the Americas*, A. L. Bryan, ed. (Orono, 1986), 115–131; Lynch, "Glacial-age man," 17.

Paleoindian. Sueva 1 has a date of 10,900 ±90, a modern fauna of mostly deer and rodents, and a meager industry of mostly simple flake tools. Subunit 3 of El Abra 2 has dates of 12,400 ±160 and 11,210 ± 90, but the thirty-seven simple flakes from that level were originally reported by Hurt as possible intrusions from the much richer layers above, which might have fallen down the rodent burrows and fissures between the boulders. Correlated levels from the neighboring shelters show no sign of human presence, and all dates on hearth charcoal at El Abra are much later. The fauna is modern, and the stone industry is of the typical Colombian Archaic pattern, made up of unifacially retouched flakes and containing no projectile points.

Once south of Colombia and into Ecuador, there can be no doubt of the technological continuity between the stone tools of the North American Paleoindians and those of their South American descendants. Even those few who would turn the origin and direction of movement around, such as Bryan and William Mayer-Oakes, do not dispute the connection. The fluted, eared, and waisted points of North America and the fluted fishtail points of South America are both too complex and stylized to have been independently invented a few hundred years apart. As for direction of movement, it is noteworthy that the best-dated fishtail point sites in South America, those in Chile and Argentina (e.g., Fell's Cave, Cerro La China, Cueva del Medio, averaging 10,600 years), date closer to the time of the post-Clovis, Folsom horizon of North America (around 10,350 years ago), than to the Clovis horizon (c. 12,000–11,200 years ago), with which the stylistic ties are most evident.[38] The simplest point styles are not necessarily the earliest, and the argument, that El Jobo points precede fishtail and Clovis fluted points, is based on a couple of fragmentary artifacts from the controversial Taima-Taima site discussed earlier.

Other fairly highly stylized artifacts of the Panamerican Paleoindians were the snub-nosed endscrapers (often with "spurs" caused by resharpening), thumbnail scrapers, gravers, notched tools, bifacial knife-scrapers on big flakes, flake scrapers with retouch from alternate sides, and large blades. If their subsistence strategies varied a bit from region to region, most Paleoindians still were using very similar tool kits.

Although it may be that not all South American Paleoindians used the

---

[38] Lawrence J. Jackson, "Junius Bird and Fell's Cave, Chile: A review of the evidence," *Arch Notes* (Ontario Archaeological Society, 1990), No. 6, 5–7.

characteristic fishtail stemmed points, and only a minority of them were fluted, virtually all archaeologists agree that these projectile points are a good marker of Paleoindian presence. Thus the distribution of this type has been much discussed. Schobinger charted their distribution across the Andean zone but also southern Brazil, Uruguay, and central Argentina. Dozens more have since been added throughout most of Argentina and, especially, central and southern Chile. In part, the known distribution surely reflects a higher level of archaeology in the Southern Cone and Central Andes of South America. However, Schobinger also speculated on a nearly complementary distribution of fishtail points in relation to that of foliate and lanceolate points in the Andean area, especially Peru, Bolivia, northern Chile, and northwestern Argentina. Unfortunately, with increasing knowledge, the neat separation of range and presumed contemporaneity has begun to break down.[39]

The first well-described sites of the stemmed and fluted fishtail tradition were in Tierra del Fuego (Fell's and Palli Aike caves) and northern Ecuador (El Inga). Subsequently, more points of the fishtail and fluted-stem type were found between the extremes, and we know more about the distribution in time and space of late Paleoindian and Early Archaic types. Tapering-stemmed shouldered points from Chobshi and Cubilán in southern Ecuador date between 10,000 and 8,500 years ago; the narrow long-stemmed points of coastal Peru appear to date between 10,300 and 8,000 years; and the "Early Archaic" triangular points (with and without stems) have a virtually continuous distribution south to Fell's Cave, where they were well stratified beneath the early Paleoindian points.[40] In general, the Central Andean large shouldered points precede the foliate (willow and laurel leaf) and lanceolate forms of the Ayampitín series. Smaller and less elongate foliate points become more common later in the Archaic. Most significantly, perhaps, these latter points have never been found in good association with extinct Pleistocene mammals – but the stemmed fishtail points have.

A common misconception, from a few years past, was that no South American kill sites (as opposed to campsites or workshops) had been

[39] Juan Schobinger, "Nuevos hallazgos de puntas 'colas de pescado,' y consideraciones en torno al origen y dispersión de la cultura de cazadores superiores toldense (Fell I) en Sudamérica," *Acts of the 40th International Congress of Americanists* 1 (Rome-Genoa, 1972), 33–50.
[40] Thomas F. Lynch, "Chobshi Cave in retrospect," *Andean Past* 2 (1989), 1–32; Mathilde Temme, "Excavaciones en el sitio precerámico de Cubilán, Ecuador," *Miscelánea Antropológica Ecuatoriana* 2 (1982), 135–164.

identified from the Paleoindian period. Kill and butchering sites are known now from Chile and Argentina, although, if one defers judgment on Taima-Taima in Venezuela, associations with mastodon are still hard to pin down. Interestingly, the most Clovis-like points yet found, at Nochaco (Osorno) in Chile, were in close proximity to mastodon remains found in fluvioglacial terrace deposits. Another unstemmed, broad lanceolate specimen (this one with typical *multiple* flutes, in the Clovis tradition) came from a glacial terrace of the Pilmaiquen River.[41] It is interesting to speculate whether the lack of stem and broader base might relate to the thickness and toughness of elephant hide or, on the other hand, to a pioneer tradition most recently derived from North America.

Since drainage for modern agriculture, the lakebed of Tagua-Tagua, in central Chile, has for several generations yielded rich data to both paleontologists and archaeologists. It is a classic lakeside kill and butchering site, at which any North American Paleoindian could have felt at home. As I reported in 1983, the lack of projectile points recovered by Montané from the lowest cultural stratum was probably a result of chance. Some of the bones (mastodon, horse, and marsh deer) showed clear butchering cuts; the few artifacts included Paleoindian scrapers; and the date (11,380 ± 320 years) was right. Now, thanks to renewed efforts by Chilean and Argentine scientists, we have three fishtail points, more artifacts (including a piece of engraved mastodon tusk), more studies of the environmental history, and two new dates: 11,320 ± 300 and 11,000 ± 170 radiocarbon years ago. Kaltwasser reports another absolutely typical fishtail point from the depths of the Santa Inés site on the north edge of the old Tagua-Tagua Lake. Further north, Quereo I (11,600 ± 190 and 11,400 ± 145 B.P.) is a similar, already well published case, where horse and extinct camelid were butchered, but no points were left behind.[42]

Another sort of Paleoindian kill site is represented at La Moderna, an Argentine site across the Andes in the province of Buenos Aires. There, some simple flakes of crystalline quartz, possibly flakes, and a single foliate piece came from the same level as glyptodon remains (*Doedicurus*,

[41] Lynch, "The Paleo-Indians," 103 and Fig. 3.5; Núñez and Santoro, "Primeros poblamientos," 112 and Fig. 4.

[42] Lautaro Núñez, Juan Varela, and Rodolfo Casamiquela, "Ocupación paleoindioen el centro-norte de Chile: adaptación circunlacustre en las tierras bajas," *Estudios Atacameños* 8 (1987), 142–185; Jorge Kaltwasser et al., "Punta cola de pescado encontrada en Chile central," *Revista Chilena de Antropología* 5 (1986), 11–16.

extinct giant relative of amadillo). These tools may have been used to butcher the beast, as claimed by Gustavo Politis, but, alternatively, the site may have been mixed up by burrowing animals. That was certainly the case at Arroyo Seco 2,135 kilometers south, where the disturbance and confusion of deposits by burrowing was compounded by intrusive burials. Still, the small industry of eighty-three stone tools includes some Paleoindian scrapers that may have been used on horse, ground sloths, camelids, deer, and ground-dwelling birds. Breakage patterns, contextual associations, and the biased presence of some body parts suggest that giant sloths and horses, at least, were the target animals. Attempts to date the degraded bone protein have been erratic, so it is not clear which human burials are intrusive, which are contemporary with the extinct Pleistocene fauna, or even which animals belong together as a fauna. Given the extent of mixture at Arroyo Seco, through thousands of years, by large and small rodents, it is likely that artifacts have migrated down from the recent level into the level containing extinct animals.[43]

The apparent association of giant sloth with human occupants at Cueva del Indio del Rincón (Mendoza) appears to have gone the way of Pikimachay in Peru. It is clear that the sloths lived there first, without human inference, until about 11,000 years ago. There is no positive sign that the sloths of Gruta del Indio were preyed upon (the first human occupation being centuries later) by a people leaving only a few tools, none distinctively Paleoindian.[44]

Stemmed fishtail points are often recovered on the Argentine *pampas* (prairies) as isolated surface finds, as were Clovis points in North America, once their significance was recognized. Similarly, in recent years, archaeologists have discovered a few sites where artifacts occur in high frequency. The most noteworthy is Cerro Sombrero, a 429-meter-high butte in the Tandilia range, from which there is a far-reaching panoramic view of the boundless *pampas* 250 meters below. It has long served as an observation point for game and, simultaneously, as a rearmament camp. So far, fifty whole and fragmented fishtail points have been collected from the summit, which covers 1.2 hectares. From one shallow 4- by 4-meter excavation, Nora Flegenheimer and Marcelo Zárate counted 2,500 flakes, 454 flaked tools, 1 core, and 4 ground stone tools, including a

[43] Gustavo G. Politis, "Quién mató al megaterio?" *Ciencia Hoy* 1(1989), No. 2, 26–35; Politis et al. "Man and Pleistocene megamammals in the Argentine pampa: Site 2 at Arroyo Seco," *Current Research in the Pleistocene* 4 (1987), 159–162; Lynch, "Glacial-age man," 23.
[44] Lynch, "The Paleo-Indians," 116; Núñez and Santoro, "Primeros poblamientos," 107.

discoidal stone with a depression in the center. The last piece is typical of the Fell's Cave or Toldense industry of Argentina and Chile, except that there is a depression pecked in the center of one flat face, just as on so many "nutting stones" of the North American Archaic. Most artifacts (94%) were made on fine-grained quartzite imported from 30 to 60 kilometers away, although cryptocrystalline silica rocks were sometimes brought from a greater distance.[45]

Although Cerro Sombrero itself has not been dated, Toldense industries often contain more triangular points, of the simple Archaic type, than fishtail or Fell's Cave stemmed points. The industry is dated now by the Cerro La China sites, just 15 kilometers south on a low hilltop, where the fishtail points have, for the first time in eastern South America, been recovered in a stratified multicomponent site. The lower level (L-2) in a small shelter contained a scute (external horny plate) of extinct armadillo (*Eutatus sequini*), a preform of a fishtail point, and enough charcoal for a conventional date (10,730 ± 150 years). A smaller sample yielded a confirmatory date of 10,790 ± 120 years, when dated by accelerator mass spectometry. Less than 300 meters away, an entirely unifacial industry at an open site (La China-3) gave an AMS date of 10,610 ± 180 years. At Cerros El Sombrero and La China, the stemmed fishtail points are only fluted on one side in 20 percent of the cases, and on both sides about 10 percent of the time, so these dates may represent a relatively late phase of the Paleoindian period.

Farther south, in Santa Cruz province, there has been much discussion about the proper date to assign to the unifacial Toldense industries from Los Toldos and El Ceibo. Some would make these small collections representative of an earlier and entirely separate flake tool tradition, in which bifacial projectile points were unknown. The justification for this assignation is a date of 12,650 ± 600 years on level 11 of Los Toldos Cave 3, but a date of 8,750 ± 480 years on the upper part of the same natural stratigraphic level is generally ignored. Level 12 at El Ceibo Cave 7 is said to have a similar industry, without fishtail points, so the oldest date sometimes is extended further yet. To me, given the few pieces in the collection and the probability that these are specialized butchering tools, an intermediate date would be more appropriate. The date of

[45] Nora Flegenheimer and Marcelo Zárate, "Paleoindian occupation at Cerro El Sombrero locality, Buenos Aires Province, Argentina," *Current Research in the Pleistocene* 6 (1989), 12–13; Zárate and Flegenheimer, "Geoarchaeology of the Cerro La China locality (Buenos Aires, Argentina)," *Geoarchaeology* 6 (1991), 273–294.

10,610 years on the unifacial industry at La China is early enough to allow for the presence of horses at Los Toldos and El Ceibo, yet late enough to allow incorporation of these specialized subindustries into the Toldense complex.[46]

Numerous Paleoindian localities have been identified and investigated in the extreme south of Argentina and Chile, suggesting that horse and mylodont sloth survived late, along with high guanaco densities, while the human population density remained low enough that the fauna was not immediately extirpated. One of the earliest sites to be investigated, in 1936–1937, was Fell's Cave, which has given its name to the stemmed fishtail point and the cultural stage (Fell's Cave I) lying under Archaic stage deposits (Fell's II and III). Because the Fell's Cave I deposit was sealed by a roof fall, the association of fishtail points with dates of 11,000 ± 170, 10,080 ± 160, and 10,720 ± 300 years on hearth charcoal, together with bones of horse, mylodon, and guanaco, is generally not questioned. Even Lawrence Jackson, who fears that some of the Patagonian associations may be secondary associations of Pleistocene fauna with later artifacts, is impressed by the Clovis-like bone foreshafts or points excavated by Bird, John Fell, Annette Laming L'Emperaire, and Henry Reichlen. Bird first described these as flaking tools, while I published an essentially identical wooden piece from Guitarrero Cave as a nocked shaft, perhaps mistaking the end of the tool from which it came. Similar North American Clovis and Folsom tools were made of ivory and bison bone, for which sloth bone was substituted at Fell's Cave. Some think they are projectile points; others see them as foreshafts on which the fluted points were hafted.[47]

One of the points found in the earliest layer of Fell's Cave clearly is a Clovis type, with no stem or waist to demarcate the base from the lanceolate blade. As it is incompletely retouched on both sides (mostly along the edges), it might be considered incomplete, but there is no doubting the Clovis base, over three centimeters wide and well fluted on both sides, derived from some unknown site in southern Chile and preserved at the American Museum of Natural History.

---

[46] Augusto Cardich et al., *Arqueología de las cuevas de "l Ceibo." Provincia de Santa Cruz, Argentina* (La Plata, 1981–1982); Lynch, "Lack of evidence," 348–355.

[47] Junius B. Bird, *Travels and Archaeology in South Chile* (Iowa City, 1988), 146–152, Figs. 57, 58, 60, 61; Lynch, *Guitarrero Cave*, 244–245, Fig. 10.11e; George C. Frison and George M. Zeimans, "Bone projectile points: An addition to the Folsom cultural complex," *American Antiquity* 45 (1980), 231–237; Larry A. Lahren and Robson Bonnichsen, "Bone foreshafts from a Clovis burial in southwestern Montana," *Science* 186 (1974), 147–150.

Another distinctive artifact type of the Fell's Cave I or early Toldense complex is the discoidal stone, of unknown use, about the size and shape of a hockey puck. At Fell's Cave, two specimens lay directly beneath the fallen rock slabs isolating Fell's Cave I material from the subsequent Archaic occupation with modern fauna. Another example comes from a less secure context at Pali Aike and a fourth from Los Toldos, found in a layer with two fishtail points. Diameters average about 10 centimeters, and thickness varies from 4 to 6 centimeters. Such stones have been found as well at Early Archaic sites farther north in the Andes. Possible uses include pigment or seed grinding, plant pulping, hide processing, or flint knapping. The resemblance to Middle and North American edge-ground cobbles, as well as a few Paleoindian grinders, has been noted. Donna Roper has cataloged the presence of ochre and grinding stones in North American Paleoindian habitation sites, where the cooccurrence suggests a relationship.[48]

Yet another trait that connects the Paleoindian and Archaic horizons is wall painting in caves and rock shelters. Stenciled hands and quadruped animals represented broadside are especially common. Even where pigment occurs in the archaeological layers, these are hard to date and analyze. However, most animals seem to be camelids and deer, hunted intensively in both Paleoindian and Archaic times. Although the cave art has been most noted in Patagonia, as at El Ceibo, it has a wide Archaic age distribution in the southern and central Andes and in northeast Brazil.

Using one or more of the marker characteristics (age, extinct fauna, fishtail points, cave art, etc.), many Paleoindian or possibly Paleoindian sites have been identified in southern Chile and Argentina. The most often discussed are Fell's, Palli Aike, Los Toldos, El Ceibo, Cueva Grande del Arroyo Feo, Cueva de las Manos, Alero Cárdenas, Alero del Buho, Cueva del Medio, Cerro Sota, Cueva del Milodón, Marazzi, Tres Arroyos, Cuyin Manzano, Traful I, Casa de Piedra, Englefield, and, of course, Monte Verde. Many show signs of both Paleoindian and Archaic occupation, sometimes mixed, but also in transition.[49] Archaic occupations are much more common, certainly because of the far longer time span (nearly to the present, here where agriculture was absent or never became important),

[48] Donna C. Roper, "Grinding stones in Plains Paleoindian sites: The case for pigment processing," *Current Research in the Pleistocene* 6 (1989), 36–37.
[49] Carlos J. Gradin, C. A. Aschero, and A. M. Aguerre, "Primeros niveles culturales en el área Río Pinturas" (Provincia de Santa Cruz, Argentina), *Estudios Atacameños* 8 (1987), 118–141; Núñez and Santoro, "Primeros poblamientos," 108–116.

and probably because population density and extractive intensity and breadth were much higher than in the brief Paleoindian florescence.

North of Argentina, in eastern South America, it is unclear whether there was a true Paleoindian stage, or whether the local sequences of Uruguay and Brazil began with what was effectively an Early Archaic adaptation. Although the sites that would prove it have yet to be dug, it would be very surprising if Paleoindians had not occupied the savannahs and open thorn forest, to say nothing of the floodplains of the major Río Uruguay system. Even at the time of European contact, savanna covered the southernmost lowlands of Brazil and the higher parts of the *planalto* (central plateau).

Lacking the resources for complex, scientific laboratory analyses, Uruguayan archaeology has concentrated on typological and terrace sequence seriation of industries such as "catalanense" and "cuareimense," once presumed to be of great age. Radiocarbon assays have not confirmed the expectations, but systematic surface collections, now adequately illustrated, demonstrate the presence of definite fishtail and Early Archaic stemmed points in the Department of Canelones. Sites are often located on slight eminences overlooking water or on the slopes of stream valleys, as in the case of Tapia (Cañada de la Totora) and Cañada Divisoria. Northwest, along the Uruguay River floodplain, serious salvage efforts were undertaken by Annette Laming-Emperaire's team from the Musée de l'Homme, in preparation for flooding of the Salto Grande Reservoir. The deepest stratigraphy was found at Site 58 near the Salto Grande Cascades, where a date of 11,200 ± 80 years was obtained from the lowest level, unfortunately not in association with either projectile points or extinct fauna, found elsewhere in reworked floodplain deposits. Pressure retouch flakes from the lowest level of Site 58 suggest that fine bifacial artifacts were made. All floodplain deposits in the Uruguay Valley are believed to be younger than 12,000 years, and no primary associations of artifacts with bones of extinct animals are known. Site 42, on the Río Arapey tributary from the east, yielded a layer combining megafaunal bones and Archaic stemmed points, in possible association, but it was capped by a layer of volcanic ash dating to about 5,000 years only. Elsewhere this ashfall had been thought to be from Chilean eruptions dating between 11,000 and 9,500 years ago.[50]

[50] Ugo Meneghin, "Arqueología en la región centro oriental del Departamento de Canelones, Uruguay," *Comunicaciones Antropológicas del Museo de Historia Natural de Montevideo* 2 (1988), No. 14, 1–32; Antonio Taddei, "Algunos aspectos de la arqueología prehistórica del Uruguay,"

The subtropical area of southwestern Brazil (the states of Paraná, Santa Catarina, and especially Río Grande do Sul) lying to the north of Uruguay, is better known. The savannah, broad-leaved forests of the valley bottoms, and fairly open subtropical mixed forest of the *planalto* were heavily settled during the period from 11,500 to 8,500 years ago, by people using medium to small stemmed points of the Uruguai phase. Deer bones and charred pits of wild fruits occur in sites at and just above shoals and rapids, suggesting an Archaic lifeway, despite the rather early dates. Two sites are assigned to an earlier Ibicuí phase, due to dates of 12,770 ± 220 and 12,690 ± 100 years ago and a possible association with *Glossotherium robustum* and *Paramilodon*, another mylodont sloth. Neither the crude "artifacts" nor the alluvial (redepositional?) contexts illustrated are particularly convincing. As aptly put by Pedro Schmitz, "We do not know how the Ibicuí and Uruguai phases originated, whether they are related, from where the populations came, how they are linked with other equally ancient hunter-gatherers in neighboring regions, where they went, or why they disappeared about 8,500 B.P."[51]

In the interior, near the geographical center of the continent, the Abrigo do Sol (MT-GU-1) presents a 6-meter-deep confusion of dates, massive rock fall, and more questionable artifacts. More than thirty dates are often out of order with the stratigraphy, or even in serious disagreement "with themselves," where the samples were divided and sent to two laboratories. The dates include several in the Paleoindian time range, but also readings of 14,470 ± 450 and 14,700 ± 195, along with a majority of Archaic age scattered throughout the strata. Although it would be convenient to have a deeply stratified cave site on the upper Guaporé, just 100 kilometers east of Bolivia, neither the dates nor the stratigraphy are trustworthy. In any event, no recognizable artifacts are illustrated from the "Dourado complex." The Periquitos complex, along the upper Madeira River, is estimated by Eurico Miller to date from 13,000 to 12,000 years ago. It would seem to have more promise, even without radiocarbon dates, given the presence of at least one bifacial lanceolate point, as well as the recovery of many fossil human and large mammal bones from the area.[52]

Estudios Atacameños 8 (1987), 62–93; Wesley Hurt, *The Paleoindian Cultures of Uruguay* (Orono, 1989); Klaus Hilbert, *Aspectos de la Arqueología en el Uruguay* (Mainz am Rhein, 1991).

[51] Pedro Schmitz, Prehistoric hunters and gatherers of Brazil," *Journal of World Prehistory* 1 (1987), 53–126, 86, 89; Eurico T. Miller, "Pesquisas arqueológicas paleoindígenas no Brasil Ocidental," *Estudios Atacameños* 8 (1987), 37–61, 45.

[52] Miller, "Pesquisas arqueológicas," 42, 59–61, Fig. 18; Schmitz, "Prehistoric hunters."

The most heavily prospected part of Brazil is the *planalto*, varying between 200 and 1,200 meters elevation, mainly in the states of Piauí, Bahia, Goiás, Minas Gerais, and São Paulo. Seasonally dry climate, moderate relief, and poor edaphic conditions keep much of the *planalto* in tropical parkland vegetation, ranging from open savannah in the highest and most poorly drained locations, through closed savannah (*campo cerrado*), to thorn forest (*caatinga*) in the driest areas. According to Schmitz, game, fish, and plant resources today are more abundant in the *cerrado* than in the *caatinga*, which would have expanded in the colder and/or drier conditions at the end of the glacial age, when Paleoindians arrived. He also notes the absence of large gregarious animals, such as the bison of the North American plains, and the guanaco and pampas deer of the south. Any Paleoindian adaptation should have changed quickly to more generalized hunting and gathering. Although extensive investigations have been conducted throughout much of the *planalto*, in the effort to establish a human association with Pleistocene animals, Schmitz reports that none has yet been successful.[53]

If there were ever Paleoindians in eastern or northeastern Brazil, they were so ephemeral as to be archaeologically invisible. The case against the Alice Boër and Lapa Vermellha IV sites is very strong. Any reasonable assessment of the Alice Boër site, churned as its deposits are, indicates that it is Archaic (Paranaiba?) in age and in the typological affiliation of its projectile points. At Lapa Vermellha, the sheltered entrance had intermittent Archaic occupation, but the nearly vertical solution tunnel is undoubtedly a secondary redeposition site for the bones of humans and extinct sloth, mixed with debris of various ages.

Still, Ruth Gruhn persists in citing dates from these and other Brazilian sites as proof of human occupation prior to Paleoindian and Archaic times. Farther north in Minas Gerais, the excavator himself (Prous) makes little of a single date of 11,960 ± 250 years at Santana do Riacho, from the same bed in which a few pieces of crystalline quartz were found. The other human remains at this site date 9,460 ± 110 years and more recent. Better hope for evidence of Paleoindians would come from Lapa do Boquette (northwest of Januária, MG) where charcoal dating of 11,000 ± 1100 years came from a layer containing a very nice industry of endscrapers, sidescrapers, and steep scrapers of the *limace* type – but

[53] Schmitz, "Prehistoric hunters," 57, 63.

also a small adze (*herminette*), typically Archaic and later, which Gruhn fails to mention.[54]

The interior of Bahia has seen brief claims of modified bones of extinct animals, sometimes accompanied by quartz or quartzite flake "tools," at Toca de Mundinho, Toca dos Buzios, and Toca de Manoel Latao. However, the Mundinho sites are secondary redepositions, now destroyed, while the two sites dug by Bryan and Gruhn lack any kind of diagnostic artifact and are disturbingly similar to the neighboring Piläo shelter, dated by radiocarbon to 9,390 ± 90 years and 9,450 ± 90 years ago. With Schmitz, I see nothing certain in the *caatinga* of Piauí before Guidon's numerous sites containing good Archaic industries of the Itaparica tradition, beginning about 10,000 years ago. The great Amazonian lowlands remain practically unexplored for Paleoindian sites, so one can only speculate about early settlement patterns there, depending on notions of Glacial-age climate and vegetation change.[55]

In South America, the Paleoindian adaptation lacks a clear-cut chronological horizon comparable to the Clovis and Folsom periods of North America. This is due not so much to lack of radiocarbon dates, or even disputes over the supposed Glacial-age sites, as it is to lack of definition of the Paleoindian culture or adaptation. In South America there are many nations, many approaches to archaeology, and few tendencies toward terminological consistency. South American archaeology has not been characterized by analytic consistency or neatly defined concepts, such as would provide a simple, continent-wide separation of Paleoindians from other, more broadly adapted peoples.

Also, although the savannahs, thorn forests, *pampas, punas,* and *páramos* were good habitats in which to hunt the Pleistocene megafauna, they were also mostly smaller, disjunctive, and less well stocked than their North American equivalents. There were no mammoths, bison, or true camels (*camelops*), although the fauna included other smaller camelids (such as *Palaeolama* and *Protauchenia*), mastodons, three genera of horses, very large megatherid and mylodont sloths, as well as various glyptodons, toxodons, and the giant capybara. All are extinct, and all but

---

[54] Lynch, "Glacial-age man," 20; A. Prous, "L'Archéologie au Brésil," *L'Anthropologie* 90 (1986), 257–306, 287–289, 294; Schmitz, "Prehistoric hunters," 60–63; Ruth Gruhn, "Stratified radiocarbon-dated archaeological sites of Clovis age and older in Brazil," in *Clovis Origins and Adaptation*, R. Bonnichsen and K. Turnmire, eds. (Orono, 1991), 283–286.
[55] Schmitz, "Prehistoric hunters," 60–73; Wesley Hurt in Ronald L. Weber, "The Amazon, Eastern Brazil, and the Orinoco (current research)," *American Antiquity* 54 (1989), 185–187, 185.

the giant capybara have been claimed, by one archaeologist or another, to be in association with human predators. It has been argued that, even allowing for excessive taxonomic splitting, South America lost more major mammals during the late Pleistocene than any other continent. Although brief, the Paleoindian exploitation may have been excessively thorough and poorly adapted to the natural ecology.[56]

On the other hand, many extant smaller animals, birds, and edible plants have been recorded from late Paleoindian or early Archaic sites, especially in the Andes. For a people that had so recently passed through lower Central America, perhaps adapting to some forest resources and less open environments, it would not be surprising if the classical western North American, big-game hunting, definition no longer fit so well.

Although it is hard to pin the South American Paleoindians down to a discrete chronological horizon, we know that they arrived quickly, perhaps only 500 to 1,000 years after the North American Paleoindian adaptation was achieved. In South America we can bracket them roughly between 12,000 and 10,000 radiocarbon years ago. The end date will have to remain flexible, because the Paleoindian tradition merges into, or evolves into, the Archaic tradition as the descendants of the earliest South Americans multiplied, diversified, broadened their subsistence strategies, and moved into new environments.

Virtually all South American Paleoindian sites have been found in what would have been relatively open landscapes, as opposed to heavy forest. In addition, most of the early sites are located near water sources, not only in desert and semidesert regions but also in high mountain regions and the far south, where fresh water is more easily available. I think that this relates more to the habits of the game animals and hunting methods employed than to the direct needs of the human beings, although we should also remember that Paleoindians were very mobile and may not have had good containers for keeping and carrying water. There are no direct indications of early hunting methods except the scattered charcoal and ash at sites like Taima-Taima, which suggests fire drives. Nevertheless, if we can extrapolate from the archaeology of their Eurasian and North American antecedents, cooperative group hunts were a distinctive feature, quite possibly an innovation, of this cultural stage.

---

[56] Thomas F. Lynch, "Paleoindians in South America: A discrete and identifiable cultural stage?" in *Clovis: Origins and Adaptations*, R. Bonnichsen and K. Turnmire, eds. (Corvallis, 1991), 255–260; Paul S. Martin, "Prehistoric overkill: The global model," in *Quaternary Extinctions: A Prehistoric Revolution* (Tucson, 1984), 374.

The location of sites near and overlooking water suggests that Paleoindian hunters, who lacked long-range weapons like bows, stalked game at watering places, hunted from stands along paths to water, or perhaps drove their prey into mires.

THE ARCHAIC STAGE

The Paleoindians did not disappear, unlike many of the animals that they hunted so efficiently and effectively. Rather, we think that they evolved, through relatively gradual changes in lifestyle, into the subsequent Archaic peoples. Although this new conception is a healthy reaction to cultural archetypes and pigeonholes, it misses an interesting trend and countertrend. The Paleoindians were relatively highly specialized hunters and gatherers, particularly in the beginning, as they entered this New World; from specialized and focused extraction, they turned, in the Archaic stage, to very generalized hunting and gathering; finally, with agriculture, American peoples focused again on a narrow range of especially productive herd animals and concentrated plants. The broad spectrum Archaic economics seem to have been more stably adjusted to the natural ecology than the narrowly specialized Paleoindian and agricultural adaptations that largely preceded and followed. In the long run of Darwinian evolution, such a development – from specialization, to generalization, then back to specialization – is unusual, counterintuitive, and worthy of further investigation.

Population rose rapidly during the Archaic stage, to judge from the far greater number of sites, found not only in the open and thinly forested habitats suitable for Paleoindian group hunting, but also in the closed forest, along the seashore, and even in extremely arid zones. Most think that the dispersal or radiation into new zones was only partly a result of demographic pressure. It was probably a response also to overexploitation and then extinction of several important prey animals, but most especially the herds of horses that had been so easily hunted. Some archaeologists and ecologists think that the major factor in the extinctions was hunting pressure, but, increasingly, paleontologists, paleoclimatologists, and population geneticists blame postglacial climate and environmental changes.[57]

[57] C. Vance Haynes, "Geoarchaeological and geohydrological evidence for a Clovis-age drought in North America and its bearing on extinction," *Quaternary Research* 35 (1991), 438–450; Vera Markgraf, "Late Pleistocene faunal extinctions in southern Patagonia," *Science* 228 (1985), 1110–

In some regions the Paleoindian open-ground hunting specialization must have continued, for perhaps thousands of years, parallel to the Archaic tradition. This epi-Paleoindian way of life – based on surviving camelids (guanacos and vicuñas), several kinds of deer (white-tailed or *Odocoileus virginianus,* brocket or *Mazama* sp., *huemul* or *Hippocamelus antisensis,* and pampas deer or *Blastoceros/Ozotoceros*) (Fig. 3.3), birds (the ostrich-like *Rhea Americana* and the *Tinamidae* especially), and smaller rodents such as guinea pigs, vizcachas, and the "desert rats" called cholulos (*Cavia* sp., *Lagidium* sp., and *Ctenomys* sp., respectively) – persisted on well-stocked *punas* of the central and southern Andes, as well as in the southern *pampas.*

The Maritime Fringe

Of the new zones into which Archaic peoples spread, the best known is the maritime fringe, where the sites, often located on coastal headlands or just back from the beaches and lagoons, have been very noticeable and accessible to urban archaeologists. On the Atlantic coast of Brazil, the northern Caribbean coasts and lower valleys, and the Pacific coast of Peru and Chile, especially, immense mounds of discarded shell mark the regular camps (and sometimes permanent villages) of middle and late Archaic collectors and fisherman. In most situations, rising sea level, caused by Postglacial return of water to the seas, has obliterated sites of the early Archaic. However, on parts of the Pacific coast, where the land rises abruptly from the sea, or where oceanic plate subduction has uplifted the coast throughout Postglacial time, we should be able to follow the entire settlement pattern. We have believed that the systematic use of maritime resources (sea mammals, fish, shellfish, algae) began only after the Paleoindian adaptation disappeared – just as in North America. However, recent work at Quebradas Jaguay and Tacahuay, Peru, suggests use of coastal resources in Paleoindian times.

The earliest dates for the maritime Archaic along the Peruvian coast were determined on shell carbonates (11,200 ± 115 years at the foot of the Amotape mountains and 10,575 ± 105 years at the Ring Site, much

1112; Paul S. Martin, "Refuting late Pleistocene extinction models," in *Dynamics of Extinction,* D. K. Elliott, ed. (New York, 1986), 107–130; Thomas van der Hammen "Cambios medioambientales y la extinción del mastodonte en el norte de los Andes," *Revista de Antropología* 2 (1986), Nos. 1–2, 27–33.

Figure 3.3. Common game animals of the Archaic Stage. These living animals have been hunted into recent times by many peoples spread throughout the continent. (A) Collared forest peccary, *Tayassu tajacu*; (B) Andean vicuña, *Vicugna vicugna*; (C) Brazilian tapir, *Tapirus terrestris*; (D) Pampas deer, *Blastoceros (Ozotoceras) bezoarcticus*. Drawings by Judy Spencer, after fig. 43 in *Splendid Isolation: The Curious History of South American Mammals*, by George Gaylord Simpson (1980), Yale University Press, New Haven.

farther south). Carbonate dates are notoriously inaccurate, due to exchange with fossil carbonates, and the Ring Site has been redated on charcoal to 8,755 to 7,415 years ago, while other sites of the north Peruvian Siches complex date around 8,000 to 5,000 B.P. The somewhat similar coastal Archaic of Ecuador may start about 2,000 years earlier, but the numerous dates on shell, bone, charcoal, and by thermoluminescence are equivocal.[58]

In Chile the Archaic adaptation to the littoral zone is dated as early as 9,680 ± 160 and 9,400 ± 160 years ago, at Quebrada Las Conchas, just a few kilometers inland, near Antofagasta. Camelid, sea lion, and dolphin bones were accompanied by the remains of twenty-four species of fish, as well as several kinds of shellfish. However, a third date of C.E. 570 ± 40 is confusing. At present, the early dates at Las Conchas are anomalous and considerably earlier than the dates on the very similar Huentelau-quén sites farther south. The earliest coastal adaptation of northern Chile otherwise begins only 7,000 to 8,000 years ago, if we exclude sites like Tiliviche, in the valleys, which have a clear inland orientation to the Andean early Archaic. Although postglacial marine transgression will have destroyed many early Archaic sites on the beaches themselves, the land rises quickly on the Pacific coast of Peru and Chile. Thus sites representing both the period and marine adaptation are preserved a few miles back from the shoreline of the period.[59]

Paijanense sites near the coast in north and central Peru sometimes contain fish and shellfish remains, as well as land snails, lizards, and other terrestrial fauna. Wherever found, the specialized long-stem points almost always date between 10,000 and 7,500 years ago. Far from the ocean, in the Andean valleys, the Paiján point type, or one very closely related, is associated with a purely terrestrial fauna of modern species, as a minority type. At Chobshi Cave in southern Ecuador, for example, the chronological range is nearly identical at 10,010 to 7,535 years.[60]

Coastal adaptation and settlement pattern along the Atlantic fringe of the continent appears, at least in the beginning, to be quite different. Whereas the western continental shelves are narrow, and even emergent where the Pacific plates subduct beneath the Andean zone, the eastern continental shelves form a broad, gently sloping plain, much of which

---

[58] Karen E. Stothert, "La prehistoria temprana de la península de Santa Elena, Ecuador: cultura Las Vegas," *Miscelánea Antropológica Ecuatoriana, Serie Monográfica* 10 (Guayaquil, 1988); Daniel H. Sandweiss et al., "Early maritime adaptations in the Andes: Preliminary studies at the Ring Site, Peru," in *Ecology, Settlement and History of the Osmore Drainage, Southern Peru*, D. Rice and C. Stanish, eds. (BAR Oxford, 1989).

[59] Agustín Llagostera Martínez, "9,700 years of maritime subsistence on the Pacific," *American Antiquity* 44 (1979), 309–324.

[60] Claude Chauchat, "Early hunter-gatherers on the Peruvian coast," in *Peruvian Prehistory*, R. Keatinge, ed. (Cambridge, 1988), 41–66; Lynch, "Chobshi Cave," 1–32.

was above sea level in Glacial and early Postglacial times. The *sambaquis* (shell middens up to 20 meters deep) of the Brazilian coast have been intensively studied for generations, but we have lost access to any occupied before 6,000 years ago. The assumption is widespread that earlier shell middens existed and were destroyed by rising sea level, but in fact, very few *sambaquis* appear to date to more than 4,500 years ago. It may be, instead, that the change in sea level combined with changing climate, drainage factors, and so forth to enlarge habitats favorable for shallow-water marine life. At the same time, growing human populations and reduction of the terrestrial habitat of the continental shelf may have forced new adaptations. Smaller shell mounds are often located in the lower river valleys, so freshwater and brackish species may, in different times and places, have been as important as marine resources.[61]

It has often been assumed that maritime shellfish gatherers and fisherman lived year-round on their middens. This is unlikely, although the Peruvian case has been well argued. Shell middens accumulate so quickly that occupations would, in the Brazilian case, have had to have been infrequent and sporadic – unless population density was extremely low. The alternative hypothesis seems more in keeping with what is known of other Archaic stage peoples – namely, that the inhabitants of the *sambaquis* moved around, probably seasonally, to secondary habitats, where they exploited complementary resources. This agrees also with the very diverse tool kits (in stone, bone, shell, teeth, wood, and other materials) that accompany the rich array of animal and plant remains, including terrestrial mammals and reptiles.

Striking features of the Brazilian littoral Archaic embrace ornamentation and use of colorants in various media, geometric pieces reminiscent of the Californian and Chilean "cog stones," and the frequency of ground stone tools – while bifacial flaking is almost unknown. Charred seeds confirm the interpretation, previously based on ground stone tools, that plants were important even to these coastal dwellers. Some seem to have been agricultural, to judge from skeletal and dental analyses that show wear patterns and many caries, characteristic of a diet high in carbohydrates.[62] The hints are tenuous, but every year more insistent, that the Archaic adaptation to South American shores is old (up to

---

[61] Schmitz, "Prehistoric hunters," 105; Prous, "L'Archéologie," 265.

[62] C. Turner and Lilia Machado, "A new dental wear pattern and evidence for high carbohydrate consumption in a Brazilian Archaic skeletal population," *American Journal of Physical Anthropology* 61 (1983), 125–130.

10,000 years), interrelated around the periphery, and rather discrete, at least in the last few thousand years, from the more strictly inland adaptations that were developing contemporaneously.

The Forests

To some extent, Paleoindians in lower Central America must have adapted to the tropical forests. Surely, they occasionally ventured into them, perhaps seasonally, or to make use of special resources. Ranere once proposed a full-time forest adaptation, much as others have proposed an elusive maritime adaptation. Once into South America, however, there are no convincing signs that Paleoindians lived in closed forests, where the nonmigrating, locally restricted game resources were meager compared to the migratory and herd animals of more open landscapes.

Nevertheless, at the close of the Paleoindian period, coincident with climate changes that mark the beginning of the Holocene conditions, there is a radiation of new Archaic traditions into various kinds of more luxuriantly vegetated forests. This process has been successfully studied by archaeologists in Brazil. Prous emphasizes the different paths followed along the southern and central littoral (the *sambaquis* and equally well used forest behind the coast, already considered), the subtropical southern interior, and the central plateau (*planalto*) and the Northeast. In reality, the second and third areas were only partly forested, and the extension of forest has changed through Postglacial time, so the reconstruction of environmental and cultural patterns has been complicated. Surely, though, broad-leaved forest covered the major valleys in the Paraná and Uruguai drainage and the slopes of the Serra do Mar and *planalto*. Humid conditions with good ground cover and relatively high but steady stream flow are indicated in the steady aggradation or valley filling, even above the lower reaches governed by rising oceanic base level.[63]

For a time the Uruguai phase, with its many bifacial and usually stemmed points, dominated in the open country of the far south. Up-

---

[63] A. J. Ranere, "Human movement into tropical America at the end of the Pleistocene," in *Anthropological Papers in Memory of Earl H. Swanson, Jr.*, L. B. Harten, C. N. Warren, and D. R. Tuohy, eds. (Pocatello, 1990), 41–47; Prous, "L'Archéologie," 259–268; Schmitz, "Prehistoric hunters," 63–105.

river, the Vinitu phase (8,000–7,000 B.P.?) similarly has many projectile points and a great variety of scrapers and is seen as a hunting adaptation in an environment with only patchy forests. But by 6,500 to 4,000 B.P., with rising temperature and humidity, broad-leaved forest had expanded to fill the Paraná, Uruguai, and Jacuí valleys. The Archaic adaptation divided, the Humaitá tradition developing in the dense forests and the Umbu tradition dominating the savannah and open subtropical forests with *Araucaria*, which bears an abundant, concentrated "pine nut." The Umbu tradition is known from some 400 sites with well-developed lithic industries featuring bifacially pressure-flaked stemmed, triangular, and laurel-leaf shaped points. Scrapers, some finely worked, are common. There are also a few ground stone axes and bolas stones toward the end of the sequence. Technologically, the relationships are clear, to the south and to the west, with other Archaic peoples living in small, nomadic groups and practicing open-country hunting and gathering of dispersed resources. Umbu sites are found in rock shelters and the open, usually near streams or rivers, occasionally near swamps and lakes, and rarely on the coast. In Rio Grande do Sul, seasonal transhumance is indicated by Umbu camps along coastal lagoons and by movement of marine products far inland. Most characteristically, sites of the Umbu tradition are found near the ecotones between savannah and forest, or in savannah mixed with patchy forest or gallery forest.

The Humaitá tradition represents an entirely novel and divergent archaeological complex, apparently adapted to zones of dense vegetation. Made usually on tough and intractable materials, the stone tools are robust and supposedly used especially in digging and wood working. The best can be classified as bifaces, picks, cleavers, and scrapers, but most are crude flakes, often unretouched. For this reason, the related Altoparanaense culture of Uruguay and northern Argentina was once assigned a great age by typological cronologists. Now, Prous assigns these sites of the Humaitá tradition, on the lower tributaries of the Paraná, to Holocene Archaic status, representative of wild plant gathering and perhaps fishing activities.

Noting that all earlier cultures occupied areas with open vegetation and used stone projectile points, Prous speculates on the origins of forest life. Hearths in the banks of the upper Uruguai, dating 9,000 to 8,000 B.P., could represent the beginnings, but typical Humaitá sites date no earlier than 7,000 B.P. The tradition becomes more elaborate and expands with the forests themselves during the climatic optimum. They are absent along the coastal strip and sparse in the fairly open *Araucaria* forest of the *planalto*, but Humaitá sites are very numerous in the forested and formerly forested valleys of the states of Sao Paulo, Paraná, Santa Catarina, and Rio Grande do Sul. Unfortunately, their very location on land that has long been plowed makes it difficult to study the suggestion that these sites may represent an early stage of horticulture. The association of Humaitá sites with pine groves is well established, but given the destruction of most sites, other aspects of subsistence (tubers and fruits, large river fish, terrestrial and riverine mollusks) are mostly inferred.

Farther north, roughly above the Tropic of Capricorn, the Itaparica tradition has well-made unifacial artifacts and only very rare projectile points. Beginning perhaps 11,000 years ago, Itaparica spread across the upland tropical parklands and into the forest itself. The archaeological record is better because Itaparica sites occur not only as camps on hilltops but also in caves and rock shelters in Minas Gerais, Goiás, Pernambuco, and Piauí. In Goiás the remains of mammals (deer and smaller), birds, reptiles, amphibians, and fish are found, with mollusks represented in Minas Gerais. From these species and the plants that have been recovered, it is clear that Itaparica people used forest, riverine, and swamp environments. Stone tools include scrapers, perforators, knives, choppers, hammerstones, ground stone anvils, bola stones, and grinders. In Piaui, Guidon believes that the Northeastern art style, formerly thought to have begun in the dim past, was initiated in sites of this tradition.

After 8,500 years ago, the archaeological subdivisions become too numerous to describe here, but the importance of hunting declined further, along with the quality of flint knapping, while plant foods and land snails became more important. Rock art grew in importance. After 6,500 B.P., large freshwater fish and birds were intensively exploited, projectile points returned to Minas Gerais and Pernambuco, but also palm nuts and other seeds are often preserved in pits and hearths. By 3,500 years ago, the Archaic people of Minas Gerais were cultivating maize, pottery had spread into the highland zone, and a new stage was under way.

Zones of Continuity

If one were to define the limits of the Paleoindian and Archaic Horizons strictly by chronology, the boundary would have to be set around 10,000 years ago. Nevertheless, in zones that were used continuously, there must have been a gradual transition from a subsistence strategy that concentrated on efficiently captured large animals, often gregarious, to one that involved a much broader spectrum of resources, both plant and animal. Most of the new artifacts, resources, and even the ways of using them, must have origins that precede the Archaic period, when they became important, characteristic, or dominant. Archaeologists may be able to differentiate the Paleoindian and Archaic patterns processually, but definitions based only on chronology, or on the presence or absence of functional classes of artifacts, are sure to fail. Archaic lifeways, by my definition at least, are highly varied, opportunistic, flexible, and locale-specific. Also, like the Epipaleolithic and Mesolithic of Europe, the two ways of life must have been partly contemporary. For all we know, Paleoindian and Early Archaic groups in areas of environmental continuity may have actually switched back and forth, at least in the topological sense, as temporary conditions caused them to change their procurement strategies.

The high Andean intermontane valleys and plateaus have been good places in which to study the continuities and transitions. Grading from open woodland and savannah through the *páramo, puna,* and *pampa* grassland formations, they have a high biomass of variegated resources that are easy to convert to human use. In fact, this region somewhat resembles the African highland zone, in which our species evolved, so it is no wonder that it was swiftly and solidly colonized. One must assume that when Paleoindians entered the Sabana de Bogotá they were pleased, successful, multiplied rapidly, and quickly perceived that the Paleoindian lifeway was not the only one possible. From the archaeology already accomplished, it would appear that the conversion from a Paleoindian emphasis on horse and mastodon, if indeed it was ever dominant, to the Abriense broad-spectrum pattern, was archaeologically instantaneous. Tibitó alone represents the classic adaptation. The simpler, Archaic-like Abriense industry was practically without stone projectile points, but it was apparently sufficient for the capture of the prolific white-tailed and brocket deer, armadillo, rabbit, paca (*Cuniculus pace*, called "spotted cavy"), guinea pig, and other rodents – to say nothing of the many plant products that were probably used, despite their lack of preservation. Some Abriense sites (including El Abra, Sueva, and Tequendama) may have dates that are "too early," but the style of life seems firmly Archaic. The later sites of Aguazuque and Chia, also investigated by Correal and his associates, show a continuation of Archaic extraction patterns until the advent of agriculture.

In highland Ecuador, the only artifacts that are intrinsically and definitively Paleoindian are the fluted fishtail points from El Inga. Unfortunately, bone was not preserved, and the radiocarbon dates, from pooled
samples and mixed deposits, do not precede 9,030 ± 144 B.P. Components of different age have been mixed at El Inga, so the date cannot be
applied to the Paleoindian component, but it is nearly 1,000 years later
than the earliest date from Chobshi Cave (10,010 ± 430 years) and even
further removed from the dates on the earliest bed at Cubilán (10,500 ±
1,300 and 10,300 ± 170 years). Here, unlike in Colombia, the rest of the
lithic industry has a Paleoindian look to it. Where bones are recovered,
though, as at Chobshi, the fauna is modern and suggests an Archaic
classification (white-tailed deer, pudu or *Pudu mephistopheles*, and possibly brocket deer – supplemented by rabbit, *paca*, opossum, porcupine,
tapir, spectacled bear [*Tremarctos ornatus*], and the *tinamidae*, popularly
miscalled "Andean partridges").

It is equally hard to separate a distinct Paleoindian horizon from an
early Archaic pattern in the Central and South-Central Andes of Peru,
Bolivia, Chile, and Argentina. Sites of the Central Andean preceramic
tradition sometimes have Paleoindian dates (7 of more than 10,000 years
from Guitarrero Cave alone), but the faunas are invariably modern at
locales securely associated with human activity. Fluted fishtail points, of
the classic Paleoindian sort, are absent. This is a controversial matter, the
sites and dates being too numerous to review here, so the reader should
consult recent analyses.[64]

In a number of thoroughly excavated and published sites (such as Guitarrero, Lauricocha, Pachamachay, and Telarmachay) the faunal associations are with deer (white-tailed, brocket, and *huemul*), camelids (guanaco
and vicuña), vizcacha, rabbit, guinea pig, other small rodents, skunk, amphibians, duck, and tinamou. Plants and organic artifacts preserved at Guitarrero also suggest an Archaic broad-spectrum existence. In point of fact,
if we knew more about the subsistence systems and perishable artifacts of
Middle and South American Paleoindians, we might not find these site
contents troubling in the least. The Central Andean preceramic tradition

---

[64] Danièle Lavallée, "L'occupation préhistorique des hautes terres andines," *L'Anthropologie* 89
(1985), 409–430; Lynch, "The Paleo-Indians," and "Glacial-age man;" John W. Rick, Dates as
data: An examination of the Peruvian preceramic record," *American Antiquity* 52 (1987), 55–73,
and "The character and context of highland preceramic society," in *Peruvian Prehistory*, Richard
W. Keatinge, ed. (Cambridge, 1988), 3–40.

made use of various triangular, lanceolate, and contracting-stemmed points. Whether one classifies it as late Paleoindian rather than early Archaic depends on the importance given to age, technological continuities in the lithic industry as a whole, or the extent of the "settling in" process implied by the organic remains and regional settlement pattern.

In parts of Peru and northern Chile, some Archaic groups are thought to have made regular seasonal migrations to secure complementary resources and weather protection. There has been much discussion as to whether transhumance in the Andes was the general rule or the exception. The best recent study was done in Chile, with the conclusion, perhaps to be expected, that the presence of transhumance varied, from place to place and time to time, depending on topography, climate, distribution of potential resources, and culturally conditioned preferences on exploitative patterns. Only in the Pampa de Junín, central Peru, have highland Archaic hunters been found to be sedentary.[65]

The issue of transhumance, or scheduled seasonal migration, is important because a number of workers have implicated it in the beginnings of pastoralism and agriculture, as observed in north central Peru, northern Chile, and northwestern Argentina.[66] To the contrary, others have found, especially in coastal Peru and Ecuador, that agriculture and social complexity arise with sedentarism and the assured productivity and protein that come from a marine diet.[67] Although the Archaic stage began as early

---

[65] John W. Rick, *Prehistoric Hunters of the High Andes* (New York, 1980); Calogero Santoro Vargas, *Settlement Patterns of Holocene Hunting and Gathering Societies in the South Central Andes* (Ithaca, 1987); Santoro and Lautaro Nùñez Atencio, "Hunters of the dry puna and salt puna in northern Chile," *Andean Past* 1 (1987), 57–109.

[66] Alicia Fernández Distel, "Excavaciones arqueológicas en las cuevas de Huachichocana, Dep. de Tumbaya, Prov. de Jujuy," *Relaciones de la Sociedad Argentina de Antropología* 7 (1974), 101–127; Peter M. Jensen and Robert R. Kautz, "Preceramic transhumance and Andean food production," *Economic Botany* 28 (1974), 43–55; Thomas F. Lynch, "Harvest timing, transhumance, and the process of domestication," *American Anthropologist* 75 (1973), 1254–1259; Lynch, "Camelid pastoralism and the emergence of Tiwanaku civilization in the south-central Andes," *World Archaeology* 15 (1983), 1–14; and Lynch, "Regional interaction, transhumance, and verticality: Archaeological use of zonal complementarity in Peru and northern Chile," *Michigan Discussions in Anthropology* 8 (1989), 1–11; Lautaro Núñez Atencio, "Hipótesis de movilidad trashumántica en la Puna de Atacama: Quebrada de Tulán (nota preliminar)," *Actas del V Congreso Nacional de Arqueología Argentina (San Juan)* 2 (1980), 19–46; Hugo D. Yacobaccio, "Must hunters walk so much? Adaptive strategies of south Andean hunter-gatherers (10,800–7,500 B.P.)," *Papers Presented at the 11th Congress of the International Union of Prehistoric and Protohistoric Sciences, Southampton and London* (1986).

[67] Robert A. Benfer, Jr., "The preceramic period site of La Paloma, Peru: Bioindications of improving adaptation to sedentism," *Latin American Antiquity* 1 (1990), 284–318; Damp et al., "On the waterfront; Quaternary environments and the Formative occupation of southwestern Ecuador,"

as anywhere in northern Chile, with dates of 10,820 ± 630 and 10,400 ± 130 years B.P. at Tuina and San Lorenzo, it must be granted that agriculture comes to this zone much later than in the Central Andes. Furthermore, when it arrives, it is based on imported crops. Even earlier, if less precise dates, based on temperature-corrected obsidian hydration, suggest that transhumant Archaic hunters of camelids were the first occupants of the Atacama *puna* and desert. A virtual depopulation of the region in middle Archaic times (roughly 8,000–5,500 B.P.) may have put the brakes on the development of agriculture, but it is possible still to argue that transhumance was associated with the local origins of camelid pastoralism.[68]

In summary, it is obvious that we are dealing with a continuous and progressive process, from Paleoindian times to the coming of agriculture, throughout the Archaic period. Certainly it is not easy, nor probably productive, to make a hard and fast distinction between the Archaic pattern and the preceding, partly contemporary, Paleoindian way of life. Common to both adaptations are features such as the capture or control of both solitary and herding animals, seasonally scheduled movements between resource zones, and at least occasional consumption of plants and maritime products. It seems now that the Archaic stage can be differentiated from the Paleoindian mostly in a quantitative way, through its broader-spectrum economies, with corresponding changes in settlement patterns and densities, altered frequencies of major classes of artifacts (grinders, polished stone tools), and increasing prominence of decorative arts, ritual, burial, exotic trade goods, mind-altering drugs, and cultivars.

AGRICULTURE AND SEDENTARISM

In most cases, Archaic peoples are thought to have been less far-ranging than the Epipaleolithic or Paleoindian peoples who preceded them. Indeed, there may have been a trend toward localization of settlement that went with Archaic intensification on the varied resources of one *region* rather than specialization on one set of behaviorally similar (and often nomadic) large *animals*. This is often called the "settling in" process,

---

Geoarchaeology 5 (1990), 171–185; Michael E. Moseley, *The Maritime Foundations of Andean Civilization* (Menlo Park, 1975).

[68] Brian Hesse, "Buffer resources and animal domestication in prehistoric northern Chile," *Archaeozoologia, Mélanges* (1986), 73–85; Lynch and Stevenson, "Obsidian hydration dating"; Santoro and Núñez, "Hunters of the dry puna."

following Braidwood's original usage. Braidwood believed that the process culminated in agriculture. Long ago, writing about Mesoamerica, Flannery differentiated nomadic hunter-gatherers from stable villagers in a somewhat similar way.[69] The former would have to exploit a wide variety of microenvironmental niches, scattered throughout their region, in a seasonal pattern; the latter, possessing effective agriculture, could concentrate on one, or only a few very efficient microenvironments lying close at hand. According to the proposal, when agriculture began in Mexico, the part-time cultivators remained seasonally nomadic for thousands of years, becoming fully sedentary only when irrigation was introduced or when rich bottom lands were tilled in coastal areas. This perspective was popular among archaeologists in South America, as well, especially among those who worked in the "nuclear" Andean area. Our presumption was that plants were cultivated and domesticated early in the Archaic sequence, and that sedentism, population concentration, class-structured society, and communal work projects (resulting in monumental constructions) came much later.

From the beginning, other scholars saw the process differently. Sauer, especially, stressed that sedentism should be a *prerequisite* for any groups that would become agricultural. They would need to live in a bountiful land and have the leisure and assured surplus that would permit experimentation with the new system. Sauer favored the rich riverine environment of northern South America as the locus and, as the method, simple vegetative reproduction (rather than sexual reproduction from seed) of plants that store carbohydrates in their underground parts. A system that began with manioc (*Manihot* sp.), along the great lowland rivers, might easily be transferred to other root crops, such as achira (*Canna edulis*), and in the higher Andes to tuber producers, like potato, ulluco (*Ullucus tuberosus*), and oca (*Oxalis* sp). A number of geographers and a few archaeologists took up Sauer's ideas and elaborated them. It is often assumed that the tropical root crops became the basis of a separate system of agriculture in lowland South America, whether earlier or later than the system based on seed crops, best known from its Mesoamerican origins.

Indian corn (maize), beans, and squash were often cultivated together in early Mesoamerica, whence they spread to North and South America,

<hr/>

[69] Michael D. Coe and Kent V. Flannery, "Microenvironments and Mesoamerican prehistory," *Science* 143 (1964), 650–655.

or so wrote Herbert Spinden long ago. In his "archaic hypothesis," this protein-rich agriculture became the basis for Native American civilization, spreading as a complex with a suite of key artifacts, beliefs, and practices. For our purposes it matters little whether Sauer or the Mexicanists are correct about the locus of the first American cultivation. The idea spread quickly into or through the Andean area of high physical and biotic diversity. Even if Sauer was wrong about the processes or point of origin of agriculture, his argument for transportation of cultivars "along the grain" of the Andes, rather than across the grain of environmental barriers, is convincing: "These interior passageways, rather than the external flanks of the Andes with their barrier zones of cloud and rain forest and of desert southward, were the avenues by which agriculture, if it spread from the lower lands, could most readily establish itself in the cold interior of the Andes."[70]

Those who have studied the archaeology of the lowland forest zone have taken it for granted, often, that Mesoamerican maize agriculture was intrusive and later than the cultivation of manioc. Thus, at the Colombian site of Momil, flat circular ceramic griddles in the lower levels are thought to be for cooking manioc "bread," but they could have been used as easily as *comales* for making maize tortillas. It is true, though, that *metates* and *manos* appear abruptly in more recent archaeological layers. These are of the Mesoamerican type used for grinding maize, and they are accompanied by a series of new Mesoamerican ceramic traits: annular (ring-shaped) bases, tripod bases, mammiform supports, and bird-shaped whistles. A similar story is told for Venezuela, where there was a shift to an economy in which corn becomes the staple crop. There, the documentation includes the charred remains of maize itself, as well as the artifacts used in its processing.[71]

Spinden started an argument that is by no means finished. Corn was an exceedingly important crop in Mesoamerica, and every year the archaeological record of its movement north and south becomes more clear. It is possible that agriculture based on manioc, and other root crops in the Andes, is the older system in South America, only supplanted in relatively recent times along the western edge of the continent by the maize complex. After all, maize was rarely the staple in South America;

[70] Carl O. Sauer, "Age and area of American cultivated plants," *Proceedings of the 33rd International Congress of Americanists* 1 (1958), 215–229, 218.
[71] Anna C. Roosevelt, *Parmana: Prehistoric Maize and Manioc Subsistence along the Amazon and Orinoco* (New York, 1980).

it was used generally for making beer (a drink of high prestige), roasted green (as a vegetable, with high sugar content), or eaten as pop corn. Where the archaeological record is good in the Central Andes, particularly Peru, we know that maize does not have a real impact until the Formative Period, about 3,000 years ago – but by then civilization, in Spinden's sense, is well on its course.

Much, perhaps too much, has been made of the importance of the maize complex (corn, beans, and squash) as an integrated dietary system and a system of harmonious cultivation (*milpa*). The Andean crops, and many of the lowland South American crops, have been neglected because little is known of them or their record in antiquity. Still, it must be admitted that the maize complex stands first – in its antiquity, its importance in a greater expanse of native America, and its importance today.

It is certain now that maize evolved from *teosinte*, a wild plant still prominent in parts of Central America. Some, following Hugh Iltis, believe that the critical changes came very quickly and simply, through feminization of the uppermost male flowers (tassels), which became cobs. More botanists follow George Beadle and Walton Galinat in believing that a number of crucial genes were involved, affecting both the floral morphology and structure. They agree that the changes, especially condensation, came rather rapidly, under heavy selective pressure during human harvests.[72]

The first archaeological record of maize comes from the Tehuacán Valley in Mexico, where small cobs were found in the Coxcatlán phase deposits of Purrón, Coxcatlán, and San Marcos caves. Associated charcoal dated as early as 7,000 years ago, but direct dates on the cobs themselves (AMS technique) have run at least 2,000 years later, with several falling after the time of Christ. Although a consistent discrepancy of several hundred years could be attributed to the C-4 carbon dioxide fixation pathway (Hatch-Slack photosynthesis), the major problem in Tehuacán must be with specimens intrusive from upper levels. The earliest Tehuacán specimens date to about 5,000 radiocarbon years ago.

At La Yeguada in Panama, the earliest unequivocal record of maize phytoliths is from a level dated to about 4,000 years ago. The four cores from

---

[72] Elizabeth Culotta, "How many genes had to change to produce corn?" *Science* 252 (1991), 1792–1793; Walton C. Galinat, "The origin of maize," *Annual Review of Genetics* 5 (1971), 447–478; Hugh H. Iltis, "From teosinte to maize: The catastrophic sexual transmutation," *Science* 222 (1983), 886–894.

La Yeguaga, fixed in time by twenty-four radiocarbon dates, surely are intact and unmixed. Macrobotanical remains of maize appear in Panama only in the last third of the first millennium B.C.E. However, Dolores Piperno and her co-workers also believe that they have identified indigenous maize phytoliths in the earliest levels of Cueva de los Ladrones and Rockshelter SE-149, at about 7,000 years ago. The same collaborators have reported maize phytoliths and pollen at an interpolated date of 5,300 B.P. (bounded by dates of 4,570 ± 70 and 7,010 ± 130) from a core at Lake Ayauch in Ecuadorean Amazonia. This date for maize cultivation would be 2,000 years earlier than any previously reported from the Amazon Basin. It is also strangely in advance of the oldest macrofossil evidence from coastal Ecuador, about 3,100 years ago. Pearsall reported maize phytoliths at Real Alto, but there are no macrofossil remains of maize at that site despite the identification of beans and cotton. It would seem that it is safe to trust in the presence of corn in the Formative level sites of La Ponga (Machalilla phase, 1200–800 B.C.E.) and Cerro Narrío, in the highland Formative. Most workers will await further refinements in phytolith identification before putting full faith in earlier reports of cultivated maize. Valdivia-phase maize at San Pablo is very dubious.

The same ambiguous situation is under contention in Peru. Alexander Grobman and Duccio Bonavia are convinced that the corn plants they recovered from silos at Los Gavilanes are dated correctly by charcoal from the midden (3,750 ± 110 years) and thermoluminescence of burnt stones of the silo structure (4,800 ± 500 years). Most specialists prefer the more recent ages obtained from the carbon of the maize plants and cobs themselves. Bonavia and Grobman defend the early dating by recourse to similarly large and advanced cob types from the Abejas phase in San Marcos Cave (Tehuacán), as well as the Aspero and Guitarrero sites in Peru. Because all sites under discussion show signs of mixture of deposits, I weigh heavily Robert Bird's argument that corn arrived in Peru only in the Early Horizon (Formative) about 3,000 years ago. Bird, a botanist, was struck first that many of the putatively preceramic cobs resembled maize otherwise dating much later, that the collections were quite variable, and that the only cobs to have been directly dated (Los Gavilanes) yielded Ceramic Period ages. As longtime observers of the Peruvian archaeological scene, Bird and I are impressed that almost all Preceramic and Initial (ceramic) Period sites *fail* to preserve corn, even where conditions for preservation and cultivation would have been good. The best evidence of Initial Period maize in Peru is the portrayal on a Kotosh phase bottle (1200–800 B.C.E.) from Kotosh.[73]

If maize agriculture, with its easily storable grain, did not arrive in coastal Peru until the Formative stage was in full bloom, modern versions of the Spinden hypothesis are in trouble. During the late or Cotton Preceramic and the first part of the Initial Period, Peruvians were organized to build immense architectural complexes, some of which clearly served ceremonial purposes and some of which covered dozens of acres. The largest of these constructions of stone and adobe are found in the lower river valleys that cross the desert to the sea. Smaller, but still elaborate, preceramic ritual sites have been found in highland valleys, presumably supported by agriculture as well as hunting and gathering.

If maize agriculture did not support the largest coastal centers, what did? Moseley and his collaborators and students have been the most effective advocates of the view that early civilization in Peru, as a pristine case, was founded not upon domesticated plants and animals but on the rich seafood of the cold coastal waters.[74] In many cases small Archaic villages seem to have become permanent year-round settlements, prosperous in their own simple way, without much benefit of agriculture. Small schooling fish, sea mammals, and shellfish were an important component of the Archaic diet, but so were land mammals and many plant products, probably increasingly cultivated, that were prolific in the river bottoms before water was removed for irrigation agriculture. While the aspect of the Archaic economy that came from the sea has been well preserved along the desert coast, most river-bottom sites of the late preceramic period have been destroyed by later farming and flooding.

---

[73] Robert M. Bird, "What are the chances of finding maize in Per dating before 1000 B.C.E.? Reply to Bonavia and Grobman," *American Antiquity* 55 (1990), 828–840; Jonathan E. Damp, D. M. Pearsall, and L. T. Kaplan, "Beans for Valdivia," *Science* 212 (1981), 811–812; Damp et al., "On the waterfront"; Alexander Grobman and Duccio Bonavia, "Pre-ceramic maize on the north-central coast of Peru," *Nature* 276 (1978), 386–387; Ronald D. Lippi, Robert M. Bird, and David M. Stemper, "Maize recovered at La Ponga, an early Ecuadorian site," *American Antiquity* 49 (1984), 118–124; Austin Long et al., *First Direct AMS Dates on Early Maize from Tehuacán, Mexico* (Atlanta, 1989); Deborah M. Pearsall, "Phytolith analysis of archaeological soils: Evidence for maize cultivation in Formative Ecuador," *Science* 199 (1978), 177–178; Dolores R. Piperno, "A comparison and differentiation of phytoliths from maize and wild grasses: Use of morphological criteria," *American Antiquity* 49 (1984), 361–383; Piperno, Mark B. Bush, and Paul A. Colinvaux, "Paleoecological perspectives on human adaptation in central Panama: The Holocene," *Geoarchaeology* 6 (1991), 227–250, 239, 240; Roosevelt, *Parmana.*

[74] Benfer, "The preceramic period"; Jeffrey Quilter et al., "Subsistence economy of El Paraíso, an early Peruvian site," *Science* 251 (1991), 277–283.

Although corn was absent or of no common importance, many crops were grown in the late Archaic stage or simply harvested in the wild state. At the single site of El Paraíso, some thirty-one plants were used. These include an abundance of tree fruits, common beans (*Phaseolus vulgaris*) and lima beans (*Phaseolus lunatus*), achira and jícama for their large edible tubers, as well as three squashes, chili peppers (*Capsicum* sp.), and the industrial plants, gourd and cotton. Many of these were also recorded at the highland Archaic site of Guitarrero Cave, with additional plants appropriate to higher elevations. Dried feces from El Paraíso revealed an expectedly high content of fish and crawfish parts but also a significant amount of mammalian meat residue and many plant remains.[75]

Sedentism and village formation occurred at the end of the Archaic and have been seen, in most of the world, as correlates of agriculture and harbingers of a Formative stage, in which class structure and civilization emerge. However, in parts of South America, sedentary coastal settlements arose that were based largely on maritime resources rather than on farming. In the Formative stage, coastal settlements in Peru, Ecuador, and Chile were superseded by more complex riverine communities, in which the economy revolved around the raising of plants and animals with Andean or trans-Andean, not coastal, origins – as well as maize from Central America. Although Andean civilization ultimately became rather conventionally dependent on agriculture and domestic animals, it has become quite clear that maritime resources, and the sedentism they allowed, were important, perhaps critically important, to the beginnings.

Andean agriculture seems to have been an outgrowth of the Archaic process in the intermontane basins themselves, but not without important contributions from and to the very different forest and coastal regions east and west. Some cultivated plants surely came originally from lower zones to the east and north – such as chili peppers, peanuts, beans, and corn – but others were thoroughly indigenous. The best known are potatoes, *quinua* (*Chenopodium quinoa*), and tarwi (*Lupinus mutabilis*). The domestic animals are native to the Andes (llama, alpaca, guinea pig) and became

---

[75] Lynch, *Guitarrero Cave*, and Lawrence Kaplan, Thomas F. Lynch, and C. E. Smith, "Early cultivated beans (*Phaseolus vulgaris*) from an intermontane Peruvian valley, *Science* 179 (1973), 76–77; Sheila and Thomas Pozorski, *Early Settlement and Subsistence in the Casma Valley, Peru* (Iowa City, 1987); Quilter et al., "Subsistence economy." Five preliminary AMS dates on common beans from disturbed contexts at Guitarrero Cave suggest late Archaic attributions as early as 5000 B.C.E. Lima beans have not dated before 2000 B.C.E. in the Callejón de Huaylas.

the basis of a rich pastoral tradition, which surely began in the Archaic stage and period, although arguments continue as to why, where, and exactly when. Only the Muscovy duck (*Cairina moschata*) seems to have been domesticated outside the Andean zone, perhaps in coastal Ecuador. In the Andean Archaic, the development of agriculture was closely related to pastoralism and the keeping of guinea pigs, much as incipiently agricultural people of the coastal Archaic depended on marine resources.[76]

Elsewhere, in greater detail, I reviewed the Archaic transition in the Andean zone, along with the process of camelid domestication and the contribution of pastoralism to Andean civilization.[77] My conclusions were that the Archaic stage represented a major change in the quality, orientation, and style of life. Broadly based subsistence systems were accompanied by experimental horticulture, varying degrees of sedentism (with seasonal transhumance in some cases), and technological proliferation, including many styles of projectile points, other artifacts for processing plant foods and industrial materials, and luxury artifacts intended to change one's personal state (objects of adornment, status, and hallucinogenic paraphernalia). The reasons for the proliferation of agriculture are an interesting problem, only partly related to Postglacial environmental changes, human population growth, and different patterns of sedentism versus seasonal mobility.[78] We know now that the process of "agriculturalization" was gradual, that it took up much of the Archaic period, and that it was different in all regions of South America, insofar as the record is known. We are coming to realize, too, that we know precious little about the process of cultural change, but that the new burial practices, ground stone tools, adornments, and artwork are more the symptoms than the essence of the process.

---

[76] Brian Hesse, "Archaeological evidence for muscovy duck in Ecuador," *Current Anthropology* 21 (1980), 139–140; Jonathan D. Kent, "The most ancient South: A review of the domestication of the Andean camelids," *BAR International Series* 349 (1987), 167–184; Danièle Lavallée, "La domestication animale en Amérique du Sud – le point des connaissances," *Bulletin de l'Institut Français d'Études Andines* 19 (1990), 25–44; John W. Rick, "Review of *Telarmachay* by D. Lavallée," *Science* 236 (1987), 1685–1686; Jane C. Wheeler, "On the origin and early development of camelid pastoralism in the Andes," *BAR International Series* 202 (1984), 395–409; Elizabeth S. Wing, "Domestication of Andean mammals," in *High Altitude Tropical Biogeography*, F. Vuilleumier and M. Monasterio, eds. (Oxford, 1986), 246–264.

[77] Thomas F. Lynch, "The Paleo-Indians," 125–132 and Lynch, "Camelid pastoralism," 1–14.

[78] For an exceptionally provocative analysis of this theme, from a selectionist and explicitly Darwinian point of view, see David Rindos, "Symbiosis, instability, and the origins and spread of agriculture," *Current Anthropology* 21 (1980), 751–772, and Rindos, *The Origins of Agriculture* (New York, 1984).

BIBLIOGRAPHIC ESSAY

For a coherent overview, reasonably up to date and representative of mainstream thought, see Brian M. Fagan, *The Great Journey: The Peopling of Ancient America* (London and New York, 1987). Chapters 3, 4, and 5 of *The Prehistory of the Americas* (Cambridge and New York, 2nd edition, 1992), by Stuart J. Fiedel, constitute another balanced review. At the other extreme of professional opinion, but less critical in its approach, is *Earlier Than You Think: A Personal View of Man in America* (College Station, 1980) by the geographer George F. Carter. *Quest for the Origins of the First Americans* (Albuquerque, 1993) by E. James Dixon is similarly personalized. The much cited volume *Ancient Man in North America* (Denver, 4th edition, 1957) has aged well, as it contains much historical and descriptive information that is still valuable. Those particularly interested in skeletal remains might refer to T. D. Stewart's *The People of America* (New York, 1973), although it is out of date in terms of theory as well as data. Similarly dated is *Prehistoria de Suramérica* (Barcelona, 1969) by Juan Schobinger, but it is the only single-author volume to focus solely on South America before the rise of agricultural civilization.

Collections of papers by various authors, even when directed to a single theme, usually are poorly integrated and difficult for the lay scholar to reconcile. However, three recent volumes stand out for their comprehensive, thematic approaches and balance: *The First Americans: Search and Research* (Boca Raton, 1991) edited by Tom D. Dillehay and David J. Meltzer; *Clovis: Origins and Adaptations* (Corvallis, 1991) edited by Robson Bonnichsen and Karen L. Turnmire; and *Method and Theory for Investigating the Peopling of the Americas* (Corvallis, 1994) edited by Bonnichsen and D. Gentry Steele. Two older collections contain a number of interesting papers: *Megafauna and Man: Discovery of America's Heartland* (Hot Springs, 1990) edited by L. D. Agenbroad, J. I. Mead, and L. W. Nelson; and *Americans Before Columbus: Ice Age Origins* (Pittsburgh, 1988) edited by Ronald C. Carlisle.

Indeed, most of the secondary literature, as well as many of the primary sources, is found in such collections and in a wide variety of professional journals. The most important of these, for our topics, are *American Antiquity, Quaternary Research, Current Anthropology, Revista de Arqueología Americana, L'Anthropologie, Geoarchaeology, Current Research in the Pleistocene*, the general journals *Science* and *Nature*, and even the newsletter *Mammoth Trumpet*. For those reading Spanish, the *Revista de*

Arqueología Americana especially has been valuable for its coverage of the issues and allowance of debate among the authors (see Nos. 1–5, 1990–1992). Between 1987 and 1990, the magazine *Natural History* (Vols. 97–99) presented a series of interesting but short essays under the rubric "First Americans." I cite several of these in my footnotes.

To a majority of scholars, a first entry across the steppes of Beringia seems most likely. The natural history of eastern Siberia, the now-submerged Bering plain, and the Yukon and Mackenzie valleys is crucial. Convenient sources include "On the mammoth's dusty trail," by R. Dale and Mary Lee Guthrie, in *Natural History* 99 (1990), 34–41, as well as a number of papers in *Paleoecology of Beringia* (New York, 1982), edited by David M. Hopkins et al. The archaeology is most conveniently summarized in a coherent volume by Frederick Hadleigh West, *The Archaeology of Beringia* (New York, 1981), but new sites and syntheses appear often in the journals. Three good reviews are *American Beginnings – The Prehistory and Palaeoecology of Beringia* (Chicago, 1996), edited by Frederick H. West; "The Upper Paleolithic of northern Asia: Achievements, problems, and perspectives, II: central and eastern Siberia," *Journal of World Prehistory* 4 (1990), 347–385, by V. Larichev, U. Khol'lushkin, and I. Laricheva; and "The 'Dyuktai culture' and New World origins," *Current Anthropology* 26 (1985), 1–20, by Seonbok Yi and G. A. Clark. More timely references and proposals are found in Michael L. Kunz and Richard E. Reanier, "Paleoindians in Beringia: Evidence from Arctic Alaska," *Science* 263 (1994), 660–662, and David R. Yesner, "Subsistence diversity and hunter-gatherer strategies in late Pleistocene/early Holocene Beringia," *Current Research in the Pleistocene* 11 (1994), 154–156.

The concept of migrations in prehistory has been controversial, as indicated by David W. Anthony, "Migration in archeology: The baby and the bathwater," *American Anthropologist* 92 (1990), 895–914. An early proponent of Paleoindian migration was John L. Cotter, "Indications of a Paleo-Indian co-tradition for North America," *American Antiquity* 20 (1954), 64–67, and "Comment on the Upper Paleolithic and the New World," *Current Anthropology* 4 (1963), 69–70. A north Atlantic migration was favored by E. F. Greenman, "The Upper Paleolithic and the New World," *Current Anthropology* 4 (1963), 41–91, and elements of Greenman's thesis still find favor with R. Bonnichsen. Although given short shrift by this author, a north Pacific coastal migration still has substantial professional support from Knut R. Fladmark, "Routes: Alternate migration corridors for early man in North America," *American*

Antiquity 44 (1979), 55–69, and Ruth Gruhn, "Linguistic evidence in support of the coastal route of earliest entry into the New World," *Man* 23 (1988), 77–100. Johanna Nichols, "Linguistic diversity and the first settlement of the New World," *Language* 66 (1990), 475–521, also eschews the archaeological record while preferring hypotheses based on dialect geography.

Some even find indications of oceanic voyaging in South American skeletons: Walter A. Neves and Hector M. Pucciarelli, "Extra-continental biological relationships of early South American human remains: A multivariate analysis," *Ciência e Cultura (Revista da Sociedade Brasileira para o Progresso da Ciência* 41 (1989), 566–575. Among archaeologists, support for early transoceanic peopling of South America is scant, but the diffusionist theories of Paul Rivet continue to be seriously considered by Annette Laming-Emperaire, *Le Problème de Origines Américaines* (Lille, 1980).

Hopeful proponents of a pre-Paleoindian presence continue to circulate reports of the latest discoveries. The most persistent has been, perhaps, Alan L. Bryan, who follows Alex D. Krieger in promoting sites that are unassociated with his own work: Krieger, "Early man in the New World," in *Prehistoric Man in the New World* (Chicago, 1964), J. D. Jennings and E. Norbeck, eds., 23–81; Bryan, "Paleoenvironments and cultural diversity in late Pleistocene South America," *Quaternary Research* 3 (1973), 237–256. The latter was the takeoff point for my review and reevaluation, "The antiquity of man in South America," *Quaternary Research* 4 (1974), 356–377, followed by "Glacial-age man in South America? A critical review," *American Antiquity* 55 (1990), 12–36. Readers of French and Spanish might consult somewhat longer versions: "L'Homme des Glaciations en Amérique du Sud: une vision européenne," *L'Anthropologie* 98 (1994), 32–54, and "El hombre de la edad glacial en Suramérica: una perspectiva europea," *Revista de Arqueología Americana* 1 (1990), 141–185. Surveying the skeletal evidence, R. C. Owen also came to negative conclusions: "The Americas: The case against an ice-age human population," in *The Origins of Modern Humans*, F. H. Smith and F. Spencer, eds. (New York, 1984).

Between the poles of Bryan's position and mine, there are all degrees of equivocation and fence sitting. For a balanced consideration of pre-Paleoindian possibilities, the reader should see Jared Diamond, "The latest on the earliest," *Discover* 11 (1990), 50; Dena F. Dincauze, "An archaeo-logical evaluation of the case for pre-Clovis occupations," *Ad-*

vances in World Archaeology 3 (1984), 275–323; Gary Haynes, "Review of new evidence for the Pleistocene peopling of the Americas," *New World Archeologist* 10 (1989), 258–262; C. Vance Haynes, Jr., "Geofacts and fancy," *Natural History* 97 (1988), 4–12; Richard E. Morlan, "Pre-Clovis people: Early discoveries of America," in *Americans before Columbus*, Ronald C. Carlisle, ed. (Pittsburgh, 1988), 31–43; and Lautaro Núñez Atencio and Calogero Santoro Vargas, "Primeros poblamientos en el cono sur de América," *Revista de Arqueología Americana* 1 (1990), 91–139.

In the footnotes to my text, I cite numerous reviews, as well as primary sources, for changing climate and environment as they affected the entry and adaptations of the first South Americans. Useful, recent reviews for the nonspecialist include Paul Colinvaux, "Amazon diversity in light of the paleoecological record," *Quaternary Science Reviews* 6 (1987), 93–114; Vera Markgraf, "Palaeoclimates in Central and South America since 18,000 B.P. based on pollen and lake-level records," *Quaternary Science Reviews* 8 (1989), 1–24; Carlos Ochsenius, "Aridity and biogeography in northernmost South America during the late Pleistocene," *Zentralblatt für Geologie und Paläontologie* 1 (1983), 264–278; and Dolores R. Piperno, Mark Brush, and Paul Colinvaux, "Paleoenvironments and human occupation in late-glacial Panama," *Quaternary Research* 33 (1990), 108–116, and "Paleoecological perspectives on human adaptation in central Panama," *Geoarchaeology* 6 (1991), 227–250.

Additional sources, especially for the southern half of the continent, are cited in Thomas F. Lynch, "Quaternary climate, environment, and the human occupation of the south-central Andes," *Geoarchaeology* 5 (1990), 199–228. See also Jorge Fernández et al., "Late Pleistocene/early Holocene environments and climates, fauna, and human occupation in the Argentine altiplano," *Geoarchaeology* 6 (1991), 251–272. For general background on the plants and animals, I recommend Carl O. Sauer, "Geography of South America," in *Handbook of South American Indians*, Julian Steward, ed. (Washington, 1950), Vol. 5, 319–344, and George G. Simpson, *Splendid Isolation: The Curious History of South American Mammals* (New Haven, 1980).

Little is known about Paleoindian culture in the Americas, beyond broad generalizations and specific descriptions of sites and artifacts. A starting point, for North America, is Robert L. Kelly and Lawrence C. Todd, "Coming into the country: Early Paleoindian hunting and mobility,"*American Antiquity* 53 (1988), 231–244. Recent thoughts by Paul S. Martin, on the classic hunting and extinction model, can be found in

"Refuting late Pleistocene extinction models," in *Dynamics of Extinction*, D. K. Elliott, ed. (New York, 1986), 107–130. In a South American context, Vera Markgraf concludes that climate and environmental changes were primarily responsible for the extinctions: "Late Pleistocene faunal extinctions in southern Patagonia," *Science* 228 (1985), 1110–1112. My chapter "The Paleo-Indians," in *Ancient South Americans*, J. D. Jennings, ed. (San Francisco, 1983), 87–137, is a general introduction for the nonspecialist. *Travels and Archaeology in South Chile* (Iowa City, 1988), by Junius B. Bird, is a vibrant personal account of the first discoveries, mixed with basic description and analysis of sites and artifacts. For an introduction to the controversial issues of Paleoindian language and genetics, see Joseph H. Greenberg, Christy Turner, and Stephen Zegura, "The settlement of the Americas: A comparison of the linguistic, dental, and genetic evidence," *Current Anthropology* 27 (1986), 477–497, including the reviewers' comments.

No attempt had been made to summarize the Archaic stage across the continent until recently: Karen O. Bruhns, Chapters 4 and 5, in *Ancient South America* (Cambridge and New York, 1994), 50–88. Detailed reviews are necessarily country by country. For Peru, see the chapters by John Rick, "The character and context of highland preceramic society," and Claude Chauchat, "Early hunter-gatherers on the Peruvian coast," in *Peruvian Prehistory*, Richard Keatinge, ed. (Cambridge, 1988), 3–40, 41–66. Another good source is James B. Richardson, III, *People of the Andes* (Montreal, 1994), and "Modeling the development of sedentary maritime economies on the coast of Peru," *Annals of the Carnegie Museum of Natural History* 50 (1981), 139–150. For the highlands of Peru, a contrasting source is D. Lavallée, "L'occupation préhistorique des hautes terres andines," *L'Anthropologie* 89 (1985), 409–430.

The Maritime Foundations of Andean Civilization (Menlo Park, 1975), by Michael E. Moseley, has been much criticized and much revised (e.g., Alan Osborn, "Strandloopers, mermaids, and other fairy tales: Ecological determinants of marine resource utilization, the Peruvian case," in *For Theory Building in Archaeology*, Lewis Binford, ed. [New York and London, 1977], 157–243). Jeffrey Quilter et al., "Subsistence economy of El Paraíso, an early Peruvian site," *Science* 251 (1991), 277–283, give a succinct rendition of the new maritime Archaic.

The maritime Archaic also has been studied well in Chile: Agustín Llagostera M., "9,700 years of maritime subsistence on the Pacific," *American Antiquity* 44 (1979), 309–324; Antonieta Jerardino et al., "Early coastal subsistence patterns in central Chile," *Latin American Antiquity* 3 (1992), 43–62. Investigations of the Brazilian shell mounds have a long history, most easily accessible through Pedro I. Schmitz, "Prehistoric hunters and gatherers of Brazil," *Journal of World Prehistory* 1 (1987), 53–126, and A. Prous, "L'Archéologie au Brésil,"*L'Anthropologie* 90 (1986), 257–306. The Archaic archaeology of the forested lowlands is covered in those sources, insofar as it is known, as well as by Anna Roosevelt in this volume.

Elsewhere, knowledge of the preceramic Archaic adaptations varies greatly from place to place. The Sabana de Bogotá is well known: Gonzalo Correal Urrego, "Estado actual de las investigaciones sobre la etapa lítica en Colombia, *Antropológicas* (*Revista de la Sociedad Antropológica de Colombia*) 2 (1980), 11–30. So also is the Santa Elena Peninsula of Ecuador: Karen E. Stothert, *La Prehistoria Temprana de la Península de Santa Elena: Cultura Las Vegas* (Guayaquil, 1988). Another environmentally marginal, climate sensitive area – especially suitable for the investigation of Archaic adaptations – is the high, dry Puna de Atacama shared by Argentina and Chile: Martin Grosjean and Lautaro Núñez A., "Late glacial, early and middle Holocene environments, human occupation, and resource use in the Atacama (northern Chile)," *Geoarchaeology* 9 (1994), 271–286; Lynch, "Quaternary Climate environment, and the human occupation of the South-Central Andes," *Geoarchaeology* 5 (1990), 199–228; and Calogero Santoro V. and Núñez, "Hunters of the dry puna and salt puna in northern Chile," *Andean Past* 1 (1987), 57–109.

The beginnings of agriculture, in both the Old World and the New, is a huge topic that has been the subject of many books and learned papers. Of recent, influential books, two of my favorites are *The Food Crisis in Prehistory: Overpopulation and the Origins of Agriculture* (New Haven, 1977), by Mark N. Cohen, and *The Origins of Agriculture* (New York and London, 1984), by David Rindos. Both have excellent bibliographies. Carl O. Sauer can be said to have begun the serious consideration of a distinctive tropical American origin for agriculture in *Agricultural Origins and Dispersals* (New York, 1952), but his best statement for the American case is "Age and area of American cultivated plants," *33rd International Congress of Americanists, Acts* 1 (1958), 215–229. References to modern work and specific problems in the development of South American agriculture are found in the footnotes to my text, as well as in the chapter by Anna Roosevelt.

4

THE MARITIME, HIGHLAND, FOREST DYNAMIC AND THE ORIGINS OF COMPLEX CULTURE

ANNA C. ROOSEVELT

Nonstate complex cultures are one of the most widespread types of ancient human societies. The complex society, or chiefdom, as some call it, was a successful way of life that hardly exists today. Accounting for the existence of such societies encourages us to look at their beginnings, florescence, and demise. We can ask what were the conditions that brought them into being? How were these cohesive and stable societies supported and integrated? What kinds of economies did they have, and how were people organized and resources used? What were the concepts embedded in their rituals and arts? And what led to their eventual replacement by other types of societies? This chapter describes the rise and development of indigenous complex cultures in South America from the late Ice Age through the Holocene, or Recent era.

THE RISE OF COMPLEX SOCIETY

Explanations of the rise of complex societies up to now have focused on five factors: patterns of environment, the impetus of human population growth, economic growth, as well as cultural diffusion, and the interaction of polities. Some theories hold that population growth in diverse, arid, circumscribed environments fostered conflict over agricultural land and ultimately led to military conquest and state organization. Statehood is thought a necessary, rational solution to living in dense, sedentary populations. Such organization came into being because central rulers and hierarchical organization were needed to run regional agricultural economies and redistributive systems. These environments possessed the rich agricultural soils to support large, sedentary populations and diverse material resources, whose exploitation and exchange were an impetus for cultural complexity. State organization is also thought to have permitted the establishment of stable societies and expansive cultural traditions; it both inspired and enabled the development of high art and monumental architecture. Finds of such cultural achievements in an archaeological culture, therefore, would be evidence of early state organization, by this reasoning.

Conversely, complex societies could not develop in tropical lowland environments, whose soils are too poor for agriculture to support population growth and whose resources are too uniform to require redistribution. The nonstate societies that could exist in the lowlands would be unstable, unable to support and organize dense, sedentary populations, and unable and indisposed to create high art and monumental architecture.

The common assumptions about the environmental and economic associations of early complex societies have been difficult to demonstrate empirically. Complex societies eventually developed in both highlands and lowlands, but they may have appeared earlier in the Andean coastal and highland valleys than in lowland forests or riverine regions. The arid regions were much less stable culturally and give more evidence of chronic human physiological stress than in humid lowland regions, where evidence of such stress was quite rare until late prehistory and in some areas not until the European conquest. These patterns suggest that expansion of populations in regions with low and variable resource productivity led to complex organizational systems long before this occurred in more productive and stable environments. It may be that where productive land that could provide a refuge was limited, "population pressure" or social conflict may have led to organizational changes that did not develop in regions where the discontented could easily leave to homestead elsewhere in the forest. Localized and circumscribed resource zones may also have been easier for élites to capture and hold than broad resource zones such as deep-sea ocean resources, very large rivers, or trackless forests.

New comparative data about cultural trajectories in the different environments reveal economic factors not seriously considered in the earlier formulations. One aspect is the continuing importance of hunting and gathering in the economies of early complex societies, alongside or even instead of agriculture. Productive aquatic resources are now recognized as particularly important in early sedentism and cultural complexity. Both on the coast of Peru and along the Amazon and Orinoco, fisheries were a key resource. In the process of settling down and developing complex cultures, fishing was intensified. In all regions, land animals were much less abundant than aquatic prey, but even in the semiarid highlands, the earliest complex societies relied more on hunting than on agriculture. Only in later prehistory did complex societies rely primarily on food production.

In American anthropology, before direct evidence of ancient economies was available, scholars looked back into the past from the reference point of contact-period states and chiefdoms, most of which were intensive maize agriculturalists. Ecologists even framed crop-determinist theories about the development of social organization. Tuberous crops were thought to mitigate against sedentary settlement, population expansion, and stratification, whereas maize stimulated such processes.

However, the evidence of cultural sequences throughout the continent and worldwide does not support this assumption. Many nonagricultural societies manifest the characteristics considered to exemplify complex culture. In South America, the earliest complex societies in the Central Andes do not show evidence of strongly agricultural food economies. The earliest horticultural complex societies in both the Andes and the tropical lowlands relied on a variety of crops other than maize, with both temperate and tropical tubers holding positions of importance. Cultivated plants enter economies more for their importance in crafts and food processing (gourds and cotton) and their ceremonial importance (maize for beer) than for their direct food value for humans. In both the lowlands and the Andes, intensive agricultural economies were created by late prehistoric complex societies, not the other way around.

On the premise that the centralization, hierarchy, and craft specialization of states exist because they are necessary to run the regional economic systems and public works projects of populous, sedentary agricultural societies, it has been assumed that archaeological evidence of public works was tantamount to evidence of state administrative organization and specialized crafts. In addition, finds of highly elaborate and accomplished, standardized crafts were taken to be direct evidence of stratified and centralized organization, and some go to the extreme of identifying complex societies solely on remains of ceremonial activity.

The archaeological record in many American regions shows that early complex societies appear long before large-scale irrigation systems and could not have been organized for the purpose of running them. Monumental construction and highly developed material culture and ritual are found in many ancient societies without any evidence of central rule or socioeconomic stratification. It is clear from both archaeological and ethnographic evidence that communal or segmentary societies are perfectly capable of organizing large public works. Further, ethnohistoric evidence for the organization of crafts in Latin America shows that some of the finest craft corpuses in the Americas were produced by élite women and men working within extended family or lineage organization, not in specialized craft groups. Thus one need not assume that the development of hierarchical and centralized organization was necessary for sedentary and complex societies to appear in such regions.

The cultural sequences of the Americas clearly show that state organization is not necessary for the persistence and growth of sedentary societies with large populations. In fact, the earlier, less highly organized complex societies are sometimes longer-lived as cultural phases than centralized and stratified bureaucratic states and empires. Early New World chiefdoms often persisted for more than 1,000 years, whereas the rarer indigenous states and empires often had lifetimes of only a few hundred years.

Chiefdoms and states have different trajectories because they have different kinds of organizational processes. States can organize differently because they possess economic control and force. Chiefdoms do not have these kinds of controls. They must organize by other means, among which the voluntary exchange of services is important.

Clearly there is a need to revise our notions of causality in cultural evolution and to reexamine questions about the origins of societies. One problem in understanding the geographic characteristics of early complex culture is that there has been a geographic bias in archaeological investigations. Thus it was assumed early on that the origins of complex culture would be found in the same regions where civilization was found at contact times, and that it would have "spread" to the lowlands. Accordingly, scholars interested in the question mainly studied nuclear areas, such as the Central Andes, where the Inkas were at contact. They have not systematically investigated the complex societies of other regions, despite the fact that complex society had a substantial development in those other regions. In fact, since the beginning of modern archaeology circa 1950, few lowland complex societies have been investigated comprehensively. This geographic bias has created an epistemological tautology. We have mostly learned about the rise of complex culture in the nuclear areas. Without evidence from the nonnuclear areas, how can the hypothesis about the geography of pristine complex societies be tested?

Therefore this chapter reviews the available comparable evidence for the development of complex society in the three contrasting environments: the maritime desert coast and highlands of the Central Andes and the tropical forest and rivers of Greater Amazonia.

THE CENTRAL ANDES

Long considered the hearth of complex culture in South America, the Central Andes appears to have had a somewhat different developmental sequence than early evolutionists imagined. They expected that indigenous South American civilization developed in the Andes from roots in sedentary, maize-farming societies of the Formative Period. We now know, however, that the earliest sedentary societies relied on wild food resources, which supported the first signs of cultural elaboration and social differentiation. Even more unexpected, the first cultures with populous settlements, monumental ceremonial constructions, and fine art seem to have combined foraging and incipient farming rather than practiced intensive agriculture. Specialized agricultural economies are not in evidence until the last 2,500 years of prehistory. These early part-time farmers focused more on nonfood production of crops like cotton for fiber and gourds for containers. Food cultigens seem to have been supplementary at this time. The craft of pottery, thought to have been invented in early Andean farming societies, actually appeared long before intensive agriculture in early Holocene foraging societies in the tropical lowlands, not in the Andes.

For earlier researchers, the Central Andean environment had an important influence on the rise of complex culture, due to its agricultural potential and regional diversity in resources. New findings confirm a role for the environment in Andean cultural development, but causality appears to have been quite different than envisioned earlier.

Key environmental characteristics include the linearly patterned diversity and the spatial circumscription of zones with high biomass. From the long, highly productive ocean margin in the west, one passes through a narrow coastal desert cut by small rivers with mountain headwaters, through cold rainy mountains and semiarid high basins, and then over the eastern Andean crest to the rainy warm lowlands to the east (see Map 4.1). From north to south, there is a progression from wetter climates and lower elevations to drier, higher land.

The Pacific coast has an inexhaustible supply of small fishes and their

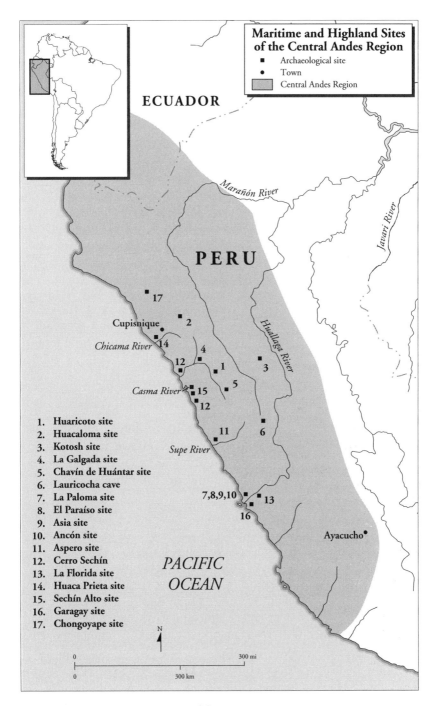

Maritime and Highland Sites
of the Central Andes Region

■ Archaeological site
● Town
▨ Central Andes Region

ECUADOR

Marañón River

PERU

Javari River

■ 17

Cupisnique ■ 2

Chicama River ■ 14

Huallaga River

■ 12

■ 4

■ 1

■ 3

Casma River ■ 15

■ 5

■ 12

■ 11

■ 6

1. Huaricoto site
2. Huacaloma site
3. Kotosh site
4. La Galgada site
5. Chavín de Huántar site
6. Lauricocha cave
7. La Paloma site
8. El Paraíso site
9. Asia site
10. Ancón site
11. Aspero site
12. Cerro Sechín
13. La Florida site
14. Huaca Prieta site
15. Sechín Alto site
16. Garagay site
17. Chongoyape site

Supe River

7,8,9,10 ■ ■ 13

■ 16

Ayacucho ●

PACIFIC
OCEAN

N

0 ——————— 300 mi
0 ——————— 300 km

Map 4.1

larger predators, as long as it is fed by cold, nutrient-bearing coastal currents coming from the southern oceans. These currents feed fisheries, but the combination of cool water temperatures and warmer land temperatures prevent rain from falling on the coast, which is a barren desert, except where fog condensing on hillsides nourishes dry forests. Marine faunas may have supported some of the earliest sedentary, nucleated communities in the Americas before the development of agriculture, according to Michael Moseley. However, their productivity is subject to periodic catastrophic drops, when weather patterns of the "El Niño" phenomenon allow warm, nutrient-poor equatorial waters to displace the cool southern currents from the coast. As their food base disappears, the abundance of marine fauna is drastically reduced. At the same time, however, rain increases on the coast, fostering more abundant vegetation on the mineral-rich desert and thus increased plant food and land game.

Ordinarily, vegetation on the coast is confined to river valleys and fog forests, both of which were probably more luxuriant and abundant in early prehistoric times, before intensive agriculture, deforestation for fuel, and overgrazing with introduced livestock. Frederic Engel has pointed out that ancient fog forests had a different species mix than modern ones, according to ancient pollen studies. In addition, some species now restricted to the tropical forests to the north and east could have lived in the richer prehistoric gallery forests. The coastal forests furnished fuel, fiber, tree fruits, edible grasses, and game for human use. The gallery forests were probably where the first Early Archaic cultigens – cotton, gourds, peppers, tubers, and tropical fruit trees and shrubs – were cultivated.

Between the rivers and fog forests, moisture in the desert coast is scarce except when the warm-current anomalies occur in the ocean. Unlike the interfluvial forests of the humid tropical lowlands, where cultivation and foraging can be practiced, the desert interfluves are barren of wild food and are uncultivatable without irrigation. Water for drinking and irrigation is available in the rivers and in fossil river channels buried in the desert, and wells and sunken agricultural fields were dug by ancient people to tap buried water, but desert soils can quickly become too saline for most crops if repeatedly irrigated.

In the highlands, temperatures and rainfall are higher than on the coasts. Rain tends to increase with altitude, except for rainshadows, and elevations above about 4,000 meters can have relatively high rainfall and perennial streams. These higher elevations have extensive grasslands (called *puna*) that supported dense populations of wild camelids, from which domestic camelids were developed by Early Horizon times. For the high grasslands, there is little evidence of major environmental change other than the descent of ice during glacials; at such times, humans may have moved downslope to warmer zones. The humidity of the *puna* varies with latitude. Thus the northern *puna* is much rainier than the southern.

At lower elevations in the highlands, between about 2,000 and 4,000 meters, rainfall lessens to below circa 500 millimeters and becomes more variable. Only a few intermontane basins have sizable areas of cultivable soils. Most of the land consists of steep, rocky hillsides clothed in thin, xerophytic vegetation. This zone has been thought to have supported the earliest maize and bean production because of the incentive to regularize and increase food production in the face of habitat instability. However, the cultigens from early sites in the area have now been dated by accelerator to the Formative or later. This zone appears to have the same limited suite of cultigens in the early Archaic as the coast.

To the east on the Amazon side of the Andes, known as the *montaña*, the mountains descend into the humid lowland climate zone, with between 3,000 and 1,500 millimeters of rainfall per year. Although it has become a cliché that these are poor soil areas where only slash-and-burn cultivation can be carried out, in fact, the geological substrate is largely dominated by limestones and volcanic rocks, which weather to comparatively rich soils under the rainy, warm climate. Preliminary research in the Amazon slopes of the Andes has uncovered the remains of numerous stone terraces and substantial buildings. Although some argue that maize cultivation in the *montaña* would have been the result of intrusions of peoples from more highly organized civilizations in the Andes, the history of staple maize cultivation in the lowlands begins about the time of Christ, long before the Andean "empires" of the Middle and Late Horizons. The Inka are thought to have been unable or uninterested in penetrating the lowland forests, and late prehistoric complex cultures of the *montaña* seem quite independent of highland cultural traditions.

Early theories of prehistoric cultural ecology in the Central Andes tended to envision extensive food interchange among regions, as adaptations to population growth and the diversity of the region. Manioc (*Manihot esculenta*), sweet potatoes (*Ipomoea batata*), chili peppers (*Capsicum* genus) and other tropical cultigens were probably introduced to the Andes from the *montaña*, which is endowed with high diversity of wild or feral relatives of the cultigens. There is little evidence of this. Ancient people seem to have exploited comparatively restricted resource areas whenever this was economically feasible. Exchange of luxury goods and ceremonial foods between the seacoast and highlands, however, is documented at least by the Late Archaic Period and intensified greatly in the Early Horizon. By late prehistoric times, many types of products from the different zones were regularly exchanged.

PALEOINDIANS

To show complex cultural developments in historical context, our review of the origins of complex culture begins with the known earliest occupations by humans. The earliest well-documented human traces belong to the final millennium of the Pleistocene, from 11,000 to 9,000 years ago. Traces of early Paleoindian hunting and fishing camps have been found all along the Pacific coast, but the only well-documented culture is Paiján.

Sites occupied by people of the Paiján culture have been found on the north coast near Cupisnique between the Chicama and Jequetepeque valleys and at the La Cumbre site and Quirihuac rock shelter in the Moche Valley. Both specialized-use sites such as quarries and general-living sites with garbage pits, hearths, and burials have been studied. Some living sites contain artifact clusters of about 200-square-meter size within an area of almost a square kilometer. Such remains suggest small but recurrent habitations. No ceremonial areas have been reported, but as yet there has been little systematic survey or test excavation.

The Paiján culture is distinguished by large (9–14 cm), finely pressure-flaked points, some stemmed, tanged, and tapered, and some leaf-shaped. None resemble Clovis or Folsom points from North America. There are also bifacial preforms for projectile points, retouched unifacial cutting tools, denticulates, and utilized flakes, but few scrapers. Most lithics are local rhyolite, with small amounts of quartz, quartzite, and dacite. Other cultural materials in the sites were milling stones, coral rasps, small round pebbles, and burial mats. The only evidence for aesthetic or ritual activity are the burials and a fish-vertebrum bead (from a child burial).

The environment was moister than it is today, with luxuriant woodland and gallery forest vegetation. Contrary to theoretical models of considerable mobility for hunter-gatherers, the sites show an ecological orientation to the coast and lack identifiable highland material.

Food remains indicate exploitation of both sea and dry forest. Diverse faunas were used, including numerous fish species, many small land vertebrates, such as reptiles, small mammals (*vizcacha* and fox), small birds, and terrestrial molluscs from moist microenvironments. Few or no medium-sized animals, such as deer, nor extinct megafauna were utilized for food at the sites, although dates on horse and mastodon specimens from paleontological sites show that they were apparently still around. The large, stemmed Paiján points thus are considered to have been for spearing large fish. At the Paiján sites, no marine molluscs were eaten, possibly because their habitats had been diminished by the lower ocean levels of the time.

The people, represented by two adults, a man and a woman, and two juveniles, were tall (168-cm male) and robust, with extremely long heads and narrow faces. Like other Paleoindians, they have been described by physical anthropologists as probably of Asian origin but not mongoloid in physique. Nineteen associated radiocarbon dates run from circa 11,000 to 8,000 B.P., suggesting that the Paiján culture lasted into the Early Archaic. Despite its contemporaneity with the Clovis and Folsom Paleoindian cultures of North America, this coastal Paleoindian culture in the Central Andean region seems focused on broad-spectrum foraging, not terrestrial big game.

John Rick's recent review of evidence from the highlands of the Central Andes suggests that there is not much indisputable evidence for Paleoindians there. In the past, the presence of pre-Clovis Paleoindians was postulated on the basis of poorly dated and undiagnostic tool assemblages from disturbed caves and rock shelters, some of which lacked evidence of fire. Perhaps the earliest discernible Paleoindian culture is Puente of the Ayacucho Basin, placed between about 11,000 and 9,000 years ago, based on five radiocarbon dates. This culture apparently adapted to a habitat not dissimilar to the present one, using a broad-spectrum hunting and gathering subsistence system. Not only deer and camelids but also birds, rodents, foxes, and various wild plant foods were consumed by the people. Their material culture includes a range of projectile points, including rare possible fluted fishtail points, as well as triangular, stemmed or lanceolate bifacial points (all of which were diagnostics of the Jaywa culture of the following early Archaic period), many types of scrapers, bone tools, and rare grinding stones. Guitarrero Cave, excavated by Thomas Lynch, is one of the few highland sites. It has numerous late Pleistocene radiocarbon dates associated with similar archaeological remains.

The lack of well-documented Paleoindian sites in much of the highlands during this period could be because unfavorable late glacial environmental conditions discouraged colonization of the area or because subsequent geomorphological processes have buried or destroyed early sites. However, site destruction does not explain why rock art sites are so much rarer in the Central Andes compared to eastern South America.

Archaeology provides little support for the hypothesis that the Central Andean highlands were a corridor for the penetration of North American big-game hunters into South America. Rather, it reveals a distinct coastal fishing and plant-collecting culture that differs from the Clovis or Folsom cultures of North America in ecological adaptation and material culture.

Early Archaic

Soon after 9,000 years ago, fishing groups occupied a fog forest at La Paloma, near the Pacific coast. The main part of the occupation dates between about 8,000 and 5,000 B.P., covering the Luz, Encanto Temprano or Corbina, and Encanto 1 periods. Major zones exploited by these people were the ocean and the fog meadows. River valleys presumably were exploited, but subsequent habitation and agriculture appears to have effaced the traces.

The foundations of numerous small, round or oval houses occur over a large area, but only a fraction was occupied at any time. The houses (often 1.5 m in diameter) look like households of nuclear families. They are of perishable materials, with shallow foundations and occasional whalebone struts or stones for holding down mats and poles. Such houses could be rolled up and easily moved. No monumental constructions have been reported, except for a few later structures with stone and mud foundations. There were hearths for warmth inside houses (the coast is chilly and humid in the winter), and outside the huts were large cobble pavements for cooking.

The Paloma people customarily left garbage in and around dwellings, a pattern more common in shifting settlements than in permanent ones. However, the many storage features and the practice of salting of fish to preserve it suggest at least partly sedentary occupation. Jeffrey Quilter, one of those who excavated at the site, suggests that sedentism is greatest in the middle period, with greater mobility in the early period, when people were moving to the site, and in the late periods, when people were relocating away from the fog meadow.

The craft technology was simple but competent, and there were various ritual practices. Burials were flexed and tied in twined reed mats and buried shallowly inside or just outside the house, usually accompanied by an object. Grave goods include pebbles, pigment, clothing, ornaments, tools, gourd fragments, grinding stones, burnt rock, and single animal bones. Objects of cut shell are found, as well as bone and stone beads and pendants. Occasionally, there is a "ceremonial" offering, such as a wad of animal hair enclosed in two mussel shells. Many burials with such objects adjoin a small, grass-lined offering pit. In contrast to Paleoindian points, early Archaic stone projectile points were rare, small (less than 10 cm), bipointed, and percussion-flaked. A few examples of knotted textiles, possibly for fishnets, mats, and twined baskets, were also made. People appear to have gone barefoot and commonly suffered broken foot bones. Their head coverings were looped fabric, down, or animal fur. They wore rush skirts and looped loin coverings.

Subsistence focused on marine resources: fish, sea mammals, and invertebrates. In the earliest period, women ate more fish and shellfish than men. As human populations increased, abundant small fish and fatty-flesh sea mammals increased in the diet. Mollusc consumption also increased but less so. These changes were accompanied by more developed upper body muscles in men and women, possibly from hauling nets, and male and female diets became more similar. Overall muscular work among males decreased somewhat with time, to the same level as that of women. Both men and women had lower-back arthritis from carrying heavy loads.

Among plant foods were cereals, fruits of cactus, guava (*Pisidium guajava*), mito (*Carica candicans*), and *algarroba (Prosopis chilensis)*, and the medicinal plants *molle* and *alberjilla*. Oca (*Oxalis tuberosa*) was also eaten as well as a tuber tentatively identified as tuberous begonia. During the middle period, more plant foods were eaten and possibly beans, gourds, and squash for the first time. Women ate more plant food at this time, to judge from the mineral content of their bones compared to men's. Plant foods decreased in the latest period, as the fog meadows diminished from overexploitation. Use of plants for fabrics increased with time, and hides and animal furs decreased.

General good health is indicated by people's comparatively tall average stature (170 cm for men and 160 cm for women) and lack of severe pathologies from infectious disease and poor diet. Teeth were worn, and caries rare (in part because the teeth are so worn down). Linear dental enamel defects (hypoplasias) indicating periodic but not chronic food scarcity or disease are relatively common, according to Robert Benfer, who analyzed the skeletons.

Changes in burial and pathology patterns through time suggest changes in human ecology, social organization, and environment. Interestingly, health improved during the intensification of subsistence, suggesting that expansion of economy was an effective adaptation. For example, stature increases from the beginning to the end of the occupation. Also, anemic pathologies in the eye sockets (*cribra orbitalia*) from parasite infection become rare through time, and life expectancy increases. Although demography of ancient cemeteries is subject to many biases, there are significant patterns in the population. Birthrates decreased through time, men were significantly more numerous in the population, and women bore children comparatively late. Taken together, these patterns suggest that population growth may have been controlled through female infanticide and late marriage.

The organization of the Paloma society appears more or less egalitarian and focused on small household groups. There were distinct differences in burial form, but nothing that could not be attributed to age, sex, and personal achievements. The lack of a separate cemetery suggests that corporate descent groups were lacking. Houses continued to be occupied after burials were put under the floor, and some burials were weighted down with stones, especially women's, suggesting some fear of the spirits of the dead. In the early period of occupation at Paloma, men and women had similar burial treatment, but near the end, men's burials become richer than those of women. Children (especially females) had the richest burials, a practice that began with the earlier Paijan culture. There is no evidence at Paloma for the uniquely elaborate burials that occur in later archaeological sites. There are no known community building projects such as earthworks or fortifications and no evidence of war traumas in the population. Overall, coastal cultures of the Early Archaic in the Central Andes seem well-adapted to the habitat and efficient at supplying the people's needs.

In the highlands, Early Archaic cultures differed somewhat from one zone to another. At intermediate altitudes in the seasonal habitats of the intermontane basins, broader-spectrum hunting and collecting were characteristic. In the Ayacucho basin, the Jaywa culture, which has six radiocarbon dates between about 9,000 and 7,800 years ago, essentially continued the cultural patterns of the Paleoindian period. Discernible changes from Paleoindian patterns consist mainly of the addition of smaller triangular projectile points.

In the cool, often rainy grasslands of the high *puna*, broadest in southern and central parts of the area, the early Archaic adaption seems specialized for hunting camelids and deer, according to John Rick. Wild grains, cactus, and medicinal plants were collected, but no plants were cultivated. It is difficult to distinguish domestic from wild camelids, but the earliest possible domestic forms are not found before the end of the period, circa 6,000 years ago. The *puna* habitat does not have marked seasonal changes that would require transhumance, and human occupations do appear permanent. *Puna* sites tend to have a narrower range of game species than basin sites.

Resources in the more arid intermediate elevations are scattered, seasonal, and subject to fluctuations. The most stable and productive zones are the river floodplains. The harvestable biomass is much smaller than in the moister *puna*. Unlike the high *puna*, the intermontane basins have been much altered recently by deforestation for agriculture, pasture, and fuel. Early Archaic human adaptations are poorly known because of stratigraphic and dating problems in the rock shelters and caves investigated. Initial publications reported early cultigens, but accelerator radiocarbon dates directly on them have shown them to be intrusions from later cultural horizons.

Highland sites usually lack fauna from the coast or tropical forest, so hunting territories may have been regionally confined, and long-distance transport of food limited. The history of plant domestication in the highlands is not well known.

Highland material culture shows some differences from coastal material. Most *puna* and intermontane basin lithics of the time included projectile points, side scrapers or knives, and large, bifacial hand tools. This tool kit changed through time. Points became more common and changed from large tanged forms to smaller leaf-shaped forms. Highland points are uniformly smaller than coastal points. They are seldom more than 5 centimeters. Generally, *puna* lithics are of local rocks. The situation for intermontane basin sites is unclear. Milling stones are scarce compared to flaked material in the highlands, although hammerstones are common. Bone items are also scarce. They include awls, needles, flakers, fleshers, and beads. Quartz crystals, paint, and beads are rare finds. Wooden fire drills, cordage, baskets, and textiles were recovered from some caves, but the disturbance of strata has made the age of some of these materials uncertain.

Small, rare domestic constructions are known from both the *puna* and intermontane basins. Only a few sites have burials. Among the side-flexed burials at Lauricocha Cave, for example, children had much richer furnishings than adults, including food, lithics, pigment, and beads. Examples of rock art associated with *puna* occupations depict camelids with geometric decoration and hunters using spear-throwers.

Based on the small amount of available information, highlanders seem to have had comparatively little interaction with people in other regions at this time, and each region seems to have had its own distinctive cultural adaptation. Human adaptation to the *puna* seems rather narrowly specialized and changed little through time. Small, apparently unstratified groups lived in relatively permanent settlements. Adaptations in intermontane basins, in contrast, are more changeable and depend on a wider set of resources. The diversity, low resource productivity, and instability of intermontane habitats are supposed to have hastened the evolution of agriculture and civilization, but, due to dating problems, the picture of human cultural development there at this time is not yet clear.

ANDEAN COMPLEX CULTURES

Late Archaic

"Dramatic cultural changes occurred in Peru during the Late Preceramic and early Initial periods," according to archaeologist J. Quilter. In this period, called the Late Archaic, between about 5,000 and 3,000 years ago, several cultures appeared as large, permanent settlements with monumental architecture, innovations in craft technology, and elaborate regional art styles. For the first time, pottery came into use in some sites. Late Archaic cultures, which occur both on the coast and in highland basins, are some of the earliest complex cultures in the Americas.

In this period, people began to live in sizable nucleated communities. These had small dwellings clustered around plazas and large platforms with larger rooms on top. The large rooms were well made and decorated and often had caches of special objects and burials. Burials commonly were richly furnished, although none are outstandingly rich. As before, children's burials were better furnished than adults'. To judge from the burials and depictions of humans, clothing and personal ornaments became more substantial, elaborate, and varied. Sites have many ritual art objects, such as unfired clay figurines. A wider range of tools and containers were made. Both pottery vessels and textiles made on looms with heddles appeared in some areas by the end of the period. Some sites, in addition, contain materials imported from afar.

Earlier, intensive maize agriculture was thought to have been the economic basis for the Late Archaic cultures. But the subsistence remains and human bone chemistry studies suggest instead that people relied mainly on hunting and fishing, supplemented with wild plants and a few crops. This general pattern is found from site to site, but the elements differ. Fish are the main protein source on the coast, and deer and camelids are the main sources in the highlands. Camelids outnumber deer at some highland sites, but domestic camelids are not identified for certain except in a few ceramic cultures at the very end of the period.

No known site of the period has any evidence of intensive maize agriculture. Most sites lack corn, and the few corn specimens from sites have not been directly dated and may be intrusive. Many sites contain the cultigens beans, cucurbits, tubers, and various fruits. The types of beans and fruits differ from site to site.

Although there are many regional variations in culture, some aspects of art, economy, and technology were shared over large areas of Peru for periods hundreds to more than a thousand years long. The shared stylistic complex was once thought to have dispersed from a single center, the monumental site of Chavín de Huántar. That site, however, turns out to be more than a thousand years more recent than the Late Archaic cultures and thus could not have been the source. Apparently, a shared culture coalesced slowly through the interaction of many local cultures, rather than through blanket influence from a center: For example, the adoption of pottery near the end of the period was not a widespread, coordinated change but a sporadic process, involving the creation of several different plain or incised wares. Despite the comparative rarity of food crops, large quantities of gourds and cotton were widely cultivated for use as materials. Gourds were hollowed out for containers. Cotton fiber, yarn, and fabric are so common in sites that the Late Archaic pre-pottery culture has been called the "cotton preceramic." In fact, it may be that Late Archaic people moved from the coast to interior river valleys in order to cultivate cotton on alluvium. Loss of marine resources presumably would have encouraged increased collection and cultivation of food plants. The cotton was used extensively for both ritual and everyday activities. The extensive cotton production at this time may have had religious and social incentives as well as economic incentives.

The Late Archaic adaptation continued substantially in the cultures that begin to make pottery near the end of the period. There were, however, some differences. Although the pottery cultures' subsistence still emphasized wild products, cultivated plants became more important, and domestic camelids appear in the highlands. In terms of technology, there were some new developments. The pottery cultures had improved fabric-making methods, such as the use of heddles to manipulate warp strings for weaving. The association of several new cultural elements in the pottery cultures suggests that the complex culture was introduced into the area, rather than locally developed, but this possibility has not been explored systematically.

Late Archaic art has many sophisticated elements that continued in all subsequent periods, such as elaborate paired animal images and trophy head appendages on anthropomorphic beings. Images of predatory fishing birds stand out among animal subjects (Fig. 4.1). Generally, architecture is more elaborately modeled and colored in early ceramic sites than in nonceramic sites. Images of central anthropomorphic figures found in some ceramic sites may have related to concepts of paramount chiefship. Several ceramic sites have architectural art designed to be seen from a distance, in contrast to the inward-turned complexes of preceramic Archaic sites. Early ceramic coastal sites, like Ancon, tend to be larger and have more mounds than aceramic sites. In the highlands, ceramic-using sites tend to have larger and fewer mound-top rooms than nonceramic sites, suggesting larger gatherings of celebrants than before.

Ceramic cultures throughout the region share many of the new elements and patterns. There is, however, no evidence of a massive supraregional initial ceramic cultural horizon. Initial pottery is very varied, unlike pottery of horizon styles. It is not particularly elaborate, being mostly plain or with incised or appliqué decoration.

Earlier scholars thought Archaic societies were centralized polities with hierarchical social classes. They assumed that monuments, elaborate crafts, and sedentary communities could not exist without central control of labor and resources. However, concrete evidence of paramount leadership or élites, in the form of possible ruler figures in art, administrative architecture, uniquely rich tombs or habitations, and so on, does not appear until the end of the period and then only at a few places. Families and local community groups seem to have been able to organize and

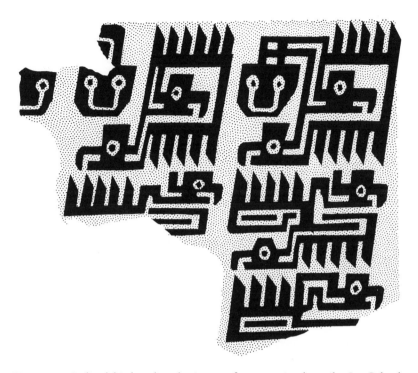

Figure 4.1. Stylized bird and snake images from a twined textile, La Galgada, Peru. From Terence Grieder, Alberto Bueno Mendoz, C. Earle Smith, Jr. and Robert M. Maline, *La Galgada, Peru*, fig. 130 (Austin: University of Texas Press, 1988). © 1988 by the University of Texas Press. Reproduced with permission.

underwrite such projects without the need for higher levels of organization. Systems of community cooperation in combination with nonhierarchical systems of communication between regions thus seem to have provided the organizational basis for the cultural achievements.

The place of origin in the Andes of Late Archaic complex culture has been debated. Some researchers thought that it must have arisen on the coast because of the rich marine resources there. Others cited the highlands' environmental diversity and instability as factors encouraging the development of cultural complexity. But there is as yet no evidence that Archaic complex cultures were earlier in one environmental zone or another. Nonetheless, coastal populations appear to have been larger and concentrated in larger settlements than highlands populations. Monumental public structures are larger and more numerous in coastal sites than in highland sites. The construction work groups and audiences thus would be expected to have been larger in coastal settlements.

Relationships between Andeans and people in the Amazon lowlands, which some scholars have seen as a hypothetical source of "Formative" culture, do not appear to have been very strong at this time. The most one can say is that there may have been sporadic trading with or travel to tropical areas. The Ecuadorian coastal lowlands just to the north seem a more likely contact area than the Amazon far to the east beyond high mountains. Several early pottery complexes in the Central Andes resembled contemporary styles in Ecuador, for example, but none looked much like Amazon pottery of the time.

The cultures of this period thus certainly had long-distance contacts but appear to be politically and economically independent societies supported primarily by local resources. There is little evidence for food exchange or regular seasonal relocation of settlements. Long-distance trade appears to have been for luxuries and industrial needs, including salt for preserving food, rather than for food itself, which was produced locally. Rather than moving from place to place as the seasons changed, people seem to have relied on the mix of resources in the immediate areas of their settlements. Accordingly, there were distinct regional differences in health and stature. People in arid highland basins were shorter and had more nutritional and/or disease pathologies in their bones than coastal people. General health status in this period appears to have been less favorable than in the Paleoindian and Early Archaic periods, perhaps because crowding, air and water pollution, lower-quality food, and fuel scarcity developed as settlements became more permanent.

In terms of human organization, the transition to the Late Archaic on the coast involved the coalescence of local corporate groups in river valleys in order to carry out substantial projects of cultivation, ritual constructions, crafts, and trade. At the same time, a shift in environmental focus of coastal populations took place. The deteriorated fog woodlands were mostly abandoned, and settlements moved to river valleys farther inland or to the very edges of the shore. Intensive cotton cultivation apparently was carried out in river valleys and the remaining fog forests, and plant collection increased. In the few littoral areas where we have such information, as near La Paloma, Late Archaic people ate less seafood and more plants, according to human bone chemistry and food remains. Cultigens were still few, however, and agriculture was not yet a major part of the diet of these peoples.

Coastal people's density and residential permanence also seem to have increased. There is much greater investment of group labor and materials in architecture. Large public ceremonial constructions appeared at living sites. River valleys have larger and more complex monuments and settlements than other parts of the coast. Where there are no valleys, as on the south coast, no large complex sites of this period have been found. The most common types of architectural monuments on the coast are large flat-topped platforms or pyramids in U-shaped arrangements around sunken courts. Large well-made rooms on top of the mounds seem to be for ritual purposes, for they have special caches and burials but not domestic remains. The courts lying between the arms of the U have been interpreted as places for meetings or outdoor rituals. (An alternative hypothesis is that they were for cultivation.) The size of community ritual structures increased in the latter part of the period, suggesting that larger groups gathered for rituals than before.

All the coastal mound sites that have been extensively investigated show dwellings grouped around them. Both small habitations for nuclear families, and large living compounds for larger residence groups, are known, but the two types usually occur at different sites. Whether there were many habitation sites without monuments is difficult to say because of a lack of evidence. No "empty" ceremonial sites without habitation, however, have been documented, in contrast to later periods.

In contrast to earlier people, coastal Late Archaic people produced substantial quantities of craft items and art objects. They had the time and skill to make elaborate cotton textiles, fancy beads, mirrors, and symbolic objects such as unfired clay figurines and trophy heads. Trophy heads, found at Asia, near Paloma, have been interpreted as evidence of warfare and human sacrifice, but they also could be interpreted as relics from funerary rites of corporate descent groups.

Let us review the findings at some specific sites. The monumental site of Aspero, situated near the coast in the Supe Valley, is one of the largest preceramic sites in Peru – about 12 hectares – and has extensive middens and various buildings: ceremonial mounds, plazas, and terraces and small constructions that include possible dwellings and stone-lined pits possibly for cooking or storage. Constructions cover about one-third of the site area.

As at other Late Archaic sites, subsistence, to judge from garbage middens near habitations, was primarily based on foraging. The excavator, Alan Feldman, writes, "Excavations in the midden failed to doc-

ument any significant dietary contribution from agricultural produce."
The main cultigens were gourds and cotton, but there were rare finds
of squash, chili peppers, legumes, and *achira* (*Canna edulis*). The many
small fish identified in the midden appear to have been the staple
food.

The seven mounds at the site have multiple levels of stone and mud
rooms that were filled in to form platforms (Fig 4.2). The interconnected
rooms were sometimes plastered and painted. Some mounds are U-
shaped and have a court between the main platform and the two arms.
Among the features of central rooms in platforms are decorations, niches,
caches, and graded access of doorways and corridors. Central rooms were
used for long periods, kept clean, and maintained by multiple refloorings,
replasterings, and rebuilding. In the later part of the occupation, the
rooms on platforms were filled in with bags of stones to create more
platforms. Among the dedicatory caches in the rooms were textiles enclosed in mollusc shells, feathers, string, and cane *ojos de dios* ('eyes of
god' made by winding a cane cross with yarn), twined cotton textiles,
twined baskets, burnt cotton seeds, and leaves. Another cache was also a
group of unfired clay human figurines deposited with leaves. The figurines, including seventeen apparent females and one male, were elaborately dressed and wore headdresses and necklaces. In another case the
offering was a carved wooden zoomorphic (froglike) bowl with what look
like painted and carved gambling sticks. On one platform was a "high-
status" infant burial deposited with a "poor" adult under a legged stone
grinder. The infant wore beads and a headdress, was wrapped in matting
and cotton textiles, and was accompanied by two bundles of textiles and
objects of stone, bone, and shell. A spondylus shell, presumably from
coastal Ecuador, also was found at the site. Some of the beads from
Aspero are like those from other Andean sites both on the coast and
highlands, indicating that finished ornaments may have been traded
between regions.

Due to the monumental constructions, ritual offerings, and elaborate
material culture, Aspero has been interpreted as the site of a chiefdom
society with central leadership by a political élite. The rooms on the
platforms suggested élite rule because they were too large to have been
built without corporate labor, lacked domestic refuse, were decorated,
and had ceremonial features. The baffled doorways were taken to be
evidence of the exclusion of commoners. Even the ornaments depicted
on figurines were interpreted as élite. According to the excavator,

the depiction of the beads on the figurines ties them more closely into the ritual complex involving ceremonial dedication of each new construction level in the mounds, and reinforces the contention that these buildings were a conspicuous use of labor designed to reflect social or political status. . . . The presence of an élite group, or group with élite functions and privileges, is one indication that we are dealing with a non-egalitarian society. As will be shown, the Aspero society was what may be labeled a chiefdom.

But many noncentralized and nonranked groups have ceremonial material culture and build communal religious facilities, so these are not in themselves evidence of ranking or central rule. Because they lack thrones, dwelling features, and garbage, the large room complexes on the platforms are difficult to interpret as administrative buildings or palaces. They could have been group ritual places, similar to the *kivas* of the southwestern United States. The baffled entrances and passages fit the custom of a wide range of societies, including politically egalitarian ones, of carrying out rituals in seclusion or restricting them to certain groups in the society.

There is thus no clear evidence for central political roles at Aspero nor evidence for social stratification. It is difficult to support a conclusion that it was a chiefdom. As the excavator acknowledges, there is "little evidence of accumulation of personal wealth" and "evidence for major social differences is not strong." Corporate residence groups, extended families, or ritual sodalities could just as well have been responsible for the ceremonial constructions and activities at sites such as Aspero.

El Paraíso is a well-known preceramic site and one of the largest complexes of early monuments in the Americas. It has eight to nine large and small complexes of stone rooms. The largest room complex covers 300 × 100 meters and was later filled in with bags of stones. It has been suggested that this room complex was an administrative center on the argument that the rooms were too large for nuclear families.

Jeffrey Quilter's excavations uncovered abundant, thick middens around the monuments, but there was little refuse other than the remains of workers' lunches of shellfish, fruits, and vegetables. A small plaza or patio had a little food refuse and, like the room floors, had been cleaned and resurfaced regularly. The large middens revealed that subsistence was based on small fish as the staple. Anchovies made up 90 percent of the animal remains. Molluscs were much less important, and there were few or no land mammals, such as guinea pigs or llamas. The seafood was supplemented with various plants: squash, lima beans, chili peppers,

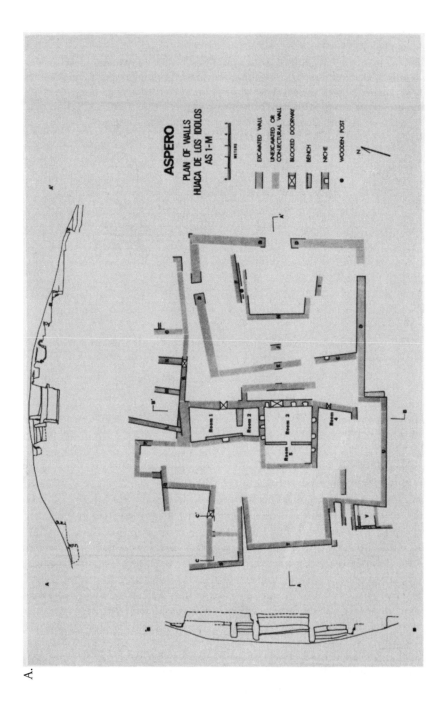

ASPERO

PLAN OF WALLS
HUACA DE LOS IDOLOS
AS 1-M

EXCAVATED WALL
UNEXCAVATED OR
CONJECTURAL WALL
BLOCKED DOORWAY
BENCH
NICHE
WOODEN POST

N

A.

B.

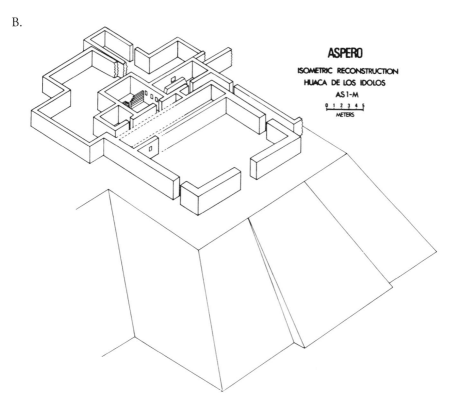

Figure 4.2. Temple of the Idols, Aspero, Peru. (A, opposite page) plan map; (B, above) isometric map. From *Early Ceremonial Architecture in the Andes*, C. B. Donnan, ed., figs. 2 and 3 on pp. 74–75. (Washington, D.C.: Dumbarton Oaks, 1985). © 1985 by Dumbarton Oaks. Reproduced with permission.

achira and *jicama*, tree fruits such as guava, *Lucuma* sp., and *pacae* (*Inga* sp.), and wild sedge roots and cattails. The remains most abundant in coprolites (dried human excrement) were squash, wild potato (*Solanum* sp.), wild ground cherry (*Physalis* sp.), and fish. The main crop was not a food but rather cotton for fishing gear and clothing. Gourds were produced for containers.

The remains at the large site were interpreted earlier by Moseley as evidence of an incipient sociopolitical hierarchy developed to supervise smaller communities in the region and to pool their resources. Recently, however, Quilter has questioned this view. The food resources come from a narrow catchment zone, not a large region, and no possible subordinate sites have yet turned up. The new interpretation suggests that the evidence does not indicate political hierarchy and centralization at the site at this time. Quilter concludes that

El Paraíso offers important lessons for those attempting to delineate the ways in which hierarchical societies came into being because the site exhibits varying degrees of elaboration of some aspects of culture and not others. Although the site is a stone architectural complex of monumental proportions it has not yielded evidence of complex political organization.

At the same time, analysis of plant and animal remains suggests a society that was knowledgeable and capable of intensive subsistence agriculture and yet chose not to conduct it, because a substantial component of the El Paraíso diet consisted of collected resources. Human energy and agricultural technology were devoted to an industrial crop, cotton, suggesting that regional economic considerations rather than local subsistence were the motivating force.

The early coastal ceramic site of Huaca de los Reyes has stone and clay architecture like the preceramic sites. The complex measures 160 × 160 meters in size and was built in increments. Structures include U-shaped mounds, porch arcades, and formal paired elements. Architectural art includes sculptured figures, including a central anthropomorphic image with animal heads on its feet. This art, not found at preceramic sites, seems designed to create a dramatic effect that could be seen from a distance.

The carefully constructed and decorated stone and clay architectural complex at Cerro Sechín is about 100 meters from the seashore in the Casma Valley. Like some other sites, it has recently been identified by Richard Burger as an early ceramic site rather than a Formative site contemporary with Chavín, as was thought earlier.

Like other Initial period pottery sites, this one has architectural amenities such as columned porches. One of the wood and cordage columns of a porch excavated at the site was radiocarbon dated to before 2,240 B.P. The architectural art is more elaborate than most preceramic art and includes formal arrangements focused on central images. Paired, herald-like figures flank apparent sacrificial victims who are nude, bloody, in tumbled posture, with streaming hair, and accompanied with disembodied eyeballs. Such images of mutilation may reflect practices associated with war ideology, such as sacrifice of captives. Animals identified in the iconography include felines and fish. Split-pupil eyes on some images are thought to indicate supernatural beings. This eye type was one of the

Late Archaic images originally thought to have been introduced from Chavín.

The site of La Florida is a huge mud and fieldstone structure still standing in a Lima residential neighborhood. The occupation at the site probably began about 4,000 B.P. in the late preceramic. The ceramic occupation has three radiocarbon dates falling around 3,610 B.P. It is a large mound constructed of stone-faced mud and fieldstone fill. The pyramid was built rapidly in superimposed stages like the layers of an onion. It is a U-shaped complex with a central pyramid and two low arms. On top of the platform are several plastered rooms. Excavation of one house floor produced traces of refuse, including fish and small mammal remains, mollusc shells, cotton seeds, and a few other plant remains. Artifacts on the floor included brown pottery jar sherds, a stone grinder for red pigment, an unfired clay figurine, and a stone spindle whorl decorated with white paint.

The excavator, Thomas Patterson, concluded that the site could have been built by a work group of about 500 to 1,000 people recruited from the surrounding area. He suggested that the community was supported by irrigation agriculture, but, as mentioned earlier, no preceramic or early ceramic site has produced evidence to support such an interpretation.

Evidence from these coastal sites has led Richard Burger, a leading specialist on the Peruvian Early Horizon, to shift focus to the highlands:

> The results of excavations at La Galgada, Huaricoto, and Huacaloma, along with the earlier discoveries at Kotosh . . . and Shillacoto . . . , should give pause for thought to those who associate the appearance of early monumental architecture and, by extension, early complex societies, with the particular environment and resources of the Peruvian coast.

The Kotosh Religious Tradition

The major highland cultural tradition during the Late Archaic is named after the Kotosh site. The tradition extended over the valleys and slopes of the Huallaga Valley in east central Peru. Many sites of the tradition are found in Central Andean intermontane basins at 1,000- to 2,000-meter elevations. The topography there is rugged, and building rock is an important natural resource. Level land is found mainly in the river bottoms. In the semiarid climate, most vegetation and cultivation are limited to river bottoms and upper hillsides that catch a little rain.

During the Late Archaic, there probably would have been more rain and warmer temperatures. Most conspicuous are the numerous sites of this tradition, located at the edges of the valleys. There, large mounds tower above large residential areas of rough mud and fieldstone houses, each about 14 square meters in area. The combination of a ceremonial nucleus and surrounding residential area makes such sites seem urban in pattern. The nature of the sites and stratigraphy suggest comparatively permanent habitation, and indeed some seem to have been continuously occupied from the Late Archaic through the Early Horizon. One possible explanation for the settlements' nucleation is that people gathered to be near a ceremonial center. Another reason could be defense. But few sites have identifiable defensive works, skeletons do not show the traumas of war, and imagery of sacrifice does not appear until the end of the tradition.

The large mounds typical of sites of the Kotosh tradition are composed of successive levels of stone and mud constructions. Each level was used for a time, filled in with rubble and garbage, and then topped with a new set of constructions. In and around the mounds are large ritual rooms and clusters of small dwellings suitable for nuclear families. The ritual rooms are carefully finished with stone slabs and plaster and have niches for offerings and painted plaster images, such as the famous crossed human hands in a preceramic level of Kotosh (Fig. 4.3).

All known archaeological sites of the Kotosh tradition appear to have ceremonial structures, so architectural ceremonialism was not restricted to a small, élite segment of the population. In addition, there is no evidence that the larger rooms on the platforms were residences for élites. The contents of their hearths and floors indicate ceremonial, not domestic, activities. The decorations, such as the prayerful hands of the Kotosh site, are also ceremonial in nature. Food remains and ordinary tools are lacking. The rooms, therefore, seem likely to have been community ritual facilities for corporate groups.

At the foot of the mound at many sites is a large circular sunken area that might have been used for open-air rituals or meetings. These cover much larger areas than the mound-top ritual rooms, so they may have been for larger groups than an extended family or ritual sodality. At some sites one or two other ritual rooms were built away from the main mound at the side of the residential area. These may have been for initiation or other special ceremonies. They do not seem like chiefly residences, for they are not in prominent positions in the layout and they lack residential refuse.

Figure 4.3. Archaic Temple of the Crossed Hands, Kotosh, Peru. From Seiichi Izumi and Toshihiko Sono, *Andes 2: Excavations at Kotosh, Peru, 1960*, color plate 1 (Tokyo: Kadokawa Publishing Co., 1963). © 1963 by the University of Tokyo. Courtesy of the University of Tokyo.

Much of the preserved material culture in Kotosh-tradition habitations consists of cotton or hard vegetal fiber fabric. The fabric is used for mats, blankets, clothing, headgear, and bags. Simple ornaments, tools, and ritual equipment such as spatulas were used by all. Gourds continue to be important containers, even after pottery starts to be made at some sites. In the highlands as on the coast, the Late Archaic sites with pottery vessels have more elaborate art and technology than the aceramic cultures. Loom weaving with heddles is associated with pottery, as is animal domestication and increased plant cultivation. Several features of these initial pottery cultures suggest the development of some kind of central rulership and ranking: the elaborate personal ornaments, the increased quantities of exotic materials, the presence of a few very rich burials, construction of a single ceremonial room, rather than many, the central anthropomorphic supernatural images, and burial paraphernalia such as litters. Kotosh imagery includes some animals, humans, human–animal combinations, and geometric patterns. Art historian Terence Grieder thinks that the rarity of the images of dominance so common later on means that there was less conflict at this time. Images of sacrificers and trophy heads are less characteristic of the Late Preceramic than of the Initial and Early Horizon periods. The humanoid deity figure, so common in later periods, has fish pendants in the Late Archaic rather than trophy heads, for example. Generally iconography suggests independence and cultural continuity at sites. The populations of the culture were large but did not rely primarily on agriculture. Confirmed domestic camelids are not found in highland valleys until Initial ceramic periods near the end of the tradition. The main phase of the tradition is preceramic and based on a mixed economy of hunting, plant collection, and incipient cultivation of a variety of plants. Later phases of the tradition have ceramics and herding and more plant cultivation. Thus intensive food production was not a factor during most of the culture's existence and cannot have been an important factor in its formation. Unfortunately, the specifics of subsistence are not well understood because of a lack of systematic collection of column samples and fine sieving of soil. Many different plants have, nonetheless, been recovered. Many were assumed to have been introduced cultigens because archaeobotanists believed that they could not grow without irrigation in such a dry environment. This conclusion is not very secure, however, because, as Frederic Engel has pointed out, there was substantial deforestation and desertification during prehistory and more since the conquest, so prehistoric flora would have been much richer. Plants from secure site contexts include small numbers of tree fruits, root crops, chili peppers, squash, and beans, but no maize. There may have been small-scale irrigation at some sites, or terraced orchards or small gardens. At sites in drier environments, there is little animal bone, but at moister sites near the tropical forest, animal bone is abundant. Representation of animals at sites differs. At Kotosh, deer bone was very important, while at other sites, camelid bone predominated.

Interregional communication is documented in material culture throughout the period. There was some long-distance trade in food, such as marine shellfish, but much less than later. A few ornamental items, such as turquoise for beads, were imported. Trade goods seem to have been valued. Many of the sites are in possible passageways between the eastern lowlands of Peru, the highlands, and the coast.

One fascinating site in the Kotosh tradition is La Galgada, at about 1,000-meter elevation on the Tablachaca River in Pallasca Province of Peru. This rich site was occupied between 4,400 and 3,900 B.P. Most of the site is preceramic, and the early ceramic period came only at the very end of the occupation.

The many mounds at the site consist of layer upon layer of semisubterranean ritual chambers rather similar to *kivas*. To accommodate progressively larger areas of construction, the main mound was enlarged three times. The mounds were faced with stone revetment walls, but there is no evidence of defensive walls. At any point in time, the tops of the mounds supported several ritual chambers carefully built of stones, adobe, and mud finished with plaster. The rooms, an average of 35 square meters in area, have central sunken hearths for burnt sacrifices and ventilators running under the doorways. Many also have benches, niches for storage or display, *dados*, and painted decoration. They were entered from above by descending stairs. Their ceilings appear to have been constructed of logs plastered with clay.

The fact that each mound level had several such chambers, the relatively large size of the chambers, their communal seating arrangements, and large central hearth, all suggest that these were ceremonial meeting places for segmentary corporate-descent groups, such as extended families, lineages, clans, or else for sodalities, according to the excavator, T. Grieder. Few differences exist between ritual rooms that could not be explained by chronology of building (the first being the central one), or by the size of the group using the chamber. This situation changes during the early pottery occupation, when the top of the mound becomes taken over by a single U-shaped sunken ritual building over 225 square meters in area. This room could probably seat fifty people along the benches. At this time, pottery vessels, the heddle loom, and Chavinoid images appear at the site. By the time of the final occupation, a U-shaped court is built.

After many years of use, during which a ritual chamber was carefully maintained and renovated, it was taken out of regular use and turned into a collective burial chamber, perhaps when an important family leader died. Men, women, and children of both sexes and most ages were eventually buried in these chambers.

The space between the burial chambers was then filled in and a new layer of ritual chambers built on top of the old, and so the sequence continued. Later in the sequence, additional collective burial chambers were constructed in the spaces between the ritual rooms. In some cases, the link between living and dead was maintained by running cotton cords from the chambers to the surface. Like the patterns of the architecture, the group burials suggest a communal emphasis that fits a segmentary, nonstratified organization focused on descent groups or ritual societies. Burials varied in many ways, but the variations seem related to age and sex. No burials were set apart by great wealth. The burial population was of relatively short stature (157-cm males and 145-cm females) and had considerable thoraco-lumbar arthritis and very worn teeth. The small stature of the highlanders contrasts with the substantial height of preceramic coastal dwellers enjoying access to rich marine resources. Through time in La Galgada, stature tends to decrease, suggesting increasing stress on the sustaining resources. Food from plants from secure stratigraphic contexts at the site include small numbers of tree fruits, such as guava, avocado, *lucuma, Inga* (*Inga* sp.), *achira*, chili peppers, squash, and lima and jack beans (*Canavalia ensiformis*).

The craft production of the preceramic culture consisted primarily of nonloomed cloth, single element or twined (Fig. 4.2). In the Initial ceramic period, the loom and heddle came into use. Cotton was the main material for finer fabrics, and bast fibers were used for mats and containers. Burials were wrapped in mats of *junco* or *totora* (*Typhus* sp. or *Scirpus totora*?) and/or barkcloth and sometimes encased in netted bags. Often the hair of the deceased was cut off and the head covered with a net bag. Modest personal ornaments – human bone pins, stone and shell beads and pendants – and ritual items, such as bone pins and spatulas, are found with all individuals. Bird feathers, bags of medicinal plants, gourd containers, and equipment such as awls or grinding stones are common burial furnishings and cache deposits in the chambers. Like other Kotosh tradition sites, La Galgada artists had a favorite image. Their long-term preference was for the image of raptorial birds paired with smiling snakes.

The remains of this settlement suggest a closely integrated, stable, egalitarian community with sufficient food, more than adequate material furnishings, and well-established ritual culture. Despite the extensive monumental buildings and large size of the community, it does not seem likely that this was a highly centralized or hierarchical society.

The evidence from Late Archaic sites in the Central Andes shows that people lived in permanent settlements nucleated around a ceremonial core. Architecture and crafts were very well developed, and art and ritual became quite elaborate, but sites lack clear evidence for social classes and institutionalized central leadership. Images and ritual concepts were shared over wide areas of the region, but the cultures never coalesced into a true horizon representative of supraregional political control. Despite the use of cultigens, people mainly hunted and gathered for subsistence, and although the shared art indicates some degree of interregional communication and exchange, economies were based on local resources.

FORMATIVE SOCIETIES

The Chavín Horizon

The Chavín stylistic Horizon appeared throughout the north, central, and south coasts and the north and central highlands of Peru during the Formative Period, about 3,000 to 2,000 years ago. The early archaeologist Max Uhle thought that the Chavín Horizon had originated in Mesoamerica. He believed that it had spread within Peru from the site of Chavín de Huántar, the most prominent architectural site. We now know that neither idea could be true. The distinctive style of the horizon appeared first in the Central Andes during the Late Archaic long before the Chavín site was occupied, as Richard Burger has pointed out. At this early time, no possible ancestral styles of art and architecture existed in Mesoamerica.

Julio C. Tello, in contrast to Uhle, thought the culture came out of Amazonia, because images of tropical lowland plants and animals were prominent in Chavín art. However, no art or architecture in any way like that of Chavín has turned up in the lowlands. Moreover, nearer sources of tropical motifs existed in the Pacific lowlands of Ecuador and Colombia to the north. Neither area, however, has convincing candidates for Chavín precursors. Closer to home, Peruvian coastal valleys shared more species with the tropical lowlands before intensive agriculture and cattle and could have furnished the "tropical" images. No doubt people of the Chavín Horizon had some communication and trade with the adjacent tropical lowlands and possibly other areas, but as yet there is no strong archaeological support for a primarily foreign origin.

Although, earlier, the Chavín de Huántar site was thought the center or capital of an empire, accumulating archaeological evidence suggests that the sites of the horizon were politically independent. The concept of Chavín as the pilgrimage center for a proselytizing religion was suggested by Gordon Willey and Dorothy Menzel. But we do not have clear evidence to support that model either. Supernatural human – animal creatures are indeed a focus of Chavín culture wherever it appears, but different centers do not share a monolithic corpus of religious concepts and ritual practices. As did its predecessor during the Late Archaic, the Chavín stylistic Horizon existed among distinct local cultures with often different forms of art, architecture, and material culture. This diversity suggests that the horizon was influential but not centrally administered or rigidly controlled conceptually.

Like Late Archaic monumental sites, all the major Chavín Horizon sites are habitation sites with ceremonial nuclei. The largest archaeological sites of the Chavín Horizon, however, have more imposing platforms and larger architectural complexes than earlier sites. Ceremonial material was not exclusive to nucleated centers. Many villages had abundant ceremonial artifacts rather than purely domestic material.

The ceremonial nuclei are built of earth, adobe, and/or stone onto mountain slopes or artificial terraces. In the highlands, platforms at some sites have interior stone galleries for burial and offerings. Platforms often have communal ritual chambers on top and U-shaped sunken rooms along their sides. The architecture is decorated with religious images. Both stone and clay are sculptured, and/or painted, a practice that began at Initial Ceramic Period sites. Some of the walls of galleries at the site of Chavín de Huántar were painted. Architectural art also includes rare free-standing sculptures, inset bas reliefs, and tenoned heads. Some coastal platforms have murals painted on the sides of platforms. Others are entirely sculptured in the shape of an animal.

In the distinctive art of the Chavín Horizon, animals were important icons. The art also shows anthropomorphized animals and some purely human images. Humans were presented in various guises, the most notable of which are the apparent sacrificial or war victims at Sechín Alto. Human–animal combinations are important cult figures, depicted in large scale at the center of compositions. The central anthropomorphic icons include crocodilians, raptorial birds, and felines. This proliferation of different central images suggests the existence of a pantheon. The images often are flanked by supernatural animals in attendance. The bodies of both central images and attendant animals are decorated with eye, teeth, or fang motifs, scrolls, and other symbolic elements. The snake, not the feline, is the source of the most common added elements, contrary to much of the literature. Night animals such as owls are common in the art and may have related to shamanic concepts and/or worship of spirits of dead ancestors. The presence of tropical lowland animals and plants, possibly indicating influence from tropical forest areas, has been often noted.

The styles and subjects of the monumental art also appear on portable art. Pottery of the Chavín Horizon is for the most part well-made, dark-colored, grit-tempered ware. Two quite distinct styles of decoration exist: a more or less straightforward representational style emphasizing techniques of appliqué, surface texturing, and punctuation, and another style that employs sinuous carving and broad-line incision to execute apparent supernatural subjects, such as fanged animals. In some regions, goldworking was highly developed by this time. Cloths recovered are mostly cotton plain weaves with many-colored painted designs. Bones and shells were carved and inlaid, sometimes with mosaic decoration. As in earlier times, mirrors were made of materials such as anthracite. Evidently, there was exchange in art objects between some parts of the coast and highlands. Craft materials and art objects from the coast are common in highland ritual caches.

Some patterns of iconography provide hints of the nature of Chavín Horizon social organization. The presence of central images flanked by attendants, an iconography that appeared first in the Initial Pottery phase, suggests the existence of paramount rulers with a household of retainers. Such rulers seem to have existed in the Late Intermediate Period and are described in recorded oral histories. In addition, what is known of Contact Period native symbolism in Peru suggests that the symbolic elements added to art figures relate to concepts of divine rulership. In late prehistoric and early historic times in Peru, fangs as ornaments are associated with the ancestral, supernatural power of rulers. Both raptors and felines figure in warlike kingly titles in the documents. Further, in lists of chiefly honorifics and origin stories, there is an ancestral élite caste descended from a supernatural snake. Such icons at Chavinoid sites suggest that the institution of king or paramount chief had come into being at least by this time in the Central Andes. Whether social stratification existed at the time is less certain. There is as yet no certain evidence for group differentiation of residences or burials. Platforms and ritual rooms at sites vary in size and quality, but it is unclear whether they represent the difference between domestic and religious facilities or between rich and poor. The few very rich burials could be simply the relatives of the rulers.

When archaeologists were developing the definition of the Chavín Horizon in the 1960s, they expected that such an innovative, influential, sophisticated culture had to be an agricultural society. However, sites of the Horizon show a pattern of mixed subsistence with only incipient reliance on farming and herding. For example, hunting and collecting were still more important quantitatively than herding and cultivation at major highland centers such as Kotosh during Chavín Horizon phases. Maize was not yet a major cultigen. The plant is rare or absent from most sites although already represented in art, in stone sculpture at Chavín, and on pottery at Kotosh. The role of animals varies by region. Camelids were important foods at many highland sites, such as Chavín itself, but it is not known whether the camelids were domesticated yet or not. At Kotosh, by contrast, deer make up 40 to 55 percent of faunal food. In lowland sites with coastal Chavín occupations, such as Huaca Prieta, food remains indicate a mixed subsistence, as was the case earlier, but there are some new cultigens from afar. The tropical root crop manioc was cultivated as well as potatoes originally from the highlands. Thus subsistence during this period, although not characterized by the intensive agriculture and export of staples envisioned by early theorists, appears to have been enriched by the transfer of cultigens between the three ecological zones: highlands, desert coast, and tropical lowlands.

Chavín de Huántar

One of the best-known sites is Chavín de Huántar, excavated by Richard Burger, who is responsible for new interpretation of the Horizon. Chavín de Huántar lies near the Callejón de Huaylas on the Mosna River, a tributary of the Marañón, itself a tributary of the Amazon and a possible corridor between coast and eastern lowlands. At an average elevation of 3,100 meters, its climate is cool and semiarid to rainy, depending on topography and exposure. Rainfall is low (856 cm). Vegetation ranges from dry forest to humid grassland. As this is not a good area for irrigation, rainfall agriculture on upper valley slopes predominates today. The very small floodplain is good for maize but cannot produce in quantity. Much of the rest of the zone is too high for maize cultivation. Today the greater catchment of Chavín is important for barley and potatoes and suitable for planting *oca*, *ullucu* (*Ullucus tuberosus*), *quinua* (*Chenopodium quinoa*), *achira*, *tarwi* (*Lupinus* sp.), and beans. Animal husbandry is not described in the sources.

The ancient settlement pattern of the valley included dispersed hamlets and camps with some kind of regular relationship with the center at Chavín. The outlying villages do not have as much of the fancy ritual pottery as is concentrated in offerings at Chavín. They might have been occupied by villagers who supplied produce for the center and visited it for periodic ceremonies. Chavín de Huántar itself appears to have been a 40- to 50-hectare nucleated community on a series of low terraces. During the earliest occupation, the river was canalized and a bridge built across it. Other canals were found during excavations. These waterworks may indicate that crops and pasture were grown with small-scale irrigation, but water control also had ritual and domestic functions, as lustral canals and basins and possible channels for carrying drinking water and sewage. The 5-hectare ceremonial core includes large and small truncated "pyramids," ritual rooms and galleries, and sunken plazas. Surrounding this were other, smaller platforms and small, "rustic" houses and areas of refuse fill. Like other sites of the Chavín Horizon, Chavín de Huántar is not a ceremonial center per se but a residential settlement with ritual nucleus.

Chavín had much expanded and elaborated ritual constructions and a much larger settlement area than those found in the sites of the earlier Kotosh religious tradition of the Late Archaic. The massive main "temple" was built 10 meters high into the hillsides with masonry blocks and rubble. It and other platforms are run through with narrow, stone-faced galleries, where human remains and caches of elaborate pottery were left. The platform is ventilated and drained by a complex of rectangular ducts. There are several similar "temple" structures of smaller size. At the foot of the "temples" were platforms with structures that could have been communal ritual chambers like those of the Late Archaic, or possibly dwellings of élites. These have many superimposed colored clay floors, stone-lined hearths, circular structures and niches, deposits of broken ornaments, special food, such as guinea pig and laurel fruit, and human crania. Like the remains in the galleries, the latter included women, men, and children. Because it has not been possible to excavate large areas, the exact nature of the platform structures is not clear. However, a ceremonial or élite function seems likely.

Contrary to the idea of the Chavín site as the center of the spread of the art style, Burger shows that its occupation begins relatively late in the Horizon, between 2,800 and 2,150 years ago. The three-part occupation is dynamic, and changes occur through time in architecture, habitation, pottery, and subsistence. The site had a small resident population at first and then became large and densely occupied in the late period of occupation. Burger estimates a site population of 2,000 to 3,000 people, with a larger labor force available from the hinterland villages. Settlement is continuous. There are numerous contemporary platforms, many substantial though crude house remains, abundant middens, and repeated repairs and refitting of monuments and regular maintenance of structures.

The site patterning suggests ranked social organization but not stratification, as interpreted by recent excavators. Different areas of the site differ in food and craft remains, as well as quality of construction. These differences may reflect different ranks of people, feasting areas versus habitation areas, or men's work areas versus women's. Structures near the temple were better made, with fitted stone and plaster, and were on wider terraces than those away from the temple. Food refuse there included marine shellfish and bones from young, tender camelids, probably raised for food. Temple areas had expensive, rare imports like *Spondylus* shells and jewelry. They lacked the ordinary obsidian tools and detritus found in the "rustic" houses of fieldstone and mud. These areas, in turn, lacked the elaborate pottery found in the ceremonial nucleus. The outer areas' food remains lacked the marine shellfish and had bones of aged camelids. However, the people of these areas were not poor in material goods. They commonly had objects such as earspools, needles, and anthracite mirrors. The small houses look like nuclear family residences, common in the Andes today.

The varied material culture from the site showed competence, interest in decoration, and a taste for exotic objects. Much of the architecture is decorated. On the outside of temples, rock of different colors is specially cut in decorative patterns. Important art is built into architecture, and there are also a few free-standing sculptures. Over 200 carvings have been found. Most of the sculpture is geometric, low-relief patterning. Representational images include anthropomorphic and zoomorphic supernaturals. Animals represented include jaguar, snake, monkey, raptorial birds, fish, shellfish, and cayman. Various plants are depicted, including apparent manioc shrubs. A typical inconographic device important to the rock carving style is the addition of a partial animal image, such as a snake head, animal fang, claw, eye, or jaw, to a body part of a large figure, presumably to imply a special quality, such as supernatural power or rank.

Most pottery had decoration by incision, excision, modeling, or carving. The decoration mainly appears on bottles and cups. Incised lines commonly ran below the rim and around decorative panels, like much Initial and Formative Period pottery of South and Central America. The finest pottery is found in the galleries. Its supernatural iconography, interestingly, is more closely related to coastal modeled clay architectural art than to the designs carved into stone architecture at the site. Chavín lithics included obsidian and chert flaked tools, many scrapers and projectile points, and a few grinders. Other common items were earspools, anthracite mirrors, and quartz crystals, all found in refuse. Most Chavín obsidian had been obtained from highland sources. The hamlets surrounding the site lacked obsidian, so this material may have been monopolized by the inhabitants of Chavín. Also found were bone artifacts, needles, awls, spatulas, tubes, points, beads, and ornaments. There were rare bones from condors and felines and many from cervid and camelid. Gold scrap was found, giving evidence of hammering, fusion welding, and soldering.

The food economy relied on hunting, agriculture, and herding. Root crops, tree crops, and two specimens of maize have been found, but human bone chemistry indicates major reliance on plants other than maize, which was less than 25 percent of the diet, and may have been much less, because marine food has much the same stable carbon isotopic pattern. Also, the chemistry of animal bones at the site suggest that maize was grown as camelid fodder. Potatoes and other root crops were probably an important source of starch in the diet. Most animal bones are from deer (*Odocoileus virginianus*) and camelids; deer make up 13.8 percent in the earliest phase but drop to 1.4 percent in the latest phase. Guinea pig is rare, possibly only for ceremonial food. Near the temple, marine molluscs and one were found, as mentioned.

The remains of food, arts, and crafts at Chavín de Huántar indicate extensive outside relations, including a far-flung trade network, presumably facilitated by llama trains. Relations with coastal peoples appear to have been active. The eastern Andean location of the site and the imagery in the art have been interpreted as evidence of links to Amazonia. But no Chavín cultural materials have been found in the lowland forest or vice versa. Probably, then, the lowland contacts of the community were limited to sporadic contacts.

Cupisnique

The coastal manifestations of the Chavín Horizon are dominated by the Cupisnique style, which apparently coalesced on the north coast. The coastal Horizon is distinct from the highland Horizon in many ways, but there seem to have been close relationships among people of the two zones. Burger believes that Chavín de Huántar people imported Cupisnique pottery. In fact, it is possible that the south Peruvian coast was in the sphere of influence of the highland culture, rather than coastal Chavín. The material in some south-coast Chavín artifact caches is so similar to that of Chavín de Huántar that Burger and Salazar think that it might represent material deposited by colonists from the highland site. Our interpretations, however, are hampered by the fact that most artifacts were recovered by looting. Little systematic research has been carried out and published on this important culture.

Sites of the Cupisnique culture have major monumental architecture consisting of rubble-filled, clay-surfaced or stone-faced platforms with painted and modeled decoration representing supernatural creatures, humans, or animals. Sunken, U-shaped "temples" are often associated with the platforms. At the site of Sechín Alto, major murals were painted on the platform sides, and there is an allée lined with inset stone slabs incised with the images of mutilated humans. At Garagay, an entire platform was sculptured and painted to represent a huge crab, its main claws creating the U-form enclosing the sunken area. Burger feels that the large Cupisnique sites Sechín Alto and Caballo Muerto lacked residential zones. But, as mentioned earlier in regard to Ancon, it is difficult to be certain about the lack of domestic remains without some kind of wide area excavation at the sites, which has not yet been done. Several Cupisnique sites were found to be built on the foundations of Late

Archaic Initial Ceramic sites, giving an opportunity to study the transition to the Early Chavín Horizon in future research.

Dark and grit-tempered like much other Early Chavín Horizon pottery, there are at least two main iconographic-stylistic groups. One includes numerous pots with appliqué and textured decoration depicting apparently realistic subjects, such as humans, animals, or vegetables. One pot from Chongoyape depicts a mouse eating a seed. Another shows a woman washing her hair. Another group of Cupisnique-style pots bear the sinuous formal carved designs of the Ofrendas styles of the site of Chavín. Burger has suggested that Cupisnique pottery was imported to Chavín de Huántar in considerable quantities along with the molluscs and other coastal objects, but we do not yet have technical proof of coastal – highland exchange of actual pieces. But the fact that the pottery is so similar shows a strong cultural link regardless.

Despite the lack of substantial information about site patterning and material culture, Cupisnique funerary art gives the earliest evidence of the existence of paramount chiefship in Peru in the form of uniquely rich burials with very valuable, elaborate, and varied furnishings. An outstanding example is the enormous cache of gold objects from the site of Chongoyape in the Lambayeque Valley (Fig. 4.4). Among the furnishings in this burial were three crowns. One of the crowns had a frontal-staff god central icon with crocodilian faces and snake and scroll kennings on its body and extremities. The corpse wore gold jewelry of long pins decorated with snakes and birds, huge earspools, and delicate finger rings. The goldwork was executed in repoussé shaping of heavy, very high grade gold, in contrast to later metalwork, which used the precious metal much more parsimoniously. The associated pottery dates to early and middle periods in the Chavín Horizon.

South-coast caches of artifacts have exquisitely painted cloths with motifs very similar to those of the stone sculpture at Chavín de Huántar. Burger and Salazar note that the staff-god images on the south-coast cloths are female, in apparent contrast to those at Chavín. They suggest that the southern sites were ritual centers subsidiary to the Chavín site, based on analogy with Inka practice, by which local patron deities were considered wives or children of the central Inka god. Female staff-deities occur at some highland sites as well.

The widespread Early Horizon regional interaction sphere had its roots in the Initial and Late Archaic periods and was not a new phenomenon.

Figure 4.4. Funerary goldwork, Chongoyape, Peru. (A) crown; (B) earspools.
From Frederick J. Dockstader, *Indian Art in South America*, plates 93 and 94
(Greenwich, CT: New York Graphic Society, 1967). © The Museum of the
American Indian. Courtesy of the Museum of the American Indian.

Other salient characteristics of the Chavín Horizon, such as the construction of ritual monuments and use of central anthropomorphic icons in
art and architecture, also were elaborations of earlier cultural patterns.
What seems new are the uniquely wealthy, rare élite burials and possible
evidence for preferential access to residential and burial sites for élites.
Thus, on the foundation of ritual culture and social ranking developed
by earlier societies, Chavín Horizon societies may have developed the
role of paramount leader for the first time.

The Early Central Andean Sequence

The basic sequence of ecological adaptation and cultural development in Central Andean prehistory can be summarized as follows. Tall, robust Paleoindian and Early Archaic foragers focused their subsistence on larger game species, especially water mammals, larger fish, and herd animals. The people were healthy but overworked. Their material culture seems sparse and simple but adequate for survival. In the early forager period, people lived in small and large communities of nuclear family households with varying permanence. Children were highly valued and buried with the most valuables. Although little is known of Paleoindian ritual, Early Archaic foragers routinely left offerings in their sites. Both groups buried their dead with reverence, and sometimes fear, in the case of Archaic people.

Later Archaic people specialized in the hunting of smaller game, fishing and shellfishing, and plant collecting on the coast, and camelid and deer hunting in the highlands. Coastal peoples seem taller and healthier than inland people, presumably because of the availability of abundant seafood, but overall pathologies of disease and nutritional stress increase in frequency. Sites tended to be in or near river valleys and were larger and more permanent than earlier sites. In many areas, cultivation of industrial plants began and soon was intensified, although food plants were rarely cultivated. Material culture became more elaborate than before, and nonutilitarian crafts and ritual activities became important. Most people had similar access to resources and wealth, but children were given special gifts in burial furnishings. Monumental platforms for rituals and meetings were constructed with community cooperation. During the period, styles of art and architecture spread widely through different regions. The end of the period sees a spurt of innovation and elaboration in crafts and architecture. Animals predominate in iconography, but humans are also depicted.

Early Horizon groups made the transition to substantial reliance on agriculture and animal husbandry. Their sites, although similar to Late Forager ones, are larger and more elaborate. Some sites have dramatically decorated architecture in colored mud or carved stone, and large quantities of fine pottery and other materials were produced. The formal anthropomorphic images that first appeared in the Archaic became an important focus of art in the Early Horizon. For the first time, there may have been discernible differences in quality of life within communities. Children continued to be accorded special burial status. A few adults have vastly richer graves than others and possibly more elaborate dwellings. Such individuals may have served as paramount community leaders.

The periods of Central Andean prehistory that come after the Chavín Horizon are discussed by other authors in this volume. We mention them here briefly with regard to their role in the rise of complex culture and development of the state in the Andes. Although few authors still hold to the idea that the earlier cultures, discussed previously, represent the development of bureaucratic states or empires, many do feel that following periods represented such developments.

In comparison with earlier periods, in the Early Intermediate, occupation sites grew in size and complexity, and material and ritual culture continued to be elaborated. Small groups gained access to more goods and ritual knowledge than others and were buried in special monumental sites. Most people, however, still had similar goods and ritual services available to them, so elaborate social hierarchies are not indicated. Additionally, major ritual centers may have been occupied only for periodic ceremonies. After the breakup of the Chavín Horizon interaction patterns, some local cultures extended their influence over several adjacent valleys. According to Izumi Shimada, however, central administrative control over these regions is not in evidence, and local populations seem to have continued in place. Large-scale, regional defensive works were not common, although individual settlements were sometimes fortified. Traditional animal and supernatural art imagery expanded to include complex scenes of humans interacting in various guises, a tradition that continues in Middle Horizon and Late Intermediate periods. Mythologized personages, presumably representing concepts of centralized leadership and ritual power, are depicted on litters, biers, and tall thrones, presiding over piles of fine craft items and lording over mutilated captives.

In the Middle Horizon, the Tihuanaco and Wari styles of art and architecture spread very rapidly over the Central Andes, and concurrently élite material and ritual culture was elaborated further and include devices such as string record-keeping. Although some population centers developed, there is little evidence of primacy other than in size. From the Middle Horizon on, different areas tended to specialize in different kinds of food production, which involved production of maize, potatoes, and other crops, supplemented with fish and legumes on the coast and with legumes and camelid and guinea pig meat in the highlands. Despite evidence for transport of luxury goods, long-distance exchange of foodstuffs is not in evidence.

In the Late Intermediate Period, a new set of regional cultural centers arise, each with distinctive styles, but neither archaeological remains nor ethnohistoric records indicate that there were bureaucratic administrations centered at the main sites. Rather, they indicate the existence of paramount rulers with a rather myopic focus on maintaining their households and retainers and furnishing funerary shrines for their ancestors.

Hinterland settlements appear to have been politically independent and produced most of their own food and crafts. By this time, however, some communities may have begun the custom of holding parcels of land in different ecological zones, to produce special goods, such as coca, or to take advantage of longer growing seasons. Neither at this time nor in the next period, however, was this "archipelagic" type of landholding associated with highly centralized administration.

In the Late Horizon, the Inka, employing both new and traditional methods of conquest and control, extended their influence rapidly over a large area of the Andes. For a brief time until the arrival of Europeans, they administered this large realm using methods ranging from military coercion to acculturation, resettlement, and cooption of local élites. The Inka cult of ancestors continued a long-established Andean tradition. Unlike their immediate predecessors, the Inka employed primarily non-urban settlement patterns.

Thus it can be argued that although Central Andean complex culture had its origins in very early prehistoric times, the first possible signs of bureaucratic state organization appear only at the end of prehistory and do not replace traditional patterns of social interaction. Traditionally, leaders gained preeminence through a wide variety of methods including patronage and gift giving to gain labor and exchange goods, use of force against enemies through an élite warrier group, and cultivation of numinous power through cults of ancestors, captive sacrifice, secret initiations, and impressive public ceremonies. For most of the native Andean trajectory, therefore, societies are more like classic complex chiefdoms than centralized, bureaucratic states.

TROPICAL LOWLANDS EAST OF THE ANDES

The lowlands have long been a focus of debate about the impact of the rainy tropical environment on indigenous cultural development. Many have seen Greater Amazonia (see Map 4.2) as a poor environment for human occupation, a "counterfeit paradise" that inhibited population growth and cultural development, in comparison to that of the arid highlands and coasts to the west. Accordingly, its prehistoric complex cultures have been attributed to influences and invasions from the outside, primarily from the Central Andes, whose agricultural resources were thought superior. The characteristic lifeway of living Amazonian Indians – small groups living in independent and egalitarian bands and villages

Amazonia and Orinoquia

■ Archaeological site
● Town
▨ Amazonia and Orinoquia

1. Monte Alegre
2. Taperinha site
3. Teso dos Bichos mound
4. Guajara site at
   Monte Carmelo mounds
5. Camutins mounds
6. Mina site
7. Lagoa Santa
8. Los Barrancos
9. Saladero site
10. Faldas de Sangay

Map 4.2

by shifting cultivation, hunting, and fishing – was projected into prehistoric times as the product of cultural devolution of Andean cultures in the humid tropical environment. Some scholars argued, contrarily, that the Amazon was a rich environment for human occupation, and a center of prehistoric cultural innovation and influence. But the debate was difficult to resolve because of a scarcity of basic archaeological information.

Recent fieldwork and reanalysis of older work suggest a long indigenous sequence of development, more complex than thought before, and less a product of outside influence. Contrary to previous interpretations, the tropical lowlands of Greater Amazonia were colonized at least as early as the Andes and were the hearth of significant cultural developments and innovations. The sequence begins with a Late Pleistocene occupation of nomadic hunter-gatherers. In the Holocene, some of the earliest sedentary occupations, horticulture, and ceramics in the New World developed in the floodplains. By the culmination of the prehistoric occupation in the period from the fifth to the fifteenth centuries, indigenous societies of considerable scale and cultural complexity developed in both uplands and lowlands. Native population density increased to levels not acknowledged by most earlier scholars, and large earthwork systems were built in several regions.

This new picture of Amazonian prehistory clashes with the earlier picture of Andean invaders bringing cultural innovations to an impoverished habitat. The foreign attribution for ceramics is no longer valid, because Initial Period ceramics are much earlier in Amazonia than in the Andes. Neither lowland Formative cultures nor subsequent complex societies resemble contemporary Andean cultures, and they are more likely to have originated in the eastern lowlands and spread toward the Andes. Indeed, there is a growing consensus that the lowlands influenced the adoption of pottery, horticulture, and the ideology of early complex cultures in the Andes.

For many years, the tropical lowlands were classified as resource-poor habitats unsuitable for the evolution of civilization, whose hearth was assumed to be the Central Andes. The lowlands east of the Andes, however, have several advantages over the Central Andes for human subsistence. These include year-round warmth and high solar radiation, abundant water, large river floodplains, and large plant biomass.

Average rainfall in Amazonia varies from rare highs of 4,000 to 3,000 millimeters a year in the northwest and northeast, to 2,000 millimeters over much of the region, to patches of 1,500 in the center, south, and north. Except in localized high-rainfall areas, rain tends to be concentrated seasonally from January to June.

The seasonality in the watershed causes rivers to flood seasonally. In the floodplains thus created, the abundant moisture, high solar radiation, and rich alluvium of Andean origin produce a very high harvestable plant biomass and good conditions for cultivation during the season of low water. It is the floodplains where the densest concentrations of people lived in ancient times. Floodplain vegetation of tropical forest, savannah, and swamp forest includes large groves of fruit-bearing palm trees, such as *moriche* (*Mauritia* spp. and *acai* (*Euterpe oleracea*). The backwater lakes and streams in the floodplains abound in fish, turtles, and shellfish. The herbaceous vegetation that develops on alluvium in the dry season is often edible to humans and attracts game animals such as capybara.

Fishing is primarily a dry season activity because fish congregate in the reduced volume of the rivers at that time. Species such as manatee (*Trichechus inunguis*), dolphin, *Inia geoffrensis* and *Sotalia fluviatalis*, the large fish *pirarucu* (*Arapima gigas*), numerous catfishes, and small characins, characins such as piranha (*Serrasalmus* spp.) and *Hoplias malabaricus*, all become easy to catch. In the rainy season, fishing is unproductive in the large volume of silty water, but many trees fruit at this time, and land game becomes more accessible on the islands of land created by flooding.

The quality of interfluvial or *terra firme* lands varies greatly with geology. There are poor soils on the South American shield rocks and Amazon high plains, but the soils are rich on higher river terraces, with limestones and basic volcanic rocks in both the upper and lower Amazon. The very tall, diverse, multistoryed forest called "seasonal evergreen rain forest" or "semideciduous rain forest" is found in areas with richer soils and seasonal rainfall in the upper and lower Amazon. It harbors concentrations of useful tree species such as Brazil nut (*Bertholettia excelsa*), the silk cotton tree or kapok (*Ceiba pentandra*), jutaí (*Hymenaea courbaril*), and achua (*Sacoglottis guianensis*). The trees attract varied game, including tapirs (*Tapirus americanus*), monkeys, and deer (*Mazama* spp.). In areas of the highest rainfall and low-nutrient, kaolinitic soils, as in the Rio Negro drainage of the northwest Amazon, the forest is shorter and less complex structurally and biologically. Patches of more open savannah vegetation, sometimes quite extensive, occur in most regions. These are associated with varying combinations of droughty, poor soils, seasonal as well as nonseasonal rainfall regimes, and impeded drainage of high-nutrient soils. Game is scarcer in the hyper-humid forests and upland savannahs than in the seasonal evergreen forest. In areas with richer soils, permanent agriculture has long been practiced, and even on poor soils, slash-and-burn cultivation has been widely used.

The Amazon environment has changed over time. At several times in the Pleistocene (the last 2 million years), slightly cooler and drier than today, and with the lower sea levels, surface water and floodplains were less extensive. By the late Pleistocene, however (c. 11,000 years ago), climates were tropical and rainy, and closed-canopy lowland forests and woodlands with the same species as are found today were present. (In the Andean slopes of the Amazon, the *montaña*, however, temperature gradients moved downslope at times in the Pleistocene, and in some areas tropical today some species from lower montane forests moved in with the tropical species.) From 10,000 to 5,000 years ago in the early Holocene, river levels, rainfall, and temperatures appear to have been even higher than at present. The terraces created at this time support abundant vegetation and wildlife and are an important agricultural resource for long-maturing crops and orchard trees tolerant of damp soil.

Humans have had a considerable impact upon the habitat. The archaeological sequence and biogeography of tree species shows that numerous species now very common in the Amazon forests and savannahs were introduced from other areas in late prehistoric times, when human settlement increased and interregional exchange intensified. Such species include cashew (*Anacardium occidentale*) and passion fruit (*Pasiflora* spp.). The present forest also includes numerous cultivated species, such as peach palm (*Bactris gasipaes*), and species introduced since the European conquest, such as mango and citrus trees. Ancient occupation sites and earthworks have had a major impact on the environment, by altering topography and increasing soil nutrients over wide areas.

As a habitat for prehistoric humans, then, Greater Amazonia seems richer in resources, more complex, and more variable than was realized earlier. Probably of greatest significance for understanding patterns of native adaptation and cultural development are the plentiful resources in certain areas for long-term support for hunting and gathering peoples, as well as for horticulturalists and agriculturalists.

PALEOINDIANS IN AMAZONIA

There is now secure evidence for human occupation in several parts of the Amazon Basin and its environs during the Late Pleistocene and Early Holocene (see Map 4.2). This evidence consists of numerous surface finds of finely flaked lithics, stratified preceramic deposits in caves and rock shelters, and a number of Initial Ceramic Period shellmounds. These finds document an early occupation of considerable extent and complexity, comprising Paleoindian and Early Archaic nomadic foragers and Archaic floodplain foragers using pottery.

Secure evidence for Paleoindian occupations in Greater Amazonia was hard to come by until recently. Although Amazonian archaeologists have expected that Paleoindian remains would eventually be found, Paleoindian experts specializing in North America have long believed that the tropical forest and riverine environments would have been a barrier to early foragers, who, they felt, were adapted to the hunting of large game in temperate environments. A number of Early Preceramic Amazonian cultures have, nevertheless, been defined and securely dated.

The best-documented Paleoindian culture from the Amazon mainstream is the Monte Alegre culture of the Tapajós mouth region in the Brazilian Amazon. This culture was excavated at the Caverna da Pedra Pintada, a painted cave in the Serra de Paituna on the Amazon north bank near Santarém. Related cultures are known from surface finds and rock art sites from Santarém downriver as far as Belem.

The Paleoindian deposit in this cave was a circa 30-centimeter thick black soil layer under a culturally sterile layer at the base of a circa 2-meter multicomponent cultural deposit. Fifty-six dates on carbonized seeds and wood from the layers fell between 11,200 and 10,000 years of age, making the culture equivalent in age to the Clovis and Folsom cultures of North America. Ten thermoluminescence dates on burned lithics and three luminescence dates on soil corroborated the Late Pleistocene radiocarbon dates. The lithics of the culture included twenty-three formal tools: triangular, stemmed bifacial projectile points, possibly for fish spears or harpoons, and unifacial gravers and scrapers, possibly for cutting wood. Quartz crystal, chalcedony, and quartz breccia were the primary materials in the abundant debitage of about 30,000 specimens. Abundant pigment in the layers had the same chemical composition as that in the paintings on the cave wall, mentioned earlier.

With the other materials were charcoal and numerous carbonized seeds from tropical fruit trees native to the area. They included the palm species tucuma, sacuri, and curua and the tree fruits Brazil nut (*Bertholettia excelsa*), forest muruci (*Byrsonima crispa*), jutaí (*Hymenaea courbaril*), apiranga (*Mouriri apiranga*), pichuna, taruma (*Vitex* sp.), and achua (*Saccoglottis guianensis*). Few faunal remains were recovered in the sandy soil. However, soil flotation produced carbonized fragments of mollusc shells, turtle shells, and bones of small animals and fish, such as piranha (*Serrasalmus* spp.). There were also a few splinters of decayed bone from unidentifiable larger animals (or humans), but no remains of extinct fauna were found. Stable carbon isotopes of the plants at the site indicated the presence of a closed-canopy rain forest.

In terms of the development of culture in South America, the Monte Alegre culture would appear to have been that of a band of nomadic hunter-gatherers well adapted to tropical forest and river resources. Although their social organization is expected to have been noncomplex, their material and conceptual culture was elaborate. Their lithics are highly accomplished, and the rock art depicts a wide range of motifs, including humans, animals, and geometric images.

In the Southern Amazonian uplands, the best known complex is the Itaparica tradition, dating between 11,000 and 8,000 B.P. Although the culture continued into the Archaic, it appears to start in the Early Paleoindian Period. Many of the sites of this tradition are painted rock shelters or caves. Notable tools are rare triangular, stemmed bifacial chalcedony projectile points and very large unifacial scrapers of quartzite, probably for woodworking. The abundant bones and plant remains in these sites indicate subsistence focused on a broad spectrum of modern game river fauna, and tree fruits. As in the Central Andes, the human skeleton from the sites are generalized Asian physical types.

The Dourado tradition, known from Abrigo do Sol in Mato Grosso state, Brazil, is comparable to the Itaparica tradition. Although a few discordant dates fall before 11,500, the great majority for the Dourado tradition fall between that date and 6,000 years ago.

Despite their chronological equivalence to North American Paleoindian specialized big-game hunters, the Amazonian Paleoindians appear to have adapted to seasonal humid tropical habitat by broad-spectrum hunting and collecting. Such a generalized subsistence adaptation was also characteristic of coastal and highland Peruvian Paleoindian cultures. Thus neither Amazonia nor the Central Andes provide empirical support for the hypothesis of a migration of big-game hunters from North America down the Andes, avoiding the tropical lowlands.

Early Archaic Preceramic Cultures

Perhaps because of the rapid hydrological and climate changes of the post-Glacial Period, or perhaps because of lowland archaeologists' preference for studying pottery cultures, no undoubted Early Archaic preceramic archaeological sites have yet been identified on the Amazon or Orinoco mainstreams. At or outside the margins of these river drainages, along the Caribbean coast and in the uplands south of the Amazon, several archaeological complexes have been defined for this period.

South of the Amazon mainstream, in the Archaic continuation of the aforementioned Itaparica culture (c. 10,000–6,000 years ago), the diet came to emphasize plants and smaller animal species, fish, and molluscs more than before, and a somewhat wider range of tool types come into use. Like the earlier phases of the culture, there is a stratigraphic association with pigment and rock paintings in several sites.

Several caves and rock shelters in the Carajás region south of the Lower Amazon have distinct preceramic complexes. The best documented of these preceramic Archaic cultures is that excavated from the Caverna do Gavião in Carajás, Pará, in the Brazilian Amazon. This and other caves with painted walls are located in nutrient-rich, hilly savannah overlooking lowland forests and rivers.

The culture is dated by six radiocoarbon dates between 8,000 and 4,000 years ago. Its lithics are unifacial, percussion-flaked, and primarily of quartz crystal. Most tools are simple utilized flakes. With the lithics were well-preserved carbonized plant and faunal remains, including palm and tree fruits, molluscs, and bones of fish and primarily small game, documenting again a broad-spectrum subsistence adaptation to tropical river, forest and savannah habitats. No structures have been recognized. Features in the deposits are limited to simple hearths. The preceramic culture ended when ceramics were introduced about 3,500 years ago. We can summarize simply. The immediate post-Pleistocene Period saw an expansion of preceramic cultures with broad-spectrum economies across the uplands of Amazonia.

Early Archaic Initial Ceramic Cultures

In contrast to what is known of the tropical uplands, several estuarine and riverine areas of Amazonia witnessed a marked change in economy and craft technology in Early Holocene cultures between about 8,000 and 4,000 years ago. The changes involved the simultaneous development of specialized aquatic foraging and the use of ceramic vessels. The use of pottery at this stage contrasts with the practice in Peru, where pottery does not appear until about 4,000 years later. The explanation for this contrast would seem to lie in the fact that the Amazonian cultures of the river floodplains and estuaries had a richer accessible resource base than the early Peruvians, whose comparatively arid, high-energy coasts and rocky mountain habitats may have had a lower harvestable biomass for early preindustrial technologies.

Numerous, large shellmounds remaining from the early pottery cultures have been discovered along the Amazon mainstream and its mouth, some of its tributaries, such as the Madeira and Tocantins, the Paraná

River to the south, and the Guiana coasts and the mouth of the Orinoco to the north. In the last twenty years, nine occupation sites of four of these eastern lowland shellmound pottery complexes – Alaka (in Guayana), Taperinha, and Paituna (all in Brazil) – have produced a series of forty-eight radiocarbon dates that place their beginning securely in the Early Archaic Period between 7,500 and 4,000 B.P. These dates make the pottery complexes the earliest yet documented in the Americas.

Although three of the Early Holocene pottery complexes were known to scientists in the nineteenth century, the climate of opinion during the development of modern archaeology in the mid-1900s was that pottery originated in the geographic areas of later complex cultures in the Andes and Mesoamerica. The lowland sites, therefore, were either not acknowledged or were assigned to a later date. Between 1965 and 1980, however, two of the complexes produced nineteen radiocarbon dates between 6,000 and 5,000 B.P., but most of these radiocarbon dates were not published. Two Brazilian sites, at Taperinha and Monte Alegre, have now produced seventeen more radiocarbon dates (and two corroborative pottery thermoluminescence dates) between 7,500 and 5,000 B.P., so the climate of opinion is changing, and lowland precocity in ceramic manufacture has become more widely recognized.

The early pottery consists of comparatively rare soot-covered, oxidized sand- or shell-tempered pottery made into simple bowls and direct rim jars, some with incised geometric decoration. The lithics include rare crude flakes and unshaped stones used for grinders and hearth stones. Bone and shell were used for simple tools and ornaments. Human skeletons are common in the mounds but have not been systematically collected and analyzed.

Subsistence remains consist primarily of freshwater or brackish water shellfish, fish, and turtles. Mammal and large reptile bones are rare. Plant remains other than charcoal are few, but there are possible plant-processing tools like grinders and nutcrackers at some sites. Absolutely no specimens of maize or other known cultigens have been recovered from the shell mounds.

Thus, in contrast to earlier expectations that agriculture was the economic base necessary for the development of pottery cultures, the earliest lowland pottery is associated with an economy based on fish and shellfish, whose abundance in the rivers and estuaries apparently allowed occupations that were sedentary enough to make heavy, breakable, but fireproof pottery containers worthwhile. The sedentism achieved by aquatic foraging, in turn, may have stimulated the initiation of plant cultivation, a practice that was established in the Formative cultures of the Early Horizon in the lowlands.

Most of the digging at these sites has been in the garbage middens, which are masses of only vaguely stratified shell refuse. However, at sites where adjacent surfaces have been excavated, occupation features, such as hearths, floors, artifact scatters, and post-holes have been uncovered. Some archaeologists have suggested that the larger mounds may have been elevated for ceremonial or political uses, but this has not yet been established empirically. The nature of social organization is not well documented, in the absence of wide-area excavations and cemetery studies. Although some would argue that sedentism and use of pottery may be signs of cultural complexity, the early pottery sites appear more likely to have been simple villages. Many seem to have been occupied or reoccupied for long periods. They have long, uninterrupted stratigraphic sequences.

The shell middens along floodplains and coasts range from about 5 to 20 hectares in area and from 5 to 20 meters deep, indicating relatively large and permanent settlements in those habitats. Cave or rock shelter sites have only thin, patchy deposits, suggesting briefer occupations. Just how sedentary site occupations were is difficult to tell until enough human skeletons can be collected to study for evidence of activity patterns. That some people at least spent time in the interior is suggested by the finds of contemporary sites of fishing and shellfishing cultures in caves and rock shelters near the river floodplains.

Among the most important of these sites is Taperinha, a large shell-mound near Santarém in the Brazilian Amazon that was first excavated by Charles Hartt, a geologist from Harvard University, in the 1870s. He concluded that the site was a village of early pottery-age fishing people. Subsequent excavations at the site in 1987 and 1993 have produced thirteen dates between 7,000 and 6,000 B.P., confirming the Late Archaic placement of the culture. To make certain that the early dates were not an anomaly, radiocarbon dates were run on pottery sherds as well as charcoal and shell.

Like much of the early pottery, Taperinha pottery is mostly grit-tempered. Only a small amount is shell-tempered. Despite its great age, the pottery bears curvilinear incision on and below the rims of a small proportion of the vessels. Identifiable motifs include zoned hachured areas and concentric arcs. Some of the pottery appears to have been used for cooking. The dated sherds were found to contain lipids, possibly from turtle or palm oil. Freshwater pearly mussel shells from local varieties common today, fishbones, and turtle bones made up the bulk of the midden. Other faunal remains – including bones of manatee, crocodilians, and amphibians – and carbonized plant remains and other organic materials were scarce in the layers, in contrast to deposits of both earlier and later cultures. Accordingly, subsistence seems to have been focused on aquatic collecting rather than plant collecting or horticulture. The one complete burial excavated is of a young adolescent. Like other early Amazonian skeletons, the individual's teeth were without any sign of chronic developmental pathologies, such as enamel hypoplasias.

Other finds were rare flakes of stone and unshaped stones used for grinding or hearth supports. There were also bone tools: a carved toggle, an awl, and turtle and mollusc shell scrapers.

The mound is 6.5 meters in height and appears to have been about 5 hectares in area before parts were removed by bulldozer for manufacture of lime. Geophysical surveys conducted prior to excavation mapped occupation features along the beach below the shell midden. In the flat areas surrounding the mound, excavation uncovered house posts, hearths, a burial, a wall trench, and occupation surfaces littered with artifacts and food remains. Wide area excavations at the site would be expected to uncover structures and reveal their size and spatial arrangements. Such evidence would be useful for assessing the nature of family groups and activities. Future research in these areas will be necessary to evaluate the organization of the ancient community and show its place in the history of complex culture in the lowlands.

Another early pottery culture was discovered on the Lower Amazon near Santarém at the Caverna da Pedra Pintada, a cave in the Paituna Mountains of Monte Alegre on the north bank. In levels dated by six radiocarbon and thermoluminescence dates from about 7,500 to 5,000 years ago, pottery sherds were recovered, associated with subsistence remains identical to those of Taperinha. The Paituna pottery was tempered either with sand or with shell. The pottery consisted of simple bowls, a small percentage of which bore broad, deep incised and punctated decoration on or below the rims, in patterns similar to those of Taperinha. With the pottery sherds were numerous disk beads of shell, revealing an interest in personal ornamentation parallel to coastal Peruvian Early Archaic cultures. These finds pushed the age of pottery in the Americas even earlier than that of Taperinha.

The south side of the Amazon estuary, called the Salgado, has numerous Early Archaic shellmounds. These are among the largest shell midden sites in the Amazon region. From these have come thirteen dates from about 5,500 to 4,000 years ago. All excavated levels of the sites have produced sherds of mostly sand-tempered pottery bowls and simple lithics. Surface treatment is limited to occasional corrugations or red washes. Several human skeletons were recovered. This is one of the cultures whose radiocarbon dates were for the most part not published until recently, due to the problems they created for current theories that pottery had its origins in the Andes. As at other early pottery sites in the Amazon, the age of the pottery has been confirmed with dates directly on the pottery.

The Alaka culture of Guyana was first discovered in the nineteenth century and then excavated in the 1950s by archaeologists who were proponents of the idea that pottery had been introduced to the lowlands from the Andes. Accordingly, they placed the cultures late in the prehistoric sequence, in the period circa 1,500 to 500 years ago. Their students later collected samples of shell, charcoal, and pottery from sites for radiocarbon dating. The eighteen resulting dates fell between 6,000 and 4,500 years B.P. Because of the idea that pottery in the lowlands could not be early, the sites were published as preceramic, even though pottery was found in all the levels excavated. The dating, however, showed that dates directly on the pottery came out the same as the other dates, so the conclusion emerged that these were Archaic pottery cultures. Few excavations have been pursued to the base of Alaka mounds, and future work would be expected to uncover even earlier pottery at these sites.

We can summarize then that in contrast to the Central Andes, pottery cultures appear in several areas of Amazonia in the Early Archaic, more than 3,000 years before the craft was practiced in the Andes. The economic context of early pottery making may have been different in different areas of South America. In contrast to the association of early Amazonian pottery with specialized harvesting of river or estuary fauna, in the Central Andes, and possibly parts of Ecuador as well, there is a possible though unproven association with incipient horticulture, supplemented by broad-spectrum hunting and gathering.

FORMATIVE CULTURES

In the period between circa 4,000 and 2,000 B.P., there appeared along river floodplains in parts of Greater Amazonia a way of life that seems quite similar to that of living Amazonian Indians. It coincides with the appearance of the earliest known complexes of elaborately decorated pottery in the lowlands, the Zoned Hachure and Saladoid-Barrancoid Horizons. These complexes are commonly classified as "Formative," a term that traditionally refers to early cultures of sedentary village farmers and nascent complex societies. The Amazonian cultures, nonetheless, seem not to have been fully agricultural. Rather, they appear to represent the establishment of villages of root-crop horticulturalist foragers through the riverine lowlands.

As the new way of life appeared, settlements proliferated, communication between regions seems to have increased, and a series of supra-regional lowland horizon styles of geometric-zoomorphic imagery appeared. The decoration commonly involves modeled-incised zoomorphic handles, geometric incision on vessel walls on the rim or shoulder, and sometimes red or red and white rough painting. Characteristic of the decoration is the use of rounded modeled forms defined by shallow grooves at inflections. The predominant vessel shape is the circular or oval open bowl, although griddles, composite-silhouette bottles, effigies, smoking pipes, and other shapes are also present in some styles. Temper varies a good deal and includes shell, grit, sherd, sponge-spicules, and, rarely, caraipe ash from tree bark. Grit temper, usually created by crushing rock, in contrast to the sand temper of Initial pottery, is the most common early temper.

Attempts have been made to group styles into contemporary region-wide Horizon styles, but, as knowledge increases, the variety and complexity of the styles increase, disrupting previously defined stylistic groupings. The early Horizons of decorated pottery are actually sloping horizons that have considerable geographic and temporal overlap. Confusion has arisen from attempts to treat the Horizon styles as contemporary entities that can be cross-dated by synchronous change in their specific attributes. The actual styles of the Horizons are much more variable.

For example, in some styles, such as the Tutishcainyo Phase of the Upper Amazon in Peru and the Ananatuba Phase of Marajó Island at the mouth of the Amazon, zoned hachured incision is important, and modeled incised adornos are rare or absent. In other styles, such as La Gruta and Ronquín, broad-line incision, modeling, and carving are common, and there is complex decoration in red and white paint. The former style group is called the "Zoned Hachure Horizon" and the latter, the "Saladoid-Barrancoid Horizon." The styles that emphasize red and white paint are commonly called "Saladoid," but most of these also have incision and modeling. Some Saladoid styles, such as that of Saladero, the type site in the Lower Orinoco, and of Jauarí, near Alenquer on the Lower Amazon, and Wonotobo of Surinam, combine zoned incised haching, grooving, modeled-incised adornos, and red and white painting. Later styles of the Saladoid-Barrancoid series often lack the red and white paint of Saladero. They are commonly called "Barrancoid," accordingly. Styles emphasizing zoned haching over other decoration are distributed throughout the Amazon proper, and there are some possible related styles in northern Caribbean Colombia. Saladoid-style painting seems to be confined to the Orinoco, Guianas, Antilles, and Lower Amazon, but Barrancoid styles are found throughout the Amazon, Orinoco, Guianas, and possibly northern Caribbean Colombia as well.

These early decorated styles have primarily geometric and animal iconography. The majority of recognizable motifs are of animals. The modeled rim decorations are primarily zoomorphic, and even the common geometric designs on rims and the sides of vessels often represent the features and markings of animals. There are also rare images of anthropomorphized animals. This iconography may be related to the subsistence system of starchy root crops and animal protein. In Amazonia today, such iconography is associated with a cosmology relating animal abundance and human fertility with shamans' propitiation of spiritual "Masters" of the game animals, supernatural beings combining human and animal traits. This manner of ritual complex would have been appropriate for peoples whose protein supply came primarily from fauna. Other than the iconography, the ritual complex is poorly known. Only a few burials or other ceremonial features have been excavated.

Generic characteristics of Early Horizon pottery, such as predominance of grit temper and particular bowl shapes, can be found in the preceding Initial Ceramic Period pottery styles of the Amazon. Given this historical foundation and given the lack of Andean predecessors, the conclusion is that the styles arose in the Amazon or Orinoco lowlands. Nevertheless, local chronologies are not well worked out enough to allow firm conclusions about where the Horizons first developed in the lowlands.

Styles characterized by both Saladoid and Barrancoid decoration appear to be the earliest dated Horizon styles so far, appearing first in the Middle and Lower Orinoco Basin sometime between 4,000 and 3,000 years ago. But widespread divergence of radiocarbon dates at several sites makes it difficult to decide at present when during the period these styles appear in the Orinoco. They are definitely in the area by 3,000 years ago, the firm date of the type style at the Saladero site in the Lower Orinoco. The styles persist in the Orinoco and Guianas until several hundred years after the time of Christ. Barrancoid styles replace Saladoid styles in the Lower Orinoco and Guianas between about the time of Christ and A.D. 500. Although the white-on-red painting of Saladoid styles was originally hypothesized to derive from Andean red-and-white styles of the Early Intermediate Period, the Saladero dates make the technique of red-and-white painting almost 1,000 years earlier in the tropical lowlands than in the Andes.

The earliest possible style of the Zoned Hachure Horizon, Early Tutishcainyo, has not yet been radiometrically dated. It was "guess dated" to 4,000 B.P. Zoned hachure as an integral style drops out of the Peruvian lowland sequence soon after 3,000 years ago. It is followed by vaguely Barrancoid styles until circa 1,200 years ago. Ananatuba of Marajó Island, the earliest dated style of hachure in the Amazon, seems to begin about 3,000 B.P. It also is replaced by vaguely Barrancoid styles, about 2,400 B.P.

The earliest actual dates for a Formative style in the lowlands come from the middle levels of Caverna da Pedra Pintada at Monte Alegre in the Lower Amazon. The style, called "Aroxí," is characterized by reddish-orange, grit-tempered pottery with Barrancoid shallow broad-line incision and griddles. Two radiocarbon dates on human bone and a carbonized palm seed are 3,603 and 3,230 B.P.

It is difficult to say how these Early Formative sites were organized. Few of them have been documented, and many lie under more than a meter of later sediments. The majority have been found along river floodplains, but little reconnaissance has been done in the interfluves of Amazonia. The average riverbank site is about one hectare, and often more than a meter deep, indicating appreciable size and stability of settlement. On Marajó Island, permanent domestic facilities, such as large, fired clay hearths, are found in Formative sites. In several areas, such as eastern Marajó Island and the Bolivian Amazon *llanos*, Formative pottery has turned up in the lowest levels of large artificial habitation mounds, indicating that moundbuilding began in that period. There are also smaller sites in seasonally flooded locations, which seem likely to have been temporary dry-season fishing camps.

So far, no Formative site in the Amazon or Orinoco has been excavated broadly enough to expose the layout and characteristics of the site community. Some earlier scholars expected that lowland Formative societies would necessarily be complexly organized, but the known archaeological sites do not seem different from what a tropical forest village would be expected to leave behind. The people that occupied these sites seem to have shifted from the shellfish–fish economies of Initial Ceramic Period complexes toward a mixed system of root horticulture, fishing, and hunting. Formative subsistence is inferred from pottery vessel shapes, lithics, and floral and faunal remains in sites. Cultivation of bitter manioc is inferred from the presence of griddles in Horizon pottery styles in the Lower Amazon, Orinoco, and Guianas. The thick griddles from Formative levels at sites such as Caverna da Pedra Pintada, Ronquín, and La Gruta resemble those used today in Amazonia for cooking manioc. Manioc processing is also indicated by the presence of possible stone manioc grater chips at several Orinoco sites. Ground stone axes, presumably for clearing fields, are present in Formative sites throughout the region. In addition, the Late Formative levels of La Gruta and Ronquín had numerous 7- to 9-millimeter-long flint chips similar to those used in manioc graters today. In areas like the Upper Amazon, where griddles are lacking in pottery assemblages, sweet manioc, which does not require elaborate processing, may have been the staple crop.

Fishing was an important activity. At Caverna da Pedra Pintada, well-preserved fish and turtle bones were common in Formative levels. At Tutishcainyo, the pottery has fish bones and scales embedded in the paste. Rare, triangular, stemmed quartz projectile points of comparatively small size found at La Gruta and Ronquín sites are thought to be arrow points, probably for hunting smaller animals or fish. And, although fauna were poorly preserved in the sandy soil at those sites, there were identifiable fragments of fishbones (Pimelodidae and Nematognathi), rare aquatic mammals, including manatee (*Trichechus* sp.) and dolphin (Phocaenidae), turtle, and rare large rodent and unidentified terrestrial mammal in the soil of the site. In all sites excavated so far, however, remains of aquatic fauna are much more common than terrestrial fauna.

Among the carbonized plant remains of Formative sites, tree fruits and wood predominate. The earlier levels of Ronquín and La Gruta held no seeds of cultivated crops such as maize or beans. At Corozal, Late Formative levels had only a few kernels of corn amid numerous remains of trees. The carbonized plant remains in these Orinoco sites include seeds and fruits of gallery forest trees and wood. None are common enough to be considered staple foods, but they may represent anthropomorphic site vegetation used for food supplements and/or materials.

Stable isotope analyses carried out on several human and animal bones from Barrancoid levels of sites in the Peruvian Amazon and from the Formative component at Caverna da Pedra Pintada showed intermediate stable carbon isotope ratios and high nitrogen isotope ratios consonant with mixed diets of horticulture and foraging. The stable isotope analysis of the collagen in human bones from early Corozal levels at the end of the Formative occupation in the middle Orinoco are consistent with, though not limited to, a diet of manioc, fish, and game. They do not fit the pattern expected of maize eaters, which appears only later at the site.

In many ways, the early horticultural village phase of prehistoric occupation resembles the present-day Amazonian Indian occupation. Parallels are the importance of root over seed cropping, the reliance on fauna for protein, emphasis on animals in art styles, and settlement in dispersed villages. But there is a major discontinuity between the early prehistoric and recent ethnographic versions of this lifeway. The lifeway of tribal villages disappeared from several areas between 1,000 and 2,000 years ago at the time of the establishment of intensive seed-cropping, human population growth, and the development of complex cultures.

Thus the culture of the present-day Indians of Amazonia may be an ancient way of life that has come back into importance since the dislocations and population losses incurred during the European conquest. Perhaps the history of this way of life in Amazonia is a clue to the conditions that made it viable: low population density and a comparative lack of competition over land and resources. As an adaptive complex, the goal of this subsistence system seems to have been to produce a calorie source so that the scarce faunal resources could be husbanded for protein needs. Its disappearance from the floodplains during the period of population expansion in late prehistoric times may be related to the inability of this horticultural complex to exploit floodplain nutrients for the production of protein at a lower trophic level, through plants. For that, the complex had to shift emphasis from starchy root crops to seed crops. Because the intensive cultivation of annuals is a labor-intensive procedure, it is not surprising that subsistence shifted rapidly back to slash-and-burn root cultivation after conquest.

LATE HORIZON CULTURES

The two millennia after Christ brought significant changes in activities, scale, and organization of societies along mainstream rivers, deltas, and parts of the uplands of Amazonia. Changes occurred in crafts, food economy, demography, ritual, and social organization that suggest the rise of complex chiefdoms.

No single Amazonian chiefdom has been thoroughly investigated archaeologically, making it difficult to evaluate the nature and origins of these late prehistoric societies. Because of earlier assumptions about the inappropriateness of the tropical forest as a context for cultural and demographic development, lowland societies were expected to be inferior in scale and complexity to the "high cultures" of the Andes and Mesoamerica. When high cultures were identified in the lowlands, they were attributed to invasions from outside of Amazonia, especially the Andes. But, in fact, present knowledge now suggests that these lowlands societies were of local origin and possessed of a substantial scale, complexity, and elaboration.

Heralded by the appearance of the Polychrome Horizon, around the beginning of the Christian era, the rise of lowland complex societies is late in comparison to the rise of complex societies in the Andes between about 4,000 and 1,000 B.P. Nevertheless, they were not necessarily inspired by highland contacts, for one of the earliest, the Marajoara of the Polychrome Horizon, is located at the eastern edge of Amazonia, and its elaborate art style is indisputably Amazonian rather than highland in geographic origin. Amazonian societies like the Marajoara maintained long-distance contacts, to judge by the Horizon styles and extensive trading in material such as lithics, but the extent of their reach seems confined to the Amazon and Orinoco. The later chiefdoms, of the Incised and Punctate Horizon, such as the Santarém culture, have stylistic relationships with the Orinoco and Caribbean lowlands of Colombia and Venezuela, but it is not established which area was donor because of the lack of detailed regional chronologies.

Early lowland complex societies, like Marajoara, have stylistic roots in the lowland Formative. The archaeological record for the Formative Period, however, seems not to have correspondingly substantial and complex remains and lacks the true Horizon styles, substantial settlements and earthworks, urn burial complexes, and craft elaboration of the late Horizons. It is likely, therefore, that complex societies were rare in

Amazonia until the time of Christ, as was the case in North America. But this conclusion will remain uncertain until archaeologists excavate more extensively at Formative sites.

Understanding the evolution of complex society in the Amazon is complicated by the disintegration of the chiefdoms in the seventeenth century. Survivors withdrew into the hinterlands and formed independent village societies. Many aspects of their lifeways seem a return to patterns that predate the rise of chiefdoms – subsistence of starchy crops and faunal protein, and primarily zoomorphic art styles. This discontinuity lessens the value of ethnography as a source on the Late Horizon chiefdoms and places the burden of investigation on archaeology and ethnohistory. The existing data for these late prehistoric societies is summarized later, and details are given for several sites that have recently been excavated. The records of the conquest period of Amazonia, from the mid–sixteenth through eighteenth centuries, help us frame a picture of the late prehistoric and early historic complex societies. Although by their nature, ethnohistoric acounts do not furnish definitive evidence of social and political organization or reliable quantitative information about subsistence of demography, the sources for Greater Amazonia contain indisputable evidence of large-scale, very populous societies comparable to complex chiefdoms and small states known in other parts of the world.

The archaeological record, which can be considered a more direct source on the late prehistoric societies, supports the ethnohistoric record. Its evidence of population concentrations, hierarchies of site size and functions, elaborate religious funerary art, and subsistence remains suggests that some Late Horizon lowland societies were indeed complex societies. The ethnohistoric and archaeological data suggest that such societies existed along the mainstreams of the Amazon and Orinoco rivers, the margins of the South American shields, and the foothills of the Andes and Caribbean coast ranges.

We can get some idea of these societies from chroniclers like Mauricio de Heriarte, who traversed the Amazon in 1639:

They are governed by Principales in the villages; and in the middle of this province, which is very large, there is a Principal, or their King, whom they all obey with great subjection, and they call him Tururucari, that means their god; and he considers himself so.

Based on a combination of such early historic accounts and archaeological data, Amazonian societies seem comparable in scale of chiefly domains and settlements to stratified chiefdoms or small states in other parts of the world. The Late Horizon societies had large domains covering tens of thousands of square kilometers. Some were unified under paramount chiefs. The paramount chiefdoms were warlike and expansionist, with ranked social organization supported by tribute and by subsistence based on intensive harvesting of field crops, fruit, and riverine fauna. Crafts were highly developed for ceremony and trade and were linked across regions by widespread art styles emphasizing human images in addition to the animals and geometrics of earlier styles. There was a widespread cult of urn burial and worship of the bodies and idols of chiefly ancestors (Fig. 4.5).

Populations were densely aggregated along floodplains and limestone- or volcanic-based uplands. Some settlements were recorded in the chronicles as occupied by thousands of people. Some were, in addition, fortified by earthworks or palisades. There was large-scale building of earthworks for water control, agriculture, habitation, and transport.

In both the upper and lower Amazon, some polities had societal religious ideologies enhancing the position of élites through the worship of their deified ancestors. Specialists had charge of charnel houses and ceremonies. There were numerous diviners and curers. Although women were not allowed to view certain ceremonies, high-ranking female chiefs and ritual specialists are mentioned repeatedly in historic documents. In a number of the societies observed at contact, high-ranking girls and boys were subjected to initiation ordeals and rituals that explicitly installed them in their appropriate ranks.

The economies of the ethnohistorically documented societies were complex and large-scale. There was food production by seed and root crops in both mono- and polycultural fields, hunting and fishing, extensive food processing, and long-term storage. Communities invested in substantial permanent productive facilities, such as turtle corrals, fish weirs, orchards, and permanent agricultural fields. Agriculture around population centers emphasized clear-cultivation and annual cropping in addition to slash-and-burn, which is the main method today. In several floodplain chiefdoms, maize rather than manioc was reported to be the staple food, allowing Europeans to collect quantities of maize while journeying among the Amazon chiefdoms.

Nonetheless, the role of agriculture in the development of lowland complex societies is not as clear as once thought. The appearance of the late prehistoric chiefdoms of the Incised and Punctate Horizon correlates in several areas with the taking up of intensive maize cultivation in the

Figure 4.5. Polychrome burial urn, Monte Carmelo mound group, Brazil. From Anna Roosevelt, "Lost Civilizations of the Lower Amazon," *Natural History* 2: 74–83. Courtesy of the author.

lowlands, circa A.D. 1000, but the change seems to be related to the earlier trajectory of chiefdom development. The early complex societies that have been investigated had highly diversified subsistence economies, not staple maize societies. Manioc continued to be an important food, and numerous other root crops were mentioned in early documents. In some areas, such as Marajó Island, cultivation of local floodplain grasses and chenopods may have preceded the adoption of maize as a staple. At many sites, fruit pits from trees, some of them probably domesticated, became common. Maize does not enter subsistence systems of Greater Amazonia much before the time of Christ. No maize specimens are directly dated before the time of Christ. Both archaeobotany and human bone chemistry show that maize did not become a staple food until circa 1,000 years after Christ.

By about A.D. 1000, maize had become the main source of both calories and protein in some regions of the upper Amazon, middle Orinoco, and lower Amazon. At this time, maize kernels and cobs became common in garbage deposits. Concurrently, stable isotope values of human bone show a rise to levels characteristic of diets with 70 percent of their protein and carbohydrates coming from plants such as maize. Faunal protein, according to both zooarchaeology and bone chemistry, shifts from being the main protein source to being a supplement only. And although fruit pits are plentiful in sites, the bone chemistry shows that fruit was a food supplement, not a staple at this time. Thus full-scale agriculture seems a culmination, rather than a cause or correlate, of the rise of complex societies. As in North America, earlier complex societies had eclectic food economies based on a wide range of cultivated and collected foods.

These societies had a high-quality craft tradition. Artifacts were produced on a large scale, and quantities of high-quality decorated pottery and fabrics, as well as various tools, edibles, and raw materials, were traded over long distances. There seem to have been locations like markets, where intensive trading was carried on periodically. Strings of disc beads, usually of shell, were used as a medium of exchange both in the Orinoco and Amazon, as were greenstone artifacts.

The late prehistoric horizon styles spread rapidly over territories comparable in size to those of chiefdoms described in the ethnohistoric accounts. Horizon styles with the time–space characteristics of the late prehistoric Amazonian styles are traditionally interpreted by anthropologists as evidence of the expansion of conquest chiefdoms or states. Before this period there existed only the sloping horizons – the widespread Saladoid-Barrancoid Series and the Zoned Hachure Horizon – which are interpreted as a product of the expansion of early root–crop horticulturalists throughout Amazonia. These early horizons spread slowly during several millennia. The earlier and later horizon styles seem to represent quite different processes of interregional interaction. The regional styles of the sloping horizons are very closely related to one another and seem of common origin but do not experience synchronous stylistic change. Between the true horizons, in contrast, there seems to have been continuing interregional stylistic communication during much of the late prehistoric period. One model for explaining such communication would be a network of alliances, intermarriage, and war among the élites of regional chiefly cultures.

Associated with the spread of the late prehistoric horizon styles is an increase in the size, number, and complexity of human occupation sites soon after the time of Christ. Occupation sites of this period are often several kilometers long and densely packed with cultural and biological remains to depths of many meters. Many occupation sites are artificial earthen mounds composed of numerous superimposed building stages and ruined earthen constructions. Although small, simple sites are numerous, some sites appear to be complex, multifunction deposits, with special-purpose craft areas, such as jewelry or stone tool manufacturing areas, ceremonial areas, defensive earthworks, cemeteries and mounds, domestic activity areas, and the remains of substantial domestic structures and facilities, such as dwellings and stoves. None of these large, complex sites has been yet comprehensively studied. Most general sources refer to prehistoric Amazonian settlements as nonurban, but late prehistoric Amazonian archaeological sites and earthworks are unexpectedly large and complex.

In some areas of the floodplains, earthworks and sites are the most prominent features of the topography, and raised field systems extend for hundreds of square kilometers. Many mounds are from 3 to 10 meters in height, but their height above the plain has been reduced since prehistoric times by erosion and sedimentation. A typical artificial mound in the Bolivian Llanos de Mojos is Casarabe, more than 16 meters high and 20 hectares in area. Faldas de Sangay, a multimound site in the Ecuadorian Amazon, is about 12 square kilometers in area. Several multimound sites on Marajó Island are more than 10 square kilometers in area and contain from twenty to forty individual mounds (Fig. 4.6). Areas such as

Figure 4.6. Camutins mound group, Brazil. From Anna Roosevelt, "Lost Civilizations of the Lower Amazon," *Natural History* 2: 74–83. Courtesy of the author.

the Llanos de Mojos and Marajó have hundreds of reported major mound sites and many others not yet recorded.

Even the archaeological sites produced merely by accretion of living refuse are massive and often continuous for miles, with 2 to 4 meters of deposit densely packed with archaeological remains and stained black with carbonized plant remains. On the north banks of the Amazon in the Manaus area and near Altamira in the *terra firme* south of the Amazon, there are many extensive, deep black soil sites several kilometers long. These habitation sites indicate a more intensive prehistoric occupation than the dispersed, temporary villages expected by early investigators of Amazonia. Such sites cannot be explained as accretions from long periods of sparse, shifting habitation, for chronologies indicate that refuse accrued rapidly, with periods of several hundred years represented by more than a meter of refuse. According to hearth counts and comparisons with worldwide averages of site area per population, not a few Amazonian sites represent hundreds of people, and a few are large enough to have had populations of several thousand.

Many large cemeteries with hundreds of burials have been found. The majority appear to be spatially concentrated urn cemeteries. The elaborate and varied burials are thought to represent significant interpersonal differences in rank. Few of the remarkably well preserved skeletal remains have been analyzed, but those preserved in museums and private collections show a differentiated population with a broad range of age, sex, disease, physiological condition, and robusticity.

Thus the scale and complexity of settlements in the late prehistoric societies of Greater Amazonia are more similar to the societies identified as complex chiefdoms and states elsewhere than to the settlements of the present Indians of Amazonia.

These late prehistoric complex societies of Amazonia appear to be those that had the most obvious effect on the environment. The earthworks and residential sites established in the period altered topography, soil quality, and vegetation over large areas. In addition, the trees cultivated or encouraged by these human populations became established as an integral part of the forests and savannahs and remain there today. In this way, the "virgin" forests of Amazonia still bear the stamp of these societies' intensive occupations.

The Polychrome Horizon

The first millennium after Christ saw the spread of the Polychrome Horizon style along the river floodplains and coast of Brazilian and French Guiana. The horizon is characterized by a style of pottery decorated mainly with elaborate geometric patterns executed in painting (usually red, black, and white) and incision, excision, and modeling. Examples of local Polychrome styles are Marajoara of the mouth of the Amazon, Guarita of the Middle Amazon, and Ariste of Amapa, all in Brazil, Caimito of the Upper Amazon in Peru, Napo of the Upper Amazon in Ecuador, and Araracuara of the Caquetá in the Colombian Amazon.

The best-known society so far is the Marajoara Phase of Marajó Island, the vast floodplain island at the mouth of the Amazon in Brazil. The culture predominated in the central-eastern plains of the island, a domain of about 20,000 square kilometers. It dates approximately from A.D. 400 to 1100. So far there has only been informal reconnaissance, and regional settlement patterning has not been investigated. Only two sites have been comprehensively surveyed geophysically and excavated systematically using modern archaeological methods.

The most common sites are the artificial earthen mounds, not instrument-mapped to scale until recently. The average mound is about 2 hectares and 5 meters tall, with a volume of circa 100,000 cubic meters, but multimound sites are much larger. Mounds seem to have been permanent habitation sites occupied for long periods. The amount of labor put into them was substantial, and their resident populations appear to have been relatively large. The average population was probably no less than 500 people, so multimound sites could have had many thousands of inhabitants.

The mounds give evidence of long-term, permanent habitation. They are composed of numerous, successive, superimposed occupations as in middle Eastern "tels." Most occupations that have been investigated consisted of a group of large oval or round houses with clusters of baked clay hearths inside, suggesting large, multifamily houses, a pattern found among some living Amazonian Indian groups. Mound community size varies between ten and twenty houses. So far no one has found clear evidence for a temple or other central building. Ceremonial materials are found clustered away from the houses, in areas that appear to have been open or possibly covered with pole and thatch shelters. This pattern, also, is common in present-day Amazonian societies. In addition to the mounds, there were small, nonmound habitation sites, perhaps communities of farmers and fishers or seasonal harvesting sites visited by inhabitants of the mounds.

The abundant prehistoric plant and animal remains excavated at Marajoara mounds suggest a mixed food economy of intensive seed cropping, tree cultivation, plant collection, and fishing. There is isotopic, dental, and archaeobotanical evidence for both cereals and root crops. Rare popcorn-type maize has been found at several sites, as well as smaller seeds of local species. There are numerous carbonized fruits of savannah and floodplain trees and palms; some, such as the valuable fruit palm acaí, were apparently cultivated. Others are species that thrive on disturbance. The predominant faunal remains are small catfishes and characins. These can be poisoned in pools and streams in the dry season and were probably collected by men, women, and children working in groups, as is the case today. Mammals and large fish of the type usually hunted by men in Amazonia are rare, possibly because of overexploitation or simply because small fish are more abundant in the ecosystem.

Many mounds have large urn cemeteries and were earlier interpreted as ceremonial facilities without dwellings. Archaeological excavation at Teso dos Bichos and Guajará and surveys at other sites, however, show that they also have large, deep midden areas and numerous domestic structures. Cemeteries are large, discrete groupings of 100 or more urns placed next to one another in the areas between houses. Excavations show that cemeteries were used for long periods and have several horizontal layers of urns, separated by a clean soil or sand layer. Secondary urn burial is the most common disposal method, but some very large urns appear to contain flexed primary burials.

Virtually all the well-preserved Marajoara material in museums is from the cemeteries. The material is abundant and elaborate, including items such as pottery vessels, statues, pubic covers (*tangas*) tools, and ornaments of imported stone. The hallmark of the culture is the fancy painted, modeled, incised, and excised funerary pottery in the shape of stylized humans and animals. Marajoara pottery is thick and sherd-tempered. Contrary to previous understanding, it had clear stylistic and technical roots in Formative phases and became most elaborate toward the end of the culture.

Iconography suggests x-ray portrayal of mummy bundles. Images related to shamanism are winged stools, scorpions, venomous snakes, male–female rattles, and decorated t-neck shirts still worn for special occasions in parts of the Amazon today. The art suggests a cult of ancestors, a drug complex, shamanism, and initiation rites. Interestingly, although Marajoara has numerous large female figures, it lacks the large images of male chiefs and shaman common in the complex societies of the later Incised and Punctate Horizon. These patterns could reflect the social importance of women, due to concepts of matrilocal residence or matrilineal geneological concepts, and a lack of central political rule in the society. Matrilocality and matrilineality are customary in some parts of the Amazon, but their relationship to general social organization has not been investigated systematically.

Because of the rich material, earthworks, differential burial, numerous large sites, and large territory, the culture was thought a stratified society, with political élite served by craft specialists. However, research so far has not turned up strong evidence of centralized political control or stratification. Due to the lack of studies of houses and grave contents, we know little about the possible nature of ranking, whether achieved or inherited, with economic distinctions or prestige alone. Interestingly, Marajoara males had an average height of circa 173 centimeters, or 12 centimeters taller than that of living Amazonians, possibly indicating a better quality of life. In addition, the lack of serious bone and dental pathologies in the general population do not suggest chronic nutritional lacks or infectious stress. Gum health was not very good, perhaps due to coarse food or seasonal lack of vitamin-rich food, and some people had minor anemic pathologies (*cribra orbitalia*), a disorder usually associated with parasites.

Because early investigators did not expect to encounter indigenous complex societies in Amazonia, the elaborate Marajoara culture was interpreted as an invasion and migration of a population of civilized foreigners from the Andes. Archaeologists thought that the migrants' culture deteriorated on Marajó, due to the poor environment. Evidence of the migration was found in the polychrome pottery cultures along the Amazon from the foothills of the Andes to Marajó.

This interpretation is now questioned on several counts. The Marajoara realm is seasonal floodplain land, not upland forest. The culture was not an ephemeral, intrusive culture but flourished for almost 900 years. In addition, the chronological evidence suggests that the Polychrome Horizon had a local origin in the Lower or Middle Amazon, where the earliest styles are, and spread thence to the foothills of the Andes. The styles found at the edge of the Andes are some of the latest styles, and no related styles have ever been found in the Andean ecological zone. In addition, preliminary study of the genetic morphology Marajoara crania suggests affinities with Amazonian populations rather than with Andean. All in all, the Marajoara culture seems to be Amazonian in origin and characteristics.

The Incised and Punctate Horizon

In the last millennium before the European conquest, another stylistic horizon spread in Amazonia and beyond. This was the Incised and Punctate Horizon, whose pottery styles have abundant modeled ornaments and dense, sharp incision and punctation. Styles of the horizon include Santarém of the lower Amazon, Itacoatiara of the middle Amazon, both in Brazil, the late prehistoric culture of Faldas de Sangay in the Ecuadorian Amazon, Camoruco and Arauquin of the middle Orinoco, and Valencia of the Caribbean coast range, in Venezuela. Like the Polychrome Horizon, the Incised and Punctate Horizon is distantly related to the Formative Zoned Hachure and Saladoid-Barrancoid Horizons and continues the ancient lowland preference for incised rim bowls with modeled rim handles. The Horizon also has polychrome paint, but in styles more rectilinear and repetitive than that of the Polychrome

Horizon. It introduces some new shapes, such as comparatively realistic human effigies and tableaux vessels.

The best known of the late prehistoric Amazonian complexes of the Incised and Punctate Horizon is Santarém. It is associated with the Tapajós chiefdom on the lower Amazon near Santarém, which was described by early sources as the largest and most powerful of the native Amazonian polities. It occupied a large area of savannah, forest, and floodplain at the mouth of the Tapajós River from about A.D. 1000. through the sixteenth century.

According to accounts, the chiefdom was multiethnic and populous over a domain of about 25,000 square kilometers centered on a capital, apparently at Santarém. Some settlements were very large. One of 500 families is mentioned, and the capital reportedly had 60,000 bowmen and a total population possibly as large as 250,000. The Tapajós had a warlike reputation and fought with battle axes and poisoned arrows. They cultivated maize as a staple, along with manioc, other crops, and fruit trees. They fished, hunted, raised ducks, corraled turtles, and collected a wide variety of wild plant foods. Tithes of maize were exacted for gifts to deities, apparently for the production of beer for community ceremonies. Crafts included pottery, basketry, cotton thread, hammocks, arms, lapidary works, wood, and spices. Many items were traded to other peoples. Media of exchange included shell disc beads and jade ornaments.

The people built special structures for sacred objects, and plazas for dancing and ceremonies as well as for threshing. Religion involved worship of idols stored in sacred structures. Important people's bodies were mummified and worshiped as ancestral gods. For annual ceremonies, the mummies were paraded by elders in dances and gift-giving ceremonies, and human bones were pulverized in a drink in honor of the ancestors. The gods included ancestors and gods of marriage, childbirth, crops, the sun, the moon, and rain.

People lived in communal houses led by a house chief under a higher chief while a paramount chief ruled over all. References to warlike male paramounts claiming descent from the sun god are common in the accounts. Early explorers also heard many times that the region was ruled by a female; she was never actually encountered, so it may be that this was a god. Town chiefs often were women. The society seems to have been socioeconomically stratified. There were noble and commoner groups, at least the concept of hereditary rulership, an emphasis on inheritance through the female line, and rank endogamy. Accounts mention a professional priesthood and a noble female oracle. Captives were enslaved and sometimes lived in poor conditions, but the practice seems rare. Marriage was sometimes polygynous, and (women's) adultery punished by death. There were puberty rites. Girls were isolated and scarified, and boys were subjected to an ant ordeal.

From the records it would seem that the Tapajós chiefdom was complex in organization and function, more like a small state than a ranked society. The size of its domain is comparable to that of many archaeological states, and several of its settlements, notably the capital, may have been urban in scale and function. Whether status groups in Tapajós society had differential access to resources is unclear, except for slaves. Whether tribute was for reciprocal exchange, as in ranked societies, or an élite expropriation, as in states, is not clear either. A large and effective military force seems to have been maintained.

The historic Tapajós chiefdom is usually identified with the Santarém archaeological culture, which excavations show lies buried immediately under the historic city of Santarém. Numerous large and small sites of this phase have been found throughout the region, suggesting a substantial population. The site under the city of Santarém appears to be of urban scale and complexity. It covers more than 5 square kilometers with a complex series of deposits including low mounds, pits, caches of fine pottery vessels and statues, and large black-earth middens. Geophysical surveys and excavations at Santarém have revealed floors of longhouses with bell-shaped pits. In Caverna da Pedra Pintada, a cave site near Monte Alegre, numerous posts of a large dwelling were uncovered. Bowls containing fragmentary human skeletons have been found, but so far the skeletons have not been recorded and studied. Many Santarém sites occur in defensive locations on high cliffs overlooking the Amazon floodplain. Within sites there are numerous mounds and round wells still in use today. Some sites are connected by elevated earth roads.

Subsistence has not been investigated at many sites. Small fish, turtles, and tree fruits have been recovered from archaeological refuse at Santarém. In the Santarém levels of the cave site abundant subsistence remains documented a broad-spectrum economy of maize and fruit tree cultivation, plant collecting, and hunting. Maize cobs and seeds of often cultivated fruit trees, such as the palm *acaí* (*Euterpe oleracea*), were found. All the forest fruits found in earlier sites were also found in the Santarém deposit in the cave. But in addition, the cave had examples of exotic fruit species originating outside the Amazon or species especially adapted to human disturbance, such as cashew (*Anacardium occidentale*). Such plants, very common in the forests today, appear to have spread widely in Amazonia during late prehistory due to the expansion of human population, increase in disturbance, and widening of exchange networks. The abundant sponge-tempered ceramic art is complex, with exuberant, busy decoration of appliqué, incision, and painting. Common shapes are bottles, bowls, plates, and effigies. Animal images predominate, but humans are more prominent and may have represented the genealogy of the ruling group. Most of the human images are females. There are also rare near life-sized figures of seated males and females (Fig. 4.7), and, given the historic accounts, it is tempting to interpret these as rulers or their mummies. Male figures are bulbous but somewhat skeletalized, and some hold rattles and wear shoulder bags and headdresses, possibly of shamanic significance. Females wear ornamented headbands and carry vessels or infants. Rare male or female alter-ego figures are thought to represent shamans transformed by drugs into their animal helpers. Tableaux vessels are thought to depict creation myths still important today in Amazonian initiation rites. The animals emphasized in Santarém art tend to be raptorial birds, crocodiles, and jaguars, although many other creatures are represented. Santarém pottery also includes pipes, whistles, and some small small vessels, possibly for drugs. The elaborately decorated pottery is found broken in large caches in bell-shaped pits. Unfortunately, the stratigraphic and structural context of Santarém art is not well known, on the whole, and very little is known of utilitarian wares. Santarém lithics are abundant and varied and include exotic materials, such as nephrite. There are axes, adzes, chisels, pendants, other ornaments, and beads.

Both the ethnohistoric accounts and the archaeological evidence are consonant with the interpretation of this society as a complex chiefdom or simple state, but firm conclusions about its structure and function will require more systematic investigation of its sites.

An important culture of the Incised and Punctate Horizon has been uncovered in the Ecuadorian Amazon, at the site of Faldas de Sangay, excavated by P. Porras. Its region is the volcanic uplands of the Ecuadorian Oriente, where rainfall is very high but soils are rich. Elevations range from between 300 and 100 meters. The site is a huge cluster of earth mounds reported to stretch for 12 square kilometers. Only the nucleus of the site has been mapped and published (Fig. 4.8). It includes several

Figure 4.7. Terra cotta sculpture of a woman, Santarem, Brazil. From Museu Paraense Emilio Goeldi (São Paulo: Banco Safra SA and Conselho Nacional de Desenvolvimento Científico e Technológico, 1986). Reproduced with permission.

large figurative mounds and numerous smaller mounds that appear to have been residential, based on traces of refuse and post molds. The figurative mounds at Sangay depict a man, a woman, and a feline, among other images. The man's penis band seems Amazonian in style, rather than Andean, where loincloths were more common. The woman wears a crescent headdress or hair arrangement like those on urns of the Napo style of the Polychrome Horizon farther downstream.

The varied pottery from the site includes elaborate incised, modeled, and punctated vessels with geometric, animal, and human images, as well as geometric polychromes related to the late prehistoric Cumancaya style of the Peruvian Amazon. The many stone artifacts include volcanic-rock pounders and cutting tools, some adorned with figures of monkeys and humanlike images.

No food remains from the mounds have been analyzed, but contem-

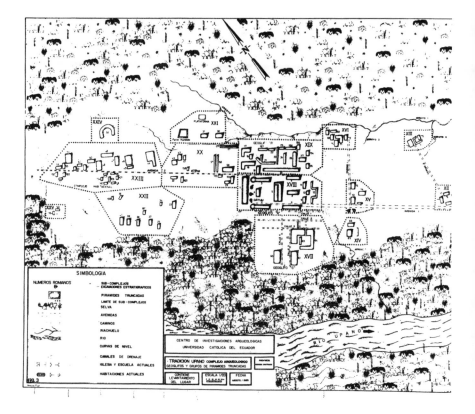

Figure 4.8. Map of mound site nucleus, Faldas de Sangay, Ecuador. From Padre
Pedro Porras, *Investigaciones Arqueologicas Faldas del Sangay*, fig. 3 (Quito, Ec-
uador: Artes Graficas Senal, Impresenal Cia. Ltda, 1987). Courtesy of Artes
Graficas Senal.

porary pollen cores from nearby *montaña* lakes contain evidence of intensive agriculture, consisting of abundant pollen from maize, weeds, and
cecropia, a tree of disturbed forests.

Several radiocarbon dates from the site suggest an age between A.D.
1000 and 1500, like other cultures of the horizon. Early Formative age
had been proposed for the complex on the basis of an earlier radiocarbon
date, but Steven Athens has pointed out that it was associated with
Valdivia-related pottery, a much earlier style than what predominates in
the mound constructions. The site was probably occupied long before
the mounds were built.

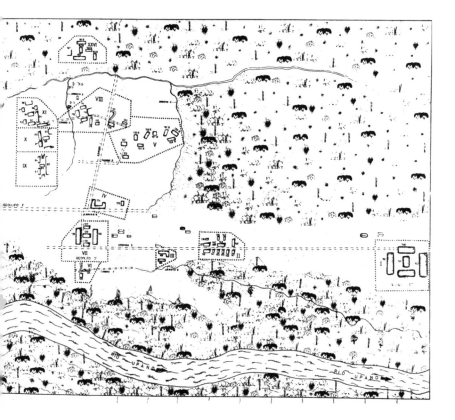

The Faldas de Sangay site is important because it is one of the few well-known *terra firme* sites of Incised and Punctate Horizon cultures. It is a good example of the cultural complexity that could develop even in the interior of the forest away from rivers, when local soils were of high quality.

Research on complex societies in Amazonia has been much less intensive than in other parts of South America. Nevertheless, what data exist document that quite a variety of different types of complex cultures and societies existed in the area, linked within broad supraregional horizon styles of varying extent and time-depth. The archaeological remains and the details of scattered historic accounts of the context period suggest that the scale and complexity of these societies were basically not much different from those of the many complex societies in other parts of the Americas in late prehistoric times. That data also reveal strong local foundations for Amazonian complex societies in cultures of the Formative Period. They do not show the types of early cultural intrusions envisioned by the theories attributing Amazonian complex societies to invasions from the Andes.

CONCLUSION

This chapter has examined the evidence for the development of complex societies in the major environmental zones of South America: the maritime coast, the highlands, and the tropical forest. For purposes of comparison, I have looked where possible at the characteristics of resources for human use, the patterns of demography and settlement, subsistence and crafts, art and ritual, and social and political organization.

With regard to the environment, there were fewer differences between the major zones in developmental trajectories, suggesting that in the long run, the environment did not cause great differences. For example, in the trajectory of cultural development, the lowlands turned out to have been less passive and marginal than thought by earlier anthropologists. Tropical lowland people developed their own types of complex societies. They also were the first to develop some very important crafts, such as pottery, and had considerable influence on art and iconography in the Andean highlands and coasts. Plants first cultivated in the tropical lowlands and certain lowland animals had a central role in the ideology of formative Andean complex cultures.

The developmental trajectories of Andean and tropical lowland cultures have both similarities and differences that seem significant for our understanding of causality. Pottery-using cultures definitely occur much earlier in riverine and coastal areas of the lowlands than in the Andean area, and people seem to have settled down earlier in permanent communities there. However, Andean communities appear to nucleate and start constructing monumental structures earlier than lowland cultures. Environmental characteristics may be at the root of both contrasts. The extensive food resources of lowland rivers and estuaries may have allowed more intensive harvesting and thus more permanent occupation, both of which could have assisted the development of the new craft. In the case of the possible earlier development of complexity in the Andes, people there may have had to organize earlier to deal with competition over the more circumscribed and limited resource base of the cool, arid environment. In the lowlands, where the rich riverine zone stretches from Andes foothills to the Atlantic and where there are enormous forested interfluves available for slash-and-burn cultivation, people could escape social conflicts by leaving to homestead elsewhere, as suggested in Robert Carneiro's circumscription theory about the origin of the state.

This explanation tends to be supported by patterns of human skeletal pathology in both areas. In the Andes, where resources are more circumscribed, stature is comparatively short and shrinks as sedentism, economic intensification, and cultural complexity develops, leading to a general pattern of comparatively low stature in late prehistoric times. In the Amazon, the few skeletons that have been analyzed are comparatively tall, as much as 15 centimeters taller than Andeans. These skeletons date to the Formative, Polychrome Horizon, and Late Horizon. In contrast, today in Amazonia, where postcolonial states hold sway, Indian height is more comparable to ancient Andeans. There seems a possible correlation of physiological stress with élite appropriation of resources in low-biomass, circumscribed environments.

In both the Andes and Amazon, the relationship of economy and technology with societal development in the archaeological record seems different from what would be expected from theories of cultural evolution. Absolute population size is difficult to estimate from archaeological remains, but it seems that the narrow river valleys of the Andes were often more crowded and urbanized than in the wide Amazon and its forests. Sedentism of settlement and complexity of organization predated intensive agriculture in both areas. In both areas hunting, fishing, and plant collecting, rather than plant and animal domestication, predominate in the subsistence of the early complex societies. Only in late prehistoric times do domestic plants or animals become the main sources of food. Although the gaps in our knowledge prevent secure conclusions, the transition to staple maize cultivation may have taken place a little earlier in the circumscribed habitats of the Andes than along the wide Amazon. The Andean Middle Horizon, A.D. 700–900, seems to be the first period when human bone chemistry reached the 70 percent maize pattern. Nothing similar appears to have happened in the Amazon until the Late Horizon, circa A.D. 1000–1500. In both areas, the most statelike societies show the greatest reliance on agriculture and/or herding. But, as described, complexity long precedes this reliance. It is a pattern developed by already existing chiefdoms.

Similarly, cultural elaboration does not turn out to have been as closely linked to complex social organization as predicted by earlier theories. Elaboration in the form of highly developed art and technology and monument building was found in both areas, without evidence of highly centralized, controlling administrations. This suggests that other forms of organization can also make such achievements. In the future, we need to inquire about what those forms may be. Periods during which regional independence was coopted or circumvented by conquest and involved administration of large areas were comparatively brief and seem not to have been a long-term adaptation.

Evidence for central rule is found earlier in the Andes than in the Amazon. Whether one chooses the Early Horizon, Early Intermediate, or Middle Horizon as the first period when images and structures for paramount chiefs or kings are recognized, it is difficult to find such evidence in the Amazon until A.D. 1000. Ranking seems evident by Early Horizon times in the Andes, with stratification probable by Middle Horizon times if not in the Early Intermediate. In the Amazon, the earliest possible ranking seems to begin in the early Polychrome societies, circa A.D. 400, and stratification seems absent until the Late Horizon, immediately before the European conquest in the sixteenth century.

Although our knowledge of settlements may be inadequate for secure inferences, there are grounds for a possible contrast between the Andes and the Amazon in structural patterning through time. We know little about early lowland residential structures, but in the Andes, both small houses, probably for nuclear families, and large compounds are known by the Late Archaic, with coastal peoples building more large compounds than highlanders. These larger dwellings cluster around platform mounds with probable communal ritual and/or political functions. Later prehistoric Andean households appear often to be composed of nuclear families. Platforms and pyramids become larger, more elaborate, more numerous, and apparently more centralized at this time. In contrast, early lowland complex societies, such as Marajoara show evidence of habitation in large, communal dwellings and do not have large-scale special structures. There is no evidence, in fact, of ritual structures much more impressive than present-day men's houses. The Marajoara mounds are actually platforms for entire villages, not specialized ritual structures or political monuments. In late prehistoric times, however, special ritual earth monuments were built in the Ecuadorian Amazon. In the Orinoco, possible élite residences are associated with large, low earthen burial mounds in the western Orinoco Basin.

The iconography of art also differs somewhat between the two areas, although there are some parallel trends. Everywhere animals appear to be more prominent than humans in art of the Early Archaic and Formative cultures. Although iconography of the earliest complex cultures in both areas includes women as central, formal images, from the Polychrome Horizon onward, there are lowland societies with a numerical predominance of female images, a pattern that is rarely found in the Andes. In the lowlands, females appear both in small figures and as the main compositional figures in important monumental pottery. Until the late prehistoric in the lowlands, no identifiable males appear in this fashion. In the Andes, both male and female images occur, but most of the central, frontally displayed, weapon-bearing figures appear to be male. Also in the Andes, images of mutilation and sacrifice are common from the Late Archaic onward, a pattern not found in Amazonian art. In late prehistoric Amazonian art, war and central leadership roles are suggested by the development of iconography of man-eating felines and raptorial birds and figures of men and women on decorated seats. In both areas, the iconography of important supernaturals and political leaders increasingly focused on males, who appear as large, frontal figures holding emblems of rank, rulership, or war. Thus, in both areas, iconography changes somewhat as social and political organization change, especially in regard to the role of humans and choice of animals. The changes are to some degree convergent in the Andes and Amazon, although local species and particular local social forms and practices remain the medium for parallel messages.

In sum, the particularities of environment and culture in the different parts of South America led to cultural trajectories that differed more in the details than in broad patterns of development. Natural resources in both areas were more than adequate to support both the development of sedentary settlement, cultural elaboration, and cultural complexity. Once established, however, complex societies in most areas proceeded to devise increasingly intensive and artificial economies based on the plants and animals domesticated by earlier societies. Along with concomitant increases in population concentration, the development of these later societies culminated in more centralized and stratified organization than is discernible for any of the earlier societies.

BIBLIOGRAPHICAL ESSAY

General sources on South American archaeology include G. R. Willey, *An Introduction to American Archaeology, Vol. 2, South America* (Englewood Cliffs, 1971) who presents an accurate summary of published knowledge at the time and a good bibliography. The recent K. O. Bruhns, *Ancient South America* (Cambridge, 1994) is more up to date but leaves out many local publications that are not in English.

Early summaries of Central Andean archaeology and ecological adaptation are E. Lanning (Englewood Cliffs, 1967) and L. Lumbreras, *The Peoples and Cultures of Ancient Peru* (Washington, D. C., 1974). A more recent survey is the anthology edited by R. Keatinge, *Peruvian Prehistory* (Cambridge, 1988). Earlier summary surveys on the lowlands include B. J. Meggers, *Amazonia: Man and Nature in a Counterfeit Paradise* (Chicago, 1971); D. Lathrap, *The Upper Amazon* (New York, 1970); A. C. Roosevelt, *Parmana: Prehistoric Maize and Manioc Subsistence along the Amazon and Orinoco* (New York, 1980). More recent surveys include the article by Meggers and Evans, "Lowland South America and the Antilles," in *Ancient South Americans*, ed. J. E. Jennings (San Francisco, 1983), and the articles by Meggers (1985) and by A. C. Roosevelt, "Resource management in Amazonia before the conquest: Beyond ethnographic projection," in *Natural Resource Management by Indigenous and Folk Societies in Amazonia*, eds. W. Balee and D. A. Posey, in *Advances in Economic Botany*, Vol. 7. (New York, 1989), 30–62; and "The Rise and Fall of the Amazon Chiefdoms," *L'Homme*, 126–128, 33(2–4) (1993), 255–283.

Still the best summary of Central Andean archaeobotany is M. Towle's *The Ethnobotany of Pre-Columbian Peru* (Chicago, 1961). More recent information can be found in the site reports. Lowland archaeobotany is relatively new and treated in the various site reports and survey articles mentioned in this essay.

On the question of early hunter-gatherer ecological adaptation and cultural complexity, there are survey articles, as well as site reports: J. Quilter's *Life and Death at Paloma: Society and Mortuary Practices in a Preceramic Peruvian Village* (Iowa City, 1989); R. A. Benfer, Jr.'s "The challenges and rewards of sedentism," in *Paleopathology at the origins of agriculture*, eds. M. N. Cohen and G. Armelagos (New York, 1984), pp. 531–558; "The preceramic period site of Paloma, Peru: Bioindications of improving adaptation to sedentism," *Latin American Antiquity* 1

(1990), pp. 284–318; C. Chauchat's "Early hunter-gatherers on the Peruvian coast," J. Rick's "The character and context of Highland Preceramic Society," both in *Peruvian Prehistory*, ed. by R. W. Keatinge (Cambridge, 1988); A. C. Roosevelt, M. Lima Costa, C. Lopes Machado, M. Michab, N. Mercier, A. Valladas, J. Feathers, W. Barnett, M. Imazio da Silveira, A. Henderson, J. Sliva, B. Chernoff, D. Reese, J. A. Holman, N. Toth, and K. Schick, "Paleoindian cave dwellers in the Amazon: The peopling of the Americas," in *Science* (1996); M. Magalhães, *Archaeology of Carajas: The pre-historic presence of man in Amazonia* (Rio de Janeiro, 1994); M. Simoes "Nota sobre duas pontas de Projetil da Bacia Tapajós (Pará)," *Boletim do Museu Paraense Emilio Goeldi [N.S.]* 62 (1976); T. Dillehay, G. Ardilla Calderon, G. Politis, and M. C. Beltrao, "Earliest hunters and gatherers of South America," *Journal of World Prehistory* 6 (1992), pp. 145–203.

For assessments of levels of cultural development during late Archaic and Initial periods, sources include J. Quilter, B. Ojeda E., D. M. Pearsall, D. H. Sandweiss, J. G. Jones, and E. S. Wing, "Subsistence economy of El Paraíso, An early Peruvian site," in *Science* 251 (1991), pp. 277–283; J. B. Bird, J. Hyslop, and M. D. Skinner's *The Preceramic Excavations at the Huaca Prieta, Chicama Valley, Peru*, in the Anthropological Papers of the American Museum of Natural History, 62 (1985); the articles in the volume edited by C. B. Donnan, *Early Ceremonial Architecture in the Andes* (Washington, D.C., 1985); R. Feldman's, "Architectural evidence for the development of non-egalitarian social systems in coastal Peru," in *The Origins and Development of the Andean state*, eds. J. Haas, S. Pozorski, and T. Pozorski (Cambridge, 1987), pp. 9–14; R. Fung Pineda's "The Late Preceramic and Initial Period," in Keatinge's book, pp. 67–96; T. Grieder, A. Bueno Mendoza, C. E. Smith, Jr., R. M. Malina, *La Galgada: A Preceramic Culture in Transition* (Austin, 1988); G. H. Weir, G. H., R. A. Benfer, and J. G. Jones, "Preceramic to Early Formative subsistence on the Central Coast," in *Economic Prehistory of the Central Andes*, eds. E. S. Wing and J. C. Wheeler, BAR International Series 427 (Oxford, 1988), pp. 56–94; F. Engel, *A Preceramic Settlement on the Coast of Peru: Asia Unit I*, Transactions of the American Philosophical Society 53, (1963); A. C. Roosevelt "Early pottery in the Amazon: 20 Years of Scholarly Obscurity," in eds. W. Barnett and J. Hoopes, *The Emergence of Pottery: Technology and Innovation in Ancient Societies* (Washington, D.C., 1995), pp. 115–131. The role of wild food resources in the development of complex culture in the Central Andes is discussed in

M. Moseley, *The Maritime Foundations of Andean Civilization* (Menlo Park, 1975).

Recent reports on Formative cultures and their ecological adaptations are those by S. Pozorski, "Chavín, the Early Horizon, and the Initial Period," in eds. J. Haas, S. Pozorski, and T. Pozorski, *The Origins and Development of the Andean state* (Cambridge, 1987), pp. 36–46; R. L. Burger, *The Prehistoric Occupation of Chavín de Hauntár, Peru*, University of California Publications, Anthropology Vol. 14 (Berkeley, 1984); "Unity and Heterogeneity within the Chavín Horizon," in *Peruvian prehistory*, ed. R. W. Keatinge (Cambridge, 1988), pp. 99–144; *Chavín and the Origins of Andean Civilization* (London, 1992); R. L. Burger and N. van der Merwe, "Maize and the origin of highland Chavín civilization," in *American Anthropologist* 92 (1990), pp. 85–95; N. van der Merwe, Roosevelt, and J. C. Vogel, "Isotopic evidence for prehistoric subsistence change at Parmana, Venezuela," *Nature* 292 (1981), pp. 536–538; A. C. Roosevelt, "Chiefdoms in the Amazon and Orinoco," in *Chiefdoms in the Americas*, eds. R. D. Drennan and C. Uribe (Lanham, Md., 1987), pp. 153–185.

Amazonian Polychrome Horizon cultures are treated in a disparate scattering of sources that summarize dissertations, recent and older fieldwork, archives, and museum collections. These include H. C. Palmatary, *The Pottery of Marajó Island, Brazil* (Philadelphia, 1950); B. J. Meggers and C. Evans, *Archaeological Investigations at the Mouth of the Amazon* (Washington, D.C., 1957); B. J. Meggers, *Ecuador* (New York, 1966); Roosevelt's *Moundbuilders of the Amazon: Geophysical Archaeology on Marajó Island, Brazil* (San Diego, 1991); C. Erickson, "Sistemas agricolas prehispanicos en los Llanos de Mojos," *América Indígena* 40 (1980), pp. 731–755.

Late Horizon cultures and contact period societies in the Amazon and Orinoco are described in Palmatary, *The Archaeology of the Lower Tapajós Valley, Brazil* (Philadelphia, 1960); S. Athens, "Pumpuentsa and the Pastaza phase in southeastern lowland Ecuador," *Nawpa Pacha* 24 (1989), pp. 1–29; P. Porras, *Investigaciones Archaeologicas a Las Faldas de Sangay, Provincia Morona Santiago* (Quito, 1987); C. Nimuendaju, "Os Tapajo," in *Boletim do Museu Paraense Emilio Goeldi* 6 (1949), pp. 93–106; Roosevelt, *The Excavations at Corozal, Venezuela: Stratigraphy and Ceramic Seriation* (New Haven, 1995); C. Spencer and E. Redmond, "Investigating prehistoric chiefdoms in the Venezuelan Llanos," *World Archaeology*

24 (1991), pp. 134–157. The relevance of archaeology and ethnohistory for Amazonian ethnology is discussed in several articles in A. C. Roosevelt, ed., *Amazonian Indians from Prehistory to the Present: Anthropological Approaches* (Tucson, 1994).

5

EVOLUTION OF ANDEAN DIVERSITY: REGIONAL FORMATIONS (500 B.C.E.–C.E. 600)

IZUMI SHIMADA

This chapter focuses on complex regional cultures that emerged on the coast and in the highlands of northwestern South America, from what is now southern Colombia through Ecuador and Peru to the Peru-Bolivian high plains (*altiplano*). In chronology it extends from the latter part of the first millennium B.C.E. to the seventh century C.E. For much of Peru, the beginning and end of this period are marked, respectively, by the spread of Chavín and Wari "horizon styles." "Horizons" are homogeneous styles that rapidly expanded over large areas.

Andean prehistory is commonly seen in terms of alternating periods of horizontal or interregional integration (i.e., religious movement or empire building) and of regional diversity. In terms of this perception, we are concerned here with cultures dating to the first era of integration (the "Early Horizon") and the following era of regional diversity. Cultures covered include: Chavín, which is associated with the Early Horizon, Paracas and Nasca on the arid south coast, Lima (also known as Maranga) on the central coast, Vicús (or Sechura), Salinar, Gallinazo (or Virú), and Mochica (or Moche) on the northern coast, Layzón, Cajamarca, and Recuay in the intermontane basins of the North Highlands, all in Peru; La Tolita, Jama-Coaque, Bahía, Guangala, and Jambelí on lush to semiarid coastal Ecuador, and Pukara (also often written Pucara) and Tiwanaku (or Tiahuanaco) in the *altiplano* or extensive, high plateau grassland around Lake Titicaca (the highest freshwater lake in the world at about 3,810 meters above sea level; Map 5.1; Table 5.1). Such cultures were variously called Mastercraftsmen, Florescent, or Classic cultures based on their material achievements, including construction of monumental adobe mounds, and the artistic and technical excellence of their metal objects, textiles, and ceramics. In this chapter, we adopt the designation "Early Regional Development" (hereafter ERD) culture, as it describes the regional character of the cultures under study without attaching undue subjective value or evolutionary implications to them.

The chapter begins by identifying a number of major biases and limitations of the available data and perspectives and by discussing their effects on the culture synthesis offered in a subsequent section. The chapter then presents a broad-stroke characterization of their natural settings and subsistence bases and strategies, emphasizing creative management of environmental potentials and limitations. The bulk of the chapter characterizes the major material, organizational, and ideological features of selected cultures. Their developmental processes and positions in the long-term trajectory of the Andean civilization are also discussed. The selection of cultures was largely based on the depth and breadth of our understanding, their long-term impacts, and specific features that help us understand the diverse cultural character of this period. The emphasis here is systemic characterization of these cultures, taking into account their broad cultural and natural contexts and long-term historical developments. In the course of discussion, various conventional views of Andean prehistory are questioned, and new interpretive perspectives are proposed.

ARCHAEOLOGICAL DATA: CRITICAL ASSESSMENT

It should be recognized that our cultural synthesis of this time span is far from complete, largely due to uneven coverage of both the vast area under study and different aspects of the cultures. Yet a whole new generation of research focused on the ERD cultures has begun after a long slack period, and conventional views are being tested, challenged, and replaced. Recent shifts in fieldwork location, research priorities, and analytical perspectives also complicate the task.

Biased Samples and Perspectives

Most of what has been written about ERD cultures has focused or been based on the artistic and technical aspects of their craft goods. These data, in turn, have been derived predominantly from analyses of looted and, to a lesser extent, excavated grave goods (overwhelmingly decorated ceramics and textiles) found in public and private collections throughout the world. Mortuary goods have been the perennial target of looters, thus scientific documentation of intact tombs has been important to the

Table 5.1 Prehistoric Chronology of Ancient Peru

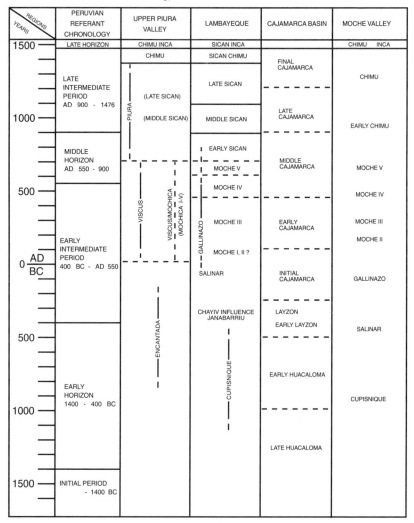

REGIONS / YEARS	PERUVIAN REFERANT CHRONOLOGY	UPPER PIURA VALLEY	LAMBAYEQUE	CAJAMARCA BASIN	MOCHE VALLEY
1500	LATE HORIZON	CHIMU INCA	SICAN INCA		CHIMU INCA
		CHIMU	SICAN CHIMU	FINAL CAJAMARCA	
	LATE INTERMEDIATE PERIOD AD 900 - 1476	(LATE SICAN)	LATE SICAN		CHIMU
1000		(MIDDLE SICAN)	MIDDLE SICAN	LATE CAJAMARCA	EARLY CHIMU
	MIDDLE HORIZON AD 550 - 900		EARLY SICAN	MIDDLE CAJAMARCA	
			MOCHE V		MOCHE V
500			MOCHE IV		MOCHE IV
			MOCHE III	EARLY CAJAMARCA	MOCHE III
	EARLY INTERMEDIATE PERIOD 400 BC - AD 550		MOCHE II		MOCHE II
0 AD/BC			MOCHE I, II ?	INITIAL CAJAMARCA	GALLINAZO
			SALINAR		
				LAYZON	
			CHAYIV INFLUENCE JANABARRIU	EARLY LAYZON	SALINAR
500					
				EARLY HUACALOMA	
	EARLY HORIZON 1400 - 400 BC				CUPISNIQUE
1000					
				LATE HUACALOMA	
1500	INITIAL PERIOD - 1400 BC				

(Vertical labels in Upper Piura Valley column: PIURA, VISCUS, VISCUS/MOCHICA (MOCHICA I-V), GALLINAZO, ENCANTADA)
(Vertical labels in Lambayeque column: CUPISNIQUE)

establishment of relative chronologies and reconstruction of rituals and beliefs. More recently, mortuary evidence has been effectively used in social reconstruction.

At the same time, heavy, persistent reliance on funerary artifacts has stymied efforts to achieve a dynamic and holistic vision of these cultures. Consider the case of Mochica art, which is one of the very few figurative,

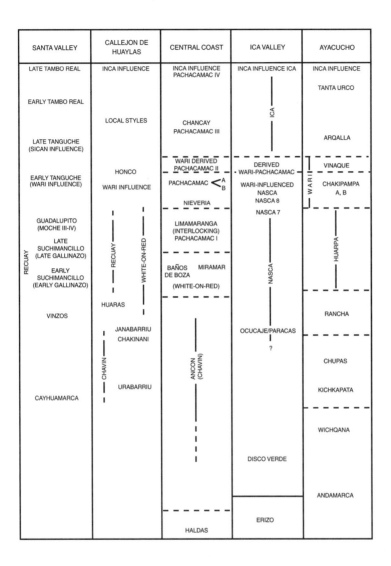

SANTA VALLEY	CALLEJON DE HUAYLAS	CENTRAL COAST	ICA VALLEY	AYACUCHO
LATE TAMBO REAL	INCA INFLUENCE	INCA INFLUENCE PACHACAMAC IV	INCA INFLUENCE ICA	INCA INFLUENCE
EARLY TAMBO REAL				TANTA URCO
	LOCAL STYLES	CHANCAY PACHACAMAC III		
LATE TANGUCHE (SICAN INFLUENCE)			ICA	ARQALLA
	HONCO	WARI DERIVED PACHACAMAC II	DERIVED WARI-PACHACAMAC	VINAQUE
EARLY TANGUCHE (WARI INFLUENCE)	WARI INFLUENCE	PACHACAMAC A / B	WARI-INFLUENCED NASCA / NASCA 8	CHAKIPAMPA A, B
		NIEVERIA	NASCA 7	WARI
GUADALUPITO (MOCHE III-IV)	RECUAY	LIMAMARANGA (INTERLOCKING) PACHACAMAC I		HUARPA
LATE SUCHIMANCILLO (LATE GALLINAZO)				
EARLY SUCHIMANCILLO (EARLY GALLINAZO)		BAÑOS DE BOZA — MIRAMAR (WHITE-ON-RED)	NASCA	
	HUARAS	WHITE-ON-RED		
VINZOS				RANCHA
	JANABARRIU / CHAKINANI		OCUCAJE/PARACAS	
		ANCON (CHAVIN)	?	CHUPAS
	CHAVIN			
	URABARRIU			KICHKAPATA
CAYHUAMARCA				
				WICHQANA
			DISCO VERDE	
				ANDAMARCA
		HALDAS	ERIZO	

RECUAY (Santa Valley, vertical)

sometimes even narrative, styles of the prehispanic New World. The realistic depictions of many subjects found on tens of thousands of looted funerary ceramics continue to entice scholars to iconographic studies, where the depictions are "read" as if they held precise and unbiased, native descriptions of their history and cultural reality. Painted and modeled representations of warriors and combat constitute a critical line of evidence for those who claim that the Mochica polity was an aggressive state led by a secular king. Though a popular view, it has not yet been adequately tested, and there is at least one equally plausible hypothesis – that they show institutionalized or ritual battles between competing social groups to capture sacrificial victims and to confirm the existing sociopolitical order or establish a new one. This debate is examined in some depth later.

This reading of art has also been accompanied by the uncritical use of ethnohistorical and ethnographic analogies. Underlying this practice is the implicit assumption of pan-Andean cultural universals – that certain fundamental organizational principles and worldviews have been widespread and persistent in spite of cultural and natural diversity and nearly 500 years of hispanization with attendant destructuration and catastrophic population decline in the sixteenth and seventeenth centuries. The notion that all Andean societies, whether coastal or highland, had moieties or dual social organization is perhaps the most common assumption found in the literature. Although there are undeniable similarities among historical and archaeological patterns, these cultural universals have neither been proven nor have their temporal and spatial parameters been specified. Yet they have been implicitly applied to ERD cultures.

Heavy reliance on funerary artifacts also has perpetuated an object-centered perspective on culture. For example, although much has been written on craft production, it has typically focused on the "best" finished products found in tombs or only on the final stages of complex, multistage production processes. Thus the range of qualitative variation among craft goods and its meaning remain poorly understood. The common tendency to equate well-made artifacts with élite or ritual use does not necessarily hold when we scrutinize scientifically excavated graves and their contents. The ceramic specialist Arnold suspects that cultures that occupied areas with a favorable climate for full-time ceramic production have greater archaeological visibility. In other words, the abundance of ceramics may not accurately reflect the culture's importance. Further, stylistic and technical homogeneity or the distribution of products is ascribed without knowledge of the location, scale, nature, or organization of production. Looted funerary-context ceramics are usually lumped together as if there were no significant regional idiosyncrasies. It has been only within the past five years that Mochica and Nasca ceramic production sites have been excavated. In other words, while lists of material diagnostics and achievements of the ERD cultures compiled in the 1940s and 1950s have been expanded, few concrete advances have been made in our understanding of how they relate to production and culture.

Excavations of burials and monumental architecture have over-shadowed all other excavations of ERD cultures. Excavation of small residential and specialized sites (excluding cemeteries) to define material diagnostics and organization of distinct activities has long been advocated as a basic field strategy in Peruvian archaeology, but it has seldom been adopted. For example, to date, only a handful of residential settlements has been excavated along the entire coast of Peru, making comparative social analysis difficult. Thus the artifact sample and data we have for Peruvian coastal cultures overrepresent ceremonial (presumably associated with élite) and funerary contexts, as well as their mythological worlds. Little can be said of the mundane with confidence.

These problems are seen in other Andean regions as well. Most ERD cultures recognized along coastal Ecuador should more accurately be described as basically distinct regional *styles* defined on the basis of looted ceramics; their temporal-spatial frameworks are still nebulous, and even the number of scientifically excavated graves is minimal. Here and elsewhere, we still face the basic question of what these styles signify.

The archaeology of ERD cultures has long tended to equate distinct art styles with distinct cultures, in spite of intermittent criticisms. The stylistic differences apparent in what have been called ''corporate'' or ''fineware'' (as opposed to folk or domestic/utilitarian) ceramics have come to be taken as the diagnostic markers of distinct cultures. Corporate style refers to the artistic expression of a powerful (e.g., political or religious) group that uses this style to strengthen and legitimize its identity and/or dogma. For example, the disappearance of the Gallinazo (or Virú) corporate style with the forceful intrusion of the expanding Mochica polity into the Virú Valley sometime around C.E. 300–350 has been implicitly regarded as the end of the associated culture. However, the disappearance of a given corporate style should not be assumed to reflect the fate of an entire regional population or broader culture. We now know that while the local polity in the Virú Valley associated with the style called Gallinazo lost its prestige and value, the biological population and many aspects of their material culture persisted. As a whole, many of the Regional Development ''cultures'' known today are more descriptions of diagnostic ceramic styles and associated sites (distribution) than holistic and systemic syntheses.

Uneven Geographical Coverage

With its many prominent prehispanic cultural developments, modern Peru has seen intense and nearly continuous archaeological research over the past 100 years. In addition to Peruvian archaeologists, scholars from some dozen nations have undertaken fieldwork there during recent decades, outdistancing archaeological advances in the surrounding countries by a large margin.

Our understanding is particularly advanced along the coast and in the South Highlands of Peru. For example, the Moche and Rímac valleys on the north and central coasts, respectively, had become the popular foci of fieldwork by the middle of this century. These are areas of easy access and convenience (near major cities), and they boast clusters of major sites with monumental constructions (regarded as the capitals of the associated Mochica and Lima cultures). These areas have received the lion's share of attention, creating a snowballing process as new findings bring about new interpretations and questions.

However, during the last two decades, a convergence of various factors has brought about notable changes in fieldwork locations and attendant research topics, many dealing with ERD cultures. This shift is partially a movement away from earlier research priorities focusing on the Chavín culture and formative era of Andean civilization. It is also a function of the significant rise in the number of archaeologists during the late 1970s and 1980s. A number of major, long-term North American research projects ended in the 1970s. This relocation was also related to widespread political violence in the Peruvian highlands during the 1980s. Many foreign archaeologists left to start new fieldwork in surrounding western Bolivia, northwestern Argentina, and Ecuador.

As a result of the preceding factors, various ERD cultures began to receive long-deserved attention. For example, a series of complementary projects focusing on Pukara, Tiwanaku, and their contemporaries in the South-Central Andes has resulted in a major advance in our understanding (discussed later). The Cajamarca culture that emerged around 200 B.C.E. in the North Highlands of Peru, with its distinctive kaolin pottery, became a focus of sustained research by the University of Tokyo team.

On the other hand, the Recuay culture (c. 300–200 B.C.E. to C.E. 600–700?), long known for stone sculptures and three-color ceramics, centered in the large, productive intermontane basin of the Callejón de Huaylas and upper reaches of the eastern and western cordilleras has remained quite obscure. Intermittent surveys and excavations conducted thus far have been largely unrelated to each other, and their results remain largely unpublished.

The state of our knowledge is even worse for the Ecuadorian and Colombian highlands, with the notable exception of the upper Magdalena drainage known for the San Agustín culture with its large, stone-lined tombs and associated sculptural idols. The extensive area between Callejón de Huaylas and the *altiplano* at the south end of our study area is yet another area that awaits focused, sustained research. This includes the zones around the important modern cities of Abancay, Ayacucho, and Huancayo. Regional styles of the time period are named and some associated sites are known (e.g., Huarpa of the Ayacucho region), but we are still a long way from being able to speak of the associated cultures in a meaningful way. Their obscurity stems from the fact that these zones coincide with the heartlands of the later Wari and Inka empires, which have been a – if not *the* – major focus of Andean archaeology for the past few decades. In general, a coherent picture of ERD cultures in the highland regions of Peru, Ecuador, and Colombia is difficult to synthesize.

On the Peruvian coast, there has been a notable reawakening of interest in the ERD cultures among both Peruvian and foreign archaeologists. These include archaeologists who left the highland region of Ayacucho with the rise of political violence and turned their attention to the adjacent Ica Valley to focus on the Nasca culture and its role in the rise of the Wari empire. With a long archaeological history dating back to the days of Max Uhle (early twentieth century) and detailed stylistic chronology ("master sequence") established for the Ica Valley by the mid-1960s, the south coast was primed for major advances. Indeed, within the last decade, south coast archaeology has seen much important research, including intensive surveys of underground canals, geoglyphs or "desert markings," and settlements in the Nasca drainage, excavation at the inferred Nasca ceremonial center of Cahuachi, deciphering of meanings embodied in Paracas textile designs, and excavation of a terminal Nasca ceramic workshop at Maymi in the Pisco Valley. However, as in the case of the Mochica culture, Nasca residential settlements and domestic contexts remain to be studied.

On the north coast of Peru, all the known ERD cultures have received varying degrees of attention. With the number of foreign projects on the decline, national archaeologists with local corporate sponsors have taken the lead in many of these advances. For example, the dramatic rescue from looters and subsequent excavations of well-preserved, early Mochica "royal" tombs at Sipán in the mid-Lambayeque Valley by the Brüning Museum team generated considerable interest worldwide. Concurrently, archaeologists at the National University of Trujillo and National Institute of Culture, Trujillo Branch, have been conducting fieldwork at major Mochica sites (Pyramid of the Moon or Huaca de la Luna at Moche and Huaca El Brujo or El Cao Viejo in the Moche and Chicama valleys, respectively) and Gallinazo sites (e.g., Tomaval in the Virú Valley). Meanwhile, the Upper Piura Project of the Archaeology Specialty of Catholic University (Lima), in conjunction with members of the Centre Nationale de la Récherche Scientifique, Paris, has begun to clarify the regional cultural chronology and the enigmatic relationship between the Vicús and Mochica cultures. A 1993 international colloquium on Mochica archaeology revealed both widespread recognition of the need to reassess conventional views on basic issues (discussed later) and continuing overemphasis on tombs and monumental architecture in Mochica archaeology. Recent advances also have underlined the importance of interaction (trade?) between southern Ecuador, on the one hand, and the North Highlands and Piura-Lambayeque zone of the north coast of Peru, on the other, for coevolution of cultural complexity in both areas.

Changing Interpretive Frameworks

An unintentional but nonetheless important outcome of the aforementioned archaeological research has been a long-overdue critical assessment of conventional conceptual schemes dating back to the 1930s. These schemes view cultural developments in terms of "Culture Areas" (or their later reformulation, "Archaeological Regions") and the related "Culture Core–Margin" dichotomy. The entire stretch of the Andes was tripartitioned into North, Central, and South Andes based on persistent, overlapping distributions of a constellation of environmental and cultural features and traits. Each Culture Area was further divided into many subareas based on the distribution of diagnostic ceramic styles of the ERD cultures and the presumed "heartlands" or "cores." Apparent stylistic homogeneity was taken to reflect political unity. Adoption of these subdivisions and assumptions inevitably invited a static core–margin dichotomy with persistent debate over boundaries. In the north coast subarea, the small Moche Valley had been long regarded as the core area of prehispanic cultural developments, while the larger, little known Lambayeque Valley, some 160 kilometers to the north, was seen as marginal to developments in this subarea. The former was treated as the cultural pace-setter and the seat of power. Situated near the northern end of the north coast, Lambayeque was believed to have been conquered late in Mochica territorial expansion (c. C.E. 500) and to have served as a refuge area at the time of the postulated Wari conquest of the north (c. C.E. 550–600). The early Mochica (c. C.E. 100–300) "royal" tombs, with singular material riches at Sipán and other sites in this "marginal area" have challenged this traditional view (discussed later). The foregoing situation is eloquent testimony to the inadequacy of not only the available survey data but, more importantly, the style–culture equation and the conventional core–margin dichotomy.

Many points just raised also apply to Peru's south coast, where the Ica Valley long has been seen as the core area. More recent fieldwork in the "peripheral" areas of Chincha, Pisco, and Acarí has brought into question the applicability of the Ica chronological sequence and cultural-historical reconstruction long used as a blueprint for the entire south coast. It has also brought into question the attribution of "state" status to the Nasca and direct cultural continuity from Paracas to Nasca (see later). The viability of some phases of the Ica sequence is especially tenuous given the small number of sherd samples and associated radiocarbon dates.

Understanding of the subsistence, economic organization, and territorial expansions of *altiplano* cultures has also improved over the past fifteen years. The South-Central Andes are now accepted as a distinct culture area. Research has defined a long tradition of an integrated *altiplano* economy with colonization of distant production zones or trade with those on the adjacent eastern and western slopes of the Andes. It was ethnohistorical data from this area that led to Murra's formulation of the "archipelago model of vertical control." This model posited a typical political system, namely, a redistributive system built on a series of long-term enclaves established in distant production zones along much of the vertical gradient of the eastern and western slopes of the Andes. Recent fieldwork suggests that such control may have been established by C.E. 550–600. At the same time, the understandable desire to emphasize the distinctiveness of the newly defined culture area has led to intellectual isolation and limited communication with those working in the neighboring Central Andes, although there is evidence of persistent interaction between these two areas.

Overall, then, the reader should keep in mind the varied effects of uneven archaeological coverage, the persistence of the static cultural core–margin dichotomy, and the skewed nature of artifact and site samples. At the same time, the recent geographical and topical reorientation of Andean archaeology will surely bring about an overhaul of basic views.

ENVIRONMENTAL SETTING, CREATIVE MAN–NATURE INTERPLAY, AND SUBSISTENCE ECONOMY

The Vision of the "Three Worlds of the Andes"

The area under consideration (Map 5.1) spans some 20° latitude, from southern Colombia just north of the Equator (2° North) to near the point of convergence of the Bolivia, Chile, and Peru borders (18° South), a north–south linear distance of over 2,000 kilometers. The dominant geophysical feature of this area, the rugged and lofty Andean range, stretches in a gentle northwest–southeast arc separating wet, lush, and vast Amazonia to the east and the mostly arid, narrow Pacific coast to the west.

Our study area has been commonly described in terms of the "Three Worlds of the Andes" – the coast, highlands, and *selva* (jungle). Travel along the west–east axis anywhere along the Andes involves vertical motion through the "tiered" environmental zones of lowland mid-valley and highland, and for this reason the present work terms this axis the "vertical" axis. Conversely, north–south movement tends to be relatively horizontal, and its axis is labeled so. These dimensions are said to provide environmental diversity and homogeneity, respectively. These are sweeping generalizations and, in many ways, oversimplify the reality. The tripartite division is adopted here only for general descriptive and heuristic purposes. In reality this is a dynamic continuum. Where applicable, the more refined ecological-ethnographic classification composed of eight zones proposed by Pulgar Vidal is employed. Archaeological remains from the period under study and indigenous folklore recorded in the sixteenth century clearly attest to the persistent material as well as cos-

---

Map 5.1. Map of the North and Central Andes showing the locations of key archaeological sites and the approximate extent of ERD cultures mentioned in the text. Based on drawing by I. Shimada.

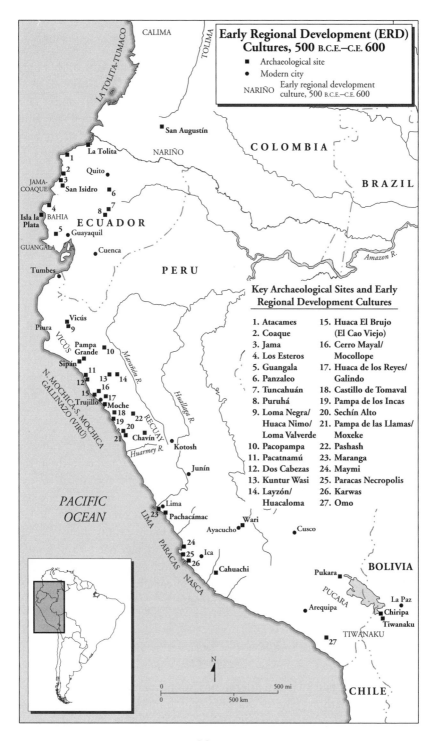

Early Regional Development (ERD)
Cultures, 500 B.C.E.–C.E. 600

■ Archaeological site
● Modern city
NARIÑO Early regional development
       culture, 500 B.C.E.–C.E. 600

Key Archaeological Sites and Early
Regional Development Cultures

1. Atacames
2. Coaque
3. Jama
4. Los Esteros
5. Guangala
6. Panzaleo
7. Tuncahuán
8. Puruhá
9. Loma Negra/
   Huaca Nimo/
   Loma Valverde
10. Pacopampa
11. Pacatnamú
12. Dos Cabezas
13. Kuntur Wasi
14. Layzón/
    Huacaloma

15. Huaca El Brujo
    (El Cao Viejo)
16. Cerro Mayal/
    Mocollope
17. Huaca de los Reyes/
    Galindo
18. Castillo de Tomaval
19. Pampa de los Incas
20. Sechín Alto
21. Pampa de las Llamas/
    Moxeke
22. Pashash
23. Maranga
24. Maymi
25. Paracas Necropolis
26. Karwas
27. Omo

Map 5.1

mological importance of all three zones for the Andean people. Highlanders have valued shells from the coast (such as *Spondylus princeps*, [spiny oyster], *Strombus galetus* [conch or trumpet shell], and *Conus fergusoni* [large spiral shell]) for their rituals at least from late Preceramic times (c. 2000 B.C.E.). Conversely, coastal inhabitants seem to have worshiped high peaks as the dwelling place of deities and the source of vital water. Although lowland–highland interaction has often been argued, there have been few detailed ground surveys linking these two zones. There exists the real possibility that during the period under study there were independent polities in the *yunka* (also spelled *yunca, yunga*), a zone of year-round warmth and sun along the valleys that connect the coast and the *selva* with highlands. Further, there is no consensus on operational definitions of coast and highlands. How and where we draw the boundaries of a study area have a significant effect on the spatial patterns (of settlements or otherwise) we may discern. The definitions used in this chapter are presented in the context of relevant discussions.

The vision of the "Three Worlds of the Andes" is also of limited value for in-depth study of man–nature interplay. Human groups usually exploit a range of highly specific resources and niches, not broadly defined "environments." Although the levels of analysis and attendant terms and concepts have been elaborated for human interaction, we have not seen concomitant advances in the human–environment relationship. For example, copper artifacts became relatively common among ERD cultures. Although copper ore was often assumed to have been mined only in the highlands, we now know that deposits individually too small or too inaccessible to be exploited by modern standards were indeed intensively exploited in the coastal foothills of the Andes. More generally, it has been a widespread practice among archaeologists to readily speak of long-distance trade upon finding what are assumed to have been exotic goods, prior to establishing secure identification and origin through detailed analysis (e.g., common misidentification of sodalite as Chilean lapis lazuli) and considering possible local sources.

Seasonal Climate, Differential Water Availability, and Cultural Solutions

ERD cultures had an agrarian economy supplemented to varying degrees by fishing, herding, and/or foraging and hunting. The availability of water in terms of quantity and timing was the key to their subsistence and physical well-being. This variable in turn is directly linked to seasonal climate. Climatically, our study area subsumes two major regimes with their division roughly coinciding with the modern Ecuador-Peru border. Nearly the entire Peruvian highlands, spanning around 15° of tropical latitude, are characterized by a single climatic regime with a pronounced wet season in the southern summer (typically between December and April), and dry season in the southern winter (June to October; Fig. 5.1). This seasonal pattern is the result of the annual northward and southward movement of the equatorial trough. During the summer, equatorial easterlies carry moisture from Amazonia up onto the highlands interacting with the equatorial trough and resulting in rain. Although varied physiography creates some local variation, annual precipitation totals are quite consistent throughout the highlands, and there is no indication of significant changes in this basic climatic regime or its geographical extent at least for the past 1,500 years.

In southern Peru, effects of the subduction of a Pacific tectonic plate under the South American plate are quite pronounced, and the Andean peaks have been pushed generally high, reaching over 6,000 meters in elevation. In fact, the eastern cordillera, a continuous high chain, acts as a highly effective barrier to the prevailing vapor-laden easterlies that make Amazonia a rain forest. Thus the extensive *altiplano* around Lake Titicaca and the western ridge are drier than in the northern highlands where the eastern range is a more punctuated chain. Consequently, rivers on the southern Peruvian coast mostly have small discharge volumes and are seasonal.

The moderating climatic effects of the cool Peruvian (also called Humboldt) Current give the initial impression that there is little seasonal difference on the coast. However, even perennial rivers show pronounced seasonal and annual variations in discharge volumes. For example, during the winter months (June–September), in the Ica–Río Grande de Nazca region of the south coast, a thick fog is formed along the Pacific shores, and the local rivers carry little or no water. Groundwater is present at varying depths throughout the year, but the water table rises dramatically from about December or January as mountain runoff reaches the coast. Thus, during the summer months, springs and rivers flow to an otherwise desiccated coastal landscape.

The Pacific coast of Peru (particularly the southern portion) and the adjoining northern coast of Chile constitute one of the driest areas of the world. Most of the moisture from the Pacific transported by the prevail-

Izumi Shimada

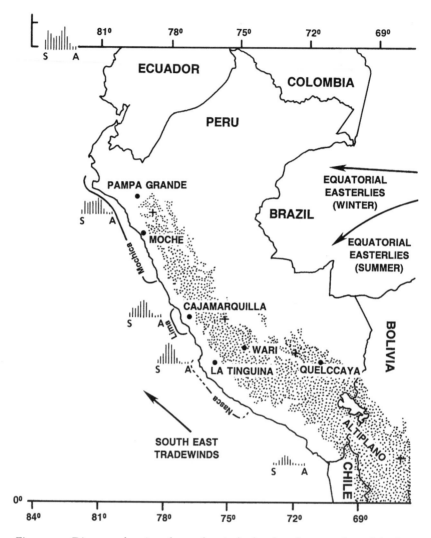

Figure 5.1. Diagram showing the trade winds that largely control precipitation in the area under consideration. Average annual rainfall at five highland sites (indicated by crosses; north to south Quito, Ecuador, Cajamarca, Huancayo, and Cusco, Peru, and Oruro, Bolivia) is shown by bar charts on a 200-mm scale running from September to August. Note double rain seasons near the Equator and the low amounts of rain during the *altiplano* wet season at Oruro. Drawing courtesy of Crystal Schaaf.

ing southeasterly tradewinds, which roughly parallel the coastline, is transported toward the Equator rather than precipitated locally. Under normal conditions, coastal precipitation is quite rare, suppressed by the atmospheric subsidence characteristic of subtropical eastern Pacific areas. Consequently, the only available surface water on the coast is carried by rivers fed with runoff from seasonal rains, particularly on the western cordillera. Of some sixty rivers on the Peruvian coast, only about a dozen of them can be considered truly year-round, and most of these are found on the northern coast. This is a critical factor in understanding the productive agrarian economy underlying a series of complex cultures that emerged on the northern coast.

With no regular rainfall to rely on, coastal ERD developed irrigation, of course, but also a range of nonirrigating water management strategies and technologies were refined. For example, in the Nasca drainage, underground canals (also called filtration galleries, *puqyu* [also spelled *pukios, puquios*, etc.]) are believed to have been developed by Nasca 5 (c. C.E. 300–400) to tap groundwater and complement the limited seasonal river flow. Not surprisingly, irrigation systems developed on the south coast pale in comparison with those on the north coast (see later).

Sunken fields (also known as *mahamaes* and other names), found widely from the north to south coasts, involve excavating planting surfaces down toward the water table, the logical opposite of "raised" or "ridged" fields (see later; Fig. 5.2). They are commonly found in natural topographic lows, such as near the mouths of side valleys with seasonal rivers or even near the Pacific coast. The excavated soil may have been used in making adobe bricks. Conversely, the large pits created by adobe brick making may have been used as sunken fields. Some of the sunken fields in the lower Virú Valley on the north coast constructed by the Salinar farmers (c. 250 B.C.E. to C.E. 1) approximate the size of football fields and may not be readily recognizable for their large sizes. In other words, contrary to widespread opinion, these fields date back at least to C.E. 0 and probably made a significant contribution to overall regional agricultural production by extending the cultivation period to year-round (as opposed to being dependent upon seasonal fluctuations of river flow) and expanding cultivation areas beyond irrigated fields.

In the northern Peruvian Andes, it is the western sierra that acts as the major barrier to moisture drifting westward from Amazonia. In southern Peru, much of the highland precipitation is drained eastward, but in the north, with greater precipitation in the western cordillera, the

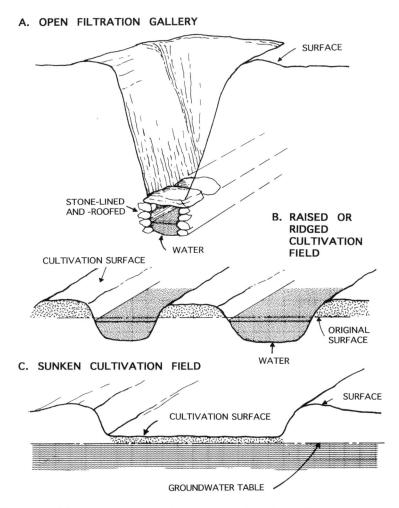

Figure 5.2. Schematic drawing of three distinct cultivation and/or water management techniques that were used by ERD cultures: (A) filtration gallery in the Rio Grande de Nazca drainage; (B) raised or ridged-field in the Titicaca and Guayas basins; (C) sunken garden on coastal Peru. Drawing by I. Shimada.

coast is blessed with perennial rivers with relatively high discharge volumes (minimum, maximum, and annual). The associated alluvial plains are extensive and have low gradients and thick, fertile soil, as well as open topography. The northerly location also offers more sunny days and overall warmth than the area farther south. In other words, the

Peruvian north coast, particularly its northern half, has conditions ideally suited for large-scale, intensive irrigation agriculture. Indeed, the largest irrigation systems in the prehispanic New World emerged there. Ceramic representations, pollen evidence, and preserved remains show that maize, beans, squash, tomato, avocado, yuca, chili pepper, and other crops were cultivated all along the coast. These cultures had constructed gravity-fed, sinuous canals that faithfully followed natural contours to maximize irrigated areas. Some impressive aqueducts were also built. No pumps or siphons were known in the prehispanic New World. By around C.E. 500, the Mochica had already achieved at least one intervalley irrigation canal that carried water from the Chancay River in the Lambayeque Valley to the north bank of the Zaña Valley, a total distance of about 45 kilometers. In fact, sometime between C.E. 200 and 500, their canals and irrigated fields either attained or approximated prehistoric maxima anywhere from 30 to 50 percent greater than the corresponding modern figures for north coast valleys (e.g., about 201 versus 128 km^2 for the Moche Valley). Sustained rainy conditions that appear to have prevailed during the fifth century C.E. most likely promoted the expansion of agricultural frontiers and productivity throughout the Andes.

Seasonal fluctuation in water availability persist despite such strategies (Fig. 5.2). The winter months when little water reaches the coast are usually the slack period of the local agricultural cycle, and many corporate undertakings such as canal cleaning and repairs (perhaps even constructions of monumental structures) were likely to have been scheduled for this period as documented ethnohistorically for late prehispanic times. Seasonal scheduling of activities was probably practiced in the highlands as well. For example, household-level production of domestic pottery and other craft items probably occurred during the winter months.

Coastal Peru benefited from the riches of the Pacific and rested on dual economic pillars of agriculture and fishing that persist to this day. At the same time, northern Peru in particular (also adjacent southern Ecuador) suffers more from the adverse effects of El Niño events – occasional intrusions of warm tropical water into the Peruvian Current that flows northward from the Antarctic along the coasts of Chile and Peru up to latitude 5° South. These events are relatively short in duration (typically 1–2 years) but vary in intensity and frequency. Severe events that may occur a few times in a century are accompanied by a wide range of environmental changes. These changes include the large-scale death or disappearance of cold-water marine organisms along much of the Peruvian coast, as well as torrential rains in both highlands and coast, causing landslides and floods that destroy roads and whole canal networks. Although the effects of El Niño events are usually described in negative terms, in reality, human populations are creative and make the most of them. Rains and floods on the coast, for example, in addition to depositing new alluvium that rejuvenates agricultural fields, soak lands well beyond irrigated fields. They can be promptly cultivated or used for pasturing. In 1983 and 1984, following an historic El Niño event, Peruvian highlanders brought their animals down to take advantage of the extensive pasture that emerged on coastal deserts, and coastal farmers cultivated soaked dunes. The fish and crustaceans that flourished in coastal rivers after the flood also helped to counterbalance the loss or reduction of agricultural harvest. Overall, it is important to remember that Andean populations have maintained a flexible, creative perception of their environment, a sort of "slide-rule approach" to broad-spectrum exploitation of a kaleidoscopic environment.

The North Andes – that is, modern Ecuador and southern Colombia – are equatorial in latitude and have a different climatic regime. Here a pervasive problem has been how to deal with too much water. Many highland areas have two wet seasons with an intermediate dry season (three seasons as opposed to two in Peru), reflecting the equatorial trough's oscillation northward and later southward during the year (Fig. 5.1). With the Ecuadorian Andes broken into relatively low (3,000–4,000 m or less in elevation), narrow ranges (c. east–west span of 250 km or less), moisture in the easterlies from Amazonia does reach the highlands and the western slope. Abundant rainfall supports tall grasslands called *páramos* in the highlands, and the landscape is generally greener than the Peruvian highlands. At the same time, rains create a widespread problem of soil erosion. Also, the high rate of evapotranspiration due to the intense equatorial sun and high temperatures often creates water shortages for highland farmers.

Reliable evidence of subsistence items and strategies in the highlands is scarce. Pollen data from the La Plata Valley, southern Colombian highlands, provide us with an important glimpse. Between 1050 and 50 B.C.E., when the climate was cooler and wetter than today, the first sedentary occupation spread throughout the valley (over 2,200–1,000 m above sea level) with clear emphasis on the temperate, humid climatic zone of about 1,600 meters above sea level with fertile soil and gentle relief. Unfortunately, hardly any pollen evidence of cultivars has been found. During the subsequent period (up to C.E. 850) with climatic improvement toward modern conditions, there was a notable population increase centered in the temperate zone between 1,400 and 2,000 meters above sea level. A much larger area of forest was cleared for agricultural and residential ends. Several population concentrations have been noted in this zone, each focused on a center marked by residences and tombs of local chiefs. Pollen data point to a wide variety of cultivars, including maize, beans, coca, yuca, sweet potato, and fruits (e.g., chirimoya and guanábana). General climatic improvements and exploitation of high-altitude production zones (up to 3,000 m above sea level for potato and *quinua*) documented in this area coincide with similar indications from Junín and other areas in Peru (see later).

The coastal region presents a range of habitats that gradually change from north to south. North of the Esmeraldas River, the Ecuadorian coast is doused with rain throughout the year (but primarily between January and July), reaching 3,000–4,000 millimeters, amid warm to hot average temperatures of around 22–25° C. Much of the region is covered by dense, humid tropical rain forest much like what is found across the Andes in Amazonia. Due to poor preservation of organic materials and limited fieldwork, little is known about the subsistence of regional ERD cultures such as the Tachina, La Tolita-Tumaco, and Calima. Carbonized food remains provide some clues but often do not accurately reflect their economic significance or relative abundance. Excavations of Illama Phase Calima residences yielded carbonized remains of maize, beans, and perhaps achiote (annatto, *Bixa orellana*) and phytoliths (diagnostic plant silicas) of calabash and arrowroot (*Maranta arundinacea*, which provides rhizomes rich in carbohydrates). These were supplemented by palms (fruits, branches for roofing, fiber for making cords) and a variety of tropical fruits including chirimoya (*Annonaceas*). Neither achira (a starchy tuber, *Canna edulis*), coca, cotton, gourd, tobacco nor yuca has been recovered, but all are suspected to have been important to the diet.

Not surprisingly, modern inhabitants of this region share many subsistence and other features (e.g., blowgun and poison dart, bark-cloth technology, manioc, and a shamanistic complex that utilizes hallucinogens) with those of Amazonia. Today, cultivation is practiced on cleared land and along rivers (maize, yuca or manioc, plaintains, as well as sugar cane, fruit trees, palms, and pineapple), but the soil is commonly high in clay and leached, necessitating mobile and scattered occupation. Game from hunting (e.g., wild pigs, deer, rodents, and birds) and fish, shellfish, and other aquatic products from both open sea and mangrove swamps or rivers are important supplements to the diet. Believing that the shared "tropical forest" lifeway mentioned previously reflects a tradition of trans-Andean migration and interaction dating back to the remote Formative times of the Valdivia culture, many prehistorians infer that the subsistence basis of ERD cultures that were centered along major Pacific-draining river systems was a mixed economy of slash-and-burn and intensive alluvial land cultivation (both seed [particularly maize] and root crops), fishing, and hunting and gathering, much as is seen today in Amazonia. A major difference from Amazonia is that this region had access to coastal food resources that added considerable diversity and productivity.

As one travels south to the wide central Ecuadorian coastal plain of Manabí, the dense tropical forest thins out, and drier, sparser vegetation appears. Macroremains and phytoliths recovered by long-term regional research in the Jama River drainage by Zeidler and Pearsall indicate that Jama-Coaque subsistence was based on cultivation of seed (maize) and root crops (arrowroot and achira) supplemented by palms and probably Canavalia beans and tropical fruits such as guava.

Farther south lies the vast expanse of the Guayas Basin that parallels the Andean range to its east and the Pacific coast to its west. This humid alluvial plain along the Daule and Guayas rivers and their tributaries has seasonal flooding and has tremendous agricultural potential, which was tapped prehistorically by means of at least 50,000 hectares of *camellones*, a local name for raised cultivation fields with similar physico-chemical and biological properties and construction to those in the Titicaca Basin over 2,000 kilometers farther south (see later). They have a roughly coterminous, parallel evolution. Raised fields are found widely distributed in swampy areas from Venezuela to Bolivia. They consist of orderly rows of elevated mounds formed by piling up soil rich in organic nutrients from the swamp bottom (Fig. 5.2). Their raised construction creates good drainage, canals possibly used for small boat transport (totora-reed boats in the Titicaca Basin) and aquaculture. Silt and aquatic plants in canals can be added to the ridged fields to increase soil depth and fertility. During the wet season, raised areas stand above the flood waters, while in the dry months, furrows or canals between the raised areas maintain sufficient moisture for cultivating a second crop. Extensive parallel tracts in the Peñón del Río sector (c. 1,700 hectares) of the basin have been investigated in depth. Here, raised fields revived for experimental cultivation of maize have registered impressive productivity of some 5,760 kilograms per hectare per year (both wet and dry seasons), or nearly double the modern national average in Ecuador. Their dating and estimates of their extent at any given point in time have been much more difficult to ascertain, and there are only a few inconclusive radiocarbon dates. Sherds found in the soil of *camellones* suggest that at least a portion of Peñón del Río was cultivated in this manner during the period under study (ERD cultures of Daule, Tejar, and Guayaquil).

Horizontal and Vertical Variation and Its Creative Exploitation

Our study area is characterized by tremendous ecological diversity and geographic extremes. An effective way to illustrate this variability is by means of east–west transects. Such a transect commonly presents an elevational difference from the arid desert along the Pacific coast near sea level to between 4,000 meters and up to almost 6,800 meters at glaciated Huascarán, the highest peak in Peru (Fig. 5.3). Impressive environmental diversity results from the tremendous elevational differences compacted in east–west horizontal distance.

The Andes differ from other alpine regions in the world by the fact that much of the total elevational span is densely occupied and/or cultivated. (Farther from the Equator, high altitudes are cold and have sparse biota.) These unique tropical alpine conditions produce marked diurnal, seasonal, and altitudinal differences. The tropical sun warms up sufficiently during the day to allow human occupation or utilization of some 60 percent of the land over 2,800 meters in elevation, the most intense use of high elevations in the world. This study shows not only how Andean farmers effectively responded to long-term temperature changes but also their longstanding effort to optimize "verticality" (i.e., access as many altitudinally differentiated production zones as possible for diverse, stable, self-sufficient subsistence).

Verticality and Altiplano Subsistence

The impoverishment of the high plains and valleys in modern times (see Chaps. 22 and 23), and the unfamiliar (to Europeans) stresses of high altitude, made it difficult for early scientists to guess at their considerable economic and demographic development in prehistory. The area has been mentioned as a possible locus of camelid and potato domestication.

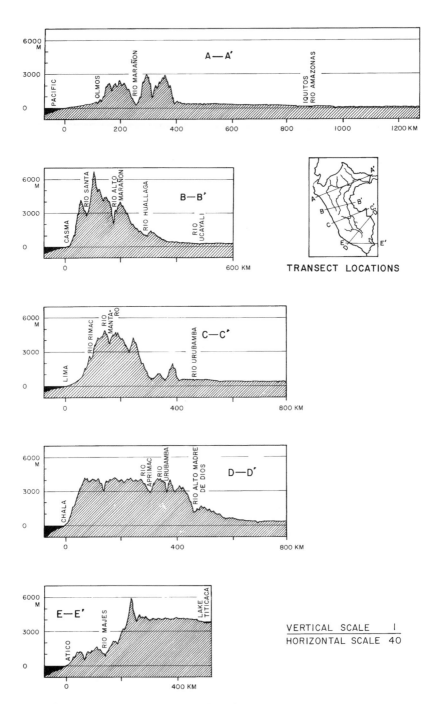

Figure 5.3. East-west transects through different parts of the Andes showing the considerable variation in height and width of mountain masses that has important environmental and cultural implications. Drawing by I. Shimada.

The "Cordilleran Complex," composed of grains (e.g., *quinua* [*Chenopodium quinoa*] and cañihua [*Chenopodium pallidicaule*]) and tubers (e.g., potato [*Solanum tuberosum*], oca [*Oxalis tuberosa*], mashwa [*Tropeaolum tuberosum*], and olluco [*Ullucus tuberosus*]) that are complementary in terms of nutrients, productivity, and growing conditions, appears to have formed the basis of *altiplano* agriculture at least since the first millennium B.C.E.

Ridged- or raised-field cultivation was critical to making the most of the Lake Titicaca environment, with its droughts, floods, hail, and frequent frost (up to 300 days per year). There are over an estimated 82,000 hectares of prehistoric ridged fields in the seasonally innundated land around Lake Titicaca. Excavations of ridged fields near Puno on the northern Titicaca shore suggest that ridged-field agriculture began around 1000 B.C.E. and was well-established by 500 B.C.E., forming a major component of the Pukara economy. These early ridges were about 2.5 meters wide, 0.5 meters high, and 5 meters apart (measuring intervals between crests of adjacent rows). Importantly, experimental construction of ridged fields using the traditional footplow has shown that the labor requirements (1 m³/hour) are relatively modest and could have been effectively managed by the traditional *ayllu*, or local-level corporate landholding group. Planting of these experimental ridges over a 5-year span yielded between 8 and 16 metric tons of potatoes (without fertilizer) per hectare. Modern field cultivation in the same area yields between 1 and 4 metric tons per hectare (with fertilizers). Overall, ridged-field agriculture was an "appropriate technology" in regard to the environmental variables, tools, manpower, and cultigens available. It also reflects the longstanding economic orientation of exploiting lacustrine resources and wetlands established by the contemporaneous (c. 1500–500 B.C.E.) agrarian Chiripa and Qaluyu (and probably Wankarani) cultures in the northern and southern Titicaca Basin, respectively. Erickson suggests that it probably underwrote the demographic and organizational growth of the Pukara and early Tiwanaku cultures.

Another "appropriate technology," freeze-drying of edibles, complemented ridged-field agriculture. This process, still widely employed in the *altiplano*, takes advantage of pronounced differences between relatively high diurnal and freezing nocturnal temperatures to produce a series of storable "freeze-dried" goods, like jerky (*ch'arki*) and potato (*ch'uñu*). The latter was found in Late Chiripa (600–100 B.C.E.) refuse at the regional ceremonial–civic center of Chiripa on the southern shore of

Lake Titicaca (Fig. 5.4). Quinua and potato (and perhaps other crops of the Cordilleran Complex as well) were found stored in baskets in the peripheral compartments within a series of sixteen rectangular adobe-stone structures that together formed an octagon at this site. The stored crop may have been used for ritual offerings and feasts or have represented the best seeds reserved for future planting, an important consideration in the *altiplano* with various unpredictable natural risks. In other words, a seemingly negative aspect of the tropical alpine conditions of the *altiplano* was productively exploited. Mohr-Chávez suggests that large temple–storage facilities at Chiripa and Pukara (Fig. 5.5) may have emerged to coordinate the rituals and cultivation of the expanding ridged fields.

Ridged fields on the northern shore seem to have been abandoned sometime after C.E. 300–350, following an inferred Tiwanaku expansion

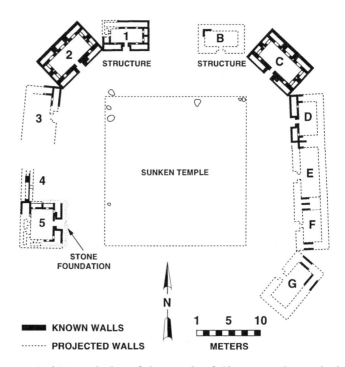

Figure 5.4. Architectural plan of the temple of Chiripa on the south shore of Lake Titicaca. Compare this plan to that of the temple of Pukara on the north shore. Redrawn by I. Shimada from fig. 3, K. M. Chávez, 1989: 19.

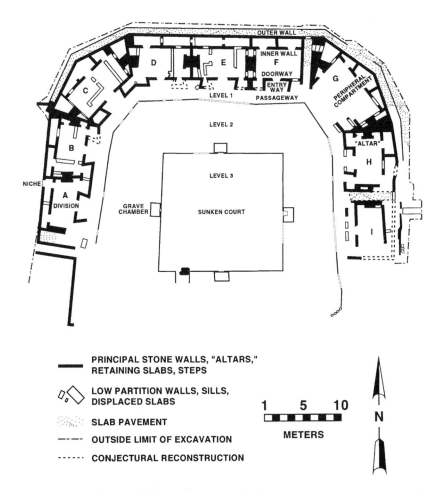

Figure 5.5. Architectural plan of the temple of Pukara on the north shore of Lake Titicaca originally excavated by A. Kidder II. Redrawn by I. Shimada from fig. 9, K. M. Chávez, 1989: 24.

and attendant demise of the Pukara polity. The initiation of large-scale land reclamation in the form of ridged-field and canal construction on the southern shore (particularly Koani Pampa), the Tiwanaku heartland, is difficult to specify. Radiocarbon dates point to circa C.E. 400–600, or late Tiwanaku III to early IV (hereafter phases are indicated only by Roman numerals). Not only the economic base but much of Tiwanaku Phases I through III, including their dates, remain to be defined.

Although domestication of the llama and alpaca is now believed to
have occurred outside of the *altiplano*, today this plateau has perhaps the
densest and highest-quality concentration of pastoral resources in the
Andes. In this sense, it is not a surprise to see that sixteenth-century
colonial tributary records for the Chucuito region (on the west shore of
Lake Titicaca) attest to impressive numbers of inhabitants as well as
alpacas and llamas so numerous that the natives were locally nicknamed
"the rich Indians." Remains of both wild and domesticated camelids
from excavations at Pukara and the earlier site of Chiripa on the southern
shore of the lake indicate that the intensive utilization of camelids as the
principal meat source was established during the first millennium B.C.E.
Agropastoralism, the symbiotic relationship between llama–alpaca husbandry and agriculture, supplemented by lacustrine resources, is commonly cited as the basic economic orientation of *altiplano* cultures, but
we are still uncertain of the relative importance of each and how they
interrelated.

Pukara and Tiwanaku IV economies were distinguished from those of
contemporary cultures farther north by the importance of vertical control. There are various competing views as to how such control was
achieved, but most scholars recognize longstanding interaction between
the *altiplano* and western slopes, with the motive of producing or acquiring warm climate crops such as peppers and maize. Relevant evidence
comes primarily from the western slopes between Moquegua, Peru,
through Arica to San Pedro de Atacama on the far north coast of Chile.

One scenario proposes waves of downward migration of *altiplano*
populations starting around 1500 B.C.E. into the Arica region already
inhabited by local populations of the Chinchorro cultural tradition with
a strong maritime economic orientation (see Chap. 9). A constellation of
new cultural features that appeared during the Early Alto Ramírez Phase
(1000–500 B.C.E.) is attributed to *altiplano* populations that coexisted
with and influenced the local population. These features include agglutinated villages based on intensive irrigation cultivation of maize, peppers,
and other warm-climate crops, ceremonial-funerary mounds, copper
working and use, woven textiles, turban-like headdresses, and trophy
heads. However, some archaeologists see many of these same innovations
as local developments pertaining to the Azapa Phase (dated to the last
several centuries before C.E. 0), which has been postulated between the
Chinchorro tradition and Alto Ramírez Phase.

More recent investigations in the middle to upper reaches of the

Osmore drainage (Moquegua region, southern Peru) suggest a gradual evolution from seasonal transhumance to a sedentary, agrarian existence in a warm zone around 2,000 meters above sea level based on irrigation by C.E. 0 (Huaracane Phase). For the period of circa 300 B.C.E. to the first centuries C.E., Feldman defines two possible ethnic groups in the mid-valley: Trapiche and Huaracane. The former may have preceded the latter and is associated with ceramics and wool textiles closely resembling the *altiplano* Pukara style. Various Huaracane sites situated on escarpments close to the fertile valley floor are associated with stone-lined, cylindrical subterranean tombs (flexed and seated position; also some chambered shaft tombs). These resemble the widespread and persistent *altiplano* burial pattern and structures. Tubular bone beads and drilled stone disks are similar to those found at Chiripa sites in the *altiplano*. Huaracane ceramics share forms and the use of organic temper with those of the Chiripa and Qaluyu in the *altiplano* and the Faldas de el Moro. At the same time, fiber-tempered ceramics seem to have been widespread in much of the South-Central Andes and may not be a reliable indicator of *altiplano* origin. In fact, Huaracane burials also contain various coastal elements as well. Thus these burials may be interpreted as representing a population composed of descendants of earlier *altiplano* settlers, or a genuinely local group who traded with the Trapiche population or emulated their customs.

The earliest indications of occupation by "settlers from Tiwanaku" (Omo Phase) are tentatively dated to circa C.E. 550–600 and are found at the flat bluff-top site cluster of Omo. Omo Phase residential occupation covered some 16 hectares and was divided into three community groups, each focused around a central plaza. The presence of a wide range of utilitarian and ritual objects in the diagnostic Tiwanaku IV style – ranging from fine ceramic vessels including flared goblets and censers to household tools made out of camelid mandibles – identifies the settlers as Tiwanaku colonists from the *altiplano*. The absence of any non-Tiwanaku plainware argues for little or no integration with local populations. Not surprisingly, camelid wool and weaving tools are found extensively. Also present is red ochre, believed to have been used for face painting, as depicted in modeled, painted ceramics, coca leaves, maize, and suggestions of *chicha* (traditional maize beer) drinking. P. Goldstein believes that Tiwanaku cultural identity was maintained among colonists through redistribution and ritual use of imported material symbols. The proximity of the site to a series of springs is seen as critical to irrigation cultivation of maize presumably for its nutritional value, storability, and making of *chicha*. Having derived from a distant land, maize and *chicha* probably conferred considerable social prestige on those who served them in social and religious events.

The foregoing data from Omo show that the simultaneous, direct exploitation of vertically differentiated zones, in a manner akin to Murra's ethnohistorical model, has considerable antiquity in the South-Central Andes. However, many crucial aspects of vertical control remain to be clarified, including the mechanisms involved in the establishment of this enclave (e.g., forceful displacement, conquest of local populations, or simply tense sharing of maize production zones). Was the cultivation of warm-climate crops the principal concern of the colonists as opposed to the exploitation of rich, local mineral resources such as sodalite and copper? Did the colonists really represent the Tiwanaku "state" as commonly assumed or just one constituent ethnic polity? How did the "state" manage the inherent centrifugal tendency of colonies to claim greater autonomy? Were these "colonists" totally isolated from local population(s)? Were they far-flung enclaves established after the emergence of the Tiwanaku state, or did they contribute to its emergence?

The models of vertical control just examined are couched in terms of a deterministic man–land relationship (i.e., the acquisition or production of nonhighland crops). But agricultural production in the Andes is not a simple function of subsistence demands and altitude or other environmental considerations; cultural beliefs and social relations definitely enter in deciding what and how much is produced. For example, to prepare for a future feast in which *chicha* is to be consumed in a large amount, maize today may be cultivated above its general elevational limit of 2,500–2,800 meters if one is willing to tolerate slow maturation or allocate extra fertilizer, land, or labor. Also, these models do not give adequate attention to the man–man relationship and noncomestible resources such as camelid fiber and hallucinogens and associated wooden snuff tablets. Given the considerable environmental and cultural variability within the South-Central Andes, there may well be correspondingly greater variability in the mode and nature of exploitation and occupation of the vertical gradient. In this sense, the model of "gyratory movements" proposed for arid northern Chile by Núñez and Dillehay is instructive. This model posits symbiosis between hunting-gathering groups practicing seasonal transhumance and agrarian communities located in dispersed oases in the highlands and in coastal river valleys starting around 100

B.C.E., when the agrarian lifestyle finally took root in this region. The former served the role of transport and exchange agents for the latter.

Horizontality and Northern Peruvian Subsistence

Related to the latitudinal variation in climate and water availability described earlier are important differences in subsistence items and strategies between the *altiplano* and northern Peruvian and Ecuadorian cultures. The east–west zone connecting the Huarmey to Supe valleys on the coast and the adjacent highlands of Junín and the eastern slope toward Huánuco has been the invisible boundary marking the major north–south subdivision within the broader physiographical-cultural unit of the central Andes. Communication across this area is physically difficult, and there have been no coastal or highland areas of major population concentrations in the past or today to promote it.

North of this zone, *puna*, or high-altitude short grassland, is largely replaced by taller grassland at a lower elevation called *jalca* and three narrow, parallel, north–south mountain chains drained by the Marañón and Santa rivers, which run northward before turning east and west, respectively. The Cordillera Blanca (middle) and Negra (west) form the intermontane basin of the Callejón de Huaylas, the home of the Recuay culture. In general, northern Peru with its narrower, lower, and more broken Andean masses has relatively small, dispersed intermontane basins, most at about 2,600–3,000 meters. Their relatively temperate and dry climate nourishes the landscape known as *quechua*. In other words, the upper end of the productive, vertical environment is truncated or greatly reduced in comparison with the areas south of the boundary. This may well have been a major factor for the lateness of the transition from deer hunting to camelid husbandry in the northern Peruvian and southern Ecuadorian highlands, in spite of relative proximity to the Junín highlands, where the earliest demonstrable llama and alpaca domestication occurred by 4000–3500 B.C.E.

In the Cajamarca Basin, during the Layzón phase (c. 600–250 B.C.E.), the shift in primary emphasis from deer hunting to domesticated camelid as the meat source was basically completed. The presence of small and large forms, presumably alpaca and llama, becomes clear during the Initial Cajamarca (c. 250 B.C.E. to C.E. 200). In contrast, data from Pirincay in the southern Ecuadorian highlands show the later appearance of a domesticated camelid form intermediate in size between the modern llama and alpaca (c. C.E. 100). The transition to full-fledged reliance on domesticated camelid(s) as the meat source had taken place throughout much of the highland region of our study area by the first few centuries C.E.

Although the spread of camelid husbandry through the North High-lands of Peru and southern Ecuadorian highlands has been commonly interpreted as an epiphenomenon of the expansion of the Chavín cult (c. 500–200 B.C.E.), the causal linkage is far from clear, and relevant pro-cesses are likely to have been more complex. Given the earlier presence of domesticated camelid (bones and dung; presumably llama) at Cupis-nique sites (c. 1500–750 B.C.E.) on the adjacent north coast and recent data suggesting inland (upward) migration of a Cupisnique population around 700 B.C.E., we need to consider why the transition from deer hunting to camelid husbandry did not take place earlier. The limited quantity of excavated bones and restricted range of environmental set-tings and cultural contexts they represent may be partially responsible for the uncertainties at hand. The initial introduction of domesticated ca-melid(s) appears to have preceded the spread of the Chavín cult and may even have come via the north coast.

Various lines of evidence support llama breeding and herding on the north coast during the period under study, including the presence of extensive and thick (over 1 m) deposits of dung at Gallinazo and Mochica settlements, representations of various life stages (e.g., coitus and caring for young), and roles played by llamas (e.g., beast of burden; Fig. 5.6) in Mochica ceramics (Phases I–III). The paucity of excavated residential sites on the coast is the primary reason for the lack of critical zooarchaeo-logical evidence that would resolve this issue.

Overall, during the period under study, throughout Peru and the South-Central Andes, llamas came to serve varied roles as a major, if not the primary meat source, sacrificial animals, sources of bones for making tools, ornaments, and flutes, and in particular, beasts of burden. Their wool and dung (as fuel and/or fertilizer) were probably utilized in many areas.

It should be remembered that in various models of the vertical econ-omy of *altiplano* cultures discussed earlier, llamas are assumed to have served as beasts of burden transporting maize and other produce from the lowlands and jerky and wool or textiles from the highlands. In other words, llama husbandry and caravans are seen to have been a critical part of the *altiplano* economy.

Figure 5.6. Mochica ceramic depiction of a llama carrying *Strombus* shell cargo. Note the young llama under the adult. Redrawn by I. Shimada from fig. 305, Kutscher 1983.

North Highland populations such as Cajamarca and Recuay also appear to have practiced some degree of vertical control, although the role of llamas in this regard remains unclear. With the rugged and snow-capped Cordillera Blanca restricting access to the eastern escarpment, the contemporaneous Recuay downward thrust emphasized the western *yunka* of the southern north coast (particularly between the Virú and Nepeña valleys). Western *yunka* (typically 300–2,300 m above sea level) is in many ways critical for both the highland and coastal populations. The year-round availability of sun and moisture allows cultivation of valued crops of not only maize and chili pepper but also coca (*Erythroxylum novogranatense var. truxillense*), which at the time of Inka domination was preferred over that of eastern *yunka* as being more potent. The zone is also where many mines of copper, iron oxides, and silver and stands of hallucinogenic San Pedro cactus (*Trichocereus pachanoi*; for shamanistic uses) are found. The lower reaches of this zone often coincide with the apex of the roughly triangular coastal river valleys. It is here that the principal intakes of major canals of coastal valleys are ideally situated. The higher the intakes, the greater the surface area in lower elevation that can be irrigated. Thus coastal populations sought to establish control over the *yunka* zone and keep highland populations from encroaching. It is a zone of critical resources and has long been the zone of contention, for example, between Recuay and Mochica.

The settlement survey data from the Santa Valley are instructive. Prior to Mochica intrusion from the north around C.E. 350 (Phase III), the local Gallinazo population focused in the lower to middle valley appears to have had a tense coexistence with Recuay settlers in the middle to upper valley, where their distinct, kaolin ceramics were abundant. However, Wilson found that the intrusion brought about not only a major reduction in the number and extent of Recuay ceramics but also a new settlement pattern that emphasized the lower valley. In other words, the Mochica seems to have subjugated the local Gallinazo population and driven the Recuay settlers out of the mid-valley. The local population was reorganized into a smaller number of larger sites that would have been well situated for agricultural maximization (i.e., intensive irrigation cultivation of maize). Recuay efforts to maintain a foothold in the *yunka* zone are also seen in the neighboring Nepeña Valley.

The suggestion of the competitive nature of the Recuay-Gallinazo and Recuay-Mochica relationships is further supported by the scarcity of north coast artifacts in the Recuay heartland of Callejón de Huaylas. Defeated warriors with distinct hair style, headdresses, and arms (e.g., star-shaped mace heads) in some of the Mochica painted battle scenes (Fig. 5.7) have been interpreted as being of Recuay ethnicity. Also, art styles of these cultures show only a few shared motifs. The popularity of the "Moon Animal" (also called "Recuay Dragon") in Mochica ceramic art was largely confined to Phases I and II, when the Mochica style emulated various other styles. The emulation was, however, without a clear understanding of the Recuay artistic canons.

The relationship between the Cajamarca culture and Peruvian north coast contemporaries appears to have had a somewhat different character and trajectory. In the Jequetepeque Valley, what Kosok aptly called a "cultural crossroads," not only the Gallinazo and Mochica populations coexisted in time and space; there are indications of longstanding interaction between coastal and highland populations at least from about 1500–1000 B.C.E. For example, the second phase occupation at the major ceremonial center of Kuntur Wasi (also called La Copa), situated about 80 kilometers inland at 2,300 meters above sea level, is attributed to an intrusive coastal Cupisnique population. For the period of circa 250 B.C.E. to C.E. 1, Layzón sites in the Cajamarca basin and on the western slope and contemporaneous coastal Salinar sites of Puémape (lower Jequetepeque Valley) and Cerro Arena (mid-Moche Valley) yielded nearly identical bowls. Unlike preceding ceramics decorated with incisions and postfiring paint, these bowls were decorated with simple geometric design in red paint applied before firing. We cannot yet specify what this means, but we cannot discount the possibility that Layzón represents an expan-

Figure 5.7. Roll-out drawing of paired combat from a Mochica Phase IV bottle. Note the clear differences in arms and dress between two groups. Redrawn by I. Shimada from plate 21 in Kutscher 1954.

sive polity based on the western slope between the north coast and highlands. Their occupation at sites in and around the Cajamarca Basin was accompanied by large-scale, intentional destruction of preceding constructions. The coastal Salinar sites of Puémape and Cerro Arena were both abandoned by around C.E. 1, just as Gallinazo and Mochica polities emerged on the coast. At about the same time, in the Cajamarca Basin, the persistent and autonomous Cajamarca ceramic tradition, characterized by a wide variety of kaolin plates and bowls with geometric and highly conventionalized, painted motifs, appears to have evolved out of the preceding Layzón.

Initial Cajamarca Phase ceramics are essentially confined to the Cajamarca Basin. However, Early Cajamarca Phase (c. C.E. 100–450) ceramics are found in much of the North Highlands, and the Cajamarca population appears to have established enclaves or traded with local populations of both eastern *yunkas* (a lushly vegetated zone along the western slope of the Marañón drainage) and western *yunkas*. In fact, at least one Early Cajamarca burial has been documented at San José de Moro (lower Jequetepeque), and a set of imported kaolin spoons has been found at the site of Moche, the capital of the Southern Mochica polity. As in the case of the Callejón de Huaylas, hardly any Mochica ceramics have been reported in the Cajamarca region, and their art styles have few commonalities. As with the Recuay-Mochica case, there is nothing that suggests the spread and sharing of a total corpus of beliefs.

A long-term perspective spanning the first millennium of our era shows that the extent and quantity of Cajamarca ceramics on the north coast is a telling barometer of the political prowess of local polities. During Phase IV (c. C.E. 450–550), when the Southern Mochica polity held sway over much of the north coast, corresponding Middle Cajamarca A ceramics were rare and confined to the upper reaches of coastal valleys. Toward the end of Phase V (final phase; c. C.E. 550–700) and immediately following the demise of the Mochica polities, Middle Cajamarca B ceramics are found throughout much of Peru, both coast and highlands. Such designs clearly enjoyed a good deal of prestige within the Wari empire and may be argued to have constituted a Horizon style. However, the rise of the Middle Sicán state on the north coast around C.E. 900–1000 saw a notable reduction in the distribution of Late Cajamarca ceramics back to the extent seen during Mochica Phase IV. In other words, the nature of the coast–highland relationship is, as expected, largely determined by the nature of ecology and sociopolitical organization of interacting populations. For example, the competitive character seen in northern Peru has much to do with the roughly comparable degrees of sociopolitical integration of coastal and highland polities, limited verticality (the upper end being truncated), and the productivity of the coast.

Gallinazo, Mochica, and subsequent Sicán and Chimú polities all had a strong littoral thrust. Their territorial expansions advanced coastwise, establishing little or no vertical complementarity. The establishment of economic self-sufficiency through extensive horizontal expansion to gain access or control of diverse coastal resources (anywhere from the western *yunka* to the Pacific and offshore islands) has been termed "horizontality."

Contrary to the common perception of the coastal environment as homogeneous, there is an impressive diversity of resources when we adopt a broader perspective to encompass a series of coastal valleys. The Southern Mochica polity, at its height around C.E. 500, had established hegemony over eleven contiguous valleys and two detached valleys, from Piura to Huarmey, a total span of some 600 kilometers (Map 5.2). This feat takes on a different meaning seen from the perspective of horizontality. Models purporting to explain Mochica expansion by imputing a desire to acquire additional productive agricultural land and tribute in response to population pressure on resources do not adequately account for situations in many valleys. For example, Mochica control of the upper Piura Valley at the northern extreme of the Mochica domain and of the small Huarmey Valley at the southern extreme existed without establishing thorough control of the closer, extensive, and productive Nepeña and Lambayeque valleys and underscores the working of other important variables. In fact, Mochica settlement patterns in valleys at the outer fringes of the domain emphasized control of the mid-valley, suggesting a major concern with control of north–south movement. We are not as yet sure if such control was achieved via diplomacy or subjugation of local populations. As seen later, the localized Mochica occupation in Piura is likely to be related to trade with Ecuador and perhaps farther north that brought *Spondylus, Strombus,* and *Conus* shell, among other exotic, prestigious goods.

Horizontally expansive strategy simultaneously accomplished other ends important to the Mochica; it assured access to good fishing grounds (e.g., around the port city of Chimbote in the Santa Valley) and offshore islands (e.g., Manabí and Lobos de Tierra islands). The latter served not

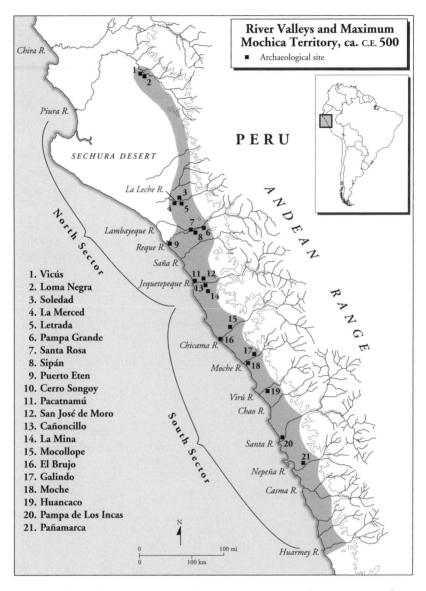

Map 5.2. Map of the north coast of Peru showing river valleys, major Mochica sites and the maximum territorial extent achieved by the Southern Mochica polity in Phase IV (ca. C.E. 500). Contour lines are at 1000 m. Based on drawing by I. Shimada.

only as hunting grounds for sea mammals such as penguins, seals, and sea lions and fishing/processing (salting and drying) bases but also as sanctuaries and guano mines. Guano, sea bird droppings rich in organic nutrients, is believed to have been mined and used as an agricultural fertilizer by the Mochica. Its use can significantly increase yields of maize and other valued crops. Hocquenghem believes that the Mochica ceramic representations of naked, bound "prisoners" and boats carrying jars, as well as the wooden figurines, necklaces and *Spondylus* found on these islands, all relate to the act of offerings for abundance of fish and guano (i.e., agricultural success). At the time of Spanish conquest, these islands were also regarded as the resting places of deceased ancestors. Thus horizontality assured Mochica physical and spiritual well-being. One can scarcely overestimate the importance of fish and other marine resources (including edible seaweed and shell heated to produce lime used in coca chewing) to both coastal and highland peoples. These resources are abundant, available year-round, and exploitable with simple technology. So Mochica horizontality meant not just removing coastal lands from Cajamarca and Recuay populations but denying their access to the Pacific.

The horizontality and verticality can be seen as a large-scale organizational response to limited resource diversity (or range of production zones) at local or regional levels. They have certain material and organizational ramifications such as the need for effective transport and distribution mechanisms. The importance of llamas as beasts of burden has been considered. Major Mochica settlements in different valleys were definitely linked by major north–south roads. As discussed later, in most valleys in the Mochica domain, there were at least three hierarchical tiers of settlements. The redistributive nature of the Mochica economy – that is, its reliance on collections of goods followed by ceremonious giveaways – is well documented for at least Phase V.

ART, CRAFT, AND TECHNOLOGY

It is evident that during the first half of the time period under study, if not much earlier, a productive, sedentary agrarian economy that combined grains and tubers was established throughout the study area. Intense, year-round exploitation of marine resources continued to be of primary importance along the Pacific coast. Favorable climatic conditions and technological advances, including the development of innovative land and water management techniques and camelid husbandry, continued to redefine "environment" in its broadest sense and its interplay with people in much of the study area. Not surprisingly, we see a notable population increase in the second half of our study period. These changes clearly went hand in hand with increasing sociopolitical complexity and concern for and sophistication in material expression of their identity, including their cosmological visions and political dogma. We now turn our attention to the technological and artistic achievements of the ERD cultures.

Although no longer employed, the label "Mastercraftsmen" was justifiable in many ways for the arts and crafts of some ERD cultures. For example, in terms of technical sophistication, virtuosity, and mastery, Mochica metalworkers and Nasca potters were unprecedented and remained to a large degree uneclipsed by later workers not only in the prehispanic Andes but in the entire prehispanic New World. In addition, the period under study saw the formalization of distinct and persistent artistic-technological traditions that characterized arts and crafts of subsequent cultures of the study area. We are speaking of distinct repertoires (or preferences) in raw materials, techniques, and technologies, as well as colors and artistic conventions that persisted in time and had a macro-regional distribution. As seen later, a rather clear difference between northern Peru–North Andes and southern Peru–South-Central Andes exists. In this and following sections, art and craft products are seen as replete with meaning, not only of technical and technological domains but also of social position and obligations and cosmology of users and manufacturers.

Textiles

In the broad scheme of prehispanic Andean arts and crafts, southern Peru and the adjacent South-Central Andes are characterized by a penchant for polychrome rendering (consistent use of three or more colors) in various media, but particularly in textiles and ceramics. When we speak of textiles, the earlier caveats regarding biases stemming from differential preservation and looting activities should be kept in mind. From the south coast of Peru to the northern coast of Chile, the extreme aridity and sandy matrix of cemeteries have facilitated exceptional preservation and intensive looting of mummy bundles wrapped in and accompanied by large quantities of textiles. In contrast, textiles in the highlands and on the Ecuadorian coast have rarely been conserved because of unfavorable environmental conditions. For example, tapestries woven with camelid fiber appear on the south coast some time around the middle of the first millennium B.C.E., which raises the likelihood that there was a notable wool-weaving tradition in the adjacent *altiplano* region even earlier. This is not surprising given that camelid husbandry was established there considerably earlier. Further, durable ceramic and stone spindle whorls, bone tools (awls, carding tools), and representations on figurines and statuary amply indicate the importance and high technical level of textiles in the Peruvian highlands even in the absence of preserved specimens.

Throughout coastal Peru, textiles were used to cover a variety of items (walls, mummies, metal objects, etc.), as backing for sheet metal ornaments and shell beads, as fishing nets, hats, bags of different sizes, banners, and, of course, clothing. The principal garments of the Andean people, such as the mantle, poncho, loincloth, turban, and other head coverings, were established by the beginning of the period under consideration. Images of men in Paracas textiles also show the use of a wraparound skirt.

Perhaps the most important function of decorated textiles in the prehispanic Andes was as a medium for visual, symbolic communication in a nonliterate world. Sixteenth- and seventeenth-century Spanish writings relate that in the Inka culture garments and headdresses indicated an individual's social position and ethnic identity, and the decorative images on them expressed the ritual obligations of the wearers. There are indications that such was the case already for the Paracas textiles, as discussed later. Also, caches of decorated textiles with and without associated human burials in coastal Peru during the period under study suggest that the decorated textiles were highly prized and that skilled weavers may have competed with each other for recognition of their expertise and social prestige. Much the same can be said about competition for social prestige among other craftsmen.

Discussion here is heavily skewed toward Paracas and Nasca textiles because the presence of numerous well-preserved specimens with informative designs, technical mastery and variability, and diverse functions has stimulated their intense study. Much of the justification for singling out the prehispanic Andes as one of the two major weaving centers of the world (the other being Persia) derives from the Paracas and Nasca textiles. Yet the reader should keep in mind that the Paracas textiles constitute virtually the only large sample of complete scientifically excavated garments for the period under study (or for that matter, for much of prehistory).

The south coast tradition of elaborately decorated polychrome textiles was established during the first millennium B.C.E., when the Paracas culture flourished in the Chincha, Pisco, and Ica valleys. From late Paracas (Necropolis phase dating to c. 300–100 B.C.E. – dating of the Paracas sequence is being actively debated) to early Nasca times (c. 100 B.C.E. to C.E. 200), south coast textiles show a remarkable artistic and technical evolution that produced what many consider to be the finest prehispanic textiles of the New World.

During 1927–1928, Tello and Mejía Xesspe excavated 429 funerary bundles (dated to c. B.C.E. 300 to C.E. 200) from a large cemetery now known as the Paracas Necropolis on the arid, sand-covered Paracas Peninsula on the south coast. Unlike the earlier Paracas Cavernas burials interred in bottle-shaped tombs (circular burial chambers at the bottoms of vertical shafts), most of the Necropolis bundles were found in subterranean square stone chambers. Both tomb types were used for multiple burials. In some Necropolis tombs, smaller bundles encircled a large, central bundle, presumably to reflect status difference. Thus far, only a handful of large bundles (that reach heights of up to about 2 m) have been unwrapped. Each has revealed a mummified adult male in fetal position set inside a basket along with foods such as maize, yuca, and peanut. Much of the Paracas Necropolis bundle volume was made up of the many layers (up to over sixty layers) of woven and embroidered cloth (including up to 10-m-long lengths of plain cloth) and clothing (e.g., turbans, shoulder mantles, ponchos, loincloths), as well as cloth-wrapped items of prestige and ritual value such as *Spondylus* shell and trophy heads. Attached to the exteriors of large bundles were such items as a headbands and simple, sheet-metal gold masks on the head of the bundle, feather tunics, leather capes, embroidered mantles, and one or two staffs. Lastly, all of these items were wrapped in a large plain cloth and sewn up. The basic organization of each bundle is the same, but specific contents differ, giving a clear indication of each individual's status and role. Given the nature and quality of accompaniments, the men in these large and elaborate bundles are regarded as the deceased political-religious leaders of regional Paracas society.

The fame of Paracas textiles is largely derived from the large, elaboratedly embroidered mantles in these bundles. We owe much of the technical knowledge about them to years of detailed analysis by A. Paul. Their sizes are typically 2.3 to 2.8 meters by 1.0 to 1.4 meters, though some are considerably bigger. These textiles have elaborate embroidered borders and orderly representational images of individuals in ritual attire, plants and animals, both terrestrial and marine, on solid-color (typically red, indigo blue, or dark green) backgrounds (Fig 5.8). Today, we think of embroidery as a technique of ornamenting small areas, but Paracas weavers employed it to cover 70 to 75 percent of the textile surface, often forming areas of solid color.

Two kinds of embroidering styles, Linear and Block Color, were used. The former preceded the latter, but both are found on the famed Necropolis textiles. In terms of manual work and the creative processes involved, they are rather antithetical: The Linear is a conservative style based on straight lines (horizontal, vertical, and diagonal), limited colors in thin lines (red, green, yellow, and blue), and highly precise, rigid,

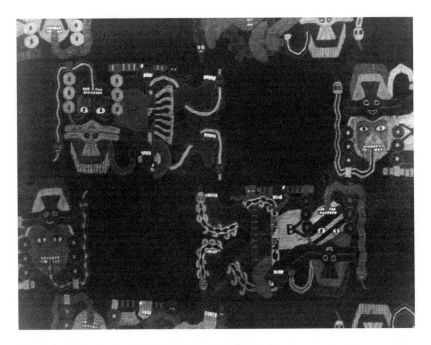

Figure 5.8. Detail of a Paracas Necropolis mantle showing personages carrying a dart-thrower and knife executed in Block Color technique embroidery. T/01661 Museo Nacional de Antropología, Arqueología e Historia, Lima, Peru. Photo by Y. Yoshii.

repetitive motifs, whereas the Block Color is characterized by curves, a wide range of colors (nearly twenty colors) in broad expanses (thus the designation), and highly variable, innovative motifs. Both are technically difficult and labor intensive, and they create in their own ways striking visual effects. Interlocking, repetitive Linear motifs such as highly stylized felines, birds, snakes, and the "Oculate Being" described in the later Iconography section, fill borders and regularly spaced columns in the center of mantles. The Block Color style is known for "ritual impersonator" motifs – outlined, curvilinear individuals wearing elaborate costumes in various positions, impersonating animals or supernaturals. Those seemingly in flight with head thrown back and hair streaming have been called "ecstatic shamans" by Paul – that is, shamans or spiritual leaders in trance state. All these motifs are filled in with intensely colored stitches.

Each Block Color embroidery is highly individualistic. Personages depicted vary from one mantle to another (i.e., one bundle to another), suggesting that embroidery was tailor-made to match specific leaders. Whether embroidered cloth was prepared while they were still alive or after their deaths (perhaps while the bodies were partially mummified), we do not know. However, inclusion of unfinished embroideries in bundles, and the thousands of worker-hours required to prepare these textiles, support the former view. We cannot ignore the possibility that some of these textiles were actually worn by leaders during their lives. Paul regards these two embroidery styles as having held complementary functions: Block Color imageries on the mantles are seen to express ritual roles or obligations that the deceased held during his life, while the Linear style motifs speak of his connection to the ideological tradition of the society to which he belonged.

Although embroidered textiles are best known, decorations on some cloth were painted. In some cases, striking visual effects were created by double- and triple-cloth, in which two or three separate layers of distinctly colored warps and wefts were woven together (over and underlying) to create combined designs. Slit tapestry weaving (in which different colored wefts are separated between warp threads) also emerged during Paracas times, as did technically difficult "discontinuous warp and weft" weaving.

By late Paracas times, weaving a textile involved systemic consideration of many variables, including range, placement, and combined effects of colors and motifs, tactile sensation, thickness, weight, and size, as well as the status and role of users. Selection of fiber, preparation of yarns, dyes, weaving techniques, and motifs also became highly structured and sophisticated. In the case of the Linear and Block Color styles of embroidery, the former was highly conservative, and designs and layout of motifs followed warps and wefts, while the latter was individualistic and ignored warp–weft structure.

Perhaps foremost among factors that contributed to the remarkable artistic and technical qualities of late Paracas textiles was the availability of camelid fiber to use in conjunction with indigenous cotton. Handfuls of unspun camelid fiber were one of various classes of goods found wrapped inside funerary bundles from the Paracas Necropolis. The wool is presumed to be of alpaca brought down from the *altiplano*, but the specific processes and agents involved in its acquisition are not understood. It is unlikely that a crucial change in raw materials (e.g., camelid fiber) would occur without concurrent adoption of other aspects of an inferred early *altiplano* weaving tradition. Camelid wool is resilient and takes and holds dyes much better than cotton; thus a search for new dyes and, more importantly, a new perception of textile art would be expected. In fact, late Paracas Necropolis textiles show a whole series of improvements in spinning and weaving techniques and an increase in the number of colors used. It is in this period that wrapping of brightly dyed camelid fiber yarns around cotton warps began. Also, the dull red color believed to have been derived from a plant (possibly *Relbunium nitidum*) was completely replaced by the intense red derived from cochineal.

Another contributing factor appears to have been integration of Chavín cult iconography (see the later discussion) presumably from area(s) farther north transmitted by portable, nonbreakable painted cotton cloth like that found at Karwa (some 8 km south of Paracas Necropolis) in Ica dating around 300–200 B.C.E. Over 200 separate, painted textiles rivaling the number and iconographic repertory of known Chavín stone sculptures were looted from tombs around Karwa. The "Staff God," "cayman" or "crocodile supernatural" "winged guardian," feline head, and other classic Chavín-style motifs were depicted in Chavín conventions. The Staff God, the Chavín's principal deity, was the most frequently depicted principal deity on the Karwa textiles. Even the layout of these motifs resembles that of the stone sculptures at Chavín as if it was meant to re-create the ritual setting of the cult center. In particular, a series of sewn pieces, when hung on walls, would produce the image of a procession of jaguars carved on the slabs that lined the sunken circular court in front of the Old Temple at Chavín (described later). At the same time, the Karwa textiles are not mere copies of Chavín stone sculptures. Simpler, local variants of these classic motifs are also found among these textiles. The painting was done in different shades of red or brown derived from iron oxides mixed with alum (a mordant) in tannic acids derived from plants. Analysis of motifs, yarns, and weaving techniques by Wallace suggests that the bulk of the lot was locally produced and that imported textiles may have come from the central or north coasts. There is no evidence of foreign enclaves in and around Karwa. Further, locally manufactured textiles show integration of the introduced Chavín iconography with local Paracas motifs, leading to the development of local substyles. In this regard, the prevalence of what Lyon calls the "Staff Goddess of Karwa," female deity figures holding staffs and associated with cotton plants not seen at Chavín, is important. Following his vision of a prestigious Chavín oracle establishing a branch oracle on the south coast around 300–200 B.C.E., Burger believes the goddess to be a wife, daughter, or sister of the Staff God at Chavín. On the other hand, Cordy-Collins suggests that the goddess represents the female half of the Staff God, who had a dual male–female existence. Stone-Miller suggests that the goddess served to assure fertility of cotton, a key coastal plant, and symbolized the association between women and weaving. Whatever the significance of the goddess, the emergence of a Chavín branch cult or Paracas-Chavín hybrid cult on the south coast undoubtedly stimulated local technical and artistic developments, including textiles for ritual use.

Although the number of preserved Nasca textiles is considerably smaller than that for Paracas, stylistic, iconographic, and technical continuities are apparent. Nasca textiles (found in Pisco, Ica, Nazca, Acarí, and Yauca), pertaining to the early to middle (of nine) phases in particular, show complex and thoughtful design composition, precise and uniform weaving and dyeing, and careful selection of raw materials and preparation of yarns to suit the different weaving techniques. Whether fine or thick, yarns are uniformly spun. Given the variability, uniformity, and stability of colors found, the art of dyeing appears to have been perfected. In comparison with Paracas textiles, Nasca weavings de-emphasized borders while maintaining other Paracas features. Difficult discontinuous warp and weft weaving also continued.

Following the tradition set by the Karwa textiles, Nasca weavers also produced painted cotton cloth that shows no evidence of use for clothing. These textiles have motifs derived from the antecedent Block Color embroideries of the Paracas Necropolis mantles but painted much larger in scale and outlined in black. They show "harvesters" or human figures holding harvested crops such as maize, yuca, and peanut; ritual impersonators; animals (e.g., Pampas cat, *Felis colocolo*); and supernaturals, some of whom carry agricultural crops as well. We have the impression that painted cloth was used as a backdrop for outdoor rituals related to agricultural fertility and/or harvest. Whether the painted and nonpainted textiles had mutually exclusive functions remains unclear largely due to the limited sample.

Overall, studies have shown that by the first few centuries C.E. south coast weavers had mastered or invented most weaving techniques known the world over, ranging from single-yarn looping to gauze, double-faced cloth, and some that are unique to the area. They used these techniques individually or in combination with cotton or camelid wool yarns dyed in a diverse range of colors and spun in different manners according to desired visual, structural, and tactile effects. Designs on textiles were achieved by a variety of means, including painting, embroidery, hanging sheet-metal pieces, sewing the trimmed feathers of bright tropical birds, and the labor-intensive technique of "structural weaving." The last means that the desired patterns and colors were created "from within" by separating and manipulating warp yarns that had been dyed and selected prior to the onset of weaving in accordance with a preconceived design configuration, composition, and colors. Thus it was during the period under study that significant improvements in raw materials, expansion in the technical repertoire, and attendant reconceptualization of the creative potential of weaving contributed to establishing decorated textiles as one of the most valued craft items of the Andean world, a position it held throughout the history.

Preserved textiles from the central and north coasts are relatively small in number but sufficient to indicate their cultural importance and impressive technical sophistication and variability. For example, Conklin has identified five distinct weave structures among Mochica textiles, including plain and compound weaves, and two forms of slit tapestry. The latter appear on "pictorial cloth" (Phase V) found in a subterranean burial chamber at the site of Pacatnamú at the mouth of Jequetepeque Valley. They were decorated with depictions of what H. Ubbelohde-Doering regards as water and fertility rites.

There are indications that brightly colored, trimmed bird feathers were anchored to plain cloth and used by Mochica élite as cloaks. We noted similar feather cloth on Paracas Necropolis bundles. Numerous fan-shaped feather head ornaments found accompanying the spectacular burial of the regional Mochica lord at Sipán (popularly known as the Lord of Sipán burial; Phase III) in the mid-Lambayeque Valley also attest to the prestige accorded to feather artifacts. It should also be noted that tatooing and facial painting complemented clothing and ornaments among Mochicas and probably among most other Andean cultures.

Ceramics

Because of its very distinctive localized developments, the prehistory of craftsmanship in pottery needs to be geographically divided. To begin with the southern portion of our study area, the south coast peoples who devised many-colored textiles also strove for polychromy in ceramics. In fact, during the period under study, polychrome ceramics came to be a hallmark of southern Peru and the adjacent South-Central Andes in contrast with northern Peruvian and coastal Ecuadorian emphasis on naturalistic, sculptural modeling and a limited palette of colors (one to three). The earlier technique of decorating the exteriors of fired vessels by means of applying pigments on an undercoat of tree resin (Fig. 5.9) was replaced with prefired, slip painting by a century or so before C.E. 0.

The southern polychrome slip-painting tradition is likely to have originated in the Marcavalle or Qaluyu styles (c. 1400–800 B.C.E.?) in the Cusco region and on the north shore of Lake Titicaca, respectively. Populations in these two areas may have been in contact, as mentioned earlier. In the case of this tradition, we are speaking of a pervasive and persistent use of more than three colors. In the Marcavalle style, the total color range reached at least eight, though only three colors may be found on a single vessel. The Pukara style continued the Qaluyu polychrome tradition that was otherwise abandoned in much of the South Highlands of Peru. It combines some modeling and painted designs outlined by carefully executed incisions. Technically, Pukara ceramics are generally well made and are commonly prefire slip-painted in red, black, white, gray, and yellow. These colors, however, are rather dull, perhaps, in part due to relatively low firing temperatures and insufficient oxidation during their firing. Common vessel forms are out flaring, incurving, and pedestaled bowls and jars. Designs include "running angels," spotted cats with modeled heads, front-facing humans, crested birds, llamas, and geometric motifs. Iconographic analysis by Chávez indicates that many motifs relate

Figure 5.9. An Ocucaje-style double spout bottle (related to Paracas) richly decorated with post-fired resin-based paint decoration of a mythical feline (probably jaguar, *Felis onca*). 0005, Fundación Museo Amano, Lima. Height: 17 cm. Photo by Y. Yoshi.

to one of two themes or two supernatural beings: a woman who leads an alpaca by rope while holding a scepter, and a man associated with trophy heads, dead bodies, and felines. Studies by Kidder and Chávez show that Pukara and Tiwanaku shared major mythical themes and deities.

A second southerly tradition is that of Paracas and Topará. Sometime before C.E. 0, Topará potters (centered in the Pisco Valley?) became quite skillful in controlling firing and began using a whitish slip. Whether or not they are indeed the source of the innovation, at about the same time, the prefire slip appears in various areas on the Peruvian coast and highlands. In fact, the introduction of white slip is regarded as the key step toward the establishment of brilliant polychrome slip painting for which the later Nasca pottery is justly famous. Once this decorative technique was established, it persisted as the south coast tradition up to the time of the Spanish conquest.

A major innovation such as the use of prefired slip does not emerge or spread in isolation from other aspects of ceramic production, which is a multistage and multifaceted process involving many decisions made on the basis of stylistic, technical-technological, and social factors. Thus it is not surprising that the Topará-style pottery also displayed considerable control over firing conditions. It was well fired, and the potters were capable of achieving subtle surface-color differences. As the largely mono-chrome Topará-style pottery achieved considerable popularity in the Ica Valley over the traditional Paracas pottery with polychrome postfired resin paints, naturalistic representations of important traditional religious motifs became largely confined to textiles (e.g., embroidering). In the Nasca drainage, Topará influence was much more limited, and there was a gradual shift from resin-painted Paracas pottery to slip-painted Nasca pottery. In Paracas pottery, designs were first outlined with fine incisions and fired, followed by application of bright-colored mineral pigments in a viscous resin base. (Fig. 5.9). With greater mastery over slip painting and high temperature firing in an oxidized atmosphere that helped to produce brilliant, colorful, and complex images, the earlier technique of outlining designs with incisions soon disappeared, and ceramics appar-ently became the primary medium of artistic expression. Concomitantly, realistic representations of religious motifs in textiles seem to disappear. Over the total span of time under consideration, execution of ceramic designs gradually shifted from rather naturalistic to highly schematic, so that their meanings cannot be readily understood without the under-standing of their evolutionary trajectories.

We now turn to the south coast's celebrated Nasca tradition. A wide array of vessel forms and intriguing representational motifs in a range of earth colors have made the Nasca style one of the most complex and intriguing of prehispanic art styles. Many scholars have focused on stylis-tic and iconographic analysis (e.g., Gayton, Kroeber, Sawyer, Proulx, and Silverman). Nasca style ceramics are primarily found in the Ica Valley and Río Grande de Nazca drainage basin just to the south on the south coast of Peru. Since its original identification by Max Uhle at the begin-ning of this century, this style has been stylistically seriated into nine phases (1–9; c. C.E. 1–700). Nasca potters utilized a wide range of slip paints with mineral pigments to produce colors such as white, gray, black, red, light red, dark red, pink, orange, light orange, yellow, brown, purple, violet, and light blue. Vessel forms included anything from bowls and cups to musical instruments (panpipes, trumpets, whistles, and drums) and effigy bottles in the form of real or mythological creatures with double spouts and bridges at the top. Some drums with cylindrical bodies and pointed bottoms reached heights of over 1 meter and weights of about 30 kilograms (Fig. 5.10).

As Carmichael has justly cautioned, the widespread high estimation of the technical and artistic qualities of Nasca polychrome ceramics is based on the carefully selected "masterpieces" that have graced publications and museums. These are pieces that exhibit a high gloss, pleasing proportions and symmetry, and complex motifs rendered in many intense colors. However, they are not representative of the general

Figure 5.10. Detail of a large, reconstructed Nasca Phase 3 (Phase 2-3 transition?) drum with a highly complex polychrome decoration. The scene may represent a mythical battle. Raúl Apesteguía Collection, Lima. Height: 1.14 m. Photo by Y. Yutaka.

quality of the Nasca ceramics. In fact, Carmichael's examination of unsorted field collections revealed considerable variation in quality as well as a relative paucity of fine pieces. Many were unslipped plainware vessels for utilitarian use, and even among painted vessels, relatively crude specimens were common.

Usually, vessels were formed using variations and combinations of coiling, drawing, and direct shaping of clay lumps placed on potters' plates. These plates are disk-shaped supports that provide a stable working surface and allow ready rotation of the vessels being formed. Shallow bowls may have been used in many cases to form vessel bottoms. Once the bottom was formed, the upper vessel body was built by drawing or coiling. In some cases, it was accomplished by simply placing a cap over the preformed walls. Carmichael observed evidence of the paddle and anvil technique in some vessels. In this technique, a hand-held anvil (usually a smooth ovoid stone) is placed against the interior of the vessel while a wooden or pottery paddle is used to strike the exterior surface in order to thin, consolidate, and shape the wall. The neck and rim were formed by shaping coils placed atop the hardened vessel body.

For the complex double-spout and bridge form, a spherical vessel body was first formed by working the shoulders of the vessel inward, until only a small opening was left that could be sealed by a plug or twisting off extra clay. Then two holes were cut, and a hand-formed double-spout and bridge was attached. This procedure is essentially identical to that used by Mochica potters for their stirrup-spout bottles. Overall, vessels were formed using a combination of techniques, rarely ever by a single technique. Unlike Mochica ceramics, Nasca potters did not employ press molds for vessel formation. The range and combinations of techniques discerned on Nasca fine ceramics are those observed on or inferred for earlier Chavín and Cupisnique pottery by Lumbreras and other scholars.

Decoration of Nasca fine ceramics was carried out primarily by means of slip painting. Incised designs that lingered on from earlier Paracas ceramics disappear by the end of Nasca Phase 1, and appliqué was occasionally used to add low-relief features. In preparation for painted decoration, a background slip, usually light beige, was first applied and the design area demarcated by bands at the rim and base. Fine-line outlines of the designs were drawn prior to or after application of slip paints, which were prepared by mixing locally available ground manganese or iron oxides (limonite, hematite, and magnetite) with fine clay in water. That the wide color spectrum employed by Nasca potters resulted from many years of experimentation is evident. For example, early Nasca pottery sometimes shows the crazing or fine cracks that result when slips shrink more than the vessel body during or after firing. Such problems largely disappear after Nasca Phase 3.

Painting was followed by thorough burnishing to assure that paints adhered securely to the vessel surface. This action aligned clay molecules, imparted a high gloss, made the vessel more impermeable, and added greater tensile strength to the vessel surface (i.e., pleasant to look at and touch and harder to break).

Information from the recently discovered terminal Nasca (c. C.E. 600–700) ceramic workshop at Maymi in the lower Pisco Valley complement the foregoing reconstruction based on analysis of finished products. Maymi is the only prehispanic ceramic workshop thus far reported on the south coast. It preserved a wide range of production debris. Although the workshop produced mainly ceremonial Wari-style ceramics, many of the tool kits and technical features appear to be indigenous. For example, Anders and her colleagues recovered potter's plates, both specifically manufactured as such (large ones 20–22-cm, small ones 10–11-cm diameter) and recycled large concave sherds. Final shaping and smoothing of interior and exterior surfaces were done using a variety of implements such as gourd fragments, large recycled sherds, longitudinal segments of split cane, and cotton rags and maize cobs. Skillful use of these implements was the key to achieving the thin walls (typically 3–4 mm) of Nasca fine ceramics. As expected, painted decorations were done with different sized brushes made by laying in parallel locks of human hair in narrow cane shafts, which were then bound with twisted cotton thread. As the brushes became worn, the hair could be pulled out further. Flat-nosed brushes made of narrow cane fibers appear to have been used for drawing design outlines. On the other hand, the use of multiple, partial molds for forming the face-neck jars and effigy bottles documented at Maymi may well prove to have been a north coast (Mochica) innovation adopted by both local and Wari potters.

The firing technique reconstructed from finished products agrees well with the independent data from Maymi. It appears that vessels were stacked or nested in layers within circular pit kilns and fired in an oxidized atmosphere. Many Nasca bowls show "ghost images" on their interiors, indicating that they were nested inside one another during firing. At Maymi, two excavated kilns (c. 3 and 1 m in diameter and 40 and 30 cm in depth, respectively) were found with sherds lining the walls and edges of the floors. A refractory sherd cover and lining would have reduced the heat loss and created a stable, closed system. The fuel and other details of firing remain uncertain at Maymi; however, the horsetail (*Equisetum* sp.) plant, which is rich in silica, was found at the bottoms of the kilns, presumably to improve air and heat circulation within the kiln.

It is clear that Nasca polychrome ceramics were widely available across social boundaries and used in habitational, ceremonial, and mortuary contexts. What is least known about them is the organization, scale, and intensity of production and distribution of products. Carmichael found that the average number of ceramic vessels interred in tombs increased over time, from one to two at the beginning of the Nasca sequence to five or six by Phase 5. Finewares were also used in votive and dedicatory offerings at such locations as the major ceremonial center of Cahuachi. Concurrently, as noted earlier, polychrome ceramics came to supplant embroidered textiles as the primary medium of artistic and religious expression. These usages and trends imply an overall increase over time in demand for fine ceramics, but we cannot readily quantify this increase. Also, many vessels in tombs show scratches, abrasions, and other evidence of use-wear, indicating that they were not made solely for burial purposes.

Northern Peru manifests a different spectrum of ceramic arts. At early dates, it is marked by the Salinar and Gallinazo styles. In a sense, Salinar ceramics found on much of the north coast of Peru (Lambayeque to Nepeña) are transitional between the earlier Cupisnique/Chavín and later Mochica. Salinar culture seems to have existed circa 200 B.C.E. to C.E. 1 following the Chavín "horizon" around 400–200 B.C.E.

In contrast to Cupisnique/Chavín emphasis on monochrome, reduced-fired wares, Salinar potters preferred oxidized-fired ceramics, as did the later Mochica. In fact, Salinar contributed to the widespread popularity of white-slipped, red-painted ceramics called the "White-on-Red Horizon," which existed about a century or so before C.E. 0 (and included Mochica and Recuay as well). Salinar potters retained many Cupisnique/Chavín vessel forms, notably stirrup-spout bottles and open bowls, but at the same time adopted new forms such as the spout-and-handle bottle and modeled-figure spout-and-bridge bottle. Decorative techniques such as appliqué, incision, and patterned burnishing persisted from Cupisnique/Chavín. Although modeling of animals and humans

occurred, it did not have the developed sculptural character of Cupis-
nique/Chavín or Mochica ceramics. Surprisingly, Cupisnique/Chavín religious motifs or derivatives are absent. In fact, Salinar decorations emphasized geometric motifs painted in white against a red-slipped
background or vice versa. It is probable that the Salinar style contributed
to the emergence of the Mochica style, but the latter in its initial phases
emphasized a fanged supernatural being reminiscent of the Cupisnique/
Chavín supernaturals. In spite of this iconographic difference, we may
eventually find that the population represented by the Mochica style
descended from a Salinar population.

Gallinazo-style pottery is characterized by unslipped utilitarian vessels,
often decorated with simple human and animal faces done by modeling,
appliqué, incising, gouging, and/or punctation, and much more rare
fineware decorated with negative painting (Fig. 5.11). Examples are widely
found on the north coast from Piura to Casma. Gallinazo ceramics were
once thought to be found primarily in the Moche-Virú-Santa valley
sector, but they are also quite common between the Jequetepeque and
La Leche valleys associated with urban sites with monumental constructions, as in the former sector.

The Gallinazo style is persistent; it probably began around C.E. 0 and
continued at least to the end of the first millennium C.E. Being iconographically and technically simple and conservative, it has not received
much attention. The ethnic population represented by Gallinazo style
ceramics coexisted in time and space with that of the Mochica style, and
issues related to their coexistence will be considered at some length later.

As Nasca and Paracas are celebrated southern styles, Mochica has been
enshrined in every museum as the glory of the north. Sometime around
C.E. 0 (or perhaps a century or so earlier), we see a distinct art style that
integrated various features of the antecedent Cupisnique, Chavín, and
Salinar styles. It combined the naturalistic, sculptural rendering and
symbolism of the Cupisnique and Chavín styles (e.g., interlocking canines) with the bichrome slip painting of the Salinar style to represent a
wide range of events, creatures, and activities of both the natural and
supernatural worlds. The resultant style, called Mochica or Moche, was
one of the few figurative or narrative styles of the prehispanic New World
art (the Maya art of southern Mexico and Guatemala is another). There
is nothing comparable in the prehispanic Andes to these informative,
illustrated records of oral narratives or "story books." In addition, the

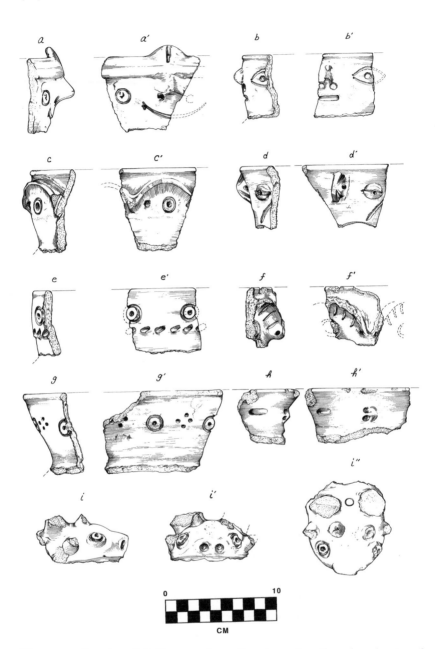

Figure 5.11. Samples of Gallinazo-style unslipped vessels collected at the site of Paredones, La Leche Valley. Drawing by César Samillán.

Mochica potters took lifelike modeling to an unparalleled level (Fig. 5.12), forming the core of what Willey labeled the "North Peruvian Plastic Pottery Tradition."

Examples of Mochica art are found in diverse media and forms: ceramics, metals, textiles, gourds, wood, bone, shell, featherwork, and human skin (painted or tatooed). The most prominent and numerous surviving component of Mochica art, accounting for over 90 percent according to Donnan, is ceramics. (Perhaps up to 100,000 whole vessels exist in collections throughout the world.) What is depicted in noncer-

Figure 5.12. Mochica Phase III "portrait" vessel (stirrup-spout bottle). Note the captivating quality of the naturalistic, full sculptural representation for which the Mochica style is justly known. Raúl Apesteguía Collection, Lima. Photo by Y. Yutaka.

amic media is invariably also found on ceramics. Besides their staggering volume, the naturalistic representations of Mochica ceramic art, and the diversity of subject matter depicted on them, have invited in-depth analysis, primarily to gain insights into intangible aspects of their world, beliefs, and customs.

Scholars such as Donnan, Hocquenghem, Golte, and others have shown that definite formal and ideological structures governed subject matter and aesthetic expression on ceramics. All these features are found on a relatively narrow range of predominantly oxidized redware-painted and modeled vessels, particularly stirrup-spout bottles. During the height of the Mochica artistic tradition (Phases III and IV of the five-phase sequence), motifs were typically painted in silhouette or fine lines in various shades of red, without any use of shading, on a well-burnished thick cream slip background. Postfired fugitive black paint was used to add details, such as mustaches, and prefired orange paint served to highlight certain features (e.g., face, costumes) of the subject. Backgrounds were often shown, typically depicted in a shorthand manner and in reduced size. Depth of field was indicated either by dividing the decorative surface into two or more horizontal panels or by placing small objects or figures in the upper area of a scene. The subject matter, human or not, was rendered schematically and in a perspective combining profile and frontal views so that it is seen from its most defining aspect. Heads, arms, legs, and feet were inevitably shown in profile, while eyes, hands, and torsos, including distinctive ornaments and tunics, were shown in frontal perspective. In a complex scene with multiple figures, the importance of a given figure was conveyed through its larger relative size and height, centrality, and elaborateness of costume. The head was commonly drawn disproportionately large to show expression and ornamentation. Supernatural beings were drawn with double-lobed ears, interlocking canines, or "winged" or comma-shaped eyes (raised, pointed outer corners; Fig. 5.13).

The two-dimensional painting technique was complemented by naturalistic, full, sculptural modeling that was unsurpassed in prehispanic Andean art. It was most effective in showing compact, static poses.

Mochica ceramics are commonly subdivided into five phases, following Larco, who seriated them largely on the basis of changes seen in stirrup-spout bottle form. Generally, over time, the stirrup increased in size relative to the vessel body. Additional Mochica gravelots excavated at the site of Moche and elsewhere have allowed refinement of Larco's

Figure 5.13. Ceramic representation of a major Mochica deity that is sometimes called *Ai-apaec* (arms are missing). Note double-lobe ears and interlocking fangs that signify supernatural origins. Probably the ears and eyes originally had inlay. Museo Banco Central de Reserva del Perú, Lima. Height: 26.5 cm. Photo by Y. Yoshii.

seriation. Donnan's stylistic seriation of fine-line drawings also complemented Larco's subdivision.

In spite of its widespread use, such chronology is far from adequate. Larco failed to publish the stratigraphic and grave-lot evidence of his seriation. The absolute dates assigned each phase, with the exception of Phase V, are still largely a matter of speculation based on scattered radiocarbon dates. In deriving his chronology, Larco relied heavily on funerary vessels from the Chicama and Moche valleys, the Southern

Mochica heartland. The applicability of his chronology to the Northern Mochica territory has not been adequately tested. In fact, in recent years, some scholars have argued that Larco's sequence is invalid for the Northern Mochica. This seems premature insofar as excavations in the La Leche Valley showed that Phases III to V are valid; Phases I and II have not been tested. Some phases span as many as 200 to 250 years, raising the possibility that two successive phases may well have coexisted in different areas of the extensive Mochica territory. "Contemporaneity" as defined by these phases is inadequate for any fine-grained cultural reconstruction and interregional comparison. Whereas Phase III saw significant territorial expansion of the Mochica polity, ceramics may well mask a series of military conquests and reconquests, rather than the implicitly assumed single successful conquest.

In terms of manufacture of Mochica ceramics, the large-scale use of two-piece press molds for vessel formation sets it apart from other ERD ceramics. Mochica potters employed single techniques and combinations of techniques such as coiling, drawing, and direct shaping (modeling) of clay lumps, stamping, paddling, and molding for vessel formation. Most commonly, more than one technique was employed. Evidence of the paddle-and-anvil technique is most apparent in large utilitarian vessels. Formation of complex, fine ceramics relied heavily on two-piece press molds or assembly of hand-shaped with mold-made components. The common construction technique of the popular stirrup-spout bottles was already described.

Larco notes that use of two-piece press molds spans the entire five phases of the Mochica ceramic sequence. In some effigy vessels, molds appear to have been made directly from real-life subjects. For example, Dunn has identified nineteen races of sculpted maize, whose molds appear to have been made from actual maize specimens. Sawyer suspected that realistic "portrait vessels" with lifelike individual features may have been made from life. Although the portrait vessels are about two-thirds of the real-life size, the size difference may be due to the volume reduction of fired clay (Fig. 5.12).

Vessel formation by using two-piece molds is a persistent technical feature that characterizes a succession of ceramic styles on the north coast of Peru. It characterizes not only the Mochica but also the subsequent Sicán and Chimú. Although formation of vessel bottoms perhaps using bowl-shaped gourds as molds is already seen among earlier Cupisnique bottles, the Mochica predilection for molds may well have been stimulated by the long tradition of mold-made figurines found in coastal Ecuador. Single-press molds were used to form the fronts of such figurines while the backs were cursorily finished into a slightly convex plain surface. These figurines have been found intentionally smashed or simply buried in caches. Cummins argues that in Ecuadorian contexts, the use of single-press molds was bound to the specific creative process of replicating important images and not employed to increase overall production of utilitarian forms or complete figurines.

Mochica potters produced a similar array of figurines with one-piece molds, but their functions are not clear. They also produced figurines using two-piece molds. Use of large, unfired mold-made sculptural figures of naked "prisoners" (for ritual offerings) with ropes around their necks and tied hands has recently been documented. Generally molds were used by the Mochica not only to replicate specific images of ritual and political importance (e.g., "portrait" vessels) but to increase greatly the production output of a wide range of complete vessels that have less ideological content (particularly face-neck jars). Mochica potters strived to balance greater availability of their products with the individuality of the subjects represented in them. Technological innovations cannot be understood apart from their social contexts.

It is difficult to overemphasize the difference in scale and complexity of Mochica society from those of their coastal Ecuadorian and Peruvian neighbors. The state-level society that held sway over a 350-kilometer stretch of the most fertile portion of the Peruvian coast demanded another magnitude of fine ceramic production to meet the demands of its political economy and religion.

Once the vessels were formed, they were covered with a slip, painted, and finally carefully burnished. Firing seems to have been done in relatively small circular pit kilns and quadricular kilns with adobe brick side walls. The fine-line drawings that decorated many fine vessels (particularly stirrup-spout bottles) show some intervalley differences in iconographic content, which suggests that production and distribution of such vessels were controlled at the regional level. There are also some differences in the relative frequencies of vessels forms. At the same time, there is considerable stylistic, technical, and morphological standardization in ceramics, suggesting a concerted, high-level effort to establish ideological and political unity among these regions, particularly on the southern half of the north coast, or the domain of the southern Mochica polity.

We now turn away from the powerful coastal centers to consider a northern Peruvian highland style, starting with Cajamarca and continuing below with Recuay. The unbroken stylistic continuity (i.e., autonomy) of Cajamarca art from its inception around 200–100 B.C.E. up to the Spanish conquest is remarkable, given the presence of powerful neighbors and the series of imperial expansions that reached this area. It is known essentially only from its fine ceramics made with locally abundant white kaolin paste fired at high temperatures (over 1,000°C) and decorated with geometric or highly stylized motifs painted in red, black (dark brown), and white against a whitish background. Prefired painting is the only decorative technique used. Shallow bowls with tripods or ring-shaped bases are the most common and best-known forms of kaolin paste ceramics. Decoration of the interior surface was emphasized over the exterior. Utilitarian jars and globular bowls were made with coarser clay.

Their ceramic tradition seems to have emerged out of an antecedent local style called Layzón, which had already shed earlier Chavín-derived motifs and featured simple monochrome geometric line decorations (dark red on whitish background). Cajamarca style ceramics are subdivided into five phases by Matsumoto: Initial, Early, Middle, Late, and Final. The first three phases pertain to the time period under consideration. Initial Cajamarca ceramics (200 B.C.E. to C.E. 200) are largely confined to the Cajamarca Basin. Early Cajamarca ceramics (C.E. 200–450) have more complex and diverse decorations and extensive distribution. They are found in much of the North Highlands as well as in *yunka* zones on both the Amazonian and Pacific sides of the Andes. Concurrently, interregional stylistic differences appear. The annular base makes its first appearance during this phase.

Middle Cajamarca phase (A and B) represents the high-water mark of this culture, and its ceramics show some degree of standardization in decoration, form, and manufacture. For example, they are well and consistently fired, and red and brown paints predominate over polychrome antecedents. Subphase A ceramics (C.E. 450–700) were once called "Cursive" or "Floral" style because of the popularity of fine-line motifs rendered in a flowing freehand. Although geometric motifs such as spirals predominate, some motifs are sufficiently representational to infer conventional meaning. Clearly the most important among them is the standing anthropomorphic figure drawn in frontal view. Some figures wear an elaborate circular or crescent headdress and hold stafflike objects in each hand (Fig. 5.14). Sometimes individuals, each with a circular object (possibly a shield) on one arm, are drawn in a row, reminding us

Figure 5.14. Middle Cajamarca A style ceramic bowl with standing personage (warrior?) in the center and cursive motifs on the interior wall. C-54402, Museo Nacional de Antropología, Arqueología e Historia, Lima, Peru. 20.5 cm in diameter. Photo by Y. Yoshii.

of Mochica representations of rows of warriors holding a rope and "dancing."

Another common icon is the "dragon," also called "Moon Animal." This is a mythical, four-legged creature with a long curled projection above the snout. It is also seen in Recuay and Mochica art, where the creature appears in association with the crescent "moon" and stars. In the Cajamarca style, the creature is found without such association, making it difficult to interpret its significance. It remained popular throughout the Late Cajamarca. Although material evidence of direct contact between Cajamarca and Mochica populations is quite limited, they may well have shared various rituals and cosmological concepts.

Cajamarca ceramics achieved their greatest prestige and widest distribution during subphase B (C.E. 700–900), coinciding with Mochica demise and dominance of the Wari empire in Peru.

The second northern Peruvian highland style is Recuay. Recuay art is known for its representational stone carvings and tricolor ceramics. Stone carvings encompass a wide range of forms: (1) heads and tenon-heads of "warriors" and "pumas"; (2) small square tablets (up to 50 cm to a side) with animals, geometric forms, or mythical creatures done in low relief; (3) "lintels" up to 2.7 meters long that typically show opposing pairs of "pumas" with bodies drawn in profile but heads in frontal view or a mythical being accompanied by a pair of pumas; (4) stelae up to 3 meters high often depicting a naked, splayed supernatural being; and (5) statues up to 1.5 meters high of men or women in a sitting position with their legs drawn up and hands on knees. The popularity of stone carvings, along with underground chambers, galleries, and stone buildings (e.g., site of Pashash), undoubtedly derived from the preceding Chavín.

Iconography on statues and ceramics is quite distinct from that of Chavín. Male warrior statues often stand in full military regalia, including war clubs, shields, elaborate headdresses, round ear spools, necklaces, and trophy heads. Most of the known examples of these sculptures have been removed from their original architectural contexts, making functional determination difficult. We are uncertain whether they were all contemporaneous and pertained to the period under study.

Recuay ceramics, like their Cajamarca counterparts, are known for their fine kaolin paste and conventionalized motifs painted in two or three colors (mostly red or brown and black). At the same time, they are quite different in decoration and form. For example, along with contemporaneous Vicús and Gallinazo ceramics on the northern coast, Recuay ceramics are known for "resist" or "negative" painting. In this case, vessels were covered first with a white slip, then a red slip, and fired. Designs were then applied in organic resist paint and fired again to produce the final product. Recuay painted motifs, however, differ from those of their northern Peruvian neighbors, and the stylized "Moon Animal" drawn in profile and geometric designs predominates.

There is also considerable variation in vessel form, including double-chambered whistling bottles and complex effigy vessels (Fig. 5.15). Bowls are common, but unlike Cajamarca examples, painted decoration emphasizes exterior surfaces. Jars with flange mouths were also popular, many with modeled human heads on their shoulders. Some jars have a semispherical or quadrangular body with slightly convex top with a modeled representation of a centrally placed "leader" encircled by smaller figures of presumably lower rank or elaborate multistory building and occupants.

Figure 5.15. Recuay effigy vessel depicting a "warrior" with shield and an elaborate headdress accompanied by a llama. C-55033, Museo Nacional de Antropología, Arqueología e Historia, Lima, Peru. Photo by Y. Yoshii.

The central personage is shown disproportionately large and wears an elaborate headdress and earspools indicating his high status. Some vessel forms (e.g., double-chambered) are surprisingly similar to those of the Vicús. What such similarities mean in social terms remains to be established.

In general, these complex modeled vessels seem to display scenes of religious or political importance in the real world. Scenic representations are not rendered in two-dimensional painting as in the case of Mochica art. Further, though modeling is a critical part of Recuay ceramic art, it emphasizes conventionalized, static forms unlike the full sculptural, naturalistic modeling of Mochica art. As in the case of Mochica ceramics, most of the known fine Recuay ceramics were looted from élite graves, limiting our understanding.

In the far north of Peru, intense looting that began in the 1960s in the Vicús region in the upper Piura Valley brought to light another distinct ceramic style. It is called Vicús, and in some ways it resembles Gallinazo. It was once called Sechura and in Lumbreras's classification Vicús Vicús. The latter term refers to those locally produced by Vicús potters (Fig. 5.16) and is distinguished from two other styles that co-existed in this region: Vicús/Mochica A and B.

Vicús Vicús ceramics are found in the Piura Valley with some examples found as far south as the Lambayeque Valley and as far north as the southern highlands of Ecuador. The best-known examples were looted from deep chambered shaft tombs (up to 12–15 meters) at Loma Negra and other cemeteries around Cerro Vicús.

Vicús Vicús ceramics are characterized by a sculptural style with negative painting (typically black, white, and yellow to light brown) like those of its Recuay, Gallinazo (north coast), and Lima (central coast) contemporaries to the south. Technically, Vicús ceramics are cruder than those of north Peruvian contemporaries; they are often asymmetrical, hand-formed (paddled), and not well fired or polished. The poor finish and firing (i.e., "primitive" appearance) are largely due to the limitations imposed by a sandy paste full of impurities. Many are cruder versions of Mochica forms. The subjects depicted are wide ranging and largely overlap with those of the Mochica. One gets the impression that Vicús potters used better-made Mochica ceramics as models. At the same time, there are unique aspects and forms – for example, whistling double-chambered bottles, human faces with hooked noses and slit eyes and mouth, and disproportionate exaggeration of selected parts of animal or human bodies.

Figure 5.16. Vicús Vicús style effigy bottle representing a jaguar (*Felis onca*). Note the body marking rendered in negative painting. A.C.E. 822, Museo Banco Central de Reserva del Perú, Lima. Height: 26.5 cm. Photo by Y. Yoshii.

The style and subject matter of Vicús ceramics exhibit a notable degree of overlap with those of the Ecuadorian and southern Colombian coasts. The possible significance of this resemblance is considered at some length later.

Vicús/Mochica A encompasses fine-quality specimens in Mochica style derived from pit tombs at Loma Negra, together with copper and copper gilt objects. Vicús Mochica B ceramics are local hybrids incorporating the features of the first two groups. Tombs associated with the hybrid ceramics have not been well defined. These two styles are confined to the upper Piura Valley.

Many of the Vicús/Mochica A ceramics are comparable to the best of the valleys farther south. For example, fine Mochica Phase I vessels recently looted from an elaborate adobe chamber tomb at La Mina in the lower Jequetepeque Valley, some 270 kilometers south of Vicús, can hardly be distinguished from some of the (A) group vessels. That the vessels in (A) display important iconographic divergence from those of the valleys farther south suggests that the former were produced by a colony of skilled Mochica artisans in the Vicús region. Recent excavations by Kaulicke documented corporate constructions at Huaca Nimo near Cerro Vicús associated with the Vicús/Mochica ceramics. As explained later, Vicús/Vicús and Vicús/Mochica ceramics are likely to have been produced by two distinct ethnic populations.

The overwhelming portion of the Vicús/Mochica (A) ceramics date to Mochica Phases I and II, whereas the metal objects appear to date to Phases III and IV. However, the north coast Mochica stylistic chronology does not apply to the (B) hybrid ceramics as features taken from different phases of the Mochica ceramics were combined. They were probably produced by local Vicús potters who used Mochica ceramics as a prestigious source for artistic inspiration. Available radiocarbon dates suggest that all three groups span circa 200 B.C.E. to C.E. 700.

Northward beyond the Peru-Ecuador frontier of today, a variety of other styles are known. Artistically and technically speaking, ceramics of the best-known coastal Ecuadorian ERD styles of (north to south along the Ecuadorian coast) La Tolita-Tumaco, Jama-Coaque, Bahía, and Guangala are similar to each other. Much the same can be said about the highland ERD styles (north to south) such as Tuncahuán, Panzaleo, and Puruhá. This similarity seemingly stems from the widespread Chorrera (1200–500 B.C.E.) cultural substratum. These styles are believed to represent regional cultural traditions with chiefdom-level social and political integration and an agrarian economy. Data on highland cultures are still largely derived from looted objects and quite sketchy. Following Chorrera precedents, artisans of the better known coastal ERD cultures continued to emphasize varying degrees of realism, sculptural modeling, particularly in figurines and effigy vessels, a diverse range of subject matter drawn from their natural and supernatural worlds, and use of one-piece molds for vessel formation. Figurines are commonly around 20 to 30 centimeters in height, though some La Tolita examples are about 90 centimeters in height. The development of a figurine tradition independent from vessel forms constitutes a significant difference between Ecuadorian coastal ceramics and the ceramic tradition on the Peruvian coast such as those of the Mochica and Nasca. Here the better-known Ecuadorian coastal styles are described.

The Jama-Coaque style centered in the moist, northern Manabí region can be characterized as the "Mochica style" of Ecuador for the features they share in common and, in some specific cases, Mochica-like sculptural vessels. Jama-Coaque represents the pinnacle of the ERD styles in Ecuador. Its figurines and effigy vessels are numerous and diverse in the subjects they represent, ranging from a superhuman head with serpents emerging from it to a pregnant woman and a standing man holding some cultivated plants. (Fig. 5.17). In general, they are quite realistic, have a good balance, proportions, and symmetry, and effectively capture the motion and emotions of individuals represented. Like the Mochica examples, many of Jama-Coaque figurines and effigies appear to represent ritual activities of the social élite.

The figures and their small accessories (e.g., shields, masks, pectorals, and head gear) were made separately by hand or with simple press molds. In most cases, only the front half of the body was mold-made, leaving the back (details of hairdo and the back) to be finished cursorily by hand. These figurines often stood on their own and were probably viewed only from the front. Their surfaces are usually smooth, but they were not covered by a slip for a uniform background color or burnished to give a high gloss. Most components were assembled together before firing, although some parts were left detachable. After firing, the figurines and effigy vessels were decorated with yellow, red, black, and blue paint. The last was produced by mixing indigo with white clay. In comparison with earlier Chorrera figurines, Jama-Coaque, Bahía, and other ERD figurines show more personal ornaments, suggesting an increase in power and material wealth of the élite.

Although there is some degree of standardization from the use of molds, there was still much to be done by hand. In addition, by altering accessories placed on the same mold-made bodies, it was possible to create numerous "variations on a theme." Thus, for example, there are many similar figurines of seated males and warriors about to throw a spear or a dart with dart-thrower. Yet organization of production or production scale, intensity, and output cannot be described, because no

Figure 5.17. Jama-Coaque style mold-made ceramic figurine. The three orna-ments on the headdress are thought to be spiral shells. The shell on his chest appears to be an open *Spondylus*. GA-1-2267-82, Museo del Banco Central, Quito, Ecuador. Height: 30 cm. Photo by Y. Yoshii.

ceramic workshop has been found to date on coastal Ecuador. In addition, like all other ERD styles on coastal Ecuador, most of the specimens we have to study have been looted, and usages of figurines and effigy vessels remain largely speculative.

A cache of Bahía-style figurines was found at the ceremonial–civic center of Los Esteros known for its numerous earthen *tolas* (mounds) in central Manabí. These figurines were found broken in pieces as if they were ritually smashed. They may well represent a votive offering intended to remove ill spirits or sickness from the individuals represented by the figurines.

Bahía is a southern neighbor to Jama-Coaque. Its figurines and effigy vessels, though not as realistic as those of Jama-Coaque, are nonetheless striking and diverse. Figurines commonly have faces with prominent, hooked noses, slightly open mouths, and almond-shaped eyes with circular perforation for the iris (Fig. 5.18). Decorations were done primarily with postfiring application of red, white, black, yellow, and green paint, though in some effigy vessels prefiring irridescent (light coat of black paint that becomes clearly visible when moistened or spotlighted) or negative painting was used. The latter two techniques are also inheritances from Chorrera ceramics.

Bahía potters also produced a wide range of utilitarian vessels common to most coastal ERD styles, such as well-known *compoteras* (shallow, open bowls on tall, flaring pedestal bases), polypod bowls, ring-base goblets, long-neck jars, round pots, and incurving and outflaring bowls. Musical instruments such as whistles and ocarinas were also made.

Decoration of these vessels in coastal and highland styles emphasized geometric abstraction. The highland Tuncahuán ceramics are noted for abstract designs done with negative painting technique.

Stamp seals similar to those in Mesoamerica may have been used to decorate cotton cloth or even bodies. Skirts of different length shown on Bahía female figurines have repetitive abstract designs that may well have been made with stamps.

Stone Sculpture, with Emphasis on San Agustín

We already noted the prominent stone sculptural traditions of the Recuay and Pukara cultures in Peru. Another important tradition is the "San Agustín" in the southern Colombian highlands. It is noted for a group of over thirty sites in and around Meseta A, B, and Alto de los Idolos in

Figure 5.18. Bahía-style whistling ceramic bottle. The two figures are decorated with resin-based, post-fired paint, while the bottle at the back is decorated with pre-fired irridescent paint. The three chambers are connected by means of a bridge-shaped handle. GA-2-918-78, Museo del Banco Central, Quito, Ecuador. Height: 12.9 cm. Photo by Y. Yoshii.

the upper reaches of the Magdalena River. Its fame lies in the over 300 stone sculptures of humans, animals, and supernaturals associated with funerary earthen mounds. Sculptures range in height from about 50 centimeters to over 4 meters. Most are carvings in the round, though low-relief carving on slabs exists. Most of the sculptures and associated tombs belongs to the Isnos Phase (c. C.E. 1–800), the period of cultural florescence, according to the regional chronology established by Reichel-Dolmatoff over 30 years ago. The last two decades have seen improvement in our understanding of the regional context of this phase, though many key sites have been damaged by years of looting.

These tombs as a whole are found in what Drennan calls small restricted ceremonial precincts near domestic settlements. The areas of tomb concentration at about 1,500–2,000 meters coincide with those zones best suited for residential and agricultural purposes. Settlement pattern data for positing the presence of several small chiefdoms are presented later.

Stylistic variation among the sculptures and associated burials may reflect social and temporal differences. The best-known burial form is the "barrow tomb," which consists of one of more burial chambers (1.5 to 3 m to a side and 1 m in height) constructed of stone slabs covered by earth. These ovoid to circular mounds reach 20 to 30 meters in diameter and 3 meters in height. Chambers may contain more than one sarcophagus. On the sides and perimeters of some mounds, simple burials have been found, presumably personal attendants or family members of the personages inside the burial chambers. Certainly the labor and materials mobilized for the stone carving and tomb construction argue not only for the considerable political power commanded by the deceased or his or her office but also the institutionalized basis for such a position. Although unlooted barrow tombs are rare, a few intact tombs have revealed sumptuary items, such as stone and gold beads, further attesting to the high status of the interred personages. Given that other tomb types (stone-slab cists and shaft tombs) of this tradition are modest in terms of labor, material requirements, and grave furnishings, San Agustín society may have had a hierarchical social organization.

The statues, in terms of placements and representations, appear to have served as markers or guardians of the tombs. The best-known statues stand next to or at the entrance to burial chambers. They often show a man with a disproportionately large head, interlocking canines, stocky torso, and short legs. One statue was found with its original paint, which accentuated its awe-inspiring visual effects. Bruhns notes that the San Agustín statues, in spite of their size, technical, and stylistic differences, are highly consistent in theme, most common being the supernatural being with fangs, as described earlier. She argues that they were an essential part of shamanistic rites that embodied concepts of ancestor worship, guardians of the dead, and even masters of animals (i.e., jaguars). There are statues that show a feline attacking a man. Another depicts a man wearing a tasseled headdress and a cat skin. As seen in later discussion on iconography, shamanistic beliefs and rituals were central to the cosmologies of the North Andean ERD cultures.

Desert Markings

Another important form of artistic expression during the ERD period, particularly on the south coast of Peru, was gigantic geoglyphs or

man-made desert markings. The idea is ancient. Sometime in the first
millennium B.C.E., a large anthropomorphic figure was made by laying
different colored stones on a visible mountain slope in the upper Zaña
Valley on the north coast. Large geoglyphs are found as far south as the
far north coast of Chile. However, by far the largest and best-known
concentration occurs on the stony desert plains around the Río Grande
de Nazca drainage (in a roughly 200-km² area). They are popularly
known as the "Nazca Lines." There, one finds some 1,300 kilometers of
straight lines of varying width, 300 geometric figures, and over 30 representational motifs (e.g., monkey, killer whale, hummingbird). Figurative
geoglyphs range from about 20 to 300 meters in length, while some
straight lines run for many kilometers. They have been made variously
by (1) removing patinated surface stones to expose lighter colored stones
and sand below, (2) cutting narrow furrows into the surface with excavated dirt mounded alongside, (3) removing stones around the figure,
like bas-relief, or (4) simply arranging stones on the surface in a continuous line to mark the image. These ground imageries have been studied
by scholars from different disciplines and nations since their initial study
by Kosok in the 1950s.

Many geoglyphs have been superimposed, indicating chronological
depth. The figural geoglyphs are concentrated in one small area of the
desert plain near the Ingenio Valley and are primarily early Nasca in style
and associated ceramics. Some of them may have been made in late
Paracas time. On the other hand, most lines and geometric geoglyphs are
superimposed over figural forms and appear to be post-Nasca in date.
Some may date as late as the time of the Inka empire.

Various ideas compete to explain these markings. Some see them as
astronomical and astrological calendars, others as markers of directions
to access points of water for agriculture. Still others see ceremonial roads
and grounds and hold the giant drawings to be works of art to be seen
from the air. Studies that are well founded on empirical and historical
data agree on certain points: (1) the lines and geometric figures were an
integral part of a complex ancient institution that encompassed religious,
ecological, and social concerns; (2) they served as pathways to ceremonial
or observation places; and (3) many point to water sources such as springs
and key points of underground filtration galleries, and "sacred" locations
such as distant mountain peaks and the Nasca ceremonial center of
Cahuachi. Reinhard, for example, argues that these geoglyphs were part
of a widespread, Andean religious practice to propitiate the deities governing the cosmos and ensure agricultural fertility. Aveni, who led an

interdisciplinary investigation of the Nasca geoglyphs, hypothesizes that they functioned in part as ceremonial pathways to be used in rituals related to bringing water to the arid Nasca region. Mountain worship, a durable Andean practice, treats sacred mountains as sources of water and controllers of meteorological phenomena.

Metal and Its Cultural Significance

One of the most significant developments in the arts and crafts of ERD cultures was the rapid evolution and spread of advanced metallurgy. This led to an attendant increase in the availability and importance of metal objects, essentially copper, gold, and copper-gold or copper-gold-silver alloys known as *tumbaga* (usually with gold concentrations considerably less than 50% [12 karats], and sometimes 10% or less). The key technological innovations and refinements that formed the foundation of the Northern Peruvian Coastal Metallurgical Tradition emerged during the period spanning a few centuries before and after C.E. 0 in northern coastal Peru (upper Piura to Zaña valleys). During this same period, important metallurgical developments appeared around the Colombia-Ecuador border, including the coastal area of La Tolita-Tumaco. The central coast and highlands of Peru and the *altiplano* in the South-Central Andes are two additional areas that may prove to have been a comparable center of metallurgical innovation or production during this period.

It should be remembered that metal objects do not preserve well in the Andean highlands. Even on the Peruvian coast with its better preservation, most of the known metal objects of this period were derived from graves, not from habitational settlements. Rather than continuing to rely heavily on data from laboratory analyses of finished products from tombs, we need much more data from habitational and production sites to resolve some of the questions and issues considered later. Further complicating the matter is the archaeologist's lack of familiarity with the material diagnostics of smelting and subsequent metalworking. Metal identifications made by archaeologists without data from technical analysis should be regarded as tentative.

The Northern Peruvian Coastal Metallurgical Tradition

We find the best-documented and in many ways the most prominent metallurgical tradition of the precolumbian world in the Lambayeque

Valley and its adjacent region. The presence of a local tradition of working with sheet gold decorated with cutout and chasing-repoussé designs during the first millennium B.C.E. is suggested by the discovery of crowns and other ornaments at Chongoyape, Morro de Eten, and Cerro Ventarrón, all in the Lambayeque Valley. Although numerous Cupisnique-style sheet-gold objects have been attributed to Cerro Corbacho in the mid-Zaña Valley, their contexts and even authenticity have not been established. Another cache of sheet-gold ornaments in a local Cupisnique variant style was recently found at Loma de Macanche near Vicús in the upper Piura Valley to the north.

The dating and stylistic identification of these finds are important, because the spread of the sheet-gold working has been viewed traditionally as part of a series of innovations to accompany the spread of the Chavín cult. As we have seen in regard to the northward spread of domesticated camelid husbandry, here too there are reasons to question conventional thinking. The Cerro Ventarrón finds are technically and stylistically nearly identical to the cache of gold crowns, pectorals, and earspools (ranging from 21 to 15 karats – 63 to 91% gold and 37–39% silver; one pendant is 70% silver and 30% gold) excavated at the site of Kuntur Wasi in the upper reaches of the nearby Jequetepeque Valley (2,300 m above sea level). Stylistically, the Kuntur Wasi find is seen to be closely related to the coastal Cupisnique and, on the basis of five radiocarbon assays, dated to circa 700–400 B.C.E. There are a number of other Cupisnique burials with gold and copper objects.

The foregoing discoveries suggest that the roots of the Northern Peruvian Tradition may well lie in precocious cultural developments in the same region dating to the second millennium B.C.E. The discoveries also call into question conventional views regarding the first metal to be worked in the Andes and the beginnings of true metallurgy (involving smelting). The copper foil (produced by cold hammering of native copper) found at Mina Perdida in the Lurín Valley on the central coast of Peru dates to the end of the second millennium B.C.E. In coastal Peru, simple working of native copper and gold may well have occurred concurrently during the second millennium B.C.E. intentional smelting of gold, silver, and copper as well as their alloying by the beginning of the first millennium B.C.E. By 400–200 B.C.E., a Salinar population was mining copper oxide ore in the upper Virú Valley (north coast) and presumably smelting, though production sites have not been identified yet. In the Zaña Valley, there are at least two Mochica sites (Phases III–

V) associated with copper oxide ore and slag lumps, suggesting copper smelting and working.

Certainly by the first centuries C.E., Mochica metalworkers were producing a diverse range of utilitarian tools and weapons (e.g., fishhooks, tweezers, needles, spindle whorls, and mace heads) in copper and ritual items (e.g., scepter-rattles, bells, and masks) and personal ornaments (e.g., head and facial ornaments, necklaces, pectorals, and earspools) in high-karat gold and silver, *tumbaga*, as well as in copper. Following the earlier emphasis, the principal Mochica manufacturing technique was cutting and shaping of sheet metal. In addition to masterful chasing-repoussé, Mochica metalworkers used inlay (e.g., shell, turquoise, sodalite) and different colored metals for decorative ends. They also hand-wrought uniform wire and carried out precise soldering and granulation (a process by which small spheres are attached to a solid surface just at the point of contact; Fig. 5.19). The indirect metalworking techniques of casting and cire-perdue, or lost-wax casting, were also employed. This last technique starts by making the desired form in wax, presumably beeswax. The modeled wax is then encased in a refractory material such as clay with an opening into which the molten metal is poured. Because wax is plastic, easy to model, and burns out cleanly, it is a preferred material for metal casting of both ancient and modern artisans the world over. Once cooled, the casing is broken and the cast object is removed.

Examples of the technical mastery of Mochica metalworkers are found among the hundreds of objects looted from several tombs in the Loma Negra cemetery in Vicús. These objects include small masks with bedangled visors, head and nose ornaments, full round figurines of "warriors," and ornamented staffs and knives. In addition, there are many realistic, repoussé copper miniatures of shrimps, scorpions, and crabs (all less than 1.5 cm in length). They are made predominantly of gilt and silvered copper and copper sheets that have been mechanically joined. Another exemplary group of objects from Sipán is described later.

With the collapse of the Mochica polity by around C.E. 700, the demand for status items probably dwindled. The Northern Peruvian Coastal Metallurgical Tradition, however, recovered during the rise of the Middle Sicán polity starting around C.E. 900, with the initiation of large-scale production of arsenical-copper (comparable to copper-tin bronze in its useful qualities) and precious metal ornaments and ritual paraphernalia.

As seen already, contemporary metal objects were relatively rare and

Figure 5.19. Ten gold ornaments that together formed a necklace found on the principal male personage in Tomb 3 at Sipán. The top of each ornament represents a spider with repoussé human face on its back. ca. 8.3 in diameter. Courtesy of the Museo Arqueológico Nacional de Brüning, Lambayeque, Peru. Photo by Y. Yoshii.

unsophisticated on the central and south coasts in spite of early native copper working on the central coast, of reports of copper mining in the adjacent highland region, and of coast–highland trade in copper by 1200–650 B.C.E. The small size and limited quantity of copper and gilded copper personal ornaments found in some burials at the necropolis at Tablada de Lurín just south of the city of Lima (dated to c. 300 B.C.E. to C.E. 100; transition to an early Lima culture) pale in comparison to what we see on the north coast.

Cross-Craft Interaction and Aesthetic Locus

In general, craft production has been studied one medium at a time. For example, ceramics are treated without considering how artistic, technical/

technological, and organizational aspects of their manufacture may be influenced by other crafts and vice versa. We are speaking of "cross-craft" interaction in which two or more crafts stimulate each other's development. In some cases, the superior development of one particular craft may inhibit concurrent development in other crafts. In addition, what Marquet calls "aesthetic locus" is quite evident in some cultures. The concept refers to one category of objects or medium of artistic expression subject to the highest quality standards of a given culture. This "aesthetic locus" may be actively emulated by other media or may be quite exclusive through control of raw materials, skilled artisans, and imageries.

Investigation into such creative interaction and differential values placed on crafts has been limited but is important for the cultures under consideration because many display such examples. This type of exploration allows us to gain insights into cultural values, the organization of craft production, and the creative processes involved.

For example, Lyon suggests that the practice of demarcating each colored area of Pukara polychrome ceramics with broad incisions may have been adopted from the incision or champlevé techniques extensively used in Pukara's well-developed stone-carving tradition. The latter produced rectangular stone slabs with flat relief carvings that, in turn, may well have influenced or conversely been stimulated by textiles. They share the shape and flatness. As noted earlier, circumstantial evidence points to a well-developed Pukara weaving tradition. In addition, Lyon suspects that the full round Pukara stone sculptures of human figures holding trophy heads may have served as the prototype modeled human and feline figures for which Pukara ceramics are well known.

Fine Mochica effigy vessels are often found with shell and stone inlays (e.g., parts of pectorals, bracelets, or earspools) and even miniature gold-alloy nose ornaments and wooden war clubs. Similarly, full-sized ear-spools such as those found in the tombs of Mochica noblemen at Sipán are as much products of lapidary work as goldsmithing. In fact, the conception, designing, and finishing of these objects required integration of crafts that are analytically segregated by the archaeologist. More likely, pottery, lapidary, and metalworking workshops were closely situated and perhaps even manned by socially related groups of specialists. Surface and excavated remains from areas around Huaca de la Luna at Moche and the two central sectors at the urban site of Pampa Grande point to spatial aggregation of metalworking, pottery making, weaving, and lapidary workshops. Such was the case also at the late prehispanic city of Chan Chan, the capital of the Chimú kingdom.

The adoption and increased use of molds for copper and copper-alloy casting and formation of fine Mochica ceramics may be yet another example of cross-craft interplay. This cross-fertilization is logical. Both involve the controlled use of heat and clay in transforming naturally occurring substances (clay and ore) to culturally valuable artifacts (ceramics and metals). Conceptually, casting of complex copper artifacts represented a refinement of making simple molds for ingots or stock forms. Yet, technically speaking, the making of mold matrices requires a great deal of skill, and in modern pottery-making communities in the Andes, this task is reserved for the most skilled potters. In this sense, press mold formation of ceramic vessels may have preceded the casting of complex copper objects. These techniques persisted on the north coast until the Spanish conquest.

As stated earlier, comparison of these metal objects with other categories of grave goods, particularly ceramics and textiles, led us to suggest that precious metals were the aesthetic locus of early Northern Mochica art. In terms of intended functions, estimated labor investment, size, iconographic originality and details, and range of materials integrated (such as feathers and cloth), high-karat gold and gilt copper clearly stand out.

High-karat gold and *tumbaga* objects, often with inlays of shells, sodalite, coral, or turquoise, appear to have been the aesthetic locus of early Northern Mochica art (Fig. 5.20). Available evidence indicates that this was also the case for the Southern Mochica. In terms of iconographic content, and labor and material costs, ceramics pale in comparison with metal objects, beadwork (primarily pectorals and bracelets), and weavings that were interred in the early élite Mochica tombs at Sipán. Not only are some imageries on metal objects unique, but certain objects are themselves unique, such as a pair of earspools with miniature portraits of the "Lord of Sipán" assembled from layers of sheet-gold components and turquoise inlay. Gold objects were emulated by *tumbaga* and copper objects. Decorated metal objects probably functioned as the artistic pacesetters. Starting late in Phase III, ceramic art appears to have become more independent with its elaboration of pictorial composition and fineline drawing.

On the south coast, late Paracas embroidered textiles can be justifiably

Figure 5.20. Gilded copper anthropomorphic "feline" found on the chest of the principal male personage in Tomb 3 at Sipán. Nose, teeth, and ears have *Spondylus* shell inlay. Note the upturned eyes indicating his supernatural power. Courtesy of the Museo Arqueológico Nacional de Brüning, Lambayeque, Peru. Photo by Y. Yoshii.

called the aesthetic locus around C.E. o. As we have seen, their relatively large size, precise control, and wide selection of weaving techniques and yarns (particularly camelid fibers that take dyes) allowed the creation of intricate designs in many bright colors. It is unlikely that these textiles were woven just to meet funerary needs, but rather, they seem to have been created to display the weaver's skill devotion to the deceased who wore them. They are unique and very labor intensive, and there is little that points to mass production or standardization. Paul suspects that weavers may have competed with each other for greater social prestige based on their skill.

As mastery of polychrome slip painting came about with the onset of the Nasca sequence, the aesthetic locus of the south coast population may have shifted to ceramics. This appears to have been the case in terms of iconographic content, particularly in regard to the pantheon of deities. Even in terms of labor and materials costs, some ceramic vessels are quite impressive. For example, ritual drums could measure over 1 meter in height and be painted with complex, multicolored images. Paracas and Nasca metal artifacts in general are rare, and the few hammered sheet-gold ornaments are relatively small and crudely made.

LONG-DISTANCE INTERACTION

Mesoamerican–Northwest South American Connections

Contemporaneity and the substantial technical and technological overlap found between the southwest Colombian and northern Peruvian coastal metallurgical traditions raise the important issue of long-distance inter-action, in spite of the widespread tendency to emphasize regionalism during the period under study. This is a longstanding issue; in this section a few well-documented cases are considered. Discussions regard-ing prehispanic connections between Mesoamerica and northwestern South America (primarily coastal regions of Ecuador and southern Co-lombia, though at times Peru is also included) have taken place since the early decades of this century, when notable archaeologists and ethnolo-gists first detected such possibilities. The debate has persisted due to the wide range of rather specific stylistic and technical-technological features and exotic items shared, ethnohistoric testimony of contact, and perhaps most importantly, the fact that relevant issues have direct bearings on the origins and evolution of complex cultures in the New World. Among the early proponents, Jijón y Caamaño, Saville, and Uhle argued for a series of migrations or waves of diffusion that transmitted specific fea-tures, such as pottery stamps or seals, stirrup-spout ceramic bottles, and gold inlay in teeth, and general features, such as stone monolith carving. As early as 1912, Verneau and Rivet suggested maritime trade as the mechanism of contact betweeen Mesoamerica and coastal Ecuador. These early views commonly postulated a southward movement of traits, ideas, and people out of Mesoamerica. Underlying this view was the implicit premise that cultures in Colombia and Ecuador were secondary and less developed than those in Mesoamerica, which served as the donors of innovations.

In 1959, in order to systematize the many studies of cultural contact betweeen Ecuador and Mesoamerica, Borhegyi listed sixty-three "parallel traits" in eight major categories that he believed were shared by both areas: (1) settlement patterns (e.g., temple and platform mound groups), (2) ceramics (e.g., tall-footed tripod vessels, whistling jars, stirrup-spout vessels, and three-pronged "incense burners"), (3) techniques (resist-dye or negative-painting decoration on pottery, rocker stamping, and use of clay molds), (4) mold-made hollow figurines, (5) miscellaneous ceramic objects (masks, effigy whistles, rollers, and flat stamps), (6) stonework, (7) advanced metallurgy, and (8) miscellaneous traits. Most prior publications focused on categories (2) to (5). Although Borhegyi did not offer any explanation of how and why these traits were carried into cultural interaction, this list is useful in providing a summary of what was considered as evidence of contact.

Over the past 35 years, efforts have been made to improve temporal and spatial placement, to flesh out cultural and environmental contexts in which these traits are found, and to address broader issues of the cultural processes involved. During this period, comprehensive regional studies by Spanish (Esmeraldas) and French (Tumaco) missions under the direction of Alcina and Bouchard, respectively, have gathered evidence to question effectively the long-held view of a Mesoamerican origin of modeled ceramics and figurines representing warriors, men with wrinkled "grotesque faces," and mythical beings composed of human and animal features. Their studies revealed continuous indigenous developments in each region starting in the first millennium B.C.E., built on the Chorrera cultural substratum and adaptation to tropical rain forest environment, including manioc-maize cultivation supplemented by riverine and mangrove exploitation. Ceramic and gold figurines are seen as outgrowths of the strong depictive and sculptural character found in Chorrera arts and crafts. As seen before, mold-made figurines can be traced back to Chorrera and Machalilla times.

In other words, archaeological attention shifted away from comparisons of isolated traits or formal similarities. Rather, it focused on the chambered shaft tomb complex, tropical *Spondylus* seashells, and clothing, items about which much was known in terms of cultural and environmental contexts. Geographically and chronologically, much attention was directed to contemporaneous ERD cultures on the central to north coasts of Ecuador (regions of Jama-Coaque, Esmeraldas, and La Tolita-Tumaco) and western Mexico (particularly the states of Colima, Jalisco, and Nayarit).

Chambered shaft tombs are widespread in northwestern South America from the southern coast and highlands of Colombia to the north coast of Peru. In Mesoamerica, they are restricted to western Mexico, most dating between circa 200 B.C.E. and C.E. 500, though some may well date back to 1500 B.C.E. Andean shaft tombs date from about C.E. 200 to the time of the Spanish conquest. Similarities include configuration (one or more side chambers and a square or circular central shaft 2–20 m deep, depending on the soil matrix), placement in elevated areas, and *claraboyas*, or narrow holes or tubes that connect the roof of chambers with the surface. The last is of particular importance because it is believed to have been used for libations (water or beer made from maize or manioc), communication, and interchange between the living and the dead. In other words, similarities are not restricted to material aspects but perhaps extended into associated religious beliefs.

Dress modes for the period under study have been extracted from figurines. Figurines from the Western Mexican shaft tombs are numerous, and the clothing shown is distinct from anything else in Mesoamerica. According to Anawalt, both Ecuadorian and western Mexican figurines show men wearing what resemble modern bathing trunks and short shirts, whereas women are dressed in short skirts and mantles. This garb is found represented in Western Mexican figurines starting around 200 B.C.E. and persisted until the Spanish conquest. In coastal Ecuador, the same garb was worn as early as Chorrera times, to judge from figurines.

Ceramic bottles with stirrup spouts, a rather unique form, can be traced in both areas to circa 1500–1000 B.C.E. but remained durably popular only in coastal Ecuador and Peru.

The foregoing data point to direct but intermittent contact between Western Mexico and coastal Ecuador, including establishment of Ecuadorian colonies during the period under study. But what would have motivated such contact? Consideration of *Spondylus* shell leads us toward one possible explanation of causal processes. *Spondylus* was believed to be the food of water-giving deities. We are speaking of a renewable natural resource that has a restricted natural habitat in the tropical waters of the Pacific. Its exploitation began along central and southern coastal Ecuador by Valdivia times (starting c. 3500–3000 B.C.E.) and continued until the Spanish conquest. Until establishment of the Chorrera substratum over much of the Northern Andes early in the first millennium B.C.E., *Spondylus* distribution appears to have been largely limited to coastal Ecuador, and its use to making beads and other ornaments.

However, in Mesoamerica and in Peru, during the period under study, along with *Strombus* and *Conus* shells from the same tropical sea, *Spondylus* had attained considerable religious and social significance. In the Tello Obelisk iconography, a key to Chavín ideas, the *Spondylus* and *Strombus* are shown as parts of a composite mythical creature that embodied concern for successful agricultural and social reproduction. These shells are thought to represent the Pacific, the source of all water. Clearly the long distance these shells traveled would have contributed to their symbolic importance, their possession both reflecting and bestowing power and prestige on the owners.

Coastal Ecuadorians were ideally suited to have been the purveyors of the prized seashells. Geographically, they occupied the middle ground between Mesoamerica and Peru. The shells were available locally and renewably but required special diving skill to harvest (*Spondylus princeps* is found at depths of 15–50 m). They were small, compact, and easily transportable. Balsa logs available on coastal Ecuador would have allowed construction of rafts necessary for long-distance navigation. The presence of deep-sea fish and shellfish remains in Valdivian refuse from the Formative Era suggests that reliable watercraft and navigation skill were long available.

Based on Sahlins' ethnographic model, archaeologist Zeidler envisioned a trade system linking Mesoamerica (through western Mexico), coastal Ecuador, and the northern Peruvian coast. He believes it to have evolved out of reciprocal exchange of localized resources, including *Spondylus*, among egalitarian societies in coastal Ecuador. As social complexity increased over time, possession of exotic commodities and control over their distribution in society at large would have become an important means by which individuals could achieve higher status and cultivate power as chiefs. The desire for exotic items having increased prestige, competition among élite for such items would have provided impetus for expanding such a system to encompass ever more distant areas yielding new and unusual goods – for example, peyote (containing hallucinogens), tobacco, and coca leaves used in shamanistic rituals. In addition, with the expansion of trade, the local supply of *Spondylus* may have been depleted, necessitating expansion farther north and south along the coast. In fact, the appearance of *Conus fergusoni*, a large spiral tropical seashell, on the north coast of Peru starting in the first few centuries C.E. may have been a response to increasing demand for tropical seashells or exotic goods. Stock copper forms may have been acquired from the Mochica and become an important component of the equation.

However, the growth of trade may have transformed the role of Ecuadorian traders from primarily serving their own élite gradually to middlemen for powerful expansive polities in Peru and Mesoamerica. In this scenario, trade would have become susceptible to the changing demands and values of these polities. Reflecting their waxing and waning, we would expect the intensity and extent of trade to be correspondingly variable. This is indeed what has been documented. For example, during much of its long tradition, Mochica art hardly depicted tropical seashells. Other than a small number of whole shells used as offerings in élite tombs, their use was limited to beads and inlay. Then in Phase V, *Spondylus* appears represented in ceramics, in ritual offerings, and in large numbers in workshops. This apparent increase in *Spondylus* use is believed to have been a response to a severe three-decade-long drought (C.E. 562–594) that significantly affected the entire Andean region. This period saw an unprecedented range of cultural changes in the Andes, as we see later. At roughly the same time, Teotihuacán intrusion altered the situation in Western Mexico. Group scenes depicted on figurines in Nayarit tombs, including representations of individuals being carried on litters, suggest the existence of chiefdoms prior to Teotihuacan intrusion. The Pacha Kamaq (also called Ichma or Ychma) polity in the central coast of Peru may have replaced the Mochica polity as a dominant trading partner until it was supplanted by the Middle Sicán polity around C.E. 900–1000.

Vicús and Trade Between the Ecuadorian and Colombian Coasts and the Peruvian North Coast

The first scientific excavations of Vicús settlements have taken place only in the past decade, and our understanding of this culture is still in its infancy. However, its understanding requires that we examine it not only from regional but also extraregional perspectives – more specifically, from the perspective of long-distance trade in exotic goods encompassing the Colombian, Ecuadorian, and Peruvian coast.

Both stylistically and technically, the Vicús Vicús ceramics show strong linkage with contemporaneous cultures of the La Tolita-Tumaco-Calima region some 700–900 kilometers farther north. For example, commonalities with the Ilama and Yotoco Phase ceramics of the Calima region are specific and numerous. They range from negative painting as the primary decorative technique and C-shaped strap handles atop vessels to the popular short single-or double-spouts, modeled anthropo-zoomorphic beings, and conical and double-chambered vessels. Some hollow human figurines found in Vicús closely resemble those of Classic La Tolita in style, form, and manufacturing technique. The discovery of two famous Classic La Tolita style gold figurines and over 200 other metal objects near Frias just inland from Vicús is not surprising in this respect. The tomb construction and associated ceramics even raise the possibility of a La Tolita colony in Frias, but details are scant due to looters' destruction. Vicús and La Tolita-Tumaco-Calima also share the tradition of chambered shaft tombs.

Recent excavation at the major Vicús site of Loma Valverde by Kaulicke and his team showed that the principal mound was constructed of earthen fill encased by walls of mud applied over the cane and log frames, in turn erected over a low *tapia* (rammed earth) foundation and perimeter. It is totally distinct from the solid platform built with rectangular adobe bricks at adjacent Huaca Nima. The former is associated with Vicús Vicús ceramics; the latter yielded Vicús/Mochica ceramics. Importantly, the technique documented at Loma Valverde is used for platform mound constructions (*tolas*) on both the coast and in the highlands of Ecuador and has not been found in areas farther south in Peru.

It is evident that the Vicús pertains to a northern Andean rather than central Andean cultural tradition. Population migration(s) out of the Ecuador-Colombian border region to Vicús sometime around 200 B.C.E. are suggested based on radiocarbon dates and the early Mochica vessels imitated by Vicús potters. The migrants seem to have served as middlemen in interregional trade between the northern Peruvian coast (Lambayeque to Piura) and coastal Ecuador and Colombia. The inferred linkage should not come as a surprise, because similar situations existed before (e.g., Chorrera and Cupisnique) and after this period (e.g., Manteño-Milagro and Middle Sicán). Thus the limited extent of Mochica occupation in the upper Piura would not represent an unsuccessful annexation of land for agricultural purposes but a foothold for trade with areas farther north.

In addition to the shells mentioned earlier, trade may have involved other goods. The relative abundance of placer gold in the coastal rivers of northern Ecuador and southern Colombia, and the scarcity of gold on the coast of Peru, suggest that Mochica metalworkers obtained at least some of their gold from there. In addition, beeswax for lost-wax casting and various perishable items such as tobacco and coca leaves and balsa wood may have been traded from the north.

In return for raw materials, the Mochica élite are thought to have offered artifacts such as copper ingots and cotton textiles. Fine-quality Mochica ceramic and metal objects from Loma Negra, however, are likely to have been the material symbols of power and status for the Mochica élite in Vicús; they probably did not pertain to the highest social echelon given that the overwhelming portion of metal objects were copper and gilded copper.

ICONOGRAPHY AND IDEOLOGY

Availability of a wide range of artifacts and architecture, richly decorated with representational designs, has spurred efforts to decipher encoded cultural meanings and thus reconstruct ancient cosmology and religion. Many scholars see the task as analogous to reading symbolic texts without appropriate dictionaries, and they have adopted a linguistic method of analysis that seeks to identify the vocabulary (different units and levels of meaningful motifs), as well as its grammar and syntax, by means of systematic comparison and contrast among contexts and forms. Ancient iconography should be studied on its own terms without imposing our own ideas and biases. The ultimate goal is to understand conventional and deeper cultural meanings of motifs and their overall configurations (semantics). This task is quite difficult and often involves making tenuous assumptions and analogies. Deep meanings embedded in iconography presumably reflect the basic character of the underlying ideologies and social and natural environments.

Chavín

The beginnings of the period under study saw, for the first time in Andean prehistory, the spread of the formalized religious ideology and associated iconography called Chavín in much of Peru. Its mecca was the impressive stone temple complex of Chavín de Huántar situated in the small Mosna Valley on the eastern escarpment of the Cordillera Blanca in the Callejón de Huaylas at an elevation of about 3,150 meters (Fig. 5.21). This location was near the confluence of two rivers, and at the midpoint in the valley was a "natural nexus" that provided access to and from the coast (via the Casma and Pativilca valleys) and highlands, on the one hand, and upper Amazonia, on the other. In addition, it is important to realize that Chavín was situated close to the invisible border that separates northern and southern Peru, the two-part macrodivision of Peruvian geography described earlier. In essence, Chavín was situated in a privileged location with relatively easy access to diverse resources and to the stimulation of important cultural developments in surrounding regions. The Kotosh Religious Tradition, which was widespread in the Central and North Highlands during the second millennium B.C.E., and contemporaneous ceremonial-civic centers on the central (e.g., Cardal and Garagay) to north coast (e.g., the Sechín and Pampa de las Llamas-Moxeke complexes in the Casma Valley, and Huaca de los Reyes), were of particular importance.

A number of scholars, including Tello, Carrión, Rowe, Lumbreras, Lathrap, and Burger, have worked at the site of Chavín de Huántar or on the associated cult and iconography. Chavín de Huántar is dominated by two juxtaposed masonry constructions called the Old and New Temples (Fig. 5.21). They represent two major construction phases that together spanned hundreds of years during the first millennium B.C.E. The site was probably established as a small, incipient agricultural village around 1000 B.C.E., or perhaps earlier during the Urabarriu Phase, which remains poorly defined in regard to its time and content. The Old Temple was built and modified during this and the subsequent Ofrendas Phase (up to about 500 B.C.E.). Temple construction incorporated various important concepts and features of antecedent and contemporary coastal ceremonial centers (e.g., U-shaped temple configuration with sunken courtyard and the use of columns). The Old Temple has an east-facing U-shaped configuration with a circular sunken courtyard at the center of the rectangular opening and a network of underground, stone-lined galleries. Originally the exterior face of the Old Temple was decorated with a series of large, carved tenon heads. The main structures at Chavín at one time may have been painted.

The focus of the early regional Chavín religion was a dagger-shaped monolith (called Lanzón) about 4.5 meters in height with a high-relief carving of the anthropomorphic "Smiling God" (Fig. 5.22). This image

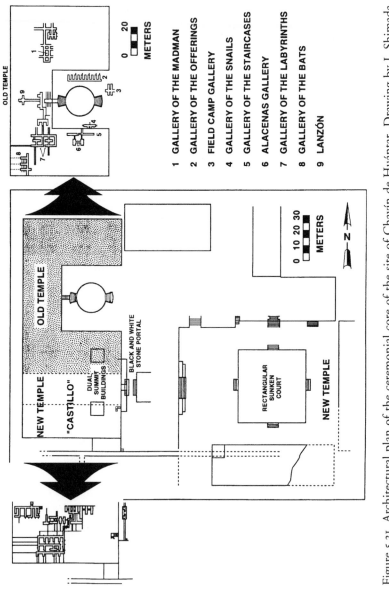

Figure 5.21. Architectural plan of the ceremonial core of the site of Chavín de Huántar. Drawing by I. Shimada based on figs. 120 and 185, Burger 1992: 131, 178 and fig. 3, Lumbreras 1993: 66.

OLD TEMPLE

1 GALLERY OF THE MADMAN
2 GALLERY OF THE OFFERINGS
3 FIELD CAMP GALLERY
4 GALLERY OF THE SNAILS
5 GALLERY OF THE STAIRCASES
6 ALACENAS GALLERY
7 GALLERY OF THE LABYRINTHS
8 GALLERY OF THE BATS
9 LANZÓN

0   20
METERS

NEW TEMPLE

"CASTILLO"

OLD TEMPLE

DUAL SUMMIT BUILDINGS

BLACK AND WHITE STONE PORTAL

RECTANGULAR SUNKEN COURT

NEW TEMPLE

0 10 20 30
METERS

N

Figure 5.22. Monolith with carved "Lanzón" or "Smiling God" image, placed at the center of the Old Temple at Chavín. Photo by I. Shimada.

may be yet another example of north coast input into the Chavín cult; such front-faced, standing human-like figures appear earlier on the north coast – for instance, the gigantic sculptured clay figures that decorated the front of a large, terraced platform mound (Huaca A) at Moxeke in the Casma Valley excavated by Tello. The Lanzón was placed at the end of a long gallery near the center of the basal part of the U-shape and stood in perfect alignment with the east–west axis of the sunken courtyard to the east. The Smiling God was not duplicated in any other context in or outside of Chavín de Huántar. It has prominent canines, hair ending in snake heads, clawed hands, and taloned feet. This supernatural image was faintly illuminated by limited light from an opening above. The deep, rumbling sounds and accompanying vibrations from rushing water in the canal below help to create awe-inspiring theatrical effects.

New Temple construction spanned the last two Chavín ceramic phases, Chakinani and Rocas, or Janabarriu (c. 500–200 B.C.E.) The Chakinani phase is defined on limited material evidence and may have had only local significance. The New Temple was formed by modifying and adding to the south wing of the Old Temple. The former has a large, rectangular sunken courtyard to the east, a black and white stone portal, and dual summit structures, all built symmetrically along the central east–west axis. The portal is one of the few stone carvings still in original context.

There is evidence of additional, auxiliary structures around both the Old and New Temples. Some associated with the New Temple have been eroded away by the Mosna River. During the Chakinani and Janabarriu phases, there was concurrent architectural expansion in the ceremonial core and residential sector of Chavín, with total site population estimated by Burger to have increased from about 500 during the Chakinani phase to about 2,000 to 3,000 in Janabarriu.

Janabarriu style (c. 400–200 B.C.E.; formerly called Classic Chavín) ceramics and images associated with the New Temple spread to much of Peru reaching the Ayacucho and Ica regions in the South-Central Highlands and on the south coast, respectively, and at least as far away as Pacopampa in the North Highlands and Lambayeque on the north coast. This style was more thoroughly diffused in the north. At one time it was thought that the Chavín cult and its iconography originated at this site and disseminated to the rest of Peru. Today they are seen as innovations based on synthesis of antecedent local developments in much of central and northern Peru. In fact, excavation of the sealed Gallery of the Offerings at the Old Temple revealed 681 intentionally broken ceremonial ceramic vessels of varied regional styles, attesting to interregional contacts and cross-fertilization over a long period of time.

Some 200 known stone carvings, mostly in the form of slabs with bas-relief designs and sculptured tenon heads, have long been the paradigm of the Chavín style. These carvings are innovative and refined in execution and style, and complex and informative in iconographic content. Many of our interpretations about the ideology underlying the Chavín cult derive from a handful of large stone carvings such as the Raimondi Stela and the Tello Obelisk, both removed from their original settings at Chavín de Huántar many years ago for display in Lima. As noted earlier, not many stone carvings remain in their original contexts, making it difficult to understand their significance fully. Chavín art, like most prehispanic art styles, was basically religious in nature, and the meaning of each carving was probably closely related not only to form and iconographic content but also to context (e.g., specific orientation and placement).

Rowe characterizes Chavín stone carvings as representational and conventional. In general, the use of multiple conventions is yet another reason why Chavín art is difficult to decipher. These conventions include symmetry, repetition, the use of standardized measures, and representation by substitution (e.g., snakes as hair), among others described later. Many of these conventions remind us of decorative textile weaving in which the design is carefully conceived before weaving begins. At the same time, the stone carvings display mastery of curves and scrolls.

In Rowe's stylistic seriation of Chavín stone carvings, the Tello Obelisk and the Raimondi Stela pertain to early and late parts of the Chavín artistic tradition, respectively – in other words, contemporaneous with the Old and New Temples. In spite of considerable temporal difference, analysis of the images on these carvings reveals strong continuity in the essence of the Chavín cult.

The Tello Obelisk is a tall (2.6-m high, 0.3-m wide), prismatic granite shaft that Carrión and Lumbreras argue originally stood in the center of the circular sunken court in front of the Old Temple as a gnomon or time-keeping device (Fig. 5.23). Stylistically, the bas-reliefs in the court and the obelisk are quite similar. The flat surfaces of the obelisk are covered by a highly complex zoomorphic representation in bas-relief. Essentially, it shows a profile view of two similar mythical creatures that possess the basic features of "crocodile" (looking more like *Crocodylus acutus* than *Alligator mississipiensis* or cayman) but with birdlike tails. Conventionalized representations of various plants and seashells are seen on different parts of their bodies. These parts are subdivided by a series of vertical and horizontal lines, suggesting a carefully planned design layout. Tello interpreted these creatures as the female and male versions of a single creator deity. The male has an L-shaped appendage ("penis")

Figure 5.23. Roll-out drawing of carving on the Tello Obelisk. Height: 2.52 m. Redrawn by I. Shimada from fig. 6, J. Rowe 1967: 99.

that ends with an anthropomorphic head with a manioc-like plant emerging out of its mouth. The female has an S-shaped motif in the genital region. Lathrap suggested that the male was associated with plants such as manioc, peanut, and achira, and the female with chili peppers and gourds. This dichotomy of root crops and legumes (underground), on the one hand, and seed crops (above ground), on the other, led Lathrap to argue that the male cayman represented the deity of the underworld, and the female, the deity of the sky. Above the head of the male is a *Spondylus* shell (undersea); a bird (said to be a harpy eagle, *Harpia harpyja*, 'sky') is shown at the corresponding location of the female.

This is a highly plausible interpretation of the obelisk. At the same time, given that the concept of complementary opposites (dualities) is an essential part of Chavín iconography, we may well see other dualities expressed in this carving (e.g., wild vs. domesticated, animals vs. plants, rainy vs. dry seasons, day vs. night, and ocean vs. sky). Tello, and later Lathrap, argued that Chavín was an important center pertaining to an eastern Andean cultural tradition diffusing out of Amazonia. This argument was based in part on its eastern location but mostly on the importance of jungle fauna such as jaguar, cayman, and anaconda in its iconography. Although Tello envisioned the Chavín religion as a "feline cult," more recent research indicates that the jaguar did not hold primary importance; rather, the jaguar is believed to represent a messenger or agent mediating earth and sky or human and supernatural worlds. (Thus shamans are said to transform to jaguars.)

It should be noted that not everyone agrees with Tello and Lathrap in holding that the reptiles, birds, and mammals depicted in Chavín art are of Amazonian origin. They may be coastal fauna such as crocodile (not cayman), migratory osprey (*Pandion haliaetus*; not eagle), and puma (*Felis concolor*; not jaguar). Similarly, the validity of plant identification has been questioned. Kaulicke interprets the manioc-like protrusion of the penis as a symbolic representation of life-giving liquids such as semen and irrigation water. The S-shaped motif is seen not as a peanut but as a marker of sexual union associated with the feline. In Kaulicke's vision, then, the Obelisk depicts the creation of life through interaction among different cosmological domains of male, female, ocean, sky, underground, and above ground; life-giving liquids are provided by the penis and sea-dwelling *Spondylus*, are absorbed by the *Strombus* or conch shell, and are then transported by the flying feline to supernatural beings and plants.

However we interpret Chavín art, it carried the beholder into alternate realities.

The Chavín cult associated with the Old Temple also had an important shamanistic component. Burger interpreted the tenon heads that decorated the exterior of the Old Temple as illustrating shamanistic transformation; shamans under the influence of hallucinogens (e.g., mescaline-bearing San Pedro cactus) could transform into jaguars to communicate with and mediate supernatural forces. Older Cupisnique ceramics from the north coast depict a head with human features on one side and interlocking canines and other feline features on the other, suggesting the persistence and pervasiveness of the notion of shamanistic transformation. After reviewing various lines of evidence, Burger concluded that the Chavín cult was based on a cosmopolitan ideology that emerged out of a fusion of tropical jungle and coastal elements. On balance, coastal (north coast) input seems more important.

The Raimondi Stela is a 2-meter high rectangular slab with low-relief carving of the frontal-faced, standing, anthropomorphic Staff God "wearing" an oversized "headdress" and holding a staff in each hand. The staffs end with a motif suggestive of a maize cob emerging out of parting husks. Like the earlier Smiling God, this divinity is shown with a set of interlocking canines, clawed hands and taloned feet, and hair in the form of snakes. How these cult images related to each other remains unclear.

When the Raimondi Stela is seen upside down, it becomes evident that the "headdress" is in reality a series of nested monstrous heads with protruding mouths and interlocking canines cayman (according to Lathrap), giving the impression of an interdependence between the earth and sky (or conversely the underworld). When we examine other representations of the Staff God, it becomes apparent that some are shown with breasts and vagina. The carvings on the black and white stone portals in front of the New Temple also show male and female winged supernatural creatures (based on eagles). In other words, the complex representations on the Raimondi Stela, and other carvings stylistically and physically associated with the Old and New Temples, embody the concept of a complementary whole or the importance of cosmic duality (male vs. female, and underworld vs. livingworld), and thus concern for reproductive success on the earth. Given the representations of cultivated plants seen on the Tello Obelisk and other Chavín artifacts, we are speaking here of an agricultural fertility cult.

The Staff God was the central icon of a late Chavín cult that spread through much of Peru about 400–200 B.C.E., perhaps by means of branch oracles (analogous to the later Pacha Kamaq oracle and its branches), pilgrims, and portable textiles decorated with religious motifs. The Staff God image itself is very rare on the north coast. Even at the site of Chavín, it seems stylistically aberrant. Its image is found, however, painted on cotton textiles from Karwa and a number of other sites on the south coast. Thus Kaulicke suggests that the image may have originated in southern Peru.

Ceramics also document the spread of the Chavín cult. In many areas on the coast and in the highlands that came to share the Chavín cosmology, pottery adopted certain new forms, motifs, and techniques that combined with those of local origin. Widely diffused Chavín forms include stirrup-spout bottles with thick spout lips and open shallow bowls. Just as distinctive are surface finishes and decorative conventions. Fine ceramics commonly have highly polished gray or black surfaces. Often an undecorated polished area contrasts with an unpolished textured area (e.g., rocker-stamped or combed). Curvilinear designs are done with broad incisions on prefired surfaces. Repetitive designs, such as rows of circles with central dots and concentric circles, were quite common. There are schematized representations of "jaguar" heads or "crested eagles" rendered in an appliqué technique that may emulate the visual effects of embossing on prestigious sheet gold, or of bas-relief carvings on stone slabs. In general, ceramics were not the prestigious medium of expression during this era, and their iconographic content was limited or truncated relative to stone carvings.

The cult with its demand for goods (e.g., used by religious élite and consumed in rituals, tribute, and temple trappings) is believed to have stimulated greater long-distance trade. Obsidian (volcanic glass) from a highland source in Huancavelica (470 km south of Chavín de Huántar), for example, became available to many areas in which the cult spread. Ritual use of cinnabar (mercuric sulfide), a bright red pigment, may have spread at the same time. The spread of tapestry and resist decorative techniques (e.g., batik and tie-dye), and an increased use of camelid wool for weaving on the coast, are believed to have been related to the Chavín cult. In metallurgy, soldering, "sweat" welding, and gold-silver alloying are believed to have been developed during the same time period. It appears that a constellation of important innovations was related to the spread of the cult.

Certainly differential funerary treatments (e.g., use of cinnabar paint on bodies and grave goods, placement of exotic goods such as *Spondylus* and *Strombus* shells, beads made of sodalite, quartz, and turquoise, and sheet-gold objects with repoussé decorations) suggest that marked social inequality had emerged by this time and that the religious élite controlled the distribution of both images and exotic goods.

Clearly the widespread, long-lasting impacts of the Chavín cult and iconography owe much to the innovative and universal character of the messages they conveyed. They boasted a new and powerful pantheon of deities, particularly the Staff God in its variant forms, that would reappear in modified form in later prehistory, particularly in the Wari, Tiwanaku, and Sicán religions (see Chap. 6).

The period of intense cultural interaction or "unification" accompanying the spread of the Chavín cult came to an end around 200 B.C.E. Not surprisingly, it was followed by a period of assimilation that involved selective integration of new and old cultural features into new overall configurations. It was a time of reasserting regional identity and setting new values and orders, away from cultural homogenization and external influences. Just such a creative process formed the basis of what we call Regional Development cultures, which began around 200 B.C.E.

Mochica

Mochica art, particularly its expression in ceramics, is characterized by an impressive range of subject matter. Unlike earlier Chavín art, ceramics were perhaps the most important means of artistic expression and symbolic comunication in the nonliterate world of the Mochica. Many subjects are shown in their broader settings – for example, sea lions on the beach or the solar deity emerging behind the mountains. As mentioned earlier, the subjects are the inhabitants of both the real/natural and mythological/supernatural worlds and their activities or roles. Real-world drawings – for example, of hand-to-hand combat between pairs of "warriors" – find their parallel depictions involving two supernatural beings. Many agricultural and natural products (including marine fauna) are depicted both naturalistically and in association with a mythic being. The omnipresence of supernatural forces in the natural world is clearly being expressed.

Subjects were carefully selected and not exhaustive in coverage. In fact, many aspects of the Mochica life and world are not depicted – for example, children and routine household and agricultural activities. Donnan and Hocquenghem have shown independently that the overwhelming portion of subject matter can be subsumed into one of a finite number of "themes" or "scenes," such as "combat," "running race," "purification," and "funerary" rites. Donnan suggests some dozen themes; Hocquenghem specifies nineteen. In other words, what is represented on most vessels is a shorthand representation or an essential part of a given theme or scene, which in turn constitutes only a portion of a complex narrative. No artifact holds more than a page or two of the implicit "storybook."

The "thematic approach" advocated by Donnan is much like linguistic analysis. The underlying premise here is that art is a form of communication, is structured much like languages, and can thus be analyzed by identifying meaningful units at various levels of organization and their interrelationships. A theme may be defined as a narrative concept or mental image translated into a visual form by recurrent configurations formed by a defined set of elements, each with specific symbolic meaning. These configurations may vary; all symbolic elements rarely occur together because artists exercise their own creativity within the boundaries set by culturally defined rules of expression. Nonetheless, they share a certain compositional integrity, and constituent elements retain the same basic function. An analogy in Christian art would be works depicting the birth of Christ or the Last Supper. Although many artists depicted the birth of Christ, there is a certain shared set of characteristic symbolic elements, such as the Christ child and the Virgin Mary. A good Mochica example is the "presentation" theme, which, according to Donnan, consists of the presentation of a goblet containing blood from a sacrificed prisoner to a presiding dignitary. This ritual is thought to relate to the combat theme, which often depicts the capture and stripping of defeated opponents, who are then tied and led away, presumably to be sacrificed.

In general, each theme is believed to illustrate important aspects of Mochica religion and associated rituals. The advantage of this approach is that it defines basic meaningful units and elucidates the underlying structural principles or "grammar" ordering them into coherent artistic expressions. Presumably, in settings where the same body of religious knowledge is widely shared, even scaled-down depictions of elements would be enough to invoke images of the complete themes in the mind of the observer. This does not come as a surprise given that decorated ceramics were made in abundance and extensively distributed, as described earlier. At the same time, it is not clear to what extent ordinary

Mochica people knew or understood deeper meanings encoded in ceramics (for example, the interplay of cosmic forces and deities to regulate the living world). Given the rarity of graphic representations of entire individual themes or scenes and their interrelationships, it is likely that small corps of shamans or priests had the role of enlightening the masses with their exclusive knowledge and communication with the supernatural world.

The foregoing approach does not readily tell us how different themes were interrelated, or the deeper meaning of the constituent themes taken together. It also has an inherent tendency to create an overly compartmentalized and static view of iconography. Given that the whole is often more than the sum of its parts, even an exhaustive delineation of themes may not provide us with full understanding of Mochica iconography.

As with Chavín and other counterparts, we can only present plausible conjectures based on historical and ethnographic analogies. Some scholars are pessimistic of reaching deep meanings. Hocquenghem is one of the few scholars who has ventured to "ferret out" encoded meaning from a comprehensive perspective. She identified the major constituent themes of Mochica iconography and related them to shamanistic traditions, mythologies, and rituals that were historically and ethnographically recorded in various regions of the Andean coast, highlands, and *selva*. These themes together are seen to form a ceremonial calendar that defined the astrological (particularly the movement of the sun, moon, and Pleiades), agricultural, and human life cycles and associated rituals. In other words, ceramic representations are believed to have depicted participants (both natural and supernatural) and their roles in each phase of the calendar. Rituals, including propitiation in the form of human sacrifice, were critical in advancing from one phase of the calendar to the next in the agricultural cycle. Thus, in her conception, Mochica iconography expressed concern for, and appreciation or celebration of, the successful maintenance of life cycles and cosmic order. Human sacrifice in the exclusive setting at the rear of the Huaca de la Luna at the site of Moche (archaeologically documented by Boguert and Uceda) appears to be related to torrential rains associated with El Niño events. These sacrifices were probably made to appease the deities and restore the normal order of their natural world.

The foregoing iconographic analysis is enlightening insofar as it offers a systemic view of the Mochica narratives. At the same time, Hocquenghem assumes persistent, widely shared pan-Andean structural principles (e.g., time-reckoning and agricultural calendar, dual and quadri-partite social divisions) and religious ideologies. If the Mochica shared "pan-Andean" calendrics, social organization, and religious beliefs with other prehispanic cultures, why then do we see so many differences, for example, between the Mochica and Inka iconographies? Berezkin, a Russian scholar, notes that there are, in fact, Mochica mythological concepts apparently without counterparts in the Cusco region. One example is an anthropomorphic deity, who supports the sky, shown as a double-headed serpent. Further, there are important differences among mythologies historically recorded in southern Peru and the South-Central Andes versus those in northern Peru and the North Andes. For example, man's acquisition of cultivated plants is explained in the south as having been unintentionally brought from the sky by fox; in the north, a cultural hero is said to have taken them from a toad or that the stolen child of the mother-goddess transformed herself into the desired plants. Thus the validity of the basic premise underlying Hocquenghem's iconographic analysis comes into question. The same kinds of questions surrounding the use of ethnographic data applies to various views of the Chavín iconography presented earlier.

Further, in lumping together examples of ceramic representations from the vast Mochica territory and its lengthy chronology, Hocquenghem assumes homogeneity of iconographic content in space and time. Actually there seems to be regional variation in the popularity of different motifs and themes, as well as indications of change in content over time.

In contrast to Hocquenghem, who believes Mochica iconography represents scenes related to their calendric cycle, Berezkin posits that it was mainly concerned with representation of Mochica mythologies. Further, he allows for the possibility that Mochica artisans consciously or unconsciously depicted their *ideas* about their social structure and its changes over time. Like Menzel, he believes that Mochica religion had a wide range of mythical beings, who may be classified into several general categories and numerous particular categories, with some overlap between them. Accordingly, Berezkin has focused his attention on the internal structure and dynamics of the Mochica pantheon through identification of the roles and status of mythological personages over time. He believes that the pantheon indirectly reflects the social reality of the Mochica culture and argues that the two opposing but complementary groups of "shamans" and "warriors" of regional populations each had their own deities. This vision differs from that of Larco and Benson, who see the existence of a supreme, creator deity referred to as *Ai-apaec* (perhaps the Mochica version of the Chavín Staff God). As Hocquenghem holds, Berezkin also believes that these two groups correspond to asymmetrical lower and upper moiety divisions. He argues that the Mochica plural pantheon seen in Phases III (c. C.E. 200–450) and IV (c. C.E. 450–550) was transformed to one with fewer major deities by Phase V. As seen later, this interpretation finds a parallel in Mochica geopolitics as reconstructed from settlement patterns and other lines of evidence; at the same time, the reader should remember that the Mochica iconography basically reflects ideology, not history, and thus should not draw any hasty conclusions regarding the coincidence. However, legitimation of the extant sociopolitical order may have acquired greater importance over time. The increased depictions of combat and warriors over time from Phases III to IV may well indicate that the "warrior" group acquired increasing power over the "shaman" group (Fig. 5.24). In other words, unlike the religious art of the Chavín, Mochica iconography seems to have increasingly served sociopolitical interests, expressing the dogma of the dominant groups. In sum, its narrative character and greater sociopolitical role set Mochica iconography apart from that of other contemporaneous ERD cultures.

In spite of differences, both analysts agree that Mochica iconography expresses the concepts of complementary oppositions, a moiety system (dual social organization), and concern with social and biological reproduction. Overall, representations of social structure, whether intentional or unintentional, set Mochica iconography apart from most other prehispanic Andean art. Narration of mythologies that in part relate to the cosmological order and origins, according to Berezkin, is yet another feature that distinguishes Mochica iconography.

The importance of shamans or curers in the Mochica world is also apparent from ceramics. In fact, some vessels show "curing sessions" with a "curer" seated next to a prone "patient" holding something in hand over the patient's stomach. Donnan has documented similarities between these and other Mochica representations of shamans/curers and modern-day practitioners on the north coast. Mochica ceramics also include modeled two-faced heads that presumably represent the transformation of shamans into felines, much like those of the earlier Cupisnique and Chavín examples. In addition, depictions of individuals with anomalies such as blindness, cleft palate, and deformed limbs are relatively com-

Figure 5.24. Moche III stirrup spout bottle representing a warrior on a throne-like seat. The stern expression and raised war club evoke a sense of power. The vessel is missing its (probably shell and/or turquoise) inlay. C-54646, Museo National de Antropología, Arqueología e Historia, Lima. Height: 22 cm. Photo by Y. Yoshii.

mon, suggesting that those individuals, like shamans, may have been perceived as possessing supernatural qualities or the ability to communicate with the supernatural world.

What is not clear is the role played by shamans in the elaborate Mochica religion and rituals linked to state-level politics. It is likely that there were differently ranked shamans, from those who played a role in folk medicine for commoners to those involved in oracular divination for crucial decisions regarding royal activities. Major personages shown in the "presentation" theme may well be "high priests" or "priestesses," as some scholars have suggested.

Paracas and Nasca

Much information pertaining to cosmology and rituals can be extracted from the complex, interrelated iconographies of the successive cultures on the south coast – namely, Paracas and Nasca. Recent evidence shows the geographical foci of these cultures to be distinct (Paracas centering on the northern south coast and Nasca, on the southern half). Nasca is no longer thought to have evolved directly from Paracas. However, iconographically, they are intimately interlinked, and they are considered together here.

An objective synopsis of Paracas-Nasca iconography is quite difficult to write. Much of the difficulty stems from (1) the dynamic character of the iconography with the changing popularity of different themes, as well as emergence of new themes, (2) the nonrepresentational and nonhistorical character of the style, and (3) the noninteractive, compartmentalized presentation of individual themes.

Like their Mochica counterpart, the Paracas and Nasca iconographies both portray inhabitants and activities in the parallel real and supernatural worlds. They are both concerned with relationships between the two worlds. However, aspects of the real world that the Nasca artisans chose to depict have no apparent basis in or reference to some significant events or personages, whether real or mythical, as they do in Mochica art. We cannot speak of specific individuals or events, as in the cases of Mochica "burial theme" or the earspools of the Warrior-Priest of Sipán, faithfully reproduced in full funerary regalia in miniature goldwork. Thus Peters characterizes Nasca art as "presentational," lacking a historical conception and emphasizing the fundamental and unchanging natural and supernatural order. Roark characterizes Nasca art as primarily "referential" and "conceptual." These terms describe art where its subject matter is identifiable as a representation of a class or member of a class of beings or objects in the "real world" or "mythical world."

In respect to the final point, mythical or natural creatures are rarely shown in Nasca art interacting with each other. Instead we see them individually in various poses from "flying" or "trance state" to "dancing." One finds neither the combat scenes nor the thematic linkages that would help us decipher the hierarchical and functional interrelationships among mythical creatures.

Whether one adopts the thematic or some other approach to understanding Nasca iconography, much is to be gained by examining the earlier Paracas art, particularly the naturalistic and detailed embroidered representations found on the Paracas Necropolis mantles. To a large extent, Nasca iconography consists of abbreviated versions of earlier Paracas themes.

In late Paracas iconography, the "Oculate Being" and his variants are the key religious figures. The Oculate Being is an enduring anthropomorphic representation with oversized head, large eyes (typically concentric circles), thick upcurved or smiling mouth, protruding tongue, and serpents placed on various parts of the head or body. He or she appears as a head or full-bodied with varied postures, and prominently hold darts, trophy heads and knive presumably used for decapitation. During the final phases of the Paracas sequence, specific features of the Oculate Being are imparted on traditional animal and human forms. Trophy heads that were earlier always associated with the Oculate Being now appear as independent motifs. Concurrently, the Oculate Being acquires attributes of the dominant predatory creatures of the land (felines), sky (raptorial birds) and sea (killer whales). The supernatural Oculate Being, by sharing these features, appears to convey the message of his supremacy over the universe as the creator and destroyer of life or "cosmic deity".

Many of the Nasca variants of the Oculate Being are subsumed under the rubric of "Anthropomorphic or Masked Mythical Beings," so named by Proulx (Fig. 5.25). They form the most complex and one of the most common themes in Nasca art. The latter are shown with a winged forehead ornament, whiskers or mouth mask, bangles, a cap, and holding a war club or a trophy head. In a few cases, this Being is associated with cultivated plants. On the basis of changes observed in this Being over Nasca Phases 3–6, Roark suggests that, whereas earlier examples may have represented a masked man impersonating a supernatural being, those dating to Phase 5 or later may actually show a supernatural being.

The presence of whiskers in the mask has led Sawyer and others to call the creature "feline deity" or "cat demon." The divergence of opin-

Figure 5.25. Nasca 5 double spout bottle depicting Anthropomorphic Mythical Being with a long tongue showing tadpoles (?). He is adorned with trophy heads and plants. Overall, the Being is imbued with the symbolism of fertility and abundance. Eugenio Nicolini Iglesias Collection, Lima. Photo by Y. Yutaka.

ions, as Proulx points out, stems in part from whether one emphasizes the human or animal side of the creature, and the different stylistic dates of images under consideration.

Another late Paracas theme that remains important in Nasca art is the "Mythical Killer Whale" (Fig. 5.26). From the late Paracas naturalistic form, it gradually becomes anthropomorphic. In the "Monumental" substyle, it is typically shown holding a "trophy head." In Phase 5, the whale becames decisively more anthropomorphic, showing lower torso,

Figure 5.26. Nasca Phase 3 effigy bottle representing mythical "killer whale" that holds a trophy head. Trophy heads decorate its body. Museo Rafael Larco Herrera, Height: 29 cm. Photo by Y. Yutaka.

breechcloth, and a pair of legs. In addition, numerous dorsal and ventral appendages between the fins add to the increasing overall complexity. However, following this anthropomorphic stage, it becomes greatly abstracted. In the final Phase 9 ("Disjunctive" substyle), the earlier symbolic version of the whale is simplified to a point where it is not readily recognizable without knowledge of its long-term stylistic evolution. In essence, the killer whale is rather typical of Nasca motifs and themes in that over time it becomes more stylized and symbolic.

Although the origin of the "trophy-head cult" remains obscure, after its initial appearance in late Paracas art, the severed-head motif comes to pervade Nasca art for its entire span. It appears as an independent motif and in association with mythical creatures (held or being eaten). The Masked Mythical Being, Mythical Killer Whales, and the "Horrible Bird" (raptorial bird with or without human-like legs) are clearly associated with "trophy heads." A general impression is that the head is associated with aggression and warfare. However, Sawyer argues that the frequent association of trophy-head symbols with the agricultural fertility cult symbol found in Phases 6–7 (e.g., fruits emerging out of a trophy head) is evidence that during this period, it was believed that the collecting of trophy heads contributed to the assurance of successful crops. In fact, trophy heads are also associated with female sexuality and fertility. Underlying the Phase 6 religion was the belief that killing and living are necessary, complementary opposites.

Many decapitated human heads have actually been excavated at the Nasca site – for example, at caches at the ceremonial center of Cahuachi. Each head has an enlarged foramen magnum, through which it is believed the brain was extracted. The depictions of mythical creatures "eating heads" may have corresponded to ritual consumption of the extracted brain. A recent analysis by Baraybar of the excavated heads with preserved soft tissues revealed superficial incisions made before death, suggesting that decapitation was preceded by intentional bleeding. Thus, in contrast to the vision of "head-hunting raids," this study argues for highly regulated ritual decapitations in special locations. If so, how were live victims captured, and who were they? Were they the conquered enemy or prisoners captured during the periodic ritual battles between two competing moeities, as Hocquenghem suggested for the Mochica? We still do not know whether the popularity of the severed-head motif and theme in Nasca art directly reflects the pervasiveness of warfare or its continuing religious significance.

Since Seler, various scholars have emphasized the close association of cultivated plants (commonly beans, hot peppers, maize, yuca, and peanut) with certain mythical creatures, particularly the "Mythical Spotted Cat" (based on the local Pampas cat, *Felis colocolo*), and later anthropomorphic variants, such as the "Feline Mythical Being." The "Harvesters" (humans drawn in frontal perspective holding stalks of cultivated plants) that appear only in Phase 5, as well as the enduring popularity of plant motifs, are another sign of concern with agricultural production. Such concern should not come as a surprise when we consider the environmental setting of the Nasca culture described earlier, particularly the limited water supply.

In some ways the symbolic meanings and functions of Nasca iconography (particularly pre-Phase 5) can be better appreciated in the complex and explicit representational art seen on late Paracas textiles. Dwyer suggests that these textiles illustrated and aided the transformation of the deceased élite from the real to the mythical world by depicting creatures and activities that were vital to the life force and regeneration. In this perspective the trophy head metaphorically relates to both death and rebirth. Killer whales, condors, and felines that take other lives to survive are commonly depicted eating or holding trophy heads. Further, humans are shown impersonating these creatures by wearing costumes (e.g., fox skins and bird dress) and masks. Burials with hammered gold masks, plumes, and other head and face ornaments, then, may represent dead priests who in their lives impersonated the mythical creatures.

Through a "direct historical approach" anchored in sixteenth- and seventeenth-century writings, Zuidema argues for continuity in the basic cosmological structure and concepts of the southern Peruvian cultures of the Nasca, Wari, and Inka. From this vantage, for example, he sees the Nasca Phase 5 variant of the frontal, standing Anthropomorphic and Mythical Being associated with two hawks, trophy head, and two small human figures as "a cosmological representation of royal power." In this view, the central standing figure and the two smaller humans represent the king and his sons; the trophy head symbolizes the conquered enemy, and the hawks the jural symbol of political dominance. Many of the comments, both pro and con, made regarding Hocqueghem's approach are also applicable here.

Pukara and Tiwanaku

We turn now to ERD cultures that arose inland, on the high plateaus and in the intermontane valleys of the Andes. The South-Central Andes developed its own distinct ideology and ritual complex, called the Yaya-Mama Religious Tradition by Chávez-Mohr and Chávez. It is dated to circa 600–100 B.C.E. and centered in the Titicaca Basin. The tradition consisted of a temple-storage complex with central sunken courts (the first public constructions in the region) associated with ritual paraphernalia, complex iconography, and large stone sculpture (a sculptural image gave the name, which means 'Father–Mother' in Quechua, to this tradition). The paraphernalia included ceramic trumpets and burners, and sculpture and iconography focused on supernaturals. The Chávezes believe that this was an enduring, indigenous religion of the Titicaca Basin that served as a catalyst in unification of various populations occupying different zones of the basin. More specifically, we can infer that ritual participation established a network of social ties and ritual obligations between the temple and participating groups. With periodic gatherings of the regional population, the temple not only assumed the role of social and ideological integration but also served as the mechanism of economic redistribution. Storage facilities, as found at the temples of Pukara and Chiripa, were crucial. This religious tradition is seen to underlie the formation of the Pukara (c. 200 B.C.E. to C.E. 200) and the later Tiwanaku cultures (c. C.E. 400?–1000?; see Chap. 6).

Representations seen on Pukara ceramics provide clues to the content and organization of Yaya-Mama religious ideology. They included anthropomorphic heads with appendages and vertically divided eyes, felines, serpents, and checkered crosses. As described earlier, many motifs relate to one of two supernatural beings – a woman who leads either a llama or an alpaca by rope while holding a scepter, and a man associated with trophy heads, dead bodies, and felines (Fig. 5.27). Oval or circular eyes divided into halves are found on supernaturals in Pukara, Tiwanaku, and Wari styles. Noting that split eyes and fangs are animal characteristics, Lyon suggests that supernaturals with such attributes represent people similar to Guardians or Masters of Animals, a widespread belief shared by various native South American groups. Generally, these supernaturals are thought to control the abundance of avian, terrestrial, and aquatic creatures under their care and to punish anyone who abuses or kills too many of their animals. Lyon suspects that supernatural beings, which combine human and animal features, or which appear sometimes in human and other times in animal guise, are such guardian beings. In this conception, the woman who leads a camelid in the Pukara iconography embodies the patron deity of all-important domesticated camelids. The meaning of the male supernatural is less certain. It is generally believed that Pukara art and associated ideology are the base upon which those of the Tiwanaku were formulated.

North Andean Cultures

Beyond the modern Peru-Ecuador border, in the orbit of the previous Chorrera tradition, some of the same ideas prevailed. The shaman is a

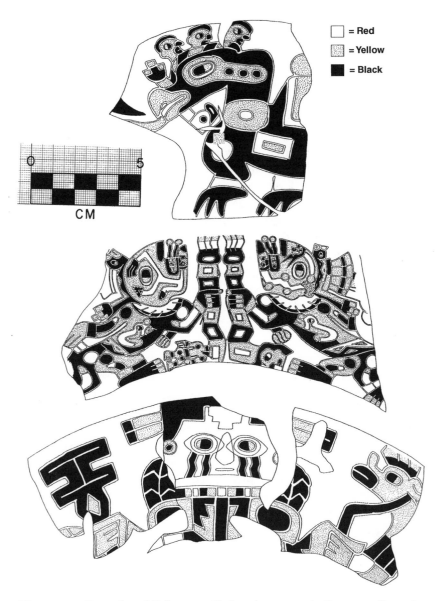

Figure 5.27. Examples of Pukara motifs found on ceramic fragments from the site of Pukara. The top piece shows what is thought to be a mythological condor. The sherd at the center displays a pair of symmetrically facing anthropomorphic figures shown in profile. Each holds a similar but not identical staff. The bottom piece shows an anthropomorphic figure holding a staff-like object in one hand and llama lead in the other. Note two parallel lines descending from the eyes. In basic form, this face is reproduced in later Tiwanaku, Wari and Sicán iconographies. Black, stippled and white areas correspond to black, yellow, and red on the original sherds, respectively. Drawing by I. Shimada based on figs. 4, 14, and 20, Rowe and Brandel 1969/70.

major focus of North Andean art, both highland and coast, and representations of what can be inferred to be shamans are common. In the case
of Mochica art, the shaman seemed secondary to anthropomorphic deities and élite personages. Agricultural and human fertility is yet another
major concern expressed in its art.

In Jama-Coaque figurines, many examples illustrate the close association between men and cultivated plants – for example, a man holding a
pineapple in each hand, or a man sitting on manioc. Figure 5.17 is said
to show a man engaged in a sowing ceremony. His detachable "hand
bag" appears to contain seed, and the staff he holds in his left hand may
represent a ceremonial digging stick.

La Tolita figurines and ceramics from the northern edge of Ecuador's
coast depict trophy heads, musicians, spinning, canoe paddling, houses,
child birth, and breast-feeding. Also included are clear symbols of fertility
– phallus, breasts, and diverse sexual activities, some with zoomorphic
creatures. Many representations of aged individuals, whose faces show
wrinkles, lost teeth, and emaciated bodies, are also found. Given that the
life expectancy inferred from a sample of contemporaneous Tumaco
burials is about 30 years, anyone of 40 to 60 years of age was rare and
probably respected. Pathologies and deformations are often depicted,
including facial paralysis, tumors, harelips, humps, and dwarfs. Depictions of physical abnormalities and sexual activities are not as common
among the Ecuadorian ERD cultures as among the better-known Mochica cases on the north coast of Peru, where such representations are
generally regarded as showing their supernatural qualities.

Classic La Tolita iconography is also replete with representations of
powerful animals of sky, land, and water (felines, serpents, cayman, bat,
and "eagle") or their diagnostic features, presumably symbolizing major
forces of different domains of the world. The importance of felines is
indicated by the abundance and diverse forms of their representations.
For example, some figurines show men wearing costumes apparently
made of feline skins with their faces visible inside the mouth, as if to
illustrate their shamanistic transformation. The appearance is much like
that of the Jama-Coaque figurines wearing feathered costumes. Among
the Desana tribe in Colombia, feline or jaguar masks are used in rituals
in which shamans transform into jaguars to mediate with the sun or the
principal deity of the tribe. The jaguar is said to possess the power of the
sun.

Other La Tolita figurines represent standing men holding objects in both hands in a trancelike state. Some are shown holding or wearing modeled trophy heads, and plenty of crania have been found at La Tolita. Perhaps these figurines as a whole represent shamans or priests in ritual acts intended to communicate with supernatural forces. We cannot discount the possibility that they represent a transformation of men into powerful animals, or vice versa.

Overall, Classic La Tolita iconography, much like that of other coastal Ecuadorian cultures, is strongly imbued with concern for fertility and natural forces. Unlike Mochica art, we do not see clearly formalized anthropomorphic beings with supernatural features or "deities" engaged in different activities critical to earthly existence. In this sense, it is still not clear whether coastal cultures had developed a separate specialized corps of priests engaged in establishment, dissemination, and perpetuation of formalized sacred dogma and related icons. At the same time, Váldez argues that clear stylistic unity and shared iconographic themes mirror social and ideological cohesion achieved under shaman-chiefs at the site during the Classic phase.

DeBoer observes that the lifeway and beliefs of modern Chachi inhabitants who occupy the region upstream from La Tolita (the population called Cayapa in older literature) are best characterized as those of the Tropical Forest Culture, as defined by Steward. Important among its defining feature is a shamanistic complex that utilizes certain hallucinogens. There is a general sense among the scholars who work on coastal Ecuador that many of the prehispanic developments there can best be understood as western extensions of the Amazonian tropical forest culture.

ORGANIZATIONAL FEATURES

In this section, the organizational features and achievements of the Mochica culture are summarized and then compared with other ERD cultures.

Mochica Organization and Polity

Mochica society grew in productive capacity, sociopolitical complexity, and territorial extent over its long existence (c. C.E. 1–700). The traditional view is that the Mochica polity, with its capital at the site of Moche, began expansion out of the Moche Valley, its "heartland," during Phase III (c. C.E. 200–400). By about C.E. 500 (Phase IV), it was thought that the Mochica had established military hegemony over the entire north coast and adjacent coastal areas (Piura to Huarmey valleys), a 600 kilometer stretch encompassing eleven contiguous coastal valleys (Map 5.2) The extent of Mochica trade and its sphere of interaction appear to have reached southward to the south coast of Peru, where Nasca artisans adopted a number of Mochica stylistic conventions and motifs. Through Vicús intermediaries, the Mochica are thought to have acquired valuable tropical shells and other exotic goods from the North Andes. To the east, the Mochica cultural frontier appears to have been the *yunka* zone shared with or contested by Cajamarca and Recuay populations.

The discovery of sumptuous early Mochica burials (Phases I–III) at the sites of Loma Negra, Sipán, and La Mina (in the upper Piura, Lambayeque, and southern edge of Jequetepeque valleys, respectively) have forced us to reconsider conventional perception of Mochica socio-political organization. The apparent stylistic homogeneity found along the north coast was long assumed to indicate political unity achieved by a single Mochica polity based at the capital of Moche. The data no longer support this monolithic vision. Rather, they suggest that, at least for the span of Phases I–III, three or even more regional polities that shared the art style we call Mochica held sway over different regions of the north coast (Fig. 5.28). We can tentatively identify regional polities centered in the upper Piura, Lambayeque, Moche, and perhaps Jequete-peque valleys. It is likely that the large productive Chicama Valley had its own but was incorporated into the Southern Mochica polity during Phase I or II. The upper Piura polity may well have met a similar fate under the Lambayeque polity, which is believed to have had its capital at the Huaca Rajada (Sipán) – Huaca Santa Rosa complex occupying the north and south banks of the Reque River (originally a large canal) in the mid-Lambayeque Valley.

In general, early Mochica style ceramics (c. C.E. 100–350) from the northern north coast valleys of Zaña, Lambayeque, La Leche, and Piura share certain idiosyncratic features, such as the occasional use of purple paint in addition to dark red and off-white, as well as the popularity of certain icons. The aforementioned sumptuous tombs at Sipán and other sites amply demonstrate the presence of a complex regional, social hier-archy during the first few centuries C.E. It is suggested here that the leaders of these valleys were politically allied through gift and marriage

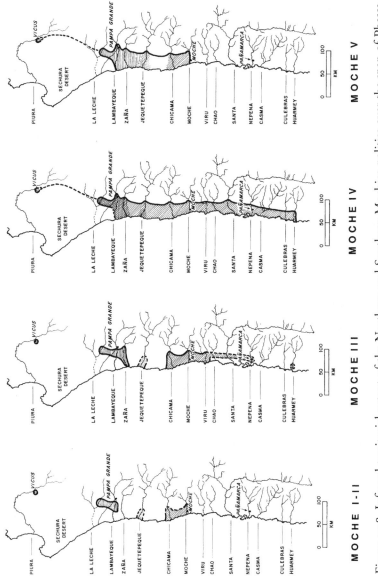

MOCHE I-II   MOCHE III   MOCHE IV   MOCHE V

Figure 5.28. Inferred territorial extent of the Northern and Southern Mochica polities over the span of Phases I to V. Drawing by I. Shimada.

exchange and shared basic religious and political beliefs. In this chapter, these polities are together called the Northern Mochica. The polity centered in the Moche Valley is referred to as the Southern Mochica.

The Southern Mochica appear to have been the most ambitious in establishing a multivalley hegemony. During Phase III (or perhaps slightly earlier), the Southern Mochica began southward military expansion by conquering Gallinazo polities in the Virú and Santa valleys. Phase III may have lasted as long as 200 years, and the limited quantities of Mochica ceramics found in areas as far south as Casma and Huarmey may well have resulted in a series of brief military incursions and attempts to establish colonies. It is quite clear that during Phase IV the Southern Mochica dominated the entire southern north coast and Huarmey Valley. In their expansion, the Southern Mochica polity came into direct contact with the Recuay, contesting control of the important *yunka* zone in the upper coastal valleys and access to the Pacific. Evidence points to a tense coexistence of two populations sharing access to *yunka* resources.

The reasons for Mochica southward expansion and associated strategy of "horizontality" have already been discussed. When we turn our attention to areas north of the Chicama-Moche region, there is no clear evidence of forcible expansion by the Southern Mochica before Phase IV. If the basic aim of Mochica expansion was agricultural maximization, then the logical strategy would have been to conquer first the northern north coast with its far greater agricultural productivity. This situation is undoubtedly related to the presence of Northern Mochica and, to a lesser degree, Cajamarca populations. In addition, in the Lambayeque and La Leche valleys, the Gallinazo and Mochica polities may have coexisted until both were incorporated into the expanding Southern Mochica polity around C.E. 500. At major sites such as Dos Cabezas and Pacatnamú in the Jequetepeque Valley, Gallinazo and Mochica style ceramics have been found together in the same tombs. In the La Leche Valley, ceramics of these styles have been found together on the same floors of ceremonial structures, and in a possible ceramic workshop at Huaca La Merced. The finer Mochica ceramics may have been adopted as a status symbol by the local Gallinazo population.

Overall, instead of viewing north coast prehistory in terms of a single dominant political center in the Chicama-Moche region, the current view of the Mochica sociopolitical organization (for Phases I to early IV) postulates parallel political development of the Lambayeque-centered Northern and Moche-based Southern Mochica polities, each with a number of conquered and allied local Gallinazo and Mochica polities. In other words, the cultural bipartition of the north coast mentioned earlier becomes quite evident during the first few centuries C.E.

Sometime in Phase IV, the Southern Mochica polity eclipsed its northern counterpart creating a short-lived pan–north coast hegemony. Most archaeologists argue that at its height, the Southern Mochica attained state-level sociopolitical integration, and that it was the first multi-valley, expansive, secular state. Larco described it as a state-level theocratic dynasty assisted by powerful military chiefs. Supportive lines of evidence include the presence of interlinked regional centers that occupied the apex of a three-tier, intrusive settlement hierarchy in the subject territories (the site of Moche occupying the top, fourth level), differential funerary treatments (presumably reflecting social stratification), and economic complexity.

However, evidence mustered in support of the Mochica state is not unequivocal. Schaedel and a few other scholars feel that the polity was a confederation of chiefdoms or in a transitional stage between a theocratic chiefdom and secular state. Questions surrounding the significance of explicit depictions of armed combat and "warriors" in ceramic art have already been considered (i.e., there is a distinct possibility that these depictions show annual, ritual battle between two ranked halves of Mochica society such as apparently existed in the Inka empire [and in some highland communities to this day], rather than indicating the importance of warfare as a means of sociopolitical integration and territorial expansion). Such battles would challenge or reaffirm the existing social order through controlled fighting. At least some defeated warriors were apparently captured as sacrificial victims. Depictions of dismembered corpses and naked "prisoners" with ropes around their necks are common. Overall, debate surrounding the level and nature of Mochica sociopolitical integration has consumed too much time and energy since the 1940s largely due to the lack of a consensus in regard to definition of the state, differential emphasis placed on different lines of evidence, and insufficient excavation of nonfunerary contexts.

This sort of classificatory or typological debate led Bawden to characterize the Andean state as a state of mind, and to argue that the term "state" is meaningless as a precise unit of social analysis. Methodologically, such perception requires identification of "well-defined material expressions of constituent social systems which are suitable for precise comparison across space and through time." However, as noted at the onset of this chapter, detailed analysis of this sort with the long-term goal of clarifying the process of social complexity has been carried out only sporadically in the archaeology of ERD cultures.

The site of Moche has received much public and professional attention largely due to the two spectacular monumental adobe constructions of Huaca del Sol and Huaca de la Luna (Fig. 5.29). These are multilevel platform mounds built with at least an estimated 143 million and 50 million adobe bricks, respectively. Only about one-third of the original construction (estimated volume of 2 million m³) of Huaca del Sol remains today, due to erosion by the River Moche, which was intentionally diverted by colonial grave looters so as to cut it away. Assuming that it had a symmetrical form, it had a cross shape with short arms and long central axis oriented northeast–southwest (345 × 160 m and 40 m in height). Huaca de la Luna, at the south base of Cerro Blanco, has a rectangular plan (290 × 210 m and 25 m in height) with its top subdivided into a series of clean, spacious courtyards that were enclosed by walls decorated with murals and friezes of religious character. One courtyard contained a complex of well-built rooms with windows. Overall, Huaca de la Luna had a sacrosanct and private character, perhaps serving as the residence of high-echelon religious personnel and the setting of exclusive rituals. Huaca del Sol is seen to have been the setting of periodic public feastings (based on the considerable quantity of food remains found), rituals, and daily administrative tasks. Depictions of feasts are relatively common and must have served as a means of gaining prestige or repaying favors – redistributive or political economy in action.

It has been observed that monumental adobe temples modeled after Huaca del Sol were built at urban regional centers in conquered territory to symbolize the political and ideological dominance of the Mochica state and to disseminate its dogma. These centers headed a regional three-level settlement hierarchy and were interconnected to each other and to the site of Moche via a network of roads. Apparently, each center had its own craft workshops to assure both an adequate supply of ceramics bearing Mochica symbolism and status goods crucial for the political economy. In addition, many, if not all, of the temples were decorated with elaborate polychrome murals or high-relief adobe friezes that conveyed Mochica religious and political dogma. The interior walls of different construction phases at Huaca de la Luna were decorated with the face of a deity with intense glaring eyes, prominent interlocking canines, and double sets of round "ears." Part of a mural showing a priestess and

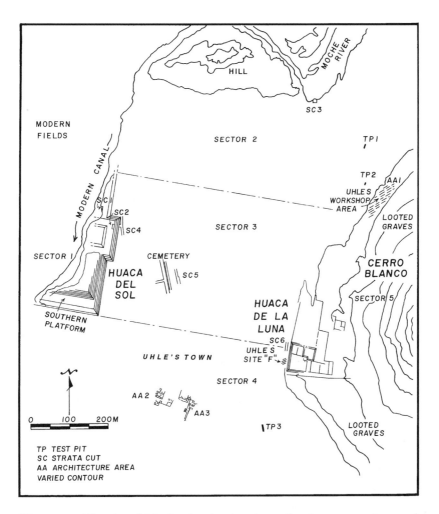

Figure 5.29. The site of Moche showing locations of major constructions and excavations conducted by M. Uhle and the Chan Chan-Moche Valley Project. An ongoing Peruvian-Canadian project is situated in Sector 4. Drawing by I. Shimada.

her companions in the "presentation" of the goblet described earlier has been found at Pañamarca in the Nepeña Valley. The facade of the Huaca El Brujo mound, near the mouth of the Chicama River, revealed elaborate friezes that correspond to at least four construction phases. Murals of the last two phases showed, among other representations, human sacrifice, a string of personages holding hands, warriors, and a procession of naked "prisoners" accompanied by victorious warriors.

Analysis of architectural forms and construction techniques has yielded valuable information pertaining to the organization and working of Mochica society. For example, Mochica monumental adobe structures were essentially built using "segmentary construction" – juxtaposition of tall, standardized (1-m wide), vertical columns of mold-made, adobe bricks mortared internally but not joined to adjacent columns. Technically it was very simple, requiring no special skill or supervision. Labor crews could build separate segments without much coordination with each other. The constituent adobe bricks were usually of a single size, shape, and soil type, suggesting that they were made at one location using a single mold form.

The segmentary construction technique was widely used by the Northern and Southern Mochicas as well as by the Gallinazo people. What distinguished the former was the practice of marking a certain percentage of constituent adobe bricks of a given segment with a simple geometric mark. In other words, there is consistent one-to-one correspondence between an individual segment and the attributes of its constituent adobe bricks (mark, size, shape [mold], and soil; Fig. 5.30). These features led Uhle, Kroeber, and Moseley to infer that each segment was built by a distinct social group who marked their bricks to identify their work. Moseley inferred that the segmentary construction illustrates a labor tax – a pre-Inka precursor of the rotating labor tax, or *mit'a* – and that each corresponding mark served as an accounting device, identifying who was fulfilling this obligation.

At Huaca del Sol, over ninety distinct marks were identified (Fig. 5.31), indicating that this structure was the collective effort of laborers representing numerous communities and other social groups from the Moche and adjacent valleys. It should be kept in mind, however, that the impressive size of Huaca del Sol and La Luna was the cumulative result of at least eight and six phases of construction, respectively, spanning nearly the entire Mochica cultural chronology, perhaps 500 to 600 years. We still do not know exactly how long a given construction phase lasted. It is possible that these structures saw numerous modifications and expansions at the ascensions of new rulers and following major victories and El Niño rains.

The modular labor organization seen in the construction of monumental adobe architecture is also found in other features of Mochica

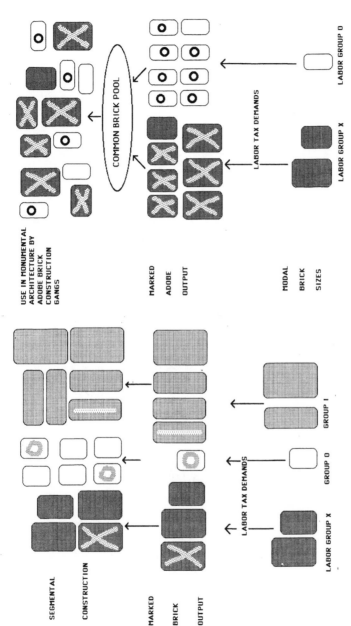

Figure 5.30. Graphic representations of (right) the model of task differentiation and centralized pooling proposed to account for the distribution of marked adobe bricks documented at the Huaca Fortaleza pyramid at Pampa Grande, and (left) the labor tax model proposed to account for the labor organization of the Huaca del Sol construction. Modified from fig. 12 in Cavallaro and Shimada 1988: 92.

Izumi Shimada

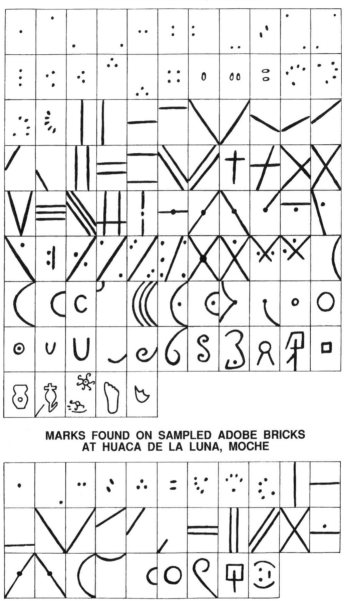

Figure 5.31. Adobe brick marks recorded at the Huaca del Sol and Huaca de la Luna mounds. Drawing by I. Shimada.

society. In construction of canals and roads, different segments of the same length were prepared in distinct manners, suggesting involvement of labor gangs from different communities. In fact, it has been argued that conscripted labor formed the basis of the Mochica economy. In craft production, this approach meant a set of similarly organized and equipped workshops in the same general area (usually interconnected by shared corridors or patios) engaged in the same craft. They produced the same whole objects or complementary parts to be assembled elsewhere. Much of the day-to-day productive activity was apparently unsupervised. However, procurement of raw materials and distribution of products are believed to have been supervised. Production thus had some degree of autonomy at the level of individual production units, but at the same time, a certain level of output and quality through replication and competition was assured. Even in ceramic production we see a balancing act between individuality and replication; molds were used extensively to assure replication of the same forms and quality as well as a good level of output; subsequent painting allowed artisans some degree of individualistic expression within the limits set by established artistic conventions and canons. Achieving and maintaining this balance probably contributed to the beauty, mastery, and longevity of Mochica arts and crafts.

Evidence from Pampa Grande in the Lambayeque Valley, the capital of the Northern Mochica during Phase V (Fig. 5.32), suggests that production at least of utilitarian craft goods in an urban setting was underwritten by "institutionalized hospitality." It is apparent that workers in metal (copper objects) and weaving (cotton cloth) workshops were provided with food and beer prepared in detached kitchens, which cooked beans and maize stored in nearby small, state-controlled storage facilities. Workers appear to have commuted daily from their residences to the workshops in other areas of the city. The status of these workers remains unclear (were they full-time state retainers or conscripted workers?), but it is evident that the principle of reciprocity governing the state–subject relationship in the Inka empire (see Chap. 10) can be traced back in time to at least circa C.E. 600. However, production of ritual and élite status goods, such as *Spondylus* beads and pendants, seems to have been much more closely supervised, with workshops set within walled enclosures with restricted access and major platform mounds. Workers involved in the latter may well have been "attached specialists" – that is, full-time state retainers producing sumptuary goods for the state's political economy.

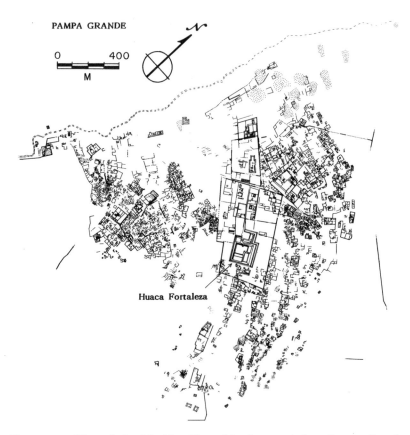

Figure 5.32. Plan of the Mochica Phase V urban capital at Pampa Grande. Dense, highly diverse architecture covered an area ca. 6 km² in extent. Drawing by J. Rosell and I. Shimada.

Economic specialization can be seen in Mochica ceramic production. This involved the large-scale use of molds for vessel formation and nucleated workshop production attached to the major ceremonial–civic centers. Such production is best seen at Cerro Mayal, a natural promontory just northwest of the major Mochica population center of Cerro Mocollope in the mid-Chicama Valley. There Russell and his colleagues found an area of about 185 × 90 meters densely covered with wasters, discarded molds, unfired vessels and figurines, ash, and other production debris, to a depth of 1.0–1.5 meters. The Cerro Mayal production area shows separate areas for different activities such as firing and vessel formation, and it was detached from the living quarters. The presence of what are believed to be storerooms containing food items may mean that potters were provided with their provisions by the Mochica state, as seen at Pampa Grande. Cerro Mayal produced primarily small decorated vessels such as flaring vases, face-neck jars, stirrup-spout bottles, bowls, figurines, and musical instruments. Although output and supervision remain to be clarified, it seems certain that products from Cerro Mayal workshops supplied the mid-valley population, including Mocollope. The degree of standardization in vessel form and size, as well as the range of vessel forms produced at Cerro Mayal and other workshops, clearly sets Mochica ceramics apart from their Lima and Nasca counterparts.

There are also indications of specialized production of fine ceramics destined for ritual and funerary uses. Workshops near the Huaca de la Luna pyramid at Moche produced mold-made figurines and large effigy vessels that formed part of the furnishings of nearby élite tombs and ritual offerings behind the pyramid. The workshop at Pampa Grande produced blackware serving dishes and effigy bottles.

The foregoing is not surprising given population size, the level of sociopolitical organization involved, and the primary role that ceramics played in disseminating religious and political visions of the Mochica élite. The associated settlements had estimated populations of several thousand to upward of 15,000. Locating workshops within major regional centers undoubtedly eased supervision of production and distribution.

Clearly, among the ERD cultures, the Mochica reached a unique high point in scale, intensity and output, sociopolitical complexity, and territorial extent. Comparison with Nasca and other cultures drives home this point.

Nasca

Let us consider the organizational implications of the Nasca ceramics. It is clear that Nasca polychrome ceramics were widely available across social boundaries and used in habitational, ceremonial, and mortuary contexts. Carmichael found that the average number of ceramic vessels interred in tombs increased over time, from one or two at the beginning of the Nasca sequence to five or six by Phase 5. Finewares were also used in votive and dedicatory offerings at such locations as the major ceremonial center of Cahuachi. Concurrently, as noted earlier, polychrome ceramics came to supplant embroidered textiles as the primary medium of artistic and religious expression. These usages and trends imply over time an overall increase in demand for fine ceramics, but we cannot readily quantify this increase. Also, many vessels in tombs show scratches, abrasions, and other evidence of use-wear, indicating that they were not made exclusively for burial purposes.

Carmichael argues for the importance of knowing the scale and complexity of the given society before we can properly understand the organizational aspects of ceramic production and distribution. Based on a systematic analysis of burials and settlement patterns, he views Nasca society as a group of agrarian villages and towns or semi-autonomous, ranked lineages that together controlled a given valley – or in other terms, an aggregation of relatively small, low-level chiefdoms. Taking into account the absence of any direct evidence of intense craft specialization or production, he suggests that Nasca pottery was produced on a seasonal basis between planting and harvesting.

This view has neither been independently field-tested nor widely accepted. In fact, various scholars such as Lumbreras, Moseley, Proulx, and Rowe see the Nasca in Phases 2 and 3 as a multivalley state with its capital at Cahuachi (Fig. 5.33), situated on the south bank of the Nazca River 50 kilometers inland. The presence of "intrusive" Nasca settlements such as Dos Palmas in the Pisco Valley and Tambo Viejo in the Acarí Valley are seen as evidence of territorial aggression. At the same time, when the known distribution of Nasca ceramics is viewed as a whole, it becomes apparent that it is concentrated in the Ica and Río Grande de Nazca drainages with only scatterings in valleys to the north or south. In addition, the nature of occupation of the Cahuachi leaves serious questions pertaining to the organization and working of the inferred state. This site has some forty low mounds of varied size and form and associated forecourts and plazas dispersed over an area of about 150 hectares. The mounds may have formed some sort of hierarchy reflecting the social ranks of the builders. Many of these mounds, including the largest, are natural promontories modified by plastered adobe facades. H. Silverman found little evidence of permanent residents. Rather, the structures that she and previous workers excavated were used as settings for human burials, cache offerings of trophy heads and textiles, and an enigmatic cluster of standing wooden posts. Over 70 percent of sherds collected on the surface and in excavations pertained to fine polychrome ceramics. In addition, a complex of geoglyphs in the adjacent plain appear to point directly at some of the principal mounds at Cahuachi.

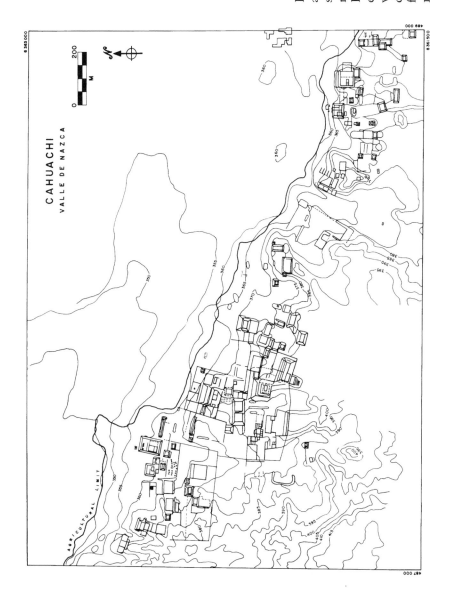

Figure 5.33. The eastern and central sectors of the site of Cahuachi in the mid-section of the Nasca River drainage. The western zone has only scant visible architecture. Redrawn by C. Samillán from fig. 2.4, Silverman 1993: 20–21.

Mustering these lines of evidence and using analogies with the famed oracle center of Pacha Kamaq near the city of Lima as well as modern sites of pilgrimage (e.g., the Shrine of the Virgin of Yauca in the Ica drainage), Silverman argues that Cahuachi was the principal Nasca ceremonial center and a pilgrimage shrine involving short-term, transient (perhaps calendrically sequential) gatherings of the regional population. In her conception, various social groups (analogous to Andean *ayllus*) of the region constructed and maintained their own mounds at Cahuachi, and periodic participation in rituals there affirmed and strengthened the Nasca corporate identity as well as their own roles and status. Silverman sees the inferred periodic gatherings as having had a function akin to the aforementioned vision of Mochica ritual battles and their role in contesting and reworking the existing social order.

Having vacillated between the competing views of the Nasca (in Phases 2–3) as a state and as a confederation of chiefdom, Silverman now sees Nasca as a fluid confederacy of independent chiefdoms. Her current position is based on the evidence summarized earlier and newly acquired settlement-pattern data. In line with Shimada's general conception of Central Andean ceremonial centers, she sees Cahuachi as the Nasca capital not in terms of population density or size but rather in centrality of interaction. In addition, most sites found in settlement surveys were small (less than 4 hectares), undifferentiated habitational sites near agricultural land with no evidence of intra- or intersite stratification. Once again, comments made earlier in regard to the level of sociopolitical integration achieved by the Mochica should be kept in mind.

Coastal Ecuador

Lastly, we consider the situation in coastal Ecuador. Here understanding of organizational achievements has greatly expanded in recent decades. We are now beginning to gain some idea of the Jama-Coaque settlement distribution, differentiation, and hierarchy. Recent surveys of the Jama Valley drainage basin have documented 150 sites of varied size, location, and inferred function (including the dwelling or ceremonial mounds called *tolas*) spanning the entire occupational sequence from the Early Formative Period (c. 1700–1650 B.C.E.) to the time of the Spanish conquest. Of particular importance are dense habitations (density of 6.7 sites per km²) in and around the relatively flat alluvial bottomland in the mid-valley around San Isidro. Groups of sites, each with a wide range of surface sizes and their own internal settlement hierarchy, cluster in discrete alluvial segments, suggesting that each site group corresponds to some significant social group. Each cluster has one large site that seems to dominate a series of nearby small sites. Most of these mid-valley sites with surface scatters of sherds cover an area of 5 or fewer hectares. A few cover about 17 hectares.

The site of San Isidro stands out. It has a surface area of some 40 hectares dominated by a large, earthen platform mound. The ceremonial precinct at the site appears to have been established during Valdivia occupation – that is, in the early years of the village-building way of life – and incremental mound building continued through the Chorrera and into Jama-Coaque I and II. The size of the site and the presence of a monumental mound are thought to attest to the role of the site as a regional ceremonial and political center, and the existence of both a substantial support population and considerable surplus production, as well as regional differentiation in wealth.

The mid-valley alluvial bottomland focus spanned the entire regional sequence, with San Isidro maintaining its primary importance in the regional settlement hierarchy. Although small sites emerged in the non-alluvial area farther inland from San Isidro during the Late Formative Period, a more generalized occupation of the nonalluvial portions of the valley does not seem to have started until Jama-Coaque II.

Overall, the sites and their distribution in space increase over time, implying an expanding regional population. The clear preference for alluvial bottomland for settlement locations argues for dependence upon an agricultural economy, though beach sites appear to have intensively exploited mangrove and marine resources. Certainly during Jama-Coaque I times, the regional settlement system consisted of a series of subsystems, each occupying a discrete alluvial segment and having its own internal (two-level?) hierarchy and presumed functional differentiation. Disproportionately large San Isidro, with its monumental mound, occupied the top of a three-level regional settlement hierarchy. Along with data from figurines, the presence of major platform mounds at large sites and the settlement data described here suggest for the Jama-Coaque I period a level of sociopolitical organization approaching that of later, historically known chiefdoms in the north Andes. No definite "administrative structures" have yet been documented to indicate clear differentiation of "sacred" and "secular" domains. The accretional expansion of the same platform mound at San Isidro, and strong continuity seen in the use and forms of the human figurines over a 2,000-year span, argue for corresponding ideological and ethnic continuity. On the other hand, it is still not clear why the "urban" ceremonial–political centers seen in the neighboring La Tolita-Tumaco and Bahía regions did not emerge in the Jama-Coaque area, particularly given the fact that these three areas share various material features.

The organization and evolution of the site of La Tolita during the Classic Phase (200 B.C.E. to C.E. 100) are relatively well known due to recent fieldwork by Váldez and his colleague. Around 200–100 B.C.E., the site began to grow with the population converging in the high (northwest) part of the island to form a large, ceremonial center with habitational structures densely built around a series of earth-refuse mounds. By C.E. 0 the nucleated site attained an extent of over 1 square kilometer, already with most of the some forty *tolas* that existed at the turn of the twentieth century.

La Tolita *tolas* were built in a specific manner that started with burning of the area where the mound was to be built to get rid of the vegetation and harden the clay-rich ground, upon which earth was piled up to a height of about 2 meters. During the succeeding Late Phase, a number of new *tolas* were built, and some extant ones were amplified from about 2 meters in height to over 5 meters. The resultant oval mound was topped with a horizontal floor covered with sherds.

Tolas of varying size and height are found along much of the Ecuadorian coast. They may occur clustered as in the cases of La Tolita, Bahía, or Atacames. The latter is found about 25 kilometers south of the city of Esmeraldas, and over seventy *tolas* are found parallel to the coast (within a 2-km² area). Along with structures built among them, the *tolas* gave an urban character to these sites. They are the most prominent prehispanic architectural features on the coast, so determination of the *tolas'* functions is of the utmost importance. However, at La Tolita and elsewhere, there is little concrete evidence that specifically tells us of their use. Widespread supposition of their ceremonial function remains only a guess. Post-holes atop the mounds indicate that there were some perishable superstructures, perhaps like the elaborately decorated, gabled-roof houses represented in modeled ceramics of the Classic La Tolita, Bahía, and Jama-Coaque. Deep cylindrical holes (c. 60 cm in diameter) dug down to groundwater level from the tops of excavated La Tolita *tolas* remain an enigma but may well relate to the widespread phenomenon of the "ceramic chimneys." For the La Tolita and Atacames examples, they did not serve funerary or any other apparent functions (e.g., drainage or wells). They may well have been used much like the ethnohistorically known *ushnu*, or ritual duct for libations, during ceremonies at the initiation of construction or modification of the *tolas*.

At La Tolita, numerous middens full of food remains and sherds and post-holes of presumably perished habitational structures have been documented around the bases of *tolas*. These remains have been interpreted as evidence of nucleated habitation by the élite and their retinues, including specialized artisans who produced ritual paraphernalia and sumptuary goods. The social élite seem to have had their power base in control of the ideology expressed in the coherent iconography. In essence, a sociopolitical organization akin to the ethnohistorically documented *cacicazgo*, or *curacazgo* (ethnic chiefdom), is inferred. In this scenario, specialized artisans would have had lower status and resided in the ceremonial core of the site close to the *tolas*. Lower still in the social scale were the masses who lived in the perimeters or detached from the site, and who were dedicated to subsistence activities. The inferred social status differences are said to be reflected in differential funerary treatment. A concentric settlement pattern organized around the ceremonial mounds at La Tolita is proposed. This view does not adequately answer the critical question of why there would be some forty *tolas* of varying size forming recognizable NW–SE alignments.

The same question is applicable to other aforementioned *tola* clusters. Given that these clusters are found close to the coast with easy access by watercraft, the *tolas* may be seen as ceremonial mounds of regional communities with internal social ranking and corresponding size differences in their respective tolas. Or, alternatively, with the "thousands" of burials said to have been interred at the ceremonial core of La Tolita, these clusters may also be seen as regional pilgrimage–funerary centers. Apparently, with increasing population settlement, the custom of placing offerings and burials, some with impressive quantities and quality of grave goods, became widespread.

In Cahuachi both ancient and modern pilgrimage centers have a strong magnetic force, affecting a large population and cross-cutting social and even ethnic differences. The convergence of pilgrims from diverse backgrounds would have offered a valuable setting for integration, communication, and establishment of social, economic, and political relations. Historically, centers have had a dual character: solemnity and uniqueness associated with the sacred, and vitality and openness associated with festivity and trade. For some centers, the latter aspect may have gained greater importance over the other. Craft production and the possible role of La Tolita as a "port-of-trade" may be more fruitfully understood in such light. The contemporaneous sites of Pacatnamú, Pacha Kamaq, and Cahuachi on the Peruvian coast also may have played a similar role as pilgrimage-trade-craft production centers.

The conventional approach delimits cultural syntheses to a single cultural area or modern nation. The present archaeological synthesis was ambitiously conceived to cover the Chavín cult and subsequent ERD cultures from southernmost Colombia to the Titicaca plateau. The approach taken here elucidates material, organizational, and ideological achievements of the ERD cultures, interregional differences and similarities, and limitations of the conventional interpretive concepts and frameworks.

This synthesis shows that much of what we can say confidently about ERD cultures pertains to specifics of their arts and crafts. For most ERD cultures, even the most basic nonmaterial issues remain to be addressed adequately. Residential settlements of all ERD cultures, including those of the Nasca and Mochica, desperately await archaeological attention. In addition, in reviewing arts and crafts, one must take into account the overrepresentation of funerary artifacts, especially among coastal cultures, with their fine preservation; the seeming paucity of certain categories of artifacts (e.g., textiles) among highland culture does not mean that they were artistically impoverished.

The attention lavished on arts and crafts is not without justification. For example, in Peru, it is during the period under study that the repertoire of techniques and media of expression both expanded and improved, offering tremendous creative potential to artisans. Consider the innovations introduced in pottery alone: use of one- and two-piece molds for figurine and vessel formation, respectively, and slip and negative painting for bright polychrome decoration. In metallurgy and weaving, we see a comparable array of major advances. Notable in this regard is the geographical spread of and technical advances in gold and copper-based metallurgy, and the wide availability of copper products throughout the Andes. In the North Andes, the La Tolita-Tumaco area on the coast and Nariño area in the adjacent highlands stand out. In Peru, the north coast was clearly the production center. Other areas enjoyed for the first time access to imported metal objects or supported local, small-scale production of primarily copper objects. In terms of important developments in weave structures, techniques, and materials, the spread of the Chavín cult was a "revolutionary" time according to Conklin. The list of innovations included looping, wrapping, discontinuous weft, tapestry, textile painting, and camelid fiber and its dyeing. Other innovations were associated with late Paracas embroidery.

All media – textiles, unfired clay including plastered walls for murals, ceramics, wood, shell, bone, stone, gourd, natural landscape for geoglyphs, and base (copper) and precious metals (perhaps with the exception of *tumbaga*) – already existed prior to 500 B.C.E., but it was the concurrent, extensive utilization of many of these media and sophisticated techniques applied that distinguish this period. In fact, technical mastery in many ways remained unsurpassed for the rest of prehistory. Thus one of the defining features of this period is the formalization (i.e., consistent use of set technologies/techniques and media) of persistent macroregional stylistic traditions (in both technological and artistic senses). These included the two-dimensional, polychrome tradition of the South-Central Andes and the south coast of Peru and emphasis on sculptural representations combined with use of one to three colors in northern Peru ("Northern Peruvian Plastic Tradition"). In coastal Ecuador, the hollow figurine tradition persisted until the time of the Spanish conquest. In general, at least in respect to the stylistic, technical, and iconographical features of material culture, we see strong continuities from the Late Formative to the Regional Development period and on until the eve of Inka intrusion into the North Andes in the fifteenth century. This is particularly true of the central and south coasts of Ecuador, suggesting ethnic continuity of the inhabitants. Interregional interaction both along longitudinal and latitudinal axes changed over time in partners and goods involved, as well as in form and intensity, but remained a critical factor in overall cultural developments in the North Andes.

In addition to the aforementioned features in arts and crafts, we see cross-craft fertilization, effective transference or blending of techniques, and movement of conventions and raw materials from one medium to another, yielding innovative and more effective representations of valued images. Many resultant products created the unique multimedia and multisense (tactile, visual, and acoustic) effect essential for rituals.

The lion's share of attention that arts and crafts have received is also a function of ideological information we have been able to extract from their iconography. In these nonliterate cultures, depictions had to communicate effectively without written explanations; shared contextual knowledge was key to understanding. There is no one "best" approach to prehispanic Andean iconography. Whether one takes a thematic, structural-historical, or some other approach, each makes its own assumptions in inferring underlying cultural meaning. Suppositions such as continuity in dual social organization or cosmologies spanning prehistoric and historic eras are difficult to verify and, in most cases, remain unconfirmed. Even the identification of geographic origins of animals depicted in Chavín art remains controversial. If they are coastal rather than Amazonian in origin, then the attendant cosmological and socioeconomic reconstruction would be significantly affected. If the bird on the Tello Obelisk is a migratory peregrine, not a harpy eagle, then its representation may be viewed as a symbol of the rejuvenating quality of life – not a sky deity. Debate surrounding the cosmological significance of Chavín iconography will undoubtedly continue.

The Mochica and Nasca iconographies differ from each other and that of Chavín. Both of the former show inhabitants of the natural and supernatural worlds. Each has its own pantheon of supernaturals but with no one enduring, dominant deity, unlike the Staff God of the Chavín cult. Like the Pukara and Chavín religions, the Mochica pantheon included both major male and female supernaturals. Mochica iconography is basically narrative – perhaps based on orally transmitted mythologies about the origins and forces of the universe as well as important sociopolitical groups (e.g., competing moieties or "shaman" vs. "warrior" groups). It was in some ways the "official art" of the social élite. Whether Nasca art was associated with any one social group is difficult to say. Concern over agricultural success and rejuvenation of life through death (human sacrifice) are found in both Mochica and Nasca art. However, in the Mochica case, the first concern was clearly a component of a much more broad cosmological conception. For the Nasca, it seems to have been the primary concern.

Pukara art appears to have been an important part of the persistent, pan-*altiplano* Yaya-Mama Religious Tradition that in turn formed the ideological foundations of the Tiwanaku and, most likely, Wari art. The female and male supernaturals of Pukara art, like their Chavín counterparts, may well embody the concept of complementary opposites essential for reproduction and cosmic order. The common representations of domesticated camelids are understandable in terms of their overall significance to *altiplano* life. Representation of trophy heads in Pukara art, as with the case of many other art styles throughout the Andes, most likely related to the view that continuation of life requires death or human sacrifice.

Clearly many features of the arts and crafts of ERD cultures emerged over a long time span, preceding the period under study. However, as noted previously, it is their convergence, consistent application, and refinement to their highest technical and artistic levels that set these cultures apart. In this sense we must consider arts hand in hand with the organizational character, scale, and complexity of societies. Settlement-pattern, mortuary, and iconographic data provide ample indication of marked social inequality and attendant differences in material wealth. Debate surrounding relevant definitions and approaches to the comparative study of sociopolitical organization (or even the worthwhileness of the typological thinking that it entails) continues. Most scholars seem to view nearly all ERD cultures, from the San Augustín and Jama-Coaque to the north to Nasca and Pukara to the south, as chiefdom-level societies with shamans serving as the nexus of ideological and social integration. The Mochica during Phases III–V with their inferred four-level, multi-valley social and settlement hierarchies, economic specialization, and other organization features are commonly thought to have been a state-level society. Major regional settlements were urban in character and appear to have had their own ceramic workshops. The construction of gigantic, multitiered platform mounds by means of contiguously placed, standardized vertical segments of adobe bricks is believed to reflect a system of labor taxation, much like the Inka *mit'a*. The marking of constituent adobe bricks is viewed as an accounting device. Data from the city of Pampa Grande, the Phase V capital, indicate that the urban economy was redistributive in character. Workers who commuted to workshops for the production of sumptuary and mundane craft goods were supplied with food and drink prepared with maize and beans from state storage facilities within the site. The Mochica polity at its height, however, was unique, at the high end of the range of sociopolitical complexity found among the ERD cultures. At the same time, its political organization was not monolithic in time and space, and its history was far from being a straight-line expansion of the polity based at the site of Moche, as was formerly thought. It involved competition between the Northern and Southern Mochica and a shifting balance of power between them, as well as the variable relationship between Gallinazo and Mochica populations. Political unification of the north coast during Phase IV probably lasted fewer than 100 years.

Monumental mounds that served as the settings for exclusive rituals, feasting, or habitation, and generally as symbols of political and religious power, were not restricted to the Mochica and Gallinazo on the north coast. The Lima culture on the central coast erected adobe-and-fill platform mounds that were comparable in size (particularly the Maranga Complex, including a mound measuring about 270 × 100 m and 15 m high), though little is known of their specific functions and associated settlements. The tradition of mound building during late Paracas times, recently documented in the Pisco Valley, seems to have lost its importance in the Nasca culture. Cahuachi with its modified natural promontories and low mounds is rather unique in this regard. It is believed to have served as the early Nasca ceremonial–pilgrimage center with only a small resident population. It differs significantly from north coast sites such as Moche and Pampa Grande, where ceremonial mounds were integrated with craft workshops and residences in urban settings. La Tolita and sites of the Bahía and Atacames cultures in coastal Ecuador, with numerous *tolas* of varying size, also indicate a significant urbanization trend. The U-shaped configuration formed by ceremonial and household mounds around the large central plaza, however, suggests continuity in the architectural embodiment of cosmological order already seen a few thousand years earlier at the Valdivia site of Real Alto.

There is no denying that during the second half of the period under study, more distinct art styles emerged than during any preceding era. Yet this stylistic diversity does not necessarily imply that we are dealing with more ethnic or cultural groups. The diversity undoubtedly combined multiple factors, including greater creative potential for varied decorations and effective representations of political and religious views. The dissipation of a Chavín ideology had once exercised homogenizing effects on regional styles and iconography and a concurrent drive to reclaim local identity visually, which involved processes such as syncretism and archaic revival. Thus much of the diversity may be more appropriately regarded as better visibility of extant groups (in kind and quality of material symbols and overall quantities) rather than substantive increase in ethnic or cultural groups.

Studies of ERD cultures suffer from tenuous equations of ceramic styles with political, ethnic, and cultural groups. The demise of the local

Gallinazo polity and disappearance of its corporate ceramic style in the Virú Valley as the result of Mochica conquest (during Phase III) has long been treated as a microcosm of the Gallinazo-Mochica relationship on the entire north coast. However, Gallinazo populations there or elsewhere were not exterminated; in fact, the Gallinazo style lingered on at least until the end of the Mochica polity in some valleys. We still do not know the political and biological relationship between the populations represented by these two ceramic styles. Although the presence of diagnostic Mochica ceramics may be an indication of their political control of the given area, it is not proof of their physical occupation. Recall the fact that the Inka state had potters of conquered ethnic groups produce ceramics in Inka style with little or no accompanying occupation by ethnically Inka people. In this sense, Mochica population increase or physical presence inferred from expanded ceramic distribution remains a hypothesis.

The spread of productive, complementary domesticates and of appropriate technologies mutually stimulated each other and continually redefined the environment's potential and limitations. We are speaking of extensive irrigation networks and associated cultivation fields, underground canals and sunken fields that utilized groundwater on the Peruvian coast, and ridged fields or elevated cultivation areas formed by mounding up organic-rich soil in swampy regions of the Guayas and Titicaca basins. Most art styles of this period, from Jama-Coaque and Bahía to Paracas, Nasca, and Pukara, express pervasive concern with the agents and forces of agricultural success and, more generally, reproduction in the natural and human worlds. Overall, during this period we see that the creative dynamism between culture and environment led to the development of basic technologies and economic orientations that persisted until the Spanish conquest.

During the period under study, cultural dimensions of major north–south differences in physiography and climate of the Central Andes became more evident. For example, greater annual precipitation, coupled with the lower elevations and dissected nature of the Cordillera Negra (Pacific range) in the northern Peruvian highlands blessed the north coast with a string of fertile, extensive coastal valleys watered by perennial rivers with relatively large discharge volumes. During the first few centuries C.E., in most of the constituent valleys of the north coast, much of their agricultural potential was harnessed by means of valley-wide irrigation systems. The complex and far-flung Gallinazo and Mochica societies were built on a productive economy that combined fishing and irrigation agriculture. The horizontal multivalley drive of the Mochica polity was much more than their drive to annex more agricultural land and tributaries; it was an institutional strategy to gain access to more diverse production zones and resources (e.g., prime fishing grounds and offshore guano islands). In addition, horizontality effectively land-locked the contemporary highland cultures of Recuay and Cajamarca.

The foregoing contrasts with the verticality seen in the South-Central Andes. Verticality refers to an institutional strategy to maximize the productive potential and resource diversity by expanding along an altitudinal gradient. In material and organizational terms, however, it accomplished for the Pukara and Tiwanaku cultures what horizontality did for the Mochica. An important difference exists, nonetheless. The contemporary coastal and highland cultures of this area should be seen as complementary dyads (Paracas-Pukara and Nasca-Tiwanaku). These pairs had something akin to "peer polity" interaction. We are speaking of pairs of populations with comparable degrees of sociopolitical complexity and political parity that engaged in trade and other mutually beneficial forms of interaction. This synergy stimulated their respective internal developments.

In northern Peru, there are only limited data to indicate that coast and highland cultures had established any sort of large-scale or lasting symbiotic interaction. Instead, available evidence points to Mochica trading for exotic goods with coastal Ecuador, perhaps through Vicús intermediaries whose material culture links them to contemporary cultures of Ecuador.

Additionally, we have seen that north–south differences in artistic and technological styles and ideologies became evident during this period and persisted until the end of prehistory. Perhaps most evident among them was the contrasting emphasis placed on two-dimensional (including geoglyphs) and polychrome expressions in southern Peru and the South-Central Andes, as opposed to the northern preference for a limited color palette and three-dimensional, sculptural expression. The latter preference clearly extended into the equatorial Andes, perhaps reflecting the persistence and importance of the Chorrera cultural substratum. As Berezkin observed, mythologies inferred from Mochica iconography bear basic similarities to ethnographically recorded folklore in northern Ecuador, but they contrast with that of southern Peru and the South-Central Andes.

What the preceding points to is that, for the period under study, the Central Andes can be bipartitioned into (overlapping) northern and southern cultural spheres. Such a bipartition would seem to be an accentuation of cultural choices harking back to the Formative Era. North Peruvian prehistory cannot be understood in isolation from developments in the equatorial Andes, particularly those on the coast. Though still poorly understood, the importance of the Vicús culture within Andean archaeology derives from the fact that it documents cultural contact between the North Andean region and Peruvian coast and contradicts the common perception that these cultures developed largely in isolation from each other. Ecuadorian coastal populations cannot be marginalized as passive recipients of cultural innovations emanating from the Central Andes. In fact, they were critical for acquisition of ritual goods valued in the latter area, such as *Strombus, Spondylus,* and *Conus* shells. The conceptual basis, and maybe the technical know-how, of Mochica ceramic production using molds and *tumbaga* metallurgy may have derived from their contemporaries on the Ecuadorian coast. The notion that La Tolita, Isla de la Plata, and other islands along the Ecuadorian coast served as "ports-of-trade" or shell harvesting cum sacred worship sites deserves further attention.

The foregoing discussion questions the widely held perception of regional cultures as having regional extent and internal focus (i.e., regional isolation and diversity). From the days of Max Uhle, the father of scientific archaeology in the Andes, the basic chronological and interpretive framework has been built on intermittent "horizon styles" (i.e., homogeneous styles that spread widely and rapidly) – namely, Chavín, Wari, and Inka and attendant cultural horizons. Since then, what have come to be called Early and Late Regional Development cultures (or their synonyms) have been defined in reference to these horizon styles; they are those cultures whose diagnostic remains show more restricted spatial distribution than those that are associated with horizon styles. Thus, in Willey's view, much of central Andean prehistory alternates periods of horizontal integration and regional diversity. Whether well-studied or not, what fell in time between any two of these horizons were labeled Regional Development cultures. The basic supposition of regional isolation persists to this day, although there is hardly any evidence that they really were isolated. As we have seen, the degree and nature of interregional interaction depends on the social segments and cultures we study. The Mochica polity during Phase IV attained a territory covering some 600 kilometers along the northern coast of Peru and interacted with contemporaneous Vicús, Cajamarca, Recuay, and even Nasca cultures. The later Middle Sicán polity (c. C.E. 1000), existing between the Wari and Inka horizons, established dominance from the Chira to Chicama valleys, and its distinct ceramics spread well over 1,000 kilometers along the coast and eastward to the Marañón River drainage. The term "regional" then becomes meaningless and only definable relative to the three well-known horizon styles and cultural horizons. This sweep-under-the-rug concept of Regional Development cultures overgeneralizes Central Andean situations and perpetuates the image of these cultures as being regional in extent and internally focused. The concept is detrimental to productive investigation into the significant variation that existed among them. The horizon-based conception of Andean prehistory has promoted compartmentalized archaeological research focused on a specific regional culture or cultural horizon rather than sustained regional studies that elucidate long-term historical developments and evolutionary processes.

What distinguished the Regional Development cultures and the Chavín, Wari, and Inka is that the latter succeeded in ideological and organizational integration, however brief, across horizontal (latitudinal) and vertical (attitudinal) dimensions of the Andes. None of the former can claim such an achievement. Even the most territorially expansive polities among them expanded along the horizontal dimension.

This chapter ends by considering the demise of the notable ERD polities. Although occurring mostly around C.E. 600–700, the demise is poorly understood in terms of the relevant factors and processes. Certainly the term "collapse" is not appropriate if it implies a widespread, synchronic event. We are speaking of political demise, not the massive death of populations. There is at least one factor that had pan-Andean impact.

Sometime in the late sixth century C.E., the Mochica culture, which had established itself as the unrivaled political and economic power on the Peruvian coast, experienced unprecedented internal upheaval. Evidence from other regions of Peru indicates that the same was happening elsewhere at the same time, suggesting that some process(es) of extraordinary scope and magnitude were at play. Traditionally the demise of Regional Development cultures such as the Mochica and Nasca has been attributed to waves of territorial expansion by the Wari based in the Ayacucho region in the South-Central Highlands of Peru (see Chap. 6).

Yet it was not clear why the Wari undertook the expansion or whether the expansion simply filled an existing political vacuum.

For the Mochica culture on the north coast, the onset of this turbulent period marked a major transition from Phases IV to V. This included near-abandonment of both the site of Moche itself and the southern half of the Mochica hegemony. The Southern Mochica lost much of their power base. The planned city of Pampa Grande (some 165 km north of Moche and 55 km from the coast) emerged as the dominant center of Phase V society. With the gigantic Huaca Fortaleza (270 × 180 by 38 m in height, 500-m long ramp; about 1.5 million m³) at its physical and symbolic center, the site covered some 6 square kilometers and was one of the largest settlements on the Peruvian coast for its time, boasting an estimated population of 10,000 to 15,000.

The northward shift of the Mochica seat of power and population nucleation at a few valley-neck sites was accompanied by major changes in the organizational, material, and even ideological domains of Mochica culture and society. Pampa Grande was by no means the predictable outgrowth of a half-millennium of Mochica cultural developments. Traditional values and institutions were reassessed and transformed, accompanied by a myriad of innovations. For example, new and revived ceramic forms, often in black or gray ware, emerged, while fine traditional painted wares manifested new iconographic emphases. Large-scale storage facilities under state control were also built. The longstanding Mochica tradition of monumental platform mounds continued in the form of Huaca Fortaleza but with altered technique. It was built by combining the traditional technique of standardized segments of stacked adobe bricks with the innovative and more rapid, pragmatic technique of refuse-filled adobe chambers. Patterns of marking adobe bricks and marked bricks also changed, suggesting corresponding modifications to labor and material mobilization.

The inferred Wari conquest does not adequately account for the variety of changes that occurred in the Phase IV–V transition or elsewhere on the coast at the same time. An alternative explanation invokes catastrophic flooding associated with a major El Niño event and coastal uplift. These are said to be responsible for sand invasion of the site of Moche and associated canals and cultivation fields, as well as downcutting by rivers and concurrent disruption of existing irrigation systems. Although this view may account for observed inland population movement, dating of the relevant events and processes is tenuous and does not fully account for the establishment of the new Mochica capital so far to the north.

There is a viable alternative explanation. Examination of a 1,500-year long precipitation record established for much of highland Peru and based on ice core samples drilled from the glacier at Quelccaya (south of Cusco) revealed a 32-year-long drought spanning C.E. 562–594 (Fig. 5.34). This climatic reconstruction is independently supported by climatic data from ice core samples from Huascarán Col in the Callejón de Huaylas, lake sediment core samples (analysis of diatom composition) from Lake Yambo in the Ecuadorian highlands, and fluvial sediment analysis in Amazonia. Significant and prolonged reduction in water reaching the coast is believed to have accentuated existing inequalities in the distribution of water and land, and to have led to population nucleation at optimal valley-neck locations. The importance and power of Pampa Grande becomes evident given that the Lambayeque Valley has one of the largest river discharge volumes and one of the most stable flows year-round of all Peruvian coastal valleys. In other words, compared to the Moche Valley, the Lambayeque probably would have fared much better during the 32-year drought.

The Northern Mochica polity took advantage of this unprecedented situation in the late sixth century C.E. Control of the valley-neck location and hence all regional canal intakes would have provided the Northern Mochica polity at Pampa Grande with enough clout not only to institute a series of major changes in land and labor use but also to reclaim the political prestige that had been degraded by the Southern Mochica hegemony. Pampa Grande is seen as a case of relatively short-lived urbanism based on integration of populations brought together by unique, stressful cultural and natural conditions through the organizational framework of earlier urban Mochica ceremonial–civic centers. In a basic sense, Pampa Grande was the Mochica's collective effort to survive a stressful period and revive the former glory and power of the Lambayeque-based Northern Mochica polity. The establishment of the capital at Pampa Grande was clearly planned with Huaca Fortaleza serving as the hub of physical growth. This structure bipartitioned the social organization of the emerging city. Most of the commoners who provided the labor services are believed to have been a lower-ranked Gallinazo population, resettled to Pampa Grande from agriculturally marginal lands in the Lambayeque and adjacent valleys. They were massed together in the physically segregated southern portion of the city, while the élite (higher-

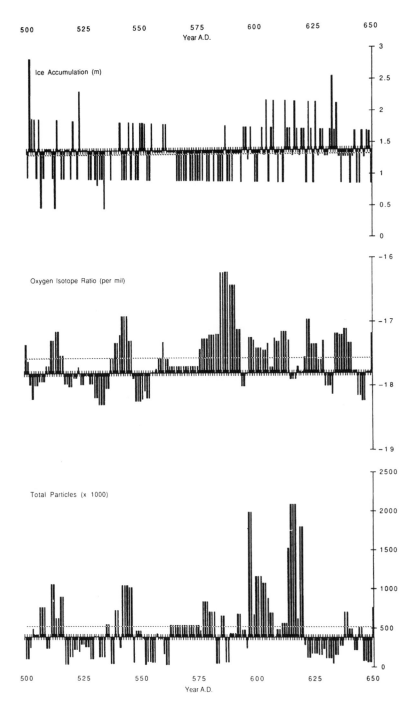

Figure 5.34. Annual precipitation record for the Central Andes (displayed around the fifteen-hundred-year mean) reconstructed from deep ice core samples taken from the Quelccaya glacier south of Cuzco. Courtesy of Crystal Schaaf.

ranked Mochica population) were on the northern and western sides of
Huaca Fortaleza within walled enclosures or other structures. The construction of Huaca Fortaleza served not only to symbolize the viability of
the Northern Mochica polity and religion but also, perhaps fortuitously,
to undergird urbanism at Pampa Grande with the permanence of a large
labor force. It was a truly unprecedented time for the Mochica élite, who
faced the complex task of managing the needs and desires of a relocated
and expanding population with varied skills, social position, and ethnicity. These unique, dynamic conditions led to the creation of new social
forms and relations, which, in turn, necessitated the increasingly complex
control measures and hierarchies that characterize a state.

At the same time, as this city and state grew, the social and administrative institutions and constituent populations that had been vital in the
formative stage of the city gradually lost their original purpose and
became too "costly" to maintain. In the long run, these conditions
created sociopolitical instability, eventually preconditioning the sudden,
violent collapse of the Moche V polity that, at least chronologically,
seems to coincide with the second wave of Wari expansion around C.E.
650–700. It is of considerable interest to note that the first definite
indication of Tiwanaku colonization of the western slope occurred about
C.E. 600, roughly the same time as the first wave of Wari expansion. In
other words, Wari and Tiwanaku territorial expansions may well have
been preconditioned by prolonged climatic anomalies of the sixth century
C.E. Clearly the issue of demise is far from resolved, requiring a long-
term and broad perspective that considers both internal and external
factors and processes.

BIBLIOGRAPHIC ESSAY

Abbreviations

AA   *American Anthropologist*
AAnt   *American Antiquity*
AP   *Andean Past*
ARA   *Annual Review of Anthropology*
BA   *Baessler-Archiv*
BAVA   *Beiträge zur Allgemeinen und Vergleichenden Archäologie*
BIFEA   *Boletín del Instituto Francés de Estudios Andinos*

CA	*Current Anthropology*
GAA	*Gaceta Arqueológica Andina*
HE	*Human Ecology*
JAR	*Journal of Anthropological Research*
JFA	*Journal of Field Archaeology*
JLAL	*Journal of Latin American Lore*
JSA	*Journal de la Société des Américanistes*
JSAS	*Journal of the Steward Anthropological Society*
LAAnt	*Latin American Antiquity*
NGM	*National Geographic Magazine*
ÑP	*Ñawpa Pacha*
WA	*World Archaeology*

General Comments

Although the references included in this bibliographic essay emphasize those written in English by North American archaeologists (who outdistance archaeologists from other nations in terms of their number, scale, and intensity of fieldwork and, accordingly, publication output), there are numerous important publications in French, German, Italian, Japanese, and Spanish. In fact, recent fieldwork by scholars from these countries has resulted in proportionately more detailed, book-length reports. Often they are bilingual or contain English or Spanish summaries, and readers are encouraged to make use of them. Non-English publications are mentioned in the absence of appropriate English sources or due to their special importance. Although North American publications are numerous, many are preliminary in nature, limited in data presentation, and written from the perspective of a specific research topic.

To gain a perspective, readers should consult "Peruvian archaeology, 1946–1980: An analytic overview," *WA* 13:358–370 by R. P. Schaedel and I. Shimada (1982); "The last sixty years: Towards a social history of Americanist archaeology in the United States," *AA* 88: 7–26 (1986), and "Political economy and a discourse called 'Peruvian archaeology'," *Culture and History* 4:35–64 (1989), both by T. C. Patterson. Also useful is *A history of American archaeology*, revised edition, by G. R. Willey and J. A. Sabloff (San Francisco, 1993).

Comprehensive, updated bibliographic sources are not available for Andean archaeology. *Introducción a una bibliografía general de la arqueo-*

logía del Perú (1860–1988) by R. Ravines (Lima, 1989) is quite comprehensive, but its organization by alphabetical order of author's name and many errors limit its utility.

A number of recent general syntheses of Andean prehistory include good summaries of Early Regional Development (ERD) cultures. *South American prehistory* by K. O. Bruhns (Cambridge, 1994) offers highly condensed but good coverage of the entire South American continent. It is organized along a chronological and geographical basis with interspersed topical chapters. It serves as an update of G. R. Willey's *Introduction to American archaeology, Vol. 2: South America* (Englewood Cliffs, 1971), which, though outdated, still represents one of the best culture-historical syntheses of the whole continent.

Informative and highly readable syntheses of the Central Andes are found in "Civilizations in the Andes" by T. N. D'Altroy in *The illustrated encyclopedia of humankind Vol. 4: New World and Pacific civilizations*, edited by G. Burenhult, pp. 78–99 (Sydney, 1994); *The Inka empire and its Andean origins* by C. Morris and A. von Hagen (New York, 1993); and *Peru* by M. E. Moseley (London, 1992). The first is a well-illustrated but sketchy characterization. The second, also with fine color illustrations, has extensive discussion of arts and crafts of the ERD cultures. The third offers more technical details of sites and settlement patterns as well as insightful discussion of cultural dynamics. However, with area coverage largely confined to Peru, important interregional interactions are not adequately considered. L. G. Lumbreras' *The peoples and cultures of ancient Peru* (Washington, D.C., 1974) is outdated but offers a Marxian perspective that emphasizes the evolutionary significance of struggles among social classes. His recent synthesis of Peruvian prehistory is found in *Visión arqueológica del Perú milenario* (Lima, 1989). The coverage is uneven, but he offers incisive comments on interregional linkages and evolutionary developments. Chapters in *Peruvian prehistory* edited by R. W. Keatinge (Cambridge, 1988) are divergent in the depth and breadth of coverage as well as in terminologies, writing styles, and theoretical perspectives adopted. The chapter on ERD cultures is brief.

A long string of well-illustrated catalogues and similar books exalt the art and crafts of ERD cultures, particularly the Mochica (Moche) and Nasca (Nazca). Most often the illustrated artifacts have been selected from museum or private collections with emphasis on superior or unique artistic and technical qualities, and thus do not represent typical examples. Illustrated items are useful for iconographic information. These include F. Anton's *The art of ancient Peru* (London, 1972); A. Baessler's *Ancient Peruvian art: Contributions to the archaeology of the empire of the Incas*, 4 vols. (Berlin, 1902–1903); W. C. Bennett's *Ancient arts of the Andes* (New York, 1954); A. Lapiner's *Pre-Columbian art of South America* (New York, 1976); *Pre-Columbian art of Ecuador from the Peggy and Tessim Zorach Collection* (Ithaca, 1982); A. Sawyer's *Ancient Peruvian ceramics: The Nathan Cummings Collections* (New York, 1966) and *Mastercraftsmen of ancient Peru* (New York, 1968); and M. Schmidt's *Kunst und Kultur von Peru* (Berlin, 1929). For the past 14 years, the Banco de Crédito del Perú has published a series, *Culturas precolombinas*, that has covered such notable cultures as Paracas, Mochica, and Nasca. Each of these books contains numerous color illustrations of artifacts, but the accompanying texts that generally focus on technical and artistic aspects of artifacts vary greatly in quality and coverage.

In the rest of this essay, publications are organized by the geographical location of the specific ERD cultures, going from north to south.

Colombia and Ecuador

As a whole, the depth and breadth of our understanding of the ERD cultures in Colombia and Ecuador are still quite restricted. Although many new publications are coming out, there is no comprehensive, up-to-date synthesis in English. *Ecuador* by B. J. Meggers (London, 1966) and *Colombia* by G. Reichel-Dolmatoff (New York, 1965) remain useful for a terminological and chronological clarification and basic material cultural characterization of the ERD cultures. "The northern Andes" by R. Feldman and M. E. Moseley in *Ancient South Americans*, edited by J. D. Jennings, pp. 139–177 (San Francisco, 1983) is outdated and coast-centric but important in its emphasis on the autonomous and innovative character of the Formative and ERD cultures. Another coast-centric summary characterization of Ecuador is offered by Ecuadorian archaeologist, J. C. Marcos, in "Breve prehistoria del Ecuador" in *Arqueología de la costa ecuatoriana: Nuevos enfoques*, edited by J. C. Marcos, pp. 24–50 (Quito, 1986). *Nueva Historia del Ecuador, Volumenes I, II: Epoca aborigen* edited by E. Ayala (Quito, 1988) is a comprehensive, cultural–historical synthesis of Ecuadorian prehistory but offers few insights into cultural dynamics. *Chiefdoms in the Americas* edited by R. D. Drennan and C. Uribe (Lanham, MD, 1987) contains a number of chapters that discuss organizational and processual issues relevant to the chiefdom-level ERD cultures of Colombia and Ecuador. Chapters rely heavily on ethnohistorical data.

The results of recent regional studies are becoming available. For example, *Calima: Diez mil años de historia en el sudoccidente de Colombia* by M. Cardale de Schrimpff, W. Bray, T. Gähwiler-Walder, and L. Herrera (Bogotá, 1992) is the result of a sustained international research effort focused on the prehistory of the Calima region. It offers a long-term environmental-cultural perspective on the Ilama and Yotoco periods. *Recherches archaeologiques dans la región de Tumaco (Colombie)* edited by J. F. Bouchard (Paris, 1984) offers a complementary picture of the region just to the south. A similar, comprehensive perspective is provided for the highland regions of La Plata and nearby San Agustín in *Prehispanic chiefdoms in the Valle de La Plata*, Vols. 1, 2 by R. D. Drennan and his colleagues (Pittsburgh, 1989, 1993). The contents are summarized in "Regional dynamics of chiefdoms in the valle de La Plata, Colombia" by Drennan et al., *JFA* 18: 297–317 (1991). The well-known San Agustín tombs and sculptural style are described by G. Reichel-Dolmatoff in *San Agustín: A culture of Colombia* (New York, 1972); by L. Duque and J. C. Cubillos in *Arqueología de San Agustín: Alto de Lavapatas* (Bogotá, 1988); by M. L. Sotomayor and M. V. Uribe in *Estatuaria del macizo colombiano* (Bogotá, 1987); and in *San Agustín 200 años 1790–1990: Seminario la arqueología del macizo y el suroccidente colombianos* edited by L. Herrera (Bogotá, 1991); among other writers. Drennan discusses burial customs and their broader implications in "Mortuary practices in the Alto Magdalena: The social context of the 'San Agustín culture'" in *Andean mortuary practices: Tombs for the living*, edited by T. Dillehay, pp. 79–110 (Washington, D.C., 1995). One of the few English publications on Cauca prehistory is *Archaeological investigations in Central Colombia: The middle Cauca and Caldas cultures of Quindío and Valle* by K. O. Bruhns (Oxford, 1995).

Regional archaeology in northern Manabí Ecuador, Vol. 1: Environment, cultural chronology, and prehistoric subsistence in the Jama river valley edited by J. A. Zeidler and D. M. Pearsall is exemplary of a new generation of interdisciplinary, regional studies on coastal Ecuador. It is yielding, for the first time, a comprehensive and dynamic picture of the Jama-Coaque culture. Its chronology is also being refined through radiocarbon dating and stratigraphy (including the use of volcanic tephra deposits). Like this book, M. Masucci's doctoral dissertation, *Ceramic change in the Guangala phase, southwestern Ecuador: A typology and chronology* (Southern Methodist University, Dallas, 1992) refines the chronology of another coastal ERD culture, Guangala, that has received little attention since the work of A. Paulsen. An important regional study by a Spanish mission focused on long-term cultural developments in the Las Esmeraldas region farther north; its results are presented in *Memorias de la Misión Arqueológica Española en el Ecuador*, Vol. 1, edited by J. Alcina Franch (Madrid, 1988). Results of investigation in the adjacent area to the north are reported in "Archaeological sequence for the Santiago-Cayapas river basin, Esmeraldas, Ecuador" by P. Tolstoy and W. DeBoer, *JFA* 16: 295–308 (1989) and W. DeBoer's *Traces Behind the Esmeraldas Shore: Prehistory of the Santiago-Cayapas Region* (Birmingham, 1995). The two preceding publications provide broader cultural and environmental contexts for *Proyecto Arqueológico La Tolita* by F. Váldez (Quito, 1987). D. Patiño's "Arqueología del Bajo Patía, fases y correlaciones en la costa pacífica de Colombia y Ecuador," *LAAnt* 4: 180–199 (1993) is helpful in making sense out of various publications that deal with ERD cultures near the Colombia-Ecuador border, such as Tumaco-La Tolita. The related issue of cultural contacts along the Pacific coast is discussed in *Relaciones interculturales en el area ecuatorial del Pacífico durante la época precolombina*, edited by J. F. Bouchard and M Guinea (Oxford, 1989). Contributing authors emphasize the indigenous developments of the coastal cultures in contrast to the earlier tendency to invoke Mesoamerican origins and long-distance diffusion. Examples of the latter view include "Pre-Columbian cultural connections between Mesoamerica and Ecuador" by S. F. Borhegyi, *Middle American Research Records* 2(6): 141–155 (1959) and "The 'Intermediate' area of Nuclear America: Its prehistoric relationships to Middle America and Peru" by G. R. Willey, *Actas del XXXIII Congreso Internacional de Americanistas* 1: 184–194 (San José, Costa Rica, 1959).

The Ecuadorian highlands are receiving more attention, although most of the recent fieldwork deals with late periods. Results of the Pirincay Project are described in "Excavations at Pirincay, in the Paute valley of southern Ecuador, 1985–1988" by K. O. Bruhns, *Antiquity* 64: 221–233 (1990) and in "Zooarchaeology at Pirincay, a Formative period site in highland Ecuador" by G. R. Miller and A. L. Gill, *JFA* 17: 49–68 (1990).

Peru and the South-Central Andes

The Salinar, Vicús, and Gallinazo cultures on the northern coast of Peru have received comparatively little attention, and accessible published sources are meager in number and limited in scope. *Pampa Grande and the Mochica culture* by I. Shimada (Austin, 1994) summarizes what is known of these cultures and their relationships with the antecedent Cupisnique and partially contemporaneous Mochica. Most of what has been published about the Vicús culture is in either German or Spanish and focuses on ceramic and metal objects from burials, most of which are looted. They include H. Disselhoff's *Vicús: eine neu entdecke altperuanische Kultur* (Berlin, 1971); H. Horkheimer's *Vicús* (Lima, 1965); and L. G. Lumbreras' *El arte y la vida Vicús* (Lima, 1979) and *Vicús: colección arqueológica* (Lima, 1987). *Vicús* edited by K. Makowski (Lima, 1995) presents recent thoughts and new data on the culture and the enigmatic Vicús-Mochica relationship, but it is still heavily based on analyses of grave goods. Results of important excavations focused on domestic areas and public architecture at Vicús sites by the Catholic University of Peru team are found in two articles by P. Kaulicke in *BIFEA* 20: 381–422 (Lima, 1991) and 21: 853–903 (Lima, 1992). See also his contribution in *Moche: Propuestas y perspectivas* edited by S. Uceda and E. Mujica (Lima, 1994).

Regarding the Salinar culture, early descriptions by G. R. Willey in *Prehistoric settlement patterns in the Virú valley, northern Peru* (Washington, D.C., 1953) and by Rafael Larco Hoyle in "A culture sequence for the north coast of Peru" in *Handbook of South American Indians*, vol. 2, edited by Julian H. Steward, pp. 149–175 (Washington, D.C., 1946) are still useful. Results of excavation at the urban site of Cerro Arena are found in "Cerro Arena: Early cultural complexity and nucleation in north coastal Peru," *JFA* 7: 1–22 (1980) and "Origins of the urban tradition on the Peruvian north coast," *CA* 23: 247–254 (1982), both by C. T. Brennan.

Without doubt, more attention has been lavished on the Mochica culture than on any other ERD culture. Book-length general treatments of the culture are found in *The Mochica: A culture of Peru* by E. P. Benson (New York, 1972); *Moche* edited by J. A. de Lavalle (Lima, 1985); and the aforementioned *Pampa Grande* by Shimada. Although most publications on this culture are heavily based on burial and iconographic data (see later) the latter is one of a few volumes that emphasizes excavational data for a more holistic understanding of the Mochica culture. This volume also offers new interpretations on sociopolitical aspects of the culture and a detailed characterization of the organization and workings of the capital city of Pampa Grande. *Moche* by G. Bawden (Cambridge, MA, 1986) is another up-to-date synthesis of this culture with a perspective complementing Shimada's. Proceedings from a recent international colloquium on Mochica archaeology resulted in the earlier mentioned *Moche: Propuestas y perspectivas* volume. The contents present a diversity of perspectives and approaches, but the persistent preference for monumental sites and burial excavations is quite apparent. "The Early Intermediate Period and its legacy" by T. L. Topic in *Chan Chan: Andean desert city*, edited by M. E. Moseley and K. C. Day, pp. 255–284 (Albuquerque, 1982) is a brief characterization of the Mochica culture as seen from the site of Moche. Larco, who was largely responsible for the systematization of Mochica archaeology had only a few English publications, including the aforementioned *Handbook of South American Indians* article. Although he did not publish detailed data in support of his views, his *Cronología arqueológica del norte del Perú* (Buenos Aires, 1948) briefly describes observations underlying his chronology. Refinements of and alternatives to Larco's ceramic seriation and classification are offered by O. Klein in *La cerámica Mochica: Caracteres estilísticos y conceptos* (Valparaiso, 1967) and C. B. Donnan in *Moche art of Peru* (Los Angeles, 1976). The former is important for its recognition of significant north–south differences in Mochica ceramics. A number of recent works expound on this difference (discussed later).

Initial characterization of the Gallinazo (Virú) culture was provided by Larco and W. C. Bennett in their *La cultura Virú* (Buenos Aires, 1945) and *The Gallinazo group, Virú valley, Peru* (New Haven, 1950), respectively. Since then, fieldwork focused on this culture has been rare, and consequently no new major synthesis has been published in English. H. Fogel's doctoral dissertation, *Settlements in time: A study of social and political developments during the Gallinazo occupation of the north coast of Peru* (New Haven, 1993) presents a three-phase chronology and argues for Gallinazo as the first multivalley state on the north coast. Her conception of the state and the city, however, are not adequately justified.

A number of publications focus on the Gallinazo-Mochica relationship. H. Ubbelohde-Doering's *Vorspanische Gräber von Pacatnamú, Nordperu* (Munich, 1983) and parts of *On the royal highways of the Inca* (London, 1967) discuss chronological problems and the sociopolitical relationship with the Mochica population. The Mochica subjugation of the Gallinazo polity in the Moche and Virú valleys is described by Willey in the *Prehistoric settlement patterns* volume and by T. Topic in her aforementioned chapter in the *Chan Chan* volume. More recently, D. L.

Wilson summarizes the Mochica conquest and administration of the Gallinazo population in the Santa Valley in "Reconstructing patterns of early warfare in the lower Santa Valley: New data on the role of conflict in the origins of complex north-coast society" in *The origins and development of the Andean state*, edited by J. Haas, S. Pozorski, and T. Pozorski, pp. 56–69 (Cambridge, 1987). I. Shimada's *Pampa Grande* volume summarizes most of the foregoing views as well as new excavation data from the La Leche Valley and offers new interpretations on the Gallinazo-Mochica relationship on the northern half of the north coast.

Increasing attention is being given to the Cajamarca culture in the North Highlands. The pioneering work of H. and P. Reichlen reported in "Recherches archéologiques dans les Andes de Cajamarca: premier rapport de la Mision Ethnologique Française au Pérou Septentrional," in *JSA* 38: 137–174 (Paris, 1949) was not followed until the late 1970s when the University of Tokyo team initiated its research. The best summary of chronological and cultural characterization resulting from the latter is provided by R. Matsumoto in "Dos modos de proceso socio-cultural: El Horizonte Temprano y el Período Intermedio Temprano en el valle de Cajamarca" in *El mundo ceremonial andino*, edited by L. Millones and Y. Onuki, pp. 169–202 (Senri, 1993). Relevant data are presented in detail in K. Terada and Y. Onuki (editors), *Excavations at Huacaloma in the Cajamarca Valley, Peru, 1979* (Tokyo, 1982) and *The Formative Period in the Cajamarca Basin, Peru* (Tokyo, 1985).

The Chavín culture has received a lion's share of attention from both Peruvian and Peruvianist archaeologists over the past half century, and there is an abundance of publications. R. L. Burger has many publications on the subject. The results of his fieldwork in and around Chavín de Huántar for his doctoral thesis are reported in *The prehistoric occupation of Chavín de Huántar, Peru* (Berkeley, 1984). By far the best and most comprehensive synthesis of the Chavín culture in English is his *Chavín and the origins of Andean civilization* (New York, 1992). This work should be compared and contrasted with *Chavín de Huántar en el nacimiento de la civilización andina* (Lima, 1989), written by the leading Peruvian authority on the Chavín, L. G. Lumbreras. Both consider the synchronous and diachronic processes leading to the florescence and collapse of the Chavín culture. They differ in terminology and chronology, among other aspects, but also complement each other. The former offers a more extensive discussion of regional and interregional contexts;

the latter provides greater detail and insights into the temple at Chavín derived from his own excavations there.

There is as yet no one good, updated, comprehensive characterization of the Recuay culture in Callejon de Huaylas. R. P. Schaedel's characterization of stone sculptures, "Stone sculpture in the Callejón de Huaylas" in *A reappraisal of Peruvian archaeology* assembled by W. C. Bennett, pp. 66–79 (1948) is still useful. *Altperuanische Kulturen IV: Recuay* by D. Eisleb (Berlin, 1987) is a photographic compilation of Recuay ceramics in the Ethnological Museum in Berlin and is useful for stylistic and iconographic studies. R. X. Reichert's doctoral thesis, *The Recuay ceramic style – A re-evaluation* (Los Angeles, 1977) remains one of the most complete treatments of the style. J. W. Smith's doctoral thesis, *The Recuay culture: A reconstruction based on artistic motifs* (Austin, 1978) is based on archaeological reconnassaince, but many of his interpretations remain untested. Reichert also examines the relationship between the Mochica and Recuay art styles in "Moche iconography – The highland connection" in *Pre-Columbian art history: Selected readings*, edited by A. Cordy-Collins, pp. 279–291 (Palo Alto, 1982). Data from excavations at Queyash by J. Gero are presented as part of a more theoretical publication, "Who experienced what in prehistory? Narrative explanation from Queyash, Peru" in *Processual and postprocessual archaeologies: Multiple ways of knowing the past*, edited by R. W. Preucel, pp. 126–139 (Carbondale, IL, 1991).

In spite of a long history of archaeological investigations, there is no good current synthesis of the Lima culture on the central coast either in English or Spanish. L. M. Stumer's work in the early 1950s yielded data critical to current perceptions of the Lima culture. For example, a glimpse of arts, crafts, architecture, and burials can be gained from "Playa Grande: Primitive elegance in pre-Tiahuanaco Peru," *Archaeology* 6(1): 42–48 (1953); "The Chillón Valley of Peru: Excavation and reconnaissance, 1952–53," Parts 1 and 2 in *Archaeology* 7(3): 171–178 and 7(4): 220–228 (1954); and "Population centers of the Rímac Valley of Peru," *AA* 20: 130–148 (1954). The results of various recent, small-scale excavations and surveys by Peruvian archaeologists remain unpublished or appear in publications with little circulation outside of Lima. I. Shimada's historical review and synthesis, "Pachacamac archaeology: Retrospect and prospect," in a new edition of *Pachacamac* by M. Uhle (Philadelphia, 1991), clarifies the nature of Lima occupation at Pacha Kamaq and its relationship to developments in the heartland in the Rímac Valley, as well as the terminological confusion surrounding this culture and its chronology. Settlement pattern and urbanization trends are discussed by J. Canziani in "Análisis del complejo urbano Maranga Chayavilca," *GAA* 4 (14): 10–17 (Lima, 1987). Cultural developments and relevant processes at the onset and end of the Lima culture are described by K. Stothert in "The Villa Salvador site and the beginning of the Early Intermediate Period in the Lurín Valley, Peru," *JFA* 7: 279–295 (1980), by P. C. Sestieri in "Excavations at Cajamarquilla, Peru," *Archaeology* 17(1): 12–17 (1964); and by D. Menzel in *The archaeology of ancient Peru and the work of Max Uhle* (Berkeley, 1977).

Much like publications on the Mochica culture, those on the successive Paracas and Nasca cultures on the south coast are numerous, but the clear majority of relevant publications focuses on burials and the artistic and technical aspects of associated ceramics and textiles. They are described under appropriate topical headings later. For a detailed description of the Paracas-Nasca stylistic tradition and ceramic sequence, see *The Paracas pottery of Ica: A study in style and time* (Berkeley, 1964) by D. Menzel, J. H. Rowe, and L. Dawson. *Paracas art and architecture: Object and context in south coastal Peru*, edited by A. Paul (Iowa City, 1991), is an informative and comprehensive introduction for anyone interested in Paracas archaeology. It brings together technical and iconographic analyses of Paracas ceramics and textiles, as well as the ecological and social contexts of their development. Chapter 7 of the *Chavín* volume by Burger is a good complement to the foregoing book in elucidating the mechanisms and nature of Chavín influence on Paracas. Other essential publications (perhaps just to glance through) are *Paracas: Primera parte* by J. C. Tello (Lima, 1959) and *Paracas, segunda parte: Cavernas y Necropólis* by J. C. Tello and T. Mejía Xesspe (Lima, 1979). They provide basic documentation of the famed Paracas mummy bundles and their original excavation.

Recent documentation of Paracas settlements in the Chincha and Pisco valleys is changing our notion of the evolution and territorial extent of the Paracas culture. Relevant evidence is discussed by D. T. Wallace in "Paracas in Chincha and Pisco: A reappraisal of the Ocucaje sequence," in *Recent studies in Andean prehistory and protohistory*, edited by D. H. Sandweiss and D. P. Kvietok (Ithaca, 1985); by J. Canziani in "Arquitectura y urbanismo del periodo Paracas en el valle de Chincha," in *GAA* 22: 87–117 (1992); and by H. Silverman in "Paracas in Nazca:

New data on the Early Horizon occupation of the Río Grande de Nazca drainage, Peru," *LAAnt* 5: 359–382 (1994).

There is as yet no comprehensive, book-length cultural synthesis of the Nasca culture in English. The forthcoming book, *Nasca*, by D. Browne and H. Silverman (Cambridge, MA, in press), should help to fill this gap. Examples of new understanding of this culture from fieldwork over the past decade emphasizing nonfunerary contexts are seen in *Cahuachi in the ancient Nasca world* (Iowa City, 1993) by H. Silverman. It is a revised version of her doctoral thesis, which interprets this site as an early Nasca religious-pilgrimage center. The book is summarized in her article, "Cahuachi: Non-urban cultural complexity on the South Coast of Peru," *JFA* 15: 403–430 (1988). She places this site within the broader context of the Nasca culture and history of its investigation. It significantly revises the traditional view of Cahuachi put forth by W. D. Strong in *Paracas, Nazca, and Tiahuanacoid cultural relationships in south coastal Peru* (Salt Lake City, 1957).

A popular research focus in Nasca archaeology has been geoglyphs or "desert markings." A good introduction is provided by the two scholars who brought them to the attention of the modern world, P. Kosok and M. Reiche, in "The mysterious markings of Nazca," *Natural History* 56: 200–207, 237–238 (1947) and "Ancient drawings on the desert of Peru," *Archaeology* 2(4): 206–215. The numerous aerial and ground-level photographs of the geoglyphs compiled by Kosok in his *Life, land and water in ancient Peru* (New York, 1965) should be studied by anyone interested in this subject. The most recent overviews of the subject are found in A. Aveni's "The Nazca lines: Patterns in the desert," *Archaeology* 39(4): 32–39 (1986) and his book review, "Back to the drawing board: Review of *Lines to the mountain gods: Nazca and the mysteries of Peru* by E. Hadingham and *The mystery of the Nazca lines* by Tony Morrison" in *Nature* 330: 278–279 (1987). The most comprehensive discussion of competing theories is offered by Aveni in Chapter 1 of *The lines of Nazca*, which he edited (Philadelphia, 1990). The following chapter, also by Aveni, presents the basic factual data and considerations that must be accounted for by any theory, and evaluates the explanation based on radial patterns of lines. The book as a whole presents the results of 8 years of interdisciplinary investigation.

As the local antecedent to the Wari culture, the Huarpa has received more attention in recent years, although our understanding is still limited. Summary characterizations of the culture, including the inferred

capital of Ñawimpukio are found in *Historia prehispánica de Ayacucho* by
E. Gonzalez (Ayacucho, 1982) and in *The peoples and cultures of ancient
Peru* by Lumbreras. The ceramic style was defined by L. G. Lumbreras
in "La cultura Wari, Ayacucho," *Etnología y Arqueología* 1: 130–226
(Lima, 1960) and by D. Menzel in "Style and time in the Middle
Horizon," *ÑP* 2: 1–105 (1964). Also useful for settlement-pattern data is
"Arqueología de la cuenca del Qaracha, Ayacucho, Perú," *LAAnt* 5: 144–
157 (1994).

There are surprisingly few substantial or accessible publications in
English on the *altiplano* cultures of Chiripa and Pukara, in spite of wide
recognition of their importance. Marcavalle, a key site in understanding
ERD cultural developments in the South-Central Andes, is detailed by
K. L. Chávez in "The archaeology of Marcavalle, an Early Horizon site
in the Valley of Cusco, Peru: Parts I, II and III," *BA* Neue Folge 28:
203–329 (1980), 29: 107–205 (1981), and 29: 241–386 (1981). Along with
her husband, S. Chávez, she continues investigation of the Chiripa and
Pukara cultures. A good introduction to Chiripa is K. L. Chávez's "The
significance of Chiripa in Lake Titicaca Basin developments," *Expedition*
30(3): 17–26 (1988). She discusses possible social and economic functions
of the site and associated Yama-Mama Religious Tradition. However,
both remain to be described fully. D. L. Browman offers a three-phase
chronology for the site in "The temple of Chiripa (Lake Titicaca, Bolivia)" in *III Congreso Peruano de Hombre y La Cultura Andina, Actas y
Trabajos*, Vol. 2, edited by R. Matos, pp. 808–813 (Lima, 1978). His
"New light on Andean Tiwanaku" in *American Scientist* 69: 408–419
(1981) discusses the role of Chiripa in *altiplano* cultural developments. In
Las culturas Wankarani y Chiripa y su relación con Tiwanaku, C. Ponce
Sanginés (La Paz, 1970) describes evidence for the newly defined Wankarani, an early agropastoral society on the southern shore of Lake Titicaca that was partially contemporaneous with Chiripa. Though sketchy,
evidence of early copper smelting in the former is presented. By far the
most comprehensive treatment of the Pukara style and culture is the
doctoral thesis by S. J. Chávez, *The conventionalized rules in Pucara
pottery technology and iconography; implications for socio-political developments in the northern Lake Titicaca Basin* (Ann Arbor, 1992). Still useful
is *Some early sites in the northern Lake Titicaca Basin* by A. Kidder II
(Cambridge, MA, 1943). The Pukara style and its relationships with
contemporaneous and later coastal and highland styles are also discussed

by S. J. Chávez in "The Arapa and Thunderbolt stelae: A case of stylistic identity with implications for Pukara influence in the area of Tiahuanaco," *ÑP* 13: 3–25 (1976); "Pucara style pottery designs" by J. H. Rowe and C. T. Brandel in *ÑP* 7–8: 1–16 (1971); and "The ancient pottery from Pucara, Peru" by E. M. Franquemont in *ÑP* 24: 1–30 (1990). Chávez has published subsequently a series of articles in *ÑP* to elaborate on Pukara stone sculptures and the significance of their iconography. R. E. Feldman's "The early ceramic periods of Moquegua" in *Ecology, settlement and history in the Osmore drainage, Peru*, edited by D. S. Rice, C. Stanish, and P. R. Scan, pp. 207–217 (Oxford, 1989) is useful for a comparative perspective seen from the cis-Andean region. E. Mujica presents a tentative outline of the evolution of vertical control and the role of the Pukara culture in "Altiplano-coast relationships in the South-Central Andes: From indirect to direct complementarity" in *Andean ecology and civilization*, edited by S. Masuda, I. Shimada, and C. Morris, pp. 103–140 (Tokyo, 1985). Drawing on the works of the Chávezes, Ponce, and others, A. Kolata offers a more current synthesis of the factors and processes leading to the florescence of the Tiwanaku culture in *The Tiwanaku: Portrait of an Andean civilization* (Cambridge, MA, 1993). His scenario for Tiwanaku collapse remains controversial.

Kolata's book also offers a succinct characterization of the site and cultural sequence of Tiwanaku. Anyone seriously interested in the Tiwanaku culture should consult A. Posnansky's monumental *Tiahuanaco: The cradle of American man*, 2 vols. (New York, 1945) and *Tiwanaku: Espacio, tiempo y cultura*, second edition (La Paz, 1977) by C. Ponce. The former, written and published by an amateur archaeologist, contains discredited interpretations of the site, but its illustrations are unsurpassed. The latter summarizes results of many years of excavations by Bolivian teams at the site under Ponce's direction as well as the associated chronology built on the problematical scheme proposed by W. C. Bennett in his *Excavations at Tiahuanaco* (New York, 1934). A good compilation of Tiwanaku artifacts is *Altperuanische Kulturen III: Tiahuanaco* by D. Eisleb and R. Strelow (Berlin, 1980). The best evidence of cis-Andean Tiwanaku colonization is provided by P. Goldstein in "House, community, and state in the earliest Tiwanaku colony: Domestic patterns and state integration at Omo M12, Moquegua, Peru" in *Domestic architecture, ethnicity and complementarity in the South-Central Andes*, edited by M. S. Aldenderfer, pp. 25–41 (Iowa City, 1993).

Iconography and Ideology

Readers interested in iconographic analysis for cultural reconstruction may find it helpful to first read the commentaries in Chapter 13 of Bruhns's *South American archaeology* book. A detailed critique of different approaches to iconography is found in Chapter 2 of Shimada's *Pampa Grande* volume. Another useful critique is offered by P. J. Lyon in "Archaeology and mythology II: A re-consideration of the animated objects theme in Moche art" in *Culture in conflict: Current archaeological perspectives*, edited by D. Tkaczuk and B. Vivian, pp. 62–68 (Calgary, 1989).

For Chavín iconography, basic readings include Chapter 3 of "Wira Kocha," *Inca* 1: 93–320, 583–606 (Lima, 1923) and pp. 615–616 of "Origen y desarrollo de las civilizaciones prehistóricas andinas," *Actas y Trabajos Científicos del 27 Congreso Internacional de Americanistas* 1: 589–720 (Lima, 1942), both by J. C. Tello, and *Chavín art: An inquiry into its form and meaning* (New York, 1962) by J. H. Rowe. The former is critical because it is the first and in many ways most comprehensive discussion to date of the meaning of Chavín art. The latter is largely reproduced in the more accessible *Peruvian archaeology: Selected readings*, edited by J. H. Rowe and D. Menzel, pp. 16–30 (Palo Alto, 1967). D. W. Lathrap's cosmological vision of Chavín iconography derives from that of Tello and is described in "Gifts of the cayman: Some thoughts on the subsistence basis of Chavín" in *Variation in anthropology: Essays in honor of John C. McGregor*, edited by D. W. Lathrap and J. Douglas, pp. 91–105 (Urbana, 1973) and "Complex iconographic features shared by Olmec and Chavín and some speculations on their possible significance" in *Primer simposio de correlaciones antropológicas andino-mesoamericanas*, edited by J. Marcos and P. Norton, pp. 301–327 (Guayaquil, 1982). *Gifts to the cayman: Essays in honor of Donald W. Lathrap*, a special issue of *JSAS* 20 (1–2, 1992) contains elaborations and critiques of Lathrap's conception of Chavín iconography by C. McEwan, R. L. Weber, and D. T. Wallace, as well as an alternative to it by T. Zuidema. Other articles of interest include "Chavín art: Its shamanistic/hallucinogenic origins," pp. 353–362 in *Pre-Columbian art history* (cited earlier) and "The dual divinity concept in Chavín art" in *Musuem of Anthropology, Miscellaneous Series*, No. 48, pp. 42–72 (Greeley, CO, 1983), both by A. Cordy-Collins. Painted textiles as a medium of dissemination of the Chavín cult are discussed by A. Cordy-Collins in "Cotton and the Staff God: Analysis of an ancient

Chavín textile" in *The Junius B. Bird Pre-Columbian Textile Conference, May 19th and 20th, 1973*, edited by A. P. Rowe, E. P. Benson, and A. Schaffer, pp. 51–60 (Washington, D.C., 1979), and by D. T. Wallace in "A technical and iconographic analysis of Carhua painted textiles" in the aforementioned *Paracas art and architecture* volume.

Relevant publications are most numerous for the Mochica and Nasca iconographies. Larco's approach to "Mochica ethnography" as well as some interesting comments are found in *Los Mochicas*, tomos 1, 2 (Lima, 1938, 1939). Recent studies are conceptually and methodologically more sophisticated. Major works include *A man and a feline in Mochica art* (Washington, D.C., 1974), *The Mochica* (cited earlier), and "The world of Moche" in *The ancient Americas: Art from sacred landscapes*, edited by R. F. Townsend, pp. 303–316 (Chicago, 1992), all by E. Benson; *Moche: Gods, warriors, priests* by E. K. de Bock (Leiden, 1978); *Moche art and iconography* (Los Angeles, 1976) and *Moche art of Peru* by C. B. Donnan (Los Angeles, 1978); *The burial theme in Moche iconography* by C. B. Donnan and D. McClelland (Washington, D. C., 1979); and *Iconografía Mochica* (Lima, 1987) by A. M. Hocquenghem. The latter and *Nordperuanische Gefässmalereien des Moche-Stils* by G. Kutscher (Munich, 1983) are the most comprehensive, published compilations of Mochica painted motifs and themes. D. Bonavia's *Mural painting in ancient Peru* (Bloomington, 1985) includes extensive photographic coverage of Mochica murals and incisive technical and cultural commentaries. It is valuable as a comparative study of style and iconography in a different artistic medium. The previously cited *Moche: Propuestas y perspectivas* volume contains descriptions and illustrations of newly discovered murals at Huaca El Brujo and Huaca de la Luna.

Donnan and Hocquenghem offer the most comprehensive iconographic analyses; the former employs a "thematic approach" described in his 1976 and 1978 books, whereas the latter applies a methodology developed by E. Panofsky in his *Meaning in the visual arts* (Garden City, 1955) and *Studies in iconology: Humanistic themes in the art of the Renaissance* (New York, 1962). Hocquenghem has written numerous articles on different aspects of Mochica iconography, including "Une interpretation des "vases portraits" Mochicas," *ÑP* 15: 131–140 (Berkeley, 1977) and "A class of anthropomorphic supernatural females in Moche iconography," *ÑP* 18: 27–48 (Berkeley, 1981). The former is important in dispelling the widely held misconception that the realistic modeled vessels of human heads are portraits. Y. Berezkin, a Russian scholar, presents a valuable approach to Mochica iconography based on comparative, structural analysis of Andean and Amazonian mythologies in "An identification of anthropomorphic mythological personages in Moche representations," *ÑP* 18: 1–26 (Berkeley, 1980). He is one of the few scholars who explores the evolutionary character of Mochica mythology and how it relates to the existing sociopolitical structure. His "Moche society and iconography" in *Pre-Columbian collections in European museums*, edited by A. M. Hocquenghem, P. Tamási, and C. Villain-Gandossi, pp. 270–277 (Budapest, 1987) is a brief summary of some of his views. D. Arsenault also explores political symbolism in "Images of power in the Moche ceremonial context: Some aspects of gesture in Moche iconography" in *The archaeology of gender: The proceedings of the 22nd Chacmool Conference – 1989* (Calgary, 1990). Although specific personages depicted may change over time, continuity in iconographic themes in North Coast prehistory is explored by A. Cordy-Collins in "Archaism or tradition?: The decapitation theme in Cupisnique and Moche iconography," *LAAnt* 3:206–220 (1992).

Like the aforementioned case of Mochica archaeology, most of what has been written about the Paracas and Nasca cultures heavily draws on stylistic and iconographic studies of polychrome ceramics and textiles primarily from funerary contexts. *The Paracas pottery of Ica* volume mentioned earlier is essential in understanding the Paracas-Nasca stylistic tradition and ceramic sequence. *Altperuanische Kulturen II: Nazca* by D. Eisleb (Berlin, 1977) and *Catalogo de la cerámica Nazca*, Tomo 1 by C. Blasco and L. J. Ramos (Madrid, 1986) are valuable compilations of Nasca ceramic art with detailed technical and stylistic information. *Culturas precolombinas: Paracas* (Lima, 1983) and *Culturas precolombinas: Nazca* (Lima 1986), both edited by J. A. de Lavalle and W. Lang, offer fine color photographs of Paracas and Nasca artifacts (primarily ceramics and textiles), respectively.

Before the reader delves into the literature on Paracas iconography, reading of the introductory essay by A. Paul and "Ecology and society in embroidered images from the Paracas Necropolis" by A. H. Peters, both in *Paracas art and architecture*, is recommended. They offer valuable background and the basic understanding necessary for further reading. Other useful publications include "Paracas and Nazca iconography" by A. R. Sawyer in *Essays in Pre-Columbian art and archaeology*, edited by S. K. Lothrop, pp. 269–298 (Cambridge, 1961); "The chronology and iconography of Paracas-style textiles" by J. P. Dwyer, pp. 105–128 in the previously cited *The Junius B. Bird Pre-Columbian Textile Conference, May 19th and 20th, 1973*; and "The ecstatic shaman theme of Paracas textiles" by A. Paul and S. A. Turpin, *Archaeology* 39(5): 20–27 (1986). Paul has written various other articles of interest, including "The symbolism of Paracas turbans: A consideration of style, serpents, and hair," *ÑP* 20: 41–60 (1982) and "Continuity in Paracas textile iconography and its implications for the meaning of linear style images" in *The Junius B. Conference on Andean textiles, April 7th and 8th, 1984*, edited by A. P. Rowe, pp. 81–99 (Washington, D.C., 1986).

Nasca style iconography is a popular but complex topic, and the reader is encouraged to compare and contrast different approaches and interpretations. R. F. Townsend provides a good introduction in "Deciphering the Nazca world: Ceramic images from ancient Peru," *Art Institute of Chicago Museum Studies* 11/12: 117–139. Another good introductory article is D. A. Proulx's "The Nazca style" in *Pre-Columbian sculptured and painted ceramics from the Arthur M. Sackler Collections*, edited by L. Katz, pp. 87–105 (Washington, D.C., 1983) and "A thematic approach to Nasca mythical iconography" in *Faenza* LXXV(IV–V): 141–158 (Faenza, Italy, 1989). Proulx has other valuable publications including *Local differences and time differences in Nasca pottery* (Berkeley, 1968) and "Nasca trophy heads: Victims of warfare or ritual sacrifice?" pp. 73–85, in the aforementioned *Cultures in Conflict: Current Archaeological Perspectives*. Readers should also consult "The Nasca creatures: Some problems of iconography" by C. J. Allen in *Anthropology* 5: 43–70 (1981); "Ecology, art, and myth: A natural approach to symbolism" by J. Davidson, pp. 331–343 in *Pre-Columbian art history: selected readings*; "The spotted cat and the horrible bird: Stylistic change in Nasca 1–5 ceramic decoration" by E. P. Wolfe, *ÑP* 19: 1–62 (1981); "From Monumental to Proliferous in Nasca pottery" by R. Roark, *ÑP* 3: 1–92 (1965); and "Meaning in Nazca art: Iconographic relationships between Inca, Huari, and Nazca cultures in southern Peru" by R. T. Zuidema, *Göteborgs Etnografiska Museum Arstryck* 1971, pp. 35–54 (Göteberg, 1972).

The interpretation of Colombian and Ecuadorian (and even Chavín) iconographies is heavily based on ethnographic analogy. Main sources of insights include the well-known works of G. Reichel-Dolmatoff, *The shaman and the jaguar: A study of narcotic drugs among the Indians of Colombia* (Philadelphia, 1975) and *Los Kogi: una tribú de la Sierra Nevada de Santa Marta, Colombia* (second edition, two vols., Bogotá, 1985), as well as *Flesh of the gods: The ritual use of hallucinogens*, edited by P. Furst

(London, 1972). Examples of how such ethnographic information is applied can be seen in "Things of beauty replete with meaning – metals and crystals in Colombian cosmology" in *Sweat of the sun, tears of the moon: Gold and emerald treasures of Colombia*, pp. 17–33 (Los Angeles, 1981); *Orfebrería y chamanismo* by Reichel-Dolmatoff (Medellín, 1988); and "The snake and the fabulous beast: Themes from the pottery of the Ilama culture" by M. Cardale de Schrimpff in *Animals into art*, edited by H. Murphy, pp. 75–106 (London, 1989). M. W. Helms offers a valuable comparative perspective in "Precious metals and politics: Style and ideology in the Intermediate Area and Peru," *JLAL* 7: 215–238 (1981).

Crafts and Technology

Much has been written about the metallurgy of ERD cultures, particularly their goldwork. A general overview of the subject is offered in "Ancient American metallurgy: Five hundred years of study" by W. Bray in *Art of pre-Columbian gold: Jan Mitchell collection*, edited by J. Jones, pp. 76–84 (London, 1985); "Traditions and styles in Central Andean metalworking" by H. N. Lechtman in *The beginning of the use of metals and alloys*, edited by R. Maddin, pp. 344–378 (Cambridge, MA, 1988); Chapter 11 of K. O. Bruhns's *Ancient South America*; Chapter 12 of Morris and von Hagen's *The Inka empire* (New York, 1993); and "Prehispanic metallurgy and mining in the Andes: Recent advances and future tasks" by I. Shimada in *In quest of mineral wealth: Aboriginal and colonial mining and metallurgy in Spanish America*, edited by R. West and A. K. Craig, pp. 37–73 (Baton Rouge, 1995).

For Colombian goldworking, good summary descriptions are *The gold of El Dorado* by W. Bray (London, 1978) and "Cultural patterns in the prehispanic goldwork of Colombia" by C. Plazas and A. M. Falchetti, pp. 47–59, in the previously cited *Art of pre-Columbian gold*. The latter and *Museo del oro* by the same two authors (Bogotá, 1992) are quite readable and well illustrated, though limited in technical details. For more information on specific regional styles and metalworking techniques, see "Two pre-Hispanic cire perdue casting moulds from Colombia" by K. O. Bruhns, *Man* 7: 308–311 (1974); "Orfebrería prehispánica en las llanuras del Pacífico de Ecuador y Colombia" by D. Scott and J. F. Bouchard, *Boletín del Museo de Oro* 22: 2–16 (Bogotá, 1988); and "Ancient platinum technology in South America: Its use by the Indians in pre-Hispanic times" by D. A. Scott and W. Bray, *Platinum Metals*

Review 24: 147–157 (1980). These studies expound on P. Bergsøe's classic, *The metallurgy and technology of gold and platinum among the pre-Columbian Indians* (Copenhagen, 1937).

J. Jones's "Mochica works of art in metal: A review" in *Pre-Columbian metallurgy of South America* edited by E. P. Benson, pp. 53–104 (Washington, D.C., 1979) is a good introduction to the artistic and technical aspects of Mochica metal objects, including those from the Vicús region. The case for electrochemical plating among Mochica copper objects from Vicús is presented by H. N. Lechtman et al. in "New perspectives on Moche metallurgy: Techniques of gilding copper at Loma Negra, northern Peru," *AAnt* 47: 3–30 (1982). Sumptuary metal objects found in élite tombs at Sipán are briefly described in *Royal tombs of Sipán* (exhibition catalogue) by W. Alva and C. B. Donnan (Los Angeles, 1993). Results of technical analysis of these objects have not yet been published.

Bits of technical information on ceramics are found sprinkled in the publications mentioned earlier in regard to iconography. Good introductions to their artistic and technical aspects are *Ceramics of ancient Peru* by C. B. Donnan (Los Angeles, 1992) and Chapter 8 of K. O. Bruhns' *Ancient South America*. Detailed discussion of technology and the organization of production based on recent excavations of ceramic workshops and archaeometric analyses of products are found in *Tecnología y la organización de producción de cerámica prehispánica en los Andes* (particularly Chaps. 5–9) and *Ceramic production in the prehispanic Andes*, both edited by I. Shimada (Lima, 1994, and Philadelphia, in press).

For Mochica ceramics, see Moche "ceramic technology" by C. B. Donnan, *ÑP* 3: 115–138 (1965) and illustrations of molds and other tools in "Arte antiguo peruano: album fotográfico de las principales especies arqueológicas de cerámica muchik existentes en los museos de Lima, primera parte: tecnología y morfología" by J. C. Tello, *Inca* 2: VII–LXII, 1–280 (Lima, 1938). For Nasca pottery, see P. H. Carmichael's "Nasca pottery construction," *ÑP* 24: 31–48 (1986). T. Cummins's fresh perspective on mold-made figurines on coastal Ecuador is presented in "La tradición de figurinas de la costa ecuatoriana: estilo tecnológico y el uso de moldes," pp. 157–171, in the previously cited *Tecnología y la organización de producción de cerámica prehispánica en los Andes*.

The body of literature on textiles of the ERD cultures is quite large. Highly readable introductions to various aspects of prehispanic Andean textiles, including those of the ERD cultures, are contained in the aforementioned textbooks by K. O. Bruhns and C. Morris and von Hagen.

Also recommended are Part 3 of *Andean culture history* by W. C. Bennett and J. B. Bird, second and revised edition (Garden City, 1964) and "An introduction to South American archaeological textiles with emphasis on materials and techniques of Peruvian tapestry" by W. J. Conklin in the *Irene Emery Roundtable on Museum Textiles, 1974 Proceedings: Archaeological textiles* edited by P. L. Fiske, pp. 17–30 (Washington, D.C., 1975). Various chapters in the proceedings of the two Junius B. Bird Textile Conferences should also be consulted. For Paracas and Nasca textiles, in addition to those cited for iconography, *Paracas fabrics and Nazca needlework, 3rd century B.C.–3rd century A.D . . . : The Textile Museum, catalogue raisonné* by J. B. Bird and L. Bellinger (Washington, D.C., 1954), and *Paracas ritual attire, symbols of authority in ancient Peru* by A. Paul (Norman, 1990) are worth reading for technical details and cultural inferences. W. J. Conklin, who has been a major figure in Andean textile studies, has written a series of important articles, including "The revolutionary weaving inventions of the Early Horizon" *ÑP* 16: 1–12 (1978), "Moche textile structures," pp. 165–184 in *The Junius B. Bird Pre-Columbian Textile Conference, May 19th and 20th, 1973*, and "Pucara and Tiahuanaco tapestry: Time and style in a sierra weaving tradition," *ÑP* 21: 1–44 (1985). The results of the detailed analysis of fine Mochica textiles from the "royal tombs" of Sipán are described in "Un tejido Moche excepcional de la tumba del 'Señor de Sipán' " by H. Prümers in *BAVA* 15: 309–369 (Mainz, Germany, 1995).

There is no single major synthesis of Andean architecture (i.e., its designs, layout, materials, and techniques) for the time period under consideration. G. Kubler's *The art and architecture of ancient America: The Mexican, Maya, and Andean peoples* (Middlesex, 1975) offers a broad stroke characterization but is outdated. The north coast of Peru is the only region that can boast any coherent body of publications. G. R. Willey's *Prehistoric settlement patterns in the Viru Valley* is full of valuable architectural data. M. Reindel's detailed attribute-morphological analysis (doctoral thesis) of monumental architecture on the north coast is published as *Monumentale Lehmarchitektur an der Nordküste Perus: Eine repräsentative Untersuchung nach-formativer Grossbauten vom Lambayeque-Gebiet bis zum Virú-Tal*, Bonner Amerikanistische Studien 22 (Bonn, 1993). Its approach and conclusions should be compared with those of I. Shimada in Chapter 7 of his *Pampa Grande* volume. The political symbolism of ERD architecture is considered in *Architecture and power in the ancient Andes* by J. D. Moore (Cambridge, 1996).

Subsistence and Economy

For Colombia and Ecuador, the regional studies mentioned earlier, such as those by Cardale de Schrimpff et al., Drenann et al., and Zeidler and Pearsall, provide the most detailed and current information on the topic. Relevant characterizations for the Chavín and Mochica cultures are found in the previously cited *Chavín* book by Burger and *Pampa Grande* volume by Shimada. For the Moche Valley, S. Pozorski offers a long-term perspective in "Prehistoric diet and subsistence of the Moche valley, Peru," *WA* 11: 413–432 (1979), though the economic significance of plants cannot be taken at face value. Useful for gaining a proper perspective on Paracas and Nasca subsistence is the aforementioned article by A. Peters in *Paracas art and architecture.*

Various agricultural and water management techniques are described in *Prehistoric intensive agriculture in the tropics* edited by I. Farrington (Oxford, 1985). *Pre-Hispanic agricultural fields in the Andean region, Part I,* edited by W. M. Denevan, K. Mathewson, and G. Knapp (Oxford, 1987), *Economic aspects of water management in the prehispanic New World,* edited by V. L. Scarborough and B. L. Isaac (Greenwich, CT, 1993). The construction, productivity, and social implications of raised or ridged fields are best discussed by C. Erickson in his articles in the three preceding edited volumes. For irrigation systems on the north coast, P. Kosok's *Life, land and water in ancient Peru* (cited earlier) is essential. It offers excellent photographs, field data, and multivalley perspective. The evolution of irrigation systems in the Moche Valley is described by M. E. Moseley and E. Deeds in "The land in front of Chan Chan: Agrarian expansion, reform, and collapse in the Moche Valley," pp. 25–53, in the aforementioned *Chan Chan: Andean desert city* volume. Impacts of El Niño-related floods and tectonic uplift on irrigation systems on the north coast are summarized by M. E. Moseley in "The good old days were better: Agrarian collapse and tectonics," *AA* 85: 773–799 (1983).

The general survey data on sunken fields provided by J. R. Parsons and N. P. Psuty in "Sunken fields and prehispanic subsistence on the Peruvian coast," *AAnt* 40: 259–282 (1975) should be contrasted with the case study of Salinar examples by M. West in "Early watertable farming on the north coast of Peru," *AAnt* 44: 138–144 (1979) and "Agricultural resource use in an Andean coastal ecosystem," *HE* 9: 47–77 (1981). Debate surrounding the antiquity of the *pukio* or filtration-gallery irrigation on the south coast is summarized by M. Barnes and D. Fleming,

"Filtration-gallery irrigation in the Spanish New World," *LAAnt* 2: 48–68 (1991). It should be read together with P. Clarkson's recent dating in "New chronometric dates for the *puquios* of Nasca, Peru," *LAAnt* 6: 56–69 (1995).

The roles and distribution of domesticated animals, particularly llamas, for the time period under study is discussed by "Our father the cayman, our dinner the llama: Animal utilization at Chavín de Huántar, Peru" by G. R. Miller and R. L. Burger, *LAAnt* 60: 421–458 (1995), "Prehistoric subsistence in the North Highlands of Peru: Early Horizon to Late Intermediate" by M. J. Shimada in *Economic prehistory of the Central Andes*, edited by E. S. Wing and J. C. Wheeler, pp. 131–147, (Oxford, 1988) and "Prehistoric llama breeding and herding on the north coast of Peru," *AAnt* 50: 3–26 (1985) by M. and I. Shimada.

The economic foundation of Tiwanaku florescence and expansion is discussed by T. Lynch in "Camelid pastoralism and the emergence of Tiwanaku civilization in the South-Central Andes," *WA* 15: 1–14 (1983) and "The agricultural foundations of the Tiwanaku state: A view from the heartland" by A. Kolata in *AAnt* 51: 748–762 (1986). The earlier Pukara ridged fields and their implications are discussed in the previously cited articles by C. Erickson.

Architecture, Settlement Patterns, Burials, and Sociopolitical Organization

There are numerous settlement pattern studies for sociopolitical reconstruction. Still valuable is G. R. Willey's original study, *Prehistoric settlement patterns in the Virú Valley, northern Peru*. It should be read with his own critique, "The Virú Valley settlement pattern study" in *Archaeological researches in retrospect*, edited by G. R. Willey, pp. 149–179 (Cambridge, MA, 1974) and that by Schaedel and Shimada in the 1982 *WA* article cited earlier.

Settlement patterns for the ERD cultures in Colombia and Ecuador are best described in the various regional studies mentioned earlier. The situation in the Chavín heartland is described in Chapters 6 and 7 of *Chavín and the origins of Andean civilization* by R. L. Burger, while S. Massey offers a case study of Paracas occupation in the Ica Valley in "Social and political leadership in the lower Ica Valley," pp. 315–348, in the aforementioned *Paracas art and architecture* book.

The most complete settlement data on Gallinazo occupation and

Mochica expansion are found in D. L. Wilson's *Prehispanic settlement patterns in the lower Santa Valley, Peru* (Washington, D.C., 1988). His data are derived from surface surveys, and many of his inferences await testing through future excavations. Mochica-Recuay competition over the coastal *yunka* is discussed by Wilson in his 1988 book mentioned earlier and by D. Proulx in "Territoriality in the Early Intermediate Period: The case of Moche and Recuay," *ÑP* 20: 83–96 (1982).

For different views on Mochica expansion and sociopolitical organization, see R. P. Schaedel's "The city and the origin of the state in America," *Actas y Memorias del 39 Congreso Internacional de Americanistas* 2: 15–33 (Lima, 1972), "Coast–highland interrelationships and ethnic groups in northern Peru (500 B.C.E.–C.E. 1980)," pp. 443–473, in the aforementioned *Andean ecology and civilization* volume; and "The transition from chiefdom to state in northern Peru" in *Development and decline: The evolution of sociopolitical organization*, edited by H. J. M. Claessen, P. van de Velde, and M. E. Smith, pp. 156–169 (South Hadley, MA, 1985). G. Kutscher's "Iconographic studies as an aid in the reconstruction of Early Chimú civilization," pp. 115–124, in the aforementioned *Peruvian archaeology: Selected readings*; Chapters 4 and 5 of *Pampa Grande* by Shimada; "Moche, Vicús Moche y el Mochica temprano," *BIFEA* 21: 835–903 (1992) by P. Kaulicke; and "Los Mochicas del norte y los Mochica del sur" by C. B. Donnan and L. J. Castillo, in K. Makowski's edited *Vicús* volume, posit a north–south division of the Mochica domain and polity contrary to the conventional view. These competing views of Mochica sociopolitical organization are critiqued in Chapter 5 of Shimada's *Pampa Grande* volume. G. Bawden points to the sterility of typological thinking in the debate surrounding the nature of the Mochica polity in "The Andean state as a state of mind," *JAR* 45: 327–332 (1989).

Pattern and process in the Early Intermediate Period pottery of the Central Coast of Peru by T. C. Patterson (Berkeley, 1966) is based on his doctoral thesis work and provides settlement pattern data and a detailed ceramic sequence. *The central Peruvian prehistoric interaction sphere* by R. S. MacNeish, T. C. Patterson, and D. L. Browman (Andover, 1975) also discusses changing settlement patterns and coast–highland interaction.

The nature of Nasca sociopolitical organization is still debated; for arguments for state-level integration, see J. H. Rowe, "Urban settlements in ancient Peru," *ÑP* 1: 1–27 (1963) and S. A. Massey's doctoral thesis, *Sociopolitical change in the upper Ica Valley, B.C. 400 to 400 A.D.: Regional states on the south coast of Peru* (Los Angeles, 1986). Evidence for Massey's position is summarized in her aforementioned article in *Paracas art and architecture*, but she does not specify the "states." The chiefdom view is supported by P. H. Carmichael in his examination of mortuary data in "Nasca burial patterns: Social structure and mortuary ideology," pp. 161–187, in *Andean mortuary practice*. It is a summary of his doctoral thesis. H. Silverman reaches the same conclusion in *Cahuachi in the ancient Nasca world*.

A major settlement shift around C.E. 550–600 affecting much of the central Andes is discussed in Chapter 6 of Shimada's *Pampa Grande* volume; "Cultural impacts of severe droughts in the prehistoric Andes: Application of a 1,500-year ice core precipitation record" by I. Shimada, C. B. Schaaf, L. G. Thompson, and E. Mosley-Thompson, *WA* 22: 247–270 (1991); and "Environment and empire: Climatic factors in prehistoric Andean culture change," *WA* 8: 121–132 (1976) by A. Paulsen. The coterminous establishment of a Tiwanaku colony in Moquegua is described by P. Goldstein in "Tiwanaku temples and state expansion: A Tiwanaku sunken-court temple in Moquegua, Peru," *LAAnt* 4: 22–27 (1993) and in his article in the aforementioned *Domestic architecture, ethnicity, and complementarity in the south-central Andes*.

The labor and tributary organization of the north coast cultures has been inferred from construction details. Incisive observations are found in *Archaeological explorations in Peru, Part II: The northern coast* by A. L. Kroeber (Chicago, 1930). M. E. Moseley followed in his footsteps in "Prehistoric principles of labor organization in the Moche Valley, Peru," *AAnt* 40: 191–196 (1975) and "The adobes of Huaca del Sol and Huaca de la Luna," *AAnt* 40: 196–203 (1975) written with C. H. Hastings. I. Shimada's "Organizational significance of marked adobe bricks and associated construction features on the north Peruvian coast" in *Architecture and civilization in the prehispanic Andes*, edited by H. Bischof (Mannheim, Germany, 1997) is a synthesis of the entire north coast situation.

Burial excavations have been a major focus of Central Andean archaeology, and their data have served as a basis for social reconstruction. Samples of scientifically excavated burials of the time period under study in Colombia and Ecuador are still too small.

Ancient burial patterns of the Moche Valley, Peru by C. B. Donnan and C. Mackey (Austin, 1978) is a compilation of photographs and drawings of Mochica, Gallinazo, and Salinar burials excavated at Moche and nearby sites. It offers few contextual and osteological details or analysis.

H. Ubbelohde-Doering's *Vorspanische Gräber von Pacatnamú, Nordperu* presents detailed descriptions by von G. and W. Hecker of Mochica and Gallinazo burials excavated at Pacatnamú. Other noteworthy publications on Mochica burials include "Finding the tomb of a warrior-god" by D. W. Strong *NGM* 91: 453–482 (1947) and "Finding the tomb of a Moche priestess" by C. B. Donnan and L. J. Castillo, *Archaeology* 45(6): 38–42 (1992). Excavations of early Mochica "royal" tombs at Sipán were reported by W. Alva in "Discovering the New World's richest unlooted tomb" *NGM* 174(4): 510–550 (1988) and "New tomb of royal splendor" *NGM* 177(6): 2–15 (1990) and by W. Alva and C. B. Donnan in *Royal tombs of Sipán*. The most complete compilation of Mochica burial data was made by Donnan in "Moche funerary practice" in the aforementioned *Andean mortuary practice*, which is largely descriptive and should be read together with comments by P. J. Lyon and J. A. Brown in the same volume. I. Shimada and T. L. Topic offer social reconstructions based on burial data in the *Pampa Grande* volume and the 1982 article in the *Chan Chan* volume, respectively.

Burials and their grave goods excavated at the major Recuay ceremonial center of Pashash are described in T. Grider's book, *The art and archaeology of Pashash* (Austin, 1978). The broader historical and cultural contexts of Pashash or sociopolitical dimensions of the burials, however, are not made clear.

In addition to the general references already cited, "The Paracas cemeteries: Mortuary patterns in a Peruvian south coastal tradition" by N. Dwyer and J. P. Dwyer in *Death and the afterlife in pre-Columbian America*, edited by E. P. Benson, pp. 145–161 (Washington, D.C., 1975) is useful for understanding the Paracas funerary customs. In all these publications, however, discussion of sociopolitical implications is quite limited.

6

ANDEAN URBANISM AND STATECRAFT,
(C.E. 550–1450)

LUIS LUMBRERAS

This chapter[1] treats the period during which great states appeared in the Andes and urbanism there reached its apex. The information is basically archaeological, although important data also come from sixteenth-century documentary sources. The first part of this process is known as the Middle Horizon (c. C.E. 560–1000); the term "horizon" signals the spread of a typical culture and social organizations across multiple regions. The second is called the "Late Intermediate Period" (eleventh to fifteenth centuries); the term "intermediate" indicates a period of diverse, regional developments between horizon cultures (see Map 6.1). Like the widely diffused culture of Chavín in remote antiquity whose traces make up the Early Horizon (see Chap. 5), the Middle Horizon showed far-flung unifying tendencies. Some of them set precedents for a third unification in the Late Horizon, or Inka era (fifteenth to sixteenth centuries). Like the Early Intermediate that followed Chavín, the Late Intermediate was an era of accentuated variety, sometimes carrying forward and reworking already-ancient cultural legacies.

THE PRECURSORS

During the fourth, fifth, and sixth centuries C.E., each region took on a particular social form, with characteristic linkages among valleys and river basins, different levels of complexity in social and economic organization, and unique ways of managing territory. Clearly the variability of the environment constituted an important factor in this process of regionalization.

The mid–sixth century witnessed an era of serious climatic alterations

---

[1] Translation from Spanish by Eileen Willingham, edited by Frank Salomon.

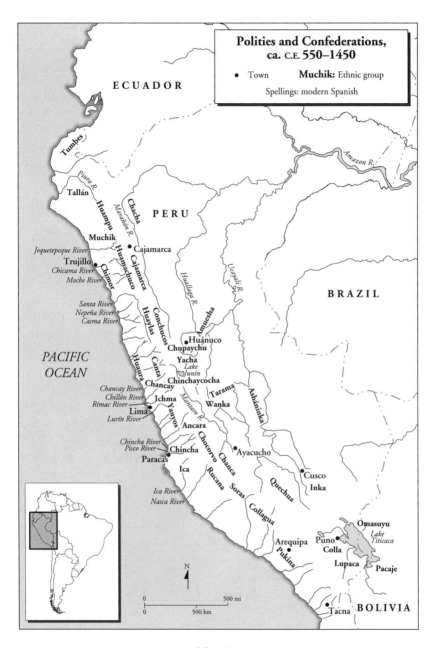

Polities and Confederations, ca. C.E. 550–1450

- Town   **Muchik:** Ethnic group

Spellings: modern Spanish

ECUADOR

PERU

BRAZIL

PACIFIC OCEAN

BOLIVIA

Tumbes

Piura R.

Tallán

Huampu

Marañon R.

Chacha

Muchik

Jequetepeque River

Cajamarca

Trujillo

Chicama River

Moche River

Chinor

Huamachuco

Cajamarca

Conchucos

Huaylas

Santa River

Nepeña River

Casma River

Huallaga R.

Ucayali R.

Amazon R.

Amuesha

Huánuco

Chupaychu

Yacha

Lake Junín

Chinchaycocha

Huaura

Canta

Chancay River

Chancay

Chillón River

Rímac River

Ichma

Lima

Lurín River

Yauyos

Mantaro R.

Tarama

Wanka

Asháninka

Ancara

Chincha River

Pisco River

Chincha

Paracas

Ica

Chocorvo

Chanca

Ayacucho

Rucana

Soras

Cusco

Inka

Quechua

Ica River

Nasca River

Collagua

Omasuyu

Arequipa

Pukina

Puno

Colla

Lake Titicaca

Lupaca

Pacaje

Tacna

BOLIVIA

N

0   500 mi

0   500 km

Map 6.1

in the Andes, which could have led to displacements of populations and to nutritional and social crises of varying magnitude. It seems that in Cusco and the Lake Titicaca area rains fell almost 30 percent below normal levels for about 30 years, between the years C.E. 562 and 594. These conditions undoubtedly affected the normal development of productive activities throughout the entire territory, possibly explaining the general tendency toward changes and dislocations in most of the populations of that period. Although paleoclimatic records indicate continual alterations in humidity throughout the whole Holocene – characterized by periods of drought and also by rains that extended over several years – this 30-year stress was exceptionally long and seemingly intense.

In the southern sierra, two processes that seriously affected the Andes as a whole emerged, although evidently not as direct consequences of such natural events. First was the formation and development of a state that expanded from the southern sierra – modern Ayacucho – throughout the entire territory of the Central Andes. This state is known by the name Wari, and it was one major component of the Middle Horizon. Many of its elements were later taken up by Tawantinsuyu, the Inka state. Another almost simultaneous process was the apogee and expansion of Tiwanaku culture in the Titicaca *altiplano* (high plain). This was the other major component of the Middle Horizon.

Tiahuanaco, or Tiwanaku, had for several centuries already proven successful at exploiting natural resources. (We use the hispanicized spelling Tiahuanaco, which persists as the name of a modern town, as a toponym only. Tiwanaku is the modern archaeological name of the culture and its type.) This regime was affected both by the altitude of the high plateau – more than 3,600 meters above sea level – and by aridity, with desert characteristics becoming more pronounced toward the Tropic of Capricorn in the south, and the Pacific Ocean in the west. The northern basin of the lake up to Tiwanaku times had seen the consolidation of a cultural development that archaeologists have called Pukara (or Pucara), an historical formation characterized by a high level of economic advance. Pukara was sustained by an agriculture based on tubers, high-altitude grains, and camelid (llama, alpaca) livestock production, along with textile manufacturing, complementary forms of extractive exploitation (metals, clays for making ceramics), and hunting and fishing in rivers and lakes. In a parallel direction at the same time, both west and south of the lake, another successful pre-Tiwanaku development materialized, identified with the name Chiripa. In both cases, agriculture played a role of primary importance. From the beginning of the process, agricultural improvement relied on soils readied for cultivation through the construction of raised fields, or *camellones*, in flood zones. Between the third and fourth centuries, both formations reached their highest levels of development. Tiwanaku grew from these roots between the fourth and fifth centuries C.E., a period variously identified as Early Tiwanaku, Qeya, and Tiwanaku III.

The sixth-century environmental crisis found the *altiplano* peoples in the ascendant, with a well-established mixed economy and a characteristic religious style strongly bound to the iconic models that had matured in Pukara, Chiripa, and Qeya. These last two, in turn, had evident connections with the coastal populations (principally Paracas) and those of neighboring sierran river basins. It is likely that peoples throughout the south followed the religious canons expressed iconographically in Paracas (in the first millennium B.C.E.) and in Qaluyu-Marcavalle (Cusco and Puno). These centered around an anthropomorphic image from whose head radiated rays whose ends were faces or figures. When the image is seen full-bodied – in Paracas and Pukara – it holds two staffs, one in each hand, and has wings and complex attributes of felines, serpents, and birds of prey, within an overall anthropomorphic body form. This personage shares attributes with a much earlier Chavín deity, visible on the Raimondi Stela (see p. 444).

It seems that the prolonged crisis of the sixth century imposed a need to amplify and intensify the practices adopted by lakeside inhabitants. They therefore adopted an expansionist policy, increasing agricultural space and intensifying local production, thereby stimulating growth of the already existing urban model. This phase of apogee and expansion, which comprises the "classic" and "decadent" phases of Tiwanaku (IV and V, according to Ponce), took place during the fifth to eleventh centuries C.E. and constituted the south's Middle Horizon.

In that same epoch, farther north, a Horizon culture called Wari (or Huari) expanded from Ayacucho throughout the coast and the sierra of most of Peru. The name Wari comes from an extensive urban settlement located in the Huarpa river basin (25 km north of the present-day city of Ayacucho or Huamanga) in a plateau whose altitude reaches between 2,600 and 3,000 meters above sea level.

Until the first half of the twentieth century, Wari type artifacts found near the Pacific were attributed to Tiwanaku, and their peculiarities were identified as a coastal variant. This style was known fundamentally from ceramic and textile iconography and dubbed "Coastal Tiahuanaco" or "Tiahuanacoide." Nonetheless, because of visible differences from Tiwanaku of the *altiplano*, beginning in the 1930s some archaeologists suggested the name "Wari." In the 1950s, above all thanks to the work of Bennett, the name "Wari" or "Huari" was adopted. The change in name expressed the hypothesis that the Wari type site, far from the coast in the Ayacucho highlands, and not the Titicaca hearth of Tiwanaku, had diffused "Tiahuanacoide." In the 1960s, scholars hypothesized that the archaeological remains bore witness to an empire similar to that of the Inka, but much earlier, with Wari as its capital.

A chronological sequence based on seriation of ceramics was formulated, proposing four phases of the "Middle Horizon." The first two showed evidence of the Wari expansion. In the third and fourth phases, local offshoots remained, of unequal duration in the diverse territories, but all associated with the Wari expansion. Some of these offshoots as well as the main stock are discussed later.

Because the terms of this theory were based on ceramics and iconography, the debate centered on the nature and meaning of pots that were vectors of images. Did they signify (1) a period of great commercial activity, or (2) a proselytizing religious movement lacking a central political power? Some researchers in recent decades in northern Peru hypothesized that urbanism was already well under way before Wari influence on the coast and northern sierra began, and therefore that Wari was not a decisive political presence. Among other reasons, they cited insufficient military artifacts to support a conquest. The information upon which these religious and unpolitical explanations rested is deficient. Extensive information that has come to light in the past two decades makes it possible to justify a third interpretation: forcible Wari expansion throughout a vast space ranging from Cusco to Cajamarca. The Wari expansion coincided with other political movements in the same region and with the simultaneous (but qualitatively different) growth of Tiwanaku to Cusco's south. The pages that follow explore both components of the Horizon in more detail and then turn to the diversity that followed their breakdown.

TIWANAKU: THE CENTRAL TO SOUTHERN ANDEAN NUCLEUS

When the Spaniards arrived in the Andes in the sixteenth century, they recorded a myth placing the origin of the gods and governors of the Inka empire in the (to them) mysterious Lake Titicaca, south of Cusco, at almost 4,000 meters above sea level. From its sacred islands and its waters, the founders of Cusco were said to have arisen, bringing with them the arts of agriculture, weaving, and other elements of a civilizing process. On the lakeshore in Tiahuanaco, one could still see the ruins of strange buildings, different from those of the Inka, and certainly empty before the sixteenth century. The Inka origin myth was then associated with them, and from the sixteenth until the late nineteenth century, Tiwanaku became the symbol par excellence of pre-Inka formation. The debate about the origins of Andean civilization began to take form around Tiahuanaco.

Archaeology was barely in its infancy, so the debate revolved around traditional accounts and philological speculations, which led to discussing the antiquity of Aymara versus Quechua language. Scholars identified Aymara as the language that the Tiwanakans had spoken, and Quechua as the Inka tongue. Max Uhle – also trained in philology but with interest in incipient archaeology – joined the debate examining artifacts that A. Stübel had collected at the site. Uhle proposed an archaeological alternative rooted in the differences in style between artifacts from Cusco and those from Tiahuanaco (Stübel and Uhle, 1894), suggesting that the Cusqueños should be considered a latecoming people. His proofs were not the most decisive. But Uhle's 1896 excavation of the great shrine and temple site of Pacha Kamaq (or Pachacámac) strengthened the point by showing that the Inka buildings there had been built on top of tombs containing objects with "Tiahuanaco" attributes. (The hispano-Quechua name Pachacámac persists as the name of a town. We use Pacha Kamaq as the Quechua name of the ancient deity and cult center.) With this proof – the only one for many years – no one doubted the origin of Tiwanaku in relation to the Inka. However, it was not until the excavations of W. C. Bennett in 1932 at the same site that evidence clarified the sequence of pre-Inka stages in the Peruvian-Bolivian *altiplano*.

Bennett's work raised questions about several of the myths that élite and popular imagination had circulated. Specifically the notion of a Tiwanaku empire had acquired force thanks to Uhle's findings on the Peruvian coast, between Nasca and Moche, during the first six years of this century. Uhle found an iconography that A. L. Kroeber (1944) and his followers called "Tiahuanacoide" or "coastal Tiahuanaco," which was taken as the trace of a Tiwanaku empire, and even as a confirmation of Inka origin myths.

The most recent research proves that such an expansion did occur but in very different terms than traditionally believed. First, it decomposed the Horizon into two separate expansions. In addition to the Tiwanaku expansion, a separate though culturally related and simultaneous one moved from Wari south toward Cusco and also north through various territories including parts of the coast. Meanwhile a true area of Tiwanaku influence covered the extreme southern coast of Peru, from Arequipa to Tacna, northern Chile from Arica to Atacama, the valleys of Cochabamba and the southern *altiplano*, including Oruro and part of Potosí, with less defined connections toward Chuquisaca, Tarija, and the Quebrada de Humahuaca and the Calchaquí valleys in Argentina's Andean margins.

Second, the Tiwanaku process differed from those of the Wari or the Inka. It appears in some places as colonization with stable occupation in agricultural zones in low-lying lands such as Moquegua, and perhaps parts of Tacna and Arica, on the coast. In other territories – such as San Pedro de Atacama and Calama – it suggests the establishment of a stable network of traffic in merchandise, moved by caravans of transhumant llama-drivers through local settlement clusters in the desert oases. The occupation of Cochabamba might have resembled that of the neighboring valleys; and the Tiwanaku influences that can be perceived more to the south, toward Tarapacá and northeastern Argentina, could be extensions of the vast network of exchange built up around the Atacama oasis.

Without dismissing the possibility of the use of some form of violence in the process of occupation of lands or of protection of the caravans, a stronger assumption is that the territory of the Tiwanakan expansion (very differently from Wari) cohered via interzonal complementarity. Tiwanakan culture grew in a region whose economic development required the agricultural integration of the *altiplano* with its eastern and western flanks, and of other forms of complementarity with the deserts and *punas* (high steppes) of the south. According to archeological data, this occurred in differing ways from the beginning of human occupation of the area, with peak periods coinciding with epochs of centralized political organization in the *altiplano*, such as those hegemonized by Pukara and Tiwanaku. One peak of integration occurred in the northern basin of the lake in the first half of the first millennium C.E. The other occurred in the southern basin, after the fifth century C.E. The inhabitants of the *altiplano* were never "outsiders" to coastal-oasis lands; they were always bound up in the same historical project.

Tiwanaku's wide spread depended on its key role in articulation, operating across a difficult landscape. It developed in the widest section of the Andean range, which is also the most arid. Lake Titicaca, at 3,800 meters above sea level, lies in the center of an immense massif more than 4,000 meters above sea level, flanked by the great ranges called the Cordillera Real and the Cordillera Occidental. Their mountains surpass 5,000 and even 6,000 meters. Both toward the south and the north, desert dominates the landscape. Dispersed oases form islands separated by stretches of rock, sand, or salt measuring tens or hundreds of kilometers. Some oases lie in lowlands, where tropical latitude affords a steady warm climate favoring agriculture; others are in the high Andean *puna*, where pastures make a pastoral life possible. Wild camelids (guanaco and vicuña) and the rhea family of American ostriches (*ñandú* and *suri*) also abounded. A very short rainy period reached up to 700 millimeters in the north and 200 millimeters in the southern part of the *altiplano*. Over immense swaths of the desert, no rain ever falls.

The richest agricultural areas of the whole highland territory border Lake Titicaca, especially in the northern (*lago mayor*) and southern (Wiñaymarka) basins, and to some degree, the western edge. There, from the Formative Period onward, an enterprising agriculture took shape combining various cultivation strategies and maximization of water and soil resources. The central problems of cultivation in this region derived from both the altitude and access to water for agricultural usage. Its high and usually rain-scarce location at the edge of the agricultural area allows only a small number of cultigens. And although rainfall is quite limited, all of the precipitation occurs during the short period that corresponds to the southern summer, so that the few all-year watercourses carrying meltoff from the heights become seasonal torrents. When they reach the plains next to the outlet, they inundate the fields and raise the level of the lake. Fields can be flooded, and crops drowned. The extent and intensity of the water rush depend on the volume of rainfall every year, which means that predictions for summer events become a topic of great importance for agricultural practices.

Obviously an agriculture that must deal with problems of both too little and too much water requires complex planning with records of multiyear cycles, corresponding to times of drought and wet periods. These oscillations comprise irregularly spaced periods of between 3 and 12 years. Annual calendric regularities had to be analyzed in the light of these longer, less regular variations. Long droughts, of 3 to 5 years, can be disastrous – as they are today – if they cannot be predicted. In the same way, short wet periods of one or two annual seasons require planned intervention aimed at confronting and benefiting from them. In this sense, specialized water-control installations and procedures were fundamental. So was cultural "software" capable of procuring and storing calendric information, and also of programming and managing the production and use of the reserves and surpluses. Had either been lacking, the *altiplano* agrarian economy would have fallen into a structural precariousness in which only products of the lake (fish, water birds, water plants) or pasturing could bolster subsistence.

Agricultural work itself used relatively simple technical resources, such as raised fields in the floodplains or terraces on mountainous slopes. These tasks can be initiated on an extended household level or with simple cooperation at community level. They do not require functionaries or specialists other than the farmers themselves, although their enlargement may demand more complex technique and management when they become parts of a supracommunal political project.

But agricultural production in Titicaca did not depend solely on the preparation of soil and hydraulic technology, which permit successful programs of productive intensification. It also required the appropriate programming of the processes of planting and harvesting, and short- and long-term planning for events and periods of excess moisture and drought. Such socioeconomic programming became the state-of-the-art productive technology. These activities, different from agricultural work per se, require different instruments and workers. Temple-like installations found from the Formative Period in the *altiplano* (Chiripa, Pukara, Tuma-Tumani) played an accentuated role in the Tiwanaku era. The religious success of such installations and their staff derived more from their effectiveness as guides to production than from myth or popular devotion. They formed the matrix of urban centers. Their regular occupants must have been specialists rather than the peasants who cultivated the surroundings.

In tracing the origin of shrine centers, we are not then dealing with normal rural settlements or villages that grew at the basic pace of demographic increase, but rather with functionally different places housing a concentrated special sector. If this argument is true, Tiwanaku buildings must have served tasks geared fundamentally to calendric production planning, concentration of information and administration, including observatories for learning about cosmic events, storage spaces, and spaces for religious communication. They called together the client population to carry out specialized services, ceremonialized or otherwise. These were permanent settlements, which little by little acquired a clear urban definition. Thus the farming population lived, in each valley, in small clusters of houses or in villages directly associated with farmland but also were connected to local urban nuclei. At the urban level they found specialized services, which in turn depended on a principal center – a capital – namely, Tiwanaku. This implied a pyramidal set of power relations.

The cultivation of raised fields (today called *camellones* or *waru waru*) took ingenious advantage of the flood-prone lacustrine environment. Both in the low zones in the valleys of Tiahuanaco and Catari, and along the western and northern fringe of the lake, swaths of fertilized soil were raised above flood stage by removing soil from adjacent ditches (or swales) and were annually improved by adding silt. The swales made habitat for edible water birds, invertebrates, and fish, and the water's effect as a heat reservoir helped crops endure nocturnal frosts. This technique is common to many other parts of the continent, from Mesoamerica to the Central-South Andes; particularly notable in the Andean environment are the wet zones of the Caribbean coast of Colombia, the Guayas river basin in Ecuador, and the Mojos plains in eastern Bolivia. Platforms of 1 to 3 meters high and 5 to 15 meters wide were usual. Their high level of productivity in the *altiplano* has been confirmed by recent experiments. Plants resistant to the cold and altitude were cultivated there, especially grains such as *quinua* (or *quinoa, kinwa*) and *cañihua* (or *kañiwa*) (*Chenopodium quinoa* and *Ch. pallidicaule*, respectively) and tubers such as the potato (*Solanum tuberosum*) and the ulluku or olluco (*Ullucus tuberosum*). Because the limit for corn cultivation falls between 3,400 and 3,600 meters above sea level, this habitat was not appropriate for it. The raised-field system was abandoned partially beginning in the twelfth or thirteenth century C.E. and completely abandoned from the sixteenth century on.

The agricultural high plain is tiny compared to the vast *punas*, or high semiarid steppes that surround it from 4,000 meters upward. There, cultivation is minimal. But it is a region of valuable natural pasture land, sheltering grasses highly resistant to drastic daily temperature changes, and these grasses nourish camelids both wild and domesticated. Although we do not know the productive capacity of the Titicaca pastures in Middle Horizon times, it is known that during the sixteenth century tens of thousands of animals pastured on the *puna* around Titicaca. The animals provided meat, wool, and hides, as well as fertilizer, and a good fuel in the form of hot-burning, almost smokeless dried dung. If fish from the lake and certain birds are added to all this, it becomes clear that the seemingly bleak land could sustain a considerable population.

Nonetheless, the *altiplano* lacks a set of resources that are found in the surrounding lowlands. Tens and hundreds of kilometers of mostly desert space separate Titicaca from the nearest river-valley agricultural zones, and the valleys from each other. Diversification, therefore, entailed days or weeks of walking. Highlanders did traverse such spaces to obtain corn, fruits, condiments, stimulants such as coca, or perhaps fine woods such as *chañar* from the Tarapacá desert, or semiprecious stones and metals. All of these are "nonessential," to be sure, but they supported social reproduction by contributing to the betterment of the quality of life.

With crops and the protein provided by the camelids and lake fauna, as well as the flora and fauna of the *puna*, lake-basin residents were adequately fed. Thus *altiplano* expansion cannot be explained by sheer subsistence need, although we might be dealing with a strategy aimed at making available "external" products to reinforce subsistence in periods of prolonged droughts, while carrying out a complementary function the rest of the time. In reality it seems that the territorial occupation beyond Titicaca does not correspond to an expansionist model with a political will or origin. Rather the *altiplano* and its area of expansion in the lowlands appear to be parts of a regional economic articulation.

In order to understand the occupation of the coastal valleys, we may turn to evidence of coast–highland articulation in one seaward valley, around Moquegua, always remembering that pre-Tiwanaku occupations of each valley showed their own singularities. In Moquegua the evidence points toward a colonization carried out by migrants from the *altiplano*. It seems to have been a territorial occupation, with Tiwanakan farmers whose settlements were of village-like character, accompanied, in at least one case, by functionaries who worked in a complex of special buildings at the Omo site. Settlers cultivated corn, peppers, cotton, squashes and legumes, and perhaps coca. The occupation of the Cochabamba and Mizque valleys, to the east on the other side of the Andes, was probably above all a quest for maize lands. There agricultural work was less demanding of irrigation, and settlers already knew the relevant seasonal changes.

Urban complexes were a distinguishing feature of the productive infra-structure erected by Tiwanaku. Although the agrarian base required a great deal of work and ingenuity, as a whole it could hardly have equaled the investment in factors of production and workforce necessary to carry out the urbanistic projects such as Tiwanaku or those of its satellite settlements. Tiwanaku's cyclopean stones and gigantic proportions make a statement audible even today about the supreme cultural importance of what went on inside it. There the gods lived and myths were born. Some of them are engraved on the stones of the temples, on the sculptures, the porticos or "gateways," and stone slabs brought from distant quarries. Their songs and festivals are lost but have left traces in the form of ceramics and polychrome weavings bearing emblems that transmitted religious and mythic memory. The gods were the ones who revealed the secrets of time and weather. Their functionaries meticulously recorded signs in the stars and the heavens, the winds, and other natural phenomena. The gods transmitted their power to the functionaries. The latter, in their name, could intervene in collective decisions with all the force of faith and political-religious coercion.

Tiwanaku, according to some scholars, must have housed a population numerous enough to be truly urban between the fourth and tenth centuries C.E. The profile of the city as a cultural center is clear from nondomestic buildings constructed with fine finishes of crafted stone, generally on platforms. But dwellings and utilitarian buildings were made of clay, adobe, or other less durable materials. Their poorer preservation has tended to focus archaeological attention on monuments.

The walls of Tiwanaku's sacred precinct make a titanic architectural impression amid the flat landscape of the Titicaca high plain. The site as a whole is made up of two sections. The main urban nucleus lies to the north, with most of the public buildings. To the south stands the relatively isolated Pumapunku complex, which could have been a temple or special place. It is almost a kilometer away from the center. Especially elegant, Pumapunku is the monument that suffered most from the site's long neglect. All the buildings are oriented on an east–west axis. In the northern section – the principal one – the axis is clearly defined by a corridor that separates the more important buildings. To the north of this road-axis stands the Kalasasaya platform, aligned with those of Putuni and Kherikala, and a large sunken patio (28.5 m in length and 26 m in width) known as the "semisubterranean temple." To the south is the huge tiered platform called Akapana, with six levels and a sunken patio on its eastern edge. Akapana is about 200 meters on each side and 15 meters high. Excavations on the upper platform of Akapana yielded traces of diverse ritual activity. Unfortunately, reports on the excavations of the other platforms are scarce, and inferences about their possible functions rest on what is architectonically visible.

All are agreed in assuming a ceremonial function also for the associated and somewhat smaller (126 m × 118 m) and lower (3 m) platform called Kalasasaya. There, anthropomorphic statues have been found. In the same spot, a famous monolithic portal bears carved imagery of what seems to have been the principal Tiwanaku divinity – a personage seen from the front who carries two rods or staffs, one in each hand. He (or She?) is accompanied by a group of secondary, winged personages, who seem to be in attitudes of adoration. Doubts about the original location of this stone have little justification, although admittedly there is uncertainty about the provenance and original placement of all the structures now on the platform. No such uncertainty attaches to the sunken patio next to the Kalasasaya access-way. It was adorned with numerous sculptures of human heads, each anchored like a nail into the wall of the patio. The center of the patio also contained an immense obelisk-like stone statue, more than seven meters high, apparently associated with another, smaller sculpture from an earlier epoch. The latter bears the image of a personage who had a muzzle that looks like a beard. Without a doubt, all of this is part of a Tiwanakan liturgical paraphernalia.

Putuni, a small platform behind Kalasasaya, is thought to be another temple, and Kherikala is thought to be a "palace" – that is, a living quarters. To the east of the entire complex, at the beginning of the central east–west axis, lies a complex called Kantatayita, with a large carved rock in the center. It too seems to have had a purely ritual role. Living quarters and other structures made of clay were found around all of these buildings. A certain amount of ceramics debris seems to show where domestic activities took place.

In secondary settlements such as Lukurmata, Putuni, or Khonkho, some of the monumental components of the buildings of Tiwanaku recur – specifically, platforms and sculptures with Tiwanaku icons. What spread from Tiwanaku to all of these settlements was this iconography, evidently standardized by a central authority. Wherever Tiwanaku people had some presence, the same occurred in ceramics, textiles, and carved wooden or turquoise objects. Engravings are also found on gold or copper objects from the era.

In sum, the evidence shows a society capable of guiding peoples who lived in an immense, predominantly desert territory toward a productive and distributive project that by all accounts was successful from the fourth to the twelfth centuries C.E. Tiwanaku is identifiable as a population of farmers and herders organized around an élite of specialists who lived in the environs of the southern basin of Lake Titicaca. Their principal center was Tiwanaku itself, in the central valley of the basin, complemented by settlements of smaller size such as Paqchiri and Lukurmata in the valley of the Catari River, or Wankani in the lakeside area of Desaguadero. Their colonies went to the low-lying valleys to the east and west. A network of merchants linked the center with an extensive periphery both to the south and to the east. Connections with the north, beyond the Vilcanota ridge, which had been solid during the Formative Period, were interrupted by the expansion of a parallel state moving into those territories – the Wari power.

THE WARI EMPIRE, PRECURSOR OF THE INKA

Wari's original sphere is the Ayacucho region, a sierran basin occupied before the sixth century C.E. by a prehistorical formation that archaeologists identify as Huarpa. Huarpa was a village-based way of life, still only partially known. In Huarpa times, the entire Ayacucho-Huanta basin was occupied by a large quantity of small villages and hamlets, scattered over the mountain slopes and associated with terraces to provide cultivable space and to forestall erosion. These villages tilled lands up to the edge of the *puna*. Huarpa prehistory is long and probably begins toward C.E. 0. The most numerous settlements were villages built with tree trunks or clay, coexisting with towns made up of rough stone houses, generally round or oval in shape, sometimes accompanied by rectangular structures and platforms that might have had a communal or ceremonial use. The largest sites were near irrigated fields. They do not show evidence of defensive systems or fortifications, which suggests few conflicts.

With the exception of rectangular structures that could have carried out special functions, such as housing the *kuraka* (ethnic lord) or perhaps serving as communal space, the settlements do not reveal significant internal differences. There are no indications of social divisions beyond those that could have existed within the heart of small, simple communities. The stone houses are plain, of homemade construction, with irregular stonework held together by mud. Walls were only a meter high and must have supported conical roofs of branches and straw. The towns were not planned or ordered in any way. Houses follow the irregularities of the terrain, and many of them take advantage of natural rock shelters, closing them off with small joined walls.

Over time one observes growth in the number and size of the settlements, along with an increase in the quality of the constructions. They become bigger, better built, with a predominance of rectangular structures. This indicates an increase of population and internal changes, which permitted some sites to stand out from their contemporaries. One such is Ñawinpukyo, and another is Wari. These inequalities indicate changes in access to subsistence resources, affecting agricultural and livestock production.

Ayacucho's native agriculture fits the "polycyclical" model described by Golte. In such systems, villages optimize the productive value of their labor force by applying it to multiple crops in multiple ecological niches, with staggered peaks of labor demand. The system prioritizes autarchic management of food production, combining small-scale irrigated cultivation with dry land farming – whether in terraces or on flat land – and the raising of llamas and alpacas, in various contiguous ecosystems. This system requires great effort by a constant and numerous workforce, but it did not reward workers richly. Its low agricultural yield only assured a precarious subsistence economy. This was structurally insufficient for sustaining the population required for its production. It certainly did not provide a surplus capable of financing tasks above and beyond subsistence.

Among the options this situation foreclosed were agricultural intensification by means of the creation of suprahousehold agricultural infrastructure with long canals or elaborate irrigation terraces like those found in Cusco. Land suited for irrigation was in short supply, and irrigable areas could be worked only at the communal level. Likewise, laboriously maintained dry terraces, which were made necessary by the danger of flash-flood avalanches, did not justify a greater investment than a domestic or communal effort could provide, even if improved with soil carried from the valley floor. The slopes were so steep that only monumental and costly retaining walls, beyond Huarpa means, would have been required to produce wide terraces. Given these limitations, hydraulic specialists and construction specialists were unnecessary. Work boiled down to indispensable technical tasks solved by community members with experience and ability.

Ayacucho conditions differed from those of the coast, where fundamental requirements for agriculture included a sector of specialists dedicated to creating the infrastructure, planning production, carrying out hydraulic projects, and organizing the workforce, as well as regulating coexistence among distant peoples that shared common interests with respect to water. In Ayacucho, agriculture was principally dry land farming, or small-scale irrigation, with little division of labor beyond what a community could manage, and did not require complex relationships among peoples with common interests in the means of production. To expand the means of production required an increase in population. But at the same time, its low yield dictated a low population.

In the Huarpa era, therefore, we assume a subsistence agriculture, not privileging any special product, and also a self-sufficient manufacture, in which consumption needs could be supplied through barter. If a greater level of efficiency were attempted, all would be caught in a whirlwind of contradictions. If population growth was regulated in order to increase the efficiency of the rate of possible food production, production declined because of an insufficient workforce for maintaining the base infrastructure. In this way, a food crisis would be generated. It would surely sharpen if external factors such as drought, increase in frosts, or hailstorms came into play.

An important compensatory activity for these difficulties was livestock production. Its nutritional function could not have been as important as its worth as the source of primary material – wool, which turns each animal into a means of production rather than a consumption good – and its role in providing llama transport. It was the camelids' wool, along with the diverse dye-producing plants of Ayacucho's dry scrub land, and abundant deposits of good-quality clay, that converted manufacturing into an important component of production. Of course, it could only have compensatory economic capacity if it were possible to integrate it with a distributive network capable of guaranteeing efficient placement of manufactures as goods for exchange.

This was forthcoming, because when Wari emerged from Huarpa one of its standout features was diversified manufacturing and expansive exporting. The most notable industries were ceramics and textiles, but wood, bone, and fine stone products were also important.

The last phase of Huarpa is distinguished by the appearance of polychrome ceramics, which we attribute to an intensification of the contacts with the neighboring valleys of Ica, during Phases 5–7 of Nasca (see Chap. 5). Nasca influences are not perceptible in iconographic or stylistic terms. Nasca's contribution was the pigments for polychrome ceramics,

because until then Huarpa had only used white, black, red, and sometimes Okros orange in ceramic decoration. Apparently late Huarpa Ayacuchans obtained polychrome pigments through barter or direct access
to Nasca sources. This practice intensified in the following phase (Middle
Horizon 1A), which witnessed the formation of the Wari style, when
significant changes in the organizational behavior of the local population
were still rare. (Notable exceptions are Wari and Conchopata, which
underwent a transformation from village-based to urban centers, by evident external contacts.) The other villages, of which 300 are known,
differ from the older ones only in the use of polychrome ceramics
alongside the traditional Huarpa. In addition, in Wari and in Conchopata, a ceramic style related to the cult of Tiwanaku appeared, along with
a clear population growth.

The increased population, polychrome ceramics, and Tiwanaku iconography were parts of a beneficial process of changes in Ayacucho. The
process rested not on agrarian intensification but rather on contacts with
distant territories and developments in manufacturing. Scholars conjecture that at the beginning of the sixth century a series of events induced
the most important towns of the basin, with Wari at their head, to
develop an economic project transcending the structural deficiencies of
the local "polycyclical" autarchy. Its cultural likenesses to Tiwanaku form
a leitmotif examined in the following paragraphs.

Wari's history belongs to the first and second phases of the Middle
Horizon. Patricia Knobloch has divided this period into six subphases:
1A; 1B–early, middle, and late; 2A; and 2B. Of these, the first is basically
local to Ayacucho and corresponds to Phase 8 of the preceding Early
Intermediate period in other part of the Andes. The three 1B subphases
represent the epoch of Wari's great territorial expansion and its greatest
urban, economic, and political development. Phase 2A is still an era of
expansion and development, and 2B encompasses its decline.

A novelty of epoch 1A was the construction in Wari of the only
Tiwanaku-style buildings known outside the Titicaca *altiplano*. It is very
likely that this interval also saw the sculpting of the Wari site's volcanic
rock statues. All, with the exception of a seated feline, represent human
beings. If they were divinities, nothing distinguishes them from humans;
there are three couples who could be culture-heroes like the mythological
couple said to have founded the Inka dynasty of Cusco (see p. 773).

Nasca and Tiwanaku differed from both Huarpa and Wari in the
sphere of production; Nasca was based on irrigation agriculture sup-

ported by fishing and other maritime pursuits, a ceramics enriched by mineral pigments from the desert, and textile manufacturing based mainly on the cotton of its oases. Tiwanaku was sustained by agriculture, with support from livestock production. It practiced a strategy of ecological diversification and articulation among zones. It, too, was associated with a wide spectrum of manufacturing based on access to rich deposits of stone, to the hardwoods of the neighboring southern desert oases, to copper and its derivatives, and so on. By contrast, Wari, like Huarpa, sustained itself through a precariously structured economy. Its manufacturing certainly could not compete with Nasca or Tiwanaku in refinement but was more productive in the local sphere than agriculture. Contacts with Nasca and Tiwanaku therefore cannot be interpreted exclusively as exchange relationships, although surely these were initiated in the Huarpa epoch.

The Tiwanakan-style buildings of Wari were similar to those of Lukurmata and Tiwanaku itself. There is a semisubterranean temple, or sunken patio, and a few chambers or subterranean cavities that duplicate designs at the site of Tiwanaku itself. All of this was built by expert stonecutters with knowledge of Tiwanakan joining, structure, and style. The question is who made them, and how did they appear in Ayacucho?

The Moquegua Valley on the seaward western slope of the Titicaca *altiplano* was occupied continuously by *altiplano* peoples since before C.E. o and certainly during the "classic" period also known as Tiwanaku IV. At some moment, perhaps at the beginning of the sixth century C.E., contemporaneous with Huarpa and Tiwanaku IV, the Ayacuchans entered this valley. Their traces are Huarpa ceramics of the Cruz Pata style, found at Cerro Trapiche. Later, toward the end of the sixth century, in the early phase of Middle Horizon 1B, Waris settled in strategic valley sites: Cerro Baúl and Cerro Mejía, building an urban center of a more formalized style than Ñawinpukyo and perhaps resembling Conchopata or Wari. It broke completely with the Tiwanaku settlement patterns. Goldstein indicates that in the transition from the Omo phase to the Chen phase (Tiwanaku IV to V), in Moquegua, a disjunction arose in the ceramic sequence. According to him it coincided with Wari intrusion. If so, it means that the Wari presence altered the conditions of Tiwanaku existence, perhaps through war. Cerro Baúl is a strongly protected place, fortified with ramparts to reinforce its naturally inaccessible position. Relations with surrounding Tiwanakan populations must not have been peaceful.

It does not seem to be simple coincidence either that in Ayacucho of
that period, Tiwanakan workers participated in the construction of buildings and perhaps in the carving of sculptures of important personages.
Isbell believes that the workforce must have been Tiwanakan but that
the directors of the project were Ayacuchan Wari. It is tempting to
propose the hypothesis that Ayacuchan invaders could have reached as
far as Tiwanaku and brought Tiwanaku stone cutters and sculptors back
to Ayacucho, where they would have participated in the construction of
sacred spaces required, for example, to sacralize and legitimize the new
power, incorporating origin myths that revolved around Lake Titicaca.
Possibly of similar origin are the Tiwanaku iconographic elements in
Wari ceramics and weaving that caused such confusion in the first half
of this century. Analogously, gods and heroes from Titicaca centuries
later legitimated the power of the Inka at Cusco. The Inka also brought
master artisans to Cusco as servitors, so that there they could make what
their state needed.

The Tiwanakan "fashion," however, did not last long in Wari. In the
first epoch, Tiwanakan features were very much sought after, but later
others displaced them. Very quickly, buildings of carved stone were
surrounded and covered by buildings that corresponded to an architectonic model based on walled enclosures. They show large proportions, a
preferably rectangular floor plan, and plastered and painted high walls.
The architectonic plan differed dramatically from that of Tiwanaku and
entailed a whole new urban model. Isbell, Brewster-Bray, and Spickard
and Topic believe that this new architecture could have been learned in
Huamachuco. This is perfectly possible, because in phase IB the Ayacuchans had already reached Huamachuco and could have learned to build
in its local style while integrating what was new with their old traditions.
Nonetheless, the architectonic space has other regional antecedents associated with the Late Paracas phase of the Chincha and Pisco valleys. It is
made up of fenced quadrangular sites, which in conjunction form an
orthogonal urban space. The overall disposition resembles village complexes in these valleys as of the second century B.C.E. to the second
century C.E.

Wari, in short, constituted a synthesis of the advances that the Andean
culture had achieved up to the sixth century, both in the north and
south. Multiple currents converged in a territory where receptivity was
very great. This was so because of a lack of elite traditions strong enough
to reject innovations; on the other hand, Wari welcomed innovations

that favored the advance of their projects of conquest and expansion. Those projects did not include powerful priests, but they did include religion; Wari surely retained traditional gods, but it had no reason to exclude other gods. Through eclectic coordinating practice, Wari began many of the institutions that later sustained the Inka empire.

Wari had a precariously structured food-producing base. It could be partially reinforced by livestock production, but a durable solution was only possible by developing manufacturing and trade as dominant activities. A first priority, therefore, was access to primary materials. Another was the building of a trade network centered on the structural needs of Ayacucho. This required a redistributive strategy rather than a strictly mercantile one.

Artisan production occurred primarily on the local level, yielding goods for domestic use (clothes, ceramics, and simple adornments). A second level was specialized, geared toward the production of luxury or mass-produced goods. This level departed from the domestic sphere, allowing the separation of some workers from their communities, and turning them toward specialized productive tasks. This does not necessarily imply the formation of a different social class. Judging by the materials used and the standardized codes of forms and decoration, it seems that the base units of production were workshops, overseen by masters or officials specialized in quality control and productive flow.

The availability of primary materials for manufacturing imposed at least three levels of work. The first was dedicated to bringing in local factors of production at domestic level. The second was geared toward tasks beyond those of the household unit – for example, extracting local or regional factors of production for dyeing, and mining of metallic or nonmetallic minerals (which might imply the need for bartering at the regional level). The third was directed toward attaining factors of production rare or nonexistent at local level. It involved exchange activities or extractive work in distant territories.

The first level could be resolved by household units directly; the second and especially the third levels needed an extradomestic work sector, and extraeconomic supports (military or ideological) to assure success.

The economic success of this chain of labor did not depend on its efficiency but rather on shrewd choices about who would receive the supply of exchange goods, and on establishing some form of mediation in relationships with recipients. This mediation – more political than economic – set the rules of the game between the Wari and other peoples, permitting wide and sustained circulation of prestige goods and agricultural products. Access to food goods would be assured. Manufacturing could be expanded or limited to determined items, and – as actually occurred – the laborious Ayacuchan dry agriculture could be abandoned. Wari people then worked only irrigated zones or those that were not demanding of low-profit infrastructure. This strategy held no guarantee of stability, because everyone was free to participate in or stay out of the give and take of supply and demand. Wari could not reliably prosper in the context of societies where all parties strove for autarchy. A guarantee of sustained stability, with direct benefit for the promoting agent, was only possible through a redistributive system, managed from the promoting center. It would utilize the traditional resources of reciprocity and complementarity, legitimated by a state, and reinforced by a powerful military apparatus and a solid religious base.

For these reasons, Wari had to construct an ever-widening strategy of conquest, finally consolidating an imperial state. Wari conquest was initiated in the south and later continued toward the center and north. The oldest evidence comes from the valleys of Ica, but the route seems mostly to have followed the territory committed to "polycyclical" agriculture, from Cusco and Cotahuasi in the south, to Huamachuco in the north, extending also westward and downward toward neighboring coastal valleys. This agrarian conquest strategy yielded excellent results in Cusco, the Mantaro Valley, and the Callejón de Huaylas (an intercordilleran region of central Peru). The evidence indicates an intensification of agriculture in conquered territories. Even with an agriculturally based state revenue, Wari continued to rely on extension of its manufacturing production.

We assume that the economic scheme originated in order to mobilize the workforce for agricultural intensification in the conquered territories, the products being in part directed toward state revenue earmarked for Ayacucho's capital and the capital's redistributive obligations on behalf of the state. This redistribution must have included a quota for buildup of state manufacturing, necessarily of a prestigious and privileged nature.

The best known of these manufactures was ceramics. Wari characteristic traits are multicolor design and fine finish. Wari pottery consists predominantly of small bottles and vessels, along with large and small bowls for food and drink. There are also large amphoras and urns, frequently associated with ceremonial use and as containers for grains, cloth, and certainly drinks. Polychrome pottery had been introduced throughout the territory before Wari, but it was then associated exclusively with Nasca and Tiwanaku. It seems that in the first era of expansion, 1B, only one or two of the Ayacuchan styles spread. But their example stimulated alternative local production, reworking the polychrome technique and some Wari resources, forms, and decorative designs. There arose a polychrome "fashion" including styles such as the Nievería in Lima, Mochica-Wari on the northern coast, and Santa in the Callejón de Huaylas and the neighboring valleys, among others. In Nasca, an original home of multicolor pottery, sierran standards took hold in the period known as Nasca Phase 9. Everywhere there was an active process of change in ceramics leading to the decline of traditional styles and procedures and the birth of new ones.

The new pottery took forms and some motifs from Wari ceramics, but it owed more to Wari technical resources of mass production, such as the "hand wheel" and molds to make plates or pots previously hand-shaped. At the end of the Wari epoch, polychrome ceramics disappeared, but these methods of production remained.

Textile production followed similar lines. The most significant Wari imprint lay in the prestige of the tapestries produced in workshops, the use of wool, and the large number of dyes. State weaving was exquisite. Surely it was one of the most important resources for communicating the dominant ideology. Two or three styles of élite Wari weaving existed, and the industry made varied use of almost all the techniques known in the Andes, from tapestries and brocades, to gauzes and netting, to plumed shawls, fabrics painted in positive or negative, and "similivelour." Weavings were multicolored, typically with geometric designs. Textile polychrome is associated with livestock production, because wool dyeing is technically simpler than cotton dyeing.

Another facet that stands out is varied production of ornamental or liturgical objects made of fine hardwoods, rare and showy stones (turquoise, chrysocolla, lapis lazuli, quartz, obsidian, and others), shell, horn, or bone, and to some extent metal, although items made with metal are not well documented. Craftsmanship in semiprecious stone seems to have stimulated much activity. In Wari sites there are lapidary workshops with many remains, especially of turquoise and lapis lazuli. This implies a need for travel from Ayacucho to distant places where the raw material is found, such as Moquegua or even the farther southern desert. The places show evidence of Wari presence.

But if manufacturing played a transforming role from the strictly technological and economic point of view, it is necessary to point out that its function was above all political. It encoded and enacted principal relationships that followed state ideology. Its imagery expressed a system of beliefs that sustained the legitimacy of the established power. For this reason the extensive diffusion among the local elites of fine polychrome ceramics and high-quality weavings also diffused the origin myths, the rules of conduct, and the sanctions that the religion – the divine force – established.

Both the agricultural and manufacturing tasks imposed by the Wari were possible because they were able to organize a centralized state, with a capital city and a variety of settlements hierarchically arranged. They were connected by a network of roads and obviously by a strong army. The military theme is central to Wari iconography, and it was made real in a tendency to fortify its settlements.

Wari, in short, was an urban formation that grew out of centralized power. Its most characteristic settlements were those that arose from the central political will. One can almost assert that all Wari urban settlements – with the exception of Wari itself – responded to that central will. That is to say they were extensions of the state and not products of their inhabitants' endogenous economic development. They formed part of a specific political project.

The city of Wari was unique because of its size, the size and quality of its buildings, and the high concentration of economic activity associated with it. The development of the city, however, does not appear to have advanced in the theocratic or ceremonial direction that it had appeared to be taking when it was just emerging from Huarpa under Tiwanaku stimulus. It seems that the contrary occurred. If indeed its growth denotes a constant adjustment of the urban space to the continual changes and innovations associated with conquests, the rectangular walled buildings – the "palace" type as opposed to temples – became its architectonic standard, especially during the 1B phases, when the orthogonal design of an urban model forced the remodeling of certain parts of the city, as well as its enlargement. Several buildings had to be demolished or placed on top of other constructions. The buildings appear hierarchical and functionally diverse. This is the period that witnessed the construction of the greatest part of the Wari citadels and palaces, over the huge distance from Cajamarca to Cusco, all following one underlying orthogonal plan. The city of Wari stopped functioning in the

2B period, leaving large new buildings that remained partially completed. All this shows that it was a city born of an economic-political project and destined to die with it.

The archaeologically visible city of Wari as unearthed by Isbell and others is very complex, just as complex as its history. Buildings of different styles are found, many of them readapted, superimposed, and enlarged. It has a central nucleus with large buildings that have not been examined well enough to define their function. During excavations done by Gary Vescelius on the northeastern side of the city, large manufacturing workshops were found. Workshops also turned up in several complexes of the "citadel" type, including some circular structures with stone rings inserted in the walls in such a way as to suggest textile workshops. (The rings would have been anchors for backstrap looms.) The site yielded an abundance of debris from the carving of turquoise, lapis lazuli, and obsidian, as well as innumerable fragments of ceramics, molds, and potters' tools. Other buildings are linked to religion. Many were surely living quarters and granaries connected to administrative or governmental functions.

In the 1B phase an architectonic and urbanistic style arose that was a product of contact with Huamachuco, Moche, Lima, and Recuay as well as of the singular development of the state. Its constructions were made of fieldstones of irregular size and form, locally accessible, arranged with double walls and with clay mortar. The urban design – wherever construction was carried out according to a plan – was rigidly orthogonal and agglutinative. Walled cities were built in this uniform style, sometimes far from the capital, examples being Pikillaqta in Cusco and Viracochapampa in Huamachuco. Older and less defined examples of the same phenomenon are found at Cerro Baúl in Moquegua and Honko Pampa in the Cordillera Blanca. Sometimes large isolated works, somewhat castle-like, were constructed in the country. These "citadels" of intermediate rank include Azángaro in Huanta and Jincamoqo in Lucanas. Many of these stand at the upper ends of coastal valleys and in the high parts of the sierran river basins. These walled settlements, with internal divisions of standardized size, follow a rigid orthogonal pattern without exception and without regard for accidents of terrain.

One of the orthogonal Wari building types is a walled structure – usually square – constructed by the simple joining of four very high walls to create a free space in the center. Parallel to the outer walls were built inner walls that formed long passageways or "galleries." When these were divided by transverse walls, they created rectangular spaces – that is, interior rooms. The structural problem of reinforcing these immense walls was resolved many times by tying the corners with thick ropes made of plant material. Another way of "tying" was with beams placed at two or three levels. Wooden cross-trunks that rested on rocks protruding from the walls yielded passageways or galleries with two or even three floors. According to McEwan these square structures, which he describes as "type A" in Pikillaqta, were mainly living quarters, with space for collective cooking and an extensive central patio available for multiple daily activities. McEwan indicates that several of these structures, with better finishes and other singular details, may have sheltered privileged people. In some places, such as Wari Willka in the Mantaro Valley, the only known large structure is of this type. It was obviously associated with administrative and living functions and perhaps religious ones, too. Dozens of them are found in Pikillaqta. Several other examples of this style occur in Honko Pampa.

After Wari, Pikillaqta is the next largest city. Its ruins reflect a monumental accomplishment, with walled access roads, ceremonial spaces, and a local environment evidently shaped to the economic and political demands of Wari. Pikillaqta is a formally simplistic urbanistic project, like the villages of Chincha and Pisco at the beginning of the Christian era, although its functioning may have been very complex. Pikillaqta makes up an aggregation of square structures, each with a central patio. A few avenues separate sectors. Four large sectors may be distinguished in the central urban nucleus, apart from the *canchones* (large open spaces) that surround it and that could have served for llamas or for disposing the city's waste. The northern sector, or sector 1, seems to have been exclusively residential and seems linked to a "common" class of people. The central sector, or 2, contains buildings that are hierarchical and that apparently housed people from at least two different class ranks. It is also possible that several of these palace-like structures had public and not just residential functions. The southern sector, or 3, shows an immense plaza or open rectangular space, with some houses and corrals, or *canchones*. Finally, sector 4, to the west, besides a few rectangular *canchones*, contains more than 500 small chambers, all of the same size and form (about 4×3 m), thought to be granaries. Remains of domestic use have been found in their interiors, which indicates that at some point they could have been used as living areas or shelters. But this is not likely to have been their original purpose, because the domestic remains could well reflect only temporary use.

The only settlements that do not follow these rigid patterns are rural ones. In all cases these continued traditional patterns predating Wari. In some cases, like those of the Chicha/Soras Valley, it seems that the Wari inhabitants began a sedentary tradition that had not existed earlier, with permanent villages of an agglutinative type, similar to those the Ayacuchans had built in the Huarpa epoch. The same may be said of the Cotahuasi region and many other territories occupied by highland shepherds and farmers. Arrival of Wari power did introduce important changes, especially by creating a whole new agricultural zone consisting of terraces for cultivating maize. Nonetheless, apart from the state settlement of Jincamoqo, villages remained stable.

Reaction to Wari influence was diverse in conquered regions, depending on whether the zones had seen a previous urban development or not. Of course (as occurred later with the Inka), in areas such as the coastal valleys, where a vast developed urban infrastructure had already existed, Wari installations like those built in the sierra were not necessary. Existing facilities were used, adapting them to Wari needs and introducing only what was necessary for Wari purposes. In this way, syncretic settlements were formed, with a considerable weight of non-Wari technical and urban resources. Examples include Honko Pampa and Willka Wain in the Callejón de Huaylas. The large adobe town of Cajamarquilla on Lima's modern outskirts shows a markedly Wari historical filiation. "Intrusive" Wari buildings or services were sometimes erected in non-Wari urban settlements, such as the presumptive intrusions in Pacha Kamaq and Maranga in the valleys of Lima, those of Marca-Huamachuco, and the seeming Wari interventions in the Huaca de la Luna at Moche on the northern Peruvian coast (see Chap. 5).

Occupation of the territory entailed a network of roads like those described by Schreiber, an extensive infrastructure of terraces and irrigation works, and ritual burials such as those of Pacheco in Nasca, Ayapata in Huancavelica, Maymi in Pisco, and La Victoria in Ocoña, all comparable with the several burials of Conchopata in Ayacucho. Wari cemeteries also exist at Pacha Kamaq and at Tambobamba in Ayacucho.

A warlike state-building élite held power. Armed leadership must have arisen from the necessity of guaranteeing the traffic of goods between Ayacucho and the Ica valleys, or of protecting workers seeking factors of production outside their territory. The commissioning of professional military personnel was unnecessary. Military functions went to Huarpa ethnic lords or some group of warrior specialists comparable to the *quechas* of the Colombian Muisca. A Huarpa tribal confederation could have underwritten the power of warrior leaders. Within it the greater wealth of the Wari and Huamanga zones could have played an important role in promoting their respective military figures. Their incursions outside the Ayacuchan ambit appear from the start to have occurred in the course of war.

This sociological sketch is speculative, but the evidence does not allow many other possibilities. There were two social classes, one of common people and another of militaristic and managerial élite supported by religious authorities. The military élite arose without direct connection to the cult, unlike what must have occurred in Moche or Tiwanaku, where priests occupied the key position. The sacralization of power and its consequent legitimation appear as a progressive syncretism between local ideological sources, related to Nasca and constantly enriched by relationships with the valleys of Ica, and the ideologies of Tiwanaku and other peoples, with whom the Ayacuchans entered into contact. Elite ceramics and textile art displayed an iconography that changed from phase to phase. It reflected a process of constant ideological adjustments, while retaining allusions to Tiwanaku precedents. Initially limited to an ornamental geometric iconography, Wari design added figures and symbols linked to the sea and to the earth, and finally introduced the images of a central divinity with associates and human beings.

This principal Wari personage is a being with a semirectangular head, seen from the front. Rays project outward from it. When seen in full-body form, the god holds a staff or rod in each hand. This deity matches the image on distant Tiwanaku's so-called *Puerta del Sol* ('Gateway of the Sun'). Both the principal god and the "angels" are themes that the Wari for a time reproduced in state textiles. In Phase 1 the Wari textiles approximated Tiwanaku patterns, but less so in phase 2, and they disappear from the Wari iconographic corpus later on. It was probably the image, not the core concept, that originated with Tiwanaku, because the same basic deity has more general iconographic precedent as far back as Chavín and also the pre-Tiwanaku Pukara culture.

This staff-bearing god could well have originated on the south coast, where Cordy-Collins associates it with cotton and the sea. If we remember the longstanding relationships linking Titicaca, Cusco, and Ayacucho to the south-coastal Paracas culture, it should not surprise us that during this entire time – which begins at least in the first millennium B.C.E. – the cult of the staff god spread far and early. In the *altiplano* it could well be associated with Lake Titicaca and livestock and agricultural production. In Wari it is associated iconographically with maize and other plants. It seems to be a god of agriculture and water, perhaps the same one whom the Inka later called Wira Qucha.

Wari's political project relied on two other infrastructures: roads and information systems. The road system was probably well developed; if we reconstruct paths connecting the principal Wari settlements, the road network appears to have reached as far as Cajamarca in the north and Cusco and Arequipa in the south. A large part of it must have been incorporated into the *Qhapaq Ñan*, or royal road of the Inka. The information system used the oldest known *khipus*, or knotted-cord records. Wari *khipus* described by Conklin differ from Inka ones insofar as they register data on cords not with knots but with windings of many-colored thread.

The Wari empire began to decline around the tenth century C.E. Its duration was hardly a period of stability; many groups seem to have fought their way loose of domination. But its epoch of expansion and dominion did achieve its goal of unification, and Wari decline marked the beginning of a new regionalization in the Central Andes.

THE REORGANIZATION OF THE ANDEAN PEOPLES, TENTH TO THIRTEENTH CENTURIES C.E.

We turn now to the Late Intermediate. With Wari, the urban pattern of life became generalized, but in a new version of the city. Ayacuchan "lay" urbanism was less centered on temples and religious spaces than on palaces, workshops, and living quarters with defense systems. "Lay" cities or urbanizations appeared in places where they had not existed earlier; and where theocratic urbanism had existed, settlement designs were modified.

The expansion of the Wari system, paradoxically, led to the liquidation of Wari's economic and political project, as empire and as city. In agriculturally rich zones like the larger coastal river valleys, cities grew rapidly and generously. The urban system in force during Wari occupation (Phases 1 and 2 of the Middle Horizon) continued to exert power even more markedly, in phases 3 and 4, but now free from direct Wari pressure. Instead they were connected by the systems of regional articulation that are discussed shortly. When Ayacucho lost its military and ideological power, for whatever reason, other systems of regional articulation favored the growth of divergently urbanizing social forces.

The urban system met with great success on the Pacific coast, where products from the sea, the valleys, and the desert were traded along overland links or by navigation. Long-distance traffic satisfied demands for luxury items but was not vital to the survival of these peoples. This made the rapid growth of coastal cities possible. The same did not occur in the sierra. There many populations sloughed off Wari urbanism, and as the political axis imposed by Wari crumbled, communal forms of articulation with village-like characteristics were resumed. The eleventh through thirteenth centuries C.E., corresponding to Middle Horizon 3–4, saw the abandonment of many Wari settlements or their readaptation to local purposes. In a large part of the sierra, perhaps with the exception of Cusco, there are no indications of an alternative large-scale political project. Moreover, one notes a tendency toward local circumscription, with fortified village settlements founded on high-altitude agriculture or on simple reproduction of "polycyclical" agriculture.

During Middle Horizon 2 (ninth through eleventh centuries C.E.), coastal cities grew to differing sizes, depending on the possibilities of their local or regional economic circuits. As coastal groups weakened the Wari political controls that had become obstacles, some Wari-based economic ties had to be broken. Wari, it seems, had hegemonized the supply of certain prestige primary materials, such as pigments for polychrome ceramics. For peoples of the northern coast or sierra, competing with such a hegemony was very costly because they were far from the sources of primary materials. After Wari they tended to abandon polychrome technology in pottery and return to pre-Wari productive habits, better suited to accessible resources. Archaeologists, following Uhle, identified these residual post-Wari styles, which insisted on using three and even four colors in the ceramics, with very poor results, as "epigonal." Post-Wari textile production on the coast, consisting almost exclusively of cotton, also shows a decrease in the quality of colors.

After a few years – we do not know how many – the city of Wari was abandoned. Ayacucho had already lost even the productive infrastructure that the Huarpa had constructed over centuries; the area was left destroyed and desolate. Peasants took refuge in high areas and did not undertake new projects of agricultural development. Economy returned to a more pastoral than agricultural rhythm. Their settlements appear marked by signs of war. Village living quarters on the mountain heights acquired roughly made fortification walls. The economy seems to have been one of camelid herding with support from dry-land subsistence farming.

Wari had exerted only a brief presence along the northern coast, perhaps limited to part of Phase V of the Moche culture, a time period perhaps equaling a generation or one or two political reigns. However, it was a period of great and important changes in the northern population. According to Schreiber, Moche then received imports linked to the Ayacuchan Wari style, more than to the long-familiar coastal one steadily connected with Pacha Kamaq and his cultic sites. The northern pole of power seemingly moved from the valleys of Trujillo to those of Lambayeque, perhaps because of war or the economic supremacy of the latter (see Chap. 5). This shift very shortly became associated with a notable northern development of irrigation infrastructures.

During the thirty, fifty, or perhaps more years that the Wari presence lasted in the old Moche world, much changed, including the urban model of life. A few southern beliefs and practices acquired prestige, as nearly as we can deduce from the strange and new mythological personages in the northern iconography. Gone were the artistic and artisan models of the old lords of Moche. They were replaced by a system organized around mass production of consumption articles. After the Moche V period, which likely coincides with Middle Horizon 1, the visible aspects of Moche, such as ceramics, radically abandoned their traditional models. Wari "epigonals" such as tricolor ceramics, which cover the period of Middle Horizon 3 and 4, arose in association with other local styles.

According to the available evidence, long before Wari declined, during Middle Horizon 2, a regional state was consolidated in Lambayeque, now identified with the name "Sicán." Its wealth and capacity for large agricultural and industrial projects reflect the high agrarian production of the Lambayeque valleys, and also a generous supply of metal. What seems to have been its principal city, the complex of Batán Grande, in many respects resembles the older center of Pampa Grande, dating to the Moche V period.

Sicán or Lambayeque must have been organized at the beginning of Middle Horizon 2, a little before the decline of Pampa Grande. It is assumed that the polity (chiefdom, kingdom, or confederation) of Lambayeque was consolidated little by little. In the middle phase of Sicán – which must correspond to Middle Horizon 3–4 – we find along with a notable growth in urbanism an enlargement of agrarian infrastructure. Indeed it yielded the greatest single achievement of prehispanic water engineering, the multiriver canal system that turned the whole area from the Reque to La Leche rivers into a single greater Lambayeque irrigation valley. Batán Grande was the urban center that acquired greatest prominence during Middle Sicán, with immense adobe buildings. Batán Grande's cultural profile owes much to both Moche traditions and Wari. Its urban plan is closer to the Moche V city of Pampa Grande than to the "lay" Wari model. Batán Grande's strong emphasis on large platforms with almost vertical ramps, and the use of adobe with marks registering labor teams' respective contributions to sacred construction, reveal the force of the local theocratic sector. Also within the Moche precedent is the considerable use of exotic raw materials in manufacturing: turquoise and lapis lazuli from the south, emeralds and *Spondylus* shells from the north, feathers from jungle birds, and so on. However, other customs such as burying the dead in squatting position recall Wari more than Moche.

The truly novel feature in the development of Batán Grande was a spectacular production of copper for all types of utensils and adornments. One fascinating product is the so-called playing cards (*naipes*) made of copper. These are flat sheets some 5 to 7 centimeters long, in shapes resembling small hatchets. They are found in tied packets, generally as funeral offerings. Other similar objects, found in the Milagro phase of the Ecuadorian region of Guayas, are known as "axe money" though they are actually far too thin, soft, and dull to cut anything. Sometimes the packets group these objects in multiples of ten. They could have been units in the circulation of copper through what is known mineralogically to have been an extensive network. In Batán Grande, Shimada found evidence of copper work at all stages from mining through refining, smelting, and shaping.

A related reorganization must have happened to the south of Moche, in the valleys of Santa, Nepeña, Casma, and perhaps Huarmey. There Wari had made itself felt in a drastic way. Moche powers were occupying these valleys when the sierran conquest took place, and Wari became overlord to the overlords. In this region new urban design was instituted. It went with a large growth in population and production, both of which had been losing ground in the lesser valleys since the Formative Period. All the archaeologists who have studied these valleys agree that population reached its prehispanic maximum in this period, with the full occupation of agricultural zones, beaches, and fishing coves. A strong net of intervalley roads existed, and its extensions also articulated contacts with the sierra. Although our knowledge is weak, it appears that during this time sustained cultural unity developed between the valleys of the coast and the Callejón de Huaylas. This lasted until the era of the "Tricolor ceramics," which must correspond to Phase 4 of the Middle Horizon (twelfth and thirteenth centuries C.E.).

At almost the same time as the kingdom of Sicán was formed in Lambayeque, between Chicama and Casma another culture entity was being formed; Wilson calls it the "White-Black-Red State," in reference to its dominant ceramic adornment. Clearly the Wari impact was much stronger here than in Sicán. Either Wari lasted longer here, or it met with more receptivity. Ceramics correspond to the style that was labeled "Epigonal or Northern Tricolor." Urban settlements such as Galindo, a settlement of Middle Horizon 1–2 in Moche, had fewer traditional elements from the northern coast than Pampa Grande or Batán Grande. The area of domain stretched at least from Casma and maybe Huarmey to the valley of Chicama. Its "capital" could have been in Casma. The dispersion of "tricolor" ceramics is uniformly evident in this stage of Middle Horizon 3–4, but conditions causing its diffusion are not clear yet. Wilson's hypothesis of a centralized state, though still incompletely supported, is the only one that attempts to give an historical explanation. After the Wari incursion during Middle Horizon 1–2, and after the abandonment of Galindo, a serious political disarticulation took place in the Moche Valley. The area was only reunified with the formation of the kingdom of Chimú. For the time being the southern valleys were left as politically autonomous, essentially rural, territories. Ceramics of this hypothetical "White-Black-Red State" also occur in the site of Chan Chan, where north coast urbanism and statecraft took on its most spectacular expansionist momentum.

THE YUNKA PEOPLES AND THE KINGDOM OF CHIMOR

The name Chimú, or Chimor, attaches to a major post-Wari social formation arising after the Middle Horizon in former Moche lands –

namely, the Trujillo valleys – between the twelfth and thirteenth centuries C.E. It expanded to other valleys of the north and south during the thirteenth and fourteenth centuries.

During their first incursions – the early sixteenth century – Spaniards heard news about a powerful "kingdom" or "lordship" named Chimo or Chimor, with its seat in the valley of Moche or Santa Catalina. Sixteenth-century chroniclers and Church records written under Archbishop Toribio Mogrovejo give the Chimú culture, though prehispanic, a place in the document record. Chroniclers, historians, officials, and travelers who knew Peru in the seventeenth century still had the chance to learn much about its culture. Especially noteworthy are references by Garcilaso de la Vega and Father Antonio de Calancha. Also from this period comes the only known grammar of the "Yunga" (Yunka, i.e., coastal or tropical) language, extinct today. It was written by the parish priest of Reque, Fernando de la Carrera.

The immense wealth found in northern tombs stirred a frenzy of Spanish looting starting shortly after 1532. Indeed, *huaquería* (treasure hunting) was until recently the principal source of knowledge about the area. At the most famously rich tombs, which are also the most looted, archaeologists were able to find only bare remains. The immense but ill-documented collections built up by looters and their customers form rich resources for imagery and design of artifacts but are lacking in contextual information. In the first third of the twentieth century, pioneer archaeologists, especially Uhle and above all Kroeber and Bennett, began the scientific study of whole sites.

Archaeological data have confirmed in large measure the sixteenth-century writers' claims. Chimú – whose archaeological "signature" is a predominantly black sculptural ceramics, which continued in monochrome the old Moche tradition – did, as Spaniards thought, develop in the Trujillo valleys and later spread to the north and south. The "nuclear" territory of the Chimú is the zone stretching between the valleys of Chao and Chicama. The area of expansion goes from the valley of Santa to perhaps Supe or Chillón in the south, and from Jequetepeque to Tumbes in the north. Different languages or dialects were spoken over this area, but archaeological remains reveal common customs within a margin of variation. A few references here and there claim Chimor advanced over the Cajamarca sierra. Although there are some Chimú artifacts in such areas, and others even farther north, among the Manteños of Manabí, Ecuador, the signs are that these extensions reflect exchanges or exports.

The inhabitants of Chimú territory in the fifteenth century spoke a language that was totally different from Quechua or Aymara, the two large linguistic trunks of the Central Andes. It was identified as the "Yunka language" by Quechua speakers, but this term identifies only a linguistic family and not the variety of languages or dialects spoken in each of the valleys or in sections of them. In the Moche Valley, the Chimú nucleus, the language spoken was locally called Quingnam according to Father Calancha, who also indicates that it was known from Pacasmayo to Lima. He also maintains that farther to the north another language was spoken, called Muchik (basically in the Lambayeque valleys), and finally, in Piura, at modern Peru's northern edge, Sec was spoken. All of these, according to Calancha's commentaries, seemed to be dialectal variations of one language. This language may also include the obscure "fishing language" (*la [lengua] pescadora*), which seems to have been associated with the fishermen of the coves of Pacasmayo and Chicama (Magdalena de Cao). We do not know how extensively this language or languages diffused before the Chimú expansion. Some of its extent overlays the apparently earliest hearth of Quechua.

The Chimú expansion, then, can be studied in at least four different sections. One is linked to the Chimú proper, speakers of Quingnam. A second concerns the Lambayeque people, who spoke "Muchik." A third covers the Piura population (called "Tallanes") who spoke "Sec." A fourth comprises the perhaps autonomous valleys to the south of the Santa River, as far as the northern periphery of Lima, where the bearers of the Chancay culture dwelled. These last also reputedly knew Quingnam. Differences were related to their respective material conditions of production – namely, water, soils, and population.

Peru's coast desert littoral widens to the north of the Santa Valley. Topography becomes flatter and coastal ranges are no longer found. More isolated desert hills appear, such as Campana in Trujillo, Puémape in Pacasmayo, or the Eten promontory, near the port of the same name. The widest, flattest part of the whole coast begins to the north of Jequetepeque, from the La Leche River onward. One effect of this widening is the absence in the north of the so-called *lomas*, a fog-moistened vegetative formation that lends the southern coast a veil of seasonal greenery suitable for pasture. In the north, Pacific mist and drizzle does not penetrate far enough inland to condense on the Andean slopes; on the other hand, summer rains occur at intervals of 6 to 12 years or more, regulated by the fluctuation of the Humboldt marine current known as "El Niño." North or south, vegetation grows densely only on river banks. Some appears around underground springs. Agriculture depends fundamentally on irrigation. Spectacular successes in ancient water management permitted the extension of green and highly productive areas partway across what would naturally be desert plains.

The fact that fresh water comes only from runoff from the mountains made the management and administration of this flow into the most important activity in the life of the coastal peoples. Everything except maritime extraction depended on it. This set a different baseline from that of highland "polycyclical" agriculture, such as that which generated the Wari. It does have a partial highland analogue in the lakeside agriculture that Tiwanaku administered.

The north coastal economy rested on extensive irrigation, with hydraulic works of monumental size. The already-mentioned Lambayeque multiriver system, begun before Chimor, united the canals of Taymi, Racarumi, Chaname, Talambo, and others to create an irrigation district of up to 100,000 hectares. The canals make a chain some 100 kilometers long. This great system had a later rival in the canal of La Cumbre, connecting the valleys of Chicama and Moche. Smaller projects created the Fortaleza-Pativilca-Supe system, between Lima and Ancash, and the Chillón-Rímac in Lima.

The La Cumbre canal, which seems to have been a Chimú state project, runs about 84 kilometers. Its intake lies about 44 kilometers inland from the mouth of the Chicama, at 350 meters above sea level. Specialists debate the operation and construction of this immense canal because apparently it never became completely operative. Some see it as a giant boondoggle to keep the labor force occupied. Others suspect errors in the engineering calculations. For whatever reason a large part of La Cumbre collapsed.

According to Ortloff, the archaeological remains of the north coast hydraulic system reflect the needs of a gradually and continuously increasing population with growing social complexity. The works required a progressive increase in specialized technical knowledge. Apart from the possibility that some projects failed for technical reasons, one may infer that the northern coast's economic development needed a central power able to control irrigation, including engineering, labor management, and use rights. The enlargement and coordination of the workforce, obviously bringing together units much larger than minimal communities, implied the existence of a corps of specialists separate from manual laborers. To mobilize large crews for long jobs also required borrowing in the form of tribute or some other levy. And it demanded storage places for the products to sustain crews as well as predictable availability of land, fertilizers, and so forth. Differences in level of hydraulic complexity must have had correlates in many other aspects of social activity.

As mentioned earlier the Chimú (c. thirteenth–fifteenth centuries C.E.) organized a state that comprised the whole northern and central coast of Peru. Nevertheless, there is little information about Chimú government, its rules of succession, or social structure. Even less is known about the relationships that the Trujillans maintained with the subjugated valleys. Based on legendary history, surely ideologically tinged by its tellers and by the Spaniards who relayed it, some information may be gleaned about the sacredness of the rulers, their successions, élite polygamy, and the "court" that surrounded the apex of power.

Traditional history maintains that the founder of the royal dynasties of Chimor was a personage named Tacaynamo, whose son Guacricaur undertook the conquest of the lower Moche Valley. The son in turn was succeeded by his son Ñançenpinco, who increased the dominions by conquering the whole Moche Valley and the neighboring valleys of Chicama, Pacasmayo, and Zaña to the north, and Virú and Santa to the south. Still, in his reign only the nuclear zone of Chimú and the southern part of Lambayeque would have been under Chimú control. The rest – reaching north to Tumbes, incorporating the Tallanes and Tumbesinos, and south to Carabayllo (Chillón), incorporating Chancay – was conquered by seven rulers who led up to the most important Chimú hero: Minchançaman, the Chimor sovereign whom the Inka had to face in the fifteenth century.

A similar history exists about the "Muchik" of Lambayeque, whose sovereigns purportedly descended from a legendary hero named Ñam-lap or Ñaymlap. According to this legend, relayed by the chronicler Cabello Valboa, Ñam-lap arrived by sea together with his wife Ceterni (or Sotenic), a harem, and a group of courtesans, with an idol of green stone named "Yam-pallec." His court comprised Pituzofi (the player of the shell trumpet), Niñacola (in charge of the litter and the throne), Niñaguintue (the royal chancellor), Fonga (in charge of the road), Occhocalo (the royal cook), Xam-muchec (the specialist in facial painting),

Ollopcopoc (in charge of the bath), and Llapchillulli (the provider of plumed weavings). Ñam-lap established himself in a place called Chot, which is perhaps the settlement known as Chotuna. At his death he was succeeded by his brother Cium, who married Zolsdoñi (or Ciernum-cacum). The third sovereign was Escuñain, then Macuy, Cunti-pallec, Allascunti, Nofan-nech, Mulumslan, Llamecoll, Llanipat-cum, and Acunta. The twelfth and last governor, Fempallec or Fempellec, after a series of magical events brought on by a woman who seduced him, gave up power. After a few years of obscurity, the Chimú conquest occurred. It established a new dynasty of governors, constituted by Pong-massa, Palles-massa, Oxa, and Llem-pisan. During this last administration, the Chimú were conquered by the Inka, and Lambayeque with it. The Inka put four rulers into power: Chullem-pisan, Cipromarca, Fallem-pisan (or Efquen-pisan), and Xecfuin-pisan, during whose reign the Spaniards appeared.

Apparently the governors of Chimú, like those of Lambayeque, prac-ticed a hereditary succession in which brothers of the deceased as well as sons could compete. Some propose a dual form of power, with a diarchy at the pinnacle of power. The head of the whole Chimú system was a Great Lord – "Cie-quic" – representative and center of the "royalty," which also included the rank of the "Alaec." Around them were a group of "courtesans" known as "Pixllca," whose prestige perhaps liberated them from manual labor and in some degree from tribute paying. There is a resemblance to the Inka privileges belonging to the high-born resi-dents of Cusco. Under these advantaged strata were a "popular" class called the *paraeng*, apparently meaning the common workers of the country. Another term, *yana* (also used in Inka parlance), referred to a kind of subordinated worker. Workers "from the city" were likely to be country dwellers who, either because of their manufacturing talent or because of obligations to the state, were made to live in the city either permanently or temporarily. (The Inka also did this with those they claimed as *yana* or rotating *mit'ayuq*.) Spanish documents refer to the *paraeng* as "vassals." The Spaniards equated *yana* with "domestic ser-vants." We speculate that such servitors lived in both the city and the countryside, alongside their masters.

Mythology implies that people were separated socially based on their origins, from which one may deduce that there was limited social mobil-ity. The origin myth said that nobles descended from two stars and the commoners from two different ones, which suggests a caste concept of inequality. A caste model fits the design of residential quarters and the inequalities in ways people were buried. We do not yet know how this putative caste system operated outside the Chimú cultural sphere proper, unless the Chimú worldview was common to the whole northern coast. The little that we know of the Chimú religion does not seem to indicate a dominant role in social relationships. The Chimú pantheon was headed by "Si," the moon, with the sun in second place. Later it was linked to the stars. The deified stars seem close to the cosmic divinities who served the interests of fishermen and agriculturalists throughout the Andean area.

An examination of the urban spaces of the great cities of the north, such as Chan Chan, shows a hierarchical architectonic model, with four basic urban units: citadels, intermediate architecture, ceremonial platforms, and popular living spaces. Because of their magnitude, elegance, and restricted distribution, the so-called citadels must have been linked to the highest levels of power – that of the Cie-quic. Intermediate architecture includes uniformly luxurious walled spaces, but of a lower standing in the hierarchy, and can perhaps be associated with the "courtesans" or persons related to or close to Cie-quic, such as the Alaec. Ceremonial platforms, funerary or otherwise, seem associated with the priestly sector, although their role is less perceptible than it was in the Moche or earlier eras. In Chan Chan, platforms occupy only a complementary urban space, reflecting a diminution in priestly power. The so-called popular neighborhoods, formed by some small and irregular agglutinated structures, which surrounded or bordered the walled buildings, contained the homes of commoners, including artisans, merchants, and servants. Outside the cities, in hamlets and villages of differing size, lived peasants, fishermen, and other nonurban workers. There are some indicators of differences between urban and rural customs.

In fact, the greater part of the population lived outside the cities. The monumental cities do not seem to have been as populous as one might guess from analogies with industrial cities. The immense city of Chan Chan, capital of the Chimú, may have had between 15,000 and 30,000 occupants or perhaps a maximum of 70,000. Most of it was occupied by buildings used for purposes other than living quarters. Nor did most of its occupants need to live in it on a permanent basis.

Like Wari, Chan Chan was a gradually built city and does not show a unified constructive plan. Indeed, it almost seems a "disorganized" settlement, difficult to follow with respect to the particular history of each one of its buildings. Harvard University's research project, directed by M. Moseley, made several attempts at chronology, either based on typology of the settlements or on variations in the form and proportions of adobe bricks used in construction. Thanks to this method we recognize at least two great building periods, with a series of intermediate phases.

In the city of Chan Chan there are nine to eleven citadels, or large walled palaces. They have been attributed to the nine (or eleven) sovereigns who governed Chimú in the aforementioned traditions. Each one would have ordered the construction of his palace both for use in life – as a residence and palace of government – and for preserving his body and eternal memory. In keeping with this hypothesis, the successive sequences of construction have been interpreted as a reflection of a dynastic sequence similar to that of the Inka kings of Cusco. Nonetheless, other archaeologists doubt this interpretation, above all because of the difficulties in fixing the precise chronology of each building.

The citadels are walled precincts with one entrance apiece, generally on the northern side. The idea was restricted access, with a checkpoint at the door, and protection from external incursions. The citadels are divided internally into three or four sections, connected by a series of passageways and patios without roofs. Certain internal structures in the form of a "U," formed by three walls at right angles, have been labeled *audiencias* (reception areas). Storage areas stood close to them, suggesting an administrative function.

Roofed rooms, funerary platforms, and in several cases *wachaques*, or wide wells dug down to the water table, are also found within. The inclusion of granaries and large storage areas makes it unlikely that citadels were simply élite living spaces. Granaries and big patios allowed the gathering of large numbers of people. The citadels also had a funerary function, lodged in raised platforms. Many walls of these buildings were adorned with figures in bas-relief, with geometric or figurative motifs organized in handsome visual harmony. These were perhaps designed as backdrops to ceremonious gatherings.

Examination of the funerary platforms lends support to the hypothesis that the palaces were each associated with one of the rulers. At least one platform housed a deceased personage surrounded by many women who were sacrificed in his honor. Burials occupy numerous rectangular subterranean chambers, arranged around a central and much larger one, in the form of a "T." In the platform known as "Huaca Las Avispas" inside the citadel labeled "Laberinto" (Labyrinth), it was estimated that a minimum of 300 individuals were buried. All of those whose skeletons permitted identification by sex were adolescent girls or young women. They were buried at different times, not all at once upon the death of the central personage. This invites speculation that the cult of the buried personage in the large T-shaped chamber was maintained over time, and that sacrifices of young women were offered to him at different times. (The Inka, too, maintained costly routines in honor of deceased rulers; see Chap. 10.)

Thus it seems that in the citadels a very exalted personage was housed and idolized. Nothing like this occurred in the palaces of lesser size classed as "intermediate architecture." There are about thirty-five of these, also walled and having only one access. Many of them even have the characteristic division in three sectors, with patios, corridors, reception areas, rooms with storage areas, and wells, but they were not as elegant as the citadels, nor as large, nor did they include funerary platforms. They seem secondary to citadels, perhaps lodging people whose rank was next to that of the inhabitants of the citadels.

Both the citadels and these lesser palaces have domestic spaces for living quarters and cooking as well as spaces used for public activities and storage. Evidently élite people lived and worked in both kinds of places. Where Chimú state buildings appear outside of Chan Chan, both in base territory and in subjugated valleys, they fit the intermediate architecture type.

The living spaces of Chan Chan's popular neighborhoods differ from the first two types of architecture. Their architecture is rustic, with walls generally made of pebbles or compacted earth, strengthened with cane or reed and roughly plastered. The walls formed irregularly shaped rooms, built one atop the other. Their remains suggest that the inhabitants were artisans dedicated to working metals, fiber, and wood. Metals came to them in ingot form to receive the refined decoration that was one of the dominant activities. Manufacturing was common to both the city and the rural sphere. Goldsmithing, however, was exclusively urban.

These popular living quarters were not all organized in the same way. Some formed neighborhoods, whereas others were isolated, or formed lesser groupings, or even perched atop platforms. It seems that the platform-top living quarters were occupied by people of a higher though not élite status. The archaeologist John Topic conjectures that some very special ones, with numerous rooms containing stools and many storage spaces, a communal kitchen, and no evidence of manufacturing work, could have served as inns, perhaps to lodge merchants and their llama caravans.

The neighborhoods, which had their own fenced-off cemeteries, seem to consist of basic domestic units. Each neighborhood apparently housed kinship groups and not just people thrown together by work. Little is known about family and marriage; Rowe has managed to infer a few points based on filiation and kinship names. Polygyny existed among the nobility. Kinship terms distinguished the husband, wife and children, older brothers or sisters, younger relatives (cousins or younger brothers or sisters), the wife's parents and brother, and the sister-in-law (sister of the spouse), as well as establishing adultery as an offense.

Chimú thus was clearly a strongly stratified society, with social classes whose inequalities approximated a caste system. It had an economic structure recognizing certain forms of ownership of land. A very strong state sustained great hydraulic projects and a complex exchange network. Artisans and merchants probably constituted a socially differentiated sector within the "popular" domain.

The special standing of the artisans and merchants makes sense in light of the fact that manufacturing burgeoned. When the Chimú were conquered by the Inka, the latter regarded its artisans as so valuable that they levied a quota of goldsmiths to be removed to Cusco as *mitmaq* ('transplanted persons') – a tribute payable not in manufactures but in manufacturers. Special objects made of gold and silver or those elaborated with exotic primary materials (e.g., turquoise, imported woods, feathered blankets) were particularly beautiful and unique. Ordinary consumption goods were mostly mass produced. Copper, alloys, and silver products were made in series, using very complex techniques of welding, lost-wax casting, and molding. Plating, stamping, embossing, and pearling gave showy finishes. Metals were mainly used for making ornaments but also went into instruments such as *tumi* (crescent-bladed) knives, needles, and fishhooks.

Ceramic production was even more definitely for mass consumption. Workshops used molds to mass-produce tableware and utensils for food preparation and preservation. The usual style was black ceramic with elaborate sculptural three-dimensionality, but other styles also occurred. Other workshops made textiles using a great variety of techniques and decorations, including painting and structural variations like tapestry. Some Chimú textiles bear adornments of dazzling featherwork or sparkling metal sequins. The usual material was cotton, with alpaca wool used on a lesser scale, sometimes with dyes such as cochineal. These last two materials had to be imported from the sierra. Significantly, it seems that some artisans such as fabric painters traveled from town to town exercising their specialty.

The Chimú state achieved a spectacular expansion in comparison to other parts of the Andes during the Late Intermediate, which was for the most part an era of relatively localized developments. It was the latter sort of development that prevailed in the neighboring highlands of Cajamarca and Ancash, where the urban process did not flourish. There a system of nonurban discrete chiefdoms was maintained. Their leaders were the people the Spanish later recognized as "native lords" (*señores naturales*) in Huamachuco, Cajamarca, Conchucos, and Huaylas. Urban experiments like Wari were not repeated, except perhaps at Huamachuco, which did have walled environments around plazas. It would be unsafe to assert that any state polity existed or that any polity exerted a sphere of influence beyond its own valley. It is probable that the "nations" or "kingdoms" to which Spanish chroniclers of the sixteenth century referred, denoted ethnic collectivities and not unified political structures.

POLITICAL CHIEFDOMS OF THE CENTRAL AND SOUTHERN PERUVIAN COASTAL VALLEYS

To the south of Chimú, including its probable zones of coastal influence in Huaura, Chancay, and Chillón, evidence does indicate local urban development, and one may infer chiefdoms or states of regional scale. In this area's development the great cultic center of Pacha Kamaq, whose ruins still stand just south of Lima, played a key role. The Wari empire seems to have highlighted the role of a cluster of roads in the valleys of Lima, thus elevating the regional rank of the Pacha Kamaq oracle to ever wider scope. This temple's prestige eventually reached to the limits of the Inka empire. Lima was always a central point of convergence for the peoples of the north and south, from the Formative Period onward. It was closely linked to Chavín in Early Horizon times, and also to Cupisnique and Paracas. It never lost contact with these regions or with the sierra of Junín and the neighboring jungles. In Middle Horizon times the Wari empire enhanced the possibility of extending those contacts, spreading the network of the god Pacha Kamaq and the attendant priests.

When the Wari state declined, Pacha Kamaq did not. Its prestige rested on its own perceived achievements; unfortunately we do not know just how it operated or how far its influence spread after the Wari era. The urban way of life was maintained and developed at Pacha Kamaq, although it abandoned Wari's lay organization (which in any case may not have taken hold beyond Cajamarquilla) in favor of a theocratic organization. Urban centers strongly affected by temples appeared around it, such as the one belonging to Maranga, and others in Armatambo, Mangomarca, and Lurigancho (today neighborhoods of urban Lima). Apparently in Late Intermediate times, Pacha Kamaq maintained a discrete regional sphere of influence through the so-called Ichma polity (*Señorío de Ichma*) with dominion over the Rímac and Lurín valleys. Only when a new pan-Andean state was reorganized, that of the Inka, did it once again enjoy the importance it had in Wari times.

In the same way, north of Lima, a spectacular urban phenomenon arose in the nearby Chancay Valley and apparently also in the Huaura Valley. The urban centers of Chancay, such as Lauri, Pisquillo Chico, Makatón, and Lumbra are large, based on pyramidal platforms with ramps and plazas, and show emphasis on ceremonial buildings. Textile and ceramic production indicate strong workshop regimens, stressing techniques of mass production. Domestic manufacturing was considerably reduced. The "Black on White" ceramic characteristic of Chancay marks an area of influence reaching at least to the Chillón Valley, including Ancón.

The other valleys of the central coast, south of Lima, do not seem to have stood out much. Southward to the Cañete and Mala valleys there is no evidence of sustained urban development. According to references by sixteenth-century chroniclers, a centralized political chiefdom existed in the Valley of Cañete or Huarco, governed by a lord named Chuquimanco, who would have exerted influence over the neighboring valleys of Mala and Chilca.

Farther to the south, the Chincha Valley reached its greatest splendor after the twelfth century C.E., based on a well-defined urban development. At least three great urban centers were formed at Tambo de Mora, Lurinchincha, and Las Huacas, associated with strong agricultural and fishing economies. An army of merchants, navigators, and travelers from Chincha traded throughout the coast and into the sierra. Chincha had an old urban tradition, which began in the times of Paracas. Despite Wari incursions the local urbanistic models did not change in the Ayacuchan direction, though there were expansions and modifications. The whole arable valley was occupied, and its nearby marine wealth was exploited intensively alongside mercantile activity. Rostworowski indicates that the range of Chincha's mercantile operations covered both the sierra to the Titicaca *altiplano* and the coast all the way to distant Puerto Viejo, in Manabí, Ecuador. Deepwater sailing by balsas, and inland expeditions by llama caravans, carried the goods. Chincha traders seem to have brought *mullu* shells (*Spondylus princeps*, a necessary sacrifice to the divine owners of rain) from the warmer northern seas off Ecuador, where they also obtained emeralds and gold and dealt in fabrics, preserved foods, and metals. Chincha's ceramics, like its textiles, are not particularly notable. They demonstrate a certain familiarity with the more southerly styles. In Chincha, unlike Chimor, it seems that there was no association between mercantile development and manufacturing development. Many tombs exhumed by Uhle contain scales, probably the kind Chinchanos used to weigh metals, according to sixteenth-century documents.

The population of the Ica valleys, after a decline in the sixth century C.E. (Nasca 8), reactivated considerably, widening its dominion over the environs and making possible the post-Wari emergence of a series of local chiefdoms that urbanized in a fashion similar to that of Chincha. Settlements like Tacaraca in Ica were organized around pyramidal platforms. However, these settlements may have carried out only a ceremonial function, perhaps similar to that which Cahuachi (see p. 456; also called Kawachi) had exercised in an earlier time in the Nasca Valley. Colonial documents refer to the ethnic lords of Ica as very wealthy people, important consumers of the merchandise mobilized by the Chinchanos.

THE QUECHUA PEOPLES OF CENTRAL PERU

In the sierran territory where "polycyclical" (multicrop, multiniche) agricultural practice is necessary – an immense territory that begins to the south of Huamachuco and reaches to Cusco – no states like those of the coast formed. This does not necessarily imply a decline. In Huánuco it seems that important local lordships formed in Tantamayo and Llata, endogenously, without much kinship to the prevailing central Andean development. A less localized constellation took shape in the central massif of Junín, which shares some traits with the Titicaca *altiplano,* where a political organization of local lords arose, with considerable powers, but distinguishable from formal states.

This area, generally identified in Peru as the Central Sierra, comprises the high middle basin of the Mantaro and Tarma rivers, as well as the extensive plateau of Junín where both rivers originate. Soon to be known as the Inka provinces of Chinchaycocha, Tarama or Taruma, and Wanka, it housed ethnic groups known by their territorial names. The common language was Quechua. Quechua of this region has been linked by historical-linguistic methods to the language's original hearth, somewhere on or near the central Peruvian coast, and it is most likely that central highlanders had already used it centuries before the Inka state began to promote it.

The Wanka (also written Huanca) constituted the biggest and strongest group; they occupied the Mantaro Valley between Huancayo and Jauja as well as the fertile zones along tributaries. The Sausa (related to the toponym Xauxa or Jauja), who occupied the widest part of the valley, seem to have reached the highest levels of development. Chinchaycocha occupied the environs of Lake Junín in the *altiplano*, which is primarily pasture land and *puna* environment. The Tarama or Taruma lived on the eastern slope of the Junín plateau in the Tarma river basin. Their territory included the border with the Amazonian peoples, including the Amuesha and Asháninka (previously called "Campa") in the basin of the Chanchamayo River beyond the mouth of the Tarma River.

All these highlanders were agropastoralists. The territory is surrounded by *puna* on three sides. Four major zones served production: valley lands, mountain slopes, plateaus, and the high *puna*. Dry-land farming predominated at all altitudes, although irrigation occurred in the valleys and slopes near sources of water. This is a relatively rich zone, with access to diverse environments at conveniently short distances. The population was concentrated in middle-altitude zones between valleys and *puna*. There is a clear association between higher density and the agricultural side of the agropastoral way of life. The Wanka settlements, especially those of the Yanamarca Valley, which was associated with a highly productive agriculture, were bigger and denser. The Tarama and Chinchaycocha settlements, which are associated with more difficult productive conditions, clearly had a low density and smaller population. Economy rested on a "polycyclical" agricultural base. In addition, the Wanka advanced toward the jungle, presumably for a coca production, perhaps building a "vertical archipelago" of diversified outliers. Wanka settlements grew in the basin of the Tulumayo, a tributary of the Amazonian Chanchamayo.

Archaeologically, one may distinguish the Wanka from their neighbors in Junín and Tarma based on the latter group's typical ceramics with red decoration, and the smaller size of their settlements, located in hard-to-reach places. Both in documentary sources and in the archaeological record, the Tarama and the Chinchaycocha show strong ethnic unity. The main contrast is that the Wanka lived in agricultural zones and the Tarama and Chinchaycocha groups were essentially herders. In other aspects, they were much alike.

Wanka archaeology shows a different ceramics, and much larger settlements, 15 to 20 hectares and sometimes up to 100 hectares in size. Two well-defined phases exist, the first characterized by small settlements and low population, and the second by large settlements, walled and situated in the mountain heights, with a notable growth in population. The greater part of the lowland settlements were abandoned during the late phase. Some were reoccupied in the Inka era.

In the early phase – Wanka I (C.E. 900–1350) – the tendency was to construct settlements toward the edges of the valleys. Of the thirty-six sites of Wanka I occupation, a third were created anew, although the houses show design continuity with those preceding them in the Middle Horizon. Adobe walls were built on top of stone foundations to form buildings with circular floor plans. Ceramics acquired greater stylistic variability than in Middle Horizon times, and there were changes in agricultural tools such as the use of stone spades. Evidence shows agricultural intensification and a reduction in herding activity as well as a certain amount of exchange activity. There are indications of a probable increase in the consumption of maize, but the overall diet seems to be about the same as that of earlier eras. Settlements stood near fields or pastures. There is no evidence of political tensions, in comparison with what happened in other places at this same time. Production and consumption apparently developed only within the domestic sphere. There was considerable continuity with the Middle Horizon in settlement patterns. This continuity was broken in Wanka II, when strong conflicts in the region began.

During Wanka II (C.E. 1350–1460), ending with the Inka expansion, changes in production and interchange seemingly went together with a new inequality among the population. Conditions of insecurity led to fortified settlements in the higher parts. At the same time, the population increased, with greater concentration in hierarchical settlements. Warrior activity increased.

According to ethnohistorical sources, the Wanka were one of the ethnic groups who offered the greatest resistance to Inka expansion in the mid–fifteenth century C.E. (Later they allied themselves with the Spaniards against Tawantinsuyu). As far as we know, however, the Wanka and their Tarama and Chinchaycocha neighbors were not organized on a level higher than that of villages, even in the struggle against the Inka. Archaeological evidence does not support long-distance exchange or any external political influence on them until Inka conquest. The overall process is reminiscent of Huarpa before the formation of the Wari state, albeit on a greater scale.

When they established themselves in the higher lands, the Wanka had to adopt new cultivation strategies. The highlands are not as fertile as their valley homelands. In order to maintain population, it was necessary both to work fields at great distances and to develop methods of intensive cultivation near settlements. There is evidence of an irrigation canal that carried water toward the northern zone of Sausa, and agricultural terraces have been located near the settlements. Intensification brought a laborious agriculture, but not necessarily a more productive one because the harvest in higher-lying areas is less reliable.

The absence of planning of the population centers is a general characteristic. Among the Wanka, as among the Chinchaycocha and Tarama, the towns were compact and nuclear, with a well-defined residential architecture. The settlements are of an irregular organization, normally with a distribution of houses according to the irregularities of the terrain; in some cases several houses are located together around small patios sometimes associated with storage spaces and tombs.

In the late phase of the Wanka, along with a tendency toward a greater concentration of the population, one also notes evidence of the fusion of villages that until that time had been separate. This must have generated greater interaction among a greater number of people. The size of the settlements suggests certain differences of hierarchy. The area of occupation was 8 to 10 hectares during Wanka I, with perhaps 1,000 to 2,000 inhabitants, but the later sites of Tunanmarka (23 ha.) and Hatunmarka (95 ha.) sheltered perhaps 8,000 to 16,000 inhabitants. Around each of these two centers clustered a constellation of small villages. There is also evidence of differentiation in the inhabitants' activities. Although outwardly massive and fortified, the centers had internally open public areas within their walls. In Tunanmarka two walls divide the site transversely in half. A central space has two patios or plazas to which several rectangular structures adhere. This space suggests the emergence of public rituals of a new type, and managerial forms evolving amid dense cohabitation.

Walled patios demarcated residence units that each included one or more circular structures around an open space. There were differences in the construction and size of the houses. Taking into account advantages such as proximity to the center, the size of the patio, and the number of circular structures, it is possible to identify richer houses. But there are no indicators of drastic social differentiation like that expressed in the walled structures of Wari, Chimú, or Inka.

Ceramic production indicates a minimum of specialization. Both fine and common ceramics were produced by the common people in the settlements themselves. Some special types may have been made by specialized producers or settlements. For example, cooking pots were produced in Tunanmarka, while its satellite Umpamalca produced bowls and other vessels. Élite houses had more ceramics per area, more variety, more fine types, more kinds with intensive work, and more nonlocal ceramics. They also had more large vessels for storage and maize beer. These same houses boast a great concentration of spindle whorls, reflecting the documented importance of weaving.

Late Wanka was a basically pastoral and agricultural economy, with extensive pastures both in the *altiplano* and in the *punas* overlooking the high Andean valleys of Mantaro and Tarma. According to document information, Chinchaycochans paid tribute to the Inka in the form of maize and coca. Because it is not possible to produce these crops in the region, we may assume, at least in Inka times, that the herders got them either through interchange with farmers from the temperate and hot valleys, or through colonies that worked in such places. The latter seems to be the case with the Wanka, who had settlements on the fringe of the jungle, in Tulumayo. The Tarama-Chinchaycocha had them in Ulcumayo. Archaeological evidence also points to exchange between the peoples of the sierra and their Amazonian neighbors; sierran ceramics appear in their territory and vice versa.

Wari times proved a durable influence on the Wanka. Sixteenth-century documents note that when war chiefs remembered the feats of their grandfathers, they spoke of *sinchikuna* (strong persons), emphasizing protection and defense of the community. When such leaders triumphed, they received captured women and land. Warrior chiefs were chosen based on their personal ability. Occasionally, when the son of a warrior demonstrated appropriate qualities, he could become the next leader. Documents also suggest that these leaders operated as governors, but only sporadically and with limited authority. There are grounds for suspecting dual or moiety organization throughout the region (that is, polities self-interpreted as consisting of complementary halves).

THE AYMARA POLITICAL CHIEFDOMS

At the southern limits of the central Andean area, including some of what is now highland Bolivia, the dominant languages were of the "Aru" trunk: Aymara, Pukina, and Uruquilla or Urukilla. This South-Central Andean area has its developmental nucleus in the Titicaca *altiplano*. In the Late Intermediate this area saw the rise of predominantly pastoral peoples, who also practiced some high-altitude agriculture. They created the "lacustrine kingdoms" that both Inka and Spanish conquerors considered notably rich. The area that circles Lake Titicaca is over 3,800 meters above sea level. Its immense mass of water does produce micro-climates that allow agricultural production of many plants well above their normal altitude limits. It takes technological effort, however, to make use of this opportunity, and after Tiwanaku's decline (tenth to eleventh centuries C.E.), Late Intermediate people, possibly affected by continuous droughts, made less use of its agricultural capacity. They oriented society definitively toward herding.

The South-Central Andes as a whole – that is, considered as a gamut of different ecological settings – was always linked to the Titicaca *altiplano*. Systems of complementary economic articulation between high and low lands are crucial to understanding social developments. In contrast to the more northerly sierra with its "polycyclical agriculture," which concentrates on moving worker power through short diverse spaces and seasons, this system implied the necessity of establishing complementarity over great distances. At a strictly domestic level, this would have been very difficult. The area of greatest development and best economic possibilities, around Lake Titicaca, always relied on supra-household access to lower, ecologically distinct, zones in order to provide resources absent in its habitat. Given that distances among different productive zones were very great in this area, the requirement of complementarity implied the establishment of a system of exchange, or conquest, or direct forms of production of the required goods, by relocating a part of the *altiplano* population in distant productive enclaves. Perhaps striving to maintain an autarchic model similar to the ideal of "polycycli-cal cultivation," the *altiplano* dwellers opted for the last. Some of them went down to the valleys to cultivate products requiring warmth – notably, maize, coca, and peppers.

This does not seem to have been a free choice. The pre-Tiwanaku history of the western slope of the South-Central Andes indicates an agricultural and demographic development that was quite limited until the arrival of the *altiplano* people. In fact, it seems that they shifted toward agrarian development only when stimulated by contact with the Titicaca *altiplano* and the eastern slope. The small west-slope population was more dependent on a maritime and hunting economy than on agriculture, and it lacked the capacity to satisfy the demands of *altiplano* folk. This may explain why colonization and not exchange came about. It may also explain the nonviolent nature of the colonization, because many valley lands may not have been cultivated by the local inhabitants at all. In west-slope Moquegua, there are no indications of conflict until the Wari appeared in the valley. (This explanation may not apply to early times in the valleys of the eastern slope. In Cochabamba, Bolivia, for example, a local population achieved more developed formations than those of the desert coast.) In any case, the westward-looking *altiplano* population found itself forced to deal with agrarian formations of lesser productive potential, and perhaps without enough population to respond to the demands of complementarity with Titicaca communities.

If the proposed outline is valid, there are no grounds to hypothesize expansionist *altiplano* state dynamics similar to the Wari, Chimú, or Inka. The Late Intermediate lakeside peoples' concrete political sphere seems limited to their respective Titicaca nuclei, plus outlying productive "islands" adding up to what Murra styled productive "archipelagos." More than one lakeside polity might have outliers at a given resource. Conflicts derived from land tenure or water rights must have been solved among the "home" lacustrine chiefdoms or states rather than among the colonists. This would allow us to understand why in Inka times, when the system continued, the "islands" could retain a multiethnic character even though the lacustrine parent-states were in conflict among them-selves. Without a central power of the type the Tiwanaku probably had, or the one that the Inka built later on, the system worked.

Documents written in the sixteenth century describe at least two great kingdoms or chiefdoms to the west of Titicaca: Qulla (also written Colla, Qolla) and Lupaqa (Lupaca). Other pre-Inka ethnic groups whose politi-

cal structure we know less well were the Canas, Canchis, and Chumbivilcas of Cusco's highlands; the Collaguas and Condesuyus of the western
slope; and the Pacaje from south of the lake. Nor do extant records
anatomize the Umasuyu to the northeast of the lake, Ubina to the south
of the Collagua, the Calaguaya (Kallawaya, Callahuaya) to the east of the
altiplano, the Uru in the lake basin, and their more southerly relatives
the Chipaya, the Charcas, the Chichas, or other local groups. It is known
in general that they were predominantly pastoral populations with support from highland agriculture. In the sixteenth century, both the Qulla
and the Lupaqa polities had hierarchical structures, presided over by local
chiefs (*Mallku*) each of whom commanded a "province." Such divisions
presumably reproduced the territory of earlier states.

Archaeology indicates some areas of unity among the diverse groups:
for example, technology, settlement patterns, burial in tower-shaped
tombs (or *chullpas*) or in cists, and ceramics of the *altiplano* tradition. It
is difficult to mark out the ethnic groups archaeologically short of referring to very detailed ceramic variations.

The best-known region is that of the Lupaqa, in the southeastern half
of the lake. Thanks to Hyslop's studies we know that after Tiwanaku's
decline, an increase in the population came about. The number of
settlements grew as did their area, which in some cases surpassed 150
hectares. These population centers were built in very high locations –
some of them, the biggest ones in fact, stood at altitudes over 4,000
meters above sea level. These locations only make sense assuming a
pastorally based economy. There is a striking spread in the sizes of
settlements, which vary from those greater than 100 hectares of occupied
space to those measuring less than 10 hectares. This hierarchy is also
reflected in the size and quality of many of the buildings. Many settlements were abandoned in Inka times, so we know that differentiation
was not just a side effect of imperial stratification.

Hyslop also suggests that the Lupaqa pioneered the building of elite
tombs in the form of towers. If so it could imply a change in the religious
sphere, with a relative diminution of temples' importance and an enhancement of ritual investments in tombs for the élite. Indeed, Lupaqa
settlements and others of this period on the *altiplano* show no places of
worship that stand out architectonically.

We do not know if the *Zapana*, rulers of the Qulla, or the paired *Cari*
and *Cusi* lords of the Lupaqa, were kings before the Inkas, but colonial

terminology indicates – most clearly among the Lupaqa – that power was dually divided. Lupaqa informants insisted on dividing the peoples into *maasaa* and *alasaa* (upper and lower moieties) and also on dividing their home polities into two sections. Apparently, the "higher" half was of greater prestige and power than the "lower," according to what is known from the early-colonial *vistas* (administrative field inspections) by Garci Diez. The *mallkus*, or rulers, occupied a social sphere superior to that of the "commoners," who labored (under the Inka, and probably before) as rotating contingents in the service of the state. Others became *yanakuna*, permanent servitors of the "lords."

Sixteenth-century testimonies suffer Inka and Spanish distortion, but they do allow a non-Inka and preexisting structure to show through. These sources present the Lupaqa economy as based first of all on camelid livestock. The sheer size of the flocks that won the Lupaqa the epithet of "rich Indians" in the mid–sixteenth century, though impressive at the time, already reflected colonial depletion. Garci Diez de San Miguel, the 1567 *visitador* of Chucuito, registered tens of thousands of animals. Some "rich" Lupaqa owned up to 50,000 head each, whereas commoners only possessed a few animals. This important economic differentiation must have begun in pre-Inka times. Ownership gave access to wool, leather, meat, and, above all, beasts of burden for long-distance transport.

THE QUECHUA PEOPLES OF THE SOUTH

In the southern sierra, between Junín and Lake Titicaca, the situation seems different. In the first place, we do not know with any certainty to what degree the post-Tiwanaku and post-Wari peoples of Ayacucho, Apurímac, Huancavelica, Ica, and the Lima sierra, were Quechua speakers. On the one hand, Quechua seems to have originated in this area, probably near Lima or inland from it. On the other hand, Quechua seems to overlie languages of the Aru group, to which Kauki (still spoken in modern times in the upper basin of the Cañete River not too far from Lima), as well as the still-widespread but now largely Bolivian Aymara and the extinct Pukina, all belong. What is certain is that in this territory, many Aru toponyms are found, along with a few Aru-speaking "islands." Some think the diffusion of Aru languages had occurred in the Wari epoch. In Inka and more recent times, Quechua became the politically dominant native tongue, but in some cases we may be looking at "Quechuafied" populations who used non-Quechua tongues among themselves.

As noted previously the breakdown of the Wari state in Ayacucho impelled return to a Huarpa-like economy based on pasturing and highland agriculture, with very limited use of irrigated zones. The characteristic settlements of this epoch in Wari's former heartland are a few villages located in the high part of the mountains, each with 30 to 100 circular and agglutinated houses of the Arqalla type. As in Huarpa houses, the walls of these houses are less than 1 meter high. Interior space was created mostly by conical roofs of sticks and straw. Textile or ceramic manufacturing was domestic both in its production and its use. In Wari's former provinces, Wari urban centers were not occupied by the local population. When Wari fell and these citadels were abandoned, certain mechanisms of class-differentiated political and economic life may have remained, but not the Wari form of urban life.

On the other hand, by all accounts, the post-Wari people did retain a warlike cast. Defensive walls and forts say as much. As the "Pax Wari" disappeared, sacking and invasion must have become commonplace. Native lordships must have dealt with them through alliances and compromises in their intracommunal relationships. It is not clear how much of the class hierarchy obviously imposed by the Wari remained, although it does seem evident that the highest sectors of the elite became totally destabilized and disappeared. Local lords about whom we have documented evidence seem to have derived their power from communal choice and personal achievement, or perhaps factional victories, but not from a consolidated class privilege. It seems that peasant "generalists" remained on the scene, carrying out whatever crafts existed on the domestic level.

This fits well with the Cusco tradition, which speaks of a great disorder before the appearance of Inka kings and the civilizing mission that the legendary Inka founders undertook. This warlike existence apparently was shared by the Chanca, Chocorvo and Anqara, Rucana, Sora, and Quechuas.

Out of this scene one must trace the dawn of Inka power and the emergence of the last prehispanic Horizon, the Inka state. This process took place in a period that seems, archaeologically, like the blink of an eye, and the reasons why Cusco should give rise to such a sudden and decisive development are not obvious. But let us sketch an hypothesis.

Cusco has one of the most generous valleys of the southern sierra and is surrounded by a vast zone of pastures. Before the Wari empire, Cusco does not seem to have had a settled agricultural economy, but it did foster great pastoral activity. From Wari's arrival onward, Cusco began to find ways to surpass the domestic system of production. One threshold factor could have been a state policy of promoting high-quality agricultural production around Cusco. Maize production is possible in Cusco, but it requires a special treatment of the agrarian infrastructure. This project of intensification, including construction of agricultural terraces, became the regional axis of agricultural production. The possibility of combining an irrigation-based agriculture for maize in the Urubamba Valley with dry-land farming of potatoes on the nearby slopes and flats, together with livestock production on the heights, converted Cusco's "polycyclical" agriculture into a first-class engine of wealth. This permitted sustained growth of the population. Its labor power was liberated from the need to pay tribute to an outside force after Wari's dissolution.

Cusco does not have pre-Wari urban antecedents, but in contrast to Wari, whose agricultural environment was very poor in soils and water, Cusco was a privileged region. The Wari city of Pikillaqta near Cusco (described earlier) was frankly a Wari colonial enclave and did not encourage local emulation of its structure. Wari rather promoted village life, suitable for imperial expropriation, as is visible in Lucre, Anta, and other settlements surrounding Cusco. But the character of agrarian production could not be reproduced, much less widened, within a domestic economy ensconced in autonomous and free communities. To create an infrastructure for the production of maize, taking advantage of the slopes and rechanneling rivers to stabilize fertile flat lands banks, implied a concerted collective work on a scale above domestic level. Specialists in maintenance and enlargement were also needed. In Cusco this had to be the base for local centralized power, with or without urbanism. It seems to have developed in one or several sections of the Vilcanota-Urubamba valleys.

After Wari's fall, towns of differing size began to appear. Some were organized like Pikillaqta (for example, Choqepukyo, which began in the Middle Horizon). These developed urban organization of a local type. Dwyer found that settlements of this period in the Valley of Cusco, attributable to the immediately pre-Inka Killke culture, were generally found on slopes. Their forms did not indicate conditions of conflict, because they were not protected, and in this they prefigured the city of

Cusco itself. The same cannot be said of the neighboring Lucre Valley, where almost all the settlements stood atop hills and built defensive systems. In the Urubamba, settlements bearing Killke ceramics also stood on hills, although in a later phase they relocated near the bottom of the valley, in the same sites the Inka later continued to use. This could indicate that some center guaranteeing the stability of Cusco and the Urubamba existed by the later Killke phase. It could have been a pre-Inka city of Cusco, later covered by the imperial city.

Killke population centers, both in Cusco and in Lucre or Urubamba, were relatively small, village-like, with generally round agglutinated houses and a few rectangular rooms. Cusco, in contrast to Wari and Chan Chan, developed at first as an agrarian urban formation. Perhaps because of this the Inka "feudalized" the economy, restricting the circulation of products and peoples, reducing the range of markets, and regulating barter. Before the formation of Tawantinsuyu in the fifteenth century, Cusco's manufacturing development, as far as we know, did not surpass the limits of domestic production.

When Cusco emerged, it shared with the ancient theocratic urban centers like Tiwanaku the function of housing the kinship corporations formed around lords and the specialized officials who were at their service. In contrast to the theocracies, however, in Cusco the palaces were as important as the temples. The whole system centered around the kings or governors and not the priests. It was a class society, heir to long experience in the management of Andean resources. Cusco also inherited an agricultural technology refined over time, chiefly by promoting an infrastructure that elevated rural productivity. The agricultural frontier expanded through construction of terraces and extensive irrigation programs. Myth aside, the Inka did not settle a virgin land. Inka traditions and legends that say otherwise appear to be appropriations of Wari ideas or memories of a putatively foundational Wari epoch. (These myths are discussed on pp. 773–775.)

The Inka and their relatives, whose distinction as a class was shown by distinctive bodily practices and insignia, were Cusqueños who saw themselves as different from other Cusqueños, alleging a unique and almost divine lineage or ethnicity. Nonetheless, their language, their family organization, and their customs were not so different from other local peoples'. Perhaps at some point they became a distinctive social class among their countrymen. It could have occurred during the times of Wari domination, or during the Wari decomposition.

Historians have absorbed the tradition that the Inka state began modestly, as a confederation of tribes inhabiting Cusco, under the rule of warrior leaders. After a quasi-mythical war with the Chanka, the hero-king Pachakuti purportedly began the organization of an empire. The culminating point of this process must have occurred around 1430 C.E. – that is, only a century before Spaniards arrived in the Andes. Archaeologically speaking, a state already existed earlier at the local level in Cusco, where the Killke culture had developed. It probably corresponded to the legendary age of the Inka. Perhaps this precursor-state also existed in Lucre, where the Pinagua ethnicity dwelled, or in other areas such as Canchis, of which we know very little. The legendary war with the Chanka, from which Inka expansion was launched, expresses the idea of Cusco as surrounded by confrontational "barbarians" on whose defeat the future of the valley turned. In Inka myth the crucial moment was a war with the Chanka. This concept must have some relation to the Wari, because the mythic Chanka homeland corresponds to Wari territory. The legendary war could express memory of the process of Wari's decomposition and Cusco's emergence as a conquest state. It is hard to tell. But somewhere in this obscure penumbra of prehistory, the origins of the last Horizon (see Chap. 10) must be sought.

BIBLIOGRAPHIC ESSAY

The last 30 years have witnessed a very large and varied new literature on the antecedents of the Andean state and urbanism. In the present review we mention only the most recent and most general works, which also contain the most convenient bibliographic references for further reading. Among the most informative general essays, and one with an extensive bibliography, is James R. Parsons and Charles M. Hastings's "The Late Intermediate Period" in *Peruvian prehistory*, edited by R. W. Keatinge (Cambridge, 1988). For environmental factors that supposedly affected the Andes in the sixth century C.E., see Michael E. Moseley's "Punctuated equilibrium: Searching the ancient record for El Niño," *Quarterly Review of Archaeology* 8:3 (1987), 7–10; C. R. Ortloff and Alan L. Kolata's "Climate and collapse: Agro-ecological perspectives on the decline of the Tiwanaku state," *Journal of Archaeological Science* 20 (1993), 195–221; and also J. Grodzicki's *Nasca: Los síntomas geológicos del fenómeno El Niño y sus aspectos arqueológicos* (Centro de Estudios Latinoamericanos, University of Warsaw, Warsaw, 1994). Despite its datedness, no one studying the Tiwanaku should omit reading W. C. Bennett's pioneering "Excavations at Tiahuanaco," *Anthropological Papers of the American Museum of Natural History* 34 (New York, 1934). The same can be said of Carlos Ponce Sanjinés's reports, especially his synthesis *Tiwanaku: Espacio, tiempo y cultura* (Academia Nacional de Ciencias, La Paz, 1972). A summary of recent work is included in Kolata's book *The Tiwanaku: Portrait of an Andean civilization* (Cambridge, Mass., 1993), and also in *Tiwanaku: Arqueología regional y dinámica segmentaria* by J. Albarracin-Jordán (La Paz, 1996). See also Linda Manzanilla's *Akapana, una pirámide en el centro del mundo* (Instituto de Investigaciones Antropológicas de la Universidad Nacional Autónoma de México, 1992). Paul Goldstein's works on Tiwanaku's extensions include "Tiwanaku temple and state expansion: A Tiwanaku sunken-court temple in Moquegua, Peru," *Latin American Antiquity* 4:1 (1993), 22–47. *Gaceta Arqueológica Andina* 18–19 (Lima, 1990) contains an extensive bibliography on the region of the western valleys. A synthesis on the Tiwanaku occupation of the west slope can be found in José Berenguer and Percy Dauelsberg's "El Norte Grande en la órbita de Tiwanaku" in *Culturas de Chile, Prehistoria* (Santiago de Chile, 1989), 129–180.

On Wari, see Dorothy Menzel's "Style and time in the Middle Horizon," *Ñawpa Pacha* 2 (1964), 1–105. For Wari's antecedents in Huarpa, see Luis G. Lumbreras's *The peoples and cultures of ancient Peru* (Washington, D.C., 1974), 133–138. Two excellent compilations of reports and essays exist on Wari. One is *Huari administrative structure. Prehistoric monumental architecture and state government* (Washington, D.C., 1991), edited by William H. Isbell and Gordon F. McEwan. The other is *The nature of Wari: A reappraisal of the Middle Horizon period in Peru*, edited by M. R. Czwarno, F. M. Meddens, and A. Morgan (British Archaeological Reports, International Series 525, 1989). One should also consult Katherine J. Schreiber's "Wari imperialism in the Middle Horizon, Peru" (Anthropological Papers 87, Museum of Anthropology, University of Michigan, 1992) and *Wari y Tiwanaku: entre el estilo y la imagen* by A. G. Cook (Lima, 1994). Polycyclic agriculture is explained by Jürgen Golte in his *La racionalidad de la organización andina* (Lima, 1980). Reforms about other agricultural and technological systems from the Andes can be found in Heather Lechtman and Ana María Soldi's edited volume, *La tecnología en el mundo andino* (México D.F., 1981), and in María Rostworowski's *Recursos renovables y pesca, siglos XVI y XVII* (Lima, 1981).

With regard to the Yunka (coastal) peoples, and especially northern

Peru's Chimor, two collaborative volumes present good information in their own right and also facilitate access to other sources. They are Michael F. Moseley and Kent Day's *Chan Chan: Andean desert city* (Albuquerque, 1982) and *The northern dynasties: Kinship and statecraft in Chimor*, edited by María Rostworowski, Michael F. Moseley, and Alana Cordy-Collins (Washington, D.C., 1990). For literature about the coastal valleys to Chimor's south, the bibliography is more dispersed. Information tends to be amalgamated with work on older periods. For Chancay, work on textiles and ceramics was done in the nineteenth century; a summary is given in Samuel K. Lothrop and J. A. Mahler's *A Chancay-style grave at Zapallán, Peru* (Papers of the Peabody Museum of Archaeology and Ethnology 50(1), 1957). Document-based information appears in various works of María Rostworowski, including *Etnía y sociedad. Costa peruana prehispánica* (Lima, 1977), *Señoríos indígenas de Lima y Canta* (Lima, 1978), and *Estructuras andinas del poder* (Lima, 1983). For Chincha, Dorothy Menzel and J. H. Rowe's "The role of Chincha in Late pre-Spanish Peru," as well as Menzel's "The pottery of Chincha," are both recommended; both came out in *Ñawpa Pacha* 4 (1966). Menzel also published a detailed analysis of Ica pottery in *Pottery style and ancient Peru, art as a mirror of history in the Inca Valley 1350–1570* (Berkeley, 1976). D. T. Wallace contributed a report on "Sitios arqueológicos del Perú, valles de Chincha y Pisco" to *Arqueológicas* 13 (Lima, 1971). Daniel Sandweiss published his report on Chincha in "The archaeology of Chincha fishermen: Specialization and status in Inka Peru," *Bulletin of the Carnegie Museum of Natural History* 29 (1992).

Many short pieces cover the peoples of the central Peruvian highlands. Substantial information can be found in Timothy Earle's *Economic and social organization of complex chiefdoms* (Anthropological Paper 63, Museum of Anthropology, Museum of Anthropology, University of Michigan, 1978). Earle collaborated with Terence D'Altroy and others in "Changing settlement patterns in the Upper Mantaro Valley, Peru," *Journal of New World Archaeology* 4:1 (1980). See also Christine A. Hastorf's "One path to the heights: Negotiating political inequality in the Sausa of Peru," in *The evolution of political systems*, edited by Stuart Upham (Cambridge, 1990) 146–176. A volume edited by Ian Farrington and entitled *Prehistoric intensive agriculture in the tropics* (British Archaeological Reports, International Series 232, 1985) contains Hastorf and Earle's "Intensive agriculture and geography of political change in the Upper Mantaro region of central Peru," pages 569–595. Danièlle Lavallée and Michèle Julien have provided information about a different part of the central sierra in their *Asto: Curacazgo prehispánico de los Andes Centrales* (Lima, 1983).

For the Titicaca high plains, a synthesis is available in Luis G. Lumbreras's essay, "Los reinos post-Tiwanaku en el área altiplánica," *Revista del Museo Nacional* 40:55–85 (1974). See also Catherine Julien's *Hatuncolla, a view of Inca rule from the Lake Titicaca region* (University of California Publications in Anthropology 15, Berkeley, 1983), and many works of Charles Stanish, including his book *Ancient Andean political economy* (Austin, 1992).

Information on Cusco just before the Inka remains weak despite the existence of a series of articles about archaeological remains that probably belong to this era. Still important is J. H. Rowe's chapter on Killke ("Canchón"), which he included in his report on Cusco, *An introduction to the archaeology of Cusco* (Papers of the Peabody Museum of American Archaeology and Ethnology 27(2), 1944). Susan Niles printed news on "Pumamarca, a Late Intermediate Period site near Ollantaytambo" in *Ñawpa Pacha* 18 (1980), 49–62. Ann Kendall's "Preliminary report on ceramic data and the pre-Inca architectural remains of the (Lower) Urubamba Valley, Cuzco" appeared in *Baessler-Archiv* 24:1 (1977), 41–159. Miguel Rivera Dorado published a synthesis in "La cerámica Killke y la arqueología del Cuzco (Perú)," *Revista Española de Antropología Americana* 6 (1971), 85–123. The many essays on ethnohistorical context to pre-Inka Cusco tend to have a heavy speculative bent.

7

CHIEFDOMS: THE PREVALENCE AND PERSISTENCE OF *"SEÑORÍOS NATURALES"* 1400 TO EUROPEAN CONQUEST

JUAN AND JUDITH VILLAMARÍN

Chiefdoms, the polities most often referred to by sixteenth-century Spaniards when they spoke of *señoríos, curacazgos* (from the Quechua, *kuraka*), and *cacicazgos* (from the hispanicized Arawak, *cacique*), were autonomous societies in which there were permanent, centralized political hierarchies headed by chiefs. The chieftainship was institutionalized and hereditary, with the rule of succession usually specified and restricted to élites. Chiefdoms constituted a persistent sociopolitical form in South American prehistory, occupying a great range of environments including highland and lowland basins, marshlands, desert, coast, islands, lagoons, floodplains, and piedmont. At the time of European contact, chiefdoms were widespread throughout the continent.

In this chapter we discuss chiefdoms/*señoríos* in four sections. The first considers what Europeans saw and reported at contact, and how their views and categorizations of societies correspond to models of sociopolitical organization that anthropologists and others use today – models that have been developed in the context of a very long-term set of inquiries regarding the development of complex societies. In the second section we discuss structure and process in Chibcha chiefdoms of the Colombian *altiplano*. The analysis, which is based on a variety of primary sources, aims to delineate how a particular set of political hierarchies were organized and integrated, how they functioned, and how centralization operated with respect to them. The third section is a general overview of chiefdoms in regions that remained independent of Inka rule – the areas encompassed by Colombia, Venezuela, the Ecuadorian coast, and Greater Amazonia. Emphasis is on political centralization. Primary focus is on societies that had paramount chiefs and multiple levels of political hierarchy in contrast to the broad array of independent regional chiefs with fewer political levels. Political centralization in sections two and three is looked at with respect to internal processes – patterns of interaction by which a given people resolve a number of social, political, and environmental stresses, and in so doing optimize hierarchical links, as well as external factors – activities such as exchange of goods and ideas, and participation in alliances and warfare with other groups, all of which affect individual polities and give rise to large interactive geographical regions. The fourth section deals with chiefdoms that lost autonomy as they were overrun by the Inka in the fifteenth century and integrated into the empire. Because indirect rule was widely used by the Inka, outlines of many chiefdoms were still discernible in the sixteenth century; however, loss of independence meant redirection of portions of tribute and labor to the empire as well as manipulation of chiefly office to fit the state's needs. In this section the South Andean (Bolivia, Chile, northwest Argentina), Central Andean (Perú), and North Andean highlands (Ecuador) are covered.

We have organized the information to give the broadest sense of chiefdoms' prevalence throughout South America prior to the Inka and Spanish conquests, and of the variations in their histories, always aware that the data on chiefdoms are neither uniform nor always comparable.

WHAT THE SPANIARDS SAW/WHAT WE SEE

Between 1498 and the 1550s, Europeans came in contact with hundreds of different native societies as they made their way from coastal South America inland. Some explorers, such as Federman, Jiménez de Quesada, Cieza de León, Vivar, and Carvajal wrote descriptions of the people they met. Their accounts and those of others were drawn on and supplemented with data obtained from direct observation by chroniclers such as Fernández de Oviedo, Aguado, and Castellanos. In addition crown officials wrote about indigenous people in early regional reports. Despite sixteenth-century European biases, misunderstandings, exaggerations, and flights of imagination, the early works contribute substantially to our knowledge of contact-period South Americans, often with incisive and pertinent descriptions particularly regarding contrasts in political complexity of different groups. Sometimes they are the only remaining documentation on people who succumbed to the depredations of conquest and early colonial settlement. Accounts note the absence or presence of permanent centralized political systems among the different societies encountered, as well as impressions of population size, descriptions of settlement, subsistence and other economic patterns, and religious and social practices.

A working understanding of indigenous societies was vital to explorers' survival and success. Knowledge of native potential with respect to taxation and labor was of primary interest to European colonizers. In the course of establishing systems of taxation thought to fit native South Americans, crown officials spent considerable attention on *visitas de tierra*, tours of inspection of societies that had survived the first periods of contact. *Visitas* emphasized areas of native life that corresponded most to Spanish economic interests. In addition to *visitas* thousands of documents were written in the course of administration, petitions, transfers of property or rights, and litigation that directly and indirectly touched on native life. Modern researchers extricate data about contact-period societies from these materials, evaluating testimonies, and organizing information in the context of the scholarly communities to which they belong, hopefully aware of their own cultural biases, misunderstandings, exaggerations, and flights of imagination.[1]

If we focus on the European interest in the political and economic components of native societies, accepting the utilitarian view at face value, we see that early narratives and documents suggest categorization of Indian societies into two major types with respect to internal organization and usefulness to the Europeans: those that had no permanent political hierarchy and were referred to as *behetría*: "There are no caciques nor native lords and thus all are *behetría* [without permanent leaders];"[2] and those that had – *señoríos, cacicazgos, curacazgos,* and *reinos* (kingdoms). For the most part Europeans could not depend on provisionment by people in the first category, *behetría*, while they could obtain food, labor, and tribute from those in the second. Groups of the second type had large populations, had high-yield food production techniques usually with surpluses, and were accustomed to more intensive patterns

---

[1] See Chap. 1 of this volume, where Salomon explores issues involved in dealing with the early texts and probes the distortions in European and Indian narratives and testimonies as well as those that arise as a result of the multiple challenges to modern scholars' perceptions.

[2] Anonymous, "Visita de 1560," in Hermes Tovar Pinzón (ed.), *No Hay Caciques ni Señores* (Barcelona, 1988), 32, 20–121. Occasionally an author used the term *behetría* in a relative sense to emphasize lack of control over a large region by a paramount lord. Cieza de León did so in the context of comparing chiefdoms – *cacicazgos,* as he himself described them – of the Gobernación of Popayán to the Inka, in his *Crónica del Perú* [1550s], 3 vols. (Lima, 1986–1989), I, 58.

of labor and individual output than those in the first. Europeans found them easier to manage and extract benefit from, so tended to make their locales major centers of colonial settlement.

The centrality of chiefs in multiple arenas of politically complex *señoríos* or *cacicazgos* is a theme that we follow through this chapter. Chiefs' association with bountiful production was repeatedly noted in early Spanish reports. Chronicler Castellanos (1601) echoed observations of earlier explorers when he said, "In the Indies, abundance of food/Tidings of very great caciques."[3] In the course of various kinds of postconquest litigation and testimony, Indians also spoke about the importance of chiefs. Frequently mentioned was their deferential treatment by commoners as well as by élites and members of the political hierarchy, demonstrated in behaviors as simple as bowing or as elaborate as carrying chiefs about on litters so as to prevent their touching the soil. Sumptuary rules involving clothing, ornamentation, and foods separated chiefs and élites from the rest of the population. Chiefs received tribute and generally had greater access to labor and goods than all others. Residential differentiation was observed, with chiefs' compounds being the largest and most elaborate. Early writers reported that they were built and maintained by their subjects as were public buildings, storage facilities, plazas, platforms, and in many instances large-scale public works such as roads, canals, causeways, ditched fields, and terraces. They saw that chiefs accumulated valued goods and materials, including gold and gold objects. They reported that chiefs had special training for office, as well as polygamous marriages, and that their burials were elaborate – their tombs contained not only a large number of valuable objects but often wives and other attendants who accompanied them or were sacrificed in their honor. Europeans cited chiefs' central roles in political organization and referred as well to their management of aspects of production, trade, religious celebrations, war, peace making, and relations with other ethnic groups.

Generally, groups that the Spaniards called *behetrías* would be identified by anthropologists today as egalitarian societies, bands, and tribes. Bands had as their basic unit of organization the nuclear or extended family. Many such groups were nomadic, dependent on hunting and gathering, and maintained no formal or specialized political, economic, or

[3] Juan de Castellanos, *Elegías de Varones Ilustres de Indias* [1601], 4 vols. (Bogotá, 1955), I, 446.

religious structures. Social scientists would agree with earlier writers that such people were very difficult, if not impossible, for the Europeans to control effectively. Spaniards also had great difficulty in subjugating and utilizing the labor of tribes, sedentary societies without permanent hierarchies such as many groups in the lowland regions of northern South America, Paraguay, and the area south of the Bío Bío River in Chile. Tribes had large descent groups – lineages and clans originating in real or fictive ancestors – through which claims and counterclaims to labor were generated and accumulated as natural resources were acted upon or transformed for subsistence purposes. There was no systematized *corvée* system nor tribute in such societies, and labor exchange was based primarily on kin and friendship determinants. In egalitarian societies labor was, as Eric Wolf has pointed out, " 'locked up' or 'embedded' in particular relations between people," and thus not easily captured by outsiders.[4]

The situation was quite different in most polities that explorers and chroniclers called *señoríos, cacicazgos,* or *reinos,* and that anthropologists call complex societies – chiefdoms and states. Labor service and tribute were already institutionalized in these polities. It was with these societies that systems were organized so that people worked to satisfy demands that they did not initiate or in some cases did not benefit from materially. Chiefdoms in South America as elsewhere varied in the degree to which chiefs were bound by kinship in rights and obligations to their use of labor. At one end of the spectrum, simple chiefdoms, kinship ties, and environmental conditions limited chiefs' access, creating tensions when their demands went beyond customary allocations, giving rise to unstable situations and short-lived tenures. At the other end of the spectrum, in complex chiefdoms (which tended to be quite stable), labor had been pried away from the rights and limitations set on it by kinship in such a way as to favor chiefs and their families, staffs, and offices. Traditional social arrangements and resources were manipulated so as to strengthen their position continually, thereby diverting a considerable amount of

---

[4] Eric Wolf, *Europe and the people without history* (Berkeley, 1982), 91. For an example of how Spaniards did draw on such labor, see Elman Service, *Spanish-Guarani relations in early Colonial Paraguay* (Michigan, 1954). Interaction between Europeans and the Guaraní was noteworthy for its demonstration of the enmeshment of labor in multiple sectors of tribal life. In the 1530s Spaniards became Guaraní allies in their fight against Guaycuru and Payagua groups. The Europeans married Guaraní women, whose relatives then worked for them as part of their kinship obligations. By forming a large number of polygamous unions, Spaniards increased their access to labor.

labor and wealth and transforming "divisions of rank into divisions of class."[5] The results were demonstrated in larger housing facilities for chiefs and élites, more elaborate dress, accumulation of goods, elaborate life-cycle ceremonial, and impressive burials with valuable and exotic objects. Many of these characteristics are often observable in the material remains of chiefdoms' long archaeological records and in ethnohistorical data such as can be put together on the Chibcha of the eastern highlands of Colombia and other groups treated here.

Passage from chiefdom to state involves intensified centralization of power, greater inequality between population sectors, expanded scale of labor appropriation by élites, increased administrative and labor specialization, codification of laws, and a formal juridical system. In states labor is organized, deployed, and allocated through the exercise of political or military means. Patterns of socioeconomic differentiation as manifested in social classes and in the monopoly of legitimized force are more intensive. The division of complex societies into chiefdoms and states is fairly well accepted, although the boundaries between the two may not always be as clear as one would want. Nor should it be assumed that complex chiefdoms naturally tend to become states. To the contrary, there is good evidence that in some areas, such as in sections of Colombia's Cauca and Magdalena river valleys, chiefdoms were much less complex at the time of Spanish contact than those that had been there in previous centuries.

Political centralization may have brought people more dependable food supplies (chiefly via coordination of many tasks associated with intensification or accretion of conquered territories), access to a greater range of products and materials (via markets and long-distance trade carried out by élites or traders), better protection against enemies, more effective control and management of internal conflict, and wider participation in festivities, religious celebrations, and rituals. Ideology played an important role in the general acceptance, legitimation, and maintenance of hierarchical structures, and in the process tribute became an accepted means of deploying labor and goods. The routinization of work, the extraction of services, and appropriation of goods appear to have been carried out with some degree of consent, as appears to be the case at the regional and subregional levels of Chibcha communities, for example. This does not preclude the likelihood that as centralization increased, so

[5] Wolf, *Europe and the people*, 97.

did demands on workers and the need to use a modicum of threat and coercion to make them comply with provisionment of their hierarchies. People also revolted and overthrew political élites in response to repeated failure in performance, such as when chiefs' labor utilization conflicted repeatedly with subsistence needs.

Chiefly organization has considerable time-depth in South America. The earliest known chiefdoms are found at Real Alto in coastal Ecuador (Valdivia V, 2970–2755 B.C.E.) and at Cerro Narrío in the highlands (c. 2500 B.C.E.). On Peru's northern and central coasts, and possibly in the highland regions, chiefdoms are first discernible between 2500 and 1800 B.C.E. In the late second millennium and early first millennium B.C.E., peoples of the Chiripa, Wankarani, Qaluyu, Pukara, and early Tiwanaku cultures formed chiefdoms in the Bolivian *altiplano*. In northwest Argentina, northern Chile, and southwestern Colombia, chiefdoms are evident in the last millennium B.C.E.

In the first and second millennium C.E., chiefdoms were the predominant type of political organization in some areas of Greater Amazonia and in most of Colombia, Venezuela, Ecuador, and northwest Argentina. They were also present in coastal and highland Peru and in the Bolivian *altiplano*. In the latter two regions, chiefdoms coexisted with states that developed between 1200/800 and 200 B.C.E. to the fifteenth century C.E. Many were affected by them and came under their rule. In Peru and Bolivia before Inka annexation, some chiefdoms, such as Lima, Chincha, Ica, Quillaca, and Caracara, were settled in areas where states had been before. Most of the chiefdoms annexed by the Inka empire reemerged with chiefdom-like structure during the period between the empire's collapse and Spanish imposition of control, indicating the level of adaptability to change in social and environmental conditions that this form of organization had.

Centralization processes that were at work over great areas and very long spans of time are highlighted by first looking at the Chibcha of the eastern highlands of Colombia, a group on which there is sufficient documentation to work out the patterns of progressive levels of centralization in a setting unaffected directly by state or empire. Northernmost South America, the zone within which Chibcha polities were located, was characterized by its great numbers of chiefdoms; many of them were quite complex, and most were interactive with others beyond their own borders.

CHIBCHA CENTRALIZATION AND EXPANSION

Chibcha[6] polities have been classified as great chiefdoms, unusually large chiefdoms, an incipient state, nascent state, and kingdom. We understand them to have been complex chiefdoms; some of them were expansionist with tendencies in the direction of stratification and state formation but without bureaucratic infrastructure. The Chibcha occupied the *altiplano*, a natural subregion of the Cordillera Oriental, containing some fourteen highland basins that extend north of Bogotá for about 240 kilometers at elevations of 2,500 to 2,800 meters above sea level in the modern departments of Cundinamarca and Boyacá. The area has been covered by Pleistocene lakes, some quite deep, as well as by swamps and marshes. During the past several hundred years, Indians and European colonizers have tried to control flooding over the very fertile lacustrine soils. The Sabana de Bogotá is the first and largest of the basins north of the Páramo of Sumapaz, measuring about 350 kilometers in length and 200 kilometers in the widest area. Small transverse ranges border the basins north of the Sabana – Ubaté, Chiquinquirá, Tunja, Santa Rosa, and Sogamoso.

Although most Chibcha settlements were in the *altiplano*, there were also a number located at lower altitudes (elevations of between 1,200 m and 1,500 m) toward the Magdalena River in the east and the *llanos* in the west. In 1537 when the Spaniards arrived in Colombia's central highlands, they found two major Chibcha divisions that they called kingdoms. The southern part, the Sabana de Bogotá and Valley of Ubaté, was the realm of the Zipa, who had his capital in Bogotá (modern Funza): "The Bogotá [Zipa] is the highest lord in this land because subject to him are many other lords including very prominent ones."[7]

---

[6] We use the term *Chibcha* rather than *Muisca* in part to distinguish the ethnic group from the archaeological phases, which use the latter term. In addition, although *Muisca* (*Muysca*) was translated in Chibcha dictionaries as 'person', 'a man', early usage often was *Mosca* instead. *Mosca* appeared in the title of the first grammar published in 1619 (Fray Bernardo de Lugo, *Gramatica en la Lengua General del Nuevo Reyno, Llamada Mosca*, Madrid, 1619). According to two colonial writers, Fray Pedro Simón (*Noticias Historiales de las Conquistas de Tierra Firme en las Indias Occidentales* [1626], 5 vols. (Bogotá, 1882–1892) and Juan Rodríguez Freyle (*El Carnero* [1636], Bogotá, 1968), the appellation was understood by Spaniards to mean that the people were as numerous as flies (*moscas*), as Simón put it (II, 117) "los campos tan espesos como moscas sobre miel"; and Freyle (p. 90), "Se les pegó este nombre de moscas, que primero se acabarán todos ellos que el nombre." Given colonial conditions, it seems fairly likely that *Muisca/Mosca* had derogatory connotations.

[7] Juan de San Martin and Antonio Lebrija, "Relación Sobre la Conquista del Nuevo Reino de Granada [1539?]," in *Descubrimiento del Nuevo Reino de Granada y Fundación de Bogotá (1536–39)*, Juan Friede (Bogotá, 1960), 185.

The northern part was the domain of the Zaque, whose capital was Tunja. He was also described by the first Spanish observers as, "a very great lord with many lords subject to him."[8] The Zipa and the Zaque exercised control over large regions and were in the process of further political centralization. Although they had expanded their zones of control by forming alliances with other Chibcha chiefs, they were increasingly resorting to force or the threat of force in growth and rule. Father Aguado described the process:

Since their beginnings in antiquity there were always particular caciques and lords who had natives subject to them by pueblos or valleys and by and large they governed peaceably, after which the forces of two of these caciques and lords, called Tunja and Bogotá in this Nuevo Reino [de Granada] grew by tyrannical means, each one striving to subjugate the other chiefs in his locality . . . by force of arms.[9]

As they annexed territories both usually kept the structure of existing hierarchies intact, placing themselves at the top. A small area in the northeast, mainly in modern Boyacá, served as a refuge area where a few groups persisted in maintaining their independence during the Zaque's and the early Spaniards' conquest.

Subject to the Zipa at the time of European contact were between 90 and 100 dispersed Chibcha communities of varying size and political complexity, as well as groups of non-Chibcha peoples including Panches in the west and natives of the Orinoco *llanos* in the east.[10] The Zaque's domain included roughly the same number of Chibcha communities. Nucleation in highland communities occurred around the elaborate homesteads of the heads of the political hierarchies. Chiefs' and other high-level lords' compounds were described by Jiménez de Quesada, leader of the first European expedition to reach the area:

They are like castles with fortifications, with many fences around them as the labyrinths of Troy are customarily painted. They have large courtyards, houses of great proportions with very large carvings and also paintings on all of them.[11]

---

[8] San Martín and Lebrija, "Relación," 187. Anonymous, "Visita de 1560," 84, 77. (In Tunja it was observed, "A este cacique y señor obedecían y tenía subjetos a todos los demás caciques que ay"; and in the Zipa's region, "Todos los demás caciques le respetavan y obedecían por señor.")

[9] Fray Pedro de Aguado, *Recopilación Historial* [1581?], 4 vols. (Bogotá, 1956–1957), I, 259, 407–408.

[10] Anonymous, "Visita de 1560," 77: "Respetaban y obedecían . . . algunos Panches de la cibdad de Tocayma y algunos yndios de los llanos y le trayan cada año sus tributos."

[11] Gonzalo Jiménez de Quesada, "Epitome de la Conquista del Nuevo Reino de Granada" [1539] in Friede, *Descubrimiento del Nuevo Reino de Granada*, 265, 253–273.

In most cases each community was under the authority of a single lord to whom leaders of the several distinct kinship-territorial units that made up the community were subject. The officer at the apex of the community's political hierarchy was referred to generically in Chibcha dictionaries as *sijipcua* and in Spanish documents and chronicles as *cacique*. *Sijipcuas'* names were the same as the communities over which each presided, a usage found consistently in colonial documents, albeit in hispanicized versions, now standard in the literature (e.g., the Bogotá, the Guatavita, the Duitama):

> And each lord has his valley, and the name of the lord and the valley is the same; and the importance of the lordship varies. There is a lord of ten thousand vassals, and such that have twenty thousand.[12]

The office of *sijipcua* (chief, *cacique*) was permanent and was the political, ceremonial, and judicial focus of the community. Occupants of office were afforded great respect and obedience. They could not be looked at in the face, were carried about on litters, and were set above all others by a series of sumptuary rules. Preparation for succession to office included long periods of seclusion and training in civil and religious matters. Jiménez de Quesada spoke at some length of the chiefs:

> The reverence that subjects have toward their caciques is very great, for which reason they never look at them in the face even if they are in ordinary conversation; so that if they enter where the cacique is they have to enter with their backs toward him, making their way backwards; and now seated or on foot they must remain so, because as a mark of respect they always have their backs turned.

Regarding their preparation for office:

> And there is a man that for seven years . . . must not see the sun . . . and once out, they can pierce their ears and noses for gold [ornaments], which is a matter of great honor among them. They also wear gold on their breasts which are covered with [gold] plates. Likewise they wear some gold engraved helmets like mitres, and they also have their arms covered with engraved gold.[13]

Sijipcuas headed religious activities and were in control of temples, priests, and a large number of sacred artifacts. Paths were built from their compounds, where there were special shrines or sanctuaries, to other

---

[12] Gonzalo Fernández de Oviedo, *Historia General y Natural de las Indias (1514–48)*, 5 vols. (Madrid, 1959), III, 125.
[13] Jiménez de Quesada, "Epitome de la Conquista," 266, 267.

locations in their territories. Along the paths processions, races (*carreras*), offerings, and religious festivities were carried out. The political position of *sijipcua* was underwritten by religious ideology. A Chibcha creation story recounts that the first chief of Sogamoso and his nephew, the lord of Tunja, created man from yellow earth and woman from a tall hollow reed. They then created the light-giving sun and moon to which people had the duty to pray, and *sijipcuas* to serve as intermediaries. Aguado reported that Chief Sogamoso, whom the Spaniards met, was:

a man of great veneration and religious reverence, considered by virtue of their superstitions the son of the sun, who as a result of being a person of such great esteem possessed vast riches which he had not only in his house but in his temples and oratories.[14]

Castellanos wrote that Sogamoso was believed to be able to "Change the seasons / [to make it] rain and hail, and send frosts."[15] In the Sabana de Bogotá, Bochica (Xue, the sun god) communicated with *sijipcuas* and *sivintivas* (officials under them) and was their private god.

Sijipcuas coordinated the agricultural round, presiding over celebrations having to do with cultivation, harvest, and the general well-being of the community. They administered justice, organized for defense or war, and received tribute and labor service from their subjects. Local and most likely long-distance trade were coordinated by them. Most markets took place in the chiefs' quarters. The largest and most important were in the major political centers, as described by Aguado:

It is a very ancient custom in the town of Tunja that every four days a market is held in the cacique's own compound, to which an infinite number of people of all ranks come to traffic and trade, to sell and buy, to which even many caciques and prominent lords come, as much to see the Cacique of Tunja in whose pueblo it takes place as for their particular interests and profits which these barbarians never neglect, no matter how great and prominent lords they might be.[16]

The chronicler, in expressing the colonial Spanish bias against engagement of élites in commerce, pointed out that the Chibcha political

[14] Aguado, *Recopilación Historial*, I, 293. Simón, *Noticias Historiales*, II, 312–313.
[15] Juan de Castellanos, *Elegías de Varones Ilustres de Indias* [1601], 4 vols. (Bogota, 1955), IV, 160.
[16] Aguado, *Recopilación Historial*, I, p. 341. Anonymous, "Visita de 1560," 77:"Los yndios desta provincia [Sabana de Bogotá] an tenido y tienen costumbre de hazer sus mercados como en España, cada día de la semana en poblazon de un cacique principal a los quales mercados acude gran cantidad de gente."

hierarchy was deeply involved in trade. Despite their disdain, Spaniards were quite impressed by the natives' economic activity, more so than by their military skills. It is likely that chiefs had specialized traders in their service, particularly for exchange of salt and emeralds, products for which Chibcha people were known far outside the region. Simón mentions that traders' groups had their own god, Chibchachum, who was also the god of the province of Bogotá. Common people probably also traveled to local markets, bringing their own produce and exchanging it for other goods. Gold, emeralds, cloth blankets (*mantas*), and other products were accumulated in *sijipcuas*' compounds under the conservation of a steward. Although they retained substantial wealth, *sijipcuas* were known for their beneficence. In testimony elicited in *visitas* during the 1590s, numerous *caciques* stated that the offering of special feasts for their people was a traditional obligation of office on the occasion of tribute payment, work on chiefs' fields, celebration of victories or religious festivals, and in times of need. Zorita, in setting the scene for his *Lords of New Spain*, mentions the Chibcha chief, Sogamoso:

> He came to see me from his pueblo which was more than thirty leagues away and he brought a great entourage; and as he came to each pueblo the first thing he commanded was to find out if there were any poor people, Indians or Spaniards, and he ordered that they be provided with food and firewood because it is very cold territory.[17]

Sijipcuas lived apart from their people in fenced-off areas (*cercados*). Succession to office was matrilineal, the preferred heir being the oldest son of the *sijipcua*'s oldest sister. The rules and practices of succession linked lineages and diverse communities, as we discuss later.[18] Chiefs had a number of women in their service – wives, mistresses, and preparers of food and drink for the periodic ceremonies and festivities that they offered. Jiménez de Quesada stated that Bogotá, "who was king of all the caciques," had more than 400 women in his entourage. Aguado estimated that twenty or thirty of them were wives.[19]

Subject to the *sijipcua* were heads of the territorial and kinship units that made up the community, officers called *capitanes* by the Spaniards

---

[17] Alonso de Zorita, *Los Señores de la Nueva España* [1584] (Mexico, 1963), 20.

[18] Matrilateral cross-cousin marriage was prescribed, potentially reinforcing loyalties and allegiances through lineages as well as across them. Over the course of three generations, it was possible for the office to pass from the *sijipcua*'s nephew to his grandson.

[19] Jiménez de Quesada, "Epitome de la Conquista," 267. Aguado, *Recopilación Historial*, I, 273.

and *sivintiva* (zybyntyva) in Chibcha dictionaries. *Sivintivas* administered the lands of their kinship units (*sivin*), which often were dispersed over several square kilometers and included from several hundred to several thousand people.[20] They were responsible for transmitting the *sijipcua*'s commands to the people and for organizing their payment of labor and tribute to him. The following native testimony regarding tribute payment to the chief, one of several hundred similar ones, was given in 1594:

He had heard from the old and aged Indians that before the Christians entered this land all the Indians paid tribute to their caciques and every year each capitan gave his chief seven or eight ordinary *mantas* and with that some gold, and the other Indians one small *manta* and in addition to this they cultivated his fields and built his houses and fences and they paid him the said tribute when they went to do work for him and the caciques gave the Indians food and drink and to each of the capitanes they gave a *manta* of good quality and they did this after the Spaniards came for some time until the custom began to be lost.[21]

Tribute payment was rewarded with the honor of being anointed with red pigment by the *sijipcua* and by his providing a feast on the occasion. Political hierarchies stored a large measure of tribute, part for the aggrandizement of their offices, part for trade, and part for provisionment during short times.[22]

Subject to the *sivintivas* were headmen of local kinship units, lineages, called *utas*, a term translated in early dictionaries as *capitanías menores*. The unit itself was also called *uta*. *Utas* linked commoners and *sivintivas* by carrying out commands at the grass-roots level, as well as overseeing and probably protecting lands. Little is known regarding the succession of *uta* headmen who carried out the same round of work as all others and were not given tribute or labor service. *Sivintivas*, however, like *sijipcuas*, succeeded to their offices matrilineally and had privileges that

[20] Chiefdoms' incorporation and transcending of local communities or villages have been used as defining characteristics of this mode of organization (see Robert L. Carneiro, "The chiefdom: Precursor of the state," in Grant Jones and Robert Kautz, eds., *The transition to statehood in the New World* (New York, 1981), 37–79 and Timothy K. Earle, "Chiefdoms in archaeological and ethnohistorical perspective," in Bernard J. Siegel (ed.), *Annual review of anthropology* (Palo Alto, 1987), XVI, 279–308). The concepts of "community" and "village" are recalcitrant, however, and, at the very least, variable with respect to the views and purposes of the observer. In the Chibcha case, the *sivin* might justifiably be viewed as the local community, one of several encompassed within the *sijipcúa*'s (chief's) domain, the larger unit that we refer to as community.

[21] Archivo Histórico Nacional de Colombia (AHNC), Visitas de Cúndinamarca, vol. 4, fol. 44r (Cucunubá-Bobota).

[22] AHNC, Visitas de Cúndinamarca, vol. 11, fol. 147v (Chocontá, 1593). Castellanos, *Elegías de Varones Ilustres*, IV, 235.

distinguished them from commoners including deferential treatment, tribute, labor, and gifts of special red and painted blankets from their *sijipcuas.*

In 1537, when the Spaniards entered the area, there were a few small, autonomous communities headed by *sijipcuas* that were not politically connected to any other. Such independent communities may have been more commonplace at one time. In 1572 Saquencipa, a community that had resettled in a refuge area of Boyacá, was described as never having been

subject to any other chiefs besides the one of their pueblo to whom they gave some *mantas* and pieces of gold, and they built his fences and huts and tilled his fields and hunted deer and rabbits for him.[23]

Beyond *sijipcua*-led communities, there were a number of political linkages that had been formalized prior to the Zipa's and Zaque's expansion. In the Zipa's area, there were ties between communities through marriage, focusing on *sijipcua* succession. Bogotá and Chía, for example, were linked: The chief of Chía was designated as heir to the office of *sijipcua* of Bogotá. A similar arrangement existed between Tuna and Suba. In the Zaque's region the chief of Ramiriquí succeeded as head of Tunja, and the chief of Tobasía succeeded as head of Duitama, or Sogamoso. Sogamoso's chieftainship alternated between Tobasía and Firavitova. Succession was supervised by four other *sijipcuas* who were also under Sogamoso. In difficult cases Duitama was invited to participate in selection of the heir. Tobasía linked the powerful Duitama and Sogamoso realms. It is possible that similar arrangements for political succession had been worked out among communities that the Spaniards identified as single units, such as Chocontá, Simijaca, or Ubaté in the savannah (*sabana*), but that the Indians considered to be two or three separate communities with distinct *sijipcuas* and *sivintivas.* Whereas these arrangements were primarily of a kinship-administrative nature, their effect was to create political units that were larger and had greater resources than most, particularly favoring the dominant community. Their linkage afforded advantages in dealing with political, economic, and environmental stresses. In some cases the position of *sijipcua* in the larger, more dominant community was ascended to by the *sijipcua* of the smaller one, underscoring not only the lineage bonds involved but the complementar-

---

[23] AHNC, Visitas de Boyacá, vol. 7, fol. 562r.

ity of the communities' material needs and resources. Such blocs involved populations of several thousand.

A higher level of centralization and expansion, one that involved almost all the communities in Chibcha domain, was characterized by regional alliances of *cacicazgos* based on politics, kinship, marriage, economic relations, and religious belief and practice. In these blocs several neighboring communities, each headed by its own *sijipcua*, were under the authority of one who commanded greater resources, prestige, and ritual powers than all the others. Divine power, evident in the *sijipcuas'* positions, was further heightened and reinforced in the regional lords' roles by their dominion over important sacred centers and centrality in key ceremonial practices. In the Zipa's domain, the Bogotá presided over one such confederation, and the Guatavita over another. Ubaté headed a third, and just outside the savannah, Ubaque (subject to the Zipa) a fourth. Guatavita had authority over twelve to fifteen communities in the valleys of Guatavita and Guachetá. Their combined territory ranged from *tierra caliente* to *paramo* and contained an important source of salt, as well as Lake Guatavita – a major sacred center.[24] Ubaque also held a sacred lake as well as the fertile Cáqueza Valley connecting the savannah with the *llanos*. Bogotá had a major temple in Chía and possibly controlled the salt mines of Zipaquirá. In addition Bogotá had control and use of warmer-climate lands at lower altitudes and gave access to them to other highland communities under its domain, such as Subachoque, Bosa, Fontibón, and Tenjo.

In the Zaque's region Duitama's authority extended over twenty-five pueblos and Sogamoso's over more than twenty-one; Tunja had fewer in its zone of influence. Sogamoso was a major religious center and, as noted previously, was linked to Duitama.

Commoners gave tribute and labor service to regional paramounts through their *sijipcuas*, who linked communities to the higher political levels. The process of creating large regional associations permitted dominant communities – Bogotá, Guatavita, Duitama, Sogamoso, Tunja – to gain control over territory in a great variety of ecological zones at different altitudes. Subordinate communities gained entrance into a cycle of exchange of goods from a greater range of climates than they might

---

[24] Aguado, *Recopilación Historial*, IV, 63. Aguado wrote that Guatavita "was famous among the natives for once having been a rival of the cacique of Bogotá, and some still hold that he was lord over more people than was Bogotá."

otherwise have had, as well as access to ritual services on the part of the dominant community. Regional groupings permitted stronger defense against enemies, more effective organization of trade, and specialization in crafts and agricultural products. They involved tens of thousands of people. At both the small and large regional bloc levels, multiple lineage rights and obligations were managed in part through successive layers of political hierarchy, creating larger, more diverse polities with emphasis, although not exclusive dependence, on proactive alliance. Both the small and the regional associations appear to have been integrated as whole entities by the Zipa and Zaque.

Expansion beyond the regional level was carried on by outright military conquest. It was by force that Bogotá overpowered Guatavita and others in the savannah and proclaimed himself Supreme Lord, Zipa. Zipa Nemequene was in armed conflict with the Zaque just prior to the European invasion, and he lost his life in that attempt. When the Spaniards came, his successor, Zipa Tisquesusa, was in the process of organizing a second expedition. He had built fortifications on the boundaries with the Panches, sending some of his best military men (*guechas*) there. The battle between Bogotá and Tunja was well entrenched:

> They strove to win each other's domains
> to which effect at various times
> there were great armed encounters and battles
> in which neither could attain
> the fulfillment of his claims.
> They were ancient, these contests.[25]

When Bogotá gained military control over the savannah and adjacent areas, he did not dismantle hierarchical structures but built on them, arranging marriages for his sisters and other relatives with the traditional political leaders. Bogotá as Zipa made his confirmation of new chiefs mandatory, with ceremonies that involved reciprocal exchanges. There are indications that *sijipcuas* and other important military-political leaders were graded in rank with reference to the Zipa, and that a warrior corps and perhaps a permanent army were in the process of being established, as well as overseers for tribute collection. The Zipa constructed storage facilities in communities other than his own for food and weapons in preparation for war with the Zaque. Further underscoring the centrali-

---

[25] Castellanos, *Elegías de Varones Ilustres*, IV, 141. In Anonymous, "Visita de 1560" (84), Bogotá and Tunja are noted to each have had "en los con(n)fines de su tierra su capitán general y guarnición."

zation process, Zipa Nemequene gave a code of laws applicable in the whole of his domain after his conquest of Guatavita and Ubaque. The Zaque may have done the same. Major conflicts, however, remained between the Zipa and some *sijipcuas*. They were brought to light when the Spaniards arrived in 1537. Dissenting *sijipcuas* formed alliances with the newcomers, using their presence to challenge the Zipa.

The Zaque incorporated conquered communities in some cases but also drove out populations or caused groups to leave their territories for areas not under his control. His rule was challenged by the powerful Sogamoso and Duitama. Although the two insisted on their own importance, the *cacique* of Sogamoso stated in 1566 that Tunja and Bogotá had greater authority and sovereignty than any of the other *caciques*. It is possible that Tunja strengthened his position and gained Sogamoso's and Duitama's fealty in the process of stopping the Zipa's expansion into the area. The Zipa and the Zaque each had populations of several hundred thousand within their dominions. Conquest by either would have consolidated most of the *altiplano* Chibcha into one unit at a yet higher level of centralization, or alternatively might have caused sufficient pressure for groups to break apart, as they did when the Spaniards interrupted the process.

An in-depth regional archaeological approach is needed to see whether the processes of centralization among the Chibcha that we describe were of a cyclical nature. Wright has suggested that complex chiefdoms tend to "cycle between one and two levels of control hierarchy" above the local community.[26] In the Chibcha case perhaps such cycles occurred between the lords of regional alliances (Guatavita, Sogamoso) on the one hand, and the supraregional Zipa or Zaque on the other. Chibcha people had a long history in the area and are clearly linked to eighth-century *altiplano* residents. Their ancestors may have occupied the region since the first centuries C.E. or earlier.

Sixteenth-century Chibcha polities were the most highly centralized in northeastern Colombia. To their north in the Cordillera Oriental, there were other Chibcha-speaking groups – Guane, Lache, and Tunebo – that had chiefdom organization without paramounts. To the west in the Magdalena Valley were "Panches," "Muzos," and other groups, probably all Carib speakers. The polities called "Panches" by Spaniards constituted

---

[26] Henry T. Wright, "Prestate political formations," in Timothy Earle (ed.), *On the evolution of complex societies* (Malibu, 1984), 43.

a number of independent groups with a wide range of degrees of political centralization from tribal, with charismatic leaders, to chiefdoms, with hereditary officers presiding over local hierarchies. The names, Muzo, Pantágoras, Yareguí, and Carare, also encompassed a large number of independent groups, probably with weak centralization. The Chibcha traded and fought with some of them.

Long-distance trade linked Chibcha chiefdoms with other areas, some with highly centralized paramount-headed polities such as those in the Cauca River valley, Caribbean Colombian coast, coastal Ecuador, and Amazonia, the regions we consider next. Although many different types of societies were involved in long-distance exchange, in chiefdoms it provided élite access to scarce and valued goods that could be used to buttress hierarchical power, as Helms has pointed out in the context of her discussion of exchange of esoteric goods and information between Panamanian and Colombian chiefs.[27] Exotic products were important in religious functions and heightened the chiefs' and élites' distinction. Marine snails from the Caribbean coast and gold from the Magdalena and Cauca valleys, for example, were significant parts of Chibcha chiefs' paraphernalia. A document of 1559/60 refers to another outcome resulting from long-distance contact, noting that "some natives of the [Orinoco] Llanos" where the Chibcha traded salt were subject to the *cacique* of Bogotá, "the foremost lord of this land."[28] The *llanos* apparently were an arena not only for Chibcha trade but for Chibcha expansion, affording them a markedly different ecology from the highlands.

Sijipcuas gave local élites special gifts acquired via long-distance trade or crafted locally in manufactures that they controlled (such as dyed *mantas*), in addition to titles and marriage exchanges. Bestowal of such gifts and rights to members of chiefly hierarchies was common throughout the chiefdoms discussed in this chapter. Whether or not redistribution was characteristic of chiefdoms has been recently discussed at some length. What we find in looking at the Chibcha case is that chiefly redistribution was most important at the level of *sijipcua*-headed units and less so as one passed to regional and paramount levels. Eyewitnesses reported that there were substantial accumulations of wealth and food in chiefs' compounds. Such stockpiles were larger in the regional lords'

---

[27] Mary W. Helms, *Ancient Panama. Chiefs in search of power* (Austin, 1979).
[28] Anonymous, "Visita de 1560," 76, 77. According to this document Chibcha traders carried salt to the Llanos, Popayán, Neiva, Mariquita, and Saldaña, "Y se tiene entendido que van por via de rescate duzientas leguas la tierra adentro."

compounds (for example, in those of Guatavita and Sogamoso) and largest in those of the Zipa and Zaque. Paramount and regional chiefs' redistribution of goods to people outside their own communities appears to have been less significant than chiefs' to their subjects, despite displays of generosity by the former in times of need, and feasting in the course of religious celebrations, completion of public works, or warfare.

OTHER COMPLEX CHIEFDOMS

Major trade networks in which Chibcha participated were located in the Cauca River valley and Caribbean regions, zones with many chiefdoms of different degrees of centralization in the sixteenth century. In the Cauca Valley unusually long and elaborate routes – some with bridges and stone roads, which Spanish explorers described as impressive – connected different polities. Markets were established, and specialists were employed in production of goods and possibly in carrying out exchanges. Cauca peoples' engagement in trade although intense was shared by chiefdoms such as the Chibcha and many others. What was distinctive in the Cauca Valley was the role and frequency of warfare, the ideology attached to it, and the overall effects that it had on regional culture. Although little is known as yet regarding the process of prehispanic centralization in the Cauca or Caribbean regions, the general outlines of hierarchical structures can be discerned from materials dating to the Spanish conquest and early colonial period. We look at paramount-headed groups first, moving north to south through the Cauca region and then back to the Caribbean.

Colombian Cauca and Patía Valleys and Adjacent Highlands

The numerous chiefdoms of the León, Atrato, Cauca, and Patía river valleys, tributary valleys, and surrounding mountain areas of the Cordilleras Occidental and Central (see Map 7.1) were actively involved in extensive trade as well as in warfare for expansion, defense, and acquisition of slaves.[29] Unlike the Chibcha, Cauca Valley chiefdoms and those of nearby valleys and highlands had slaves on a large scale that they

[29] In prehispanic America slaves varied from one society to another with respect to treatment accorded them and access to resources. Generally speaking slaves were individuals who had lost their rights of inheritance, resource use, succession, and protection by kin and community.

Colombia, Venezuela and Coastal Ecuador
ca. C.E. 1400–1550

Map 7.1

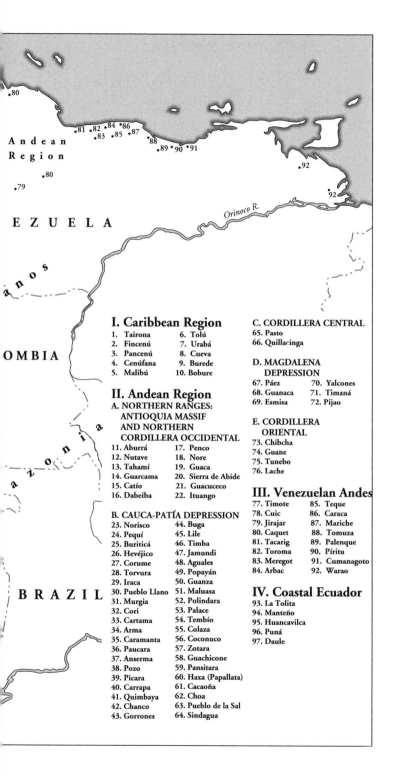

.80

A n d e a n
R e g i o n

.81 .82 .84 .86
.83 .85 .87
.88
.89 .90 .91
.92

.80

.79

.92

Orinoco R.

E Z U E L A

a n o s

O M B I A

a z o n i a

B R A Z I L

I. Caribbean Region
1. Tairona
2. Fincenú
3. Pancenú
4. Cenúfana
5. Malibú
6. Tolú
7. Urabá
8. Cueva
9. Burede
10. Bobure

II. Andean Region
A. NORTHERN RANGES: ANTIOQUIA MASSIF AND NORTHERN CORDILLERA OCCIDENTAL
11. Aburrá
12. Nutave
13. Tahamí
14. Guarcama
15. Catío
16. Dabeiba
17. Penco
18. Nore
19. Guaca
20. Sierra de Abide
21. Guacuceco
22. Ituango

B. CAUCA-PATÍA DEPRESSION
23. Norisco
24. Pequí
25. Buriticá
26. Hevéjico
27. Corume
28. Torvura
29. Iraca
30. Pueblo Llano
31. Murgia
32. Cori
33. Cartama
34. Arma
35. Caramanta
36. Paucara
37. Anserma
38. Pozo
39. Picara
40. Carrapa
41. Quimbaya
42. Chanco
43. Gorrones
44. Buga
45. Lile
46. Timba
47. Jamundi
48. Aguales
49. Popayán
50. Guanza
51. Maluasa
52. Polindara
53. Palace
54. Tembío
55. Colaza
56. Coconuco
57. Zotara
58. Guachicone
59. Pansitara
60. Haxa (Papallata)
61. Cacaoña
62. Choa
63. Pueblo de la Sal
64. Sindagua

C. CORDILLERA CENTRAL
65. Pasto
66. Quillacinga

D. MAGDALENA DEPRESSION
67. Páez
68. Guanaca
69. Esmisa
70. Yalcones
71. Timaná
72. Pijao

E. CORDILLERA ORIENTAL
73. Chibcha
74. Guane
75. Tunebo
76. Lache

III. Venezuelan Andes
77. Timote
78. Cuic
79. Jirajar
80. Caquet
81. Tacarig
82. Toroma
83. Meregot
84. Arbac
85. Teque
86. Caraca
87. Mariche
88. Tomuza
89. Palenque
90. Píritu
91. Cumanagoto
92. Warao

IV. Coastal Ecuador
93. La Tolita
94. Manteño
95. Huancavilca
96. Puná
97. Daule

utilized for their labor, as important items of exchange, and for sacrificial and cannibalistic purposes. Cannibalism and acquisition of trophy heads and other body parts were characteristic of the Cauca region and of neighboring Cenúfana groups in the Caribbean zone, suggesting a substantially distinct worldview from the Chibcha, other Caribbean chiefdoms such as Tairona, and even other Cenú groups that did not engage in these practices.

Levels of political complexity varied in Cauca region chiefdoms, but at least fourteen of fifty-four ethnically distinct polities had paramounts whose domain extended over other lords and principales. We discuss three: Guaca, Buriticá, and Popayán, each from a different region.

In the 1530s Guaca, Dabeiba, and Nore chiefdoms as well as many others occupied the ecologically complex northwestern Antioquia region between the Cauca River to the east and Río Sucio and the Penderisco River to the west and southwest.[30] The Guaca paramount, Nutibara, was described as "a lord or great and powerful cacique."[31] He succeeded his father to office while the latter was still alive but probably too old to carry out some of the duties of chief such as command in warfare. Nutibara received gold, jewels, *mantas*, food, and peccary in tribute, was carried on a litter covered with gold by individuals of high rank, and had "many wives." In addition to attendants he had specialized individuals in his service, such as messengers and interpreters who knew several languages. Nutibara had a large, well-organized army that was under the field command of his younger brother, Quinuchú. Preparation for war was backed up by an amply provisioned fort capable of sustaining a sizable population.

Chief Nutibara annexed the gold-rich Sierra de Abibe area, appointed Quinuchú as its governor, and collected tribute from its people. Territorial expansion brought the Guaca polity into open conflict with Nore peoples, who were involved in hostilities on multiple fronts. Throughout the region warfare was important for expansion and defense as well as for the capture of laborers and sacrificial victims. Trophy heads were collected and displayed on the doors of Nutibara's compound and on those of his officer-nobles, as well as at cannibalistic feasts, which early chroniclers such as Cieza de León reported. In war neither women nor children

---

[30] It is difficult to pinpoint exact locations of Cauca Valley chiefdoms until further study is done and consequently to assay the degree to which they were or were not geographically circumscribed.

[31] Cieza de León, *Crónica del Perú*, I, 51.

were spared. Women accompanied men to battle and to the feasts that celebrated victory.

The complex exchange network that linked groups in Antioquia, Central America, the Colombian coast, and other parts of modern Colombia and Venezuela included the Guaca polity. Paramounts like Nutibara may have been in command of long-distance trade in which among other goods slaves, gold, and *mantas* were exchanged, items that Guaca chiefs and their officers had in abundance. When chiefs died, opulent gold offerings were placed with them in the temples where they were buried. One such sanctuary, sacked and burned by *conquistadores*, yielded a treasure valued at 10,000 to 30,000 pesos (some estimates go as high as 100,000 pesos). The paramount chiefs of Nore and Dabeiba also had great wealth, and the latter was known to employ 100 people in a gold workshop. In 1513 in one of the few reports on the region, Nuñez de Balboa wrote that Chief "Davaive" was

a very great lord of considerable territory with a great many people; he has gold in bountiful quantity in his house, so much that it would be quite unlikely to believe for someone who didn't know the affairs of this land.[32]

Buriticá, Pequí, Corume, Caramanta, Paucura, and Carrapa – all paramount-headed chiefdoms – were located in the northern Cauca River Valley, the eastern flanks of the Cordillera Occidental, and the western flanks of the Cordillera Central, a zone characterized by wide variations in relief, temperature, rainfall, and vegetation. At least thirteen other ethnic groups with a multiplicity of somewhat less centralized chiefdoms also occupied the region (see Map 7.1).

Buriticá, located between the Cauca, Sucio, and Tonusco rivers, was an important center where several major trade routes converged. Trimborn, one of the earliest scholars to emphasize the importance of long-distance trade in the region, worked out the four most important routes that linked it to other areas in northern South America and Central America. One headed northwest, connecting Buriticá with the Nore, Guaca, Dabeiba, and others. It appears to have gone on further to parts of Panamá and Central America. On this route Antioquian gold as well as goods obtained afar such as Chibcha emeralds, were traded for slaves,

[32] Vasco Nuñez de Balboa, "Cartas Dirigidas al Rey 20 de Enero 1513 y 16 Octubre de 1515," in *Obras de Don Martín Fernández de Navarrete* (Madrid, 1964), II, 218 (215–230).

peccary, fish, cotton, textiles, salt, and objects made of gold and metal amalgam.

The second route went north to the Sinú River, the Sierra Nevada de Santa Marta, northern Venezuela, and the Antilles. Gold and gold objects were moved northward along it while slaves, fish, peccary, salt, cotton textiles, and some manufactured products such as gold goblets were conveyed to Buriticá.

A third route connected Buriticá with the upper valley of the Porce. From there one branch went to the southeast to areas of the Rio Negro and Nare River. Another went northeast to the Yolombo region; then both headed toward the Magdalena River, where they were united with a trade route that came from the Chibcha of the Cundinamarca-Boyacá zone. Gold that was moved out of the Antioquia area was exchanged for salt, *mantas*, and emeralds.

The fourth route headed south along the Cauca River. Gold and gold objects and food moved southward, while salt, foods, and textiles moved north.[33] The four major routes and their lateral connectors linked many ethnically and linguistically distinct populations, including macro-Chibchan, macro-Caribbean, and Arawakan speakers. Along the routes markets and fairs were held, arenas in which some degree of immunity from hostilities was most likely maintained, as the entire region in the sixteenth century was witness to active and intense warfare.

In 1537 Vadillo wrote that the paramount of Buriticá, Tapeepe, was "very prominent . . . he is a man of great stature . . . he has more than one hundred thousand Indians."[34] He added that Tapeepe had a gold mine in his domain that his subjects worked for him which he allowed other chiefs to exploit as well. It was located at some distance from the main settlement where gold was smelted and gold jewelry and other objects were manufactured. Tapeepe held large amounts of the precious metal, a major item of trade.

Tapeepe and his hierarchy managed military activity, the capture of slaves, and cannibalism that was involved in war. He lived in a fortified

---

[33] Herman Trimborn, *Señorío y Barbarie en el Valle del Cauca* (Madrid, 1949), 175–189, 191–192, 126, 160, 162, 166.

[34] Juan de Vadillo, "Cartas del lycenciado Xoan de Vadillo a su majestad, dándole cuenta de su vysita a la Gobernación de Cartagena, (1537)," in *Colección de Documentos Inéditos Relativos al Descubrimiento, Conquista y Organización de las Antiguas Posesiones Españolas de América y Oceanía* (Madrid, 1884), XLI, 404 (356–420).

settlement in the flattest section of a hilly area. Spanish soldiers took his fort after some skirmishes and found abundant food and *mantas* stored there. Some gold jewelry was also uncovered, but Tapeepe, who escaped, had taken most of it and buried it.

The southern part of the Cauca-Patía Valley, Popayán, the highest region of the depression (at 1,500 m–1,700 m above sea level), also had a great many chiefdoms. The area, crossed by rivers that flow from the Cordillera Central, has been filled by alluvial deposits and volcanic ash and lava. Best known among the chiefdoms in the region is Popayán, subject to a celebrated paramount, also called Popayán. Described as "one of the foremost lords that there was in those provinces,"[35] Popayán had domain over communities in the valley of Pubenza and the ranges nearby. His brother, Calambás, appears to have been the chief of a number of pueblos populated by a different ethnic group in the indigenous "province" of Guambía, most likely recently conquered by Popayán at the time of contact. Chief Popayán's fort was made of bamboo, where Spaniards found abundant supplies of food and well-appointed lodgings, which suggest his readiness for involvement in warfare. Guambiano groups had been under attack by the Indians of Tierra Adentro, a situation that persisted through colonial times, as groups from east of the cordillera moved into the Popayán region.

Chiefs of Popayán, like those in the rest of the Cauca region, coastal Ecuador, and the Colombian Caribbean and *altiplano*, were polygamous. When they died they were buried in their compounds with wives, servants, food, clothing, and in many cases large amounts of gold and jewelry. Here as elsewhere in the regions mentioned, there were close ties between chiefs, the gods, and their cults, with chiefs' courtyards, plazas, and designated buildings (as in Popayán) serving as major loci of religious ceremonies and human sacrifice.

Warfare among Cauca Valley chiefdoms and the role of war in the process of centralization has recently been discussed by Carneiro, who writes that the evidence

points to the fact that chiefdoms were born out of war, were powerfully shaped by war, and continued to be heavily involved in war as they evolved. Furthermore, the evidence marshalled by Trimborn supports the view that states, in

[35] Cieza de León, *Crónica del Perú*, I, 102. On Popayán, see also Castellanos, *Elegías de Varones Ilustres*, III, 351, 353.

turn, arise as the culmination of a process in which stronger chiefdoms, continuing their successful military careers, defeat, incorporate, and assimilate weaker ones.[36]

Possibly warfare and the cannibalism that accompanied it bolstered political centralization processes by affording opportunities for élites and warriors to demonstrate bravery, skill in headhunting, and defense against other chiefdoms and invaders from the eastern flanks of the Cordillera Central. Acquisition of territory, goods, and slaves, and subsequent strategic allocation of at least part of them, must have served to build up their positions. Although warfare may have strengthened political hierarchies, its implication as a causal factor in their development is not certain in our view. In the Chibcha case warfare was important in late phases of centralization leading to paramountcy, a type of organization shared by only a quarter of the Cauca polities. Yet all of the Cauca chiefdoms were engaged in hostilities. Warfare also caused political fragmentation, as occurred with the Aburrá chiefdoms of the Antioquia massif shortly before European contact. Conquistador Robledo wrote:

Along this whole route there are large sites of ancient towns and of very large buildings, of carefully constructed and sizeable roads through the mountains and along the slopes, of which there are no better in Cuzco. And all of this is lost and destroyed.[37]

Aburrá population had dispersed, but their territory was not occupied by any other groups nor had they come under the control of any other polity.

Robledo spent several weeks in the area looking for a settlement. Instead he found "one hut and at two leagues' distance, another, and each [household] had cultivated its own crop of corn and yucca."[38] Whatever political organization remained was not discernible to him. Puzzled about the scattered population and the contrasting remains of large public works such as the roads and buildings, Robledo made inquiries as he moved toward Tahamí territory. A chief told him that "there was a very large population ahead ... the provinces of Nutave

---

[36] Robert L. Carneiro, "The nature of the chiefdom as revealed by evidence from the Cauca Valley of Colombia," in A. Terry Rambo and Kathleen Gillogly (eds.), *Profiles of evolution* (Ann Arbor, 1991), 181 (167–190).

[37] Jorge Robledo, "Descripción de los Pueblos de la Provincia de Ancerma (1540–1541)," in *Colección de Documentos Inéditos*, III (1865), 402–403 (389–413).

[38] Juan Baptista Sardella, "Relación del Descubrimiento de Las Provincias de Antiochia por Jorge Robledo (1540)," in *Colección de Documentos Inéditos*, II (1864), 316–317 (291–356).

[and] Urezo where the lord who had caused such destruction was to be found."[39] Previous to the devastating war, Aburrá had been an important political center with a large population, and one of the most important links in trade routes that connected the east and west of today's Colombia.

Fragmentation had occurred earlier as well. For example, in the Cauca Valley, Calima chiefdoms flourished between C.E. 100 and 1200. Smaller, less-complex polities succeeded them and continued to occupy the territory until European contact.

Chiefdoms of Colombia's Caribbean Coast

Sixteenth-century Cenú and Tairona chiefdoms of the Caribbean coast although quite complex may also have been descendants of larger, more centralized polities. The two groups inhabited quite different regions of the Caribbean coast: The Cenú occupied a low-lying area with flat basins and soft, undulating hills that rise to 300 meters, and the Tairona occupied sections of an isolated triangular-shaped mountain massif, the Sierra Nevada de Santa Marta, which pierces the northeast coast about 40 kilometers inland. Surrounded by tectonic depressions, and measuring about 150 kilometers on each side, it has peaks that rise close to 5,800 meters above sea level. With the exception of the Sierra Nevada, the Caribbean region is hot, averaging temperatures over 27° C.

Cenú polities occupied the lowland basins of the Sinú and upper San Jorge rivers, a region containing extensive savannahs, some of which are periodically flooded to form great marshes. This was also a region where chiefdoms had developed during the first three centuries C.E. Sixteenth-century Cenú were culturally related to people of the San Jorge River basin who built large-scale earthworks – raised fields, drainage systems, and artificial canals over an area of about 5,000 square kilometers – between the second and eleventh centuries C.E., a time when the area's greatest population density was attained. From the eleventh century on, people gradually abandoned the area for higher, unflooded zones. There is evidence that between the fourteenth and seventeenth centuries Malibú groups moved into the area and settled at higher elevations, having nothing to do with the raised fields.

During the Spanish-contact period, Cenú chiefdoms were described

---

[39] Sardella, "Relación del Descubrimiento," 318. Robledo, "Descripción," 402–403.

as having large numbers of people. Some, particularly the Fincenú, lived in nucleated areas with streets, plazas, and well-built houses. They grew abundant maize, beans, sweet manioc, sweet potatoes, and fruits, hunted a variety of animals, and fished. There were three major Cenú political divisions, each of which encompassed multiple communities and extensive territories not unlike Chibcha paramountcies, with the important exception that one of the paramount chiefs at the time of Spanish contact was a woman, preeminent not only in her own domain but in Cenú religious activity in general. The three polities were Fincenú in the Sinú River basin, Pancenú along the lower San Jorge River and its valley, and Cenúfana in the lower Cauca and Nechi regions (see Map 7.1). Their paramounts were identified as two brothers and a sister. It was reported in the 1530s that the chief of Cenúfana was the most powerful of the three, followed by the Cacica of Fincenú, "highly revered by her subjects," and finally the chief of Pancenú. In the 1530s élites of all three groups were buried in large mounds in Fincenú territory with the most abundant fine gold that the Spaniards would find interred in Colombia – 10,000 pesos' worth in one tomb alone. Tombs also held chiefs' attendants, *chicha*, and food; men's burials contained armor and weapons, and womens' had metates. In Fincenú there was a temple of major proportions in the corner of a plaza that, according to chronicler Castellanos, could easily accommodate 2,000 people. According to an eyewitness, it was "more than 100 paces long and consisted of three naves."[40] Spaniards collected 15,000 pesos of fine gold at the site.

When Spaniards raided the stockpiles of the Cacica of Fincenú in 1533, they collected 20,000 pesos of fine gold. She had a monopoly on the manufacture of gold objects, which were widely exchanged on the coast and in the interior for gold, salt, *mantas*, and other goods. Cenúfana traders also participated in the exchange routes that led to the powerful Cauca chiefdoms of Buriticá and Aburrá, with a substantial road connecting their settlement to Aburrá. Cenúfana warriors, engaged in hostilities with neighboring groups, appear to have been organized in an army and, as noted, to have acquired some of the characteristics of nearby Cauca River valley people such as cannibalism, which was not reported in the other two polities. Robledo (1540/41) wrote that in Cenúfana

---

[40] Pedro de Heredia, "Relación de Pedro de Heredia [1533]," in Hermes Tovar Pinzón (ed.), *Relaciones y Visitas a los Andes Siglo XVI. Tomo II Región del Caribe* (Bogotá, n.d.), 371–372, (367–373).

houses there were accumulations of "many skulls and piles of bones, the remains of people who had been eaten or who died in battle."[41]

In the sixteenth century, Cenú chiefdoms were highly centralized and stratified, as was reflected in their burials. Chronicler Aguado noted that there were great variations in wealth in the tombs. Fincenú with its large temple, chiefly burial grounds, and intensive gold manufacture may have been the center of earlier expansion by the Cenú as a whole. The friendly relations among the three major Cenú groups at the time of European contact suggest longstanding connections that crosscut strictly territorial ties. Within 25 years of European contact (1510–1535), the chiefdoms and their populations were decimated by warfare and disease.

In the Sierra Nevada de Santa Marta, some "Tairona" chiefdoms had a very long history of political complexity and were ruled by well-defined hierarchies with paramounts, although with no central figure who held authority over the entire territory.[42] Chroniclers speak of provinces at the time of European contact such as Betoma, Tairona, and Taironaca, but it is not known whether they corresponded to native political divisions. Valleys were mentioned as well (Buritacá, Tairona, de la Caldera, and others), giving a vague sense of political unity within each. Early writers spoke primarily of large settlements, which some modern scholars have termed cities: Bonda, Pocigueica, and La Ramada. There were numerous other settlements of varying size and prominence in the region, described as a place where "centers of population were large and the people numerous."[43] In the province of Tairona, Buritacá 200, a site until recently hidden by jungle cover, was continuously occupied from about the ninth century C.E. until the sixteenth. It was a major urban center, surrounded by other settlements of varying size and complexity. In it and its environs, extensive stonework projects modified the area's rugged terrain. Stone terraces with retention walls were built for habitation sites and to contain fields for cultivation. Canals, stairways, plazas, ceremonial locales, and roads leading to water sources and to secondary areas near Buritacá 200 have also been found, as well as roads connecting this region with others.

Paramount chiefs presided over Bonda, Pocigueica, Taironaca, Buritacá, Valle de la Caldera, and Valle del Coto. All had political hierarchies,

---

[41] Robledo, "Descripción," 402.
[42] Tairona, so-named by Spaniards, were actually a number of politically and culturally distinct groups who had some features of material culture in common.
[43] Anonymous, "Relación de Santa Marta [ca 1550]," in Tovar (ed.), *Relaciónes y Visitas*, 149 (123–188).

with most of their subjects living in large settlements, in contrast to some other groups in the region whose populations were dispersed and political systems only weakly centralized.

The more complex groups, such as those headed by Bonda, Pocigueica, and Tairona, had specialists who produced excellent gold objects, ceramics, and textiles, which were exchanged with coastal people for salt, cotton, and fish. They were alluded to early in the colonial period: "There are craftspeople in this valley who produce green and red beads. The valley [Tairona] is very rich in gold."[44] Tairona traders may have moved quite far along the coast, as well as along the Magdalena River, bringing luxury goods to other regions of the Caribbean, the interior of Colombia, Central America, and Venezuela. Chiefs managed long-distance trade and exchange of luxury goods (accumulations of which appear in their tombs), and they were important in organizing festivities and warfare, which was waged against both ethnically related and unrelated groups. A chief's territorial domain included multiple vertical, and in some cases, horizontal ecological zones. Chiefs' organizational and managerial activities probably were essential in coordination of labor for the building and maintenance of the complex settlements and agricultural fields. In some areas where soils were poor and arable land was scarce, local production was supplemented with foods obtained in exchange with surrounding groups.

In the Colombian Caribbean, there were other complex, paramount-headed chiefdoms such as the Tolú, as well as ethnic groups (Urabá, Cueva, Malibú) with a multiplicity of chiefdoms that had marked social stratification and a great deal of interaction with each other. Helms has proposed that northern Colombia and Panamá formed a primary area of religious, aesthetic, political, and economic interaction, bringing élites into contact with each other during the 500 to 1,000 years prior to European arrival. She points out that exchange of gold, gold products, and esoteric knowledge was élite-dominated with political, ideological, and religious implications. The material available on Caribbean coastal groups bears out the Colombian side of the discussion. Further, it suggests that the abundance of locally crafted fine gold items, such as was found in the Cenú and Tairona chiefdoms, in the Cauca Valley, and in Chibcha settlements, can be interpreted as a mark of very complex chiefdoms. Much as Helms suggests, it was the élite who had access to

[44] Anonymous, "Relación de Santa Marta," 139.

gold. Very large accumulations were in the hands of members of political hierarchies who made claims to dominance on the basis of sacred as well as secular authority.[45]

Northern Colombian and Panamanian chiefdoms were linked to broader areas of exchange and interaction, much as were those of the Cauca region and the Colombian *altiplano*. The general picture of complex, highly interactive polities that we find in northernmost South America belies descriptions of chiefdoms there as for the most part small, restricted to mini-areas, settled in unfavorable microenvironments, and marked by cultural isolation, regionalism, and discontinuity in occupation.[46]

Coastal Ecuador

The Ecuadorian coast, sierra, and Amazonia constituted another broad zone of interaction peopled by chiefdoms of various levels of political complexity among other polities. Ecuador's coast, home to very complex, paramount-headed chiefdoms, begins our tracking of this extensive area. Highland chiefdoms are discussed in the context of Inka rule, which had encompassed them by the time of Spanish contact.

The coast is an irregular lowland plain with two major river basins. In the north the Esmeraldas and its tributaries have formed narrow tropical valleys. There is rapid transition southward to dry, tropical savannah and hot steppe climate as a result of the effects of the Humboldt Current. In the south the Guayas River and its tributaries have formed a broad fertile basin, most of which has tropical monsoon climate. The basin's southern section is flooded during the rainy season, and a wide estuary has been formed where the Guayas empties into the Gulf of Guayaquil.

The Manteño, Puná, and Daule polities of Ecuador's coast (see Map 7.1) were among the most complex chiefdoms in contact-period South America. Paramounts and élites were set apart from commoners by elaborate pomp and great wealth. Unlike most chiefs the Manteño paramount was sovereign over diverse ethnic groups. All three chiefdoms were centers of long-distance trade that had exceptionally long spatial

---

[45] Helms, *Ancient Panama*.

[46] Gerardo Reichel-Dolmatoff, "The agricultural basis of the subandean chiefdoms of Colombia," in Johannes Wilbert (ed.), *The evolution of horticultural systems in Native South America. Causes and consequences* (Caracas, 1961), 88–89 (83–100). On this matter also see Frank Salomon, *Native lords of Quito in the Age of the Incas* (Cambridge, 1986), 28–29.

and temporal dimensions as well as a substantial variety of fine crafts and highly valued exchange goods.

In this region, unlike that of the Chibcha or other groups discussed, independent histories of great time-depth have been partially reconstructed. The island of Salango, center of the Manteño domain, has yielded cultural sequences that extend from 3360 B.C.E. to the C.E. 1500s. Chiefdoms occupied various parts of coastal Ecuador for over four millennia. During C.E. 500–1530 (the Period of Integration), politically complex groups waged war for territorial expansion; built mounds (*tolas*), stone platforms, ceremonial centers, plazas, and temples; carved stone stelae and heraldic wooden posts; had different-size residences indicating social rank; and had special cemeteries for the élite, with more elaborate types of burial offerings than in ordinary graves. They constructed irrigation systems, drained swamp areas, utilized extensive terracing and raised fields, and executed fine metalwork (particularly south of the Cojines River). Long-distance trade, important since the Machalilla Period (2259–1320 B.C.E.) and through the Chorrera (1300–500 B.C.E.), continued to be so until European contact, linking this region with the Sierra, Amazonia, Colombia, Peru, and possibly Central America and Mexico. There were important marketplaces on the coast in the sixteenth century such as Ciscala, and market-sanctuary-ceremonial centers on the islands of La Tolita, Salango, La Plata, and Puná.

The Manteño polity extended from the Esmeraldas to the Ayampe rivers and was under the control of the Lord of Salango (also known as Calangone, Calango) at the uppermost level of at least three tiers of officers. Salango dominated culturally and linguistically diverse populations. The large towns in his domain were headed by chiefs who presided over local political hierarchies, all with hereditary offices. Differential status and wealth were expressed in house size and burial contents. Élite men were accompanied to their graves by wives and retainers. Dense populations were supported by intensive agriculture, with terracing in some areas where maize, sweet manioc, beans, squash, a variety of potatoes, chili peppers, tomatoes, cotton, cacao and tobacco were cultivated. Llamas, guinea pigs, honeybees, and ducks were kept, and fishing as well as hunting were pursued. Manteño territory may have included enclaves in the *ceja de la montaña*, and thereby access to products of different ecological zones.

Long-distance waterborne trade via rafts (*balsas*) was far reaching. The goods carried by Manteño traders suggested connections with different locales, as well as local craft specialization. A European eyewitness, Bartolomé Ruyz described the opulent cargo on one raft in 1526:

They carry many articles of silver and gold used as personal adornment to exchange . . . crowns and diadems . . . armour . . . strings of beads . . . [also] cups and other vessels . . . many woolen and cotton *mantas* and shirts . . . and many other dry-goods and clothes, most of them highly embellished with rich embroidery of scarlet and brown and blue and yellow and all other colors worked in different ways with figures of birds and animals and fish and forests; and they bring some small balances to weigh gold similar in design to the *romana* [steelyard], and many other things; on some strings of beads there were small stones of emerald and chalcedony and other stones and pieces of crystal; and all of this they carry for the purpose of exchange for some sea shells [*conchas de pescado*] of which they make beads of a reddish and white color.[47]

The *conchas de pescado* – *Spondylus* and *Strombus* shells – had social, economic, and ceremonial value locally and far beyond. Exchange of the shells among élites had gone on for over 2,500 years. Salango's domain, where elaborate workshops have been found, was a major center of *Spondylus* processing. Manteño products were traded as far as Chincha in Peru, possibly along the coast of Colombia, and into the interior of Peru, Ecuador, and Colombia. Trade items included luxury goods such as those described earlier, as well as items of daily use. Craft specializations associated with trade included work in textiles, ceramics, metal, stone, and shell. Traders themselves may well have been a specialized group in the service of the Lord of Salango.

In Ecuador's coastal chiefdoms as in those of the Chibcha, Cauca, and Colombian Caribbean, religious practice and belief were closely associated with chiefs. Salango controlled important sanctuaries, priestly hierarchies, and temples, where abundant animal sacrifices and occasional offerings of prisoners were made. Some chiefs, such as the lord of Manta (subject to Salango), had esoteric objects that were used for curing. Cieza de León wrote in the 1550s:

In this district they attest that the lord of Manta has or had an emerald of great size and opulence, which emerald was greatly revered and esteemed by his ancestors who held and possessed it. And some days they placed it in public, and they worshipped it and revered it as though it had some deity enclosed in it. And should any man or woman be ill, after making their sacrifices they went to pray to the stone: for which they affirm that they presented gifts of other

---

[47] Reported in Juan Sámano, "La Relación Sámano-Xerez (1527)," in Raul Porras Barrenechea (ed.), *Las Relaciones Primitivas de la Conquista del Perú* (Paris, 1937), 66, (63–68).

stones [emeralds] . . . the sick came from many places in the interior to the town
of Manta to make their sacrifices and offerings.[48]

Some of the stones used in the sacrifice were destroyed at the ceremony's
conclusion. Emeralds had importance all along the coast. North of Manteño the province of Esmeraldas was so named by the Europeans because
of the abundance there of emeralds imported from the Chibeha region.
The island of Puná (measuring about 919 square kilometers at the
mouth of the Guayas River) was described as very fertile at the time of
European contact, containing what appeared to be artificial lagoons,
where rainwater was held. Puná's large population was under the domain
of a paramount chief whose office was inherited patrilineally. Chronicler
Jerez wrote that the polity had "many settlements, and seven caciques
rule them, and one is lord of all of them."[49] The paramount was the
focus of substantial ceremonial, probably not unlike that in many other
complex chiefdoms. Retainers accompanied him, and when he left his
house, it was with great pomp to the sound of trumpets and drums. He
had a large number of wives, some possibly his sisters, guarded by
eunuchs whose noses and mouths had been mutilated. Hoards of gold,
sliver, and textiles were held by him. He coordinated warfare including
campaigns against groups on the mainland where his warriors may have
made some inroads, possibly enabling establishment of Puná settlements.
Warfare was also waged with the Tumbez and Inka. Captured men and
women were taken as slaves and were used as sacrificial victims or
agricultural workers.

Puná craftspeople were renowned, and their products formed part of
long-distance trade goods. Salt, on which the chiefdom had a monopoly,
was exchanged in the highlands. Puná subsistence was based on maize,
beans, sweet manioc, chile, and fruits, along with game (peccary, deer,
ducks) and dried fish. The llamas that they had were most likely utilized
in their trade with the sierra.

The Daule (Chono) *señorío* occupied a large territory closely associated
with the archeological Milagro-Quevedo Phase (C.E. 400–1500) along the
basins of the Daule and Guayas rivers and their tributaries. Its paramount
chief coordinated military campaigns and possibly long-distance trade.
He had about sixteen distinct units in his domain, each headed by a

---

[48] Cieza de León, *Crónica del Perú*, I, 161–162.
[49] Francisco de Jerez, "Verdadera Relación de la Conquista del Perú y Provincia del Cuzco, Llamada
la Nueva Castilla (1534)," in *Historiadores Primitivos de Indias* (Madrid, 1947), II, 322 (319–348).

chief who presided over a political hierarchy. Local and regional lords received tribute in products from their subjects and in turn passed on considerable amounts to the paramount, who accumulated stores of high-quality exchange goods such as textiles, metal objects (gold, copper, some silver), and thin copper axes that had economic and ceremonial value. Daule mariners and warriors were known for their expertise. In their own territory, Daule workers built and maintained extensive raised fields where maize and other crops were cultivated.

It has been suggested that an association or league of merchants was formed within sovereign political units or among distinct coastal groups such as the Manteño, Huancavilca, and Puná chiefdoms. Although the purposes of the league, its organization, and function have not yet been discerned, it is clear that there was considerable regional interaction among different polities as well as long-distance contact with trade partners who came from many different types of societies including coastal and central Andean states.

Coastal societies remained politically independent of the Inka. For the Daule people, independence cost great loss of life in the course of military engagement. Inka expeditions into the region were unsuccessful in establishing either control or a significant presence. According to Cieza de León, the Inka lacked interest in the territory, "holding it in low esteem."[50] Even so, traders under Inka rule exchanged goods with a number of groups in it.

On the coast in the sixteenth century, there were also a number of chiefdoms of differing levels of political complexity. They included Huancavilca (Southern Manteño) chiefdoms without paramounts, and in the northern coastal area, a number of groups of recent arrival and lesser political complexity: the tropical forest Malaba, Cayapa, Lacha, and possibly other linguistically related people.

Mechanisms for maintaining highly centralized and stratified political systems in the Daule, Manteño, and Puná cases appear to have been related to chiefs' managerial activities in the economic sphere, the polities' maintenance of horizontal diversity whereby coastal, inland, and riverine zones were exploited, and (in the Manteño example) by vertical expansion as well. Chiefs probably had a primary function in the building and maintenance of raised fields given their preferential access to communal labor. Diversified exchange made possible by extensive local and

---

[50] Cieza de León, *Crónica del Perú*, I, 157.

long-distance seagoing, landborne, and riverine trade connected these
groups with other peoples in varied ecological regions, sources of both
luxury and commonplace exchange goods. Waterborne transportation
and llama caravans permitted the exchange of staple products. Local-level
economies appear to have been fairly generalized, but craft specializations
such as metallurgy, weaving, and shell processing were associated with
some communities, diverting workers from subsistence activities and
possibly requiring some arrangement with other units within the polity
for provisioning.

The economic roles of chiefs were of considerable consequence but
cannot be separated from their social, political, and ideological functions,
as was also true of Chibcha chiefs. Further, chiefs' control in the religious
sphere over paraphernalia, temples, and priests was critical for maintenance and enhancement of chiefly office among people whom Cieza de
León (referring to coastal chiefdoms) described as "extreme believers in
prophecy, and highly religious, so much so that in most of Peru there
were no people who practiced sacrifice so much as these, as it is well-
known."[51]

Greater Amazonia

Connected with the coast and sierra via exchange were societies in the
Ecuadorian Oriente, part of Greater Amazonia, a vast region inhabited
by indigenous groups of many different sociopolitical levels including
chiefdoms in the sixteenth century. Greater Amazonia, an area that until
recently was considered by most scholars to have been lacking in locally
evolved politically complex prehispanic groups, includes all the tropical
lowlands and plateaus east and south of the Andes and north of the
Tropic of Capricorn, excluding the Gran Chaco. Research of the past
two decades has shown that densely populated chiefdoms of varying
levels of complexity were located throughout the region at the time of
European conquest or shortly before – in Amazonia (the Oriente of
Ecuador, Peruvian *montaña*, and Brazilian and upper Amazon), the Orinoco Llanos of Colombia and Venezuela, and the Llanos de Moxos of

[51] Cieza de León, *Crónica del Perú*, I, 157. Earle has spoken cogently of the interlocking, mutually
dependent roles that chiefs play. See Timothy K. Earle, "Preface" and "The evolution of chiefdoms," in *Chiefdoms: Power, economy and ideology*, edited by him (New York, 1991), 9 (xi – xii
and 1–15).

Bolivia – and that political complexity there had a history extending at least as far back as the beginning of the first millennium C.E.

In the Ecuadorian Oriente, the Quijos region encompasses about 8,400 square kilometers at elevations primarily between 300 meters and 2,000 meters above sea level. Bordered on the north and northeast by the Coca River, on the south and southeast by the Napo, and on the west by the Cordillera Real, the region and its inhabitants have been identified as Quijos since European contact in 1535 despite sociocultural and, most likely, linguistic diversity. It was continuously occupied by 400 B.C.E. or earlier; groups in it practiced intensive ridged-field agriculture, built roads, and carried on active trade with the sierra by the seventh century C.E.

At the time of Spanish contact, populations at elevations of 1,000–2,000 meters were reported to be dense, with subsistence based on cultivation of maize, sweet manioc, beans, potatoes, and fruits. Europeans encountered a considerable range of sociocultural complexity among Quijos societies. Some such as the Hatunquijos, Cosanga, Sumaco, and Avila polities, located close to the sierra or on major trade routes, had centralized political structure with chiefly offices that were inherited patrilineally. There may also have been paramounts, as for example in Hatunquijos groups. At the time of European contact, the chief of the Hatunquijos had among his wives the sister of the paramount of the highland Latacunga chiefdom, suggesting sociopolitical ties between the two. A multiplicity of chiefdoms, as well as of other less complex societies, existed in areas near Quijos in the regions called Provincias del Coca, de los Algodonales, and de la Canela. Inka armies made three expeditions into Quijos territory but failed to integrate it into the empire, thus having little direct influence on local political systems.

Long-distance trade from Quijos extended to the coast, the sierra, and other parts of the oriente. Esoteric knowledge, gold, coca, medicinal plants, dyes, and slaves were exchanged for cotton, *mantas*, salt, and dogs. Quijos populations also traded with people to the south in the Peruvian *montaña* and upper Amazon. They in turn were connected via exchange to other areas of Amazonia as well as to the Peruvian highlands and coast.

The Peruvian *montaña* and upper Amazon, very complex areas ecologically and culturally, were inhabited at the time of European contact by Cocama, Conibo, and Piro chiefdoms, among other groups. The eastern flanks of the Andes, or *montaña*, have heavy rainfall and dense forests.

Below the open valleys of the *selva alta* (400–1,000 m) are highly dissected areas, followed at descending elevations by terraces that are varied in relief as well as in rates of erosion, types of soils, and patterns of vegetation. The *selva baja* (below 400 m) receives over 4,000 millimeters of rain annually, with precipitation occurring throughout the year. There is an extraordinary variety of vegetation and animal life. Very important exchanges of products and ideology were carried on among peoples of the *selva baja*, the sierra, and the coast.

Conibo and Piro populations had large permanent settlements governed by chiefs and in some cases by paramounts. Both were known for their military prowess and for participation in a wide trade network along the Amazon River (with Omagua, Machiparo, and Solimões chiefdoms), the Napo River (with Quijos), and Ucayali affluents (with Setebo, Shipibo, and Remo groups). Piro trade extended into the Andes as well. Piro chiefdoms had colonies in areas at a distance from their main settlements and at different altitudes where there were resources of importance to them. Some were located several hundred kilometers away. European impact, disease, interethnic warfare, and emigration to refuge areas resulted in greatly reduced populations, as well as modification of settlement patterns and sociopolitical decentralization.

Upper Amazonian Omagua, Machiparo, Solimões, and Tapajós River Tapajós chiefdoms (see Map 7.2) were also involved in extensive networks of exchange with peoples in other sections of the region and the Peruvian *montaña*. Early European writers commented on floodplain chiefdoms' population density and abundant crop production here as in many other sections of the Amazon Basin. The ability to produce abundant crops, a feature not often associated in modern times with Amazonia, was due in large measure to differential potential of soils. In the Amazon Basin, an area of about 7 million square kilometers drained by the great river and its more than 1,100 tributaries, soils of the two major landforms – *terra firme* and *varzea* – are quite different from each other. A combination of high temperatures, heavy rainfall, and ancient soils make *terra firme*, land above flood level, relatively nutrient-poor, generally viewed as adequate only for slash-and-burn agriculture and not for intensive cultivation by any known indigenous methods. In contrast the *varzea*, or floodplains, are inundated annually, receiving deposits of recent alluvium along the Amazon and some of its tributaries, as well as providing the locus for the intermingling of aquatic and terrestrial fauna

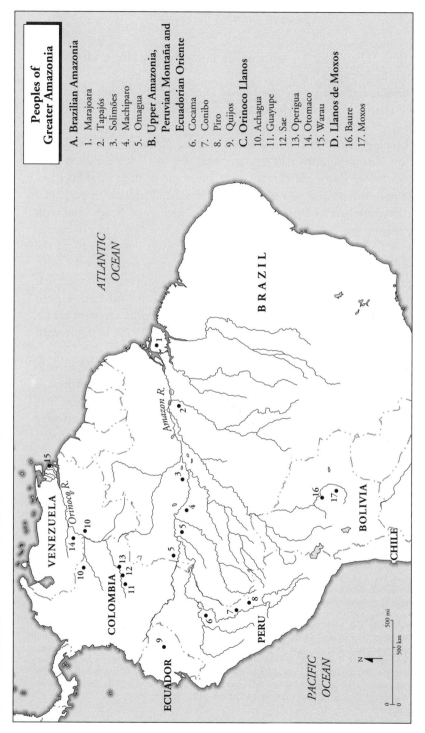

Map 7.2

Peoples of Greater Amazonia

A. Brazilian Amazonia
1. Marajoara
2. Tapajós
3. Solimões
4. Machiparo
5. Omagua

B. Upper Amazonia, Peruvian Montaña and Ecuadorian Oriente
6. Cocama
7. Conibo
8. Piro
9. Quijos

C. Orinoco Llanos
10. Achagua
11. Guayupe
12. Sae
13. Operigua
14. Otomaco
15. Warau

D. Llanos de Moxos
16. Baure
17. Moxos

and flora. These soils are suitable for intensive agriculture adequate to support large populations.

Omagua settlements occupied a very long stretch of the upper Amazon in the sixteenth century, dominating the floodplain for more than 700 kilometers west of an area midway between the Jutaí and Juruá rivers, and keeping strictly to the river banks and the islands in it. Descendants of Tupi-Guarani groups that migrated into the area a few hundred years at most before European contact, they and some of their neighbors had dense populations and powerful chiefs. Omagua chiefdoms in particular were characterized by Europeans as having "such good people and with such reason and political organization, and such a rich and prosperous land."[52] Carvajal, writing in 1541 about the Omagua to the east of the Juruá River, who may have differed somewhat from groups to the west, spoke of great lords, each the ruler of many people. He mentioned that twenty-six *señores* were subject to Aparia, "their principal lord, a great lord," in the area west of the river. Cristobal de Acuña reported on his trip to the region in 1639 that the Omagua were still "the best governed of all the indigenous people along the river."[53]

Contact-period Omagua were continually engaged in hostilities with inland groups and took prisoners of war as slaves.[54] Island settlement provided defense against attacks, and some of the floodplain villages may have been stockaded. In the sixteenth century, Omagua chiefdoms were expanding by means of force and had established colonies or outposts outside of their territory.

As noted, Omagua and neighboring Machiparo communities were observed to have a great abundance of food. They cultivated maize, bitter

[52] Captain Altamirano, "De la Entrada que el Gobernador Pedro de Ursua . . . (1559–61)," in Antonio Vázquez de Espinosa, *Compendio y Descripción de las Indias Occidentales* (Washington, D.C., 1948), 383 (381–396). Also see Gaspar de Carvajal, *Relación del Nuevo Descubrimiento del Famoso Río Grande que Descubrió por muy Gran Ventura el Capitán Francisco de Orellana* [1541] (Quito, 1942), 34–35, 37–38, 60, 177, 181–184, 190.

[53] Cristóbal de Acuña, "Nuevo Descubrimiento del Gran Río de las Amazonas," in *Informes de Jesuitas en el Amazonas 1660–1684*, Francisco Figueroa, Cristobal de Acuña y otros [1641] (Iquitos, Perú, 1986), 72 (25–102). Carvajal, *Relación del Nuevo Descubrimiento*, 12, 17, 20, 24.

[54] Slaveholding had both indigenous and colonial components and may have been part of a developing "class society" in the precontact period (Alfred Métraux, "Tribes of the Middle and Upper Amazon River," in Julian H. Steward (ed.), *Handbook of South American Indians*, 6 vols. (Washington, D.C., 1948), III, 698 (687–712). Missionary Samuel Fritz (1686–1723) reported that slaves were also obtained in trade and that they were utilized in domestic and agricultural labor (Fritz, *Journal of the travels and labours of Father Samuel Fritz in the river of the Amazons between 1686 and 1723*, George Edmunson, trans. and ed. (London, 1922).

manioc, sweet manioc, sweet potatoes, peanuts, kidney beans, peppers, pineapples, avocados, tobacco, achiote, gourds, and cotton on the islands, beaches, and banks of the river. Crops were harvested in January and February before the high floods of March through June. Maize was stored in houses or elevated granaries, and manioc was buried in pits in the floodplain. Turtles were corraled in great numbers in holding pens, and fish were important elements of the diet as well.

Omagua artisans were well known for their painted cloth and ceramics. Early European witnesses described their pottery as extremely fine, "of the best that has been seen in the world . . . glazed . . . with all colors and of great intensity."[55] In colonial times both the cloth and the pottery were in great demand by other indigenous groups. They most likely were also traded extensively in the precontact period for silver, gold, and other products.

Two other sectors of Greater Amazonia that had complex societies involved in broad trade networks, connecting them with other Amazonian areas and the Andes, were the Orinoco Llanos and the Llanos de Moxos. At the time of contact, the Orinoco Llanos were occupied by Jirajara, Warau, and other groups (see Map 7.2). Some chiefdoms had paramounts, but there is little information on most.[56] By the time documentation on them began in the colonial era, they had already been greatly altered and depleted by slave-raids and disease.

Significant links between the Orinoco Llanos and the Colombian highlands are mentioned in early reports. As noted previously, some groups in the *llanos* considered themselves subjects of Bogotá. Others knew of the Chibcha polities. Federman, leader of one of the earliest European expeditions to Chibcha territory, wrote in 1539 that he learned of them in the *llanos*. After leaving the city of Coro on the Venezuelan coast, he traveled several hundred leagues

until arriving at a very large settlement of a nation called the Bayupas [Guayupe], and because this witness found a large sample of fine gold, which until then he

---

[55] Carvajal, *Relación del Nuevo Descubrimiento*, 36.
[56] Warau chiefdoms in the Orinoco delta and along nearby rivers, for example, were mentioned by Jorge Griego, who came to the region in the 1580s and who reported that there were two *caciques* at the mouth of the Orinoco – Morequito, lord of Chucopare with 4,000 people, and Carapana with 2,000. See Neil L. Whitehead, *Lords of the tiger spirit. A history of the Caribs in Colonial Venezuela and Guyana 1498–1820* (Dordrecht-Holland, 1988), 13. It most likely was the same Carapana referred to by Raleigh as "the king of this land" (Sir Walter Raleigh, *The discoverie of the large, rich and beuutiful empyre of Guiana . . .* , London, 1596, 29).

had not found, he learned from the Indians that they brought it from the other side of the mountain range [Chibcha territory].[57]

Federman set out to find the wealthy highland people, reaching their domain after an expedition lasting about 40 days.

The *llanos*, great alluvial plains that slope gradually from the Andean ranges to the Orinoco River, have elevations of 10 to over 200 meters. In the higher plains, the Colombian *llanos arriba*, rivers flowing from the Andean mountains have formed great alluvial fans, some with fertile, moist soils and fairly good drainage. Clusters of forest are supported in such areas, as is agriculture. The lower plains in Colombia (*llanos abajo*) are annually flooded grasslands. Annual flooding also occurs in Venezuela, inundating large tracts of land below elevations of 80 meters. Along permanent rivers, plant cover varies from dry scrub to palms to gallery forest, and at the Orinoco Delta, to mangrove swamps and marshes.

Mound-builder chiefdoms may have existed in the *llanos abajo* of Colombia. In Venezuela, where more extensive archaeological work has been done, the remains of raised roads of considerable length, extensive agricultural terraces, and mounds for house sites and ceremonial platforms suggest that by the beginning of the second millennium C.E. there were complex sociopolitical groups in areas such as the Middle Orinoco and the region between it and the Andes. There was also considerable population movement and exchange of goods within Venezuela and possibly between it and northern Colombia.

In northeastern Bolivia's Llanos de Moxos, there were a number of chiefdoms including Baure and Moxo, and perhaps other polities (see Map 7.2). Moxo people were known for their extensive trade with the Chiriguano of the Santa Cruz area for salt; with the Mosetén at the headwaters of the Río Bení for salt, beads, and knives; and with groups in the Andean foothills and Chiquitos uplands for stone, which was lacking in the savannah. Archaeological and ethnohistoric data indicate that trade intermediaries were important in Moxos exchange networks. Mosetén people and the Arawak-speaking Mariquiono linked the savannah with the Eastern Andes, highlands of Cochabamba, and Titicaca Basin, where silver items, metal, stone ax heads, and salt were obtained. Chroniclers and early visitors reported that Moxo crafts in bark, cotton

---

[57] Nicolás Federman, "Declaración de Julio 4, 1539," in Juan Friede (ed.), *Documentos Inéditos para la Historia de Colombia*, 10 vols. (Bogotá, 1955–1960), V, 204 (203–206).

cloth, feathers, and pottery were of high quality. Although elaborate painted pottery was reported, very little has been found to date.

Little is known of Moxo chiefs, called *achichaco*. Baure chiefs, *arama*, had hereditary positions and were supposed to marry the daughters of other chiefs, a marriage preference suggesting the forging of social and political links evident in so many chiefdoms. Chiefs commanded respect, obedience, and labor services, and they had slaves. Baure people were reported to be more warlike than Moxo. Jesuits also described them as "more civilized," and their villages were well built "with streets and plazas," raised settlements, palisades, ditches, causeways, and canals.[58] The magnitude of the earthworks that have been found in the region suggest centralized polities with the ability to carry out significant public works projects. The Llanos de Moxos may contain the most extensive prehistoric modifications of landscape known, as Erickson has pointed out, but their connection with polities in the region at the time of conquest is unclear.[59]

Situated in the center of the district of Bení, the *llanos* region has been calculated to cover between 120,000 and 180,000 square kilometers at elevations of between 275 meters in the south to 180 meters in the north. Terrain is very flat, and about 80 percent of the area is low-lying savannah. The rest is dense forest at slightly higher elevations. Flood and drought alternate annually. The savannahs are inundated to a depth of between 0.3 and 1 meter for several months during the summer. As the flood recedes, only the lowest spots retain water, and drought ensues during the warm, dry winter.

Nordenskiold excavated three mounds in southwestern Bení during 1908–1909. His work suggested the presence of "advanced cultures" in the region. Not until aerial photographic surveys were carried out between 1958 and 1961, in conjunction with oil exploration, was the extent of earthworks in the *llanos* known. Canals, causeways, drained fields, settlements, houses, and burial mounds could be distinguished, covering up to 20,235 hectares. Denevan proposed that raised fields and other earthworks were built and used by large, stratified groups in the *llanos* in response to population and territorial pressures.[60] Raised fields here, as

---

[58] William Denevan, *The aboriginal cultural geography of the Llanos de Mojos of Bolivia* (Berkeley, 1966), 46, 49.

[59] Denevan, *The aboriginal culture.* Carl L. Erickson, "Sistemas Agricolas Prehispánicos en los Llanos de Mojos," *América Indígena,* 40 (1980), 740 (731–755).

[60] Erland Nordenskiold, *L'archeologie du bassin de L'amazone* (Paris, 1930). Denevan, *The aboriginal culture,* 64–89.

elsewhere in lowland South America, would have elevated crops above flood level, provided a means of draining off water, and also improved the soil by loosening and aerating it and concentrating the humus. In the absence of stone in the area, it may have been more efficient to build the fields than to practice large-scale slash-and-burn agriculture in the forests. Landscape modifications were made not only in the plains, as Erickson has pointed out, but in forested areas where "pozos" and dams, more difficult to perceive by aerial photography, were constructed to retain fish in dry times, probably making this very important source of protein available through the year.[61]

Questions regarding the dating of the earthworks and the relation of the people who built them to contact populations need to be examined. Whether dense, politically complex groups survived for extended periods in the prehispanic past has been raised by Dougherty and Calandra; research by Erickson and Bustos Santelices supports Denevan's views that they did.[62]

A tendency to discount the existence of chiefdoms in Greater Amazonia can be seen as part of a tradition that predominated through the late 1960s and early 1970s, which saw complex organization in the region as aberrational. Steward wrote in 1948 that Amazonian villages "were large and numerous, but the social and political concomitants of a dense population are not recorded." In 1949 he added that these were "sociopolitical groups which were based on kinship and lacked classes" and that "political units that transcended the community were exceptional." By 1959 Steward among others expressed what came to be known as the "limiting factor theory." He and Faron wrote:

> Subsistence techniques in this environment barely provided enough food, particularly proteins, to meet daily requirements, and it was impossible to accumulate surpluses that could support full-time occupational specialists or ruling classes.[63]

Concomitant with this view, shared by many, was the thinking that lowland precontact groups were of necessity small and scattered, practic-

---

[61] Erickson, "Sistemas Agricolas Prehispanicos."

[62] Bernard Dougherty and Horacio A. Calandra, "Prehispanic human settlement in the Llanos de Moxos, Bolivia," in *Quarternary of South America and Antarctic Peninsula* (Boston, 1984), II, 163–199. Erickson, "Sistemas Agrícolas Prehispanicos," and Bustos Santelices in Alcides Parejas Moreno, *Historia del Oriente Bolivano. Siglos XVI y XVII* (Bolivia, 1979), 53–54.

[63] Julian H. Steward, "Cultural areas of the tropical forest," in *Handbook of South American Indians*, III, 886 (883–899); "South American cultures: An interpretative summary," in *Handbook of South American Indians*, V, 697, 760, 762 (669–772). Julian H. Steward and Louis C. Faron, *Native peoples of South America* (New York, 1959), 298.

ing slash-and-burn agriculture on soils that could not support more intensive cultivation. Manioc was the staple, and maize, a plant of higher protein value, was secondary, if grown at all. The limiting factor view is also compatible with the argument that in those areas where prehispanic technical or political complexity existed, they did so as a result of intrusions from other regions, such as the Andes or the circum-Caribbean, rather than of in situ development. Meggers and Evans, who did pioneering work in Amazonia, argued that pottery and pottery types had spread eastward from Andes, that urn burials were intrusions from Colombia and Venezuela, and that the origins of the complex mound-builder Marajoara Phase (C.E. 400–1300) on Marajó Island were not in situ developments but intrusions. In contrast Lathrap contended that complex cultural traditions, Marajoara included, were firmly grounded in the lowlands, and that upriver complex cultures such as the Cocama and Omagua derived from east–west migrations along the Amazon. Roosevelt describes the direction of spread of polychrome pottery as being westward from Marajó, and the origins of the Marajoara Phase, where she has recently done intensive research, as autochthonous.[64]

Whatever the predominant direction of flow of people, ideas, and goods, there were clearly prehispanic longstanding exchanges between the Andes and Amazonia. Amazonian influences are found in the iconography of the Andean cultures' mythology and religious and ceremonial practices. Plants, dyes, medicines, animal skins, and feathers of Amazon origin were incorporated into use by Andean societies as well. Amazonia received Andean gold, textiles, and other goods. Trade, migrations, and warfare were important arenas for interaction of groups along the Amazon, and between the Amazon and other regions. There is evidence of long-distance trade, possibly carried out by specialists, linking groups over distant areas via major waterways. Gold, pottery, greenstone (jade and other stones), stone for tools, salt, cloth, and other goods were traded

---

[64] Betty J. Meggers and Clifford Evans, *Archeological investigations at the mouth of the Amazon* (Washington, D.C., 1957) 7–30. Betty J. Meggers, *Amazonia. Man and culture in a counterfeit paradise* (New York, 1971); "Environment and culture in Amazonia," in Charles Wagley (ed.), *Man in the Amazon* (Gainesville, 1974); "Aboriginal adaptation to Amazonia," in Ghillean T. Prance and Thomas E. Lovejoy (eds.), *Key environments. Amazonia* (New York, 1985). Donald W. Lathrap, *The upper Amazon* (London, 1970). Anna C. Roosevelt, *Parmana: Prehistoric maize and manioc subsistence along the Amazon and Orinoco* (New York, 1987); "Resource management in Amazonia before the conquest: Beyond ethnographic projection," in D. A. Posey and W. Balée (eds.), *Resource management in Amazonia: Indigenous and folk strategies* (New York, 1989); *Moundbuilders of the Amazon. Geophysical archaeology on Marajo Island, Brazil* (New York, 1991).

along the rivers, where the major complex Amazonian polities were located, and into the hinterland as well. Exchange may have served to maintain systems of alliance. Hostility and trade were not mutually exclusive, and possibly some of the same (or similar) circumstances that motivated war, such as local scarcity of valued resources, also motivated trade.

SOME GENERAL CHARACTERISTICS OF CHIEFDOMS

In each of the regions that we have discussed, there were many societies of varying levels of sociopolitical complexity at the time of European contact. Smaller, less centralized chiefdoms with fewer levels of political hierarchy and more limited chiefly authority and power were, in some cases, settled near groups that had paramounts. It would have been unlikely for any to be isolated. These were areas of intense regional activity, and any given polity would likely be affected by nearby societies via trade, exchange of esoteric knowledge, political alliance, marriage, raids, or warfare within and across ethnic boundaries. Most were also linked through long-distance exchange to people who were culturally, linguistically, and politically different from themselves.

Powerful regionally dominant chiefs were not so different from para-mounts in terms of their position within polities, use of sumptuary rules, and deferential treatment, but by and large they lacked their extent of domain, intensity of control, and scope of resources. Spaniards observed chiefs with regional authority throughout Colombia, Ecuador, and Greater Amazonia at the time of contact. In Ecuador Huancavilca people of the Santa Elena peninsula region and portions of the Guayaquil gulf had several regionally dominant chiefdoms. The Guayupe and possibly the Tapajós chiefdoms in Amazonia, as well as the Malibú, Urabá, and "Cueva" chiefdoms in Colombia's Caribbean coast could be described in this way (see Maps 7.1 and 7.2). In Colombia's Cauca River valley, there were regional chiefdoms among the Guarcama, Norisco, Hevéjico, and others (see Map 7.1). Some Páez chiefdoms in Colombia's Magdalena Valley had regional dominance, as did some Pasto and Quillacinga chief-doms in the Pasto Plateau (Cordillera Central). In the northern Cordi-llera Oriental, Guane, Tunebo, and Lache polities were regionally domi-nant, and in the Segovia highlands and surrounding areas of Venezuela, so were Caquetío and Jirajara chiefdoms. In Venezuela's central high-lands, Sierra de Cumaná, and central coast, Toromaima, Cumanagoto,

Warao, Mariche, and Palenque polities had chiefdoms with regional authority among them.

Smaller "simple" chiefdoms with minimally structured hierarchies, in which chiefs were at less of a status distance from the general populace than were regional chiefs and paramounts, also were present throughout the areas under discussion. On Ecuador's coast such chiefdoms included those of the Cayapa people, who had recently migrated to the region; in Colombia's Pasto Plateau, Abades chiefdoms; in the Magdalena Valley, Pantagora and Yarequí groups; and in coastal Venezuela, Bobures and Buredes among others.

Yet less politically centralized at the time of Spanish conquest were what we might call incipient chiefdoms such as Chitarreros and Muzos in the eastern Cordillera, and some Panches in the Magdalena Valley. Under Spanish colonial rule, Panches, Chitarreros, and Muzos all adapted to imposed centralized governance as their traditional provisional leaders were made permanent officers, albeit without internal support or broad recognized authority among their own people.

Finally, there were complex societies that had splintered apart and lost most if not all of their formal centralized political organization under the impact of other chiefdoms, as did Aburrá in the Antioquia massif. Less extreme situations may have resulted from warfare – for example, the perpetuation of large numbers of mutually hostile chiefdoms in the Cauca and Magdalena regions. We discuss a few better-known groups of those mentioned from the far north.

Regionally Dominant Chiefdoms

Malibú people had no centralized supraregional political system but rather an array of chiefdoms, some more important than others. For the most part they occupied the extensive savannahs of the northern Magdalena Basin in Colombia, a region that alternates between dry periods and annual seasonal flooding (see Map 7.1). Abundant fish and other fluvial fauna were staples of the Malibú diet along with maize, sweet manioc, bitter manioc, and fruits. There were some cultural and dialectic differences between the Malibú who inhabited the lagoons and those along the rivers. Some chiefs controlled territories with settlements that the Europeans found unimpressive, whereas others were perceived as quite imposing, such as that of Chief Tamalameque on the island of Parabuy in the César River. Oviedo referred to the place with awe – "it's something that must be seen" – and wrote that there were as many as 600 houses on the island.[65] Chronicler Simón described it as a "gracefully designed city," with a large plaza surrounded by three triangular-shaped neighborhoods of about equal size. People from the surrounding areas, most of them under Tamalameque's jurisdiction, came to the plaza to exchange goods.[66] Macalamama, another important chief, who held sway in the Tenerife region of the Magdalena River, was also noted: "even though each pueblo has a chief, and some have two or three, this lord, Macalamama, was the high chief [*cacique grande*] over all of them."[67] Macalamama received agricultural products, fish, cotton thread, and hammocks in tribute. His subjects planted large fields of maize and sweet manioc for him. He, in return, provided a great feast at the time of tribute payment, presiding in rich gold adornments.

In the Cauca-Patía depression, Lile chiefdoms were located in the environs of today's Cali. As Cieza de León described the larger region:

All this valley from the city of Cali to these narrow sections [the entire valley between Cali and Cartago] was densely populated with very large and beautiful settlements, the houses near each other and very large.

He continued, saying that the Valley of Lile, about five leagues from Cali, was very flat: "and they are always cultivated with many maize and yucca fields, and they have large orchards and many palm groves." Cieza counted six *caciques* in the Valley of Lile, and he noted that their command was limited: "They are held in little regard by their people."[68] However, bordering on the valley was a powerful Lile chief, Petecuy (Petequi), lord over a number of chiefs. Cieza described a large house in Petecuy's compound, located in the center of his settlement, that contained a number of specially prepared corpses placed together with their weapons on a high shelf. A large number of hands and feet were also displayed. Next to that house was another with

a great number of cadavers and heads and piles of bones, so many that it was terrifying to see . . . with which they [chiefs] secured honor and were understood to have shown great bravery, saying that they learned this from their fathers and elders.

---

[65] Oviedo, *Historia General*, III, 102.   [66] Simón, *Noticias Historiales*, II, 70.

[67] Bartolomé Briones de Pedraza, "Descripción de la Villa de Tenerife de las cosas que mando azer el muy ilustre señor Don Lope de Orozco . . ." [1580] in Tovar Pinzón, *Relaciones y Visitas a los Andes*, 329.

[68] Cieza de León, *Crónica del Perú*, I, 88, 94.

Asked by Cieza de León about the collection, an Indian responded

that it was the glory of the lord of that valley, and that not only did he want to have the Indians that he had killed before him, but he even ordered that their weapons be hung from the beams of the houses as a commemoration.[69]

Petecuy led in battle, commanding disciplined squadrons. He was accompanied by one of his wives, who was an active participant on the battlefield. Petecuy also managed religious celebrations that were carried out in the plaza in front of his house, and he had command of seers, or *agoreros*. His court was composed of relatives, and his compound was run by a steward.

Not far to the north of Lile, communities were Quimbaya chiefdoms that, according to Cieza de León, had entered the area in the not too distant past, displacing and annihilating the people there at the time.[70] Quimbaya chiefdoms occupied an area that extended from the Cauca River to the Cordillera Central between the Guacaca River and Río La Vieja, with about half the territory above 1000 meters. Some Quimbaya had access to multiple ecological floors from cold climate to hot, with concomitant variety in fauna and vegetation from *paramo* to humid tropical forest. Food staples included maize, beans, sweet manioc, and other roots (possibly potatoes), supplemented with fruit, fish, meat, and honey. Conquistador Robledo reported that at the time of contact there were a great number of Quimbaya *caciques* with independent territories:

There are more than eighty chiefs [*caciques*] in this province . . . there are five or six prominent lords here . . . none of them is lord over more than his territory, and none of the other chiefs obey him.[71]

Some chiefs were very wealthy in gold and salt, products of the area, and were probably involved in their trade. They had special use of chairs, crowns, and jewelry, were carried about on litters or in hammocks, and had women servants and men slaves in their compounds. Chiefs were polygamous, and the most important ones (as well as others most likely) married into each other's families. When chiefs died, their slaves were buried with them in tombs that were reputed to be very large and rich in gold and *mantas*.

Quimbaya chiefs were noted by Spaniards to be strictly obeyed and to

---

[69] Cieza de León, *Crónica del Perú*, I, 96.   [70] Cieza de León, *Crónica del Perú*, I, 85–86.
[71] Robledo, *Descripción*, 398–399. Cieza de León, *Crónica del Perú*, I, 135.

have important roles in warfare, especially in battles with the Pijao and Anserma peoples. Their compounds were fenced with bamboo on which trophy heads and other parts of their enemies were exhibited.

Simple and Incipient Chiefdoms

Contrasting with the more politically complex Malibú or Lile were simpler chiefdoms of the Maracaibo lowlands and the piedmont of the Venezuelan Andes. In the early 1500s these regions had great linguistic and cultural diversity, although a very limited number of ceramic styles. Two major styles were utilized by the seminomadic Quiriquire (Carib speakers) and Ona (Arawak speakers), the more sedentary groups like the Chinato and Zorca (all Carib speakers), and the Chitarrero and Lache (Chibcha speakers).

Bobure and Burede polities of the western Maracaibo lowlands and Perijá mountains probably were chiefdom-like in organization (see Map 7.1). Both had access to multiple vertical and horizontal ecological zones. As agriculturalists, they raised maize, manioc, and coca in abundance and exchanged them with Ona and Quiriquire people for salt and fish, which they in turn appear to have traded inland. A series of exchange links connected them with other groups at least as far as northern Colombia, where they obtained gold objects and jewelry. Chiefs probably managed the long-distance trade in luxury items and acquired esoteric knowledge, which served to bolster their standing and authority at home, as Helms has proposed for exchange between Colombians and Panamanian élites. Burede and Bobure chiefs were succeeded in office by close relatives.

Several culturally distinct but linguistically related groups whom Spaniards called Chitarreros inhabited northern regions of the Cordillera Oriental (Colombian Santander and Venezuelan Táchira regions). Each group had access to multiple ecological floors where they raised guinea pigs and cultivated maize, sweet manioc, potatoes, and beans. The Chitarrero people were involved in exchange of cotton and red vegetal dye (*bija*). During the Spanish conquest and under colonial rule, chiefs were imposed on what had been "big man" or charismatic leader systems. Chronicler Aguado wrote that at the time of contact

the natives . . . did not have a cacique nor in all the province of the Indians that Spaniards called Chitarreros did they have them. The mode of government that they had was that in each pueblo they obeyed the wealthiest and bravest Indian, and this person is their commander in war.[72]

War chiefs were converted into permanent officers by colonial officials, but they became functionaries with little support on the part of their own people.

The Temporal Dimension

Chiefdoms varied in distribution, complexity, and domain not only spatially but over time as well. More centralized polities than those the Europeans encountered had existed in prior epochs in the Moxos region of lowland Bolivia, Marajó Island, and the Orinoco Llanos. In Colombia sociopolitical and material complexity in the upper Magdalena mountainous region and in the Cauca Valley, particularly El Valle, may have been most highly developed between the last centuries of the first millennium B.C.E. and the eleventh century C.E., with larger cultural units and political entities than existed thereafter. A period of regional development then followed and lasted until the arrival of the Europeans, with further late precontact-period simplification in some places. In the Calima River area, peoples of the Yotoco-Calima culture (C.E. 100–1200) appear to have been more politically and technologically complex than the unrelated groups that followed in the Sonso Period or the culturally related sixteenth-century Gorrones. Similarly, in the Cundi-Tolimense portion of the Magdalena River, people of the Tolima culture (first millennium C.E.) had more complex polities than did the Pijao groups encountered by Spanish expeditions in the sixteenth century.

In the Pasto region of southern Colombia, differential burials indicating the presence of commoners, specialists, and élites with access to exotic goods suggest a more highly ranked set of polities during the time of Piartal culture (C.E. 750–1250) than those that followed in the Tuzo phase or in the sixteenth-century Pasto chiefdoms met by Europeans.

In contrast, in the Cordillera Oriental of Colombia, a tendency toward increased centralization patterns began to occur in the second millennium C.E. among the Chibcha, Guane, Lache, and Tunebo peoples and continued until the sixteenth century. The course that centralization and

---

[72] Aguado, *Recopilación Historial*, I, 465.

simplification took in different regions and among different peoples strongly points to the importance of placing attention on particular local histories and regions of sociocultural interaction in tracing out the broad patterns of evolving processes.

CHIEFDOMS AND EMPIRE IN THE ANDEAN REGIONS

In the Andean regions a great deal of attention has been focused on the origins, development, and spread of states and empires. The emphasis has tended to divert attention from the great many nonstate societies that these regions held. In the South, Central, and North Andean highlands alone, several hundred societies were under different degrees of subjugation by the Inka at the time of European contact, and they had themselves been at diverse levels of political complexity ranging from incipient chiefdoms to expanding states at the time of conquest. In the Ecuadorian highlands, northwest Argentina, and northern and central Chile, chiefdoms had been prevalent. In Peru and the *altiplano* of Peru and Bolivia, chiefdoms coexisted with states or were dominated by them.

Inka expansion and control were directed primarily toward highland and coastal complex societies with political hierarchies and routinized tribute or labor service. Under Inka rule, tribute demands were exacted in labor and increased for both men and women. Work was directed into agriculture, construction, road building, maintenance, military service, mining, and crafts. Subject populations concurrently became segments of a markedly stratified society, different from chiefdoms in that use of time, land, and possessions could be regulated by state edict.

Inka rulers found it difficult to extract labor from egalitarian societies, and such groups by and large remained marginal to imperial interests much as they would for the Europeans. Amazonian societies also remained on the periphery of the empire except for a few Inka outposts, even in areas such as the Quijos region where there were complex societies. Although at least three military expeditions were launched there, it was never integrated into the empire. Trade with these areas was permitted to continue, however.

Recent studies indicate that the Inka expanded first into the area around Cuzco (also written Cusco) and to the rest of the southern Peruvian highlands, then southward into portions of the Bolivian-Peruvian *altiplano*, and possibly to the southernmost Peruvian coast. Expansion followed into the rest of the *altiplano*, northwestern Argentina, northern Chile, and the unconquered sections of the southern Peruvian coast. Areas added to the empire at about the same time or somewhat later were the northern Peruvian coast, the central and most of the northern Peruvian highlands, and the southern and some central portions of the Ecuadorian Andes. The last phase of conquest added the eastern portion of the northern Peruvian highlands and the rest of the central and northern Ecuadorian highlands to the empire.[73] Our discussion follows the Inka path, focusing first on the Southern Andes and then the Central and Northern zones.

The South Andean regions had long histories of interaction among each other, including having been under the influence or control of expansionist states previously, such as the Tiwanaku/Wari (C.E. 1–1200). Similarly the Central and South Andes (Peruvian-Bolivian *altiplano*, northern Chile, and northwest Argentina) formed an area of economic, social, ideological, and, at certain times, political interaction prior to the Spanish conquest. Exchanges among these areas took shape by as early as 1000 B.C.E. and were of large scale and persistent. Camelid herding produced pack animals that permitted caravan transportation not only of luxury items but of food and goods from the coasts to the *altiplano* and other areas back toward the coast and *altiplano*.

Southern Sierra of the Central Andes and Southern Andean Region

In the South Andes, complex societies appear to have evolved first in the *altiplano*, the hub of the region's trade networks. Chiefdoms there had agricultural and pastoral bases. Cereals such as *quinua* (*chenopodium quinoa*) and *kañawa* (*chenopodium pallidicaule*) were cultivated productively up to 4,450 meters, as were potatoes and other tubers. Livestock – llama, alpaca, and guinea pigs – were also capable of being raised at great altitudes (up to 5,000 m). Foods were freeze-dried by the heat of day and frost of night, turning the dry, intensely insolated, high-altitude characteristics of the *puna* (3,800–4,800 m) to the benefit of storage and potential accumulation of foods. In addition early chiefdoms such as those associated with the Chiripa (1300–100 B.C.E.), Qaluyu (1300–500 B.C.E.), and Wankarani (1200–250 B.C.E.) cultures utilized multiple ecological zones, including temperate western valleys. Qaluyu people living on the northern shores of Lake Titicaca practiced a sophisticated mode

[73] María Rostworowski de Diez Canseco, *Historia del Tahuantinsuyo* (Lima, 1988), map in Ch. 1.

of cultivation that met the challenge of water control, temperature, and soil maintenance problems. Raised fields and canals were used to manage the lake plain's annual inundation and waterlogging, and the effects of killing frosts were ameliorated by the presence of water surrounding cultivated fields. Productivity was increased by using fertile mud from the canals to build up the planting areas.

Qaluyu was succeeded by Pukara culture (c. 300 B.C.E.–C.E. 400). Pukara groups – agriculturalists and pastoralists – expanded the use of ridge agriculture and appear to have supplemented production by participating in trade caravans and by having colonies on the coast. They also maintained close relations with contemporary maritime Paracas culture communities of southern Peru. Pukara groups also exercised influence or control in the northern highland areas of Puno and Cuzco. Warfare probably played an important role in their organization, as is indicated by carved sculptures with humans wearing or holding trophy heads. The settlement of Tiwanaku, which was contemporaneous with the Chiripa, Wankarani, and Pukara, was located on the southern shores of Lake Titicaca. Having grown from a small village to a substantial city with monumental architecture and art by the first century C.E., Tiwanaku became a major power for over a thousand years (C.E. 1–1100/1200), forming an empire that encompassed many different ethnic groups in the *altiplano* and adjacent regions. In its later stages, Tiwanaku ruled over several million people in an area of several hundred thousand square kilometers, and it had a hierarchical arrangement of administrative centers. Ridge agriculture was employed extensively, and massive land-reclamation projects were undertaken. It is possible that populations were moved from one place to another as well. Some authors have proposed that Tiwanaku had colonies at different ecological floors, including the edge of the *selva* and the Peruvian and Chilean coasts. Others emphasize the importance of trade and hypothesize that the state-controlled caravan traffic to the coast, northern Chile, and northwestern Argentina. It is possible that Tiwanaku did all of these things, experimenting as it expanded with different ways of integrating diverse peoples and obtaining resources not available in the immediate *altiplano* area. The spread of Tiwanaku religion and art is associated with increasing trade of hallucinogenic drugs brought from the *selva* and distributed in the highlands and coast of Peru, Chile, and northwest Argentina.

Tiwanaku exercised considerable influence over Wari (C.E. 550/600–1000), a powerful state to the north. It is not known presently whether Wari was an emulator, ally, or dependent of Tiwanaku, but its political influences were felt all along the Peruvian coast (although more weakly north of Lambayeque), and in Peru's northern, central and southern highlands. Wari established provincial and regional administrative centers and built roads, aqueducts, irrigation canals, and ceremonial centers.

Soon after the decline of Tiwanaku and Wari, a number of kingdoms and chiefdoms (*reinos y señoríos*) emerged, most, if not all, Aymara speakers, with enclaves of Pukina and Uru in the *altiplano*, and with ethnically and linguistically diverse groups in the Peruvian area. There was a great deal of movement and warfare within and between different populations. This flux was brought to an end by Inka conquest, although coexistence may have been tense among formerly belligerent groups.

The area that the Inka first expanded into, the southern highlands of the Central Andes, was richly multiethnic. Located near Cuzco was the powerful Quechua polity (see Map 7.3), a complex chiefdom or state with substantial territory until some time during the fifteenth century when it lost a considerable amount to enemies of the Inka, the Chanka confederation. Thereafter Quechua entered into alliances with the Inka and helped in the final defeat of Chanka polities. For their services they were made "Inca by privilege," recognition also granted to other people in the southern highlands – Lare, Yanahuara, Cavina, Chillque, Masca, and Tambo. According to a recent detailed study, the latter three groups (in what is now the province of Paruro) may have been united "in some form of early Cuzco (also spelled Cusco)-based polity, or proto-state" in the Killke or early Inka period (C.E. 1000–1400). Their subsistence and settlement patterns, which were characterized by small communities, with each exploiting multiple ecological zones, continued through Inka times.[74]

Chanka territory (Pampas and Mantaro basins) was located opposite the Inka on the Apurímac River in what had been the nuclear zone of the Wari empire. Defeat of Chanka was critical to further expansion by the Inka. Although apparently a small ethnic group, the Chanka had formed an alliance referred to in the literature as the Chanka confederation with Huanca, Willca, and others for the purposes of defense and expansion. Chanka polities themselves have been described as *señoríos* with dual organization and a hierarchy of chiefs.[75] Some of their settle-

---

[74] Brian S. Bauer, *The development of the Inca state* (Austin, 1992), passim, 145. Bauer considers the Inka to have already been a state when they defeated the Chanka, and not, as traditional models have it, a state as a result of the conquest and Pachacuti Inka Yupanqui's role as organizer.

[75] Polities with dual organization were bisected into two complementary groups. Although the chiefs of each were of the same general hierarchical level, one frequently had superior status and power.

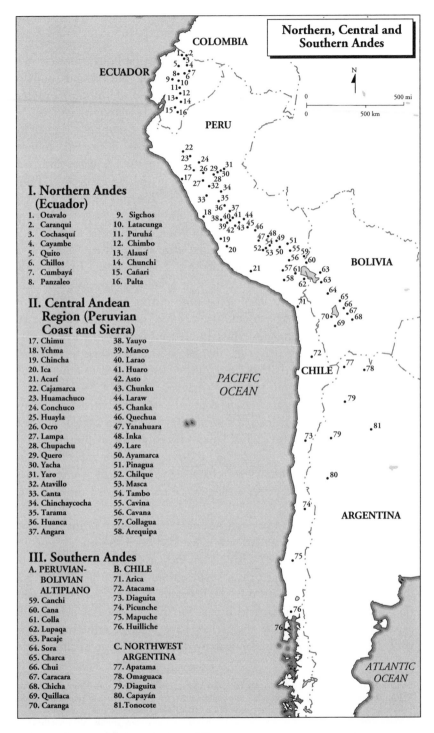

Northern, Central and Southern Andes

COLOMBIA

ECUADOR

N

0   500 mi

0   500 km

PERU

I. Northern Andes (Ecuador)

1. Otavalo	9. Sigchos
2. Caranqui	10. Latacunga
3. Cochasquí	11. Puruhá
4. Cayambe	12. Chimbo
5. Quito	13. Alausí
6. Chillos	14. Chunchi
7. Cumbayá	15. Cañari
8. Panzaleo	16. Palta

II. Central Andean Region (Peruvian Coast and Sierra)

17. Chimu	38. Yauyo
18. Ychma	39. Manco
19. Chincha	40. Larao
20. Ica	41. Huaro
21. Acarí	42. Asto
22. Cajamarca	43. Chunku
23. Huamachuco	44. Laraw
24. Conchuco	45. Chanka
25. Huayla	46. Quechua
26. Ocro	47. Yanahuara
27. Lampa	48. Inka
28. Chupachu	49. Lare
29. Quero	50. Ayamarca
30. Yacha	51. Pinagua
31. Yaro	52. Chilque
32. Atavillo	53. Masca
33. Canta	54. Tambo
34. Chinchaycocha	55. Cavina
35. Tarama	56. Cavana
36. Huanca	57. Collagua
37. Angara	58. Arequipa

BOLIVIA

PACIFIC
OCEAN

CHILE

ARGENTINA

III. Southern Andes

A. PERUVIAN-BOLIVIAN ALTIPLANO	**B. CHILE**
	71. Arica
	72. Atacama
59. Canchi	73. Diaguita
60. Cana	74. Picunche
61. Colla	75. Mapuche
62. Lupaqa	76. Huilliche
63. Pacaje	
64. Sora	**C. NORTHWEST ARGENTINA**
65. Charca	
66. Chui	77. Apatama
67. Caracara	78. Omaguaca
68. Chicha	79. Diaguita
69. Quillaca	80. Capayán
70. Caranga	81.Tonocote

ATLANTIC
OCEAN

Map 7.3

ments were located in high, strategically defensible locations. They did not have urban centers. After their defeat by the Inka, some Chanka retreated to the *montaña*. Others were employed for military purposes by the expanding empire. Chanka territory was depopulated and resettled along a decimal system (modular units of tax-paying households organized on a base of ten) with settlers introduced by the Inka, *mitmaqkuna*, from different parts of the empire. Major Inka centers were built (Vilcashuamán, Intiwatana) and became the residences of provincial officials as well as of Cuzco élites.

The population of the Titicaca Basin, south of Cuzco, has been calculated at between 2 and 3 million at the time of Spanish contact. It contained an array of chiefdoms and kingdoms of varying degrees of complexity: Cana, Canchi, Colla (Qulla, Qolla), and Lupaqa in the northern section; and Caranga, Quillaca, and Caracara among others in the southern basin.

Colla, a polity with hereditary dynasties, expanded to form a very large state in the *altiplano* and then fragmented prior to Inka conquest. When the Inka army entered the area, some of the remaining Colla groups, possibly chiefdoms, formed an alliance with Lupaqa peoples, their former enemy. The Lupaqa polity, which has been called a kingdom and a high-level chiefdom (macro-etnia) most likely shifted from chiefdom to state with dual organization shortly after it regained independence from Colla domination and before conquest by the Inka. The Qari (Cari) lineage of Chucuito headed Lupaqa and remained seated through Inka and Spanish conquest at least until the 1560s. Under Inka rule the Lupaqa population was organized with respect to tributary households (numbering about 20,000 in the sixteenth century) in units arranged along decimal guidelines and presided over by local officials. Inka administrators relied heavily on indirect rule to integrate polities into the empire, maintaining traditional political hierarchies and utilizing them for their own purposes, a pattern employed in the region earlier and well-understood by Spaniards. Cieza de León wrote:

So as not to be abhorred by the natives they never took away the lordly prerogative of becoming chief [*cacique*] from those who had the natural right to it by inheritance. And if by chance any of them committed an offense, or was found guilty to the extent that he merited being divested of the lordship that he possessed, they gave and entrusted the chieftainship to the chiefs' sons or brothers; and ordered that everyone obey them.[76]

[76] Cieza de León, *Crónica del Perú*, I, 135.

This tactic, used wherever the empire expanded, gave permanence to families of officeholders while allowing removal of individuals who resisted or rebelled. As a general rule succession of officers under Inka rule was patrilineal, passing through eldest sons to the degree possible. Inka officials could and did manipulate traditional inheritance patterns even at low levels of hierarchy. Materials from the *altiplano* show that they redrew boundaries as well, with attention to the smallest settlements. Traditional hierarchies were subject to multiple levels of officers, headed by a provincial governor (often an "Inka by blood") and backed by military units directly representing Inka authority and interests. Important chiefs had to spend part of the year in or near Inka administrative centers.

Inka rule could also result in strengthening of local leadership positions, as was the case with Pacaje groups. Pre-Inka Pacaje in the northern Titicaca Basin were described in a sixteenth-century document as having been a bellicose people without permanent rulers: "They lived in a state of *behetría*, not acknowledging anyone's lordship nor paying tribute."[77] Their leaders were those who proved the most valiant and wise among them. According to these writers who cited older Indians, and who referred to the contemporary Pacaje domain as a kingdom, Tupa Inka Yupanqui appointed Pacaje chiefs and other functionaries, establishing a permanent and hereditary hierarchy: "[Some] of the successors of the chiefs appointed by the said Inka are currently those who command these Pacaxes."[78] Inka officials also reorganized the Pacaje land tenure system and divided up their large camelid herds, appropriating half for the Sun. Lands for cultivating maize were designated in Cochabamba and Cavari, as well as on the coast at Arica and near Arequipa, where harvests may have been destined in part for the Inka army.

Multiple ecological floors were utilized in the fifteenth and sixteenth centuries by indigenous groups in the region. Verticality probably evolved as a result of autochthonous internal and regional development and was expanded under Inka rule. Under the same rule populations were moved in and out of areas. Approximately forty-two different ethnic groups were brought as *mitmaqkuna* to settle in the peninsula of Copacabana, an important religious center in the Lake Titicaca region. People

---

[77] Pedro de Mercado de Peñalosa et al., "Relación de la Provincia de los Pacajes," in Marcos Jiménez de la Espada (ed.), *Relaciones Geográficas de Indias* [1570s?] (Madrid, 1965), I, 338 (334–341).
[78] Mercado de Peñalosa, et al., "Relación," I, 338.

from the *altiplano* were moved permanently and resettled in the warmer valleys of Cochabamba, Sipesipe, Pocoma, Mizque, and Larecaja.

In the Southern Titicaca Basin, it was noted in 1582 that Caracara, Charca, and Caranga chiefdoms had each been capable of contributing an army of 10,000 men to the Inka, suggesting quite large populations. At the time of Spanish contact, Caracara, Charca, and Quillaca polities had paramount chiefs, but little is known of their political hierarchies.

Prior to Inka conquest, Sora, Charca, Caracara, Chui, and Chicha lords formed a military alliance under the paramount of Charca, probably in defense against the expansionist Colla and Lupaqa. When the Spaniards came, the Charca lord apparently attempted to make permanent what had been a somewhat fluid ranking, by claiming that Caracara, Chui, and Chicha groups were under his political jurisdiction. Members of the alliance suffered differential damage in the course of military campaigns against Inka armies. The Charca appear to have fared best and the Chui population, in contrast, to have been almost annihilated. After Inka conquest, Charca, Caracara, Chicha, and remaining Chui people formed a close association with the Inka providing military service, the only tribute demanded of them.

Ethnic lords' military contributions were rewarded with highly valued gifts corresponding to their level of service and given to them at certain festivities, a symbolic and material sharing or redistribution of the benefits of an expanding empire that bound them to the Inka. Depending on their services and the number of warriors they contributed to the army, local lords received titles, privileges, and gifts, as well as prestigious sumptuary goods, certain allocations of subsistence goods, and people for their service. Inka Huayna Cápac gave one of his daughters as wife to the son of the lord of Caracara. He permitted the Charca chief to be carried by 100 people. Other chiefs received shirts woven with gold or silver or other special fabrics that were treasured and passed from generation to generation. Lupaqa and Caranga people also became close allies of the Inka, and through them the empire expanded into northern and central Chile and northwest Argentina.

With the collapse of the empire in the sixteenth century, a wide range of autonomous polities, from chiefdoms to states, reemerged in the *altiplano* before Europeans took over. Levels of political complexity varied among the chiefdoms. Some chiefs made claims to the large territories and populations that their ancestors had domain over before Inka conquest. Spanish reorganization usually simplified hierarchies and curtailed chiefs' power and authority.

Chile and Northwest Argentina

The Inka gained control over northern Chile by the early 1470s and over central Chile probably a few decades before the arrival of Spanish expeditionaries. Inka domination extended into the region mainly via administrative centers in the Bolivian *altiplano* and via *mitmaqkuna* and officers from *altiplano* polities such as Caranga and Lupaqa. Chuqi Cambi of Turco, a Caranga lord, held jurisdiction over Chief Cayoca, whose domain included several petty chiefs in Chile's Lluta and Azapa valleys and along the coast. Other Caranga lords also had subjects there, as did Lupaqa lords in the Lluta Valley. An Inka administrative center was placed in Catarpe near Quitor.

Northern Chile is traditionally divided into two major subareas, the Norte Grande, or arid north, and the Norte Chico, or semiarid north. Over 70 percent of the Norte Grande has little or no rain as a result of the effects of the Humboldt Current. In the Norte Chico desert, conditions gradually give way to better-watered zones, with rain increasing southward. By 500 B.C.E. villages and semiurban centers such as Caserones – known for its metal works, high-quality textiles, and basket weaving – grew in number in the arid north. Chiefdoms existed there from that time on. Southward chiefdoms developed later: in the semi-arid north between C.E. 800 and 1200, and in central Chile, a long, narrow, fertile strip that extends about 1,000 kilometers from north to south, between C.E. 900 and 1470. Chiefdoms in central Chile were less politically complex than those to the north.

Considerable interaction took place between peoples of northern Chile and the *altiplano* of Bolivia and Peru for several thousand years and continued through the period of Inka expansion. Tiwanaku exerted varying degrees of control over different parts of the region beginning about C.E. 200, having greatest overall impact between C.E. 600 and 1000. Its influence in the arid north is evident in settlement patterns, cemeteries, pottery, iconography, tools, textiles, hallucinogenic equipment, and other material goods. Tiwanaku appears to have taken control of some trade caravans that originated in northern Chile, an area that was connected via trade with the *altiplano*, northwest Argentina, and possibly some of the coastal societies of Peru. There is evidence as well that people from the Bolivian *altiplano* settled in the region, following a pattern of multiple zone use already established there. Settlers also entered from northeast Argentina and the tropical forest, a course that would continue in times to come.

Tiwanaku may have established administrative centers in the arid north. Under its influence, roads were built, as were aqueducts, irrigation canals, and ceremonial centers. It also seems to have brought some degree of stability, a Pax-Tiwanaku, prior to which there is evidence of interpolity hostilities (500 B.C.E.–C.E. 300). At the same time, it stimulated or permitted local societies such as San Pedro de Atacama to increase trade in Chile and northwest Argentina and to expand into other ecological zones, some at quite a distance from the parent settlements.

With Tiwanaku's decline between C.E. 1000 and 1200, complex independent chiefdoms (Arica, Atacama, and Pica) reemerged in Chile's arid north (see Map 7.3). There was notable simplification in crafts and the arts and an escalation of conflict and warfare. Forts were built, and abundant remains of war materials were left, as were pictorial representations of violence. Hostilities may have affected the volume of trade but did not bring an end to local and interregional exchange nor to some migrations of *altiplano* groups such as the Lípez and Chicha into the region. Diverse ethnic groups continued to maintain access to multiple ecological zones. Alliances of varying scope and length developed among different populations during the thirteenth through fifteenth centuries C.E.

In the fifteenth century, Inka conquest and utilization of indirect rule permitted continuation of some of the sociopolitical and cultural characteristics of chiefdoms in northern Chile but made their political hierarchies and economies subservient. Local production was integrated into the empire's movement of goods and people. Marine resources, crops, copper and gold, semiprecious stones, and lumber were all used for Inka projects. In Viña del Cerro (Copiapó Valley), an Inka copper foundry had a number of buildings and twenty-six smelters. According to chronicler Vivar (1558), Inka officials established a settlement in the northern part of El Chañar Valley to manage the movement of Chile's products, "and they were posted there for that purpose alone."[79] Existing roads were expanded, new ones were introduced in the Atacama desert, and

---

[79] Gerónimo de Vivar, *Crónica y Relación Copiosa y Verdadera de los Reinos de Chile* [1558] (Berlin, 1979), 27.

tambos (roadside inns) were built as well. Settlements were modified to serve as military and administrative centers. Specialized production of goods developed based on locally available resources. The *mitmaqkuna* who were settled in diverse ecological zones brought with them Inka architecture, tools, new forms of ceramics, metallurgical techniques, and textile and ceramic ornamentation. Under Inka administrators intensification of agriculture, enlargement of irrigation systems, and placement of new areas under cultivation using various water management strategies all took place. Exploitation of multiple vertical and horizontal ecological zones probably expanded, and new fishing techniques were introduced. Long-distance caravans, especially those between the arid north and the *altiplano*, were taken over by Inka officers to move foods, metals, cloth, and semiprecious stones, while native chiefs maintained control of local and regional traffic.

Of the independent polities that emerged from Inka rule in the European contact-period arid north, Atacama chiefdoms are the best known. Centered in Quitor, Atacama people controlled the oasis of San Pedro de Atacama, where lands were irrigable using the brackish waters of the Vilama and Atacama rivers, and nearby areas. Spanish chroniclers commented at the time of early contact (c. 1540) on the great number of "canals (*acequías*) that were utilized to water their fields" and the abundance of maize, *algarrobo*, *chañar*, and llama.[80] Atacama groups supplemented local production with trade, moving goods in caravans to the Bolivian *altiplano* and northwest Argentina.

In the semiarid north, chiefdom-type organization is evident in the Las Animas period (C.E. 800–1200), with social status differences reflected in burials and offerings. Diaguita chiefdoms (from C.E. 1200) displayed a degree of cultural continuity with Las Animas peoples in terms of subsistence, sociocultural complexity, burial practices, and ceramics. By the 1300s, there was a greater variety of material goods than in earlier periods, including very refined pottery. Some bone snuff spatulas were decorated with depictions of people in elaborate headdress and rich garments, probably representing members of a political hierarchy.

Diaguita chiefdoms opposed Inka troops and paid for it with their partial removal from the region. At the time of Spanish contact in 1540, the Diaguita lived in valleys of the semiarid north and northern central Chile. In each valley chronicler Vivar identified two major chiefs (*ca-*

[80] Vivar, *Crónica y Relación*, 20. Also see Oviedo, *Historia General*, V, 148.

ciques), each with specific territories possibly indicating dual organization. Other documents of the 1540s provide similar information. In some descriptions, such as of the valleys of Huasco and Aconcagua, chroniclers refer to the two major lords as brothers. In general the two chiefs appear to have been close but to have governed independently:

> The lords of this valley [Aconcagua] are two. Their names are these: the one, Tanjalongo, he has command over the half of the valley toward the sea. The other cacique is called Michimalongo, he has command and rules the half of the valley toward the mountains.[81]

Under them were lesser chiefs (*capitanes, principales*). Chiefs were distinguished from the rest of the population by deference and sumptuary rules and received service and tribute in return for which they offered their subjects feasts with abundant food and alcoholic beverages. Vivar reported temple-priest complexes in some valleys.

Hostilities among chiefdoms occurred as the *Pax-Inka* was weakened by civil wars at the highest level of the empire and the arrival of the Spaniards. Cooperation of unrelated chiefs against common enemies occurred first to expel Inka officials and their people, and later to attempt the same with Spaniards as they posed an increasing threat. Chiefs of different valleys united temporarily, forming a larger alliance and more inclusive level of organization than they formerly had, with Michimalongo as war chief: "He was the most esteemed lord that has been found in all the valleys."[82] Chiefs of Aconcagua, and particularly Michimalongo, emerged as powerful leaders. Vivar wrote about Aconcagua: "that it was the head of this territory, and seeing that if this valley or its people submitted the others would follow, the general [Valdivía] decided to engage them in battle."[83]

South of Diaguita territory, in central Chile, were Mapundungun-speaking Picón, Mapuche, and Huilliche groups at the time of European contact. All had a time-depth of several hundred years in the region. The northernmost, Picón (Picunche), occupied an area extending from the Mapocho Valley to the Maulé River in the central valley. In this region during the Aconcagua Period (C.E. 900–1470), settlement patterns varied from semipermanent to permanent depending on resource availability and use. Some degree of status differentiation is indicated by the distri-

---

[81] Vivar, *Crónica y Relación*, 50, 80.   [82] Vivar, *Crónica y Relación*, 50.
[83] Vivar, *Crónica y Relación*, 88.

bution of mortuary goods, which included semiprecious stones. How people of the Aconcagua period were related to the subsequent Picón (Picunche) whom Spaniards encountered is problematic. Inka armies conquered the northernmost Picón by the 1480s. *Mitmaqkuna* from Arequipa, the Bolivian *altiplano* (possibly Lupaqa), and the semiarid north (Diaguita) were brought in, some apparently assigned to mining work. Inka imperial control was strongest in and around the territory of the Picón people who, unlike Mapuche and Huilliche groups, had the formal, hereditary office of chief. There were several Picón chiefs along the Mapocho River and in adjacent valleys at the time of European contact. They headed political hierarchies, and some had domain over multiple ecological zones. Populations to the south of them without permanent chiefs were difficult for the Inka, and later Spanish officials, to control or exploit for their labor.

In northwest Argentina as in northern Chile, Inka rule was administered for the most part by *altiplano* officials, who were well-acquainted with the area when Spaniards arrived. The Inka empire encompassed the northwest by 1480, but its influence varied from area to area. Patterns of management were similar to those utilized in northern Chile. Control over major local trade routes and those that connected the region with Chile and Bolivia were secured. *Tambos* were built as were military and administrative centers. Settlements were established for the exploitation of minerals. Religious and craft centers were founded or, if they already existed, were augmented, and craft specializations (ceramics, metallurgy) were concentrated in towns. Ecological verticality appears to have expanded, llama herds increased, products previously not in the area were made available, and large storage facilities were built. Inka styles and planning influenced local architecture and the remodeling of some towns already in existence. Local ceramics showed Inka motifs, and the use of bronze in daily activities was expanded. Inka administrators settled *mitmaqkuna*, possibly from Chile and Bolivia, moved indigenous populations out, reorganized production, and modified economies, redirecting labor to produce goods for the state.

The northwest, which encompasses about 600,000 square kilometers, is usually subdivided geographically into four regions – the Puna, Valliserrana and Humahuaca Quebrada, the Sierras Subandinas or western *selvas*, and Santiago de Estero. The area has probably been occupied continuously since 10,000 B.C.E. Chiefdoms had a long tradition throughout the northwest, the result of local evolution and influences from nearby as well as from northern Chile and the *altiplano*. Centralization processes took place in the Formative Period (200 B.C.E.–C.E. 1000) in Puna and Valliserrana among groups connected with Condorhuasi, Ciénaga, and Aguada cultures. Aguada iconography, ceramics, and stonework were strongly influenced by Tiwanaku in the course of trade or political control.

During the Late or Regional Development Period (from C.E. 1000 to Inka conquest in the 1480s), complex societies associated with Humahuaca, Santa María, Tafí, and other cultures developed in the region's heartland of chiefdom formation, Valliserrana and Humahuaca Quebrada. During that time irrigation techniques and widespread intensive agriculture with terraced fields were refined, and new varieties of crops were introduced. Surplus products were held in storage facilities. Agriculture was complemented by large-scale llama and alpaca herding. Metal was used not only for personal adornment and ceremonial purposes, as it had been earlier, but also for tools and weapons. As populations grew and settlements became more concentrated, towns developed. Many were situated outside arable zones in places of difficult access, which, along with defensive constructions, fortifications, and depictions of trophy heads, indicate some frequency of warfare. Under Inka rule, peace was maintained throughout the area where chiefdoms had previously fought with each other as well as against encroachment from other ethnic groups. With the collapse of the empire, warfare was renewed. As in the Bolivian-Peruvian *altiplano* and Chile, independent chiefdoms reemerged: Apatama (Atacama) in the *puna*, Omaguaca (also written Humahuaca), and Diaguita in the Valliserrana-Humahuaca and Sierras Subandinas, Capayán in Valliserrana-Humahuaca, and Tonocote in Santiago de Estero (see Map 7.3). None, however, had the degree of centralization that would facilitate control of any one whole subarea. Apatama communities were predominant in the *puna*, where there were also enclaves of Chicha groups as well as of Omaguaca, who were politically dependent on the principal chief of the Omaguaca Valley. It is not known whether Inka officials brought them there or they were already in place as a result of caravan exchange systems or ecological diversification. Each Apatama community had a chief. Possibly some multitiered political hierarchies were in place, given the large size of some of the settlements. Salt from extensive salt flats was actively traded for ceramics from Valliserrana, for mollusks from the Pacific, and for other products, such as foods. Agriculture included the use of extensive *andenes* (raised long, narrow, parallel plots, supported with stone walls, and built up along hillsides). Llama herding was practiced above 4,000 meters.

Omaguaca (Humahuaca) chiefdoms with a number of independent local-level hierarchies and regional paramounts were located in the Valliserrana-Humahuaca and Sierras Subandinas regions. Spaniards noted that some burials, probably those of chiefs, were very rich in imported and local goods. In times of war, the Omaguaca formed large confederations with other ethnic groups, as they did against the Spanish in the sixteenth and seventeenth centuries.

Their territories were reported to be densely settled. Agricultural intensification included the use of large-scale irrigation systems, terracing, and stone walls to prevent erosion. In some places along rivers, narrow ditches were excavated that filled with water when first dug and provided ample fish. When they dried up, they were planted with maize, the yields of which were abundant, according to Spanish observers. Communities raised crops at multiple elevations, gaining control of varied horizontal and vertical niches. Major crops included maize, potatoes, *quinua*, beans, squash, oca, olluco, ají, mate, maní, and *algarroba*. Surplus food was kept in storage facilities. Llama were herded extensively and were used for local and regional transportation, as well as for their products. Local production was supplemented with goods obtained in long-distance exchange that connected the local economy with those of other regions. Items thus obtained included hallucinogenic drugs and coca from the tropical forest.

Spaniards had great difficulty in subjugating Omaguaca chiefdoms. Increased colonial control in the seventeenth century brought severely negative consequences to native economy and population.

Valliserrana-Humahuaca and the Sierras Subandinas were also inhabited by large Diaguita populations. In the literature the Diaguita have been divided into three groups, probably with dialect and cultural differences: Pular (valleys of Calchaquí and of Salta), Calchaquí (Calchaquí and Yocavil valleys), and Diaguita proper (in Catamarca and La Rioja). Chronicles and historic accounts list numerous communities whose names correspond mainly to geographic locations, usually valleys. Each appears to have been under one or two chiefs, perhaps a dual-organization system. Some archaeologists have identified dual organization in the Formative Period, with village and, later, town growth developing around two clusters in each case.

Chiefly position was inherited patrilineally, passing from father to son, and in the absence of sons, to the chief's brother. Social and material differentiation of Calchaquí chiefs included multiple wives and possession of specific kinds of jewelry. A chronicler reported that the Indians believed when *caciques* or *principales* died their souls went to the planets while the souls of common Indians and of animals went to the stars, maintaining status differentiation in death as well as in life. Chiefs' importance was such that Spaniards tried to capture or kill them early in battle as a means of defeating all of their subjects.

By the fifteenth and sixteenth centuries, the northwest was under threat of Guarani-speaking Chiriguano and Lule groups, who were semi-nomadic hunters. These two peoples were expanding from El Chaco into the region where they caused considerable damage to settled populations. In the period between Inka and European rule, chiefly organization reemerged and, in some areas where European settlement was sparse, retained autonomy by resisting Spanish control. Omaguaca peoples did so until the late 1590s, and Diaguita until the 1660s. Atacama chiefdoms in Chile maintained independence until the early seventeenth century, but Diaguita, Picón, and others in the fertile central region and some northern portions came under Spanish rule shortly after the sacking and burning of the city of Santiago.

Chilean and northwest Argentine chiefdoms that emerged from Inka rule were of varying size and political complexity. There were no paramount-headed blocs until the second half of the sixteenth century, when Calchaquí polities appear to have been united under the leadership of *cacique* Juan Calchaquí in the course of resistance against the Europeans. Once colonial rule was established, there was drastic decrease in native populations as a result of war, disease, overwork, loss of land, and related conditions.

Central Andes

Inka expansion north of Cuzco and the southern Peruvian highlands involved the domination of more than one hundred *grupos, behetrías, curacazcos,* provinces, etnias, *señoríos,* kingdoms, nations, and tribes in the Central Andean cordillera and on its eastern and western flanks. Chiefdoms of many different levels of sociopolitical complexity most likely constituted a substantial portion of them. Here, as in the South Andes, the Inka incorporated such polities into larger administrative units. Consolidation did not totally obscure the outlines of pre-Inka political units. Data on particular groups, however, is uneven; some are no more than mentioned by early writers or modern scholars, and others are dealt with more fully. We look at the highland regions first and then the coast.

The sierra, which has an average elevation of 3,000 meters, widens toward the south and forms fairly uniform plateau surfaces in the course of its 2,400-kilometer span through the Central Andes. Rivers have cut deep tropical canyons into it, and in the southern region, tectonic activity and volcanism have been important forces. Descending eastward the *ceja de la montaña*, an 80–160-kilometer wide ecological belt at about 1,800 meters separates the sierra from the forested plain, the *montaña*, which lies at elevations between 400 and 1,800 meters. Westward of the sierra the coast, primarily desert, has been crossed by rivers that flow from the mountains and have formed fertile valleys, important sites of prehispanic development. Throughout these regions, there is a great deal of geomorphological and climate variation and consequently great contrasts in ecology and vegetation. Chiefdoms had a long history in the Central Andes. Simple ones developed by 2500–1800 B.C.E. along the region's northern and central coasts, and possibly in the highlands. Complex chiefdoms appeared by 1800–1200/800 B.C.E. Chiefdoms, some of several hundred years' duration, are identifiable thereafter throughout the region.

We look at two of the many chiefdoms subjugated by the Inka in the central Sierra and see two quite different examples of reorganization: Huanca, where emphasis is on the process of integration of a polity into the empire; and Yacha Chupachu, and Quero, where Inka-imposed centralization is on distinct groups that may have been moving in the direction of hierarchy.

The Huanca, a people that inhabited the province of the same name (Department of Junín), exploited multiple ecological floors, where they cultivated a variety of root crops and maize and herded llama. The Huanca polity has been variously described as a state, a "macro-chiefdom," and most convincingly, a moderately complex chiefdom with dual organization at the time of Inka conquest. Prior to development of hierarchical ranking with very weakly centralized political bodies, numerous corporate descent groups of varying size, some quite large, were engaged in constant hostilities with each other over land and other resources – "those of one bank of the river ... against those of the other."[84]

---

[84] Andrés de Vega, "La Descripción que se hizo en la Provincia de Xauxa por la Instrución de S. M. . . . (1582)," in Jiménez de la Espada, *Relaciones Geográficas*, I, 169. Native declarations.

Centralization and the formation of chiefdoms had taken place or was taking place in the 1460s, the result of consolidation of power that had been in process for some time. Nevertheless, competition among political leaders was strong and was manipulated by Inka officials in attracting a number of lords to their camp. The Huanca capitulated after strong resistance by some chiefs. Inka administrators resettled those who had opposed them and divided the area into three *sayas*, or sections – Jatunsausa (Jatunjauja), Lurinhuanca, and Ananhuanca – apparently with correlation to a previous tripartite division. They also shifted some of the population to lower elevations. In each section natives and *mitmaqkuna* introduced by the Inka were organized along the decimal system into *pachacas* and *guarangas*, administrative units of approximately 100 and 1,000 taxpayers, respectively. Inka administrators drew on local élites in appointing paramount lords of the Huanca *sayas* and heads of *pachacas* and *guarangas*. As élites, officeholders continued to have special privileges in the form of services, private lands, and special cloth (*qumpi*). Some heads of *ayllus* kinship/territorial units were permitted to remain in their preconquest positions. Huanca officials provided the Inka with soldiers for the campaigns in Quito but turned against them when Spanish expeditions arrived and became allies of the Europeans.

In the province of Huánuco (Department of Huánuco), there were several distinct native groups, among them, Quero, Yacha, and Chupachu. The Quero and Yacha were organized by Inka Huayna Cápac into one *guaranga*, but by the late 1520s or early 1530s, Inka Huáscar had reorganized Quero populations, grouping them with Chupachu into four *guarangas*. Spanish *visitas* of 1549 and 1562 indicate that Quero and Chupachu were closely connected as parts of one overarching native political unit. Although the two had political leaders prior to Inka conquest, their positions were not inherited, and their influence was only local: "The Indian followers of the deceased gave the lordship to another who was praiseworthy and not to the son."[85] The two chiefs whom the Inka placed at the head of each *guaranga* were probably traditional leaders, but by virtue of the new organization, their positions could now be inherited by their sons. A more inclusive level of political organization, involving all the *guarangas* and headed by a *cacique principal*, emerged after the Europeans established themselves in the area. In the *visita* of 1562, a *cacique* of Auquimarca stated that Paucar Guaman had been an

---

[85] Iñigo Ortiz de Zúñiga, *Visita de la Provincia de León de Huánuco en 1562*, 2 vols., (Huánuco, 1967–1972), I, 65–66. Declaration of the *principal*, Masco, of the pueblo of Chupa.

influential person who made himself *cacique principal* when all the *caciques* of the *guarangas* died leaving heirs of minor age. In 1562, two years after Guaman's death, it was not clear whether his minor son would eventually succeed him. In each *guaranga* there were sons of *caciques* who were able to assume office, and the successor would need to be properly authoritative.

Yacha people were organized into one *guaranga* by Inka officials. There is information on four of its *pachacas*, or subunits. Each had a lord referred to as *cacique* in the *visita* of 1562. Below them were local chiefs in charge of pueblos. *Pachaca* lords' positions were inherited by their sons, who, according to one informant, had to serve the Inka for one or two years to confirm that they had the appropriate qualities for office. Native lords were subject to a provincial Inka governor who oversaw the region and had the power of capital punishment. Such an official was based in Huánuco Pampa, a political, ceremonial, and festival center. *Mitmaqkuna* were also organized into *pachacas*, each with its own chief, and all subject to one *cacique principal*.

In the northern sierra the Inka encountered a number of states and chiefdoms, among them Cajamarca, which has been called a *señorío*, or chiefdom, but was probably a kingdom. It had established control over territories in multiple ecological zones on the coast and in the highlands, and it was described as having very fertile, well-cultivated lands and excellent crafts, especially in textiles, silver, and gold. Cajamarca's territorial domain was maintained under the Inka.

Also in the northern highland regions were Huamachuco, Conchuco, and Huayla (Huaylla) polities identified as local chieftainships. There is little information on them. Language, religion, clothing, and other characteristics of Huamachuco were the same as those found among people of Cajamarca. Conchuco groups were known for their wealth in silver and gold and for their bellicosity. The Huayla polity, whose officers made claims in the sixteenth century to be descendants of the Huari, had dual organization. The two sections each had a paramount chief who organized resistance against the Inka. Once conquered (probably in the 1460s after at least two campaigns), Huayla populations, like those discussed earlier, were regrouped by the Inka into *guarangas* and *pachacas* and also divided into sections. By the time of Spanish arrival, chiefly office had been assumed by Añas Colque, daughter of the deceased paramount of one section. She occupied the office with the approval of Inka Huayna Cápac, to whom she was a secondary wife.

The northern Peruvian coast was dominated by the Chimú empire prior to Inka conquest (late 1460s to 1470s). Chimú's domain extended from the Tumbes to the Chillón River, encompassing some twenty-one major coastal valleys and diverse political systems, among which were chiefdoms. Chimú officials utilized indirect rule in some areas with minimal local structural change. In sections of Piurá, for example, political officers (who happened to be women) were retained. Women were still in office at the time of European arrival. In other areas, such as Lambayeque, Chimú administrators established new leaders. Similar patterns of management were later followed by the Inka, but layers of administration were added to those already existing. Populations were also regrouped and moved from one place to another; people formerly under Chimú dispersed along the coast and resettled as *mitmaqkuna*.

South of the Chillón Valley, the House of Ychma ruled the Rimac (or Lima) and Lurín valleys. Pachacamac, the Ychma ruling seat, was also the site of a famous Andean oracle and a major pilgrimage center. The two Ychma brothers were installed by Inka Huayna Cápac. One of them had been *yanakuna* (also written *yanacona*) to a wife of the Inka, and the other the Inka's own attendant.[86] Subject to the Ychma were a number of small, chiefdoms that may have been independent until then, although involved at various times in alliances for protection and defense. The aggregation or confederation and break up of particular units was played out within intervalley and intravalley political contexts, as well as between them and contiguous mountain groups who controlled their sources of water. Ychma lords controlled a number of groups; some may have been halves of a pair – for example, Lima and Amancae, Maranga and Guala. Each *señorío* had several dispersed pueblos that could be identified by name, probably had their own officials, and occupied the banks of defined portions of major streams. Some of their populations were within domains of other *señoríos* at the time of European contact as a result of Inka social engineering, as were Chimú *mitmaqkuna*, mentioned earlier. Under Inka rule local lords had specific lands, as did commoners; lands within their territories were also assigned to the Inka himself and to the support of state religious sectors: the Sun (*huacas*, 'holy place') and *mamakuna* (selected women who were trained to work and perform rituals in their service).

There is less information on valleys to the south before and after Inka

---

[86] *Yanakuna* were selected individuals without rights or duties in their communities of origin, who served as personal retainers to Inka élites, performing a wide variety of domestic and public duties.

conquest. Recent work indicates that groups such as the Chincha and Ica were similar to the Chillón, Rimac, and Lurín *señoríos* and were polities of "rather loosely integrated entities of small 'ethnic' groups dependent upon a major 'lord' whose own base of operations was in the irrigated coast" and whose territory included one or two adjacent valleys.[87] The degree of centralization among them varied.

Northern Andes (Ecuador)

Chiefdoms in the highland areas of Ecuador came under Inka control in the late fifteenth century. Inka armies inflicted great losses on the people of this region, who tenaciously resisted conquest and who subsequently proved difficult to integrate into the imperial system. Here as elsewhere, the state moved populations out and introduced new ones into it. As they did elsewhere, Inka administrators appropriated lands for the royal family and the state, apparently compensating local groups by increasing their access to subtropical or tropical zones. Ecuadorian Andean chiefdoms tended to have great ecological diversity within relatively close range of primary settlements prior to conquest, a feature that Inka lords maintained and expanded. Maize, beans, tubers, and fruits were basic crops. In some areas, such as in the southern part of the Quito Basin, a highly productive raised-field agriculture was practiced.

In Ecuador the two major Andean ranges, the Cordillera Oriental (or Real) and the Occidental, are quite close to each other for about 640 kilometers north to south. Between them is a deep valley (25–40 km wide) divided into ten to fifteen basins at elevations ranging from 750 to 2900 meters and bordered by about thirty volcanos, some of which are still active.

Local and long-distance trade were important here as on the coast, and by 2500 B.C.E. at the latest, there is clear evidence of exchange, especially of exotic products, among people of the Andes, the coast and Amazonia. Cerro Narrío in the southern Ecuadorian Andes, near today's city of Cañar, was an important trade center. In the second millennium B.C.E., its influence spread as it sent *Spondylus* shells to Peru and controlled exchange of exotic products from Amazonia. By 550 B.C.E.–C.E. 550, the people of Cerro Narrío, possibly organized in complex chief-

---

[87] Jeffrey R. Parsons and Charles M. Hastings, "The Late Intermediate Period," in Richard W. Keatinge (ed.), *Peruvian prehistory* (Cambridge, 1988), 219–220 (190–229).

doms, were intruding into the Ecuadorian coast. A chiefdom, or a series of chiefdoms, occupied Cerro Narrío until the Inka conquest. Complex societies probably existed elsewhere in the Andes of Ecuador from early times. There is greater information on chiefdoms in the period C.E. 550–1530, when ridged fields, extensive areas of platforms, funeral mounds, and pyramids were built by them. Outlines of a number of chiefly polities were still discernible under Inka rule when the Spanish arrived. At the time of European contact, there were several whose paramounts the Inka had retained, such as Otavalo and Caranqui. There also were less centralized chiefdoms such as Chillos and Cumbaya (see Map 7.3), none of which developed more complex centralization while part of the empire or after its collapse.

Among the earliest to be subjugated by the Inka were the Cañari in the basins of the Cañar, Paute, and Jubones rivers. When Inka conquest occurred, there had been complex societies in the region for at least 500 years. According to native declarations made in the 1580s regarding pre-Inka times, lords of communities received food, beverages, and labor for the construction of their compounds and cultivation of their crops "by virtue of their recognition and lordship."[88] Their houses were larger than others and had special ornamentation. Chiefs in the Cañaribamba region were reported to have a great deal of power, with control over other lords and extensive territories. Men and women of high rank accumulated large amounts of gold and silver jewelry, textiles into which feathers were incorporated, and special ceramics. These were buried with them when they died, along with food, drink, and various attendants. Chiefs were polygamous; their offices were inherited by sons of principal wives. Some Cañari communities were situated in regions with good access to varied ecological zones.

In the fifteenth century, Cañari chiefdoms of varying size were waging war against each other as well as against other groups for territory and access to trade routes. A number of chiefs entered into alliances with each other to fend off Inka armies. They resisted conquest at considerable human cost. Many Cañaris were sent to different parts of the empire as *mitmaqkuna* and *yanakuna*. Possibly over 50 percent of the local population was moved; some resettled along roads. Cañari men were used in the Inka's personal guard and as soldiers. Inka Huayna Cápac brought a

---

[88] Antonio Bello Gayoso (ed.), "Relación que enbió a Mandar su Magestad Hiziese desta Ciudad de Cuenca y de Toda su Provincia," [158], in Jiménez de la Espada, *Relaciones Geográficas*, II, 275.

large number of *mitmaqkuna* into the region, and Inka officials rebuilt or expanded some Cañari settlements, such as Tomebamba, Cañari-bamba, and Hatuncañar. Irrigation and terracing were also expanded, and in some cases possibly so was access to diverse ecological zones. Cañari groups were permitted by Inka officials to be involved in long-distance trade. They exchanged gold, ceramics, deer meat, fish, wood, wood products, and *mantas* for salt on the coast and in the sierra and for tropical materials, feathers, cotton, and coca in the *yunka* (also written *yunga* or *yunca*) (the western subtropical flanks of the cordillera) and in Amazonia.

Cañari communities again incurred population losses in the sixteenth century, when Atawallpa (also spelled Atahualpa) punished them for not supporting him against his brother, Waskhar (Huáscar), and in the 1540s, when they fought on both sides of the Spaniards' civil wars.

Northward, in the Riobamba Basin, Inka armies encountered Puru-háes polities, a number of small chiefdoms with multitiered political hierarchies of limited domain, some with more renowned leaders than others. Inka administrators introduced or fostered dual organization among local populations and settled large numbers of *mitmaqkuna* organized along the decimal system and headed by their own leaders. Highland chiefs appear to have been given access to the *yunka* in compensation for loss of territory, and they received half of the coca, cotton, maize, and other goods that were produced there. Sumptuary rules and special services distinguished chiefs. They may have been the only ones who could use cotton. Traders who exchanged various products including salt and textiles over long distances were probably subject to them. A symbol of chiefly office was a chair in which the chief ultimately was buried with his arms, jewelry, and food, accompanied by some wives.

Further north in the basins of Ibarra and Quito, some of the last groups conquered by Inka armies shared a common history as reflected in their material culture. At the time of European arrival, there was still a great deal of cultural, social, and linguistic similarity among them. Most writers, beginning with the late eighteenth-century chronicler, Ve-lasco, have referred to these groups as one complex sociocultural unit, called Cara, a name that has also been used for a late archaeological phase. Treatment of these polities as a single people has been challenged by a number of scholars, including Caillavet and Moreno, who find on the basis of archival and other data that there were at least four chiefdoms in the region in the late fifteenth century: Otavalo, Caranqui, Cochisquí, and Cayambe.[89] They were partially subdued by the Inka in the 1470s, and possibly in the 1490s joined together in an uprising. The rebellion was very costly in terms of lives lost, and it may have lasted for as long as two decades until the chiefdoms suffered a bloody defeat at the Laguna of Yaguarcocha.

Cayambe appears to have assumed a leadership role during the revolt. A paramount lord (*ango*) of Cayambe presented documentation on the matter in early colonial times and made claims to political control over the people of Otavalo and Cochasquí. At the time of European contact, the *ango* of Otavalo seems to have had more authority in the region, resulting from either Inka political organization or indigenous sociopolitical order. There may well have been a certain fluidity in predominance of one chiefdom over others through time.

In the sixteenth century, Cayambe and Otavalo polities had close relations with the *ango* of Cayambe growing up in the household of the paramount chief of Otavalo. The practice of chiefs raising other chiefs' children may not have been uncommon and may have strengthened affinal ties among them. The élites of Cayambe and Caranqui intermarried, a practice conducive to producing larger sociopolitical blocs. Also both before and after Inka times, there appear to have been close linguistic, economic, social, cultural, and possibly political ties between chiefdoms of the highlands and tropical and semitropical region societies such as the Intag, Quilca, Caguasquí, Pimampiro, and Chapi. During the Inka and Spanish periods, highland chiefdoms established direct control over them. Otavalo, Caranqui, and Cayambe people shared lands in the basins of the Guayllabamba and Mira rivers, although it is not clear whether this was a pre-Inka practice that resulted from the exchange networks between them, or a result of Inka policy. All three were involved in long-distance trade carried on by specialists (*mindaláes*).

In the Quito Basin south of the Pisque and Guayllabamba rivers, there were a number of subregions occupied by chiefdoms, some with mutually similar political structure and organization, such as Quito and Panzaleo. Paramount office was permanent and inherited. The incumbent presided

---

[89] See Juan de Velasco, *Padre Juan de Velasco (Historia del Reino de Quito (1789)*, 2 vols. (Quito, 1960); Chantal Caillavet, "La Adaptación de la Dominación Incaica a las Sociedades Autóctonas de la Frontera Septentrional del Imperio: Territorio Otavalo – Ecuador," *Revista Andina*, 2 (1985), 403–423; Segundo E. Moreno, "Introducción, La Epoca Aborigen," in Moreno (ed.), *Pichincha: Monografía Histórica de la Región Nuclear Ecuatoriana* (Quito, 1981), 15–174; and Moreno, "Formaciones Políticas tribales y Señoríós étnicos," in Enrique Ayala (ed.), *Nueva Historia del Ecuador* (Quito, 1988), II, 9–134.

over a hierarchy of officials, had authority and power over his subjects and their belongings, and could mete out punishment. Paramounts settled disputes, organized and directed warfare, controlled trade, allocated labor and strategic resources, and sponsored and led ceremonies. Served by attendants, they had sumptuary privileges, amassing large quantities of luxury goods and foods. They lived in special compounds that were the ceremonial centers of the society.

Quito's main settlement, also called Quito, was in the process of modification by Inka officials who were rebuilding roads, inns, and possibly fortifications. Dual division was established, Quechua was introduced, and some groups were moved from Quito to the shores of Lake Titicaca. Diverse *mitmaqkuna* were brought into the Quito region where they formed enclaves organized along the decimal system. A labor tribute was established, and lands were taken for various purposes, including assignment to Inka royal households. Quito lords still maintained active trade, including their long-distance routes westward to the Yumbos, eastward to Quijos, and possibly to the coast. Quito was the location of one of the most important markets for specialized traders (*mindaláes*) who exchanged exotic goods throughout the northern regions.

The 1562 Huánuco *visita* in Peru make it clear that Inka officials were in the process of standardizing political bureaucracy throughout the realm to the degree possible, crosscutting cultural heterogeneity in inheritance guidelines, and possibly in other features as well, while utilizing local *principales* to fill positions. Under Inka rule patrilineal succession to office by eldest sons was the preferred course. If the proper son were not of age, office could pass to the brother of the deceased chief and revert to the heir after such time as he was capable of doing the job and receiving state approval. Women were not excluded from holding office, as evidence from the Peruvian coast and highlands indicates.

In societies where centralization was already underway, Inka officials accelerated the process by making positions of appointed leaders hereditary, although the status of some such lords was in question at the time of European arrival. In the brief period between the collapse of the Inka empire and imposition of European control, states and chiefdom-type organization emerged. In the case of the many chiefdoms that did so, most leaders were descendants of the families that held chiefly office before their integration into the Inka empire. Others, related to administrators imposed by Inka officials outside the indigenous systems, also made claims to office.

Throughout the former Inka realm, there remained enclaves of *mit-maqkuna* who had their own officers, remained independent of local political organization, and claimed rights to the areas to which they had been brought to live. To further complicate the postempire picture, many polities had lands and populations in territories of others, in some cases as a result of resettlement by Inka administrators. Clearly the social fields of interaction of chiefdoms had been changed on the large scale by Inka rule. The same was so of their societies and cultures. The decimal system impinged on social organization. Resettlement, reapportionment of lands, and demands for labor all affected economic structures. Incorporation of local lords into the state system altered chiefs' political status. Acceptance of Inka gods altered the ideological sphere, and acceptance of Quechua altered the linguistic domain. As a result the autonomous societies that briefly reemerged in the sixteenth century were different from those that existed prior to Inka rule despite political, social, and ideological links with their fourteenth-century ancestors.

CONCLUSION

The considerable time-depth and broad distribution of chiefdoms throughout the regions discussed here call attention to the adaptability of this mode of sociopolitical organization, even in areas where states and empires emerged. South American chiefdoms varied considerably with respect to levels of centralization and long-term trajectories. The larger sociopolitical, economic, and ideological fields of interaction in which they developed also shifted through time, as we have seen in the context of Andean empires, in changes in constellations of Cauca Valley chiefdoms, and in the rise and fall of complex polities in Amazonia among other areas. The identification of different levels of sociopolitical complexity as well as of chiefdoms' histories and spatial contexts are important in understanding their autochthonous development and fragmentation as well as modifications in them brought about by contacts of varying intensity with other groups – from exchange activities with neighbors, to regional alliances and hostilities, to conquest and incorporation by empire-building states.

The Chibcha case, presented to illustrate the complexity of sociopolitical organization in a polity that had been moving toward concentration of power when the Spaniards arrived, covers a relatively short-range record of centralization as it traces processes of social, political, and economic articulation that may be analogous to those undergone by other complex chiefdoms at various times prior to European conquest. The Chibcha were among a great many chiefdoms that occupied northernmost South America (Colombia and Venezuela), Amazonia and coastal Ecuador, territories that did not come under the rule of empire. Chiefly polities ranged from almost statelike to minimally centralized at the time of Spanish contact. In complex chiefdoms division between chief (or chiefs) and commoners was very marked in the political, social, economic, ideological, and ritual arenas; the greater the demarcation, the more concentrated positions of power and authority. Chiefs' roles were many and multifaceted, overlapping with each other. Political and economic functions, for example, were more often than not deeply interconnected with symbolic and social ones. The South American material supports the thesis that the authority of the office of chief was augmented with power obtained in three major areas: economic, with increased control over land, labor, goods, storage, or trade; ideological and/or ritual; and warfare, with increased concentration of force and control over a warrior elite. Rather than there being dominance of any one base, there was manipulation to concentrate power in such a way that there was interlocking dependency of available options.[90]

In some groups such as the Chibcha at the time of European contact, there may have been the beginnings of internal specialization of political hierarchies and creation of governmental offices with different functions in decision making and areas of control, characteristic features of states. Nonetheless, without studies of further historical depth, it is not possible to say whether these processes were part of a cycle of centripetal and centrifugal forces or a definitive trend toward state organization. Although chiefly office was occupied primarily by men, women succeeded to the position in a number of societies in Colombia, Peru, and possibly elsewhere as well.

Numerous chiefdoms were composed of communities that had access to multiple ecological zones situated at varying distances, sometimes involving several days' travel. Others were made up of single-zone communities in areas with diverse climates and resources. Ecological complementarity – an important adaptive characteristic throughout South America among a great number of polities from tribally organized eastern

---

[90] Earle, *Chiefdoms*, xi – xii, 1–15.

Colombian Chitarerros to the Inka empire – though not a distinguishing feature of chiefdoms, appears nonetheless to have been very important in the structure and organization of many. Methods of use of multiple zones, allocation of personnel, and intensity of exploitation and distribution of produce most likely differed from one political level to another and bear further description and analysis. Indeed, attention to basic food production technologies and resource orientation of complex groups still is called for given that methods of landscape modification and agricultural intensification (as in raised fields, terracing, ditches, and irrigation) as well as harvesting of riverine and marine products continue to be discovered and discussed – for example, in the Moxo region (Bolivia), San Jorge Basin (Colombia), the Orinoco Llanos (Colombia and Venezuela), and Amazonia.

Throughout South America, societies developed complexity locally while benefiting in their growth from intensive trade and contact with various other groups. Chibcha communities in Colombian *tierra fría*, (2,000–3,000m above sea level) for example, depended on access to cotton-producing lowlands as well as trade for cotton in large quantities that was used locally, in tribute, and in further trade. Chibcha people participated directly and indirectly in exchange along trade routes southward all the way to coastal and highland Ecuador, north to the Atlantic coast and the Sierra Nevada, west to Antioquia, and east to the Orinoco Llanos. Chiefdoms in the Antioquia region were connected to several trade routes and major trade centers. In coastal Ecuador, chiefdoms were linked by exchange activities with Peru to the south, the *yunka*, sierra, and Oriente inland to the east, and possibly by sea with Panama and Central America to the north. Trade connected northern Chile and northwest Argentina to the Bolivian-Peruvian *altiplano*, Peruvian coastal areas, and Amazonia. The Orinoco and Amazon rivers and their tributaries were also vital routes of travel and exchange. Over time chiefdoms involved in trade no doubt underwent changes as a result of power struggles, the making and breaking of alliances, or antagonistic relationships with respect to control of goods, routes, and related matters.

Networks established via exchange may have been important in stimulating the formation of large, macrochiefdom political units, but warfare and resistance to regulation from outside strengthened the maintenance of political entities that, given their antiquity and ubiquity, may have had greater sociopolitical and ecological adaptability than states or empires. From the vantage point of areas where chiefdoms predominate, the question is not so much why states and empires did not form but why they should form in a sort of lock-step unilineal evolutionism.

The role of warfare in political centralization and fragmentation is still difficult to discern. At the regional level it may have promoted centralization processes, but there are ethnohistorically documented cases, such as that of the Colombian Pijao, where warfare that continued for over half a century did not promote centralization. Persistent hostilities in most cases did not create the conditions for supraregional centralization in the prehispanic Cauca-Patía or Magdalena valleys, nor did it in many areas of the Andean highlands from Ecuador to Bolivia prior to Inka expansion. Warfare was highly destructive in some areas of Colombia, but that was also true of the Central Andes and *altiplano* prior to the successes of Inka conquest and rule.

For traditional chiefs incorporation into the imperial Inka bureaucracy involved, above all, loss of political autonomy, followed in some cases by changes in succession pattern, and in most cases by modifications in former domains to accommodate Inka social and economic engineering. Many Andean chiefdoms briefly regained autonomy between the period of Inka collapse and Spanish domination, but they were then faced with very different sets of social, economic, and political concerns from those of the fourteenth century. In the sixteenth and early seventeenth centuries, they, like other indigenous societies throughout the continent, were confronted with issues of basic survival in the maelstrom of European-introduced epidemics, harsh labor demands, and colonial rule.

BIBLIOGRAPHICAL ESSAY

Julian Steward's pioneering work on native South American sociopolitical organization and ecology still has a great deal of well-deserved influence among scholars, although there have been important departures from his views as discussed in the section on Amazonia. See his introductions in Julian H. Steward (ed.), *Handbook of South American Indians*, 6 vols. (Washington, D.C., 1946–1950), and Steward and Faron (1959), already cited in the chapter. Kalervo Oberg, in "Types of social structure among the lowland tribes of South and Central America," *American Anthropologist* 57 (1955), 472–487, was among the first to bring the term "chiefdom" into modern anthropological usage, employing it for societies composed of multiple villages governed by a paramount chief and a hierarchy of subordinate chiefs. It was with the work of Elman Service in *Primitive social organization* (New York, 1962) that chiefdom as type and evolutionary level became important in archaeological and anthropological analysis. Service characterized chiefdoms as "redistributional societies with a permanent central agency of coordination." The centrality of redistribution has been strongly challenged, but Service still holds to it. See his "Political power and the origin of social complexity," in *Configurations of Power*, edited by John S. Henderson and Patricia J. Netherly (Ithaca, 1993), 112–134. Other early works of importance on the theoretical aspects of chiefdoms include Morton Fried, *The evolution of political society* (New York, 1967), in which the author discusses chiefly societies within his category of "rank societies." Marshall Sahlins, like Service and Fried, emphasized redistribution in his classic work on Polynesia, *Social stratification in Polynesia* (Seattle, 1958). In 1963, in comparing "big men," or leaders of Melanesian groups and chiefs of Polynesia, in "Poor man, rich man, big-man, chief: Political types in Melanesia and Polynesia," *Comparative Studies in Society and History* 5 (1963), 285–302, Sahlins moved away from that emphasis. Sahlins saw chiefs as masters of their people and "owners" of group resources. As they increased their power, chiefs tended to divert a considerable amount of the general wealth, usually by exacting tribute, for the maintenance of chiefly office. Work on societies that could be identified as chiefdoms proliferated over the following decades. On chiefdoms' potential variety in sociopolitical and economic organization and differences in pathways of political evolution, see, for example, Patrick Kirch's *The evolution of the Polynesian chiefdoms* (New York, 1984). Regarding some of the difficulties and strategies involved in identifying chiefdoms, see Gary Feinman and Jill Neitzel, "Too many types: An overview of sedentary prestate societies in the Americas," in *Advances in archaeological method and theory*, VII, edited by Michael Schiffer (New York, 1984), 39–102, and Christopher Peebles and Susan Kus, "Some archaeological correlates of ranked societies," *American Antiquity* 42 (1977), 421–448.

Recent discussions on the possible origins, characteristics, and correlates of chiefdoms can be seen in the following works and their extensive bibliographies. Various factors (ideological, economic, political) and processes (warfare) have each been emphasized as primary in chiefdom formation; however, recent trends are toward multifactor analyses. See Robert Carneiro, "The chiefdom: Precursor of the state," in *The transition to statehood in the New World*, edited by Grant Jones and Robert

Kautz (Cambridge, 1981), 37–79; and Timothy Earle (ed.), *Chiefdoms: Power, economy and ideology* (Cambridge, 1991); Timothy Earle, "Chiefdoms in archaeological and ethnohistorical perspective," in *Annual review of anthropology*, edited by Bernard Siegel et al., XVI (Palo Alto, 1987), 279–308; and Allen Johnson and Timothy Earle, *The evolution of human societies. From foraging group to agrarian state* (Stanford, 1987).

Regional archaeological studies on the development of chiefdoms have been carried out very productively in recent years, some with broad international collaboration. Important examples are *Calima* (Bogotá, 1992) by Marianne Cardale de Schrimpff, Warwick Bray, Thérès Gähwiler-Walder, and Leonor Herera; *La Sociedad Hidráulica Zenú* (Bogotá, 1993) by Clemencia Plazas, Ana María Falchetti, Juanita Sáenz Samper, and Sonia Archila; *Prehispanic chiefdoms in the Valle de la Plata, Vol. I, The environmental context of human habitation*, edited by Luisa Fernanda Herrera, Robert Drennan, and Carlos Uribe (Pittsburgh, 1989); and the second volume, *Prehispanic chiefdoms in the Valle de la Plata, Vol. II*, edited by Drennan, Mary Taft, and Carlos Uribe (Pittsburgh, 1993). On regions in Ecuador, see José Alcina Franch, *La Arqueología de Esmeraldas (Ecuador): Introducción General* (Madrid, 1979); and David Stemper, *The persistence of prehistoric chiefdoms on the Río Daule, coastal Ecuador* (Pittsburgh, 1993). The evolution of sociopolitical complexity in northwest Argentina is dealt with by Rodolfo Raffino in *Poblaciones Indígenas en Argentina. Urbanismo y Proceso Social Precolombino* (Buenos Aires, 1988); and in Chile in several studies, among them *Diaguitas, Pueblos del Norte Verde, Museo Chileno de Arte Precolombino* (Santiago de Chile, 1986); Carlos Aldunate's *Cultura Mapuche* (Santiago de Chile, 1978); Gonzalo Ampuerto's *Cultura Diaguita* (Santiago de Chile, 1978); Bente Bittmann, Gustavo le Paige, and Lautaro Núñez's *Cultura Atacameña* (Santiago, 1978); as well as in several works by Tom Dillehay and Lautaro Núñez, including Dillehay's *Araucania: Presente y Pasado* (Santiago de Chile, 1990); Núñez's *Cultura y Conflicto en los Oasis de San Pedro de Atacama* (Santiago de Chile, 1991); and Núñez and Dillehay's *Movilidad Giratoria. Armonía Social y Desarrollo en los Andes Meridionales: Patrones de Tráfico e Interacción Económica* (Antofagasta, Chile, 1979). Also see Calogero Santoro and Liliana Ulloa (eds.), *Culturas de Arica* (Santiago de Chile, 1985).

On the Peruvian-Bolivian *altiplano* region, see *The Tiwanaku: Portrait of an Andean civilization* (Cambridge, Mass., 1993) by Alan Kolata; *Tiwanaku: Espacio, Tiempo y Cultura* (La Paz, 1981) by Carlos Ponce Sanginés; and *Ancient Andean political economy* (Austin, 1992) by Charles Stanish.

Archaeological sequences of development that include materials on chiefdoms have more often been worked out by countries than regions. Most of the following contain good bibliographies and references to regional work and results. Very useful general treatments and overviews, they include Alvaro Botiva, Gilberto Cadavid, Leonor Herrera, Ana María Groot de Mahecha, and Santiago Mora, *Colombia Prehispánica* (Bogotá, 1989); Alicia Eugenia Silva (ed.), *Arte de la Tierra (Colección Tesoros Precolombinos)*, 9 vols. (Bogotá, 1988–1992); María Victoria Uribe and Santiago Mora, "Colombia Prehispánica," in *Gran Enciclopedia de Colombia*, I (Bogotá, 1991), 1–38; José Cruxent and Irving Rouse, *An archaeological chronology of Venezuela*, 2 vols. (Washington, D.C., 1958–1959), and their *Venezuelan archaeology* (New Haven, 1963); Mario Sanoja and Iraida Vargas, *Antiguas Formaciones y Modos de Producción Venezolanos* (Caracas, 1979); Enrique Ayala Mora (ed.), *Nueva Historia del Ecuador*, I (Quito, 1988); Donald Lathrap, *Ancient Ecuador* (Chicago, 1975); Jorge Marcos (ed.), *Arqueología de la Costa Ecuatoriana: Nuevos Enfoques* (Quito, 1986); Pedro Porras, *Nuestro Ayer. Manual de Arqueología Ecuatoriana* (Quito, 1987); William Denevan, Kent Mathewson, and Gregory Knapp (eds.), *Prehispanic agricultural fields in the Andean region*, Proceedings, 45th International Congress of Americanists (Oxford, 1987); Duccio Bonavia, *Perú: Hombre e Historia. De los Orígenes al Siglo XV* (Lima, 1991); Richard Keatinge (ed.), *Peruvian prehistory* (Cambridge, 1988); Luis Lumbreras, *Visión Arqueológica del Perú Milenario* (Lima, 1990); Alan Kolata, "The South Andes," in *Ancient South Americans*, edited by Jesse Jennings (San Francisco, 1983), 241–285; Carlos Ponce Sangines, *Panorama de la Arqueología Boliviana* (La Paz, 1980); *Recent studies in pre-Columbian archaeology*, edited by Nicholas Saunders and Oliver de Montmollin (Oxford, 1988); Alberto Rex González and José Pérez, *Argentina Indígena, Visperas de la Conquista* (Buenos Aires, 1972); David Browman (ed.), *Advances in Andean archaeology* (The Hague, 1978); Jorge Hidalgo et al. (eds.), *Culturas de Chile – Prehistoria* (Santiago de Chile, 1989); Clement Meighan and D. True (eds.), *Prehistoric trails of Atacama: Archaeology of Northern Chile* (Los Angeles, 1980); Mario Rivera, "Panorama de las Investigaciones Arqueológics en Chile," in *La Antropología Americanista en la Actualidad. Homenaje a Raphael Girard*, Francis Polo Sifontes et al. (eds.), I (México, 1980), 163–181; Betty Meggers and Clifford Evans, "Lowland South America and the Antilles," in

Ancient South Americans, cited earlier, 287–335; Betty Meggers, "Cultural evolution in Amazonia," in *Profiles in cultural evolution*, edited by A. Terry Rambo and Kathleen Gillogly (Ann Arbor, 1991) 191–216; and Anna Roosevelt (ed.), *Amazonian Indians* (Tucson, 1994). Several regions in different parts of the Americas are discussed in the collection *Chiefdoms in the Americas* (Lanham, Md., 1987), edited by Robert Drennan and Carlos Uribe, as well as issues regarding the concept of chiefdom.

Early European perceptions of and reports on the Americas are both invaluable and highly debated. On the subject, see Frank Salomon, this volume. For general introductions and reference work on historiography of the area, see the still useful but dated work by Francisco Esteve Barba, *Historiografía Indiana* (Madrid, 1962) and the second, revised edition by Hortensia Esteve, 1992. Also see Horacio Larrain Barros, *Cronistas de Raigambre Indígena*, 2 vols. (Otavalo, 1980); *Los Cronistas del Perú (1528–1650) y Otros Ensayos* (Lima, 1986) by Raúl Porras Barrenechea; and *Las Crónicas y los Andes* (Lima, 1995) by Franklin Pease.

Chroniclers' works should be read and assessed in conjunction with primary materials from local archives and the Archivo General de Indias (Seville). Samples of such materials have been published, and although they do not replace basic archival work, they are most useful. See, for example, Marcos Jiménez de la Espada, *Relaciones Geográficas de Indias*, 3 vols. (Madrid, 1965); Juan Friede (ed.), *Documentos Inéditos Para la Historia de Colombia*, 10 vols. (Bogotá, 1955–1960); Hermes Tovar Pinzón (ed.), *Relaciones y Visitas a los Andes*, 2 vols. (Bogotá, n.d.); Antonio Arellano Moreno (ed.), *Relaciones Geográficas de Venezuela* (Caracas, 1964); José Alcina Franch and Remedios de la Peña (eds.), *Textos Para la Etnohistoria de Esmeraldas* (Madrid, 1974); Pilar Ponce Leiva (ed.), *Relaciones Histórico-Geográficas de la Audiencia de Quito. (Siglo XVI–XIX)*, 2 vols. (Quito, 1992–1994).

There is a wealth of *visitas*, most in national archives and the Archivo General de Indias. A few have been published. See *Las Visitas a Cajamarca 1571–72/1578*, 2 vols., edited by María Rostworowski and Pilar Remy (Lima, 1992); *Visita de los Valles de Songo, en los Yunka de Coca de la Paz (1568–1570)* by Diego Dávila de Cangas and Bartolomé de Otazu, edited by John Murra (Madrid, 1991); Garci Díez de San Miguel's *Visita Hecha a la Provincia de Chucuito por Garci Díez de San Miquel en el Año 1567*, edited by Waldemar Espinoza Soriano and John Murra (Lima, 1964); *Visita de la Provincia de León de Huánaco en 1562* by Iñigo Ortiz de Zúñiga, 2 vols., edited by John Murra (Huánaco, 1967–1972); and

Visita y Numeración de los Pueblos del Valle de los Chillos 1551–1559, edited by Cristobal Landázuri (Quito, 1990).

Our interpretation of conquest-era Chibcha comes primarily from archival work carried out over the last 25 years in parish records of the Sabana de Bogotá, Archivo Histórico Nacional de Colombia (Bogotá), and the Archivo General de Indias. Some of the material has appeared in Villamarín and Villamarín, "Kinship organization and inheritance patterns among the Chibcha of the Sabana de Bogotá at the time of the Spanish conquest," *Ethnology* 14 (1975), 173–179, and "Chibcha settlement under Spanish rule: 1537–1810," in *Social fabric and spatial structure in Colonial Latin America*, edited by David J. Robinson (Syracuse, 1979), 25–84. Also see the work of Sylvia Broadbent, *Los Chibchas. Organización Socio-Política* (Bogotá, 1964), and "The prehistory of the Muisca area," in *Arte de la Tierra. Muisca y Guanes*, edited by Alicia Silva (Bogotá, 1989), 88–91. Valuable for the Tunja region are the studies by Ana María Boada Rivas, *Asentamientos Indígenas en el Valle de la Laguna (Samacá – Boyacá)* (Bogotá, 1987), and Neyla Castillo Espitia, *Arqueología de Tunja* (Bogotá, 1984).

Studies of Cauca Valley and coastal Colombian complex chiefdoms are scarce; however, information can be found in *Los Cacicazgos de Popayán a la Llegada de los Conquistadores* by Hector Llanos Vargas (Bogotá, 1981); *La Encomienda en Popayán* by Silvia Padilla, María Luisa López, and Adolfo Luis González (Seville, 1977); and in *Die Spanisch-Indianische Auseinandersetzung in der Nördlichen Sierra Nevada de Santa Marta (1501–1600)* (Bonn, 1971), and "Indígenas y Españoles en la Sierra Nevada de Santa Marta – Siglo XVI," *Revista Colombiana de Antropología* 24 (1982–1983), 76–124, both by Henning Bischof.

An excellent overview of coastal Ecuador at the time of Spanish conquest is provided by Segundo Moreno's "Formaciones Políticas Tribales y Señoríos Étnicos," in Enrique Ayala (ed.), *Nueva Historia del Ecuador*, II (Quito, 1988), 9–134. Other very useful studies of the region and of preconquest trade include José Alcina Franch's "El Modelo Teórico de 'Jefatura' y su APlicación al Area Andina Septentrional," *Miscelánea Antropológica Eucatoriana* 6 (1986), 265–288; the collection of essays edited by J. F. Bouchard and M. Guinea, *Relaciones Interculturales en el Area Ecuatorial del Pacífico Durante la Época Precolombina*, Proceedings of the 46th International Congress of Americanists (Oxford, 1989); Dorothy Hosler, Heather Lechtman, and Olaf Holm, *Axe-monies and their relatives* (Washington, D.C., 1990); Birgit Lenz-Volland and Martín Volland, "Algunas Noticias Acerca de los Caciques de Daule Durante el Siglo XVII, Estudio Preliminar," in Segundo Moreno (ed.), *Antropología del Ecuador* (Quito, 1989), 211–222; Olaf Holm, *Cultura Manteña-Huancavilca* (Guayaquil, 1986); and studies by Jorge Marcos and Presley Norton, including Marcos's "Economía e Ideología en Andinoamérica Septentrional," in Enrique Ayala (ed.), *Nueva Historia del Ecuador*, II, (Quito, 1988), 167–188; Marcos and Norton's "Interpretación sobre la Arqueología de la Isla de la Plata," *Miscelánea Antropológica Ecuatoriana* 1 (1981), 136–154; the collection of essays edited by them in *Primer Simposio de Correlaciones Antropológicas Andino-Mesoamericano* (Guayaquil, 1982); and Norton's "El Señorío de Salangone y la liga de Mercaderes (El Cartel Spondylus-Balsa)," *Miscelánea Antropológica Ecuatoriana* 6 (1986), 131–144.

The literature on Greater Amazonia is growing steadily. In addition to works such as those by Métraux, Denevan, Nordenskiold, Erickson, Meggers, Lathrap, and Roosevelt cited in the text, studies that warrant consultation include Waltraud Grohs's overview, *Los Indios del Alto Amazonas del Siglo XVI al XVIII* (Bonn, 1974); Thomas Myers's "Aboriginal trade networks in Amazonia" in Peter Francis, F. Kense, P. Duke (eds.), *Networks of the past: Regional interaction in archaeology* (Calgary, 1981), 19–30; essays in D. A. Posey and W. Balée (eds.), *Resource management in Amazonia: Indigenous and folk strategies* (New York, 1989); and in Ghillean Prance and Thomas Lovejoy (eds.), *Key environments. Amazonia* (New York, 1985). Anna Roosevelt provides an overview of the evolution of complex societies in the region in "Chiefdoms in the Amazon and Orinoco," in Drennan and Uribe's *Chiefdoms in the Americas*, 153–184. See F. M. Renard-Casevitz, T. Saignes, and A. C. Taylor, *Al Este de los Andes*, 2 vols. (Quito, 1988) on Amazonian regions east of the sierra from Ecuador to Bolivia. Hilgard O. Sternberg's *The Amazon River of Brazil* (Wiesbaden, 1975) is an elegant and instructive treatment of the river and the region. Regarding the Ecuadorian Amazon, see José Rumazo, *La Región Amazónica del Ecuador en el Siglo XVI* (Quito, 1982); and Udo Oberem, *Los Quijos. Historia de la Transculturación de un Grupo Indígena en el Oriente Ecuatoriano. 1538–1956*, 2 vols. (Madrid, 1970–1971). On Marajó Island, see Betty Meggers' critique, "Review, moundbuilders of the Amazon: Geophysical archaeology on Marajó Island, Brazil," *Journal of Field Archaeology* 19 (1992), 339–404; on the Tapajó, Helen Palmatary's *The archaeology of the Lower Tapajos Valley, Brazil* (Philadelphia, 1960); "The Tapajó, by Curt Nimuendajú," translated and edited by John

Rowe in *Kroeber Anthropological Society Papers*, Spring (Berkeley, 1952), 1–12; and on the Omagua, Antonio Porro's "Os Omagua do Alto Amazonas: demografía e Padrões de povoamento no século XVII," in *Contribuições á Antropologia em Homenagem ao Professor Egon Schaden* (Sao Paulo, 1981), 207–232.

Information on the spatial and temporal diversity of complex societies over very long spans of time and great distances must be culled from monographs and essays. Many of the works already mentioned lend themselves to time-depth analysis, as do the following studies. For coastal Ecuador, see Emilio Estrada, *Los Huancavilcas. Ultimas Civilizaciones Pre-Históricas de la Costa del Guayas* (Guayaquil, 1957); and Segundo Moreno, "De las Formas Tribales al Señorio Étnico," *Miscelánea Antropológica Ecuatoriana* 6 (1986), 253–263. On Greater Amazonia, in addition to works already cited, see J. Jorna, L. Malaver, and M. Oostra (eds.), *Etnohistoria del Amazonas* (Quito, 1991); Nancy Morey, "Ethnohistorical evidence for cultural complexity in the Western Llanos of Venezuela and the Eastern Llanos of Colombia," *Antropológica* 45 (1976), 41–69; Fernando Santos, *Etnohistoria de la Alta Amazonia. Siglos XV–XVIII* (Quito, 1992); Alberta Zucchi and William Denevan, *Campos Elevados e Historia Cultural Prehispánica en los Llanos Occidentales de Venezuela* (Caracas, 1979).

On Colombia, see Juan Friede, *Los Quimbayas Bajo la Dominación Española. Estudio Documental (1539–1810)* (Bogotá, 1963); Jorge Morales and Gilberto Cadavid, *Investigaciones Etnohistóricas y Arqueológicas en el Area Guane* (Bogotá, 1984); Kathleen Romoli, *Los de la Lengua Cuiva* (Bogotá, 1987); María Victoria Uribe, "Asentamientos Prehispánicos en el Altiplano de Ipiales, Colombia," *Revista Colombiana de Antropología* 21 (1977–1978), 57–195; and on the Chitarreros, German Colmenares, *Encomienda y Población en la Provincia de Pamplona (1549–1650)* (Bogotá, 1969). For Venezuelan sequences, see Walter Coppens (ed.), *Los Aborigenes de Venezuela. Etnología Antigua*, I (Caracas, 1980); Charles Spencer, "Coevolution and the development of Venezuelan chiefdoms," in Rambo and Gillogly's collection, *Profiles in cultural evolution*, 137–165; Iraida Vargas and Mario Sanoja, "Cacicazgos del Noroeste de Venezuela," *Gens* 1 (1985), 52–63; Erika Wagner, "Arqueología Andina Venezolana," *Revista Colombiana de Antropología* 13 (1964–1965), 227–237, and by the same author, *The prehistory and ethnohistory of the Carache area in western Venezuela* (New Haven, 1967).

A number of collected works with important articles on areas that came under Inka domination are valuable both for their texts and their extensive bibliographies. They include the book edited by George Collier, Renato Rosaldo, and John Wirth, *The Inca and Aztec states, 1400–1800* (New York, 1982); Tom Dillehay and Patricia Netherly (eds.), *La Frontera del Estado Inca*, Proceedings of the 45th International Congress of Americanists (Oxford, 1988); Jonathan Haas, Shelia Pozorski, and Thomas Pozorski (eds.), *The origins and development of the Andean state* (Cambridge, 1987); D. P. Kvietok and D. H. Sandweiss (eds.), *Recent studies in Andean prehistory and protohistory* (Ithaca, n.d.); M. A. Malpass (ed.), *Provincial Inka* (Iowa City, 1993); Shozo Masuda, Izumi Shimada, and Craig Morris (eds.), *Andean ecology and civilization* (Tokyo, 1985); Segundo Moreno (ed.), *Antropología del Ecuador* (Quito, 1989); Segundo Moreno and Frank Salomon (eds.), *Reproducción y Transformación de las Sociedades Andinas. Siglos XVI-XX*, 2 vols. (Quito, 1991); Michael Moseley and Alana Cordy-Collins (eds.), *The northern dynasties: Kingship and statecraft in Chimor* (Washington, D.C., 1990); John Murra, Nathan Wachtel, and Jacques Revel (eds.), *Anthropological history of Andean polities* (Cambridge, 1986); Rodolfo Raffino (ed.), *Inka, Arqueología, Historia y Urbanismo del Altiplano Andino* (Buenos Aires, 1993); D. H. Sandweiss (ed.), *Andean past* (Ithaca, 1987); Elizabeth Wing and Jane Wheeler (eds.), *Economic prehistory of the Central Andes* (Oxford, 1988).

Altiplano chiefdoms of the fourteenth and fifteenth centuries have been treated by Thérèse Bouysse Cassagne and Catherine Julien, who offer excellent panoramic views of the complex societies and their connections with other groups. See Bouysse Cassagne, "Pertenencia Étnica, Status Económico y Lenguas en Charcas a Fines del Siglo XVI," in *Tasa de la Visita General de Francisco de Toledo*, edited by N. D. Cook (Lima, 1975), 312–328, and *La Identidad Aymara: Aproximación Histórica Siglo XV, Siglo XVI* (La Paz, 1987). By Julien, see "The Uru tribute category; ethnic boundaries and empire in the Andes,"*Proceedings of the American Philosophical Society* 131 (1987), 53–91, as well as "How Inca decimal administration worked," *Ethnohistory* 35 (1988), 257–279. Also very valuable are essays by Waldemar Espinoza Soriano, "Copacabana del Collao, un documento de 1548 para la Etnohistoria Andina," *Bulletin Institut Francais D'Etudes Andines* 1 (1972), 1–16, and "El Señorío de Ayanca en el Reino Lupaca, Siglos XV–XVII," in *Actas del Congreso Nacional de Investigación Histórica*, edited by Humberto Rodríguez Pastor, III (Lima, 1991), 51–108; María B. LaLone and Darrell E. LaLone's, "The Inka state in the Southern Highlands: State administrative and production enclaves," *Ethnohistory* 34 (1987), 47–62; Luis Lumbreras's "Los Reinos Post-Tiwanaku en el Area Altiplánica," *Revista del Museo Nacional* 40 (1974), 55–85; John Murra's "An Aymara kingdom in 1567," *Ethnohistory* 15 (1968), 115–151; and the study by Nathan Wachtel, *Le Retour des Ancestres: Les Indiens Urus de Bolivia, XXe–XVIe Siecle, essai d'Historie Regressive* (Paris, 1990).

Jorge Hidalgo presents an overview of Chilean indigenous societies in "Culturas y Etnias Protohistóricas: Area Andina Meridional," *Chungara* 8 (1981), 109–153, which has been translated with changes as "The Indians of Southern South America in the middle of the sixteenth century," in *CHLA*, I, 91–117. Also see Louis Faron, "Effects of conquest on the Araucanian Picunche during the Spanish colonization of Chile: 1536–1635," *Ethnohistory* 7 (1960), 239–307.

Rodolfo Raffino's general overview of preconquest northwest Argentina, *Los Inkas del Kollasuyu* (Buenos Aires, 1981) should be consulted on the region, as should his essay with Eduardo Cigliano, "Un Modelo de Poblamiento en el N. O. Argentino," in *III Congreso Peruano de El Hombre y la Cultura Andina*, edited by Ramiro Matos, II (Lima, 1978), 673–707. Also see Alberto Rex González's "Las 'Provincias' Inca del Antiguo Tucuman," *Revista del Museo Nacional* 46 (1982), 317–380. For information on particular complex societies and their interaction in northwest Argentina, see Margarita Gentile's "Evidencias e Hipótesis sobre los Atacamas en la Puna de Jujuy y Quebrada de Huamahuaca," *Journal de la Société des Américanistes* 74 (1988), 87–103; the essay by Pedro Krapovickas, "La Economía Prehistórica en la Puna," *Runa* 14 (1984), 107–121; Ana María Lorandi's "Los Diaguitas y el Tawantinsuyo: Una Hipotesis de Conflicto," in *La Frontera del Estado Inca*, cited earlier, pp. 235–259; and Anibal Montes's "Encomiendas de Indios Diaguitas Documentadas en el Archivo Histórico de Córdoba," *Revista del Instituto de Antropología* (Universidad Nacional de Córdoba, Argentina, 1965), 2–3, 7–29.

Some recent works on the Central Andes (Perú) are very useful for their focus on local societies rather than on the traditional subjects of states and empire. For global views of early complex societies, see Rogger Ravines's "Reinos y Señoríos Locales de los Andes Centrales: 800–1476 DC," in *Historia del Perú*, II (Lima, 1980), 93–184. Data on particular complex societies, their relationships to the Inka, and their transformations under empire are provided by the following very well-crafted essays and monographs, including *Etnohistoria y Antropología Andina*, edited by

Amalia Castelli, Marcia Koth de Paredes, and Mariana Mould de Pease (Lima, 1981); Terence D'Altroy's "Transitions in power: Centralization of Wanka political organization under Inka rule," *Ethnohistory* 34 (1987), 78–102, as well as his *Provincial power in the Inka empire* (Washington, D.C., 1992); Tom Dillehay's "Tawantinsuyu. Integration of the Chillón Valley, Perú: A case of Inca geo-political mastery," *Journal of Field Archaeology* 4 (1977), 397–405; and Dillehay's "Relaciones Pre-Hispánicas Costa-Sierra en el Valle del Chillón," in *III Congreso Peruano, El Hombre y la Cultura Andina*, cited earlier, pp. 120–140; Waldemar Espinoza Soriano's "Los Huancas, Aliados de la Conquista," *Anales Científicos de la Universidad del Centro del Perú* 1 (1972), 9–407, and his monograph, *Huaraz. Poder, Sociedad y Economía en los Siglos XV y XVI* (Lima, 1978). Also see Enrique González Carre, *Los Señoríos Chankas* (Lima, 1992); Christine Hastorf, *Agriculture and the onset of political inequality before the Inka* (Cambridge, 1993); William Isbell and Anita Cook, "Ideological origins of an Andean conquest state," *Archaeology* 40 (1987), 26–33; Terry Yarov LeVine, "Inka labor service at the regional level: The functional reality," *Ethnohistory* 34 (1987), 14–46; Dorothy Menzel, "The Inca occupation of the south coast of Perú," *Southwestern Journal of Anthropology* 15 (1959), 125–142; John Murra, "La Visita de los Chapachu Como Fuente Etnológica," in *Visita de la Provincia de León de Huánuco en 1522*, I (Huánuco, 1967–1972), 383–406; Franklin Pease (ed.), *Collaguas I* (Lima, 1977). Several of the works of María Rostworowski de Diéz Canseco should be consulted, including *Curacas y Sucesiones, Costa Norte* (Lima, 1961), *Señoríos Indígenas de Lima y Canta* (Lima, 1978), and *Estructuras Andinas del Poder* (Lima, 1983). Also see Katharina Schreiber's *Wari imperialism in Middle Horizon Perú* (Ann Arbor, 1992); John Rowe's classic essay, "Inca culture at the time of the Spanish conquest," *Handbook of South American Indians*, II, 183–330; Rafael Varón Gabai's *Curacas y Encomenderos. Acomadamiento Nativo en Huaraz. Siglos XVI y XVII* (Lima, 1980); Tom Zuidema's *Reyes y Guerreros. Ensayos de Cultura Andina* (Lima, 1989); and Gordon Willey's instructive and insightful "Horizontal integration and regional diversity: An alternating process in the rise of civilizations," *America Antiquity* 56 (1991), 197–215.

On Ecuador, Segundo Moreno and Udo Oberem's *Contribución a la Etnohistoria Ecuatoriana* (Otavalo, 1981) should be read. Frank Salomon's *Native lords of Quito in the age of the Incas* (Cambridge, 1986) is a key work both for its ethnohistoric content and for its methodological clarity in identifying and dealing with the various political, cultural, and economic overlays on indigenous patterns and structures in Andean regions. Excellent works on highland Ecuador that provide information from a variety of conceptual approaches include Chantal Caillavet's "Etnohistoria Ecuatoriana: Nuevos Datos Sobre el Otavalo Prehispánico," *Cultura* (Quito) 11 (1981), 109–127, and "Caciques de Otavalo en el Siglo XVI. Don Alonso Maldonado y su Esposa," *Miscelánea Antropológica Ecuatoriana* 2 (1982), 38–55; Juan Carrera's "Apuntes Para una Investigación Etnohistórica de los Cacicazgos del Corregimiento de Latacunga ss XVI y XVII," *Cultura* 2 (1981), 129–179; Waldemar Espinoza Soriano's *Los Cayambes y Carangues: Siglos XV–XVI. El Testimonio de la Etnohistoria*, 2 vols. (Otavalo, 1983), his *Etnohistoria Ecuatoriana* (Quito, 1988) and *La Etnía Chimbo al Oeste de Ríobamba. El Testimonio de la Etnohistoria* (Guayaquil, 1988); Niels Fock and Eva Krener's "Los Cañaris del Ecuador y Sus Conceptos Etnohistóricos Sobre los Incas," in *Amerikanistische Studien*, edited by Roswith Hartmann and Udo Oberem (St. Agustin, 1978), I, 170–181. Also see Roswith Hartmann's essays, "Mercados y Fería Prehispánicos en el Area Andina," *Boletín de la Academia Nacional de Historia* (Quito) 54 (1971), 214–235, and "Comercio y Economía Durante la Ocupación Incaica," in *Historia del Ecuador, Salvat*, II (Quito, 1980), 161–164; and in the same volume, Jorge Lara's "La Resistencia del Reino de Quito contra la Expansión Incaica," 129–149. Valuable sources as well are Horacio Larrain Barros's, *Demografía y Asentamientos Indígenas en la Sierra Norte del Ecuador en el Siglo XVI*, 2 vols. (Otavalo, 1980); and Galo Ramón's studies, *La Resistencia Andina. Cayambe 1500–1800* (Quito, 1987), and *El Poder y los Norandinos. La Historia en las Sociedades Norandinas del Siglo XVI* (Quito, 1990).

8

ARCHAEOLOGY OF THE CARIBBEAN REGION

LOUIS ALLAIRE

Nature has often raised the most formidable barriers ever experienced by humans in their developments; oceans, deserts, forests, and mountains have served to divide and isolate peoples from the very beginnings of human existence. Landscapes have also presented situations that on the contrary have favored and even encouraged human interaction over vast areas. Maritime basins surrounded by continuous stretches of coastline are likely to have had this stimulating effect not only around their coastal periphery but also directly between various points across their shores, when adequate seafaring technology had become available. This is not a matter of environmental determinism but more properly of opportunistic circumstances.

The Mediterranean is a classic example. Peoples and civilizations emerging around its shores were bound from the earliest prehistoric times, not only by the uniformity in climate and landscape but culturally by a common Palaeolithic substratum, and later by a shared subsistence basis of wheat, olives, sheep, and marine fishes. Although political integration was only once and briefly accomplished by the Romans, the area never escaped a cultural interdependency that at times bounded France to the Holy Land, or Spain to Morocco.

GEOGRAPHICAL AND CULTURAL CONDITIONS

In the New World the only geographical setting that could have led to a similar situation is the Caribbean Sea. This unique maritime basin is essentially a division of the Atlantic Ocean that overlaps both North and South America; indeed, a true maritime basin even extends as far north as the Gulf of Mexico (see Map 8.1). The more precise boundaries of the Caribbean Sea originate in the north at the Yucatan Peninsula of Mexico

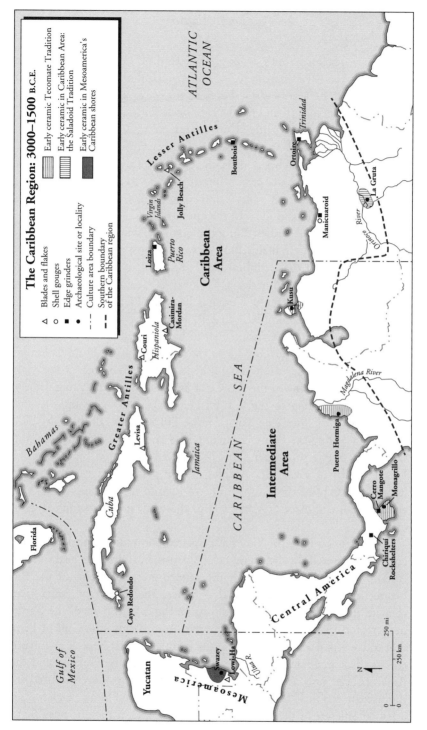

The Caribbean Region: 3000–1500 B.C.E.

△ Blades and flakes
○ Shell gouges
▥ Edge grinders
■ Archaeological site or locality
—·—·— Culture area boundary
— — Southern boundary of the Caribbean region

▤ Early ceramic Tecomate Tradition
▥ Early ceramic in Caribbean Area: the Saladoid Tradition
▓ Early ceramic in Mesoamerica's Caribbean shores

ATLANTIC OCEAN

Lesser Antilles

Boutbois

Ortoire
Trinidad

La Gruta

Manicuaroid

Orinoco River

Virgin Islands
Jolly Beach

Loiza
Puerto Rico

Caribbean Area

Kusu

Couri
Hispaniola

Casimira-Mordan

Greater Antilles

Levisa

Bahamas

Jamaica

CARIBBEAN SEA

Cuba

Florida

Gulf of Mexico

Cayo Redondo

Intermediate Area

Puerto Hormiga

Magdalena River

Cerro Mangote
Monagrillo

Chiriqui Rockshelters

Central America

Yucatan

Swazey
Lowe-Ha
Ulua R.

Mesoamerica

N

0   250 mi
0   250 km

Map 8.1

and Belize, reaching south as far as the island of Trinidad and the delta of the Orinoco River in Venezuela. The mainland of the South American continent set the Caribbean's shores to the west, and the West Indian islands mark its eastern and northern boundaries in the form of a massive barrier to the open Atlantic. Continuous communication was at least potentially feasible all around its periphery even before European contacts, and despite stretches of difficult coastlines, simple open boats could progress along the coasts even without sails. Overland communication along coastal plains and valleys must also be considered in spreading peoples, commerce, and ideas to the entire region.

At the time of the earliest European contacts, communication by land or by sea was regularly maintained between almost all contiguous points of the periphery of the Caribbean Sea. The highlands of Guatemala were in touch with Central America as far away as Costa Rica, mainly across well-traveled overland trails. Contacts between Panama and the Caribbean lowlands of Colombia – that is, between lower Central America and South America – are also known to have existed, albeit infrequently, by either land or sea, possibly across the Gulf of Darien. From Colombia to western Venezuela, a long-established overland route out of the Magdalena lowlands followed the Río Cesar and Río Rancheria along the foot of the Andes leading to the Goajira Peninsula, and bypassing the high mountains of the Sierra de Santa Marta. Further east, all the Caribbean islands, including the Bahamas, maintained continuous and regular contacts with simple watercraft. This is also well illustrated by the historic Island Caribs of the Lesser Antilles, whose peoples are well known to have regularly plied the sea from Puerto Rico to the Guianas in the east, and the Cumana Area of Venezuela to the west, in their simple dugout canoes.

The Orinoco River in Venezuela opened communication beyond the coast from not only the Venezuelan Llanos but also the heart of the Amazonian Basin itself through the interconnected systems of the Rio Negro and the Casiquiare Canal – hence, the important Amazonian element in the development of cultures in the eastern parts of the Caribbean region that must never be ignored. Accordingly, the Gulf of Paria that today separates Trinidad from the mainland must be seen as a major crossroad of trade and influences reaching far into the Guianas and the Amazon. The only areas where contacts seem to have never occured are the narrow channels between Cuba and Yucatan or Florida, each within a few kilometers of the Greater Antilles. Likewise, it may be possible to identify an area of less frequent communication between the Maracaibo area of Venezuela and its central and eastern coast, where the aridity of the coastal region seems to have been a major impediment to regular coastal navigation. Yet the historical situation suggests that communication in the ancient Caribbean consisted of little more than a linear coasting navigation; there are no historical records of circumnavigation or direct crossings ever taking place among its native peoples between the mainland and the islands.

The Caribbean Sea

As the unifying element of this entire region of the New World, the Caribbean Sea is recorded as the world's second largest sea (with its surface area covering some 1,900,000 km², about two-thirds the size of the Mediterranean). It expands in the form of a broad T-shaped configuration, which from east to west reaches 2,735 kilometers, and 805 to 1,287 kilometers from north to south, the widest distance being between Haiti and Panama. Its deep ocean floor (an average 2,400 m) is noted for its extremely deep trenches (7,685 m in the Cayman Trench south of Cuba) and for broad basins separated by submerged ridges and platforms, which are at the origins of many smaller islands and reefs, located mostly near its mainland coasts or its major islands. There are no major isolated islands in the middle of the Caribbean sea, if we except the smaller Cayman Islands south of Cuba, which seem never to have been occupied in prehistoric times, and a few major gulfs or peninsulas along its coasts. The small Jamaica keys that stretch from Nicaragua to Jamaica are a series of barren and waterless sand bars and reefs unfit for human occupation.

Of particular importance for early marine transportation is the nature of its winds and currents. The entire area is dominated by easterly trade winds that push warm surface currents west, then north through the Caribbean Sea; water flows out through the Yucatan Channel to the Gulf of Mexico. A general east to west pattern dominates the flow of the Caribbean. The hurricane season from August to November makes it unlikely that the period was favored for island-oriented voyages; an element of seasonality is therefore indicated in the area's potential for voyages at sea. During the periods covered by this chapter, climate and environment were stable and comparable to modern conditions. Sea levels stabilized around 5000 B.C.E., but local variations, possibly in the order of several meters, may have occurred because of tectonic activity or shore erosion in areas most likely to have been occupied by human settlements. No land bridges ever existed between any points of the Caribbean Basin within the time of its human occupation.

A Caribbean Landscape

There is something undeniably unique and distinctively "Caribbean" that is shared by the region as a whole, be it the coast of Yucatan in Mexico, the island of Antigua in the Lesser Antilles, or Cartagena in Colombia. Like the Mediterranean, one associates the Caribbean with distinctive characteristics of climate and landscape, natural resources, and basic nutrition. This reality should not be ignored, but it certainly over-simplifies the actual diversity in its environment. The entire area lies within the tropics, where temperatures average 27° C on the islands and seldom fall below 24° C. Temperatures vary in altitude, however, for those areas with major mountain ranges; this is especially the case for Central America and northern South America, where it is usual to differ-entiate between the hot *tierra caliente* of the lowlands, the temperate *tierra templada* above 750 meters, and the *tierra fría*, or "cold" area above 1,800 meters. Various regions are affected differently by a seasonal pattern of rainfall, felt more especially on the mainland where rain occurs mostly between June and October. This period is the hurricane season in the northern part of the region, especially on the Atlantic watershed. This serves as a reminder that the potential for catastrophic events is ever present throughout the Caribbean region. Volcanism is still active along an axis that runs from Guatemala through Central America with a more or less parallel counterpart through the Lesser Antilles; major earthquakes may occur anywhere at any time. Exposure and topography affect precip-itation in the islands, producing drier ecological systems on lower islands where seasonal water shortages are a problem even today.

Environmental diversity is well represented in Central America, where five major vegetation zones are represented. This ranges from dense tropical rain forest on the Caribbean lowlands to the mangrove belt along its coastline, in sharp contrast to the Pacific littoral, which is much drier with its deciduous woodlands and patches of grasslands. Cooler high altitudes are covered with a more temperate pine and oak vegetation that degrades into scrub and cactus in arid sectors of the uplands.

The Caribbean coastline of northern South America also displays a marked contrast between the humid conditions of the Magdalena Basin in the lowlands of Colombia to the arid climate of the coast of Venezuela. Humid conditions prevail throughout most of the Caribbean islands, which are in many ways similar to Central America, with the exception of those without sufficient relief. Once covered by a lush tropical rain forest, the islands today suffer from extensive deforestation; Cuba, however, is mostly dominated by grasslands.

The coastal areas of the Caribbean Basin offer a rich variety of natural resources and raw materials significant for prehistoric populations both on the mainland and the islands. These include essentially minerals, such as copper and gold, and rocks, such as flint and obsidian for making tools, as well as many types of semiprecious stones (amethyst, carnelian, jade, crystals), hard rocks for making axes, and even salt. All these had the potential for the development of extensive trading networks. Obsidian, while widely traded in many parts of the world, was limited to Mesoamerica and Central America; it never reached the islands, thus depriving archaeologists of a valuable index of long-distance relationships. Jade, however, may have been more widely circulated, certainly between Mesoamerica and Central America, as well as potentially between Venezuela and the Greater Antilles and even out of the Amazon Basin. Salt, likewise, may have been traded widely through the Greater Antilles.

Whereas the more humid tropical areas of the Caribbean were associated with dense vegetation and an overwhelming fertility, enhanced in many places by deposits from a long history of volcanic eruptions, faunal resources in their distribution display a contrasting pattern between the mainland, where large mammals such as deer and peccaries were at all times prized as valuable suppliers of much needed and often scarce proteins, and the islands, which beyond Trinidad only supported an impoverished fauna that never allowed the dispersal of large animals. The islands' land fauna was limited to small rodents or reptiles, such as the iguana; this paucity was somewhat balanced, however, by the richness of marine and shore resources, which the islands shared with other parts of the Caribbean coasts where shallow waters have allowed the development of mangrove swamps, reef formations, and their abundant populations of fish and shellfish, or crustaceans. The less common sea mammal, the manatee, whose hard woodlike ribs were traded all across the Caribbean, was valued everywhere not only as food but as raw material for small carvings.

Cultural Divisions

Anthropologists have long speculated on the cultural-historical significance of the geographical situation particular to the Caribbean region.
By the 1940s the concept of a circum-Caribbean area as a distinctive
cultural phenomenon, or type of culture, was introduced by Paul Kirch-
hoff and developed by Julian Steward in the now classic *Handbook of
South American Indians*, which was published by the Smithsonian Institution. The hypothesis sought to explain the many striking sociocultural
similarities encountered around the entire periphery of the Caribbean
region, dominated in early historic times by chiefdom-level societies, as
the result of common origins and shared history, which everywhere
revealed intriguing features that appeared to be derived from the distant
highland societies of the Central Andes.

The circum-Caribbean hypothesis may have been an oversimplified
theory in the light of more recent evidence, especially on the earlier
prehistory of the area, and the more varied potential for influences that
now challenges the preeminent role formerly attributed to the Andes.
Indeed, a considerable amount of diversity must not be ignored among
the original human populations of the Caribbean region, especially as
they appeared at the eve of European contacts. Three major culture areas,
each characterized by different levels of cultural and social developments,
converged on its shores: (1) the *Mesoamerican Area* in Mexico and Belize
and the part of Central America most influenced by Mesoamerica – that
is, El Salvador and northern or western Honduras, with what proved to
be a shifting frontier through the centuries; (2) the *Intermediate Area*,
which includes those areas that lie between the high civilizations of
Mesoamerica and those of the Central Andes, and which in the Caribbean region include lower Central America as well as the lowlands of
Colombia and the western and central coasts of Venezuela; and (3) the
Caribbean Area proper, which includes not only the West Indian islands
and the Bahamas but the eastern coast of Venezuela and the lower
Orinoco River. The latter area witnessed the highest degree of diversity,
ranging from the sophisticated Taino chiefdoms of the Greater Antilles
to simple agricultural village societies, and ultimately to "marginal"
groups of hunters and collectors, best represented by the Warraus of the
Orinoco delta. This diversified situation also characterized much of the
earlier periods of Caribbean prehistory. One must not ignore either,
because of its influential and fundamental role, the *Amazonian or Tropi-*

cal Forest Area, which also lies at its doorstep to the south. Amazonian contribution to the Caribbean area proper is fundamental and may be the source of many features once attributed to the Andes. The Andean area, a center of high powerful civilizations, is the most remote, and it seems to have had little direct effect on the Caribbean region.

Because both Mesoamerica and the Intermediate Area extend much beyond the Caribbean region proper, the mainland boundaries of the Caribbean region must be set arbitrarily, as they are for the Mediterranean. For this purpose a coastal zone of approximately 200 kilometers may be a reasonable limit. Thus defined, the area includes in the north much of the hinterland of the Maya area of the Yucatan Peninsula and practically all of Belize. Further south and eastward it encompasses the entire area of Central America, even including its Pacific coast, which only extends 200 kilometers into the central part of Nicaragua. Beyond Darien and the Ataro River in South America, the Caribbean region is usually limited to the Caribbean lowlands of Colombia and the lower basin of the Magdalena River and its tributaries (excluding the Colombian highlands, which belong geographically and culturally to the Andes). Further east along the northern coast of South America, the Caribbean zone further includes the high Sierra Madre de Santa Marta, veritable gateway to Venezuela and the Maracaibo area with essentially the Guajira Peninsula, the Gulf of Venezuela, and the central coast and its Caribbean mountains. The entire east coast of Venezuela to the delta of the Orinoco and to Trinidad, as well as the lower reaches of the Orinoco River, traditionally belong to the Caribbean culture area proper. Northward along the eastern boundaries of the Caribbean Sea, the Lesser Antilles and Barbados stretch like stepping stones between Trinidad and Puerto Rico. The Greater Antilles, long with the Bahamas, bring us to the northwestern edge of the Caribbean region in western Cuba. Florida, standing just north of western Cuba and the Bahamas, is not included, however, in the Caribbean region by anthropologists.

Archaeological Perspective

The geographical unity of the Caribbean, as opposed to the Mediterranean, is a phenomenon that has been largely ignored by archaeologists, even within the context of the circum-Caribbean theory. The task may have appeared as amounting to an idle collage of disjuncted local sequences of unrelated prehistoric peoples and cultures with little more than a documentary interest to offer. Yet the potential for a more comprehensive approach is enticing and well worth exploring but without any preconceived ideas about distant interaction or claims of trans-Caribbean contacts, which have been occasionally raised but which are more often spurious and unsubstantiated by facts.

The story to be told is an anonymous history, without names of rulers and their peoples and nations. The prehistoric past, with the exception of areas of civilization in Mesoamerica, evolves before the formation of major states and ruling dynasties, when class struggles and political decisions were not yet the basis for social changes and economic developments. It is more a material and domestic history that archaeologists are able to unravel, more akin to a natural history in which the documents may be mute yet remain relatively unbiased, and in which social and cultural changes and progress in technology and subsistence play the major roles. These realities are often reflected in cases of human expansion in search of new lands to colonize, leading at times to a degree of militarism and warfare, as well as to the hazards and vagaries of human interaction and communication over vast distances and varied environments through the ages. It is in such events that archaeologists hope to be able to detect the interplay of new ideas and new peoples acting on particular environments that leads to all those cultural and social changes that make the backbone of human prehistory.

In the Caribbean region proper, more of the story concerns three basic phenomena: (1) the spread of agricultural colonization to island environments, and the intensification of these systems to support larger populations; (2) contacts with and role of neighboring great powers in challenging local adaptations; and (3) the distinctive rise of chiefdom societies and their varied, sophisticated, and often enigmatic art forms.

This ancient past may appear as an historiography without writing, yet it is not entirely without its inscriptions; as a history of form, very much an art history, archaeology seeks to identify changes in style and meaning recorded on the otherwise mute material remains revealed in these innumerable potsherds and ceramic styles that may seem to appear too frequently and in such fastidious manner throughout this chapter. Their role is no mere display of worthless erudition; it testifies to our only mute messages from the past. The native voice of these ancient Caribbean peoples may have been silenced; they nevertheless have left their very own images and symbols, certainly to be variously interpreted and understood by archaeologists, yet never to be distorted as historical documents might have been. They remain as the only testimony for changes and interaction whose other dimensions may have forever vanished. They are still vividly present as a global recollection of the dynamic trajectory of these populations, who for more than 5,000 years existed in a closed universe left entirely to their own devices until the fatal years that brought Europeans to their shores.

In this perspective, the Caribbean region may be looked at as part of a "World System" – that is, as a part of the world that may have been affected by events which occurred among the most developed and more powerful of its elements, under the assumption that more developed peoples, qualifying as centres of cultural developments, are more likely to have sent influences to greater distances than is the case for peoples of more modest achievements distributed around their periphery, without inferring necessarily any economic interdependency. Certainly the powerful Mesoamerican states that bordered the Caribbean region had a profound influence on their immediate neighbors, as illustrated by Central America. The more precise role of the powerful Andean civilizations and their complex periphery, which rises above the Caribbean region proper, is still more difficult to assess. There are suggestions that it may also have been active, perhaps even as far as the Greater Antilles, and there are hints that the Caribbean area is the ground where the two centers of civilization may have overlapped, albeit ever so briefly.

Although political integration was certainly never achieved in the Caribbean, except perhaps at the very dawn of the colonial period under Spanish rule, it may still be worthwhile to look at this geographical phenomenon as an integrative force in the hope of understanding better its role in the course of human interaction and cultural diffusion throughout its considerable and complex prehistoric past, as the following survey of its major prehistoric events illustrates.

Villagers and Colonists: 4000/3000–1500 B.C.E.

The emergence of a circum-Caribbean reality dates to the peopling of the Caribbean islands and to the beginnings on the mainland of sedentary village life and its close association with pottery making and eventually agriculture. This may be seen as nothing less than a major revolution in the early prehistory of the Caribbean region because sedentarily marks the beginnings of population growth and its impact on the later course of social developments. The earliest peopling of the Caribbean Islands is also the last major human expansion to a significant part of the world.

An approximative baseline for this phenomenon may be set anywhere betweeen 4000 and 3000 B.C.E., as suggested by the most recent radiometric dating evidence. Human groups had by the beginning of the fourth millennium B.C.E. aleady occupied the entire mainland shores of the Caribbean region for at least 7,000 years, during the Paleoindian and Archaic (or Preceramic) ages. The Archaic Age especially is the period of the first experimentation with plant domestication, especially the two major staples of the Caribbean region, corn in the west and manioc in the east. Although precise knowledge of these significant events is still far from satisfactory, it may be assumed that domestication had developed through most of the mainland by 3000 B.C.E.

The beginning of the third millennium B.C.E., or the end of the fourth millennium, also witnessed the development and spread in coastal areas of the first shell middens – that is, heaps of empty seashells mixed with other archaeological remains that became a type of site closely associated with Caribbean archaeology until much later times, as well as a subsistence resource that will remain important to all coastal adaptation throughout the region's prehistory. The appearance of the first shell middens is often attributed to the stabilization of the oceans' shorelines by 3000 B.C.E., which now allows for the development of stable and abundant shellfish populations. A new orientation toward more permanent resource bases and settlements could thus be achieved even before full agriculture had spread.

Another distinctive achievement of this period was the appearance of pottery making, which in the Caribbean region is among the earliest in the New World, earlier than in either Mesoamerica or the Andes. Ceramics first appeared in the same context as the intensification of food-gathering techniques, and perhaps of incipient cultivation. This marks the time of the Archaic Age, with its relatively mobile lifeways and dependency on wild resources for subsistence, as well as on simple tools made of chipped or ground stone or of bone and hard shell, representative of conditions of life that survived in many coastal areas of the Caribbean alongside the rise of the first Ceramic Age villages until historic times.

Colombia and Central America

The origin of pottery making in the New World is a subject usually discussed around two early centers. Valdivia, on the coast of Ecuador, belongs to the Intermediate Area and is outside the Caribbean region proper. The Valdivia people, dated to circa 3000 B.C.E. or just before, may have already grown some maize, and they also exploited fish and shellfish on the dry coast of Ecuador, as their shell middens demonstrate. It is the ceramic tradition however, dating to around 3000 B.C.E. (and perhaps even to 4000 B.C.E.), found at several coastal sites on the Caribbean coast of Colombia and in the flood plain and adjacent hills of the Magdalene River, that is of greater significance for the development of pottery making in the Caribbean region.

The best-known manifestation is Puerto Hormiga. The site is a ring-shaped shell midden, a pattern characteristic of early midden sites, which may be suggestive of village occupations, and it is composed of oyster shells and fish bones. Ceramics were relatively sophisticated there from the very beginning. Shapes are characterized by an emphasis on large globular bowls, or *tecomate*, and the clay is tempered with plant fibers. The pottery is elaborately decorated with incisions and punctations; small modelings in the form of human and animal heads, known as *adornos*, are frequently attached to vessel rims. This type of ornament remained closely associated with Caribbean ceramics both on the mainland and the islands throughout most of their prehistory.

Other evidence for technological advances is limited to large stone flake tools and perhaps basketry. In this context the true nature of Puerto Hormiga subsistence is still difficult to determine. The local environment is unsuited to agriculture, but artifact types may indicate the processing of wild plant food. Other ceramic sites in the general vicinity of Puerto Hormiga, some with a more interior location, such as Monsu and Turbana, have recently been reported with radiocarbon dates predating 3000 B.C.E. San Jacinto, located still further inland in the interior hills of the Magdalena Valley, claims a 4000 B.C.E. antiquity. This may support the idea that pottery first appeared in interior sites before spreading to coastal areas. Yet all these early sites share many basic features: They are ring-shaped shell mounds, they include many preceramic tool types, and they all belong to a same tradition of shapes – that of the *tecomate* (globular) – despite decoration styles that varied but always within a modeled and incised tradition. Subsistence might have consisted essentially of coastal

or lagoon fishing and shellfish collecting, complemented by riverine
fishing. Although digging of wild tubers and plant collecting is suggested
by stone artifacts, it is still impossible to ascertain the presence of food
production.

The significance of this early pottery-making center in Colombia for
the further spread of ceramics in the New World must not be underrated.
Whether this early fiber-tempered pottery is also at the origins of the
earliest pottery of North America – which is also fiber tempered and
dates to before 2000 B.C.E. in various sites of Florida and Georgia – is a
matter that calls for more substantial evidence and the solution of considerable geographical and chronological problems. The idea, which has
some serious supporters, involves a direct diffusion all across the Caribbean Sea and the Gulf of Mexico; it may be supported by the presence
on the Gulf coast of Florida of a linguistic family (Tucuma) believed to
be related to the distant Warraus of the Orinoco delta. The Warraus
were expert seafarers but practiced neither agriculture nor pottery making.

The further spread of pottery making from Colombia leads directly
north to a neighboring area of Central America, where another early
center of pottery making has been identified in the Paria Bay area of the
Pacific coast of central Panama and its adjacent foothill area. The region
was already well known from its earlier preceramic occupation dating to
circa 5000 B.C.E., a practically unique occurrence in Central America as
best represented by the coastal Cerro Mangote culture, and many rock
shelter sites of the hilly interior. The earliest ceramics are represented by
the Monagrillo culture, currently dated to circa 2900 B.C.E. and lasting
until about 1300 B.C.E. Known essentially from the Monagrillo shell
midden site, and such inland rock shelters as the Cueva de los Ladrones,
ceramics are found in sites that have revealed a continuous occupation
dating to earlier Archaic times, and where ceramics only appear in the
midst of earlier technology represented by such artifact types as edge
grinders, milling stones, and pestles.

Monagrillo pottery is sand tempered, and only a few late specimens
are decorated with incisions, excisions, and punctations as well as simple
painting in single red bands. The simple style differs markedly from
Puerto Hormiga and other traditions from Colombia. Vague similarities
with Valdivia in Ecuador, however, have been noted. The ecological
context of this coastal shell midden is one of unfertile mangrove swamps,
but conditions suggest that some maize may already have been grown as

a pot vegetable. Edge grinders and milling stones may have been used for processing wild tubers such as manioc, as well as palm nuts and other seeds, but this idea is still speculative. Conditions were more suitable for maize agriculture inland, near rock shelter sites, where the earliest experimentation with plant domestication, including both maize and manioc, may actually have taken place. Indeed, Central America, judging from an evidence so far limited to central Panama, may have been instrumental in spreading maize cultivation to Mesoamerica and even perhaps to South America, as suggested by the dating and distribution of plant pollens and phytoliths found there (c. 5000 B.C.E.). Yet the Monagrillo people are not believed to have resided in permanent settlements; instead, they seem to have engaged in a pattern of seasonal transhumance between coastal camps near marine resources and inland rock shelters, where they practiced slash-and-burn agriculture. Pottery itself does not seem to have been associated with the introduction of any new conditions of life; it was simply added to existing technologies.

The later spread of pottery making in Central America after circa 2500 B.C.E. may still appear somewhat erratic. At first, both ceramic and nonceramic occupations tended to occur in the Parita Bay area of Panama before pottery had established itself everywhere toward the end of the third millennium. Further north in Costa Rica, early ceramics are represented by the Tronadero culture, dated to circa 2000 B.C.E. or before in the hinterland of the Atlantic watershed of that region. Tronadero origins, based essentially on ceramic evidence, show no definitive affiliations with either Colombia or Mesoamerica, but the culture is certainly ancestral to later developments in that part of Central America after 1500 B.C.E. Both Tronadero and the interior ceramic caves of Panama may suggest that ceramics were first introduced among inland hunters and collectors, who perhaps already had incipient maize cultuivation but whose more precise traces still remain to be found.

Venezuela

The spread of pottery making eastward from Colombia also betrays some delays. In Venezuela, and within the boundaries of the Caribbean region, the earliest Ceramic Age people belonged to the Kusu culture on the western coast, known from the earliest occupation levels at the La Pitia site on the Goajira Peninsula, around circa 2000 B.C.E. Not unexpectedly, its pottery is consistent with the *tecomate* tradition, which must have spread there through the Río Ranchería. As in Colombia, the Kusu people were not yet agriculturalists; at least, no clay griddles, a distinctive clay artifact used for processing bitter manioc, are associated with their ceramic production. Their simple pottery decoration included incision and punctation, consistent with the *tecomate* tradition, but some white painting is also found. Fish bones are abundant in their site, where catfish alone accounts for 90 percent of the faunal remains; turtle hunting also seems to have been important. Some burials near the site are the only indication of semipermanent habitations, but no sedentary villages are suggested at that early stage.

In the middle Orinoco, however, the situation is somewhat different and more complex at the onset of the second millennium B.C.E. This fertile riverine area, which appears to have been largely unpopulated until then, witnessed the beginnings of both pottery making and agriculture. Of particular significance is the Ronquin locality, where a series of sites and cultures initiated an uninterrupted local sequence of related traditions that lasted until historic times. The earliest pottery at Ronquin appears in the La Gruta culture, dated to the very beginnings of the second millennium B.C.E., or to shortly before. Its excavators, however, favored a calibrated radiocarbon date of 2750 B.C.E., which has been received with some controversy. Until the issue is further substantiated, it is nevertheless safe to assume that La Gruta initiated a long series of ceramic and cultural developments that remain distinct from the *tecomate* tradition. Instead of globular vessels, new styles of shapes emphasize keeled or composite vessels also often associated with elaborate flanged rims. Decoration is still essentially plastic with modelings and *adornos* as well as an emphasis on finely incised, or hachured, designs. Of greater significance is the first emergence of a painted pottery tradition associated with the distinctive white-on-red decoration that survived locally for an extended period and became the hallmark of early ceramic styles in the eastern Caribbean until the beginning of the Common Era. With its composite, or bell-shaped, vessels, decorated with white-on-red painting or fine incisions, the La Gruta occupation of Ronquin marks the earliest appearance of the Saladoid series (named after the later Saladero site on the Lower Orinoco), which held such a prominent role in later events in eastern Venezuela and the Caribbean islands.

As opposed to early ceramic occupations of Colombia and Central America, the phenomenon in the middle Orinoco is now firmly associated with agriculture at La Gruta, in the form of bitter manioc cultivation

(*Manihot esculenta*), a root crop widely distributed as a staple in the tropical lowlands of South America to this day. The evidence itself is of a secondary type, because the plant itself is not likely to be preserved, but it is unmistakable. It consists of numerous fragments of *budares*, or clay griddles, and small stone chips used in making grater boards, both being essential instruments in the processing of this toxic root crop for human consumption.

The origins of La Gruta suggest a homeland in the Amazon Basin, where related ceramic styles are widely distributed after 2000 B.C.E. within the so-called Zoned Hachured Horizon. Because the Amazon and the Orinoco are joined by the Casiquiare Canal, the river system allows for possible cultural connections between the tropical lowlands and the Caribbean region through the middle Orinoco. The question bears also on solving the problem of the origins of manioc agriculture. An Amazonian origin favors the La Gruta ancestry. The alternative would involve the fertile Magdalena Basin in Colombia, an early population center far in advance of its neighbors by 2000 B.C.E., where a wild endemic form of manioc (*Manihot carthaginensis*) is still found on mountain slopes. This wild manioc may possibly have been more widespread in the Caribbean lowlands of Colombia in the prehistoric past, when it may have been the staple food among peoples of the *tecomate* tradition.

Initiated by La Gruta at Ronquin, the Saladoid series further evolved in the lower middle Orinoco toward 1500 B.C.E. into the Ronquinan Saladoid, which spread farther down river taking full advantage of the agricultural potential of the river levees, which became small islands in flood season and received annual deposits of fertile alluvium, not unlike the situation, as Rouse has oberved, in the Nile Valley. Permanent villages were widespread on the middle and lower Orinoco. Their ceramic art elaborates upon the previous painted and modeled-incised techniques of La Gruta to which they contributed painted cross-hatching, a powerful motif that achieved more prominence, as an incised design, on the coast and the islands a millennium later.

While agricultural and pottery-making villages were developing in the middle Orinoco and the Maracaibo Basin, coastal peoples further east in Venezuela, as well as on the offshore islands of Cubagua and Margarita, remained the same Archaic Age shellfish gatherers who had developed there before 3000 B.C.E. They reached their modest cultural climax around the middle of the second millennium with the Manicuaroid cultures. Archaic peoples, whose sites are now exclusively shell middens, emphasized shell – especially the large and very common conch *Strombus gigas*, itself a major food resource – in the manufacture of their simple artifacts. Tools made from shells, such as axes, adzes, and especially gouges made from the inner whorl of a large conch, were probably used for woodworking and perhaps canoe manufacture. Some shell beads and pendants were produced as ornaments, and a distinctive type of small bipointed bone artifact was probably used as spear or harpoon barbs. Ground stone artifacts, typical of Archaic Age technology, include some edge grinders, essentially a flat smooth rock deeply ground along one or two edges, not unlike similar artifacts from preceramic and early ceramic sites of Panama.

Similar bone points and edge grinders are also associated with the earliest known occupation of Trinidad, as represented by the Ortoiroid cultures. This large island must be considered more representative of mainland events than those of the Caribbean islands proper; it was attached to the mainland until the recent past, and the development of the Gulf of Paria still keeps it within easy reach of Venezuela and the Orinoco. Earliest traces of human occupation in Trinidad date to the sixth millennium B.C.E. for the Banwari Trace culture (actually 5230 B.C.E. for the earliest of many radiocarbon determinations), which produced a typical Archaic Age technology that included conical ground stone stone pestles and crude flake and cobble tools, including the edge grinders, suggestive of the processing of wild plant food along with shellfish collecting. Other small Ortoiroid sites have been reported from other areas around the Gulf of Paria, and they are representative of the preceramic occupation of this part of eastern Venezuela after 3000 B.C.E. Relationships with coastal Manicuaroids further west in Venezuela are suggested by some artifact types, but the lack of emphasis on shell tools (including the lack of shell gouges) in Ortoiroid technology, as well as an emphasis on amorphous stone flakes, justifies a separate classification. Ortoiroid sites are certainly earlier and may ultimately prove to be the Manicuaroids' ancestors.

The Western Caribbean

West of Costa Rica little is known about the early archaeology of Central America and adjacent parts of Mesoamerica until circa 1500 B.C.E. The evolution of a maize-based agricultural adaptation in central Mexico, well documented in the Tehuacan Valley by MacNeish, would have had little direct effect on the Caribbean region despite the fact that maize agriculture might have also developed early in a parallel manner between the two areas in lower Central America. The earliest pottery manifestations in Mesoamerica belong to the Pacific coast of Guatemala, and they seem unrelated to developments further south except for the presence of smaller *tecomate*-shaped vessels in the Barra culture, dating to circa 2000 B.C.E.

Of far greater significance is the Archaic sequence recently uncovered by MacNeish in coastal Belize. Although the successive cultures believed to have developed there since 7500 B.C.E. (the Lowi-Ha phase) are poorly dated, the presence of a developed and diversified lithic industry – which includes finely made large prismatic blades (10–15 cm in length), a technology uncommon in the New World and more reminiscent of the Upper Paleolithic of Europe, as well as many other types of artifacts such as scrapers, adzes, and even bifacial projectile points, and which culminates between 4000 and 3000 B.C.E. in the Sandy Hill phase – offers intriguing similarities with the earliest archaeological remains later to be found in the Greater Antilles. Grinding stones and *manos* (hand-held grinding stones), reliable indicators of the growing importance of maize agriculture, also appear at that time, predating the rise of the first sedentary villages and the first ceramics around 2000 B.C.E. Unfortunately, the lack of faunal remains in the sites leaves us with little evidence on the adaptation and subsistence of these unique preceramic peoples of the Mesoamerican area. A distinctive inland orientation is indicated by artifact types, and there is no evidence of any seafaring technology. Yet the Belize preceramic sequence offers the most attractive similarities with the earliest technology revealed in the archaeology of the Caribbean islands. No preceramic occupation is known otherwise for the remaining Caribbean coastal areas of the Yucatan Peninsula in Mexico.

THE PEOPLING OF THE WEST INDIES

The origins of a human population in the West Indies – that is, in all the islands between Cuba and Trinidad – is a phenomenon that represents the last major human expansion in a major part of the world. As such, the subject has attracted considerable attention, but the research often has proved inconsistent and the data frustrating. The issue is far from being entirely resolved. Accordingly, theories still vary about the actual date of the first human colonization, its precise mainland origins (whether single or multiple) and the number of separate migrations, and the processes responsible for its occurrence, not the least being whether it involved an accidental or deliberate crossing of the Caribbean Sea.

On the basis of current models of biological dispersals in the Caribbean region, it appears that the West Indies flora and fauna are essentially South American in origin. Biologists explain the introduction of these species as a series of accidental drifts mainly from South America toward various locations of the West Indies. This theory has been attractive to archaeologists who have adopted a similar model to explain the apparently erratic distribution of preceramic sites and artifact types around the Caribbean periphery. The most obvious natural route of entry into the West Indies from South America are the Lesser Antilles, which form stepping stones between Trinidad and the Greater Antilles. Unfortunately, the lack of supportive evidence in the Lesser Antilles makes this corridor unlikely. Alternative routes have been sought along a mid-Caribbean chain of islets and cays that stretches between Nicaragua and Jamaica, especially at the time of potentially lower sea levels, but the suitability of this route is questionable because preceramic remains are notoriously lacking in both Jamaica and Nicaragua.

The earliest radiocarbon dates so far available for the West Indies (excepting Trinidad) as a whole are from both Cuba and Hispaniola. A recent radiocarbon date for Haiti of circa 3600 B.C.E. is the earliest. It appears to support the long hypothesized date of 4000 B.C.E. for the event as postulated by Rouse. The date, however, comes from a shell sample retrieved from a surface scattering of shells and a few stone flakes. A date of 3100 B.C.E. had already been known for the Levisa site in eastern Cuba, in association with a substantial assemblage of stone blades and flakes, is reminiscent of Old World Paleolithic archaeology, as in the preceramic of Belize. Otherwise, sites associated exclusively with lithic remains are known mainly from the Dominican Republic (the Barrera-Mordan culture) where they appear generally later than 2500 B.C.E. Remains at Casimira, also in the Dominican Republic, are responsible for the Casimiroid series of Archaic cultures whose emphasis on large blade tools survived in many areas until the introduction of agricultural peoples. The presence of sites on the more substantial river systems of these large islands indicates the importance of terrestrial resources (essentially small rodents and iguanas) in Casimiroid subsistence. An extinct giant ground sloth may even have survived to the last millennia B.C.E. and have been hunted by these early island colonists. Bypassing Puerto Rico toward the Lesser Antilles, early dates in excess of 2000 B.C.E. for the small island of Antigua in the Leeward Islands, where the Jolly Beach culture has revealed an Archaic Age blade technology based on the abundant local supply of flints and cherts, may be the Casimiroids' easternmost distribution.

The addition of new artifact types and raw materials in the preceramic technology after 2000 B.C.E. becomes more characteristic of an Archaic Age. This includes ground stone and shell and bone tools, as well as the first ornaments. Whether this innovation reflects a second, Ortoiroid wave of migration out of Trinidad through the Lesser Antilles is still conjectural.

The search for a continental homeland to this original West Indian population, based on cultural similarities, has encountered all kinds of difficulties. If we consider the artifact evidence alone, we must exclude such a likely population center as the Caribbean lowlands of Colombia in the Magdalena Basin, because pottery was already known there by 3000 B.C.E., and because the area lacks a developed lithic technology comparable to the fine Casimiroid blade tools. It is true, however, that large stone knives and daggers, practically identical to Casimiroid specimens from Hispaniola, are also known from Central America, and this lent support to the idea that the chain of small mid-Caribbean islets may have been the most likely route of entry in times of lower sea levels. Unfortunately, stone knives and daggers in Central America, as in central Panama, date to a later Ceramic Age context. Moreover, no archaeological remains have yet been found on the barren mid-Caribbean islands, and no preceramic remains are known for Jamaica.

More attention has recently been focused on the shores of Belize, where MacNeish has brought to light the early preceramic sequence described above earlier, but despite tantalizing similarities, the islands' technology lacks many diagnostic features common in Belize, such as chipped adzes, scrapers, and bifacial projectile points. Preceramic remains on the northern coast of South America beyond the Magdalena lowlands tend to appear later than 3000 B.C.E., with the notable exception of the Paleo-Indian Jobo tradition, whose fine bifacial lithic technology is on the one hand too early to be ancestral to the islands, and on the other is more complex than the technology evidenced among the Casimiroids.

Much of the problem depends on understanding more precisely and realistically how human groups could have reached the islands from the mainland across substantial spans of ocean. This long-neglected problem has recently been addressed in Richard Callaghan's computer simulation study for the potential of various accidental drifts from the mainland to have landed successfully on the Greater Antilles. Results show that the most likley successful crossing would originate from the coast of South America, from Colombia to central Venezuela, in a westerly direction conditioned by prevailing winds and currents, aimed toward Cuba, Jamaica, and Hispaniola. Unfortunately, no obvious homeland may yet be identified on that part of the coast on the basis of artifact type similarities or compatible radiometric dating.

After 2000 B.C.E., Archaic sites began to show a greater diversity, as well as a wider distribution. New cultural complexes appeared in western Cuba as represented by the Cayo Redondo and Guayabo Blanco cultures, which emphasize ground stone tools, some ornamental, and shell tools including the ubiquitous shell gouge. Unusual new ground stone artifacts are "gladiolitos," a dagger-like implement possibly associated with ceremonial activities. Fishing, hunting, and wild plant collecting provide the subsistence basis. Settlements had likewise spread with these innovations in Hispaniola, as represented by the Couri culture of Haiti and El Porvenir in the Dominican Republic, which display the most diversified and elaborate remains in stonework (such as fine stemmed daggers made on large prismatic blades), and ground stone artifacts, including distinctive conical pestles certainly associated with the preparation of plant food, as well as small incised bowls and occasional pendants. No shell gouges or much emphasis on shell tools are found there, however. None of these cultures are known in Puerto Rico, where the period is still poorly known, and where preceramic sites are usually associated with a simple inventory of hammerstones and crude flakes, as in the Coroso culture.

THE SPREAD OF VILLAGE LIFE, AND THE DEVELOPMENT
OF A MESOAMERICAN FRONTIER (1500–500 B.C.E.)

The Western Caribbean

The Formative Age marks the time of the first farming villages and early chiefdoms in the Mesoamerican side of the Caribbean basin (map 8.2). The phenomenon is introduced rather suddenly around 1500 B.C.E. near the coast of Belize with the simple Swazey culture, which is believed to be ancestral to the later Maya civilization of this area. Still identified with *tecomate*-shaped pottery, ceramic production adds large flat-bottom ba-

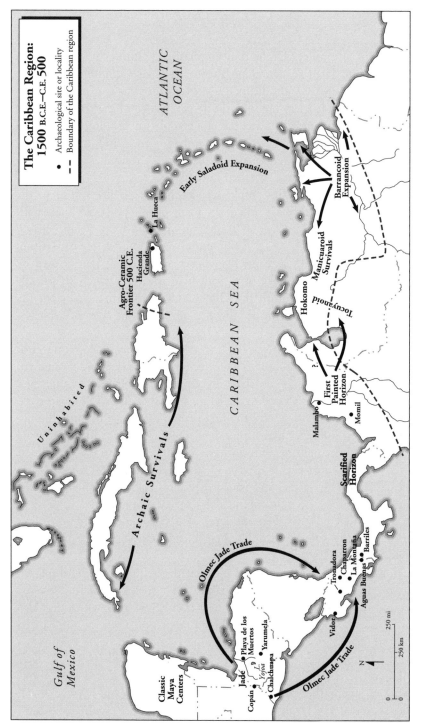

Map 8.2

The Caribbean Region:
1500 B.C.E.–C.E. 500

• Archaeological site or locality
-- Boundary of the Caribbean region

ATLANTIC
OCEAN

Early Saladoid Expansion

Barrancoid
Expansion

La Hueca

Agro-Ceramic
Frontier 500 C.E.
Hacienda
Grande

CARIBBEAN SEA

Manicuaroid
Survivals

Hokomo

Tocuyanoid

?

First
Painted
Horizon

Momil

Malambo

Scarified
Horizon

Uninhabited

Archaic Survivals

Olmec Jade Trade

Tronadora
Chaparron
La Montaña
Barriles

Vidor

Aguas Buenas

Playa de los
Muertos
Yarumela

Yojoa

Classic
Maya
Centers

Jade
Copán
Chalchuapa

Olmec Jade Trade

Gulf of
Mexico

N

0   250 mi
0   250 km

sins to its inventory. Decoration emphasizes painting in simple linear patterns, unrelated to contemporaneous styles of Colombia and Venezuela. Other artifacts are distinctively Mesoamerican and include finely worked chert bladelets but not the larger blades of earlier preceramic sites. *Manos* and *metates* (essential stone tools for grinding corn) are a certain indication that maize agriculture had been introduced from central Mexico. Simple ceremonial structures may already have been standing at the center of small thatched-hut villages.

Shortly thereafter, this simple agricultural village life spread to the Pacific coast of Guatemala, where the Ocos people practiced maize agriculture with sedentary lagoon fishing in the low-lying Pacific coastal plain as early as 1500 B.C.E. Their pottery also emphasizes flat-bottom bowls decorated with a distinctive rocker stamping design, created by impressing the jagged edge of a seashell in the clay, which stylistically links the Ocos people with the Olmec and as such may represent the further effects of their seminal influence on the Pacific coast of Mesoamerica.

The Olmec civilization was the first in Mesoamerica to develop a great and complex art style as well as major ceremonial centers and monumental architecture. It may also have developed the religion, writing, and calendrical systems ancestral to the Maya and other areas of Mesoamerica. Because the Olmec also were the first people to engage in long-distance trading, their influence may have extended as far as Costa Rica in Central America. Olmec culture seems to have first developed on the Gulf Coast of Mexico, an area that was poor in stone and other raw materials but was agriculturally fertile, and where they built elaborate centers and the earliest pyramids, often surrounded by carved monuments. Some hold that they had only reached the level of a theocratic chiefdom; others insist that the Olmecs had by then already developed the first great civilization of Mesoamerica.

The Olmec can be identified by their distinctive art style, displayed on massive monuments such as large stone stelaes or statues erected around their ceremonial centers or near trading colonies, which may also have been the focus of elaborate religious activities. Their art emphasized a "were jaguar" iconography, combining human and feline features associated with a number of deities that may be the prototype for the later Mesoamerican pantheon. It is the Olmec who introduced the prominence of jade, rather than gold, as the highest valuable in Mesoamerican élite symbols. As a result, small jade or pottery figurines with "baby-face" characteristics were widely distributed in the regions influenced or controlled by the Olmec.

Central America

Because of their wealth and their need for jade, the Olmec were in a position to have been the first people to engage in long-distance trade, which is known to have extended over most of Mexico and Guatemala as well as to Central America and as far south as the Gulf of Fonseca in Nicaragua. On the Atlantic coast, however, and near the base of the Yucatan Peninsula, Olmec influence bypassed the western Caribbean to reach directly south into Honduras, revealing their early presence at such sites as Playa de los Muertos or Yarumela, or Chalchuapa in El Salvador, soon after 1000 B.C.E. Planned settlements, artificial mounds, and small pyramids built around courtyards, as well as stone monuments, mound burials, stone columns, and carved stelaes and altars, all testify to the Olmec's direct interference. The phenomenon is reinforced by the prevalence of the jaguar motif in local arts; by "baby-face" figurines, distinctive styles of pottery decoration, and stone axes, all associated with jaguar, birds, and serpent themes; and even calendrical inscriptions. Beyond all these cultural manifestations, the Olmec are believed to have also been responsible for the early introduction of jade and social stratification.

The situation is well represented at the site of Chalchuapa in El Salvador, which is interpreted as an important, distinctively Olmec trade center dominated by a 20-meter-high conical pyramid. A question remains: What were the Olmec seeking in El Salvador, some 850 kilometers from their homeland? If not jade, they may have been after cacao beans, a form of exchange currency in prehistoric Central America, while also trading for obsidian from the local volcanic interior mountains. Cotton textiles may also have figured in Olmec trade. Chalchuapa is the earliest known occupation of El Salvador, yet archaeologists are still uncertain whether it was an actual Olmec colony, or whether it represented the effects of trade with a local population, in view of some apparent relationships with the Pacific coast of Guatemala and its Ocos culture. Specialists are tempted to speculate that, as possible colonists, the Olmec might have introduced their original Mixe Zoque languages to Central America, more especially to El Salvador and Honduras, languages that were still spoken there in historic times. There is no evidence that the Olmec engaged in a maritime trade, however; in Honduras overland trails along the Ulua River were their major thouroughfare, largely avoiding the Caribbean watershed.

The first known human occupation of Honduras dates to around 1000 B.C.E.; it is as expected related to the Olmec presence of El Salvador, and it likewise exhibits similarities with Ocos. At Playa de los Muertos, a major settlement and cemetery located in the drainage of the Río Ulua, pottery decoration displays even more distinctive Olmec features (straight-sided bucket-shaped pots, bottles, effigy vessels, etc.), which do not occur in Guatemala, and whose nearest similarities are with central Mexico. Indeed, their clay figurines show similarities with figures carved on Olmec stelaes. Platforms and defensive features, in the form of ditches surrounding settlements, were erected. Being associated with elaborate jade jewelery and differential burials, the remains suggest a stratified, probably chiefdom-level society thriving at Playa de los Muertos.

This must have been the case at Los Naranjos in the region of Lake Yojoa, and also in Honduras, where a settlement dominated by a 6-meter-high platform was surrounded by a deep ditch. Elsewhere, the caves of Cuyamel in central Honduras have preserved an ossuary associated with artifacts and ceramics decorated in typical Olmec style. The site, dated to just after 1000 B.C.E., may relate to the Yarumela site for its pottery reminiscent of the Ocos culture. These similarities serve to reinforce the significant role of the Pacific coast as a center in Olmec trading with its Central American frontier.

Lower Central America

Beyond the Ulua River and western Honduras, we leave the Olmec world and the first manifestations of a Mesoamerican frontier. Further east into lower Central America, the earliest ceramic occupation of the Atlantic watershed of Costa Rica, as represented by the Tronadora culture, had evolved locally by 1500 B.C.E. into more diversified farming-village societies, of which La Montaña is a good example. At La Montaña the ceramic assemblage contains at least 40 percent *tecomate* vessels, although only a few are painted with simple red lines. Plastic decoration dominates; it includes punctations, pellets, cord markings, and the widespread rocker stamping. One particular shape of vessel may belong to *budares*, or clay griddles, because of a very distinctive raised rim similar to manioc-baking griddles of South America. Also distinctive are *manos*, but these and *budares* are unrelated to earlier assemblages of the area or of Panama. Relationships instead point toward northern South America and the north coast of Colombia, as suggested the finding of *budares* and the distinctively small *manos* stones that may have been used for pounding manioc rather than for grinding corn. No sets of *manos* and *metates* are present, suggesting a lack of both maize and relations with Mesoamerica. The La Montaña culture, already established by 1000 B.C.E. in Costa Rica, may thus be an example of early manioc cultivation in Central America, originating in South America, only later to be replaced by the maize-based subsistence typical of later periods.

The intermediary situation of Central America is well reflected in other simple village societies of Costa Rica that are contemporaneous with La Montaña. The Chaparron culture, which developed on the Atlantic watershed after 1000 B.C.E., is somewhat anomalous. As opposed to La Montaña, the bichrome-painted decoration of its pottery, and the major presence of *tecomate* vessels (85 percent) as well as the lack of *budares* griddles, is interpreted as a Mesoamerican manifestation that well reflects the fluctuations of this cultural frontier. None of the more elaborate developments already encountered further north in Honduras and El Salvador, nor any Olmec influences, have been detected in these two Central American cultures.

The situation may be different on the Pacific coast, more precisely in the Greater Nicoya area of Costa Rica, where close to 800 B.C.E., the Loma B culture, despite clear relationships with La Montaña, had yielded larger settlements, such as the Vidor site, and a more sophisticated painted ceramic decoration style, which may be ancestral to the later "Zoned Bichrome Horizon" cultures that developed in that area after 500 B.C.E. Low-level chiefdom societies may be indicated. This phenomenon raises the possibility of a more direct Olmec influence into this region of lower Central America that to this day remains a controversial issue. Olmec influences are usually discussed around the identification of jade objects that may have reached Nicoya from Olmec centers to the north, as suggested more especially by the so-called Olmec heirloom of jade artifacts from Tibas. Jade sources have not been identified in Central America, and it is generally assumed that all local jades must have come from sources in the Motagua Valley of Mexico. Jade obviously may have been worked locally from imported blanks or fragments.

Northern South America

In the Caribbean lowlands of Colombia, after more than a millennium of Puerto Hormiga cultural tradition, and through a sequence of related

styles (essentially Tesca and Barlovento), the most significant innovations
are represented by the Malambo culture (c. 1100–1000 B.C.E.). Its people
lived in simple villages, and their subsistence was based definitively on
the cultivation of bitter manioc as indicated by the many griddle fragments in their sites. The Malambo site itself is located in the delta and
lagoons of the Río Magdalena. The new ceramic style emphasizes plastic
decoration that includes deep incisions, modelings, *adornos*, and clay
masks, suggesting some continuities with Puerto Hormiga. Malambo was
eventually followed by another significant culture, that of Momil I (at c.
1000 B.C.E.), represented by a small sedentary farming village adaptation
oriented to the lagoons of the Río Sinu, and where bitter manioc was
also the staple crop as evidenced by *budares* and possibly stone chips
from manioc grating boards. Momil I pottery may still belong to the
tecomate tradition and perhaps is also distantly related to Puerto Hormiga. New shapes were introduced, later to become more widespread,
such as footed and keeled (composite) vessels, while plastic designs and
painting in red, white, and black were added to the decoration inventory.
Figurines were introduced. In search of distant relationships, some archaeologists go as far as suggesting a link between the Momil I culture
and the manioc-growing La Montaña people of Atlantic Costa Rica, on
the basis of similarities in ceramic decoration.

Manioc cultivation also extends further east into western Venezuela to
the shores of the Guajira Peninsula, where the Hokomo style (1000
B.C.E.) at La Pitia develops out of the earlier plastic decorated Kusu
pottery, and still hints at connections with Colombia and the Puerto
Hormiga tradition; this is indicated by broad incisions, curvilinear designs, and punctations. But Hokomo is also associated with the earlier
patterned painted designs in red, white, and black, utilizing earlier broad-
lined incised curvilinear designs that forshadow the later developments
of painted traditions in other parts of Venezuela and Colombia (respectively, the Tocuyanoid cultures and the First Painted Horizon).

Hokomo ceramics may in fact be the earliest expression of polychrome
pottery in northern South America. This is not without significance for
the fact that polychrome painting is usually associated with more developed cultures appearing in Mesoamerica and later found in Central
America. It was first believed that polychrome painting derived from
Mesoamerica, but radiometric dating now indicates that Central America
and northern South America were either earlier or as early as Mesoamerican developments. Hokomo subsistence still emphasized fish and shell-

fish. On the evidence of *manos* and *metates*, some maize cultivation, as opposed to manioc, might have been introduced there early. Villages may have been semipermanent, but more complex burial patterns, including funerary urns, argue for more sedentarity. In the Venezuelan *llanos* to the south, the prehistoric Cano del Oso pile dwellers (dated to c. 920 B.C.E.) may also claim to have produced some of the earliest polychrome pottery in northern South America. Otherwise, Cano del Oso villagers simply lived on collecting snails and growing maize in their poorly drained areas of the Venezuelan *llanos*.

In Eastern Venezuela beyond the *llanos* and the coast, the valley of the middle and lower Orinoco, an earlier cradle of the Saladoid cultures, brings us further away from a Caribbean reality and closer to the Amazonian universe. In the last millennium B.C.E., the area witnessed the development of the Barrancoid culture, whose settlements were typically always closely associated with the best agricultural lands near river banks and levees. The distinctively sculptural Barrancoid pottery emphasizes bucket-shaped vessels with a predominant flange usually at the rim. Decoration involved broad incisions and curvilinear designs as well as a distinctive emphasis on modeled and incised elements. Beginning with the more simple initial Barrancas culture around 1500 B.C.E., the long evolution of pottery style led to the more elaborate designs after 700 B.C.E. of the Los Barrancos style, on the lower Orinoco at the head of the delta. Bowls, bucket-shaped vessels, and boat- or hammock-shaped containers are typical of the basic shapes, but noteworthy are some unusual double-bridge handles and stirrup spouts, which are usually associated with Andean ceramics, and in Mesoamerica with the Olmec. Monochrome red or black painting is the only Barrancoid venture in ceramic painting, in sharp contrast to their Saladoid neighbors and predecessors. Barrancoid subsistence was based on slash-and-burn manioc cultivation, and the people resided in large permanent villages where they also left dense shell middens.

Barrancoid origins have been a longstanding matter of controversy in Caribbean archaeology and is not yet fully resolved. It has been argued that the Barrancoids were the original introducers of manioc cultivation into Venezuela. This theory is favored by Meggers and Evans, who trace Barrancoid origins through the Malambo in Colombia, because of similarities in the modeled-incised pottery decoration, from the Andean highlands area before spreading to Venezuela. Others believe, like Rouse and Rooseveldt, that the Barrancoid cultures developed in situ in the Orinoco

Valley out of the previous Saladoid occupation, as represented by the Ronquin Sombra culture established there around 1000 B.C.E., before expanding toward the delta area and the coast of Venezuela and even further west into the Guianas. If so, the Orinoco peoples may have been ancestral to the Malambo in Colombia; this idea is still speculative but would account for striking similarities, in pottery decoration. Ultimately, like the Saladoids, the Barrancoids may trace their deepest roots out of the Amazonian area, which may still be the cradle of manioc cultivation. What is certain, however, is that once established on the lower Orinoco, the Barrancoids had rapidly displaced the short-lived occupation of the Saladero style, later to reemerge on the coast, thus initiating a pattern that persisted in other coastal areas, including Trinidad and possibly even the Lesser Antilles, near the time of the European contact.

Despite the relative antiquity of these events, archaeologists have long speculated on the intriguing linguistic implications of these stylistic developments and the ethnic diversity they are likely to reveal. Linguistic reconstructions and the distribution of historic languages in northern South America suggest that Saladoid peoples were the ancestors of the Arawakan language family, as speakers of proto-Arawakan introduced from the Amazon Basin. Later archaeological changes are likewise believed to reflect the further history of this linguistic family. In this context the Barrancoids have been associated with the Maipuran branch of Arawakan languages, to which belong many dialects still spoken today. The implications of these identifications are far reaching and involve directly the later Ceramic Age archaeology of the West Indies, where developments have often been discussed in terms of linguistic changes.

The coastal area of eastern Venezuela, in comparison with the dynamic conditions encountered further west from the Goajira Peninsula east of Maracaibo to the Llanos and the Orinoco Valley, is associated with the spread of agriculture and village life, as well as substantial population increases. This area lingered in the hands of Archaic Age peoples, essentially those same Manicuaroid fishermen and shellfish collectors, with their distinctive artifacts, such as shell gouges, inherited from the previous millennium. This is also true of Trinidad and the Paria area, where Ortoiroid peoples survived with their old lifeways and simple lithic technology.

The West Indies

Regional developments characterized the surviving Archaic Casimiroid cultures during much of the period between 1500 and 500 B.C.E., until they were replaced by Ceramic Age peoples. The period nonetheless witnessed the first peopling of Puerto Rico and possibly also some of the Lesser Antilles south of Antigua.

The Coroso culture of Puerto Rico may have appeared by 1000 B.C.E. It boasts a few artifacts from cave or shell midden sites, such as Cayo Cofresi; simple tools include edge grinders as well as some conical pestles and crude flakes and choppers. Lacking a fine-blade technology, the Coroso were influenced by their Casimiroid neighbors in Hispaniola, judging by their decorated pendants and pieces of stone bowls. Despite the lack of good diagnostic artifacts, archaeologists tentatively may assign them an Ortoiroid connection suggestive of a Trinidad origin, despite much evidence still missing from the Lesser Antilles.

As in the Greater Antilles, some diversity in artifact types still hampers attempts at more precise cultural classifications. The Virgin Islands, for instance, immediately east of Puerto Rico, are best represented by the Krum Bay culture and its distinctive chipped and ground celt blades, unique to the region. Other sites have revealed edge grinders similar to those of the Coroso in Puerto Rico. An Ortoiroid context may even be more speculative in their case. This only illustrates how blurred the Lesser Antilles route still appears when trying to trace the origins of Archaic cultures in the West Indies.

Within the Lesser Antilles, well beyond the Virgin Islands, the Jolly Beach culture in Antigua (c. 2000 B.C.E.) seems to have taken advantage of rich supplies of flint deposits on its beaches for developing a blade-and-flake technology that is reminiscent of Casimiroid remains. Ground stone artifacts have been found, but no shell gouges. South of Antigua, the Windward Islands are the major population area. The only known Archaic sites between Antigua and Trinidad have been found in the interior hills of Martinique; this Boutbois culture is undated, but it includes the typical inventory of edge grinders, crude flakes, and grinding surfaces usually associated with other edge-grinder sites in Puerto Rico, Trinidad, Venezuela, and even Panama. Could this be the missing link in the Ortoiroid expansion toward the West Indies, if indeed such was ever the case?

THE FORMATIVE MILLENNIUM (500 B.C.E. TO C.E. 500)

The period beginning in 500 B.C.E. was marked by almost universal changes. In the Caribbean region, human groups had now colonized all areas including the islands, and agriculture had established itself almost everywhere on the mainland. Nonagricultural Archaic Age peoples were by now simply relegated as "marginal" groups. Times were ripe for a population explosion. The idea may be simplistic yet it is not without reality. The year 500 B.C.E. may therefore be regarded as a convenient baseline for a wave of new technologies, cultural differentiation, and social evolution, well reflected in Gordon Willey's concept of a *Regional Developmental Period*, whose significance extends far beyond the Caribbean region.

The Western Caribbean

In distant Mesoamerica this seminal period is known as the "Middle Formative" or "Preclassic." The coasts of Belize and Honduras witnessed the rise of monumental architecture in settlement centers ruled by powerful chiefs and their élite in key areas later to be associated with the Maya civilization. This is especially well illustrated by the early prominence of Kaminaljuyu in the highland valleys of Guatemala, near the Ixtepeque volcano, an economically important source of obsidian.

The florescent Miraflores phase at Kaminaljuyu developed out of the Formative highland cultures with the first evidence of monumental religious architecture. Step pyramids built around large courtyards were not only erected as temple platforms but were also used for élite burials associated with objects of great value, an unmistakable indication of rising complex social stratification. The deceased were covered with cinnabar, a red pigment obtained through long-distance trade. That women and children were offered as sacrifice in the burials reinforces the impression of authoritarian rule. Wealth was expressed everywhere through an abundance of jade objects. The major ceremonial center at Kaminaljuyu, the nearest proto-metropolis to the Caribbean region, has no counterpart elsewhere in Mesoamerica or Central America. Following the demise of Olmec influences, Kaminaljuyu's aura was felt more strongly on its immediate neighbors in Central America.

The evidence comes from a distinctive type of Central American ceramics known as the Usulatán Ware (a decoration of bundles of combed or wavy lines done in negative painting), which serves as a time marker for the Middle Formative, and which was traded to Kaminaljuyu as well as throughout Central America. Also typical of Miraflores is a distinctive style of monumental carving consisting of large heads that were once thought to be Olmec but which are now believed to be different stylistically. Carvings are set on pillars or pedestals, and themes include jaguars, humans, and mushroom stones with a carving at the base. The theme of the toad is pervasive on the pottery; along with mushrooms, toads may also have been used as hallucinogenic substances. The Miraflores culture may have been a source of influence for monumental architecture and especially stone sculpture well throughout Central America.

Central America

Beyond the immediate cultural boundaries of Mesoamerica, the parts of Central America most directly under Mesoamerican influence were Greater Nicoya, Costa Rica, and the Gulf of Chiriqui in Panama, where a substantial development in ethnic diversity was beginning to emerge, certainly concomitant with a population explosion. The phenomenon is subsumed archaeologically under a "Zoned Bichrome Horizon," which (as on chronological charts) overlaps with a "Scarified Horizon" that reached well into Panama, as revealed by distinctive styles of pottery decoration.

Zoned Bichrome ceramics, with their red and black painted areas surrounded by incised lines, emphasize feline and serpent motifs. Zoned rocker stamping also occurs on the pottery, as well as on clay figurines that retain some degree of Olmec features; some figurines may even perhaps have been traded from Mexico. Zoned Bichrome peoples probably maintained contacts with distant areas through trade for the obsidian or salt produced on the Pacific coast. Exterior influences derived essentially from the north. They eventually spread to the Atlantic coast of Costa Rica, as represented by the Early Diquis culture. Subsistence still involved manioc cultivation, but maize was also extensively grown as indicated by *manos* and *metates*. Beans, avocado, chili peppers, fish, and shellfish complemented their diet.

Zoned Bichrome society seems to have belonged to low-level chiefdoms built around federations of large sedentary villages. This is certainly suggested by their finest cultural manifestation, the Aguas Buenas culture of Panama, which became one of the most widespread cultures of coastal Central America between 500 B.C.E. and the beginning of the Common Era. Their original ceramics, however, were not entirely similar to the Zoned Bichrome styles of northern Central America; they associated plastic decoration with some painting, and their distinctive tall-footed vessels had flaring elbow-shaped legs. Their particular significance is in the first truly monumental sculpture that they produced in Central America, well represented at the Barriles site, a major ceremonial center believed to have been the capital of a large chiefdom. Ceremonial architecture typically included artificial mounds with stone cobble facing and shaft grave burials, whose surroundings are often associated with massive and enigmatic stone spheres, a unique type of Central American monument. Aguas Buenas artists were also the first to produce large carved, hammock-shaped ceremonial *metates*. They are often decorated with trophy heads, indicating warfare and competition between rival chiefdoms, and with Atlantean figures for legs. These *metates* were more likely used as ceremonial seats for powerful chiefs whom the Aguas ·Buenas people may have deified and may have represented in free-standing statues. Ceremonial seats of various kinds as symbols of political powers are common to many chiefdom societies throughout the Caribbean region, including the Greater Antilles.

Cultural diversity is well illustrated by the contemporaneous Concepción culture, centered on the Pacific coast of Panama, which by contrast is assigned to a "Scarified Horizon" based on a distinctive style of ceramic decoration. The Concepción were not as highly developed as the Aguas Buenas; they were essentially coastal oriented and seem to have avoided the highlands. Maize agriculture was practiced as indicated by *manos* and *metates*. The Concepción people are mostly remembered for their elaborate stone-lined shaft graves with a distinctive shoe-shape, which are distributed in cemeteries probably adjacent to large villages that have yet to be identified. This burial practice was likely reserved for a powerful elite. They manufactured "Scarified" pottery marked by deep incisions set in rows. This culture is also associated with the beginnings of sedentarism and maize cultivation on the Pacific coast of Central America. These cultural traits differ from Aguas Buenas and are believed to indicate a more direct influence from Colombia.

Northern South America

The Caribbean lowlands of Colombia became the scene after 500 B.C.E. of an economic event of consequence, as revealed by the upper levels of the Momil site (Momil II, c. C.E. 0), where manioc was replaced by maize as a staple, and where there was more potential for a substantial surplus accumulation, which could support higher populations and more elaborate public works. This event is marked, somewhat more modestly, at Momil by the disappearance of clay griddles and the appearance instead of *manos* and *metates* in the remains. Maize agriculture, which has no local antecedents in the Magdalena Basin, must consequently have been introduced fully developed, along with its processing technology, from the north in Central America. New pottery shapes, such as tripod vessels, also suddenly emerged, which despite locally developed decoration techniques hark to Central America and possibly even to Mesoamerica as a more direct inspiration. Parallels with contemporaneous cultures of Costa Rica have been suggested, including the Atlantic littoral, which would have played an important role in the diffusion of these innovations to lower Central America and Colombia from Mesoamerica. There is no question that the introduction of maize cultivation allowed for the later diversification of Formative cultures in this region. Archaeologically, this new development belongs to the "First Painted Horizon," as represented by the La Loma and El Horno cultures of the Río Ranchería, east of the Magdalena Basin, and on the major route to Venezuela. Similarities between the Hokomo culture at La Pitía and its polychrome pottery on the Guajira Peninsula, and the early polychrome Tocuyanoid cultures of Venezuela, as opposed to the rest of Colombia, have been noted. Elaborate curvilinear designs in red and black, such as scrolls and the typical and ubiquitous comb motif, were painted over a cream or white slip background. Simple farming villages that left deep shell middens suggest an essentially riverine adaptation. Maize was undeniably the staple crop, but remains of large clay griddles may indicate the survival of bitter manioc in the diet.

In Venezuela, contacts with Colombia certainly followed the most obvious route east of the Magdalena Basin through the Río Ranchería and the Río Cesar, which bypass the formidable Sierra Nevada de Santa Marta and the coastal region, thus spreading the "First Painted Horizon" directly into the Guajira Peninsula. Yet beyond the Maracaibo Basin and the coastal mountains, the northern *llanos* and the central coast remained in the Archaic Age at the beginning of the Common Era. Northwestern Venezuela, however, soon gave rise to the influential Dabajuroid cultures, whose initial Guasare style is at the origin of many later developments all over the area. Simple plastic and simple red-painted decoration were by then typical of the pottery; fabric impressions, or corrugation, were also common decoration techniques.

In the northern *llanos* behind the Caribbean mountains, polychrome pottery spread with the long-lived Tocuyanoid cultures. Tall Tocuyanoid globular vessels display a distinctive curvilinear design, painted in red and black on white, that emphasizes the ubiquitous snake motif with a human face. Black paint is applied over white (like Momil II in Colombia), indicating that the Venezuelan Tocuyanoid may also be considered the eastern expansion of the "First Painted Horizon" of Colombia, its western frontier reaching even further into Central America. Little else is known of Tocuyanoid culture besides the pottery, and simple villages are the only types of settlements known. None of the more complex ceremonial developments of Central America are thus in evidence anywhere in northern South America.

On the eastern coast the Archaic Manicuaroid series survived practically unchanged until the first centuries C.E., until at least when contact with Ceramic Age peoples of the Orinoco Valley contributed some intrusive pottery to their remains. The Orinoco is where Barrancoid cultures developed and multiplied and became even more elaborate in their ceramics, as represented by the ornate Los Barrancos style. The lower Orinoco must indeed have been the center of much prosperity and demographic growth in view of the Barrancoids' relatively sudden expansion to many parts of Venezuela, beginning before C.E. 500. Barrancoid peoples introduced the first Ceramic Age on the central coast of Venezuela and the highland basin of Lake Valencia, bringing with them manioc cultivation, pottery making, and sedentary villages, in the process replacing existing Archaic settlements on the coast. To their distinctively ornate and complex pottery, which includes double-spout and bridge vessels, the western Barrancoids added such unique and exotic objects as clay earplugs and clay pipes. Yet there is otherwise little evidence of complex society or social stratification. Their burials, for instance, were simple and lacked valuable or luxury grave goods. Detailed studies of Barrancoid settlement patterns are still lacking, but the unusually large size of their archaeological sites, and the distinctive abundance of their ceramic remains, warrant further investigation into the nature of their society.

Further Barrancoid expansion followed the Orinoco down to the eastern coast of Venezuela into adjacent territories of Guyana (beyond the Caribbean region proper) as far away as Suriname. Their presence there is more difficult to identify precisely because of the close relationship they seem to have maintained with the existing Saladoid peoples. Vanishing from the lower Orinoco, Saladoid peoples reappeared several hundred years later on the eastern coast of Venezuela, replacing earlier Archaic (Manicuaroid and Ortoiroid) populations. Radiometric dating shows no indication of an occupation before circa C.E. 100, but much research remains to be done in this remote area of Venezuela. The earliest sites (the El Mayal culture) are typical of the Cedrosan Saladoid cultures already present in the West Indies at that time. By C.E. 500, however, following a pattern that is also encountered in the islands, their pottery increasingly betrays a significant degree of Barrancoid influences (Chuare culture), which has prompted some archaeologists to be hesitant in assigning some sites a cultural label or to make reference to a Saladoid-Barrancoid phenomenon. Sites were essentially coastal, and although manoic cultivation was practiced, fishing and shellfish gathering contributed to their subsistence, in the same manner as on the islands.

In this context the situation on Trinidad is the most significant, albeit still poorly investigated, considering the cross-road situation of this major island on the Gulf of Paria that is practically an extension of the mainland rather than a truly oceanic island. The Cedros culture there dates to the first century C.E., and it is stylistically close, as the label Cedrosan Saladoid indicates, to the styles encountered on the coast and in the islands. Close contact with eastern Venezuela and efficient seafaring technology must be assumed, but this Early Ceramic Period of Trinidad is still poorly known otherwise. The same phenomenon observed for the mainland reappeared after circa C.E. 300, when the Saladoid Palo Seco culture began to display unmistakable Barrancoid influences and actual Barrancoid trade sherds – to such a degree that by C.E. 500, a distinctively Barrancoid occupation predominated in Trinidad, making the island a veritable gateway to the West Indies (the Erin culture).

The West Indies

The period that follows 500 B.C.E. emerged as particularity dynamic both culturally and demographically in Venezuela and the lower Orinoco, being dominated by population expansions. It may not be surprising then, on the basis of several recent radiocarbon dates, that it is precisely in this period that the original migration of agricultural and pottery-making peoples into the Caribbean islands through the Lesser Antilles is known to have taken place. The process was certainly well underway around 250 B.C.E., and the event belongs essentially to Cedrosan Saladoid peoples. Saladoid colonists apparently pushed out into the islands from their lower Orinoco homeland, likely under ongoing Barrancoid pressure, practically at the same time they were establishing themselves on the coast (radiocarbon dates are actually earlier in the islands), Trinidad, and the Guianas. Sometime before 100 B.C.E., they were able to colonize all intervening islands between eastern Puerto Rico and Trinidad, before spreading out to eastern Hispaniola in the first centuries C.E., their westernmost occurrence in the West Indies.

We must assume that before reaching the islands, Saladoid colonists first had to adapt to a coastal situation to which they were already predisposed by the earlier riverine environment of their homeland, where they must also have been able to develop a fishing technology as well as canoe navigation. The islands, however, offered no great incentive for many resources abundant on the mainland; their impoverished fauna was limited to a few land animals, such as rice rats (Megalomys), agoutis, and iguanas (now all extinct), while lacking such major game animals as deer and peccary common in Trinidad and the mainland. This scarcity was certainly compensated by the abundance of marine and riparian resources available in the islands. Indeed, the earliest Saladoid sites are generally associated with such dense layers of the remains of land crab, in particular, that the culture itself was originally designated as the "Crab Culture." Saladoid subsistence, nonetheless, remained essentially based on manioc cultivation from the earliest beginnings, as evidenced by the abundant remains of clay griddles, and by a close association with the most fertile areas in the choice of their settlements.

That such a phenomenal migration was able to take place within hardly 200 years is an indication that the process must have involved a substantial population, or that considerable mobility between all the islands must have been the rule. Each island from Grenada (the Pearl style) to Puerto Rico (at Hacienda Grande) has yielded substantial remains of these early colonists, who seem to have selected the best agricultural regions. Their distinctive pottery is decorated with fine incisions, modelings such as *adornos*, and the diagnostic white-on-red painted designs. We know much less about their technology. They left few artifacts other than fragments of clay griddles and small crude stone chips from local jaspers and chalcedonies. Ground stone tools are uncommon and consist of petaloid celts; other axe blades, which must have been essential for clearing land, were fashioned out of the thick outer lip of the conch shell *Strombus gigas.*

When they are associated with shell middens, Saladoid sites reveal more evidence about subsistence practices where fishing and shellfish collecting was a major complement to manioc cultivation. The prominent role of the land and sea crabs in their diet is still enigmatic, however. It may have provided them with a means to withstand the stress of early colonization of an unfamilar environment. Their taste for crab subsided in the first centuries C.E., however, perhaps because they had partially depleted the local populations. We know about the ceremonial aspect of their culture from the elaborately decorated ceramics and modeled-incised *adornos* in the shape of small anthropomorphic or zoomorphic heads or effigy vessels. Many animal species can be identified; prominent are the frog, the bat, and the turtle, but parrots, manatees, and even dogs were occasionally represented. Of the ceremonial artifacts, the most distinctive and the finest are the so-called incense burners, hollow cylinders open at both ends and elaborately decorated. Uncommon on the mainland, these unusual objects may have been an invention of the first island colonists.

This simplified scenario of the agricultural colonization of the Lesser Antilles and Puerto Rico has recently been disrupted by the discovery in the northernmost parts of the area (eastern Puerto Rico and its small offshore island of Vieques) of an early distinctively aberrant ceramic style despite obvious relationships with Saladoid pottery. Dated to circa 200 B.C.E., the La Hueca style is currently a subject of much bitter controversy among specialists, and its true role in events remains to be more precisely determined. La Hueca pottery emphasizes the same fine incisions and cross-hatching as the Cedrosan Saladoid but with the further exception that it has yielded none of the distinctive white-on-red painted decoration common everywhere else. Motifs and designs in their details also vary from Cedrosan types. Distant similarities with a much later style of the central coast of Venezuela, Río Guapo, have been singled out to suggest a direct initial migration from the mainland. The style is not known elsewhere on the mainland or in Trinidad and the Windward Islands. It may have spread to the Leeward Islands, however, and as far south as Guadeloupe and Marie-Galante. Whatever its true significance, La Hueca is also associated with an unusual development of lapidary work in semiprecious stones (amethyst, carnelian, greenstone) and mother-of-pearl. Besides many types of beads, carved pendants were produced including a type of birds head (probably parrots rather than condors) that has received much attention. Other early Cedrosan sites of the Lesser Antilles have also yielded evidence of lapidary work (in Montserrat and Grenada), and the situation is suggestive of an early trading network throughout the islands that included the mainland potentially as far away as the Amazon.

The Huecan presence was short-lived. By the first centuries C.E., all the Lesser Antilles were bearers of a more typical Cedrosan Saladoid style, with its elaborate white-on-red painted and zone-incised cross-hatched decoration. This is also true of eastern Puerto Rico with its Hacienda Grande culture. That interaction with the mainland is still active is well illustrated by the fact that after C.E. 100, Saladoid styles on the east coast of Venezuela are so similar to those of the Lesser Antilles as to justify their classification as a single cultural manifestation. The more precise nature of this interaction has not yet been explored fully. The entire area was certainly part of a common interaction sphere.

This situation only serves to emphasize that the role of the mainland must at all times have been instrumental in relation to cultural change in the islands. This is especially true after C.E. 350 of the strong influences over the Saladoid ceramic styles of the Lesser Antilles, derived from the thriving Barrancoid population of eastern Venezuela, that led toward a more baroque expression of ceramic decoration and the appearance of a local manifestation of polychrome painting. That ceremonialism also developed in this particular context is further indicated by the early appearance, and perhaps even "invention," of small three-pointed stones, later to become so much a part of Taino art and religion in the Greater Antilles.

It may still be premature to assess the proper role of the mainland Barrancoids in the archaeology of the Caribbean islands. Their presence on Trinidad, well established by C.E. 500 may well justify the concept of a "Barrancoid of Saladoid Tradition" in the Lesser Antilles, suggestive of deeper sociocultural and possibly also linguistic and demographic changes in the entire West Indies than is warranted by the usual reference to a "Saladoid with Barrancoid influences" in the current literature. The particularly dynamic conditions of the period were also marked by the first peopling of the small but remote island of Barbados, and by the spread of the Puerto Rican Saladoid to eastern Hispaniola, that became the westernmost frontier of ceramics and agriculture in the Greater Antilles, a position it maintained for several centuries.

THE PROTO-HISTORIC MILLENNIUM (C.E. 500–1500)

Early Developments

The entire 1,000 years that preceded the fateful coming of the Europeans in the New World may be qualified in the Caribbean region as the Proto-Historic Period because of the first rise of strong continuities that led it to the ethnic situation encountered by the Europeans around 1500 (Map 8.3). Although this was especially true after the year 1000, historical documents now begin to be useful for acquiring a deeper knowledge about these prehistoric peoples. Indeed, the full realization of many of the developments previously ongoing in the Caribbean region, especially outside Mesoamerica, during the preceding millennium now fully manifest themselves. This became the time for the achievement of the greatest degree of cultural and social complexity in the form of advanced theocratic and militaristic chiefdoms and even proto-urban societies, essentially the period with which the former concept of a Circum-Caribbean phenomenon is most closely attached.

Mesoamerica and its southeastern frontier experienced after C.E. 500 some of the most consequential series of cultural, social, and political events yet to have happened there since the collapse and demise of the Olmec, almost a millennium earlier. The powerful city of Teotihuacan had sent far-reaching influences that extended as far away as the Maya, who were themselves approaching the height of their own civilization. Major Maya centers like Tikal were thriving, and the magnificent site of Copan represented a Maya metropolis at the very edge of Central America and the Caribbean region. By C.E. 900 both Teotihuacan and the Maya centers were devastated, terminating their potential political influence beyond the boundaries of their realm.

To the south, however, and beginning soon after 500 B.C.E. powerful chiefdoms in the highlands of Guatemala, following the demise of the Olmec, had taken over an extensive trading network that reached to the Pacific coast, perhaps involving some degree of maritime ventures. A major volcanic eruption in El Salvador led to the sudden abandonment of the area, fatally disrupting trade with highland Mexico. The highland Maya of Guatemala soon collapsed, however, preparing the rise of the

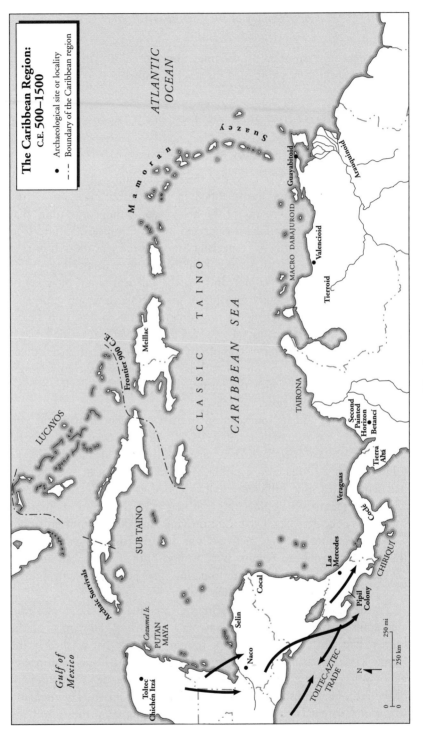

The Caribbean Region:
C.E. 500–1500

• Archaeological site or locality
--- Boundary of the Caribbean region

Map 8.3

lowland Maya who, in turn, took over the trade with Central America, using cacao beans as a form of currency, and for this reason giving preferences to those humid regions more favorable to growing the precious plant, especially in Honduras and El Salvador.

After C.E. 700 most Maya sites began their decline and collapse, leading to the depopulation of the central areas. Copan itself was abandoned early, around C.E. 800. A vacuum in Mesoamerican influences was thus created over the southeastern frontier and Central America, whose major consequence was symbolically reflected in the disappearance of jade ornamentation as far away as Costa Rica. As the most prestigious material and symbol of wealth and status, jade was replaced locally by gold objects and a technology derived from Colombia. This marks the end of the "Age of Jade" in vast areas of the western Caribbean region. Lost wax, soldering, casting, hammering, and "mise en couleur" with acids, are typical of this complex new metallurgy, which also produced the distinctive *tumbaga*, a gold-copper alloy, whereby only the surface was transformed into pure gold.

During the first half of the millennium under consideration, the Mayoid area of Central America extended to the Ulua Valley of western Honduras, where mound sites have been found. This area of Mesoamerican "veneer," as revealed in artistic decoration, remains quite limited, however, not extending even to eastern Honduras. The Mesoamerican frontier follows a southern line that reaches south into the Nicoya Peninsula, more or less hugging the Pacific coast. The entire Atlantic watershed is consequently entirely outside its sphere of influence.

Mesoamerican styles are reflected archaeologically in the fine ceramics of the "Early Polychrome Horizon" and its distinctive Maya inspiration. Nothing there is truly Maya, yet local ceramics were traded with Copan. In the Greater Nicoya area (the Rivas region and the Nicoya Peninsula), the remarkable "Nicoya Polychrome" ceramics developed independently and were less derivative of the Maya sphere, with tripod and tall annular-based vessels. Colors consisted of light orange, white, red, and dark orange, with the addition of black and brown. Monkeys, serpents, birds, and humans were represented. Influences on the so-called Tepeu pottery of the central Maya area have been noted. This artistic phenomenon in painted pottery decoration is associated with the development of elaborate stone carvings, such as those found in the Isthmus of Rivas region of Nicaragua. These tall stone columns, on which are supported sculptured figures, are perhaps even more reminiscent of the San Agustin "alter ego" statues in the highlands of Colombia. The carved columns seem to have belonged to ceremonial structures built on platform mounds. Similar large stone sculptures, in the style known as *Chontales*, are also found on the eastern shores of Lake Nicaragu. A man holding a spear and wearing a prominent headdress is typical of the iconography. The style, which is believed to have survived until C.E. 1000, may be more closely related to the Caribbean watershed.

The centuries between C.E. 500 and 1000 are those of the most sophisticated cultures of lower Central America, in which the Coclé culture of central Panama is the best known and the most spectacular. Coclé, which still belongs to the extensive Polychrome Horizon, is known from the site of Sitio Conte, a river bank burial complex. The culture is highly representative of the powerful and wealthy theocratic chiefdoms that ruled over Central America. Wealth was reflected in sophisticated polychrome pottery, such as their famous painted plates, and their metalworking reached new heights. Coclé is indeed the first major culture to have replaced jade with goldworking, probably derived from Colombia, as symbols of political authority and status. The painted pottery remained essentially different from Mesoamerican styles; stylized alligators, birds, humans, or monsters, painted in white, purple, red, and black, decorated the inside of flat plates or the walls of tall urns and jars. Gold was used in the form of the *tumbaga* alloy, derived from the Quimbaya technology of the Colombian highlands. Colombian emeralds also decorated their gold jewelry, essentially represented by varieties of alligators, frogs, or bat pendants worn as insignia of rank and status by a powerful élite. Burial practices were highly developed at Coclé, where most of the fine artifacts were found in chiefly graves, often also associated with sacrificed wives and retainers laid to rest in deep pits.

Interestingly, on the Atlantic watershed from Costa Rica to northeastern Honduras, a somewhat original contemporaneous cultural development preserved a stronger element of Mesoamerican influences. This Curridabat culture in Costa Rica (and its Selin counterpart in eastern Honduras), for instance, built stone-faced mounds and stone walls in the rain forest and lagoons where they lived, and where they erected carved stelae and monoliths. Whether their structures were ceremonial or defensive is still undetermined. Likewise, their ceramics are still revealing of distant Maya influences.

THE WESTERN CARIBBEAN AND CENTRAL AMERICA
(C.E. 1000–1500)

At the end of the first millennium C.E., a series of profound changes appeared throughout the Caribbean region. The collapse of major Mesoamerican societies, the Maya especially, could not have failed to have had serious repercussions over Central America where the frontier of Mexican influences tended to shift repeatedly in response to the intensity of trading activities.

While Guatemala and western Honduras were reduced to a power vacuum, the mighty Toltec ruled out of central Mexico and their new capital at Tula, after taking over many Maya cities in Yucatan, especially the famous Chichen Itza. After the collapse of the Toltec in the thirteenth century, the Maya people were allowed to experience a cultural revival, known archaeologically as the "Decadent Period" because of a marked artistic decline. This led them immediately, however, to renew their involvement in a maritime trade with their neighbors, which was based essentially on a coasting navigation in conjunction with the old Toltec networks, which they may have simply revived.

By now, ethnohistorical documents reveal that trading became more especially the role of the Putun Maya, who occupied the Caribbean coast of Mesoamerica. Although the Putun Maya originated on the Gulf Coast of Mexico, they were able to extend their commercial activities through various ports-of-trade around Yucatan, perhaps as far south as Honduras. They are remembered as the "Phoenicians of the Caribbean" due to their large seagoing canoes and large cargo rafts. The presence of sails has been suggested, but there is no definitive evidence of its use. Maritime transportation would have made dealing in bulk commodities far easier and cheaper than overland trade routes. Their Caribbean trade operated out of the island of Cozumel as well as the nearby coastal site of Tulum, where they flourished until Spanish times.

In the hands of the Putun, long-distance trade dealt essentially in Mesoamerican resources such as salt, obsidian, jade, copper, quetzal feathers, cacao beans, cotton, and copper bells and axes. Moreover, they mainly supplied Honduras not only with mass-produced pottery but also with slaves for the local élites. The effect of this Maya revival in Central America is well represented by the Naco culture, and more especially the Naco site on the Ulua River of eastern Honduras. This site must have been a substantial town with a population estimated at 10,000 inhabitants, which also boasted one of the few Mesoamerican ball courts of Central America. The local population may have been a trading colony of ethnic Maya or even Nahua-speaking Pipil from central Mexico.

On the Pacific coast of Central America, Toltec trade had been traced through the distribution of a characteristic type of monochrome pottery known as Plumbate Ware, a veritable horizon marker, which because of particularities of the clay developed a metallic sheen reminiscent of glazed ceramics (a technique otherwise unknown to the New World). Pacific coast trading networks survived the Toltec, when later revived by the Aztec through the intervention of their specialized class of merchants, the famous *pochteca*, who established colonies as far away as Costa Rica, from where they were responsible for supplying Nicoya Polychrome pottery and Panama goldwork to Mesoamerica.

That this unsettled period was a time of widespread conflict and warfare is well reflected in the relatively sudden appearance of hilltop fortresses in Guatemala and Honduras. Putun traders, who had introduced Plumbate Ware, obsidian, and the theme of the feathered serpent, may well have been regarded as fearsome "Caribbean raiders" against whom these defensive structures had been built. This is especially true of the Cocal people of eastern Honduras and northern Nicaragua, who lived in such fortified hilltop villages as in the Río Claro site. Their Central American roots, however, are clearly revealed by stone cist graves and carved giant grinding stones.

An unexpected glimpse of the kind of trading activities in which the late Maya of the western Caribbean area were engaged can be found in Columbus's diaries, in which he recorded having observed a probably Putun trading raft, laden with resources, plying the ocean between Belize and the Bay Islands of Honduras. Further south, in the Nicoya Peninsula, the Nahua-speaking Pipil ethnic group, with their distinctive monolithic stone axes, bark beaters, and large carved and complex table-like *metates*, may have been descendants of *pochteca* traders or of even earlier Toltec merchants. The colorful Nicoya Polychrome pottery was replaced locally by the more linear and graceful Luna Polychrome (after c. C.E. 1100), reflecting a curious admixture of central Mexican with local styles.

In Panama and eastern Costa Rica, new more powerful chiefdoms, such as the Chiriqui, had emerged, revealing exterior associations with the Pacific coast, although essentially based on the Atlantic watershed. The Chiriqui people built large burial sites and ceremonial centers of a scale unknown previously; the most famous is at Las Mercedes in Atlantic

Costa Rica, where a group of mounds was erected according to a planned layout on the banks of a large river, a rather unique architectural feat in Central America. Large stone statues of various humans and animals are representative of their monumental art; trophy heads, however, are still often depicted along the edges of ceremonial *metates*, an unmistakable sign of militaristic pursuits. Chiriqui pottery is complex; it emphasizes negative painting, a technique new to Panama despite a long history elsewhere in Central America.

On the Caribbean shores of Panama, the Veraguas people had re-placed the sophisticated Coclé culture. They are best known for their deep shaft tombs with side chambers dug into hill sides. Breaking away from the Polychrome Tradition of the Pacific coast, Veraguas ceramic art emphasized instead modeled monochrome vessels with tall legs carved in the shape of alligators, frogs, or reptilians. The technique is more consis-tent with the Atlantic ceramic tradition in Central America. Their large stone *metates* were carved as jaguar effigies or three-legged ceremonial seats, as expected of Caribbean chiefdoms. It is their metallurgy, however, that distinguishes the Veraguas people, especially their unusual use of gilded copper rather than purer gold for their metal ornaments.

Northern South America and the Greater Antilles (C.E. 500–1000)

In the Caribbean lowlands of Colombia, the fertile and now densely populated Magdalena Valley became the home of a "Second Painted Horizon" characterized by bichrome rectilinear designs, as in the wide-spread Zambrano culture and its large villages built on the banks of major rivers. Strong stylistic affinities with the much earlier Machalilla culture of coastal Ecuador (c. 1500 B.C.E.) have been noted by Colombian archaeologists but without solutions to the extreme chronological gap. Cultures also diversified regionally. The Crespo culture located in the lagoons and mangroves of the Caribbean littoral, for instance, is known for its diversified use of conch shell for the manufacture of axes as well as a variety of pendants and ornaments. The technology is reminiscent of the West Indian islands' shellwork across the Caribbean Sea, but no direct links can be reasonably established.

Perhaps of greater significance was, by the end of the first millennium, the formation of the Tierra Alta culture in the same areas of the Magda-lena lowlands. Its pottery, essentially flat bowls and pedestal vessels, has been characterized as a "real international style" because of similarities with the northern ceramics of Darien and Panama, certainly along the Atlantic coast. Gold became more common, an unmistakable index of wealth and power. The first evidence of public work in the form of small hillside agricultural terraces (a form of intensive agriculture) and artificial mound platforms in this part of South America is also attributed to Tierra Alta chiefdoms.

The last few centuries before European contacts are marked by the late spread of deep shaft graves, which seemed to occur as a cultural horizon when the lowlands of the Magdalena Basin became the home of the Betanci chiefdoms with their distinctive ceramics. To an even greater extent than Tierra Alta, the Betanci people built artificial mounds everywhere, including temple platforms 8 meters high, and some 40 to 60 meters at the base; entire villages were also built on mounds. All these features serve to classify Betanci in the sub-Andean cultural pattern in spite of its lowland distribution. Burials were also repositories for gold artifacts, as well as a distinctive type of carved shell ornament. Following upon earlier practices, labor-intensive agricultural techniques produced extensive ridged fields, which are today the most distinctive and visible remains of the Betanci people. What was grown certainly included maize and perhaps also sweet manioc as a staple. It is believed that the Betanci people were directly ancestral to the historic Sinu chiefdoms, builders of impressive temples, encountered by the first European explorers of the Magdalena Basin of Colombia.

Even by the standards of the Betanci's notable achievements, the cultural climax of this part of South America is to be found further to the east of the Magdalena Valley in what are the foothills and upper valleys of the high Sierra Nevada de Santa Marta, an impressive mountainous formation that rises directly above the Caribbean Sea and that is separated from the Andes by the Río Ranchería. These mountains were the home of the famous Tairona culture. Probably derived from lowland groups, as suggested by their shaft tombs with side chambers in which they deposited their urn burials, the Tairona, while living mostly in small villages, also built towns of elaborate masonry structures temples, and palaces, from where the chiefs of large village federations ruled. This is the case at their major site at Pueblito with its 3,000 dwellings and public buildings of dry stone slab masonry, in addition to bridges of stone slabs and stepped mounds. These Tairona still represent the most complex architectural remains ever built in northern South America and, as such, must be representative of the highest degree of social complexity ever achieved there, or anywhere outside Mesoamerica and the Andes. Accordingly, the qualification of "proto-urban" has been assigned to these advanced chiefdoms, despite the lack of clear Andean antecedents.

Tairona technology provides further evidence of their developments. They were sophisticated goldworkers, and their pottery emphasizes plastic decoration rather than painting. Their monolithic axes are similar to those of lower Central America and, to some degree, those of the Greater Antilles. Central Mexican influences, especially from the Toltec, were once suggested on the basis of similarities in the iconography of their many decorated artifacts, in which the image of Tlaloc, the Mesoamerican rain god, had been recognized. This theory has not recently been revived; it would certainly raise the question of the extent of earlier Maya trading at the time of Toltec rule, or the possibility that the Tairona might have ventured out to sea toward the western Caribbean and Mesoamerica.

In Venezuela, however, a radiation of more modest cultural developments that began its spread after C.E. 1000 is in sharp contrast with the more uniform and more advanced cultures of the Colombian lowlands. Based on the central areas of the coast and adjacent coastal mountains, the phenomenon resulted in such stylistically varied cultures as the Tierroid, Ocumaroid, Valencioid, Guayabitoid, Dabajuroid, and Arauquinoid, as well as some isolated styles. Old Barrancoid enclaves still survived, but Saladoid groups were virtually gone. These diverse peoples and their cultures were essentially the direct descendants of earlier groups such as the Tocuyanoid and early Barrancoid; some also had a long local history of development. None achieved the level of development of the Tairona or Betanci of Colombia, and few left any forms of structural or architectural remains.

The more developed among the Venezuelan peoples were found near the Andean area and the coastal mountains. This is the case of the Tierroid cultures (named after the site of Tierra de los Indios), which dominated western Venezuela after C.E. 1350. The Tierroid were likely descendants of the Tocuyanoid because of their distinctive polychrome pottery, which hints at closer relationships with Colombia, and even with some late painted ceramics of Panama (the Herrera style), as suggested more specifically by the presence of a distinctive comblike motif in their pottery decoration. Tierroid structural remains are limited to low platform mounds. None of the Tairona architecture seems to have filtered east from the Santa Marta area.

In the more centrally located area of Lake Valencia, an inland lake basin rising above the Caribbean coast, the contemporaneous Valencioid cultures may have been the most influential. They are known for a famous style of female figurines with prominent buttocks. Their unpainted ceramics include the use of the "coffee bean" element especially for eyes, and they used human faces modeled on the upper parts of urnlike pots as ceramic decoration. Some urns were actually used for burying the dead under earth mounds, which are their only structural remains. The Arauquinoids were located toward the east coast and Orinoco Valley, and they replaced the Barrancoid. They reveal a degree of Valencioid influences with their "coffee-bean" pottery decoration. Their Barrancoid ancestry is not universally accepted however; their distinctive pottery belongs more properly to a pan-Amazonian horizon (the Incised and Punctate Horizon) distinguished by rows of incised or punctated geometrical motifs and more especially by the use of sponge spicules as temper in the clay, a practice then widespread in the Amazonian lowlands for the production of a fragile, greyish ware.

One still wonders at the reasons for this unique cultural radiation in central and eastern Venezuela at the eve of European contact, and at its social, political, ethnic, and linguistic implications. The ethnic and linguistic diversity it reflects may even raise the specter of a "Balkanization" of this part of the Caribbean region, a situation that may not be entirely unrealistic. Indeed, the situation appears to have been extremely dynamic everywhere in Venezuela, resulting in a significant amount of late culture changes that are not yet fully understood. This may be especially true of the series of cultures grouped into a "Macro-Dabajuroid phenomenon," according to an expression developed by Oliver, and which affected more directly the western and central coasts of Venezuela. Without much evidence for social complexity or chiefdom formations, these cultures more likely consisted of village farmers; nevertheless, they were responsible for the population growth and expansion reflected in the peopling of the small islands off the western coast of Venezuela (Curacao, Bonaire, and Aruba), and which may have had far-reaching repercussions as far away as the eastern fringes of the Caribbean region, even to the Lesser Antilles and Barbados. The further association of this Macro-Dabajuroid expansion with the spread of Arawakan languages, so widely spoken in that part of South America, reinforces the importance of their role in the late prehistory of the eastern Caribbean region, and the formation of the diverse historical ethnic groups encountered there by the Europeans.

The Greater Antilles

In sharp contrast to the mainland, the entire area of the Greater Antilles – from Puerto Rico to Cuba, including Jamaica – experienced shortly after C.E. 500 a single uniform evolution that resulted in the local emergence of chiefdom societies among the Taino, encountered there by Columbus on his first voyage of 1492. This unique event follows upon the demise of the earlier Saladoid colonists, who after expanding to eastern Hispaniola (the La Caleta culture in the Dominican Republic) had established a long-lasting frontier with their Archaic (Casimiroid) neighbors, who still occupied the greater part of that island as well as all of Cuba. The earliest manifestations of these changes have now been traced to eastern Hispaniola, where the Late Saladoid Cuevas culture developed into an Ostiones culture which may have been seminal to the sequence of events that led to the formation of the sophisticated culture of the historic Taino. Whereas the Saladoid had maintained obvious traces of their earlier mainland origins, the new developments appear to have been entirely the result of local processes, and no clear influences from the mainland can be satisfactorily identified in their archaeology.

Ostiones ceramics differ from previous Saladoid wares by their simplicity in shapes as well as in their incised and modeled or painted decoration. The Ostiones' initial contribution was twofold: (1) They were the first to colonize Jamaica, while introducing pottery and agriculture to Cuba before expanding eastward toward Puerto Rico; and (2) they were the first to have systematically colonized the forested and mountainous interiors of these large islands. The origins of this new manifestation must have involved some population increase to justify such an expansion; the reasons for the changes are unclear. We can reasonably assume that no actual migration from a mainland origin can be detected from the archaeological remains to account for these events. What is not clear either is the nature of the Ostiones people's relationship to the Archaic population they encountered in their expansion, except in Jamaica where they seem to have been the original human colonists.

The rise of the Ostiones culture is further associated with the emergence of cultural diversification and social complexity in the Greater Antilles, not only within the Ostiones pattern but also regarding the somewhat enigmatic Meillac culture, which replaced them in the fertile Cibao Valley of northern Hispaniola. There the Meillac people introduced artificial ridged fields before following the steps of the Ostiones to

Jamaica and Cuba, where they appear to have survived until historic times; the Meillac culture remained marginal in Puerto Rico. As opposed to earlier styles, Meillac pottery was never painted; it is highly distinctive by its decoration technique of texturizing vessel surfaces with incised lines, punctations, appliqué clay ridges and trellis, and a few small modeled lugs. The almost exclusively rectilinear style of the incised decoration is also in sharp contrast to all other pottery decoration in the Greater Antilles, before and after the Meillac.

Although many other types of artifacts seem to belong to an Ostiones background in the Meillac culture, the unusual ceramic style has led to a variety of interesting speculations about a possible exterior origin of this culture in the Greater Antilles. One theory favored by Dominican archaeologists emphasizes strong similarities with a contemporaneous late ceramic culture of Guyana (the Taruma phase), which are indeed intriguing. Venezuelan archaeologists propose instead an origin in the middle Orinoco and adjacent *llanos* (the Memoid series), outside the Caribbean area proper. It is difficult, however, to determine how such a stylistic diffusion or migration could have spread over vast areas of both sides of the Caribbean Sea without intermediary connections in the Lesser Antilles. One would have to infer direct contact across the Caribbean Sea, bypassing the Lesser Antilles and most of Puerto Rico, by peoples aiming directly at the northern coast of Hispaniola, where the Meillac culture first appeared. It would have been more difficult to migrate from Guyana, even though it is suggested by many uncanny stylistic similarities. Interestingly, Callaghan's simulation studies of marine navigation on the Caribbean tend to indicate that direct crossings between Venezuela and Puerto Rico (where the Meillac culture is only marginal) might have been nautically easier than hopping along the Lesser Antilles, where winds and currents would have made sailing conditions more perilous.

As an alternative theory, Meillac origins may be attributed to contacts with local preceramic peoples, who are known to have decorated small stone bowls with incised chevrons and hatchings, reminiscent of Meillac pottery decoration. The Meillac culture survived in an uneasy relationship (at least from the viewpoint of archaeologists) in northern Hispaniola, where it existed alongside later cultures until historic times, and where it may have been ancestral to the Ciguayos, a somewhat marginal Taino-speaking group encountered in eastern Hispaniola by Columbus.

The native population that first saw Europeans in the New World is known today as the Taino. Their culture was found throughout the

Greater Antilles and the Bahamas. Their greatest achievements, however, were centered in Hispaniola and Puerto Rico, and to some extent in eastern Cuba; in comparison, other areas are characterized by a sub-Taino culture. Archaeologically, these Taino were distinguished by their particular ceramic style (known as Chican Ostionoid), which almost entirely lacks painted decoration, emphasizing instead elaborate modeled and incised vessels reaching sculptural proportions in the finest specimens such as their effigy vessels. Although their pottery belongs to a stylistic tradition introduced by the Ostiones people, their work is unlike anything in the Caribbean region, and it displays no obvious connections with ceramic styles of Central America or South America. Distant Barrancoid influences, perhaps even a Barrancoid revival, have been noted, however, because of the emphasis on modeled and incised decoration including the ubiquitous *adorno* rim decorations.

Taino developments were first noticeable in the eastern part of Hispaniola, more precisely on both sides of the Mona passage between that island and Puerto Rico, where they began to emerge from the previous Ostiones culture just before C.E. 1000. This initial Atajadizo style developed locally before spreading westward, around C.E. 1200, as a fully developed Taino culture to eastern Cuba, then eastward to Puerto Rico, before reaching its easternmost outposts in the Virgin Islands, and as far as Saba, their gateway to the Lesser Antilles.

Population increase and the rise of a complex of the chiefdom type, as encountered by Columbus, as well as diversified art forms of a complexity unknown elsewhere in the islands and eastern Venezuela, are everywhere associated with the phenomenon. Prominent in their art is their unique development of small stone carvings that are free-standing statuettes, all portable in size, characterized by three basic types of object unique to the Greater Antilles: (1) three-pointed stones or trigonoliths; (2) stone collars; and (3) elbow stones. These stone objects may be simple or plain; most are elaboratly carved to represent zoomorphic beings identified with the deities or "zemies" they worshiped.

The only structural remains of the Taino consist of a number of unique ball courts, which are vast open spaces, lined with standing stones or earth embankments, in places associated with causeways or "roads" found throughout Puerto Rico and Hispaniola. A ball game described by the early Spaniards may have been played in these courts, which may also have held religious ceremonies and dances. Some of the stone paraphernalia, the collars especially, may have been used in the ball game, a striking parallel with Mesoamerica. Indeed, Maya influences have often been cited in connection with the introduction of ball courts in the Greater Antilles. Because of the total lack of other evidence to argue for contacts or influences from Mesoamerica in the Greater Antilles, and because of great differences in scale and structure, it may be more reasonable to trace the ball courts to a local development out of earlier plazas or courts simply delineated by dwellings that may have developed since Saladoid times. This would be more consistent with the simple ball game played in the lowlands of South America. It is also interesting to note that the ball game and ball courts never spread to Central America, an area otherwise strongly and unmistakably affected by the Mesoamerican civilizations.

Usually located in the hilly interior valleys of the islands, these ball court sites may have been the seat of major chiefdoms; large ceremonial buildings or chiefly residences of perishable materials may have been built near the courts. Another major evidence of rank among the Taino is the large wooden *duho* seats, hammock-shaped and carved, which survived the period of initial European contact. We can only speculate about the true nature of Taino woodcarving, which must have been quite sophisticated, based on the few remains. The technique of black polished wood carvings is common to many areas of the Caribbean region, including Central America; it has often been claimed to be one of the few genuine circum-Caribbean features.

Although Columbus seems to have encountered full evidence for similar chiefdoms in Jamaica, the incomplete archaeological evidence reveals instead a sub-Taino pattern beginning with what appears to be the initial colonization of that large island by Ostiones peoples (the local Little River culture) after C.E. 500. The later White Marl culture, a typical representative of the Meillac pattern, survived until historic times. This is essentially what happened in Cuba, where the classic Taino culture had simply crossed over the Windward Passage into the eastern part of that island to replace an earlier Ostiones occupation. In central Cuba as in Jamaica, the Meillacoid Bani culture was that of agricultural colonists expanding after C.E. 1200 among existing Archaic groups remembered as Ciboney, who may have survived on the more barren eastern tip of Cuba until European times.

On the outer northern frontier of the Caribbean region, the small Bahamas islands, essentially those offshore from Cuba, are the site of the first European landing in the New World. They were occupied at that time by a sparse population of agricultural natives known as the Lucayo, who were closely related to the people of Cuba. An Ostiones origin, somewhat after C.E. 500, has been suggested for this island population. Beginning after C.E. 900, however, most of the archaeological remains belong to a distinctive culture named after its plain and scarce pottery, the Palmetto, who represented the Lucayo's most direct ancestors from the Greater Antilles, and who may have been attracted to such barren islands by salt quarries and a favorable climate for growing cotton, both important trading commodities, as well as by fishing and shellfish collecting opportunities.

The Lesser Antilles and Trinidad

The climax reached in the Lesser Antilles, from Trinidad to Puerto Rico, by the Barrancoid trends that characterize local ceramic styles around C.E. 500 gave way probably no later than around C.E. 650 to the same phenomenon of stylistic simplification evidenced earlier in the Cuevas culture of the Greater Antilles. So many hallmarks of Saladoid decoration, the white-on-red painted designs in particular, had disappeared that a new classification of a Troumassoid series is warranted. Yet it must be emphasized that no migration from the mainland is evidenced by the remains, and culture changes must be regarded as entirely indigenous to the islands. They are not without parallels, however, with events occurring in Trinidad and the mainland, where Barrancoid peoples had established themselves practically everywhere after C.E. 500. Indeed, the new Troumassoid cultures may still have shared similarities with some of the more simple Barrancoid manifestations of the mainland. No further evolution took place in the Lesser Antilles, however, and this degenerative trend lasted until the very end of prehistoric times, giving rise after C.E. 1100 to the distinctive Suazey culture of the Windward Islands and Barbados.

The general coarseness of Suazey pottery, with its plain and roughly shaped cooking pots often decorated with finger indentations around the rim, contrasts sharply with the earlier ceramic technology of the islands. The style includes finer decorated vessels that hint at the earlier Saladoid and Troumassoid continuities. The Suazey favored areas of mangroves and sand beaches, and their sites consist essentially of scattered shell middens that reveal a diet based on shellfish, fish, and turtle hunting. The presence among the Suazey and their neighbors of the Leeward

Islands of a type of large clay griddle attached to three sturdy legs, which they seem to have invented, and which will always remain unique to the Lesser Antilles, nevertheless indicates the importance of manioc cultivation in their subsistence.

Although no Suazey remains have been encountered in Trinidad or the mainland, it is possible to detect contacts and interaction with their neighbors at both ends of their distribution. For instance, the Suazey's simple art and pottery decoration includes evidence of direct Taino influences, and many carved three-pointed stones have been found in their sites. Likewise, the presence of footed vessels, griddles, and painted Caliviny linear designs may hint at influences from the mainland, especially the widespread Macro-Dabajuroid peoples then expanding all along the Venezuelan coastline from the west and rapidly colonizing offshore islands such as Curacao and Bonaire.

The hope of finding the ancestry of the Island Caribs, also known to the Spanish explorers as Canibales, has been the focus of much of the archaeology of the late Lesser Antilles. Because the Island Caribs are so closely associated with an area of the New World, which after all still bears their name, and because they have long been considered the prototype of the fierce New World native populations that the Europeans encountered and were meant to conquer, it has often been argued that most archaeological remains of the Lesser Antilles might have belonged entirely to them, especially the latest ones, represented by the Suazoid cultures.

Recent research, however, warrants a more sober perspective. Historical documents reveal that, first of all, Island Carib pottery was entirely different from Suazoid ceramics; their cooking pots and pans instead belonged to a widespread tradition of the Guianas from where the Caribs claimed to have recently migrated to the Lesser Antilles. A late migration is thus the best interpretation for their sudden appearance in the Lesser Antilles, from where they were relentlessly raiding Puerto Rico as well as the mainland when encountered by the Spaniards.

CONCLUSIONS

The Caribbean region was the first part of the New World ever to be seen by Europeans, if we exclude the extreme northern edges of the continent. Columbus practically touched on all four corners of the Caribbean Sea between the time of his initial voyage of 1492 and his fourth and last venture of 1503. This included all the islands from Martinique northward to Cuba, which Columbus appears, however, never to have circumnavigated himself. He later explored the coasts of Trinidad and the Gulf of Paria, as well as the entire Caribbean coast of Central America. Later Europeans were soon to intrude on the coast of Venezuela and Colombia, not visited by Columbus, who had also entirely missed the coast of Yucatan and thus failed to reach the Maya. One can only speculate about what a landing by Columbus at Tulum would have meant for the later course of European colonization in the West Indies.

The events that followed upon this European discovery of 1492 belong to another era of world history better left to historians. The Caribbean world described by archaeologists from their incomplete evidence soon came to a sudden end; disease, displacement, forced labor, failure to reproduce, slave raiding, and warfare, all contributed to a collapse everywhere of the native societies and cultures that had evolved there at least since 3000 B.C.E. The case of the Taino is the most dramatic, with a practically total depopulation within a single generation of initial European contact.

But were the greatest achievements of this archaeological world exactly the scene encountered by Columbus and his immediate followers? It cannot be denied that inconsistencies have been pointed out often. The Caribs of the Lesser Antilles, for instance, have left no identifiable prehistoric archaeological remains, and the local Suazey culture must therefore have belonged to an earlier, probably ethnically different, population that shows closer ties to the Greater Antilles than to the Guianas. It is still difficult to correlate with any precision the cultural, linguistic, and ethnic complexity encountered in Venezuela between late prehistoric and early historic times. The most advanced peoples outside Mesoamerica, the Tairona, were never described while still thriving in their masonry towns; likewise many chiefdoms of Central America no longer produced the sophisticated arts of earlier centuries, or they had simply vanished. The Maya, certainly, were no longer anything more than a back province of the Aztec-dominated Mesoamerican civilization, having long lost aspects of their original writing and calendrical systems. We may argue that the Taino of the Greater Antilles had probably already experienced a decline because few of their more distinguished remains, including the ball courts, are included in European descriptions. Almost everywhere on the Caribbean coast of South America by the end of the fifteenth century, the sophisticated and highly decorated pottery styles had given way to plain, coarse, and poorly decorated wares, even in the Lesser Antilles. The situation encountered all around the Caribbean region unmistakably suggests that the world of 1492 was not the time of the climax of any of the most developed cultures or the height of these chiefdom societies. Likewise it may not have been the time of the highest population densities either. The Europeans had missed out by a few centuries a Caribbean world at its most populous and powerful.

It is intriguing to wonder if these general events are in any way related, an issue that raises the question as to whether there ever was in reality anything that could qualify as a true prehistoric Caribbean unity. Even today the vision of a unified Caribbean region remains unfulfilled; this brief and somewhat simplified chronological survey leads to the same conclusions. Yet a pattern emerges which demonstrates that although the existence of a prehistoric Caribbean region is very real, it was never a truly circum-Caribbean phenomenon – that is, a self-contained "cultural" basin.

That communication and contact always existed between neighbors at all times along the Caribbean coastline cannot be doubted, but it existed in a linear rather than circular manner, as if we were to stretch out along a single plane the coastline of the Caribbean sea from the tip of Yucatan to western Cuba, with contact extending from one extreme to the other in a chain-link fashion. There is no evidence that mainland peoples had any knowledge of the islanders, except perhaps for Carib marauders near the Gulf of Paria and adjacent coast of Venezuela; the people of the Greater Antilles, however, may have had some vague ideas about the existence of a distant mainland represented by the hostile Caribs that appeared to them as foreigners from a distant, quasi-mythological land. After all, the fleur-de-lis–shaped gold ornament observed by Columbus around the neck of a chief from Jamaica, so highly suggestive of the winged ornaments favored in Colombia and Central America, must have made its way there from the mainland.

Yet the lack of evidence for direct crossings across the Caribbean Sea is most intriguing in view of the fact that it must have been responsible for the earliest peopling of the islands at a time of primitive technology and sparse population everywhere. There are no recorded historic trans-Caribbean voyages and no archaeological evidence, despite some weak theories favored by Venezuelan archaeologists. The problems raised by the origins of the Meillac culture of Haiti may also be cited in this context. That crossings were feasible has been demonstrated; had they occurred at all, we must conclude that they would have been of practically no consequence to later cultural developments in the islands.

We may wonder whether the people themselves visualized their world as that of an enclosed maritime basin or as the "Center of the World," like on the Mediterranean. No cultures, even the most advanced, have left any cartographic documents or mental maps of their Caribbean territories. We may also question the reality of a common, earlier prehistoric substratum. Certainly the initial peopling of the mainland in distant Paleoindian times was divided between apparently unrelated traditions: the Clovis Tradition, present as far south as Panama, and the Joboid series, also known as the "Andean Biface Horizon," in northern South America and western Venezuela. Neither seem to have contributed directly to the earliest completed peopling of the Caribbean Basin that was first achieved in Archaic times with the first human migration to the Greater Antilles. We may be able to find the best case for regional unity within a pattern of diversity that included shell middens and a subsistence based on fish and shellfish, as well as a technology that somewhat erratically spread flint blades from Belize to Cuba, edge grinders to Panama, Venezuela, Trinidad, Martinique, and Puerto Rico, and shell gouges from Venezuela to Cuba.

Later events belong to the agricultural colonization of the entire area that proceeded between 2000 B.C.E. and, in some places only a few centuries before, the coming of the Spaniards. The basic dichotomy between maize and manioc was established early almost everywhere, except perhaps in Colombia and the Orinoco, but its impact on later developments endured just as the world of the Mediterranean remains divided between Islam and Christianity. Eventually it was the rise and spread of chiefdom societies around the periphery of the Caribbean Sea that most distinguished the prehistory of the area. The phenomenon is not without diversity, especially between the militaristic societies of Central America and the more theocratic groups of South America and the Caribbean. Beyond typology, which may be a simplification, the levels of development varied greatly, especially from an archaeological perspective. Art, monuments, and architecture were variously distributed, as were population densities and wealth; many of these features were distinctively absent from the lowland areas of northern South America, and to a degree from the islands, where, nevertheless, thriving chiefdom societies were observed in early historic times.

Lacking a true maritime orientation, and the technology necessary for its development, peoples around the Caribbean were by necessity bound to their shores and to their island chains, mainly for fishing and limited trading. No true "sea peoples" ever developed to engage in massive long-distance migrations (if we exclude Carib marauders in their attempt to reach the Greater Antilles). The more developed societies of the Tairona and the Cinu of the Magdalena lowlands were not oriented toward the sea in either their economy, subsistence, or settlements. They left no major harbors or ports-of-calls and no evidence for territorial expansion outside their sierras. Even their arts lacked emphasis on maritime themes and iconography. Maritime trade was therefore always limited, and technology prevented the use of ships for the transportation of commodities in bulk. Was there even a need or a demand? Resources and materials may not have been regularly distributed but were nevertheless accessible within a restricted network that cannot qualify as long-distance trade. Luxury items – jade especially – may have been more extensively distributed, and this may have been true of the islands. The Taino in the Greater Antilles were the most significant peoples to contact across the Caribbean; yet we still cannot determine precisely if they ever were aware of the presence of other chiefdom societies on the mainland. There is no record of Taino contact with South America, as opposed to the Caribs' frequent incursions as far away as the coast of the Guianas, and they may have had only a vague idea of quasi-mythical land masses to the southeast through their interaction with their Carib enemies.

Trying to find similarities with the Mediterranean, where cultural developments were allowed to follow their natural course well into their own historic times, may be a hopeless task for archaeologists. Indigenous Caribbean developments were brutally interrupted between 1492 and 1517, and any comparison must be made with an earlier more properly Neolithic Mediterranean, when Egypt was only beginning to radiate toward the eastern coast of the Levant as the earliest and only civilization on its shores. The Maya, with their pyramids and hieroglyphs, are perhaps too facile an analogy to be meaningful, yet they were also beginning to venture timidly along the neighboring littoral while Aztec *pochteca* were establishing trading colonies in lower Central America. We can hardly doubt that the process would have pushed even further southward (if we ignore the illusion of Toltec influences on the Tairona) and that direct contacts with South America and the chiefdoms of the Magdalena, or more likely the sub-Andean chiefdoms of the highland areas, would have been the scene of the first encounter between the Mesoamerican and Andean worlds, an event that would have had revolutionary conse-quences on the future course of social and cultural developments in the New World.

Influences from other geographical as well as cultural areas were in-strumental in the process. Whereas Mesoamerica radiated toward Central America along its Pacific coast, and only marginally on the Caribbean littoral itself, its influence was to become more profound toward North America. In contrast, northern South America displays more originality in the lowlands of Colombia, but further east and throughout the West Indies it was the Amazonian area that ruled supreme and was at the origins of half the area. This part may be qualified as an offshoot of the lowlands, and potential from Mesoamerica, both in Central America and ideally toward Cuba, was left unfulfilled.

Ultimately we may wonder whether the concept of a "world system" would apply to the ancient Caribbean region as revealed in its prehistoric archaeology? Far from seeking the interplay and economic dependencies of a center on its less developed periphery, we may still question what effects such powers as Mesoamerica might have had on its nearest neigh-bors (e.g., Central America) as well as on more distant peoples, all linked through a chainlike relation. The particular geography of the Caribbean region may have served to diffuse these repercussions along its shores not in a circular manner, as a maritime basin would suggest (because the gap to Cuba was never filled), but in a linear way, like a domino effect. Did the collapse of Teotihuacan in the sixth century C.E., or that of the Maya in the tenth century, send shock waves all the way to Hispaniola or Barbados, not to forget Venezuela all along continuous shorelines? Inter-connected disruptions of trade, depopulations, collapses of local chiefly centers, and displacement of populations, all may offer a still largely unexplored and still tentative model for explaining the rise of chiefdoms in the Greater Antilles or the Barrancoid expansion in Venezuela in manners unsuspected before. We are only now beginning to understand this process, and the more precise details of the complex relationships remain to be determined.

BIBLIOGRAPHICAL ESSAY

No single book or article covers the archaeology of the Caribbean region as presented in this chapter. Cultural and political boundaries have im-posed their own divisions on the region that have even affected geographical works, such as *The atlas of Central America and the Caribbean* (Macmillan Publishing Co., New York, 1985). The basic reference for the physical and oceanographic aspects of the Caribbean region remains the volume edited by A. E. M. Nairn and F. G. Stehli, *The ocean basins and margins: Volume 3, The Gulf of Mexico and the Caribbean* (Plenum Press, New York, 1975), whereas E. C. F. Bird and M. L. Schwartz's *The world's coastline* (Van Nostrand Reinhold Company, New York, n.d.) is another valuable reference. The concept of a circum-Caribbean cultural phenomenon, exclusive of Mesoamerica, was developed by the anthropologist Julian Steward as editor of the *Handbook of South American Indians*, published between 1946 and 1950 by the Smithsonian Institution, especially its Volume 4, *The circum-Caribbean tribes* (Washington, 1948), which still remains an essential reference for ethnography and much archaeology as of 1945. The entire *Handbook* was later condensed by Steward and Faron in a single more theoretical work, *Native peoples of South America* (New York, 1959), whose chapter on the circum-Caribbean chiefdoms may be more useful. The same subject also receives more recent coverage in the *Cambridge history of Latin America* (1984), with emphasis on postcontact native populations; the complex subject of primary sources on the early historic native populations of the region are not included in this essay. For archaeology alone, there is no recent detailed summation of New World prehistory that supersedes Gordon Willey's earlier massive two volumes of *An introduction to American archaeology* (Prentice-Hall, Inc., New Jersey, 1971), now obviously in need of revisions after 25 years. The question of the first New World ceramics receives a definitive discussion in the recent volume edited by W. K. Barnett and J. W. Hoopes, *The emergence of pottery* (Smithsonian Institution Press, Washington, 1995), especially the paper by Augusto Oyuela-Caycedo for Colombia, and those of Richard Cooke and John W. Hoopes for Central America.

Because the Mediterranean has been used as a source of analogy in this chapter, and its study also served as a model for its organization, it may be worth citing a useful summary of early Mediterranean prehistory by D. H. Trump, *The prehistory of the Mediterranean* (Yale University Press, New Haven, 1980), or Sarah Arenson's *The encircled sea* (Constable, London, 1990) for the beginnings of the historical period and for many insights on how the region was ever unified in antiquity. The historical period in the perspective of a fundamental unity is discussed by Fernand Braudel in *La Méditerranée: l'espace et l'histoire* (Flammarion,

Paris, 1977). Articles and reports on the Caribbean region outside of Mesoamerica number in the thousands since the turn of the century. These bibliographical notes must therefore be selective; they emphasize recent book-form publications and only a minimum of very recent articles of particular interest published in major journals. Other publications of historical significance are also cited, as are a very few unpublished Ph.D. dissertations. Early historical populations are not the major topic of this chapter, and the complex issue of references to primary sources is not included in these notes.

Major publications on Mesoamerican civilizations are presented in the chapter covering this particular area; it may nevertheless be worth citing a recent volume on the Olmec phenomenon and its influences on Central America, edited by R. J. Sharer and D. C. Grove, *Regional perspective on the Olmec* (Cambridge University Press, New York, 1989), as well as a volume on late Maya maritime trade and navigation edited by Elizabeth P. Benson, *The sea in the pre-Columbian world* (Dumbarton Oaks Research Library and Collections, Washington, D.C., 1977). The frontier area itself, from Copan and the highlands of Guatemala to Honduras, is thoroughly covered in several articles published in a recent volume edited by P. A. Urban and E. M. Shortman, *The southeast Maya periphery* (University of Texas Press, Austin, 1986). There are finally the recent reports on the preceramic sites of Belize by Richard S. McNeish, *Third annual report of the Belize Archaic archaeological reconnaissance* (Phillips Academy, Andover, Mass., 1983) for their significance for the earliest peopling of the West Indies.

Besides Mesoamerica, Central America and especially lower Central America is the most advanced of the entire Caribbean region in the state of archaeolgical research, and for this reason bibliographical notes must be more drastically selective. Several well-illustrated books and edited volumes are devoted to this area as a whole, and to lower Central America in particular. I list them here alphabetically: C. Baudez, *The ancient civilizations of Central America* (London: Barrie and Jenkins, 1976); Elizabeth P. Benson, *Between continents/Between seas: Pre-Columbian art of Costa Rica* (N. H. Abrams, New York, 1981); F. W. Lange and D. Stone (eds.), *The archaeology of lower Central America* (University of New Mexico Press, 1984); Doris Stone, *Pre-Columbian man finds Central America: The archaeological bridge* (Mass.: Peabody Museum Press, 1972). On the Preceramic Period of Panama, recent research is presented in Olga Linares and Anthony J. Ranere (eds.), *Adaptive radiations in prehis-*

toric Panama (Peabody Museum Monograph 5, Harvard University, Cambridge, 1980). The rise and nature of Central American chiefdoms is fully discussed in F. Lange (ed.), *Wealth and hierarchy in the Intermediate area* (Dumbarton Oaks Research Library and Collection, Wash., 1992), as well as in several papers published in *Chiefdom in the Americas*, edited by R. D. Drennan and Carlos A. Uribe (University Press of the America, New York, 1987). For more details on the elaborate Coclé culture, one has to turn to Samuel Lothrop's original description of his excavations at Sitio Conte in *Coclé: An archaeological study of Central Panama* (Parts 1 and 2, Memoirs of the Peabody Museum of Archaeology and Ethnology 7–8, Harvard University, Cambridge, 1937 and 1942). The anthropologist Mary Helms has written extensively on the ethnohistory and native populations, especially in her book *Ancient Panama: Chiefs in search of power* (University of Texas Press, Austin, 1979).

In the context of Atlantic or Caribbean Colombia, for many years the basic reference to the complex archaeology of Colombia was the book by Gerardo Reichel-Dolmatoff, *Colombia* (Ancient Peoples and Places, Praeger Publisher, New York, 1965); an updated revised edition of the book, *Arqueologia de Colombia: un texto introduciones* (Funbotanica, Bogotá, 1985) seems to have been published only in Spanish. For want of more varied sources, one may be reluctantly tempted to cite a recent book by Sam Enslow, *The art of prehispanic Colombia: An illustrated cultural and historical survey* (McFarland and Co. Inc, Publishers, London, 1990), for a useful comprehensive overview, if readers ignore the author's obsession with transoceanic contacts and other esoteric theories! More reliable is Armand J. Labbé's *Colombia before Columbus: The people, the culture, and ceramic art of prehispanic Colombia* (Santa Ana, Cal.: Americas Foundation and Bowers Museum, 1986). The intriguing problem of the earliest ceramics perhaps in the entire New World deserves special attention; original publications on the Puerto Hormiga and related early styles are those of Reichel-Dolmatoff, "Excavaciones arqueologicas en Puerto Hormiga, Departamento de Bolívar," *Publicaciones de la Universidad de los Andes, Antropologia 2* (Bogotá, 1965); and *Monsu: un sitio arqueologico* (Biblioteca Banco Popular, Bogotá, 1985). The famous Tairona culture is fully described in an early publication by Alden Mason, *Archaeology of Santa Marta, Colombia* (Anthropological Papers, Vol. 20, Nos. 1–3, Filed Museum of Natural History, Chicago, 1931–1939), as well as several papers by Reichel-Dolmatoff published in Colombian periodicals. More recent papers can also be found in the Boletins series published by the Museo del Oro in Bogotá.

Venezuela has a long history of research by American archaeologists. A basic reference, albeit now somewhat out of date, is the two-volume technical report by Jose Cruxent and Irving Rouse, *An archaeological chronology of Venezuela* (Social Science Monographs, Pan American Union, Washington, D.C., 1958); a later updated summary version, *Venezuelan archaeology* (Yale University Caribbean Series, No. 6, New Haven, 1964), was also published by Rouse and Cruxent. A different theoretical perspective is offered by Mario Sanoja and Iraida Vargas, *Antiguas Formaciones y Modos de Produccion Venezolanos* (Monte Alban Editores, Caracas, 1978), who emphasize Barrancoid and Saladoid occupations of eastern Venezuela and the preceramic period, as well as by Sanoja in his monograph on the Barrancoid series, *Las Culturas Formativas del Oriente de Venezuela: la tradicion Barrancas del Bajo Orinococ* (Biblioteca de la Academia Nacional de la Historia, Caracas, 1979). A more recent book by Anna Roosevelt on her middle Orinoco research, *Parmana: Prehistoric maize and manioc subsistence along the Amazon and Orinoco* (Academic Press, New York 1980), is also relevent to the region. I must also include Jose Oliver's recent Ph.D. dissertation, *The archaeological, linguistic, and ethnohistorical evidence for the expansion of Arawakan into northwestern Venezuela and northeastern Colombia* (University of Illinois, Urbana, 1989), which has contributed significant new ideas about the late prehistoric dynamics of the entire coastline. Recent views on the possibility of cultural contact across the Caribbean Sea from Venezuela are discussed in a brief publication edited by Erika Wagner, *Relaciones Prehispanicas de Venezuela* (Acta Cientifica Venezolano, Caracas, 1984).

The West Indies area is represented by a scattering of short publications that go back to the turn of the century. These are found in a very recent bibliographical essay published by John M. Weeks and Peter J. Ferbel, *Ancient Caribbean* (Garland Publishing Inc., New York, 1994), which suffers from poor organization and lacks authoritative editorship but remains useful for the Greater Antilles, especially Cuba. The most recent summary of the entire area, with special emphasis on the Greater Antilles, is still Irving Rouse's *The Taino: Rise and decline of the people who greeted Columbus* (Yale University Press, New Haven, 1992). The recent volume *Taino: Pre-Columbian art and culture from the Caribbean* (The Monacelli Press, 1997) is so far the best illustrated account of this intriguing art. A simulation study of the feasibility of cross-Caribbean human passage to explain the original peopling of the Caribbean islands from various points of its shores is the subject of a recent unpublished Ph.D. dissertation by Richard T. Callaghan, *Mainland origins of the preceramic cultures of the Greater Antilles* (University of Calgary, 1990). The period of agricultural colonization is covered in several papers edited by Peter E. Siegel, in *Early ceramic population lifeways and adaptive strategies in the Caribbean* (BAR International Series 506, Oxford, 1989). From a historical perspective, works by Fewkes on the Dominican Republic and the Lesser Antilles, published by the Smithsonian Institution, are still useful references. Numerous important papers and reports have been published over the years in the series *Yale University Publications in Anthropology*, and more recently works by Ricardo Alegria *Ball courts and ceremonial plazas in the West Indies* (No. 79, New Haven, 1983), and by Rouse and Alegria, *Excavations at Maria e la Cruz Cave and Hacienda Grande Village site, Loiza, Puerto Rico* (No. 80, New Haven, 1990). Various series and collections of the Museo del Hombre Dominicano, especially their Boletin series, include many significant reports and monographs, among which the most representative are those of Marcio Veloz Maggiolo, *Las Sociedades arcaicas de Santo Domingo* (Serie Investigaciones Antropologicas, No. 12, Santo Domingo, 1980), and Veloz Maggiolo, Ortega, and Caba Fuentes, *Los Modos de vida Meillacoides y sus posibles origines* (Santo Domingo, 1981). The Lesser Antilles are a major subject of the sixteen published proceedings of Caribbean archaeological congresses held biannually since 1961; their entire contents are listed in the *Ancient Caribbean* volume cited earlier. Accounts of the Taino include those of Sven Loven, *Origin of the Tainan culture, West Indies* (Goteborg, 1935), and more recently, Samuel N. Wilson *Hispaniola: Caribbean chiefdoms in the age of Columbus* (University of Alabama Press: Tuscalosa, 1990). The Bahamas have received a theoretically and methodologically sophisticated treatment in a provocative book by William F. Keegan, *The people who discovered Columbus: The prehistory of the Bahamas* (University Press of Florida, Gainesville, 1992). The archaeology of the Lesser Antilles is still represented by a multitude of journal articles or proceedings papers that go back to the turn of the century. It may be worth citing for its influence on later work a short report by Ripley and Adelaide K. Bullen, two archaeologists closely associated with the archaeology of the Lesser Antilles in the 1960s and 1970s, on their work on Grenada, authored by Ripley Bullen, *The archaeology of Grenada, West Indies* (Gainesville, 1964).

Recent books include a detailed account of the late prehistory of the Leeward Islands as seen from the small Dutch island of Saba by Corinne L. Hofman, *In search of the native population of pre-Columbian Saba* (Part I, Leiden 1992); recent work on Montserrat coauthored variously by investigators David Watters, James Petersen, John Crock, and their colleagues, in several recent issues of the *Annals of Carnegie Museum* (Pittsburgh,) and an overview of the archaeology of Barbados by Peter L. Drewett and colleagues, *Prehistoric Barbados* (London, 1991). The most recent account of the Lesser Antilles for nonspecialists is found in Samuel M. Wilson's (ed.), *The indigenous people of the Caribbean* (University Press of Florida, Gainesville, 1997).

9

PREHISTORY OF THE SOUTHERN CONE

MARIO A. RIVERA[1]

The Southern Cone is the great triangular landmass extending from the edges of the Central Andean high plateaus southward to Tierra del Fuego (see Map 9.1). Under familiar social-evolutionist assumptions, this vast space has often been called "marginal" because nearly all of it lay outside the political realm of the Inka and because, in general, its native societies operated with simple technologies and small populations. In suggesting more nuanced images, we differentiate among five component spaces. First, at the northern edge of this macroregion, we distinguish a region that we call the South-Central Andes. It comprises northern Chile, northwestern Argentina, and part of southern Bolivia. Here social complexity took shape relatively early (1500 B.C.E.–C.E. 1450), and here too Inka rule eventually penetrated. It makes sense to consider the South-Central Andes's prehistory over the long term as dynamically linked with Andean developments proper. On the other hand, groups living in the huge spaces south and east of the South-Central Andes experienced different processes and produced social forms fundamentally dissimilar from those of the Andes. These are the peoples to which the "marginal" rubric has most stubbornly adhered. They inhabited four spatial units comprising the Southern Cone proper: the Chaco, the Pampas, Araucania, and Patagonia.

The purpose of this work is to afford a prehistoric vision of the peoples of these territories, starting from the moment when their societies began to build social complexity by using a technology that allowed domestication of the environment. In absolute chronological terms, this includes a period from 1000 B.C.E. up to the fifteenth century C.E. The extreme environmental diversity of the Southern Cone – which includes every-

---

[1] Translation by Frank Salomon.

734

Archaeological Regions of the
Southern Cone

1. Arid North Chile
2. Semi-Arid North Chile
3. Central Chile
4. Southwest Bolivia
5. Northwest Argentina
6. Araucania
7. Pampas
8. Chaco
9. Patagonia
10. Chilean Fjords
    and Channels
11. Tierra del Fuego

South-
Central
Andes

Chaco

Araucania

Pampas

PACIFIC
OCEAN

ATLANTIC
OCEAN

Patagonia

N

0   400 mi
0   400 km

Map 9.1

thing from high deserts to forested fjords – and the far-from-obvious relations between its environments and cultural processes, make a unitary treatment inappropriate. The processes that led to agriculture and animal domestication in the South-Central Andes occurred differently or not at all in the rest of the Southern Cone. Ceramic and copper metalwork developed briskly in some of its areas, but in Patagonia they were unknown. Copper metallurgy, which in the arid north of Chile took shape about as early as it did in the Old World (more than 1,000 years B.C.E.), arose there not out of any obvious adaptive process but as part of a sumptuary complex reinforcing rituals. In some cases although people knew of these techniques and could have practiced them, their adaptations did not require incorporating them. Other prehistoric processes were no less uneven.

Broadly speaking, the present chapter divides the Southern Cone regionally. But the regionally separate sections share a common argument against the traditional usage of "marginality." The South-Central Andes housed a wide spectrum of cultures that built up complex structures over long periods of development. These societies' early phases were created by hunters and gatherers, both high-Andean and coastal, whose cultures gradually came to reflect the foreign customs and values that successively affected the area. These influences arrived via direct contacts, group migrations, and cultural diffusion. The most important early ones came from the tropical forests, and later ones from the high Andes. The latter eventually gave the South-Central Andes their predominantly Andean cultural profile. But to treat it as a fringe of the Andean civilization is a half-portrayal of its prehistoric synthetic process.

Farther south the societies that inhabited Araucania, the Pampas, and Patagonia have generally been considered as simpler societies, shaped amid a marginality that approached actual isolation. At least where the southernmost members of this set are concerned, there is room for doubt about the term "marginal." It misleadingly implies that the periphery generates cultures that are deficient or declining versions of those nearer to civilizational centers. Luis A. Orquera holds to the contrary that Fuegian and Patagonian prehistoric groups had reached what could be called a successful equilibrium with their environments "with slow drift toward greater emphasis on resources that provided equivalent return for least effort." The strength of this adaptation becomes clear when one notes evidence that "the high productivity of the Fuegian and southwestern Magellanic environment permitted a population density some thirty

Table 9.1. *Chronological Chart for Southern Cone*

Central Andean Periods	Southern Cone Periods	South-Central Andes	Chaco	Pampas	Araucania	Patagonia	Time
Late Horizon	Late	Inka Inka			Neo-Araucanian (Valdivia)	Ona/Tehuelche/Alakaluf/Yahgan	1400
Late Intermediate	Late — I N T E R M E D I A T E	Gentilar San Miguel Diaguita (Regional Development)	Riberenos Plasticos				1200
			Las Mercedes		Vergel		1000
Middle Horizon	Middle	Maytas Animas Chiribaya			Paleo-Araucanian (Pitren)	Magellan V/Patagonian II	800
		Alto Ramirez III — San Pedro Atacama II					600
		Cabuza				Classic Patagonian	400
Early Intermediate	Early — A T E	San Pedro Atacama I El Molle				North Patagonian II	200
Early Horizon							0
			San Francisco				200
		Alto Ramirez II		North-Patagonian III			400
		Alto Ramirez I					600
Initial Period	Transition II	Chinchorro III				Proto-Patagonian	800
						Shell Knife Culture	1000

times higher than recorded on the Pampas and continental Patagonia prior to Araucanian penetration."[2] Moreover the basic coastal adaptation was reached rapidly, as early as 5000 B.C.E. Only from the viewpoint of intruders or latecomers does this formation need to be considered "marginal."

The concept of marginality also misleads insofar as it implies isolation. It is important to appreciate factors connecting each area with others across the Southern Cone. Demographic dynamics and migrations help explain some prehistoric developments. The early inhabitants of Patagonia, arriving probably during later Paleoindian times (see Chap. 3), were succeeded many times over by other newcomers. The recent population of hunters that travelers of the sixteenth century observed in southern mainland Patagonia were the latest of many immigrant waves. The more recent movements by the Chilean Mapuche Araucanians, who drove eastward into the Pampas' southern territory, and into northern Patagonia, well into the eighteenth century and later (see Chap. 16), constitute extensions of these continual movements and displacements of people over enormous spaces. Similarly it is a mistake to assume that areas we know poorly are poorly known because they were "marginal." The intermediate areas between high Andean lands and the tropical lowlands (borderlands between Bolivia and Paraguay in modern times), forming the region of the Chaco, characterized by semisedentary lifeways, are a case in point. Although the scarcity of archaeological information about its peoples has exaggerated images of social simplicity, the Chaco area seems to have been a transitional area, over which most of these movements passed. Its importance in the tracing of cultural movements derives from its closeness to the Amazon Basin, one of the main centers of early dispersion of people and cultural traits.

Finally, although the Southern Cone is in some respects a residual category, in other respects it has culturally unifying attributes of its own. The knowledge that enabled people to deal with its generally harsh environments included specific technologies shared among neighboring groups. At the most general level, the Southern Cone has common cultural features from the Chaco to Patagonia, and from late prehispanic to recent times. If there is within it a major discontinuity, it is the one

[2] Luis A. Orquera, "Advances in the archaeology of the Pampas and Patagonia," *Journal of World Prehistory* 1 (1987), 405.

between the South-Central Andes and the four regions of the Southern Cone proper.

THE SOUTH-CENTRAL ANDES

Isaiah Bowman, a modern student of Chile's arid north, wrote:

On my first pack-train journey into northern Chile where the nitrate desert begins I was delighted to find all my expectations of desert scenery realized. For the first fifty miles there was but a single spot where a natural growth of green could be seen from the trail and but one other where there was any green growth at all, and that beside a desert well about which were clustered a few low huts. All the rest was naked rock and sand, brown and yellow in color yet appearing stark and colorless in tone in the midday sun when the whole landscape is over-lighted; glowing with color as the sun declines and the shadows of the ravines come out.[3]

Partly because this extremely arid landscape offers spectacularly favorable material preservation conditions, we have a relatively complete and finely calibrated 10,000-year chronological sequence.

The Chilean north shows three major cultural traditions. They are:

1. Pacific littoral hunters and gathering cultures;
2. Chinchorro, a unique early culture of probable tropical forest or lowland origin; and
3. Andean cultures originating in the high plains of Bolivia.

Each of these traditions has characteristics tending to create internal diversity, especially as they developed regionally. Leaving aside precer-amic hunter-gatherers (who are treated in Chap. 3), we begin with the later phases of Chinchorro (Transition Period II). This culture displays decisive cultural changes, such as the beginnings of agriculture, metal-lurgy, and pottery. Chinchorro is notable for a mortuary complex that involved making elaborately dressed and painted mummies. Chinchorro's transition to complexity ran from about 1,500 to 500 B.C.E. In discussing post-Chinchorro times we periodize in a fashion keyed to the well-known "Horizon"/"Intermediate" system elaborated by Rowe, Willey, Lum-breras, and others for the Peruvian Andes. This scheme's cardinal periods are the Early, Middle, and Late Horizons. The Early Horizon consists

[3] *Desert trails of Atacama* (New York, 1924), 13.

chiefly of the Chavín development (Chap. 5), the Middle Horizon equated with Tiwanaku and Wari (Chap. 6), and the Late with Inka (Chap. 10). The intervals known as the Middle Horizon and Late Horizon in Peru are respectively termed the Middle Intermediate and Late Periods in the northern Chilean sequence. The Chilean periodization used here is essentially chronological, and it is based on the archaeology of the Azapa Valley, located in Arica.

Archaeological remains in the deserts of northern Chile suggest the introduction of ceramics toward the end of the Archaic stage as the culmination of a process that also included domestication of several animals (llamas [*Lama glama*], alpacas [*Lama pacos*], and guinea pigs [*Cavia porcellus*]) and plants including *quinua* (*Chenopodium quinoa*), squashes (*Lagenaria siceraria*), pumpkins (*Cucurbita moschata, Cucurbita maxima*), cotton (*Gossypium barbadense*), and possibly maize (*Zea mays*). These occur in deposits overlying those of the ancient hunters.

The Andean or "altiplanic" tradition radiating from the high plateaus of Bolivia down the western parapets of the Andes appeared after C.E. 1000. It brought a group of traits in sharp contrast to the lowland-influenced late Chinchorro. The altiplanic tradition reflected the arrival of an early (pre-Pukara and pre-Tiwanaku) Andean influence on the coast, initiating Formative development. The Formative culminates in a process of sedentarization and the building of a series of villages. Sites like Alto Ramírez and Caserones demonstrate the achievement of economies that produced surpluses beyond subsistence.

Within the Andean tradition, much of the development at Alto Ramírez occurred during the early part of the Early Intermediate (600 B.C.E.–C.E. 500). It brought a new sociopolitical system, with an economy based on reciprocity and complementarity. Rationally managed surplus and the adoption of new agricultural and livestock techniques allowed the population to grow. This brought demographic stabilization, and with it, villages that held irrigated fields. Their leading products were *quinua*, maize, hot peppers, beans (*Phaseolus vulgaris*), squashes, and gourds. This set of products, together with access to bird-guano fertilizer and to salt, made up a complement to highland products like camelid wool, meat, leather, and fat, as well as durable foods like *quinua* grain and freeze-dried potatoes. The newer technology included rectangular-platform blowguns with many long darts to improve hunting, and improved metalwork, especially gold and silver ornaments, which reinforced ritual prestige. Material products included double-handled spoons; equipment for taking hallucinogenic snuff such as tablets, spatulas, sniffing tubes, and little boxes; artfully made basketry; ceramics; camelid-wool textiles with techniques including tapestry and *kelim* (also called slit tapestry) in a complex variety of colors and designs. A cult of human sacrifice is attested by trophy heads and sacrificing axes in treasures buried with the dead. Burials were usually in small mounds.

Exchange and complementarity apparently took place within a unified ideological frame, whose most important nodes were the urban centers around Lake Titicaca up on the high plains. These developments gave rise to a sociopolitical and economic organization whose climax was the expansion of the Tiwanaku state in the Middle Horizon contemporaneous with the Chilean Middle Intermediate Period (C.E. 500–900). Tiwanaku political unification also seems, with some variation, to have covered all the north of Chile, the Argentinian northwest, and southern Peru. At Azapa (a valley in Arica, northern Chile) the beginnings of Tiwanaku can be seen in the Cabuza Phase (C.E. 300–700), although we do not know what the social link between highland state and coastal valleys was. The Maytas Phase (C.E. 700–1000) and, with lesser connection, the Chiribaya Phase, can be taken as regional variants of Tiwanaku.

The Andean Late Intermediate Period (C.E. 900–1350) corresponds to a northern Chilean period of Regional Development. It was characterized by ethnic groups that maintained contact with the highlands, especially economic contacts contributing to a system of resource complementarity. The end of the Tiwanaku Horizon produced a redistribution of peoples throughout the Andean south. Groups identified with black-on-red decorated ceramics occupied the upper part of the western valleys, the *precordillera* or foothill ranges near the Pacific, and the high plains. Meanwhile in the lower valleys and along the shore, groups that made polychrome ceramics predominated. The continual movement of peoples from the high plains down into the lowlands forced many local groups to defend their lands by building the kind of fortresses known (from a Quechua word) as *pukaras*. The best-known examples of Regional Development cultures are San Miguel, Gentilar, and Pocoma, all showing pre-Tiwanaku influences as well as locally developing styles. San Miguel (C.E. 1000) is typified by ceramic large globular vases that have narrow necks and vertical handles and bear geometrical decoration in black or red over white. Gentilar (C.E. 1350) displays a ceramic with more elaborate finishes and pitchers with everted necks adorned in black and white designs over red. Pocoma style is transitional, with its designs distributed in soft red color-panels, separated by vertical lines. The Chilpe style is contemporaneous with Gentilar. It represents a Qulla expansion (Qulla, also called Qolla, and Colla, being one of the Aymara polities growing on the Lake Titicaca shore), and it initiates the "Aymarization" of the seaward western valleys.

Around C.E. 1450 Inka influences began to overlay these diverse regional developments. The area of Azapa came directly under Inka hegemony. Many sites show the force of state-controlled economy: waystations, forts, segments of Inka roadway, cemeteries, and mines.

In the oasis region of the Atacama desert, the best sequence is the one from San Pedro de Atacama. Ceramic-making agricultural groups appear around C.E. 800, to develop fully at dates close to the European invasion. This part of Atacama prehistory has been divided into an Early Intermediate Period (500 B.C.E.–C.E. 400), a Middle Period (C.E. 400–1000), a Late Intermediate Period (C.E. 1000–1470), and a Late Period (C.E. 1470–1535).

During the Early Intermediate, at least three demographic currents contributed to the making of the early Atacameño (Atacames) culture (also called San Pedro I). The first came from the high plateaus of the southern Andes, just south of Lake Titicaca. It brought a polished red and gray ceramic, as well as advanced techniques in agriculture and camelid pastoralism. It introduced an urbanizing trend, to judge from the first villages of the oases of Tulor, Calar, Chiu-Chiu 200, and Guatacondo. A second current came from tropical forests on the far side of the Andes. It is traceable in modeled ceramics with incised and impressed designs, ceramic urns, clay pipes, lip plug ornaments (labrets, *tembetá*), and a hallucinogen complex. These movements from the tropical forest seem to make up a backwash from earlier waves that had originated the Chinchorro tradition of the farther north coast. A third current was made up of the descendants of the ancient hunter-gatherers.

The Middle Period, or San Pedro II Phase, displayed intensively developing agriculture based on artificial irrigation, which allowed populations to grow even with the limits of the oasis situation. During this same period caravan traffic to the coast, the highlands, the Titicaca Basin, and the Argentinian northwest throve. The typical ceramic of the period is burnished black. From C.E. 600 onward Tiwanaku influence on San Pedro de Atacama is notable in a series of luxury goods, such as textiles, carved Andean-style wooden beakers (for formal drinking), gold beakers, engraved bones, and hallucinogenic snuffing gear. These objects sometimes have figurative designs. Iconography emphasized the figure of the sacrificer, winged figures, felines, and condors. Toward the end of the period, Tiwanaku influence faded. An apparent crisis produced a re-regionalization, which brought declining and finally mediocre technical work.

The Late Period is characterized by the rise of chiefdoms and independent kingdoms, just as in the highland regions. Political frictions obliged Atacama groups to build a line of fortresses in the area of highland-desert contact and along the Loa River. Ceramic of this period shows a thick red slip, usually unpolished and of poorer quality than the burnished blackware. During this period people from Atacama won back control of some of the desert caravan circuits. The most important Inka sites in the region are Catarpe and Peine, on the road that connected Cusco (Cuzco) with central Chile.

The semiarid mid-north of Chile to the south of the Atacama Desert, as opposed to the true desert of the far north, is a region crossed by transverse (east–west) river valleys. It makes up a transition from the extremely dry region where only oases, narrow riverbanks, the well-watered lands of central Chile, and ocean coves support life. This transitional band is limited by the Andean mountain wall on the east and the Pacific on the west.

Within it, ancient hunting societies yielded to formative developments around C.E. o. Early manifestations of the developments make up the El Molle complex (C.E. 50–700), which centered for the most part around the northerly Salado River and the southerly Choapa Valley. It was characterized by some tropical forest elements such as lip plugs and *cachimbas*, or stone pipes in the shape of an inverted T. Technology included copperwork and, rarely, gold or silver, as well as worked shell and bone, basketry, cotton cloth, and especially a distinctive style in ceramic and rock art. The diagnostic ceramic style shows cylindrical beakers, globular forms, and basins, together with less common forms such as double-spouted jars with a bridge handle. There are animal and human likenesses of high technical quality. Sophisticated decorations were commonly made with incised or engraved fields, and less commonly with negative painting, postfire painting, smoking, and double firing.

In the last few years studies have increasingly addressed work sites. The results identify the villages as farming-herding settlements sharing a common plan despite their varied settings. The villages used their areas in diversified ways, but always with an emphasis on herding.

As farmers they developed irrigation techniques that improved production of cultigens such as maize, beans, large squash, and probably cotton and *quinua*. Blades of shovels and stone hoes are evidence of agricultural work. Large amounts of camelid bones indicate herding. Agropastoralists filled out their diets by collecting wild fruits such as carob (*Prosopis dulcis*), carbonillo (*Cordia decandra*), and chañar (*Gourlica decorticans*). The distribution of Molle sites tends to follow interfluves with favorable herding conditions. But there are also sites in valleys, possibly housing important enclaves of stable population able to intensify agriculture. Following the distribution from north to south, a "River Huasco" phase has been defined for the north. The burials there are generally in mounds, and the ceramic is simple and almost unadorned. A contemporary phase seems to have grown farther south, in the Elqui-Limarí interfluve, with more complex burial forms in tumuli and common graves. These same sites show a more sophisticated ceramic, including the most complex of the known Molle techniques. Still farther south this complex came into contact with the prehistoric peoples of central Chile. The Molle population disappeared abruptly toward C.E. 700, replaced by the first indications of the Diaguita.

Diaguita emergence is important because the Diaguita were to become a major cultural group that alone dominated the semiarid northern region for over 700 years. Their distinctive organization and ethnic separateness outlasted Inka dominance and even endured Spanish intervention (see Chap. 14). The Diaguita were sometimes referred to as a "nation" in colonial times. Las Animas, which follows Molle, is the beginning of the Diaguita sequence. Las Animas forms part of what is called the Middle Agro-ceramic (*agroalfarero*) Period (C.E. 800–1200) in the semiarid north from the Copiapó Valley to the Limarí. Although the type site is located in the Elqui Valley near the city of La Serena, a much larger area can be characterized by the same traits. Las Animas is typified by herding societies that moved between coastal and up-valley sites. The herders also farmed maize, exploited carob and *chañar* forests, ate camelid meat, and took both shellfish and fish from the ocean. Their ceramics show zoomorphic decorations, or red-line decoration on white, or simple red slip on bowls of conic-trunk shape. A slightly different kind of ceramic abounds in subglobular forms, usually without slip, and with an application of red, white, and black paints made of specularite. Paint was applied right over the paste, in a pattern of linear designs. Las Animas made increased use of copper in tools but made little use of silver. Its crafts also included finely polished bone spatulas and wooden tubes much like those used in the northern Chilean hallucinogenic kit. From cemeteries it is possible to detect a complicated funeral rite including llama sacrifices. At the site of Plaza de Coquimbo, llamas have been made to embrace the dead with their front legs, surely a gesture of magico-religious sentiment.

Diaguita culture suffuses the period of agro-ceramic development through the Late Period of this region. It was defined in the 1950s by Francisco Cornely using postulates first suggested by Ricardo Latcham and filled out by evidence from the many excavations in Atacama and Coquimbo. The result of these researches allowed Cornely to propose a sequence based on a typology of burials and of ceramics. He distinguished three periods: Archaic, Transitional, and Classical. Recent studies have redefined this periodization by including data from habitation sites. The new periodization includes a phase called Diaguita I or Initial, which starts where the Animas Phase ends; Diaguita II Phase, corresponding to Cornely's Classical; and Diaguita III, which coincides with the era of Inka influences and acculturation.

It is important to appreciate that this acculturation did not occur farther north, even though in these more northerly zones the native peoples faced a more complete Inka organization of power. Although the Diaguita population put up stiff resistance to Inka conquest, its political-administrative arrangements were modified in the direction of Inka norms. The Diaguitas had devised a traditional system of dual chiefdoms controlling each valley. These organizations with their double lordships constituted through alliance one unitary system along the coast, and a separate system along the upper and middle parts of the respective river valleys. The Inka invasion brought a forcible imposition of a different system. One of the Inka novelties was the designation of *kuraka*s or local chiefs (as they were called in Quechua) representing Inka central administration. Another was the transporting of Diaguita people to central Chile and to Argentina, apparently in fulfillment of *mit'a* (cyclical labor obligations).

The Diaguita were basically agropastoralists. As agriculturalists they cultivated maize, beans, potatoes, quinoa, large squash, and (especially in the Copiapó and Huasco valleys) cotton. They preferred to dwell in the fertile alluvial valleys, their upper reaches, and stretches along the coast. As herders they moved between the lower valleys and the montane high valleys, also occupying the interfluves. In the Late Period, they increasingly became armed agropastoralists and produced settlements of two types related to political conditions. Some sites were peacetime settlements situated along the richly cultivable alluvial terraces. Others were fortified establishments set up at strategic but hard-to-reach locations, suitable for territorial defense. Diaguita weaponry commonly included long lances, darts, bows and arrows, slings, clubs, shields, leather breastplates, and heavy rocks to roll down on the foe.

The absence of a complex administrative organization, a servile class, and a professional army indicate that the Diaguita "nation" did not undergo state centralization. The political structure was rather a federation of lordships. This mechanism retained potential for resistance under Inka rule, and at various moments during the Spanish conquest, various Diaguita lordships succeeded in organizing jointly to meet the foreign menace. They even chose a single war commander in 1541, when Michimalonco sought to beat back Spanish incursions led by Pedro de Valdivia.

THE CHACO

The Chaco region comprises territories in northeastern Argentina (known as the Central Chaco), along with parts of eastern Bolivia and western Paraguay (known as the Boreal or Southern Chaco). It makes up a huge ecological unit throughout which similar adaptive processes took place. The environmental conditions are those of a vast alluvial plain, whose landscape alters dramatically between wet and dry seasons. The major rivers that cut across the area are the Pilcomayo and the Bermejo. They flow from the Andes into the Paraguay River, which runs from north to south. The Paraguay River also divides the savannah landscape of the east from the true Chaco to the west. Alcides D'Orbigny, who traveled the area between 1827 and 1830, described it as a land of forced mobility, where people had no choice but to move periodically as the dust of the dry season and the mud of the rains drove them.

To some degree recent Chaco material culture is of ethnoarchaeological relevance. As in the remote past, wild food plants such as carob seeds and palm fruits were of primary importance. Carob, which contains sugar, proteins, and starch, was used to make a paste of ground flour mixed with water, or it was enjoyed as a drink. Palms (*Copernicia australis, Copernicia alba, Bactris gasipaes*) furnished many foodstuffs; the heart, shoots, and seeds were eaten, and the sap was brewed into a fermented beverage. Other wild products include honey, fruits, seeds, and tubers. Groups living near the rivers fished with nets, spears, and bows and arrows. Wild animals such as peccaries (*Pecari tajacu, Tayassu pecari*), marsh deer (*Dorcelaphus dichotomus*), and ostrich-like rheas (*Rhea americana*) were also hunted. Soon after the Europeans' arrival, most Chacoan peoples acquired horses, and with them, powerful hunting techniques eventually including firearms.

According to Willey, nearly all Chaco populations practiced some agriculture by C.E. 1800 if not earlier. Harvests included maize, sweet manioc (*Manihot esculenta*), beans, tobacco (*Nicotiana tabacum*), and cotton. Farming must have been difficult in the face of seasonally dry soil, high concentration of clay, floods, and animal damage by birds and peccaries. We hardly can guess the real subsistence value of agriculture to Chaco natives, but it never displaced gathering.

Chaco dwellers built small circular or oval houses made of poles and covered with palm leaf thatch. In some cases, large communal houses were built the same way. Dwellings were usually arranged in a semicircular shape, open on one side, facing a central plaza. The Chaco dwellers made textiles by twining fibers from cotton and wild plants, as well as net bags and rush mats. Basketry, however, was not known to all of them, and according to Métraux, it was introduced by groups of Amazonian origin. Gourds, some engraved, served as containers.

Because warfare was a main concern, weapons like bows and arrows, spears, and clubs, mostly made of wood, were quite common. Among the historic Tobas, *bolas* (stones connected by cords, thrown to entangle and fell prey or the enemy) were a typical weapon. Stone was imported for some special purposes, like the making of ground stone axes. Metallurgy was unknown before the Spanish invasion. But pottery made by coiling was widespread among all Chaco people. Shapes included water jars with narrow necks, cooking pots, and bowls, and occasionally urns. Generally, pottery of the Chaco is plain, but there are some instances of decoration either with paint, fingernail incision, or cord impression, the last being the most characteristic all over the Chaco. Individual cords were pressed into the fresh unfired clay surface. The most distinctive pottery of this type is that of recent Mbayá potters, who also painted the zones between cord-impressed lines with red and black pigments.

Recent material culture of ethnographically known Chaco peoples featured featherwork in personal adornments. For clothes, especially hot-weather garments, the most common material was *caraguatá* (a silky fiber from the agave-like plant *Bromelia argentina*). On colder days Chaco-dwellers wore robes of leather. In some places, for example among the Chané, old women in recent times still used the Guaraní-style *tipoy* (sleeveless tunic), while men used *tembetá* labrets in their lips.

In general, Chaco archaeological data remains limited. Almost nothing is known from the preceramic. Most ceramic stages are known from sites located in the southwestern Chaco, close to Salta, Jujuy, and Santiago del Estero provinces in Argentina. In the Bermejo drainage, particularly along old watercourses, Fock has located several ceramic sites with peculiar burial types. In Lomas de Olmedo, a site located near Embarcación in Salta's upper Bermejo, Fock found urn burials, with incised, punctated, and cord-impressed necks, and rounded-base pottery. This style resembles the Mbayá ceramics, particularly the single-line impressions. But Lomas de Olmedo also shows a pottery tradition related to the South Andean highlands, especially in pots with flat bases and handles.

This combination of local with Andean-derived features is common to many Chaco sites. Las Mercedes (Salta, Argentina) is the most characteristic style in this respect. R. Gómez, in associating its ceramics with settlement patterns, concludes that Las Mercedes shares features of the Andean cultural tradition with traits coming from the tropical lowlands.

A related complex is San Francisco, first studied by the Swedish pioneer prehistorian Erland Nordenskiöld (1902–1903), and recently studied again by Dougherty (1977) along the San Francisco River, a tributary of the Bermejo, near Orán in the Salta and Jujuy provinces. Willey suggests that it may have a marginal affiliation to the South Andean area, particularly through traits that relate it to the Candelaria culture of Southern Salta. But here, too, alleging Andean derivation explains only a part of the picture. San Francisco is defined by a dispersed settlement pattern with economic activities including grazing and incipient agriculture with irrigation. Also, there was an incipient use of ceramic urns for interment, especially in the ware called polished San Francisco. Two dates are registered: one of 620 B.C.E. from the locality of El Piquete, Jujuy, and a second date of C.E. 300 from the Palpala site.

San Francisco pottery shows traits related to tropical forest lowlands, particularly corrugated and modeled techniques, thick rims, modeled figurines, cord impression, and finger-impressed techniques. Cord-impressed techniques are also known among the Mbayá-Caduveo, Guana, and Ribereños Plásticos styles in the littoral area of Paraná. Of these, the finger-impressed technique is associated with Tupí-Guaraní and Taquara traditions of Eastern Brazil. Corrugated style is found, without interruption, from northwestern Argentina to the Tupí-Guaraní orbit. Ground pottery temper forms part of the general technology of pottery known throughout the tropical lowland, including San Francisco and the Chaco-Santiago regions. Other traits like twisted handles on pots, "coffee-bean" eyes, and corncob-impressed decoration seem to derive from later waves of people entering from the tropical lowlands. On the other hand, the San Francisco bicolor red-on-white pattern also seems to be present in the so-called Vaquerías style of the Andean part of northwest Argentina. It is characteristic of early pottery stages in the South Andean area, developing later into the Candelaria style.

Willey's Lower Paraná and Uruguay subarea can also be related to these developments. This unit is treated as the littoral (coastal) region among Argentinian scholars influenced by ethnological traits. It includes the provinces of Misiones, Corrientes, and Entre Ríos, as well as the lower Paraná and Paraguay rivers into the Río de La Plata. The reason for including this region in the Chaco is indirect but plausible. Environmentally it constitutes a transitional zone from the tropical lowlands into the Pampas, but it is connected to the Chaco by tropical rivers, and culturally it represents an extension of Chaco complexes, borne by waves of Guaraní people who carried techniques such as cord-impressed pottery and pipes. Guaraní demographic surges continued to arrive during the sixteenth and seventeenth centuries.

Later influences from Arawak people touched the existing groups. The result was the configuration of the Ribereños Plásticos phase, dated between 860 and 1200 at Salto Grande. Its main development is located in the Lower Paraná and Uruguay rivers.

THE PAMPAS

Pampa is a Quechua word meaning 'flat place,' and the pampean landscape is typified by oceanic expanses of what was, before cattle ranching and agroindustry, open grassland broken only by rivers. The Pampas area includes the Argentine plains, or *pampas* proper, from the Paraná and Paraguay rivers, across the plains of Uruguay, south to about latitude 43° South. It encompasses parts of the provinces of Córdoba and San Luis, and the entire provinces of Buenos Aires, La Pampa, and Rio Negro, as well as much of Chubut. South of this area lies Patagonia.

Looking more closely, the landscape can be differentiated between the river lowlands and alluvial plains of the north, and the more truly flat plateau to the south. According to Orquera the Pampas is characterized by "a gently sloping plain interrupted by low hills [Tandilia, Ventania, Lihue Calel]. The elevation does not exceed 500 m over most of its extent but rises gradually to 1000 m in the west."[4]

The archaeology of this area reflects differences between the two subareas: the northerly Paraná-Uruguay lower drainage, and the true Pampas to the south.

Willey profiles a Paraná-Pampean cultural tradition that represents a cultural synthesis already in process after 4000 B.C.E. This combined an Andean hunting-collecting tradition with riverine fishing and gathering in southeastern Brazilian style. This tradition came to produce pottery only in late periods, especially from the Paraná drainage southward. Throughout this diffusion area a late wave of Tupi-Guarani from the Amazon left its mark.

The Lower Paraná-Uruguay Drainage

The earliest known pottery of this region is a type that resembles the Periperi phase of Eastern Brazil, dated to 880 B.C.E. But the best-known ceramic tradition in the lower Paraná-Uruguay region is the already-mentioned Ribereños Plásticos, whose motifs include geometric designs such as parallel lines, zigzags, modeled ornaments in the shape of parrots' heads fixed to the rims, and so-called bells. "Bells" are modeled ceramic objects open at both the upper and lower ends. Probably they were used as clay andirons (supports for burning logs). At Malabrigo, findings also included secondary human burials with bones sometimes painted with red ochre. The dead were accompanied by their *bolas*, and by food offerings whose remains include fish bones, shells, reptile and bird bones, and palm nuts. There are no C-14 dates for this complex. However, it seems to have been a durable tradition lasting into historic times. At one site, Arroyo Las Conchas, near Paraná, Venetian glass beads (an item of Spanish trade that caught on among natives all over South America in the sixteenth century) are found with Malabrigo-style burials.

---

[4] Luis A. Orquera, "Advances in the archaeology of the Pampas and Patagonia," *Journal of World Prehistory* 1 (1987), 340.

Buenos Aires and La Plata Drainage

The ceramics of northern Buenos Aires, including the delta of the Río de La Plata, are also prehistorically related to Ribereños Plásticos, especially its drag-and-jab punctated and incised designs. Based on the scant data available, Willey's suggestion of an earlier El Cerrillo Phase followed by an Arroyo Sarandí Phase lasting until the Tupí-Guaraní and Spanish contacts still seems appropriate.

The Uruguayan side of the La Plata shows rather different characteristics. Here, pottery bears no more decoration than incised zigzag lines, punctations, and fingernail impressions. These characteristics resemble examples from sites south of Buenos Aires. Serrano argued for an earlier stratum of pottery-making people in both areas, but the whole matter remains underresearched.

South Buenos Aires and the Pampas

The southerly plains show elements of the north-Patagonian complex with its typical triangular projectile points, found from the sub-Andean region all the way to the Atlantic. This phase is similar to González' Intihuasi II. A later phase, north-Patagonian III, with small points and microliths, milling stones, and ceramics has also been defined. In the northwestern corner of La Pampa province, a culture called Pampeano-Atuel developed; its campsites and workshops on marshlands have been recovered.

On the Atlantic coast of southern Buenos Aires Province, F. Outes studied the site of Puerto San Blas, in San Blas Peninsula, as early as the 1900s. He defined an assemblage of lithic artifacts: knives, scrapers, and large stemless and stemmed points. Those without stems resemble Magellan III projectile points in Bird's sequence from the far side of the Andes, and the stemmed ones resemble those from the Magellan IV period. In association with these points, Outes found mortar stones, pitted hammerstones, and engraved stone plaques of rectangular shape, with engraved rectilinear designs. The pottery is unpainted, similar in texture and manufacture to that from northern Buenos Aires Province. However, the designs differ in that these are fine-line incisions and small-dot punctations. Incised geometric designs were filled with punctations.

ARAUCANIA

Within Chile "Araucania" is used to refer to a heartland of the Araucanian peoples whose later expansions spread far into Argentina. Alonso de
Ercilla apparently coined the term in his 1589 epic poem about the war
against the Mapuche. A common archaeological definition of Chilean
Araucania is the territory south of the Bío Bío River down to the large
Island of Chiloé, just south of Puerto Montt. Heavy rainfall supports
exuberant forests of cedars and beeches, whose density increases southward. Under these conditions agriculture without steel tools to clear fields
was very difficult. The area is also quite steep, bounded on the east by
the South Andean cordillera, which rises to an average of 2,000 meters.
However, within the Araucanian heartland there are also gentler environments along the coast, where climatic conditions are much milder than
in the cordillera. A coastal range running parallel to the Pacific is of
much lower altitude than the main range. The central valley, the historic
core of Mapuche settlement, is the space between the Andes and the
coast range.

Araucanian subsistence depended on *piñones* or "pine nuts" of the
Araucaria tree, around which gathering activities were organized in sum-
mertime. Historic Araucanians hunted, and more recent ones keep some
livestock. In the central valley both horticulture and agriculture are
important. The coast offers excellent fishing and shellfish gathering.

The prehistory of Araucania is still poorly understood. One problem
is that archaeological ceramic sequences remain insufficiently defined
because of scarce stratigraphic excavations. Only two sites (the Cave of
Los Catalanes, and Pucón VI) have been properly studied, and they
contain limited information. The chronology, such as it is, rests largely
on comparison with data from outside areas, particularly ceramic complexes from northern and eastern territories. This uncertainty encourages
different interpretations, none yet amounting to a secure profile of regional development. However, the pottery record does seem to portray
the transformation of Mapuche subsistence from pure horticulture to a
fully agricultural and sedentary way of life. It is clear that the Araucanian
regional cultures developed from the Andean Formative ceramic
traditions. The Araucanian Formative can be considered a late regional
process, of which the Pitrén Phase represents the earliest development.
Technical similarities link Pitrén to the somewhat earlier El Molle Formative complex from farther north. Menghin has pointed out that con-

nections with northwest Argentina are possible, particularly with the Candelaria culture. Because the latter is in turn related to the tropical forest, Pitrén may represent a regional variant of a much broader Formative development also including Vergel I, Tirúa, Pucón VI, and Neuquén in Argentina. A single C-14 date from the Huimpil site gives C.E. 660 as a possible Pitrén date. Additional dates from the Moquehue-1 site, in Neuquén (C.E. 1050), and from Mallín del Tromen (C.E. 1040) confirm a chronological framework between C.E. 0 and 1000 for early Araucanian development.

The other ceramic tradition that characterizes the area is Valdivia (not to be confused with a similarly named Formative Ecuadorian culture), which, according to Menghin, shows Inka influences. Menghin refers to this complex as Neo-Araucanian because it developed in historic times, as opposed to early Pitrén, which is sometimes called Paleo-Araucanian. Chilean Valdivia pottery is characterized by linear red designs on white slipped vessels.

PATAGONIA

For our present purposes Patagonia includes all of South America south of latitude 43°. It comprises the Argentinian provinces of Chubut and Santa Cruz, and in Chile, the territories south of Chiloé all the way to Tierra del Fuego (part of which is governed by Argentina). Thus at least three different types of landscape are involved.

First, east of the Andes, the flat, dry, and windy open grassland, known as the "Patagonian steppe," mostly in Argentinian Santa Cruz Province. It was settled in relatively recent times by Tehuelches, an expanding Araucanian population. The second type of landscape, on the western side of the Andes, is the area of the channels of southern Chile. It is characterized by fjords, small channels, isles, and a rugged landscape of dense forests. The landscape astonished the archaeological pioneer Junius Bird when he surveyed it in 1934:

The shoreline at the western base of the mountains is well described as one of the most irregular and broken in the world. It is only 870 statute miles in a straight line from Puerto Montt to Cape Froward, yet the shore measures 4,500 miles according to existing surveys, which are incomplete and lacking in detail. It would be useless, if not impossible, to measure the shoreline of the offshore islands; but if we include western Tierra del Fuego, and the mainland, we obtain a rough estimate of 12,000 miles of shore on a direct line of 1,000 miles. In all this distance there is no place where one can walk along or near the shore without the greatest difficulty. The reason lies not only in the densely tangled forest that clings wherever it can secure foothold, but also in the rough nature of the country – mountains and hills that drop precipitously beneath the sea with little or no foreshore. Beaches are few and widely separated. Glaciers and swift-flowing rivers offer further obstacles.[5]

Here, Alakaluf and Chono natives developed a canoe-based way of life exploiting the marine resources and forest products.

The third type of landscape, Tierra del Fuego, with its cluster of islands and channels, forms the wintry and stormy southern tip of the continent. The varied landscape of inland forest, glaciers, and fauna-rich ocean supported the historic (now extinct) Ona and Yahgan peoples.

Two different types of adaptation occurred in these settings. The Atlantic side provided the requirements for the development of land hunting societies from very early times. On the Pacific side, the main adaptive mechanism was fishing and sea hunting, complemented by shellfish gathering and the hunting of sea birds.

Hunting traditions in northern continental Patagonia, an expanse of cold steppe shading northward into the southernmost part of the Pampa territory, goes well back into Paleoindian times. Their traces make up the earlier phases of Junius Bird's Magellan sequence at Fell's Cave and Palli Aike. The southern hunting adaptation enjoyed amazingly long persistence, with local and temporal variants accommodating changes of fauna and climate over time. Several sites such as Casa de Piedra in the Río Colorado drainage contain interesting sequences. The upper levels of this site show an occupation widely distributed in the area and known as *norpatagoniense costero* ('coastal North-Patagonian'). It includes an earlier, preceramic phase with triangular stemless projectile points, probably connected with the Andean Intihuasi II complex. This early pattern is distributed along the valleys of the Diamante, Atuel, and Colorado rivers. By the beginning of the Common Era, such points are associated with pottery, particularly in the extensive shell middens along the Atlantic shore. This second phase is known as north-Patagonian II.

Environmental change seems to have fueled the change in economic activity from pure hunting to a diversified hunting-gathering that left behind microliths and grinding stones. The later development of ceram-

---

[5] Junius Bird, *Travels and archaeology in South Chile* (Iowa City, 1988), 3.

ics is probably also related to this shift. Apparently readaptation was contemporaneous with the neoglacial, which ended by 2000 B.C.E. and which produced a period in the far south characterized by increasingly arid conditions. During the shift Patagonians apparently moved toward riverine environments.

From about the middle of the third millennium B.C.E. up to the sixteenth century C.E., the critical resources of the north-Patagonian area were mollusks, vegetables, birds, and rodents. Large mammals did not constitute a major resource.

The sequence for southern continental Patagonia rests on the stratigraphy provided by Bird at Fell's Cave and later by his own and others' work at Palli Aike, Las Buitreras, and Los Toldos. The early part of the sequence is treated in Chapter 3 of this volume. Fell's Cave Period IV has been dated between 1775 and 1525 B.C.E. It is characterized by stemmed Patagonian triangular points, *bolas*, beads and ornaments, incised bones, and bone awls, as well as side, end, and shafted scrapers. According to Bird stemmed points replaced stemless points of the preceding period. Burials assigned to this period are found in stone cairns; the bodies are extended.

Period V of the Fell's Cave sequence saw the use of small arrow points similar to the ones that the historic Ona used. By C.E. 1265 these traits were associated with other artifacts also typical of the Ona inventory, such as combs and beads. It is interesting to note that both periods also contain a large percentage of guanaco bones. Guanaco hunting was important to historic Fuegians as well.

Sites of the type named Patagoniense proper are found in almost all of continental southern Patagonia, with some signs of diversification along with specialization for exploiting particular environmental niches. Sites along the dry lakes and canyons of the Rio Negro are excellent examples of this situation. Between Casapedrense, the previous industry, and Patagoniense proper, there was a transitional stage, whose contexts have been defined as Proto-Patagonian and dated 1500 B.C.E. to C.E. 0. Its main features are a high percentage of blades, the predominance of knives and scrapers, and the complete absence of projectile points.

The appearance of the stemmed projectile point, similar to Bird's Period IV points from Fell's Cave, marks the beginning of the Classic Patagonian (also known as Preceramic Patagonian I), dated between C.E. 0 and 600. The most common economic activity in this area was hunting of guanacos, rheas, and smaller birds, combined with increasing plant gathering. A notable flowering of rock art features styles known as "footprint engraved" (*grabado de pisadas*) and curved geometric designs.

Patagonian II, also called Tehuelche, is the material record of the period from C.E. 600 to the sixteenth century. Pottery appeared in the area probably by C.E. 600, according to evidence from the site of Shequen. It appears associated with small stemmed points similar to those of Fell's Cave Period V. Rock art became more abstract, with a predominant style using step-frets (*estilo de grecas*). By the time Spaniards arrived, horses had already diffused into the area, and with them a variety of influences from the Pampas.

Farther south, on the western side of the Andes, adaptive process took two distinct lines: land hunting in continental Patagonia, and sea hunting along with fishing and gathering in the channels and isles of southern Patagonia. The latter gave rise to what Bird called the "shell knife culture" typifying both Yahgans and Alakaluf.

In the extreme south, among the Fuegian channels, a sequence has been devised based on work at the sites of Túnel and Lancha Packewaia in Ushuaia. (Ushuaia, Argentina, is the southernmost modern city.) Its second component already reveals a marine-oriented adaptation. The cultural assemblage included many-toothed harpoons with cruciform bases and bone points. Often they were incised with geometric designs. The harpooners ate sea lions and much smaller amounts of guanaco meat, birds, and fish. Abundant food remains suggest a solid adaptation already stabilized in the third millennium B.C.E. During Túnel's third component (around 2000 B.C.E.), the adaptive process became more complex, with a much more elaborated bone industry. Sites at the extreme south of Patagonia, such as Englefield, Bahía Buena, and Punta Santa Ana, indicate a long and stable marine adaptation. The low population density of the groups amid enormous potential marine resources underpinned stability and laid the basis for about 6,000 years of continuity, ending with the historic Yahgans.

CONCLUSIONS

Southern Cone prehistory is characterized by similar processes taking place with different emphases in the four areas. These initial processes each built up adaptations to very harsh environments. They were followed by migratory waves, both from the eastern tropical forest and from the Andes.

Although the technology that southern South Americans developed was fairly simple, it reflected, along with the development of long cultural traditions, a uniquely achieved fitness for the environment. Whether in the seasonally hot and humid tropical environment of the Chaco region, the extreme cold of the Patagonian steppe, or along the expanses of Pampas and Araucania that connect these extremes, prehistoric populations clearly did master subsistence and built a stable economy supporting specific forms of social organization.

In the case of the Chaco, tropical forest traits associated with the Tupí-Guaraní are detectable. Even today it is possible to see some of these ethnic groups as parts of a Tupí-Guaraníian sphere of influence. Tupí-Guaraní tradition spread from the upper Paraná and Uruguay rivers to the Río de La Plata, in a north–south direction. It reached westward through the Chaco region, expanded into the Mojos region in Bolivia, and up to the Andean foothills. Despite spatial disconnection, Tupí-Guaraníian features characterized socioeconomic systems of this diffusion. Over this vast area dwelled horticulturalists who practiced slash-and-burn techniques to cultivate maize, manioc, tobacco, and cotton. They also practiced hunting and gathering, and in some cases they took advantage of river resources. They formed villages with large communal houses. They made hammocks, and they navigated along rivers in canoes made of tree trunks. Their weapons were the mace and bow and arrow. Ceramic urns were also very common.

Migrations also influenced the prehistory of northern Chile, where a synthesis of a different sort occurred. Hypothetically we envision preceramic migrations out of the Amazon Basin toward the Pacific and Atlantic coasts formerly occupied only by Paleoindian hunters and gatherers. This development entailed two different processes: an adaptation of foreign populations to the coast, valleys, and oases of the desert, and later a second process of regional differentiation.

In regard to Araucania, there is consensus that the historic population of the area derives from waves of peoples who spoke a Mapuche-like language and not from development of the earlier Paleoindian cultures of Monte Verde (near Puerto Montt) or San Vicente de Tagua Tagua (south of Santiago). Araucanian roots lie in the first developments of pottery-making culture, to which Pitrén is fundamental. This complex built toward the more agriculture-oriented complex of El Vergel, and to Valdivia ceramic style, which lasted into the historic era. The makers of Chilean Valdivia developed a sustained agriculture of potatoes, maize, and probably beans and quinua, which together formed a basis for stable nucleated settlements by families. Mapuche culture is a posterior development of these elements, unified by the spread of a language (Mapudungun or Mapuche; see Chap. 16). from the coast across the Andes to Neuquén.

The Pampas and Araucania seem to form a nexus between the respective cultural processes of the Chaco to the south and that of Patagonia to the north. The Pampas as a transitional area bore many traits and influences from both. In fact, the late Araucanian or Tehuelche expansion that settled in the Pampas was but the last of these waves.

Araucania, too, shows characteristics derived from Formative and later complexes in the Central Andean area, including traits characteristic of Inka development. These are complemented by others from the Amazon tropical forest.

Both the Pampas and Patagonia show cultural continuity based on an enduringly stable foot-nomad adaptation to hunting and gathering. With a simple technology that took up pottery late or not at all, its social organization attempted no scale larger than small bands with recognized territories. In this process one can distinguish continental Patagonian groups, who developed an economy based on hunting, from coastal groups of the channels and islands of the west coast and the extreme south. These latter peoples relied on a basically maritime economy of hunting and gathering. The canoe was their fundamental technology, balanced by land hunting for guanacos and *huemul* deer (*Hippocamelus bisulcus*). Recent research indicates that coastal groups took to the sea when more specialized hunting groups displaced them from the mainland environments, so that they had to adapt to maritime conditions from 5000 B.C.E. onward. Nonetheless their maritime technology seems advanced right from the start of the process. So it is possible to hypothesize that the area was also populated by a migratory current of ancient canoe hunters who arrived from a more northerly stretch of the Pacific shore.

In all four areas that make up the Southern Cone proper, once equilibrium with the environment had been achieved, and because of relative protection from violent and massive changes, the material elements of cultural development remained almost unchanged for millennia.

This situation was interrupted with the arrival of the Europeans, first along rivers and coasts and in later times throughout the Chaco area.

But a slow historic rhythm is not the same as stasis, nor does it imply isolation. The peopling and cultural development of the Southern Cone shows interrelation with neighboring regions in the form of a slow interactive cultural exchange going both north–south and east–west. This is especially noticeable in the first Formative Periods in the South-Central Andes, where interaction created the base on which Tiwanaku exercised its influence later.

The first millennium C.E. in the northern deserts of Chile and in the Argentinian northwest is characterized by the coexistence of economically interlaced groups. Until Tiwanaku domination each of the interacting valley, oasis, coastal, desert, and highland polities showed some autonomy. The South-Central Andes made up a mosaic of small polities in whose coherence ideology played an important role, as it did in the Formative. Interdependence is visible in combinations of Andean with tropical forest components, each contributing, both before and after Middle Horizon unification, to a process of regionalization different from the process of urbanization propelled by state societies in the Central Andes. In this way the South-Central Andean region became unusual for its diverse experience of ways to achieve cultural complexity. Openness toward the eastern lowlands and local autonomy fostered its processes of microregionalization and discontinuity.

Archaeological research is beginning to reveal interesting problems in this part of the Southern Cone. We know that a long time before the rise of Tiwanaku, networks of exchange and ecological complementarity were facilitated by a common ideological frame. These groups may also have shared a linguistic frame, formed by an early expansion of the Pukina language, which touched the ethnic groups of the Atacama Desert among others. The later Aymara expansion that was related to Tiwanaku submerged this Pukina substratum.

Post-Tiwanaku times saw a balkanization of the territory. Local chiefdoms maximized their autonomy without any one of them developing preeminence. Only later, in the Inka era, does Quechua seem to enter the area and even then in a limited and conditional form.

This period of fragmentation corresponds to the Late Intermediate in Andean terms. It was characterized in the South-Central Andes by demand for renewed ideological frameworks capable of organizing exchange among heterogeneous and mobile groups with limited economic resources. In this conjuncture the Tiwanaku sphere of influence, broken up and reconfigured, assumed a new importance to the South-Central Andean agropastoral peoples. They show a shared iconography and a net of economic interchange whose ideological and political concepts still centered on Lake Titicaca. Atacama groups were influenced by their experience as hegemonically regulated native lordships under Tiwanaku, while the more Aymarized farther north had been directly affected by the presence of Tiwanaku enclaves or colonies.

In northwestern Argentina, the site of Aguada also expresses a regionalization of the Tiwanaku legacy. It can be thought of as a "reprocesser" of Tiwanaku culture, favored by a geographic situation allowing reception of information from the high Andean north and from the eastern tropical forests. Such sites developed sociopolitical and economic systems that allowed population growth, metallurgical technology, and artistic development exploiting the influential Tiwanaku feline icon. This process made Aguada an important node in a regional network whose exact operation is still little-known.

One important aspect of archaeological research on the regional developmental period, in the northwest of Argentina, no less than in the north of Chile, is the effort to define local chiefdoms preceding Inka rule. This period is generally characterized by growing populations, the creation of irrigation networks attached to important productive establishments, major works of architecture, and the building of strategic defenses. All these elements contributed to the design of settlements at sites in northwestern Argentina (Hualfín, Calchaquí, Santa María) and in the Atacama Desert oases and the valleys of Azapa, Tarapacá, and Camarones in northern Chile. These establishments made up hierarchical structures dominating networks of exchange. They display a shared type of chiefdom, with signs of social stratification, industrial manufacturing, and long-distance distribution, particularly of exotic or prestigious products such as those made of copper and bronze.

It seems that major transitions correlate with contacts between societies of different organization. At the period when it developed complex society, Araucania was in a state of contact with more Andean societies. In the Chaco-Santiago area and in Uruguay, the later establishment of agricultural villages may be related to a still-hypothetical influence via Guaraní-speaking migrations out of the eastern tropics into the Pampas and Araucania. We still do not know the role of agriculture in the growth of complexity and connectedness through these zones, so it is hard to specify the mechanisms of change. We do know that in addition to relationships of ecological complementarity, political units built connections of marriage exchange among élites. Mechanisms of exchange may have included élite participation in preexisting markets. The caravaneering abilities of high Andean society may have exerted an independent force in shaping wide-ranging social nets after Tiwanaku.

In the scheme of interregional relations, environmental changes and especially drought that alternated with rainier periods could have played a key part. Very little is known about climate change, but preliminary studies show periods of lesser humidity in the Amazon Basin, periods of drought in the high plains, and other periods when the Atacama Desert received more moisture. These situations are likely to have influenced migrations and the politics of resource access.

Such a view of prehistory in zones related to the Andean sphere may serve as a guide for sounding the prehistories of societies farther south. Questions remain for the future. What kept Patagonian populations at a distance from these more dynamic interactions? What common traits can be detected between incompletely sedentarized societies and those partaking of Andean developments? Did the less stationary hunting-gathering societies in any way influence processes farther north? To what degree can the development of Andean civilization be correlated with processes of interaction across the tropical lowlands? The Southern Cone, as an area with prehistoric characteristics of its own, offers opportunities to investigate how social change and environmental adjustment took shape over time in the absence of imposed or hegemonic foreign systems like Chavín, Moche, Wari, and Inka. Its enormous space and the large number of groups inhabiting it offer chances for local studies that could exploit local "natural laboratories" of adaptation, while at the same time illuminating change in great macroregional webs of influence over long intervals of development.

BIBLIOGRAPHIC ESSAY

Some scientific travelers who journeyed in the Southern Cone furnish prehistorically relevant information on landscape and resources. Among them are Alcides D'Orbigny, *L'Homme Américain (De l'Amérique Meridional) Consideré Sous Rapports Physiologiques et Moraux* (Paris, 1839); Isaiah Bowman, *Desert trails of Atacama* (New York, 1924); Annette

Laming-Emperaire, *Tout au bout du monde* (París, 1954; translated as *Patagonia confín de mundo*, Santiago, 1957).

The pioneering and now classic syntheses include José Toribio Medina, *Los aborígenes de Chile* (Santiago, 1882); Ricardo Latcham, *La Prehistoria de Chile* (Santiago, 1928), and his *Alfarería indígena chilena* (Santiago, 1928); Aureliano Oyarzún, "Los Aborígenes de Chile," *Revista Universitaria* (Santiago), 11 (1927), 1092–1115. Other pathfinding studies include Stig Rydén's *Contributions to the archaeology of the Río Loa region* (Gothenburg, 1944), and Richard Schaedel, *Arqueología chilena: Contribución al estudio de la región comprendida entre Arica y La Serena* (Santiago, 1958).

Alberto Rex González set a landmark with "Cultural development in northwest Argentina" in *Aboriginal cultural development in Latin America: An interpretative review*, Betty Meggers and Clifford Evans (eds.) (Washington, 1963), 103–117. Detailed information on sequences for ceramic-making agricultural peoples can be found in Juan Schobinger, *Prehistoria de Sud América* (Barcelona, 1969), and in Gordon Willey's *An introduction to American archaeology. Vol. 2. South America* (Englewood Cliffs, N.J., 1971). In Willey, see especially chapters 4, "The South Andes," (194–253), and 7, "Eastern and southern South America," (434–481). Grete Mostny, *Prehistoria de Chile* (Santiago, 1974), affords an overview of prehistory in Chilean territory. The Southern Cone is placed in a wider context in Luis G. Lumbreras, *Arqueología de la América andina* (Lima, 1987); see also Alberto Rex González and José Antonio Pérez, *Historia argentina. Argentina indígena: Vísperas de la conquista* (Buenos Aires, 1972).

A more recent work in handbook format is *Introducción a la arqueología y etnología, Diez mil años de historia argentina*, by Marta Ottonello and Ana María Lorandi (Buenos Aires, 1987). Rodolfo Raffino's *Poblaciones indígenas en Argentina* (Buenos Aires, 1988), and the collective volume edited by Jorge Hidalgo, Virgilio Schiappacasse, Hans Niemeyer, Carlos Aldunate, and Iván Solimano under the title *Culturas de Chile, Prehistoria desde sus orígenes hasta los albores de la conquista* (Santiago 1989), and more recently Mario Orellana's *Prehistoria y etnología de Chile* (Santiago 1994), offer the most complete panoramas.

There exists a small literature on the history of archeology in the area. See Betty Meggers (ed.), *Prehistoria de Sud América, Nuevas perspectivas* (Taraxacún/Washington, 1992); Tom Dillehay, "Archaeological trends in the Southern Cone of South America," *Journal of Archaeological Research*

1 (1993), 235–266; Gustavo Politis, *Arqueología en América Latina hoy* (Bogotá, 1992); Hugo Yacobaccio, Luis A. Borrero, Lidia García, Gustavo Politis, Carlos Aschero, and C. Bellelli, *Arqueología argentina contemporánea, Actualidad y perspectivas* (Buenos Aires, 1988). Mario A. Rivera and Mario Orellana (1994) contributed a national survey: "Chile: Institutional development and ideological context," in *History of Latin America archaeology*, Augusto Oyuela-Caycedo (ed.) (Aldershot, UK, and Brookfield, Vermont, 1994), 36–48. A work of similar scope is Mario Orellana, *Investigaciones y teorías en la arqueología de Chile* (Santiago, 1982). Also useful is Jorge Fernández, *Historia de la arqueología argentina* (Mendoza, 1982). Alberto Rex González offers a memoir and regional focus in "Cincuenta años de arqueología del nor oeste argentino (1930–1980): Apuntes de un casi testigo y algo de protagonista," *American Antiquity* 50 (1985), 505–518.

The largest share of monographic and specialized studies covers northern Chile and the northwest of Argentina. Good sources are the journals, *Chungará* (Arica), *Diálogo Andino* (Arica), *Estudios Atacameños* (San Pedro de Atacama), and *Estudios Arqueológicos* (Antofagasta). Several Chilean museums publish *Boletines*: the Museo de Arqueología de La Serena, the Museo de Arte Precolombino, and the Museo Nacional de Historia Natural. Other academic journals include *Revista Chilena de Antropología* and *Relaciones de la Sociedad Argentina de Antropología, Comechingonia* (Córdoba), *Revista del Instituto de Antropología* (Córdoba), *Revista del Instituto Nacional de Antropología* (Buenos Aires), *Revista del Museo de La Plata* (La Plata), and the *Anales del Instituto de Arqueología* (Cuyo/Tucumán/Salta). Detailed information useful for both prehistory and intellectual history often appears in the *Anales* of the Congresos de Arqueología Chilena y Argentina, which have run steadily for 30 years.

Outside Chile and northwestern Argentina, Southern Cone literature is rather scarce. The Chaco region is an extreme case, almost lacking in important publications. For adaptive processes in Patagonia, the works of Luis A. Borrero are interesting: "Replanteo de la arqueología patagónica," *Interciencia* 14:3 (1989), 127–135. See also Luis A. Orquera, "Advances in the archaeology of pampas and Patagonia," *Journal of World Prehistory* 1 (1987), 333–413, and Luis A. Orquera, Ernesto Piana, and Alicia Tapia, *Lancha Packewaia, Arqueología de los canales fueguinos* (Buenos Aires, 1975); Mauricio Massone, *Cultura selknam (Ona)* (Santiago, 1982); and Omar Ortiz-Troncoso, "Arqueología del estrecho de Magallanes y canales del sur de Chile," *Culturas indígenas de la Patagonia*

(Madrid, 1984). A broader view of the area, including environmental studies and excavation reports, is found in Joseph Emperaire, *Los nómades del mar* (Santiago, 1963).

Among prehistorically relevant ethnographies of the Fuegian south, a 1982 Buenos Aires translation renders Martín Gusinde's *Los indios de Tierra del Fuego* from the original *Die Feuerland Indianer* (Vienna, 1939). It is a world-class ethnographic classic. Junius Bird, *Travels and archaeology in South Chile* (Iowa City, 1988) evokes the career of another pioneer. See also the journals *Anales del Instituto de la Patagonia* (Punta Arenas), *Rehue* (Concepción), and *Etnia* (Olavarría).

The origins of the Mapuche were an axis of debate in the 1930s. Ricardo Latcham wrote in 1927 on "El problema del origen de los Araucanos" in *Revista Universitaria* (Santiago), 12, 1116–1129. Tomás Guevara refuted some of his ideas in *Chile prehispano* (Santiago, 1925). Osvaldo Menghin in "Estudios de prehistoria araucana," *Acta Praehistorica* 3–4 (1959/60), 49–120, once again hypothesized on Araucanian origins while offering a sequence for Mapuche prehistory. Also important are Tom Dillehay's contributions in his compilation *Araucania, pasado y presente* (Santiago 1990) and Carlos Aldunate's *La cultura mapuche* (Santiago, 1978).

For the Atacama, the Diaguita region, and the Aymara-influenced parts of northern Chile, see Gustavo Le Paige, "San Pedro de Atacama y su zona: 14 temas" in *Anales de la Universidad del Norte* 4 (1965), 5–29. Bente Bittmann, Gustavo Le Paige, and Lautaro Núñez in 1979 synthesized *Cultura atacameña* (Santiago); see also Clement Meighan and Delbert True, *Prehistoric trails of Atacama* (Los Angeles, 1980); José Berenguer, "San Pedro de Atacama: Espacio, tiempo y cultura" in the catalogue *Tesoros de San Pedro de Atacama*, from the Museo Chileno de Arte Precolombino (Santiago, 1984), 3–34; and finally, Gonzalo Ampuero, *La cultura diaguita* (Santiago, 1979).

The following are monographic and synthetic works on northern Chile: Gonzalo Ampuero and Jorge Hidalgo, "Estructura y proceso en la Pre-y Proto-Historia del Norte Chico de Chile," *Chungará* 5 (1985), 87–124; Mario A. Rivera, "The prehistory of northern Chile, a synthesis," *Journal of World Prehistory* 5:1 (1991), 1–47; Mario A. Rivera (ed.), *La problemática tiwanaku-wari en el contexto pan-andino del desarrollo cultural*, as a special issue of *Diálogo Andino* 4 (1985). Hans Niemeyer and Virgilio Schiappacasse offer a pioneering study of a coastal Andean transect through southern Chile in "Padrones de poblamiento en la Quebrada de Camarones," *Actas VI Congreso de Arqueología Chilena* (Santiago, 1972–1973). Lautaro Núñez in 1974 published a complete analysis of archaeological materials on cultivation in *Agricultura prehistórica de los andes meridionales* (Santiago, 1974). This work complements the same author's "Desarrollo cultural prehispánico del norte de Chile," *Estudios Arqueológicos* I (1965), 37–115. Recently Mark Aldenderfer has edited a set of studies on the domestic architecture of the South-Central Andean in *Domestic architecture, ethnicity, and complementarity in the South Central Andes* (Iowa City, 1993). Percy Dauelsberg's 1982 "Prehistoria de Arica," originally published in *Diálogo Andino* I, 31–82, and recently reprinted in *Diálogo Andino*, 11/12 (1992/1993), 9–31, furnishes a synthesis for the Arica area. Carlos Aldunate and Victoria Castro, *Las Chullpas de Toconce y su relación con el poblamiento altiplánico en el Loa Superior, período tardío* (Santiago, 1982) focuses on funerary architecture.

Alberto Rex González' works are important for northwestern Argentina, particularly "La cultura Condorhuasi del nor oeste Argentino," *Runa* 7 (1956), 37–85. For the Argentinian Andes, see also Pedro Krapovickas, "Subáreas de la Puna" in *37 Congreso Internacional de Americanistas*, Vol. 2 (Buenos Aires, 1968), 235–271, and his 1984 "Relations between the Argentina puna and its eastern border zones" in *Social and economic organization in the prehispanic Andes*, David Browman, Richard Burger, and Mario Rivera (ed.), (London, 1984) published as British Archaeological Reports, International Series 194, 171–192. Related studies include Myriam Tarragó, "La historia de los pueblos circumpuneños en relación con el altiplano y los andes meridionales," *Estudios Atacameños* 7 (1984), 116–132, and Mario E. Cigliano and Rodolfo Raffino, "Un modelo de poblamiento del Nor Oeste Argentino," in *Obra del centenario del Museo de La Plata* (La Plata, 1977), vol. 2, 1–25.

Rodolfo Raffino has analyzed Inka establishments, especially in respect to Argentina, in *Los Inkas del Collasuyo* (Buenos Aires, 1983). A comparable study for the Atacama Desert in Chile is Hans Niemeyer and Mario A. Rivera, "El camino del Inca en el despoblado de Atacama," *Boletín de Prehistoria de Chile* 9 (1983), 91–193. Two excellent recent works on metallurgy in the Southern Cone are Alberto Rex González, *Las placas metálicas de los andes del Sur, contribución al estudio de las religiones precolombinas* (Munich, 1992), and Eugene Mayer, *Vorspanische Metallwaffen und Werkzeuge in Argentinien und Chile* (Munich, 1986), published as Materialien zur Allgemeinen und Vergleichenden Archaeologie Band 38.

All these works are in some degree complements to the classic studies: Max Uhle, *Fundamentos étnicos y arqueología de Arica y Tacna* (Quito, 1922); Ricardo Latcham, *Arqueología de la región atacameña* (Santiago, 1938); Junius Bird's 1943 *Excavations in northern Chile* (New York), published as American Museum of Natural History Anthropological Papers 38: 4; and Francisco Cornely, *Culturas diaguita chilena y cultura El Molle* (Santiago, 1956). Other works setting the baseline for modern archaeology are Wendell Bennett, E. Bleiler, and F. Sommer, *Northwest Argentine archaeology* (New Haven, 1948), and Éric Boman, *Antiquités de la région Andine de la République Argentine et du désert d'Atacama* (Paris, 1908). Jorge Iribarren, *Nuevos hallazgos arquelógicos en el cementerio indígena de la Turquía-Hurtado* (Santiago, 1958), and his 1957 "Nuevos aportes sobre la arqueología de la cultura El Molle," *Revista Universitaria* (Santiago), 42 (1958), 175–185, offer more locally focused views. So does Fernando Márquez Miranda, "Los Diaguitas," *Revista del Museo de La Plata*, Nueva Serie 3 (1946), 5–300.

For the Chaco, modern research begins with Erland Nordenskiöld, *Praecolumbische wohn-und Begrabnisplätze an der Sudwestgrenze von Chaco* (Stockholm, 1902–1903). Niels Fock's *Chaco pottery and history, Past and present* appears in the 34th International Congress of Americanists (Vienna, 1962). Other broad-based works are George Howard, *North east Argentina* (New Haven, 1948); George Howard and Gordon Willey, *Lowland Argentine archaeology* (New Haven, 1948); and Antonio Serrano, *Arqueología del Litoral* (Paraná, 1931), published as Memorias del Museo de Paraná 4. See also his 1972 "Líneas fundamentales de la arqueología del litoral (una tentativa de periodización)," in *Revista Universidad Nacional de Córdoba* 32, 3–79. A more recent study is Bernardo Dougherty and Elsa L. Zagaglia, "Problemas generales de la arqueología del Chaco occidental," *Revista del Museo de La Plata* 8:54 (1982), 107–110. Jehan Vellard's, "Notes sur la céramique pré-columbienne des environs d Asunción" appeared in *Journal de la Société des Américanistes* 26 (1934), 37–45.

Important works on the Pampean region include those of Guillermo Madrazo, "Síntesis de la arqueología pampeana," *Etnia* (Clavarría), 17 (1973), 13–25, and Antonio Austral, "Prehistoria del sur de la región pampeana," *Actas del 37° Congreso Internacional de Americanistas* (Buenos Aires, 1968), vol. 3, 325–338. An updated synthesis appears in Gustavo Politis, "Paradigmas, médelos y métodos en la arqueología de la Pampa bonaerense," *Arqueología argentina contemporánea, actualidad y perspecti-*

vas, Hugo Yacobaccio et al. (eds.) (Buenos Aires, 1988), 59–107. See also Orquera (1987), cited previously.

Problems of chronology and sequence have produced interesting contributions. See Carlos Gradín, "Secuencias radiocarbónicas del Sur de la Patagonia Argentina," *Relaciones de la Sociedad Argentina de Antropología* 14:1 (1980), 177–194, Omar Ortiz-Troncoso, "Nuevas dataciones radiocarbónicas de Chile austral," *Boletín del Museo Arqueológico de La Serena* 17 (1979), 244–250; Virgilio Schiappacasse, Alvaro Román, Iván Muñoz, Angel Deza, and Guillermo Focacci, "Cronología por Termoluminiscencia de la cerámica del extremo norte de Chile," *Actas del XI Congreso de Arqueología Chilena* (1991), vol. 2, 43–59; José Berenguer, Angel Deza, Alvaro Román, and Agustín Llagostera, "La Secuencia de Myriam Tarragó para San Pedro de Atacama, un test por termoluminiscencia," *Revista Chilena de Antropología* 5 (1986), 17–54; and Mario A. Rivera, *Prehistoric chronology of northern Chile*, Ph.D. Dissertation, University of Wisconsin (Madison, 1977). Site-focused reports include Carlos Aldunate, J. Berenguer, V. Castro, L. Cornejo, L. Martínez, and C. Sinclaire, *Cronología y asentamiento en la región del Loa Superior* (Santiago, 1986), and Myriam Tarragó, "Secuencias culturales de la etapa agroalfarera de San Pedro de Atacama," *37° Congreso Internacional de Americanistas* (Buenos Aires, 1968), vol. 2, 119–144.

Biological anthropology clarifies some problems in northern Chilean and Patagonian archaeology. See Juan Munizaga, "Antropología física de los andes del sur," *Prehistoria de Sud América*, Betty Meggers (ed.) (Washington/Taraxcún, 1992), 65–75; Francisco Rothhammer, Alberto Cocilovo, Elena Llop, and Silvia Quevedo, "Orígenes y microevolución de la población chilena," *Culturas de Chile, Prehistoria*, Jorge Hidalgo et al. (eds.) (Santiago, 1989), 403–413. See also Marvin Allison, "Las condiciones de salud prehistóricas en el Norte Grande" on pages 221–226 of the same volume. Bernardo Arriaza, Marvin Allison, Guillermo Focacci, and Enrique Gerszten studied "Mortalidad materna y de la niñez en el área de Arica prehispánica y conceptos asociados," *Chungará* 12 (1984), 161–172.

The following studies offer interesting material on migration and multizonal adaptations: Tom Dillehay and Lautaro Núñez, "Camelids, caravans, and complex societies in the South Central Andes," *Recent studies in pre-Columbian archaeology*, W. Saunders and O. Montmollin (eds.), British Archaeological Reports International Series 421 (Oxford, 1988), 603–634; Thomas Lynch, "Regional interaction, transhumance and verticality archaeological use of Zonal complementarity in Peru and northern Chile," *Multidisciplinary studies in Andean anthropology*, V. J. Vitzthum (ed.), published as *Michigan studies in anthropology* 8 (1988), 1–11; Elías Mujica, Mario Rivera, and Thomas Lynch, "Proyecto de estudio sobre la complementaridad económica tiwanaku en los valles occidentales del centro sur andino," *Chungará* 11 (1983), 85–109; Alberto Rex González, "La metalurgia precolombina de Sud América y la búsqueda de los mecanismos de la evolución cultural," *Prehistoria de Sud América Nuevas perspectivas*, Betty Meggers (ed.) (Washington/Taraxacún, 1992), 45–61; and Mario A. Rivera, "Hipótesis sobre movimientos poblacionales altiplánicos y transaltiplánicos a las costas del norte de Chile," *Chungará* 5 (1975), 7–31.

The role of living languages such as Guaraní, Quechua, Aymara, and Mapudungun (Mapuche), as well as extinct ones like Atacameño, Diaguita, Kewhaskar, Tehuelche, and Ona, is clarified in a number of historically and prehistorically oriented linguistics works. For the Andean languages influencing the northern part of the Southern Cone, see Alfredo Torero's "La Familia Lingüística Quechua," *América Latina en sus lenguas indígenas*, Bernard Pottier (ed.) (Caracas, 1983), 61–92, and his 1974 monograph *El Quechua y la historia social andina* (Lima). Louisa Stark comments on Argentinian Quechua in "History of the Quichua of Santiago del Estero," in Louisa Stark and Harriet E. Manelis Klein (eds.), *South American Indian languages* (Austin, 1985). On languages beyond the Quechua-Aymara orbit, see Stark's and Klein's "Indian languages of the Paraguayan Chaco" in the same volume. See as well, Christos Clairis' "Indigenous languages of Tierra del Fuego," and Robert A. Croese's "Mapuche dialect survey."

In regard to iconographic and ideological studies, see José A. Pérez Gollán's 1986 "Iconografía religiosa andina en el nor oeste argentino," *Boletín del Instituto de Estudios Andinos* (Lima), 15 (3–4), 61–72; Alberto Rex González, "Notas sobre religión y culto en el nor oeste argentino prehispánico," *Baessler Archiv* 31 (1983), 219–282; José Berenguer, "Relaciones iconográficas de larga distancia en los Andes – Nuevos ejemplos para un viejo problema," *Boletín del Museo Chileno de Arte Pre Colombino* 1 (1986), 55–74; Mario A. Rivera, "Alto Ramírez y Tiwanaku, un caso de interpretación simbólica a través de datos arqueológicos en el área de los valles occidentales, Sur del Perú y Norte de Chile," *Diálogo Andino* 4 (1985), 39–58; and Tom Dillehay, "Mapuche ceremonial landscapes, social recruitment and resource rights," *World Archaeology* 22:2 (1990), 223–241.

10

THE FOURFOLD DOMAIN: INKA POWER AND ITS SOCIAL FOUNDATIONS

MARÍA ROSTWOROWSKI AND CRAIG MORRIS

At the time of the Spanish invasion (C.E. 1532), the Inka ruled the largest empire the New World had ever seen.[1] It extended from the sacred center of Qusqu, now called Qosqo, Cusco or Cuzco,[2] northward along the spine of the Andes through what are today Peru, Ecuador, and southernmost Colombia, as well as southward into Bolivia, northern Chile, and northwestern Argentina (Map 10.1). Its domains also covered the Pacific seaboards of nearly all these lands, and parts of western Amazonia. From a European perspective many areas ruled by the Inka looked inhospitable, even marginal. Yet the Inka controlled a land rich with varied natural resources and domesticated plants and animals. Andean peoples developed the sophisticated management and redistribution mechanisms required to utilize this wealth effectively centuries before the Inka rose to power. Although the Inka based much of what they wrought on technologies and institutions developed centuries earlier, the size of the Inka enterprise made it unique in the Americas.

Inka wealth in its owners' eyes consisted supremely of richly woven textiles, herds of llamas and alpacas, and thousands of storehouses. To the Spanish invaders, however, gold was the most immediate and measurable sign of Andean wealth. The last Inka emperor, Atawallpa[3] (written

---

[1] This chapter contains additional editing and material by Adriana von Hagen and Frank Salomon.

[2] Transcribed by the Quechua method, which the Peruvian government promulgated in the 1970s, the name would be Qusqu. This volume uses the form Cusco because it avoids the misleading suggestion that the second consonant is a voiced "z", and because it appears on Peruvian government maps.

[3] In dealing with Quechua and other Andean words, we adopt the following conventions. Toponyms appear in the officialized form so as to facilitate reference to atlases and so forth. Names of persons appear in manuscripts and print in varied and inaccurate transcriptions. Where possible we supply a reconstructed version of the Quechua using Gonçález Holguín's 1608 *Vocabulario de la Lengua Qquichua* as a guide to the colonial Cusco form, then use the Peruvian "official" 1973

Map 10.1

Atahuallpa, Atawalpa, etc.; his name may mean 'Fortunate in Creative Works'), sensed the Spaniards' gold lust and amassed vast quantities of gold and silver in a vain attempt to buy his freedom. Eyewitnesses recorded the amount of the ransom to have been nearly ten tons of gold and seventy tons of silver. But the Spanish conquistadors, led by Francisco Pizarro, killed Atawallpa shortly after the delivery of the great treasure. Even this was only a fraction of the total amassed by the Spaniards.

The rapid rise of Tawantinsuyu (written Tahuantinsuyu, etc.), as the Inka called their empire, was as spectacular as its geographic extent. The Quechua name could be glossed 'four parts united among themselves' or 'fourfold domain'. From their center in Cusco the Inka built a logistics network of administrative centers, waystations manned by relay runners, storehouses, and religious shrines, all linked by daringly constructed roads. As they expanded, by diplomacy or by force, if necessary, the Inka encouraged ethnic diversity. At the same time, they propagated their administrative language, Quechua, and superimposed their solar religion and their administration onto the older societies whose heterogeneity is emphasized shortly.

In the early fifteenth century the Inka were one of several large Andean societies scattered across the Andes. Population estimates for Tawantinsuyu in 1520, just before the arrival of the Spaniards, range from 6 to 13 million.[4] The Inka were at first smaller and apparently less powerful than several other polities, most notably the Chimú state of Peru's northern desert coast (see Chap. 6). But the Inka spread rapidly from their base in Cusco, and expansion and consolidation were still underway near the Ecuadorian and Colombian borders when Atawallpa's father, Huayna Cápac or Wayna Qhapaq ('Youthful Majesty') died, probably in early 1528, during an epidemic of European-introduced smallpox that preceded the arrival of the Spaniards by several years. A civil war between Wayna Qhapaq's sons, Atawallpa and Waskhar (Huáscar, etc.), was near its conclusion when the Spanish invaders led by Pizarro landed in northern Peru in November 1532. Shortly after that, the Spaniards captured Atawallpa at the highland center of Cajamarca.

To understand this sweep of events in the fifteenth and sixteenth

---

alphabet as orthographic system. Many Quechua onomastics consist of an adjective and a head word. Where a common hispano-Quechua jargon form existed, it is mentioned as well. When a Quechua word occurs in a direct quote, we do not modify the form given in the quote.

[4] Verano 1992.

centuries, we explore a series of Andean religious, social, political, and economic institutions. The Inka borrowed and adopted these institutions from those who came before, adapting them to suit their needs and the situations they encountered. Many of these institutions were quite divergent from European ones. Their properties help explain the nature and rapid rise of the Inka state, as well as its fragility on confronting the foreign invaders.

The data we use here come from two sources: written records and the archaeological record of material remains. In the decades following the invasion, Spanish observers, administrative officials, and clergy kept several kinds of paper records. These range from systematic descriptions of the Inka realm by a series of chroniclers, such as the young soldier Pedro de Cieza de León, to more specific administrative inspections (*visitas*), litigations, ecclesiastical documents, and dictionaries (see pp. 19–49, pp. 121–142). Although native accounts, such as Felipe Guaman Poma de Ayala's 1,200-page illustrated "letter" to the king of Spain, began appearing in the early seventeenth century, nearly all of what the documents describe had already been filtered through the Spanish language and biased by Spain's cultural and religious perspective. Information on topics such as Inka kingship and origins are, in addition, frequently based on the official Inka version of their "history" passed on by the native elites to their Spanish conquerors.

Archaeological remains such as buildings, refuse, and landscape modifications left by native peoples have been altered and sometimes obliterated by centuries of use, deterioration, and ransacking. Although the archaeological remains are free of the linguistic and cultural filters that characterize the written accounts, archaeological reconstruction and interpretation are subject to a different range of biases and filters, and their use also requires care. Our approach is to bring together these disparate and sometimes contradictory sources of information. It is not yet possible to write a satisfactory "history" of Tawantinsuyu, but the written fragments and the material remains play both together and against each other to produce a better understanding of the last episode in a purely native Andean history.

THE RISE OF TAWANTINSUYU

The Spaniards recorded several versions of the Inkas' own ideas about their origins. One describes how the founding Inka and his siblings emerged from a cave at Pacarictambo (Quechua *Pakariq Tampu* 'origin station'), near Cusco. The other cycle of origin myths focuses on Lake Titicaca, far to the south of Cusco, and tells of a god, Wira Qucha[5] (written Viracocha, etc.), and his role in the birth of the sun, moon, and stars. Some chroniclers present a hybrid version of the legend and describe the Inka ancestor-founder Manqu Qhapaq (Manco Cápac, etc.) and his sister-consort emerging from the waters of Lake Titicaca and traveling to Pakaria Tampu and on to Cusco.

The myth of the four Ayar brothers is a sixteenth-century native account of Inka origins. It tells how four brothers, accompanied by their sisters, emerged from the cave of Tampu T'oqo (Tambo Toco, etc.) at Pakariq Tampu in search of fertile land where they could settle. Their wanderings were fraught with many complications, and three of the brothers never made it to Cusco. The first brother to leave the group was Ayar Kachi ('ancestor salt'). His brothers envied his magical powers and shut him up in the cave from which they had emerged. Later, a second brother, Ayar Uchu ('ancestor chili pepper'), transformed himself into a stone on Wanakawri Mountain, where he became the principal *wak'a*, or shrine, of the Inka. (The Quechua word *wak'a* – also spelled *guaca* or *huaca* – refers to any place, person, or object considered sacred. Some *wak'a*s can reasonably be called deities.)

The third brother, Ayar Awka ('ancestor enemy'), was the first to arrive at what would become Cusco (later the Inka capital), but he too was turned into stone. In this mythical narrative, one of the two wives of the fourth brother, Ayar Manqu ('first ancestor'), played a special role as leader of an army. Upon arriving in Cusco, then called Akamama and inhabited by various peoples, Mama Waqu picked up her *boleadora* (a weapon made of cords with stone or copper weights attached to the ends) and wounded a man. With her stone knife she cut open his chest, removed his lungs and blew into them. Mama Waqu's violent character terrified the people, who abandoned their settlements. Mama Uqllu (written Oclllo, etc., and meaning approximately 'nurturing mother'), Ayar Manqu's other wife, was the female prototype of the subordinate woman dedicated to household chores. It is interesting that the wives represent the two female archetypes found in the Andean tradition.

---

[5] The gloss is problematic. *Wira* means 'fat' or 'grease', and *Qucha* 'lake' or 'ocean' or 'reservoir'. Some think the names allude to this deity's having disappeared by walking over the ocean, floating on water like oil. Others, noting that in Andean folk medicine fat is taken to be the essence of bodily vitality, think the name 'Ocean of Fat' means something like 'Boundless Vitality'.

It is thus that Ayar Manqu settled in the region along with his four sisters. From then on Ayar Manqu became known as Manqu Qhapaq and lived in the temple of the sun in lower Cusco, becoming a member of *urin*, the lower half or moiety of Cusco (these divisions are explored further on). According to the myth, on settling in Cusco, Manqu Qhapaq fought the remaining people living in the area.

Like the origin myths of other cultures, Inka myths were a kind of official social and cultural template that shed light on the political, social, and ideological foundations of the Inka state. In some cases, such as the Titicaca origin myths, the legends mix mythology with political ideology and propaganda, linking the emergence of the sun and moon with that of the founding Inka. In the case of the Ayar brothers, their tale tells us how the Inka used folk memory to explain their origins and as a political resource to structure their society.

The Inka and other Andean people worshiped the hills, caves, rocks, and springs where their mythical ancestors were believed to have originated and called these origin places *pakarinas*. The Inka built an especially elaborate temple at Tampu T'uqu (written Tambo Toco, etc.), the cave where Manqu and his siblings were said to have emerged.[6] Wanakawri Mountain, the site of Ayar Uchu's magical transformation into stone, became one of the most important *wak'a*s in Tawantinsuyu, and sacrifices and pilgrimages to it were part of Qhapaq Raymi, "the most serious and solemn festival of the whole year,"[7] when noble Inka youths were initiated into manhood. The Island of the Sun on Lake Titicaca was also one of the most sacred and powerful sanctuaries in the Inka empire.

Archaeology fills in some details of the preimperial period that perhaps corresponds to the epoch of the mythical accounts. Unfortunately, archaeological research has been limited. John H. Rowe in 1944 identified the pottery style associated with the preexpansionist early Inka. That style, called Killke (see pp. 571–573), uses many design elements that would later be standardized, more finely executed, and incorporated into the imperial late Inka ceramic style, found in varying quantities throughout most of Tawantinsuyuyu. The shapes of Killke pottery, however, are very different from those of late Inka imperial pottery.

Only when archaeologists identify the styles of pottery made and used

---

[6] For the political consequences, see Urton 1990; Bauer 1991, 1992.   [7] Cobo [1653] 1990: 134.

by the non-Inka groups in the area and study their distribution and stylistic interrelationships will we be able to understand who lived in the pre-Inka Cusco region. We may then be able to detect the supposed arrival of the Inka from outside Cusco and to document any changes in location and relative hierarchical position of local peoples who may have accompanied the Inka and founded an important new polity. Some have suggested that preimperial Inka supremacy and consolidation over the Cusco Valley took place as early as C.E. 1400.[8]

The second part of Inka oral history begins with the legend of the wars against the Chanka, a people who lived north of Cusco beyond the Apurímac River. These events cover a later time, perhaps around the mid-fifteenth century. The Chanka attack on Cusco may have been preceded by a series of battles. In the final clash the Chanka besieged the city during the reign of Inka Wira Qucha. The ruling Inka, along with Urku (or Urqu?), his son and co-regent, feared the Chanka and fled the city. This is when Kusi Yupanki, another son, took on Cusco's defense and after prolonged fighting defeated his enemies. Following several victories Kusi Yupanki assumed power and took the name Pacha Kutiq ('Turns or changes the Age', also spelled Pachacuti, etc.). This event has traditionally been interpreted as marking the onset of Inka expansion and the formation of the state.

The first part of Inka "history" is purely mythical and possibly covers more time than that suggested by the list of Inka sovereigns in the written sources. Indeed, there is considerable debate over how the king lists should be interpreted. Do they record real individuals who reigned in succession or parallel chiefs who ruled simultaneously, or do they express the social organization of Cusco?[9]

In the Andes, some Spaniards thought they had found a land where people lacked the true concept of history – understood at that time to be a biblical history reinforced by Greco-Roman learning.

They did not count their age in years; neither did they measure the duration of their acts in years; nor did they have any fixed points in time from which to measure historical events, as we count them from the birth of our Lord Jesus Christ. . . . When they are asked about things of the past . . . what they usually

---

[8] Bauer 1992.
[9] For some elements of the debate, see Rowe 1946; Zuidema 1977; Rostworowski 1988; and Urton 1992. See also Chap. 1 of this volume.

answer is that the incident occurred *ñaupapacha*, which means "a long time ago" . . . when the thing is very ancient, they express this by a certain accent and ponderation of their words.[10]

Anthropologists reading Inka testimony tend to see the Inka view of the past as cyclical, rhythmic, repetitive, and patterned. Such discourse is hard, maybe impossible, to render into "history" as a series of unique events. Because of the cyclical way in which the Inka regarded their past, assigning dates before the European invasion is risky. Rowe in 1946 suggested "plausible" dates for the reigns of the last four Inka rulers, Pacha Kutiq, Thupa Yupanki, Wayna Qhapaq, and Waskhar, and these dates have been widely accepted. If one is willing to use plausible longevities of putative monarchs as guideposts to chronology, one can estimate the onset of Inka expansion around C.E. 1438, the year of the Inka's alleged defeat of the Chanka. We propose that early on, the Inka formed alliances in the Cusco area and that Inka expansion in the region was the result of transformations of social, economic, and religious institutions rather than of outright military conquests.[11]

There is as yet no archaeological evidence to confirm the legends of the Chanka wars or to verify the abrupt beginning of Inka expansion during the rule of Pacha Kutiq. Nonetheless, the highly standardized Late Inka pottery style does appear in the archaeological record with little suggestion of gradual transition between it and the earlier Killke style. Perhaps the best interpretation of the ceramic sequence, given current evidence, is that Killke was replaced rather rapidly with an officially mandated corporate style backed by a centralized state authority.

Resuming our account of the Inka legends, the chronicles tell us that the Inka, after defeating the Chanka, hoarded considerable spoils, seized during their wars in the Kunti Suyu region (one of the territorial divisions of Tawantinsuyu, discussed later). This plunder allowed Pacha Kutiq to initiate reciprocal relations with neighboring *kuraka*s (local chiefs), thus establishing the ancient mechanisms of Andean reciprocity. The Inka victory over the Chanka saw the beginnings of an incipient balance of power in Cusco. Although Pacha Kutiq had acquired military prestige and many allies, he did not wield absolute power or control over the other *kuraka*s. He could neither order nor carry out public works without their approval and support, and thus he did not have direct access to his neighbors' labor force. At the onset of Inka expansion,

---

[10] Cobo [1653] 1979: 252–253.   [11] See Rostworowski 1978, 1988.

authority was not carried out directly; it functioned through the mechanisms of reciprocity and "entreaty." Reciprocity is a socioeconomic organizational system that regulates labor service at several levels. It served as the lever that propelled the production and distribution of goods. It was a way of ordering relationships among members of a society whose economy was a nonmonetary one. In the Andes it acted as a link among distinct models of economic organization.

Inca Yupanqui [Pacha Kutiq] ordered in the city of Cuzco that all the important cacique lords, [*kurakas*] who had pledged obedience to him and were living in the provinces and neighboring lands around the city of Cuzco, attend a meeting on a certain designated day because he had certain things to communicate to them. . . . It seemed to him that each one of them should have designated and recognized lands to be farmed and maintained for each one by the people of their house and their friends. . . . And thus all together, having received this great favor that he did for them by giving them lands that would be recognized in perpetuity for each one of them, all together they gave him many thanks.[12]

Betanzos goes on to describe in detail how Pacha Kutiq first constructed storehouses in Cusco "for all the foods such as maize, *agi* [chili peppers], beans, *choclo* [tender maize], *chuño* [a variety of freeze-dried potato], *quinua* [a grain], dried meat, and all the other dried provisions and foods that they have." In an Andean system of reciprocal relationships, these accumulated goods translated into wealth. One by one, Pacha Kutiq asked the *kurakas* to come to Cusco. First, he entertained them with feasts, public banquets, gifts, and the exchange of women.

It seemed to Inca Yupanque [Pacha Kutiq] that it was proper for him to do them some favors and do something to please them. In the assembly he gave them many jewels of gold and silver. . . . He also gave each one two sets of garments he wore, and to each one he also gave a lady born in Cuzco and of Inca lineage. . . . Because of these family ties, they would never rebel. There would be perpetual friendship and confederation between them and those of the city of Cuzco.

Then Pacha Kutiq delivered his entreaty – the request to carry out the necessary public works before embarking on his conquests. This allowed the young ruler to consolidate and expand his territories and begin negotiations with the peoples of the *altiplano* surrounding Lake Titicaca to the south.

Reciprocity was the key to the rapid expansion of the Inka state: The empire made an overture with initial gifts and offered potential vassals a

---

[12] Betanzos [1551] 1996: 50.

tempting series of exchanges should they accept and make a return – but it was understood that exchange of "gifts" entailed losing autonomy. When a reciprocal entreaty was not accepted, the Inka launched wars of conquest. The *kurakas* of other regions feared engaging in wars that spelled certain defeat, death, or their replacement by others partial to the lords of Cusco. It was preferable for the *kurakas* to accept the gifts offered, begin kinship ties by exchanging women, and submit to Inka supremacy. "In this way, and with other good methods they employed, [the Inka] entered many lands without war."[13]

The Inka entreaty may have been refused if it was not carried out in the established manner or if it did not satisfy the *kuraka* because the Inka was not sufficiently generous. Local lords may have refused the Inka entreaty if they were discontent or offended by some omission. To avoid such situations, the Inka was obliged to display lavish generosity, and negotiations may have involved offers and counteroffers.

Perhaps the rulers of fledgling Tawantinsuyu encountered obstacles in the mechanisms of reciprocity. Such obstacles could have delayed their plans and they may have, at least on occasion, disregarded the entreaty and the obligation, acting directly instead. No doubt this jeopardized the close ancestral ties that linked the Inka to the lower-ranking lords, as is evident during the peak of Inka power.

Archaeological evidence confirms that Inka expansion occurred late in the long prehistory of the Andes. Archaeologists identify it by a series of distinctive styles in ceramics, architecture, textiles, and metalwork that are found lying above and sometimes mixed with the remains of immediately pre-Inka societies in much of what became Tawantinsuyu. The distribution of late Inka pottery, the imperial style associated with the Inka state, is uneven. In some areas there is no material evidence for an Inka presence. All of this leads most archaeologists to believe that Inka expansion took place in fewer than 100 years, beginning with Pacha Kutiq's consolidation of the Cusco region and the nearby Urubamba Valley and followed by his conquests in the Soras and Vilcas regions of Kunti Suyu and the kingdoms of Qulla Suyu on the shores of Lake Titicaca. It is generally thought that the imperial style that marked the onset of expansion began during the reign of Inka Pacha Kutiq in the mid–fifteenth century.

[13] Cieza [1553] 1959: 159.

CUSCO AND THE RULING ÉLITE

What was the structure of Cusco's ruling élite? At the apex sat the Inka ruler, who traced his ancestry to the sun and was sometimes referred to as "the child of the sun." Although today the word Inka is used to describe the king, the dominant people of Tawantinsuyu, and the art style associated with the Cusco rulers, Inka "rightly means king, and it is the name applied to all the *orejón* lords [lords who wore ear ornaments] of Cusco and to each one of them. In order to distinguish between the *orejones* and the *inca* king (and when one wants to talk to him) he was called Çapa Inca, which means unique king."[14]

As a descendant of the sun, the Inka king was regarded as a living god and divine monarch, and he was treated accordingly.

No one was allowed to appear before him with shoes on, no matter how important a lord he might be, not even his brothers; rather, they came barefooted and with their heads bowed all the time they were speaking before him or bringing him a message. He always ate alone, without anyone daring to touch the food he was eating. Lords carried him in a litter on their shoulders. If he went out to the square [of Cusco], he sat on a golden seat under a parasol made of ostrich [i.e., rhea] feathers dyed red. He drank from golden tumblers, and all the other service dishes of his household were of gold.[15]

The Inka ruler was in charge of war, religion, and the administration of the empire. But the vast size of Tawantinsuyu and the rapid pace of conquest meant he could not be everywhere at once. As a living god he was considered too omnipotent to deal with his subjects directly, and, as Gose observes, this required him to authorize a whole range of stand-ins. Thus he often delegated his powers to his generals, to the high priest of the sun, and to the *Inkap rantin*, or "Inka's substitute" (often a half or full brother of the Inka), some of whom served as high-ranking administrators of the four *suyus*, or territorial divisions of the empire. At the same time, the Inka had a statue made of himself:

They would take the statue for their brother, calling it *guauque*, which means brother. . . . Some of the statues were made of gold, others of silver, wood, stone, or other materials. The kings gave their *guauques* a house and servants.

---

[14] Betanzos [1551] 1996: 123.   [15] Betanzos [1551] 1996: 27–28.

They also assigned some farmland to support those who were in charge of each statue.[16]

From the reign of Thupa Yupanki onward, the sovereign Inka, like divine kings in a few other dynastic societies (pharaonic Egypt, pre-Christian Hawaii), was expected to marry his full sister (Fig. 10.1). The spectacular deviation from ordinary incest rules dramatized the gulf separating his divinity and purity from the common lot, and it served politically to differentiate close heirs from the many other potential contenders for succession whom his numerous secondary wives might bear.

Cusco's nobility was organized into corporate descent groups of royal *ayllus* (written *ayllo*, etc., in colonial times), or *panakas* (*panaca*), and nonroyal *ayllus*. (The word *ayllu*, which had numerous and puzzling usages, seems basically to have meant an ancestor-focused descent group at any given level of aggregation. With reference to a relatively small kindred, the focused ancestor might be a recent forebear, while some large – perhaps ethnic – segment of humanity might be imagined as the *ayllu* founded by a mythic being of remote times.) These nonroyal *ayllus* were composed of so-called Inkas-by-privilege, non-Inka peoples from the Cusco area whose *kurakas* were accorded the hereditary status of provincial nobility. Because the Inka considered these people loyal and they spoke Quechua, many were resettled as *mitmaq* colonists throughout the empire (a policy discussed in detail later).

Each *panaka* included the male and female descendants of one former Inka but excluded the person currently in power, whose descendants would in time form their own *panaka*. The chroniclers say that these corporations tended the mummy of the dead ruler, keeping the memory of him and his exploits alive with songs. They recorded these on *khipu*, multicolored knotted cords used to keep track of numbers and possibly oral history. They also commemorated his deeds on painted cloth, which was passed on from generation to generation. For a nonliterate society, it was extremely important to maintain such traditions.

Upon the death of the king, the prince did not inherit his house and treasure, but it was handed over along with the body of the deceased king to the family that he had founded. This entire treasure was used for the cult of his body and the sustenance of his family. After having the body of their father the king

---

[16] Cobo [1653] 1990: 37.

331

Figure 10.1. Litter bearing Thupa Inka Yupanki and Mama Uqllu. From Felipe Guaman Poma de Ayala, *Nueva Coronica y Buen Gobierno* (Paris: Institut d'Ethnologie, 1936 [1613]).

embalmed, they kept it with all his dishes and jewelry; the king's family and all of his descendants adored the body as a god. The body was handed down to the most prominent members of the family, and they did not make use of the king's dishes, except when the town or place where the body was deposited held an important fiesta. And the successor to the crown set up his house anew, accumulating for it a treasure to leave to those of his ayllo and lineage.[17]

The mummy of the Inka continued to enjoy all his possessions just as he had during his lifetime. He represented a living ancestor whom the people revered during Cusco's great festivals. On these occasions the members of his *panaka* carried the mummy on a litter into the great plaza of Cusco, where he was surrounded by his kinfolk and servants.

The bodies were brought out with a large retinue for all solemn festivals, and for less solemn occasions, in place of the bodies, their guaugues [brother statues] were brought out. In the square they were seated in a row according to their seniority, and there the servants and guardians ate and drank. A flame was kindled before the deceased of a certain firewood that was carved and cut all the same length. The food set before the dead bodies was burned in this flame. Also placed before these bodies were large tumblers made of gold and silver like pitchers, which were called vilques. Into these tumblers they put the chicha, with which they would drink a toast to their deceased, but before drinking they would show it to the deceased. The deceased would toast each other; the deceased would toast the living, and vice versa.[18]

The *panaka*s enabled the deceased rulers to maintain an active role in Cusco politics, creating a large entourage that was incorporated into the Inka administrative class. According to Sarmiento de Gamboa, writing in 1572 from Inka testimony, ancient "custodian *ayllus*" along with the *panaka*s formed Cusco's élite and aristocracy. As we see later, the *panaka*s could undermine or enhance the power of living kings and created factions and alliances that influenced various events in Inka history, especially the prolonged squabbles over succession that followed the death of a ruler. Each ruler sired many children with his various wives, resulting in a large ruling class. The *panaka*s of the last Inka rulers were the most important and had access, since the onset of the Inka conquests, to large tracts of private land. In addition to their estates, worked by innumerable *yana*, or retainers at the service of the Inka, they also had augurs, persons who foretold the future by observing the flight of birds, as well as diviners, women, and servants responsible for the upkeep of the estates.

---

[17] Cobo [1653] 1979: 111.   [18] Cobo [1653] 1990: 40.

In the final decades of Tawantinsuyu, the large number of people involved in *panaka* affairs and the labor investment tied up in managing their landholdings, as well as those of the state religion, kindled considerable resentment. Waskhar, who ruled Cusco briefly before civil war broke out between him and his brother Atawallpa, declared that "so many nobles were involved in serving these dead bodies, and their lives were so licentious" that the dead should be buried and all their riches should be taken away from them. "The dead should not be a part of his court, only the living, because the dead had taken over the best of everything in his kingdom."[19] Betanzos tells us that Waskhar

went out into the square [of Cusco] and declared that henceforth the lands of coca and maize production that had been owned by the Sun and the bodies of the dead rulers, including those of his father, Huayna Capac, would be taken from them. All these he took for himself, saying that neither the Sun nor the dead nor his father who was now dead ate. Since they did not eat, he had need of their lands. This action horrified the lords. And they were saddened because they had permitted him to become lord.[20]

What did the royal mummies look like? The chroniclers relate that the bodies of the deceased kings were elaborately embalmed and prepared "with great skill."[21] When Wayna Qhapaq died in Quito (probably in early 1528),

the nobles who were with him had him opened and took out his entrails, preparing him so that no damage would be done to him and without breaking any bones. They prepared and dried him in the Sun and the air. After he was dried and cured, they dressed him in costly clothes and placed him on an ornate litter well adorned with feathers and gold. When the body was prepared, they sent it to Cuzco.[22]

Cobo, who claims he saw one of the royal mummies, said it was "so well preserved and adorned that it looked as if it was alive. The face was so full and with such a natural skin complexion that it did not seem to be dead, though it had been for many years."[23]

As noted earlier, in addition to the traditional *panaka*s, the chroniclers refer occasionally to other *panaka*s that may have been protagonists in earlier times but whose authority was checked by more powerful antagonistic groups. We are obviously not dealing with mythical groups because there is abundant information about them in the archives. Records tell

---

[19] Cobo [1653] 1979: 41. [20] Betanzos [1551] 1996: 189. [21] Cobo [1653] 1990: 31.
[22] Betanzos [1551] 1996: 185. [23] Cobo [1653] 1979: 42.

Centers, Routes and Peripheries of the Inka State ca. C.E. 1530 (Modern Vernacular Spellings)

■ Inka site
● Modern town or city
▲ Town or city over Inka site
–·–·– National boundary
——— Inka road system

Quito ▲ Huaca
ECUADOR
Hatun Cañar ■
Tumbes ▲ Tomebamba ■

Putumayo River
Napo River
Tigre River
Marañón River
Javari River

Sechura Desert

Cajamarca ▲

Chiquitoy Viejo ■
Moche Valley and Chan Chan
PERU
Huánuco Pampa ■

Ucayali River

BRAZIL

Madeira River

Pumpu ■
Hatun Xauxa ■
Lima ■
Pachacámac ■
Inkawasi ■
La Centinela ■
Tambo Colorado ■
Nasca
Vilcas Huaman ▲

Cusco ■

Urubamba River

Beni River
Mamoré River
Guaporé River
Grande River

Hatun Colla ■
Lake Titicaca
Arequipa ● Chucuito ■ Chuquiabo (La Paz) ▲
Cochabamba ●
Paria ■ BOLIVIA

Lake Poopó

PACIFIC OCEAN

CHILE
Catarpe ■
San Pedro de Atacama ●

Tupiza ■
Tilcara ■
Salta ●
La Paya ■

ARGENTINA
Copiapó ■
Pucara de Andagala ■
Chilecito ■

Salado River

Ranchillos ■
Mendoza ●
Santiago ▲

Desaguadero River

N

0 ——— 300 mi
0 ——— 300 km

Map 10.2

where these people lived and what fields they owned before the sixteenth century. The books of the Real Hacienda of Cusco (Archivo General de la Nación, Lima) and the parochial books of Cusco are a font of information. If we add every *panaka* mentioned there to the list of traditional ones, they form a total of eight on either half or moiety. Because the number eight is a multiple of dualism and quadripartition, it appears often in Andean *ayllu* organization.

Dualism may be a very old Andean (and also Amazonian) tradition, but we cannot be sure of its extent. Long before the rise of the Inka, local lords organized their communities into two halves, upper and lower, or right and left. The division, however, was not limited to two halves; instead, each half was ruled by two chiefs, forming a quadripartite organization.

If this was the sociopolitical organization of the pre-Inka period, it is understandable that the Inka continued this system. It allowed two Inka rulers to rule simultaneously, one in upper Cusco and the other in lower Cusco. In other words, the ruler who wielded power and leadership belonged to the upper, *hanan*, moiety and had an "assistant." The second Inka, of the lower, *urin*, moiety, was generally a priest of the sun religion who also had his "companion." Thus, instead of comprising a chronological listing of successive monarchs, the king list discussed earlier would seem to represent parallel chiefs – what Duviols has called a "diarchy." This hypothesis would, of course, disallow an absolute chronology that assumes monarchical succession (see pp. 54–55, 138–139).

This dual system is confirmed at the provincial level by two documents that refer to the southern Andes, one from La Paz, Bolivia, the other from Capachica on Lake Titicaca. The documents speak of a principal lord and a secondary lord, who served as the principal lord's "companion" or "assistant."

Quadripartition is evident in the *visitas*, or inspections, of Viceroy Toledo (1571) in the southern Andes, where we find many references to societies ruled by four chiefs. During colonial times the Spaniards found these multiple lords an obstacle and allowed only one for each moiety, excluding the "companion." The head of the lower moiety was called the *segunda persona*, or lieutenant. Over time the role of the *segunda persona* fell into disuse.

Archaeology has so far shed no light on how parallel rule actually functioned, but the layout of archaeological sites often suggests the dualism, which was such an important organizing feature in Andean societies.

Indeed, dual patterns of planning and organization can now be traced back at least 2,000 years before the Inka. Several settlements built immediately before the Inka expansion are divided into two parts. These include Auki Marka ('Princely Village') in the Huánuco region, pre-Inka Pacha Kamaq ('Animator of Space and Time', after the great deity resident there), and Hatun Marka ('Great Village') in the upper Mantaro.

Cusco: Center of the Realm

The patterns of dual and also quadripartite divisions of society and space are evident in Cusco. The city's ceremonial core consisted of upper, or *hanan*, and lower, or *urin*, divisions. Like the empire itself, Cusco was divided into four *suyus*. *Hanan* Cusco included Chinchay Suyu (written Chinchaysuyu, etc.) and Anti Suyu (Andesuyo, etc.), while Kunti Suyu (Condesuyo, etc.) and Qulla Suyu (Collasuyo, etc.) lay in *urin* Cusco. These divisions were further intersected by a complex network of conceptual lines or sightlines that originated at the Quri Kancha, Cusco's sun temple. (Some scholars locate the center at other points in the city.) These lines are recorded as *ceques* in colonial renderings of Quechua, probably representing a word *siqi* or *siq'i*. Forty-one or forty-two such lines radiated out from the Quri Kancha. The orientations of these lines were determined by some 328 *wak'as* (or shrines) – natural features in the landscape such as outcrops, springs, caves, or mountain passes – or by artificial features such as houses, fountains, or canals. Zuidema, the first modern researcher to interpret this arcane pattern, has identified many of them.[24]

From the temple of the Sun [Qori Kancha] as from the center there went out certain lines which the Indians call ceques; they formed four parts corresponding to the four royal roads which went out from Cuzco. On each one of those ceques were arranged in order the guacas [*wak'as*] and shrines which there were in Cuzco and its district, like stations of holy places, the veneration of which was common to all.[25]

Chinchay Suyu, Anti Suyu, and Qulla Suyu contained nine lines each, and Kunti Suyu had fourteen or fifteen; the number of *wak'as* along a

---

[24] The question of whether the lines were straight rays, as Zuidema has maintained since he rediscovered the complex (*The Ceque System of Cuzco*, 1963), or whether, as Rowe held in "La Constitución Inca del Cuzco" in 1985, they followed less geometric paths, is still debated; see, for example, Bauer and Dearborn 1995.

[25] Cobo [1653] 1990: 51.

given *ceque* line ranged from three to fifteen. The lines in each quadrant were ranked by a tripartition as *qullana* (often written *collana*), *payan*, or *kayaw (cayao)*. The first term alludes to royalty, the second to nonroyal status, and the third to mixed royal/nonroyal origin. The hierarchy of Cusco's *ayllus* and *panakas* in the sociopolitical organization of the valley was indicated by each group's association with a particular line, quadrant, and moiety. The groups were responsible for rituals on their *ceques'* respective *wak'as*. Some of the shrines were associated with events in Inka mythology, others marked boundaries between Cusco's social groups, and still others pinpointed locations such as mountain passes or summits.

About a third of the *wak'as* were water sources or the origins of principal irrigation canals. Thus not only did the *ceques* organize political and ritual space, they also appear linked to Cusco's economic base – its water and productive farmland.[26] The *panakas* apparently controlled better canals and richer lands than the *ayllus*.

Some researchers, including the archaeoastronomer Aveni,[27] have suggested that the *ceque* system had astronomical functions beyond those noted by Cobo, arguing that the lines aligned with celestial events on the horizon. Zuidema sees the total *ceque* wheel as an inhabitable calendar, linking each shrine of the system with a day of the year. We explore Inka astronomy and the calendar in more detail later.

The putative center of the *ceque* system, Quri Kancha ('Golden Enclosure'), was not only Cusco's sun temple but also the empire's holiest and richest shrine. No other structure incited Spanish gold fever like the riches plundered there in 1533. By the time Cieza de León reached Cusco in the 1540s, the sanctuary had been stripped of its treasures, but those who had seen it before its ransacking told him that it was "one of the richest temples in the whole world . . . there was an image of the sun, of great size, made of gold, beautifully wrought and set with many precious stones." Below the temple "was a garden in which the earth was lumps of fine gold, and it was cunningly planted with stalks of corn that were made of gold . . . there were many tubs of gold and silver and emeralds, and goblets, pots, and every kind of vessel all of fine gold."[28] The temple's finest surviving construction is a curved wall built of blocks of

---

[26] Sherbondy (1982) first identified the relation between *ceque* ritual and water control; see also Hyslop 1990 and Bauer and Dearborn 1995.

[27] See Aveni 1981, 1987.   [28] Cieza [1553] 1959: 146–147.

shimmering dark grey andesite. Recalling this sight the same witness wrote, "In all Spain I have seen nothing that can compare with these walls and the laying of these stones."

Cusco is the most storied of all the Inka cities. As the ceremonial, political, and administrative center as well as the architectural showcase of a rapidly expanding empire, it was designed to dazzle and impress visitors with the virtuosity of its stonework, the pomp of its ceremonies, and the holiness and wealth of its shrines. Pizarro's secretary, one of the first Spaniards to see Cusco, remarked on its size and beauty, noting it "would be worthy to appear even in Spain."[29] "Nowhere in this kingdom of Peru is there a city with the air of nobility that Cusco possessed. . . . Compared with it, the other provinces of the Indies are mere settlements," wrote Cieza de León, who saw a city partly in ruins – the aftermath of the 1535 Inka siege against the Spanish invaders. Nonetheless, such was the fame of Cusco's wealth that even the usually levelheaded Cieza de León confessed himself "amazed . . . that the whole city of Cusco and its temples were not of solid gold."[30]

The city's population waxed and waned to accommodate pilgrims attending the city's numerous religious feasts or workers engaged in Cusco's monumental building projects. Eyewitnesses reported seeing many houses on the hillsides surrounding the city, and others described it as "very large and very populous."[31] Population estimates, notoriously unreliable, range from 40,000 to 100,000 for greater Cusco.

Cusco's population mirrored the ethnic makeup of the empire. Some twelve districts of what Cieza de León called "foreign tribesmen," many of them laborers and artisans, lived in districts surrounding the ceremonial core. "This city," noted Cieza de León, "was full of strange and foreign peoples, for there were Indians from Chile, Pasto and Cañar Chachapoyas, Huancas, Colla, and all the other tribes to be found in the provinces . . . each of them established in the place and district set aside for them by the governors of the city."[32]

Cusco's residents also included provincial lords, required to set up lodgings in the city and live there for 4 months a year. Their sons were brought to the capital and educated in Quechua, the political language of the realm. The Inka also took the idols of newly conquered peoples to Cusco, where they were regarded as honored hostages. If "some province

---

[29] Pedro Sancho de la Hoz, cited in Rowe 1968: 63.   [30] [1553] 1959: 156.
[31] Cristobal de Molina, in Gasparini and Margolies 1980: 49.   [32] Cieza [1553] 1959: 148.

rebelled against them, the Incas ordered the protective native gods of the rebellious province to be brought out and put in public, where they were whipped ignominiously every day until such province was made to serve the Incas again."[33]

Despite its importance, however, relatively few archaeological excavations have been carried out in the city itself. Much of what we know of Inka Cusco comes from the often contradictory descriptions of the chroniclers, none of whom, curiously, left us with a plan of the city as they first saw it. This, coupled with the Spanish remodeling of Inka Cusco, has stimulated considerable debate about the city's layout and the identification and functions of certain buildings.

Some chroniclers noted that Pacha Kutiq, often called the architect of imperial Cusco, "named the whole city lion's body, saying that the residents of it were limbs of that lion."[34] Based on these accounts, some researchers[35] have suggested that the city's founders laid out the ceremonial core of their capital in the form of a puma (the Spaniards often used "lion" to refer to the puma), with Saksay Waman (written Sacsayhuaman, etc.), the temple-fortress perched above the city, serving as the puma's head, and the sector where the rechanneled Tullu Mayu (written Tullumayo, etc.; 'Bone River') and Saphi Mayu (written Sapphi, etc.; 'Root River') came together, forming the tail. This area is still called *pumap chupan* ('puma's tail'). Others, however, propose that Cusco's puma shape should be read metaphorically rather than literally, and that it explained social structure, royal succession, and borders,[36] with reference to an area that extended far beyond the confines of the city's ceremonial core.[37]

Other early Spanish accounts of Cusco note that Pacha Kutiq used models to design his city, ordering "clay figures made just as he planned to have it built."[38] No matter who designed Cusco, careful planning is evident. The scheme embraced scattered hamlets and agricultural estates set among cultivated fields, storehouses, terraces, and irrigation canals extending many kilometers beyond the city.

The focus of Cusco's central sector and its ceremonial core was a large plaza open to the southwest and later covered over in part by Spanish constructions. Smaller plazas also graced the ceremonial core, but in

[33] Cobo [1635] 1990: 3–4.   [34] Betanzos [1551] 1996: 74.
[35] Rowe 1967; Gasparini and Margolies 1980.   [36] Zuidema 1983.   [37] Hyslop 1990.
[38] Betanzos [1551] 1996: 69.

antiquity, the main plaza, called Aucaypata in a Hispano-Quechua rendering, formed, along with the adjoining Kusi Pata, an enormous dual plaza divided by one of the city's rivers, the Saphi. The river was "covered with broad beams, and great flags . . . laid over them to make a floor."[39]

The plaza served as the setting for ceremonies that punctuated the Inka ritual calendar. "In neither Jerusalem, Rome, nor Persia, nor anywhere else in the world, did any republic or king ever bring together in one place such wealth of gold and silver and precious stones as in this plaza of Cusco when these feasts . . . were celebrated."[40] Cusco's main square was also the nexus of the four principal roads leading to the empire's territorial divisions: Chinchay Suyu, Anti Suyu, Kunti Suyu, and Qulla Suyu. Although more than twenty other roads linked Cusco to its hinterland, the four main ones are important because they represented and connected the four *suyus* to Cusco.

Around the plaza lay the finely built palace-compounds, or "splendid buildings" of the ruling monarch and the lineages of deceased rulers, public buildings, temples, and shrines, "all made of stone, so skillfully joined that it was evident how old the edifices were, for the huge stones were very well set."[41] Pedro Sancho, Pizarro's secretary, noted that "most of the buildings are built of stone and the rest have half their façade of stone. There are also many adobe houses, very efficiently made, which are arranged along straight streets on a cruciform plan. The streets are all paved, and a stone-lined water channel runs down the middle of each street. Their only fault is to be narrow; only one mounted man can ride on either side of the channel."[42]

Palace-compounds included the Hatun Kancha ('Great Enclosure'), many of whose walls are still visible, and the Aqlla Wasi ('House of the Chosen'), which housed the *mamakuna* or 'chosen women' who served rituals, brewed maize beer, and produced fine cloth. Among the shrines surrounding the plaza was one on the southeast side of the plaza dedicated to Wira Qucha, the invisible deity who combined the attributes of Trickster and Creator. (Today it is the site of Cusco's cathedral.) The Kasana (written Casana, etc.) compound on the northwest side of the plaza may have served as the palace of Wayna Qhapaq. Spanish accounts are not very precise about whether these compounds served as palaces of the reigning monarch, the lineages of deceased rulers, or as *kallanka*, the

---

[39] Garcilaso [1604] 1987: 428.   [40] Cieza [1553] 1959: 183.   [41] Cieza [1553] 1959: 144.
[42] Quoted in Hemming 1983: 119.

great halls designed to house visitors or stage official and religious functions in rainy weather. One of these *kallanka* was so large "that sixty
mounted men could easily joust with canes in it."[43]

Religion, astronomy, and the calendar

Inka religion, like some other aspects of the culture, can be considered
on two levels: the state and the local. The official state religion was in
theory imposed on the newly conquered territories, but not to the exclusion of the older, local ones. Imperial Inka religion declined rapidly in
importance in the aftermath of the Spanish invasion, partly because it
was indeed imperial religion and relied on the now destroyed state
infrastructure, and partly because it was the first and obvious brunt of
efforts by the Spanish clergy to stamp out "idolatry." Local beliefs fared
somewhat better and proved more resilient to Spanish efforts to destroy
them, often surviving into the seventeenth century when they became
the targets of a new and vigorous campaign against "idolatry" (see Chap.
14).

Inka religion is not well understood, partly because it was so foreign
to the Spaniards that they lacked concepts to comprehend it.[44] The
confused and contradictory accounts reflect attempts by the chroniclers
to simplify what was an extremely complex Andean religion. The Inka
articulated and merged pan-Andean folk beliefs and religion with their
own cosmology, into which they incorporated regional *wak'as* and
weather/sky gods.

Sometimes the devil told them he was the Sun, and at other times in other
places he said he was the Moon. He told others he was their god and creator.
He told others he was their light who warmed them and shined on them, and
thus they would see him in the volcanoes of Arequipa. In other places he said
he was their lord who had made the world and that he was Pachacama, which
means maker of the world. Thus, as I have said, he had deceived and blinded
them.[45]

Much of the confusion surrounding Inka religion stems from the fact
that the Spanish clergy, in the aftermath of the invasion, created a many-

---

[43] Garcilaso [1604] 1987: 426.
[44] On the Spanish effort and (by 1600) failure to conceptualize it, see Sabine MacCormack's *Religion
in the Andes* (1991).
[45] Betanzos [1551] 1996: 44–45.

faceted godhead to explain the Catholic holy trinity. In this scheme three deities – Wira Qucha (creator), Inti (sun), and Illapa (thunder) – shared the main altar at Quri Kancha. In their zeal to explain Catholicism to Andean converts, the clergy even invented new deities, such as Inti-Illapa.

The Inka state religion concentrated on Inti, the solar deity, whose principal temple was Quri Kancha in Cusco. "Although this temple was dedicated to the Sun, statues of Viracocha, the Thunder, the Moon and other important idols were placed there."[46] The Inka and other Andean peoples did not merely worship the heavenly bodies themselves but focused on their movements, such as the appearance of the Pleiades or the daily passage of the sun from east to west or the sun's yearly solstitial movement.[47] "Since they boasted of being children of the Sun, the Incas made every effort to legitimize and enhance Sun worship with more brilliant services, a larger number of priests, and more frequent offerings and sacrifices."[48] In his role as tutelary god, Inti served as both an ancestor for the ruling Inka and as a symbol for the expanding state. This imperial manipulation of religion was apparently gradual and began after the Chanka wars and the onset of Inka expansion. In doing so, the Inka created a mythology to legitimize their rule and a rationale for expansion.

As noted, the Inka rulers traced their ancestry to the sun, which they believed emerged from Lake Titicaca. The sanctuaries on the Island of the Sun and Moon in Lake Titicaca ranked third in importance after Pacha Kamaq and Quri Kancha. Their "veneration was so widespread that people came to this place on pilgrimages from everywhere."[49] The shrine on the Island of the Sun boasted a large plaza flanked by a sacred rock where Inka myths relate that the Sun itself emerged. The side of the rock facing the plaza was covered with plaques of gold, and the side facing the lake was covered with finely woven textiles.

Illapa, the lightning god, was regarded as the sacred force controlling thunder and, by extension, all celestial bodies and forces, such as rain, hail, and the rainbow. "They imagined that he was a man who lived in the sky and that he was made up of stars, with a war club in his left hand and a sling in his right hand. He dressed in shining garments which

[46] Cobo [1653] 1990: 49.   [47] Demarest 1981.   [48] Cobo [1653] 1990: 25.
[49] Cobo [1653] 1990: 96.

gave off the flashes of lightning when he whirled his sling, when he wanted it to rain."[50]

Inka ritual emphasized the readings of omens and divination. Oracles and their predictions played a central role in the Andes and in Cusco politics. Not only did Inti have an oracle, but major and minor provincial *wak'a*s as well as dead kings, represented by their *panaka*s, spoke through oracular shrines. Inka rulers often formed alliances with provincial oracles, such as Pacha Kamaq, one of the most powerful and influential of all oracles. "In magnitude, devotion, authority, and richness, the Temple of Pachacama was second only to the magnificent [Cusco] Temple of the Sun."[51] The Inka built a sun temple at Pacha Kamaq and called it P'unchaw Kancha ('Daylight Enclosure').

After they conquered the Valley of Pachacama, they saw the grandeur, antiquity, and veneration of this temple and the way the neighboring provinces were so devoted to it. And they decided that it would not be easy to change this because the authority which the place commanded over everyone was so extraordinary. It is said that the Incas conferred with the local caciques and lords of this valley and with the priests of this god or devil. Thus the Incas decided that the temple would remain with the majesty and service that it had before, on the condition that another building or chapel be built there and that a statue of the Sun be placed in the chapel and worshiped. . . . This arrangement did not displease the devil; in fact, it is said that from then on he showed he was very pleased by his answers.[52]

Ethnohistorical sources and archaeological evidence have pinpointed Pacha Kamaq as the center of a vast ceremonial network that, centuries before the Spanish invasion, had expanded throughout much of the central and north coast (see Chaps. 5 and 6). A much feared deity, Pacha Kamaq was thought to punish offenders by sending earthquakes. Tribute to him came from as far away as Esmeraldas in Ecuador and included cotton, maize, coca leaf, dried fish, llamas, and guinea pigs, as well as finely woven textiles, ceramic drinking vessels, and raw materials such as gold, all stockpiled in the sanctuary's storehouses.

Pacha Kamaq gave public pronouncements and predictions. But before they could visit the sanctuary, pilgrims had to abstain from salt, chili pepper, dried meat, and sex for twenty days. A private consultation with the oracle involved abstaining for a year. Although oracular communica-

---

[50] Cobo [1653] 1990: 32.   [51] Cobo [1653] 1990: 85.   [52] Cobo [1653] 1990: 89.

tion could be public, it was more often private, with a priest consulting the *wak'a* in private and conveying the reply to the public. Inka rulers often conferred with Pacha Kamaq's oracle; Wayna Qhapaq, for instance, consulted Pacha Kamaq about his health shortly before his death. Waskhar also consulted the oracle and was told he would emerge victorious in the war against his brother, Atawallpa. Because the oracle made a mistaken prophecy, even Atawallpa lost respect for it and apparently encouraged the Spaniards to ransack it. Such was the renown of Pacha Kamaq that Pizarro sent an advance party from Cajamarca to plunder its riches. Describing its oracle, Miguel de Estete, one of the first Spaniards to see Pacha Kamaq in 1533, wrote:

It was in a good house, well painted, in a very dark chamber with a close fetid smell. Here there was a very dirty Idol made of wood, and they say that this is their God who created them and sustains them, and gives them their food. At the foot of the Idol there were some offerings of gold, and it was held in such veneration that only the attendants and servants, who, as they say, were appointed by it, were allowed to officiate before it. No other person might enter. . . . The Captain [Hernando Pizarro, a younger, half-brother of Francisco] ascertained that the Devil frequented this Idol, and spoke with his servants, saying diabolical things, which were spread all over the land. . . . They come to this Devil from distances of three hundred leagues, with gold and silver and cloth.[53]

Provincial *wak'a*s also played an important role in the administration of the realm. During the all-empire sacrificial cycle, which the Spanish recorded as "Capacocha" (Qhapaq Qucha?), the cult objects of every important provincial *wak'a*s were taken to Cusco where they were consulted by the ruler in a "congress of oracular deities" (as Gose calls it) and asked to make predictions. This was "a very special and solemn festival [which] was also celebrated after the death of the Inca when his successor took the fringe, which was the insignia of the king. The purpose of this festival was to pray to the gods for the health, preservation, and prosperity of the Inca who was to be crowned."[54]

Kurakas from all over Tawantinsuyu gathered together at the court, including a deputy representing each *wak'a* and shrine of the empire. Although the *kurakas* accompanied their *wak'a*s, the rulers preferred to communicate with the provinces through their *wak'a*s rather than through their chiefs. During the "Capacocha"

[53] Report of Miguel de Astete on the expedition to Pachacamac, in Markham 1872: 82.
[54] Cobo [1653] 1990: 154.

the things that were to be offered in the sacrifice were brought [to Cusco's main square], namely, two hundred children from four to ten years of age, a large amount of gold and silver made into tumblers and figurines of sheep [i.e., alpacas or llamas] and other animals, much very well made cumbi [fine cloth], both large and small, a large amount of seashells of all kinds, colored feathers, and up to a thousand sheep [llamas] of all colors.[55]

Then, according to Cieza,

They encircled the entire square of Cuzco with a great cable of gold, and inside it they placed all the treasure and precious stones . . . after this was done, they went through the annual ceremony, which was that these statues and images and priests came together and announced what was going to happen during the year, whether there would be abundance or scarcity; whether the Inca would have a long life, or might, perchance, die that year; if enemies might be expected to invade the country from some side, or if some of the pacified peoples would rebel . . . And this was asked not of all the oracles together, but one by one.[56]

Later, according to Cobo, "the Inca ordered the distribution . . . of the sacrifices that had to be offered at the *guacas* of the city and at the provincial *guacas* from throughout his kingdom." Cobo says that the *wak'a*s were included in the sacrifice because if any *wak'a* "did not receive an offering, it would become angry with the Inca and take his vengeance on him." Once all the *wak'a*s of Cusco had been lavishly served with sacrificial offerings, Cobo continues, the "provincial priests took what had been allotted to the *wak'a*s of their lands." Processions accompanied the young children who had been designated as offerings to the provincial *wak'a*s. Some children, dressed in fine garments and accompanied by pottery and figurines of gold and *Spondylus* shell were sacrificed on the summits of snow-clad volcanoes. Such is the origin of the "Ampato Maiden," a girl in Inka garb found frozen on the snowcapped peak of a mountain near Arequipa in 1995. Duviols interpreted the injunction to carry these sacrifices to their destinations in straight lines as meaning the sacrificial caravans cut rectilinear paths across the landscape, and thereby enacted the ritual triumph of the ideal over the actual.

In his discussion of Cusco's *ceque* system, Cobo detailed the sacrifices that had to be made to each shrine on each line, variously including gold, clothing, seashells, llamas, and, occasionally, children. In addition to the regular sacrifices for the Cusco shrines, llamas were sacrificed every day in the main square at sunrise, noon, and sunset.

---

[55] Cobo [1653] 1990: 154. [56] Cieza [1553] 1959: 191.

"Capacocha" was only the most spectacular of many ways in which the Inka state systematically coopted local and regional cults, thereby attaching local sacred authority to Inka edicts. Huarochirí's non-Inka villagers, who gave testimony to the writer of an anonymous 1608 Quechua book about their deities, were impressed by the thoroughness of the Inkas: "the Inca would have offerings of his gold and silver given according to his *quipo* account, to all the *huacas*, to the well-known *huacas*, to all the *huacas*. He used to have them [officials and local worshipers] give gold and silver . . . all this exactly according to *quipo* counts."[57] When Lanti Chumpi, a young woman of this community, discovered the new deity Llocllay Huancupa and the villagers built him a shrine, Inka authority immediately set out to coopt Llocllay's cult. An Inka-sponsored augury speaking on behalf of the otherwise mute Llocllay made him declare himself to be a "child" – that is, an affiliated cult – of the great state-sponsored shrine of Pacha Kamaq:

At that time there existed in the village named Llacsa Tampo another *huaca*, called Cati Quillay, an emissary of the Inca. Cati Quillay was a *yañca*, one who could force any *huaca* that wouldn't talk to speak.
    Saying "Who are you?"
    "What is your name?
    "What have you come for?"
    He started to make the *huaca* called Llocllay Huancupa talk.
    Llocllay Huancupa answered saying, "I am a child of Pacha Camac Pacha Cuyuchic, World Maker and World Shaker. My name is Llocllay Huancupa. It was my father who sent me here, saying 'Go and protect that Checa Village!' "

For many years the villagers served Llocllay, but there came a time when their devotion no longer sufficed in the eyes of his Pacha Kamaq – oriented managers. Inka authority then had the deity, in effect, go on strike by retiring to the home of Pacha Kamaq:

At one time, maybe because people didn't take good care of him, Llocllay Huancupa went back to his father Pacha Camac and disappeared.
    When the people saw this happen, they grieved deeply and searched for him, adorning the place where Lanti Chumpi had first discovered him, and building him a step-pyramid.
    But when they still couldn't find him, all the elders readied their llamas, guinea pigs, and all kinds of clothing, and went to Pacha Camac.

---

57 Salomon and Urioste 1991: 100.

So by worshipping his father again, they got Llocllay Huancupa to return. People served him even more, with renewed fervor, endowing him with llama herders.[58]

The story as a whole, though clothed in mythic idiom, is typical of Inka politics. By a modest investment of initial reciprocity, the local Inka representatives positioned themselves to later leverage a major increment in state-supervised infrastructure (temple), productive goods (herds), and labor (herders).

The annual cycle of religious festivals as well as the agricultural year was regulated by an extremely accurate calendar. Sun, moon, and star observations were used to program the most important rituals in Cusco and, by extension, Tawantinsuyu: "and they know the revolutions the sun makes, and the waxing and waning of the moon. They counted the year by this, and it consists of twelve months, by their calculations."[59]

The Inka, like other Andean peoples, observed rising and setting celestial bodies and used their 12-month calendar to mark the onset of the planting or harvesting seasons and rituals related to these events. Some village specialists used shadow or light-casting devices (gnomons) to determine the timing of certain celestial events, such as solstices. When the non-Inka villagers of Huarochirí explained their rites, they said that "this man [a priestly officiant] observes the course of the sun from a wall constructed with perfect alignment. When the rays of the sun touched this calibrated wall, he proclaimed to the people, 'Now we must go'; or if they didn't, he'd say 'Tomorrow is the time.' "[60]

Several chroniclers note that the Inka placed sets of tall stone pillars on hills flanking Cusco. Called *sukanka* (in colonial spelling, *sucanca*, these gnomons marked the movement of the sun along the Cusco horizon and the times of specific sunsets, such as on solstices and equinoxes. When Cieza de León saw them, they were "in a state of neglect" but still numerous. Because of their links to imperial religion, zealous Christian priests probably destroyed the *sukanka*s early in the Spanish occupation of Cusco, and archaeological evidence for these pillars is slim. The chroniclers offer conflicting accounts as to the numbers and exact locations of the *sukanka*s. Important sunsets were probably observed by hundreds of people congregated in Cusco's central plaza. More private

[58] Salomon and Urioste 1991: 112.   [59] Cieza [1553] 1959: 172.
[60] Salomon and Urioste 1991: 72.

rituals involving shadow and light-casting devices may have been attended only by Cusco's political and religious élite. The main fiestas were related to the sun and agriculture, such as Inti Raymi, the June solstice, and Qhapac Raymi, the December solstice, which probably marked the onset of the new year as well. The beginning of the planting season in August and the harvest in April were similarly fêted.

As Tawantinsuyu grew ever larger, it became increasingly important for the Inka to coordinate ritual activities across the realm. According to Zuidema and Aveni, the Inka reckoned multiple calendars, taking into account solar, lunar, and planetary rhythms for different purposes. There are hints that as sun worship spread, the traditional lunar calendar was being replaced by or merged with a new calendar based on months determined by solar observations. This not only entrenched centralized ritual authority in Cusco but also underscored the special link between the reigning Inka and the sun. "When the Inca co-opted the power of the sun, they took control of time itself."[61]

CONQUEST AND CONSOLIDATION

Pacha Kutiq's principal concern after he defeated the Chanka and consolidated his hold over the Cusco Basin and the nearby Urubamba Valley was to subjugate the ethnic lords who ruled the high plains around Lake Titicaca. As discussed in the previous section, Lake Titicaca figured prominently in Inka mythology as the origin of the sun and the birthplace of the founding Inka in one version of the Inka origin myths. From the onset, relations between the Inka and the lords of Chucuito and the chief of the Hatun Qulla (written Jatun Colla, etc.) were hostile. But rivalries and internal disputes among the Lupaqa and Qulla eased the Inka conquest of the area. After they defeated the Titicaca lords, the Inka not only took over the region and its vast herds of alpacas and llamas but also opened the way to the Pacific via the various highland enclaves established by these ethnic groups in the temperate coastal valleys to the west of Lake Titicaca. These enclaves were the first contact between Inka and the coast. The lakeside kingdoms continued to function semi-independently under the Inka, but frequent rebellions made the region problematic.

[61] Bauer and Dearborn 1995: 155.

Conquest Strategies

As the Inka expanded they used a variety of conquest and administration strategies, adapting them to the situation at hand. When possible, Inka emissaries negotiated peaceful submission, especially among societies that did not have the resources to resist. Incentives to join rather than fight the expanding Inka no doubt also included the Inka policy of ruling through the existing, local leadership rather than imposing their own appointees on their new subjects. When military action was necessary, the Inka relied on a large, well-disciplined army with a very well-organized supply system. Late in Inka times it may have become a professionalized standing army. In the following section we explore by way of example how the Inka dealt with three of the regions it encountered. It annexed Chincha by peaceful means; it subjugated neighboring Guarco (Cañete) by force; and it established the provincial center of Huánuco Pampa from scratch in a marginal, sparsely populated area.

The Chincha case displays predominantly political strategy. Castro and Ortega Morejón's account[62] tells how a brother of Inka Pacha Kutiq appeared in the valley oasis of Chincha on the southern Peruvian coast accompanied by a large army. The general asked only that he be recognized as lord of the Chincha people. The highlands general handed out gifts, and women were exchanged. He requested that a palace be built and that certain lands be handed over to the Inka, and he chose *mamakuna* – women who wove cloth and brewed maize beer, the vital fluid of ceremony – to serve the Inka. Some time elapsed before the arrival of Thupa Yupanki, who commanded his father's armies. After the usual festivities, the Inka began to establish the Cusco organizational model and ordered that the population be divided into *pachaka* groups (100 households), ten of which formed a *waranka* (1,000 households) with a local chief assigned to each. (This decimal system of administration is explored later.)

Inka construction works increased in Chincha as did the lands designated for the Inka. Land endowments for the state were very important to the Inka because produce from these filled state warehouses. Local lords, however, were not pleased because they saw their portion of the harvests decreasing. Wayna Qhapaq, the son of Thupa Yupanki, was the

---

[62] Castro and Ortega Morejón [1558] 1936.

third Inka to appear in the Chincha Valley. He asked for even more land
and requested women and servants to serve the solar religion. These
events show that by then central power, though initiated by entreaty,
had become firmly entrenched to the detriment of the native population.
Even so, the Inka "did not strip the caciques and headmen of their
power, they sent out their representative or high steward to the valley,
and ordered the worship of the sun."[63]

The people of Chincha accepted Inka impositions as long as they did
not interfere with Chincha's exchange relationships with two regions:
first, maritime long-distance barter with the far north (today Ecuador),
and second, overland barter with the highlands and Cusco. A vital part
of their exchange (discussed in more detail later) was based on obtaining
the coral-rimmed Ecuadorian *mullu* shell (*Spondylus* sp.), used as offerings for the gods.

Archaeological research in the Chincha Valley graphically shows the
outcome of the peaceful incorporation of a rich *señorío* into Tawantinsuyu. (*Señorío*, 'lordship', is a Spanish term that denominates polities of
varying political complexity and territorial extent. A *señorío*'s territory
could include one valley, as in the case of Chincha, or a larger region,
such as Huarochirí in the highlands east of Lima. Spaniards, perhaps
following the Inka, regarded any political aggregate recognizing one
leader as a *señorío*, regardless of how tightly or loosely structured the
entity was.) The Inka achieved the substantial economic gains described
by Castro and Ortega Morejón by carefully inserting themselves into the
local patterns of control. The Chincha capital, today the archaeological
site of La Centinela, is a group of impressive adobe compounds built in
the local style but continuing to function during Inka domination. In
their midst the Inka built, or had built, a compound of their own that
included what was probably a palace.

The Inka compound was constructed of adobe bricks, in contrast to
earlier Chincha constructions, which were of coursed adobe (*tapia*). It
also contained a rectangular plaza and the trapezoidal niches and doorways so characteristic of their architecture. Alongside the buildings that
may have served as an Inka palace lies a truncated pyramidal platform
more reminiscent of Chincha architecture, although it was constructed
of adobe bricks and formed part of the Inka compound. The compound
is unmistakably Inka, but the truncated pyramidal platform mimics the

[63] Cieza [1553] 1959: 347.

similar central features of the ethnically Chincha compounds that dominate the site. It is almost as if the Inka had made a conscious attempt to recognize and legitimize local patterns within the very compound from which they controlled the polity.

The Inka modified several Chincha compounds: sun-dried adobe bricks were added to *tapia* constructions, niches were incorporated into some public spaces, and traffic flow into at least one compound was altered to align it with the Inka compound. The archaeological evidence, however, suggests that the activities carried out in the Chincha compounds were not drastically changed by the Inka overlords. The Inka intent was to change the façade and the orientation but not the function. The *tapia* compounds with their pyramid-like architecture clearly served public and ceremonial ends, but because of their size and traffic capacity, they seem to have been related to small and probably tightly structured groups. We speculate that they were the scenes of important ceremonies of political legitimation and rites of passage, such as initiation and marriage.

Here as everywhere in Inka political architecture, there are suggestions of state hospitality related to conquest and administration. The scale of the hospitality and the way much of it appears to have been channeled through local authorities, however, differs from the plan at Huánuco Pampa, which began from a clean slate. Because of the centralization of power in pre-Inka Chincha, Inka reciprocity such as feasting was probably constricted and channeled through the existing power structure.

As Dorothy Menzel noted in 1966, Inka-period pottery from Chincha combines local styles with a heavy borrowing of the elements of imperial Inka pottery as known from Cusco. Mingling of local and Inka elements in pottery continued into the Spanish colonial period, even while in most areas the symbols of Inka governance were being abandoned. Inka designs in Chincha had apparently been sufficiently incorporated into the local style of pottery so that they were no longer seen as insignia of alien rulers.

In Chincha peaceful incorporation into Tawantinsuyu apparently led to a relationship of mutually advantageous collaboration, in part because of the importance of *mullu* shell to feed the ever-growing number of state-endorsed cults (as in the Huarochirí example cited on pp. 796–797). The relationship between Chincha and the Inka became so close, and the prestige of Chincha's lords so high, that when Spanish invaders first laid eyes on the Inka king Atawallpa, the lord of Chincha was riding in a litter right behind him. The Inka exerted control indirectly, with local officials in charge of most activities. Nevertheless the Inka were obviously not content to leave the mechanisms of control entirely in local hands. Elements of Inka identity were pressed upon local people at the same social and political ceremonies that served to hold the upper levels of local society together. The Inka had inserted themselves carefully, but effectively, into the heart of local rule.

The second example of Inka conquest strategy that we explore is that of the *señorío* of Guarco, today Cañete, a little farther north along the Pacific shore. This example highlights the importance of military force. During the immediately pre-Inka period, the people of Guarco defended their valley with fortresses and a wall that protected them against any attack from the highlands or from the sea. So confident were they of their defenses that they did not accept Inka offers of reciprocity and preferred to fight. "Since the natives did not want to become their vassals, for their forefathers had left them free, they displayed such bravery that they carried on war . . . for more than four years."[64]

Because the Inka did not at that stage have permanent armies (armies being composed of peasant conscripts on rotational *mit'a* duty), and because the heat of the coastal summer forced the highland armies to repair to the cooler sierra, the conquest of Guarco took three or four campaigns. Even then, force was not enough; various chroniclers, including Acosta and Cobo, report that in the end the Inka won thanks to a ruse played on Guarco's ruler by the *Quya*, or wife-consort of Thupa Yupanki. At the time, a woman ruled Guarco. The *Quya's* emissary told Guarco's ruler that the Inka wished for peace and that they would respect Guarco's independence. The people of Guarco believed the *Quya* and to celebrate the peace treaty organized a ceremony in honor of the sea. On the appointed day all the people of Guarco boarded their balsa rafts and went to sea, accompanied by the music of drums and flutes. When they were far from the coast, Inka armies invaded the valley and took over Guarco.

Inka reprisals were very cruel; they hanged many men from the walls of the fortresses. Cieza de León saw piles of bones, which he understood to be those of murdered Guarco nobles. They handed over much land to people from neighboring valleys. These people, called *mitmaq*, were

[64] Cieza [1553] 1959: 338.

sent from their place of origin to work land elsewhere as part of their obligation to the state.

During or following their conquest, the Inka built two important centers in the Cañete Valley. One of these lies near the modern town of Cerro Azul on high bluffs overlooking the sea. The structures at the top of the bluff are built of adobe, but they employ trapezoidal doorways and niches in the clearly recognizable imperial Inka style. A long stairway of finely dressed stone blocks once led from the cliffs to the sea, and the foundations of fine masonry walls can still be seen. "To celebrate his victory, [the Inka] ordered built on a high hill of the valley the most beautiful and ornate citadel to be found in the whole kingdom of Peru, set upon great square blocks of stone, and with very fine gates and entrance ways, and large patios. From the top of this royal edifice a stone stairway descends to the sea."[65]

There are no historical accounts that independently link the cliff-top structures and the fine stairway, one of the very few examples of dressed stone construction on the coast, to the legend of the *Quya*'s deception. The Inka did, however, sometimes build fortresses or other monuments to commemorate their conquests, and Cerro Azul with its stairway to the sea may relate to the legend.

The other important Inka site in Cañete is known as Inka Wasi ('Inka House', written Inkawasi, etc.), located 27 kilometers inland near the town of Lunahuaná. It is a major installation, one of the largest coastal centers built by the Inka. Its builders used local stone and covered the walls with a layer of earth plaster. Originally Inka Wasi may have been painted, as were most Inka sites, especially on the coast. Inka Wasi also has the diagnostic trapezoidal niches and doorways that point to its planning by Inka architects.

Cieza de León notes that Inka Wasi was built by Thupa Yupanki during his campaign to conquer Guarco. "The Inca was determined to bring [the war] to an end . . . and built a new city, to which he gave the name of New Cusco."[66] Cieza de León implies that the Inka probably abandoned the installation before the arrival of the Spaniards. If this is correct, Inka Wasi served as more of a temporary, military center than as an administrative center charged with the continuing control and management of the region.

---

[65] Cieza [1553] 1959: 339.   [66] Cieza [1553] 1959: 339.

Hyslop, who mapped and surveyed the still well-preserved ruins of Inka Wasi, proposed that astronomical alignments played an important role in the planning of the site. He also tentatively identified probable storage and barracks areas at the site, all consistent with a military role. Excavations are needed to identify firmly activities associated with state hospitality, such as brewing or the communal serving of food and drink. Both the quantity and the percentage of imperial-style Inka pottery on the surface of the site are very small, however. We often associate large quantities of state-style pottery with reciprocal activities related to the state. At Huánuco Pampa, for instance, the state stamped with its distinctive style the containers used to serve the food and drink it distributed, thus underlining the source of generosity. If this evidence and line of reasoning are correct, state hospitality was not an important function at Inka Wasi. The state had apparently chosen other, more coercive means for the incorporation of Guarco into Tawantinsuyu.

The third case study in conquest strategy shows how the Inka sometimes built whole new regional centers from the ground up. These places did not replace established social structures; rather they served to articulate the state with them, bolstering organization on age-old traditions of the late pre-Inka period, and adapting these practices to the needs of an ever-growing government. Prominent ethnic lords, especially in the early years, maintained their privileges and status if they adapted to the mechanisms of reciprocity and accepted Inka supremacy by having their subjects receive "gifts" – actually stored tribute, redistributed after processing through the state – at such centers. Archaeological evidence supports the important role that reciprocity played in the growth of the state. Huánuco Pampa was one of the largest and most important administrative centers. Located along the *Qhapaq Ñan*, or royal highland road, its ruins show the enormous investment the Inka state made in facilities and goods to provide the state hospitality essential in a system of "entreaty" and "obligation."

Although Cieza de León apparently never visited Huánuco Pampa, he did leave a description, drawn from an unknown informant:

In what is known as Huánuco [Huánuco Pampa] there was an admirably built royal palace, made of very large stones artfully joined. This palace or lodging was the capital of the provinces bordering on the Andes, and beside it there was a temple to the sun with many vestals and priests. It was so important in the times of the Incas that there were always over thirty thousand Indians to serve it. The stewards of the Incas were in charge of collecting the regular tributes, and the region served this palace. When the Lord-Incas ordered the headmen of these provinces to appear at the court of Cuzco, they did so. They tell us that many of these tribes were brave and strong, and that before the Incas brought them under their rule many and cruel battles were fought between them, and that in most places the villages were scattered and so remote that there were no relations between them except when they met for their gatherings and feasts.[67]

Huánuco Pampa lies on a barren plateau at more than 3,800 meters above sea level, 700 kilometers northwest of Cusco on the main highland road. The center's emphasis was neither military nor bureaucratic, as might have been expected for a center of state control in an expanding empire. Instead the emphasis was on the rites and feasting related to reciprocal administration. Although Huánuco Pampa probably housed only a small permanent population, the center's nearly 4,000 structures provided lodging for the thousands of people who came periodically for the ceremonial festivals of state.

The great central plaza, measuring 500 × 300 meters, and the buildings around it all served these public ceremonies, including the festivals of the elaborate ritual calendar. Perhaps ritual battles also helped define relations among regional groups. Although we have no eyewitness accounts of ritual battles at Huánuco Pampa, several chroniclers described such encounters in Cusco, and through their words we can imagine a similar ritual at Huánuco Pampa:

One day when the new moon could be seen . . . those who had been knighted [in an initiation rite for Inka nobles] came to the square with new clothing, black tunics, tawny mantles, and bunches of white feathers, and with their slings in their hands, they divided into bands, one composed of those from Hanancuzco and the other of those from Hurincuzco. They threw a certain fruit at each other. . . . Sometimes they would come to blows to test their strength. This would be done until the Inca stood up and made them stop. This was done so it would be known who among them were the bravest and strongest.[68]

Royal dwellings and temples formed a compound at the city's eastern edge. Thousands of beer jars and serving plates found in buildings around smaller plazas lying between the royal compound and the central plaza suggest that public feasts took place there. About 500 warehouses held food and other supplies to support the center's elaborate feasts. A compound of fifty houses provided work and living space for a group of weavers and brewers who turned out cloth and maize beer, which con-

---

[67] Cieza [1553] 1959: 109. [68] Cobo [1653] 1990: 135.

ferred prestige on recipients and imbued the Inka providers with respect and power. Huánuco Pampa was "another Cuzco," not because of its very minor physical resemblance to the capital of the empire, but because it was the Inka's reciprocal center, where he could entertain and fulfill his obligations to those he sought to incorporate into the realm – as if he were in Cusco.

Huánuco Pampa's layout provides perhaps the most complete architectural expression of the principles of division and organization used by the Inka in conquered provinces. Based on principles similar to those used in the capital, the site is divided into two main parts by the Inka road running northeast to southwest through the site. One of these divisions contains more elaborate and finely made buildings and probably can be conceived of as *hanan*, or upper. The two main divisions are in turn subdivided, creating a quadripartite pattern around the large rectangular plaza. The four divisions may have been further subdivided into three divisions each, creating twelve zones.

Huánuco Pampa's plan may have reflected the basic Inka organizational principles that permeate several aspects of Inka ideology. The best documented expression of these principles is found in the organization of the shrines located along *ceque* lines around Cusco. These were conceived of as lines that created spatial divisions. There is no written evidence for such a set of divisions at Huánuco Pampa; however, the similarity to the patterning of the Cusco shrines seems too close to be coincidental. Similar principles of division and organization pervade other aspects of Inka organization and ideology.

The elaborate set of divisions expressed in Huánuco Pampa's plan is probably related to its role as an administrative center. To function effectively the Inka would have found it more efficient to establish a hierarchical order among the small local groups that populated the region, allowing the state to deal with fewer local leaders. Could the city plan have been used not just as an abstract expression of important ideological principles but to actually place groups of people in a physical relationship to each other that mirrored the hierarchical relationship the Inka state wanted them to assume? These relationships could then have been reinforced through participation in the ceremonies prescribed by the ritual calendar. Seen in this way, the city plan becomes a model for sociopolitical ideology and a template for the creation of social, political, and economic organization. It was a way of defining, maintaining, and sometimes rearranging the social segments that are the building blocks of state society. Relationships, often involving conflict among and between the various divisions, were probably mediated and manipulated through reciprocity. In this way a more coherent state organization could be created and administered.

Quechua, the "Language of the Inka," and Cultural Unification

At places like Huánuco Pampa, varied ethnic groups came together under Inka auspices: multiple neighboring native populations, people arriving from afar on their rotating labor service, state transplants, servitors, and guests. How did the idiom of reciprocity in politics, which depends so much on eloquence and persuasion, overcome the problems of linguistic diversity? Writing for Spaniards a lifetime after the conquest, the half-Inka literary genius Garcilaso de la Vega enshrined in European thinking the erroneous idea that Inka conquest entailed a forced linguistic unification of the Andes via the imposition of Quechua. Garcilaso was probably not consciously distorting linguistic facts; Quechua in fact was and still is the most widely spoken of all Native American languages, and its geographic range actually did roughly coincide with that of Tawantinsuyu. It is also well confirmed that the Inka state used Quechua as its administrative tongue, encouraging or forcing vassal lords to be sure their heirs learned it. However, two mistaken ideas have become fused with these valid ones: first, that Quechua originated among the Inka and spread as a result of their victories; and second, that the dialect spoken by the Cusco Inka was the one early Spanish grammarians like Fray Domingo de Santo Tomás had in mind when they wrote of a "General Language," which members of the innumerable Andean ethnic groups used in common. Rather the Inka linguistic system, like most Inka policy, worked to articulate the preextant diversity of Andean culture while keeping outright imposition at a minimum.

A series of historical-linguistic studies by Torero and others[69] have made it increasingly clear that the parent language of Quechua's many dialects arose in central coastal Peru, not in the south-highland Cusco area, and that it took form at least a millennium prior to Inka ascendancy. Its nearest descendants are the "Quechua I" dialects, which have spread, with considerable internal diversity, through the central Peruvian highlands. These dialects as a group differ widely from the "Quechua II"

[69] Notably Rodolfo Cerrón-Palomino, Willem Adelaar, Gerald Taylor, and Gary Parker.

dialects, which make up most of the vast Quechua orbit. Quecha II also diffused long before the Inka, spreading immense distances both northward and southward in the sixth through tenth centuries C.E. Torero associates the northward spread in good measure with deepwater navigation and calls the variety that probably served as the maritime *lingua franca* Wampuy or 'floating' Quechua. The southward spread may have been related to the far-flung influence of the great central Peruvian shrine Pacha Kamaq. A northern Peruvian dialect called Cañaris (Quechua IIA) may have taken shape in this era; in grammar and sound system, it bears a likeness to what Spaniards later called the "General Language." The northern (Ecuadorian) and southern (Bolivian) variants of Quechua II seem on lexical grounds to have separated from their common ancestor quite recently – perhaps about C.E. 1230.

All this suggests that the symbiosis of Inka administration with the Quechua language forms part of a third wave of Quechua expansion. The Inka themselves probably spoke an ethnic tongue of their own, perhaps Pukina, which is not closely related to Quechua, and like other ethnic groups they used Quecha as a *lingua franca*. When Inka armies entered remote domains, they probably found that the local peoples, speakers of numerous other languages (for example, Aymara, Muchik, Uru, Puruhá, and many more) also used Quechua. It was thus opportune to build up Quechua as an administrative tongue and perhaps also a cultic one. Virtually all Inka administrative jargon is Quechua, but religious terminology contains some words of possible Aymara or otherwise non-Quechua origin.

A very few samples of Quechua as it may have sounded in Inka royal discourse survive via colonial manuscripts. The villagers of Huarochirí embedded in their 1608 Quechua narratives a remembered sample of a religio-political harangue by a reigning Inka, in which the Inka tongue-lashes the *wak'a*s of the realm (and of course, through them, their respective political communities) for not reciprocating with sufficient military support when routed Inka armies needed it:

Then the Inca began to speak: "Fathers, *huacas* and *villcas*, you already know how wholeheartedly I serve you with my gold and my silver. Since I do so, being at your service as I am, won't you come to my aid now that I'm losing so many thousands of my people? It's for this reason that I've had you called together."

But after he said this not a single one spoke up. Instead they sat there mute. The Inca then said, "Yao! Speak up! Shall the people you've made and

fostered perish in this way [i.e., in warfare], savaging one another? If you refuse
to help me, I'll have all of you burned immediately!"

"Why should I serve you and adorn you with my gold, with my silver, with
basketfuls of my food and drinks, with my llamas and everything else I have?
Now that you've heard the greatness of my grief, won't you come to my aid? If
you do refuse, you'll burn immediately!"[70]

The villagers who remembered this rare sample of Inka political language were probably native speakers of a non-Quechua tongue related to
Aymara. In the early days of the Spanish conquest, Spaniards too were
one of the many small non-Quechua ethnic groups using the "General
Language." The Quechua described by Fr. Domingo de Santo Tomás in
1560, and that used by the unknown writer of the Quechua mythological
manuscript of Huarochirí, have strong affinities to dialects from Peru's
far north and thus suggest that up to 1600 a non-Inka "general" Quechua
was widespread. But as the Spanish monopoly on power took form, an
influential faction of largely Jesuit scholars succeeded in persuading the
Archbishopric of Lima that royal Spanish policy ought to propagate the
royal (and therefore supposedly most sophisticated) variety of Quechua –
namely, the kind spoken by Inka descendants in Cusco – as its missionary tongue. Thus the fourth wave of Quechua spread. This colonial
ecclesiastical wave (see Chap. 15) had the effect of delegitimating both
"general" and ethnic Quechua and canonizing (but not widely inculcat-
ing) an Inka-like Quechua with an Aymara-like sound system.

Peeling back these phenomena, we can guess that in Inka times,
Cusco's courtly and bureaucratic Quechua coexisted with many other
dialects in a "mosaic" (as Mannheim calls it) of differentiated Quechuas
– both with a "General Language" that was millions of people's second
tongue, and with many local ones of dissimilar antiquity and prestige,
some of which were themselves certain groups' first and native tongues.
At places like Huánuco Pampa, speeches and songs in honor of Inka and
native lords were almost certainly heard in "the language of the Inka" –
but also in the Quechua and non-Quechua languages of the peoples.

The Administration of Tawantinsuyu

Inka administration varied according to the political complexity of the
societies it encountered, the availability of resources, the proximity of

[70] Salomon and Urioste 1991 [1608]: 114.

each region to Cusco and the royal highland road, and how big a security threat each conquered polity posed. Policies were flexible and developed as new areas were incorporated into Tawantinsuyu.

Societies most similar to the Inka assimilated more easily, whereas those that were less politically complex (such as those of far southern Chile and far northern Ecuador) or more politically sophisticated (such as the Chimú), created administrative problems. Peoples whose systems fit less than neatly into Tawantinsuyu saw the most substantial changes in local political administration. The Chimú posed a considerable threat to Inka power, and the Inka decentralized rule and took Minchançaman, the last independent Chimú ruler, as an honored hostage to Cusco. In other regions, especially those rich in resources such as the territory of the Lupaqa and the Qulla in the Titicaca Basin, the Inka dovetailed the power of the local *kuraka*s into the political and economic machine of Tawantinsuyu. On the south coast, where populations were smaller and generally less politically complex than their northern neighbors, the Inka ruled indirectly. Sometimes the Inka resettled local populations, such as in the Mantaro Valley, where the Wanka, who lived in dispersed hilltop settlements, were brought down into the valley. Tawantinsuyu's vast size created innumerable administrative problems. To facilitate administration, the Inka divided the empire into four territorial divisions, or political units, called *suyu*s. Centered at Cusco, Chinchay Suyu, which lay to the north and west of Cusco, and Qulla Suyu, located to the south and east, formed the largest *suyu*s; Anti Suyu to the northeast and Kunti Suyu to the southwest were much smaller.

Who was responsible for the day-to-day running of Tawantinsuyu? Many officials and individuals oversaw its administration, managing and conducting the affairs of state. Positions of greater rank and responsibility were filled by members of the Cusco élite, and these held power over the provincial native lords. Each *suyu* was governed by an administrator and divided into many provinces, which usually corresponded to pre-Inka polities. These were administered by provincial governors, called *tukuy rikuq* or *tuqriquq* (the title seems to derive from a Quechua phrase meaning 'all-seeing'), usually Cusco nobles. These in turn, governed the local élites. Provinces were often divided into two or three units, called *saya*s, that included a number of *ayllu*s.

A new class of leaders emerged parallel to the formation of the state, including the administrators responsible for the functioning of Tawantinsuyu. They controlled state revenue, the proper storage of accumulated goods, the procurement of labor from ethnic lords, and the mobilization of people from determined regions to join the Inka armies. The administrators had to oversee the construction of roads, bridges, *tampu* (way-stations), and administrative centers. They were aided by keepers of knot records, and also by the runners who relayed messages along the royal road, or *Qhapac Ñan*. All this involved great effort and challenged the organizational capacity of Tawantinsuyu's administrators.

Some parts of the empire, basically the highland core area, were organized into a decimal administration that facilitated the recruitment and organization of permanent labor (*mitmaq* colonists, *yana* retainers, and full-time craft specialists) or temporary, rotational (*mit'a*) labor.[71] The system was comprised of tributary households organized into decimal units ranging from 10,000, headed by a *hunu kuraka*, or lord of 10,000 households, to *kuraka*, who headed up 5,000, 1,000, and 500 households, and so on. It may be that at the time of Spanish invasion the decimal order had not been realized fully in districts beyond the imperial core. The decimal system of administrative divisions was probably coordinated with the *khipu*, the knotted-string recording device (discussed later). These ideal numbers from the chronicles, however, do not generally match the demographic numbers found in Spanish bureaucratic documents. This discrepancy could be a reflection of the demographic collapse suffered by the native population in the aftermath of the Spanish invasion.

An enormous array of lords of distinct ranks and attributes flourished along with the state. These lords ruled over various *señoríos*, some small and insignificant. As the state consolidated its power, it created new categories of lords, chiefs, or sometimes even rewarded *yana* (retainers at the service of the Inka) by granting them lordships. Several documents refer to chiefs or lords with prior *yana*, or servant status. Among the chiefs, we also find female *kuraka*s. Many women ruled and controlled *señoríos*, including one "Contar Huacho," a secondary wife of Wayna Qhapac, and lord of four or six *waranka* (4,000 or 6,000 households) in Huaylas. She was the mother of the *ñusta* or princess "Quispe Sisa" (Qispi Sisa, 'Crystal Flower'), who was given by her brother Atawallpa to the conquistador Francisco Pizarro. At her christening Qispi Sisa was

---

[71] Julien 1982.

renamed *doña* Inés Yupanki Huaylas. Women rulers were more common on the north coast of Peru, where they were called *capullanas*. Even their *segundas personas* (lieutenants) were women.

How did the Inka keep track of such a vast territory and its resources without some sort of writing system? Instead of writing as we know it, the Inka used a system of knotted strings called *khipu* to record the numbers so vital to Tawantinsuyu. It is difficult to imagine Tawantin-suyu without the *khipu*. Cord records were the means by which rulers and administrators managed their people and their wealth. By these knots, explained Cieza de León, "they kept the account of the tribute to be paid by the natives of that district in silver, gold, clothing, flocks, down to wood and other more insignificant things, and by these same quipus at the end of a year, or ten, or twenty years, they gave a report to the one whose duty it was to check the account so exact that not even a pair of sandals was missing."[72]

Each *khipu* consisted of pendant cords attached to a main cord and studded with knots and clusters of knots to indicate numbers. The position of the knot clusters signified the number's position in a decimal system of notation. Secondary cords and summary cords allowed the keepers and readers of these records, the *khipu kamayuq* ('khipu master', also written *Quipocamayo*, etc.), to record complicated numerical infor-mation. The order in which the cords were attached to the main cord probably referred to traditional categories of information and their rela-tive importance. *Khipu* were portable and could be rolled up and stored and carried from one place to another (Fig. 10.2).

It is worth noting that *khipu* recorded only the results of mathematical operations, not the process. Calculations were made using a kind of abacus.[73] These were made of carved wood or clay and divided into compartments. The compartments corresponded to decimal units, and sums were tallied with the aid of small stones or grains of maize. Both Quechua and Aymara include words to express this kind of accounting tool. In one of his illustrations of a *khipu kamayuq*, Guaman Poma shows such a device.

The first *khipu* are known from Wari times, about 500 years before the Inka, and these may have served as models for the Inka ones. Several kinds of *khipu* existed. The most sophisticated ones were large and summarized the accounts of an entire *suyu*, one of the four territorial

[72] Cieza [1553] 1959: 174.   [73] Wassen 1931.

Figure 10.2. 'Principal accountant and treasurer of Tawantinsuyu,' who was the authority in charge of the *khipus* of the realm. From Felipe Guaman Poma de Ayala, *Nueva Coronica y Buen Gobierno* (Paris: Institut d'Ethnologie, 1936 [1613]).

divisions of the Inka state. They were kept by a high-ranking individual who received the accounts sent from the various ethnic divisions or provinces that made up each *suyu*. Many minor accountants and assistants served the chief *khipu kamayuq*. Guaman Poma refers to one of these, illustrating a *khipu kamayuq* holding a *khipu* so large he stretches his arms to hold it. Much larger ones are known archaeologically.

Besides these large and complicated *khipu*, there were also smaller ones that recorded the accounts of each province. The lower-ranking *kurakas* also tallied population figures and the contents of storehouses. On the social scale, everyone, even humble peasants and herders, kept knotted accounts, ranging from the simple to the sophisticated. *Khipu* were used to figure out the number of camelids belonging to the state herds and to the religion. At the same time, the ethnic lords or even simple herders, members of *ayllu*, used these knotted recording devices to track how many animals grazed the grasslands.

State accounting involved gathering already-processed figures into totals, such as the number of inhabitants in a region or a polity, or how many *mitmaq* had been sent to one place or another. State administrators also kept accounts of how many men from a given area were incorporated into the army, or the number of girls sent to the *Aqlla Wasi*. Perhaps their most important use was in keeping track of the goods stored in the warehousing system. Stored goods were classified according to the type of goods. So important were the numbers themselves that a good part of the state's wealth could be calculated via the goods stored in the warehouses. Apparently all the state warehouses had *khipu kamayuq* who were essentially bookkeepers, and who kept strict accounts of incoming and outgoing foodstuffs and manufactured goods.

Many chroniclers marveled at the efficiency of the *khipu*, although some questioned their accuracy and even considered them "fables." One convert was Cieza de León, who noted that he was "dubious about this accounting" until he interviewed a *kuraka* in the Mantaro Valley in the central highlands of Peru, home of the Wanka. Cieza de León asked the *kuraka* "to explain the system in such a way that I could understand it and make sure that it was exact and dependable." The Wanka were early allies of the Spaniards and kept detailed *khipu* accounts of all the goods and services given to Francisco Pizarro when he entered the valley in 1533. Like many other Spaniards, Cieza de León found the system not merely credible but authoritative. "I saw the account of the gold, silver, and clothing that had been given, the llamas and other things . . . without a single omission . . . and I was amazed thereby."[74]

Researchers such as M. and R. Ascher, Conklin, and Urton have shown how cords could convey nonnumerical formal relationships such as "tree" hierarchies and matrices. There are some suggestions that *khipu* may also have been used to record oral history, but how this was done is unclear. Cieza de León tells us that during his reign an Inka ruler selected "three or four old men . . . skilled and gifted for that purpose . . . to recall all that had happened in the province . . . whether prosperous or adverse, and to make and arrange songs so that thereby it might be known in the future what had taken place in the past." Possessed of "great memory, subtle wit, and lively intelligence," the men were ordered to "learn the songs . . . and to prepare new ones of what took place . . . what was spent, what the provinces contributed, and put all this down in the quipus, so that after his death, when his successor reigned, what had been given and contributed would be known."[75] Colonial and modern attempts to reconstruct cord-verbal codes posit either color-coding of semantic categories (e.g., red for cities, the cities in turn being number-coded) or else the use of standardized keywords as sources for a syllabary that could be referred to in numbers. None of these decipherments can be taken as confirmed.

WEALTH IN TAWANTINSUYU

Because money in the sense of currency did not exist in Tawantinsuyu, wealth in the Inka state was measured by tallies of commodities. Access to and control of these commodities allowed the state to plan its future. One of the few points on which all Spanish witnesses agreed was that the sums were vast. What prosperity allowed the Inka to dominate and control the state's economy and politics?

Inka wealth rested on access to three sources of revenue: labor, land, and herds. Together these ultimately were turned into goods accumulated in state warehouses and redistributed for state purposes. Commodities enhanced by state power were the most sought-after signs of wealth. The "value added" by ceremony, warehousing, and the cachet of power gave the state the control of reciprocity, key to Andean organizational systems.

[74] Cieza [1553] 1959: 174.   [75] Cieza [1553] 1959: 172–173.

This mechanism underpinned not only territorial expansion but also routine state maintenance. If, for any reason, the state lacked accumulated goods, it could not meet the requisites for administration or the constant gifts and "donations" required by the institution of reciprocity.

For many years the Inka organizational model, so admired by sixteenth-century Europeans (see pp. 121–142), was extolled by later Europeans as a utopia. It was believed that the accumulation of foodstuffs and goods of all kinds had a humanitarian purpose intended, for example, to assist people after a natural disaster, such as drought or famine. These themes were elaborated in Louis Baudin's *L'Empire Socialiste des Incas* (1928), which saw the Inka empire as a predecessor to the twentieth-century socialist state. Related ideas infused Peruvian indigenism from the 1920s onward.

The concept of redistribution as employed here also privileges politics, presupposing a model of institutional centralization, but explaining it in terms of relations with local endogenous systems rathern than with royal ideology. In societies where redistribution is the norm, production and distribution of goods are conducted on behalf of a chief, a lord, a temple, or a despot. A centralized authority amasses products and redistributes them to his compliant subjects and agents, thus ensuring the upkeep and the continuation of common services and maintaining the social and political order, as, for example, during the celebrations of public feasts. The principles of chiefly redistribution organized production, the provision of services, the periodic distribution of lands and the distribution of products, gift giving, and so forth.

A great part of redistribution was expended by the reciprocal system, which obliged the state to constantly bestow gifts to the many ethnic lords, military chiefs, shrines, and so on. As discussed earlier, these goods were stored at the storehouses that the state maintained to guarantee access to vast quantities of accumulated goods – goods that symbolized and indeed constituted power for Tawantinsuyu. Within these broad principles, Inka policy varied to meet regional realities.

Tawantinsuyu's economic model as applied in the southerly domains has been studied by John Murra as well as by other scholars. To acquire goods from a variety of ecosystems, the people of the heights depended on a system of discontinuous enclaves, which Murra dubbed "vertical archipelagos." By means of multiethnic colonies, these highland centers controlled patches of different ecosystems located in areas distant from one another. We underscore "distant" to emphasize that these enclaves lay at distances of more than a day's walk from each other. Enclaves enabled lords or villages to obtain warm-valley maize and exotic products not available in the *altiplano*, such as coca leaf, fish, cotton, tropical fruit, honey, feathers, and so forth. It might take weeks of walking to reach remote enclaves, which were located in temperate valleys both to the west and to the east of the *altiplano*. Such great geographical spans mark the southern Andean model and differentiate it from the central highland one.

A very different situation prevailed in Peru's Central Andes. There, more closely spaced microclimates allowed a compact plan manageable on a smaller scale. This distinct application of the "verticality" model shows that it was not rigid but that it varied according to the circumstances and environment. This is apparent in the *visitas*, or inspections, carried out successively in 1549 and 1553 in Canta, a valley just northeast of Lima. Both of these early testimonies offer a glimpse of the area's economic makeup. The people of Canta did not need to establish distant enclaves because within a short range the valley's microclimates afforded its inhabitants access to a variety of resources. The eight communities that made up the *señorío* of Canta got together to cultivate coca in the temperate and sunny mid-valley areas and to shear camelids at higher altitudes.

Given that the highland economy was linked to the environments of the Andean valleys and *altiplano*, it follows that the geography of the coast also produced a different model. Despite its aridity, the coast was a region rich in renewable natural resources, especially fish and shellfish. Moreover, as the rivers tumbling out of the highlands form slower courses toward the sea, their margins form irrigable plains of year-round fertility. Since early times two different subsistence patterns had emerged: fishing and farming. These were carried out by separate societies, governed by their own chiefs. Products were exchanged between the two societies. Fishermen, however, ensconced in their beaches and coves, remained subordinate to the lords of the farming communities. The first inkling that such divisions existed came from the *Relación de Chincha*,[76] which describes a society of 30,000 "tribute payers" including 10,000 fishermen, 12,000 farmers and 6,000 *mercaderes*, or merchants, living in

[76] Analyzed in Rostworowski 1970.

the same coastal valley of Chincha whose conquest was discussed previously. These numbers suggest clear divisions of labor among the inhabitants, distinct from the patterns we see elsewhere in the Andes. The fishing surplus that was not consumed locally was dried and conserved. This surplus promoted barter not only with other communities in the valley to obtain farm produce but with highland communities as well for their products. The document also describes other specialists, such as dyers, carpenters, and cooks. The most prestigious artisans appear to have been the metalsmiths. This and other archival research has revealed that the labor situation on the coast was highly specialized. Each speciality was seen as a distinct profession and was carried out by specific persons; people could not switch their roles.

On the coast, reciprocity and redistribution were combined with barter. Barter was based on established equivalencies (rather than negotiated prices). This mechanism compensated for the lack of some local products. Exchange mechanisms among the coastal societies of ancient Peru occurred at two very different levels. The first was carried out by farming or fishing communities to procure everyday products. The other was carried out by several categories of people in charge of barter and exchange. The Spaniards called these specialists *mercaderes*, or merchants. The document from Chincha refers to 6,000 *mercaderes* who sailed their balsa rafts between Chincha and Manta and Puerto Viejo in Ecuador. Accompanied by llama caravans and porters, these specialists also traded overland for goods such as wool from the high plains and Cusco. The merchants of Chincha exchanged copper for sacrificial *mullu*, the coral-rimmed shell from the warm waters off Ecuador. The importance of this shell was great, for it was the favored offering to the gods, and it was used in propitiatory rites to summon rain and to feed the waters of springs.[77] Long-range *mullu* trade is also mentioned in a document on Atico in southern Peru dating to 1549. It notes the existence of expert carvers who fashioned wooden statues inlaid with *mullu*. According to the artisans the shell came from Huancavilca in the north, today Ecuador. At places like Huancavilca, Chincha navigator-traders probably came into contact with their counterparts from far-northern polities (some beyond Inka control), where politically authorized traders were called *mindala*.[78]

Inka managers adroitly manipulated both the highland "archipelago"

[77] Murra 1975.   [78] Salomon 1986, 1987.

model and the coastal system of agro-maritime interpendency. In the former case, Tawantinsuyu helped its allies encroach on valleys and widen their "archipelagoes" but also required allies and subjects to supply labor for the building and staffing of outlier islands belonging to the state, its cults, and its royal descent groups. These latter would fill warehouses and subsidize pump-priming reciprocity with peoples yet to come under Inka control. In the latter case, Inka policy allowed politically sponsored specialist long-distance operations to continue, under vigilance, perhaps as a way to tap resources of remote peoples beyond the reach of the state. But Tawantinsuyu seems to have been leery about letting plebeian tributaries travel or trade beyond their lords' immediate domains, because such relative free-lancing offered an undesired alternative to dependence on state largesse.

Land

As in other societies land was a highly valuable good in Tawantinsuyu. Land tenure mechanisms followed established Andean patterns. According to the chroniclers, the lands were divided into those of the Inka, those of the state religion, and those of the communities. But this scheme falls short of capturing a multifaceted practice:

When the Inca settled a town, or reduced one to obedience, he set up markers on its boundaries and divided the fields and arable lands within its territory into three parts, in the following way: One part he assigned to Religion and the cult of his false gods, another he took for himself, and a third he left for the common use of the people . . . it is known that in many places the division was not equal, but depended on the availability of land and the density of the population. In some provinces, the part assigned to Religion was greater; in others, that belonging to the Inca was greater. . . . Accordingly, in some regions, there were entire towns, which with their territory and all that it produced, belonged to the Sun and the other gods . . . and in other provinces (and this was more usual), the king's share was the largest.[79]

Local laborers worked state-held lands, and their produce filled the state warehouses. When the Inka began their conquests, one of the first measures they carried out was to designate lands for the state. Local chiefs were obliged to provide labor and watch over these lands. As Inka power increased, so did the extent of its landholdings. Unpublished

[79] Cobo [1653] 1979: 211.

archival sources suggest that the last Inka rulers held private lands and that their produce became the personal revenue of the Inka. These estates included farmland and grassland, where the ruler's personal herds grazed. To a lesser extent, the *Quya*, or queen, also had access to private property.

It was an established custom in the Andes that each idol or sanctuary, large or small, had a piece of endowed land. Produce from these lands was used as offerings, above all to brew the maize-based beverages that were offered to both the divinity and the celebrants at feasts. Documents on Spanish efforts to stamp out idolatry provide ample information on the land tenure system as applied to the idols. Important deities like the sun had access to much land scattered around the empire. "The lands dedicated to the gods were divided among the Sun, Lightning, and the rest of the idols, shrines and *guacas*[*wak'as*] of general worship and *guacas* belonging to each province and town; the amount belonging to each god and *guaca* was specified, and these fields were cultivated before the others of the Inca and the community."[80]

Lands used by the communities, along with grazing land and water, allegedly made up the smallest tracts. The chroniclers relate that all members of a community had access to a *tupu* (a relative unit of land measure, which took the quality of the land into account) of land. With the birth of every child, a tributary farmer's, or *hatun runa*'s, land allotment grew. This system took into consideration both the permanent qualities of the land and its current condition (i.e., the length of its last fallowing) to calculate the measure that would cover the needs of the household. Each year, according to Cobo, "the caciques [*kurakas*] distributed these lands among their subjects, not in equal parts, but proportionate to the number of children and relatives that each man had; as the family grew or decreased, its share was enlarged or restricted."[81]

Labor

An array of social categories existed among the people of Tawantinsuyu. Craft specialists played an important role on the coast, where their labor specialization formed part of the organizational model. In the highlands craft specialists such as silversmiths and potters also existed, but in the early years of Tawantinsuyu they were not full-time artisans.

At its apogee the Inka state required increasing amounts of sumptuary

---

[80] Cobo [1653] 1979: 212–213.   [81] Cobo [1653] 1979: 213.

and manufactured goods. This called for full-time craft specialists. The Inka took advantage of craft specialists from the main coastal valleys such as Moche, Chincha, and Ica by sending them to Cusco to work for the state. Goods then went from Cusco to the administrative centers governing compliant polities, and thence to consumers. In addition, specialists like the *mamakuna* lived and worked in some administrative centers.

Most of the population was comprised of tribute-paying plebeians, called *hatun runa* (or 'big men') once they married. The *hatun runa* were not only farmers but also herders who took care of the camelid herds belonging to the Inka, the sun, and the religion. They lived in scattered communities or isolated homesteads. In addition to the agricultural labor they provided to their communities and to the state, they were mobilized by the state to form armies and public works crews, postal runners, and so on. Their ranks made up the enormous *mit'a* workforce that was so indispensable to the building and running of Tawantinsuyu. Women's political work duties emphasized textiles; although both sexes knew fiber technology, women spun and wove for the state until their old age, as well as laboring in the fields. People with bodily handicaps were assigned labor taxes commensurate with their abilities. Special endowed fields were designated to support orphans (who lacked family networks to guarantee subsistence) and other helpless persons.

Fishing communities lay scattered along the coast of Tawantinsuyu. Fisherfolk lived near their coves and bays, or near the lagoons that once existed in all the coastal valleys. Not everyone had access to coastal fishing areas; rather each community exploited designated fishing grounds. Fishing communities did not have access to farmland. Only in later colonial times do we see a change in this pattern. Along with their fishing grounds, these coastal communities had lagoons where they hunted birds and harvested reeds to build their boats and their huts. They also planted *totora* (*Scirpus*) reeds along the shores of the lagoons. Some practiced pisciculture in special ponds, producing domesticated fish in quantities that excited Spanish greed.

In each valley fishing communities maintained close relations with farming villages, exchanging fish and shellfish for produce. Fishing communities had their own lords, but before the sixteenth century, fishing communities depended on the principal lords of inland polities.

Llama and alpaca herds followed the same divisions and customs as land tenure. Like land, herds were managed as multiple endowments: Some herds belonged to the state, others to the Sun, still others to the idols. Privileged herds grazed on the private pastures of the Inka ruler. At the lowest level were the herds of the *hatun runa*.

> The Inca had the same division made of all the domesticated livestock, assigning one part to the Religion, another to himself, and another to the community, and not only did he divide and separate each one of these parts, but he did the same with the grazing land and pastures. . . . The herds belonging to Religion and to the Inca were named *capac llama*, and the herd owned by either the community or privately were named *huacchac llama*, which means "rich herds" and "poor herds."[82]

In addition to their importance as sources of meat and fiber and, in the case of llamas, as beasts of burden, camelids also had ceremonial value and were frequently sacrificed. Up to 300 or 400 llamas were sacrificed on some feast days in Cusco. The remains of llama and alpaca corrals in the Cusco countryside point to the enormous investment the state lavished on these herds.[83]

In the Andes local chiefs (*kurakas*) organized the labor force of farmers and *hatun runa* into *mit'a* (or rotational labor) contingents at the community level. *Mit'a* labor sustained the religious cults and, in Inka times, the state. The labor demands of the state increased with each successive reign. To what extent did the generosity of the Inka compensate for the divestment of the labor and land of the *kuraka*? Did access to wealth from remote parts of Tawantinsuyu make up for sacrifices in basic local resources? Was it merely an enticement to keep them satisfied? Were they truly satisfied? Resentment among the provincial ruling classes did contribute to the startlingly rapid collapse of the Inka empire as local lords mistakenly sought a better deal from the Spaniards (see Chap. 12).

Mit'a (provision of rotational labor) was an Andean institution used to carry out cyclical enterprises at predetermined times. All labor undertakings presupposed the idea of *mit'a*, or periodicity. A variety of labor-intensive projects were carried out under the system of rotational labor. This Andean form of service was found at several levels within the same group, including labor for communal tasks, for the fields of the local lords and for the lands of the idols, and as support for local *kuraka*. In Tawantinsuyu, state lands and those of the religion were worked by *mit'a* labor. These occasions were festive ones, lightened by state-provided music, songs, and banquets.

---

[82] Cobo [1653] 1979: 215.   [83] Flores Ochoa 1987.

The taxpayers came to these jobs by turns or *mita* (as they say), when each person was called; and they all took part in the occupations and chores that the Inca and his governors assigned to them, and the most common and ordinary ones were the following. In the first place, they provided what was needed for war, and the numbers of men that commonly served was very great, both in the armies that were formed and reassembled, and in the garrisons and presidios that were in the capital cities of the provinces and on enemy borders. . . . Another part of the *mitayos* was employed in the service of the Inca and his kinsmen and all of the governors and caciques [*kurakas*] of the provinces, as well as in the care and upkeep of all the *guacas*[*wak'a*s] and temples . . . some of these *mitas* provided the labor for the mines of gold, silver and other metals. . . . [Others] worked on the construction of fortresses and royal palaces.[84]

In addition to such temporary levies, the Inka state often transplanted whole colonies of subject peoples to permanent postings afar. Such transplants were called *mitmaq* (written *mitimaes*, etc.). The origins of the *mitmaq* institution are obscure but could be based on the more ancient southern Andean tradition of highland colonists who established enclaves far from their homeland to grow crops on the warmer western and eastern flanks of the Andes. Under the Inka the *mitmaq* formed part of a large class of people who were transferred, along with their families and their subordinate ethnic chiefs, from their place of origin to other regions. There they carried out specific tasks or missions, such as growing maize or manning garrisons. In spite of the distances that separated them from their native villages, they maintained reciprocal ties and kinship links with their place of origin. This is the fundamental difference between *mitmaq* and *yana* (see p. 825), who lost all claims to their place of origin.

[Mitmaq] were transfered to another town or province of the same climate and nature as that which they left; if they came from a cold climate, they were taken to a cold climate, and if from a warm climate, to a warm. . . . They were given land to work and sites on which to build their homes. And these mitimaes were ordered by the Incas to be always obedient to what their governors and captains ordered, so that if the natives should rebel, and they supported the governor, the natives would be punished and reduced to the service of the Incas. Likewise, if the mitimaes stirred up disorder, they were put down by the natives.[85]

Mitmaq could not exchange the clothing or headdresses that distinguished them from others, and when they received orders to move they took their household furnishings, seeds, and other personal effects with

[84] Cobo [1653] 1979: 231–233.   [85] Cieza [1553] 1959: 57.

them. They might ritually transfer soil from their home villages to the plazas of their new stations. Because they maintained their customs and costumes, state administrators could recognize and easily distinguish the *mitmaq* from the local populations.

According to Cieza de León, there were three kinds of *mitmaq*, all of whom "contributed greatly to the upkeep and conservation of the kingdom, and even to its settlement. First, there were those who colonized a recently conquered area, to "teach the natives and inhabitants how they were to serve and comport themselves." Second, the Inka sent *mitmaq* to guard frontier regions, such as the rebellious Chachapoyas area or the recently conquered areas north of Quito, "so that no tribe should be in a position to make war or quickly organize a rebellion or conspiracy." Third, *mitmaq* were sent to a conquered area that was "fertile and had a good climate, and was empty of people."[86]

Although at the onset the *mitmaq* worked lands close to their places of origin, this custom changed during late Inka times, as increasing numbers of people were mobilized ever greater distances to fulfill the state's needs. In its final years Tawantinsuyu was a kaleidoscope of *mitmaq:* peoples from as far away as Guayaquil in Ecuador or from Piura and Trujillo in northern Peru worked fields in the Abancay Valley near Cusco, where they cultivated chili pepper, coca, yuca (sweet manioc), and cotton. In the Urubamba Valley there were Qulla from Lake Titicaca, Cañari from Ecuador, and *mitmaq* from Chumbivilcas. Some areas such as Ecuador's Cañar province (whose natives were often sent as police troops), or Ayabaca and Cajabamba provinces in northernmost Peru, sent out so many contingents – virtual involuntary diasporas – that one wonders how their home economies survived at all.

The most ambitious *mitmaq* project of all, however, was that of Wayna Qhapaq in the Cochabamba Valley, today Bolivia. The emperor reorganized the valley, claiming large tracts of prime land for the state and ordering 14,000 *mit'a* and *mitmaq* laborers brought in to engage in large-scale maize production. According to sixteenth-century land litigation documents studied by Wachtel, the maize was intended to feed Wayna Qhapaq's army, then engaged half a continent away in conquering the northernmost reaches of Tawantinsuyu. Although some local groups such as the Sipa Sipa, who served the Inka as llama herders, were allowed to remain in the area, others were displaced to make way for the

---

[86] Cieza [1553] 1959: 57–62.

colonists. *Mit'a* laborers were rotated in on a yearly basis to work the fields, while permanent *mitmaq* labor maintained the 2,400 *qolqa* (storehouses) at Cotopachi, where the maize was stored before being shipped out on llama caravans.[87]

Sometimes *mitmaq* status was considered a sign of confidence and a mark of distinction; other times it was imposed on ethnic groups who rebelled against the Inka. After the Spanish conquest, many *mitmaq* and *yana* tried to return to their places of origin. But such an exodus would have proven chaotic for the Spanish administrators, and they prohibited it.

An archaeological identification and survey of several former *mitmaq* villages in the upper Huallaga Valley inspected by Iñigo Ortiz in 1562 confirms the rather independent nature of *mitmaq* groups. However, their architecture and ceramics do not show any such obvious connections with those of their home region as the written sources would lead us to believe. Unfortunately, systematic archaeological studies of contemporaneous village settlements in the regions from which the Huánuco *mitmaq* populations were drawn have not been made, so this fact remains hard to interpret. The Huánuco findings suggest only indirect influence of the Chupaychu communities indigenous to the region where the *mitmaq* settled. The sites are well enough preserved to make reconstruction of settlement forms possible. These consisted of household units aggregated in what appear to have been separate communities.

The most radical way of attaching labor power to the state was by totally detaching it from community systems. Such detached individuals were called *yana*. Unlike *mitmaq, yana* laborers were not subject to normal reciprocal relations, and the Inka was not obliged to hold public banquets or offer gifts or entreaties to curry their favor. Some authors influenced by subsequent Spanish abuse of the institution and the term have mistakenly described *yana* as slaves. It was probably considered an honor to be a "servant" of the sun, the Inka, or the *Quya* (queen). In addition to the *yana* lords referred to earlier, there was also a class of artisan or peasant *yana*. Although their social status was different, they were not chattels or captives. As for *yana* lords, this status was conferred when a provincial chief refused to engage in reciprocity and opted to go to war against the Inka. When the Inka defeated one of these recalcitrant chiefs, a *yana* was designated as his replacement.

[87] Wachtel 1982.

The female counterparts of the *yana*, described earlier, were the *mamakuna*, women taken from their places of origin as young girls to serve the cloistered *Aqlla Wasi*, the great compounds where the *mamakuna* lived. Although the daughters or sisters of the Inka led a privileged life, other women were seen by the Inka state as a font of labor to produce textiles and brew *chicha* for rituals. They were also handed over as wives in reciprocal arrangements when the Inka wished to ingratiate himself with lesser nobles.

Ordinary activities [of the *mamakuna*] included taking great care in the service and worship of the temple. They spun and wove clothing of wool, cotton and vicuña which was very fine and delicate, of excellent quality. . . . This clothing was used to dress the idols, and it was offered in the sacrifices; it was also used for the garments of the Inca. These women made large amounts of high-quality *chicha* which was for offerings to the gods and for the priests to drink. Every day they cooked the food that was offered to the sacrifices and was eaten by the priests and attendants of the idols.[88]

Eight-to ten-year-old girls from all over Tawantinsuyu were chosen for the *Aqlla Wasi*. They were divided into categories according to their beauty and skills. Women known as *yuraq aqlla* ('white chosen') were of Inka blood and consecrated to the cult as wives of the sun. These were followed by the *wayrur aqlla*, generally the most beautiful women, from whom the Inka chose his secondary wives. The *paqu aqlla* ('reddish chosen') eventually became the wives of lords and chiefs whom the Inka wished to please. The *yana aqlla* (with *yana* to be taken in its sense 'dependent servant', though a homonym means 'black') were those who did not stand out for their rank in society or for their beauty, and they worked as servants for the others. The final category was the *takiq aqlla* ('singing chosen'), who were chosen for their musical skills; they played the drums and flutes and entertained the court.

Archaeological evidence confirms the critical economic role of the *mamakuna* and gives new insights into the pervasive use of these women for state goals, particularly in the last decades of Tawantinsuyu.[89] A large group of *mamakuna* apparently lived and worked north of the central plaza at Huánuco Pampa. In a compound of fifty structures surrounded by a wall, archaeologists found the remains of hundreds of vessels used to prepare maize beer. They also unearthed spindle whorls and other tools used to produce cloth and copper stickpins used to fasten women's

---

[88] Cobo [1653] 1990: 174.   [89] Morris and Thompson 1985.

garments. Finally, the cloistered nature of the compound itself with its tightly controlled access ties in with chroniclers' descriptions of *Aqlla Wasi*. "These women were not totally confined. They did go out at times, not only to the temple but also to other places. However, this was only so they could be present for the sacrifices made to the Sun wherever he might go. And they were not allowed to leave their cloister for any other occasion."[90]

The fifty structures provided more than 6,000 square meters of roofed space. Stone benches under the eaves of many of the buildings suggest that many activities took place out of doors. The total space within the compound walls was about 15,000 square meters. It is difficult, however, to translate these working and living areas into numbers of women. Judging by the quantity of ceramics and the number of hearths, the area was probably intensively used and occupied year-round by scores of women. In contrast, much of the rest of the city was used only periodically.

The foundations of earlier structures beneath the walls of the women's compound show that it was not part of the city's original layout but a renovated, more carefully planned zone. Does this imply an increased need for *mamakuna* as Tawantinsuyu expanded? The *mamakuna*, removed from the context of reciprocal obligations like their male *yana* counterparts, may have played an increasingly important role in supplying the growing labor needs of the expanding empire. In this manner, the Inka addressed their need for the goods that supplied their ever-growing reciprocal obligations by using labor mechanisms that they could control more directly.

Direct control over production also allowed the state to regulate design of artifacts embodying reciprocal generosity of the Inka. Some goods, especially cloth, incorporated the signs and symbols of rank and membership in various social groups. Control of production and the distribution of such signs and symbols is of obvious importance for a growing state engineering new forms of social order.

The State Warehouses

The substantial surplus garnered from fields and the meat and wool from state herds not only fueled redistribution and covered the demands of

[90] Cobo [1653] 1983: 174.

reciprocity at the state level but also conferred on the state an accumulation of invested, revenue-producing goods that symbolized its political might. The storehouses filled with manufactured goods and foodstuffs, all accounted for by the *khipu kamayuq*, never ceased to amaze the Spaniards. Yet the Spaniards, oblivious to the political indispensability of the storehouses, squandered what the Inka had so painstakingly accumulated (Fig. 10.3).

In earlier times spoils of war seized by the Inka from the Chanka may have marked the beginnings of Inka glory. Everywhere the "gifts" that gratified neighboring lords signaled the initiation of reciprocal relations and, consequently, Inka preeminence. Both the chroniclers and archaeology confirm that great wealth was accumulated in storage throughout Tawantinsuyu. The sixteenth-century sources noted the enormous numbers of Inka storehouses and their rich contents of fine textiles, weapons, and a vast array of foodstuffs. In one storage facility, noted Cieza de León, "there were lances, and in another darts, and in others, sandals, and in others, the different arms they employed. Likewise, certain depots were filled with fine clothing, others, with coarse garments, and others, with food and every kind of victuals . . . nothing, from the most important to the most trifling, but could be provided."[91] Spanish eyewitnesses also pointed out that the storage buildings were typically located in long rows above Inka settlements. This observation allows archaeologists to identify Inka storage facilities, to study their distribution and storage capacities, and to excavate them to see what they once held.

The massive Inka storage system was sophisticated both in terms of using natural environments that extended the shelf life of stored goods and in engineering artificial environments. Maize and tubers were some of the main foodstuffs stored in Inka storehouses. One of the major advantages of maize and other grains is their storability. As long as grains are kept dry and relatively cool, they remain dormant and useful as food. Stored grains must be guarded against moisture and warm temperatures, which trigger germination or consumption by bacteria, insects, or rodents. Inka storehouses typically had thick walls and thatched roofs that kept their interiors cool. Maize excavated at Huánuco Pampa was found shelled and stored in large jars. Such conditions assured a dry and cool storage environment. The jars protected against rodents and probably offered some defense against insects as well.

[91] Cieza [1553] 1959: 68.

335

DEPOCÍTODELÍNGA
COLLCA

topaynga
yupanqui

administrador
suyo yoc
apo poma chaua

depocitos del ynga

como

Figure 10.3. Sections of two rows of Inka storehouses, or Qolqa, showing Thupa Inka Yupanki and an administrator with a *khipu*. From Felipe Guaman Poma de Ayala, *Nueva Coronica y Buen Gobierno* (Paris: Institut d'Ethnologie, 1936 [1613]).

Tubers pose a much more challenging storage problem. Because tubers carry part of their own water supply for germination, they sprout easily and are subject to bacterial and fungal damage. Temperature and humidity must be maintained within a relatively narrow range to retard sprouting and prevent the formation of sugars. Andean peoples developed two radically different procedures for extending the storage life of tubers. One of these was a prestorage processing strategy; the other involved controlling the storage environment. The prestorage processing, a kind of freeze-drying, converted the tubers into an essentially new substance with far superior storage qualities to newly harvested tubers. These included *chúñu, muraya,* and other light, dry products still common in the Andes. They differ drastically, however, in taste and other qualities from the tubers from which they were made. Production involves alternately freezing, drying, and sometimes soaking tubers to take advantage of the daily temperature oscillations in the South Andean dry season. These products can be kept routinely for a year, and they played a major role in Andean subsistence, particularly in tiding the population over years of poor harvests.

Excavations at Huánuco Pampa and at Hatun Jauja in the Mantaro Valley have revealed that most of the storehouses were probably used to store food. Huánuco Pampa's storehouses show that some foods, particularly maize and potatoes or other tubers, were often stored separately.

Places with especially large stores also tended to be settlements, such as Huánuco Pampa, where the Inka expended much effort on state hospitality. The prominent hillside locations of most storehouses helped take advantage of prevailing winds for ventilation, but they also made them visible from a distance. Thus storage became a visible symbol as well as an infrastructure for Inka wealth and credibility throughout Tawantinsuyu.

ART AND TECHNOLOGY

The Inka employed complex technologies to solve a series of problems related to food, shelter, clothing, warfare, transportation, communication, and the production of nonsubsistence goods. The archaeological record, in demonstrating the march of technology over several centuries, makes it clear that the Inka achievement lay in the refinement of previously developed technologies and, especially, their application on a much larger scale. There is no evidence for a flood of new inventions. There is, however, evidence that the sophisticated management of existing technologies amid a new and larger sociopolitical arena was itself inventively done. The combination of advanced methods of manipulating the material world with the Inka genius for managing human energy resulted in impressive achievements.

In its final years, the rulers of an ever-expanding Tawantinsuyu intensified production of sumptuary goods by specialists, allowing the state greater control over production and distribution and ensuring the quality of goods. Many of these sumptuary goods, especially textiles, were dispensed in settings of political and religious rituals intended to teach the populace a new, imperial level of social and political order. Inka-style architecture set the centers built by the state apart from existing local settlements; these state centers provided the settings for rituals, ceremonies, and administrative activities where visitors were served from ceramic, metal, and wooden vessels made in the Inka style.

As in most nonwestern societies, there is no evidence that the Inka had a category of objects thought of as art. Most of the things beautiful to the modern eye had functions in Inka society beyond display. Some were utilitarian objects: pottery or metal vessels to hold food and drink or textiles for clothing. Others functioned mainly in the symbolic realm, such as figurines of gold, silver, or *Spondylus* shell used as offerings or carved stones that related peoples and society to the natural and supernatural worlds.

Inka art has sometimes been described as rigid and standardized, uninspired and plain, and is often considered a classic case of artistic imperialism and political authority exerting strong sway over creative output. Many objects made under state supervision were indeed standardized. Yet because the Inka state did not extend its control to the lower, local levels in most of the realm, much of life and art continued under local traditions. And some state-sponsored art escaped standardization, reflecting local traditions or interplay between local traditions and those of the rulers from Cusco.

The art of Tawantinsuyu, as usually defined, refers to those objects produced in the Cusco style of the ruling élite beginning sometime toward the middle of the fifteenth century. It is a style characterized by the use of relatively simple, bold geometric designs with a strong emphasis on symmetry, particularly in textiles. It "is classic in its formal clarity, balanced proportion and clean outline. It is compact, integrated and simple."[92] The level of technical excellence is high, and the repetition of designs and motifs suggests mass production.

The visual strength and clarity of Inka art, as well as its repetitiveness, can be understood as the result of its official nature. Most of the bold architecture, metalwork, ceramics, and textiles were produced by artisans working for the state, such as specialized women *aqlla* or male *qumpi kamayuq* (master luxury weavers) who produced cloth. The state controlled production not just to provide itself with substantial quantities of necessary and valuable goods but also in part because it wanted to stamp those objects and buildings with its own identity. Its goal was to create an image of the state and its rulers as providers of hospitality and givers of valuable gifts.

But uniformity was not the whole picture. The diversity of objects whose production escaped imperial control reflects the patchwork variety of the Inka empire. Sometimes local artisans combined elements of imperial style into local products, and in other cases they ignored the Cusco style almost entirely. Not surprisingly, some of these stylistic relationships are related to the extent of local resistance to Inka rule. Chimú potters, for instance, occasionally imitated Inka ceramic shapes but otherwise continued to produce the sculptured basic blackware they made before they were conquered by the Inka. In textiles the emphasis was also on stylistic continuity. The Inka did not or could not drastically change the principal features of Chimú art. Accomplished artisans such as metalsmiths, however, were taken to Cusco, where they produced objects in the style of their Inka masters. "As the [Chimú] were so skilled at working metals, many of them were taken to Cusco, and the capitals of the provinces, where they wrought jewelry, vessels, and goblets of gold and silver, and whatever else they were ordered."[93]

In other regions, such as the south coast valleys of Ica and Nazca, the peaceful Inka conquest was marked by the appearance of innovative new styles that combined a strong degree of artistic independence with a liberal borrowing of Cusco Inka elements. These new eclectic styles were most marked in ceramics and textiles.

---

[92] Jones 1964: 5.   [93] Cieza [1553] 1959: 328.

Architecture

The Inka are famed for their remarkable buildings of closely fitted stone. Inka architecture combined ambitious concepts of function with an almost sacred reverence for stone, creating constructions of great eloquence. The massive labor available to the Inka state to quarry stone and carry it great distances enabled the Inka to build extensively. There was considerable standardization of forms and stylistic elements, such as trapezoidal doorways, windows, and wall niches. Inka architecture appears to have clearly and deliberately stamped its builders' identity on its structures in such a way that "one should think that a single architect has built this large number of monuments."[94] The symbolism of the easily identifiable Inka architectural style seems clear. It associated entire settlements with the state, contrasting them with all settlements occupied by other groups in the same region. In some cases, such as in Chincha, the Cusco style identified Inka compounds or sectors within settlements built by other peoples. As the "architecture of power" (in Gasparini and Margolies' phrase) such buildings symbolized the state, its rulers, and its activities.

In spite of standardization, each center had an individual character. Although architecture was involved in critical ways with the identity of the state, it was less standardized than textiles or pottery. Town plans included many common elements, but the combinations were quite distinct; no two Inka towns match the way cookie-cutter Spanish "reduction" villages match. Frequently this individuality comes from the way Inka architects took advantage of a site's natural setting. Machu Picchu, which is shaped by and echoes the mountains that surround it, is the most famous example of the justly admired Inka sense of harmony between setting and architecture.

As ubiquitous as elaborate Inka stonework may seem, however, this masonry style was reserved for the most important buildings in and around Cusco, the Urubamba Valley, and a dozen or so provincial capitals. Most Inka constructions are of fieldstones set in mud mortar with plastered walls. Even some of the surviving finely built stone walls we see today were covered in a thin layer of plaster. On the coast the Inka usually built in adobe, reserving stonework for only the most important structures, such as at the site of Cerro Azul in Guarco (Cañete).

[94] Humboldt 1850.

Knowing that the Inka had access to battalions of *mit'a* laborers makes the magnitude of their constructions comprehensible; in less than a century this labor force created scores of cities and hundreds of waystations. Cieza de León, discussing the building of Saksay Waman near Cusco, described a workforce of "four thousand [men who] quarried and cut the stones; six thousand hauled them with great cables of leather and hemp; the others dug the ditch and laid the foundations, while still others cut poles and beams for the timbers."[95]

Saksay Waman is one of Tawantinsuyu's most imposing monuments. Cyclopean limestone blocks, many weighing almost a hundred tons and fitted together without mortar, form the foundations of Saksay Waman's three zigzagging, rampart-like walls. "This was such a magnificent construction that it could be considered one of the marvels of the world."[96] To the Spaniards, as to modern popularizers, these walls resembled those of a fortress. Saksay Waman apparently served both a religious and a military function, although its military role may have been mostly symbolic. The wide esplanade between its lower and upper ramparts, and a large carved stone outcrop, may have served as a setting for ritual battles, such as those that took place in the city below.

Some scholars have suggested that the Inka used log rollers to move stones, but the principle of the wheel, linked to rollers, was never used by the Inka. Rollers in any case seem to be of dubious value on the steep ramps, roads, and chutes that confronted Inka engineers. The real answer is probably much simpler: The Inka used their highly organized work crews to drag the stones using ropes. The Spaniards saw similar large stones moved by native laborers during the construction of Cusco's cathedral, using "much human labour and great ropes of vine and hemp, some as 'thick as a leg'." Like so much of Inka technology, transporting stone was based more on keen human skills, strength, and organization than on technical ingenuity.

Stone possessed special – in a sense sacred – qualities for the Inka.[97] This is seen in the unusual treatment of individual stones incorporated into the walls of buildings and terraces and especially in the treatment of "living" rock. (The locution is not metaphorical in Andean context, because Andean cultures treat minerals as "grown" material.) In many cases Inka masons incorporated living rock into structures; in others they shaped outcrops into free-standing sculpture. Although they did not

[95] Cieza [1553] 1959: 154.   [96] Betanzos [1551] 1996: 157.   [97] Hyslop 1990; van de Guchte 1984.

produce sculpture with the elaborately detailed carving characteristic of some earlier Andean cultures such as Chavín and Tiwanaku, the Inka did sculpt living stone into strikingly modern-looking monuments. These sculptures also served as boundary markers and symbols of the Inka presence. Frequently they commemorated important events in Inka myths and legends – for example, places of ancestral origin.

Reverence for stone extended to the quarries, such as the limestone outcrops dotting the hills around Cusco, where the Inka extracted the enormous blocks that form Saksay Waman's zigzagging ramparts. Other stones – for instance, the smaller andesite blocks that the Spaniards removed from Saksay Waman to build their churches and mansions in the city below – came from Rumiqolqa (*Rumi Qulka* 'rock warehouse'), a quarry 35 kilometers southwest of Cusco.[98] At Rumiqolqa Inka roads and ramps lead to the ancient quarry area, but traces of Inka quarrying are largely obliterated because the quarry is still worked today. The Inka quarriers followed natural fractures to extract the stone and may have used bronze pry bars to break out stones or used wooden sticks, as modern quarrymen do. The quarries are littered with stones in different stages of production. Stonecutters shipped finished stones to construction sites in Cusco, where we find them in the finely wrought walls of Loreto street or at Quri Kancha, the city's holiest shrine.

Another even more impressive source of Inka building stone was the rockfalls of Kachiqata in the Urubamba Valley, as described by Protzen. The Inka used blocks from this quarry to build the cyclopean yet graceful walls of Ollantaytambo, 5 kilometers upstream from Kachiqata on the opposite bank of the Urubamba River. Unlike the Rumiqolqa quarries, Kachiqata is not a quarry in the true sense. Rather quarrymen picked blocks from rockfalls, preshaped them, and dispatched them to Ollantaytambo. Kachiqata's highest rockfall rises 900 meters above the valley floor. The entire area is crisscrossed by the remains of an elaborate 9-kilometer-long network of ramps and roads along which the quarrymen dragged the stones – some weighing close to 100 tons – from the rockfalls to a chute or slide overlooking the Urubamba. One block is still wedged in the chute. The steep chute drops 250 meters to the valley floor. Suddenly, perhaps during the 1536 Spanish siege of Ollantaytambo, the quarrymen, masons, and rock-dragging crews stopped work at Kachiqata and abandoned some forty blocks in different stages of transport. Frozen

[98] Protzen 1985.

in time, the blocks lie scattered along the ramps leading from the rock-falls to a chute overlooking the Urubamba River, in maize fields on either side of the river, and along the ramp leading up to Ollantaytambo's temple hill.[99]

The Road System

More than 25,000 kilometers of roads formed the backbone of the empire. Much of the road system incorporated roads built in pre-Inka times. Nevertheless the scale of the Inka road system was much larger than any previous road network, and it clearly ranks among the world's major public works achievements. In addition there were hundreds of bridges, causeways, drainage canals, and other features, many difficult to build and complicated to maintain because they spanned chasms or had to withstand flash floods. The roads and state installations were probably planned as a unit. Together they display Inka state planning on a grand scale. Key to the system were two roads, the *Qhapaq Ñan*, or main highland royal road that ran north–south along the spine of the Andes, and a north–south coastal road. Dozens of lateral roads connected these two roads. The road system linked Cusco with administrative and storage centers throughout the realm, such as Huánuco Pampa. *Tampu*, or waystations, and other roadside installations lay along the roads. Road walls kept herds in transit out of adjacent fields. Inka-era suspension bridges, made of thick grass-fiber cables and amounting to vast textile webs anchored to boulders, spanned abysses such as the Apurímac River canyon (Fig. 10.4).

The roads did more than facilitate travel. They moved goods, people, and information and served as physical and conceptual links between the hinterland and Cusco, center of the realm.[100] Not everyone could travel along these roads. Access was at least theoretically restricted to those engaged in state business: the elaborate entourages accompanying the Inka emperor as he inspected his farflung domains, armies engaged in wars of conquest or in quashing the frequent rebellions, llama caravans carrying produce and goods to stockpile storehouses, provincial adminis-trators and bureaucrats occupied in matters of state, and the *ch'aski* runners conveying messages throughout Tawantinsuyu.

Cieza de León, who traveled along many of the roads, called them

---

[99] Protzen 1993.   [100] Hyslop 1984.

Figure 10.4. Drawing of an Inka suspension bridge and the administrator or "governor" in charge of bridges. From Felipe Guaman Poma de Ayala, *Nueva Cronica y Buen Goierno* (Paris: Institut d'Ethnologie, 1936 [1613]).

"splendid highways." "There were many of these highways all over the kingdom, both in the highlands and the plains. Of all, four are considered the main highways, and these are those which start from the city of Cusco, at the square, like a crossroads, and go to the different provinces of the kingdom." He marveled at the road Wayna Qhapaq built to Quito:

[Can] anything comparable be said of Alexander, or of any of the mighty kings who ruled the world, that they built such a road, or provided the supplies to be found on this one! [The road ran] through deep valleys and over high mountains, through piles of snow, quagmires, living rock, along turbulent rivers; in some places it ran smooth and paved, carefully laid out; in others over sierras, cut through the rock, with walls skirting the rivers, and steps and rests through the snow; everywhere it was clean-swept and kept free of rubbish, with lodgings, storehouses, temples to the sun, and posts along the way.[101]

Tampu were placed strategically along the roads. Some *tampu*, spaced 6 to 9 kilometers (or up to a day's walk) apart, were manned by messengers who ran in relay delivering messages from one end of the realm to the other. Cieza de León wrote that news could move in a week from Quito to Cusco. Cobo, who traveled the same roads several decades later, noted that messages carried by relay runners could cover 50 leagues (approximately 250 kilometers) in a day. While the Inka emperor was in Cusco and "felt a desire for some fresh fish from the sea, his order was acted upon with such speed that, although the city is over seventy leagues [roughly 350 kilometers] from the sea, the fish was brought to him very fresh in less than two days."[102]

Agriculture

Some foods were singled out for both technological improvement and ritual emphasis. The sociopolitical importance of maize and the beer brewed from it spurred Inka efforts to increase its production. As we have seen, these efforts combined population movements and other labor and land-tenure strategies with technological improvements in irrigation and terracing to increase production per unit of land.

Terracing greatly increased the amount of level land. Many terraces were constructed with underlying levels of stone, clay, and sand to assure proper drainage. Irrigation had been vital on the desert coast for millen-

---

[101] Cieza [1553] 1959: 136–138.   [102] Cobo [1635] 1979: 230.

nia already. In the highlands the Inka expanded the land under irrigated cultivation; Earls has suggested that the amphiteater-shaped terraces of Moray served as test beds for agricultural technique. Many deep highland valleys' rainfall is insufficient for cultivation without canals. In some higher regions irrigation shortened the growing season, reducing the risk of frost damage.

The Inka invested their most monumental agricultural technology in the high-status crop, maize. They moved thousands of *mitmaq* and *mit'a* cultivators to work the production enclaves in the so-called breadbasket valleys of Urubamba, Abancay, Cochabamba, and the Mantaro.

Outside such enclaves centuries-old agricultural systems assured basic subsistence. Farmers used simple tools such as clod breakers and the Andean foot plow, or *chaki taklla*, often illustrated by Guaman Poma and still used because it is efficient on fields too steep for oxen. Except when the Inka took land for state purposes, they usually interfered little in the management of local agriculture.

Andean farmers cultivated some forty species of plants, including a wide range of tubers and grains, using irrigation, dry farming, raised fields, and combinations of techniques that varied widely among the different Andean ecosystems. Domesticated animals included the llama, the alpaca, the "muscovy" duck, dogs, and the guinea pig. (For species and domestication information, see Chaps. 3–6.) Agriculture and animal husbandry allowed people to exploit areas ranging from the coastal desert to steep mountainsides and frigid high plateaus.

Andean wealth was based on the management and redistribution of a wide variety of products and resources. The Inka role, once again, was to increase the scale, range, and integration of this control. They were also able to mobilize effectively the labor needed to build terraces, irrigation canals, and other public works. These investments made it possible to finance partially the state élite and state expansion, so as to extract only part of the high costs from locally controlled production.

Weaving, Metalwork, and Ceramics

For the Inka, as for Andean peoples before them, cloth was the most valued of all goods. The link between cloth production and the principles of reciprocity has already been emphasized. The great virtuosity and technical range of Inka weaving grew from millennia of experimentation in weaving technology. In the age-old Andean tradition, cloth carried society's most important symbols and was used in all of the important rites and turning points in life – and death. The preeminence of textiles continues among many contemporary Andean peoples.

The Inka state, as we have seen, invested enormous resources in the production of cloth. Part of the state's interest in cloth production related to textiles' economic and symbolic values. But the state also held a vested interest in creating and controlling a series of essential signs and symbols. The sociocultural importance of Inka cloth is matched by its technological virtuosity and variety. By Inka times Andean peoples had developed essentially the full range of weaving techniques and structures of cloth known today.

Cloth was given or exchanged to celebrate all of life's turning points. Elaborate gifts of cloth to newly conquered peoples elevated this custom to political importance.[103] Designs on cloth were richly symbolic, and distinct patterns signaled differences in group membership. Some patterns may have symbolized the royal *panaka*s. Certain garments, such as those woven from the silky fiber of the vicuña, a wild relative of the domesticated llama and alpaca, were reserved for the ruler. Francisco de Jerez' eyewitness description of the Inka ruler Atawallpa and his retinue as they entered the plaza of the Inka city of Cajamarca gives an impression of the brilliance and color of the Inka court. It also shows how people dressed according to their status and duties.

Soon the first people began to enter the plaza; in front came a group of Indians in a colored uniform with checks. They came removing straw from the ground and sweeping the road. Another three groups came after them, all singing and dancing, dressed in a different way. Then many people advanced with armor, medallions, and crowns of gold and silver. Among them Atawalpa entered in a litter covered with colorful parrot feathers and decorated with gold and silver plaques. Many Indians carried him up high on their shoulders, and after this came two other litters and two hammocks in which two other important people rode. Then many groups of people entered with gold and silver crowns. As soon as the first entered the plaza, they went to the side and made room for the others. Upon arriving in the middle of the plaza, Atawalpa made a sign for silence.[104]

Inka garments show considerable standardization of design, particularly in *unku*, the tunics worn by men.[105] The designs of these tunics possibly were related to the status of the wearers, such as the "Indians in

---

[103] Murra 1962.   [104] Jerez [1536] 1917: 56.   [105] Rowe 1979.

a colored uniform of checks" described by Jerez. The use of brightly and highly visible designs would tell knowledgeable observers at a glance the ethnic identity and other essential social and political facts about the people they encountered. This capacity to communicate social information rapidly was essential, given the variety of people who made up Tawantinsuyu. Such ethnic markers extended to headdresses:

If they were Yungas, they went muffled like gypsies; if Collas, they wore caps shaped like mortars, of wool; if Canas, they wore larger caps. . . . The Cañari wore a kind of narrow wooden crown like the rim of a sieve; the Huancas, strands that fell below their chin, and their hair braided; the Canchis, broad black or red bands over their forehead.[106]

The state devoted much of its cloth production to dressing its armies, often reserving the finest garments, especially feather cloth, for its soldiers. Indeed, cloth played an important role in all aspects of warfare. The focus on metal weapons so important to Old World militarism was not, as Lechtmann observes, a concern for the Inka. Inka troops protected their bodies by wrapping them in cotton cloth or wore quilted cotton tunics and covered their heads with quilted or wooden helmets or caps of plaited cane. "Over this defensive gear they would generally wear their most attractive and rich adornments and jewels. . . . And they generally wore the finery and jewels with which they customarily dressed for their festivities."[107] They fought with slings made of camelid wool, agave fiber, or rawhide, and they carried shields of woven palm slats and cotton, sheathed with deerskin and decorated with fine cotton, wool, or feather cloth. As we see later, such weapons and "armor" proved no match for the lances and swords of Toledo steel wielded by Spaniards on horseback.[108]

Precious metals, specifically gold, were of primary interest to the invading Spaniards. Yet for the Inka, gold and silver had not become the universal measure of value that they were in Europe. The importance of metals in the Andes was symbolic. Precious metals, especially gold, which was associated with the divine Sun, conveyed status, wealth, and political and religious power in life as well as in death. The Spaniards' insatiable appetite for precious metals baffled the Inka, who regarded cloth as a more valuable commodity. In one telling exchange illustrated by Guaman Poma, a native asks a Spaniard whether he ate gold. The Spaniard

---

[106] Cieza [1553] 1959: 71.   [107] Cobo [1653] 1990: 216.   [108] Hemming 1983.

"answered in the Spanish language and by signs . . . that he ate gold and silver."[109]

Although gold and silver were imbued with ritual and political significance throughout Andean prehistory, this symbolism reached new heights under the Inka, in part because of the association between precious metals and the origin myths of Tawantinsuyu's rulers. Sumptuary laws restricted the use of precious metals to the nobility. Élite Inka males, for instance, wore earspools, and the Spaniards referred to men of high status as *orejones* ('big ears') because these heavy ornaments elongated the ear lobes. Inka rulers apparently wore ear ornaments of gold.

Inka metalworking was based on pre-Inka technology; indeed much of Tawantinsuyu's metal output was produced by Chimú smiths whose mastery of metalworking, especially alloys, underscored a north coast metalworking tradition dating back several thousand years before the rise of the Inka (see Chaps. 5 and 6). The Inka borrowed tin-bronze technology from the southern Andes. It soon replaced arsenic bronze in the former Chimú heartland and throughout Tawantinsuyu. The widespread use of this alloy made it the "stainless steel" of the Andes.[110] It was used for ornaments and for cast and hammered implements, such as axes, chisels, tweezers, and women's stickpins. Some implements fashioned from cold-hammered tin bronze can be as hard, or harder, than iron. They may have been used by Inka masons to dress stone.

Like other natural resources, especially those imbued with ritual significance, the Inka theoretically had sovereign rights over all the mines and a monopoly on their output.[111] There were two types of mines in Tawantinsuyu: those belonging to the Inka and worked by local people, often supplemented by *mitmaq* and *mit'a* labor, and smaller, less important mines that belonged in practice to communities. The output of the latter went to the *kuraka*, and the labor involved was not regarded as tribute to the Inka but part of the local reciprocal arrangements. The *kuraka*, in turn honored the Inka with gifts of precious metals as part of a reciprocal arrangement with Tawantinsuyu.

In ceramics as in almost everything they created, the Inka built on millennia of technological and artistic achievements. Centuries before the Inka the potters of Chavín, Moche, Nazca, and Wari had reached pinnacles of artistic creativity on a par with those of the Old World. Inka pottery was made in standardized forms and designs. In most areas it

---

[109] Guaman Poma [1614] 1980: 268–269.   [110] Lechtman 1980.   [111] Berthelot 1986.

represented a technical improvement over immediately pre-Inka vessels. Technical standards were high, and the clean geometric polychrome designs, though rather limited in range, are vibrant and appealing. Modeled ornaments took the shape of puma heads, and bird heads often served as handles of plates. Rare pieces modeled the human form.

The role of pottery in the material culture of the state was relatively narrow. Of course, its primary use was in the preparation, serving, and storage of food and drink. The brewing and storage of maize beer required great quantities of jars. Pottery was provided as containers for offerings of food, including offerings placed in graves.

Ceramics in standardized Inka styles are found mainly in Cusco and the centers built by the Inka along their road system. In some cases the Inka established ceramic manufacturing enclaves, uprooting skilled potters from one part of the realm and resettling them in others, such as at Hupi or Milliraya near Lake Titicaca and at El Potrero-Chaquiago in Argentina. During the reign of Thupa Yupanki, potters from Collique in the Lambayeque Valley in northern Peru were resettled in Cajamarca.[112]

THE FALL OF THE INKA EMPIRE

Reciprocity-based policy fostered a rapid pace of conquest right from the onset of Inka expansion. This mechanism, however, carried with it unforeseeable consequences. The need to accumulate enormous quantities of agricultural produce and manufactured goods to fuel the constant demands of reciprocity forced the Inka to increase agricultural production. This in turn obliged the Inka to mobilize vast numbers of *mit'a* workers, *mitmaq*, and *yana* to work the state lands and, consequently, fill the state warehouses. They also had to mobilize artisans to produce pottery, cloth, and objects in metal.

The state felt pressured by the constant stream of gifts it was forced to lavish on the greater and lesser lords, the military chiefs, the priests, and the powerful *wak'as*. The constant demands for compensation required by the mechanisms of reciprocity became a never-ending expense for the state. Tawantinsuyu's solution was to embark on new conquests and territorial annexations, but these in turn promoted more entreaties and gifts. This compelled the Sapa Inka to acquire ever-greater sources of production to fulfill the demands of the system. Use of better technol-

---

[112] Espinoza Soriano 1973; Rowe 1982.

ogy and efficient organization, such as the growing deployment of skilled *mitmaq* specialists to increase production, only partially offset these growing demands. Unfortunately for the state, the later war frontiers – the campaigns against the Caranquis and Pastos of the Ecuadorian and Colombian north, and those against the Mapuche in the Chilean south – generated extremely effective anti-Inka resistance, stalling the growth of Tawantinsuyu.

Faced with stalled growth a state such as the Inka empire easily became fragile and vulnerable on many fronts. In addition, the lack of an adequate mechanism to govern successions left the field open to the "most competent" of the pretenders to the throne. Although this practice allowed the succession of three highly qualified individuals, as were Pacha Kutiq, Tupaq Yupanki, and Wayna Qhapaq, it also contributed to the outbreak of civil war. And because of Tawantinsuyu's vast size, the war took on continental proportions, easing the Spanish conquest.

How did a small band of Spaniards overthrow the lords of Cusco in the space of only a few months? The Inka state's easy fall to the Spaniards can be attributed to two types of factors: the obvious causes and the underlying, or more profound, causes. The obvious ones include the fratricidal war that divided power between two brothers, the surprise factor of the Cajamarca ambush; the superior firepower of the Europeans' weapons, including the arquebus, small primitive cannons, steel swords; and, finally, the horse.

By European standards the Inka armies were lightly armed, and their strength lay in numbers not weapons. Like the costumes of their troops, Inka battles were imbued with symbolism and ritual. The Spaniards took advantage of Inka battle tactics, noting that the Inka forces launched their attacks during the full moon and paused at the new moon to honor the lunar deity. This highly structured and ritualized code of Andean warfare provided few answers to the ambush tactics of the Spanish troops.

The marquis [Pizarro] . . . made his signal to the artillerymen. When they saw it they fired their cannon and the harquebuses. Then everybody came out at once and fell upon the Inca's men. The horsemen lanced them and the foot soldiers cut with their swords without the Inca's men putting up any resistance. Given the suddenness of the attack and never having seen a similar thing in all their days, the Indians were so shocked that, without defending themselves and seeing the great slaughter that they were undergoing, they tried to flee.[113]

[113] Betanzos [1551] 1996: 164–165.

When Inka troops clashed for the first time with Spanish soldiers in Cajamarca, they discovered that their quilted cotton armor could not thwart the steel lances and swords wielded by Spaniards on horseback.

Among the underlying reasons for Tawantinsuyu's fall are its fragile design, exacerbated by the speed of the Inka conquests, and the empire's large size. Did Tawantinsuyu become increasingly unwieldy and impractical to govern from Cusco alone? The more profound factors that weighed heavily also included the fact that the Andean peoples, who regarded each other and the Inka as rivals or even enemies, did not cohere against Spain. At the same time, growing discontent among powerful provincial lords toward the policies of the Cusco sovereigns, whose ever-increasing demands for *mitmaq* and *yana* translated into great losses of the *kurakas'* local labor forces, made it easy for Spanish invaders to find anti-Inka allies among the Wanka, Cañari, and other peoples (see Chap. 12).

A review of Andean civilization at the end of the fifteenth century shows a hierarchical society that, on the eve of Inka domination, had been composed of *señoríos* ruled by local lords who, in turn, controlled a series of smaller polities. Although in this sense the structure did not change, Inka overlordship spelled for these peoples a loss of their power and a goodly part of their wealth. For these reasons Andean identity was expressed only at the *señorío* level, which the Inka state, perhaps because it was so short-lived, was unable to mold into a cohesive all-Andean unit.

The arrival of the Spaniards spurred the more powerful local lords to rid themselves of the Cusco yoke. From their perspective we can understand why many gave their full support to Pizarro's army. Not only was the provincial nobility pleased by the turn of events, but their people thought well of the alliance with the foreigners. The people had suffered during the prolonged wars of succession.

Furthermore, the lack of rules governing succession to the throne kindled intrigue among the Cusco *panakas*, embroiling the nobility in periodic power struggles. To maintain the royal estates of the *panakas* consumed considerable energy, detracting from more serious matters of state. The civil war that followed the death of Wayna Qhapaq rocked the foundations of Tawantinsuyu's carefully orchestrated social, political, and economic institutions.

Finally, another more insidious evil dealt the death knell to an already beleaguered Tawantinsuyu. European diseases such as smallpox and measles, to which indigenous peoples had no natural immunities, had begun making their way through the Americas shortly after Christopher Columbus's 1492 landfall. A decade before Atawallpa's fateful encounter with Pizarro, a major epidemic, probably smallpox, spread into Tawantinsuyu from the north. Among its first victims was the sovereign who had ruled over the apogee of empire, Wayna Qhapaq. The disruption that beset Tawantinsuyu in the wake of the Spanish invasion, combined with a series of epidemics, led to a major decline in Andean populations, especially in the more densely populated coastal valleys.[114]

One cannot blame only a handful of foreigners for the downfall of the Inka. The end of Tawantinsuyu was also fostered by discontent among subject peoples who saw the arrival of the Europeans as an advantageous time to recover their independence. If their calculations failed, it was because of their ignorance of what foreign rule would bring, of the imperialist designs of the Spanish crown, and of Spain's extensive conquests in Mexico and the Caribbean. Only later (see Chap. 22), battered by the misery and suffering wrought by colonial administration, did Andean peoples long for their Inka past.

BIBLIOGRAPHICAL ESSAY

On the history and archaeology of Tawantinsuyu, the Inka empire, John H. Rowe, "Inca culture at the time of the Spanish conquest," in Julian H. Steward (ed.), *Handbook of South American Indians*, vol. 2 (Washington, 1946), 183–330, although long out of print, is considered a classic. Rowe has stressed chronology and brought a strong historical tradition to the material. For a similar treatment, see, for example, Richard P. Schaedel, "Early state of the Incas," in H. Claessen and P. Skalnik (eds.), *The early state* (The Hague, 1978), 289–330.

John H. Rowe's "An introduction to the archaeology of Cuzco," *Papers of the Peabody Museum of American Archaeology and Ethnology*, 27/2 (1944), identifies Killke as the pottery style associated with the preexpansionist, early Inka; see also Brian S. Bauer and Charles Stanish, "Killke and Killke-related pottery from Cuzco, Peru, in the Field Museum of Natural History," *Fieldiana Anthropology* 15 (1990), 1–17. More recent archaeological research in the Cuzco region by Brian S. Bauer, *The development of the Inca state* (Austin, 1992) posits a less linear reading of Inka "history" as proposed by Rowe and suggests that preimperial

[114] Verano 1992.

consolidation over the Cusco valley took place as early as 1400; see also Edward B. Dwyer, "The early Inca occupation of the valley of Cuzco" (Ph.D. dissertation, Berkeley, 1971).

Several recent books on the archaeology of the Central Andes include chapters on the Inka. Michael E. Moseley's *The Incas and their ancestors* (New York, 1992) begins with the Inka and works back through time, using the Inka model of statecraft as a template to analyze the Andean societies that preceded Tawantinsuyu. Other authors use a more traditional, chronological approach, tracing the development of Andean civilization from the earliest recorded settlements and culminating with the Inka empire; see, for example, Karen Olsen Bruhns, *Ancient South America* (Cambridge, 1994), which touches on the prehistory of areas beyond the Central Andes, while Craig Morris and Adriana von Hagen, *The Inka empire and its Andean origins* (New York, 1993), and the *People of the Andes* (Washington, 1994) by James B. Richardson, focus on the archaeology of what is today Peru. *The peoples and cultures of ancient Peru* (Washington, 1974) by Luis G. Lumbreras (Betty J. Meggers, trans.), although somewhat dated, remains an authoritative text on Central Andean prehistory.

Travelogues by nineteenth-century writers, for instance, Charles Wiener's *Pérou et Bolivie, Récit de Voyage* (Paris, 1880) and *Peru: Incidents of travel and exploration in the land of the Incas* (New York, 1877; reprint, Cambridge, Mass., 1973) by E. George Squier are lively narratives with many descriptions of Inka monuments.

Eyewitness accounts by Spanish chroniclers written in the early years of the European invasion include the testimony of the young Spanish soldier Pedro de Cieza de León, whose *La Crónica del Perú* (Part I) (Madrid, 1962 [1553]) and *El Señorío de los Incas* (second part of *La Crónica del Perú*) (Lima, 1967 [1553]) are regarded among the most reliable and least biased of all the Spanish writings; *The Incas of Pedro de Cieza de León*, Harriet de Onis (trans.) and Victor W. von Hagen (ed.) (Norman, 1959 [1553]). Juan de Betanzos spent many years in Cusco as a Quechua interpreter for the viceroyalty of Peru. His marriage to a former wife of Atawallpa, the last Inka emperor, afforded him an insider's view of the Cusco nobility, and he recorded his impressions in *Suma y narración de los Yngas* (Madrid, 1987 [1551]); *Narrative of the Incas*, Roland Hamilton and Dana Buchanan (trans. and eds.) (Austin, 1996 [1551]). The mestizo chronicler Inca Garcilaso de la Vega, son of an Inka noble woman and a Spanish conquistador, cast the Inka as benevolent rulers in

Comentarios Reales de los Incas (Madrid, 1963 [1604]) 2 parts; *Royal Commentaries of the Incas and General History of Peru*, Harold V. Livermore (trans.), (Austin, 1987 [1604]), 2 parts.

A compelling, illustrated account addressed to the king of Spain is that by the native chronicler Felipe Guaman Poma de Ayala, *El Primer Nueva Corónica y Buen Gobierno*, John V. Murra and Rolena Adorno (eds.) and Jorge I. Urioste (trans.) (Mexico City, 1980 [1614]), 3 vols. On the life and times of Guaman Poma, see Rolena Adorno, *Guaman Poma: Writing and resistence in colonial Peru* (Austin, 1986), and *Guaman Poma de Ayala: The colonial art of an Andean author* (New York, 1992).

Visitas, or inspections by Spanish officials, recorded, house-by-house, census data and information on resources to be tapped for colonial tribute. Although the data registered in the *visitas* was filtered through interpreters, these documents remain valuable fonts of information on peoples who lived in conquered areas far beyond the empire's heartland; see, for example, Iñigo Oritz de Zúñiga, *Visita de la provincia de León de Huánuco en 1562*, J. V. Murra (ed.) (Huánuco, 1967 [1562]), analyzed by John V. Murra in "An archaeological 'restudy' of an Andean ethnohistorical account," *American Antiquity* 28 (1962), 1–4; and "Visita hecha a la provincia de Chucuito por Garci Diez de San Miguel en el año 1567," in *Documentos Regionales para la Etnología y Etnohistoria Andina*, Vol. I (Lima, 1964 [1567]), 1–299, discussed by John V. Murra in "An Aymara kingdom in 1567," *Ethnohistory* 15 (1968), 49–62.

On the conquest of Peru, see John Hemming's *The conquest of the Incas* (Harmondsworth, 1983; revised edition London, 1993), and the classic, William H. Prescott, *History of the conquest of Peru* (New York, 1847) 2 vols. Hemming also portrays the life and times of Francisco Pizarro in "Pizarro: Conqueror of the Inca," *National Geographic* (February 1992), 90–121. On Inka militarism, see Joseph Bram, *An analysis of Inka militarism* (New York, 1941) and discussions by John H. Rowe (1946) and by George Kubler, "The Quechua in the colonial world," in Julian H. Steward (ed.), *Handbook of South American Indians*, Vol. 2 (Washington, 1946), 331–410.

For an account of the early decades of Spanish colonial rule, see James Lockhart, *Spanish Peru, 1532–1560* (Madison, 1968) and *Men of Cajamarca: A social and biographical study of the first conquerors of Peru* (Austin, 1972). The impact of the Spanish invasion is explored by Nathan Wachtel in *The vision of the vanquished* (New York, 1977). For discussions on the effects of western diseases in the New World, see John W.

Verano and Douglas H. Ubelaker (eds.), *Disease and demography in the Americas* (Washington, 1992), particularly, John W. Verano, "Prehistoric disease and demography in the Andes," 15–24; and Noble David Cook, "Impact of disease in the sixteenth-century Andean world," 207–214, and by the same author, *Demographic collapse, Indian Peru 1520–1620* (Cambridge, 1981), as well as C. T. Smith, "Depopulation of the Central Andes in the 16th century," *Current Anthropology* 11/4–5 (1970), 453–464.

The interplay of archaeology and ethnohistory is addressed by Donald E. Thompson, "An archaeological evaluation of ethnohistoric evidence on Inca culture," in B. J. Meggers (ed.), *Anthropological archaeology in the Americas* (Washington, D.C., 1968), and by Catherine J. Julien, "Finding a fit: Archaeology and ethnohistory of the Incas," in M. A. Malpass (ed.), *Provincial Inca: Archaeological and ethnohistorical assessment of the impact of the Inca state* (Iowa City, 1993), 177–233.

For analyses of Inka origin myths, see Gary Urton, *The history of a myth: Pacariqtambo and the origin of the Inkas* (Austin, 1990), and Brian S. Bauer, "Pacariqtambo and the mythical origins of the Inca," *Latin American Antiquity* 2 (1991), 7–26, which reports on Bauer's excavations near the legendary origin place of the founding Inka. Much of our survey of early Inka preeminence in the Cusco Basin is drawn from María Rostworowski's *Historia del Tahuantinsuyu* (Lima, 1988) forthcoming in English as *History of the Inca realm* (New York, 1998), which discusses how the Inka transformed social, economic, and religious institutions, establishing reciprocal relationships with rival groups rather than embarking on outright military conquests. Rostworowski explores the Andean institution of reciprocity in "Reflexiones sobre la reciprocidad andina," *Revista del Museo Nacional*, XLII (1976), 341–354.

On the structure of Cusco's ruling élite, see accounts by chroniclers Betanzos (1996 [1551]: 27–28), and Pierre Duviols, "La dinastía de los Incas: ¿Monarquía o Diarquía?," *Journal de la Société des Américanistes* 66 (1979), 67–83, as well as "Succession, coöption to kingship and royal incest among the Inca," *Southwestern Journal of Anthropology* 16/4 (1960), 417–427, by María Rostworowski. Much of Tom Zuidema's large body of research (for example, *Inca civilization in Cuzco*, Austin, 1990) takes a structuralist approach, seeking broad principles of order and structure that crosscut Inka sociopolitical organization, ritual, the calendar, and many aspects of ideology; see also "The Inka kinship system: A new theoretical view," in R. Bolton and E. Mayer (eds.), *Andean kinship and marriage* (Washington, 1977), 240–281; "Hierarchy and space in Incaic social organization," *Ethnohistory* 30 (1983), 49–75; and Geoffrey W. Conrad and Arthur Demarest, *Religion and empire: The dynamics of Aztec and Inca expansionism* (Cambridge, Mass., 1984).

On Inka religion, see Arthur A. Demarest, "Viracocha: The nature and antiquity of the Andean high god," *Peabody Museum Monograph* No. 6 (Cambridge, Mass., 1981), and John H. Rowe, "The origins of creator worship among the Incas," in S. Diamond (ed.), *Culture in history, essays in honor of Paul Radin* (New York, 1960), 408–429. The most authoritative colonial account of Inka religion is that by the Jesuit priest Bernabé Cobo, *Historia del Nuevo Mundo* (Madrid, 1964 [1653]), parts of which are translated into English: *History of the Inca empire*, Roland Hamilton (trans.) (Austin, 1979 [1653]), and *Inca religion and customs*, Roland Hamilton (trans.) (Austin, 1990 [1653]). Although Cobo wrote in the seventeenth century, he based much of his account of Inka religion on the earlier writings of Polo de Ondegardo, for example, "De los errores y supersticiones de los indios, sacados del tratado y averiguación que hizo el Licenciado Polo," in Horacio H. Urteaga, (ed.), *Colección de Libros y Documentos Referentes a la Historia del Perú* (Lima, 1916 [1571]), 1–44.

Reports by zealous Spanish priests bent on stamping out "idolatry" provide valuable insight into the religious beliefs of peoples conquered by the Inka; see, for example, *The extirpation of idolatry in Peru* by Father Pablo Joseph de Arriaga, L. Clark Keating (trans.) (Lexington, 1968 [1621]) (José de Arriaga, *Extirpación de la idolatría del Pirú* (Madrid, 1968 [1621]); Pierre Duviols, *Cultura andina y represión: procesos y visitas de idolatrías y hechicerías, Cajatambo, siglo XVII* (Cusco, 1986); and "Un inedito de Cristóbal de Albornoz: La instrucción para descubrir todas las guacas del Pirú y sus camayos y haziendas," *Journal de la Société des Américanistes* 66 (1979), 67–83; as well as Frank Salomon and George L. Urioste (trans.), *The Huarochirí Manuscript: A testament of ancient and colonial Andean religion* (Austin, 1991). The late prehistory and early colonial occupation of the Huarochirí are sketched by Karen Spalding, *Huarochirí, an Andean society under Inca and Spanish rule* (Stanford, 1984).

Cusco's *ceque* system, *wak'a*s, and the sacrifices carried out at its shrines are described in detail by Cobo (1990 [1653]: 47–84). Cobo's account of the *ceque* system is translated and analyzed by Rowe in "An account of the shrines of ancient Cuzco," *Nawpa Pacha* 17 (1979), 2–80. See also Tom Zuidema, "The Ceque system of Cuzco: The social organization of the capital of the Inca," *International Archives of Ethnography*,

Supplement to Vol. 5 (Leiden, 1964); and Brian S. Bauer, "Ritual pathways of the Inca: An analysis of the Collasuyu ceques in Cuzco," *Latin American Antiquity* 3/3 (1993), 183–205. The *ceque* system's relationship to Cusco's irrigation network is explored by Jeanette Sherbondy, "The canal systems of Hanan Cusco," (Ph.D. dissertation, University of Illinois at Urbana-Champaign, 1982) and "Los ceques: Código de canales en el Cusco Incaico," *Allpanchis* 27 (1986), 39–60.

Peter Gose, "Oracles, divine kinship, and political representation in the Inka state," *Ethnohistory* 43 (1996), 1–32, discusses the role of oracles in Inka religion and politics. Miguel de Estete, one of the first Spaniards to see the temple and oracle at Pacha Kamaq, described his impressions in "Relación del viaje que hizo el señor capitán Hernando Pizarro por mandado del señor gobernador, su hermano, desde el pueblo de Caxamalca a Pachacamac y de allí a Jauja," (Madrid, 1947 [1534]). Thomas Patterson, "Pachacamac: An Andean oracle under Inca rule," in D. P. Kvietok and D. Sandweiss (eds.), *Recent studies in Andean prehistory and protohistory* (Ithaca, 1985), addresses Pacha Kamaq's widespread influence and its network of shrines. The Inka sanctuary on the Island of the Sun in Lake Titicaca is examined by John Hyslop in *Inka settlement planning* (Austin, 1990), drawing on the seventeenth-century account by Alonso Ramos Gavilán, *Historia de Nuestra Señora de Copacabana* (La Paz, 1976 [1621]), and on the excavations by Adolph F. Bandelier, *The islands of Titicaca and Coati* (New York, 1910 [reprint 1969]).

For accounts of the all-empire sacrificial cycle, see Pierre Duviols, "La Capacocha: Mecanismo y función del sacrificio humano, su proyección geometrica, su papel en la politica integracionista en la economía redistributiva del Tawantinsuyu," *Allpanchis* 9 (1976), 11–57, and Colin McEwan and Maarten van de Guchte, "Ancestral time and sacred space in Inca state ritual," in Richard F. Townsend (ed.), *The ancient Americas: Art from sacred landscapes* (Chicago, 1992), 359–371, as well as Tom Zuidema, "Bureaucracy and systematic knowledge in Andean civilization," in G. A. Collier, R. I. Rosaldo, and J. D. Wirth (eds.), *The Inca and Aztec states, 1400–1800* (New York, 1992), 419–454.

The discovery in 1995 of a young woman sacrificed on the summit of Ampato, a volcano near Arequipa, as part of the sacrificial cycle, is retold by Johan Reinhard in "Peru's ice maidens: Unwrapping the secrets," *National Geographic* 189/6 (1996), 62–81. On mountain worship and human sacrifice, see Reinhard, "Sacred peaks of the Andes," *National Geographic* 181/3 (1992), 84–111, and "Sacred mountains: An ethnoarchaeological study of high Andean ruins," *Mountain Research and Development* 5/4 (1985), 299–317, as well as Juan Schobinger, "Sacrifices of the high Andes," *Natural History* 4 (1991), 63–69.

Brian S. Bauer and David S. P. Dearborn's *Astronomy and empire in the ancient Andes* (Austin, 1995) is the most recent survey of Inka astronomy and calendrics. See also Mariusz S. Ziolkowski and Robert M. Sadowski (eds.), *Time and calendars in the Inca empire*, BAR International Series 479 (Oxford, 1989); Gary Urton, "Orientation in Quechua and Incaic astronomy," *Ethnology* 17/2 (1978), 157–167; Anthony F. Aveni, "Horizon astronomy in Incaic Cuzco," in R. A. Williamson (ed.), *Archaeoastronomy in the Americas* (Los Altos, 1981), 305–318; David S. P. Dearborn and Raymond E. White, "Archaeoastronomy at Machu Picchu," in A. F. Aveni and G. Urton (eds.), *Ethnoastronomy and archaeoastronomy in the American tropics*, Annals of the New York Academy of Sciences, 385 (1982), 249–259; and David S. P. Dearborn and Katharina J. Schreiber, "Here comes the sun: The Cuzco-Machu Picchu connection," *Archaeoastronomy* 9/1–4 (1986), 15–37.

On the layout of Inka Cusco, "What kind of a settlement was Inca Cuzco?," *Ñawpa Pacha* 5 (1967), 59–76, by John H. Rowe, is a portrait of the imperial capital, based on the author's surveys and early colonial accounts. Both John Hyslop's *Inka settlement planning* (Austin, 1990) and Graziano Gasparini and Luise Margolies' *Inca architecture*, Patricia J. Lyon (trans.) (Bloomington, 1980) devote chapters to Inka Cusco, drawing on early Spanish eyewitness reports and architectural and archaeological evidence, as does John Hemming's *The conquest of Incas* (Harmondsworth, 1983). Tom Zuidema's "The lion in the city: Royal symbols of transition in Cuzco," *Journal of Latin American Lore* 9/1 (1983), 39–100, suggests an alternative reading of early colonial accounts of Pachakuti's remodeling of Cusco (for example, Betanzos 1996 [1551], 74), proposing that the city's alleged layout in the shape of a puma should be read metaphorically rather than literally.

Much of what we know about the archaeology of the Inka is based on research beyond the imperial capital – for instance, Susan A. Niles, *Callachaca: Style and status in an Inca community* (Iowa City, 1987); and Ann Kendall, *Proyecto Arqueológico Cusichaca, Cusco*, Vol. 1 (Lima, 1994), an Inka settlement in the lower Urubamba Valley. Excavations by José Alcina Franch at Chinchero, a "royal estate" near Cusco reportedly founded by Thupa Yupanki, are detailed in *Arqueología de Chinchero* (Madrid, 1976), 2 vols. For descriptions of other "royal estates" near

Cusco, see Susan A. Niles, "Looking for 'lost' Inca palaces," *Expedition* 30 (1988), 56–64; and Ian S. Farrington, "The mummy, palace and estate of Inka Huayna Capac at Quispeguanca," *Tawantinsuyu* 1 (1995), 55–64.

On the discovery of Machu Picchu, the most famed Urubamba Valley site, see Hiram Bingham's own account of his 1911 expedition, for example, *Machu Picchu – A citadel of the Incas* (New Haven, 1930; reprint, New York, 1970) and the biography by his son, Alfred M. Bingham, *Portrait of an explorer: Hiram Bingham, discoverer of Machu Picchu* (Ames, Iowa, 1989). Rowe's "Machupijchu a la luz de los documentos del siglo XVI," *Kuntur* 4 (1987), 12–20 discusses evidence from colonial land tenure documents which hint that Machu Picchu may have been built by the emperor Pachakuti or his lineage to commemorate Inka conquests in the region. Anthropologist Johan Reinhard, *Machu Picchu: The sacred center* (Lima, 1991), links Machu Picchu to mountain worship and the sacred geography of the region.

On exploration in the area following Bingham, see Paul Fejos, "Archaeological explorations in the Cordillera Vilcabamba," *Viking Fund Publications in Anthropology*, No. 3 (1944); and Gene Savoy, *Antisuyu: The search for the lost cities of the Amazon* (New York, 1970), which includes chapters on Vilcabamba la Vieja, the capital of the neo-Inka state founded by Manqu Inka, a son of Atawallpa; and Vincent R. Lee, *Chanasuyu: The ruins of Inca Vilcabamba* (Wilson, Wyoming, 1989).

Farther afield, Craig Morris and Donald E. Thompson, *Huánuco Pampa: An Inca city and its hinterland* (London, 1985), and "Huánuco Viejo: An Inca administrative center," *American Antiquity* 35/3 (1970), 344–362, details excavations at this administrative center on the *Qhapaq Ñan*, the royal road that connected Inka administrative centers strung along the spine of the Andes between Cusco and Ecuador. Morris' "The infrastructure of Inka control in the Peruvian Central Highlands," in G. A. Collier, R. I. Rosaldo, J. D. Wirth (eds.), *The Inca and Aztec states, 1400–1800* (New York, 1992), 153–172, discusses the nature of the Inka settlement at Huánuco Pampa. Morris's Arquitectura y estructura del espacio en Huánuco Pampa *Cuadernos del Instituto Nacional de Antropología* 12 (1987), 27–45, looks at the planning of space. The same author's "State settlements in Tawantinsuyu: A strategy of compulsory urbanism," in Mark Leone (ed.), *Contemporary archaeology* (Carbondale, 1972), 393–401, describes the artificial nature of Inka settlements built on virgin ground. "Reconstructing patterns of non-agricultural production in the Inca economy: Archaeology and ethnohistory in institutional analysis," in C. Moore (ed.), *The reconstruction of complex societies* (Philadelphia, 1974), 49–60 looks at evidence for the mamakuna at Huánuco Pampa. Northeast of Huánuco, Inge Schjellerup, "Cochabamba – An Incaic administrative center in the rebellious province of Chachapoyas," in Ann Kendall (ed.), *Current archaeological projects in the Central Andes*, BAR International Series 210 (Oxford, 1984), 161–189, reviews Inka rule in an area plagued by rebellions.

South of Huánuco Pampa, research by Ramiro Matos Mendieta, *Pumpu: Centro Administrativo Inka de la Puna de Junín* (Lima, 1994) highlights excavations at the Inka administrative center of Pumpu (Bombón) on Lake Junín. Terence D'Altroy's *Provincial power in the Inka empire* (Washington, 1992) draws on the author's work in the Mantaro Valley (*Empire growth and consolidation: The Xauxa region of Peru under the Incas*, Ph.D. dissertation, New York, 1981) and takes a comparative look at Tawantinsuyu in relation to other ancient empires. His viewpoint grows out of an archaeological focus that stresses ecological, technological, and military factors, much of it based on research conducted by D'Altroy and his colleagues in the Mantaro Valley of Peru's central highlands. See, for instance, Terence N. D'Altroy, "Transitions in power: Centralization of Wanka political organization under Inka rule," *Ethnohistory* 34/1 (1987), 78–102; Timothy Earle et al., *Archaeological field research in the upper Mantaro, Peru, 1982–1983: Investigations of Inka expansion and exchange*, Institute of Archaeology, Monograph XXVIII (Los Angeles, 1987); Earle et al., "Changing settlement patterns in the upper Mantaro Valley, Peru," *Journal of New World Archaeology* 4/1 (1980), 1–49; Terry LeVine, *Inka administration in the Central Highlands: A comparative study* (Ph.D. disseration, Los Angeles, 1985).

In the Lake Titicaca region, Catherine J. Julien, "Hatunqolla: A view of Inca rule from the Lake Titicaca region," *University of California Publications in Anthropology* 15 (1983), describes Inka rule around Lake Titicaca, one of the first regions far beyond Cusco conquered by the Inka. For the Inka and early colonial administration of the Kunti Suyu administrative division, see Julien's "Condesuyu: The political division of territory under Inca and Spanish rule," *Bonner Amerikanistische Studien* 19 (1991).

On the Inka conquest and administration of Peru's south coast, Dorothy Menzel's "The Inca occupation of the south coast of Peru," *Southwestern Journal of Anthropology* 15/2 (1959), 125–142, sketches the nature of Inka rule in its southern, coastal domains. The Inka occupation of the Acarí Valley is detailed by Dorothy Menzel and Francis Riddell in *Archaeological investigations at Tambo Viejo, Acarí Valley, Peru* (Sacramento, 1986).

John Hyslop, "Inkawasi: The new Cuzco," *British Archaeological Reports*, International Series 234 (Oxford, 1985), describes the author's research at this Inka garrison in the Cañete (Guarco) Valley, while Joyce Marcus, Ramiro Matos Mendieta, and María Rostworowski report on the excavations at Cerro Azul in "Arquitectura Inca de Cerro Azul, Valle de Cañete," *Revista del Museo Nacional* XLVII (1983–1985), 125–138; see also María Rostworowski, "Guarco y Lunahuaná: dos señoríos prehispánicos de la costa sur central del Perú," *Revista del Museo Nacional* XLIV (1978–1980), 153–214. Graziani and Margolies (*Inca architecture*, Bloomington, 1980) portray the ruins at Tambo Colorado, an administrative center in the Pisco Valley and one of the best preserved Inka sites on the coast.

On the archaeology of Chincha, see Dorothy Menzel and John H. Rowe, "The role of Chincha in late pre-Spanish Peru," *Nawpa Pacha* 4 (1966), 63–76; and Daniel H. Sandweiss, "The archaeology of Chincha fishermen: Specialization and status in Inka Peru," *Bulletin of Carnegie Museum of Natural History* 29 (1992), 1–162. A colonial account of Chincha is that by Cristóbal de Castro and Diego de Ortega Morejón, "Relación y declaración del modo que este valle de Chincha y sus comarcanos se governavan antes que oviese Ingas y despues q(ue) los vuo hasta q(ue) los Cristianos entraron en esta tierra," intro. in Juan Carlos Crespo, *Historia y Cultura* (No. 8, Lima, 1974 [1558]), 91–104; on the "merchants" of Chincha, see María Rostworowski, "Mercaderes del valle de Chincha en la epoca prehispánica: un documento y unos comentarios," *Revista Española de Antropología Americana* 5 (1987), 135–177. "Merchants" in the empire's northern domains are explored by Frank Salomon, "A North Andean status trader complex under Inka rule," *Ethnohistory* 34 (1987), 63–77.

Tom D. Dillehay, "Tawantinsuyu integration of the Chillon Valley, Peru: A case of Inca geo-political mastery," *Journal of Field Archaeology* 4 (1977), 397–405, looks at Inka rule on Peru's central coast, while the reprint of Max Uhle's landmark excavations at Pacha Kamaq, with an introduction by Izumi Shimada, "Pachacamac archaeology: Retrospect and prospect," in Max Uhle, *Pachacamac, a reprint of the 1903 edition,*

University Museum of Archaeology and Anthropology (Philadelphia, 1991), xv–lxxvi, discusses archaeological research at this famed oracle and pilgrimage center.

The Inka occupation of Peru's north coast is less well documented archaeologically, in part because the Inka built little, especially in the former Chimú heartland, where they imposed their rule through local lords. Nonetheless the Inka presence is apparent in their integration of earlier roads into the Inka coastal road system, parts of which are described by John Hyslop in *The Inka road system* (New York, 1984). See also Geoffrey W. Conrad, "Chiquitoy Viejo: An Inca administrative center in the Chicama Valley, Peru," *Journal of Field Archaeology* 4 (1977), 1–18 and Thor Heyerdahl, Daniel H. Sandweiss, and Alfredo Narvaez, *Pyramids of Túcume: The quest for Peru's forgotten city* (London, 1995). On the ethnohistory of the north coast, see Susan Ramirez, "The Inca conquest of the North Coast: A historian's view," in María Rostworowski and Michael E. Moseley (eds.), *The northern dynasties: Kingship and statecraft in Chimor* (Washington, 1990), 507–537.

On Inka dominion of its southern fringes, see Alberto Rex González, "Inca settlement patterns in a marginal province of the empire: Sociocultural implications," in E. Z. Vogt and R. M. Levanthal (eds.), *Prehistoric settlement patterns: Essays in honor of Gordon R. Willey* (Cambridge, Mass., 1983), 337–360. Tawantinsuyu's administration of its northern frontier is discussed by Frank Salomon in *Native lords of Quito in the age of the Incas* (Cambridge, 1986), while excavations at Inka outposts in Ecuador are detailed by José Alcina Franch, "Ingapirca: arquitectura y áreas de asentamiento," *Revista de Antropología Americana* (1978), 127–146, and Antonio Fresco, "Arquitectura de Ingapirca (Cañar-Ecuador)," *Boletín de los Museos del Banco Central del Ecuador*, 3/3 (1983), 195–212, as well as "Excavaciones en Ingapirca (Ecuador): 1978–1982," *Revista Española de Antropología Americana* 14 (1984), 85–101. John Hyslop reviews Inka garrisons and forts on the fringes of the empire in chapter 6 of *Inka settlement planning* (Austin, 1990).

Our own viewpoint on the nature of Tawantinsuyu has grown out of ethnographic studies of non-Western societies and traditional economic anthropology. It draws from the pioneering work of Marcel Mauss and Karl Polanyi and links to the focus on reciprocity and redistribution of John V. Murra, particularly his *The economic organization of the Inka state* (Greenwich, Conn., 1980 [1956]). As we have pointed out, the Andean economy was a nonmonetary one and was not influenced by market institutions; see, for example, Timothy K. Earle, "Commodity exchange and markets in the Inca state: Recent archaeological evidence," in Stuart Plattner (ed.), *Markets and exchange* (Lanham, Md., 1985), 369–397; Timothy K. Earle and Terence N. D'Altroy, "The political economy of the Inka empire: The archaeology of power and finance," in Carl C. Lamberg-Karlovsky (ed.), *Archaeological thought in America* (Cambridge, 1989), 183–204; and Darrell E. La Lone, "The Inca as a nonmarket economy: Supply on command versus supply and demand," in J. E. Ericson and T. K. Earle (eds.), *Contexts for prehistoric exchange* (New York, 1982), 291–316.

On Inka "wealth," see Craig Morris, "The wealth of a Native American state: Value, investment and mobilization in the Inka economy," in J. S. Henderson and P. J. Netherly (eds.), *Configurations of power: Holistic anthropology in theory and practice* (Ithaca, 1993), 36–50; and Terence N. D'Altroy and Timothy K. Earle, "Staple finance, wealth finance, and storage in the Inka political economy," *Current Anthropology* 26/2 (1985), 187–206; Timothy K. Earle and Terence N. D'Altroy, "Storage facilities and state finance in the upper Mantaro Valley, Peru," in J. Ericson and T. K. Earle (eds.), *Contexts for prehistoric exchange* (New York, 1982), 265–290; and Sally F. Moore, *Power and property in Inca Peru* (Westport, Conn., 1958).

In one way or another, many modern works are also influenced by the theoretical frameworks centering on the idea of a society supremely influenced by its state. Thomas Patterson's *The Inka empire: The formation and disintegration of a pre-capitalist state* (New York, 1991) emphasizes class structure in Inka society and sees it, in a Marxist perspective, as heavily exploitative. See also Martti Parssinen, *Tawantinsuyu: The Inca state and its political organization* (Helsinki, 1992); and studies by Peruvian historians, for example, Franklin Pease's, *Del Tawantinsuyu a la Historia del Perú* (Lima, 1978), and "Los Incas," in Fernando Silva Santisteban (ed.), *Historia del Perú* (Lima, 1980), 185–293.

On Inka conquest strategies, especially in the final years of Tawantinsuyu, see John V. Murra, "The expansion of the Inca state: Armies, war and rebellions," 49–58, and on Inka conquest and administration in Ecuador, Frank Salomon, "Vertical politics on the Inka frontier," 89–117, both in J. V. Murra, N. Wachtel, and J. Revel (eds.), *Anthropological history of Andean polities* (Cambridge, 1986).

Inka decimal administration is discussed by Catherine J. Julien, "Inca decimal administration in the Lake Titicaca region," in G. A. Collier,

R. I. Rosaldo, and J. D. Wirth (eds.), *The Inca and Aztec states, 1400–1800* (New York, 1982), 119–152; and by the same author, "How Inca decimal administration worked," *Ethnohistory* 35 (1988), 257–279; see also John V. Murra, *The economic organization of the Inka state* (Greenwich, Conn., 1980 [1956]), 89–119, and John H. Rowe, "The age grades of the Inca census," pp. 499–522 in *Miscellanea Paul Rivet Octogenario Dicata*, XXI Congreso Internacional de Americanistas (México, 1958).

Craig Morris explores Inka warehousing and the processing of stored foodstuffs in *Storage in Tawantinsuyu* (Ph.D. dissertation, Chicago, 1967). See also T. Y. Levine (ed.), *Inka storage systems* (Norman, 1992), particularly Craig Morris, "The technology of highland food storage," 237–258, and "Huánuco Pampa and Tunsunkancha: Major and minor nodes in the Inka storage network," 151–175. See "The archaeological study of Andean exchange systems," in C. Redman et al. (eds.), *Social archaeology: Beyond subsistence and dating* (New York, 1978), 315–327, as well as "Storage, supply and redistribution in the economy of the Inka state," in J. V. Murra, N. Wachtel, and J. Revel (eds.), *Anthropological history of Andean polities* (Cambridge, 1986), 59–68. On Inka storage facilities in the Mantaro Valley, see Terence N. D'Altroy and Christine A. Hastorf, "The distribution and contents of Inca storage facilities in the Xauxa region of Peru," *American Antiquity* 49 (1984), 334–339.

John V. Murra discusses llama and alpaca herd management in "Herds and herders in the Inca state," in *Man, culture and animals* (Washington, D.C., 1965), 185–216, while Jorge Flores Ochoa describes the llama and alpaca corrals maintained by the Inka near Cusco, in "Los corrales del ganado del sol," *Kuntur* 5 (1987), 2–10.

Tawantinsuyu's economic model, especially the "archipelago" model of its southern domains, has been explored by John V. Murra in "El 'control vertical' de un máximo de pisos ecológicos en la economia de las sociedades andinas," in *Visita de la provincia de León de Huánuco en 1562* (Huánuco, 1967). On coastal lifeways on the eve of the Spanish invasion, see María Rostworowski, *Etnía y Sociedad: Costa Peruana prehispánica* (Lima, 1977), and by the same author, *Recursos naturales renovables y pesca, siglos XVI y XVII* (Lima, 1981). Rostworowski also examines land tenure in Tawantinsuyu in "Nuevos datos sobre tenencia de tierras reales en el Incario," *Revista del Museo Nacional* XXXI (1962), 130–164 See John V. Murra, "Rite and crop in the Inca state," in Stanley Diamond (ed.), *Culture in history, essays in honor of Paul Radin* (New York, 1960), 393–407; on the production of *chicha*, the maize beer so indispensable to Inka ritual, see Craig Morris, "Maize beer in the economics, politics, and religion of the Inca empire," in C. Gastineau, W. Darby, and T. Turnek (eds.), *Fermented food beverages in nutrition* (New York, 1979), 21–34. On the role of rotational (*mit'a*) labor and craft specialists in the economy of the Inka empire see Terry Yarov LeVine, "Inka labor service at the regional level: The functional reality," *Ethnohistory* 34 (1987), 14–46; Mary B. LaLone and Darell E. LaLone, "The Inka state in the southern highlands: State administrative and production enclaves," *Ethnohistory* 34 (1987), 47–62; G. Y. Franklin Pease, "The formation of Tawantinsuyu: Mechanisms of colonization and relationship with ethnic groups," in G. A. Collier, R. I. Rosaldo, and J. D. Wirth (eds.), *The Inca and Aztec states, 1400–1800* (New York, 1982), 173–198; John V. Murra, "The mit'a obligations of ethnic groups to the Inka state," in Collier et al. (eds.), *The Inca and Aztec states, 1400–1800*, 237–262.

Nathan Wachtel discusses Wayna Qhapaq's ambitious *mitmaq* project in Cochabamba, Bolivia, in "The mitimas of the Cochabamba Valley: The colonization policy of Huayna Capac," in Collier et al. (eds.), *The Inca and Aztec states, 1400–1800*, 199–235; John H. Rowe, "Inca policies and institutions relating to the cultural unification of the empire," in Collier et al. (eds.) *The Inca and Aztec states, 1400–1800*, 93–118.

For descriptions of *mitmaq* drawn from the archives, see studies by Waldemar Espinoza Soriano, especially, "Los mitmas yungas de Collique en Cajamarca," *Revista del Museo Nacional* 36 (1970), 9–57; "Los mitmas huayacuntus en Cajabamba y Antamarca, Siglos XV y XVI," *Historia y Cultura* 4 (1970), 77–96; "Las colonias de mitmas múltiples en Abancay, siglos XV y XVI," *Revista del Museo Nacional* 39 (1973), 225–299; and "Los Mitmas Cañar en el Reino de Yaro (Perú) Siglos XV y XVI," in R. Hartmann and Udo Oberem (eds.), *Amerikanistische Studien: Festschrift für Hermann Trimborn anlässlich seines 75. Geburtstages* (St. Agustin, 1978–1979).

On the *khipu*, the system of knotted strings used by the Inka to keep track of their wealth and to manage their subjects, see Marcia Ascher and Robert Ascher, *Code of the quipu: A study in media, mathematics and culture* (Ann Arbor, 1981); Leland L. Locke, *The ancient quipu or Peruvian knot record* (New York, 1923); and Carol Mackey et al. (eds.), *Quipu y Yupana – Colección de Escritos* (Lima, 1990). On the abacus, see Henry Wassen, "The ancient Peruvian abacus," *Comparative Ethnographical studies* 9 (Göteborg, 1931), 189–205; and María Rostworowski, "Mediciones y cómputos en el antiguo Perú," in Heather N. Lechtman and

Ana María Soldi (eds.), *La Tecnología en el Mundo Andino* (Mexico City, 1981), 379–405. Waldemar Espinosa Soriano discusses the Wanka *khipu camayoc*, or *khipu* keepers and readers, in the Mantaro Valley in "Los huancas aliados de la conquista: tres informaciones inéditas sobre la participación indígena en la conquista del Peru, 1558, 1560 y 1561," *Anales Científicos de la Universidad del Centro del Peru* I (1972), 9–407; also described by D'Altroy (1992) and Cieza de León (1959 [1553]), 174.

Quechua and its origins are explored by Alfredo Torero, "La familia linguistica Quechua," in Bernard Pottier (ed.), *America Latina en sus lenguas indígenas* (Caracas, 1983); see also Bruce Mannheim, *The language of the Inka since the European invasion* (Austin, 1991).

Julie Jones examines Inka aesthetics in *Art of empire: The Inca of Peru* (New York, 1964) as does Craig Morris, "Signs of division, symbols of unity: Art in the Inka empire," in J. A. Levenson (ed.), *Circa 1492: Art in the age of exploration* (Washington, New Haven, and London, 1991).

The best survey of Inka architecture is still Graziano Gasparini and Luise Margolies's *Inca architecture* (Patricia J. Lyon, trans.) (Bloomington, 1980). John Hyslop's *Inka settlement planning* (Austin, 1990) covers more territory than Gasparini and Margolies, especially settlements founded by the Inka on the fringes of their realm. John Hemming and Edward Ranney, *Monuments of the Incas* (Albuquerque, 1982) focuses on Inka settlements and monuments in Cusco and beyond. For a comparative look at Andean urbanism, with a chapter on the Inka, see Adriana von Hagen and Craig Morris, *Cities of the ancient Andes* (forthcoming).

Susan A. Niles explores Inka architecture in the environs of Cusco in "Inca architecture and the sacred landscape," in R. F. Townsend (ed.), *The ancient Americas: Art from sacred landscapes* (Chicago, 1992), 347–358, and in "Style and function in Inca agricultural works near Cuzco," *Nawpa Pacha* 20 (1982), 163–182, as well as "The provinces in the heartland: Stylistic variation and architectural innovation near Cuzco," in M. A. Malpass (ed.), *Provincial Inca: Archaeological and ethnohistorical assessment of the impact of the Inca state* (Iowa City, 1993), while Ann Kendall reviews Inka architecture in "Aspects of Inca architecture – Description, function and chronology," *British Archaeological Reports*, International Series 242 (Oxford, 1985) and, by the same author, "Architecture and planning at the Inca sites in the Cusichaca area," *Baessler Archiv* 22 (1974): 73–137. See also Elizabeth L. Moorehead, "Highland Inca architecture in adobe," *Nawpa Pacha* 16 (1978), 65–94; and Vincent R. Lee, "A study of function, form and method in Inca architecture,"

(Wilson, Wyo., 1988). Jean-Pierre Protzen investigates the construction history of Ollantaytambo in the Urubamba Valley, in *Inca architecture and construction at Ollantaytambo* (Oxford, 1993); see also J. Lee Hollowell, *"Precision cutting and fitting of stone in prehistoric Andean walls and reassessment of the Fortaleza, Ollantaytambo, Peru,"* National Geographic Research Report No. 3284 (Washington, 1987), and "Reassessment of the Fortaleza, Ollantaytambo, Peru," *Willay* 32/33 (1989), 7–10.

On Inka stone masonry and quarrying, see Jean-Pierre Protzen, "Inca stonemasonry," *Scientific American* 254/2 (1980), 94–105, which discusses how the Inka quarried stone and used hammerstones to shape their building blocks. "Inca quarrying and stonecutting," also by Protzen, *Nawpa Pacha* 21 (1983), 183–214, reviews the Inka quarries of Rumiqolqa near Cusco and Kachiqata near Ollantaytambo. Inka reverence for stone is described by Maarten van de Guchte in "Carving the world: Inca monumental sculpture and landscape," (Ph.D. dissertation, Urbana, Ill., 1990); and "El ciclo mitico andino de la piedra cansada," *Revista Andina* 2/2 (1984), 539–556.

Vincent R. Lee examines how the Inka may have roofed their buildings, especially the large halls, or *kallanka*, in *The lost half of Inca architecture* (Wilson, Wyo., 1988) and proposes an alternative theory on how the Inka fitted the megalithic stones of Saksay Waman, the temple-fortress perched high above Cusco, in *The building of Sacsayhuaman* (Wilson, Wyo., 1987).

On weaving, John V. Murra's "Cloth and its functions in the Inca state," *American Anthropologist* 64 (1962), 710–728, is still the best overview of the symbolism and uses of Inka weavings. On analyses of Inka weaving structure and design, see John H. Rowe, "Standardization in Inca tapestry tunics," in A. P. Rowe, E. P. Benson, and A. L. Schaffer (eds.), *The Junius B. Bird Textile Conference* (Washington, 1979), 239–264, and Anne P. Rowe, "Technical features of Inca tapestry tunics," *Textile Museum Journal* 17 (1978), 5–28.

Inka ceramic production in the Lake Titicaca region is discussed by John V. Murra in "Los olleros del Inka: hacia una historia y arqueología del Qollasuyu," in *Historia, Problema y Promesa: homenaje a Jorge Basadre* (Lima, 1978), 415–423; while pottery manufacture on the southern fringes of Tawantinsuyu is analyzed by Terence N. D'Altroy, Ana Maria Lorandi, and Veronica Williams, "Producción y Uso de Ceramica en la Economía Politica Inka," in Izumi Shimada (ed.), *Tecnología y Organización de la Producción de Ceramica Prehispánica en los Andes* (Lima,

1994), 395–442. Frances M. Hayashida provides a synthesis of Inka ceramics, touching on her work on the north coast of Peru in "Producción
Ceramica en el Imperio Inca: Una Visión Global y Nuevos Datos," 443–
476, in Izumi Shimada's text just cited. For ceramic production under
the Inka in the Mantaro Valley, see Terence N. D'Altroy and Ronald A.
Bishop, "The provincial organization of Inka ceramic production,"
American Antiquity 55 (1990), 120–138; and Cathy L. Costin, Timothy K.
Earle, Bruce Owen, and Glenn S. Russell, "Impact of Inka conquest on
local technology in the upper Mantaro Valley, Peru," in Sander E. van
der Leeuw and Robin Terrance (eds.), *What's new? A closer look at the
process of innovation* (London, 1989), 107–139.

    Heather N. Lechtman surveys Andean metalworking in "The Central
Andes: Metallurgy without iron," in T. A. Wertime and J. D. Muhly
(eds.), *The coming of the age of iron* (New Haven, 1980), 267–334, as well
as "Traditions and styles in Central Andean metalworking," in R. Maddin (ed.), *The beginnings of the use of metals and alloys* (Cambridge, 1988),
344–378. In "Technologies of power: The Andean case," in J. S. Henderson and P. J. Netherly (eds.), *Configurations of power: Holistic anthroplogy
in theory and practice* (Ithaca, 1993), 244–280, Lechtman contrasts the
production of Inka textiles and metals, noting that the value of precious
metals in Tawantinsuyu lay in the realm of the symbolic; see also, by the
same author, "Andean value systems and the development of prehistoric
metallurgy," *Technology and culture* 25 (1984), 1–36. On Inka mining
practices, see Jean Bertholet, "The extraction of precious metals at the
time of the Inka," in J. V. Murra, N. Wachtel, and J. Revel (eds.),
Anthropological history of Andean polities (Cambridge, 1986), 69–88. Samuel K. Lothrop describes the treasure amassed by the Spanish conquistadors at Cajamarca and what they missed, in *Inca treasure as depicted by
Spanish historians* (Los Angeles, 1938).

    John Hyslop followed sections of Inka roads throughout Tawantin-
suyu, reporting his findings in *The Inka road system* (New York, 1984).
Earlier studies on Inka roads include those by Alberto Regal, *Los Caminos
del Inca en el Antiguo Perú* (Lima, 1936), and by Victor W. von Hagen,
Highway of the sun (New York, 1955) and *The royal road of the Inca*
(London, 1976). Alberto Regal also reviewed Inka bridges in *Los Puentes
del Inca en el Antiguo Perú* (Lima, 1972), and Donald E. Thompson and
John V. Murra discuss bridges near Huánuco Pampa in "Inca bridges in
the Huánuco Pampa region," *American Antiquity* 31/5 (1966), 632–639.
The Inka incorporated earlier road systems into theirs, especially those

roads that formed part of the earlier, Wari, network; see, for example, Katharina J. Schreiber, "The association between roads and polities: Evidence for Wari roads in Peru," in Charles D. Trombold (ed.), *Ancient road networks and settlement hierarchies in the New World* (Cambridge, 1991), 243–252, and "Conquest and consolidation: A comparison of the Wari and Inka occupations of a highland Peruvian valley," *American Antiquity* 52 (1987), 266–284. On Inka roads on the empire's southern reaches, see Rubén Stehberg and Nazareno Carvajal, "Road system of the Incas in the southern part of their Tawantinsuyu empire," *National Geographic Research* 4/1 (1988), 74–87; and Rodolfo Raffino, "Inka road research and Almagro's route between Argentina and Chile," *Tawantinsuyu* 1 (1995), 36–45.

On agricultural terraces and farming, see R. A. Donkin, "Agricultural terracing in the aboriginal New World," *Viking Fund Publications in Anthropology* 56 (1979), and Ian S. Farrington, "Prehistoric intensive agriculture: Preliminary notes on river canalization in the sacred valley of the Incas," in J. P. Darch (ed.), *Drained field agriculture in Central and South America*, Proceedings of the 44th International Congress of Americanists, Manchester, BAR International Series 189 (Oxford, 1983). Domesticated plants of the Andes are reviewed by the National Research Council, *Lost crops of the Incas: Little known crops of the Andes with promise for worldwide cultivation* (Washington, D.C., 1989).

11

THE CRISES AND TRANSFORMATIONS OF INVADED SOCIETIES: THE CARIBBEAN (1492–1580)

NEIL L. WHITEHEAD

The native populations of the region that the Europeans came to call Caribbean were the first to negotiate the new realities to which this encounter gave rise, as well as to endure the ecological and demographic consequences of that arrival. The Caribbean was thus center stage in the crises and transformations of the indigenous societies of the Americas during the fateful years 1492–1580. The Caribbean is defined here as equivalent to the old Spanish administrative region of the Audiencia de Santo Domingo. This comprised the Spanish-occupied islands of the Caribbean Sea and also included the littoral region known as *Tierra Firme* (see Map 11.1).

THE CULTURAL FORMS AND SOCIAL INSTITUTIONS OF CONQUEST

In the islands of the Caribbean a series of brutal occupations, particularly in the Greater Antilles, meant that the native population had all but disappeared from view within a few decades of the initial encounter. In the Lesser Antilles, autonomous native society persisted much longer and developed in a more convoluted fashion because the inhabitants fiercely resisted the establishment of colonial enclaves. Similarly the variable impact of the Europeans on the native societies of the mainland, although it could be locally disastrous, also allowed for more extended interactions to develop, as in the Lesser Antilles. This meant that a wide range of novel political and economic responses emerged amongst the native population. Obviously many of the political and cultural strategies that developed showed continuity with the traditions of precolumbian times. But none of the societies of the Caribbean region that were extant in 1492 could be said to have survived unscathed. Whether fated for

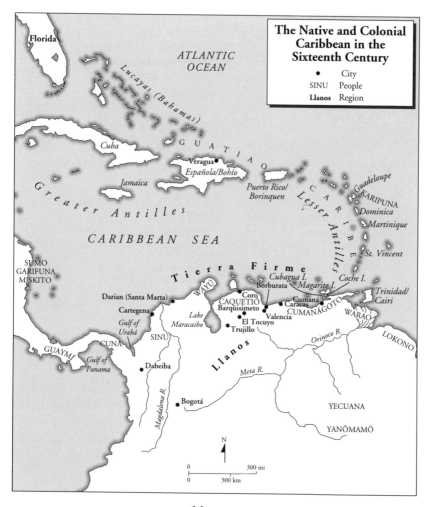

Map 11.1

extinction or florescence, autonomous historical development certainly continued among Amerindian societies, even if the issue of how to respond to the Europeans became central to the native political agenda.

Impact on indigenous regional trade and alliance systems was fundamental even where contacts with the Europeans were not physically direct, inducing change amongst groups well before they ever encountered the invaders. This pattern of effect outrunning cause is particularly evident in the spread of Old World diseases on an epidemic scale.

Epidemics proved lethal to the biologically pristine human populations of the New World and encouraged a rapid and widespread migration away from the epicenters of disease dispersion. However, it is not sufficient to explain all population loss from given locations by this means, and the consequences of the introduction of European disease differed greatly between the concentrated settlements on the littoral and some of the islands and the more scattered settlements of other continental regions; although on the islands the virulence of diseases could be enhanced by the geographical circumscription of the native population. It should again be emphasized that this by no means precluded migrations by sea, toward the southern continent.

The effects of the introduction of new flora and fauna also provoked crisis and transformation in native societies. Rats, cats, dogs, sheep, goats, and cattle flourished in the domestic sphere, which especially in the circumscribed ecotones of the islands sometimes led to the extinction of native species of small mammals and birds as well as dramatic changes in the island flora. For example, on the island of Margarita the introduction of livestock by the Spanish led to a dramatic change in the vegetation cover through the persistent browsing on the young flower-bearing shoots. The vegetation gap was then filled by cactus-like plants, drastically upsetting the precolonial ecology. Similar processes occurred on the neighboring islands of Cubagua and Coche.

On the mainland the introduction of European fauna took longer to show its effects, but the introduction of cattle to the Orinoco *llanos* (seasonally flooded savannahs) and Caribbean littoral upset the existing *llanos* ecology and was later reflected in the use of native labor as *vaqueros* (cattle hands). More immediate affects were apparent in the way that the neglect or abandonment of native agricultural sites allowed the spread of forest cover. As the Amerindians died, migrated, or were physically relocated by the Spanish, so their systems of agricultural production fell into disuse. At the same time, the encroachment of forest cover reduced the habitat for certain species critical to native diet, such as deer and peccaries, already negatively impacted by the increasing presence of European livestock. Moreover it must be appreciated that in a parasite-and predator-free context the reproductive rates of Old World species was explosive in these initial years, compounding the competitive advantage over indigenous flora and fauna and disrupting the native ecologies that were attuned to them.

In the investigation of this general historical context, the very first encounters with the natives of the Caribbean islands have always loomed largest in the subsequent historiography of the region. The manner of this encounter and the judgments that sprang from it are also inscribed in the ethnological schema of subsequent anthropologies, both colonial and modern. This has resulted in a situation where those initial observations that the Europeans made of the native population have become enshrined in the general literature concerning the Caribbean region and even in the standard anthropological accounts. Consequently our historical perceptions of the native Caribbean are heavily prejudiced by the distinction, inaugurated by Columbus, between the fearsome *caribes* of the Lesser Antilles and the tractable *aruaca* or *guatiao* (*taíno*) populations of the Greater Antilles.

In point of fact the term *taíno* as an ethnic ascription, although derived from the native terminology *ni'taíno* (meaning 'my lord'), was only coined in the nineteenth century by the antiquarian C. S. Rafinesque. Naturally this leant a spurious authority to the ethnographic dualism of the early Spanish accounts. A number of other terms, such as *aïtij, bohio, boriqua, caribe, canima, ciboney*, and *ciguayo*, as well as the honorific titles of *caciques* (meaning 'king' or 'chieftain') frequently occur in the early sources, and these may have carried overt ethnic implications; so there is no particular reason to privilege the term *taíno*. The rapid destruction of the polities of the Greater Antilles means that it is not possible to elucidate all the subtleties of the usages of these terms, but it is possible to examine the consequences of those associated with some of them, such as *caribe, guatiao*, or *aruaca*. Eventually the colonial political distinction between the *caribe* and the *aruaca* was generalized across the whole of the northern part of the continent. The derivation of the term "cannibal" from the native terms reported by the Spanish (such as *caribal, caniba*) has often been noted, but the ethnic plurality this concealed was forgotten due to the European elision of such concepts for political ends.

Recent scholarship on the native population of the Antilles has begun to correct this fallacy, but its centrality partly stems from the historical reason that this ethnological dualism was directly adopted into Spanish colonial law by a decree of Queen Isabella of Spain. As early as 1504 *caribes* had been juridically defined as any and all natives who opposed Spanish occupation in the Caribbean. The royal decree of Queen Isabella intones thus:

If such Cannibals continue to resist and do not wish to admit and receive my Captains and men who may be on such voyages by my orders, not to hear them in order to be taught our Sacred Catholic Faith, and to be in my service and obedience, they may be captured and are to be taken to these my Kingdoms and Domain and to other parts and places to be sold.[1]

As a result *caribes* were "discovered" on *Tierra Firme* as well as on the islands, and the colonial logic of directly enslaving those who could not be brought within the system of *repartimiento* – a forced distribution of native lands and peoples into *encomiendas* – was widely applied.

By contrast with the wide-ranging license given for the hunting down of *caribes*, the *repartimiento* and *encomienda* were applied against native peoples in situ. Rather than an institution for the organization of slave labor, the *repartimiento* and *encomienda* placed the native population in a "feudal" relation to its putative conquerors. Indeed, having wasted the population of the Greater Antilles within a few years of their arrival, the Spanish had to turn quickly to the coast of west Africa to ensure a new supply of labor to support the mining and sugar growing that formed the basis of the island economy of Cuba and Española. For example, on Española between 1492 and the *repartimiento* of 1514, the overall Amerindian population declined from perhaps 1 million or more to around 30,000. By the middle of the sixteenth century, only a handful of Amerindians could be found.

The *encomienda* was not universally used in the Caribbean region, however, being principally associated with locations where the Spanish themselves actively colonized with a civilian population. It was meant to ensure due rewards for those who had taken part in the discovery and conquest. Very broadly the institution operated by requiring that a section of the native population under their *cacique* ('headman') work for their designated *encomendero* ('owner of the *encomienda*') in return for "protection" and instruction in the Catholic faith. In the idiom of feudalism then, a tribute was due to the *encomendero* in the form of agricultural produce or money. Although such a system transposed the idiom of a feudal relationship between "lord" and "vassal" to the novel context of the Caribbean, the content of such relationships was vastly different. In the first place the whole system rested on the assumed political authority of the native leaders whose "villages" were assigned to the *encomendero*. That is, the system distributed not land and natural resources but people. It thus left the day-to-day control of the native population in the hands of native individuals, who often had their élite

[1] *Collleción de Documentos Inéditos*, Vol. 31 (Madrid, 1864–1884): 196.

status recognized in these arrangements. Native complicity was therefore fundamental to the success of any given *repartimiento* because the resources simply did not exist to maintain Spanish authority continuously by direct military means. As a result the viability of *encomiendas* as economically productive was highly variable but could be offset by the use of the *mita* ('work party'). The *mita* was a small labor force, garnered from any number of villages, that could be rented out by the *encomendero*. This proved a very attractive option because a calculable money profit could be made through Amerindian labor, which was not dependent on the vagaries of agricultural or tributary production. But, by the same token, the system was subject to abuse, and ferocious exploitation of the *indios encomendados* was often the result. This possibility was offset by both the rules of inheritance, which did not allow the bequeathal of an *encomienda*, and the formal structures of colonial bureaucracy. The *corregidores de indios* and the *curas doctrineros* were individuals who also had responsibilities toward the native population that cut across the untrammeled authority of the *encomendero*. The *corregidor* was responsible for overseeing the use of *mita*, for trade between the native population and the Spanish *vecinos* (settlers), and for protecting the natives from exploitation by the *encomendero*. This may have been an elegant theory, but in the close-knit world of the Spanish colonizers, it was quite possible that the *encomendero* could make arrangements with the *corregidor* to the detriment of the native population.

Set against the *encomendero* and the *corregidor* was the authority of the *curas doctrineros*, responsible for overseeing the induction of the indigenous population into the mysteries of the Catholic faith. But the effectiveness of such individuals was dependent on the broader missionary effort as a whole, which, while often antagonistic to lay authority over the native population, was nonetheless overtly connected to the Spanish project of empire. The Amerindian villages granted in *encomienda* did have their own elected officials – *alcaldes, regidores*, and *aguaciles* – who collectively formed the *cabildo*. But because these elections had to be approved by the *corregidor* and the *cura doctrinero*, there was generally little room for Amerindian autonomy through these officials, and so little potential threat from them.

In this context the type of native societies the Europeans encountered strongly conditioned their choice from amongst these possible political responses, which ranged from diplomacy through military conquest, *repartimiento*, and evangelization to outright slaving. The initial diplomacy exercised toward the *caciques* of Española in 1492 thus contrasts with the summary military invasions of Puerto Rico or Trinidad and the Venezuelan littoral in the 1530s, because these latter regions were the first hunting grounds for slavers seeking labor to replace the wasted population of Española and Cuba. In these situations ethnological expectations and definitions became critical political factors, as is shown in the great public debates in Madrid between the clerics Las Casas and Sepúlveda, concerning the dimensions of humanity and rationality in the New World population. But these ethnological definitions were also responsive to the unfolding needs of the emergent colonial system, and Isabella's original decree proved insufficient to these ends. So in the case of the *caribes*, it was finally necessary for the Spanish crown to dispatch a special legal mission, under the *licenciado* (judge) Rodrigo de Figueroa, to make an evaluation as to the *caribe* nature of the native populations of the Caribbean islands and Venezuelan littoral. Figueroa's depositions of 1520 indicate that this process was indeed highly political. Populations were assigned to the *caribe* category in a way that directly reflected the interests of the planters and slavers of Española. Figueroa's classification was therefore only related to a few specific ethnological markers, the principle one among these being the practice of anthropophagy, or cannibalism. The centrality of this issue for Spanish colonial policy is shown by the way it ranks alongside the refusal of Christian teaching as the reasons for populations that were previously *guatiao* being declared *caribe*. This is evident enough in Figueroa's own usage of the term *caribe*, in which the eating of human flesh was one of the key criteria he cites for so classifying a population:

All of the islands which are not populated by the Christians, except the islands of Trinidad, the Lucayas, Barbados, Gigantes, and Margarita they declare themselves to be and I declare them to be *caribes* and barbarous people, enemies of the Christians, repudiating their conversion, and such that they eat human flesh, and have not wanted and do not wish to receive Christians for their conversion, nor priests of our Catholic faith.[2]

It is notable that at this time there is still a latitude of reference contained in the term *caribe*, such that it is not yet equivalent to the accusation of eating human flesh. With the progress of colonial occupation, the identity of *caribe* with "cannibal" became complete.

[2] *Collecíon de Documentos Inéditos*, Vol. 1 (Madrid, 1864–1884): 380.

In such a highly charged political context, the native population was itself polarized around the question of how to meet and deal with the European invaders, some favoring appeasement, others confrontation. In fact no single political strategy proved invariably successful over time, and particular responses often mixed such stratagems right down to the village or longhouse level. In short the encounter with Europe was a fundamental disjuncture in native patterns of historical development – crises – and it is the nature of that disjuncture and the new historical trajectories that were born of that encounter – transformations – that are considered here. In order to explain these developments, I include a chronological narrative of external contacts with the Europeans, followed by an examination of the internal effects these contacts had on Amerindian modes of life and thought.

THE COURSE OF CONQUEST AND ITS HISTORIOGRAPHY

Columbus first sighted the islands of the Caribbean in October 1492. He immediately made a second voyage in 1493–1449, a third in 1498, and his last in 1502–1503. But within a year of his second voyage, the Spanish crown had sent a royal governor, Francisco de Bobadilla, to try to stabilize the nascent colony on Española. In the intervening years Columbus, his family, and their opponents had all but destroyed the indigenous population in a series of brutal military campaigns. Only some of these campaigns were waged against the indigenous opposition directly. But others carried out against dissenting Spanish factions took their toll on the native population.

The critical moment in these events was a large-scale military confrontation in 1495 between the Europeans and the natives of the valley of Maguá (or La Vega Real), the largest and most densely populated native province on the island. Here 200 heavily armed Spanish troops confronted the combined forces of the principal *caciques* of Española, numbering tens of thousands of warriors. However, the military technology and organization of the Europeans, which included armored cavalry, steel weapons, guns, and attack dogs, utterly devastated the native warriors, whose leaders were captured and tortured to death. The pro-Indian Spanish chronicler, Bartolomé de Las Casas, informs us:

The Christians fell upon them suddenly, at midnight, for the Indians do nothing by night, neither attack or even prepare for war – they did not even have time to get their weapons. All in all, they could do nothing against the Spaniards, who did them great damage. The Christians captured the King Guarionex and many others; they killed many of the captured leaders . . . burning them alive.

Las Casas is credited with an important role in the formation of the so-called black legend of the Spanish occupation. His writings condemning Spanish treatment of the native population were the starting point for an anticatholic, anti-Spanish historiography of the Americas.

Out of the destruction that he chronicled in the valley of Maguá, the native leader Guarionex emerged as the principal mediator of Spanish demands for food, labor, and, above all, gold. But by 1497, following famine and the first outbreaks of epidemic disease, this brief appeasement ended. Francisco de Roldán induced rival chiefs to support his opposition to the Columbus family, and Guarionex was also won over to the cause. However, Bartolomé Columbus preempted this conspiracy by a night attack on Guarionex's villages to seize the rebel *caciques*, most of whom were executed. Guarionex himself was allowed to live, but he functioned essentially as a puppet of the Columbus family until his death by shipwreck, en route to Spain in 1502.

By 1500 most of the complex native polities of Española had ceased to operate autonomously. This was also true of the rest of the Caribbean islands following Ponce de Léon's conquest of Puerto Rico in the following decade. The fate of the few native survivors of this first decade or so of European occupation has therefore become a key historiographical issue. It is unclear whether they were simply incorporated into the burgeoning colonial settlements of the region, with the need for their labor answered by the importation of black Africans as slaves, or, whether their disappearance from the historical record represents a physical liquidation through disease or slavery. It is entirely an open question as to what percentage of the aboriginal population had fled the Greater Antilles or had died there. But the overall consequence, as the colonial processes that initially unfolded on Española repeated themselves in Cuba, Jamaica, the Lucayas, and Puerto Rico, was the dispersion and virtual disappearance of the native element by the 1530s.

These issues are very prominent, for example, in the native history of Puerto Rico, proximate both physically and culturally to Española. Juan Ponce de León first led an expedition of reconnaissance there in 1508. Although native military resistance on the island itself was short-lived, it was fierce, being supported by *caribes* from the Lesser Antilles. Continuing attacks on the Spanish in Puerto Rico throughout the sixteenth century may then be directly related to a wider alliance among native populations dispersed and driven out by Ponce de León's initial occupation of the island.

Further key historiographical issues also come to the fore in this period on Puerto Rico. The Spanish ethnological dualism of *caribe* and non*caribe* naturally identified this region as the "frontier" between these antagonistic identities. Yet this dualistic framework of *caribe/guatiao* and *caribe/aruaca* has been uncritically transposed to modern archaeological and historical accounts. It is evident that many modern anthropological approaches to the archaeology, history, linguistics, and ethnography of the region have taken the colonial ethnological schema as their starting point, especially because native testimony as to their own cultural origins, as far back as the seventeenth century, was itself already partly expressive of this dualism. The combination of "authentic" native testimony, the epistemological priority of the "pristine" Spanish descriptions of the native Caribbean, and the unusually rich ethnography of the French missionaries that was carried out in the seventeenth century, offered what appeared to be an unarguable basis for an analysis of the origins and evolution of native society on the islands. But as already suggested, the relation of the *caribes* to the aboriginal societies of Cuba, Española, and Puerto Rico was certainly more complex than such dualistic models have allowed. This dualistic analysis of Spanish colonial policy has persisted into modern archaeological and ethnological usage, and it is still maintained by some that "Island Carib" origins are totally extraneous to the islands themselves.

Not surprisingly therefore, the first modern efforts to give this old colonial schematic a scientific footing – by attempting to correlate the data of archaeology with that of linguistics – produced wildly contradictory results as to the possible time-depth of an "Island Carib" presence in the Lesser Antilles, which remain unresolved. Further research on the peoples of the Caribbean continues to reveal data that, from the viewpoint of these standard schema, are anomalistic. A less dualistic, more polythetic conceptualization of native society and polity in the Caribbean therefore seems fundamental to any advance in the historiography and ethnology of the region.

On the Lucayas, the most northerly of the Caribbean islands, no resistance, and so no *caribes*, were encountered. The population there lacked some of the natural refuges available to the inhabitants of the larger islands and was simply "harvested" by slavers during the period

1509–1512. The subsequent "discovery" of Florida by Ponce de León might therefore be rightly characterized as little more than "an extension of slave hunting beyond the empty islands."

Few records have been left concerning the occupation of Jamaica, which was initiated by Diego Columbus and completed by Juan de Esquivel in 1509. According to Las Casas the natives were not evangelized and were put to hard labor in the production of foodstuffs, cloth, and hammocks. As a result, when the new governor, Francisco de Garay, took over from Esquivel in 1515, the royal factor, Pedro de Mazuelo, complained of the tiny number of natives left on the island, and their total disappearance within a couple of years was confidently predicted.

Although Columbus had surveyed the coast of Cuba during his first voyage, official interest did not manifest itself again until 1508, when the then royal governor of Española, Nicolás de Ovando, sent Sebastián de Ocampo to circumnavigate the island – rumors of gold quickly followed. In 1511 a license to occupy Cuba was given to Diego Velázquez de Cuéllar, a veteran of the brutal combats on Española. Cuéllar assembled 300 troops on the southwestern peninsula of Española and was then joined on Cuba by troops fresh from the conquest of Jamaica, as well as a further contingent from Española. This latter contingent included the future Indian apologist, Bartolomé de Las Casas, for whom this was to prove a critical experience in the formation of his negative views about the European treatment of the native population. With brutal efficiency the two parties of invaders had overrun the island completely by March of the following year.

These rapid conquests in the Greater Antilles contrast strongly with the situation that unfolded on the Lesser Antilles, which became a refuge not just for native populations but also for the *cimarrones* (escaped black slaves). In this way Puerto Rico certainly emerged as a southern frontier of Spanish settlement in the Caribbean islands, with the Lesser Antilles being occupied during the seventeenth century by Spain's imperial rivals, the French, Dutch, and English. In this way the necessities of colonial occupation were read into the native ethnology of the region. And in turn the "frontier" between the Greater and Lesser Antilles was represented as proceeding from native political structures, or at least from the intractable "caribness" of the populations on these latter islands; a very apt metaphor for Madrid's view of the incursions of the English *piratas* (pirates) and the Dutch *corsarios* (corsairs).

NATIVE RESPONSES TO INVASION

During the hiatus between the end of new Spanish colonization and the onset of the French, Dutch, and English permanent occupation, in the early seventeenth century, the native populations of the Lesser Antilles were able to use their geographical position on the main shipping lanes between Europe and America to their advantage. This enabled them to practice a profitable trade with the European vessels that stopped to replenish their drinking water and supplies after the Atlantic crossing. The following passage vividly illustrates the content of this relationship and also communicates something of the developing European attitudes to the *caribes* and how Spanish perceptions influenced even those of their rivals. At the same time, it is clear that the *caribes* had adapted themselves to many of the new realities produced by the Spanish presence. The passage is taken from John Hawkins' voyage of 1564–1565 along the Venezuelan coast:

The Captaine . . . saw many Caribes on shore, and some also in their Canoas, which made tokens unto him of friendship, and shewed him golde, meaning thereby that they would trafficke for wares. Whereupon he stayed to see the manners of them, and so for two or three trifles they gave such things as they had about them, and departed: but the Caribes were very importunate to have them come on shore, which if it had not bene for want of wares to trafficke with them, he would not have denyed them, because *the Indians which he saw before were very gentle people, and such as do no man hurt.* But as God would have it, hee wanted that thing, which if hee had had, would have bene his confusion: for these were no such kinde of people as wee tooke them to bee, but more devilish a thousand partes and are eaters and devourers of any man they can catch, *as it was afterwards declared unto us at Burboroata, by a Caravel comming out of Spaine with certaine souldiers.* And a Captaine generall . . . , who sayling along in his pinnesse, as our Captaine did to descry the coast, was by the Caribes called a shoore with sundry tokens made to him of friendshippe, and golde shewed as though they desired trafficke, with which the Spaniard being mooved, suspecting no deceite at all, went ashore amongst them: who was no sooner ashore, but with foure or five more was taken, the rest of his company being invaded by them, saved themselves by flight, but they that were taken, paied their ransome with their lives, and were presently eaten. And this is their practise to toll with their golde the ignorant to their snares: they are bloodsuckers both of Spaniards, Indians, and all that light in their laps, not sparing their owne countreymen if they can conveniently come by them. Their policie in fight with the Spaniards is marvelous: for they chuse for their refuge the mountaines and woodes where the Spaniards with their horses cannot follow them, and if they fortune to be met in the plaine where one horseman may overunne 100 of them, they have a devise of late practised by them to pitch stakes of wood in the ground, and also small iron spikes to mischiefe their horses, wherein they shew themselves politique warriers. They have more abundance of golde than all the Spaniards have, and live upon the mountaines where the Mines are in such number, that the Spaniards have much adoe to get any of them from them, and yet sometimes by assembling a great number of them, which happeneth once in two yeeres, they get a piece from them, which afterwards they keepe sure ynough.[3] (emphases added)

Relations with the Spanish were thus usually hostile, and the farms and ranches of the Venezuelan coast and Puerto Rico were frequently raided by the *caribes*. The Spanish in turn suspected that the *caribes* held not just African and European captives (including the son of the governor of Puerto Rico) but also a vast treasure of gold and silver taken from wrecked and plundered shipping. In this context the testimony of Luisa de Navarrete, who was married to a prominent rancher, Luis Hernández, on the island of Puerto Rico, is a brief window onto the quality of Spanish relations with the surviving indigenous population. A particularly important feature of her account is that it reveals the extent to which both blacks and whites had already been absorbed into the native society.

Taken in 1580 following her escape from captivity in Dominica, the political utility of her testimony on the *caribes* is evident enough. But she also mentioned that the Amerindians on Dominica had a store of gold and silver that they had collected from their raids, no doubt enhancing the prospects that the Spanish crown would consent to more extensive counterraids against the *caribe* population. At the same time that Luisa's testimony was recorded, the authorities also interrogated a young *caribe*, called simply "Pedro," who had deserted Dominica. The inclusion of this native testimony undoubtedly augmented the authority of the petition and the accuracy of its claims as to the barbarity of the *caribes*.

The following extracts from the petition of Bernáldez de Quiroz, procurator general of Puerto Rico, are not a verbatim transcript of Luisa de Navarrete's testimony or of that of the caribe Pedro, but his rendition of their verbal testimonies under oath:

She said that what is known is that . . . the said Indian *caribes* in past times robbed the town of Guadianilla and Humacao and Maunabo and other areas.

---

[3] Hulme and Whitehead, *Wild Majesty* (Oxford, 1992), 49–50.

And when they robbed Humacao they took away this witness and left her in Dominica as the captive of an Indian *casique* of the aforementioned Dominica, where it was four or five years that they held her captive. And this witness has seen that in the time that this witness was in this island [Puerto Rico] and in the time that she was in Dominica, without giving offence to the *caribes* nor causing them any harm, they arm themselves every year and cross to this island of San Juan [Puerto Rico] and rob and destroy whatever they can. And this witness has seen that the three times they have come to this island while this witness was captive, they have carried away a great quantity of negroes and left some in Dominica and distributed the rest amongst the Indians of these islands, which they take to their lands in order to serve them. And this witness saw that one of these times that they carried off a quantity of negroes that they had stolen, they took from Luysa a white boy, son of one Domingo Pinero. And another time that their armada came this witness saw that they took from this island two other negroes that this witness knew, and the aforementioned Indians said that they had carried off another to another island. And the said Indians always used to go boasting and making great fiestas saying that they had burnt and destroyed many farms in this island and killed many people. And this witness saw that in the Dominica passage a ship appeared . . . and they attacked and overcame and burnt and robbed it . . . , carried off and killed three or four of the principal Spaniards . . . , and captured six principal women and ten or twelve men, among whom this witness saw one called Doña María and another Doña Juana, who was her sister . . . They held all these people captive, and many more from before this witness was captured . . . and treat them very roughly, making them work and go about naked by day and night. And they paint them like themselves, making them sleep on the ground, not allowing them to eat meat except lizards and rats and snakes and some fish. And they do not let them roast this nor cook this [meat], but they are made to eat it raw. And they tell them to eat human flesh. And when they want to make wine they make the Christians chew cassava at night to make it, with which wine they get drunk, take the female captives and force them, knowing them carnally, making them do as they wish. And the wives of the said Indians, seeing this, shoot arrows at the other captive women in parts where they do not kill them. And when the said Indians want to eat others that they have captured they make their *areytos* [heroic ballads] and call to and speak with the Devil. And there in their *areytos* they agree to kill one, and so they kill him and eat him. And when it is agreed that they kill some Christian of another nation, they kill him and throw him in the sea, and when some Indian who holds captives dies, they kill some of his captives and say that they kill them in order that they should go on serving him. If it were not for this there would be many more captives than there are. And among the captives that they have this witness saw that there is Don Garcia Troche, son of Juan Ponze de León, resident of this city, Governor and Captain General, who was in the island of Trinidad. When this witness was taken prisoner, he was already captive in the said island of Dominica for the said Indians had captured him when going to the conquest of Trinidad. And later the said Indians spread it around that they had killed him. And so the said *caribes* carried him away because they took him from the Indians of the said island of Trinidad in a war that they and those of the other island had between them. And this witness knows that the said Indians have much gold and worked and unworked silver, and Reales and silver collars and plates and much merchandise that they have taken from the ships, . . . this witness knows and saw in the said island of Dominica that there are two women and a man who were already as much *caribes* as the rest of them, and the women say that they no longer remember God, and the man neither more nor less so, and he eats human flesh and they do just as the Indians do, neither more nor less. And another man comes with these said Indians that has now become as *caribe* as them and likewise eats human flesh. And this witness and other Christians speaking with this man asked him why he did not remember the mother of God, since he was a Christian, and the said man replied that since the mother of God had not remembered to take him from here in forty years, neither did he wish to remember her. And this witness saw the same among the other negroes who eat human flesh and do as the Indians do, and what she has spoken is the truth. . . . This passed before me, Andrés Goncales public notary.[4]

The issue of the *caribes* therefore remained a preoccupation of the Puerto Rican colonists throughout the sixteenth century, and evidence continued to be collected as to their lawlessness and cannibalism in the hope of persuading the crown to permit the slaving of the Lesser Antilles. But Spanish imperial ambition had turned its attention to the marvelous possessions of the Inkan and Aztec empires, as well as the rich plunder that was to be had all along the Central American isthmus. The struggle with the *caribes* of the Lesser Antilles little troubled Spain, until the *caribes* made alliances with the French *flibustiers* (freebooters) and the English *pirates* who, by the end of the sixteenth century, were already actively seeking sites for colonial establishment in the Americas. Following their expulsion from Brazil, the French redoubled their efforts to gain a settlement in the Caribbean (see Chap. 20), which project began in earnest by the 1630s, principally on Martinique and Guadeloupe. In a similar manner the English, partly stimulated by their expulsion from Surinam in the 1650s, joined the scramble for islands in the Lesser Antilles, centering themselves on Barbados and St. Lucia. In most of these locations, the fate of the native population was the same, and despite initially peaceful contacts the *caribes* were driven out or marginalized. On St. Vincent and Dominica, however, the occupation of the islands was fiercely contested on all sides, and the native population was alternately courted by French and English rivals. This meant that native

---

[4] Hulme and Whitehead, *Wild Majesty* (Oxford, 1992), 39–43.

political autonomy persisted into the eighteenth century, because they had become valuable allies in the intercolonial rivalry that beset these tiny islands. In any event, following a full-scale war in the 1790s, the English carried out a mass deportation of a large part of the indigenous population of St. Vincent, which had thoroughly mixed with *cimarrones* to form the "Black Caribs," leaving only a remnant population of "Red Caribs."

The Dominican *caribes* therefore well exemplify this history of transformation, rather than extinction, that resulted from a close adaptation and opposition to the Europeans and their successors in the Caribbean. As a result many of the native cultural and social features that were a product of European intrusion into the Caribbean islands and *Tierra Firme* are to be seen in microcosm in the history of the native population of Dominica.

EASTERN *TIERRA FIRME* – THE LURE OF THE PEARL, THE
PROMISE OF GOLD

Physically proximate to the Antilles and culturally integrated with them were those regions that the Europeans referred to as the Costa das Perlas, Paria, and Trinidad. All these locations had been seen by Columbus in 1498, but only the Pearl Coast was exploited initially, following the information gathered during the armed reconnaissances of Alonso de Hojeda and Cristobal Guerra. With the discovery of the vast pearl fisheries off the island of Cubagua in 1512, European interests centered on the Venezuelan coast rather than Trinidad, and it was not until 1531 that any sustained attempt was made to occupy and explore Trinidad and the Orinoco delta to the south. Eventually both these locations were simultaneously occupied by Antonio de Berrio at the end of the sixteenth century.

Meanwhile the Spanish town of Nueva Cádiz became the center of a booming pearl economy, and the local population was declared non-*caribe*, probably to preserve some sort of labor force in situ, just as was the case when gold was discovered on Trinidad. Moreover, as elsewhere, the Spanish colony needed Amerindians to supply foodstuffs and water. The production of the pearlbeds was prodigious for some 20 years. But by 1534 overexploitation had exhausted the supply, and by 1537 the Cubaguan pearlbeds were all but finished.

In the intervening period the status of the local native populations, as *caribe* or *guatiao*, was closely debated. In this context the classificatory exercise of Figueroa (discussed earlier) is revealed as deeply political. For example, Trinidad was declared *caribe* in 1511, but that decision was reversed, following the intervention of Las Casas, in 1518. This decision was itself reversed again in 1530, in order to facilitate the occupation of Trinidad by Antonio Sedeño. In a similar way the initially favorable classification of the native populations in the vicinity of the Cubaguan pearl fisheries as *guatiao* was reversed in 1519 once commercial extraction of the pearls had got underway. In the period between these decisions, it was the hapless Lucayans who supplied the majority of Amerindian slaves to act as divers for the pearl fisheries.

   This hiatus in the onset of Spanish exploitation of the local populations of the Venezuelan littoral allowed the foundation of the first Franciscan monastery in the New World at Cumaná, as well as a Dominican mission at Chirichirivichi. But these pacific contacts were not to last, and in 1519 the activity of the slavers recommenced, the coastal population having been declared *caribe*. The native response to these renewed encroachments was decisive. The religious foundations were destroyed and the Spanish settlements besieged. But the Spanish reoccupied the region in 1522, waging a deadly war – *a fuego y sangre* ('by fire and blood'). Thereafter followed a period of virtual anarchy during which various *doradistas* (searchers for El Dorado) vied for access to the fabled wealth south of the Orinoco from their bases in the Cumaná and Trinidad. This episode was duly described in the rhetoric of Las Casas:

> From the shore of Paria, to the Bay of Venezuela . . . the Spaniards committed most wonderful depopulations; for they gave themselves wholly to their wanton robberies, enslaving also infinite numbers of men . . . against all pledges which they had given them for their security.

   The pearl fisheries of Cubagua themselves had been exploited to the point of total exhaustion by 1540, and the once flourishing town of Nueva Cadiz was then virtually abandoned. Even as new pearlbeds were opened up off the island of Margarita, the lure of those discovered in the Gulf of Panama proved far stronger. Along the Venezuelan coast the rule of the missions was gradually reestablished, but only with the support of a series of military campaigns amongst the Cumanágoto and other groups. It was not until the 1630s that the campaigns of Juan de Orpín definitively established Spanish dominance in this region.

   The native networks of gold trading that the *doradistas* so eagerly hoped to intersect ultimately connected both the Caribbean islands and the western coasts of *Tierra Firme* to the heartland of the Colombian sierras. It was here that the dreams of encountering an El Dorado were indeed realized, and the occupation of the coastal region in order to gain access to those goldworking cultures was correspondingly brutal. An understanding of the native ritual and symbolic context for the exchange of goldwork, with Europeans as much as among the native population itself, must begin with a consideration of the native use of gold on the Caribbean islands. Recently various scholars have examined the early sources and independently produced similar schema of native belief surrounding the magical metal *guanin*. The words "golden," "gold," and "goldwork" are used here, unless otherwise indicated, in a very general sense. This is because the precise amount of gold in native objects varied somewhat, the absolute purity in terms of gold content not being a primary consideration for the native metalsmith. However, a composition of 2 to 3 parts gold to 1 part copper, with silver traces varying up to 25 percent of the whole, could be considered typical. The Mazaruni pectoral was assayed at 12 carats, precisely agreeing with the "triall of an Image of copper" made by Walter Raleigh in Guayana in 1595. The melting point is much lower and the malleability much greater for such alloys, and the modern jewelery business has now accepted such native wisdom, predominantly using 18-carat alloys, as a result of which "the whole world adorns itself with *guanin*."

Based on Father Ramón Pané's sixteenth-century account of native conceptions on Española, they point out that Guahayona, the first "Man," took all the women from Española to Matinino (Martinique) and then traveled on to the island of Guanin, origin of metal alloys. In this way a close connection is established between the ancestors, marriageable women, and golden metals. *Caona* is the native term for pure gold, and *guanin* is the term for gold/copper alloys. This is also a reason for the link between the honorific titles of the élite and these terms for golden metals. Among the chieftains of Española we can recognize Caona-bo, 'He who is like gold', as well as his wife Ana-caona, and also the honorific of the *cacique* Bohechio, Turei-ga Hobin, 'King as dazzling and heavenly as *guanin*'. On Puerto Rico among the names of the native provinces (which were often treated as equivalent to the personal names of *caciques* by the Europeans) we find Guaynia, Guaynabo, Guayama, and Guayaney, all containing the radical for *guanin* and the ancestor Guahayona. On Trinidad the title of the paramount chief of the Yao,

Anacajoury, reflects both the name of the ancestor who accompanied Guayahona to the "isle of *guanin,*" Anacacuya, and the meaning of that name as 'brilliance that guides'. Moreover, because the natives of Española could not find or produce *guanin* (there being no copper ore deposits), and given that *guanin* is much harder yet more malleable than pure gold, as well as producing a distinct smell when heated or rubbed, its "magic" was very evident in these physical properties. In the islands the *caracoli,* a croissant-shaped chest plate, was the preferred form of *guanin.* The *caracoli* was representative of the rainbow, a shamanic bridge for communication with the gods. Such pieces were also associated with masculine authority, especially for the *caribes,* for whom such objects were intimately linked to patterns of warfare with their fellow Arawakans of the Guayana coast, the Lokono.

It is therefore important to note that in praxis, as well as in myth, the Europeans were directed by the *caciques* of Cuba and Hispaniola toward the Lesser Antilles (isla de Carib, Matinino) and Guayana (isla de Guanin) as the source of gold. They also indicated that in this direction lived the *canibales.* Thus the first ancestor, Guayahona, when he left Española for Matinino, persuaded the women to accompany him, abandoning their husbands but bringing with them their children and a cargo of the drug *digo.* At Matinino they saw beautiful seashells (*cobo*), which, following the example of Guayahona's brother-in-law, they descended into the sea to admire. Here they were left by Guayahona who then returned with the first *guanin* and *cibas* ('magic stones', Cariban *takua*). In the version of this mythic history recorded by Pedro Martir, the fate of the children is slightly different to that in the account of Pané, who says they were simply abandoned in a ditch on Martinique; Martir says they were turned into frogs, precisely the shape into which *takua* were customarily carved.

Thus there are grounds for understanding Guayahona to be not only the ancestor of the *guatiao* but the first *caribe* as well. This emphasizes how a close interpretation of native conceptions is vital to avoiding the errors of a transposed colonial ethnology. Indeed, this whole myth cycle may be interpreted to represent the ideological underpinning of an élite exchange in which drugs, seashells (shell necklaces), and persons (women and children) were exchanged for gold and the magic *takua* stones carved in the form of frogs. In this interpretation the physical location Matinino, "the island of women," represents the site of these exchanges, just as seems to have been the case on the continent. Thus a further connection of Matinino with the Amazon myth cycle is evident in the manner of origin of the *ciba* (i.e., from female water spirits), just as the continental *takua* were said to be made by the "water-mama," who to this day still supplies the stones for smoothing pottery among the Pomeroon Kariña (Carib).

In this symbolic and mythic context, it is not difficult to see why the Amerindians of Martinique, Dominica, and Guadeloupe were constructed as consumers of persons, or cannibals in the chiefly ideologies of the Greater Antilles. Nor is it necessary to follow Spanish colonial presumptions in seeing this as primarily a gastronomic consumption rather than an economic one. For example, in the first Spanish description of Guadeloupe by Dr. Chanca, it is clear that cottonwork was a major item of production, the cloaks being said to rival those of Spain. We are also informed about the "captive women" that were held there, and it seems plausible to suggest that the use of such women for the *caribes* was primarily as producers of such items, not as victims for a cannibal feast. They would have been of far greater significance to the political ambitions of men in this former capacity than in the latter (see also the testimony of Luisa de Navarrete, quoted previously). Cannibalism, insofar as it can be established in native custom, was intimately linked to the conduct of warfare in a way that would have made women an entirely inappropriate object of such a practice. Certainly it would appear that some men who were captured by the *caribes* as a result of armed conflict may well have had their bodies subjected to ritual forms of dismemberment and dispersion. But this sphere of exchange runs parallel with that of the *guanin* – warfare here being expressive of the interdependence of the different groups, not their isolation. Suggested earlier was the case for the conflict of the mainland Lokono and island Karipuna in the seventeenth century, which also revolved around the capture of persons and the possession of *caracoli*. It should also be noted that Caonabó, one of the principal *caciques* of Bohio (Española), was himself a *caribe* according to Hernando Colón. This underlines the point that this designation was a political as much as cultural or ethnic designation for native and European alike.

This Caribbean trade nexus was in turn linked to the Orinoco and Meta rivers, at whose headwaters the Muisca offered gold for *mojas* (a term possibly related to Arawakan *macu*, 'slave', 'barbarian'). It is notable that Caonabó was, like the *cacique* of the Dabeiba mines in Colombia, a *caribe* and that, like the Muisca and *caribes* of the islands, all were

controllers of gold sources or finished goldwork and known as anthro-
pophages. In this context we can say that the exchange of persons for
gold was a key element in chiefly ideologies, which underlay not just the
Caribbean exchange between *guatiao* and *caribe* but also stretched across
the whole of northern South America – just as the conquistadors intuited
from the intelligence they gathered on their armed reconnaissances into
the interior.

WESTERN *TIERRA FIRME* – THE TEUTONIC *CONQUISTADORES* AND THE GREAT SOUTH SEA

As Spanish interests moved west from the pearl fisheries, the first substantial occupation of the Gulf of Venezuela region was carried out by
Germans under license from the Spanish crown, an event unique in the
annals of Spanish colonialism. Ambrosio Alfinger, Jorge Spira, Philip von
Hutten, and Nicolas Federmann were the principal *conquistadores* who
initiated this enterprise, under the auspices of the House of Welser –
merchant-bankers who were creditors of the Spanish king, Charles V.
Alfinger, who was chosen to be the first governor, arrived at Coro in
1529, where the existing Spanish governor, Juan de Ampués, deferred to
the authority of the newcomers.

Initial reconnaissance by Alfinger was to the west and the regions
around Lake Maracaibo. In subsequent years the valley of the Río Magdalena was penetrated, and the true wealth of the native cultures was
uncovered; Alfinger's final expedition returned to Coro at the end of
1533. Alfinger was then succeeded by Jorge Spira (known in German
sources as George Hohemut), who pushed into the region to the south,
there garnering reports of a fabulous land called Meta, but losing many
men before his final return to Coro. During his absence Nicolas Federmann, Spira's lieutenant, lead an unauthorized *entrada* (armed reconnaissance) also to the south. He crossed some of the major rivers that
ultimately drained into the Orinoco Basin and at length managed to
ascend the cordillera and enter the plains of Bogotá. However, he found
that he had been beaten to this objective by an expedition approaching
from the Magdalena Valley, led by Jiménez de Quesada.

Last in this line of German adventurers came Philip von Hutten. He
spent 4 fruitless years in journeying from Coro across the great *llanos* of
Colombia and Venezuela in search of the fabled lands of Meta and El
Dorado, only to be hacked to death with a blunt machete on his return

journey to Coro at the behest of his rival, Juan de Carvajal, founder of the Venezuelan city of El Tocuyo.

This long succession of adventurers left a violent mark on the native societies they encountered. When the coastal Venezuelan territories became the direct responsibility of the Spanish crown once again, the new administration of Juan Pérez de Tolosa found a population chastened and resentful of the treatment they had received from the *doradistas*.

Nonetheless Spanish occupation crept out inexorably from these early coastal enclaves, southward into the *llanos* of Orinoco and westward along the Venezuelan littoral toward the Gulf of Urabá and the province of Darién. In the next few decades, the cities of Borburata, Barquisimiento, Valencia, Trujillo, and, in 1567, Caracas itself were founded. From these slender beginnings the province of Venezuela and the captaincy of Caracas rapidly grew in economic significance. By 1600 up to forty-five ranches were established in the *llanos*, and by the mid–seventeenth century some 75 percent of exports to Spain were of cattle hides, much of this having been achieved through the forced labor of the native population.

Further to the west, the information that had been gathered during the voyages of Guerra and Hojeda, which had led to the discovery of the Cubaguan pearl fisheries, revealed also the existence of the Caquetío and Wayú (Goajiro), who occupied the region around the Gulf of Venezuela. Over time the Wayú in particular were to develop an active accommodation with the Europeans, based on their skill as cattlemen, and as traders with the imperial rivals of Spain, especially the Dutch and English. This legacy, similar to that of the *caribes* of the islands, preserved their autonomy from the Venezuelan state and given them a reputation for hostility to outsiders that persists right up to the present day.

Exploration of the Gulf of Venezuela region also indirectly led to the discovery of the Gulf of Urabá and the province of Darién by Juan de la Cosa and Rodrigo de Bastidas in 1500–1501. The return to this region was almost immediate, and the native town of Urabá was captured and looted in 1504 by Juan de la Cosa. There were many indications here of the rich goldworking cultures of Colombia, particularly the Sinu. However, the slaving activities of the Guerra brothers to the east, around Cartagena, and the subsequent foray by Alonso de Hojeda into this region in 1505, as well as Cosa's own attempts to take slaves during his return from Urabá, produced yet again a legacy of hostility to further European intrusions.

The Spanish crown, in order to regulate the occupation of this region, issued two concessions. One was to cover the area to the west of Urabá, the other to the east. The former concession was named Veragua, following the usage of Columbus who had first sighted the region during his fourth voyage, and was given to Diego de Nicuesa. The latter region was known as Urabá, following native usage, and was given to Hojeda, with Cosa as second in command.

Just as was the case in the occupation and exploitation of the Pearl Coast, the natives of the coast west of Cartagena were declared to be *caribes*. This opened the way for a summary military conquest and a seizure of the population as slaves. However, the martial abilities of the natives were considerable, and Juan de la Cosa himself was killed, along with another seventy of the Hojeda expedition, on attempting their landing at Cartagena. The survivors were saved by the arrival of Nicuesa's fleet, en route to Veragua. The Spanish then fortified a position at Urabá, from where a series of plundering raids were conducted into the interior. But Hojeda himself, still suffering from his wounds received at Cartagena, returned to Española, leaving the nascent colony in the charge of Francisco Pizarro, later conqueror of Peru. The Spanish held on in Urabá for a few more months but then abandoned the site in favor of the native town of Darién in the land of the Cuna to the west. Initially the Cuna proved more tractable to their purposes.

Nicuesa, meanwhile, had landed in the next native province beyond Darién, called Careta. Here the expedition split into two groups, but as Nicuesa pushed ahead he became lost, while the slower party tried to fortify a position on the Río Belén, following the earlier example of Columbus. But they were eventually forced to evacuate, having rescued the remnant of Nicuesa's group. A second expedition the following year achieved little more than to confirm the undesirability of European occupation in the eyes of the native population of the region – the Cuna, Guaymí, and Sumo.

These initial acts of possession had done little to establish the royal concessions of Urabá or Veragua. It was the pragmatism of Vasco Nuñez de Balboa, in illegally taking command of the survivors of the Hojeda and Nicuesa expeditions, that allowed the Spanish to forge ahead with the project of colonization from their base of Santa María, founded on top of the native town of Darién in 1511. Balboa proved an altogether more able strategist in regard to the native population, and he was able to use local rivalries to his advantage. The fruits of this policy were a more stable food supply and a firmer political basis for the control and exploitation of the hinterland, particularly the gold-rich chiefdom of Dabeiba. But perhaps his greatest prize was the sighting of the "South Sea" (Pacific Ocean) on September 27th, 1513.

In response to this momentous discovery, as well as the rising fortunes of the Spanish in Veragua and Urabá, the two concessions were united and renamed "Castilla del Oro" with royal authority being vested in Pedrarias Dávila. This was to prove a total disaster. Contemporary records are unanimous in their description of the brutality of Dávila's governorship toward the Amerindians, even in the case of Las Casas and Oviedo y Valdes, otherwise at odds in the matter of the European treatment of the native population. At the beginning of the sixteenth century, the native population of the Panamanian isthmus region was estimated to have been over 2 million. By 1607 the Audiencia of Panama was reporting a desolate and impoverished scene, and the dominant cultural group, the Cuna (then known as the Cueva), were reduced to a fraction of their original population. Many also had retreated away from their previous coastal and downriver locations. This utter devastation of the native population was also dramatically reflected in the changed ecology of the coasts and immediate hinterland, which was overgrown with thick forest by the mid–sixteenth century, where once the savannahs and fields of native agriculture had dominated. Like the remnant *caribes* of Dominica and St. Vincent, the Cuna eventually adapted to the presence of large numbers of fugitive black slaves and provided alliance for the French and Scotch colonies that existed in Darién from 1690 to 1757. In contrast the other major grouping of this isthmian region, the Guaymí, though also initially withdrawing from the anarchy of the coastal region, were brought into missions in considerable numbers during the latter part of the sixteenth and early part of the seventeenth century.

In considering the fate of the native populations in the northernmost areas of the Veragua region, it is important to note that the impact of European colonialism on native society came full circle here, in that the postcontact culture of the Miskito, Sumo, and Paya was significantly influenced by that of the "Black Caribs" who were transported there by the British in the 1790s. So too the specialized military organization of the Miskito seems to have been a legacy of their close alliance with the English planters and woodcutters who settled the Nicaraguan and Honduran coastline in the early seventeenth century, as was the redevelop-

ment of hierarchial social organization from the wreckage of the Spanish
entradas.

THE CONSEQUENCES OF INVASION FOR NATIVE PEOPLES

Having outlined the initial manner of the Amerindian encounter with
the Europeans, it now remains to explore the effects of these often violent
occupations on Amerindian lifeways. The discussion is organized so as to
consider change in three related spheres; the sociopolitical, the economic,
and the cosmological. Each aspect is examined in terms of both the crises
in native forms and their transformations. However, it would be well to
emphasize that this procedure is adopted only as an expository device,
because the crises provoked by European invasions obviously upset existing patterns of society and culture in differential ways. Crudely put,
while specific sociopolitical arrangements might quickly dissolve as a
result of direct conquest and the dispersion of a population, cultural
repertoire remained potentially recoverable and an important idiom for
the organization of resistance to the Europeans. Such a cultural repertoire
was inevitably shared amongst a far wider range of persons than those
organized into specific social or political arrangements and so was a
continuing locus of resistance, even where political and economic autonomy had been eradicated through slavery, the *encomienda*, or epidemic
disease. The vitality of a cultural repertoire was clearly dependent on the
existence of certain forms of social relations, but then cultural transformations are direct evidence of new and emergent social formations.

Despite the complexity and variability of the processes of European
occupation, as well as the wide diversity of native cultures and polities
that the Europeans encountered, recent theoretical work in anthropology
suggests that the categories that need to be employed to explain and
analyze these processes are relatively few. This is done by focusing on the
zone of mutual interaction that emerges as colonial state formations
encounter a range of indigenous organization, rather than counterposing
discrete native and non-native "worlds." In this way it is possible to
classify the myriad of differing forms of encounter so that it brings out
some of the constant features of the colonial process as they affected
native groups in crisis and transformation.

The zone of mutual interaction can be characterized as a "tribal zone,"
a shifting region that stretches out from the points of European entry
into the, as yet, uncontacted hinterlands. It should be emphasized again

that the activity of the Europeans was often manifest well within this area before any direct encounters occurred. In the Caribbean, as elsewhere, such effects are most obviously made evident through the spread of African and European diseases, such as smallpox and measles, to which the native population had no resistance. However, as has already been indicated, the question as to the exact scale and severity of depopulation, both on the island and mainland, remained the subject of dispute. Certainly the scale of population loss is rightly considered to have been large given the first reports on the size of native populations, and the role of epidemic disease in that population "loss" was significant. But as most secondary commentators indicate, the issue of precise numbers is probably intractable. The point is perhaps less the absolute starting figure for the Amerindian population before contact than the unchallengeable figures of the size of the remnant population and the virulence with which disease struck in known contexts. There is considerable variation in the early documentation, even within a single author's own writings, as to "contact" populations. But they all agree that the end result was a dramatic diminution in the presence of native peoples in the vicinity of Spanish settlement. One contemporary chronicler observed that at the time when Columbus discovered the islands he found a million or more inhabitants. By 1548 this number had declined to barely 500 persons.

So although there is still extensive debate on the timing and severity of epidemics, there can be little doubt that this was a significant factor in inducing new kinds of social and political organization among the native population. Dramatic population losses, through either war or disease, provided the demographic context for the emergence of new leaders and new visions of how Amerindian people might respond to the crisis of European invasion. For example, the emergence of the Kariña (mainland *caribes*) as a significant political force in the eastern Caribbean region, as well as reports of the appearance of prophetic leaders among them, can be related to the physical extinction of a number of élite families that had previously ruled the lower Orinoco.

In a wider sense the implantation of alien flora and fauna upset existing economic relationships, necessitating changes in native ecological practices. But the consequences were not always negative, and dogs, pigs, chickens, plantains, and sugar cane all were adopted into native ecologies. At the same time, those native ecologies were reorientated to trade with the Europeans. The supply of foodstuffs, as well as fresh water and wood for shipbuilding, was a constant feature of early relationships between

Amerindians and Europeans. For example, the supply of *aru* (manioc flour) and fresh water to the pearl-fishing colonies off the Venezuelan coast in the early sixteenth century engendered extended alliances between the Spanish and certain native groups – principally *aruacas* (Lokono) from the Guayana coast. The alliances formed during these exchanges then heavily influenced the pattern of European and Amerindian settlement for decades to come. In like fashion, the *caribes* of the Lesser Antilles were repeatedly visited by ships in the last stages of the Atlantic crossing seeking to replenish their food, water, and wood supplies, as this account taken from *The Primrose Journal* of Drake's second voyage to the Caribbean illustrates (note that the *caribes* already have plantains and chickens to trade):

The 21 of December wee fell with an Iland called [Dominica]. The people ar all as redd as Scarlet, Wee ankered there to refresshe our men. Wee fownde verie goodlie rivers there, & there wee tooke in water for our neede. Wee woulde have tarried there longer for to have refresshed our men but wee coulde finde no convenient place to keepe them in from the people of the countrie, for they ar great devowrers & eaters of men. And the Ile is all woodes. Wee withe our boate met with 8 of these men at sea who as soone as they espied us waved us unto them & put forthe a flagg of truce beinge a cake of Cassado bread, Wee borded them presentlie, there boate was a Cannow that is made like a hogges trowghe, all of on [e] tree. These people go naked withowte anie manner of clothe abowte them. There manner is when they kill anie of there enemies they knocke owte the teethe & were them abowte there neckes like a chaine & eate flesshe for meate.

When wee had borded them as before they gave us a kinde of Bottle full of water & Cassado bread that is made of a tree & wee gave them Bisket & a can of Beare, which they did presentlie bothe eate & drinke & then wee Departed from them & went rowinge close aborde the shore where the people of the countrie came runninge to the water side wounderinge greatlie at us. Then we came to a goodlie river of fresshe water & thither came 6 men of the countrie unto us & emongst them ther was on [e] that commaunded the reste. On [e] broughte a cocke & a henne a nother browght Potatos, an other, Plantaine fruite. They did swime over the River to us & came to our boate.[5]

In a similar fashion the introduction of metal tools by the Europeans was an opportunity for Amerindian leaders to reformulate political networks. The possession and distribution of such desirable items was the source of significant political authority. The European colonizers also used the exchange of metal tools in a political fashion, themselves trading

[5] Hulme and Whitehead, *Wild Majesty* (Oxford, 1992), 53–54.

with those Amerindian leaders who were tractable to their designs, excluding others who were more troublesome.

Of particular significance to European influences on Amerindian ecologies was the way the supply of metal tools could allow a more extensive practice of swidden agriculture. Both the supply of foodstuffs to the Europeans and their slaves, as well as the ability to become autonomous from the more sedentary and established chiefdoms, were powerful reasons for the adoption of slash-and-burn modes of horticulture. This became an economic context for the emergence of new political leaders, referred to previously. The trade in metal tools therefore also had significant impacts on native horticultural practices, because the efficiency of cutlasses and axes permitted the extensive clearing of forest for slash-and-burn agriculture. It also permitted a commerce in cut wood, which like the supply of tobacco, gold, animal products (such as jaguar pelts and live birds), and various gums and resins, were all facets of the burgeoning Amerindian-European economic relationship. Economic relationships and the trade in foods, metal tools, and forest products thus strongly affected native ecological practices and resource usage. But they were also used to foster close political relationships with selected Amerindian leaders and to influence autonomous native societies in a variety of ways.

In political terms the mere presence of Europeans could spark latent conflicts. As the Spanish occupied the Venezuelan coastal region in search of gold, their *entradas* to the south left a trail of destruction that radiated out, upsetting the existing relationships between the various native polities, provoking migrations away from the points of contact and causing secondary conflicts among the native population. A good example of this process was the migration of the 'ancient rulers' of Trinidad, the Yao, down the Atlantic coast almost as far as the mouth of the Amazon. Here they settled amongst an extant native population. But they were unable to reestablish their political authority and were repeatedly raided by local groups. Even alliance with various English and Dutch expeditions failed to preserve them, and they disappeared from the historical record altogether by the mid–seventeenth century.

Similarly, as the Spanish moved into the Guayana coastal zone, they became aware of the existence of shipwrecked Spaniards who had been living amongst the Lokono for some years. Theirs was not, therefore, the "first contact" that the Lokono had with the Europeans, and we can only infer the possible consequences of this for subsequent Lokono political strategies toward the Europeans. But in view of the sustained trade in *aru* (manioc flour) as well as the gift of black slaves to Lokono chiefs for the production of tobacco on the lower Orinoco, we must assume that these contacts were important.

Similar examples can be found easily throughout the history of the European occupation of the Caribbean region. However, a regularity in the form of transformation in native society and culture, as a result of even these tentative attempts at colonization, does emerge. Principal among these was the "tribalization" of extant native sociopolitical structures. Such tribalization essentially consisted of the formation of increasingly closed and endogamous social groups and a development of hierarchical political authority expressing the emergence of new ethnic divisions.

At issue was usually native strategies for dealing with external invasion. The analysis of Maya and Aztec responses to the Europeans would only partly fit such a model, but it is most relevant to understanding native responses when applied to the Caribbean region. Essentially the term "tribalization" became a shorthand for expressing the commonality of effect that European contact induced. We have already seen how this operated in that part of political life concerned with leadership, and how ecological and economic factors could reinforce these tendencies. At the level of the family household, further consequences can be traced.

Marriage and kinship relations, where they did not actually incorporate Europeans and Africans, certainly were altered in their structure and quality in a number of ways. For example, marriage exchanges as part of the indigenous political process were inevitably altered by the changing political conditions. Stable patterns of exchange between élite families, as well as established exchange patterns between tribal clans or moieties, rapidly broke down, as in the case of Española, Puerto Rico, and the Lesser Antilles. The roles these types of exchanges had in cementing both local and regional relationships therefore ceased or were supplanted by new ones. A good example of this process would be the emergence of intense patterns of intermarriage between the Amerindians of the Antilles and the mainland. Although it is unlikely that there were no such exchanges in precolumbian times, the history of the island *caribes* is particularly marked by the intense relationships they developed with the *caribes* of Orinoco. Given that the Orinoco *caribes* were themselves, par excellence, a group that had their origins as a regional political force in the conditions of European contact, the specifically colonial context of this pattern of marriage alliance seems undeniable.

At the interpersonal level we can certainly trace one particular change in quality of kinship relations directly to the effects of European intrusion. The category *poito* or *macu* in Cariban and Arawakan kinship terminologies now designates a range of statuses: son-in-law, trade client/partner, servant, or slave. But the roles of client and slave seem to have been greatly expanded as the Europeans introduced a commercial trade in Amerindian war captives and took Amerindian women and children as domestic servants. Alongside of this the enhanced trading opportunities in metal goods, slaves, and guns for those politically favored by the Europeans meant that the category of trade client (carrying the connotation of "debtor") was a prevalent means of forming political solidarity and dependency by the new wave of Amerindian leaders that supplanted the ancient élites.

In a more passive way the incorporation of native groups into *encomiendas* had profound consequences for the integrity of native political forms, which based themselves on specific marriage practices. Quite simply Spanish political control was facilitated by breaking down native marriage practices – through a requirement for settlement endogamy, a valorization of patriliny over matriliny, and intermarriage with non-natives. The latter could undermine the basis of both affinal relations and consanguineal groups – important building blocks for native polity.

In the sphere of military behaviors and institutions, the effects of European intrusion were acute. The historically compelling reason for this is that warfare and plunder were all too often the primary form of interaction between would-be colonizer and colonized. Nevertheless, as outlined earlier, the effects of trading relationships, especially where this involved steel tools or guns, could have an equally profound effect on native autonomy and sociopolitical organization in the longer term. But the consequences of a rising tide of military conflict for the native population were not always negative, in that many native groupings acted as "ethnic soldiers" or "martial tribes." Such individuals or groups acted as mercenaries recruited on the basis of their "tribal" loyalties. In just this way the *caribes* soon became military specialists fighting without regard to the putative distinction between native and colonizer.

One might therefore make the following analytical distinctions among the political trajectories of native groups in the Caribbean for the period we have been considering. This also provides us with a means of summarizing the regularities in the various forms of Amerindian-European contact. First, there were those groups that emerged in large part as a result of the European presence and their own situation in a tribal zone. Classically this category would be represented by the *caribes*. Such groups are sometimes called "colonial tribes" to indicate this connection, but it should not be thought that these indigenous groupings were created for the natives by the Europeans – in the way village "captains" sometimes were. On the contrary, while these products of ethnogenesis in the tribal zone were certainly predicated on the presence of the Europeans, the degree of political control that was exercised over them by the colonial regimes of the region was highly variant through time. For example, the *caribes* were not a homogenous political entity, and the disposition of particular populations varied accordingly, sometimes allying with the French or the English, and cooperating with the Spanish on the mainland, even as they opposed the *vecinos* of Puerto Rico.

Second, Amerindian groups that were aboriginally powerful, perhaps exemplifying a chiefdom-style of political incorporation of many villages, often failed to survive the new conditions of initial European occupation and so were reduced to "tribal" status by direct military campaigns. For example, such was the fate of the Cumanágoto and Warao of the Orinoco delta and Venezuelan littoral. Both groups showed significant degrees of social hierarchy at the time of contact. But this made them all the more attractive to Spanish adventurers because such political forms suggested they might be controlled effectively through the manipulation of the ruling élite. However, these attempts to manipulate native leaders to Spanish ends were inconsistent and usually frustrated by precipitating attempts to extract goldwork, or the theft of their *naborias* (native "slaves"), or the sexual assault of the women. As a result the Cumanágoto and the Warao were militarily crushed in the 1530s following renewed attempts to occupy eastern Venezuela. Although other such chiefdom-level groups (such as the Cuna, Wayú, and Guaymí) did make a successful transition into the colonial period, others were nevertheless tribalized in the longer term as a direct consequence of their wider involvement with the Europeans.

Finally it can be seen that other groupings emerged as an indirect and longer-term consequence of the European presence, although a consideration of their case does not strictly concern us here because such transformations continued into the twentieth century. These "tribes" were the end result of a series of relocations and changing marriage exchanges in the hinterland. Their transformation often took place without any direct contact with Europeans until the seventeenth or eighteenth century. However, there were important contacts with Africans. The relationships developed between freed black slaves and native groups were often critical to colonial development, as in the Dutch West India Company's use of such freed blacks as traders into the interior.

This latter type of transformation was not seen in the coastal and island locations we have been considering but certainly relates to groups who are treated by contemporary ethnography as if they had existed untouched since 1492. The Yanomamö or Ye'kuana (also Yekuana, Ye'cuana) of the Venezuelan Amazon are examples of such groups currently accorded this iconographic status as "pristine" or "uncontacted" until the advent of recent ethnographic study.

In each of the foregoing cases, specific ethnic identities were influenced by the rhythm of expansion and contraction on the part of the colonial states in this region, regardless of a group's geographical distance or relative isolation from these states. In this sense no modern native groups can be seen as exemplifying precolumbian patterns of existence, as has sometimes been the assumption of ethnographers and archaeologists.

These kinds of sociopolitical distinctions are also reflected in the way in which ethnic identities were ideologically derived. In the case of groups like the *caribes*, political authority was derived largely from competence in trade and war, kinship boundaries becoming commensurately negotiable as both 'clients' and 'captives' (*poitos*) were tribally incorporated. In the case of the aboriginally dominant groups, befitting those who displayed complex polity at the time of contact, political authority was originally derived from some form of dynastic social charter, or genealogical positioning and kinship boundaries were correspondingly inflexible as a result. For example, the *caciques* of Puerto Rico and Española differed in their responses to the emerging political significance of *caribes* in the Antilles. This had already been a critical issue in the period of the earliest Spanish occupation, as the fate of Caonabó shows. As the European presence persisted, such dynastic chiefdoms came more and more to approximate the *caribes* in their modes of incorporation and leadership. In any case the Spanish proscription of Amerindian identity had itself become a powerful factor in the native construction of ethnic sentiment, as native political conceptions came to reflect those of the conquerors. In the final category, political authority emerges from positioning in exchange relationships, both marital and economic, within the surviving indigenous political economy of the region, "tribalization" thus being only indirect and tenuous.

In sum, the European occupation provoked demographic collapse, predation from slavers, repeated immigrations, and large-scale amalgamations of previously independent groups throughout the whole of northern South America and the Caribbean region in particular. In turn these forces provoked a fundamental reorientation of patterns of ecology, marriage, and intergroup relations, which had the overall effect of tribalizing indigenous lifeways. This meant an increased isolation between different ethnic communities (once a phase of amalgamations had ceased), an end to many long-range trading relationships, and a shrinking of the demographic base of political leadership. This continuing process effectively produced the kind of small-scale, linguistically homogeneous and endogamous social grouping that is familiar from the more recent ethnographic record. However, it should now be clear that the nature of this style of tribal organization is both historically contingent and intimately linked to the European occupation.

It remains to suggest how native thought and cosmology reflected these radical processes. In general terms the advent of missionary work, within a few years of the first arrival of Columbus, most obviously challenged existing native categories. But the fact that the missionaries were not mere purveyors of ideas, but were often actively and openly supported by the military capabilities of the *conquistadores*, put this exchange of ideas on a thoroughly inequitable basis. Because the élite of native political leaders often derived their authority from putative divine genealogies, or from arcane procedures for intercession with the spirit world, the political conquest was inevitably inseparable from the spiritual one – as the Spanish themselves so clearly enunciated.

It is all the more remarkable then that "conversion" to Christianity remained an uncertain process, evidenced more in the acceptance of the temporal power of the church and the political and economic influence of the missionaries than in a respect for their spiritual authority. Indeed, due to the vitality of native spiritual traditions up to the present day, it was not until the nineteenth and twentieth centuries that significant syncretic religious idioms emerged, even in those areas that were in the forefront of the first attempts at conversion.

Principal amongst these native traditions is *piaii-sang* ('shamanism'), by which practice those adept or skilled in techniques of trance, vision, prophecy, and song directly encounter the denizens of the spirit world. It was this class of native spiritual leaders that was most directly attacked by missionary endeavors. But given the fact that shamanic practice in these regions was essentially open to those who could master the techniques, it did not offer up an institutional target for religious extirpation, as did the temple and ancestor cults of the Aztec, Maya, and Inka.

Certainly the European invasion prompted all kinds of specific vision and prophecy as native leaders struggled to explain and control the unpredictable consequences of a European encounter. But no millennial tradition emerged until the nineteenth century, unlike in Peru or coastal Brazil, not least because the autonomous persistence of native society was so severely curtailed in the Caribbean context. On the Lesser Antilles, for example, vigorous shamanic practices are recorded down to the present day, but they did not underwrite a particular movement of opposition to the Europeans. In this way the tribalization of native political and economic structures was reflected in the cosmological sphere by a shrinking role for the shaman in the ordering of political decision making. This now largely fell to the warriors and traders. Rather the shaman became a figure associated with curing, healing, and the symbolic ordering of change through mythic narratives. Even in these more limited roles, however, the authority of shamanic vision was compromised by the succession of epidemics that eventually swept most coastal and island societies. In this context indigenous theories and beliefs about death and contagion were proved inadequate or irrelevant.

Something of the way in which the Europeans were incorporated into native thought may be understood from their common designation as *paranaghiri* ('spirits from the great water'). Although there has been much speculative writing about the extent to which the Europeans may have been prefigured in native thought – either as returning culture-heroes, such as Amalivaca in Venezuela, or as fulfillments of specific prophecies, as for the Aztec and Maya – most assimilations of the Europeans in native thought proved to be far more closely connected with political strategy. For example, at the end of the sixteenth century, *caribes* in Trinidad and Orinoco were stirred by the apocalyptic visions of one of their number who, claiming the authority of Wattopa ('spirit of fire'), prophesied the liberation of the Amerindians from the oppression of the Spanish through the imminent military intercession of the Dutch and English. The pragmatism of this vision and the use of prophecy as historical commentary is underlined when we remember that it was at precisely this moment that Walter Raleigh was arming the Trinidad natives, following his capture of the Spanish governor, and coasting Orinoco and the Guianas in search of an entrance to El Dorado. His open appeal for alliance with the Amerindians was thus culturally translated into the vision of this Kariña seer.

In material and bodily representation, the artistic expression of the Amerindians was very much altered by the European hunt for gold and silver. Native goldworking seems to have effectively ended at the point of European arrival and only persisted in the most marginal regions of the Caribbean until the end of the sixteenth century – partly explaining the frustrations of the search for El Dorado in Orinoco. In short, knowledge of the sources of gold or of the locations of artifacts became highly dangerous knowledge because the Spanish did not scruple at torture and execution in order to discover its whereabouts. Certainly native leaders specifically enjoined their followers to withhold such information and invented tales of great dragons that guarded the golden ores in order to discourage the curious. At the same time, the observed willingness of the Amerindians to exchange goldwork at rates the Europeans perceived as laughably favorable to themselves was less an expression of native naiveté than that of alternative cultural values in regard to brilliant metals. Gold alloys were therefore valued not for their financial "value" but for their brilliance and smell. *Guanin* objects were thus sometimes referred to as *taguagua* after the odoriferous Caribbean plant of the same name, and their absolute gold content was strictly irrelevant. Accordingly, European alloys, especially brass, appear to have been valued as much or more than their native equivalents because they displayed the properties of brilliance, malleability, and smell that was a source of the symbolic significance of *guanin*.

The production of highly decorated ceramics, once a central part of native plastic arts, declined as the ritual uses of these objects disappeared with the destruction of the élites who had employed them for complex burial rituals and display. Plainware continued to be produced for everyday use, and even increased as it became an item of trade with the colonial settlements of the Europeans. By the same token the introduction of metal pots and griddles further discouraged the continuing practice of native pottery.

In a less tangible way, the native experience of radical difference in styles of dress and bodily presentation certainly altered the native aesthetic. The metal-armored *conquistadores* perfectly displayed the brilliance that was the property of native élites, and many European items were incorporated into native dress. For example, the following is a description of the "wild majesty" of a *caribe* chieftain of Dominica. The extract relates to George Clifford, Earl of Cumberland (1558–1603), who was one of the most active English privateers, having organized twelve expeditions to the Caribbean between 1587 and 1598, and spending a small fortune in the process. The following account, written by Clifford's chaplain, Doctor Layfield, is taken from an extensive description of this last voyage and includes a surprisingly detailed description of the native Dominicans at the end of the sixteenth century. The phrase "wilde majesty" occurs as a marginal note made by Samuel Purchas to this account:

> They came to a Towne of these poore Salvages; and a poore Towne it was of some twenty cottages rather than Houses, and yet there was there a King, whom they found in a wide hanging garment of rich crimson Taffetie, a Spanish Rapier in his hand, and the modell of a Lyon in shining Brasse, hanging upon his breast. There they saw their women as naked as wee had seene their men, and alike attired even to the boring of their lippes and eares, yet in that nakednesse, they perceived some sparkes of modestie, not willingly comming in the sight of strange and apparelled men: and when they did come, busie to cover, what should have bin better covered. The Queene they saw not, nor any of the Noble wives, but of the vulgar many; and the Maidens it should seeme they would not have so squeamish, for the King commanded his Daughters presence, with whom our Gentlemen did dance after meate was taken away. It seemeth that themselves are wearie of their nakednesse, for besides the Kings apparrell, they are exceeding desirous to exchange any of their Commodities for an old Waste-coate, or but a Cap, yea or but a paire of Gloves.[6]

Given the centrality of defining native ethnicity and culture to the European conquest and occupation of the Caribbean, it is unsurprising that native habits of speech and the political significance given to the use of various language forms by native groups reflected these processes. The need to produce well-defined units of administration, the exigencies of using native informants to supply information on the vast southern continent, and the self-perception of the Europeans as mediators of native conflicts and civilizers of their societies, all produced a deep interest in issues of native linguistic competence and usages. In turn the politically dangerous status of *caribe*, the construction of mythic charters to underwrite the political products of ethnogenesis, and the pragmatic business of a burgeoning trade with the polylingual European adventur-

---

[6] Hulme and Whitehead, *Wild Majesty* (Oxford, 1992), 60.

ers, all were important factors for indigenous societies that favored an internal emphasis on monolingualism, as a means for defining authentic ethnic affiliation, and an external emphasis on pidgin dialects in order to facilitate that trade.

The burgeoning trade, involving such items of native manufacture as boats, sails, hammocks, and pottery, in turn resulted in intensified production. The same was true in the horticultural sphere because foodstuffs and items of direct export to Europe, such as dyes, woods, oils, and tobacco, were produced by native plantations, not European ones. The planting of sugar by the Europeans thus effectively eclipsed these earlier markets.

Such phenomena provoked reflection on the meaning of cultural identities, just as it did for the Europeans. If the reported words of various Amerindians are to be accepted as accurately reported, then it would seem that they were no less active in debating the significance of the encounter with the *paranaghiri*; just as the Europeans themselves were divided in many ways over the import of this "new world," so too Amerindians were eager to travel to Europe and learn of the context from which the invaders sprang.

The difference in this common experience stems from the European consciousness of their relative unity as 'Christian' and in their initiation of the encounter with the peoples of the native Caribbean. Amerindian responses were severely constrained by having to react to those colonial initiatives and were not organized by a common cosmological or ideological order, as in the case of the Christians. As such the inequity of understandings is obviously symptomatic of the inequity of all colonial relationships. But the vigor, inventiveness, and endurance of native strategies for dealing with the European conquest of their sociocultural forms clearly evince the reality of historical process and the consciousness of native peoples in directing that history. Through the crises of invasion, native peoples were not just transformed; they also transformed themselves.

BIBLIOGRAPHIC ESSAY

The first century of European occupation in the Caribbean, and especially the early encounters between Columbus and the natives of the islands, stimulated a great variety of publication and commentary on the indigenous population. The recent commemoration of the Columbian

Quincentennial likewise was the occasion for much republication of original sources, as well as secondary comment on their meaning and credibility. The latter debate will obviously continue, and the reissue of many of the early works enables a wider participation in those debates. Special interest must therefore always attach to the writings of Columbus and his contemporaries. However, issues as to the authorship of materials supposedly written by Columbus are very complex, because much of the manuscript material has been lost or only survives in versions edited by his contemporaries. This corpus has been collected by Consuelo Varela in *Cristóbal Colón. Textos y documentos completos* (Madrid, 1982) and Juan Gil and Consuelo Varela in *Cartas de particulares a Colón y relaciones coetáneas* (Madrid, 1984). Bibliographical commentary on this material, especially the Las Casas transcription of Columbus's *Diario* account of the first voyage, is given in David Henige's *In search of Columbus* (Tucson, 1991) and in Margarita Zamora's *Reading Columbus* (Berkeley, 1993). Among the English translations of Columbian accounts of the early voyages are Cecil Jane's *The voyages of Christopher Columbus* (London, 1930) and Oliver Dunn and James Kelley's *The Diario of Christopher Columbus's first voyage to America* (Norman, 1989). A contemporary account of Columbus's life was written by his son Hernando Colón – *Vida del Almirante Don Cristobal Colón* (Mexico City, 1946) – and translated by Benjamin Keen as *The life of the Admiral Christopher Columbus* (New Brunswick, 1992). All this material contains important first descriptions of the native Caribbean and arguably the first ethnographic document on the Americas; *An Account of the Antiquities of the Indians* (Durham, 1998), written by the Hieronymite cleric Ramón Pané, was produced on the orders of Columbus himself.

Sixteenth-century documentation published as the *Colleción de Documentos Inéditos relativos al descubrimiento, conquista y colonización de las posesiones españolas en América y Oceanía*, 42 vols. (Madrid, 1864–1884) contains the day-to-day reports sent back on the new discoveries, and works by Spanish chroniclers go on to give a fuller picture of the native inhabitants. Although the larger Caribbean islands were soon depopulated, the reasons for this are themselves an issue for debate as outlined by David Henige's 1978 article "On the contact population of Hispaniola: History as higher mathematics," *Hispanic American Historical Review* 58 (2): 217–237. However, this uncertainty also reflects contemporary sixteenth-century controversy over the exact impact of Spanish colonial policies, as can be seen from the writings of the cleric Bartolomé de Las

Casas in *Historia de las Indias* (Mexico City, 1951) and *Brevísima relación de la destrucción de las Indias* (Buenos Aires, 1966), which castigated the Spanish for the excesses of the colonial occupation. A more sanguine view of the exigencies of Spanish policy, as well as detailed description of the native population, is contained in Gonzalo Oviedo's *Historia General Y Natural de las Indias* (Seville, 1535). Also among the early sources are Pedro de Aguado's *Historia de Santa Marta y Nuevo Reino de Granada* (Madrid, 1581), Juan de Castellanos's *Elegías de varones ilustres de Indias* (Madrid, 1944), Pedro Simón's *Noticias historiales de las conquistas de Tierra Firme en las Indias Occidentales* (Cuenca, 1627), and Pedro Martyr's *De Orbe Novo* (Madrid, 1530).

An excellent critical overview of the ethical ambiguities and policy debates that Columbus's encounter with the people of the Caribbean provoked in Spain is given by Anthony Pagden in *The fall of natural man* (Cambridge, 1982), which also considers the origins of ethnology in the Western tradition. More exclusively focused on the insular Caribbean area is the literary study by Peter Hulme, *Colonial encounters*, which, as with Pagden's volume, traces the continuing relevance of the first encounters for Western intellectual development.

The course of early Iberian voyaging to the mainland as well as the islands is outlined by Louis Vigneras's *The discovery of South America and the Andalusian voyages* (Chicago, 1976). Carl Sauer's *The early Spanish main* (Berkeley, 1992) gives an overview of the human geographic consequences of these impacts. Alfred Crosby's *The Columbian exchange* (Westport, 1972) outlines the biological and epidemiological consequences of the introduction of European flora and fauna into the Americas. *The meeting of two worlds* (Oxford, 1993), edited by Warwick Bray, contains a number of articles on the early contacts between Europeans and the native population of the Caribbean.

As a result of the extensive historical documentation and persistent debate surrounding the early encounters of natives and Europeans in the greater Caribbean region, there are a number of anthropological studies devoted to the history of native peoples, especially those that eventually survived the initial crises of invasion. *Wolves from the sea: Readings in the anthropology of the native Caribbean* (Leiden, 1995), edited by Neil Whitehead, provides an overview of the current debates about native ethnicity, society, and political structure with particular reference to the way in which colonial policy fed into anthropological thinking about the Caribbean. More specific studies include Marc de Civrieux's "Los Cumanágoto y sus vecinos," in *Los Aborigenes de Venezuela, Volumen I, Etnologiá Antigua* (Caracas, 1980), edited by A. Butt Colson; Inga Clendinnen's *Ambivalent conquests: Maya and Spaniard in Yucatan, 1517–1570* (Cambridge, 1987); Charles Gullick's *Myths of a minority: The changing traditions of the St. Vincentian Caribs* (Assen, 1985); Nancie Gonzalez's *Sojourners of the Caribbean: Ethnogenesis and ethnohistory of the Garifuna* (Urbana, 1988); Jalil Sued-Badillo's pioneering study *Los Indios Caribes: Realidad o Fabula?* (Rio Pedras, 1978); and Samuel Wilson's *Hispaniola: Caribbean chiefdoms in the age of Columbus* (Tuscaloosa, 1990). Peter Hulme and Neil Whitehead's anthology of historical documentation on the natives of the Lesser Antilles, *Wild majesty: Encounters with Caribs from Columbus to the present day* (Oxford, 1992), contains a number of new translations and transcriptions of the early Spanish documentation as well as a collection of sixteenth-century English accounts of the native Caribbean.

Although the French missionaries did not arrive in the Caribbean until the 1620s, the philological and ethnological studies they made have been seen as important sources for the reconstruction of native Caribbean society. They themselves quite consciously collected information that they deemed to refer to the "originary" state of native society and culture, as did their secular and Protestant rivals. For these reasons any historical understanding of the first century of contacts will necessarily use such sources. They include Sieur de la Borde's *Voyage qui contient une Relation . . . de les Caraïbes* (Paris, 1674); Raymond Breton's *Dictionnaire Caraïbe-François* (Auxerre, 1665) and *Dictionnaire François-Caraïbe* (Auxerre, 1666); Pierre Pelleprat's *Relation des missions des pères jésuites* (Paris, 1655); Jean Baptiste du Tertre's *Histoire générale des Antilles habitées par les François* (Paris, 1667): Jean Baptiste Labat's *Nouveau Voyage aux Isles Amérique* (Den Haag, 1724); and Cesar Rochefort's *Histoire naturelle et morale des îsles Antilles de l'Amérique* (Rotterdam, 1665).

12

THE CRISES AND TRANSFORMATIONS
OF INVADED SOCIETIES:
ANDEAN AREA (1500–1580)

KAREN SPALDING

As a European historian has observed, historians "have a soft spot for conquest," which provides a neat, defined chronology in which to fit an intractable past.[1] That is particularly true in the Americas, where the conquest of the native states has been generally accepted as marking the beginning of modern history. But conquests can provide only a chronology for the winners, for like many defining "events," they become clear only with the passage of time, and only as long as they are seen from a single perspective. The Spaniards who moved into the Andes in 1531 regarded themselves as conquerors, and their own versions of what happened in the region between that date and the 1560s remains unchallenged. After all, after 1532, it became impossible to deal with the region without taking into account the European presence. The Andes became part of an expanding Europe, and more specifically, of the Spanish empire, the most powerful European political structure of the sixteenth century (Map 12.1). But it would be very poor history to view the events of the sixteenth century through the focus of the twentieth, and to assume the absolute victory of Spaniards over Andeans simply because, centuries later, the relationship between people who defined themselves as European and people who were defined (and often defined themselves as well) as Andean was one of almost total domination of the latter by the former.

The pages that follow attempt to examine the period from 1500 to

---

[1] This chapter began as a revised version of chapter 4 of my book *Huarochirí: An Andean society under Inca and Spanish rule* (Stanford, 1984). I would like to thank both Stanford University Press for permission to use that material, and my editors, Frank Salomon and Stuart Schwartz, for urging me to undertake the revision, which has become a very different piece from the original. It is seldom that an author gets the opportunity to rewrite what has already been "set in print," and it has been both exciting and humbling to have the opportunity to take stock of how much the discipline and my own ideas have changed in the course of the last decade.

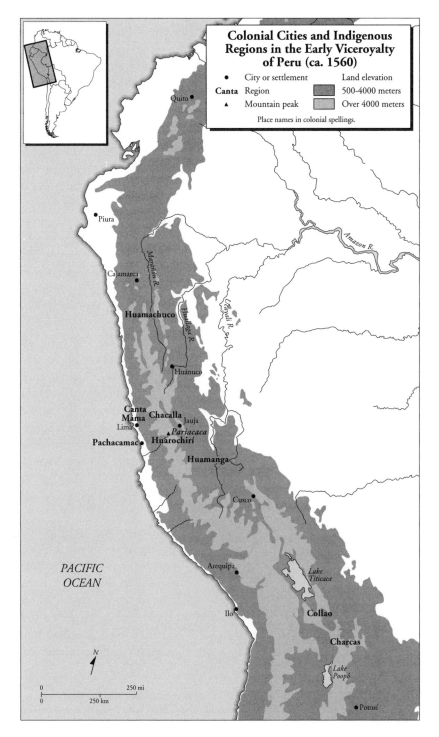

Colonial Cities and Indigenous Regions in the Early Viceroyalty of Peru (ca. 1560)

- City or settlement
- **Canta** Region
- ▲ Mountain peak

Land elevation
- 500-4000 meters
- Over 4000 meters

Place names in colonial spellings.

Quito

Piura

Cajamarca

Marañón R.

Amazon R.

Huamachuco

Huallaga R.

Ucayali R.

Huánuco

Canta
Mama Chacalla
Lima Jauja
      ▲*Pariacaca*
Pachacamac Huarochirí

Huamanga

Cusco

PACIFIC
OCEAN

Arequipa

Lake Titicaca

Ilo

Collao

Charcas

Lake Poopó

N

Potosí

0   250 mi
0   250 km

Map 12.1

1580 – the period usually classified as the Spanish conquest – from a somewhat different perspective. The task is not easy because the appearance of the Spaniards in the Andes also means that the sources for the study of the region change massively. Before 1531, the only direct records available to a student of Andean history are those read by archaeologists; the Europeans who came to the Andes after 1532 generated the kind of record used by scholars who traditionally depend upon written materials. That change is both useful and misleading, because the standard bias of the written word, which is a bias toward the view of an élite, is multiplied by the fact that all our data about Andean people undergoes a process of translation and interpretation through a different culture. Even sources generated by Andeans are constrained by the differences between oral and written traditions. So we must use data about Andeans generated by Spaniards cautiously, and appreciate that the data has made it possible to learn a great deal not only about Andean societies since 1532 but before as well.

We have learned a great deal in the last decade alone. Ten years ago the present author set about the study of how members of Andean societies "responded to or resisted the political structures imposed upon them, and how they dealt with, were exploited by, or benefited from the Europeans who occupied their land and made it their own."[2] I would not frame the issue in those terms today. It is becoming increasingly possible to see the members of Andean societies as active participants in the events that transformed their lives. The Spaniards did not have an entirely free hand in the Andes; like all other conquerors, they had to deal with people who had their own ideas about what was going on, and who defined their own agendas and objectives.

Nor can we look at the encounter between Europeans and Andeans simply in terms of opposing forces, even opposing forces in which many Andeans chose for their own reasons to ally with the invaders. Beneath the umbrella of the Inka[3] state (see Chap. 10), itself in disarray when the Spaniards appeared, there were many different societies, some of them complex state systems in themselves and others smaller and less stratified (see Chap. 6). All the respective leaders had their own agendas. It is becoming increasingly clear that, whereas Andeans and Spaniards un-

---

[2] *Huarochirí*, 8
[3] The term "Inka" signifies a member of an ethnic group that expanded from the Cusco Valley to conquer the Andean region from what is today Ecuador to Chile and Argentina. It also refers to the ruling élite of the Inka state, as well as to the head of state or ruler.

doubtedly did not understand a great deal about one another, this fact hardly kept them from trying to use one another for their own ends. Andean leaders used Spaniards to buttress or advance their positions in their own societies; they participated actively – and successfully – in European markets; they took part in the political definition of the colonial system. There is no longer any need to choose between the two standard – and equally unsatisfactory – versions of this period: either portraying the Indians as passive victims or the Spaniards as all-powerful. Members of Andean society were full participants in the struggle to define what the European presence would mean. This effort to broaden our perspective is still in its initial stages, but it is already possible to see some of the exciting prospects opened by the work of those who have made the effort.

THE SPANISH INVASION AND THE KILLING OF THE SOVEREIGN INKA

The conquest of the Andes began from Panama. In 1524 the governor of Panama, Pedrarias de Avila, gave Francisco Pizarro, a captain and veteran of the Indies who had been in the New World since 1502, authority to explore and conquer toward the south. After a first unsuccessful expedition south, in which the explorers were forcibly beaten off by the people they met, and the insects took all the booty that was to be had, a second expedition reached the settled area of what is today northern Ecuador. The members of the expedition, most of them hungry and ill, holed up on Gallo Island off the coast of Colombia. Thirteen remained there through the winter while the rest went back to Panama. The pilot who took the group that withdrew back to Panama returned a few months later with fresh supplies, and the tiny group explored the coast by ship, penetrating the Inka empire as far south as Túmbez. They saw evidence of a settled, prosperous society along the coast, and they met and captured a seagoing raft with a crew of twenty people. The cargo included objects of gold and silver and finely woven cloth of many colors. Pizarro also obtained two young boys from a coastal chieftain, or *kuraka*, whom he trained to become interpreters for the Spaniards.

From Panama Pizarro went to Spain, with the evidence of the rich lands lying to the south of the territory then claimed by Spain, in order to obtain legal authority for further action. He returned in 1530 with full authorization from the crown to establish Spanish rule over the territory

he had discovered and a title of governor and captain-general of the lands
he conquered. The crown gave Pizarro full military command and direction of the enterprise, which contravened the terms of the partnership
Pizarro had formed in Panama before leaving for Spain with a younger
man, Diego de Almagro, and a priest-investor, Hernando de Luque.
Almagro's anger at his exclusion almost ended the partnership, but relations were patched up, and the first band of conquerors left for Peru
under Pizarro's command in January 1531, with about 180–200 men and
thirty horses, to be followed by Almagro with the rest of the men who
signed up for the operation. Pizarro's band disembarked on the coast of
northern Ecuador, occupying a large settlement and sending their plunder in gold and silver objects back to Panama.

The expedition entered the Inka empire early in 1532. The first Spanish
settlement in Peru, San Miguel de Piura, was founded in August. There
the Spaniards learned about a civil war over succession to the leadership
of the Andean state. Warfare had raged since the sudden death of the
last Inka, Huayna Cápac (Quechua: Wayna Qhapaq). Following rumors
that Atawallpa (hispano-Quechua: Atahuallpa) the Quito-based con-
tender who was then winning the civil war, was in the northern Inka
center at Cajamarca, the Spaniards moved into the Andean highlands in
search of him. They entered Cajamarca in November and requested a
meeting with Atawallpa. After an initial delay, the Inka sovereign (whom
his people titled Sapa Inka) agreed to the meeting, and with a small force
of some several thousand men, mostly unarmed, he entered the square at
Cajamarca. What he met was an ambush from the Spaniards, who had
hidden in the long buildings surrounding the square. The ambush went
according to Pizarro's plan, and the Inka was taken prisoner while his
forces, unable to move within the enclosed space when the horses charged
directly into them, died by the thousands.

In an effort to regain his freedom, Atawallpa offered to collect a
ransom of a room filled with gold and silver as high as he could reach.
The Spaniards agreed. Atawallpa sent messengers throughout Inka territory to collect gold and silver objects, using the opportunity to revenge
himself upon regional deities or *wak'as* that had failed to support him
during the civil war, and respecting only the mummies of past Inka rulers
who were guarded by their descendants. The Spaniards settled in Cajamarca to wait for the treasure, uncertain what to do with their dangerous
and powerful captive if and when he met the ransom. Waskhar (hispano-
Quechua: Huáscar) Atawallpa's half-brother and rival in the civil war,

was already dead, killed by Atawallpa's forces on his order. The war for succession was over – or would have been if it had not been for Francisco Pizarro.

The ransom was collected and melted down into bars of gold and silver by the spring of 1533. At the same time, the Spaniards condemned Atawallpa to death on the basis of rumors that he was organizing his forces in the field to move against the Spaniards; they thus removed a figure whose presence had become steadily more inconvenient to them. The treasure of Cajamarca totaled more than 1.5 million pesos when it was melted down. After the traditional "royal fifth" was set aside for the king, the remainder was divided into shares and distributed among the men. The share of the plunder that fell to a horseman in the distribution of the treasure was some 90 pounds of gold and 180 of silver.[4] The share of a foot soldier was about half that amount, and Pizarro himself took thirteen shares. The initial investment in the expedition paid off beyond the wildest dreams of everyone in the Americas, and it sparked a rush of men to Peru in the hope of making their fortunes.

Groups of hopefuls captained by men who had participated in earlier expeditions began to descend on Pizarro almost immediately. Diego de Almagro, Pizarro's original partner, and the force of 150 men he brought to Peru, reached Cajamarca while the ransom was being collected. In October 1533 the authorities in Panama wrote excitedly to Madrid that "the wealth and greatness of the provinces of Peru increase so greatly every day that it is becoming impossible to believe, and in truth, to those of us who are here and see it most closely, virtually within our reach, it seems a dream." Almagro was followed by Pedro de Alvarado, Hernan Cortés's erstwhile lieutenant in the conquest of New Spain (Mexico), who brought a force of 500 men from Guatemala to Ecuador in the hope of finding another Peru in the northern reaches of the Inka state. One of Pizarro's lieutenants, Sebastián de Benalcázar, reached Ecuador first, staking out his own claim to Quito and making himself effectively independent of Pizarro. The conquest of Quito was long and hard and produced little plunder, but the rumors of immense wealth were a magnet drawing

---

[4] Some 13,420 pounds of gold and 26,000 pounds of silver were melted down at Cajamarca. Calculations of their worth in contemporary terms do not take into account changing currency values or prices, whose fluctuations limit the value of any estimate. Still, the figure of over half a billion dollars provides an approximate yardstick against which a reader can estimate the plunder of the conquest. See John Hemming, *The conquest of the Incas* (New York, 1970), 74, 556; and James Lockhart, *The men of Cajamarca* (Berkeley, 1972), 13.

Spaniards from Central America and the Caribbean whose years in the new lands had brought them little more than hard times.

From 1533, when the first of the men present in Cajamarca returned to Spain with the crown's and their own shares of the treasure, word of the great event spread rapidly. The first eyewitness reports of the conquest, by Cristóbal de Mena and Francisco de Jérez, were read and translated and read again, encouraging growing numbers of people to consider seeking their fortunes in Peru. In October 1533 an official in Panama reported that "the numbers and quantity of people mobilizing to pass through these parts en route to the provinces of Peru are so numerous and so sudden that here we have not been able to provide for them."[5] Early in 1533 an authority in Panama informed the crown that "here everyone is up in arms about leaving for Peru, and if Your Majesty does not send authority to restrain people, . . . this province will be entirely deserted."[6] A few days later the authorities in Santo Domingo wrote anxiously that "with the enormous news of the riches of Peru, we are hard put to stop the people of this island and even of all the surrounding areas . . . because all the people are aroused with plans to go to that land."[7] The officials in Puerto Rico added that "with the news from Peru, not a citizen would remain if he were not tied down."[8] The gold rush was on.

The history of the European invasion of the Andes, like the history of any struggle for power, has more than one dimension, and not only the interpretation of events, but the chronology – and even the facts themselves – shift according to the perspective from which we view the struggle. From the European perspective – the one with which we are all familiar – the capture of the Inka ruler and his death a year later at the hands of the Spaniards mark the conquest of Peru. But if we try to see the events of this period from an Andean perspective, there is little evidence that the Andean combatants saw what happened to Atawallpa as anything more than another part of the long civil war that rent the Inka state from the 1520s. Atawallpa's death was a setback to the aspirations of the factions backing him, and a reprieve for the factions that

[5] El Lic. Espinosa al Emperador, Panamá, 10 de Octubre de 1533," in Raúl Porras Barrenechea, *Cartas del Perú (1524–1543)* (Lima, 1959), 68.

[6] "Francisco de Barrionuevo al Emperador, Panamá, 19 de Enero de 1534," *Cartas del Perú*, 96.

[7] "La Audiencia de la Isla Española al Emperador, Santo Domingo, 30 de enero de 1534," *Cartas del Perú*, 99.

[8] "Los oficiales de Puerto Rico al Emperador, San Juan, 26 de febrero de 1534," *Cartas del Perú*, 100.

mobilized around Waskhar, leader of the opposing side in the war, killed only days before the Spaniards appeared in Cajamarca. As Pizarro was well aware, Atawallpa's death left the opposing Inka factions intact in the field. Despite the enormous advantage attributed by European scholars to Spanish military skill and technology, Pizarro himself was acutely aware that his future depended on how he managed Spanish fortunes in the struggle among Inka factions for control of the state. Our sources depict Pizarro as selecting a puppet Inka to replace Atawallpa, but from an Andean perspective, the Spaniards can be seen as one more among the multitude of groups negotiating in the confused field of a war in which the leaders of both major factions had been eliminated, and no resolution had been made. Pizarro was acutely aware that the safety of the Spaniards depended upon some Inka faction gaining control of the situation, for as the Pizarran version of events sent to Madrid put it, Pizarro's principal concern was that there be a single ruler. "For if that were not so, there would be great confusion, for each [lord] would revolt along with those who obeyed him, and it would be very difficult to bring them to friendship with the Spaniards and service to His Majesty."[9] From the Spaniards' perspective, it mattered little which Inka faction won, as long as they were on the winning side, so when one claimant died as the Spaniards, with their current Inka allies, were en route to Cusco (Quechua: Qusqu, also written Cuzco), they allied themselves quickly with the next.

The version recorded by Pizarro's secretary presents the story of Pizarro's support of Manco Inca (Manqu Inka), who intercepted the Spanish/Andean force outside of Cusco, as a Spanish tactic. But even the secretary cannot hide the fact that Manco initiated negotiations with the Andean/Spanish forces as a Cusco lord "who was the rightful leader of that province, and the one who all of the chiefs [*caciques*] of the area wanted as their lord." He offered an alliance with the Spaniards "in order to expel from the land all those from Quito, for they were his enemies."[10] It seems obvious that, as far as the Inka factions in Cusco were concerned, their primary focus was the elimination of what they regarded as a revolt against Cusco by Quito and its allies, and the reconstitution of the Inka system ruled from Cusco. One of the ethnic groups that favored the venture was the central Peruvian Wanka or Huanca (see pp. 561–566).

[9] Pedro Sancho, *Relación de la conquista del Perú* [1534] (Madrid, 1962), 20.
[10] Sancho, *Relación*, 61.

An Inka/Huanca/Spanish force succeeded in driving the Quito forces that threatened Jauja out of the central highlands and back to the periphery of the Inka state. From an Andean perspective, that victory made it possible to define the civil war as over, and to open the door for a new Inka to rebuild the authority of the Inka system. Manco was crowned in Cusco in a ceremony where the Spaniards occupied the position of valued allies. Perhaps the Inka now evaluated Spaniards as somewhat analogous to the status of the Cañari – that is, as "foreign" but recognized warriors of the Inka state. During the ceremony the Spanish read and translated the *requerimiento*, that odd bit of legalistic bombast that demanded that the hearers acknowledge, without question, the supremacy of the Christian God in heaven and the Spanish monarch on earth. Manco embraced Pizarro, and "with his own hand offered drink to the Governor and the Spaniards." And with these two examples of political ritual, probably meaningful only to Spaniards, both Spaniards and Andeans "withdrew to eat because it was already late," neither understanding the meaning assigned the performance by the other.[11]

THE VIEW FROM SPAIN

It is virtually impossible to comprehend the 3 years between Manco's coronation in Cusco and his attack on the Spaniards in 1536 without making a serious effort to read "behind" our sources. From the death of Atawallpa on, Pizarro moved through the Andes founding Spanish cities and assigning control over Andean polities to Spaniards in recognition of their services in the region. The sources contain abundant evidence that during these years, the Spaniards looted and plundered with impunity, providing abundant material for later Spanish portrayals of the conquerors as ravening wolves among sheep. The depredations of some of the Spaniards in the Andes were so extreme that those men were tried later for excessive violence despite their "services" to the crown. Pedro de Alvarado faced such charges in 1545, and witnesses testified that "he warred against [the Indians] by both fire and sword, as is normally done

---

[11] Both quotes can be found in Sancho, *Relación*, 67–68. This incident, I suggest, offers a great deal more meat to scholars interested in analyzing cultural misunderstandings and disjunctures between Spaniards and Andeans than the "battle of the book" between Valverde and Atawallpa, which has been the subject of several articles to date. For examples of these articles, see the chapter-end Bibliographical Essay.

with Indians."[12] In the same proceeding, another Spaniard who "robbed in the province of the Chupachos [Huánuco] and other provinces, and in the royal *tambo* [*tampu*, 'waystation'] of the province of the Chupachos," was charged, with his Indian allies, who were more than 400 in number, of having "killed the principal cacique of the Chupachos, and bound and carried off many Indians, men and women, and robbed the natives of their llamas and shawls and gold and silver, leaving them in such misery and poverty that they will never recover." The Spaniard, it was alleged, "told the caciques and Indians to give him gold and silver because he was a son of Huayna Capac."[13]

But such testimony only reinforces the image of the Andean population as passive witnesses to their own destruction, unable to prevent the Spaniards from doing whatever they chose. If we accept such images, we cannot escape the tendency to see the Spaniards as superhuman marauders and the Andeans as passive victims. If we are to get beyond this vision, we need to develop a vision of Spaniards and Andeans alike as people who sought to work out their futures in terms of their own cultures.

As might be expected, we have much more information about the culture of the Spaniards than we have about the Andeans. The Spaniards who entered the Andes in 1531 were products of a culture that was in a process of rapid change. European societies, organized around commodity production and an expanding market economy, were rapidly moving toward a social structure in which social position was closely related to material wealth, which in turn was tied to the accumulation of precious metals. And the seeds of that transformation were present in the 1530s; the clash of the two cultures was a clash not only of productive systems but of the entire complex of law and custom that structured social relations and defined the patterns of distribution and access to goods and resources.

The European invasion of the Americas took place against a background of economic and social tension in Europe. The growing demand of the Spanish state for money to finance its European designs, and the doctrinal revolts against the power of the Church that took the form of a political revolt against the Spanish-Hapsburg claims in central Europe,

---

[12] Carlos Sempat Assadourian, "La gran vejación y destruición de la tierra": las guerras de sucesión y de conquista en el derrumbe de la población indígena del Perú," in his *Transiciones hacia el sistema colonial andino* (Lima, 1994), 30.

[13] Sempat, "La gran vejación," in *Transiciones*, 32–33.

are the most obvious factors in that tension, and the ones that most directly affected Spanish policies in the Andes. By the sixteenth century, European political struggles were increasingly defined by the financial capacity of the combatants. The "new monarchies" rested upon the abilities of the monarch to "buy" loyalty by offering lucrative privileges to the nobility or, on the other hand, by offering privileges to the towns that threatened noble income. The armies of the sixteenth century fought for cash, and the monarch who could field the largest mercenary force was generally the victor in a conflict. But if contracts were not met, that same army would take its pay by plundering the local population. It took increasing amounts of money to maintain and protect political power; even crowns were up for auction. The three candidates for the office of Holy Roman Emperor in 1519 all supported their claims with bribes, and the election went to Charles, soon to be Charles I of Spain, because his bribe was backed by precious metals coming from the new American lands. From the time of the regency of Ferdinand of Aragón, Charles's grandfather, it was increasingly clear to the people surrounding the Spanish monarch that the "Indies" offered an unparalleled source of income that could be used to bolster and extend the power of the crown in Europe, and the demand for remissions from the Americas was a major, and steadily increasing, factor in all decisions regarding the new colonies made in Spain.

Nor was the search for wealth limited to the newly expanding states. Wealth was increasingly important for ambitious individuals as well. The driving force of the rapid Spanish expansion in the Americas was the search for wealth that could be traded for rank and position in contemporary Spanish society. The Spanish conquerors themselves were essentially pirates: organized gangs of men who, under a thin cover of legality that consisted of little more than titles of authority over the unknown, drawn up in Madrid or wherever the royal court happened to be, robbed and plundered in search of the precious metals that were in short supply in the rapidly expanding European economy. The men who came to America were the heirs of a culture that equated status and privilege with warfare. The society that men left for the Indies was highly aristocratic, dominated by the power and the values of the great noble families built during the Reconquest – that is, the long process of expansion of the northern Iberian Catholic principalities southward into lands occupied by the Muslim principates in the eighth century C.E.

The Catholic kingdoms expanded rapidly toward the south in the thirteenth century, and the conquest of Muslim territories opened vast areas of land for Christian occupation. Control over newly occupied territories was assured, however, not only by military victory but by occupation. The social prestige of the aristocracy depended on its role as warriors, a function honed in the battles of the Reconquest. Those battles were the source of the material wealth that made possible the profession of arms. From the tenth to the fourteenth centuries, the Christian principalities in the north of the Iberian peninsula pushed south, occupying the rich lands held by the Muslim principates. Unlike the more organized and static societies to the east of the Pyrenees, where feudalism was more solidly established, the Iberian peninsula from the tenth to the fourteenth centuries was a frontier, a land of opportunity for the ambitious individual willing to risk his life for great rewards.

The life of El Cíd, the eleventh-century figure who became a legend shortly after his death and the hero of an epic known and referred to by the Spaniards when embarking on their own adventures in the sixteenth century, represents the model of the horizons open to the man with sufficient skill and audacity. From a beginning as a member of the minor nobility of Castile, Rodrigo Díaz, "El Cíd," turned the profession of arms to such advantage that he died the independent ruler of a principate that he won for himself in eastern Spain, with its capital in the city of Valencia.[14] Within a few years after his death, the life and exploits of this man were familiar enough to people all over the Iberian peninsula that authors could refer to him simply as *meo Cíd*, a term meaning simply 'my leader', 'my commander', or 'my boss'. Until the fourteenth century, the Muslim territories offered a chance for an ambitious noble to become wealthy and powerful by taking control of a more prosperous area. The security of the newly conquered territory could be assured by quickly attracting other people. The bargain was to let them establish their own town government in exchange for the payment of a tax to the new lord. These towns became the other pole of the complicated combination of aristocratic and popular values characteristic of early modern Spain: a society in which the "self-made man" was a dream on which many would stake their lives.

The majority of the men who participated in the invasion of the Andes came from Castile, and the largest proportion of those hailed from

---

[14] For a discussion of the career of Rodrigo Díaz and his later transformation, see Richard Fletcher, *The Quest for El Cíd* (New York, 1989).

Extremadura, a less-developed, primarily rural region of Castile. That region was primarily a wool-producing area, providing the raw material that supplied the great textile-producing areas of Flanders and France. In the course of the fifteenth century, the great military orders, which played an important part in the Reconquest and had amassed vast areas of land, were gradually brought under royal control. But economic expansion from the late fourteenth century meant that wealth, rather than lineage or service, increasingly became the measure of rank and status. By the late fifteenth century, 2 or 3 percent of the population of Castile owned 97 percent of the land, and over half of that 97 percent belonged to a handful of great families. Sixty-two noble houses in the kingdom of Castile controlled the vast majority of the wealth of the kingdom.[15] The authority of the monarch over this group rested more on alliance than authority, with the *grandes* (upper-tier nobility) providing for both the monarch's and their own interests through their participation in the definition of royal policy.

Few of those great families, however, were in Extremadura, which was in many ways a less-developed backwater of Castile, and in any case, the *grandes* of Castile did not contribute to the number of those who went to the Indies. The lineage of a *grande*, founded on wealth, might be relatively recent in contrast to the generally less wealthy but illustrious *caballeros* ('men on horseback'). The latter traced their ancestry and privileges to their participation in the Reconquest, in the tradition of El Cíd, but their wealth might not have lived up to their status. Below the *caballeros* were the individuals and families who lacked titles but were exempt from taxation or had some privilege, real or honorary, that separated them from ordinary taxpayers subject to fiscal and military levies. These exempt individuals were the *hidalgos*, a group that was not homogeneous in either wealth, social standing, or political influence. The economic development of Castile, reflected to a less but real degree in Extremadura, introduced disjunctures in the criteria that were once united in the élite, blurring the boundaries of rank and privilege and presenting opportunities to those eager to improve their position.

The Indies presented vast new horizons of opportunity, especially to members of this group. The poor *hidalgo* – or in some cases even a commoner with sufficient military skill to become part of a conquest

---

[15] John H. Elliott, *Imperial Spain*, (New York, 1963), 109.

company – who became wealthy in the Indies could turn that wealth into higher status at home through the purchase of land, a position on the *cabildo* ('council') of his town, and social connections that could be parlayed into association – even marriage – with the nobility. The whole concept of nobility and *hidalguía* was changing during the sixteenth century, as wealth made it possible to behave in ways that were hardly possible before the entry of Spain in the Americas. The gradual expansion of the Spanish wool trade from the thirteenth century became a flood that made it possible for the newly wealthy to exchange a part of their wealth for the privileges and social position that went with a title, even a relatively minor one. Ferdinand and Isabella began to create new *hidalgos* liberally in the fifteenth century. By the 1520s the privileges of *hidalguía* were being freely offered for sale despite numerous complaints.[16] A proverb of uncertain origin but accurate insight that was repeated in Latin America during the colonial period described a title as equivalent to a zero. Alone it was worth nothing, but combined with money it multiplied the value of anything placed in front of it.[17] The cynicism of the proverb, whatever its actual provenance, fits the mood of the sixteenth century, with its inflation of titles and scramble for the wherewithal to obtain them.

The values of *hidalguía* were prominant in the men who came to the Americas in the years following the first voyages of Christopher Columbus, as well as in the 1530s and 1540s when the Spaniards entered the Andes. These values explain much about the conduct of the conquerors in Peru. As an historian of Spain has pointed out, noble values could appear quite contradictory: qualities of honesty, charity, generosity, and justice were ranked equally with horsemanship, military skill, wealth, success – and a conviction of the right and justice of one's claim whatever it might be. The *hidalgo* insisted upon his loyalty to his sovereign but ignored law and royal officials when either conflicted with his own interests or objectives. Violence and defiance of authority were common among these men, who saw themselves as the natural leaders of their society, fully justified in expecting to be obeyed while at the same time defying all efforts to control them.[18] The same attitude is evoked by Steve

---

[16] *Imperial Spain*, 113.
[17] My memory of the proverb dates to graduate lectures by Robert Padden; a poem of similar import is found in Sergio Bagú, *Estructura social de la colonia* (Buenos Aires, 1952), 125.
[18] Ida Altman, *Emigrants and society: Extremadura and America in the sixteenth century* (Berkeley, 1989), 73–78.

Stern with the saying "nobody gives me commands, I'm the one to command others."[19]

Somewhat less than a quarter of the men present at the capture of Atawallpa could use the elevating title *don* in 1533, but all of them shared the values and the ambitions of the *hidalgo* class to which they aspired, no matter how recently they had gained the means to fulfill those aspirations.[20] They, as well as floods of people who followed them to Peru, hoped to amass a fortune by force of arms and trade it to the crown for a reward that matched what they regarded as their service to the monarch in adding new lands and vassals to his patrimony. And for the first generation of the conquerors, that was true; from the 1530s through the 1560s, those present at the capture of Atawallpa were indisputably the upper nobility of Peru. Moreover, members of the Iberian nobility came to Peru in increasing numbers after the first years, often as part of the household entourage of officials sent from Spain, and all of them expected to be rewarded in accord with their social rank at home. Their social position and their rapid accommodation in the new kingdom overseas fixed the aristocratic values developed in Spain at the summit of Spanish colonial society in Peru.

Although the men who came to the Indies to seek their fortunes and social position subscribed firmly to the concept of a society led by an aristocracy supported by income from land worked by commoners, they saw no contradiction between that concept and active participation in commerce. The aristocracies of both Castile and Aragón were actively involved in maritime trade from the thirteenth century. In addition to supplying the international trade in wool, wealthy nobles were also directly involved in trade. Whereas association with petty trade might have carried a stigma, there was no such attitude toward international commerce. In fact, one of the most powerful aristocrats of Spain, the Duke of Medina-Sidona, owned ships, negotiated directly with Genoese merchant houses for the sale of his grain, and was dubbed "the tuna king" for the fisheries he controlled off the Atlantic coast west of Cadiz. Despite the alleged antagonism between nobility and trade, the great noble families took quick advantage of the opportunity to increase their wealth presented by exploration and settlement overseas. They financed at least

---

[19] "Nadie me manda a mí; yo soy el mandón de otros." Stern, "Paradigms of conquest," Prologue to the 2nd edition of *Peru's Indian peoples and the challenge of Spanish conquest* (University of Wisconsin, 1993), xxix.

[20] Lockhart, *Men of Cajamarca*, 32.

some of Columbus's expeditions and advanced capital to merchants outfitting ships to send to the Indies in exchange for a percentage of the gains.

At least some of the new Spanish aristocracy in Peru increased their wealth by mercantile activities in Peru; a man who used his opportunities in America to buy and sell in the course of amassing a fortune drew no adverse comment. In doing so they sometimes took commercial advantage of the *encomienda*, which was a grant of authority over a group of Indians, most commonly defined as all of the people under the authority of a designated native leader, or *kuraka*. A grant of *encomienda*[21] in Peru could provide the goods and labor needed to produce commodities for international trade. Precious metals mined and refined by the Andean people were shipped to Spain, and cloth requisitioned from Andean households was shipped to distant centers such as Chile to clothe Spanish settlers. The search for additional wealth was not scorned by members of the Spanish nobility, and the accumulation of profits from commerce was characteristic of Spanish society in the Americas as well as in Spain. Trade, like conquest, was a mechanism for the accumulation of wealth, a means to gain income that could be used to buy social status. Mercantile fortunes bought titles and land and entailed estates to maintain family status and position. The values of the nobility were shared by the people who dealt in merchandise – at least by those who did so on a large scale. Making money, in short, never undermined the predominance of the aristocracy in Spain or in Peru. (The *encomienda* is further discussed on pp. 935–942).

In the Indies both plunder and commerce were part of the search for the wealth necessary for social ascent. The expeditions that explored and took possession of the new lands in the Americas were private enterprises organized for personal gain. The men who joined an expedition "invested" their persons and equipment in the enterprise; the goods appropriated in the course of their operations were distributed among them in proportion to their initial investment and their participation. The crown granted the right to undertake an expedition to designated leaders who petitioned for that authority, carefully reserving specific rights and incomes for itself. The agreements that were concluded between the prospective leader of an expedition and the crown, usually called *capitula-*

---

[21] The recipient of the grant, the *encomendero*, was charged with the responsibility for the natives' conversion to Catholicism in return for the privilege of using their labor essentially as he saw fit.

ciones, specifically reserved for the crown the legal authority over any
territory claimed in its name as well as the royal fifth – a tax of one-fifth
of all plunder taken on the expedition. Because the crown rarely provided
any financial assistance to the operation, the bargaining was usually hard,
and the expedition leader came away with extensive authority.

As might be expected, the initial objective of the Spaniards in the
Andes was openly and frankly the appropriation of treasure. The members of the expedition outfitted themselves at their own expense, buying
their horses if they joined as horsemen as well as their arms and equipment. Pizarro contracted for the ships and other supplies, paying for
them from his own income or taking out loans against expected plunder.
The proto-company that was the expedition to Peru was financially a
gamble; many similar expeditions brought little besides illness and defeat
for the warrior-entrepreneurs. It is hardly surprising under the circumstances that the people who followed the lucky few who shared Atawallpa's ransom and the later plunder collected in Cusco among themselves were ready recruits to factions whose members felt that they, too,
should receive a share of the spoils of conquest. And Pizarro, who meant
to insert himself as ruler, was undoubtedly frustrated and upset by the
behavior of his countrymen.

Despite his wealth Pizarro, like other leaders of conquest expeditions,
sought far more than riches alone. These men sought to establish new
realms, new political entities under their ultimate supervision and command. Their dreams were of power and authority – political objectives
rather than primarily economic ones. The capitulations between the
crown and Pizarro gave the latter the rank of governor and captain-
general of all territories that he conquered; he was to enjoy the full
prerogatives of government, including military authority and the right to
grant land and assign vassals, together with responsibility for organizing
the institutions of Spanish society in the newly claimed lands. Pizarro
had no intention of grabbing the plunder and running for Spain to buy
a title of nobility and a permanent seat on the *cabildo* of his home town.
His primary concern was the authority and command he exercised as
governor, and he insisted to his death that any infringement of his
authority, even by the crown, was unjust and unfair. Pizarro's jealous
defense of what he regarded as his right to order and govern the lands he
held was echoed, interestingly enough, not by his elder brother, a titled
member of the nobility, whose entire concern seems to have been obtaining and protecting the fortune and position that went with his title, but

by his half-brother Gonzalo, who claimed that "rather than live forty years he would prefer to live ten and be governor of Peru."[22]

THE VIEW FROM CUSCO

Just as the behavior of the Spaniards must be understood in terms of their own culture, we cannot understand the behavior of the Andeans – particularly of Manco Inca as the head of a state system that spanned the Andes – without taking a closer look at the Inka state. According to Inka informants the Inka expansion had brought peace and security to the Andes by imposing order upon a chaos of warring local communities, translated by the Spaniards as *behetrías*. But this Hobbesian imagery of the Andes as existing under conditions of unremitting war hides the fact that these *behetrías* were not fragmented local societies but organized polities of varying size and extent. The Inka state was simply the latest and most successful polity to expand rapidly enough to become a power that could not be easily opposed, while incorporating other more local states under its authority. In central Peru, archaeologists have found a decline in the evidence of high-status activities and goods in Inka-period sites occupied by local people. The high-status remains were found instead in Inka-constructed *tampu* ('way stations') in regional centers such as Huánuco Pampa and in storage complexes that stood apart from local communities.[23] This evidence supports the argument that the Inka appropriated the goods that fueled and maintained the reciprocity expected of those who held authority. The Inka élite used these goods to create new relationships that tied local élites to Cusco by a chain of gifts, feasting, wives, and other honors (see Chap. 10). The highly visible constructions pointed to by those who have argued for Inka power and stability may in fact be evidence of the ephemeral quality of power built on ritual and ceremonial as a substitute for open conflict. There is little evidence of a bureaucratic or military presence in Huánuco Pampa, the only Inka provincial center that has been systematically excavated. Instead the archaeological evidence points to the use of the center for feasting and public display in which local élites received gifts and participated in ceremonies renewing their allegiance.[24]

---

[22] Altman, *Emigrants and society*, 44.
[23] Christine A. Hastorf, *Agriculture and the onset of political inequality before the Inka* (Cambridge, 1993), 227.
[24] Craig Morris and Donald Thompson, *Huánuco Pampa* (New York, 1985).

The Inka presence in the Andes, particularly on the peripheries of the state, was relatively recent – it is estimated that the region of Quito (now Ecuador) was not controlled from Cusco until the 1460s – and local sources published since the 1950s have made it clear that there was considerable variation at the local level in the relations between the Inka and the peoples under their control. This is not to deny the extent of Inka demands. The huge extent of material construction that took place during the relatively short period during which Inka élites ruled the Andes bears witness to the enormous amount of labor appropriated by the state. The lavish expenditure of labor not only in construction but in war, the displacement of entire populations, and the elimination of others, all indicate that under the Inka, the reciprocities based on kinship were in the process of transformation into the deeper and more long-standing inequalities based on the monopoly of resources by a ruling minority in the Andes. The Inka still formally "begged" labor services and retained the figment of reciprocity with lavish feasts and "gifts" to local élites, but the threat behind the gifts was clear not only to the Inka but to the people absorbed into the state as well.

But despite all of this, the Inka system in the 1520s was hardly a monolithic state. Franklin Pease has suggested that, rather than a central-ized authoritarian state that collapsed with the death of its ruler, the Inka system can be better understood as a network of asymmetrical relation-ships, ritually confirmed, that were established between the Inka and the polities that made up the empire self-denominated Tawantinsuyu (his-pano-Quechua: Tahuantinsuyo).[25] Those relationships, established both with local élites and with the more important regional deities, were not abstract but were continually renegotiated, as evidenced by the "rebel-lions" inside the frontiers of the state throughout its existence. Local sources indicate that, despite Inka willingness to use brutal tactics against enemies, internal or external, the authority of the state rested on a carefully structured web of alliances with regional deities and the élites of the polities that made up the Inka system. The war over the succession in Cusco opened the entire network of alliances for a process of renego-tiation that might have been accomplished by Atawallpa but was reini-tiated and prolonged by the appearance of the Spaniards in the Andes. The conclusions reached by the archaeologists responsible for the exca-

[25] Franklin Pease, *Curacas, Reciprocidad y Riqueza* (Lima, 1992), 21; and his general history, *Perú, hombre y historia, II, Entre el siglo XVI y el XVIII* (Lima, 1992), 65–77.

vation of Huánuco Pampa suggest that Inka power may well have been "bought" with lavish ritual and ceremonial activity.

It is rather ironic that the great centers and monuments constructed by the Incas in similar styles in far-removed parts of the Andes have created the impression of a powerful, stable, and relatively uniform state. When we narrow our focus to the actual operation of a specific region the picture changes to one of diversity and a system of government almost impossible to conceive of in terms designed for European nation states. The Inca political and economic achievement was based in large part on principles so dynamic they almost ensured that the state itself would be ephemeral.[26]

The Inka maintained and perhaps even promoted cultural and linguistic diversity among the various societies that were included in Tawantinsuyu, and the regional deities played an important part in tying them to Cusco. The Inka courted the regional deities, honoring them with gifts of valued objects as well as productive resources. Among the regional deities favored by the Inka were Pacha Kamaq, whose shrine was on the central coast at the mouth of the Lurín River; Paria Kaka (known by his colonial name Pariacaca), who watched over his people from a snow-capped mountain at the watershed of the western Andean range in Jauja; and a northern deity, Catequil, in Huamachuco. The Inka alliance with Pacha Kamaq permitted the regional deity, and the polity associated with it, to aid the expansion of the Inka and serve its own interests at the same time. The Inka built shrines for "sons" of Pacha Kamaq in areas not yet under the direct control of the state, as well as in other areas that were within the southern core of Inka territory nearer to Cusco.

Regional deities took an active part in Inka politics. The traditions of Huarochirí record that Pariacaca sent a "son" to help the Inka put down a series of rebellions during the rule of the Inka Tupa Yupanqui (also written Thupa Yupanki). In return, the Inka gave offerings and support to Pariacaca, assigning him retainers and accepting the ritual responsibilities of a descendant of the regional deity. Catequil, in the north, was reported by the Augustinian friars who entered the region in the 1550s to be "adored and revered from Quito to Cusco, the *huaca* [regional deity] most feared by the Indians."[27]

The regional deities were crucial to Inka power because their predic-

---

[26] Morris and Thompson, *Huánuco Pampa*, 166.
[27] Augustinos, [1561], *Relación de la religión y ritos del Perú hecho por los padres agustinos*, ed. Lucila Castro de Trelles (Lima, 1992), 18.

tions could buttress the power of an Inka, or they could undermine it. As long as the regional deities foresaw victory and success for the Inka, challenge to Inka authority was less likely, and his power was real. The regional deities' participation in Inka state politics could facilitate their own expansion as long as their predictions came to pass, but if they, and their priests, failed to chart the course of events successfully, their failure could have serious consequences. If they predicted that an aspirant to power would fail, and he turned out to be successful, he was likely to take action against the regional deity for its "lies." The civil war that devastated the Andes after the death of Huayna Cápac gave rise to several cases of retribution against regional deities. The shrine of Catequil was ransacked by Atawallpa in retribution for its prediction of a victory by his half-brother and rival, and Atawallpa also abused the priests of Pacha Kamaq for the "lies" of the regional deity. Pacha Kamaq had not only failed to predict Huayna Cápac's death but had first sided with Atawallpa's foe in the civil war by predicting his victory, and later dismissed the threat of the Spaniards, predicting that Atawallpa would eliminate the strange invaders.[28]

Amid the invasion crisis, then, Inka prospects for recovery seemed to depend on forging new alliances. Manco Inca's faction hoped to coopt the still little-known Spanish army. Manco's first priority after gaining the support of the Huanca/Spanish forces outside Cusco was to end the war that had divided the Andes for a decade, driving the forces that had supported Atawallpa from the core area of the Inka state. The Inka's forces joined the Huanca/Spanish force, returning to Jauja to attack the warriors of Quito. They arrived too late, but the Huanca repelled the invaders, and the combined Spanish/Inka force drove them out of the central Andes. From an Andean perspective, the victory at Jauja marked the end of the civil war, after which the Inka would proceed to consolidate his control by reestablishing the ritual ties and gifts that bound the Andean polities to Cusco. In 1532–1535 it seemed by no means unrealistic to hope that Cusco could fashion a manipulative alliance to steer Spain, as it had steered much bigger military forces before.

Seen from this perspective, the Inka's behavior during the 3 years that followed the withdrawal of the forces of Quito makes more sense. Pizarro's distribution of *encomiendas*, granting virtually unlimited authority

---

[28] Agustinos, *Relación*, 19; Pedro Pizarro, *Relación del descubrimiento y conquista de los reinos del Perú* (Lima, 1978), 34.

over Andean people to Spaniards, meant nothing unless the Spaniards could exercise that authority, and it is not difficult to understand how the Inka could see the Spaniards and their actions, violent and brutal as they were, as tools for the reprisals that Manco meant to conduct in the process of reestablishing his own Cusco-based authority. Violent reprisals were a common part of Inka tactics. When the Spaniards moved into the highlands from the coast to meet Atawallpa, they were amazed to find most of the settlements destroyed as a result, they were told, of the war between Waskhar and Atawallpa. Francisco de Jerez was told by a local chief that Atawallpa had killed 4,000 of a total 5,000 men under the chief's authority, and Carlos Sempat, using the *khipu* ('knotted cord') records of local polities interpreted later for the Spaniards, has estimated that the loss of adult men to Atawallpa's forces in Jauja was approximately 75 to 80 percent.[29]

The new Inka's initial support of the Spaniards' projects makes even more sense if we can see the Spaniards from an Andean perspective as useful auxiliaries, not unlike the Cañari whom the state had used in its expeditions to the peripheries. Expansion north was at least temporarily blocked by a strong force in Quito that would not be taken easily; southern explorations might result in campaigns that could be more easily won. Manco had no way of knowing that other Spaniards commanded by Sebastián de Benalcázar, aided by local polities antagonistic to the Inka, had taken on the Quito warriors. With the Cusco faction temporarily compliant, Spaniards were able to enter the Inka's sacred center, Cusco, in 1535. There a few witnesses beheld the innermost rites of the "children of the Sun," including the "feeding" of the mummified deceased Inka, before pillaging dismantled the holy city.

The data from this period leave the impression of two very different scripts, telling different stories, that have been mixed together. Francisco Pizarro acted as the governor of a conquest society in the process of organization and consolidation, while at the same time Manco – operating in the same physical space – was attempting to rebuild the complicated alliances that supported the system of rule from Cusco. Pizarro's next act was the foundation of Lima. If the Spaniards were not to remain entirely dependent on the good will of the Andean polities among whom they moved in the highlands, they had to have ready access to the sea, their only means of communication with other Spanish foundations and

---

[29] Sempat, "La gran vejación y destruición," *Transiciones*, 35.

the source of news, goods, and reinforcements if necessary. Increasingly mindful of that, Pizarro determined to move to the coast the capital of the new state he claimed to rule. He sent out parties to determine a proper site, and in January 1535 the city of Lima, originally named "City of the Kings," was formally established. The city was built and supplied by the Andean polities who lived in the area, at least one of whose leaders became an important supporter of the Spaniards.

The Spanish faction was expanding, not only as a result of the arrival of more Europeans but also as a result of its alliances with other Andean polities. It is hardly surprising that Manco Inca finally decided to rid himself of his now obviously sacreligious and untrustworthy allies. In the spring of 1536, Inka forces gathered in response to messages from the Inka to his kinsmen serving as governors and representatives of the Inka in other parts of the Andes. They resolved to win the holy city back by siege. The Spaniards estimated that the Inka force that attacked and besieged Cusco consisted of from 100,000 to 200,000 men. The first attack was almost successful, and the Andeans besieged the city for more than 4 months, cutting Cusco off from all contact with the coast. Other forces were sent down to the coast to attack Lima, but the Andean polities of the valley, seeing a chance to repel Cusco's demands, defended the city against the attackers. Pizarro sent desperate messages back to Panama pleading for help; in July 1536 the authorities in Panama reported to Santo Domingo that "the rebellion of Cusco has spread from province to province and [the Indians] continue to rise in rebellion; rebel chiefs will soon be within forty leagues [about 120 miles] of the City of the Kings [Lima]."[30] The siege of Lima was not broken until August, when Manco's forces, no longer maintained by the vast system of state storehouses, began to drift off to prepare their fields for planting.

The failure of Manco's attack meant the end of the Inka system. In 1539 Manco and those loyal to him withdrew into the eastern part of the Andes, establishing themselves in the broken jungle region that slopes gradually down to the Amazon Basin at a place known as Vilcabamba. There he followed the pattern characteristic of the people who traditionally harassed the Inka. His troops raided the highland areas once controlled by his ancestors. The Spaniards as well as Andeans who were

[30] "Pascual de Andagoya y el Lic. Espinosa a la Audiencia de Santo Domingo, Panama, 27 de julio de 1536," *Cartas del Peru,* 218–219.

either actively or passively loyal to them were harassed by Manco's forces. Manco became, in reality, the leader of a small polity on the periphery of the Andes. The vast territory once ruled from Cusco became, as it had been before the expansion of Cusco, a collection of *behetrías*, or self-governing polities of varying size, whose élites competed with one another for lands, resources, and power. In this fragmented situation the Spaniards had become important players, and ambitious native élites moved to assure their relationships with the new, rising power in the Andes.

LOCAL POLITIES IN THE PLUNDER ECONOMY

From 1536 on, the history of the Spanish invasion can no longer be told from Cusco, but it is also misleading to accept the story as told from Lima. European versions of this period describe the civil wars among the Spaniards, but all of these sources, valuable as they are, emphasize the fratricidal struggles between Spanish factions. Spanish sources, however, contain evidence that the Andean polities took active parts in power struggles in their own rights. The Europeans focused only on their own motivations, yielding oversimplified political interpretations.

From the outbreak of the struggle for power among the Inka factions to the end of the battles among the Spaniards, the majority of the fighting forces on all sides were Andean, not Spanish. Losses to the Andean polities in lives and resources were enormous. And while many groups did respond to Manco's call for warriors to attack the Spaniards, there were factions among the Inka lineages, notably that of the noble called Paullu Inca in hispano-Quechua, who refused to join the attack against the Spaniards in 1536. The Spaniards were well aware of how much their survival – let alone their ultimate victory – depended upon the continued rivalries among the Inka lineages. Years after the attack on Cusco, a Spaniard wrote to the crown that Paullu was "a true friend of the Christians and Your Majesty, . . . and it is the truth that he has been a great pillar of support in these parts, for if he had fallen and tried to destroy things, the extinction of all the Spaniards living in Peru, little by little, would have begun."[31] Mancio Sierra, who was present at the

---

[31] Luis de Morales, quoted by Carlos Sempat Assadourian, "Dominio colonial y señores étnicos en el espacio andino, *Transiciones*, 153, note 3.

capture of Atawallpa in Cajamarca, commented that "if the Inkas had not favored the Spaniards, it would have been impossible to win this kingdom."[32]

Throughout the years that Europeans called the civil wars between the Spaniards, Spaniards and Andeans fought – and died – together. The Spaniards saw the struggle as a battle among Spaniards; no one ever asked the Andean polities who made up the majority of the fighting forces on both sides what they thought. In all of the battles of these years, ostensibly fought by Spaniards, Andean forces made up the majority of the combatants, as well as all of the maintenance personnel. Paullu supported the Pizarrist side in the conflict, blocking access to the coastal valleys with warriors armed with slings, and a Spanish witness later testified that in the final battle between the two forces, "the Indians on both sides gathered, and fought, and Paullu's warriors proved to be a great advantage to us because of their much greater numbers . . ."[33] Years later the great soldier-chronicler Pedro Cieza de León, author of the official chronicle of the wars between the Spaniards, said of the destruction caused by these wars among the natives of the coastal valleys of Ica and Nasca that "some trustworthy Spaniards told me that the greatest destruction to these Indians has come from the struggle between the two governors, Pizarro and Almagro."[34]

It is also clear that polities that had once been part of the Inka state did not wait upon the Inkas to develop their own strategies. Well before the Inka system was eliminated, the local polities were acting not only to ensure their survival but also to gain what they could from the struggle for power among the Inka factions. Some of the Spaniards' most loyal allies faced certain retribution for their earlier support of Waskhar and therefore stood only to gain if the Spaniards eliminated their nemesis. The Huanca polity of Jauja chose the wrong side in the struggle between Waskhar and Atawallpa and had only Atawallpa's vengeance to look forward to when the Spaniards appeared in Cajamarca. Others had already suffered from Atawallpa's forces.

In other cases Andean polities seem to have chosen to side with one or another Spanish factions with more positive objectives in mind. Some

[32] Cited by Sempat, "Dominio colonial," *Transiciones*, 153.
[33] Cited by Sempat, "La gran vejación y destruicción," *Transiciones*, 54.
[34] Sempat, "La gran vejación y destruicción," *Transiciones*, 54.

sources suggest that the conflicts between first the Inka and then later the Spaniards provided opportunities for polities to renew longstanding enmities. In a quarrel over coca lands between the polities of Chaclla and Canta near Lima that was carried to the Spanish courts in the 1550s, the response of each side to the Inka seems to have been dictated primarily by the choices made by the local ethnic adversary. Witnesses in the case stated that Canta used Manco Inca's call for support to draw Chaclla leaders to a meeting place where people of Canta killed them. Other witnesses testified in turn that Chaclla accused Canta leaders of performing rites to kill Tupa Inka Yupanqui, the father of Huayna Cápac, for which crime the Canta leaders were killed and their lands assigned to Chaclla.[35] Here the Inka, and the Spaniards later, seem to be external forces used by the local polities in their longstanding conflict with one another. This case, as well as others, makes it clear that at least in the Central Andes, local groups continued their struggles with one another under the cover of the enforced truce imposed by the Inka, even seeking when possible to use the power of the state against their neighbors.

In suppressing the warfare that seemed to have been expanding before the Inka arrived, prehispanic Inka rule also had frozen the structure of authority, together with access to additional goods and labor that underwrote and legitimated authority, at the state current when the Inka, with their access to coercive force far beyond the means of any local group, took control. But the effect of removing the negotiation of rank and status from local control was, circa 1532, recent enough for local societies, trained in their own histories through the songs of the deeds of their ancestors and heroes, to remember their pre-Inka past. And the disintegration of Inka power in the 1530s removed the coercive threat that maintained the artificially static organization of local polities. The Spaniards had unintentionally opened the playing field for the renegotiation of rank and authority.

As the Spaniards gradually took control of the Andes, and as the polities that once comprised the Inka state negotiated their relationships to the new power, it soon became clear that there was considerable variation in the internal organization of local polities. That variation was recognized by the Spaniards, who were attempting to define the relation-

---

[35] See María Rostworowski de Diéz Canseco, *Conflicts over coca fields in XVIth-century Peru*, Memoirs of the Museum of Anthropology, University of Michigan, No. 21. (Ann Arbor, 1988), 145, 180.

ships of these societies to a new central authority. Like the Inka before them, they wanted to define a fixed social order in the local polities in order to make it easier to tie that order to the colonial system.

The Spaniards later made strenuous efforts to impose upon the Andes a vision of a highly stratified social system in which access to authority was restricted to a specific group of people who could be defined and codified according to European images of hereditary authority. However, a close examination of Spanish sources from the period before the 1560s suggests strongly that the prosperity and success of societies of varying scale in the Andes depended upon the abilities of those who held authority to negotiate successfully with the forces that affected the security and prosperity of the group. Authority and leadership in Andean societies was a complex process of interaction among many people. The local elders who spoke for the lineages and segmented kin groups, or *ayllus* functioned on a more minimal level, together with the variety of specialists whose function it was to communicate with and interpret the messages of the regional deities and the ancestors to their descendants. Authority was negotiated and adjusted as people dealt with the conditions of their lives. This characteristic of Andean polities played an important part in the ability of these groups to respond rapidly, and often effectively, to the cataclysmic changes that affected their world during the conquest period.

Those changes constituted a major challenge to the capacity of Andean societies to maintain and reproduce themselves. Perhaps the most immediate evidence of that challenge was the demographic disaster that affected the Andes in the sixteenth century. After the first massive expropriation of the accumulated goods of Andean society that the Spaniards took as plunder, they too depended upon their access to Andean labor for the wealth they accumulated. But within a few decades after the Spaniards appeared, the fundamental differences between European and Andean cultures began to undermine the basic organization of Andean societies. The cataclysmic drop in the population of the Andean area, especially in comparison with the growing demands of the Spanish population, put severe strains on the capacity of the societies of the region to reproduce themselves.

The preconquest and early colonial demography of the Andean area has been a subject of dispute since the sixteenth century. The evident wealth of the Inka empire had to rest upon a dense population, particularly in view of the limited sources of energy beyond that of the people themselves. The miles of abandoned terraces that strike any traveler in the Andes are witness to a large population sometime in the past. But many of those terraces are difficult if not impossible to date, which only increases controversy regarding the time of their construction and abandonment. The size of the population of the Inka state in 1532 has been estimated as high as 32 million, although other scholars regard that estimate as exaggerated. Maria Rostworowski has pointed to the devastation of the Inka expansion, the slaughter and relocation of entire populations, and the abandoned terraces and fields noted by the first Spaniards to enter the Andes as evidence that the population of the Andean area may well have reached its maximum prior to the establishment of the Inka empire and have declined under the rule of the Inka.[36]

The Inka insisted that they had brought prosperity to the polities they conquered, ending the constant warfare that prevailed before they appeared. Inka rule may have blocked local conflicts, but the continued expansion of the state, as well as risings and rebellions within the core of the Inka system, exacted a heavy toll in lives and other resources lost to their societies. But whatever the demographic cost of constructing and maintaining the Inka system, the toll of death that accompanied its destruction were enormous. It was acknowledged to be devastating by eyewitnesses as well as by succeeding generations, and the loss of population to war and famine was multiplied by the introduction of European diseases. Smallpox, measles, and even the common cold were deadly to people who had no immunological resistance, and epidemics spread rapidly, each leaving thousands of dead in their wake. It is generally assumed that the sudden death of Huayna Cápac, which began the war for succession that ended with the disintegration of the Inka state, was due to his having contracted smallpox.

The first epidemic, estimated to have swept through the Andes about 1525, has been diagnosed on the basis of descriptions of the appearance of people who contracted the disease as smallpox, although the penetra-

---

[36] On Andean demography in general, see Noble David Cook, *Demographic collapse. Indian Peru, 1520–1620* (New York, 1981). For the high estimate of Andean population before the appearance of the Spaniards, see Henry Dobyns, "Estimating aboriginal American population: An appraisal of techniques with a new hemispheric estimate," *Current Anthropology* 7(4) (1966), 24–31; and for a discussion of Andean demographic history that points out some of the problems with current estimates, see Carlos Sempat, "La gran vejación y destruición," *Transiciones*, 19–24.

tion of that epidemic, documented only as far south as Panama, to Peru has been questioned.[37] A second major epidemic hit in 1546, originating in Cusco and moving north. A third, again smallpox, spread through the Andes from Lima in 1558–1559. Finally at the end of the century, the area was devastated by three waves of different illnesses. The first was another wave of smallpox that began in Cusco in 1585 and moved north, reaching Lima a year later. Then a new disease, probably either typhus or bubonic plague, came from the area of Panama, reaching Peru about 1590; at the same time, an epidemic of grippe originating in Potosí moved north through the Andes.[38] Smallpox and measles ravaged Quito in the northern Andes in every decade between 1531 and 1560, and again during the last decade of the sixteenth century.[39]

There has been a great deal of controversy over the demographic patterns of the Andes in the sixteenth century – and indeed in the Americas as a whole – but there seems to be little question that the population fell sharply through the sixteenth century. The coastal population was hardest hit. Between 1525 and 1575 it has been estimated that the population of the coastal societies in central Peru fell to about 4 percent of its preconquest size. Many depopulated villages were completely taken over by outsiders.

The catastrophe was less extreme in the highlands, but even there two-thirds to three-fourths of the population is estimated to have died during the first 40 years following the entry of the Spaniards.[40] The depopulation of the Quito region has been estimated at 85–90 percent in the 50 years between 1520 and 1570.[41]

People died – of war, of disease, of famine – and other people left their communities in enormous numbers during this period. In some cases it is possible to reconstruct a fairly accurate estimate of the loss to specific polities of their people. The Huancas of the Jauja area kept a record of their losses in human and other resources from 1533, which was presented to the Spaniards in 1561, in support of their claim for restitu-

---

[37] See Sempat, "La gran vejación y destruicción," *Transiciones*, 20–21.

[38] Dobyns, "An outline of Andean epidemic history to 1720," *Bulletin of the History of Medicine* 37 (1963), 493–515.

[39] Karen Powers, *Andean journeys: Migration, ethnogenesis and the state in colonial Quito* (Albuquerque, NM, 1995), 17.

[40] The standard work on Andean demographic history is Noble David Cook, *Demographic collapse*; see also C. T. Smith, "Despoblación de los Andes centrales en el siglo XVI," *Revista del Museo Nacional del Perú* 35 (Lima, 1969), 77–91.

[41] Powers, *Andean journeys*, 17.

tion. The province of Jauja at the time of the Spanish invasion was reported to have 27,000 warriors. This category, equivalent to the first group of the Inka census categories, was described by Guaman Poma (de Ayala) as "valiant men, soldiers," between the ages of 25 and 50 – in other words, adult male heads of households. The Spanish took thousands of these men and additional women with them in the march to Cusco as warriors, bearers, and servants. Over 3,600 warriors accompanied the Spaniards to Cusco, to Lima, and into the provinces between 1533 and the Inka rising in 1536. About 5,000 more men and some women accompanied the Spaniards to carry provisions and booty, build fortifications, repair bridges, and otherwise maintain the fighting forces.[42] If these numbers are compared to the fighting forces available at the time of the conquest, it appears that nearly one-third of the total adult male population of Jauja left the province in the company of the Europeans between 1533 and 1548. Many of these men died in battle. All but a few hundred never returned to their homes. Using the same kind of records, Carlos Sempat calculated the loss of people to three Huanca groups from the time of Huayna Cápac to 1548 at between 79 and 86 percent.[43]

This is not to say that Andean people did not leave their communities under normal conditions, voluntarily as well as involuntarily. Even in normal times the Andean population was – and is – a mobile one. People moved from one ecological zone to another to plant and harvest their crops; they did labor service, or *mit'a* (hispano-Quechua: *mita*), in peripheral areas or in warfare for the Inka; and they were sent as colonists to specialized resource areas for their own polities or for the state.

But in the crisis of the conquest period, migration took on other forms. *Entradas*, or expeditions of exploration and conquest to other areas, forced large numbers of people out of their communities to accompany the Spaniards. Almagro's expedition to Chile in 1535 took at least 12,000 warriors from the polities of Cusco, Collao (Qullaw), and Charcas under the command of Manco Inca's brother, Paullu, in addition to the *yana* (retainers) appropriated by the Spaniards.[44] Gonzalo Pizarro's ill-fated expedition into the Amazon drained Quito of between 6,000 and

[42] Waldemar Espinosa Soriano, *Destrucción del Imperio de los Incas* (Lima, 1973): 68, 97, 129, 154, 182.

[43] Andres de Vega, "La descripción que se hizo en la provincia de Xauxa por la instrucción de Su Majestad," in Marcos Jiménez de la Espada (ed.), *Relaciones geográficas de Indias, I* (Madrid, 1881), 79–95; Carlos Sempat, "La gran vejación y destruicción," in *Transiciones*, 47.

[44] Sempat, "La gran vejación y destruicción," in *Transiciones* 55–56.

10,000 native people.[45] Other migrations were part of strategies of survival initiated by the Andeans themselves. In many cases individuals seeking to escape the demands made on them simply fled to other areas to become 'outsiders', or *forasteros*, cut off from their communities and seemingly safe from levies. But in other cases migration was orchestrated by community leaders. In the northern Andes the Andean population in the region around Quito moved away from the area of Spanish settlement, diffusing into the *montaña*, the lower slopes of the Andes to the east and west, whose population seems to have increased between the 1530s and the 1560s. From the 1560s, however, the native population near urban Quito increased enormously, putting severe pressure on the land and other resources around the Spanish city.

Karen Powers has suggested that the complicated and unusual demographic patterns of the area of Quito were the product of not only Spanish depredation and European epidemics but also Andean initiative. The close proximity of ecological zones in the northern Andes, where people can travel from the Pacific coast into the Andean valleys to the eastern lowlands in a few days, made possible a network of politico-economic relationships that linked local groups through both outlier colonies and specialized trade, and people seeking to escape Spanish demands moved to the less accessible areas familiar to them. Migration not only provided a refuge to individuals; it was a strategy used by local élites to limit exactions on the community by hiding people from the Spaniards. During the second half of the sixteenth century, highland leaders in Quito even competed with one another for population.

The Andean people responded to the demographic disasters of the conquest period by drawing on Andean precedents and traditions to deal with the new conditions they faced. The same pattern can be seen in their reaction to the primary Spanish institution of the conquest period, the *encomienda*, through which the Europeans drew upon the resources of Andean societies to provide them with the goods that they could translate into wealth, status, and power in their own culture. Adapted from the Reconquest, the *encomienda* was formalized and codified in the Caribbean at the end of the fifteenth century, when the native population of the islands was parceled out among the Spanish colonists for their virtually unlimited use. The first governor of Hispaniola, Juan de Ovando, regularized and institutionalized the practice, which bore a

---

[45] Powers, *Andean journeys*, 16.

striking resemblance to the medieval tradition of frontier administration of the same name. The people of the area newly claimed for Spain were distributed among the conquerors by the leader of the expedition "in *encomienda*" as part of the division of the spoils of conquest. The grantee, or *encomendero*, received full authority to use the Indians as he saw fit. In return he was charged with providing his people with religious instruction and the other benefits of European civilization. He was also obligated to keep horse and arms prepared for the defense of the land, whether against outside invaders or the people under his charge. Part of that obligation included residing in the city within whose jurisdiction his *encomienda* fell, and housing and feeding people in times of emergency.

The first *encomiendas* in Peru were distributed by Pizarro to the men present at the capture of Atawallpa in 1533 and were grants of authority over thousands of people, assigned in terms of a *kuraka* (indigenous ruler) and all of the people subject to him. As all the Europeans in the Andes admitted openly, the wealth that could be extracted from the new territory depended entirely upon the native Andean population; the importance of the right of jurisdiction over men and women was basic to the *encomienda*. The *encomienda* altered the initial plunder of the Spaniards' first forays among the local people, refining the practice to a more institutionalized and regular form of plunder in which the right to appropriate the goods and labor of the native population was restricted to one man alone: the *encomendero*. A grant of *encomienda* defined the legal rights of particular Spaniards – the grantees – who were authorized, in reward for their services to the crown and the conquest, to assume and exercise whatever authority they could make effective over the people assigned to them. This included making virtually unrestricted use of Indian labor and goods, to the extent that they were not limited by the resistance, passive or active, of the Indians themselves.

Although the grants of *encomienda* define the rights of the *encomendero* in relation to other Spaniards, they say little about the relations expected or established between the *encomendero* and the people assigned to him. Those relationships were hammered out between the 1530s and the 1550s as *encomendero* demands were accepted by the people or resisted until a modus vivendi – often an uneasy one – was reached. In the course of that often violent bargaining process, a rough political system emerged and lasted for more than three decades. Particularly when the Spaniards moved into lands in which there already existed a political system that Spanish culture recognized as such, the relationships that permitted an *encomendero* to extract surplus from the local population were the product of negotiation between the Spaniard and the local élites. Local "native lords" or "natural lords" (*señores naturales*), who often regarded themselves as allies of the Spaniards, used the new relationship to gain advantages for themselves, and sometimes for their people as well. The resulting system was a partnership – albeit what at this distance looks like a highly unequal one – between the Spaniard who made demands and the Andean élites who passed them on to their people.

There were enough similarities between the *encomienda* as it functioned in the Andes, and the pattern of redistribution to privileged élites employed by the Inka, to make the acceptance of the Spanish institution by local polities understandable. Andean institutions could have provided some precedent for the relations between the Spanish *encomendero* and the *kuraka*s under his authority. The Inka governor was also an outsider with authority over the *kuraka*s. The *encomendero*'s demands for labor could be defined in terms of the state's similar demands, and the external similarities between the generosity expected of Andean leaders and the lavish table that was traditional in medieval noble households cannot be overlooked. Many of the leaders of ethnic groups maneuvered skillfully in the complicated political scene engendered by the war for succession and the Spanish presence. These same leaders, at least initially, chose to accept the *encomienda* structure; however, they defined it for themselves and their people. Without their cooperation the *encomienda* as a mechanism for extracting goods and services from the Andean population would have been worthless.

The *kuraka* who accepted the Spanish *encomendero* as his local overlord often built up a relationship with him reminiscent of the ties of ceremony, reciprocal gifts, and feasting that linked the local ethnic élite to the representatives of the Inka state. The *kuraka* of Huarochirí, Ninavilca, apparently built up a close relationship with the Spaniards, who praised him as among the most able and acculturated of the *kuraka*s within the jurisdiction of Lima. Ninavilca, baptized Don Antonio, was one of two *kuraka*s charged with the administration of the Indians living around Lima, a position that brought him the title of Regidor de Indios ('magistrate of Indians'), with power to enforce the orders of the Spaniards and supervise the affairs of the people under his authority. His daughter was brought up in the household of his *encomendero* – a practice reminiscent of the education of young *kuraka*s in Cusco or in the provincial capital under the Inka – and was later married to a Spaniard.[46] All of this undoubtedly represented an extension of Don Antonio's prestige and status within his own community. On the local level the *encomendero*, with his lavish table to which the *kuraka* was often invited, could be equated with the Inka governor. According to a Spanish official some years later, "[T]hese encomenderos each set themselves up as an Inka, and appropriated by virtue of the encomiendas all of the rights, tributes, and services granted by that land to the Inka."[47] And Guaman Poma, also writing later, had some vivid comments to make about the *encomenderos'* adoption of the panoply of Andean society. The *encomendero*, he complained, "has himself carried in a litter like the Inca with drums and dances [taquies] when he arrives at [his people's] communities."[48]

All of this demanded the presence of the *encomendero* in the Andean communities, and successful *encomenderos* spent much of their time in their *encomiendas*, returning to the urban centers to oversee the conversion of the goods they extracted from the Indians into merchandise for sale to other Europeans. The *kuraka*, with whom the *encomendero* maintained a close relationship, transmitted the *encomendero*'s demands to his people and organized the production of the goods he wanted. Initially the Europeans adapted themselves to the structure of Andean society, itself well organized to produce a wide variety of goods by utilizing social relationships. These social relationships permitted the *encomendero* to lay claim, through the *kuraka*, to the goods he wanted to maintain his household and to enter the European economy with the surplus he extracted from the Indians. It was possible to translate the Spaniards' demands for goods in terms of the traditional claim of political authority, to labor services from the local community. It was the task of the *kuraka* to make that claim for the *encomendero*, translating the latter's demands into labor time invested in producing the goods Europeans demanded, generally on the lands once assigned to the state and the regional deities, and appropriated by the conquerors as successors to the Inka authorities.

[46] Waldemar Espinosa Soriano, "El alcalde mayor indígena en el virreinato del Perú," *Anuario de Estudios Americanos* 17 (Seville, 1960), 202; Biblioteca Nacional del Perú, doc. A-36, Libros Notariales de Diego Gutiérrez, 1545–1555, Lima, August 7, 1550.
[47] Fernando de Santillán, "Relación del orígen, descendencia, política y gobierno de los Incas," in *Tres relaciones de antiguedades peruanas* (Asunción del Paraguay, 1950), 57.
[48] Felipe Guaman Poma de Ayala, *Nueva corónica y buen gobierno (Codex peruvienne illustre)* (Paris, 1936), 554.

The *encomenderos* made lavish use of the fine craftsmen of Andean society. The first buildings of Lima were erected by Huanca craftsmen sent from Jauja by their *kurakas* with Francisco Pizarro, and other conquerors followed that example.[49] The members of Andean society erected the palaces of their *encomenderos* and sent men to plant their fields and guard their herds – both llama and alpaca herds expropriated from the Inka state and cattle and sheep imported from the Caribbean. The Spaniards also used native labor as servants and household help. The *kurakas* of the Chupachos of Huanuco testified in 1549 that they sent forty people to serve in the household of their *encomendero*, Gómez Arias.[50] Skilled tapestry weavers prepared the cloth that decorated the palaces of the conquerors, and skilled craftsmen carved the new coats of arms awarded by the crown in stone over the palace doors in Cusco.

Although the conquerors could live luxuriously in Peru on the contributions of the people they held in *encomienda*, they could not found a lineage and gain the wealth that assured social position without exacting goods from the Indians that could be converted into commodities – goods valued for the price they could bring rather than the use that could be made of them. The exploitation of silver and gold mines in the first years following European invasion is one of the best examples that can be found of the use of Andean forms of production for the benefit of the Europeans – a use that also permitted Andean élites to accumulate resources of their own. From the 1530s to the 1580s, members of the Andean élite mobilized the productive mechanisms of their own society to produce the precious metals demanded by the Europeans as well as to feed and clothe both the Europeans and members of their own society at work in the mining centers. In doing so they adapted quickly to the European market system, rapidly monopolizing not only the production of ore itself but also the supply of foodstuffs and other necessities that maintained the growing mine city of Potosí (now in Bolivia).

The *kurakas* of the southern highlands sent *mitayos* or rotating labor quotas, to mine silver in Potosí, using traditional Andean techniques of production. The friable surface ores were easily extracted and were rich in silver that could be purified by melting the silver free of embedded ore in a wind-heated furnace called a *huayra* (Quechua: *Wayra*), fueled

---

[49] Espinosa Soriano, *Destrucción*, 154.
[50] Marie Helmer, "La visitación de los Indios Chupachos: Inka et encomendero, 1549," *Travaux et Memoires de l'Institut Francais d'Etudes Andines* 5 (Lima-Paris, 1955–1956), 42.

by llama dung. But despite the use of traditional Andean methods, the scale of the operation was far beyond that of mining under the Inka state. It worked by drawing large amounts of unskilled labor from the local communities. The laborers, working their *mit'a* turns under the direction of their *kuraka*s, excavated ore and sold it to skilled miners, who reduced it according to the traditional techniques of their craft, taking a share of the metal for their services. The *kuraka* then passed the metal to the *encomendero* in payment of the tribute assigned his community, retaining any residual metal for the community.[51]

In these early decades the Europeans held only the mine claims themselves, turning to the Andean miners for the extraction and processing of the ores. Many of the miners sent to the mines by their *kuraka*s remained there, paying the entire tribute assessment of their communities in silver through their labor – a clear adaptation of the traditional Andean *mitmaq* colonists sent to exploit particular resource oases. The *kuraka*s sent foodstuffs and other goods to the market in Potosí, trading them for silver. Cloth, maize, *chuñu* (freeze-dried potatoes), jerked meat, chili peppers, and coca obtained from resource areas held by the communities were sent to Potosí on llama trains, where they were sold to European and Indian peddlers. The *kuraka*s also rapidly adopted the cultivation of European products such as grapes (for wine) and cattle, which found a ready market in Potosí.[52] The trade was not a small-scale affair; in the 1560s, when Potosí had already entered into a crisis of production and its population had begun to decline, a Spanish official noted that the trade in cloth and foodstuffs amounted to about 300,000 pesos, most of which was in the hands of the members of Andean society.[53]

Although in most cases the *encomenderos* depended upon the Indians to produce the tribute goods however they saw fit, in some cases the Spaniards became active entrepreneurs, introducing new goods and new techniques of production and using their access to Indian labor. Sometimes they enjoyed the participation of their *kuraka*s, and sometimes they operated independently. *Mit'a* laborers assigned to an *encomendero* household could also be used for other purposes by enterpris-

---

[51] Andean mining techniques of the conquest period are described in Carlos Sempat Assadourian, "La producción de la mercancía y dinero en la formación del mercado interno colonial," *Economía*, I, 2 (Lima, August, 1978), 9–55.

[52] John V. Murra, "Aymara lords and their European agents at Potosí," *Nova Americana*, I(1) (Turin, 1978), 231–243.

[53] Juan de Matienzo, *Gobierno del Peru (1567)*, ed. and prologue by Guillermo Lohmann Villena (Lima-Paris, 1967), 132.

ing Spaniards, and the conquerors found many people, voluntarily or involuntarily cut off from their own communities, who were ready to adapt to the culture of the invaders and learn the skills that helped them survive in a new milieu. It is not easy to distinguish between a labor force that still functioned according to traditional norms and a labor force that was mobilized on European terms, but a few examples should suffice to give an idea of the variety of activities initiated by the *encomenderos*.

A list of the *encomiendas* of Cusco prepared for Pedro de la Gasca in 1542 offers some insight into the sources of *encomendero* income. The document lists about sixty distinct grants, many of them originally assigned by Francisco Pizarro and later transferred, fused, or split among new holders in the course of the civil wars. It ranks the grants by estimated value to the holder, listing the number of people in each *encomienda* and the use made of them. The major sources of income for the *encomenderos* of Cusco in the 1540s were mining and coca leaf. The *encomenderos* demanded a fixed number of baskets of coca from their people per season, and they then sold the leaf to merchants who sent it to the mining areas. The people of Cusco provided about 10,000 baskets of coca per harvest to their *encomenderos*, and some of the most highly valued *encomiendas* were those in which the sole source of income noted was in coca. Other *encomenderos* regularly sent people to mine silver in Porco, or gold in Carabaya and Guallaripa – the latter mines in the *encomienda* of Francisco Pizarro. The income from ten *encomiendas* came solely from gold mines worked by the populations in their own respective lands.[54] In other cases the *encomenderos* drew upon Indian labor to introduce productive activities that reproduced those they knew in Europe. In 1539 Nicolás de Ribero, an *encomendero* and councilman of Lima, formed a fishing company with another Spaniard to provide fresh ocean fish for the city. Ribero contracted to provide eight fishermen to his partner, Juan Quintero, who agreed to run the operation and oversee the costs of the enterprise. In 1543, Doña Inéz Muñoz, the widow of Martín de Alcántara, gave power of attorney to Ribero and a companion to use the Indians of her *encomienda* as miners. That same year, 1543, Francisco de Ampuero, another *encomendero* of Lima, set up a partnership with a blacksmith, who sold the lands and the shop equipment to his new partner. Ampuero was to provide ten Indians to work in the

---

[54] Rafael Loredo, *Alardes y derramas* (Lima, 1942), 126–131.

shop, and the two agreed to share all profits equally.[55] Lucas Martínez Vergazo, holder of a large *encomienda* in Arequipa, organized an integrated productive operation centering around the mines he controlled in Tarapacá that included a mill, a cordage manufactory, a vineyard, a ranch, and several ships that plied the coast between Quilque, the port of Arequipa, and Ilo, in northern Chile, and that probably reached Lima as well.[56]

By the 1550s the organization of production through the *encomienda* was working smoothly. The *encomenderos* appropriated goods produced by the Indians as tribute and turned them into profits through the intermediartion of merchants, without fundamentally altering the productive system of Andean society. The great majority of these goods were traditional products of Andean society that could be converted into merchandise by transporting them to the new Spanish urban centers, particularly Potosí, where they were sold to the European population and its Andean employees permanently attached to these centers. Even transportation was provided through tribute assessments, in the form of requisitions of llamas that first packed the goods to market and were then transformed into merchandise themselves for their meat. A closer look at one of these traditional Andean goods, cloth – a product highly valued by Andean and European society alike – provides insight into the commercialization of traditional goods for European profit. Andean clothing consisted of straight panels that when shorter and narrower were turned into breechcloths and sleeveless shirts for men, and when longer and wider were wrapped around the body and pinned for women. *Cumbi* (a hispano-Quechua form of *q'umpi*), fine tapestry cloth woven by skilled weavers, was a prized gift – a mark of honor and status to receive and to use. It was also prized by the Spaniards. The rougher cloth worn as workaday clothing found a ready market in Lima, in the mining regions, and in the settlements of Chile to the south, where it was bought by Spaniards to clothe the native people working as household servants, as miners, and in other activities. Some of the Europeans established *obrajes* (mills or workshops) to produce cloth, sending Indians to work at looms brought from Europe. But in the decades immediately following the

[55] *The Harkness Collection in the Library of Congress. Documents from Early Peru. The Pizarros and the Almagros (1531–1578)* (Washington, D.C., 1936), 101, 110, 128.
[56] Efraín Trelles Aréstegui, "Lucas Martínez Vergazo: funcionamiento de una encomienda peruana inicial," thesis (Department of History, Pontificia Universidad Católica del Perú, 1980), 32–41. The thesis was published by the Catholic University of Lima (1983) under the same title.

Spanish invasion, a far more common way of obtaining piece goods was to get them directly from the native peoples as tribute, relying on traditional household production.

The activities of María Suárez, wife of an *encomendero* in Huánuco, provide a clear picture of the transformation of Andean cloth into a European commodity. In 1567 the Indians of her husband's *encomienda* brought her 100 pieces of women's clothing in tribute. She sent them to a merchant, Salvador Reyes, who had contracted to give the Indians 250 pesos in a marked bar of silver for the cloth. The Indians were ordered to turn the bar of silver over to her upon delivery of the cloth to Reyes. Reyes regularly bought tribute goods from Suárez. On January 17, 1567, a few days after the transaction just described, he paid the *kuraka*s of her husband's *encomienda* 375 pesos in a bar of silver for 150 pieces of tribute cloth, which the *kuraka*s delivered to María the same day. A few days later a merchant from Geneva arrived in Huánuco and picked up the tribute clothing as well as cotton cloth and *cumbi* in order "to bring it from this city to the City of the Kings [Lima] and from there to the kingdom of Chile in the first ship leaving for those kingdoms and there sell it at the best prices I can obtain."[57]

But the fit between the *encomienda* and the organization of local societies was far from exact. Even under the Inka many Andean polities were large, with a population that rivaled that of many contemporary European states. Their size made possible the accumulation that underlay the lavish public display that was part of the role of the leaders of Andean societies. As the numbers of Spaniards demanding *encomiendas* grew, Pizarro, as well as the authorities who succeeded him, often divided the subjects of a *kuraka* among several Spaniards. The greatest spokesman for native interests in Peru, Fray Domingo de Santo Tomás, complained in 1550 that the Spanish often divided a polity, which he called a province, into as many as three or four *encomiendas*. He railed about "the injustice against human and divine law and right that is done by taking away the vassals and towns of a supreme lord, because they are divided into as many lords as there are Spaniards receiving [an *encomienda*], and each of the leaders who were once subject to the supreme lord becomes himself an independent lord, and neither he nor his Indians obey [the supreme lord] any longer."[58]

---

[57] Libro Notarial de Hernando de Caçalla, Archive of Guillermo Gayoso G., Huánuco, Peru, Book 4 [1567], folios 1, 44.

[58] Quoted in Carlos Sempat Assadourian, "Dominio colonial y señores étnicos en el espacio andino," *Transiciones* (Lima, 1994), 157.

In order to understand how the events of this period affected the productive capacities of Andean societies, we have to look at the intimate connections between their political and economic organization. The Inka state limited the authority exercised by the "supreme lords," or rulers of local polities before the expansion of the Andean state, and there is considerable evidence that the disintegration of the state was seen by many as an opportunity to reassert past authority, or even expand it.

The key to how the fragmentation of Andean polities occurred is precisely the fact that Fray Domingo noted: The Spaniards were able to find native aspirants to power with whom they could operate effectively. Europeans would function with any leader who could assure them a regular supply of goods and resources; they were not concerned with the social and political mechanisms that governed the extraction of those goods and resources.

Spanish descriptions of the functions of the *kuraka* in Andean societies emphasized the managerial function of these figures. According to Juan de Matienzo, "their function is to be idle and drink, and to count and divide up; they are very capable at this – more so than any Spaniard."[59] On his (or, more rarely, her) managerial ability depended the prosperity of the group, which was reaffirmed in the generosity that kept community members responding to his "requests" for support and service. Generosity created obligations, which in turn made it easier for a leader to expand demands for service. Ultimately, the ability – and the support – of a *kuraka* was measured by the prosperity of the people he ruled. A leader who was truly worthy of the support of others was expected to demonstrate his wisdom and skill not only to the people from whom he claimed labor but also to the ancestors who were the guardians of the group's patrimony, and who expressed their opinions through the forces that affected everyone's lives: nature and climate, even accident and chance.[60] Such a person could become, according to tradition, not only a powerful *kuraka* but even an ancestor, revered, mummified, and honored after death (like the one mentioned at the beginning of Chap. 15).

The tale of Tutay Quiri (Jaqaru? Tutay Kiri?), an ancestor-deity of Huarochirí, is an example. Tutay Quiri was a son of Paria Caca, one of the regional deities or *huacas* honored by the Inka. He was a successful

---

[59] Matienzo, *Gobierno del Perú*, 21.
[60] The stories collected in Huarochirí contain examples of this kind of largesse, which can also be found throughout the colonial period. See also Susan E. Ramírez, "The '*Dueño de Indios*': Thoughts on the consequences of the shifting bases of power of the '*Curaca de los Viejos Antiguos*' under the Spanish in sixteenth-century Peru," *HAHR* 67(4) (1987), esp. 586–592.

war leader, who led his people in the conquest and incorporation of coastal polities before Huarochirí was incorporated in its turn into the Inka state. His success as a war leader multiplied his own and his descendants' access to productive resources and labor; his deeds were celebrated in songs and rituals; and after his death he became a revered ancestor to whom his people turned for guidance. The story appears to be a myth, but there may have been a real Tutay Quiri. In 1611 a Spanish priest described what he was told was the mummy-bundle of Turauquiri [sic], which "although he died more than 600 years ago was so intact in body that it is amazing."[61] Such were the horizons open to the successful leader.

A leader who failed to protect the people he or she represented was held responsible for that failure. In a situation like that of the conquest period, with social disruption, war, epidemics, and the demands of the Spanish invaders, it was not easy for a leader to buffer his people against the forces that assailed them. The traditions also included stories of *kuraka*s whose decisions brought ill fortune rather than prosperity, and who were punished by their people for their failure. Miguel Cabello Balboa relates the story of a *kuraka* of Lambayeque on the north coast who attempted to move the image of his ancestor, founder of his line, to another settlement. His act was followed by 30 days of rain and a year of sterility and hunger – a good description of the shift in oceanic currents called "El Niño," which periodically devastates the normally rainless coastal plain in Peru. The priests of the ancestor/regional deity, with the elders of the community, deposed the *kuraka* and killed him by throwing him into the ocean with his hands and feet bound.[62] The penalty for a leader's failure to retain the support of his community remained high during the conquest period. The Augustinian missionaries in Huamachuco reported in the 1560s that "every year a cacique [kuraka] is eliminated [by poison], and some they don't let live even a year."[63] And even when people did not express their rejection in so final a manner, a leader could find himself unable to claim the support of his people just when

---

[61] The exploits of Tutay Quiri are the subject of chapters 9 and 12 of *The Huarochirí manuscript*. The comment on the preservation of Tutay Quiri's body is contained in the "Carta del padre Fabián al arzobispo," José María Arguedas (ed.), *Hombres y dioses de Huarochirí: narración quechua recogida por Francisco de Avila (1598?)* (Lima, 1966), 252.
[62] The story is told by Miguel Cabello Balboa, *Miscelánea Antártica: una historia del Perú antiguo* [1586] (Lima, 1951), 327–329, and also by María Rostworowski, *Curacas y sucesiones, costa norte* (Lima, 1961), 44.
[63] Agustinos [1561], *Relación*, 37.

he needed it most. There were many complaints from *kuraka*s that their people no longer obeyed them as they had in the time of the Inka, and a *kuraka* on the north coast specifically linked that unwillingness to his inability to maintain the largesse and display that he associated with high rank. In his view it was because of the limits imposed by the Spaniards that his people no longer obeyed him.[64]

The leaders of Andean polities were increasingly caught between the expectations of their own people and the demands made by the growing Spanish population. A *kuraka* who failed to cooperate with the Spanish *encomendero* could find himself replaced by a more compliant aspirant, and those in turn might find themselves caught in the same bind. A *kuraka* of Reque, who gained his position through the intercession of a faction of the people with the Spaniards, held it no more than 5 or 6 months, because the rest of the people refused to obey him, saying that he was a tyrant. They killed him, replacing him with the son of the deposed leader.[65]

We can clearly see a scramble among the members of the Andean élite to maintain or extend their authority during this period, at the same time as other aspirants to power tried to take advantage of new circumstances to replace them. When Guaman Poma complained of a "world upside down," he was describing a situation in which people who held to more traditional definitions of rank and status were scandalized by others whom they saw as usurpers flourishing on disorder.

But in this general picture of confusion and changing avenues of access to power, one shift remains striking in its consistency: the elimination of women from power. It has been argued that the expansion of the Inka state turned parallel gender hierarchies in Andean societies into hierarchical ones in practice despite preserving ideologies of gender equality.[66] But while it can be argued that a woman's role in the Inka state did not include access to authority and power, there is clear evidence of women who held and exercised authority in their own right when the Spaniards entered the Andes. In the north, incorporated into the expanding state late in that state's relatively short history, there were female *kuraka*s who held and exercised authority on their own rather than providing legiti-

[64] Ramírez, "The '*Dueño de Indios*'," 600.
[65] Rostworowski, "Testimony of Dona Maria Atpen, cacica of the village of Collique," *Curacas y sucesiones*, 65.
[66] Irene Silverblatt, *Moon, sun, and witches: Gender ideologies and class in Inca and colonial Peru* (Princeton, 1987), esp. 40–108.

macy to power exercised by their husbands or male kin. A dispute over the position of *kuraka* in Reque at the beginning of the seventeenth century described several female *kuraka*s who governed and administered their communities. In two of these cases, witnesses testified that the women succeeded their fathers, exercising full authority. Another woman who was *kuraka* of her settlement in the 1590s noted that she was received by other – male – *kuraka*s and was given the hospitality due her by virtue of her rank.[67] In the case of one who married a man who did not share her status, the *encomendero* obtained a provision from the viceroy to permit her husband to govern along with her. But by the seventeenth century, women who claimed the title of *kuraka* no longer exercised authority or power. Although women could inherit the position, it was actually exercised by their husbands, and even their claim to the position was made by male guardians in their name. Access to authority seems clearly to have been open to both genders in at least some Andean polities in the conquest period, but to have been eliminated within a half-century after the European invasion. The elimination of women from access to positions of authority was clearly a priority for the Spaniards. (Beyond the bounds of Inka power, but within the Andes of what is now Colombia, colonial rule also undid the matrilineal political order of the Bogotá savannah.)

The paucity of information on the relationship between authority and gender in the decades following the Spanish invasion does not necessarily lead to the conclusion that Andean societies, like the Spaniards, regarded authority as inherently a male role. In fact there is considerable evidence of women exercising political authority. The lack of data may suggest rather that gender was not of major importance in an individual's ability to claim – and enforce – authority. A leader had to be able to elicit the support of others for activities that increased the prosperity of the group as a whole. A leader was a kinsman, one who claimed the role of family elder by virtue of his or her abilities. Principles of social organization, or the rules of interaction that are described by anthropologists, are not followed automatically by the people who profess them. The members of any society use the rules or principles that define how people should behave toward one another as strategies, not prescriptions. A member of the society who used these principles creatively and skillfully could take advantage of the opportunities offered by daily life to increase the rewards

---

[67] Rostworowski, *Curacas y sucesiones*, 32, 65.

defined as desirable by the culture. The language itself expresses the assumption that prosperity and success is part of and equivalent to the size of the kin group. People owed service and support, including labor time, to the senior members of their household, as well as to their *ayllu*. Guaman Poma added that a man who had numerous children became a leader, or *mandoncillo*, and those who could claim a family of fifty or more (a number also described as an *ayllu*) became lords of their communities.[68] According to Guaman Poma, such success in maintaining the unity of an extended household was rewarded by the Inka, but the traditions of Huarochirí make it clear that before the Inka appeared, family groups also secured the same things for themselves and their descendants by conquering other groups.[69]

Successful leadership in the Andean societies of the fifteenth and sixteenth centuries can be seen as the ability of the leader to negotiate effectively in the complicated web of human – and extrahuman – interaction. In the absence of the ability to call upon coercive force, the individual who hoped to be remembered in her society had to be able to convince others that personal support was in the interest of the group as a whole. A leader reflected in his or her own person the behavior and values seen as desirable and productive in Andean society. If we look closely at the kind of behavior expected of a family member by Guaman Poma, as well as that of political leaders and even deities, there is a real overlap. Again the language provides evidence for this equivalence. *Kuraka*, the Quechua term used by the Spaniards to designate a political leader, also referred to both age (eldest) and rank, suggesting that people applied the same norms to the behavior of their leaders as to their kin. Kin should be able to expect maintenance and support from one another, and the ability to provide that support could raise a lower-ranked brother to a position of authority in the group.[70] And if he or she were able to negotiate the complicated social interactions necessary to gain support from human and superhuman alike, he could become a *villca* (Quechua or Aymara *willka*), a person so powerful that he is accorded the status of a regional deity or deity. Such a person understood the reasons for accident and misfortune and the ways to prevent them, in contrast to the

---

[68] Huaman Poma de Ayala, *Nueva Corónica*, 188.
[69] See *The Huarochirí manuscript*, chapters 11 and 12 (79–83).
[70] In *The Huarochirí manuscript*, 79–80, the exploits of the ancestor-leader of a putative "younger" lineage raised his group's status by conquering and incorporating other groups, who in turn recognized his lineage as senior.

false *villca* described in one of the myths of Huarochirí, who "spent his life deceiving a whole lot of people with the little that he really knew."[71] The terms *villca* and *camac* (Quechua *kamaq*, 'able to impart specific spiritual force') were applied to human beings as well as deities or natural forces, and they carried the sense of a being whose true ability and power was sufficient to command authority in human and superhuman society alike.[72]

I suspect that the importance to the Spaniards of defining what kinds of authority were legitimate in Andean societies had little to do with the internal structure of those societies and the ways in which people gained and exercised authority. If we want to understand the "career paths" followed by Andean political leaders, we would do better to look more closely at the ways in which people responded to the crisis of the sixteenth century. The Spaniards made strenuous efforts to impose a vision of a highly stratified social system in which access to authority was restricted to a specific group of people who could be defined and codified according to European notions of hereditary authority. But a close examination of the evidence on the internal organization of Andean societies at the time of Spanish contact suggests that the prosperity and success of societies of varying extent in the Andes depended heavily upon the abilities of those who held authority to negotiate successfully with the touchy, competitive, status-conscious members of the world they inhabited, a world that included both beings who moved in the society of the living and those that existed elsewhere. To be successful in this task, leaders needed all the help they could get.

There is considerable evidence to suggest that authority and leadership in Andean societies was a complex process of negotiation and interaction among many people. This process included the local elders who spoke for the lineages and nested kin groups, or *ayllus* on a more minimal level, as well as the variety of specialists whose function was to communicate with the regional deities and ancestors and to interpret the messages transmitted to their descendants. Authority did not inhere in a specific individual or lineage but was constantly negotiated and adjusted as people dealt with the conditions of their lives. This characteristic of Andean societies made it extremely difficult for the Europeans to transform these

---

[71] *The Huarochirí manuscript*, 55.
[72] The term is defined by Frank Salomon in *The Huarochirí manuscript*, 46 (note 44); see also 55–56.

societies into a docile peasantry on the European pattern, but it also played an important part in the ability of Andean groups to respond rapidly, and often effectively, to the cataclysmic changes that affected their world during the sixteenth century.

It has been suggested that the authority of a *kuraka* in his or her community was rooted in that figure's function as mediator between the community, however defined, and the powers outside that community.[73] Despite the efforts of the Spaniards to limit that function to a few clearly defined and specified individuals, many members of local Andean societies seem to have played a part in achieving consensus. The Spaniards were told that a *kuraka* was selected by the other recognized leaders and had to show evidence of personal ability.

All those who were lords showed great zeal that they be succeeded by a person who was sufficient enough to command and who would conserve his authority [señorío], and thus during their lifetime they would choose from among all the *principales* of their jurisdiction the one who was most capable and of the best customs.[74]

As we might expect, authority was not unqualified; a *kuraka* had to retain his ability to claim support from his people. Authority in Andean society was conditional and dependent upon performance. The Inka state seems to have tried, with some success, to limit the exercise of authority to particular lineages or groups, but while the state supported the *kuraka*s in most cases, it also tried to assume the function of protector of community interests when needed. The skills described as part of the attributes of a "good *kuraka*" – management, mediation, persuasion, mobilization, and provision of support – were the same skills expected of a family elder, and of the regional deity priests who interpreted the messages of the ancestors to their descendants. Under normal circumstances, there was probably agreement in general on the qualities of leadership, and even the personnel. But under extraordinary conditions, when the world turned "upside down" and normal behavior failed to ensure prosperity or even survival, the social organization that structured access to authority was open-ended enough to permit the emergence of a variety

---

[73] The comment has been made by Franklin Pease, *Curacas, Reciprocidad y Riqueza*, 38–40, as well as by Ramírez, *"Dueño de Indios,"* 587–592, although Ramírez limits herself to the *kuraka*'s role in the material world.

[74] Santillán, "Relación del orígen, descendencia, política y gobierno de los Incas," *Tres relaciones de antiguedades peruanas*, quoted by Susan Ramírez, *"Dueño de Indios,"* 590 (my translation).

of responses to the new circumstances. Rather than attempt to determine whether the "social climbers" bitterly denounced by Guaman Poma were better or worse than the traditional *kurakas* who could trace their authority to the period of Inka rule or even prior to Inka expansion, I suggest that we recognize the capacity of Andean social organization to permit – or even foster – the emergence of a wide variety of responses to the crisis of Inka disintegration and European invasion.

INNOVATION AND STRATEGIES OF UNITY

People interested in the native response to the European invasion of the Americas frequently marvel at what they see as the inability of the native societies to unite against their invaders. The European conquest of the Americas succeeded only because the Europeans were joined by formidable native forces, it is argued; the Native Americans – in this case, the Andeans – "should" have realized the threat posed by the outsiders and set aside their internal squabbles to repel the invaders. Such an argument, offered with a variety of refinements by people whose training and sophistication ranges from that of college freshmen to historians and other scholars with decades of research experience, is not only pointless but ignores the fact that human beings learn by experience, making sense of new situations in terms of the explanations available in their own culture. There is evidence that during the period between 1531 and the 1570s, there were efforts, albeit limited, among members of Andean societies to develop strategies that involved setting aside dominant cultural patterns of competition and rivalry in order to forge alliances across ethnic groups.

Some of the story of those strategies can be told, although we still lack the kind of detail that can be obtained from the letters and memos of royal officials and other Spaniards. The strategies do not tell a story of pan-Andean ethnic unity, any more than the actions of local polities during the Spanish invasion reflect a uniform attempt by local polities to rid themselves of Inka domination; such interpretations view the sixteenth century through the matrix of the twentieth. On the basis of the written sources, the most that can be argued is that tentative attempts to argue an all-Andean position were developed in alliance with the faction of the Church that sought to eliminate the *encomienda*.

Individual clerics reached the Andes with Francisco Pizarro, and the secular struggle among the Spaniards monopolized both local attention and the historical record for more than a decade after 1533. By the 1540s, however, a number of men in the Andes, primarily members of religious orders, had become fluent in Andean languages, primarily Quechua and Aymara, and had developed relationships with members of Andean societies. Domingo de Santo Tomás, the great Dominican associate of Las Casas and later bishop of Charcas, was in Peru by the 1540s and took a vocal and active part in the complicated struggle to define the relationship between Andean and Spaniard that continued to the 1580s. A cultural as well as political champion of Andean societies' capacity to function as polities worthy of crown recognition, he had already published a dictionary and a grammar of Quechua at the strikingly early date of 1560.

Carlos Sempat Assadourian, who has subjected the data from this period to a searching cross-examination, argues that an alliance was developed in Peru during the 1550s that brought together members of the religious orders, primarily Dominicans and Franciscans, and a few members of the *audiencia* (board of governing judges), with members of the Andean élite in an effort to limit and contain the demands of the *encomenderos* for goods and labor from native communities.[75]

It fell to the "Pacifier" Pedro de la Gasca to reorganize Peru after the crown finally suppressed the wars among Spaniards. In order to make it possible for him to regain royal control of the Andes, La Gasca had been granted unlimited authority, even to the extent that the crown provided him with signed decrees that he could fill in as he felt necessary. Although Gasca's primary task was the defeat of the Spanish rebels, there is some evidence that he – and the king himself – had listened to the complaints of native exploitation. While Gasca bought the allegiance of the rebels with grants of *encomienda*, he also moved to limit exploitation by putting ceilings on what the *encomenderos* could demand from the people under their authority. His choice of pro-indigenous assistants for the task of counting the native population and assessing tribute is an indication of his sympathies.[76]

As Sempat has pointed out, however, Gasca's sympathies did not translate into any real change for the members of Andean societies. Gasca

---

[75] The articles by Carlos Sempat, published between 1982 and 1987, are included in *Transiciones hacia el sistema colonial andino* (Lima, 1994). See esp. "Dominio colonial y señores étnicos en el espacio andino" (151–171), and "Los señores étnicos y los corregidores de indios en la conformación del estado colonial" (209–292).

[76] The general *visita* was done by Santo Tomás, the head of the Dominican order in Peru, Tomás de San Martín, Archbishop Loayza, and Hernando de Santillán, a lawyer of the colonial high court, or *audiencia* – all people known to historians as "defenders" of the Indians.

paid a high price for peace, and continuing pressure from armed and
vocal Spaniards who insisted upon what they saw as their "rights" in the
Andes convinced him of the necessity of moving slowly and cautiously,
postponing reform for the future. Tributes left intact many of the practices denounced as excessive. Even so, regulation still provoked opposition from resident Spaniards, not only *encomenderos* but also the large
numbers of people who depended for their livelihoods on the *encomenderos*.

Other aspects of Gasca's reorganization of Peru added to the burden
carried by members of Andean societies. Gasca multiplied *encomienda*
grants by dividing native ethnic groups among several *encomenderos*,
which fragmented Andean holdings as well as undermining the authority
of the Andean élites. He also found employment for potential Spanish
rebels by sponsoring new expeditions of exploration and conquest despite
general agreement that the expeditions were among the most important
contributors to the destruction of the Andean population. He stated
openly that he saw no immediate alternative to his actions, informing
the crown that while the tribute assessments specified in 1549 were still
excessive and unjust, even these limited reductions provoked resistance
from the "citizens" (*encomenderos*) and from "all the other people supported by the *encomendeors* from their extortion of the Indians of their
encomiendas." He further counseled that in the future, tribute adjustments no longer be done in a block but "in response to the protests of
the *repartimientos* against their current assessments, little by little and one
by one, with new information, reducing the tributes for one citizen at a
time and not for all."[77]

We have as yet no specific data that describes the activities of the
Andean members of the anti-*encomendero* coalition. It is clear that the
alliance between Spaniards and Andeans was limited, and that many of
the objectives that emerge from letters and reports were not shared by
all. Some friars in orders like the Dominicans enlisted the support of the
Andean élite because they were well aware of the authority of the *kurakas*,
and they hoped to enlist them in converting the members of native
society to Christianity. The orders' hopes of building a power base
sheltered from the power of the Archbishopric of Lima may also have
played a part. Some *kurakas* were initially favorable to the Christian

---

[77] *Documentos relativos a don Pedro de la Gasca y a Gonzalo Pizarro* I, 506–507, cited by Sempat,
180.

missionaries; however, they tested the Christian God (or, if we include the other denizens of the Christian pantheon, the Virgin, Christ, and the Saints) against the regional deities in an effort to determine how best to ensure the prosperity of both themselves and their communities. And when the Christian Gods failed to protect against epidemics or end exploitation, the *kurakas* returned to the ancestors and the regional deities. Within a few decades their erstwhile allies would be reviling them for apostasy and idolatry (see Chap. 15).

Still, for a few years, some *kurakas* struggling to prevent the fragmentation of their societies together with the loss of their own authority and privileges joined the clerics to petition the Spanish crown to defend the natives against the heirs of the *conquistadores*. Leaders of a large number of ethnic groups, some of them traditional enemies, met in 1562 at the site of San Pedro Mama near Lima, the location of an important female regional deity also described as the wife of Pacha Kamaq. Of that meeting we know only that the *kurakas* gave power of attorney to eight Spaniards, one of whom was Domingo de Santo Tomás, to represent their interests in Madrid.[78]

Leaders of Andean communities agreed to act together in this instance in an effort to convince the Spanish authorities to drop their project of resettling and reorganizing local communities. The *kurakas* tried to present a united front to the Spaniards on other issues as well. In 1558 the *kurakas* of the northern Andean coast met to try to reduce the movement of people from the jurisdiction of one lord to that of another. Their objective in this case was to prevent people from leaving their communities and to prohibit other *kurakas* from luring them away.[79] The best-known example of united action is the offer in 1560 by a group of *kurakas*, through the intermediary of Santo Tomás, of a donation of 800,000 pesos if only the crown would reject efforts of the *encomenderos* to turn the *encomienda* into perpetual grants.[80]

It is easier to discern the signs of some common purpose in the Andean élite, who had access to Spaniards with status and authority in their own society, than to find any such evidence among those members of Andean society not seen as powerful by the new rulers. The clear evidence of large-scale migration, sometimes along pre-Spanish routes of

[78] Sempat, "Los señores étnicos," *Transiciones*, 227–228; John V. Murra, "Waman Puma, etnógrafo del mundo andino," in Guáman Poma de Ayala, *Nueva corónico y buen gobierno* (Mexico City, 1980), xviii – xix.
[79] Ramírez, "El '*Dueño de Indios*'," 603.   [80] Spalding, *Huarochirí*, 149.

contact and exchange and sometimes not, is a sign that all sorts of people were engaged in efforts to improve their situations rather than passively awaiting their fates. But where should we look for signs of a more conscious effort to develop common strategies?

Ideological forces could still bring together people of distinct ethnic groups. Important regional deities drew people seeking advice and counsel from distant areas. The priests of these regional deities received the offerings on behalf of the deity, transmitted the question, and, often in a trance, interpreted the regional deity's response. At the apex of Inka society, Spanish destruction moved fast. By the 1550s little was left of Cusco's great solar temple, and its complex galaxy of aligned shrines could be served clandestinely at best. But the crisis of the disintegration of the Inka state and the Spanish invasion apparently brought in its wake a multiplication of regional deities. New regional deities were recognized by ritual specialists, who defined for people the sacred qualities of stones or other odd objects. In Huamachuco the Catholic missionaries reported that after the initial destruction of Catequil, the primary regional deity, stones that were defined by local ritual leaders as sons of the regional deity began to appear, until there was no settlement without two or three of them. The harassed missionaries burned more than 300 of these "sons of Catequil" in the short decade following their arrival in the region in 1551.[81]

In the 1560s there were indications that several of the most important regional deities began to emerge as foci around which people gathered, convinced that a return to traditional ways might protect them from the Spaniards. In 1564 a Catholic priest reported a religious movement in the southern highlands that was given the name Taki Unquy (colonial spelling: Taqui Oncoy) in the region of the city of Huamanga (today Ayacucho). Our only information on the phenomenon is contained in four reports of service to the state, submitted by a Spanish priest named Cristóbal de Albornoz in support of his four – successful – petitions for promotion. It is perhaps unfortunate that data on the movement are contained only in a kind of record that by its very nature is often of dubious veracity, and in fact some doubt has been cast on the truthfulness of Albornoz's depiction of his own role in the discovery and sup-

---

[81] Agustinos [1561], *Relación*, 21.

pression of the Taki Unquy.[82] Almost surely he exaggerated its strategic potency against the viceroyalty.

But while much of the testimony on the movement was offered by Spaniards whose understanding of Andean practice can be questioned, at least one witness, a local priest named Gerónimo Martín, who served as Albornoz's interpreter and interrogator of the Indians, was referred to by both Albornoz and all witnesses as one of the finest linguists in the Andes. Martín's description of Taki Unquy omits many statements that have drawn scholarly attention, among them assertions of speaking in tongues, possession, and other actions that bring to mind contemporary European discourses on witchcraft.[83] He simply describes a movement spread by "many natives" who counseled their fellows to abandon belief in God and his commandments, to avoid the Spanish churches, confess with native priests rather than Catholic clerics, and follow the customs of penance used in the time of the Inka, including not eating salt, chili pepper, or maize, and avoiding intercourse with their women. The native priests predicted that "Titicaca," "Tiahuanaco," and other major regional deities were about to defeat the Christian God and create a new world, punishing all who did not support the regional deities by turning them into guanacos, deer, vicuña, and other animals – transformations described in the only description of Andean religion written from a perspective that is at least partially non-Christian.[84] I suspect that the Taki Unquy may well prove to be an example of the efforts of the priests of major regional deities, who had dealt with pan-Andean issues and strategies in the past, to develop a multipolity strategy.

[82] Gabriela Ramos, "Política ecleciástica y extirpación: discursos y silencios en torno al Taqui Onqoy," in G. Ramos and Henrique Urbano (eds.), *Catolicismo y Extirpación de Idolatrías, Siglos XVI–XVIII* (Cusco, 1993), 137–165. The article also appeared in the *Revista Andina* 10(1) (1993), 147–169.

[83] The European model and probably the inspiration for accusations of idolatry in Europe from the fourteenth to the eighteenth centuries was a manual for inquisitors written in 1486 by the Dominican inquisitors Heinrich Kramer and Jacob Sprenger, entitled *The Malleus Maleficarum* [*The Hammer of Witches*], which provided detailed descriptions of possession and other practices. Originally written in Latin, there are various translations of *The hammer of witches*; see, for example, the translation by Montague Summers (London, 1928).

[84] Testimony of Gerónimo Martín, "Informacion de Servicios (Huamanga, 1570)," in Luis Millones et al., *El retorno de las huacas. Estudios y documentos sobre el Taqui Onqoy, siglo XVI* (Lima, 1990), 130; for a myth in which people are punished by being transformed into animals, to be eaten by humans, see *The Huarochirí manuscript*, 59.

DESTRUCTURATION AND DISINTEGRATION

Whether from the perspective of Andean societies or European invaders, scholars have generally agreed that Andean colonial society was in crisis by the 1560s. Despite the external efficiency of the plunder economy, which seemed to permit Spaniards to use the Andean productive system for their own benefit through the *encomienda* without destroying the productive capacity of local societies, the relationship between Andean and European societies was both conflictive and fragile. The value of an *encomienda* to an enterprising and creative *encomendero* was undeniable, and it is clear that members of Andean society also accumulated goods – particularly coined silver – from their activities. *Kuraka*s in particular became wealthy in European terms; by 1588 Don Diego Caqui, the son of a *kuraka* of Tacna, owned four vineyards and a winery, a llama train to transport wine to Potosí for sale, and two frigates as well as a small sloop for commerce between Tacna, Arica, and Callao.[85] There were enough accumulated resources in the Andean communities for the *kuraka*s to be able to offer the crown a huge sum in 1560 to reject the *encomendero* petitions to make their *encomienda* awards permanent. And the accumulated resources of the local communities by the end of the sixteenth century were large enough to attract the attention of the colonial authorities. They appropriated them, using them to form the *caja de censos de indios*, which functioned as a mortgage fund for Europeans, providing low-interest loans, the income from which was officially supposed to be used to help the local communities that had provided the capital to meet their tribute payments and other expenses.[86]

Although it is obvious that the Andean productive system, reoriented to European objectives, could generate considerable surplus, the plunder economy was not self-sustaining. The continued production of goods that the Spaniards could turn into commodities for a European market depended upon the capacity of Indian societies to reproduce their own numbers and continue to meet the demands of the Europeans. But that capacity depended heavily upon the labor of all members as well as upon

---

[85] Steve J. Stern, "The variety and ambiguity of native Andean intervention in European colonial markets," in Brooke Larson and Olivia Harris (eds.), *Ethnicity, markets, and migration in the Andes: At the crossroads of history and anthropology* (Durham, 1995), 77.

[86] Vilma Ceballos López, "La Caja de Censos u su aporte a la economía colonial (1565–1613)," *Revista del Archivo Nacional del Perú* 26(2) (1962), 269–352. As might be expected the Spanish borrowers often failed to make interest payments, as well as defaulting on repayment of the principal, leaving the *Caja de Censos* depleted by the end of the seventeenth century.

the careful husbanding of goods and resources. It could be undermined by the loss of resources in labor through either death or failure to participate in the reciprocity that was the organizing principle of the productive system. Accumulated resources that were withdrawn from the Andean economy to the European also undermined the capacity for the redistribution that made it possible to claim labor. And the rapid growth of the Spanish population in the Andes, all of it either supported, directly or indirectly, by the *encomienda* system or else in direct competition with it, made these problems even more acute. All of these factors, as well as political conflicts among various Spanish factions involved in defining the colonial system, played important parts in the developing crisis of the 1560s.

The demographic disaster of the sixteenth century has been largely explained as the result of the absolute decline of the native Andean population, decimated by war, overwork, abuse, and most importantly, epidemic disease. Despite the evident drop of the Andean population, the crisis was due not as much to the alarming decimation of the native Andean population as to the squeeze between falling Indian population and the rapidly growing numbers of Spaniards in the new kingdom. This in turn was not absolute, because the number of Spaniards was and remained tiny in comparison to the native populations among which they moved. Rather, the Indian population drop was social – the product of the fact that the plunder economy functioned on the basis of the exploitation of many people by a few, and of the assignment of thousands of people to be used by one *encomendero* for his own and his household's profit. From the time of the initial assignments of *encomiendas* by Francisco Pizarro, the total number of *encomiendas* changed little while the number of Europeans competing for them multiplied. The *encomienda* offered a promise of riches to the recipient who managed it well, but it excluded those who did not enjoy those grants from access to wealth in excess of that which they could gain by their own efforts and personal skills and labor. Save for those few people satisfied with a modest living – and they were few in the gold-rush atmosphere of the conquest period – access to an *encomienda* was the major (and in most cases the only) avenue to wealth and position.

In this context the flood of Spaniards to Peru from the Caribbean, from the Isthmus, and from Spain takes on new meaning, for it put pressures upon an economy organized on the basis of the exploitation of many people by a privileged few. In 1536 there were approximately 500 *encomenderos* in a total Spanish population of about 2,000 in Peru. In the following two decades, the total number of *encomenderos* remained constant while the Spanish population grew rapidly: by the 1540s the *encomenderos* accounted for only about one-eighth of the total Spanish population, and by 1555 they made up only slightly more than 6 percent of all Spaniards in Peru.[87] The growing volume of Spanish hopefuls was accompanied by an inflation in the social status expected of an aspirant to an *encomienda* or its equivalent in Peru. Men who could prove their presence in Peru during the first few years after the European invasion were generally assured of *encomiendas*, although those who chose the losing side in the civil wars lost theirs in the redistributions made by Vaca de Castro and Pedro de la Gasca. These redistributions incorporated newer arrivals, generally with claims to social status in Spain; also, the viceroys who came to Peru from the middle of the century brought kinsmen and clients whose social rank in Spain inflated their claims for consideration. By 1556 the only men eligible to receive *encomiendas* were court nobles from Spain, men who had served the crown in the civil wars, the first conquerors, or men in Peru before 1540.[88]

The authorities in charge of the political structure of the plunder economy following the civil wars were well aware of the dangers represented by the growing numbers of ambitious and often unruly men of arms in Peru, even though they themselves brought additional kinsmen and clients with them to the new kingdom. When these people could not find employment or support from the *encomenderos*, they turned to raiding and plundering. The Marqués de Cañete, viceroy from 1556 to 1560, wrote the crown from Seville before his departure for Peru complaining, "I am informed that there are more than 3,000 men in Peru, all well armed, who expect to be rewarded for their services."[89] His sources informed him well.

But despite the threat to political authority posed by Spaniards who were prepared to fight one another over *encomiendas*, many of the Spaniards who emigrated to the Andes by 1540s sought their livelihoods without reference to the *encomienda* system. By the 1560s there was a substantial Spanish population in Peru that not only did not live from the surplus extracted through the *encomienda* system but was also in open

---

[87] James Lockhart, *Spanish Peru, 1532–1560: A colonial society* (Wisconsin, 1968), 12.
[88] Lockhart, *Spanish Peru*, 18.
[89] Carta de S. M. del Virrey Marqués de Cañete, Panamá, 11 de marzo de 1556," in Roberto Levillier (ed.), *Gobernantes del Perú*, I, 259.

and often antagonistic competition with the members of traditional Andean society. In Lima there were only 32 *encomenderos* in a Spanish population of 2,500 in 1569 – between 1 and 2 percent of the total population. In Potosí, the second-largest urban center in Peru, there were none at all.[90] And Lima and Potosí together contained more than half the total Spanish population of Peru in 1569, offering a market for goods and services that was greater than all of the other centers combined. The people who sought to make their living by producing for that market were not part of the conquest élite. They held no *encomiendas* and could hope for none. They were settlers of all kinds: small farmers, peddlers, merchants, professionals, and even priests trying to make enough to support their families and kin and retire in comfort. And by the 1560s they were finding it very difficult to make a living.

The factional struggles among the Spaniards in the Andes focused the attention of Spanish authorities upon the *encomienda* system, and they drew people with widely varying objectives and agendas into the debate over whether or not to build the colony around an élite whose power rested in its control of the native population. Whatever their other characteristics and failings, the royal officers sent to the Andes between 1544 and 1560 all seem to have been instructed to try to limit the exploitation of the Andean population. Definitions of what that exploitation consisted of varied wildly, however. Núñez Vela brought the New Laws. Gasca, whose primary charge was the defeat of Gonzalo Pizarro, seems to have favored the anti-*encomienda* faction, championed by a vocal segment of the religious. The Marqués de Cañete, third viceroy of Peru, took further steps to reduce tribute payments and eliminate personal services provided by Indians, although he limited his measures to *encomiendas* that had fallen vacant, avoiding confrontation with the *encomenderos* who took arms to defend their "rights" against the crown once again in 1554, only 4 years after Gasca left Peru to assume a position in the Council of the Indies. Until King Charles I abdicated and passed the crown of Castile and Portugal to his son Philip II in 1556, the forces concerned with the condition of the native peoples seem to have remained important in Spain.

Philip II was faced with a government in bankruptcy, however, as well as expensive political projects of his own, and he initially seemed willing

[90] Juan de Salinas Loyola, "Las encomiendas del Perú, 1569," in Marcos Jiménez de la Espada (ed.), *Relaciones geográficas de Indias* 1 (Madrid, 1881), 56.

to augment his finances by granting authority over distant people to their Spanish overlords. He asked a council of theologians in 1553 to determine the justice of selling the vassals of the Church to raise moneys for the war against the Turks. Philip's interest was further stimulated by an offer presented by a representative of the Peruvian *encomenderos*, promising 5 million ducats in exchange for making *encomienda* grants permanent, with full civil and criminal jurisdiction – in other words, transforming them into feudal principalities. Despite royal pressure and the guarded and conditional approval of the clerical lawyers, the Council of the Indies resisted the project.[91]

In several articles Carlos Sempat has laid out the basic outline of the campaign against the *encomienda* in the Andes, as well as the fragile alliance between the *kurakas* and the Church in that campaign. The story is an extremely complicated one, not least because the agendas of the allies were contradictory. The clerics, or at least some of them, initially supported the *kurakas*' efforts to gain Spanish recognition and protection of their own privileges, as well as protection against challenges to their authority from other members of Andean society. The *kurakas* petitioned the Spanish authorities to "preserve our good customs and the laws that existed and continue to exist, and are just for our government and ourselves, as well as the other customs from before our conversion."[92] Domingo de Santo Tomás and other clerics initially supported the efforts of the *kurakas* to enlist the Spaniards in preserving and reinforcing their authority. The clerics argued that the *kurakas* were the foundation of local social order, arguing that their authority should be confirmed and reinforced. The Church even went so far as to use the confessional to reinforce chiefly authority as they saw it. In the instructions to clerics on how properly to interrogate the Indians in the confessional prepared by the Peruvian Church, the priest was instructed to include a question about proper respect for the *kuraka* in the questions relating to the observance of the fourth commandment: "Thou shalt honor thy father and mother."[93] Some *kurakas* were appointed to positions of political authority, holding the of-

---

[91] The story is told in Sempat, "Los señores étnicos," *Transiciones*, 221–225. I suspect that the role of Gasca in the Council of the Indies may be important here; in any case the council felt the issue to be important enough to oppose their sovereign's expressed wishes.

[92] Sempat, "La renta de la encomienda en la década de 1550: piedad cristiana y desconstrucción," *Transiciones*, 160; see also John V. Murra, "Waman Puma, etnógrafo del mundo andino."

[93] *Doctrina Christiana y catecismo para instruccion de indios* [1584]. Facsimile of the trilingual text issued by order of the III Provincial Council of Lima (Madrid, 1992).

fice of *alcalde mayor de Indios* ('superior native magistrate') in specified urban areas. The *kurakas* actively solicited positions of this kind from the 1550s, and Cañete made a couple of appointments, but most appointments of Andeans as native magistrates were made only after the *kurakas* lost the chance to influence the overall political outlines of the viceroyalty.[94]

For a decade after the defeat of the *encomenderos'* revolt captained by Gonzalo Pizarro and the imposition of a formal tribute system by Pedro de La Gasca, the alliance of clerics, members of the *audiencia* of Lima, and *kurakas* held together and, with the support of the superior authorities – governors and viceroys – sent from Spain, began to cut back the sum of goods and labor legally granted the *encomenderos*. As Gasca himself had recommended, the tribute assessments set by Gasca in 1549 were gradually reduced, on a piecemeal basis, frequently as a result of *kuraka* petitions.[95]

The *encomenderos* did not submit calmly to the reduction of their income or power, however, and an armed rebellion in 1553–1554 captained by Francisco Hernández Girón, while quickly defeated, was blamed by the authorities on the Indians and their supporters for pushing the *encomenderos* too far and too fast. The *audiencia* of Lima, governing as interim between the death of Viceroy Antonio de Mendoza and the arrival of his successor, suspended tribute reassessments and reinstated the exactions set by La Gasca in 1549.[96]

The Marqués de Cañete, third viceroy of Peru, renewed the process of tribute revision, although his instructions warned him to proceed with caution. But while the authorities in Madrid still appeared to be focused on the threat to royal control represented by the *encomendero* faction, the alliance between the *kurakas* and their Spanish allies disintegrated in the course of the decade. The *kurakas* did not prove to be the means to introduce Christianity in the Andes for which the clerics had hoped. Even those whose conversion to Christianity was sincere – and there is

[94] See Spalding, *Huarochirí*, 220–222; also Walder Espinosa Soriano, "El Alcalde Mayor Indígena en el Virreinato del Perú," *Anuario de Estudios Americanos* 17 (1960), 183–300.

[95] See Sempat, "La renta de la encomienda," *Transiciones*, 178–90, for a comparison and discussion of the tribute assessments of Gasca and later assessments.

[96] Sempat, "La renta de la encomienda," *Transiciones*, 182–184. Sempat notes that the Indians participated actively in the suppression of the Hernández Girón revolt, as evidenced by the petitions for reward for services later presented by various *kurakas* in support of the request for privileges or other rewards. A careful reading of these petitions, several of which are specified by Sempat, might throw additional light on the strategies of the members of Andean societies during this period.

evidence that the new faith drew real converts in the Andes – were often rejected by the people. Philip II's succession to the throne, and his demand for a profitable resolution of the political conflict in the Andes, undoubtedly contributed to the tendency of the clerics to pull away from a cause that seemed increasingly doomed, in order to salvage something of the main cause for which they had fought. Complaints about abuse of the members of local communities by the *kuraka*s grew. Many insisted that local élites had taken advantage of the defeat of the Inka to appropriate to themselves powers they never held under Inka rule. Some even argued that it was useless to reduce tribute assessments because the *kuraka*s took everything the natives saved, treating them worse than the *encomenderos* had earlier.[97]

The political shift initiated by Philip II became clear with Viceroy Cañete's replacement by the Conde de Nieva in 1561. In 1555 the royal instructions given the Conde de Nieva stated that the major priority of the crown was the christianization of the natives, but by the time Nieva received his instructions, the crown expressed concern only about the state of the treasury and sent a royal commission to Peru to investigate the question of granting perpetual jurisdiction to the *encomenderos* for a price.[98]

The *kuraka*s' meetings and their efforts to present their case to the crown in Spain through the clerics, especially Domingo de Santo Tomás, could not reverse the political shift underway in Peru and in Spain. The attack upon Andean traditions by the representatives of royal authority was clear long before the arrival in 1569 of Francisco de Toledo, fifth viceroy and official author of the colonial system in the Andes. Openly contradicting longstanding orders against permitting the imposition of personal services by the natives, Nieva argued in 1562 that the Indians should be "encouraged" to work in the mines, as long as they were well treated and paid, saying that "without the mines there [is] no Peru." And because Indians were "naturally lazy," they would have to be forced to go to the mines. He also insisted that it was useless to reduce tribute assessments, because any reductions would reduce the natives' incentive to work, and they would be appropriated by the *kuraka*s for themselves.[99]

---

[97] See the statements of the first Archbishop of Lima, Rodrigo de Loayza, in Sempat, "Señores étnicos," *Transiciones*, 210.

[98] Spalding, *Huarochirí*, 149–155; Sempat, "Señores étnicos," *Transiciones*, 229–235.

[99] Sempat, "Señores étnicos," *Transiciones*, 229–231.

Nieva attacked all who opposed him, insisting that the *kurakas* were thieves seeking to rob the state and that the friars were attempting to usurp royal authority. His own greed, however, exceeded the limits of past practice and brought down the hopes of the *encomenderos* with him. The crown discovered that the viceroy, as well as the royal commissioners, had accepted bribes, sold *encomiendas* and offices on a vast scale, and even attempted to smuggle their new fortunes back to Spain piecemeal to conceal them. The commissioners were arrested as they left their ship in Seville, and orders were given for the arrest of Nieva in Peru, who conveniently died before he could be arrested.[100]

Viceroy Francisco de Toledo has gone down in Peruvian historiography as the great organizer, the architect of the colonial system, but the destructuration of Andean societies was largely accomplished by the time he reached the region. Toledo left a body of bureaucratic decrees that have been lauded from his day to the present as a model of centralized and efficient political organization. He organized the forced labor that underlay the silver production of the mines of Potosí, and he decreed the resettlement of the members of native societies in concentrated settlements from which tribute and labor service could be more easily extracted. He reinforced the system of rural governors (*corregidores*) that his predecessor had begun. But within a decade of Toledo's departure, the new Indian settlements were losing their population, and the Spanish officials appointed to represent the interests of the colonial government were becoming famous for their exploitation of the people they administered. Throughout the seventeenth and eighteenth centuries, proposals for reform referred to the "golden age" of political centralization under Toledo and insisted upon the need to reimpose his organization. But the proof of Toledo's accomplishments has been limited to descriptions of the laws and decrees issued under his signature, with little evidence of their enforcement. It can be argued that Toledo, a political realist, understood the dilemma of the crown. In order to maintain royal authority in the Andes, either the representatives of the crown had to be rewarded with incomes that met their expectations, or the crown had to turn a deaf ear to what, three centuries later, would be defined as corruption and share both its authority and its income with those responsible for

---

[100] Ismael Sánchez Bello, "El gobierno del Peru, 1550–1564," *Anuario de Estudios Americanos* 17 (1960), 497.

enforcing its rules. The choice was to share both royal income and royal authority with the Spaniards in the Andes, at the expense of the members of Andean societies.

While the Andean societies of the sixteenth century were gradually transformed into subordinate, "colonial" societies during the decades of struggle that followed the European invasion, the image of what native societies were like, not only before but after that invasion, is the product of the virtually complete control of the record by the colonial authorities. Beneath the official record that portrays the members of Andean societies as a peasantry on the European model but with a few exotic differences, such as language, dress, and certain customs, the members of those societies absorbed their defeats and discovered other strategies (see Chap. 15) to advance or defend their interests.

BIBLIOGRAPHIC ESSAY

Although the Spanish penetration of the Americas has never lacked its historians, until the last several decades, the perspective from which events have been seen has been almost exclusively European. In recent decades, however, there has been a growing body of work seeking to understand the crisis of the sixteenth century from an Andean perspective. Many studies that are primarily concerned with Andean societies before European contact, discussed in previous essays, also contain valuable insights on the interaction of Europeans and Andeans in the sixteenth century. In particular, see the work of María Rostworowski, whose contributions, carefully built on a solid foundation of careful, clearly presented documentary research, promise to remain indispensable while more theoretical and interpretative studies are replaced by new contributions. Fifteen valuable articles on Inka and regional élites, land tenure, and local ethnicities that originally appeared between 1960 and 1990 have been collected and published as *Ensayos de historia andina: élites, etnías, recursos* (Lima, 1993). The collection includes studies of the *visitas* and tribute assessments imposed by Pedro de La Gasca in 1549, the first systematic data on the structure of Andean societies in that Francisco Pizarro's first *visitas* have not appeared.

Other material that deals with the European invasion from the perspective of the Andean societies include Steve J. Stern, *Peru's Indian peoples and the challenge of Spanish conquest: Huamanga to 1640* (Wisconsin, 1982, 1993), and Karen Spalding, *Huarochirí: An Andean society under*

Inca and Spanish rule (Palo Alto, 1984). For a fine introduction to recent research on native societies, see Stern's Prologue to the second edition of *Huamanga*, "Paradigms of conquest: History, historiography, and politics." Also see Vol. II of the luxury edition of the history of Peru financed by the Banco Continental: Franklin Pease, *Peru, Hombre e Historia: Entre el siglo XVI y el XVIII* (Lima, 1992). And for a narrative introduction to the story of the European invasion that makes good use of the published sources available at the time it was written, see John Hemming, *The conquest of the Incas* (New York, 1970).

For the chronology of the European invasion, Hemming remains useful, but the most rewarding sources continue to be the chronicles and other materials produced by the Spaniards. The first generation of conquerors in particular saw things and reported incidents that, when reread in the light of assumptions different from the more "official" interpretations of events imposed from the 1580s, offer evidence for new interpretations. New editions of these sources, sometimes including material absent from earlier editions, have made these standard sources more available. See in particular the description of events prepared by Pedro Sancho, the secretary of Francisco Pizarro, carried to Spain by Sancho, undoubtedly with Pizarro's consent, *Relación de la conquista del Perú* [1534] (Madrid, 1962), and Pedro Pizarro, *Relación del descubrimiento y conquista de los reinos del Perú* (Lima, 1978). The officially approved version of the conquest and the struggles that followed was that of Pedro Cieza de León, *Crónica del Perú*, extremely valuable for the effort Cieza made to include as much information obtained from Andean sources as possible. Parts of his history that were thought to be lost have been recently discovered, and the entire chronicle was edited and published in four parts by the Catholic University of Peru between 1984 and 1992.

On the "battle of the book," a favorite topic of recent postmodernist interpretations, see Sabine MacCormack, "Atahuallpa y el Libro," *Revista de Indias* 48 (1988), 693–714; Patricia Seed, " 'Failing to marvel': Atahuallpa's encounter with the word," *Latin American Research Review* 26(1) (1991), 7–32.

On Spain there has been much new and exciting work published since 1984. The work of John Elliott, Jaime Vicens Vives, Pierre Vilar, and Guillermo Céspedes del Castillo remains invaluable; see, for example, John Elliott, *Imperial Spain, 1469–1716* (New York, 1963), 66 and the essays in his *Spain and its world 1500–1700* (London, 1989). See also John Lynch, *The Hispanic world in crisis and change, 1598–1700* (Oxford, 1969,

1992). The Reconquest is examined from both sides (Christian and Muslim) by Richard Fletcher in *The Quest for El Cíd* (New York, 1989) and *Moorish Spain* (Berkeley, 1992). Since the death of Francisco Franco, there has been a flowering of scholarly research as restrictions on access to archives and official support for particular historical interpretations were relaxed, and that work has begun to reexamine traditional positions on Spanish society and the nature of the Spanish state. See Juan Ignacio Gutiérrez Nieto, *Las comunidades como movimiento antiseñorial (la formación del bando realista en la guerra civil castellana de 1520–1521* (Barcelona, 1973) and Stephen Haliczer, *The comuneros of Castile: The forging of a revolution, 1475–1521* (Madison, 1981); also Helen Nader, *Liberty in absolutist Spain: The Hapsburg sale of towns, 1516–1700* (Baltimore and London, 1990). Idea Altman has provided an invaluable study of the reciprocal relations between Spain and America in the period of the invasion of the Andes in her work on the movement between Extremadura and America, *Emigrants and society: Extremadura and America in the sixteenth century* (Berkeley, 1989). On the transfer of Spanish institutions to the Andes, and the internal organization of Spanish societies in the Andes, the standard source is James Lockhart, *Spanish Peru, 1532–1560: A colonial society* (Madison, WI, 1968), and for the biographies of the men from Spain, his *The Men of Cajamarca* (Berkeley, 1972).

Despite the attention devoted to the Spaniards, we still know far more about their quarrels with one another than about their interactions with the people they encountered in the Andes. While much still remains in the archives, some historians have published document collections that contain material on the relations of Spaniards and Andeans before 1560. See especially, Roberto Levellier, *Gobernantes del Perú: cartas y papeles, siglo XVI. Documentos del Archivo de Indias*, 14 vols. (Madrid, 1921–1926). See also the edition of Francisco Pizarro's actions as governor by Guillermo Lohmann Villena, *Francisco Pizarro, Testimonio. Documentos oficiales, cartas y escritas varios* (Madrid, 1986).

On Inka society and the Inka state, there is an immense literature, as well as a growing body of research that offers new light on the organization of the native state and the dynamics that underlay both its expansion and its rapid disintegration. See Franklin Pease, *Los últimos Incas del Cuzco* (Lima, 1972, 1976); John V. Murra, *Formaciones económicas y políticas del mundo andino* (Lima, 1975); Nathan Wachtel, *Sociedad e ideología: ensayos de historia y anytropología andinas* (Lima, 1973); John V. Murra, Nathan Wachtel, and Jacques Revel (eds.), *Anthropological history of Andean polities* (Cambridge, 1986); an English-language translation of a special issue of *Annales (ESC)*, 33, 5–6 (Paris, 1978); María Rostworowski, *Historia del Tahuantinsuyu* (Lima, 1988); R. T. Zuidema, *Inca civilization in Cuzco* (Austin, TX, 1990); and Thomas C. Patterson, *The Inca empire: The formation and disintegration of a pre-capitalist state* (Oxford, 1991). Archaeological research has also made important contributions to the debate on the mechanisms that underlay the rise and decline of centralized political systems in the Andes. Christine A. Hastorf, *Agriculture and the onset of political inequality before the Inka* (Cambridge, 1993), relates the distribution of material remains of consumption to political organization and the consolidation of power in the Central Andes. Craig Morris and Donald Thompson interpret the archaeology of a provincial Inka administrative center in *Huánuco Pampa* (New York, 1985). On the Inka state outside of the valley of Cusco, see Frank Salomon, *Native lords of Quito in the age of the Incas: The political economy of North Andean chiefdoms* (Cambridge, 1986); and Michael E. Moseley and Alana Cordy-Collins (eds.), *The northern dynasties: Kingship and statecraft in Chimor* (Washington, D.C., 1990). Also see the articles in George A. Collier, Renato I. Rosaldo, and John D. Wirth (eds.), *The Inca and Aztec states, 1400–1800: Anthropology and history* (New York, 1982), especially John H. Rowe, "Inca policies amd institutions relating to the cultural unification of the empire"; Craig Morris, "The infrastructure of Inka control in the Peruvian Central Highlands"; and Nathan Wachtel, "The Mitimas of the Cochabamba Valley: The colonization policy of Huayna Cápac." The relation between the Inka state and the Andean regional deities is discussed by Thomas C. Patterson, "Pachacamac: An Andean oracle under Inca Rule," in D. Peter Kvietok and Daniel H. Sandweiss (eds.), *Recent studies in Andean prehistory and protohistory* (Ithaca, 1985), 159–176. The collection of articles written by Carlos Sempat Assadourian between 1982 and 1987 on the transformation of Andean societies in the sixteenth century and published under the title *Transiciones hacia el sistema colonial andina* (Mexico City and Lima, 1994) are extremely important contributions to our understanding of the Inka state, as well as the interactions of the members of Andean societies with the Europeans from the European invasion to the 1580s. This collection is the only publication dealing specifically with the period covered by this chapter. On the participation of the Inka in what the Spanish defined as the conquest, and the Inka saw as the war for control of the state, see the suggestive discussion in the first article, " 'La gran vejación u destruición de la tierra': las guerras de sucesión y de conquista en el derrumbe de la población indígena del Perú," 19–62.

One of the most important developments in the research on Andean societies since the 1980s is the growing attention given to the local polities that were drawn into the Inka state. The publication of the great *visitas* of local polities made between 1535 and the 1570s has sparked a great deal of work on the organization of local Andean societies, and these sources will continue to be invaluable. See Iñigo Ortíz de Zúñiga, *Visita de la provincia de León de Huánuco en 1562*, 2 vols (Huánuco, 1967–1972); and Garci Díez de San Miguel, *Visita hecha a la provincia de Chucuito por . . . en el año 1567* (Lima, 1964). The diversity of language and culture in the Andes is persuasively argued by Bruce Mannheim, *The language of the Inka since the European invasion* (Austin, TX, 1991), and the great Aymara and Quechua dictionaries prepared in the sixteenth century contain much on social organization embedded in the translations offered of both Andean and Spanish terms. See Diego González Holguín, *Vocabulario de la lengua general de todo el Perú llamado lengua qquichua o del Inca* (Lima, 1952); Fray Domingo de Santo Tomás, *Gramática o arte de la lengua general de los indios de los reynos del Perú* (Lima, 1951); and Ludovico Bertonio, *Vocabulario de la lengua aymara* [1612] (Cochabamba, 1984). Enrique Mayer offers a reading of a portion of the *visita* of Huánuco that applies an ethnographer's eye to the evidence collected in 1567 in "Los atributos del hogar: economía doméstica y la encomienda en el Perú colonial," *Revista Andina*, 2(2) (1984), 557–590. María Rostworowski has devoted a great deal of attention to the ethnohistory of regional polities, especially those of the central and northern coasts of Peru. See *Etnía y sociedad. Costa peruana prehistórica* (Lima, 1977), and *Señoríos indígenes de Lima y Canta* (Lima, 1978). Her work on the northern coast contains invaluable data on the presence – and elimination – of female *kurakas*. See her discussion of the documents in *Curacas y sucesiones, Costa Norte* (Lima, 1961). Irene Silverblatt published a ground-breaking and thought-provoking study of gender relations in the Andes that expands Rostworowski's earlier study; see *Moon, sun, and witches: Gender ideologies and class in Inca and colonial Peru* (Princeton, 1987). Susan Ramírez also examined the polities of the north coast in a valuable study of the pressures on the local élites and the disintegration of their authority, in "The 'Dueño de Indios': Thoughts on the consequences of the shifting bases of power of the 'curaca de los viejos antiguos' under the Spanish in the sixteenth century," *HAHR* 67(3) (1987), 575–610. Rostworowski's contributions are valuable not only for their hypotheses but for their full and careful presentation of documentary evidence; see, for example, *Conflicts over coca fields in 16th century Peru* (Ann Arbor, MI, 1988), a case from the Archive of the Indies that provides a vivid example of the ways in which local polities used both the Inka state and the Spaniards that succeeded it in their pursuit of their conflict with one another. Waldemar Espinosa Soriano has also studied the actions of local polities during the sixteenth century. See, for example, "Los señoríos étnicos de Chachapoyas y la alianza hispano-chacha," *Revista Histórica* 30 (Lima, 1967); *Lurinhuaila de Huacjra: un ayllu y un curacazgo Huanca* (Huancayo, Peru, 1969); *Destrucción del Imperio de los Incas* (Lima, 1973); "Los señoríos étnicos del valle de Condebamba y provincia de Cajabamba," *Anales Científicos de la Universidad del Centro del Perú* 3 (Huancayo, Peru, 1974). A valuable study of the Ecuadorian Andes that contains insights into this early period is Karen Viera Powers, *Andean journeys: Migration, ethnogenesis, and the state in colonial Quito* (Albuquerque, NM, 1995), as well as her "Resilient lords and Indian vagabonds: Wealth, migration, and the reproductive transformacion of Quito's chiefdoms, 1500–1700," *Ethnohistory* 38 (Summer 1991), 225–249; see also Chantal Caillavet, "Caciques de Otavalo enel siglo XVI: don Alonso Maldonado y su esposa, *Miscelánea Antropológica Ecuatoriana* 2 (1982), 38–55; also the studies included in Vol. I of Segundo Moreno Yáñez and Frank Salomon (eds.), *Reproducción y transformación de las sociedades andinas, siglos XVI a XX* (Quito, 1991). For the southeastern Andes, see Thierry Saignes, *Los Andes Orientales: historia de un olvido* (Cochabamba, 1985).

The materials on Andean religion can also reveal a great deal about social organization. One of the best treatments of the collision between European and Andean beliefs is Sabine MacCormack, *Religion in the Andes: Vision and imagination in early colonial Peru* (Princeton, 1991); see also "The heart has its reasons: Predicaments of missionary Christianity in early colonial Peru," *HAHR* 65(3) (1985), 443–466, and "Pachacuti: Miracles, punishment, and last judgement: Visionary past and prophetic future in early colonial Peru," *American Historical Review* (1988), 960–1006. Our only source on Andean religion in an Andean language is the collection of myths and tales from the province of Huarochirí collected at the beginning of the seventeenth century and published in various editions; the English-language edition also contains valuable notes by Frank Salomon, *The Huarochirí manuscript: A testament of ancient and colonial Andean religion*, transl. Frank Salomon and George L. Urioste

(Austin, TX, 1991), but the records of the activities of priests involved in the campaign to convert the Andean peoples to Christianity also contain invaluable information on both Andean conditions and European assumptions. See Lucila Castro de Trelles (ed.), *Relación de la religión y ritos del Perú hecha por los padres agustinos* [1561?] (Lima, 1992); also Luis Millones et al., *El retorno de las huacas. Estudios y documentos sobre el Taqui Onqoy, siglo XVI* (Lima, 1990). And on the relationship between ideological and political structure, María Rostworowski, *Estructuras andinas del poder. Ideología religiosa y política* (Lima, 1983).

The great "Letter to the King," by Felipe Guaman Poma de Ayala, is in a class by itself. The facsimile publication of this wonderful source, *Nueva corónica y buen gobierno (Codex peruvienne illustré)* (Paris, 1936), is long out of print, but see the fine edition prepared by John V. Murra, Jorge L. Urioste, and Rolena Adorno, *Nueva Corónica y buen gobierno* (Mexico, 1980). See also Rolena Adorno's study of Huamán Poma's life and writings, *Guaman Poma: Writing and resistance in colonial Peru* (Austin, TX, 1986).

The standard source on the demography of sixteenth-century Peru is Noble David Cook, *Demographic collapse. Indian Peru, 1520–1620* (New York, 1981). Later contributions have contested Cook's data; see, for example, Carlos Sempat Assadourian, " 'La gran vejación y destruición de la tierra': Las guerras de sucesión y de conquista en el derrumbe de la población indígena del Perú," *Transiciones hacia el sistema colonial andina* (Mexico City and Lima, 1994), 19–63. Other authors have reinterpreted Cook's data in light of other evidence on social structure and migration; for a fine example of this, see Karen V. Powers, *Andean journeys*, as well as Sempat's article, cited earlier. For other sources dealing with Andean demography, see the Bibliographical Essay accompanying Chapter 15 by Thierry Saignes, this volume.

Despite the obvious fact that the study of the transformation of Andean societies after the 1530s must be read through the lens of Spanish sources, historians have tended to deal with Andeans and Europeans as operating entirely independently of one another. Some older sources, however, remain a fine introduction to the arena of forces within which all residents in the Andes, Andean and Spanish alike, developed their tactics and strategies. For a survey of that arena, see Guillermo Lohman Villena's "Etude préliminaire" to his edition of Juan de Matienzo, *Gobierno del Perú (1567)* (Paris and Lima, 1967), v–lxix. Carlos Sempat's detailed examination of the participation of members of Andean societies in the struggles over the *encomienda* and the organization of colonial rule views Andeans and Spaniards alike as skilled and determined political actors. See, especially, "Dominio colonial y señores étnicos en el espacio andino," in *Transiciones hacia el sistema colonial* (Mexico City and Lima, 1994), 151–170; "Los señores étnicos y los corregidores de indios en la confirmación del estado colonial, in" *Transiciones hacia el sistema colonial andina* (Mexico City and Lima, 1994), 209–292. In addition to his role in ending the open political conflict between Spanish factions and imposing royal authority, Pedro de La Gasca clearly played a very important part in the political struggles among Andeans and Spaniards, making a close look at his life an important part of the story. See Teodoro Hampe Martínez, *Don Pedro de La Gasca, 1493–1567* (Lima, 1989). See also the essays by Luis Miguel Glave, published under the title of *Trajinantes: caminos indígenas en la sociedad colonial, siglos XVI/XVII* (Lima, 1989).

It has been clear for some years that the economy of the conquest period not only rested on the labor of the members of Andean societies but upon Andean technology and productive techniques as well. For a fine analysis of an Andean *encomienda* that makes such dependence entirely clear, see the model study by Efraín Trelles Aréstegui, *Lucas Martínez Vegazo: funcionamiento de una encomienda peruana inicial* (Lima, 1983; 2nd ed., 1991). Andean productive technologies and their appropriation by Spaniards are described in Carlos Sempat Assadourian, "La producción de la mercancía dinero en la formación del mercado interno colonial," *Economía* 12) (Lima, 1978), 9–55; see also the essays collected in *El sistema de la economía colonial: Mercado interno, regiones y espacio económico* (Lima, 1982). See also Karen Spalding, "Kurakas and commerce: A chapter in the evolution of Andean society," *HAHR* 50 (November 1970), 645–664. The active part taken by members of Andean society in the colonial economy of the sixteenth century is well-known by now. See John V. Murra, "Aymara lords and their European agents at Potosí," *Nova Americana* 11 (Turin, 1978), 231–243. Steve Stern discusses the problems of interpreting the data on Andean market activity in "The variety and ambiguity of native Andean intervention in European colonial markets," in Brooke Larson and Olivia Harris (eds.), *Ethnicity, markets, and migration in the Andes: At the crossroads of history and anthropology* (Durham, 1995), 73–100.

The political shifts in both Spain and the Andes that undermined the *kurakas'* efforts to find a place for themselves in the colonial system are indicated by Sempat in his articles in *Transiciones hacia el sistema colonial andino,* but further study of the period between Gasca and Toledo from this perspective will undoubtedly clarify this story of political defeat and throw new light on the ways in which the members of Andean societies understood, and dealt with, the Spanish invaders. I made an initial attempt to see the period from this perspective in *Huarochirí,* 136–156, but the picture is far more nuanced and complex than I understood at that time. Carlos Sempat has come closer in the essays in *Transiciones,* especially chapters 4 and 6; the petitions in the Archive of the Indies for reward of services submitted to the crown by Andean *kurakas,* which he cites, may well prove invaluable in reconstructing the history of the participation of the members of Andean society in the political struggles that preceded the administration of the fifth viceroy, Francisco de Toledo, and made possible the exclusion of the members of Andean societies from the colonial system.

13

THE CRISES AND TRANSFORMATIONS OF INVADED SOCIETIES: COASTAL BRAZIL IN THE SIXTEENTH CENTURY

JOHN M. MONTEIRO

"It is impossible either to enumerate or comprehend the multitude of barbarous heathen that Nature has planted throughout this land of Brazil," wrote Portuguese chronicler Pero de Magalhães Gandavo, around 1570.[1] To be sure, the enormous cultural and linguistic diversity of lowland South America presented a stiff challenge to sixteenth-century Portuguese observers, in spite of their considerable experience with the intricate political configurations of coastal Africa, South Asia, and the Far East. Even so, early European writers left relatively abundant, detailed descriptions of coastal populations. Portuguese, French, German, and English chronicles and reports, along with the massive letters and relations penned by Jesuits, constitute a wide array of sources for the reconstruction of indigenous social organization. However, although this material has been central to Brazilian ethnological debates over the development, dispersion, and structure of Tupi culture for much of the twentieth century, it has been all but abandoned by mainstream Brazilian historiography for over a century. Indeed, the historical dimension of indigenous societies and of their relations with the European invaders remains a glaringly neglected facet of the history of Portuguese America.

Although rich in information and detail, the early literature on indigenous Brazil showed some difficulty in discerning territorial divisions, political organization, and religious institutions in terms familiar to the Western experience. Sixteenth-century writers sought to simplify the intricate mosaic of languages and societies by dividing the native population into broad generic groups. Most of the coastal societies, sharing practically identical cultural attributes, came to be called Tupi, and their

[1] Pero Magalhães Gandavo, *Tratado da Terra do Brasil e História da Província Santa Cruz* (São Paulo and Belo Horizonte, 1980), 52.

language the *lingua geral da costa* ('common language of the coast'). But
the cultural affinity between Tupi societies failed to correspond to any
sort of political unity: From the European perspective, the most remarkable characteristic of the Tupi lay precisely in the constant warfare
between competing segments. Referring to the Indians of Porto Seguro
and Espírito Santo in his important treatise on the peoples of Brazil,
Gabriel Soares de Sousa illustrated this apparent paradox: "And even
though the Tupinikin and Tupinambá are enemies, between them there
is no greater difference in language and customs than that between the
residents of Lisbon and those of Beira."[2]

This portrait of acute and persistent political fragmentation was enhanced further by the presence of a great number of non-Tupi societies
interspersed among the Tupi peoples along the coast, occupying vast
expanses of the interior of Portuguese America as well. These societies,
in effect representing dozens of unrelated language groups, were assembled by early writers as a second generic category, the Tapuia. Also
referred to as *nheengaíbas* (those who spoke badly), the so-called Tapuia
were defined in contrast to what was known about the Tupi. Although
this designation sought to classify the many groups possessing an apparently simpler material culture than that of the coastal Tupi, it also
became a descriptive term for societies about which little was known;
indeed, the remarkably sophisticated classification schemes and the complex social organization of the "simple" Gê-speaking groups began to call
for closer attention only in the twentieth century. Gabriel Soares de
Sousa openly admitted the limitations of his knowledge with reference to
the Tapuia: "Since the Tapuias are so many and so divided in bands,
customs and languages, in order to say much about them it would be
necessary to collect meticulously much information about their divisions,
life and customs; but at present this is not possible." Basically relying on
Tupi informants, early writers projected Tapuia groups as the antithesis
of Tupi society, thus describing them ordinarily in negative terms.

Although grossly oversimplifying the cultural makeup of coastal Brazil,
the Tupi-Tapuia dichotomy did reflect fundamentally different traditions
as well as distinct forms of social organization. In his interesting account
of the Indians of coastal Bahia, Soares de Sousa outlined the historical
dimension of the Tupi-Tapuia relationship. Relying on "information

---

[2] Gabriel Soares de Sousa, *Tratado Descritivo do Brasil em 1587* (São Paulo, 1971), 88.

taken from the oldest Indians," Soares de Sousa asserted that the first inhabitants of the region were the Tapuia, "who are an ancient caste of heathen." At a certain point in the remote past, the Tapuia were expelled from the coast by the Tupiná, a Tupi group, "who came from the backlands in search of the reputed abundance of the land and sea of this province." After many generations, "when the Tupinambá learned of the greatness and fertility of this land," this new group invaded the lands of the Tupiná, "destroying their villages and fields, killing those who re-sisted, sparing no one, until they managed to expel the Tupiná from the edge of the sea." In conclusion Soares de Sousa wrote: "Thus the Tupi-nambá have remained lords of this province of Bahia for many years, waging war against their enemies with great effort, until the arrival of the Portuguese; this information was taken from the Tupinambá and Tup-iná, in whose memory these stories pass from generation to generation." Of course, one might argue that Soares de Sousa simply sought to elaborate an historical framework within which the Portuguese conquest would fit harmoniously. But the Tupinambá's rise to prominence in coastal Bahia probably stands as one of the most significant events in the precolonial history of Brazil, coinciding with the emergence of other Tupi and Guarani groups throughout eastern South America.

While most sixteenth-century observers showed little interest in the historical relationship between Tupi and Tapuia, they all pointed out obvious fundamental differences that justified this typology. Gabriel Soares de Sousa, for example, in his description of the Guaianá of southern Brazil, clearly set them apart from the coastal Tupi:

They are people of little work, much leisure, they do not work the land, they live from the game they hunt and the fish they take from the rivers, and the wild fruits that the forest yields; they are great archers and enemies of human flesh. . . . These heathen do not live in villages with neat houses, like their neighbors the Tamoios, but in hovels in the fields, under the ground, where they keep a fire burning night and day and make their beds of twigs and of skins taken from the animals they slay.

This description stands in stark contrast to Tupi societies, who had a more sedentary settlement pattern, developed a varied and productive horticultural base, and placed great importance on activities related to warfare, sacrifice, and cannibalism. These differences were to play an important role in the patterns of Indian – white relations that emerged following the arrival of the Europeans (Map 13.1).

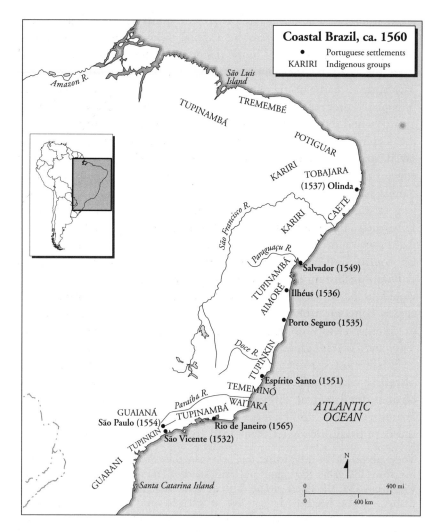

Map 13.1

INDIGENOUS POPULATIONS OF THE BRAZILIAN COAST

The Tupi-Tapuia dichotomy may have helped the Portuguese organize their perception of the cultural configurations of indigenous Brazil, but it also masked an ethnic complexity that remains difficult to sort out to this day. In linguistic terms, societies belonging to at least forty distinct language families flourished during the sixteenth century within the present territorial limits of Brazil. Many of these families have been classified as belonging to three language trunks: Tupi, Macro-Gê, and Arawak. The coastal Tupi, speakers of the *lingua geral*, as well as the southern Guarani, all spoke related dialects of Tupi-Guarani, one of nine known language families in the Tupi trunk. Peoples identified as Tapuia in the sources in many cases spoke variants of Gê, a language of the Macro-Gê trunk. Often little was known about these groups, however, and several non-Gê peoples were listed as Tapuias in the early literature, including the Kariri of the northeast, the Waitaká (Goitacá) of the east, and the Puri of the southeast, whose respective languages later came to be classified as isolated. Finally, Arawak-and Karib-speakers, as well as members of other specific linguistic affiliations, though having sporadic contact with isolated European expeditions in the sixteenth century, were to become more fully engaged with Portuguese America only in the seventeenth and eighteenth centuries.

Because early Portuguese colonial activities remained tied basically to the Atlantic coast, Tupi-Guarani peoples became the central protagonists of sixteenth-century Portuguese-Indian relations. Strikingly similar in terms of language, social organization, and ritual activities, a large number of local groups covered an extensive, though discontinuous, area ranging over 4,000 kilometers, from the Amazon to the River Platte Basin. Archaeologists and ethnohistorians, concerned not only with the origins and dispersion of Tupi-Guarani culture but also with significant differences in historical traditions, divide this enormous whole into two, broad parts. The many groups inhabiting the coast between the future captaincy of São Vicente and the mouth of the Amazon came to be known collectively as the Tupinambá, though early sources attribute a much greater variety of ethnic designations in reference to the coastal Tupi. The second subdivision of the Tupi-Guarani, the Guarani, occupied vast stretches of river floodplains and subtropical forests to the south of the captaincy of São Vicente, between the Atlantic coast and the Paraná-Paraguay river system.[3]

The territorial boundaries of Tupi groups remain difficult to ascertain from existing evidence, especially when one considers that spatial mobility was one of the central characteristics of Tupi-Guarani culture. Nonetheless the early literature often identified groups specifically in terms of

---

[3] For a fuller treatment of the Guarani and their relations with the Portuguese, see Chapters 14 and 18 in this volume, as well as John Monteiro, "Os guarani e a história do Brasil meridional," in M. Carneiro da Cunha (ed.), *Historia dos Índios no Brasil* (São Paulo, 1992), 475–498.

their hostile relations with other Tupi groups or with Tapuia enemies. For example, in the southernmost captaincy of São Vicente, the Tupinikin maintained constant hostilities with the Karijó (Guarani) to the south and the Tamoio (Tupinambá) to the north. These same Tamoio, residing along the coast of Rio de Janeiro, also held as enemies the Tememinó, who occupied the coast between the southern Paraíba and Doce rivers. Other Tupinikin groups dominated much of the eastern seaboard between Espírito Santo and the Bay of All Saints, where they clashed with the Tupinambá, located between the bay and the mouth of the São Francisco River. The Tupinaé also were enemies of these Tupinambá, engaging in persistent warfare along the Paraguaçú River. In the hinterland along the São Francisco River, there lived another populous Tupi group, the Amoipira. Between the São Francisco and northern Paraíba rivers, the Caeté faced the Tupinambá to the south and the Tobajara to the north. Farther up the coast, beginning at Itamaracá Island and almost reaching São Luís, the powerful Potiguar maintained hostile relations with the Caeté, the Tobajara, and, finally, with the Tupinambá, who came to occupy the island of São Luís and much of the coast to the southern shore of the Amazon.[4]

Groups identified as Tapuia in colonial times also may be located tentatively in terms of their relations with Tupi groups or with Portuguese colonists, though their mobility was even greater in historical times. In the far south, the Guaianá, probably a reference to the Kaingang, were in permanent contact with Karijó, Tupinikin, and Tamoio groups. Near the southern Paraíba River, the Waitaká established firm opposition to Tupi expansion in the region, remaining a steady base of resistance to the Portuguese in colonial times. Farther north, in the interior of the future captaincies of Espírito Santo, Porto Seguro, and Ilhéus, another group showed an even more aggressive posture toward Tupi and Portuguese alike, becoming an archetype for the barbarous Tapuia: the Aimoré. Many other Tapuia groups inhabiting the northeastern backlands were known to the Portuguese already in the sixteenth century: The Jesuit Fernão Cardim found little trouble in listing seventy-six distinct Tapuia peoples in his 1583 relation. However, most of these groups became involved with Portuguese colonial activities only during the sec-

---

[4] It seems likely that the Tupinambá of ãMaranhao were late arrivals, migrating northward in retreat from Portuguese expansion along the northeast coast during the sixteenth century. See Florestan Fernandes, *Organização Social dos Tupinambá* (São Paulo, 1948), 29–44.

ond half of the seventeenth century, when the expansion of the cattle industry along the São Francisco River and throughout the interior of the northeastern captaincies resulted in drawn-out conflicts with the Indians.

If identifying the geographical distribution of the native peoples of sixteenth-century coastal Brazil remains an imprecise science, calculating their population faces many of the same challenges and problems. Spatial mobility, the repetition of generic names in different places and at different times, and the poor quality of population reports in the early sources, all have contributed to the incipient character of the demographic history of indigenous Brazil. Although most global appraisals have taken into account multiple factors, including eyewitness colonial accounts, territorial and ecological considerations, and the size and density of current indigenous societies, results have been widely divergent, often distorted – either upward or downward – by projections based on population density estimates.

The most complete example of this exercise in "educated guessing" may be found in John Hemming's *Red Gold* (1978), which shows both the advances and limitations of historical demography as applied to sixteenth-century Brazil. Listing all groups known in the historical and ethnological bibliography, Hemming assessed the so-called original population case by case, arriving at the figure of 2,431,000 Indians, among which the coastal Tupi (not including the Guarani) accounted for about 625,000. Hemming's figures, though generally held to be the most reasonable, inspire some reservations. Some specific cases need to be revised in light of current research; for example, his estimate of 6,000 for the Paiaguá recently was brought into question, based on evidence describing large concentrations of war canoes along the Paraguay River.[5] Another problem emerges in the compression of five centuries of widely varying information into the single historical moment of 1500. Some groups are in effect double-counted, such as the Tupinambá of Maranhão and Pará or the Tobajara of the Ibiapaba Hills, because they had migrated during the sixteenth century in retreat from Portuguese slaving activities and were once again contacted and counted in the early seventeenth. A more serious case is that of the Canoeiros of Goiás, a group that simply did not exist in 1500 because this society in effect was reconstituted in the

---

[5] Barbara Ganson, "The Evueví of Paraguay: Adaptive strategies and responses to colonialism, 1528–1811," *The Americas* 45(4) (1989), 468.

eighteenth century by runaway slaves possibly of Guarani origin. In short, Hemming's perspective assumes the stagnation of population size and dynamics in 1500, after which indigenous populations began to suffer an almost inexorable decline. As a result the history of these "peoples without history" becomes the chronicle of their extinction, which appears to be the perspective adopted throughout the pages of *Red Gold*. It is true that the impact of contact was universally negative on aboriginal peoples, but the essential question should not be limited to how contact decimated native populations. More importantly one must consider the role and significance of indigenous demographic change in the early history of the colony. Indeed, precolonial population dynamics, as well as the multiple transformations that occurred following contact, were much more complex and varied than a simple numerical decline.

Although the debate over the size and density of preconquest populations remains an open question, one important assertion may be established. The information in eyewitness accounts, which is supported by a growing number of archaeological investigations, convincingly suggests that both the size and density of coastal and river floodplain populations of the early sixteenth century were significantly greater than what is found among modern forest peoples. Indeed, early reports on the Tupinambá along the coast, the Tupi-speaking Omágua on the upper Amazon (Solimões River), and the Guarani near the Paraná-Paraguay Basin describe villages with well over a thousand inhabitants. This should hardly be surprising, considering two major effects of colonial expansion on native populations: radical demographic decline and strategic retreats to less accessible regions. Nonetheless it does raise compelling questions about the development of precontact social and political organization *before* the arrival of Europeans. Did larger populations necessarily involve more complex political structures, not unlike the chiefdoms of the circum-Caribbean? Was the constant warfare noted by all early observers a function of territorial competition moved by population pressures? In short, were early sixteenth-century Tupi societies more "sophisticated" than their postconquest descendants?

Recent research on the evolution of lowland cultures, refuting environmental circumscription theories and evaluating the agricultural potential of tropical floodplains areas, has injected new blood into the debate. Antonio Porro, for one, through a critical analysis of early Spanish sources, offers a strong case for the development of Omagua chiefdoms, while Anna Roosevelt, in her exhaustive appraisal of Amazonian archaeology, presents an even bolder argument in favor of the emergence of floodplain chiefdoms, whose development would have been abruptly cut off by the European "conquest" of the Amazon.[6] Whereas fresh archaeological evidence may come to confirm or dispel hypotheses concerning Amazonian chiefdoms, the ethnohistorical record on the coastal Tupi-Guarani societies during the sixteenth century appears to point in a different direction.

THE COASTAL TUPI PEOPLES

Thoroughly described in the early colonial literature, the coastal Tupi-Guarani societies also came to occupy a distinguished position in Brazilian anthropology. The classic studies of Alfred Métraux and Florestan Fernandes, based on systematic readings of sixteenth- and early seventeenth-century sources, remain essential reference points for both ethnological and ethnohistorical studies of native Brazilian societies. Writing from different theoretical perspectives – the first diffusionist, and the second functionalist – these two authors provide valuable, detailed analyses of Tupinambá social organization, belief systems, migrations, and warfare. However, precisely speaking, both Métraux and Fernandes have produced ethnographic studies of past societies based on written accounts; neither is preoccupied with Indian history, as such. Fernandes's historical ethnography, for example, in identifying the internal dynamics of Tupinambá social organization and reproduction as a closed system, limits Tupinambá actions during the conquest to a series of "reactions" attempting to restore precontact tribal integrity.[7] In short, while Métraux and Fernandes enrich our knowledge of extinct coastal societies, they leave open a series of issues concerning the impact of colonial expansion on the coastal peoples, as well as the relevance of Tupinambá history in shaping patterns of Indian – white relations.

Tupi history has much to do with the reconstruction of coastal societies from the available record, but it also involves the ways in which past events and processes informed native actions both before and after the arrival of the Europeans. Although specific historical experiences were as

---

[6] For cogent summaries of their respective positions, see the articles by Anna C. Roosevelt and Antonio Porro, in *História dos Índios no Brasil*, edited by Manuela Carneiro da Cunha (São Paulo, 1992), as well as Roosevelt's contribution to this volume (Chap. 4).

[7] This position is made explicit in Florestan Fernandes' "Os Tupi e a Reação Tribal à Conquista," *Investigação etnológica no Brasil e outros ensaios* (Petrópolis, 1976), 11–32.

fragmented as the political makeup of indigenous Brazil, coastal Tupi societies all shared common trends, which help explain the logic underlying the political responses and strategies adopted in the face of European expansion during the sixteenth century. Contemporary sources, while allowing for brilliant reconstitutions of coastal Tupi social organization in ideal terms, also shed light on the dynamic that moved Tupi societies over time and space. As we see in this section, the fragmentation and regeneration of local units, the role of political and spiritual leaders, and the critical importance of warfare, all formed central aspects of this dynamic.

Early sources clearly identify what may be considered tribal agglomerations, but the basic organ of social and political organization among the coastal Tupi was the multifamily village. Several villages could be linked by kinship or alliance networks, but there is no reason to believe that these relations involved the development of larger political or territorial units. In effect specific historical circumstances could expand or shrink the association of local groups as the constantly shifting scenario of alliances and animosities determined the nature and extent of multivillage bonds. Sixteenth-century observers often failed to recognize this flexibility, describing groups of villages as if they formed a wider political whole. For example, in reference to the Potiguar, "masters of over 400 leagues of this coast," an anonymous Jesuit depicted them as "the largest and most united of any [heathen] in Brazil."[8] This Potiguar "unity," however, certainly was conditioned by their alliance with the French and their common defense against the advance of the Portuguese conquest along the coast of Paraíba. Furthermore, later on, several Potiguar groups forged alliances with the Portuguese, and during the Luso-Dutch war (1630–1654) they were to be found on both sides of the conflict.

Just as the multivillage networks proved mutable over time, individual Tupi villages also did not constitute fixed, permanent settlements. According to sixteenth-century accounts, villages usually consisted of four to eight multifamily residential lodges *(malocas)* and varied considerably in size, ranging from a few hundred to a few thousand inhabitants. In part at least, this variation resulted from the disparity of colonial observations, but it also reflected the recurrent pattern of village fragmentation and regeneration: Every few years established villages were divided, dis-

---

[8] Anonymous, "Sumário das armadas que se fizeram e guerras que se deram na conquista do Rio Paraíba," *Revista do Instituto Histórico e Geográfico Brasileiro* 36 (pt. 1) (1873), 8.

solved, and recreated at new sites. The widespread and frequent reference to *taperas*, or abandoned settlements, in land documents of the sixteenth and seventeenth centuries, suggests the spatial dimensions of this process. These moves were stimulated by various possible factors, including decline in horticultural productivity, depletion of game reserves, internal factional disputes, the emergence of a charismatic new leader, or the death of a headman. Whatever the precise motive, the repeated creation of new units of settlement constituted important events, involving the reproduction of the principal bases of indigenous social and political organization.

The original composition and proliferation of any given village was associated intrinsically with the role of its founding headman. Consequently, the community's identity – both historical and political – also corresponded to the personal trajectory of its leader. The settlement of independent villages occurred when an emergent political leader managed to mobilize a significant following of relatives and friends. This following was attracted essentially by one's fame as a warrior but also could be consolidated through marriage strategies, including the selection of sons-in-law (subject to brideservice obligations) and the adoption of several wives. During the conquest these strategies proved critical in the early development of Luso–Indian relations.

The headman's principal source of authority grew out of his capacity to lead warriors against traditional enemies, but his responsibilities also had much to do with the organization of social and material life. According to Gabriel Soares de Sousa, it was he who determined the relocation of a faction or whole village and who chose a site for the new settlement. He then would organize the construction and occupation of the *malocas* and select the ideal location for the garden plot that was to provide the community's subsistence. Significantly the headman not only labored alongside his followers but also set the example: "When the *principal* (headman) prepares the *roça*, with the assistance of his relatives and followers, he is always the first to begin work."[9]

Thus, in spite of the headman's greater responsibility and prestige, he remained essentially equal to his followers in the productive sphere. In effect, among the coastal Tupi, political leadership did not correspond to any sort of economic privilege or differentiated social status. To be sure the authority of headmen always remained subject to the consent of his

---

[9] Soares de Sousa, *Tratado Descritivo*, 303.

followers. In describing leadership in Tupinambá communities, Pero de Magalhães Gandavo commented: "These people do not have a King among them, or any other sort of justice, except for a *principal* in each village, who is like a captain, whom they obey by choice and not by force." According to German gunner Hans Staden, "they also obey the chiefs of the huts, in what they order; this is done without any compulsion or fear, but from goodwill only."[10] The peculiar characteristics of Tupi headmanship thus posed a considerable challenge to early observers. The sixteenth-century literature projected three distinct levels of political leadership, designating the term *principal* for each type of leader. The term applied to *maloca* headmen, to village headmen, and finally to pan-village leaders. This last category remained restricted to the context of warfare, when several villages formed alliances in the face of a common enemy. For example, on several occasions in the sixteenth century, Tupinikin headman Tibiriçá and Tupinambá headman Cunhambebe led warriors from several villages to battle, each enjoying widely recognized reputations as valiant and respected leaders.

But headmen also commanded other significant attributes. For one, oratory skills figured in the making of a great leader among the Tupi. The Jesuits, outstanding communicators themselves, frequently commented on the effectiveness of native speakers. What caught their attention was not only the rhetorical methods but also the contents of the frequent speeches. According to Fernão Cardim, every day before dawn, the headman "preaches during half an hour, reminding [the villagers] that they will work as did their ancestors, and distributes their time among them, telling them what they are to do."[11] Father Manuel da Nóbrega, writing from São Vicente in 1553 and probably referring to the Tupi or Guarani peoples of the interior, observed: "Every day before dawn from a high place [the principal] sets out the day's tasks for each household, and reminds them that they must live communally."[12] These suggestive comments, reproduced by many other early writers, indicate perhaps the central nonmilitary attribute deposited among headmen. The headmen acted as guardians of tradition, expressing and organizing the

---

[10] Gandavo, *Tratado da Terra*, 124; Hans Staden, *The captivity of Hans Stade of Hesse* (London, 1874), 134.

[11] Fernão Cardim, S. J., *Tratados da terra e gente do Brasil* (São Paulo, 1978), 105.

[12] Jesuit letters, cited frequently in this chapter, are from the following sources: Serafim Leite (ed.), *Monumenta Brasiliae*, 5 vols. (Rome, 1956–1960); Alfredo do Valle Cabral (ed.), *Cartas Jesuíticas*, 3 vols., 2nd ed. (São Paulo and Belo Horizonte, 1988); Hélio Viotti, S. J. (ed.), *Cartas: Correspondência Ativa e Passiva* (São Paulo, 1984).

tasks of daily life in terms of what had been set down in the past. Tupinambá headman Japiaçú, in submitting to French pressures to eradicate prisoner sacrifice and cannibalism, explained how tradition dictated practice, when his will was vetoed in a meeting of elders:

I well know that this custom is bad and contrary to nature, and for this reason I have sought many times to extinguish it. But all of us, elders, are much alike and with identical powers; and if one of us presents a proposal, even if it is approved by a majority of votes, all it takes is someone to declare that the custom is ancient and that it is not right to modify that which we have learned from our fathers.[13]

Although not in the same way, this role of guardian of tradition was shared by shamans, or *pajés*, who sometimes wielded political authority as well. "Mediators between the spirits and the rest of the people," according to Yves d'Évreux, Tupi-Guarani shamans exercised multiple functions, such as healing the sick, interpreting dreams, and warding off the many outside threats to local society, including spirits and demons.[14] Their authority, respected by headmen and followers alike, derived primarily from the esoteric knowledge they possessed, resulting from long years of apprenticeship with experienced shamans. Their importance and prestige was emphasized by Tupinambá headman Porta Grande of Bahia, who informed Jesuit Pedro Rodrigues in 1551 that the *pajés* "gave them all the good things, that is, their food."

The spiritual life of the coastal Tupi also was marked by the appearance of wandering "prophets," known as *caraíbas*. According to Jesuit Manuel da Nóbrega, writing shortly after his arrival in Bahia, "From time to time witches appear from distant lands, feigning holiness; and at the time of their arrival, they order the Indians to clear the paths, and are received with dances and festivities according to custom." Thus, unlike the resident shamans, the *caraíbas* were not permanent members of the community, though they commanded considerable influence over its residents. Early accounts frequently equated *caraíbas* with shamans, often describing them as *pajé guaçú*, or great shaman. But these figures played quite a different role, preaching a prophetic message to all who would listen. According to Nóbrega:

---

[13] Claude d'Abbeville, O. F. M., *História da Missão dos Padres Capuchinhos na Ilha do Maranhão* [1614] (São Paulo, 1975), 234.
[14] Quoted in Hélène Clastres, *Terra Sem Mal. O Profetismo Tupi-Guarani* (São Paulo, 1978), p. 35.

Upon arriving . . . the sorcerer enters a dark hut and sets a human-shaped gourd in the place best suited for his deceptions, and altering his voice to that of a child . . . , tells [the villagers] that they should not work or go to the roça, that the crops will grow untended and come to the houses by themselves, and there will never be a lack of food; and the digging sticks will break the earth, arrows will fly into the woods to hunt for their masters and to kill many enemies, and will capture many to be eaten.

Gifted speakers, the *caraíbas* supposedly persuaded followers to join them on distant peregrinations in search of an earthly paradise, a "land without evil," of abundance, eternal youth, and successful warfare and cannibalism. In his excellent recent synthesis of Tupinambá history and culture, anthropologist Carlos Fausto cogently identifies this concept on both a horizontal (spatial) and vertical (temporal) plane. In spatial terms this land was the object of collective migrations, which sought both material and spiritual renewal. In temporal terms it was not only the land of the ancestors but also the future destination of brave warriors who killed and ate human flesh.[15] Thus the quest for the "land without evil" cannot be explained simply as a messianic reaction to conquest (as Alfred Métraux and Maria Isaura Pereira de Queiroz have argued) or as a politico-religious manifestation in radical opposition to traditional authority (as Hélène Clastres contends). In effect the prophet's message addressed the basic elements that placed the coastal Tupi within an historical dimension: spatial movements, headmanship, shamanism, and, above all, warfare and prisoner sacrifice.

Indeed, the central importance of warfare among the coastal Tupi, before and after the arrival of the Europeans, was not lost either on early observers or later anthropologists; of all the aspects of indigenous society they described, this activity occupied the most space. In his lengthy description of indigenous social organization, Gabriel Soares de Sousa summed up best the position of warfare in Tupi society : "As the Tupinambá are very bellicose, all of their foundations are directed towards making war on their enemies." In spite of differences in treatment or degree of detail, the early accounts, taken together, pointed out three significant features that played crucial roles in internecine and, subsequently, Euro-indigenous warfare: the vengeance motive, the practice of prisoner sacrifice, and the complex configuration of intervillage alliances and rivalries.

---

[15] Carlos Fausto, "Fragmentos de história e cultura Tupinambá," in Manuela Carneiro da Cunha (ed.), *História dos Índios no Brasil* (São Paulo, 1992).

The ongoing conflicts between Tupi groups assumed gigantic proportions by the mid–sixteenth century, though mainly because of their colonial implications. During that period eyewitness accounts reported battles involving literally hundreds and even thousands of warriors on land and at sea. Pero Magalhães Gandavo, in his description of the Tupinambá, declared that "it seems strange to see two or three thousand naked men on each side, howling and whistling noisily, shoot one another with arrows." And José de Anchieta, while on his peace mission among the Tamoio, reported that these Indians had prepared some 200 canoes for their war against the Portuguese, each capable of carrying between twenty and thirty warriors, along with weapons and victuals.

Although the circumstances of the Tamoio conflict were exceptional, the observations of Hans Staden, Jean de Léry, and the Jesuits, all of whom lived for substantial periods among the Indians during this period, do reveal significant aspects of Tupi warfare that must have existed before the arrival of Portuguese and French allies and enemies. All accounts agree that the principal, if not single, motivation for the constant fighting between groups lay in the thirst for vengeance. "These people have the feeling of vengeance firmly rooted in their hearts," wrote Léry of the Tupinambá. Shortly after arriving in Brazil in 1549, Father Nóbrega observed that "they do not go to war in search of gain, because no one has any more than that which he fishes and hunts, and the fruits that the land yields, but only for hate and vengeance." Staden, for his part, describing the raids carried out and attacks suffered by his captors, held that revenge alone moved warriors to set out against their enemies. In explaining "why one enemy eats the other," Staden reported several provocations called out in the course of battle, including "To revenge my friend's death on thee, am I here!"

In spite of the emphasis placed on vengeance by contemporaneous observers, most modern authors have tended to dismiss revenge among the Tupi as the single factor motivating warfare, one which supposedly obscures other, more significant causes, ranging from territorial to ecological to magico-religious. But the revenge motive in itself does explain a lot. In defining traditional enemies and in reaffirming social roles within local groups, vengeance, in particular, and warfare, more generally, played important parts in situating Tupi peoples within a spatial and temporal dimension. Jean de Léry, during his stay among the Tupinambá of Rio de Janeiro, recorded an interesting speech, suggesting the significance of warfare in preserving the collective memory of the local group.

Tupinambá elders, according to Léry, constantly reminded their fellow tribesmen of their traditional duties with respect to warfare, particularly on the eve of battle:

"Our predecessors," they repeat one after another without interruption, "not only fought valiantly but also subjugated, killed, and ate many enemies, thus leaving us honored examples; how, then, can we remain in our houses like cowards and weaklings? Will it be necessary, to add to our shame and confusion, for our enemies to come get us in our homes, when in the past our nation was so feared and respected that no one could resist us? Will our cowardice allow the Margaiá [Tememinó] and the Peró-angaipá [heartless Portuguese], who are worthless, invest against us?'

The orator would then answer his own exhortations, exclaiming, "No! No! People of my nation, strong and valiant young men, this is not how we should proceed; we must seek out our enemy even if we all die and are devoured, but that our fathers be avenged!"[16] Indigenous warfare, it would appear, fueled by a universally perceived need to avenge past injuries, thus provided an essential link between the past and future of local groups.

Revenge itself was to be consummated in one of two traditional ways: through the death of an enemy on the battlefield or through his capture and subsequent ritual sacrifice. In either case the preferred mode of execution was by smashing the enemy's skull with a heavy wooden club. Enemies spared on the battlefield faced an often long captivity within their captors' village, culminating in a great local feast, when captives were killed and eaten. The taking of prisoners was directed singularly toward these events, though colonial observers, for obvious reasons, sought to equate captives to slaves. In effect these captives were neither exploited nor treated as slaves, even though they performed certain productive tasks. Léry noted that the Indians "treat their prisoner well and satisfy his every need," feeding him and providing him with a female companion, often one's sister or daughter. Although most captives were male prisoners-of-war, many colonial observers registered the presence of women and even child captives, evidently taken in raids of enemy villages. These captives also were submitted to a ritual sacrifice and were eaten. The same fate awaited the offspring of the captives' companions.

The role of prisoner sacrifice and cannibalism among the Tupi has stirred considerable controversy since the sixteenth century. Early chroni-

---

[16] Jean de Léry, *Viagem à Terra do Brasil* (São Paulo and Belo Horizonte, 1980), 184.

clers showed great disgust with the cannibalistic ritual, while the Jesuits and colonial authorities expended much energy in trying to abolish this practice. Modern authors, for their part, in favoring ecological, demographic, or even nutritional factors, have tended to remove Tupi cannibalism from its immediate cultural and historical contexts. An exaggerated focus on cannibalism, naturally abhorrent to Western sensibilities, in effect has distorted the warfare–sacrifice complex. It is interesting to note, for example, that while the Jesuits managed to persuade many groups to give up eating their sacrifice victims, they failed miserably in their attempt to curtail the ritual sacrifice. This suggests, once again, that the consummation of vengeance, whether or not cannibalism was included, constituted the driving force behind indigenous warfare in coastal Brazil.[17]

The importance of the sacrifice rite also extended, significantly, to the sphere of intervillage relations. The ritual feast marking the end of captivity often served as an event that brought together allies and relatives from diverse villages. According to Nóbrega, in his letter to Coimbra College in 1549, when the victims were to be killed, "all the inhabitants of the district assemble to attend the festivities." Even when the influence of the Jesuits was beginning to be felt among the Tupinikin of São Vicente, one group refused to suspend a "great slaughter of slaves" in spite of Jesuit pleas to stop the ceremony. "The Indians excused themselves by saying that this could not be halted because all the guests were already assembled and all the preparations had been made with wines [cauim] and other things," wrote Brother Pedro Correia, in 1554.

Warfare, the taking of captives, and prisoner sacrifice thus provided one of the bases for relations between villages in precolonial Brazil. Battles often joined warriors from various villages; in São Vicente, for example, even in the presence of Jesuits, the Tupinikin would host warriors from other local groups in preparation for coming battles against the hated Tamoio. And the aftermath of victories or of defeats brought together allies and relatives in host villages – in victory, to savor the consummation of vengeance; in defeat, to rebuild raided homes or reconstitute shattered populations. The dynamics of intervillage relations, whether expressed in terms of conflict or alliance, in turn provided one of the keys to European success – or failure – in gaining control over the native population.

---

[17] Manuela Carneiro da Cunha and Eduardo Viveiros de Castro, "Vingança e Temporalidade: Os Tupinambá," *Journal de la Société des Américanistes* 79 (1987), 191–208.

THE PATH OF CONQUEST

Far from a uniform, swift process, the Portuguese conquest of the east coast of South America involved a complex scenario of trade, alliance, warfare, slavery, and conversion, as indigenous groups were drawn in at different times and in different ways. During the first three decades of the sixteenth century, the sporadic presence of European navigators along the Brazilian coast had little impact on indigenous lifeways. European interests remained restricted to periodic reconnaissance missions and to the modest extraction of dye woods, as Portuguese and French traders dispatched irregular shipments of wood and small numbers of Indian slaves to the Old World. But the initial project that began with the expedition of Martim Afonso de Sousa in 1530–1532 steadily gave way to the more ambitious, if still tentative, design of populating the coast with European colonists, which was to project Luso–Indian relations into an entirely new direction.

Encouraged by the results of Sousa's voyage, which planted the first permanent European colony on the southern coast at São Vicente, the Portuguese crown sought to stimulate further settlement by dividing the coast into fifteen parcels, called "captaincies," distributed among twelve proprietors between 1534 and 1536. But the captaincy plan proved a resounding failure in almost all cases. Although lax management and insufficient investment certainly retarded their development, most captaincies faltered when faced with mounting native resistance to the invasion of their lands. To be sure, the land question proved thorny from the start, in both its logistical and juridical dimensions. The Europeans themselves recognized that the act of "discovery" did not confer territorial rights, as influential Iberian jurists began to assert that the Indians were the "natural lords and owners of the land." For their part the Indians remained indifferent to papal briefs and international treaties signed in faraway lands, challenging European settlement designs in a rather more direct fashion. In the words of eighteenth-century historian Sebastião da Rocha Pita, it was necessary for the Portuguese "to gain span by span that which had been granted in leagues."[18]

If, from the Portuguese standpoint, the Brazilian Indians began to pose a threat to colonial development, they at the same time repre-

---

[18] Sebastião da Rocha Pita, *História da América Portuguesa* (São Paulo and Belo Horizonte, 1976), 60.

sented a solution for the same problem, constituting a considerable source of labor for emerging European enterprises. From the start, however, the recruitment of native workers proved problematical, because it remained subordinated to indigenous patterns of production, exchange, alliance, and warfare. Over time increased colonial demands began to erode these patterns, touching off a seemingly endless series of conflicts throughout coastal Brazil. Exacerbated by the ravages of epidemic disease, these conflicts led to a relatively rapid devastation of coastal populations. The main dilemma for the Portuguese, then, lay in the delicate balance between the exploitation and destruction of the native population.

Not surprisingly the most successful early Portuguese settlements were precisely those where significant alliances had been struck between European adventurers and native headmen. Characteristically these alliances were cemented by marriage strategies, as headmen "adopted" outsiders as sons-in-law. One notable case occurred in the captaincy of Pernambuco, where the proprietor's brother-in-law Jerônimo de Albuquerque married Tobajara headman Arcoverde's daughter. Although this Luso-Tobajara alliance broke down later in the century, when a native headman was enslaved by an unscrupulous Portuguese, it explains why the captaincy prospered from an early date. In the long run these unions favored Portuguese designs, though native interests were served initially, because European sons-in-law brought advantages, which proved extremely valuable in the context of indigenous warfare: firearms and the prospect of a broader alliance. According to Rocha Pita, the Portuguese castaway Diogo Alvares, known to the Tupinambá as Caramurú, achieved great success among the Indians through his use of firearms. Married to an influential local headman's daughter, widely respected for his military feats, Caramurú became an indispensable agent in Luso–Indian relations, especially during the establishment of royal government in the Bay of All Saints after 1549.

Farther south, in São Vicente, another castaway named João Ramalho played a similar role as cultural broker between the Tupinikin and the Portuguese. Stranded on the coast long before the establishment of São Vicente, Ramalho became integrated into the Tupinikin of the interior plateau through his marriage to headman Tibiriçá's daughter Bartira. By mid-century, when Jesuits and colonists began to settle the plateau, Ramalho had accumulated considerable prestige among the Indians. Jesuit Manuel da Nóbrega, though at first disapproving of Ramalho's heathenish ways, admitted that his role was essential to the Portuguese, "since he enjoys great fame and has many kin among the Indians." Indeed, according to Ulrich Schmidl, a German traveler who visited Ramalho's Luso-Tupinikin village in 1553, he "could assemble five thousand warriors in a single day."[19] Thus Ramalho clearly had appropriated the attributes of a Tupinikin headman. Not only was he a respected warrior and founder of a village; he also followed native traditions in having "his daughters married to the principal men of the Captaincy," as Nóbrega observed. Intermarriage, and more significantly the generation of mixed offspring, contributed in no small way to the early transformation of native populations and political structures in the captaincies where alliances prospered.

As European settlement advanced along the coast, these initial alliances were put to a serious test. The growth of the Portuguese communities and the establishment of permanent sugar plantations created a new demand for food supplies and labor, particularly in the 1540s. Tupi swidden agriculture, though oriented almost exclusively toward local subsistence needs, produced copious amounts of manioc, other assorted roots, and maize. Several sixteenth-century sources reported that the Tupi maintained supplies within their villages, but these surpluses usually were limited to short-term storage strategies related to military expeditions. Occasionally headmen showered their European neighbors or visitors with plentiful stores of manioc or maize, but to the dismay of the colonists, the supply of foodstuffs came only sporadically, even if the Europeans offered iron tools and other imported items in exchange. In effect barter failed to develop more fully because each party attached radically different meanings to it. The supply of foodstuffs by the Indians was not – as Alexander Marchant and subsequent authors have asserted – simply an economic response to a market situation. Rather, both the acquisition and supply of goods had more to do with their symbolic value than their commercial significance. For example, in 1552, the Jesuit Antonio Pires thus explained the offer of foodstuffs by a Tobajara headman in Pernambuco: "He hopes that we supply him with much life and health and provisions as his sorcerers have promised." In short, cordial relations with Tupi headmen could reap immediate positive benefits, though to a limited extent. Eager to acquire iron tools and especially firearms, in exchange headmen organized work crews (*mutirões*) who were

---

[19] Ulrico Schmidl, *Relato de la conquista del Río de la Plata y Paraguay* (Madrid, 1986), 106.

used by the colonists to cut and drag brazilwood logs, or to clear forested areas to make subsistence *roças* (garden plots).[20]

The food problem found a partial solution in alliance relations, but the quest for permanent, plantation labor posed quite a different problem, with far-reaching consequences for native societies. While some of the larger enterprises, such as that of the Flemish Schetz family in São Vicente, sought to develop a West African slave labor force from an early date, most sixteenth-century sugar planters turned exclusively to the local Indian population. Indeed, at least until the end of the century, the imperatives of sugar and slavery strongly marked the shape and direction that relations between colonists and Indians were to take along the coast. Once again alliance strategies proved critical: The Portuguese soon perceived that the permanent state of war between Tupi groups offered a potentially unlimited source of Indian captives. The Indians, for their part, took on Portuguese and French allies with an initial enthusiasm, because they introduced new weapons and methods and fit comfortably within the logic of Tupi warfare. However, to their dismay, the new allies' insatiable appetite for captives – though not in the traditional sense – threatened to undermine the main objective of indigenous warfare: ritual prisoner sacrifice.

But war captives were not transformed into chattel slaves so easily. The Europeans found resistance to the sale of slaves not only among their captors but also among the captives themselves. For example, in 1551, when the Jesuit Azpilcueta Navarro offered to purchase a Tupinambá war prisoner about to be sacrificed, he was surprised to learn that the Indian refused to be sold, "because he would rather keep his honor in meeting such a death as a valiant soldier." And the Calvinist Jean de Léry, writing about the Tupinambá during the French occupation of Rio de Janeiro, expressed the internal conflicts experienced by the Indians in facing changing patterns of warfare and sacrifice, in his account of French attempts to buy Maracajá (Tememinó) captives recently taken in battle:

In spite of our efforts, our interpreters succeeded in purchasing only a few of the prisoners. I noticed that this was not to the contentment of the captors when I bought a woman and her two year-old son, who cost me three francs in merchandise. The vendor told me: "I do not know what will happen in the future, for ever since Pai Colá [Nicholas Villegaignon] arrived here we have not eaten even half of our prisoners."[21]

---

[20] Alexander Marchant, *From barter to slavery* (Baltimore, 1942).   [21] Léry, *Viagem*, 190–911.

Indeed, the Europeans found it difficult to undercut the social and ritual significance of captivity and cannibalism. Often, Portuguese participants themselves failed to collaborate; describing the Paraguaçú War in 1559, Father Nóbrega remarked that certain Portuguese captains were behaving in indigenous fashion, complete with the ritual sacrifice of captives and the adoption of the victims' names. Allied Tupi headmen, pressured by elders, shamans, and other tribesmen to preserve traditions, also came into conflict with Portuguese authorities and Jesuits when resisting colonial orders to cease these practices. Even João Ramalho's father-in-law Tibiriçá, of the São Vicente Tupinikin, considered by the Jesuits as an exemplary case of conversion, at one point shocked and disgusted Brother Anchieta when he insisted on slaying a Guaianá war captive "in the heathenish fashion." Perhaps the most disconcerting aspect of the incident – from the Jesuit point of view – was the enthusiastic approval manifested by all the Indians present, "even the catechumens, since this was exactly what they wanted, shouting as one that he should kill."

Although the coastal Tupi clung dearly to the ritual practices of sacrifice and cannibalism, the increased participation of Europeans in the assaults on traditional enemies began to alter the form and content of indigenous warfare. Without the Europeans, raiding parties would travel hundreds of miles to bring back a precious few captives, while mid-century battles involved far greater numbers of warriors, producing scores and even hundreds of captives. Over time indigenous warfare gradually assumed the character of *saltos*, or slave raids. By the end of the sixteenth and beginning of the seventeenth century, colonial writers began to assert that the allies eagerly waged battles against their enemies only to produce captives for sale to the whites. But the war for slaves in fact had begun in the 1540s, as the Portuguese managed to incite their allies to intensify ongoing conflicts with traditional rivals. With the escalation of hostilities, enemy groups sought to offset these alliances with alternative strategies of their own: Tupinambá groups in Rio de Janeiro and Itamaracá formed alliances with the French, while others articulated pan-village military forces, often referred to as "confederations."

Certainly the most important of these emerged in southeastern Brazil, where Tupinambá groups along the coast from Cabo Frio to São Vicente formed a powerful resistance movement, calling themselves the Tamoio, a Tupi term for grandparent or ancestor. According to Father Manuel da

Nóbrega, writing in 1557, the origins of the Tamoio War followed a common pattern in the context of Indian – white conflicts: the frequent Portuguese and Tupinikin raids on Tupinambá villages, the sack and destruction of *roças*, and the taking of Indian slaves. Active from the late 1540s to the mid-1560s, the movement demonstrated the presence of powerful Indian resistance even in the most successful colonies. More importantly, perhaps, it showed clearly that Indian hostility was directly proportional to European provocation.

By the 1550s the struggle for slaves threw practically the entire Brazilian coast into intense conflicts involving not only traditional rivals but also Portuguese and French military forces as well. The wars were tremendously costly to native populations, in terms of lives lost, captives taken, and homelands destroyed. To a certain degree these conflicts reflected important changes in the structure of indigenous warfare that were accelerated during this period. But even within this context of repeated and decisive defeats, warfare remained rooted in the logic of precolonial relations and rivalries. The role played by the Jesuits of São Paulo in the "pacification" of the Tamoio illustrates some of the apparent contradictions that indigenous warfare posed to the Europeans. The Jesuits did manage to reach an agreement with certain Tamoio groups, suspending hostilities against the Portuguese. But it was not a peace agreement, as Brazilian historiography conventionally has held; according to Anchieta's account, the Tupinambá were willing to negotiate precisely because of the changing alliance situation of the war. Aware of the fact that certain Tupinikin factions had rebelled against their Portuguese allies near São Paulo in 1562, the Tupinambá saw an opportunity to form an alliance with the Portuguese against their traditional rivals. Indeed, Anchieta admitted that "the principal reason that has moved them to want this peace was not their fear of the Christians, but their great desire to make war against their Tupi enemies, who until now were our friends, and recently rebelled against us." In spite of the persistence of this internal dynamic, however by mid-century it was clear that indigenous warfare had become subordinated to the pressures and demands of a nascent colonialism. As the Indians now began to resist European advances more aggressively, colonial reprisals, tied to an increasingly repressive Indian policy, became all the more violent. Facing this critical challenge, the Portuguese crown itself became more intimately involved in the Indian question.

INDIAN LAND AND LABOR IN A RAPIDLY CHANGING
COLONIAL WORLD

At mid-century Luso–Indian relations along the Brazilian coast began to
enter a critical phase. Two decisive new actors were at the center of this
shift, both arriving in the 1549 fleet: royal government and the first Jesuit
missionaries. Shortly after arriving at the Bay of All Saints, Governor-
general Tomé de Sousa and his small retinue of royal bureaucrats erected
the new capital at Salvador, establishing the roots of a centralized government that was to tie together the loosely articulated captaincy system.
Although hereditary proprietors maintained many of their original privileges, the crucial questions of defense and labor appropriation became
the immediate concerns of royal authorities. Tomé de Sousa's standing
orders (*regimento*), issued by King João III, in fact outlined the first
formal statement of Portuguese Indian policy, inaugurating a long series
of legislative acts that sought to protect "peaceful" Indians but to enslave
or destroy those who refused to submit to European control. Thus the
regimento openly recognized that native resistance in most captaincies was
a direct result of slaving activities and ordered the governor to curtail
these abuses in protection of oppressed indigenous groups. At the same
time, it bared the other edge of the sword in recommending that he
destroy enemy villages, punishing, killing, and enslaving their inhabitants
as necessary to subdue refractory natives.

The new policy had an immediate impact on indigenous warfare, with
disastrous effects on native populations. While the struggle for slaves
continued to fuel conflicts at the local level, Portuguese military activities
during the second half of the century also expressed the explicit goal of
political domination. The first two governors remained concerned mainly
with the consolidation of Portuguese settlement in the Salvador area, but
during Mem de Sá's long tenure (1558–1572) a brutal policy of armed
conquest spread up and down the coast. In 1558–1559, though promoting
the formation of mission villages with "peaceful" Indians, he conducted
a bloody campaign against the remaining independent Tupinambá and
Tupiná groups near the Bay of All Saints and particularly along the
Paraguaçú River, where he supposedly burned 160 villages.[22] In 1559 he

---

[22] The reference to 160 villages appears in the anonymous account (probably by José de Anchieta),
"Informação do Brasil e de suas capitanias," *Revista do Instituto Histórico e Geográfico Brasileiro* 6
(1844); according to Frei Vicente do Salvador, *História do Brasil*, written in 1627, 70 villages were
destroyed.

led a powerful contingent of Tupinambá allies against the Tupinikin of Ilhéus and Espírito Santo, who had raised arms against Portuguese slavers and sugar planters, sacking and burning plantations. According to a Jesuit chronicle, 300 villages were burned near Ilhéus, leaving the beaches "covered with bodies." The campaign in Espírito Santo was slightly less successful, because native resistance was strengthened by the alliance between Tupinikin and Waitaká factions, but the captaincy was "pacified" (a term that was to stay with Brazilian Indian policy well into the twentieth century) by the early 1560s.

Certainly the most important of Mem de Sá's initiatives was the conquest of Río de Janeiro, which also illustrates the considerable transformations in indigenous warfare during this period. As we have seen, the Tamoio of the southern coast developed a powerful resistance movement in the 1540s and 1550s, which drew together many local groups under the military coordination of Cunhambebe and other influential headmen. Battles reached new proportions: Contemporary observers described pitched battles involving hundreds of warriors and canoe fleets with as many as 180 canoes. Perhaps more significantly, although prisoners continued to be sacrificed and eaten, many confrontations degenerated into wholesale slaughters, which struck at the very logic of Tupi warfare. If at first carried out within the context of traditional vendettas between Tupinambá, Tupinikin, and Tememinó factions, the so-called Tamoio War gained further colonial overtones with the involvement of the French. In 1555, departing from the prior policy of maintaining strictly trade relations, a French Calvinist adventurer named Nicholas Durand de Villegaignon established the colony of Antarctic France on an island in Guanabara Bay, which provided a significant military boost to the Tamoio, especially in terms of European weaponry. The Portuguese, already at war with the Tamoio, now had all the more reason to destroy them. After a long battle with many losses on both sides, Mem de Sá's forces managed to storm Villegaignon's fort in 1560, but it took several more years of fighting, Jesuit diplomacy, and epidemic crises before the French were expelled and the Tamoio defeated. By 1567 Guanabara Bay was "restored" to Portuguese control and the city of Rio de Janeiro established, while the surviving Tamoio either retreated to the interior or submitted to the conquerors.

While the military conquest made decisive progress during this period, the other side of Portugal's double-edged Indian policy also advanced through the energetic efforts of the Jesuits. Few in number, the first

Jesuits dedicated themselves to itinerant missionary activities among the many Tupi villages near the principal Portuguese settlements. By the late 1550s, with the active support of the governor, they began to establish mission villages of their own, in many cases concentrating several separate villages into one, while also sheltering the victims of colonial wars. The mission villages, or *aldeias*, sought to offer a peaceful, alternative solution to the problems of domination and labor recruitment, thus consciously subscribing to the collective colonial ideal of development. However, for a number of reasons, this project failed to produce its desired results, in part because of native resistance but mainly because it created a bitter relationship between Jesuits and private colonists, each vying for the control of the Indian population.

Amidst the theological and economic controversies that grew out of the struggle over Indian labor, the Jesuits began to organize their system of mission villages in several captaincies. The *aldeias* substituted for the rapidly disappearing independent Indian villages near the Portuguese settlements, transferring the control of coastal Indian land and labor into European hands. In Bahia, where Jesuit activities were most intense, at least twelve *aldeias* were created in the late 1550s, concentrating over 40,000 Indians in the immediate area of Salvador by the early 1560s. The early figures indeed were promising; writing to the crown in 1560, Governor Mem de Sá reported that 437 Indians had been baptized in a single day at the *aldeia* of Espírito Santo, near Salvador. This early success was repeated in other captaincies, particularly in Espírito Santo and São Vicente, where several villages were established among the local Tupinikin.

From the outset the crown was anxious to support the Jesuit enterprise, seeing this as a desirable means of reconciling the freedom of the Indians with the more general goal of developing the colony. To be sure, a healthy *aldeia* system was intended to serve not only Jesuit and crown interests but also those of the settlers themselves. From the royal point of view, the establishment of *aldeias* seemed a sensible way of protecting the nascent sugar economy from the external threat of European interlopers, as well as the internal threat of attacks by Tapuias and, later, by runaway African slaves. In this sense the *aldeias* could serve as buffers between the plantation zones and the unsettled interior, as well as providing a military force that could be mobilized quickly. Perhaps most importantly, though, the sustained growth of the *aldeias* was to proportion a reserve of free labor for colonial enterprises.

For their part, in the early years at least, private colonists also lent support to the *aldeia* plan, hoping that it would solve some of the practical obstacles holding back agricultural development. For instance, these reconstituted indigenous communities, often much larger than traditional Indian villages, offered a seemingly reliable and cheap alternative to slavery, through a system of contract labor. At the same time, the formation of *aldeias* redefined the land question by confining indigenous populations to spaces determined by colonial interests. New villages received extensive land grants, conveniently located on the outskirts of zones most suited to sugar production, which imposed a radical transformation in the definition of territorial and property rights. The legal instrument conferring title to the villages was the *sesmaria*, which made it clear from the start that Indian lands were to have special characteristics. Unlike the *sesmarias* distributed among private individuals, these lands were designated as collective property belonging to the Indians of the village, which could not be alienated under any circumstances and which was to be exploited exclusively by the *aldeia* residents.

Another ostensible advantage of this new form of land tenure lay in the prospect of foodstuff production, destined to support not only the Indians but the Luso-Brazilian population as well. Stuart Schwartz, in his book on sugar plantations in Bahia, suggests that part of the Jesuit strategy was to mold an independent indigenous peasantry out of the detribalized peoples thrown together in the *aldeias*.[23] But this paper peasantry never materialized because the *aldeia* residents rarely produced enough to maintain themselves, let alone supply the colonial economy. In short, the *aldeia* scheme failed to produce the structures necessary to sustain and reproduce a reserve labor force sufficiently large to meet settler demands, in part because native response once again frustrated colonial expectations.

The *aldeias*, though designed to protect the declining Indian population and at the same time make the Indians useful if dependent subjects, in effect hastened the disintegration of indigenous societies. Perhaps the most significant disruptive factor was disease, which also served as an important ally to the Europeans on the battlefield. By concentrating the native population – some individual *aldeias* had over 5,000 residents – and restricting its customary mobility, the Jesuits unwittingly contributed to the conditions favoring the spread of epidemics. Other Jesuit innova-

---

[23] Schwartz, *Sugar plantations in the formation of Brazilian society* (Cambridge, 1985), 41–43.

tions, as Luis Felipe Baeta Neves has pointed out, such as the use of clothing and the burial of contaminated persons within the villages, also contributed to the spread of disease.[24] To make matters worse, with persistently high mortality rates, the *aldeias* only survived through their constant replenishment with new groups of previously uncontacted Indians. Although consistent with the Jesuit strategy of reducing members of varied societies to a single ideal Christian type, the constant influx of new catechumens had the more serious effect of aggravating the epidemiological situation, because recently contacted peoples were far more susceptible to the imported diseases.

Disease struck all segments of the Indian population, including independent villages in the interior, and it hit the young and unstable *aldeias* especially hard. Isolated outbreaks already had been registered, but the first large smallpox epidemic – possibly introduced by African slaves who participated in the campaigns against the Tupinikin – raged along the east coast in 1559, carrying off over 600 Indian slaves in Espírito Santo alone. By 1562 the disease was claiming victims from São Vicente to Pernambuco. The following year measles broke out in the wake of the smallpox epidemic, certainly intensified by the arrival of new Indian slaves taken in the Caeté campaigns. In Bahia the impact of these epidemics was sudden and powerful: According to contemporary Jesuit accounts, 30,000 Indians and Africans perished in the brief interval of 3 months. Modern authors have estimated that between one-fourth and three-fifths of the *aldeia* population perished. Over a longer period, between 1560 and 1580, the total population of the Bahia *aldeias* was diminished from over 40,000 to less than 10,000 residents. This gloomy balance was pronounced by the Jesuit Anchieta in the early 1580s: "The people that have been wasted in Bahia over the last twenty years is something incredible; because no one considered that so many people could ever be expended, especially in so short a time."

Under these adverse conditions the Jesuits meticulously sought to dismantle some of the fundamental elements of indigenous social organization, substituting these elements with radically different patterns. For example, the creation of fixed, permanent villages with restricted land rights stood in stark contrast with the irregular patterns of fragmentation

---

[24] Luís Felipe Baêta Neves, *O combate dos Soldados de Cristo na Terra dos Papagaios* (Rio de Janeiro, 1978).

and regeneration, which characterized precolonial village formation. The spatial orientation of the *aldeias*, based on European models featuring a church and central plaza, also departed somewhat from the organization of non-Christian Indian villages. The replacement of extended-family living units with nuclear households and the prohibition of polygamy affected some groups greatly, while the suppression of most ceremonial activities and their substitution with Christian rituals sought to restructure the basic contours of Indian existence. Finally, and perhaps most significantly, the Jesuits attempted to inculcate a totally new concept of time and work discipline into their Indian subordinates, where a new sexual division of labor and a rigid schedule of productive activities clashed with preconquest patterns.

The Jesuit program centered its fire primarily on three areas: the conversion of the headmen, the indoctrination of youths, and the elimination of the shamans, or *pajés*. At each step, however, they met varying degrees of resistance. The Jesuits, along with other Europeans, counted naively on the blind acceptance of Christianity by their Brazilian flock, and their accounts are filled with reports of mass baptisms, supposed miracles, and dramatic professions of faith by Indian leaders. But their teachings were not always heeded uniformly, and even the conversion of a local leader did not guarantee that the tribesmen would follow. For example, referring to one of the first native villages approached by the Jesuits in Bahia in 1549, Father Nóbrega reported the case of a headman who came to be ostracized by all of his relatives because of his adherence to Christianity and his collaboration with the Jesuits. Another exemplary collaborator was Garcia de Sá, headman in São Paulo *aldeia* near Salvador, who adapted traditional forms to the new rhetoric. According to Nóbrega this leader would amble throughout the village before dawn, as in precolonial times, only the content of his speech was diametrically opposed to tradition: Instead of urging his tribesmen to fight as valiant warriors and eat human flesh, he attempted to persuade them to "become Christians and leave behind the customs of the past." Nóbrega detected a sure sign that customs indeed were changing in that Garcia had convinced his followers to sell all their feather adornments and with the proceeds buy Western garments. However, when the power of speech failed to persuade the Indians to change their ways, the Jesuits were not averse to adopting disciplinary measures, following Mem de Sá's policy of harsh law enforcement. Indigenous bailiffs were appointed in each village, and stocks were erected for exemplary punishment of relapsed converts who engaged in prohibited acts, such as fornication, cannibalism, and drunkenness.

The first Jesuits also dedicated much energy to the instruction of Indian youths, in part because of the resistance that older generations offered, but also because of the persistence of traditional forms of instruction that they sought to undermine. "Those who are already adults," wrote Anchieta in 1560, "and who follow the evil customs of their parents most naturally, cover their ears so as not to hear the healthy word and become converted to the true cult of God." Initially the fathers found it difficult to make their efforts compatible with the daily obligations facing the boys of the village. Referring to the *aldeia* of São João near Salvador, Nóbrega reported that he was able to teach the boys a curriculum of religion, literacy, and music only 3 or 4 hours each afternoon, because the students first had to carry out other obligations, such as hunting and fishing. After the formal school sessions, the Jesuits would assemble all the members of the *aldeia* for mass, which included hymns executed by a boy's choir. Finally, to round out activities, they would ring the church bell at a determined hour in the middle of the night, when the boys would relay the day's teachings to their elders. But even these efforts often proved short-lived, according to Anchieta; initial success with young boys often was undone when they reached adolescence, when they would take up the customs of their elders.

Pajés, or shamans, constituted perhaps the last line of resistance to European domination, particularly with respect to the work of the Jesuits. The Jesuits were quick to launch an all-out offensive against the "sorcerers" because the continued presence and charismatic influence of the *pajés* among the Indians threatened to undermine the conversion efforts of the Padres. In 1557 Anchieta observed that the work of the Jesuits in São Paulo was being rivaled by a shaman who was attracting many followers, who "venerate him as a Saint" and who intended to destroy the Christian Church. Anchieta offered no further information on this specific case, but other Jesuits mentioned the emergence of *santidade* (holiness or saintliness) cults, evidently responses to the conversion efforts of the priests. One such movement attained great prestige in the backlands of Bahia later in the century.

Within the specific context of the native villages, Father Nóbrega reported in 1549 that the *pajés* were telling the Indians that the baptismal water was the cause of the diseases that were beginning to afflict the villages at that time. Later, in another village near Salvador, sick children were hidden from the Jesuits, "because the sorcerers say that we kill them through baptism." Curiously this association of epidemic disease with the work of the Jesuits extended beyond the actions of *pajés*. Referring to a village near Salvador in 1559, Brother Antonio de Sá remarked that in his *aldeia* "there is nothing on our part that will move the old women to accept baptism, because they are certain that baptism will bring them death." This fear was not totally unfounded in that the Jesuits themselves tended to reserve baptism to Indians on their deathbeds. Several of the padres harbored suspicions as to the efficacy of baptism, having witnessed countless examples of Indians reverting to their decidedly non-Christian practices after conversion. Father Afonso Brás, working among the Tupinikin and Tememinó in Porto Seguro and Espírito Santo, reported in 1551: "I dare not baptize the heathen here so readily, unless they plead for it repeatedly, because I am wary of their inconstancy and lack of firmness, except in the case of when they are at the point of death."

In short, to be truly effective, it was not enough simply to discredit the *pajés*; the Jesuits also would have to appropriate for themselves the traditional role of charismatic spiritual leader. Indeed, in their mission activities and on their visits to Indian villages, the Jesuits adopted practices thought to be effective because they emulated precolonial practices. It was common, for example, for Jesuits to preach before sunup, as was the practice of headmen or *pajés* who harangued their fellow tribesmen. Anchieta, in spreading the gospel among Tupinambá villages along the coast of São Vicente in 1565, expressed his message in a fashion closely modeled on the rhetoric of the charismatic leaders whom he so despised. Speaking "in a loud voice throughout their houses, as is their custom," Anchieta preached that "we wanted to remain among them and teach them about God, so that He could give them abundant crops, health and victory against their enemies and other such things." Perhaps with this in mind, the Jesuits soon perceived baptism, with its apparently magical implications for the Indians, to be an effective method of subverting certain rituals, especially the cannibalistic rite. For example, when visiting a Tupinikin village in 1554, the Jesuits Nóbrega and Pedro Correia attempted to intercede on behalf of prospective sacrifice victims. The Tupinikin villagers refused to allow the baptism of the victims, "saying that if they killed them after having been baptized, all those who had killed and eaten that flesh also would die." And in 1560 the Indians of a village near São Paulo killed two captives, one a small boy aged two or three and the other a youth of fifteen, but declined to eat them as planned because Father Luís da Grã had baptized them first. Finding it difficult to eliminate prisoner sacrifice altogether, Anchieta recognized the limits of Jesuit success when he remarked in 1554 that "among such a multitude of infidels, a few of our flock at least have abstained from eating their fellow man."

Day-to-day resistance certainly wore down the Jesuits' patience, but the *aldeia* project also was jeopardized by more radical actions. In Bahia the *aldeia* plan met considerable native opposition from the start. Some local groups refused to submit to colonial rule, as in the case of Chief Cururupeba, who openly defied the governor's prohibition of cannibalism. Others, once converted and settled in mission villages, soon after abandoned their new ways. In 1557, in the Rio Vermelho village, the Indians rebelled against the Jesuits, who had pressured their headman to abandon polygamy. But the most common form of resistance was flight from the *aldeias*. According to Nóbrega, "many flee the subjection of our doctrine and live like their ancestors, eating human flesh as before." In 1560, during a religious procession, many of the residents of the São João *aldeia* followed headman Mirangoaba into the interior. Mirangoaba sported a long record of insubordination, though the main reason for his abandoning the *aldeia* emanated from a factional dispute that had developed within the settlement. Indeed, while the Jesuits were quick to attribute such actions to the Indians' inconstancy, this served conveniently to mask problems that they themselves had created.

In short, unable to meet the labor needs of the settlers and frustrated by their incapacity to transform the recalcitrant tribal Indians into loyal Catholic subjects, the Jesuits and their *aldeia* program quickly lost ground to alternative forms of labor recruitment and political control. To be sure, along with the devastating effects of epidemic disease, the cultural modifications imposed by the Jesuits served mainly to hasten the disintegration of native societies. Instead of producing Christian Indians able and willing to work for the development of the colony, the *aldeia* system succeeded only in creating marginal communities of sickly, morose, and unproductive residents, hardly able to provide for their own survival. It was within this context, then, that the colonists sought increasingly to take the labor question into their own hands.

Dissatisfied with the results of the *aldeia* experiment, and stimulated by the repeated demographic crises that punctuated the second half of the sixteenth century, both private settlers and enterprising colonial authorities intensified the search for new sources of slave labor. As we have seen, the tenure of Governor Mem de Sá marked a critical turning point in Luso–Indian relations. Although Mem de Sá openly supported the Jesuits and their missions – his own Sergipe plantation near Salvador eventually passed to them in a bequest from his daughter – the need to pacify the coastal regions surrounding the Portuguese settlements and the attendant development of the sugar industry inevitably resulted in a series of wars of conquest, which in turn were to produce a rich booty in Indian captives. Indeed, while the king's counselors discussed the ethics of "Just War" from a moral and theological perspective, Mem de Sá and his immediate successors adopted a more practical stance, organizing powerful military columns that were to squash Tupi resistance in Rio de Janeiro, Bahia, Pernambuco, Sergipe, and Paraíba.

Mem de Sá's willingness to resolve the defense and slavery issues in single strokes became evident in 1562, with the prosecution of a "Just War" against the Caeté, who 6 years earlier had slain and devoured Brazil's first bishop. In his proclamation, the governor authorized the enslavement of all Caeté, which evidently pleased the colonists of Bahia, who faced their first serious labor crisis as a result of the great smallpox epidemic that raged along the coast. But not all Caeté were enemies; some, in fact, lived in Jesuit missions, while others traded peacefully with the Portuguese. Nonetheless the colonists and their Tupinambá allies seized the opportunity with relish, attacking and enslaving any Caeté to be found, including those living in the Jesuit villages. And when the declared enemy proved insufficient, the slavers launched attacks against other Tupi groups, claiming that they were Caeté. According to the Jesuit Anchieta, within a few months over 50,000 captives were taken in the war, but only 10,000 lived on to serve as slaves in the Salvador area, the others falling victim either to ruthless massacres or uncompromising disease.

The Caeté case set a dangerous precedent, which subsequently was incorporated into Portuguese legal codes dealing with the Indian question. Evidently preoccupied with the indiscriminate and illegal enslavement of native peoples, the Portuguese crown issued its first major legislative statement on the Indian question with the Law of 20 March 1570. This law specifically sought to regulate both Indian slavery and freedom. The new statute designated the legitimate means of acquiring Indian captives, restricting these to "Just Wars" duly authorized by the king or governor, and to the ransom (*resgate*) of captives destined to perish in cannibalistic rituals – the so-called *índios da corda*, or bound Indians. All other Indians captured unjustly were declared free. This code may have had little effect on the actual relations between colonists and Indians – illegal slaving expeditions were difficult to repress in practice – but it did reflect the conciliatory tone adopted by an ambivalent crown caught between Jesuit and settler interests. The posture in favor of the freedom of the Indians most likely came from pressures by the Jesuits Luís da Grã and José de Anchieta, who sat on a commission organized by the crown in 1566 to discuss the Indian question. On the other hand, the "Just War" clause, while falling within the limits accepted by the Jesuits, also answered settler demands because they saw a need for new supplies of slaves to replace those who perished in the frequent epidemics.

Even had the settlers observed crown regulations strictly, the concession of rights to the enslavement of certain groups through "Just Wars" would not have resolved the labor problem even as a supplementary source. As the century wore on, with the defeat of Tupi groups surrounding the Portuguese settlements, many of the remaining coastal groups who qualified as indomitable and subject to "Just Wars" were Tapuia; the Law of 1570 explicitly singled out the Aimoré, a denomination that included various Gê peoples who were particularly resistant to Portuguese expansion in eastern Brazil. The colonists were interested mainly in Tupi labor, though, and with the collusion of royal officials would invent flimsy pretexts for the prosecution of wars against Tupi peoples, as in the Caeté case of 1562. Part of the problem lay in the difficulties posed by the very different pattern of Gê warfare: Rather than the intricate web of alliances and constant movement of captives, the frequent, effective raids by Gê groups made them at the same time formidable adversaries and objects of Portuguese reprisals. But the main Portuguese objection resided elsewhere. Referring to the Gê-speaking Guaianá of São Paulo, Gabriel Soares de Sousa summed up a consensus view on the labor issue: "Anyone who buys a Guaianá slave expects no service from him, because these people are lazy by nature and do not know how to work."[25]

The military defeat of a significant number of coastal peoples also opened the way for the rapid expansion of the sugar industry during the final quarter of the sixteenth century. Between 1570 and 1600 the number of *engenhos*, or large mills, on the Brazilian coast grew threefold: the northeastern captaincies alone, with 24 mills in 1570, boasted 100 *engen-*

---

[25] Soares de Sousa, *Tratado Descritivo*, 115.

hos 30 years later. Many planters tied their fortunes to the growing supply
of African slaves, but most counted on the increased flow of Indian labor
to guarantee the production and local transport of the sugar crop. Stuart
Schwartz, in his pioneer analysis of the gradual shift to African labor on
Bahían plantations between 1570 and 1620, has documented the persistence and complexity of Indian labor arrangements – particularly slavery
– during this period.[26] Although few studies exist for the other captaincies, it now seems clear that not only the origins but also the early
development of the colonial sugar economy were closely tied to the
expansion of Indian slavery. In addition subsidiary economic activities,
notably foodstuff production and distribution, also depended heavily on
the supply and exploitation of forced native labor.

The forced relocation of indigenous societies, often involving great
distances, contributed to the depopulation of vast stretches of coast and
hinterland alike. These movements also aggravated the epidemiological
problem in zones of European settlement, because the introduction of
large numbers of captives with little or no immunity to a new disease
environment kept mortality rates always at high levels. Writing in 1583
Anchieta produced a grim picture of the fate of 20,000 captives taken in
the Aribó backlands 6 years earlier, claiming that only 2,000 had survived: "Go now to the mills and plantations of Bahia and you will find
them filled with Guinea blacks and very few native blacks, and if you ask
what happened to so many people, they will tell you they have perished."
The deadly epidemics in turn stimulated new slaving expeditions to
increasingly distant lands, in a destructive cycle that persisted until Indian
slavery no longer remained a viable economic proposition. This cycle
played out on the sugar-growing coast sometime during the first half of
the seventeenth century, but it lasted well into the eighteenth century in
other areas, particularly the colonies of São Paulo, Goiás, Mato Grosso,
Maranhão, Pará, and Rio Negro.

Part of the demand was filled through the formal prosecution of "Just
Wars." Thousands of Tupinambá captives were marched to Bahia during
the first conquest of Sergipe in 1575–1576, and many Tobajara and Potiguar where enslaved during the Paraíba campaigns of the 1580s, linked to
the expansion of the Pernambuco sugar industry. Another source of slaves
came from the Indians who sold themselves into slavery, which raised an

---

[26] Schwartz, "Indian labor and New World plantations: European demands and Indian responses in
northeastern Brazil," *American Historical Review* 83 (1978).

interesting moral and ethical question about the legitimacy of slavery. According to Fernão Cardim, a severe drought drove many Indians to the plantations of Pernambuco, where they offered themselves and their children to the planters as slaves.[27] Most slaves, however, were submitted to captivity by the many private, informal expeditions that began to penetrate the *sertão* (backlands) regularly during the final years of the century. Precursors to the seventeenth-century *bandeiras*, these slaving expeditions often operated with the open consent of local authorities, though clearly violating the precepts of royal legislation, which prohibited unauthorized attacks on native peoples. But the law had other gaping loopholes, especially that which permitted the ransom of war prisoners taken to be sacrificed and eaten. The expeditions often adopted the term *resgate* to describe their operation, which came to mean not only ransom but also any other sort of trade with the Indians. Outfitted by planters, who supplied weapons, provisions, and Indian warriors, individual expeditions "ransomed" hundreds of slaves at a time, usually turning over half to the financial backer and dividing the remaining half among the participants of the expedition.

Many colonists, mainly half-breed *mamalucos* (usually spelled *mamelucos*), emerged as slaving specialists during this period. Raised by their Indian mothers, these backwoodsmen were fluent in Tupi and well versed in the ways of the *sertão*. The anonymous Jesuit who described the conquest of Paraíba remarked on

the boldness and impertinence with which the slavers allow themselves to enter that great wilderness, at great cost, for two, three, four or more years. They go without God, without food, naked as the savages and subject to all the persecutions and miseries in the world. These men venture two or three hundred leagues into the *sertão*, serving the devil with such amazing martyrdom, just to barter or steal slaves.[28]

One such "martyr" was Domingos Fernandes Nobre, also known as Tomacaúna, a *mamaluco* from Pernambuco. In 1591 Tomacaúna told his fascinating life story to the Holy Office of the Inquisition, during its first visitation to Brazil.[29] This Christian subject no doubt startled his inquisitors as he described his life in the *sertão*, where he had relations with at

[27] Cardim, *Tratados da Terra*, 199.
[28] Quoted in John Hemming, *Red gold* (Cambridge, Mass., 1978), 154.
[29] João Capistrano de Abreu (ed.), *Primeira Visitação do Santo Ofício às Partes do Brasil: Confissões da Bahia, 1591–92* (Rio de Janeiro, 1935), 220–227.

least seven different "wives," had smoked "holy grasses," and had painted himself with dyes, all in native fashion. Evidently holding this freedom in great esteem, "often he wished that he never return from the *sertão*, because there he had many wives and ate meat on forbidden days and did everything else he wished without anyone paying notice." But To-macaúna's heathenish ways served quite another purpose: He proved indispensable to the slaving business, because he was able to penetrate native societies with great ease, at times persuading them to migrate to the coast or enticing them to attack other enemies in order to produce captives. In 1572, for example, as part of the great Antônio Rodrigues Adorno expedition to the interior of the captaincy of Porto Seguro, Tomacaúna led 7,000 Tupiguen (possibly Tupiná) to the coast, where they were divided among the colonists. The Jesuit Anchieta, witness to many slaving expeditions, remarked that the crafty *mamaluco* backwoods-men indeed were successful in persuading Indians to move to the coast, though these soon realized that they had been tricked: "When they reach the sea, the Portuguese divide them amongst themselves, some taking the wives, others the husbands, others the children, and selling them."

NATIVE STRATEGIES OF RESISTANCE: MIGRATION AND
SANTIDADE

Seeking to offset the intensification of Portuguese slaving activities during the second half of the century, native peoples developed new collective strategies based not only on precolonial traditions and patterns but also on the historical experience of conquest and domination. Some headmen, particularly in areas settled only marginally by Europeans, sought to preserve their people from a harsher fate by collaborating with Portuguese slaving interests. For example, according to Manuel da Nóbrega, the Tupinikin of Porto Seguro and Ilhéus served as brokers in the slave trade, seizing Indians who came to the sea to collect shellfish and salt, selling these captives to the Portuguese, who in turn shipped them to the plantations of Bahia and Pernambuco. Coastal Guarani headmen also gained considerable notoriety during this period as they supplied Portu-guese and Spanish traders with captives taken on raids to the interior. These relations afforded protection as long as the slavers' interests were being satisfied, but they often broke down after a short number of years, as indigenous collaborators themselves became the objects of slaving expeditions.

Migration provided the most effective method of combatting the pernicious effects of disease, slavery, and confinement to missions. Many Tupi groups abandoned coastal areas over the course of the sixteenth century and reestablished their political autonomy on lands far removed from Portuguese control. For example, after their defeat in Rio de Janeiro, several Tamoio groups settled in the interior along the southern Paraíba River, as well as along the São Francisco to the north. Various Tupinambá groups departed from Bahia and Pernambuco during the middle decades of the century; some established themselves on the east – west coast between Ceará and the mouth of the Amazon, and others came to control a significant area in the middle Amazon Valley. In the wake of the conquest of Paraíba, disaffected segments of the Pernambuco and Paraíba Tobajara came to occupy the Ibiapaba Hills in the interior of Ceará, where they continued to repel Portuguese slavers and Jesuits throughout the following century.

These movements became more frequent by the late 1550s, when coastal societies faced an increasingly aggressive Indian policy, serious epidemiological crises, and a rapid growth in the demand for slaves. According to Gabriel Soares de Sousa, within a few years the Portuguese under Governor Mem de Sá "destroyed and ruined the heathen that lived around Bahia, burning and devastating over thirty villages, and those who escaped being killed or enslaved fled to the *sertão*, removing themselves more than forty leagues from the coast."[30] In the 1580s a Tupinambá leader from the Real River explained to the Jesuits his reasons for leading a large group to the remote wilderness:

We must leave, we must leave before these Portuguese arrive. . . . We are not fleeing from the Church or your Company, for if you wish to join us, we will live with you in the forests and backlands. . . . But these Portuguese do not leave us alone, and if so few who are among us already seize our brothers, what else can we expect when the rest arrive, but to see ourselves, our wives and our children enslaved?[31]

Once established in new areas, migrant groups did not necessarily withdraw from all contact with the Portuguese, though they preserved bitter memories of their experience as betrayed allies, mission Indians, or slaves. Both the Tupinambá of Bahia, who moved to the Raripe backlands of Sergipe, and those of Pernambuco, who settled around Tupi-

---

[30] Soares de Sousa, *Tratado Descritivo*, 132.   [31] Quoted in Fernandes, *Organização Social*, 36.

nambarana Island on the middle Amazon, served as intermediaries in the Portuguese slave trade. The latter group, visited by several Spanish and Portuguese expeditions in the mid–seventeenth century, confirmed that they "were peoples who many years ago left the conquered lands of Brazil, in Pernambuco, in defeat, fleeing the severity with which the Portuguese had been subjugating them." According to Jesuit chronicler João Felipe Bettendorff, who based his account on Cristóbal Acuña, "they left in such great numbers that, in abandoning eighty-four villages, there was not a single creature that they did not bring in their company."[32]

Far from simple retreats from the coast in reaction to Portuguese advances, the many long-distance population movements registered throughout the sixteenth century also obeyed the logic of age-old patterns of rupture, migration, and recomposition of local political units. Often quoting native informants, colonial sources reveal that these journeys, even though clearly stimulated by colonial oppression, were organized under the influence of a resolute headman or a prophetic *caraíba*. In 1549, for example, a weary group of some 300 Tupinambá led by Uirar-açu appeared in the town of Chachapoyas, in the Peruvian Amazon. There they told local Spanish authorities that "they were all fleeing from the vexations they suffered from the Portuguese conquerors of that province [Brazil]."[33] Although it is not clear whether Uiraraçu was a headman or a *caraíba*, Pero Magalhães Gandavo reported later in the century that this trek was motivated by "their constant desire to seek new lands, in which they imagine that they will find immortality and perpetual ease," ostensibly a reference to the "land without evil."[34] Later in the century, according to a Jesuit report, Indian slaves of the Japacé and Paranamirim plantations in the Salvador area rebelled, "fleeing to the *sertão*, in the process burning plantations and robbing what they could." The reasons behind this mass flight, aside from unjust captivity, were linked to the prophetic message of an indigenous "saint" who urged the captives to return to their place of origin, along the Real River.[35]

This last example, evidently led by a persuasive *caraíba*, was one of many resistance movements with apparently millennarian characteristics

[32] João Felipe Bettendorff, S. J., *Crônica do Padres da Companhia de Jesus no Estado do Maranhão* (Belém, 1990), 56–57.
[33] Quoted in Hemming, *Red gold*, 195.   [34] Gandavo, *Tratado da Terra*, 144.
[35] Francisco Adolfo Varnhagen, *História Geral do Brasil*, I, 5 vols. (São Paulo and Belo Horizonte, 1981), 1:348, note by Capistrano de Abreu.

John Monteiro

that punctuated the history of Luso–Indian relations during the second half of the sixteenth century. Early on, the Jesuits adopted the term *santidade* (holy figure or saintly cult) to describe elaborate ritual ceremonies presided over by *caraíbas*, who, evoking Tupí-Guaraní myths and traditions, exalted warfare and promised abundant crops and game. By the late 1550s, however, the term acquired an explicitly subversive connotation, because in addition to their traditional discourse, the indigenous prophets also began to attack Christian institutions as well as the domination structure imposed by Portuguese slave owners. In 1559, for example, Father Nóbrega reported the outbreak of a movement on a plantation near Salvador, where an Indian from one of the Jesuit missions spread an insurgent message among a growing number of slaves who were eager to listen. A saint was to appear, transforming the master and other whites into birds, freeing the subsistence plots of caterpillers and other pests. The Jesuits were to be spared, though the Indians were to destroy the Church, dissolve their Christian marriages, and take on many wives. The movement was repressed by Mem de Sá, but the rebellious *caraíba* managed to escape to the *sertão*.[36]

Another similar movement was described later in the century by Luísa Barbosa, a white woman interrogated by the Inquisition. In 1591 Luísa confessed that she herself was drawn into a *santidade* cult at the age of 12 (c. 1566), when converted Indians told her that their god "told them not to work because food would sprout up by itself and that anyone who did not believe in that *santidade* would be converted into sticks and stones, and that the white people would be converted into game for them to eat."[37] Thus the prophetic message not only included the conventional promise of a life of ease and abundance, associated with the "land without evil," but also significantly restored the ideals of cannibalism and revenge, which practically had been eradicated in the Salvador area by the combined efforts of royal governors and the Jesuits.

Several authors erroneously have depicted the *santidade* as a single, unified movement that spread along the coast and throughout the backlands over the course of several decades in the sixteenth century. In a recent work on native "idolatries," Ronaldo Vainfas persuasively shows that many different phenomena were called *santidades*, ranging from traditional Tupi-Guarani shamanistic rituals to manifestly anticolonial

---

[36] Valle, ed., *Cartas Jesuíticas*, 1.
[37] Confession of Luísa Barbosa, in Abreu (ed.), *Primeira Visitação*, 83–84.

resistance.[38] Luísa Barbosa, in her confession to the Inquisition, asserted that the cult she was drawn into as a child was followed by many others that "after this arose also in this captaincy [of Bahia]." Indeed, given the dynamics of precolonial political and religious movements, and considering the divide-and-rule characteristics of early Luso–indigenous relations, the emergence of several small movements organized by charismatic leaders makes more sense than a large messianic cult.

Nonetheless the development of the *santidade* near Jaguaripe, a sugar and foodstuff-producing zone located just south of the Bay of All Saints, continues to raise important questions about native resistance. Although little is known about most other movements, which earned only brief mentions in Jesuit letters and other early literature, the Jaguaripe movement has come to light thanks to special circumstances; because the cult was installed on a sugar plantation and enjoyed a considerable following in the non-Indian community, it became a central concern of the Inquisition during the 1591–1592 *visita* in Bahia. Unfortunately, however, as Vainfas points out, not a single Indian was heard by the Inquisition, though white and mixed-blood witnesses furnished information on the cult in rich detail. According to these accounts, the cult emerged in the *sertão*, possibly in the Orobó Hills near Jaguaripe, sometime around 1580. Led by the charismatic Antônio, a Tupinamba who had run away from a Jesuit *aldeia* at Tinharé, to the south of Bahía, the movement began to attract a significant following of Indian and even African fugitives from mission villages and slave plantations, causing great concern among sugar planters and local authorities. In 1586 Governor Manuel Teles Barreto and planter Fernão Cabral de Ataíde hired the experienced backwoodsman Tomacaúna to organize an expedition to destroy the cult, which reputedly counted hundreds of followers. Although Tomacaúna made contact with the leader Antônio and observed some of his rituals, most of the members of the sect remained with Antônio in the backlands, avoiding contact with the Portuguese, while the expedition managed to persuade a group of sixty to settle in a village near Ataíde's mill in Jaguaripe. The cult flourished for awhile on the plantation, incorporating new members from the colonial community, but it was extinguished completely by the early 1590s; isolated vestiges of the movement persisted in the *sertão*, however.

Firmly based on traditional Tupinambá political and religious components, the *santidade* of Jaguaripe, perhaps more than any other similar movement that erupted in sixteenth-century Brazil, also borrowed heavily from the hierarchical order introduced by Jesuits and slave owners. By all accounts the leader of the movement displayed all the crucial characteristics of the charismatic *caraíba*. Based on fresh archival material, Vainfas demonstrates that Antônio was a gifted speaker, in the tradition of persuasive Tupinambá leaders, and also commanded a profound understanding of Tupi-Guarani heroic mythology. The backwoodsman Tomacaúna, himself son of an Indian mother and quite familiar with Tupi-Guarani spritual life, was impressed by the shamanistic rituals conducted by Antônio. But Tomacaúna's account, perhaps the most detailed description of the movement before part of it was coopted by Fernão Cabral de Ataíde, also suggests that Antônio was more than the spokesman of tradition and, in effect, also was the product of history.

Raised by Jesuits in the Tinharé mission, Antônio incorporated significant new elements to the prophetic experience. Declaring himself "pope" and one of his wives "mother of God," Antonio established a parallel church, complete with "bishops" and "vicars." According to Vainfas new members were accepted to the cult through a sort of reverse baptism, in which Christian names were substituted with names given by the leader. His message also mixed Tupinambá and colonial images: Beyond the usual appeal to a world of abundance, where crops would produce themselves, where arrows would shoot spontaneously through the air slaying game, and above all where the enemy would fall easily captive to heroic warriors, Antônio's message also addressed the problem of colonial oppression. According to the confession of Gonçalo Fernandes, a *mamaluco*, the cult attracted many Indian slaves and mission residents, who fled from the plantations and *aldeias*. Using an incomprehensible language invented by the members of the *santidade*, possibly in emulation of the Latin ritual of the *aldeias*, and inspired by a stone idol, cult leaders claimed that their God was to come immediately and "free them from slavery and make them the masters of the white people, who were to become their captives."[39]

The *santidade* often has been classified as a typical, syncretic "religion of the oppressed," but it remains important to recognize how this and other movements – such as the Guarani rebellion led by Oberá in 1579[40] –

[39] Confession of Gonçalo Fernandes, in Abreu (ed.), *Primeira Visitação*, III.
[40] Bartomeu Melià, *El Guaraní, conquistado y reducido* (Asuncion, 1986), 30–40.

consciously combined tradition and revivalism with historically new elements in order to forge novel strategies that aimed to restore indigenous collective identity in a dynamic fashion. The challenges of contact and conquest introduced new pressures, which, in the long run, eroded age-old patterns and contributed to the decline of indigenous coastal Brazil. Nonetheless in facing adversaries of the likes of contagious diseases, colonial armies, and, above all, an Atlantic economy in inexorable expansion, indigenous peoples reached into their own past to draw both strategies of survival as well as the will to resist the advances of colonial domination. Thus, while the indigenous history of Brazil continues to be a neglected subject, the task facing future historians is much greater than simply emphasizing the role of Indians in an essentially colonial history; it also means rethinking Indian history itself – that is, the history experienced and reflected upon by Brazil's native peoples.

BIBLIOGRAPHICAL ESSAY

Mostly dated or limited in scope, research tools dealing with sixteenth-century Portuguese America are useful primarily as guides to the early sources. The most comprehensive ethnographic bibliography on Brazilian Indians, with extensive commentaries on sources, is Herbert Baldus, *Bibliografia Crítica da Etnologia Brasileira* (São Paulo, 1954, and Hannover, 1968), which has been enriched by a third volume compiled by Thekla Hartmann (Munich, 1984). Bartomeu Melià et al., *O Guarani: Uma Bibliografia Etnológica* (Santo Angelo, 1987), is excellent on Guarani ethnohistory, with many references to the Brazilian coast during the sixteenth century. Originally published in 1949, Florestan Fernandes, "Um Balanço Crítico da Contribuição Etnográfica dos Cronistas," in *Investigação Etnológica no Brasil* (Petrópolis, 1975), 191–298, is a detailed and systematic reading of sixteenth- and seventeenth-century printed accounts. Though generally glossing over the theme of Portuguese – Indian relations, José Honório Rodrigues provides excellent insights to sources and their disparate editions in *História da História do Brasil, Primeira Parte: Historiografia Colonial* (2nd ed., São Paulo, 1979). For English-language sources, Francis Dutra, *A guide to the history of colonial Brazil, 1500–1822* (Santa Barbara, 1980) is very useful. A recent guide to unpublished sources is John Monteiro (ed.), *Guia de Fontes para a História Indígena e do Indigenismo em Arquivos Brasileiros* (São Paulo, 1994). Many sixteenth- and seventeenth-century European sources contain rich ethnohistorical information on the coastal peoples. Hans Staden, *The captivity of Hans Stade of Hesse, in A.D. 1547–1555 among the wild tribes of eastern Brazil*, translated by A. Tootal with notes by Richard Burton (London, 1874), is the extraordinary narrative of a German adventurer who spent several years as captive among the Tupinambá, containing lively descriptions of Tupi social organization, ritual activities, warfare, and cannibalism. Another German, Ulrich Schmidl, includes important comments on Guarani and Tupinikin groups in his *Wahrhaftige Historie einer wunderbaren Schiffart* (Frankfurt, 1567), also translated into English (London, 1889). The French colony of Rio de Janeiro produced two excellent, sensitive accounts of Tupinambá society: André Thevet, *Les Singularités de la France Antarctique* (Paris, 1558), and Jean de Léry, *History of a voyage to the land of Brazil*, trans. Janet Whatley (1578; Berkeley, 1990). Early seventeenth-century Capuchins from the French colony at Maranhão also contribute to our understanding of the Tupinambá: Claude d'Abbeville, *Histoire de la Mission des Pères Capucins en l'Isle de Maragnan* (Paris, 1614), and Yves d'Évreux, *Voyage dans le Nord du Brésil* (Paris, 1614). Staden, Léry, and Thevet have been issued in good, critical Portuguese translations by the Editora da Universidade de São Paulo. Finally, the Englishman Anthony Knivet, who spent several years among the Tamoios in São Vicente and even led a migration to the far southern coast, registered his "Admirable adventures and strange fortunes," in Samuel Purchas (ed.), *Hakluytus Postumus or Purchas his Pilgrimes*, (facs. ed., New York, 1965), 16, 177–289.

Portuguese sources on the Brazilian Indians begin with Pero Vaz Caminha's letter to the crown, which appears in *The voyages of Pedro Alvares Cabral to Brazil and India* (London, 1937), translated and annotated by William B. Greenlee. Portuguese–Indian relations during the first half of the sixteenth century remain poorly documented, though the records published in Capistrano de Abreu's critical edition of Francisco Adolfo de Varnhagen's *História Geral do Brasil*, 5 vols. (1854; 10th ed., São Paulo 1981), and in Carlos Malheiro Dias (ed.), *História da Colonização Portuguesa do Brasil*, 3 vols. (Porto, 1921–1924), fill the gap somewhat. Another important source for this period is the diary of Martim Afonso de Sousa's voyage, published with supplementary documents in Eugênio de Castro (ed.), *Diário de Navegação de Pero Lopes de Sousa*, 2 vols. (Rio de Janeiro, 1927), with information on early relations with the Tupinikin and Guarani of the southern coast. The picture improves markedly after 1549, with the arrival of royal government and the Jesuits.

Among the principal non-Jesuit Portuguese sources, Pero de Magalhães Gândavo, *Tratado da Terra do Brasil e História da Província de Santa Cruz* (1576; 2nd ed., São Paulo and Belo Horizonte, 1980) and English translation (New York, 1922), includes an important discussion of Indian customs, slavery, and population movements; Gabriel Soares de Sousa, *Tratado Descritivo do Brasil em 1587* (São Paulo, 1971), provides the best contemporary description of the Tupinambá, particularly in the region surrounding the Bay of All Saints; and Ambrósio Fernandes Brandão, *Dialogues of the great things of Brazil*, trans. Frederick Holden Hall (1618; Albuquerque, 1987), offers a description of indigenous and colonial societies at the beginning of the seventeenth century. In 1627 the Franciscan Vicente do Salvador penned the first systematic history of the Brazilian coast, *História do Brasil* (7th ed., São Paulo and Belo Horizonte, 1982), especially rich in its narrative of Luso–Indian relations in the northern captaincies.

Jesuit writings constitute perhaps the most important sources on native societies produced in the sixteenth and seventeenth centuries. Serafim Leite, S. J., prepared a careful edition of Jesuit letters and reports from the 1550s and 1560s, covering the critical phase of the *aldeia* experience: *Monumenta Brasiliae*, 5 vols. (Rome, 1956–1960), whose first 3 vols. were published in Brazil as *Cartas dos Primeiros Jesuítas* (São Paulo, 1956–1958). Selected letters of Anchieta, Nóbrega, and other contemporary Jesuits edited by Alfredo do Valle Cabral in the 1930s have been reissued as *Cartas Jesuíticas*, 3 vols. (São Paulo and Belo Horizonte, 1988). The complete works of Anchieta, certainly the greatest sixteenth-century authority on the Brazilian Indians, are being published by Edições Loyola, including *Cartas de Anchieta, Correspondência Ativa e Passiva* (2nd ed., São Paulo, 1984), a selection of letters edited by Hélio Viotti, S. J.; *Textos Históricos* (São Paulo, 1989), also edited by Viotti, including important treatises on the coastal Tupi; *De Gestis Mendi de Saa* (2nd ed., São Paulo, 1984), a panegyric poem in praise of Mem de Sá and his feats during the Tamoio War; and *Teatro de Anchieta* (São Paulo, 1977), consisting of religious plays in Portuguese and *língua geral* written for Indian converts. Even though of considerable ethnohistorical relevance, Anchieta's non-prose and Tupi writings have not received much scholarly attention. Another extraordinary Jesuit source is Fernão Cardim, S. J., *Tratados da Terra e Gente do Brasil* (3rd ed., São Paulo, 1978), first published in English by Samuel Purchas in 1625. The anonymous "Sumário das Armadas que se Fizeram e Guerras que se Deram na Conquista da Paraíba

(c. 1587)," *Revista do Instituto Histórico e Geográfico Brasileiro* 36(1) (1873), later attributed to the Jesuit Simão de Travassos, contains valuable information on indigenous politics during the conquest of Paraíba. Finally, the excellent chronicles of Simão de Vasconcelos, S. J., written in the mid–seventeenth century, deserve mention because of their careful study of early Jesuit–Indian relations: *Vida do Padre João d'Almeida* (Lisbon, 1658); *Crônica da Companhia de Jesus no Brasil* (1663; 3rd ed., Petrópolis, 1977); and *Vida do Venerável Padre José de Anchieta*, 2 vols. (1672; 2nd ed., Rio de Janeiro, 1943).

Several documentary sets include information on different aspects of native history and European Indian policy. Official correspondence and legislation dealing with the Indian question appear in several volumes of *Documentos Históricos da Biblioteca Nacional do Rio de Janeiro*, 110 vols. (Rio de Janeiro, 1928–1955). Mem de Sá's activities are registered in his service record along with other documents published as "Documentos Relativos a Mem de Sá," *Anais da Biblioteca Nacional* 27 (1905), 119–280. The role of Indian labor during the early years of the sugar industry comes to light in *Documentos para a História do Açúcar*, 3 vols. (Rio de Janeiro, 1954–1963). Indian–white relations in the southern captaincies were the frequent concern of municipal council meetings in São Paulo, published as *Atas da Câmara Municipal de São Paulo*, I (São Paulo, 1914) and *Registro Geral da Câmara de São Paulo*, I (São Paulo, 1917). The proceedings of the special Inquisition court installed in Bahia by Heitor Furtado de Mendonça were published in Capistrano de Abreu (ed.), *Primeira Visitação do Santo Ofício às Partes do Brasil: Confissões da Bahia, 1591–92* (Rio de Janeiro, 1935), especially useful in documenting the *santidade* of Jaguaripe. Recently, Ronaldo Vainfas edited an updated version of these documents, with rich notes based on previously unveiled manuscript sources: *Confissões da Bahia* (São Paulo, 1997). Finally, Darcy Ribeiro and Carlos de Araújo Moreira Neto (eds.), *A Fundação do Brasil* (Petrópolis, 1992), provides a good selection of document excerpts from Brazil's first two centuries, with a special focus on native actors.

Although somewhat burdened by detail, the best general work on the historical experience of the Brazilian Indians during the colonial period is John Hemming, *Red gold: The conquest of the Brazilian Indians, 1500–1760* (Cambridge, Mass., 1978). Berta Ribeiro, *O Índio na História do Brasil* (São Paulo, 1983), aimed at a general audience, is a useful guide to some of the issues. Mércio Gomes Pereira, *Os Índios e o Brasil* (Petrópolis, 1988), presents a broad overview of the question of ethnic survival in an historical framework. An important collection of essays addressing the problem of Indian history in Brazil is Manuela Carneiro da Cunha (ed.), *História dos Índios no Brasil* (São Paulo, 1992). Some of the older interpretive works on Brazilian history dedicate considerable coverage to the indigenous background and early relations between Europeans and natives. Robert Southey's pioneer *History of Brazil*, 3 vols. (London, 1810–1819) pays particular attention to early Indian–white relations, and Varnhagen's *História Geral do Brasil*, though manifestly unsympathetic toward the Indians, includes relevant information on all the captaincies. Recently translated into English, João Capistrano de Abreu's turn-of-the-century classic *Chapters of Brazil's colonial history, 1500–1800*, trans. Arthur Braekel (New York, 1997), introduced fresh insights to colonial history, though his most brilliant contributions were on the seventeenth century. The essays covering the sixteenth century in Sérgio Buarque de Hollanda (ed.), *História Geral da Civilização Brasileira*, I, 2 vols. (São Paulo, 1960), await a much-needed current revision. Among more recent works, James Lockhart and Stuart Schwartz, *Early Latin America* (Cambridge, 1983), and the articles by Harold B. Johnson, Stuart Schwartz, and John Hemming in Leslie Bethell (ed.), *Colonial Brazil* (Cambridge, 1987), provide neat syntheses on early Portuguese America.

The concise manual of Aryon Dall'Igna Rodrigues, *Línguas Brasileiras. Para o Conhecimento das Línguas Indígenas* (São Paulo, 1986), is most useful for sorting out native language groups, and Curt Nimuendaju's *Mapa Etno-histórico do Brasil e Regiões Adjacentes*, (2nd ed., Rio de Janeiro, 1981) remains a convenient research tool. Varied population estimates may be found in the following: William Denevan, "The aboriginal population of Amazonia," in W. Denevan (ed.), *The native population of the Americas in 1492*, (Madison, 1977); the appendix to Hemming's *Red gold*; and Berta Ribeiro, "Quantos Seriam os Índios das Américas?," *Ciência Hoje*, 1(6) (1983), 54–60. Warren Dean, "The indigenous population of the São Paulo–Rio de Janeiro coast: trade, *aldeamento*, slavery and extinction," *Revista de História* 117 (1984), 3–26, studies the factors contributing to demographic decline after the conquest. Specifically on the spread of disease, Dauril Alden and Joseph C. Miller, "Out of Africa: The slave trade and the transmission of smallpox to Brazil, c. 1560–1830," *Journal of Interdisciplinary History* 18(1) (1987), 195–224, furnishes fresh insights.

The Tupi-Guarani peoples of the coast have received extensive scholarly attention, though primarily from anthropological perspectives. Alfred

Métraux made pioneer contributions on Tupinambá society, religion, and migrations in his *La Civilisation Matérielle des Tribus Tupi-Guarani* (Paris, 1928), *La Religion des Tupinamba et ses Rapports avec celle des autres Tribus Tupi-Guarani* (Paris, 1928), and "Les Migrations Historiques des Tupi-Guaranis," *Journal de la Société des Americanistes* 19 (1927), 1–45. Florestan Fernandes's brilliant studies, while strongly marked by a functionalist framework, remain central to any discussion of the Tupinambá, particularly with respect to warfare: *Organização Social dos Tupinambá* (São Paulo, 1948), and *A Função Social da Guerra na Sociedade Tupinambá* (São Paulo, 1952). On political organization, Pierre Clastres develops suggestive hypotheses in *Society against the state*, trans. Robert Hurley (New York, 1977), and Tupi-Guarani shamanism and migrations are minutely dissected in Hélène Clastres, *The land-without-evil: Tupí-Guaraní prophetism*, trans. Jacqueline G. Brovender (Urbana, 1995). Not surprisingly, Tupinambá warfare, sacrifice, and cannibalism continue to stimulate scholarly debates. Donald W. Forsyth, "Beginnings of Brazilian anthropology: Jesuits and Tupinambá Indians," *Journal of Anthropological Research* 39 (1983), 147–178, challenges William Arens's thesis questioning the veracity of eyewitness sources. Isabelle Combès, *La Tragédie Cannibale chez les Anciens Tupi-Guarani* (Paris, 1992), includes a meticulous reconstruction and critical discussion of this question. Focusing on the historical dimension of Tupinambá society, two important contributions to the theoretical debate deserve mention: Manuela Carneiro da Cunha and Eduardo Viveiros de Castro, "Vingança e Temporalidade: Os Tupinambá," *Journal de la Société des Americanistes* 79 (1987), 191–208, and Carlos Fausto, "Fragmentos de História e Cultura Tupinambá," in Manuela Carneiro da Cunha (ed.), *História dos Índios no Brasil* (São Paulo, 1992). For a stimulating revision of Tupi studies, with a critical discussion of Métraux and especially Florestan Fernandes, see Eduardo Viveiros de Castro, *Araweté: Os Deuses Canibais* (Rio de Janeiro, 1986), which proposes a bridge between "ethnographic" and "historical" Tupi peoples. A revised version of this important book was published in English as *From the enemy's point of view* (Chicago, 1992). There are no solid studies of sixteenth-century Gê groups. For a synthesis of modern Gê studies, see Manuela Carneiro da Cunha, "Études Gê," *L'Homme*, 126–128 (1993).

Early European–Indian relations have been studied mainly from the optic of Portuguese policies and legislation. For general overviews of Portuguese Indian policy, see Georg Thomas, *Die portugiesische Indianerpolitik in Brasilien, 1500–1640* (Berlin, 1968), Portuguese translation (São

Paulo, 1983); and José Vicente César, "Situação Legal do Índio durante o Período Colonial: 1500–1822," *América Indígena* 45 (1985), 391–426. Though dated, Agostinho Marques Perdigão Malheiros, *A Escravidão no Brasil: Ensaio Histórico-jurídico-social*, 3 vols. (1867; 3rd ed., Petrópolis, 1976), covers Indian legislation, especially with regard to slavery, in Vol. II. A more recent compilation and discussion is Beatriz Perrone-Moisés, "Legislação Indígena Colonial: Inventário e Índice," unpublished *mestrado* thesis, Universidade Estadual de Campinas, 1990, part of which appears as an appendix to M. C. da Cunha (ed.), *História dos Índios no Brasil*. The land issue receives illuminating treatment from an ethical and legal perspective in Manuela Carneiro da Cunha, "Terra Indígena: História da Doutrina e da Legislação," in her *Os Direitos do Índio: Ensaios e Documentos* (São Paulo, 1986), 53–101. A fresh discussion on the legal principles underlying "Just Wars" is Beatriz Perrone-Moisés, "A Guerra Justa em Portugal no Século XVI," *Revista da SBPH* 5 (1989/90), 5–10.

The impact of initial contact with the Brazilian Indians on European thought has been the object of a growing bibliography, taking up many of the points introduced by Sérgio Buarque de Hollanda in his classic *Visão do Paraíso* (Rio de Janeiro, 1959). Laura de Mello e Sousa, in *O Diabo na Terra de Santa Cruz* (São Paulo, 1987) and *Inferno Atlântico* (São Paulo, 1993), discusses the Edenic and Demonic images that emerged from early colonial contacts in a fresh light. Ronald Raminelli, *Imagens do Índio* (São Paulo, 1996), focuses more specifically on European iconographic representations of the Indians. Three other innovative studies add interesting perspectives on this period: Leyla Perrone-Moisés, *Vinte Luas* (São Paulo, 1992), based on Paulmier de Gonneville's early travel account, reconstructs the life story of a Guarani Indian who was taken to Europe by the French; Guillermo Giucci, *Sem Fé, Lei ou Rei. Brasil 1500–1532* (Rio de Janeiro, 1993), examines the process of "accidental colonization" involving European castaways; and Ronaldo Vainfas, *Trópico dos Pecados* (Rio de Janeiro, 1997), casts interethnic sexual liaisons and miscegenation in a new mold, establishing a fruitful dialogue with Gilberto Freyre's 1933 classic, *The masters and the slaves*, trans. Samuel Putnam (New York, 1946). French–Indian early relations in Rio de Janeiro are placed in comparative perspective by Olive P. Dickason, *The myth of the savage and the beginnings of French colonialism in the Americas* (Edmonton, 1984). Finally, the impact of these relations on French thought is covered by Frank Lestringant, *Le Huguenot et le Sauvage* (Paris, 1990).

On native labor, Alexander Marchant's pioneer study, *From barter to slavery: The economic relations of Portuguese and Indians in the settlement of Brazil, 1500–1580* (Baltimore, 1942), remains a standard work, though his model of indigenous economic response has been questioned. Urs Höner, *Die Versklavung der brasilianischen Indianer: der Arbeitsmarkt in portugiesisch Amerika im XVI. Jahrhundert* (Zurich, 1980), focuses specifically on the development of slavery, though based mainly on legal sources. The debate over early labor relations has been considerably enriched through the study of plantation records by Stuart Schwartz in "Indian labor and New World plantations: European demands and Indian responses in northeastern Brazil," *American Historical Review* 83(1) (1978), 43–79, as well as in his larger work, *Sugar plantations in the formation of Brazilian society: Bahia, 1550–1835* (Cambridge, 1985). The conflict between colonists, Jesuits, and the crown over Indian labor is discussed in Dauril Alden, "Black robes versus white settlers: The struggle for freedom of the Indians in colonial Brazil," in H. Peckam and C. Gibson (eds.), *Attitudes of colonial powers toward the American Indian* (Salt Lake City, 1969), as well as in Stuart Schwartz, *Sovereignty and society in colonial Brazil* (Berkeley, 1973). Focusing on the southern captaincies, John Monteiro, *Negros da Terra: Índios e Bandeirantes nas Origens de São Paulo* (São Paulo, 1994), provides new evidence and fresh insights on the problem of Indian slavery.

The role of the Jesuits is exhaustively described (and defended) in Serafim Leite, S. J., *História da Companhia de Jesus no Brasil,* 10 vols. (Lisbon and Rio de Janeiro, 1938–1950). An alternative view may be found in Eduardo Hoornaert (ed.), *História da Igreja no Brasil: Ensaio de Interpretação a Partir do Povo,* 2 vols. (Petrópolis, 1979). Dauril Alden's massive *The making of an enterprise: The Society of Jesus in Portugal, its empire, and beyond, 1540–1750* (Stanford, 1996), places the Brazilian experience within the wider context of Portuguese expansion to Africa and Asia, with important new insights on the spiritual, economic, and political activities of the missionaries. For interesting discussions of Jesuit strategies of "cultural repression" in sixteenth-century Brazil, see Luiz Felipe Baêta Neves, *O Combate dos Soldados de Cristo na Terra dos Papagaios: Colonialismo e Repressão Cultural* (Rio de Janeiro, 1978), and Roberto Gambini, *O Espelho Índio: Os Jesuítas e a Destruição da Alma Indígena* (Rio de Janeiro, 1988), which provocatively seeks to analyze Jesuit thought and actions in Jungian terms. An instigating article proposing the Indian perspective on Jesuit activities and expectations is

Eduardo Viveiros de Castro, "O Mármore e a Murta," *Revista de Antropologia* 35 (1992), 21–74.

The indigenous response to conquest is outlined in Florestan Fernandes, "Os Tupi e a Reação Tribal à Conquista," *Investigação Etnológica no Brasil e Outros Ensaios* (Petrópolis, 1976), 11–32. For a different approach, emphasizing native strategies as political actions, see Mário Maestri Filho, *Os Senhores do Litoral* (Porto Alegre, 1994). There is a growing bibliography that explores the historical roots of contemporary indigenous rights movements. Interesting examples treating groups mentioned in this article include Frans Moonen and Luciano Mariz Maia (eds.), *Etnohistória dos Índios Potiguara* (João Pessoa, 1992), which traces the contact history and struggles of these Northeastern Indians over the past five centuries, and Judith Shapiro, "From Tupã to the land without evil," *American Ethnologist* 14 (1987), 126–139, which discusses the link between Tupi-Guarani religious reinterpretation in colonial times and modern Liberation Theology discourse. Finally, the *Santidade* movements are studied by José Calasans in *Fernão Cabral de Ataíde e a Santidade de Jaguaripe* (Salvador, 1952), and Ronaldo Vainfas, *A Heresia dos Índios*, (São Paulo, 1995), presents abundant new information from Inquisition records.

INDEX

Italic numbers indicate pages with illustrations.